Political Science:
The State of the Discipline

Political Science:

THE STATE OF THE DISCIPLINE

Ira Katznelson and Helen V. Milner, editors
Columbia University

W. W. Norton & Company   **American Political Science Association**

NEW YORK | LONDON   WASHINGTON, D.C.

Copyright © 2002 by W. W. Norton & Company, Inc.

Previous editions published by the American Political Science Association:
POLITICAL SCIENCE: The State of the Discipline (1983)
POLITICAL SCIENCE: The State of the Discipline II (1993)

The text of this book is composed in Electra LH
with the display set in Electra LH.
Composition by PennSet, Inc.
Manufacturing by Courier, Westford
Book design by Martin Lubin Graphic Design

For information about permission to reproduce selections from this book, write
to Permissions, W. W. Norton & Company, Inc., 500 Fifth Avenue, New York,
NY 10110

Library of Congress Cataloging-in-Publication Data
Political science : the state of the discipline / ed., Ira Katznelson and
Helen V. Milner.
     p.   cm.
   Includes bibliographical references and index.
   ISBN 0-393-05142-0
   ISBN 0-393-97871-0 (pbk)
   1. State, The.   2. Political science.   I. Katznelson, Ira.
II. Milner, Helen V., 1958–
JC11.P65   2002
320—dc21   2002025547

W. W. Norton & Company, Inc., 500 Fifth Avenue, New York, N.Y. 10110
www.wwnorton.com

W. W. Norton & Company Ltd., Castle House, 75/76 Wells Street,
London W1T 3QT

2   3   4   5   6   7   8   9   0

Contents

Ira Katznelson and Helen V. Milner
Preface and Acknowledgments   xiii

Ira Katznelson and Helen V. Milner
American Political Science: The Discipline's State and the State of the Discipline   1

1 | The State in an Era of Globalization

Margaret Levi
The State of the Study of the State   33

Miles Kahler
The State of the State in World Politics   56

Atul Kohli
State, Society, and Development   84

Jeffry Frieden and Lisa L. Martin
International Political Economy: Global and Domestic Interactions   118

James E. Alt
Comparative Political Economy: Credibility, Accountability, and Institutions   147

James D. Morrow
International Conflict: Assessing the Democratic Peace and Offense-Defense Theory   172

Stephen M. Walt
The Enduring Relevance of the Realist Tradition   197

2 | Democracy, Justice, and Their Institutions

Ian Shapiro
The State of Democratic Theory   235

Jeremy Waldron
Justice   266

Romand Coles
Pluralization and Radical Democracy: Recent Developments in
Critical Theory and Postmodernism   286

Gerald Gamm and John Huber
Legislatures as Political Institutions: Beyond the Contemporary
Congress   313

Barbara Geddes
The Great Transformation in the Study of Politics in Developing
Countries   342

Kathleen Thelen
The Political Economy of Business and Labor in the Developed
Democracies   371

3 | Citizenship, Identity, and Political Participation

Seyla Benhabib
Political Theory and Political Membership in a Changing World   404

Kay Lehman Schlozman
Citizen Participation in America: What Do We Know? Why Do
We Care?   433

Nancy Burns
Gender: Public Opinion and Political Action   462

Michael C. Dawson and Cathy Cohen
Problems in the Study of the Politics of Race   488

Morris P. Fiorina
Parties, Participation, and Representation in America: Old Theories
Face New Realities   511

Amy Gutmann
Identity and Democracy: A Synthetic Perspective   542

Randall Calvert
Identity, Expression, and Rational-Choice Theory   568

Thomas Risse
Constructivism and International Institutions: Toward Conversations across Paradigms   597

4 | Studying Politics

David D. Laitin
Comparative Politics: The State of the Subdiscipline   630

Barry R. Weingast
Rational-Choice Institutionalism   660

Paul Pierson and Theda Skocpol
Historical Institutionalism in Contemporary Political Science   693

Karen Orren and Stephen Skowronek
The Study of American Political Development   722

Robert Powell
Game Theory, International Relations Theory, and the Hobbesian Stylization   755

Charles M. Cameron and Rebecca Morton
Formal Theory Meets Data   784

Donald P. Green and Alan S. Gerber
Reclaiming the Experimental Tradition in Political Science   805

Works Cited   833

Index   A1

CONTRIBUTORS' PAGE

James E. Alt | *Harvard University*
Seyla Benhabib | *Yale University*
Nancy Burns | *University of Michigan*
Randall Calvert | *Washington University in St. Louis*
Charles M. Cameron | *Columbia University*
Cathy Cohen | *Yale University*
Romand Coles | *Duke University*
Michael C. Dawson | *Harvard University*
Morris Fiorina | *Stanford University*
Jeffry Frieden | *Harvard University*
Gerald Gamm | *University of Rochester*
Barbara Geddes | *University of California, Los Angeles*
Alan S. Gerber | *Yale University*
Donald P. Green | *Yale University*
Amy Gutmann | *Princeton University*
John Huber | *Columbia University*
Miles Kahler | *University of California, San Diego*
Ira Katznelson | *Columbia University*
Atul Kohli | *Princeton University*
David Laitin | *Stanford University*
Margaret Levi | *University of Washington*
Lisa L. Martin | *Harvard University*
Helen V. Milner | *Columbia University*
James D. Morrow | *University of Michigan*
Rebecca Morton | *New York University*
Karen Orren | *University of California, Los Angeles*
Paul Pierson | *Harvard University*
Robert Powell | *University of California, Berkeley*
Thomas Risse | *Free University of Berlin*
Kay Lehman Schlozman | *Boston College*
Ian Shapiro | *Yale University*
Theda Skocpol | *Harvard University*
Stephen Skowronek | *Yale University*
Kathleen Thelen | *Northwestern University*
Jeremy Waldron | *Columbia University*
Stephen M. Walt | *Harvard University*
Barry Weingast | *Stanford University*

ILLUSTRATIONS

Ian Shapiro, The State of Democratic Theory
    Figure 1   Ethnic Engineering Continuum   252
Morris Fiorina, Parties, Participation, and Representation in America: Old
Theories Face New Realities
    Figure 1   Trust and Faith in the National Government
                Are Down   512
    Figure 2   Turnout in the United States Has Declined since
                1960   514
    Figure 3   From Rare to Everyday: Media Coverage of
                Poll Results   519
    Figure 4   Party Activitists Have Grown More Extreme   526
    Figure 5   Popular Attitudes toward Legal Abortion since *Roe v.*
                Wade (1973)   529
    Figure 6   Turnout Has Declined Primarily among Less Partisan
                Americans (Presidential Elections)   537
    Figure 7   Turnout Has Declined Primarily among Moderates
                (Presidential Elections)   538
Barry Weingast, Rational-Choice Institutionalism
    Figure 1   Executive, Legislature, and Status Quo   662
    Figure 2   The Effect of a Presidential Veto   663
    Figure 3   Policy Choice in Chile   664
    Figure 4   The Effect of Legislative Veto in Chile   664
    Figure 5   Postauthoritarian Political Environment in Chile without
                Institutional Senators   665
    Figure 6   Postauthoritarian Political Environment in Chile with
                Institutional Senators   666
    Figure 7   The Filibuster Pivot   668
    Figure 8   Civil Rights Policy   668
    Figure 9   The Role of Courts in Interpreting Statutes   676
    Figure 10 Constraints on an Extremist Court   676
    Figure 11 Courts Facing Elected Officials with Very Different
                Preferences   677
    Figure 12 Ethnic Conflict as the Absence of Credible
                Commitment   684
Robert Powell, Game Theory, International Relations Theory, and the
Hobbesian Stylization
    Figure 1   Preferences over Outcomes and Strategies in
                Chicken   766
    Figure 2   Bargaining over Territory   774
Charles M. Cameron and Rebecca Morton, Formal Theory Meets Data
    Figure 1   A Structural Model   785
    Figure 2   Equilibrium in the Expository Example   789
    Figure 3   A Simple Comparative Static in the Expository
                Model   792

PREFACE AND ACKNOWLEDGMENTS

Ira Katznelson and Helen V. Milner

We began work on this successor to the two prior State of the Discipline volumes (Finifter 1983; Finifter 1993) in 1999 when we were selected by president-elect Robert Keohane to chair the program committee for the 96th annual meeting of the American Political Science Association in 2000. Soon after our designation, APSA inquired about our willingness to edit a volume in conjunction with our plans for the meeting. We had already selected "Political Science as Discipline? Reconsidering Power, Choice, and the State at Century's End" as our theme, so this seemed a natural fit.[1] We asked numerous colleagues for advice about the most important topics and potential authors for such a volume and remain grateful for the outpouring of useful responses. Our goal from the outset was to reflect the vibrant, often contested, diversity of political science while chronicling the past decade's scholarship and prompting thought about future directions. We asked the book's contributors to provide critical reflection on their particular fields and to indicate and advocate promising avenues of research for the future. The essays in this book are not just retrospective appraisals; they also strongly express views about where the discipline should be going. Many of the essays are quite spirited. Since each is

1. The meeting's program statement read as follows:

> Power, choice, and the state have been central concepts in political science since its founding as a self-conscious discipline. By reconsidering these orienting themes, we seek to initiate discussion about both the distinguishing characteristics and internal coherence of political science as well as late-century developments which challenge how the discipline deploys its key organizing concepts.
>
> From its founding, political science has transacted with history, its parent discipline, and the other social sciences. Once (perhaps again), the "state" defined its special focus. Arguably, "power" and especially "choice" have been more widely shared across disciplinary lines. Are there, or should there be, clear and coherent distinctions among these disciplines for the creation of knowledge? Further, do power, choice, and the state integrate political science across its own subfields and methodological variations? Will political science fragment, much as sociology has, or narrow its focus, much as economics has done?
>
> Worldly developments at century's end challenge more than the character of the discipline. They command reexamination of the concepts of state, power, and choice. Sovereign states are being pressed on many fronts, from globalization to ethnic and regional movements. Their number, scale, capacities, and competitive advantages vis à vis other forms of political organization have become open issues. Power, too, is not static. The nature of power, even what we mean by the term, has been brought into question by nuclear weapons, the velocity of financial exchanges, and new communications technologies, among other transformations. In these circumstances, the very character of choice and rationality of agents become open issues.

stamped by the author's personal voice, there is no uniformity of style or approach.

The authors first sent us short proposals in early 2000. We then had long discussions with each to ensure broad and pluralistic coverage. Each paper was presented at a panel at the APSA 2000 meeting in Washington, D.C., where it received extensive comments by at least two discussants. We added our own written comments. The authors then were asked to revise their contributions for collegial discussion and review at two conferences, held with APSA support, in December 2000. There, they were subjected to vigorous critical discussion, led off by two commentators. These sessions produced a great deal of constructive criticism and critical feedback and facilitated the development of a common sense of the mission of the volume and a shared understanding of its overall design. Following these productive sessions, we wrote the authors once again early in 2001 to summarize those discussions and point toward changes we believed should inform the final texts. The final iterations of the essays were submitted in the late spring and early summer of 2001. Each paper thus has been reviewed by at least two and often four scholars in the same field, in addition to the interventions by the editors. As it turned out, our colleagues in this venture proved uncommonly conscientious, responding quickly and thoughtfully to these various editorial entreaties. We thank them in the warmest possible terms for this service to the discipline of political science. Their, and our, only compensation will be the impact this book has on the discipline, a result now in the hands of our readers.

We also are indebted to the many nonauthors who contributed to this venture. At the American Political Science Association, Catherine Rudder and Robert Hauck, especially, provided intellectual comradeship and administrative support. We salute their leadership. At W. W. Norton and Company, we have had the dedicated partnership of Roby Harrington, Avery Johnson, and Carey Schwaber, backed by a terrific production team. We are particularly grateful to the community of scholars who have read and commented on various versions of the chapters in this book. In addition to colleagues who wish to remain anonymous, these include David Baldwin, Brian Barry, Robert Bates, Henry Brady, Gregory Caldeira, John Carey, David Collier, Gary Cox, Robert Dahl, Geoffrey Garrett, James Fearon, Russell Hardin, Robert Jervis, James Johnson, Mary Katzenstein, Robert Keohane, Claire Jean Kim, Gary King, Peter Lange, Anthony Marx, David Mayhew, Nancy Rosenblum, Sven Steinmo, Paul Pierson, Ronald Rogowski, Kenneth Shepsle, Kathryn Sikkink, Robert Shapiro, Jack Snyder, Sidney Verba, and Margaret Weir.

There are, of course, many ways to organize a volume assessing the state of the discipline. We resisted the most prominent possibility that would have divided the book into the four conventional subfields (American, comparative, international relations, and political theory), plus perhaps a methods section, because we do not think that this division best advances the discipline. The subfields increasingly inform and blend into each other. The essays confirm this proposition. Many share substantive themes such as the nature of the state, globalization and its impact, liberalism and democracy, the power of institutions, and concerns about identity, participation, and citizenship. Of course, scholars choose different approaches to these topics. But whether they privilege historical institutionalism, rational choice, or constructivism and postmodernism, they are engaged in what, broadly, is a common disciplinary discussion, as we discuss further in our introductory essay. We think that this targeted diversity is important. Given our prior views about the character of the discipline (Katznelson 1997; Milner 1998), the essays here lend support to our beliefs about the state of the discipline.

Our particular intellectual architecture focuses first on the state ("The State in an Era of Globalization"), followed by democracy ("Democracy, Justice, and its Institutions"), and then agency ("Citizenship, Identity, and Political Participation"), concluding with the means of inquiry ("Studying Politics"). In this order, the essays flow from considering the state broadly, irrespective of regime type, to the subset of liberal democratic regimes to political participation and behavior mainly within such a framework. This organization, we believe, reflects both the emphases and choices made within political science. The methodological papers that end the volume discuss alternative ways of addressing each of these political phenomena. We had commissioned a paper on courts and public law, but unexpectedly pressing demands made it impossible for its author to finish the essay before the book went into production.

Soon you will see that we think about the discipline in terms of an extended, although highly varied but coherent, intellectual conversation. May our debates long continue!

Ira Katznelson and Helen V. Milner

American Political Science: The Discipline's State and the State of the Discipline[1]

> *Political Science as a debate might be political science at its best.*
> (Lindblom 1997, 262)

■ | Political Science as a Discipline

State of the discipline implies a discipline, yet even this much about political science cannot be taken for granted. As an organized profession, political science has existed for nearly a century. However, it has been a capacious, often cacophonous, undertaking. Political scientists possess sharply divergent views about their research and pedagogy. They disagree not only about what they should study and what constitutes a persuasive argument and evidence but also about how to understand the discipline's past. By the second page of his recent history, Gabriel Almond felt compelled to note that there exist many competing alternatives to his preferred progressive-eclectic approach (Almond 1996; also see Almond 1990). Further, political scientists often lack confidence in their enterprise. Charles Lindblom's iconoclastic assessment of the discipline records its meager contributions, amateur selection of research questions, obsession with method rather than substance, and absence both of social criticism and scientific authority (Lindblom 1990, 1997). Is there a discipline at all, we might wonder, before moving on to chronicle its condition?

Readers of this volume will not miss the remarkable heterogeneity and contested qualities of political science. We choose to put them to the side, not because we are disengaged or lack particular preferences about these

---

1. We have benefited from comments on our first draft by Robert Dahl and Sidney Verba at the American Political Science Association 2000 Annual Meeting, by Gregory Caldeira, Jeffry Frieden, David Laitin, Paul Pierson, and Barry Weingast, who offered formal critiques at two meetings to discuss the volume in Washington, DC, in December 2000, and by most colleagues in this book.

matters but because we believe that clarifying the kind of discipline political science has been can offer a fresh appreciation of what political scientists possess in common despite their differences and can refocus our understanding on continuities and their implications. The essays in this book are not just markers of variety. Together, they underscore how, despite its many internal epistemological and methodological divisions, political science in the United States continues to constitute a distinct scholarly undertaking. Coming to terms with the discipline, moreover, facilitates activities that we want to encourage. These include promoting collaboration by scholars in diverse subfields, clarifying various scientific and normative debates, and expanding the reach of political science by making the discipline's historical omissions more apparent and thus more remediable. Sharing with Almond a taste for scholarly diversity, we think that the eclecticism of the discipline can most effectively produce political knowledge by becoming self-conscious about the limited but compelling sets of questions it has addressed.

In his skeptical consideration, Lindblom observes that political science "is a name given not to a field of conventional scientific inquiry but to a continuing debate" about specific subjects and claims. These, he argues, do not get resolved; "on any given big issue of fact or value, debate in political science tends to be endless rather than declining (or terminating in a finding)" (Lindblom 1997, 260–61). We agree with Lindblom that the image of a long-running debate captures well the dynamics of our discipline as a continuing process of inquiry engaged with understanding fundamental political issues. But what has this debate been about? What have been its achievements, limitations, and possibilities? These are our central questions.

For about a century, political science as an organized professional enterprise—intertwined with, but distinct from, history and the other social sciences—has set boundaries, enabled collaboration and cumulative progress, punished outliers, induced a common state of mind, and defined positions characterized by frontiers between conformity and challenge. The diverse elements in political science have formed a single broad family with recognizable features and distinguishing characteristics: a pragmatist orientation to the modern state that makes the analysis of power and choice a constitutive feature; attention to the nature and stability of liberal political regimes and, increasingly, to democracy; and a dedication to study the state and liberal democracy in ways that are transparent and systematic. Political science thus has been a discipline with recognizable content and boundaries, even if there are disputes over their exact nature. The existence of a discipline is both limiting and productive; without it we are adrift, so knowing what it consists of is a pressing matter.[2]

2. As Goodin and Klingeman claim, "the same received disciplinary traditions and practices which so powerfully mould and constrain us are at one and the same time

For better or worse, political science within and across its subfields has operated as an interwoven branch of knowledge. But this unity is a particular kind. Characterized by a wide variety of questions, methods, and borrowings from other disciplines, it is distinct from the crisp methodological individualism that marks postwar neoclassical economics or analytical philosophy. It is also less permissive and open than, say, the fields of English literature or anthropology in recent decades. Marked by an emphasis on liberal politics, a tension-ridden engagement with democracy, and conceptual bearings that rest on a nonmetaphysical view of the modern state, political science is recognizable as a clear-cut scholarly endeavor whose development has been shaped by coherent and delimited intellectual debates. As a discipline, political science may lack a defining paradigm, but not a defining identity. It has used its principal concepts and methodological tool kit to work on a limited number of core problems.[3]

But it is not mainly the enabling and confining institutional terrain of political science on which we focus. American political science has specialized in developing particular kinds of social knowledge. The modifier *American* has to be taken seriously. Clearly, biblical, as well as classical Chinese, Indian, Greek, and Roman texts, not to speak of medieval, early-modern, and modern political thought in the West, present ample evidence that methodical reasoning about political authority hardly has been limited either to the United States or produced under the auspices of the American Political Science Association. Humankind's rich lineage of political thought, however, does not constitute political science in the modern sense (even if its texts and teachings have been incorporated, albeit in

---

powerfully enabling. The framework provided by the structure of a discipline's traditions both focuses research and facilitates collaboration, unintentional as well as intentional. A shared disciplinary framework makes it possible for mere journeymen to stand, productively, on the shoulders of giants. It also makes it possible for giants to build, productively, on the contributions of legions of more ordinarily gifted practitioners. . . . Discipline, academic or otherwise, is thus a classic instance of a useful self-binding mechanism. Subjecting oneself to the discipline of a discipline . . . is conducive to more and indisputably better work, both individually and collectively" (1996, 4–6).

3. By the time the *American Political Science Review* made its first appearance in 1906, the American Political Science Association, though just three years old, had secured a membership of some 400 scholars and practitioners. Ever since, virtually all practicing political scientists have been oriented by this publication and professional association, even when they disliked them. Further, the departmentalized organization of the major research universities and liberal arts colleges and a growing number of journals and research bodies, including the National Science Foundation, have encouraged the development of peer-understood criteria for making judgments about quality, authority, and prestige. As students of professions have observed, these institutions help produce a center of gravity defined by a combination of innovation and elite standard setting (Larson 1977; Friedson 1986; McDonald 1995). In political science, as in other knowledge-based professions, such arrangements never constitute a fully welcoming environment.

mixed fashion, in the discipline). The timing and character of the self-conscious attempt to define a specific, professional domain for the study of politics that took place in the United States at the turn of the last century had a formative impact on the discipline.

Bearing the marks of its origins, the discipline has been infused by prevailing assumptions about political values and about how to conceptualize and study the modern state. Most significant has been the discipline's attention to political liberalism (not in the partisan sense but in the sense of the doctrine fashioned in early modern Europe to guide relations between states and their citizens) joined, over time, by a heightened emphasis on democracy and its requisites. American political science was born in the Progressive Era as a nonpartisan, specialist profession geared to produce new knowledge in order to understand and help sustain liberal political regimes (Kloppenberg 1986), even when their democratic character was curtailed. Its most innovative features concerned the development of a realistic and empirically oriented liberal theory of the state that takes power and choice seriously.[4] The discipline's focus on liberalism has been most pronounced, if also most taken for granted, in its studies of the United States. But this cohering thrust to systematically understand the liberal state also has been important in political theory, which is often marked by a strong contractarian bent; in comparative political studies, where attention to the differences separating liberal, democratic regimes from other forms of rule is manifest; and although to a lesser extent, even in international relations, where concerns about how liberal, democratic regimes can thrive in an anarchic world have been salient.

The character of the founding of political science further helped shape its contours by pushing certain areas of inquiry into the margins. Demarcating itself from history, political science showed a greater concern for current events. To differentiate itself from sociology, it became relatively disinterested in the social bases of political action and inequality. In distinguishing itself from economics, it mainly left issues of political economy to other scholars, at least until recent decades.[5] Further, born at the heyday of

---

4. Ever since, American political studies have been influenced by the liberal political tradition that Louis Hartz (1955) controversially signaled as the hallmark of American political culture and development. His claim that liberalism possesses an ascendant and undisputed place in the United States has not gone unchallenged, of course (Greenstone 1993; R. H. Smith 1997). Arguably, Hartz's claim has been more on the mark for the discipline of American political science (and especially studies of American politics) than for the history of the United States as a political regime.

5. In 1940, Benjamin Lippincott opened a consideration of "the bias of American political science" this way: "Political problems, as Aristotle observed, are at bottom psychological and moral. It is equally true, however, that the political activities of men, as Aristotle also pointed out, are affected in a fundamental way, often crucially, by economic factors. Yet curiously American political scientists, so far as

segregation, political science initially treated race as mainly beyond its ken.[6] Later, each of these areas became contentious inside the discipline, as dissatisfied scholars sought to bring history, social analysis, political economy, and studies of race into its core. Because they have done so with at least a degree of success, many of these issues are now important elements in the discipline.[7]

Because of the broadly shared political tradition of political science, the scope of the discipline has been deep but restricted. Much of its effort has been to understand liberal institutionalism under democratic conditions, while comparing the U.S. experience to those of others and seeking knowledge about the liberal polity in a dangerous global environment. Thus, throughout its organized history, American political science has emphasized a liberal version of the state; that is, it has searched for the identification of rules based on civic and political rights to restrict potentially predatory state actors and to make the modern state permeable to the power and choices of members of society. Democracy, liberalism's first cousin, has been treated by comparison in a more ambivalent fashion, often with distrust by political scientists for the presence of the mass public and of groups thought to be ill informed and ill prepared for citizenship, and thus available for illiberal mobilization inside the liberal polity.[8]

"Liberalism," of course, is a broad term, with many meanings. From its origins in seventeenth-century England, political liberalism has entailed

---

their writings are concerned, have been all but oblivious of this elementary truth" (1940, 125). The work of Charles Beard (1913) and Robert Dahl and Charles Lindblom (1953) are notable exceptions.

6. In the first quarter-century of the *American Political Science Review*, there are three articles that might be considered exceptions to this omission (Rose 1906; Stephenson 1909; Roach 1925).

7. For an argument that they remain more to the periphery than at the heart of the discipline, see Walton, Miller, and McCormick 1995. With these emphases and limits, the discipline's virtues and defects have tended to be mirror images. Working on preferred subjects, political science has made impressive gains, especially when measured against the achievements of its first quarter-century. Its attainments based on an intensity of focus, however, coincide with the costs of a focused set of concerns.

8. This tension is a centerpiece of the scholarship of Robert Dahl, who, more than any other political scientist in the past half-century has placed democracy and its tension-ridden relationship with key features of the liberal political order at the center of his work. The development of "polyarchy" as a central concept by Dahl was geared to grapple with just this tension (see, among other works, Dahl 1956, 1961, 1982, 1989, 1997, and 1998).

The discipline's ambivalence about democracy was crystallized by the fall of Weimar and the flourishing of fascism. For a manifestation of this uncertainty and equivocation, see the discussion of "morbific politics" in the concluding chapter of Truman 1971 [1951].

a small number of core ideas: defense against arbitrary government; nonrevocable rights to free speech, association, assembly, and property for individual citizens who are the irreducible unit of the polity; toleration for diverse beliefs and practices; protections for minorities against the power of the majority; and institutions to enable actors in civil society to represent their interests inside the state. The questions of democracy have appeared as issues about membership and as concerns for the institutions that would represent the majority and constrain the executive. Who will get to participate in the liberal polity? What forms will political participation take? How will rights and duties vary by population category? What types of institutions are best for representing the preferences and interests of the public to the political leadership? What form and organization of institutions are necessary to effectively constrain political leaders so that they cannot stray too far from the interests of civil society? By establishing rules for governance, liberalism and democracy delineate a set of contested boundaries, including those that define where the state meets its citizens, where the individual meets the community, where members of the polity meet outsiders, where sovereignty meets property, and where a liberal state meets a global system of states, empires, and other forms of rule. Each of these charged borders has been subject to controversy; each has defined key subjects for analysis and debate by political scientists.

The discipline has a distinct understanding of the modern state. It has been distinguished both from the relative inattention to the state in the cognate disciplines of economics and sociology and especially from the more unitary, less concrete, and normative continental European approaches to the state, which many of the discipline's founders encountered firsthand in their studies in Germany. By contrast, American political science has pursued a quest to understand the state at a lower, more realistic, and behavioral level of abstraction.

"State" is an awkward concept for Americans, yet, much revised from its European lineage, it has fashioned one of the discipline's main conceptual tools. Its level of abstraction was brought down to make its institutions, relationships, networks, and actors identifiable for systematic studies. Political science strives "to assemble on common ground those persons whose main interests are connected to the scientific study of the organization and functions of the state," Frank Goodnow asserted in his inaugural presidential address to the American Political Science Association, and so it remains (cited in Reeves 1929, 2). For nearly a century, political scientists have been studying, debating, refining, extending, and deploying a state-focused agenda, though often without using the word itself.

From this vantage, we can see why the most familiar periodizations of the history of political science often overlook deep continuities that have made up political science during its first century as an organized discipline. We are familiar with the typical ways in which the history of political science is told. An early legal-formal constitutionally oriented discipline was supplanted by a more scientific, behavioral impulse. In turn, behavioralism was replaced by a more heterogeneous postbehavioral period during which many approaches have emerged, some of which push toward unification of the discipline via a method-specific research program, including, most notably, one based on game theory and strategic interaction.

These histories are both too simple and too complex. Their simplicity results from a tendency to overstate the internal consistency of a given period within and across subfields. Thus, for example, even after the behavioral revolution had transformed American politics, in 1968 the founders of *Comparative Politics* lamented the relative weakness of this scientific impulse in their domain. On the other hand, these historical narratives are too complex because their periodization tends to miss the manner in which American political science has been continuous across epochs, not only with regard to its attention to a liberal political tradition and engagement with democracy but with regard to its realistic approach to the modern state, combining governance with power and choice. Underneath its flux, political science has been uncommonly continuous in its central concepts and substantive themes.

Standard disciplinary histories tend to identify the early period with studies of the state, the middle epoch with studies of power, and the latest era with studies of choice. Though each key concept has known moments when it has been featured more prominently than the others, the discipline constantly has deployed all three at the same time in order to achieve realistic and behavioral understandings of the modern state. Political science has had to come to terms with a capable U.S. national state despite a certain liberal aversion to state capacity. Recurrently, practitioners have done so by borrowing from Europe-centered state theory, which they have modified by lowering the level of abstraction, turning the big questions into mid-level researchable ones. By exploring the linkage between liberalism and democracy, moreover, political science has had to repeatedly confront issues of power. And by focusing on liberal democratic institutions, it has spotlighted the making of political choices as well as structural constraints on choosing. The repertoire of political science thus has been fixed and focused on debates about justice and membership, legitimacy and identity, the capacities of citizens and the qualities of choice, the meaning of power and functioning of state institutions, the requisites for liberal democratic states and their stability, and the relations of liberal democratic states to the international order. A century on, we continue to be challenged by the questions that most vexed our founders.

■ | Beginnings

The genesis of American political science combined a number of key elements. Its founding was an aspect of a wider trend in the history of social knowledge. At least since early modern Europe, scholars have attempted to produce knowledge, as opposed to mere information, by means of systematic thought and investigation organized in cooperative terms.[9] Later, from the 1860s to the second decade of the twentieth century, there were major advances in the West to this structured pursuit of knowledge. In this period, new forums, organized in disciplines and based on claims to rationality and science, were fashioned. The knowledge community divided into distinct specialties, eventually segmenting into the modern disciplines that we now know (Ringer 1969, 1992). At the time, a second split was under way between academic practitioners of the social sciences, located mainly in institutions of higher education, and scholars more directly concerned with the impact of knowledge on public affairs, with homes mainly in governmental bureaus or not-for-profit institutions.

As part of this reorganization of social knowledge, the American discipline of political science was founded in a double act of boundary formation. It demarcated its zone of inquiry both from those of cognate disciplines, especially history, economics, anthropology, and sociology, and from more instrumental, short-term policy studies. Though these borders were permeable to other scholarly disciplines and to policy concerns, political science came to occupy intellectual territory its members understood to be its own. The discipline's singularity and significance were recognized early in its existence.

Substantively, this arena for political inquiry shared an understanding of the modern state as a complex normative and institutional setting with other national efforts, especially German, that also were committed to study modern politics systematically. But there was a key difference. In the United States, the impulse to study the state was associated to some extent with the desire to control and contain the state by civil society. Late-nineteenth- and early-twentieth-century U.S. studies of the state went hand in hand with a concern to tame state power by liberal values and practices, including consent, toleration, representation, and individual rights. Woodrow Wilson's classic 1887 essay on public administration provides a case in point. By the late–nineteenth century, he stressed, the United States had begun to develop a robust national state. Its effectiveness re-

9. In this enlightened spirit, academies for the study of politics were founded, for example, in Paris in 1712 and in Strasbourg in 1757. In tandem with new print technologies, the creation of centralized libraries, the growth of large cities, and improvements to communication, not just the creation but the dissemination of knowledge became possible on the basis of a broadly shared standard of rationality and transparent method (Burke 2000).

quired the application of up-to-date tools of bureaucratic governance, the most-advanced examples of which could be found on Europe's continent. This importation, he cautioned, would both be incomplete and dangerous unless it were accompanied by the elaboration of ideas and institutions governing the exchanges between the state and its citizens guided by the protections promised by the liberal political tradition.

A year earlier, the statement introducing the *Political Science Quarterly*, the country's first modern political science journal, had defined "the domain of political science" similarly in terms of "the dominant position . . . the science of the state is assuming" at a moment when its scope was expanding significantly. "The conception of the state as a mere protective association against external force and internal disorder is antiquated," Munroe Smith wrote on behalf of the journal's Columbia University editors. "The state is everywhere exercising other functions than the protection of person and property and the enforcement of contract. Whether the increasing importance of the state be deplored or applauded," he concluded, "the fact remains that it is rapidly becoming, if it is not already, the central factor of social evolution" (1886, 8). Writing a half-century later, Frederick Watkins noted that "Among contemporary social scientists it is a virtually unquestioned assumption that the state forms the basic concept of political science" (1934, 1).

Wilson observed that the systematic study of the state had not yet taken root in the United States but that it had in Europe, especially in the "strong" states of France and Prussia. Yet these models, he argued, should not be imported into the United States without major modification. "We should not like to have Prussia's history for the sake of having Prussia's administrative skill; and Prussia's particular system of administration would quite suffocate us. It is better," he asserted, "to be untrained and free than to be servile and systematic." In the United States, the modern state had to balance efficient administration with popular sovereignty under a liberal constitution. He thus called for a particularly American science of politics and administration, one that filtered the knowledge and practices of other regimes "through our constitutions, only to put it over a slow fire of criticism and distil away its foreign gases" (1887, 207–19).

Characterized by a focus on formal institutions, public administration, and law, the core of the country's new political science was infused with an emphasis on the elements of political liberalism articulated by Wilson. It focused primarily on the interactions between the national state and civil society, which occurred through processes such as those governing interest representation, public opinion, and elections. The discipline also rested strongly on the premise of the modern state, which implied a global order divided into sovereign states, the separation of sovereignty from property, the demarcation of the state from civil society, a split between the ruler and the institutions of the state, and a bundle of normative justifications for public authority. On this basis, American political science began as a quest to understand and secure liberal regimes against competitors, such as monarchies and illiberal empires.

The relationship between liberalism and democracy has been a charged feature of the discipline from its Progressive Era founding. American liberalism in this period was being tested by the process of democratization. The country's massive demographic changes, occasioned by the entry of new immigrants, the organization of labor, the assertiveness of urban political machines, and the demands of populist social movements, brought new participants into American politics. As the effective size of the polity and expectations for political participation grew, the problem of how to manage liberalism and democracy together came to the fore. These pressures for participation and patterns of mobilization produced important democratizing institutional changes, culminating in votes for women and the direct election of senators that were supported by many members of the young discipline inclined toward social reform. But others were concerned about the potentially disruptive social forces empowered by expanding democracy. About liberalism, the founders of political science were rarely ambivalent. About democracy, they were more so.[10]

As a science rooted in political liberalism and mindful of the demands of democracy, members of the discipline worked from its founding on a small number of recurrent issues. These included an understanding of the features that distinguish liberal democratic regimes from other forms of public authority, whether dictatorial, oligarchic or, later, totalitarian; the manner in which a state can function in a perilous international environment often hostile to liberalism and democracy; and, most prominent of all, the rules governing relations between the state and its citizens in civil society. Thus, early on, the themes of public opinion, voting, interest representation, and legislative behavior—the central institutions of a liberal democratic political order—were placed at the forefront of domestic political studies. But it took some time for this orientation to mesh with the period's scientific aspirations that political science shared with its sister disciplines and to advance the ongoing shift from theology and metaphysics to the social sciences as sources of guidance.

In 1925, the historian Harry Elmer Barnes edited a volume of assessments of the history and prospects of the social sciences. Barnes exhorted that "we must bring [them] up to the same level of development and objectivity which have at present been attained by the natural and applied

---

10. As a consequence, as Terence Ball (1995) has observed, American political scientists have tended to oscillate between a vision of their role, on the one side, as educating the citizenry to overcome their lack of information in order to become thoughtful political participants and, on the other side, as servants of social stability and order in the face of skepticism about the hazards of mass political participation.

sciences" (1925: xv–xvi). The book's essay on political science by Walter James Shepard of Ohio State could not have given Barnes much heart. Shepard wrote to underscore intellectual progress, noting that not only had political science separated successfully from other disciplines, it now also was internally differentiated into distinct subfields. He identified the distinctiveness of political science as a concern to develop both a science and a philosophy of the state. What was different about modern political science, he averred, was that the theoretical aspects of this quest to understand the state had become a specialized branch of the discipline. Now, speculative and deductive political theory was complemented by studies of the state that increasingly were grounded in data, history, and comparison. Treating the scientific method as entailing the systematic accumulation of fact, the elaboration of data into causal sequences, and generalization from these sequences, Shepard concluded that the discipline was making "distinct progress toward a really scientific character" (1925, 427).

Read with the testimony provided by his text, however, this seems more an act of wishful thinking than a warranted conclusion. The discipline's rules of evidence and procedures for inference still were primitive. The discipline remained suspended between its nascent rejection of history (the founding of the American Political Science Association formally represented a breakaway from the American Historical Association), its ambivalence about normative theory, and its still early effort to discover a scientific character. By and large, the work accomplished in the first-quarter of the twentieth century was more descriptive; it tended to involve efforts at the semisystematic factual debunking of abstract philosophical dogma in favor of concrete, empirical descriptions of how politics actually works.

Judged retrospectively, the key element of the early years of political science was not only its nascent devotion to the scientific project but also its pragmatic view of the modern state. The discipline focused on constructing realistic portraits of how, in fact, it was linked to its own citizenry in its quest to secure liberal polities. With good reason, Almond identifies the research program at Chicago between 1920 and 1940, led by such considerable figures as Charles Merriam, Harold Gosnell, Harold Lasswell, Leonard White, and Quincy Wright, as the place where first, major advances were made in developing an empirical social science. This observation is correct; yet it misses some of the earlier pragmatic underpinnings that inspired the Chicago School.

Arthur Bentley's *The Process of Government* (1908), not cited at all in Shepard's or Almond's review essays, is exemplary of a pragmatist effort to establish the study of liberal democracy on a realistic footing; it also was a precursor to more systematic scientific ventures.[11] The key feature of this

---

11. Bentley's early work was methodological, stressing a methodological individualism he soon was to abjure (1895).

often opaque text was a reconceptualization of the state as a process of interaction between the government and its active citizens. Influenced by John Dewey, Bentley shifted our understanding of political conflict from abstract competing theories about the state, which were dominant in late-nineteenth- and twentieth-century works of political science, to clashes between actual groups with specific social interests.[12] Though in later work, Bentley documented vast class inequalities and their impact on political participation, here both the social structure and the economy were ignored in favor of group interactions within a system of transactions (Bentley 1969).[13] This "process of government," the historian of the social sciences Dorothy Ross observed, "was a liberal process" (1991, 334). By placing interest representation within a systematic framework, this practical and scientific approach to the state, focusing on institutions, power, and choice, was created to facilitate a more realistic understanding of the political order.

A significant portion of political science scholarship in the United States, ranging from neo-Marxist and neo-Weberian macroanalysis to institutional scholarship to studies of group formation and political participation, continues to approach the state by focusing on the functioning of liberal democracies, especially the one at home.[14] Ever since Barrington Moore published his major work (1966) on alternative regime pathways, macrohistorically oriented scholars have sought to figure out the causes of these alternative trajectories (e.g., Downing 1992; Ertman 1997; Luebbert 1991). The subjects considered in more microlevel scholarship—including public opinion, voting, political parties, and legislative behavior—likewise are concerned with requisites of liberal political orders. They too are extensions of the manner in which the state was operationalized in the early years of the discipline.

Subsequent work has had deep affinities with the themes and orientation of the discipline's founding period. Even though political scientists often stopped well short of methodical inquiry in the first phase of the discipline's history, it is a mistake to divorce as prescientific this moment from later efforts to create systematic political knowledge. Indeed, the empirical scholarship promoted in Merriam's review of "The Present State of

---

12. Bentley attended Dewey's University of Chicago lectures and later they were frequent correspondents (Ratner and Altman 1964).

13. To our knowledge, he never wrote about race or the exclusionary practices of Jim Crow. This silence about race and racism was quite typical even among progressive liberals.

14. There are important exceptions, of course. An older vein of work focusing on sovereignty and jurisprudence (e.g., Willoughby 1896; Merriam 1900) and more recent research at the intersection of historical sociology dealing with how modern sovereign states supplanted other forms of political rule (e.g., Tilly 1990; Spruyt 1994) consider states without placing their regime type at the center of analysis.

the Study of Politics" (1921, 21–22) and his advocacy of "a new world made over by modern science," in *New Aspects of Politics* (1925, 173–85) were intimately related to more traditional research on sovereignty and the state that had characterized his doctoral thesis on political theory since Rousseau (1900). In both, he sought to understand the requirements for a liberal political order under conditions of uncertainty, including democratic uncertainty and the insecurity generated by international relations. By turning the study of the state in an empirical direction, pre–World War II political scientists bid what they hoped would be a decisive farewell to the rarefied style of late-nineteenth-century German and French studies in favor of a focus on the two-way linkages connecting the state to its citizens.

■ | The Discipline's State

Despite the discipline's methodological plurality, virtually all its practitioners can recognize their participation in this particular kind of probe. Since World War II, political scientists have been concerned to understand the state as a bundle of norms, a site of power, and an ensemble of institutions. In the face of various illiberal alternatives and international dangers, they have tried to grasp the sources of liberal democratic stability and instability. Moreover, as Levi and Kahler point out in their essays that follow, this task has become ever more urgent with the globalization of politics. Within this context, political scientists also have sought to better comprehend the dynamics of political citizenship, participation, choice, and their consequences. They have done so in partially bounded subfields using a wide variety of tools. Notwithstanding, the agenda has continued to be well defined.

States are composed of bundles of norms, not just institutions or patterns of behavior. Hence it is hardly surprising that the character of liberal polities and the relationship between liberalism and democracy have long been staple questions of political theory. How such states can and should provide justice thus has been a core normative question. Justice is important in all political systems but especially in the liberal democratic state. Justice here concerns how to reconcile the individual citizen with the state and how to find guidelines for the distribution of key assets. Principles of justice mediate between the rights possessed by individuals and those held by the state. As Waldron reminds us in his contribution, norms of justice help define the public and private spheres, and they bind the state's ability to use or threaten to use force. Such norms also adjudicate value conflicts among individuals in civil society. In effect, they provide decision rules for how individuals should be treated by others and by the state. They also address issues of membership, cultural and group diversity, and distributions not only of welfare but of cultural assets (e.g., Walzer 1983; Kymlicka 1989; for a skeptical reading, see Barry 2001). Rawls (1971) and Barry (1995), most notably, have elaborated important and controversial decision rules for justice.

Others, of course, have been suspicious of such efforts, viewing them as insufficiently attentive to often incommensurable differences in culture and identity. As Coles observes in this volume, they have worried about the manner in which such principles can perform as hegemonic covers for hierarchy, discipline, and social control (Foucault 1971, 1977). Such thought falls, at times, within the central ambit of liberal theory, as in the case of Isaiah Berlin (1990), who made incommensurability and value pluralism the bedrock of his vision of liberty. Others find footing more in republican and communitarian traditions (Sandel 1982), strong democratic theory (Barber 1988; Barber 1998, I. Shapiro 1996), or feminist thought (e.g., Pateman, 1988; I. Young 1990). As Benhabib's and Gutmann's contributions here underscore, these bodies of work suggest that a key problem for liberal democracy is how to deal with fundamental conflicts of culture and value without resort to nondemocratic procedures and complacency about issues of membership and inclusion.

Two mechanisms that some theorists have explored to move beyond singular, universalistic guidelines are discursive processes and the contraction of claims by the public sphere to a defensible, consensual minimum. The first is associated most vibrantly with Habermas's wager on communicative ethics (Habermas 1971, 1990) and elaborated by theorists of civil society who stress the power of intersubjectivity (Cohen and Arato 1992). Since reason behind a Rawlsian veil of ignorance can neither produce widely agreed deductive principles for deciding among individual and group claims nor unmask the power they may cloak, they argue, conditions must be provided for unfettered communication to allow people to mediate among themselves through discussion and argumentation and to understand the hegemonic discourses in which they take part. Such full and free discussion is necessary if liberal democracy is to be more than a cover for the reproduction of inequality. These approaches also are controversial because they raise concerns about freedom of speech and the limits on free speech in liberal societies (Holmes 1993). The second approach, associated most importantly with recent work by John Rawls (1993) to advance what he calls political liberalism, retracts the scope of the claims made by the public sphere to an arena where an overlapping consensus exists. At issue is whether liberalism in fact can accommodate deep differences, while conforming to its own most cherished principles.

In part, this is a question of power, one of the discipline's main organizing themes. Power, of course, has been much debated (e.g., Dahl 1957, 1961; Bachrach and Baratz 1962; Lukes 1974; Polsby 1980; Gaventa 1980; Baldwin 1989). Simplifying considerably, two conceptions have been paramount. The first and dominant position, grounded in the work of Weber

(1946) who treated power as the ability of one actor to get another to do something the latter would not otherwise do, with some persons' thus causing the action of others to conform to their preferences, was announced as a core feature of political science by Watkins (1934) and famously elaborated by his student Robert Dahl (1957). A second, more critical perspective, owing more to Marx than Weber, reminds us that liberal politics can be a cover for pervasive inequality and privilege. A focus on overt conflict and behavioral causality can neglect power as agenda setting and as shaping worldviews and preferences, even language itself (e.g., Schattschneider 1965; Bachrach and Baratz 1962; Lukes 1974; Gramsci 1973; Foucault 1971, 1977). Because such nonovert forms of influence often do not have behavioral correlates, they pose dilemmas for empirical research.

Two consequences follow from this second conception of power. If power is invoked through language and ideas, then a thorough understanding of the connotations and limitations built into the discourse of the time is important for understanding how power is being exerted (Connolly 1969). Interpretations of language and the meanings of action thus are fundamental to power analysis. For this reason, constructivists and other proponents of this view believe that normal political science often is superficial. Being embedded within liberal values, many political scientists, they claim, rarely question the assumptions or language used by the actors they study. Instead, such critics argue, scholars should realize that it is less important to understand what voters think or prefer than how dominant structures and agents have shaped why they do so.[15] Scholarship in this vein is a powerful source of critique.

Gramscian ideas of hegemony often are deployed by critical theorists and constructivists (e.g., Honig 1993; Wendt 1999; R. Cox 1983). They view elites who rule, whether capitalists, men, or members of other dominant groups, as a unitary hegemonic bloc which devises and gains from enduring structures that dominate the lives of others, even shaping their very desires. Their conception of power is both subtle and blunt—subtle in that the very structures of everyday life manipulate often unconsciously, blunt in that power tends to run mainly in one direction (for a counterflow, see Scott 1976, 1990). Since, according to them, power under conditions of hegemony cannot be grasped by direct methods of observation, special methods, including deconstruction, are deployed to discern the nature of power. Such methods often, however, raise concerns about the problems of counterfactuals and the possibility of falsification.

By contrast, the more pervasive liberal conception is less bluntly encompassing and in some respects more subtle. Here, individuals are central; structures of power ultimately are traced back to individual actions. So, too, are the formal institutions and less formal rules within which they

---

15. Echoing these themes, Lindblom finds that both scholars and citizens often are impaired (1990, 1997, 267–68).

connect to each other and come to decisions. Individuals, in this approach, form and know their own desires and beliefs; false consciousness is an elusive mystification. Language can be important from this standpoint, as studies of rhetoric (e.g., Riker 1986), propaganda, and the framing of issues make clear. But as it usually is not seen as a structure of power in itself, language, especially language used by analysts themselves, can be utilized as a neutral medium of communication. This conception of power also is more subtle in its acknowledgment of mutual influence. In an environment characterized by complex social and political relations, unidirectional power relations are unlikely. Models of strategic interaction stress this interaction. When individuals cannot achieve their goals without the help or at least acquiescence of others, they are mutually bound up, even if unequally. To change the behavior of others one must alter one's own, thus allowing the other to have influence, a pattern at work in the issuing of threats and promises (Schelling 1960; Jervis 1970; Baldwin 1989). This recognition has led to counterintuitive conclusions about how to exercise power, such as those informing nuclear deterrence theory where leaving oneself vulnerable to destruction can be the best way to ensure that one stays secure.

Both approaches to power are closely linked to studies of choice that confront many of the same issues. The theme of individual choice has reappeared throughout the history of the discipline, a subject expanded on for different subfields in this volume by Calvert, Weingast, and Powell. Political science finds itself sitting uneasily between economics, where choice under constraint is paramount, and sociology and anthropology, where constraint by limiting structures or culture is fundamental. The liberal democratic vision of the state intersects this tension. For individuals to matter, there must be some capacity for choice. Voting and elections are meaningful only if some options are available.

With regard to choice, political science has been characterized both by disagreement and a division of labor. Some colleagues emphasize the structural restrictions under which any choice occurs, a theme that developed for different parts of the discipline by Thelen, Pierson and Skocpol, and Orren and Skowronek in their essays that follow. "Instead of reducing behavior to individual decision-making," Charles Tilly counsels, "social scientists urgently need to study the relational constraints within which all individual action takes place" (1998a, 34). For both historical institutionalists and constructivists, these circumstances are paramount and derive from history. Mechanisms by which the past imposes itself on the present, including path dependence (Pierson 2000a), and the weight of culture and language shape and narrow choices open for individuals. Sharing much with sociologists, historians, and anthropologists, these political scientists emphasize the constraints on behavior that institutions, among other structures, impose (e.g., Katzenstein 1996a; Hall 1986; Katznelson 1981).

Another part of the discipline places these confining structures in the background and emphasizes acts of choice. This orientation treats institutions as part of the choice set of individuals; institutions can and should be endogenized as they are not separate from individuals and their behavior. Choosing institutions goes hand in hand with making choices under particular institutional rules. Constrained choice is the only type of choice ever available, as economists are well aware. So, as Risse points out in his contribution, there is a bond between the two schools, even if it is not often recognized, just as there are potentially unrealized fruitful possibilities in encounters between the two main views of power.

The debate over choice also involves methodology. Rational-choice theory is a contested method in the discipline. It provides a core for economics, even though many economists feel "a chafing dissatisfaction with the standard neoclassical paradigm of economic analysis" (Alt, Levi, and Ostrom 1999, xv). But agreement on methods does not integrate political science as a discipline. Rather, the introduction of new methods often has been not only a source of innovation but also a cause of anxiety throughout the history of the discipline, as the essays by Cameron and Morton, and Green and Gerber in the concluding section of this book suggest. This, in fact, is one key reason why it makes little sense to periodize the history of political science by dominant scientific techniques. Indeed, as Laitin argues in his paper, in recent years there has been a growing effort to blend research methods and use their respective strengths to triangulate on the evidence.

For some colleagues, power or choice, rather than state, liberalism, or democracy, are the discipline's master concepts. They see political science as the study of "the organization of power" (Holden 2000, 3; earlier see Lasswell and Kaplan 1950) or as a set of strategic interactions producing equilibria under determinate historical conditions (e.g., Bates, Greif, Levi, Rosenthal, and Weingast 1998). But important as power and choice have been as key concepts in political analysis, they define only two of the entry points to the discipline's quest to understand politics in the modern state. The discipline's nonmetaphysical attention to the state has primarily manifested itself not with power or choice alone but with power and choice in tandem with a concern for the functioning of political institutions. The state is not studied as such but from different vantages to discern the operation of its distinct parts.

The liberal democratic state has been a recurring source of deep anxiety, a theme that Shapiro takes up in his essay on democratic theory in this volume. The fall of the Weimar Republic and, more broadly, the collapse of many other constitutional democracies with the rise of fascism and bolshevism in the interwar period alerted the discipline to the terrible consequences of unstable democracies. Later, Arrow's Impossibility Theorem (1963 [1951]), a key instance of incisive analytical work on the core problems of liberal regimes, set forth the theoretical challenge in stark terms. Instability is an immanent feature of liberal democracy. Under broad conditions, majority rule leads to the cycling of coalitions and policy; only nondemocratic practices can alleviate this deep tendency, convoking a trade-off between stability and democracy.

Determining sources of instability and ungovernability in liberal democratic institutions has been a major area of research for decades. Where some see individual voters as the problem for stable democracy, others fault the mechanisms that aggregate their preferences (e.g., Eckstein 1966). A state is a composite of institutions that may not fit well together since each was designed for a distinct task or problem. For liberal democratic states, this web is even more complex since it also requires institutions to ensure accountability and enforce limits on actors. It must provide security and justice as well as representation and restraint. The basic tasks of the state as Leviathan can collide with the elementary demands of a liberal democratic polity. The historical failure of countries to follow the relatively peaceful path to democracy charted by England defines a puzzle that still animates the discipline (e.g., Bendix 1977; Almond, Flanagan, and Mundt 1973). Interestingly, recent work by Przeworski and Limongi (1993) and Barro (1997) broadly confirms, albeit with variation in emphasis, the early studies of Moore (1966) and Lipset (1959, 1994), among others, finding that democracy is premised on certain socioeconomic requisites. These claims, too, link the state to its civil society in complex ways, as Kohli elaborates in his essay here.

The functioning of state institutions has defined a major vein of research throughout the history of the discipline, as a number of the essays in this book make clear. Institutions now are understood to provide one solution to Arrow's problem. They induce policy stability but do not overcome his concern for the loss of democracy (e.g., Shepsle 1979; Austen-Smith and Banks 1999). Recent literature on institutions shows exactly how they possess nondemocratic mechanisms that can privilege certain actors and move outcomes away from the preferences of median voters (e.g., Romer and Rosenthal 1978, 1979; Baron and Ferejohn 1989a, b; Ferejohn and Shipan 1990). This new institutionalist literature reminds us that political science always has been concerned with institutions. The study of electoral rules, for example, has been a long-standing feature of the discipline. From Duverger (1959) to Rogowski (1987b) and Cox (1997), political scientists have been theorizing about the impact produced by different ways of translating votes into office holding. Greater proportionality has a variety of consequences for democracy: more parties, more fine tuned representation of interests, more coalition governments, less policy movement, and perhaps more instability. Against these must be weighed the costs and benefits of more majoritarian systems (winner take all) that allow short-term stability within governments but longer-term instability as governments and their policies change. The stable democracies of Britain and the United States for years were our only models, and many scholars accepted their lessons. But more recent research into other stable systems has shown that this instruction is too simple. Some forms of proportionality combined with other institutions, such as corporatism, also have been consistent with representative and stable liberal democracies (Lijphart 1968, 1977; Linz and Stepan 1978; Katzenstein 1985; Rogowski 1987b).

Party systems as institutions of liberal democracy essential for connecting voters and politicians have been another area of persistent attention, one that Fiorina addresses in his contribution here. Related to the debate over electoral rules, disputation over the functioning of two-party and multiparty systems, not to mention attention to one-party systems, is long standing, as recent retrospectives on the American Political Science Association's 1950 report "Toward a More Responsible Two-Party System" and V. O. Key's landmark *Southern Politics in State and Nation* (1949) make evident. The happy conclusion initially drawn from the U.S. and British cases was in favor of two-party democracy. This finding was muddied by Downs's prediction (1957) that such two-party stability can be achieved only with a huge cost in terms of choice. Convergence to the median position by both parties reduces substantive choice even as it underscores liberal democracy's central principle of rule by the majority. Since Downs's seminal work, we have learned much more about party systems and their implications for the success of liberal democracy (e.g., Sartori 1976; Lijphart 1977; Powell 1982; Cox 1987; Aldrich 1995).

The executive branch of government also has been increasingly attended as it has absorbed responsibilities for more, and more complex, policymaking and policy implementation. Presidential and parliamentary (as well as mixed) systems define and determine the executive differently. In many ways the executive is a simpler branch in presidential systems; winning a national election gives the leader and his party control over the presidential system. For parliamentary systems, where the executive comes from the legislature, forming a government is a central issue. When the U.S. and British examples dominated discussion, this issue did not seem very pressing. But over time, the revival of liberal constitutional regimes, after the defeat of fascism and Nazism in Europe and, later, with the collapse of communism, raised this question anew. Early work predicting minimum winning coalitions and minimally winning connected coalitions (e.g., Riker 1962; Axelrod 1970) has grown increasingly sophisticated and empirical as scholars struggle with the failure of these predictions (Strom 1990). The game of government formation has been linked backward to parties' electoral strategies and forward to their policy preferences, improving our understanding of actual outcomes (e.g., Warwick 1994; Laver and Shepsle 1996; Baron 1991, 1993).

Legislatures also have garnered an enormous amount of fruitful attention, especially in American politics where Congress, whose powers are unusually enhanced by the country's separation of powers, arguably is the center of the Constitution (Wilson 1956 [1885]). Representation, of course, is the core concept of political liberalism; it lies at the heart of

Locke's *Second Treatise* (1980 [1689]) and is the core element of government by consent. By representing the preferences and interests of members of civil society, legislatures are the key institution for liberal democracy. A central puzzle, notwithstanding, is which of their activities—including legislation, legitimation, oversight, and constraint of the executive, as well as the representation of voters' preferences—enhance chances for the persistence and success of such polities. For an extended period, Congress provided the principal model, since other parliaments could not legislate or self-organize in the American manner (Polsby 1968).

As Gamm and Huber show in this volume, recent scholarship has reacted against this understanding, showing that legislatures, even if not American in organization and style, can influence policy and the executive through other mechanisms (e.g., Huber 1996a; Tsebelis 1994, 1995). Still, studies of Congress continue to dominate legislative studies. Recent work has reopened two areas of particular interest: the ability of the legislature to constrain the executive and the functions of committees. These contributions, too, place the preservation and enhancement of liberal democracy at their center. This normative value is enhanced when the legislature is able through anticipated reaction to constrain the executive and make better policy choices in a complex environment because of the informational role of its committees (e.g., Epstein and O'Halloran 1999; Krehbiel 1991, 1998).

The attention that political scientists have paid to the state includes a long-standing concern with how different institutions interact. Indeed, strategic interaction among the institutions of democracies has been a key concern from the discipline's start; the long-standing notion of checks and balances involves such interaction. How should these relations be constructed to be consistent with liberal principles that put a premium on limiting the power of rulers? Long a key concern, the topic of balance of power between executive and legislative branches today is being examined more thoroughly than in the past. In presidential systems where the executive and legislature are independently elected, the existence and character of the game defining the relations between the two branches are most apparent. Still, such strategic interaction occurs in all liberal democratic political settings as actors within the institutions vie for influence over policy. Thus both in American and comparative politics, scholars have sought to flesh out the games that arise from this interaction. Recent models and data reveal subtle ways in which legislatures delegate to the executive yet maintain control through threats to unseat governments or revoke its delegation and, in turn, ways executives use their threats of the veto or decree power to move legislatures in their preferred direction (e.g., Shugart and Carey 1992; Huber 1996a, b; Epstein and O'Halloran 1999; Cameron 2000). Some work also has extended this approach to the study of judicial systems.

This literature on institutional interaction also has returned to the key theme of gridlock that so obsessed analysts of Weimar's fall (Holborn 1982). Divided government, with the executive and median legislator in different political parties, promotes checks and balances and policy moderation but can be a recipe for policy immobility, making leaders unable to respond to a changed environment (for a skeptical view see Mayhew 1991). Moving beyond divided government, some scholars have explored the general conditions under which the strategic interaction among various institutions of democracy can lead to policy gridlock (Tsebelis 1995; Krehbiel 1998). Such policy immobility paradoxically can be a central source of democratic instability and failure. Institutions thus help solve the Arrovian problem of cycling majorities and instability in democracies but, in turn, raise serious concerns about the ability of such states to respond to changing conditions due to their status quo biases.

The question of governability under democratic conditions has been connected for decades to puzzles about the rational qualities of mass publics and their readiness for political participation. Reaching back to the work of Walter Lippmann (1922) and Lindsay Rogers (1949), one branch of research has treated the central problem of liberal regimes as residing with its citizens rather than with its rulers or rules. "Democracy is of a massive nature. Therefore it cannot function without masses," Roberto Michels (1927, 762) wrote in an early issue of the *American Political Science Review*. The beliefs, opinions, and ultimately the behavior of individual citizens either is suspect or is treated as consistent with democracy only under some conditions of political culture or civic life. The latter theme has been especially important in comparative politics, where important scholarship has focused on the correlates of democratic behavior and civic culture (Almond and Verba 1963, among others) and on the role of associations in producing the development of trust among citizens (Tocqueville 1969 [1832] to Putnam 1993a, 2000). In the American politics subfield, a robust literature on public opinion has been very important, if also subject to controversy. From Lazersfeld et al. (1944) and Campbell, Converse, Miller, and Stokes (1960) to Popkin (1991), Page and Shapiro (1992), and Zaller (1992), scholars have asked whether citizens have knowledgeable opinions about politics and whether these form a coherent (enough) system of beliefs either to permit democratic control of elites or informed participation in the public arena.

This search for, and these signs of, relatively knowledgeable and consistent citizens has also extended to voting, a theme Schlozman addresses in her essay in this volume. Together with public opinion, this work has broad implications for understanding the relationship between states and liberal values. Our knowledge about and methods for studying voters have developed greatly over time. This interest in public opinion, beliefs, and behavior is founded on a vision of the state where individual citizens, especially citizens as voters, provide the foundation for popular sovereignty. The possibility of choice by voters and the circumstances guiding that choice thus are of central importance to a liberal society (Lazarsfeld, Berelson, and Gaudet 1944; Campbell, Converse, Miller, and Stokes 1960; Nie, Verba, and Petrocik 1976). Our understanding of that public has expanded as it has come to include more diverse individuals, themes that Burns, and Dawson and Cohen take up here in their essays, respectively on gender and on race.

The public's interaction with the state also occurs in collective, not just individual, forms. Interest groups are an important element of liberal democracy, but they too pose vexing issues. Collective action by groups pursuing their interests often is seen as beneficial; how otherwise would the state know the concerns of its citizens or the intensity of their preferences? On the other hand, such groups pose grave challenges. The optimistic view of groups suggests that if all interests could form and press their demands, political leaders would know well the desires of the public (Truman 1971 [1951]). The literature on logrolling, however, has been less sanguine. If all groups act collectively in defense of their interests, a state might end up with policies different from those any one group desires and much worse than otherwise, as the Smoot-Hawley tariff demonstrated (Schattschneider 1935). Such pessimism appeared early in the discipline and was famously reinforced by Mancur Olson's demonstration (1965) that not all groups could or would act collectively; only certain privileged ones would. Worse yet, these likely would be groups that could reap highly concentrated benefits from their desired policies at the expense of the public interest. Democratic politics look very different in the presence of such active lobbies representing only parts of the public (Lowi 1964). Recently this debate has continued over the benefits given by the signaling and informational aspects of interest groups as compared to their corrosive impact on the representation of the public interest in policymaking (e.g., Chubb 1983; Walker 1991; Austen-Smith and Wright 1992, 1994; Kollman 1998).

If political science has been concerned intensely to understand the impact of institutional design and democratic participation on the persistence of liberal regimes, it also has had to consider international relations where the state appears as a nakedly coercive institution. A paradox is at work in the international relations subfield. The main tradition in international relations does not privilege the liberal democratic state, as the essay in this volume by Walt shows. Rather, the state often is conceived as a unitary dictator.[16] The realist tradition, however, has been concerned with how liberal states fare in an anarchic international system; from Morgen-

16. From one perspective, this account is consistent with key features of the history of liberal regimes that have conferred rights on members but, whether in geopolitics or in the conquest of overseas empires and their treatment of native peoples, have been prepared to act in a more severe manner.

thau (1948) to Kissinger (1957) and Waltz (1959, 1979), liberal democratic states have been viewed as dubiously able to perform the activities necessary to assure their survival in a brutal international environment. How can these states counter their enemies as effectively as illiberal regimes free from the constraints of representation and rights? In part, answers to this have focused on the role of international institutions in defusing the anarchic elements of the international system (e.g., Krasner 1983; Keohane 1984; Martin and Simmons 1998).

Both policy instability and immobility in liberal democracies have been causes for concern in understanding states' foreign policy responses. Allison's work (1971) on bureaucratic politics, for example, focused attention on the inner workings of democratic institutions, showing that competition among bureaucrats significantly affected foreign policies. Others have brought executive-legislative interaction into the picture. Trying to use models of the state from the American and comparative fields, they have shown that the strategic interaction between democratic institutions need not lead to foreign policy failure. The interaction might make foreign policy more difficult to conduct, but it might also give the democratic state an advantage in international bargaining (e.g., Fearon 1994a; Milner 1997; Milner and Rosendorff 1997; L. Martin 2000; Schultz 2001).

Most important, the literature on the democratic peace has recently had a profound impact, as Morrow argues here. Reversing the realist view of liberal states as hopeless in foreign affairs, this literature has argued that they may be far more able to conduct peaceful foreign policy and cooperative relations with other states than other regime types (e.g., Doyle 1986b; Russett 1993; Bueno de Mesquita, Morrow, Siverson, and Smith 1999). The complex internal workings of democracies actually enable them to function better in the international environment. This optimistic view is not new (Wilson 1919), but it certainly never before has captured a dominant position in international relations.

Concern with the state's relationship to citizens in civil society and to other states is complemented, of course, by an interest in the state's relationship to the economy, a theme that Geddes's contribution addresses in relation to developing countries. Here, political science has a checkered record, both attentive and neglectful. Many scholars have taken up Marx's challenge to consider the association linking capitalism, liberalism, and democracy (Schumpeter 1942; Polanyi 1944; Hayek 1994 [1944]). Some think capitalism threatens democracy. Markets may be efficient but they also produce very divergent outcomes for different individuals and groups. Yawning inequalities of wealth and market distributions can translate directly into political power (or its absence), thus threatening the robustness and meaning of majority rule. Moreover, markets left to their own devices may produce so much insecurity that individuals can become willing to sacrifice liberal rights and democratic regimes on behalf of security and more equal resources (e.g., Polanyi 1944; Katznelson 1996). If liberal democracy is to thrive or in some instances even survive, active state intervention to regulate markets and reshape their patterns of distribution becomes imperative. This requirement is the basis, of course, for the vast literature on modern welfare states (e.g., Esping-Andersen 1992; Flora and Heidenheimer 1981). Reciprocally, democracy also may threaten market-based economies. Demands for redistribution and rent seeking by interest groups can be particularly potent in democracies and thus erode the efficient operation of markets. The requirements for democracy and well-functioning markets, especially in a highly globalized environment, may pose even more very difficult issues (e.g., Garrett 1998b; Rodrik 1997).

Other scholars have underscored how liberal democracy and capitalism may be mutually supportive (Friedman 1963; Lindblom 1977). Liberalism, especially its impulse to secure private property rights and ground political rights in property ownership, may be the only foundation for the growth of capitalism. As Polanyi (1944), North and Weingast (1989), and others have argued, the operation of markets depends crucially on the political system—a point recognized as well in international political economy (e.g., Gilpin 1987). Economic growth is most likely to be robust where governments ensure private property rights and equalize social and private returns. Much current research shows that the rule of law is essential for economic prosperity (Barro 1997; Haldenius 1992). Capitalism thus is considered by some to be a bulwark for democracy (e.g., Hayek 1994 [1944]; Friedman 1963). Without private property and markets, citizens are left to the economic prey of the state. Without their own means of economic support, how can individuals resist the encroachments of the state, let alone control its behavior? As Lindblom (1977) points out in his study of the way the advantages of business can bias a political system, historically there have been no democracies without market-based economies, though the degree of market freedom has varied under liberal democratic auspices.

Issues of political economy thus have been important to the quest by political science to come to terms with the modern state in a realistic fashion. However, political economy has played less of a role in the history of the discipline than the other subjects surveyed here. Indeed, much of the theory and research in this area has been ceded to economists, leaving political scientists to focus rather more on the core zone of liberal politics where the state meets civil society. Currently, though, there is growing interaction between economists and political scientists who study political economy, in part as a result of a growing affinity of research methods, as the essays by Frieden and Martin, and Alt in this volume demonstrate. What political scientists bring to these collaborations is their long-standing concern with the state and problems of liberal democracy.

▪ | State of the Discipline: An Afterword

The state of the discipline? Contested and methodologically diverse, polit-ical science nonetheless remains focused, as it has for a century, on a particular understanding of how to study the modern state and liberal democracy. Though there have been shifts, of course, in emphasis and method, attempts to periodize the discipline's history mislead if not grounded in these powerful continuities delineating the discipline. More-over, though political science has not produced fixed findings in the strong sense of the term (Lindblom 1990), its intellectual debates have been cu-mulative and its disputations have grown more textured, more variegated, and in many respects, though not all, more capable over time.

The essays in this book, of course, record a discipline almost unrecog-nizable to its founders in method, range of inquiry, and achievement. Political theory has surmounted the descriptive history of ideas that domi-nated in the early–twentieth century. Comparative political studies have vastly expanded in scope beyond an institutional record of what foreign governments do. Americanists, deploying fresh systematic tools, have parsed the country's institutions and behavior with great analytical detail. Students of international relations have far more thoroughly grasped the tensions that confront liberal democracies in a dangerous and predatory world as they engage in trade, finance, diplomacy, and war.

Still, Goodnow, Beard, Bentley, Merriam, and the other creators of modern political science would know that they belong to this family of pragmatic, institutional, and realistic inquiries. They, too, wished to under-stand the state, and especially the liberal state, in an age of demo-cratization and globalization, to assay liberal democracy via the study of institutions and approaches to justice, to treat as privileged the study of participation and behavior by citizens in these regimes, and to improve the tools they possessed to advance the scientific study of politics. They would not have been taken aback by the character or the content of the reviews of the discipline present in this book. As practicing political scientists, we continue to carry our history with us.

This observation is no mere antiquarianism. If we focus mainly on va-riety, methodological differences, or the massive changes that have charac-terized this history of the discipline rather than these continuities, we will fail to see both its cumulative attainments and the costs, as well as the gains, that have attended the discipline's bounded set of inquiries. If the state of the discipline is good and advancing, it also still must be judged as wanting to the extent to which key vexing questions—among others, ques-tions of the robustness of democracy, the inclusiveness of citizenship, the powers of ascription and illiberalism, the varieties of legitimate political identities, the deep incommensurabilities of values and cultures, the dark side of human psychology and propensity for cruelty and violence, and the illusion that all the pieces of the liberal puzzle can neatly line up to-gether—are left unresolved.

Political science may have a particularly notable role to play in sharp-ening understandings of its landmark themes of state, democracy, justice, and participation at this historical moment. Writing about the character of global political life at the start of the twenty-first century, Geuss, a political theorist who has worked on both sides of the Atlantic, observes that there has been convergence on "a single ideal model" of "the democratic liberal state with a capitalist economy, and a commitment to a set of human rights for its citizens . . . with five distinct elements here—liberalism, democracy, the state, capitalist economy, the doctrine of human rights." He notes fur-ther that "in much contemporary thinking about politics it is tacitly as-sumed that these five items form a more or less natural, or at any rate minimally consistent and practically coherent, set" (2001, 3). As an organ-ized discipline, political science has been ahead of its time in that it has taken this group of traits and institutions as its domain for some eleven decades. No one who apprehends the field can confidently conclude that these dimensions form a stable constellation neatly or automatically. If the discipline is to successfully marshal its full potential, it must be done with an inquiring spirit that reckons with the relationship among these values and concepts in a diverse and increasingly insecure global environment.

Political Science:
The State of the Discipline

1

The State in
an Era of
Globalization

How might we best conceive of the state given its transformations over time and the pressures that shape it? The papers that consider these questions highlight such internal challenges for states as ethnic and regional conflict and such external conundrums as the anarchic state system and international conflict, and they underscore the powerful and global economic forces with which states have to contend.

This part opens with Margaret Levi's reflections on "The State of the Study of the State." Addressing definitional questions, she considers what we know about what the state does and can do and about the relationships among the institutions of state, government, and market. She then turns to analytic and methodological issues. Throughout, she addresses normative questions concerning the role states should play in the economy and polity, raising problems of democratic accountability. Nettl (1968) rightly observed that the concept "state" within the social sciences goes in and out of fashion due to the combination of problems encountered in using this bulky term in rigorous analysis and the extent to which the state seems to be a primary factor in what concerns the contemporary world. For Levi, a crucial current problem lies in the failure of scholars to develop adequate methodologies and theories of stateness. Despite a massive literature on the state developed over the course of centuries, she believes state theory to be still in its infancy. By combining an interdisciplinary perspective with adequate attention to the variations and specificities of state actions and effects, there is hope, however, that we can untangle the complex relationships within states and among states, governments, and civil societies.

Miles Kahler's "The State of the State in World Politics" argues that after decades of axiomatic importance in international relations, the somnolent theoretical world of the state has come to life. New research is diverse, but its agendas share an initial assumption that the state is a variable, not a constant in world politics. Research in political science has emphasized globalization as a source of new political and sectoral coalitions or as a constraint on government policies. Investigations of its effects on the state, Kahler underscores, have been hampered by concentration on state capabilities as the only factor of interest. Three strategies promise a more measured and accurate portrait: modeling the preferences of nonstate actors and their bargaining with the state, explaining the migration of governance functions from the national state to other public and private sites, and charting the advantages of particular institutional designs in a globalized environment.

A second research agenda on unit variation in international relations regards the modern nation-state as only one, temporarily successful, contender amid numerous competitors over the course of history. Kahler thus explores antecedent and contemporary alternatives to the sovereign, territorial nation-state. He discusses the significance of variations in the relationships linking state and nation and assesses how the emergence of particular types of units and their disappearance influence system outcomes. Finally, he shows how institutional analysis can provide means for defining and measuring variation in the characteristics of states or other units in world politics. These research agendas require theoretically informed taxonomies, a rejection of any sharp distinction between domestic and international concerns, and careful attention to the environments surrounding states and their influences on variation among states.

In "State, Society, and Development," Atul Kohli examines how varying patterns of state authority emerge in developing countries and how state authority is in turn used to push these countries along a variety of developmental pathways. These questions are of enduring interest to scholars of comparative political development. While these concerns can be addressed from multiple theoretical standpoints, he argues that over the last quarter-century, the most important research has been informed by what he labels a state-society perspective. Following a summary of the key elements of this neo-Weberian perspective, the essay reviews research in this tradition, exploring two main themes: the emergence of a variety of authority structures (revolutionary, authoritarian, and democratic regimes, as well as failed states) in the context of development and the impact of state structures and actions on such outcomes as good governance, economic growth, and redistribution. The essay takes into account some of the main criticisms of this research tradition by culturalists and rational-choice scholars, maintaining that when judged against such criteria as the capacity to generate cumulative and generalizable knowledge, to connect the deep knowledge of area specialization to social and political theory and analysis, and to attract the interest of a range of risk-taking senior and emerging scholars, the state-society perspective represents a robust research tradition in the study of comparative political development.

Jeffry Frieden and Lisa Martin review developments in a part of international relations in "International Political Economy: Global and Domestic Interactions." They observe that this relatively new field has moved from a stage of paradigmatic conflict to a more consensual approach to analysis. The biggest challenge facing the field is in understanding the simultaneous interaction of domestic and international factors as they determine foreign economic policies and international economic outcomes. Rigorous work on domestic-international interaction now is possible because it can build on well-established intellectual building blocks at the domestic and international levels. Frieden and Martin develop this argument by presenting an analytical organization of major work in international political economy and illustrate it with empirical applications drawn from international trade, monetary relations, and other issue areas. Though strong frameworks for analysis have been developed, they conclude by averring that the scope for applying them and extending them to new issues remains considerable.

James Alt considers "Comparative Political Economy: Credibility, Accountability, and Institutions." Where multilateral sanctions provide the only enforcement incentives for accountability, cooperation and coordination problems can arise and institutions can help solve them. In the literature, such institutions bestow a large role on the credibility of monetary policy and on centralization and transparency in fiscal policy. Progress in understanding monetary policy has come from analyzing strategic interactions among central banks, labor market agents, and partisan governments and legislatures. Prominent among explanations of variations in fiscal scale and balance are common pool problems and the interaction of electoral and budget process institutions. A review of this vast literature demonstrates the importance of relating policy outcomes not only to economic fundamentals but also to the ideological and redistributive goals of political parties and interest groups and the institutional contexts in which policy is made.

James Morrow's "International Conflict: Assessing the Democratic Peace and Offense-Defense Theory" examines another area of international politics in which states are fundamentally challenged by external forces. He claims that international relations was characterized by four main movements during the decade of the 1990s. First, game theory attracted attention as a way to study the microfoundations of the field. Second, interest in statistical methods revived both in international political economy and conflict. Third, the constructivist movement challenged the questions, approaches, and results of the mainstream. Fourth, the end of the cold war led to new problems for study and a shift in focus away from great power rivalry. The first three of these trends created methodological ferment, which occurred with less acrimony than in past decades. However, he observes, the field has not reconciled this ferment into a commonly accepted approach for using these methods. Seeking to advance such a development, the essay reviews progress in the game theoretic microfoundations of conflict, the democratic peace, and offense-defense theory. Each has predominantly used one of three methods: formal models, large-*n* statistical studies, and case studies, respectively. Morrow seeks to show how the three methods can be combined fruitfully, a task none of these areas has yet achieved.

Closing the section is Stephen Walt's essay on "The Enduring Relevance of the Realist Tradition." Though widely criticized, he avers, the realist tradition has yet to be supplanted by an alternative perspective with similar range or equal explanatory power. Although critics have been quick to announce the obsolescence of realist theory in the wake of the cold war, the real world seems to have paid scant attention to such academic obituaries. Major powers remain acutely sensitive to the distribution of power, are wary of developments that might leave them vulnerable, and still strive to enhance their position at the expense of potential rivals. Although states do cooperate in a variety of ways, military force remains a depressingly constant feature of international political life. As events in the Balkans, Central Africa, South Asia, and elsewhere remind us, insecurity and the struggle for survival are still important elements of the human condition. Substantively, the essay reviews the main developments in the realist tradition since the publication of Kenneth Waltz's *Theory of International Politics* in 1979, showing how recent efforts have helped refine the basic logic of the theory, broadened its range of applications, and creatively explored its implications for the future.

Margaret Levi

The State of the Study of the State

The concept of state is not much in vogue in the social sciences right now. Yet it retains a skeletal, ghostly existence largely because, for all the changes in emphasis and interest of research, the thing exists and no amount of conceptual restructuring can dissolve it.

(Nettl 1968, 55a)

Nettl's words, published more than thirty years ago, resonate today. After a period of scholarly emphasis on theories of the state, social scientific interest in the state seems to have taken a back seat to institutions, on the one hand, and social capital, on the other. Consideration of the state as a conceptual variable ebbs and flows; there are good reasons for claiming that the state is useless as a concept and equally well founded resistance to shelving it. We know that the nation-state is a problematic notion, given the number of nations without states and the number of states without nations. We know that the continental European model of the state has limited descriptive or theoretical usefulness in understanding Britain, the Americas, or the antipodes, let alone the developing world. We have found the efforts to measure the degree of stateness far from satisfactory. Even so, "The State" captures the combination of centralized, far-reaching coercion with the complex of staff, governmental institutions, and nongovernmental actors and agencies in a way that nothing else seems to.

A state, whether it arises out of or is imposed on civil society, is at the core of modern Western political theory à la Bodin and Hobbes, and it is a bedrock of comparative political and sociological analysis à la Marx and Weber. The existence within a given territory of a state apparatus that concentrates violence, coordinates regulation, and possesses a government able to make and implement public policies has long been considered a key component of economic and political development. So, why has it proved so difficult to use the concept of the state in analysis?

There are several reasons, and they have more to do with the methodology of understanding the state than with the applicability of the concept.

First, the state is a composite of factors, not a single variable. Sometimes, only one or a subset of those factors, for example, the ruler or the ruling class or the bureaucracy, is doing the crucial explanatory work. Good analysis requires differentiating among the features of the state in order to assess their relative importance; the state becomes less than the sum of its parts. Second, the state is an abstraction, but key decisions are made by state personnel or rulers not by the state per se. Once again, the analysis focuses on a particular aspect of the state, and the state becomes less than the sum of its parts. Third, the state is sometimes what is affecting a situation, sometimes the focus of action, and often what is transforming and being transformed at the same time. This requires a dynamic model with complicated feedback loops. Such models are often the stuff of caricature rather than hardheaded inquiry. Fourth and finally, the state is historically and geographically bounded; it is a notion that does not have meaning in all places and at all times. There have not always been states, and there are not states everywhere. Some of the efforts to identify it or to assess its degree of penetration may simply be misplaced. Analysts are not always careful in specifying the scope conditions of their concepts, and much state theory illustrates the problems that arise from this failure.

The concept of the state is also out of fashion because of shifts in emphasis in political practice. There is attack, from the right and from the left, of the integrative, centralizing, and coercive features of the state, and there is skepticism about the reality of the state's sovereignty and relative autonomy in the international sphere. The very model of the state that was the goal of many countries in the past three centuries is now being questioned in advanced industrial democracies as well as in the transitional postsocialist countries and the Third World. At the same time, in both developed and developing countries, there is mobilization for change and demands for popular autonomy and control. The targets are the large states and the mammoth corporations and international organizations those states support. Democratization is a major rallying cry for a wide range of groups and individuals who feel that the state is distant and, more importantly, unrepresentative of their interests, concerns, and values.

In many advanced industrial countries, there is also an attack on the large government that the traditional model of the state seems to imply. Margaret Thatcher, Ronald Reagan, and neoliberal economists who emphasize deregulation and laissez-faire have initiated a serious reconsideration of social policies and taxation levels. In developing countries and within the international banking and aid communities, the turn from government reflects the corruption, cronyism, and inefficiencies that are as likely to flow from the state's personnel as growth-enhancing policies. When the rearrangement of the global economy is added to this mix, large-scale transnational corporate decision making appears to be of far greater consequence than state-based decision making. And, of course, the emphasis on civil society by both policymakers and protesters reflects the collapse or inadequacy of governments and the very states in which they are embedded. It seems that states are not always where the action is or, for some, should be.

Among comparativists an urgent question is whether we are witnessing the end of the era of the modern state and large government.[1] These concerns are implicated with the contemporary debate over the appropriate role of government and democratic interventions, especially in Europe and in transitional and developing countries facing serious state-building and governance issues. At the very heart of state theory is how to best achieve social order, promote economic growth, and facilitate democratic expression. Thus, it is very difficult to separate the normative and institutional design questions about the state from the empirical program focused on explaining variations in state arrangements and their effects.

As this brief introduction suggests and as the following literature review makes clear, the range of subjects included in discussions of "The State" are very numerous indeed. The literature leads us to definitional issues, then to consideration of what we actually know about what the state does and can do and of the relationship among the institutions of the state, government, and market, and finally to analytic and methodological issues. Throughout I address the normative questions of what role the state should play in the economy and polity and raise problems of democratic accountability. All of these topics have received considerable scholarly attention — past and present; I apologize in advance to all authors whose important work I fail to note.

It does not worry me that the study of the state per se is currently out of fashion; swings of the pendulum are the stuff of social science. What does worry me is that we may not build usefully and constructively on the scholarship to date. I am a guarded optimist; I believe that there is a possibility for cumulative knowledge in the social sciences but only if we take into account the work that has gone before and only if we pay attention to the methods and findings currently in play. More critically, I want us to maintain a research program on the state with a healthy skepticism about the role of the state. I am most certainly not advocating that the state, let alone big government, is always a positive force in development. Douglass North, an economic historian committed to understanding the role of the state (1981, 1990) is the author of a statement I quote often: "The existence of the state is essential for economic growth; the state, however, is the source of man-made economic decline" (1981, 20). It is this anomaly of state intervention that our research must address.

1. There are a considerable number of articles on this subject. See, e.g., Evans 1997; Hagopian 2000; the symposium in *Governance* 13: 2 (April 2000), edited by Graham Wilson, pp. 233–78, which includes articles by Wilson, Sbragia, Peterson, and Michiletti.

■ | How Did We Get Where We Are?

State theory, as it is often called, has gone through several incarnations, and several quite distinct controversies have dominated the discussion at different times. The early theorists concerned themselves with the problem of social order. To understand its source, Thomas Hobbes, John Locke, and Jean-Jacques Rousseau rested their arguments on assumptions about the state of nature. Since the nineteenth century, anthropologists have been debunking these pictures of stateless or, at least, acephalous society, but one legacy is the ongoing debate about the circumstances under which cooperation and the production of public goods is possible without a state. The underlying logic of liberal theory also gave rise to another set of controversies about whether the origin and maintenance of the state is based on consent or coercion, controversies with clear links to concerns about democratic accountability. These remain lively issues among those contesting state interventions in the market or individual lives.

The classical economists, the original liberals that neoliberals revere, for example, Adam Smith and David Ricardo, and their counterparts in political philosophy, for example, David Hume, Jeremy Bentham, and John Stuart Mill, generally emphasized an important but minimal role for the state in protecting contracts and offering certain public services that would not otherwise be provided. However, the main target of the economists was the elimination of regulations and monopoly privileges that inhibited trade. For the philosophers it was the use of the state to promote individual liberty and the inhibition of state-based infringements on that liberty.

The most famous critics of classical liberalism, Karl Marx and Friedrich Engels, focused on the role of the state in promoting economic growth and improving the human condition, the "high modernist" project James C. Scott (1998) and others condemn. As depressions, inequality, imperialism, and Marxist revolutions led to the significant expansion of state power, theory was not far behind. Leninism gave a formidable role to the state in building socialism. By comparison with today, so too did the politics and economics of governments that accepted Keynsianism, social democracy, or some form of the New Deal. Mid- and late-twentieth-century literature on the state reflected the governing elite's preoccupation with the importance of the state role and with popular demand for, or resistance to, government intervention and protection. Research was generally framed around the issues of the development of modern states. Detailed historical and comparative research characterizes much of this work. This was the era of grand models of modernization, on the one hand, and of area studies, promoted in the United States by the State Department, on the other hand. This was the heyday of what are now labeled the "old institutionalists," many of whose classic works are now receiving a renewed reading (e.g., Stinchcombe 1997; Remmer 1997).

Beginning in the late 1960s, leftist scholars revisited Marxist and class analysis as a basis for the understanding and investigation of the relationships between states and capitalism. In France, Nicos Poulantzas (1968, 1969) and Louis Althusser (1971) initiated a worldwide debate. In the United States, James O'Connor (1973) raised the alarm bell about the "fiscal crisis of the state"; in Germany, Claus Offe and Jürgen Habermas discussed the "legitimization crisis" (see, esp., Offe 1973a, b, 1984; Habermas 1975), and subsequently other major scholars took up similar themes and concerns (see, e.g., Block 1977, 1980; Jessop 1990; Przeworski and Wallerstein 1982).

The capitalist state controversy was one impetus behind the outpouring of major texts that situated the state in history and used forms of structural analysis linking the form of the state to the nature of the economy. Perry Anderson (1974a, 1974b), Charles Tilly (1975, 1990), Theda Skocpol (1979), Michael Mann (1986, 1993), and other state-centered structuralists focused on the interaction between state arrangements, the holders of state power, geopolitics, and civil society, particularly its class composition. They tended to work with large-scale macro variables and to treat the state as a unitary actor. Their mantra became "bringing the state back in" (see Evans, Rueschemeyer, and Skocpol 1985). The first of these authors tended to be historians and sociologists, but they were soon joined (and sometimes preceded) by numerous political scientists in comparative politics (e.g., O'Donnell 1973) and international relations (e.g., Krasner 1978; and Katzenstein 1978, 1984). Over time, their self-identification changed from state-centered structuralists to historical institutionalists.[2]

At approximately the same time, there arose an alternative approach to analyzing the state, largely initiated by Douglass North (1981) and Yoram Barzel (1989) in economics and developed by Robert Bates (1981; also see Bates and Lien 1985) and, I like to believe, myself (1981, 1988) in political science. These models rely on neoclassical economics but bring in a strong dose of structuralism in the form of property rights or class power. All build on the microfoundation of constrained rational actors, who face collective action problems and opportunity costs, have only relative bargaining power, and must consider the transaction costs of their policies. In a literature review in my 1988 book, I labeled the impulse behind this approach as "bringing people back into the state." For the rationalist state theorists, the state per se is not the actor; the actors are the agents who compose the state and the social, political, and economic groups who make demands on the state.

The action in rational choice theorizing about the state comes from the assumptions about the maximands of the key actors and variation in

2. See Thelen 1999 and Pierson and Skocpol this volume for a discussion of the evolution and contributions of historical institutionalism.

the constraints on their action; rationalists argue over the appropriate max-imand and the most critical constraints. For example, Edgar Kiser (1994) posits power maximizing by rulers in contrast to my presumption of rev-enue maximizing; the adjudication of the power of our theories is through testable implications. After deducing a plausible set of goals for state actors, rationalist state theorists then focus on the rules and arrangements that constitute the state and on the relative bargaining power and influence of nonstate actors. The combination of the institutions that constitute the state and of power relationships within society structures the incentives on state actors to establish, implement, and enforce the policies that they do.

Battle lines were being drawn between these two very distinct ap-proaches to state theory, the one grounded in historical macrosociology and the other in microeconomics. Throughout this whole period, of course, innumerable scholars of comparative politics offered analyses of the role of the state in political and economic development that did not fit neatly into either camp. Some of the names that come immediately to mind are Alice Amsden (1989), Robert Wade (1990), and Stephen Hag-gard (1990).

The most recent research on the state comes from several perspec-tives. Carrying on the historical sociological tradition are Brian Down-ing (1992) and Thomas Ertman (1997). Both emphasize geopolitics, but Downing is focused on fiscal extraction and military mobilization while Ertman stresses the role of local governance institutions. The rationalist perspective is represented by David Laitin (1992; also, see Laitin et al. 1994), Barbara Geddes (1994), Edgar Kiser and X. X. Tong (1992, 1999) and Yoram Barzel (2001; also, see Kiser and Barzel 1991; Barzel and Kiser 1997), and Mancur Olson (1993), whose work focuses on state building, state reform, and the origins of democracy. There is also a strong tradition within international relations, represented by Henrik Spruyt (1994), Janice Thomson (1994), and Andrew Moravscik (1997, 1998a), whose concerns with sovereignty led them to think more deeply about the state itself. In ad-dition, there are numerous texts trying to synthesize the various approaches to the state and suggest new directions (e.g., Hall and Ikenberry 1989; Hobson 2000) as well as some serious efforts to test specific aspects of some of the major claims of state theorists (see, e.g., Rasler and Thompson 1985; Thompson and Rasler 1999). Finally, an important group of younger scholars is applying and improving the theoretical models of the past to understand the transitions in contemporary states (e.g., Whiting 2000; Grzymala-Busse 2002; Luong 2002; Kang 2002).

Most of the work cited above is state centered, whether defining the state or state personnel as the key actors. Another tradition, equally long in the tooth, concentrates on the alternatives to the state as a system of regu-lation and means of ensuring cooperation and social order. The contem-porary version is found in the scholarship that locates community-based and spontaneous solutions to collective action problems. Michael Taylor's seminal work (1987 [1976]), Elinor Ostrom's award-winning *Governing the Commons* (1990), and the opus of William Riker have influenced numerous researchers to search for decentralized nongovernmental, albeit often institutional, arrangements for producing collective goods and for securing cooperation and exchange. In line with this program was the final major work of the great sociologist James Coleman (1990b, 300–21) in which he reflected on how social capital, defined as the social structural resources that derive to an individual from social relationships and social organization, can facilitate individual actions. In Coleman as well as in the even more group-oriented work of Robert Putnam (1993a, 2000) on social capital, the role of the state is not condemned; it is ignored or treated as secondary.

There is another group of scholars, some of whom began with a focus on the state, whose historical researches led them to discover nonstate solutions to social order and collective action problems. The modeling of these alternative institutions for regulating markets, such as the Hanseatic League or merchant guilds (Greif 1994b; Milgrom, North, and Weingast 1990), or for ensuring social peace and economic growth where there are potentially warring factions, such as the *Podesta* (Greif 1994a, 1998), fueled the version of the new economic institutionalism that now influences comparative politics.

A very different research tradition, associated with the popularity of interpretive and Foucaultian approaches, also produces criticism of state-centric research. Joel Migdal (1988, 2001; also see Migdal, Kohli and Shue 1994) introduced the state-in-society approach in order to emphasize the importance of social groupings in delimiting the penetration and effectiveness of states in many developing countries. Scott (1998) went further. He defines the state as a "totalizing" project with grand but failed schemes to "improve the human condition" (part of his subtitle). Paul Brass (1997, 2000) makes a similar claim. Migdal, Scott, Brass, and others emphasize power relations and the resistance of the populous as the subjects of interest rather than the state.

The reemphasis on the state as a conceptual variable produced good work that in turn stimulated a dialogue with scholars who wish to deemphasize, combat, or more simply reconsider the import of the role of the state in economic and political development. But what have we actually learned as a result of the large body of work now available? It is to that question I now turn.

■ | **What Is the State?**

One of the problems scholars confront in their efforts to use the state as a conceptual variable is how best to define it. Without knowing what the state is, it is difficult to determine what role it is playing, how "strong" it is, and so on. Scholars long tended to rely on Max Weber's definition, "A compulsory political organization will be called 'a state' insofar as its administrative staff successfully uphold [*sic*] the claim to the *monopoly* of the *legitimate* use of physical force in the enforcement of its order" (1978 [1956], 54, Weber's emphasis). This definition captures several key attributes of a state: its coerciveness, its reliance on physical force, and the existence of an administrative staff. However, as the newer literature on the state teaches us, the extent to which the state has a monopoly of physical force and the extent to which the use of physical force is legitimate are variables, not elements of a definition. Moreover, Weber's definition does not capture the territorial qualities of states or, sufficiently, its regulatory capacities by means of laws and norms. His work certainly confronts such questions, but his classic definition does not seem to get us where his agile mind otherwise takes us.

Let me offer a less parsimonious but more comprehensive alternative, drawn from the literature I have just reviewed. A state is a complex apparatus of centralized and institutionalized power that concentrates violence, establishes property rights, and regulates society within a given territory while being formally recognized as a state by international forums.[3] All states share some common characteristics: a legal structure and coercive apparatus that creates and enforces property rights; a system of laws and norms that regulates interactions among those who live in the state; a mechanism for trading with, defending against, and attacking those in other states; and procedures and agencies for taxing and policing the population. A state performs these roles by means of a wide variety of institutions, agencies, social norms, and actors, some governmental and some not. This approach to conceptualizing the state leaves open the question of legitimacy and general popular acceptance; some states have these characteristics and some states do not. It also means there can be varieties of states: some large, some small; some deeply penetrative into the society, some not so embedded. Thus, each state, even states with virtually similar laws, constitutions, and governmental arrangements, is distinct, because the combination of the complex of factors is almost by necessity particular and unique.

It is with the state that governors, subjects, and citizens identify. Citizens who oppose a particular set of governmental officials may still feel loyal to the state itself. "Indeed," as Migdal argues, "what has distinguished the modern state from most other large-scale political organizations in history, such as empires, has been its insinuation into the core identities of its subjects" (1994, 13). Patriotism and nationalism are among the forms such an identity takes. The salience of the state as an identity is verified partially

3. Formal international recognition excludes statelike organizations such as the mafia.

by the existence, in the modern world, of the phenomenon of statelessness. There are those who either feel no identity with any given state or feel identity with a nation or people who lack a territorial base or have lost control over a traditional territorial base.

States are comparable to but distinct from city-states, empires, and other such alternative means of institutionalizing power and identity over a given territory. States contain but are also distinct from their laws, bureaucracies, and governments.

States can be formed, but they are not selected. Governments are selected. A government is the organization that sets and administers public policies, and types of governments are distinguished by arrangements for making and implementing law and legislation. They can be authoritarian, democratic, or some other regime type. Government is, often, the main engine of the state, for it is the government that arranges the legal waging of war, administration of justice, collection of revenue, and provision of official state benefits. But major shifts in the personnel, policies, or even form of government can change while the state remains stable. It is difficult to imagine the state changing without its government also changing.

The study of the state raises separate issues from those the study of government does. Origins of states, whether they exist at all, and questions of state building and state transformation focus scholarly attention on historical and demographic processes as well as on internal social forces and power dynamics within a particular geographical space. Of equal importance must be attention to global factors, including trade, war, and colonialism. Corporations, parties, NGOs, and classes as well as government officials and citizens (or subjects) figure into the study of the state. The analysis of government—its size, organization, policies, and regime type—focuses our attention almost exclusively on interactions among actors in very specific roles, for example, legislators, executives, organized interests, citizens, ambassadors, who are influenced by economic pressures both within and outside the country's borders and by competing ideologies and groups. These actors are constrained by the institutions and norms of the state and by the relative bargaining power of other state agents, subjects, and enemies. They are embedded within the state but are not the totality of the state.

As scholars began to systematically investigate the role of the state as repressive or facilitative of political liberalization and economic growth, the emphasis tended to switch from the state, a relative abstraction and a complex set of variables, to the particular elements of the state that were doing the work: rulers, citizens, bureaucrats, legislators. The government is most definitely a compulsory political organization, and among its central roles are extraction in the form of money and people from its populous and regulation of the economy through the creation and protection of markets. Although attention may have shifted from the state to the government, we shall soon see that a larger conception, which includes nongovernmental actors and societal norms, are a crucial part of the story.

■ | The State in Economic and Political Development

We know quite a bit about some of the roles the state plays in economic and political development although, as is evident by a quick glance at the world around us, there is no recipe book for success. In what follows, the emphasis is on the domestic responsibilities of the state and not on the part it plays in trade or war.[4]

First, the state is an enforcer of contracts. To be sure, markets can exist without states, but the kinds of markets we identify with advanced economies depend on stable government and the rule of law. What we do not know is when bureaucratic or juridical implementation is essential, and under what circumstances and in what forms coordinative (rather than cooperation or coercive) mechanisms will do the trick—although we are beginning to get some ideas (Carey 2000).

Second, the state is a provider of public goods that firms require but might not supply: standardized weights and measures, bridges, roads, education. Not all markets require state-provided infrastructure, but complex and sophisticated networks of trade certainly do. The production of these goods reduces the costs of exchange and enhances productivity by ensuring the capacity of its capitalists to locate, build up, and allocate physical capital and appropriately skilled labor.

Third, the state in the political economy provides social insurance. The debate over the welfare state is, of course, a debate over the extent of the state's responsibility for its unemployed, displaced, or poor.

We know that securing contracts, reducing the costs of exchange, and providing public goods involves the provision of information about potential trading partners and resources, education and other forms of human capital production, and the creation or protection of social relationships and networks that facilitate a variety of cooperative and exchange activities. Discussion of these issues will lead us to a possible fourth role of the state: encouraging civic-mindedness and civility within the polity.

While there is consensus on the roles of the state, or at least the first three, we do not know what it is most efficient and equitable for the state to provide directly and what the trade-offs are in having private provision, regulated or not by the state. There are lots of claims of knowledge about this, especially by neoliberal economists, but there is only beginning to be hard evidence. And some of what we think we know is now up for grabs. Perhaps this current period of neoliberalism, by creating a basis for compari-

---

4. See Kahler this volume for a discussion of more international issues involving the state.

son with past practices, will generate sufficient research to enhance our understanding of these issues.[5]

LEVIATHANS AND PREDATORY STATES

Part of why the state is in such bad odor among many political analysts and policymakers has to do with the extent to which it has proved a significant ". . . source of man-made economic decline" (North 1981, 20) and an inhibitor of democracy and equality. Given that the recent resurgence of interest in the state focused on problems such as revolution, taxation, and the inefficiencies created by state corruption, public ownership, and so on, it is not really surprising that the state becomes identified as the problem rather than the solution.

The perception of the state as a threat to liberty is embodied in the notion of the state as Leviathan. Hobbes used this term as a descriptor of the amassing of the population into one grand commonwealth: "This is the generation of that great Leviathan, or rather (to speak more reverently) of that *Mortall God*, to which wee owe under the *Immortall God*, our peace and defence" (Hobbes 1985 [1651], 227, Hobbes's spelling and emphasis). According to the OECD, the term derives from two earlier usages: a mythical and gigantic aquatic sea creature and a man of enormous power and wealth. It has come to represent the idea of the state as huge in size, long in reach, and vast in power. While presumably beneficent, at least in Hobbes's view, the Leviathan is meant to act in the interests of the aggregated populace whether individuals concur with its policies or not.

For Hobbes, the existence of the state enhances liberty by providing physical security of person and property. It also ensures economic prosperity by enforcing property rights and thus security of production and trade. But in its very formulation, the Leviathan is a nondemocratic, even antidemocratic institution. Who does and should control the state were and continue to be subjects of investigation and contestation. I have already rehearsed the outlines of important normative arguments, but the empirical question of what states do and under what conditions remains.

Models, particularly models derived from public choice and rational choice perspectives, have clarified the reasons why states may be inclined to rent seeking, overtaxation, and other so-called predatory practices. Rents are returns "in excess of a resource-owners opportunity costs" (Tollison 1982, 30), and rent seeking refers to behavior that generates social waste because of socially unproductive activity dedicated to winning licenses, official monopolies, or other economic rights. The work of Anne Krueger,

---

5. The model of what I have in mind is Waterbury's book (1993) on the Egyptian state; Smith and Lipsky's comparison (1993) of government versus private provision of social services in the United States; or Snyder's investigation (2001) of deregulation in Mexico.

Robert Bates, and others (Krueger 1974; Bates 1981; Bates and Krueger 1993) provides evidence that rent seeking exists and is wasteful. And there is little doubt that government agents can be corrupt, using their control over economic resources as a means to enhance their personal wealth. Nor is there much question that rent seeking and corruption can prove highly inefficient for economic actors who must bribe and lobby to survive as well as for the economy as a whole.

By conceiving of government decision makers as rational actors, it is possible to see how such outcomes might arise. In my initial account of the state, rulers are always predatory in the sense that they will seek to maximize the revenues of the state, but their predation is subject to the constraints of their relative bargaining power, their transaction costs and their discount rates (1988, 10, pass.). Rulers who are relatively unconstrained, who are captured by particular sets of powerful actors, who are unable to control their agents, or who are faced with crises that require huge additional funds are likely to tax in ways that may damage long-term economic growth. The documentation of such rulers and policies is legion. Rulers may be personally efficient in terms of extending their length of office but disastrous for the economy as a whole or for the rights of groups within the polity.

Even so, as North (1981), Evans (1992), and many others have argued, the state may be the means of solving the very problems it creates. Adam Smith, more than 200 years ago, emphasized the need for very different state policies. What more contemporary scholars claim and have begun to investigate systematically are the conditions for transforming and constructing the institutional arrangements of a developmental state.

A GROWTH-ENHANCING AND DEMOCRATIC STATE

As destructive as states can be of well-being, economic and political, they are also "essential for economic growth" (North 1981, 20) and can facilitate democratization. The contribution of an effective state is more than defense against the Hobbesian "war of all against all." It is also, as is universally accepted, the production of public goods that enhance physical and human capital. But infrastructure and a well-educated polity are not sufficient conditions for political and economic development. Increasingly, it is becoming apparent that also essential are an array of social relationships and norms that serve as resources for individual activity—what some analysts label social capital. The question here is the extent to which government activity facilitates social capital that then makes not only the market but also the government and society work better.

The argument that a centralized state destroys the social cohesion and social networks of traditional communities and thus undermines the potential for cooperation is a claim with a distinguished pedigree (see, e.g., Scott 1976; Taylor 1982; Gellner 1988; Ostrom 1990). But centralized states may also help build social networks and relationships of trust and authority that may serve the populace well. It can be key in providing the resources and targets for facilitating the growth of organizations and voluntary associations that generate a flourishing civil society. For example, the creation of the U.S. post office was not only essential for commerce and savings (Carpenter 2001); it was also a critical factor in building and sustaining the potential for civic engagement in the very period that Tocqueville observed (Skocpol 1997, 459–63). This institution of central government made possible social, political, and economic relationships across time and space by cementing information exchange by building canals, railroads, ports, and roads and through the circulation of newspapers, documents, and people. Kevin Costner's film *The Postman* may have been off the money but on the mark.

There is a considerable literature on how national states create the "opportunity structure" and other resources that enable groups to engage in collective action, sometimes in opposition to the state, sometimes in its support, and sometimes to achieve its own ends vis-à-vis other societal actors.[6] In her presidential address to the Social Science History Association, Theda Skocpol argued that "the early national U.S. State created a framework that encouraged widespread voluntary association," (1997, 476) and she traces the evolution of that framework as well as the state-society symbiosis that led to translocal organizations capable of active participation in national policymaking. She limits her analysis to the United States, but the underlying point is relevant to a wide range of societies and eras (see, e.g., McAdam, Tarrow, and Tilly 2001).

There are numerous examples that make this point, but here I will offer up a few illustrations of how state policy provides an opportunity structure for citizen action networks, even when that may not be the intention. Central and colonizing states may well have transformed linguistically, religiously, and racially distinct groups into minorities, but such states also offer a new basis for power relationships and definitions of ethnic status and languages (e.g., Hechter 1975, 2000; Laitin 1992; Laitin et al. 1994). The antipoverty programs of President Lyndon Johnson did, at least for a time, offer resources to poor people who then mobilized to change local governmental policies (Bachrach and Baratz 1980). Sidney Tarrow (2000), a scholar closely associated with the theory of contentious politics, provides a compelling account of how the very rules that states establish may enable and legitimize citizen action and aid the formation of networks of activists, as happened around the Mad Cow disease controversy in Europe. Several authors (Rothstein 1990, 1992, 39–46; Western 1997) have documented how variations in the administration of public unemployment insurance affect unionization; in those countries where the scheme is administered by unions, union density is higher.

6. For a useful review of this concept and of the social movement literature generally, see McAdam, Tarrow, and Tilly 1997.

We may today question the positive aspects of patronage, which is often a form of corruption and cronyism, but it is also, as Robert Merton (1949) so astutely observed, a means of creating both human capital and social capital (although he used neither term) in the form of a network that linked government actors to neighborhood, especially ethnic, residents. Robert Michels (1962 [1919], 185–89), even longer ago than Merton, noted how the state provides jobs that buy off discontent by creating bonds of dependency and loyalty as well as by offering a livelihood. There is some evidence for both of these propositions and considerable room for pinning them down even further.

Attention to the civil norms that facilitate law-abidingness and civic engagement need not be insulated from attention to the way states help produce as well as benefit from such norms. I am following Ensminger and Knight (1997, 2) in delineating social norms as "informal rules that structure behavior in ways that allow individuals to gain the benefits of collective action." There are numerous examples of ways in which the establishment of certain government laws and policies promote norms which then change the way people think and which also promote collectively beneficial outcomes. Changes in thinking about slavery (Engerman 1997) clearly had extrastate sources, but the resulting changes in the law seemed to have an effect of changing peoples' conception of slavery over time. I find a similar process in my own work (1997a, 103–6, 205–8, 211) on the evolution of conscription practices and the search for a more equitable draft; I find that changes in conscription practices reflect but also alter what constitutes the perception of a fair and equitable draft. Bo Rothstein (1998) analyzes how the creation of universalistic welfare policies at an earlier period in Swedish history continues to affect the beliefs of Swedes about what is fair and thus the kinds of legislation they will accept and which can be implemented at relatively low cost. Finally, in a quite different realm, Robert Keohane (1999, 236–37) explores how government bureaucracies help generate the creation of transnational networks that become the carriers of ideas that secure international cooperation.

As important as the social networks, organizations, and norms a state nourishes are the relationships of trust it cultivates.[7] Laws, enforced by the state, provide insurance and sanctions against illegal opportunism; trust, on the other hand, lubricates both exchange and governance. Interpersonal trust is essential to economic growth because it facilitates the making of contracts, reduces the costs of exchange, and eases renegotiation when the situation changes. Tocqueville noted how important trust is to business relationships (1990 [1835], 387–90), and many subsequently have emphasized the importance of trust in the development of complex capitalist economies. Only a few (e.g., Fukuyama 1995), however, have recognized

7. This section draws heavily from my "A State of Trust" (1998). Also see my *Consent, Dissent, and Patriotism* (1997a).

the major role the state plays in creating the kinds of trust that lead to both better government and a more productive economy.

States can also help to produce interpersonal trust and reduce transaction costs through regulations directed at reassuring consumers that they are getting what they believe they are paying for and that they will be safeguarded against a wide variety of human-created dangers. Technically these regulations often constitute a form of contract enforcement, and abuses by the seller are subject to the courts. However, the effect is a kind of generalized trust or, more correctly, confidence in the market and a greater willingness to engage in productive trade. Whether the public is aware of it or not, it is government regulations that provide the backdrop to consumer willingness to give out credit card numbers over the phone, use ATMs, get on and off airplanes, even buy property. Those countries with less trustworthy and transparent governments tend to have significantly higher transaction costs of exchange and dead weight loss, as empirical studies are beginning to demonstrate (see, e.g., DeSoto 1989; Campos and Root 1996).

The ability of a state to generate interpersonal trust may rest largely on the trustworthiness of the state itself. What trustworthiness means in this context is the extent to which its decision making, policies, and implementation procedures are considered fair and nondiscriminatory by the standards of the era, but it also and even more centrally means that government actors credibly convey that they will act in the interests of the citizens they are meant to serve.[8] Thus, widespread incompetence or corruption is usually an indicator of untrustworthy state agents, and so, too, generally is behavior that favors a particular class, racial, ethnic, linguistic, or racial group.

One of the major findings of my research on the state (1988, 1997a, 1997b) is that cost-effective means to extract revenue and men depend on low-cost mechanisms for increasing compliance among taxpayers and that even the most autocratic rulers depend on a certain amount of quasi-voluntary compliance. The creation of quasi-voluntary compliance, let alone consent, requires a trustworthy government, in particular one that meets current standards of fairness in both its decision making and policy implementation. Citizens and subjects are in a kind of tit-for-tat arrangement; each cooperates as long as there is some assurance that the others will.

The implication is that certain kinds of states are likely to be better able to extract resources, in money and men, from their populations. There are two necessary conditions. The first is sufficient capacity to penetrate deep in the society, a capacity that rests on the power of the state to pacify the countryside and to build an adequate bureaucratic apparatus. The second is the existence of a government, which may be more demo-

---

8. This conceptualization of a trustworthy state comes largely from my own work (1997a, 1998) but also from that of Russell Hardin (2002).

cratic but certainly is more likely to be relatively consensual and fairer in the way it inaugurates and implements policies. At the least it will be more credible (Whiting 2000). But the implication is also that, without trustworthy government, the polity will feel betrayed and will be more likely to resist or rebel. Indications of considerable citizen free riding that government could but is not controlling are likely to provoke additional citizen noncompliance. So, too, is evidence of discriminatory government practices, violations of policy bargains, or poor bureaucratic treatment of citizens. States enforce rights and rules other than those associated with economic and material property contracts. By protecting minority rights, states facilitate cooperation among individuals who have reason to be wary of each other. By legalizing trade unions or enforcing child labor laws, states reduce the costs to workers of monitoring and sanctioning employers, and thus may raise the likelihood of both trust and productivity.

The amount of socially and economically productive cooperation in the society affects, in turn, the state's capacity to govern and the vitality of economic exchange. Confidence in the trustworthiness of the state has additional consequences for governance as well. It affects the level of citizen of tolerance of the regime and also the degree of compliance with governmental demands and regulations.[9] Destruction of the belief in the state's trustworthiness may lead to widespread antagonism to government policy and even active resistance, and it may be one source of increased social distrust. Research on eastern Europe adds additional credence to this claim (see, e.g., Rose 1994; Mishler and Rose 1997; Sztompka 1999). The effect can be the breakdown in state capacity, even where there is strong governmental infrastructure.

Once confidence in the trustworthiness of the state has been destroyed, its rebuilding often requires extraordinary efforts, as we are learning on the ground in numerous parts of the world. In fact, the current moment in history provides a remarkable laboratory for understanding state destruction, transformation, and rebuilding. There are numerous scholars right now producing the in-depth research that will provide a basis for generating and testing hypotheses and contrasting their explanations with the alternatives.[10] And many of them believe in and are committed to cumulative knowledge.

9. This point is increasingly well documented by scholars using both quantitative and qualitative methods. See, e.g., Tyler (1990, 1998), Peel (1995), Levi (1997a), Scholz (1998), Rothstein (1998).

10. Any list I provide will neglect important work of which I am not aware or have simply forgotten to include. So, let me just list some of the relevant recent and forthcoming books in the Cambridge Studies in Comparative Politics series: Kitschelt et al. 1999, Bunce 1999, Easter 2000, Migdal 2001, Stokes 2001a, Stokes 2001b, Snyder 2001, Kreppel 2001, Beissinger 2001, Murillo 2001, Jones Luong 2002, Kang 2002, Grzymala-Busse 2002, Franzese 2002, Lehoucqu and Molina forthcoming.

At one level, in fact, we know quite a lot about this process. Here is where the historical and sociological literature on the origins and development of states really comes into its own, as well as the work of the quite considerable number of comparativists who have been tilling the fields for some time. But despite all the detailed accounts and despite considerable advances in understanding the pathways to any particular configuration under study, we still lack an adequate dynamic understanding of how to resolve issues of corruption, improve poverty, and ensure the well-being of populations by means of the state or, for that matter, by other means. But, as I said earlier in this essay, I am a guarded optimist.

STATE-PRODUCED DEFICITS IN TRUST AND DEMOCRACY

A growth-enhancing state is not, even if achieved, a sufficient condition for political democracy. A centralized state does not necessarily ensure against descent into political violence and economic dissolution, nor is it the only or even best way to promote positive economic and political cooperation at the local level. Nor, for that matter, does the reduction in the size and interventions of government necessarily enhance democracy.

There is a huge literature on democracy, its origins, fragility, and sustainability, and comparativists have made considerable progress in understanding certain features of democratization as well as in acknowledging the need to analyze the particularities of each case (see Bunce 2000 for an excellent review). According to Bunce, there are at least two things we know about the relationship between the state and the survival of democracy. First, the maintenance of democracy generally requires "rough agreement on the composition of the nation and boundaries of the state" (2000, 712). Second, "A strong state, in short, is a guarantor of democracy—much as it is a guarantor of capitalism" (715). Democracy has a chance of stability only where there is a stable rule of law.

But even with a strong state and democratic institutions in place, democracy can come under pressure. This can occur as a result of a reduction in democratic accountability, state capture by particular interests who do not serve the general welfare, and failures of government to deliver what the polity believes it wants and deserves. The analysis of the state as composed of actors with goals that are constrained by and respond to trustworthy governmental institutions begins to get at the answer to several puzzling issues in contemporary social science: why democracies tend to be more productive of economic growth than authoritarian regimes, and why we are witnessing what appears to be an increase in citizen skepticism about government and politics in the established democracies.[11]

Mancur Olson (1993) argues that the more encompassing the interest

---

11. There is, of course, some serious question as to whether they really are. See, especially, Przeworski and Limongi 1993; Przeworski et al. 2000.

of the ruler in the polity, the more likely the tax system will provide the proper incentives for growth and the rulers will provide public services in return for their extractions. An alternative, more-compelling, and better-substantiated view is that sophisticated rulers and elites create or take advantage of political institutions, such as parliaments, that not only facilitate bargaining over taxes but also provide a means to sanction rulers who renege on agreements; in other words, such institutional arrangements make the promises of rulers credible (Levi 1988, 117–21; Root 1989; Brewer 1989; North and Weingast 1989; Ertman 1997, 221). Credible commitments and self-enforcing institutions significantly reduce the citizen's need to make a personal investment in sanctioning and monitoring state agents and thus enhance citizen trust of state and government. This is, of course, theorizing that permits explanations of specific actions. It lacks the grandeur or sweep of the Olson conjectures, but it is observable and falsifiable.

There is little question but that what Scharpf (1999) calls the "input-oriented mechanisms" are under considerable pressure as a result of global market forces, the creation of regional government in Europe, and the scope of government just about everywhere. Increasingly, important sources of power reside in private organizations or in nonmajoritarian organs of the state. The problem is not as Karen Remmer (1997, 52) and others have argued that "the activities, resources, and relative weight of the state are being reduced." But rather, as Peter Evans argued, "The danger is not that states will end up as marginal institutions but that meaner, more repressive ways of organizing the state's role will be accepted as the only way of avoiding the collapse of public institutions" (1997, 64, in the article immediately following Remmer's in *World Politics*). The question of the effects of the changing locus of power and policies of the state deserves the theoretically informed empirical investigation that is beginning to occur.

But there are some things we know already. We know that the state is often the captive of economic pressures—international and domestic—and powerful societal actors that influence the range of options available to state actors. The Marxists long asserted this proposition, and it is part of the canon of scholars of development. Only fairly recently, however, have scholars disaggregated and tested key components of this claim. Przeworski and Wallerstein (1988; also see Przeworski 1985, 1991) helped initiate a whole spate of sophisticated formal and quantitative work on the structural dependence of the state on capital. Work on tariffs and cartels by economic historians, comparativists, and IPE scholars are beginning to reveal some determinant conclusions about the interplay between domestic and international factors (see, e.g., Bates 1997b; Moravcsik 1998). Many of the authors of recent research on the social policies and economic regulation within the changing global and regional economies are engaged in real debate about the role of globalization, the effects of partisan politics, and the influence of labor unions and corporations on the state. They are testing and falsifying each others' hypotheses while also offering alternative accounts (see, e.g., Garrett 1998b; Boix 1998; Iversen 1999; Scharpf and Schmidt 2000b; Swank 2002; Hall and Soskice forthcoming).

But it is not only the lack of popular input or the inordinate influence of business or corporate interests that accounts for the democratic deficit. There are also real problems of "output oriented legitimatization" (Scharpf 1999). Part of the story lies in the reduction of welfare or other social benefits that characterized so many European governments, particularly the social democratic governments, of the post–World War II era. Part of the story is also the increased costs of governance combined with politically driven reductions in tax income that make it extremely difficult to pay for what citizens want and need. So, we have a new version of the "fiscal crisis of the state."

Of equal or perhaps greater significance in "output legitimization" is the fact that national governments must find ways and rules that inhibit "the race to the bottom" and convince citizens to share in the commitment to this new vision of the collective good.[12] This is no easy task.

▪ | Methodological and Conceptual Issues

To maintain a program of research about the state is one thing, and there are still many attempting to do just that. To improve the quality of that research is quite another. The state shares many characteristics with the elephant so misdescribed by the blind men of Chelm. It is vast yet full of parts whose connections only make sense if you can grasp the whole—difficult to do if your perspective permits a view only of certain elements. The problem intensifies if you are interested in the origins of the state or its likely future, let alone its institutional design or best practice.

My argument is that the strategy of the men of Chelm is wrong. As we know from other stories about them, their real deficiency is the lack of reason, not sight. The state is too complex and too varied to grasp the whole, even if it were possible to offer a static picture of the exterior of the beast with all its peculiarities and particularities. Some scholars react by providing rich and detailed accounts of state processes and governments, and others offer grand theories derived from either wide reading or formal logic. We must go beyond thick descriptions of specific states at specific times to develop models and falsifiable hypotheses derived from realistic and logical presuppositions about the state and the interactions of its agents with each other and with the larger society. Good theory requires understanding the relationships between the parts, how they connect. At best, we can develop only partial theories, which will increase our under-

---

12. I am loosely paraphrasing and strongly building on Scharpf (1999).

standing and leverage. I concur with Barbara Geddes (her paper for this volume) when she argues, "The tradition that most impedes the development of a body of knowledge in comparative politics is . . . our selection of big, inadequately defined outcomes to explain."[13] Although my long-term goal is to further our capacity to understand the large outcomes of political and economic development, the approach I take is to consider pieces of the puzzle, model the situation as best I can through a combination of rationalist deduction and inductive investigation, and use comparative statics to produce falsifiable hypotheses, which are then tested against empirical evidence.

I am also arguing for generating testable hypotheses from models that may have high predictive power but that ". . . are likely to be of limited scope and will only represent certain subsets of the complex multiarena and multilevel interactions that are characteristic of real world processes" (Scharpf 1997, 31; also, see Moravcsik 1998a, 17, pass.; Bates et al. 1998). This turns much of what has been claimed about rationalist theory on its head, especially its pretention to universalism. The universalism rests on the assumptions of rationality or the general theory of interest, not in the models of particular interactions or the findings about them.

What I have just said suggests that a lot of the debate about state origins and impact will remain unresolved because the scope of the enterprise is too large. There is another reason as well. The adjudication of theoretical claims, be they deductively or inductively derived, involves getting down to the nitty-gritty of data collection and hypothesis testing. The hypotheses must, of course, be derived logically, and the assumptions must be defensible. It is more than appropriate to criticize failures on either of these dimensions, and, of course, theories can be superseded by alternatives that account for more of the variation. Yet, despite the detailed evidence often gleaned and the rich narratives offered, many authors do not in fact derive and test hypotheses. Rather, we have witnessed ". . . the multiplication of plausible claims. . . . Where hypotheses are rarely discarded, they are rarely confirmed" (Moravcsik 1998a, 17; also see Remmer 1997).[14]

But another question immediately arises: How do we most effectively go about deriving these hypotheses? Here there are a myriad of strategies, many of which are equally productive of good model building in the service of cumulative knowledge. I shall outline mine (shared by others) with the recognition that it is hardly the only possible route, although, of course, I believe it is the best.

13. As John Carey will no doubt realize, I benefited immensely from his comments on my earlier description of appropriate methodology.

14. Now, I should add, with the possible exception of legislative research in the United States, there are probably no areas of political science that have met these criteria.

Whether the subject is the government or the state, three similar analytic problems arise. The first is that state and government institutions, are, as Stinchcombe (1997, 1) puts it, "staffed." Even if one accepts, as I do, the definition of institutions as rules of the game as opposed to "the process by which organizations and procedures acquire value and stability" (Huntington 1965, 394), someone still has got to see to it that the job gets done. There are individuals involved who are making purposive decisions and upholding values as well as interests. Stinchcombe is quite right when he critiques many of the "new economic institutionalists" for neglecting the role of individuals in their accounts just as the rationalist state theorists were correct to take the structuralists to task for treating states as depersonalized.[15]

The second major analytic point is that it is inappropriate to treat the state as a unitary actor. There can, of course, be spokespersons who reflect the aggregated preferences of the key players in the state or government apparatus. It is not enough, however, to disaggregate to the component organizational parts; it is essential to provide a microfoundation based on individuals and groups. This brings us immediately into the world of preferences, motivations, collective action, and coordination problems.

The third and final point is it is essential to understand state actors as persons responsive to other domestic or international players and sources of pressure, as actors engaged in strategic interaction. There can be states and their representatives more autonomous from society or more powerful internationally than others. But the best extant theories of the state take seriously these factors and model the strategic interactions among state actors, between state and societal actors, and among the representatives of various states. In the process, they bring to bear the role of institutions, transaction costs, collective action, contentious politics, and social movements.

Note I have not yet said anything about rational actors, although that is clearly an assumption in virtually all the most-interesting theories of the state. However, not all such theories are by rational-choice scholars. Thelen (1999) emphasizes the "creative borrowing" and the learning that has gone on between rationalists and historical institutionalists. Many of the latter now explicitly discuss collective action and agency problems; they have also learned that accepting actors as rational does not preclude them from also presuming that actors are ideological, emotional, altruistic, and so on. Rationalists, meanwhile, are learning that the recognition of the

---

15. Stinchcombe's other major point—and it is one of Migdal's (1994) as well—is the importance of values. Yet, part of what the state is all about, at least for many state theorists, is gaining authority and credibility and making coordination possible. Parchment and constitutions are good because they coordinate members of the polity around certain norms, values, and rules (see, e.g., Carey 2000; Hardin 1999). So part of this debate is more terminological than real.

role of ideas and values does not preclude rationality in the form of strategic or self-interested behavior, and they are taking on board interpretive materials. Historical institutionalists tend to embed actors in frameworks of meaning and provide them with nuanced identities that affect their preferences; this is only beginning to happen among rationalists (Bates et al. 1998).

Over time, as several scholars have noted (Hall and Taylor 1996; Levi 1997b; Thelen 1999) there has been some convergence in the research programs and tools of analysis of what were once extremely distinct and competitive approaches to institutions and the state. For some the major difference between these two approaches is "the relative centrality of 'equilibrium order' versus 'historical process' in the analysis of political phenomena" (Thelen 1999, 381; also see Orren and Skowronek 1994). Undoubtedly, those within the historical institutionalist school are more likely to be interested in instances of state transformation, revolution, and civil war; with how preferences arise and are altered; and with dynamic explanations. Undoubtedly, rationalists tend to be more concerned with stability, to take preferences as given, and to rely on comparative statics. But even this distinction is breaking down.

There is, nonetheless, a theoretical and methodological divide that continues to be the subject of symposia and debate.[16] What matters for my purposes here, however, is not the arguments among the state theorists and the varieties of institutionalists but what we have collectively learned that informs the burning research and policy questions we currently face.

■ | Conclusion

We come full circle. In the '70s and '80s, a new generation of social scientists argued for "bringing the state back in." In this era of "taking the state out," the mantra carries considerable appeal, at least to me. But with some provisos. The state needs to be constituted or reconstituted in those countries operating without the rule of law and institutional or, perhaps as Stinchcombe (1997) might have it, institutionalized mechanisms of coordination. In those countries with functioning states, there must be some attention to the democratic deficit produced by the reorganization of state responsibilities. What has changed most markedly is the role of government and the public sphere. Government, properly instituted, is a major impetus to economic growth, political development, and collective goods.

16. For example, see Kiser and Hechter 1991 and the subsequent 1998 "Symposium on Historical Sociology and Rational Choice Theory" in the *American Journal of Sociology*, with articles by Somers, Kiser and Hechter, Boudon, Goldstone, and Calhoun. Also see the symposium on *Analytic Narratives* in *Social Science History* (2000) with articles by Carpenter, Skocpol, Parikh, and Bates et al.

Government, badly instituted, is a major font of poor economic performance, elitist privilege, and social waste. The antigovernment ideology embodied in neoliberalism may prove an antidote to reliance on the state for inappropriate tasks and may prove a corrective to inefficient and inappropriately costly regulations. However, the effect of this ideology has been to obscure the important roles the state can and often does play in promoting a productive economy and a participatory polity. These are roles the state plays not only historically or in developing countries but also in the most-advanced industrial and democratic countries in the contemporary world. And these are roles the state can and should continue to play.

But I do not want to end on a normative note. Although I think the normative issues are critical, no normative program can be effected without real understanding of what is actually happening, why it is happening, and what is possible. I have followed Nettl in claiming that the state goes in and out of fashion as a social science construct due to the combination of the problems encountered in using the concept in rigorous analysis and the extent to which the state seems to be a factor in what concerns the contemporary world. Nettl, for example, argues that the loss of interest in the state reflected the combination of the growing influence of American social science (1968, 560) and the growing importance of third world countries (1968, 560). A concept like nation-state was not applicable, and the concept of the state had almost as little meaning. It was neither adequate as a descriptor of processes taking place in those countries nor useful in theory building about those processes. For Nettl geography is determinative. In my view, the failure of scholars to develop good methodologies and theories leads practitioners to search for alternative concepts as the basis for explanations and policy.

What I have offered, I hope, is an outline of the research that still needs to be done based on an assessment of what we, as scholars, have accomplished thus far. Despite the multicentury literature on the state, despite all the thinking and writing that has been addressed to the consequences—positive and negative—of state intervention in the economy and of the problems of democratic accountability, state theory remains in its infancy. The blind men of Chelm looked only at the exterior. We have begun to delve into the interior, to understand how the pieces fit together, what are the sources of change and dynamism, and what makes for a healthy or diseased state. However, the tools of investigation and the body of careful case research necessary for adequate theory building and testing are only just becoming available. By combining an interdisciplinary perspective with adequate attention to the variations and specificities of state actions and effects, there is hope that we shall untangle the complex relationships within the state and among the state, government, and civil society.

Miles Kahler

The State of the State
in World Politics[1]

The career of the state in international relations research has been a peculiar one: central as a matter of faith but often taken for granted, a theoretical sideshow. That core belief in the central role of sovereign states in world politics has been repeatedly challenged during the twentieth century. World War II—a monumental clash of militarized states—paradoxically brought a wave of doubt about the state system. With typical prescience, E. H. Carr (1941) questioned the untrammeled application of the principle of self-determination, pointing out that military and economic trends called for larger units in world politics, not a host of small ones. He was largely wrong on the military threats to small or weak states in the postwar decades, but he clearly framed the looming conflict between economic interdependence and political autonomy. A decade later, John Herz predicted the end of the conventional territorial state as its "hard shell" of defensibility was stripped away by the instruments of total war, particularly nuclear weapons. He later retracted this stark prediction in the wake of decolonization and the birth of dozens of new states. Like many others in the 1960s, however he pointed out the "synthetic" quality of these states and argued for an international role in their "hardening" over time (Herz 1976, 114–18, 242–43).

These lines of inquiry were set aside as a long peace among the great powers persisted and economic integration among the industrialized countries deepened. The research agenda of international political economy initially questioned the unitary and coherent internal ordering of the state. State-society relations figured prominently as a determinant of foreign economic policy; multiple transnational channels connected societies

1. The author wishes to thank Robert O. Keohane, Kathryn Sikkink, Jeffry Frieden, Margaret Levi, David Lake, the editors of this volume, and the participants in the State of the Discipline conference for comments on earlier drafts of this paper. The author also acknowledges the valuable research assistance provided by Pablo M. Pinto.

(Katzenstein 1978; Keohane and Nye 1977, 24–25). Its emphasis on the roots of state policy in society was subsumed by a call to "bring the state back in" during the 1980s, however. The distinction between strong and weak states dominated other variation on the state-society dimension.[2] Competition from other international actors faded, in theoretical debates at least, and the agenda of complex interdependence was set aside (Keohane and Nye 1987). By the end of the 1980s, the state as an unproblematic, uniform, unitary, and rational actor seemed to satisfy conventional realists and neorealists (who saw homogeneity imposed by international competition) as well as those of a more game-theoretic and rationalist bent.[3] Even those sharply critical of the individualist assumptions of neoliberalism and neorealism accepted that "states are the principal actors in the system" and defined states in a way that was completely familiar (Wendt 1996, 1999).

Since the importance of the state was taken as axiomatic, a careful definition of statehood was seldom offered. Nonetheless, the outlines of the ideal-typical state in world politics were clear if not always explicit. States were territorial: they claimed to rule over a carefully delimited space. Within that space they were sovereign: they reserved for themselves core political functions of internal order and external defense (war making)[4] The result was a system of "defensible units, internally pacified and hard-shell-rimmed" (Herz 1976, 111). These material characteristics could be defined as a normative identity as well, framed by mutual recognition, sovereignty, and territoriality (Van Creveld 1999, 1, 416). The state was "the basic, irreducible unit" of international relations, "equivalent to the individual person in a society" (Nettl 1968, 563).

The somnolent theoretical world of the state exploded in the 1990s. The comfortable bipolarity of the cold war ended in the collapse of one superpower state. Old preoccupations with interstate war (military and economic) dissolved into an awareness of widespread violent internal conflicts and the encroachments of globalization. Predictably, although many of these developments were hardly novel, they quickly produced one last twentieth-century wave of proclamations that the state was endangered, in decline, or eclipsed.[5] In the earlier alarms described, the principal threat to the state was modern military technology. In the 1990s, collapsing internal capabilities and global economic integration were the designated threats.

2. This distinction in the U.S. case pervades Ikenberry, Lake, and Mastanduno 1989, for example.

3. In the debate between neoliberals and neorealists, both sides accepted without question this prevailing consensus (Baldwin 1993). Reasons for this convergence are discussed in Kahler 1997.

4. On the definition of the state, compare Waltz 1979, Van Creveld 1999, 1, and Wendt 1999, 201–14.

5. See Guéhenno 1995; Van Creveld 1999; Evans 1999.

The international environment, which had propped up the state, now seemed less supportive and possibly subversive of its role (Evans 1997, 65).

These alarms also paralleled and in some measure stimulated a wave of serious scholarly attention to the state in international politics. The new research was diverse, a marriage of different theoretical and methodological interests. These agendas intersected on one point: the state had for too long been taken as a constant in the study of world politics; it was past time to consider it as a variable. Like any good marriage, this one contained something old, something new, and something borrowed.

The *old*, or at least familiar, was the initial agenda produced by the "new" phenomenon of globalization. Economic integration at the global level (a narrow definition of globalization) had been underway among the industrialized societies for decades. The characteristics and scope of integration and the political issues it raised have changed over time, but research on globalization recast an earlier agenda in international political economy, when sovereignty also appeared to be at bay. Attention centered on decline in territorial control by the state—the rise of dense cross-border channels for economic, political, and cultural exchange—and the resultant competition with other economic and political actors, international and domestic, that were labeled international civil society. The state's *centrality* was challenged and, in some cases, its *capabilities* as an autonomous agent.

A *new* research agenda on the state in world politics is based on a growing awareness that the state has too often been defined as the modern European state, a species delimited in both time and space. Our familiar ideal type emerged from competition with other units organized very differently. As a description of units, it is hardly characteristic of many of the polities labeled states in the contemporary world. Governance functions are concentrated in the nation-state, delegated to international institutions, and devolved to smaller units within the state in different regional patterns. *Variation* among political units and in the relations among them defines this new attention to the units in international politics. The norm is no longer assumed to be the modern European state in one type of anarchic setting. This line of research is the most subversive of the conventional view of the state and the most significant for political science.

Finally, students of world politics have also *borrowed* in their renewed investigation of the state. Institutional analysis, absorbed from the study of American and comparative politics, has played two roles. Treating the state as a composite of institutions allows a more refined analysis of how states and other political units vary and a more accurate estimation of the consequences of that variation for foreign policy and international politics. Institutional analysis has also offered common methodologies for examining political actors of different kinds, undermining the assumption that international anarchy draws a sharp line between domestic and international politics. One can examine the state through a lens that permits its comparison with other political units. This third avenue of research decomposes the *unitary* character of the state and considers the consequences of different institutional combinations.

Each of these old, new, and borrowed elements is considered in the following sections. None has yet produced a coherent research agenda on the state in world politics. Each could be aligned productively with other ongoing research in the discipline. Whether this new interest in the oldest concept in international relations will persist is hardly certain in a faddish field. What follows should confirm, however, that the questioning itself has reopened and refreshed a once-familiar subject.

■ | Globalization and the State

Growing economic interdependence in the 1960s directed attention to many of the same political outcomes that are prominent in the contemporary globalization debate: the growing power of nonstate actors and the emergence of political networks and coalitions that cross national boundaries. The central concerns of those analyzing interdependence also differed from those evaluating the effects of globalization, however. For those writing in the shadow of the 1930s and the realities of the 1970s, the consequences of interdependence for interstate cooperation were most important. Maintaining regimes of economic openness was a primary goal in the face of growing spillovers that hampered policy autonomy and created political conflict (Cooper 1968). Others emphasized the effects of interdependence on interstate bargaining through increased vulnerability to the policies of other states (Keohane and Nye 1977). Policymaking within and between states had changed, but the state itself was not called into question.

Political scientists have developed a successful research agenda on the political effects of globalization, but they have not emphasized the effects of globalization on the state or a particular configuration of political institutions. Instead, researchers have treated globalization as either a source of new political and sectoral *coalitions* under conditions of increasing economic integration or a *constraint* on government policies. Effects on national policy autonomy have been found to vary with the size of the economy, which is associated with economic openness; issue area (for example, monetary policy versus industrial policy); and other concurrent policy choices (for example, adopting a fixed exchange rate under conditions of international capital mobility) (Garrett 1998a, b; Frieden 1991b; Mosley 2000). Those who examine the effects of internationalization on domestic coalitions and policy outcomes often accept intermediation by domestic political institutions as an important explanation for national variation. They have treated the state and other domestic political institutions as significant intervening variables that offset or amplify the effects of internationalization (Keohane and Milner 1996). The effects of globalization on those institutions have received less attention.

Claims that globalization has direct effects on the state and its role in world politics are often based on a definition of globalization that incorporates cultural, environmental, and social networks, as well as economic interdependence (Keohane and Nye 2000). Even defined in more narrowly economic terms, contemporary global economic integration may be substantially different from and, on several dimensions, deeper than earlier periods of economic openness (Baldwin and Martin 1999; Bordo, Eichengreen, and Irwin 1999). Underlying many of these differences is technological innovation: large and continuing reductions in the costs of cross-border communications, which promote cross-border financial flows, facilitate international production networks, and underpin the emergence of new forms of transnational political organization.

These novel features of the contemporary international economy could in turn threaten or transform the role of the state in ways that earlier interdependence did not. Interstate conflict that resulted from growing economic interdependence drove the older agenda of international political economy. The anxieties surrounding globalization emphasize potential conflicts between democratic accountability—located in the state or its subordinate political units—and private actors, particularly economic agents, whose bargaining leverage in domestic political systems has been inflated. The bargaining power of these private actors—particularly mobile capital or multinational corporations—is assumed to increase because they have a more credible exit option from the confines of a single state. Exit is eased in part by technology, in part by the adoption of investor-friendly policies by other states. Observed mobility is not required for the political effects on the state that have been claimed for globalization; a credible threat of exit is sufficient to shift the balance between state and private economic actors.

The logic of expanded transnational political action is similar. Although the exit option is less significant, democratization, coupled with more open borders and lower communication costs, produces possibilities for political arbitrage or leverage that did not exist in the past. Margaret Keck and Kathryn Sikkink describe the strategies of transnational advocacy networks and a "boomerang pattern" that capitalizes on these developments to increase the influence of nongovernmental organizations that have international allies (Keck and Sikkink 1998).

This assumption of a shift in bargaining power between states and nonstate actors leads those pessimistic about the effects of globalization on the state to emphasize declining state capabilities, whatever the national policies pursued. Capabilities could be undermined through several avenues: downward pressure on state revenues, technological disadvantages for hierarchical organizations, a loosening of the identities that link citizens to states, and a reduction in state scale.

Globalization may reduce state capabilities by placing downward pressure on revenues. As taxable economic actors become more mobile and shop for low-tax jurisdictions, the resource base of the state could decline. Taxes on mobile capital are likely to become ineffective. As highly paid individuals become more mobile and more capable of constructing international strategies of tax avoidance, the income tax base of the state could be further eroded. A more-refined view of the effects of globalization suggests that overall revenues need not decline but that the incidence of taxation is likely to shift to less mobile factors, such as labor and more regressive forms of indirect taxation. These distributional effects, rather than a necessary decline in total revenues, create a political limit on state revenues. Revenues may also be shifted toward subnational or local governments, since their tax base would be less affected by capital and labor mobility. If such a shift occurred, it could also affect the internal political balance between levels of government (Rodrik 1997; Tanzi 1998).

Technological innovation and diffusion have lain behind the economic transformations of globalization. Those information and communications technologies may have an independent effect on states and other hierarchical organizations by supporting networked organizations in economics and politics, organizations that are "neither hierarchical nor reducible to market relations" (Keck and Sikkink 1998, 200). Globalization and its technologies, a world of markets and networks, is interpreted as hostile to the hierarchical world of the state and its bureaucratic mode of organization.[6] New transnational organizations, whether economic or political, use the new network technologies far more effectively than traditional states or corporations. Thus, technologies can appear to have an affinity to the competitors of states, directly reinforcing the second-order effects described earlier.

In one popular view, globalization's homogenizing effects on national and local cultures, like the exit options that it provides for key political actors, undermine an important tie that binds states and populations. Both advanced industrial societies, such as Canada and France, and many developing countries portray large-scale, unrestricted trade in cultural products as incompatible with indigenous national cultures. More directly, a renewal of large-scale migration (although substantially smaller than in the pre-1914 era) calls into question existing notions of citizenship and conceptions of national identity (M. Weiner 1995).

Finally, theoretical arguments suggest that economic openness renders large-scale political units unnecessary: as barriers to trade and investment decline globally, the advantages of a large internal market can be

6. On the relationship of networks and markets, see Rauch and Casella 2001.

captured directly through participation in the world economy (Alesina and Spolaore 1997). A similar argument underlies Richard Rosecrance's "virtual state" (1999), in which territorial rule is replaced by economic access. Such pressures, even if unmatched by other countervailing trends, would only produce more states of smaller size rather than units that are different in kind. The historical record also undermines the claim of an association between smaller scale in political units and economic openness: in the decades before 1914, the last period of global economic openness, large-scale units dominated world politics.

The preferences and behavior of nonstate transnational actors over time, the persistence of strong border effects that indicate the importance of different national policy regimes, and alternative explanations for any observed reduction in state capabilities have all been marshaled to counter claims that globalization systematically undermines states. The modern state and global capitalism originated at the same time, and they have co-evolved for centuries.[7] Their relationship might best be described as symbiotic or complementary rather than competitive. The strategies of nonstate actors support this view of complementarity with the territorial state. Modern multinational corporations, however globalized their production networks, maintain close and dependent relations with particular states (Hirst and Thompson 1996). Multinational corporations also display the traits of distinctive national capitalisms. Nationality in the operations and strategies of these corporations "is given by historical experience and the institutional and ideological legacies of that experience, both of which constitute the essential structures of states" (Pauly and Reich 1997, 4). In similar fashion, leverage within the political systems of powerful states largely determines the influence exercised by transnational political networks, even as their activities undermine conventional views of state sovereignty (Keck and Sikkink 1998).

The persistence of strong border effects also suggests that globalization is far from producing a single market in goods, capital, or labor. In other words, the policy regimes created by states—admittedly only one source of border effects—remain influential. Although trade has grown faster than global national income during the past half-century, trade (measured by sales of goods) within OECD national economies remains approximately ten times greater than trade between those economies.[8] Border effects are even higher for international migration, even between two neighboring countries with a history of substantial migration, such as the United States

7. The dependence of capitalism on a fragmented international political system (the modern state system) has been argued by Robert Gilpin, with reference to Jean Baechler.

8. Helliwell 1998. This estimate excludes the effects of common membership in a trade bloc, such as the EU or NAFTA, and a common language. Both of these reduce border effects.

and Canada (Helliwell 1998). Although international financial markets are more integrated than goods markets, at least among the industrialized countries, several indicators suggest the incomplete nature of that integration: national savings and investment rates remain highly correlated (the Feldstein-Horioka effect) and national investment portfolios remain highly concentrated on national assets (Obstfeld and Rogoff 2000). The barriers to a borderless world are not only the discontinuities and risks imposed by national states and their policy regimes. Information discontinuities, emphasized by Rangan and Lawrence (1999), depend on language and other features that differentiate national societies. The combination of increasing economic specialization, an often-overlooked consequence of globalization, and national policy regimes may slow the erosion of border effects by global economic integration.

Finally, alternative explanations may account for evidence that state institutions have changed or state capabilities have weakened. Peter Evans calls into question the evidence itself, claiming that pressure for a diminished state role in economic policy reflects the international dominance of the United States and a politically driven "Washington consensus." The power of that Anglo-American consensus, not the demands of globalization, has shifted normative discourse and policy against state-centered options (Evans, 1997). Geoffrey Garrett argues that globalization, in the form of increased capital mobility, does not explain weaker economic performance in social democratic corporatist states during the 1990s (Garrett 1998b). Expansion of the state's role in insurance against economic insecurity has often been linked to growing economic openness; demands for a welfare state expand at the same time that globalization may undercut national abilities to finance such a state (Rodrik 1997). Recent research suggests, however, that technologically driven processes of deindustrialization—not globalization—may better explain the growth of the welfare state (Iversen and Cusack 2000).

The alleged effects of globalization on the state have too often sustained logical but contradictory arguments that have not been investigated systematically. Concentration on state capabilities as the principal outcome of interest has also narrowed and distorted an investigation of globalization's effects. Without a more careful accounting of the dimensions of institutional change and how central they are to the units that we label states, generalizations of the kind that have pervaded debates over globalization are futile.

This requirement is easily illustrated in the effects of global financial integration, which has progressed further than integration in the markets for goods or labor. The constraints imposed on monetary and exchange rate policy by increased capital mobility are summarized in the "trilemma": fixed exchange rates, an autonomous monetary policy, and capital mobility cannot be realized simultaneously. Given increased global financial integration, the trilemma has been translated by Barry Eichengreen into a sharp dilemma for small, open economies: completely fixed exchange rates (including currency unions or the adoption of another national currency) or exchange rate flexibility are the only sustainable choices in the longer run (Eichengreen 1994, but see Frankel 1999). Even if one accepts this "hollowing out" thesis, global financial integration substantially constrains national policy choice; it does not eliminate the role of states in monetary policy. In similar fashion, Eric Helleiner questions widespread arguments that regulatory arbitrage on the part of financial institutions has undermined that dimension of state capabilities vis-à-vis private actors. Rather, it has changed the location of regulation and the need for interstate coordination (Helleiner 1999).

Benjamin J. Cohen argues that globalization has intensified currency competition within national borders, undermining the Westphalian model of territorial money. Rather than a sweeping assertion of the state undermined, however, Cohen confirms two more qualified findings. The model of exclusive national currencies was only established in the nineteenth century, at a time when international economic integration was growing. This contemporary marker of state sovereignty is of fairly recent vintage and developed concurrently with a first stage of global financial integration. In this regard it resembles the regulatory and macroeconomic roles that have also been constrained by financial integration. Renewed currency competition in recent decades has not undermined the ability of all states to supply money, one of their core functions. It has instead established a clear hierarchy among states based on demand for their currencies. A more fundamental threat to the state itself only lies in an uncertain future: the possibility that purely private money may begin to compete with and eventually overtake national (state-supplied) currencies (Cohen 1998).

If supply of a national currency is usually regarded as a core state function, then a central bank—closely associated with autonomous national monetary and financial policies—is a key state institution. Its autonomy and influence within the state has been influenced by global financial integration through at least two avenues. An independent central bank provides a path to monetary policy credibility for countries with liberalized capital movements and flexible exchange rates. Sylvia Maxfield (1997) suggests a second connection between globalization and central bank independence for developing economies: the belief that such institutions are a useful signaling device in attracting foreign capital. Maxfield's evidence does not suggest a necessary connection between global financial integration and central bank independence, however: institutional change is based on political perceptions, conditioned by national need for capital inflows.

Clark and Hallerberg (2000) offer a similar contingent model of the relationship between globalization (in the form of international capital mobility) and choice of state institutions. Governments change the instruments by which they may attempt to influence electoral outcomes when they choose an exchange rate regime in an environment of mobile capital. Given that monetary policy becomes the effective instrument under a flexible exchange rate regime, governments may be reluctant to give up that instrument to a more independent central bank. This model of electoral competition predicts an institutional choice (central bank independence) that is not determined by globalization per se, but rather by a political calculus that still allows considerable government discretion.

These more complex and contingent models of the effects of globalization on the state point to three avenues that would permit more systematic empirical investigation. Explicit or implicit bargaining between the state and nonstate actors represents the microfoundation of many arguments about the effects of globalization. Better models of that bargaining relationship and how it changes as economic integration deepens would provide a useful grounding for research on globalization and its effects on the state. Such modeling would force more attention on the preferences of nonstate actors and the credibility of their exit or cross-border options.

Economic integration may produce a concentration of core governance functions in the state or their selective dispersion to other sites of governance at the international, regional, or subnational levels (Kahler and Lake 2000). If such deconcentration proceeds far enough, a "hollowing out" of state functions might occur, although that is far from inevitable. Growing cross-national spillovers or economies of scale in the production of public goods may point toward a transfer of some state functions to international or regional institutions. At the same time, intervening political dynamics, often based on transnational political organizations, may create externalities that are less easy to identify and explain. The influence of globalization on governance transfers requires additional exploration and explanation. Such transfer, in the European case and others, may produce alternative institutional bundles that make up units distinct from and potentially in competition with states.

Thinking of the state as an institutional composite—an institutional profile that changes over time—offers a third perspective on globalization and its effects on the state. Without such institutional specification, estimating the effects of globalization on the state quickly becomes an argument over how to define the state. An evolutionary model does not ask whether globalization brings about a generalized eclipse of the state. Instead it enquires whether particular *types* of states are likely to be successful in a new economic environment. In order to contend with an unevenly integrated international economy, certain state institutions will expand or decline over time. Comparative research has often found little evidence of overall institutional convergence among highly integrated economies (Berger and Dore 1996). Nevertheless, the preceding discussion of central bank independence suggests that globalization may create common incentives—under specific political conditions—for adopting particular institutions.

The State Displaced: Unit Variation in World Politics

If globalization could threaten the central position of the state in world politics, that threat would arise from a redefinition of territoriality, a permanent loosening of control over boundaries. Its competitors in world politics derive their power from cross-border economic and political arbitrage. This prospect, if it exists, is based on their *lack* of territoriality, their freedom to shift with ease between political jurisdictions. Although private actors might claim governance functions from the state or press for a different institutional design, they do not attempt to displace the state.

Usurping the state's role as sole territorial unit in world politics would represent an agenda far more radical than the familiar (if unproven) effects of globalization. Such an agenda questions the monopoly that the modern state has exercised on imaginations and research agendas in the study of world politics. Instead of taking the state and stateness as given in international relations (the use of *international* suggests how taken for granted both are), the state and its key characteristics become variables. The contemporary nation-state becomes only one political competitor, albeit a central one, that is a dominant unit in world politics at the turn of the century. J. P. Nettl (1968) urged social scientists to consider stateness as a conceptual variable (while claiming that the external role of the state was invariant). In recent research the political constituents of world politics—the external dimension of the state and its attributes—are assumed to change over time and across political space. Rather than a simple Ptolemaic world politics with the state at its center, a galaxy of alternative political forms claims our attention.

At the center of the new agenda are explanations for the modern nation-state's evolution and its systemwide spread, taxonomies of other units and the systems that they once dominated, and investigations of the consequences of unit variation on external behavior and system outcomes. One key unresolved theoretical issue runs through this research. Recent scholarship on nationalism has emphasized the constructed quality of national identity and nationalist ideologies. From this conception of nationalism, it is a few short steps to the view that the units in world politics themselves are constructed, a corollary of the assault on the invariant nature of the state. But constructed by whom and for what purposes? Is this construction by the other units in the system or by individual agents within the units? Is it primarily normative (infusing sovereignty and other attributes with meaning) or is it based on rational calculation of material interests such as military power or wealth? Within each part of the new agenda, these theoretical disagreements remain. Whatever the response, however, the state will never be the same again.

The neorealist conception of the state claimed that the type of unit engaged in strategic interaction was irrelevant so long as the units were functionally equivalent. On that claim rested neorealism's concentration on capabilities as the only significant unit-level variable within anarchic systems. John Ruggie opened debate over unit variation by attacking this assumption, arguing that neorealism did not accommodate the possibility of systems—such as feudal Europe—in which units were differentiated (Ruggie 1983). In response, revisionists attempted to incorporate differentiated units into a structural realist frame, deriving different anarchies from that unit variation (Buzan, Jones, and Little 1993). Others have rejected a neorealist frame and extended their search for unit variation back in time and into the non-European world.

PRESTATE AND ANCIENT SYSTEMS

One method for capturing unit variation and its effects is to extend the range of theorizing historically, far past the norm in international relations (typically the twentieth century). This strategy permits examination of the links between states and particular behaviors (such as war making) through units that share only certain attributes with states. These approaches also shed light on the evolution of states and the reasons for their relative success among other competing political forms.

Although political scientists have seldom examined the practices of prestate societies toward one another, anthropologists have debated whether war, often taken as a fundamental attribute of state systems, is characteristic of societies without states. Lawrence Keeley, Steven LeBlanc, and others have discovered widespread evidence of violent (rather than ritualistic) warfare among prehistoric and prestate societies (Keeley 1996; LeBlanc 1999). Drawing on the patterns of warfare among such societies, Keeley suggests that interstate conflict may be lower by comparison because of better control over members of society (preventing the outbreak of revenge cycles) and a higher level of interunit institutionalization. The importance of such institutions is illustrated in those prestate societies that have constructed resilient security institutions, such as the Iroquois federation (Crawford 1994).

Ancient polities and their interaction have also attracted attention. Although most analysis is at the system level, unit characteristics provide one explanation for system outcomes that diverge from the modern state system. Christian Reus-Smit (1999) contrasts the fundamental institutions of the society of Greek city-states with those of later societies of states. He explains those institutional differences by constitutional structures that are grounded in beliefs about the moral purpose of the state. Early Mesopotamian systems and the interaction of Mayan polities have been investigated (Cioffi-Revilla and Landman 1999; Cioffi-Revilla 2000). Patterns of state formation and decline or dissolution have been traced to growing status or income inequality under a wide range of conditions (Midlarsky 1999). Fine-grained analysis of one long-lived system—the Amarna system of the ancient Middle East—has illuminated the relationship between diplomatic practices and norms on the one hand and the construction of a system among culturally dissimilar units on the other (Cohen and Westbrook 2000).

Data limitations have shaped research on the relations among prestate and ancient societies. Systems are more easily investigated than units, even though the units diverge from modern states in interesting ways. Only a careful reading and interpretation of historical and ethnographic data—requiring skills that are often beyond the reach of political scientists—can generate an accurate portrait of the self-understanding of these societies and their external relations. In an interdisciplinary dialogue regarding the Amarna system of the ancient Middle East, political scientists were quick to discover practices analogous to those in the contemporary state system; scholars trained in ancient languages and history were more attentive to the risks of anachronism. Both methods could be deployed to considerable effect: historical and linguistic techniques to "get inside" the historical agents and their world-view and social scientific methods to compare their self-understanding with actual practices and with modern patterns of interaction (Cohen and Westbrook 2000).

EVOLUTION AND VARIATION IN THE WESTPHALIAN SYSTEM

Gaining purchase on variation in the units of world politics does not require such distant historical investigation. The modern state itself has evolved over time, and it emerged in competition with other units that enjoyed considerable military and economic success. Unit variation can be captured by examining that evolution over time and by analyzing its now-extinct competitors. This emergent-actor approach to variation has most often relied on historical and comparative approaches. Lars-Erik Cederman (1997), however, has applied a class of models used for other complex systems to simulate the emergence of state systems and nationalism.

Charles Tilly (1990) and Hendrik Spruyt (1994) have challenged the assumption of a unilinear development from feudalism to the modern European state. Both have constructed a wider taxonomy of political units that emerged from the feudal order (city-states and city-leagues), unit types that competed for dominance with the sovereign territorial state. Both have also emphasized a selection mechanism centered on military competition to explain the ultimate dominance of the modern territorial state. In Tilly's case, evolving military technology and the development of capitalism in larger territorial states eroded initial financial advantages of the city-state. Spruyt emphasizes the internal institutional advantages of the state in the competition with other units. He also suggests other, nonevolutionary mechanisms: the mutual empowerment of states through practices of recognition and legitimation and the institutional choices of influential social actors.

One difficulty with such selection models is the incomplete outcome in Europe: other types of units survived for centuries into the era of the modern state. Also, the European state itself was not a constant. The external and internal attributes of sovereignty have evolved over time. Stephen Krasner disaggregates sovereignty into four dimensions and demonstrates that two of these—Westphalian sovereignty (domestic political autonomy) and legal sovereignty (recognition by other sovereigns)—have had different content (measured in state practices) in different historical periods. Westphalian sovereignty in particular has been "frequently transgressed" (Krasner 1999, 224). Although Krasner finds the source of this variation in the preferences and practices of dominant states, others trace different understandings of sovereignty to an evolving process of collective social construction (Biersteker and Weber 1996).

STATES AND NATIONS

More than any other contemporary events, the dissolution of the Soviet Union and Yugoslavia underlined the transience of apparently secure states. A decline in the frequency of interstate conflicts relative to domestic insurgencies and civil wars placed the question of state collapse and ethnic identity at the center of the comparative politics research agenda. As Barbara Geddes and David Laitin describe in this collection, explanations for the mobilization of ethnic identity into politics and the collapse of political order into violent conflict have been sought using an array of methodologies. Both international relations and comparative politics have spent much less time considering the political units within which identity and order are constituted.

The demise of modern states drew attention to nationality, an attribute of those units that had been largely ignored in international relations (Lapid and Kratochwil 1996a). The manufacture of new nationalisms in the 1990s brought to the fore the constructed character of both national identity and the states to which it attached itself. Nationalism necessarily concerns the state, since nationalism is usually defined as a theory of political legitimacy that requires a congruence between ethnic and political (state) boundaries (Gellner 1986; Hobsbawm 1992). In an authoritative compendium of nationalist movements, John Breuilly (1994) claims that nationalism is a "form of politics" that has "possession of a state" as its "major objective." These definitions themselves imply invariance in nationalism, however, an invariance belied by the historical record. The attachment of ethnic movements to a claim for statehood has varied over time; unless one classifies only movements with such a claim as nationalist. Conventional definitions divert attention from this important fact.

Nationalism and the state have varied over time, as has the link between the two. The first assumption (variable nations) is now the centerpiece of research on ethnicity and nationalism; the second lies at the core of renewed interest in the units of world politics. The link between the two has received much less attention. As Cederman notes, however, if both state and nation are treated as variables, the possible outcomes are multiplied: groups may choose to define their ethnic identities according to particular criteria, those identities may find political expression (or not), that political program may or may not include the demand for a fully sovereign state that is associated with a nationality, and states may define themselves as mono- or multiethnic political entities.

Consider the Scots and Scottish nationalism. Creeping union with England was largely a constitutional process in 1707; its economic benefits increased over time but were not a major motivation for union. Expression of Scottish local identity shifted over time, from North Britain, to Caledonia, to Greater Britain, and then back to Scotland (without rejecting other, broader identities). By the nineteenth century, Scotland was a "melting-pot of different, overlapping identities" (Lynch 1991). Political claims for a more exclusive Scottish identity began in that century but did not take the form of demands for a sovereign state until well into the twentieth century. The link of that national identity to familiar ethnic characteristics such as language or religion remained tenuous. In response to recent political assertiveness by Scottish nationalists, the British state devolved power to both Wales and Scotland, creating a more decentralized state. Whether such an institutional response, well short of sovereign statehood, will satisfy nationalists (or the median Scottish voter) is uncertain.

Why states define themselves in national terms, and why and when ethnic groups determine that their identity requires a state are research questions that are central to a definition of political units in contemporary world politics. Answers to the first question—why states choose nation building—often rely on military competition, which creates demands for the extension of direct rule and top-down nationalism on the part of state elites (Tilly 1996). This reading of the benefits of a nation-state are drawn in part from the experience of the French Revolution, when a citizenry mobilized by nationalism appeared to provide the military means for the French state to defeat its dynastic rivals (Posen 1993a). The politics of incorporating this "knowledge" into the practices of rival states was uncertain, however. The success of citizen armies required interpretation by other political elites, and the exclusion of mercenaries and other noncitizen soldiers did not emerge rapidly as a point of state identity (Avant 2000). The extension of direct rule and concomitant nation building by the state could also be attributed to an ideology of "state simplification" that attempted to transform multilingual and disorderly societies into "something more closely resembling the administrative grid of [the state's] observations" (Scott 1998, 82). Whatever their source, the extension of direct rule and programs of nation building that aimed to inculcate uniform language and culture in turn produced resistant nationalisms within the state (Hechter 2000).

Resistance to nation building, which can be violent, drives up the costs of such programs. The potentially high costs of nation building demand a fuller explanation for projects to construct a link between state and nation. Presumably a perceived reduction in administrative costs (costs of resource extraction, use of a conscript army) more than offsets the estimated costs of nation-building programs and containing resistance. Over time some states have been transformed into relatively successful nation-states in which national identity becomes hegemonic—"common sense" for the population in David Laitin's terms (1986). In other cases, persistent and costly efforts to meld national identity with existing states have failed. The reasons for the record of success and failure across states and over time represent another puzzle in the adoption of the nation-state model.

The second question linking nation and state—why some nationalist movements claim statehood and not others—also remains unanswered. Mobilized ethnic groups may stop short of demanding a sovereign state because of invested economic interests or an inability to overcome collective action problems (Hechter 2000). Questioning the link between state and nation casts that most familiar of actors in world politics as a far more problematic construct. As the nation-state model expanded outside Europe, the connection between state and nation became more tenuous as a basis for international politics, and the gap between the empirical and juridical state widened.

THE EXPANSION AND FAILURE OF THE NATION-STATE MODEL

During World War II, E. H. Carr recalled the failures of blanket self-determination and the misguided creation of nation-states after the previous conflict. He warned against experiments in state building across ethnically diverse territories in the non-European world, arguing instead for "balkanisation" as a positive outcome, "a far greater measure of devolution and an immense variety of local administration rooted in local tradition, law, and custom" (Carr 1941, 56). Two world-historical surprises occupied the second half of the century: first, the rapid demise of one unit type—empire—that had persisted for millennia, quickly succeeded by postcolonial imitation of a nation-state model imported from former colonial masters. "The state, once a rare political construct confined to the western extension of a rather small continent, has spread its rule all over the world" (Van Creveld 1999, 334). An emerging consensus now recognizes that the export of the nation-state model (and its willing import by elites in the developing world) has often been a failure, producing rather than preventing internal disorder and external weakness (Badie 2000).[9]

The disappearance of empires has been treated historically and comparatively, but rarely theoretically.[10] The existing literature has concen-

9. For similar judgments, see Van Creveld 1999, 332; Tilly 1998b, 407.

10. For example, comparisons of the collapse in the Soviet empire with earlier imperial disintegration: Dawisha and Parrott 1997.

trated on long-standing debates over why empires emerge, rather than the question of how they have varied in their institutional design and why they have persisted or failed. Much of the debate surrounding the underpinnings and end of the European colonial empires has contrasted models based on self-interested actors motivated by material or political interests and explanations that emphasize normative change at the global level.[11]

Empire had required the stripping of sovereign recognition from many of the sovereign territories; winning such recognition from the European powers offered some measurable insurance against forceful incorporation. That lesson in state selection explains only part of the widespread adoption of the Western nation-state model in the aftermath of decolonization. Given resistance to European rule and availability of both precolonial models and postcolonial rivals (such as pan-Arabism), adoption of the ill-fitting template remains a puzzle. Recent research on pre- and postcolonial state systems offers both a deeper understanding of the consolidation of new states and competing explanations for the hold of this European import on their elites. Two types of explanation dominate: on the one hand, reinterpreted international norms of sovereignty and territorial integrity and, on the other, the calculus of domestic elites.

In their consideration of regional politics in the Middle East, Malik Mufti (1996) and Michael Barnett (1995) offer different interpretations of the consolidation of a regional state system whose units were in question as the colonialists departed. Barnett gives greater weight to emerging norms of sovereignty and Arab nationalism in the region; Mufti, to the self-interested strategies of political elites, whose interest in pan-Arabism as a domestic prop declined as their hold on state power strengthened. Paralleling Barnett's normative explanation, Robert H. Jackson (1990) argues that quasi-states in the developing world are actively sustained by an international regime of negative sovereignty that differs from both the preimperial sovereignty regime and the positivist doctrines that reinforced European colonialism. In his recent analysis of the African state system, Jeffrey Herbst (2000), on the other hand, awards an important role to the "importers" of the sovereignty regime, the new political elites in Africa who rejected more differentiated precolonial units and welcomed an inherited regime of fixed borders. A supportive international environment, in Herbst's view, diminished the incentives for constructing internal rule over the national territory and laid the basis for today's failed states.

UNITS WITHIN UNITS: VARIATIONS ON A THEME OF HIERARCHY

Renewed interest in empires and their demise points to a final theoretical shortcoming in the view of units that has prevailed in international relations. The conventional view of the modern state system incorporated a

11. For the former, Davis and Huttenback 1986; Kahler 1984. For the latter, Jackson 1993.

particular model of the state as well as an assumption that normal relations among those units were anarchic. Just as the state has been deposed from its position as an invariant feature of world politics, the assumption of anarchy has also been reexamined. With reexamination has come an awareness that international relations and domestic politics display a spectrum of relations among units that is wider than a simple divide between anarchy and hierarchy. Anarchy has not been the defining characteristic of all world politics; hierarchy within domestic politics has often been uncertain as well. States and other units have engaged in hierarchical relations (involving more or less coercion), as well as consensual unions and cooperative arrangements, of greater and less formality. Clusters of international or interunit relations may in turn become units of a different sort, engaging in their own relations with one another. Rather than Herz's conventional view of hard-shelled states of a single type within a competitive, anarchic setting, one begins to perceive units of different types managing an array of relations, both internally and externally. The sharp divide between domestic and international politics breaks down.

David Lake (1999) has used this core insight to reexamine the foreign policies of the United States, a powerful state during the twentieth century, when military competition was often intense. He develops a model of interunit contracting to explain a "rich tapestry" of security relationships. Lake's model is based on joint production economies (which determine whether security cooperation or unilateralism will dominate) and two additional variables that determine the anarchic or hierarchical form of any security relationship: costs of opportunism (in turn influenced by relationally specific assets) and governance costs. This approach not only captures a greater degree of variation in security policies, beyond decisions to ally or not ally; Lake also provides explanations for those policies over time.[12] Units defined by internal relations of greater or lesser hierarchy among constituent units also characterized the antebellum Philadelphian system in the United States, an alternative to both federation and empire that has been described by Daniel Deudney (1995). The richest territory for exploring the array of relations within and between units can be found in the burgeoning literature on the European Union (EU), however.

THE EUROPEAN UNION: ECONOMIC INTEGRATION AND UNIT VARIATION

The institutions of European integration draw together economic integration (globalization) as a source of unit variation and the extension of that variation beyond nation-states. The EU was defined from its beginnings by conflicting models of European institutions—a trajectory toward federalist hierarchy versus a setting for intergovernmental bargains. Whether its constituent political elites were motivated primarily by economic interests in

12. For a similar argument, see Weber (1997).

the face of growing trade and investment flows or wider foreign policy and political goals has also remained controversial.[13]

By the 1990s, analogies to other intergovernmental organizations were weakened by more extensive delegation to European institutions, the wider scope of European bargains, and dense political linkages between European and national institutions (Kahler 1995). Although development of the European legal system and constitutionalization of the European Union permitted comparison to a domestic legal order, the EU did not approach the foreign policy and security powers of any existing federation in its outer face.

The study of European institutions has gradually been liberated from comparison with the singular benchmark of the nation-state. Postliberation, research on the European Union illustrates the value that is added by expanding the field of unit variation. The EU is best captured in a wider array of institutional models that sidesteps the earlier concentration on attaching a statelike label to its institutions. Its recent development and political processes have been characterized as a regulatory structure based on efficiency gains as well as a parliamentary model based on democratic legitimacy (Caporaso 1996; Dehousse 1998). Policy networks, rather than more hierarchical or state-centric models, have also been advanced as characteristic of European political processes (Risse-Kappen 1996). Even the external relations of the EU, usually portrayed as the failure of a common foreign policy, have been subjected to revisionist scrutiny. Instead of a failed superstate, the European Union is portrayed as an "exclusive international club," creating its own network of partners and clients through negotiation and the incentives of prospective membership (Zielonka 1998). In evaluating the EU's performance in the sphere of foreign and security policy, as in other policy domains, observers now realize that the appropriate units of comparison must be specified precisely (Jørgenson 1998).

The European Union provides a final example of the historical and theoretical limitations of conventional conceptions of the state and the benefits of embracing the agenda of unit variation that has been described. Research on the EU also demonstrates that empirical investigation of unit variation requires the specification of unit dimensions and a means for measuring them. When the state was unquestioned, this dilemma did not exist. Now that the state has become a variable, taking the measure of that variable becomes essential. Institutional analysis has begun to play that role in the case of the EU. The next section suggests how that borrowed set of tools can be applied to other analytical tasks.

13. For a strong statement that economic motivations were dominant, see Moravcsik 1998a.

FORGING A CONCEPTUAL TOOL KIT: THE STATE AS AN INSTITUTIONAL COMPOSITE

More precise analysis of the consequences of globalization for the state or the effects of unit variation on world politics requires an ability to identify and measure variation within the category of states or the larger field of political units. In system-dominant approaches, such as neorealism, the assumption of institutional convergence under conditions of international competition obviated the need for such institutional analysis. Although some still use the state as an unproblematic starting point, most neorealists now concede the need for unit-level variables in order to explain international outcomes. Stephen Van Evera's treatise (1999) on the causes of war, for example, includes polities as diverse as ancient Rome, ancient China, and modern European states as implicitly similar units.[14] His core explanation for war, however, is misperception regarding the international structure of power. Most of those misperceptions are, in turn, caused by variations in state institutions and policies.

Alternative approaches to institutional analysis could be used to both enrich the dimensions of variation in states and other units in world politics and sharpen the measurement of that variation (Hall and Taylor 1996). When the state was "brought back in" during the 1980s, historical institutionalism framed the state as an institutional endowment, slow to change, imposing relatively fixed constraints on political actors within its borders. The degree to which those constraints were binding over time measured state strength vis-à-vis domestic society, a distinction with implications for foreign policy and international outcomes.[15] A second conception of the state was more compatible with rationalist and game theoretic approaches to political institutions and international politics. The state was defined as an actor, represented by "politicians and administrators in the executive as independent participants in the policy process" (Ikenberry et al. 1988, 10). Each of these approaches to the state had its drawbacks. State strength represented a single dimension of state institutions, and one that proved difficult to measure. The state-as-executive view often eliminated any political model of how state preferences were formed and removed the state from wider domestic political processes.

Development of institutional analysis during the past decade has allowed reconstruction of conceptions of the state (and other units in world politics), enriching the dimensions applied and sharpening their measurement. In an admirable survey of institutionalist approaches to foreign policy, Ronald Rogowski suggests one set of institutional dimensions based on

14. The causes include dominance of professional militaries over policy; construction of "chauvinist myths," largely through state educational systems; failure of bureaucratic evaluation of key policy ideas; and vagueness in official strategy (Van Evera 1999, 256–57).

15. For a recent example of state-centered realism that awards a central place to state strength, see Zakaria 1998.

principal-agent theory: a franchise (defining the set of principals), rules and mechanisms for representation of those principals, and decision rules that govern those agents or representatives (1999, 119–22).

Although these dimensions are limited to the internal ordering of the state, they add two key features to earlier typologies of the state. In contrast to those who limited the state to the executive and bureaucratic apparatus (and implicitly viewed legislatures and their power as signs of a weak state), legislative institutions are central to rational-choice institutional analysis. In addition, explanation requires attention to the composition of the constituents or principals who can retain or remove state officials. These may be a democratic electorate, politicians (in the case of bureaucratic personnel), or, in nondemocratic regimes, a selectorate. The state and its institutions are firmly embedded in a wider domestic politics.

In its application to the state, rationalist institutional analysis displays strengths and shortcomings. Both are illustrated in one of the most active research agendas in political science: the democratic peace. The finding that democracies rarely, if ever, make war on one another has produced a large and growing body of research that both documents and contests that finding. The distinctiveness of both the foreign policies of democratic states and dyads of those states have been extended to other foreign policy domains as well.[16] Two alternative explanations are advanced for the democratic peace and related observations: normative and institutional. Institutional explanations now appear to fit existing observations of democratic states, their foreign policy behavior, and international conflict with greater accuracy.

The institutional attributes that explain the democratic peace remain in dispute, however. At least three institutional alternatives have been advanced. The first emphasizes the information environment of democracies, and particularly the reduction in information asymmetries that result from greater transparency and clearer signaling between democracies. The second regards democratic institutions as constraints on leaders who make the decisions for war or peace, altering their incentives (through the threat of removal) and permitting easier mobilization of opposition to conflict.[17] A third alternative builds on two of these constraints—the breadth of the democratic franchise and the criteria for selection of democratic leaders— to argue that democratic leaders who opt for war are likely to try harder to win and to avoid conflicts they believe cannot be won (Bueno de Mesquita et al. 1999). Discrimination among different institutional arguments in this instance, as Schultz points out, is difficult because the institutional variables in question are highly correlated (1999, 238).[18]

16. These findings are summarized in Bueno de Mesquita et al. 1999.

17. These two models of institutional influences are summarized by Schultz 1999.

18. Schultz does devise a research design that permits such discrimination, although he cannot conclusively rule out the competing institutional argument.

The testing of increasingly sophisticated institutional models against foreign policy data has produced a cumulative research agenda on democratic states and their foreign policies that is unmatched in international relations. Despite its accomplishments, this agenda includes a limited set of institutional dimensions: the franchise and rules of representation. Institutional analysis in this instance borrows heavily from the study of contemporary advanced industrial democracies, which may limit its usefulness for investigating a wider array of units. Another avenue of institutional analysis may be more promising in this regard: the role of institutions in promoting credible domestic and international commitments. Peter Cowhey (1995) has described how divided powers in the United States and Japan's parliamentary system offer contrasting obstacles in the form of veto gates to initiating new policies and reversing existing commitments. Both within the group of stable democracies and across democratic and nondemocratic regimes, institutional design will typically grant a greater ability to change policy to meet external circumstances only at the cost of lower accountability and reduced credibility of commitments.[19] By measuring veto gates and other institutional devices that enhance credible commitments, one could construct a spectrum of states between poles of credible states and flexible states.[20]

Delegation is a third feature of political institutions that may be used as a commitment technology. As described earlier, independent central banks may provide such an anchor for national monetary and exchange rate policies. Delegation to institutions or units *outside* the national state, however, provides the basis for additional dimensions of state and unit variation: the centralized state versus the deconcentrated state. Whether produced by the pressures of economic integration or other causes, national states display considerable variation in their willingness to delegate key governance functions to international and regional institutions on the one hand or subnational units on the other. Cross-regional variation on this dimension is striking: European states have delegated considerable powers to the European Union and other regional and global institutions; they have also instituted significant devolution to states, regions, and localities within their borders. In other regions, such as the Middle East, states remain highly centralized and are reluctant to delegate any significant functions to regional institutions. Research on international institutions and on federalism have seldom been joined to determine whether and how these two types of delegation might be related.

19. This trade-off and the question of how institutions reinforce the credibility of commitments figures prominently in Auerswald 2000, MacIntyre 2001, Martin 2000, and Mansfield, Milner, and Rosenthal 2000. On veto players, see Tsebelis 1995, 1999.

20. Compare this distinction to the trade-off of decisiveness and resoluteness in Cox and McCubbins 2001.

The institutional analysis described thus far is individualist and ratio-nalist in its assumptions; self-interested actors construct state institutions through strategic interaction. An alternative sociological view of institu-tions emphasizes their normative content and the role of the institutional environment in constituting actors and their interests.[21] Peter Katzenstein (1996a) has argued that key security institutions in the Japanese state are circumscribed by a normative consensus, one that has been shaped by po-litical contestation over the postwar decades. Military institutions and poli-cies have also been shaped by distinctive and persistent strategic cultures (Johnston 1995). Martha Finnemore documents institutional and norma-tive importation from the international environment in the spread of sci-entific research bureaucracies. In this case there is little evidence of financial or other incentives offered by the external actors; the construction of these institutions seems to be related to a particular normative identity of the state as "engine of progress and modernity" (Finnemore 1996a, 129).

A normative approach to defining state institutions faces different ob-stacles than rationalist strategies. The most familiar is that leveled by Kras-ner in his analysis of the central norms of sovereignty as "organized hypocrisy," persistent, resilient, but with shifting effects on state practice. The multiplicity of norms and their empirical specification over time is also source of uncertainty. Post hoc explanation is a serious risk without clear definition in advance of the norms and their content (Kowert and Legro 1996). Finally, the political process through which certain norms define state institutions and others fail remains obscure. The model of norm dynamics proposed by Finnemore and Sikkink (1998) provides one model for norm-driven politics, but its scope is unclear.[22]

Whatever the approach to institutions taken, reconstructing the state as a composite or bundle of institutions would require changes in the di-rection of institutional research. A taxonomy of institutional composites or bundles is required in order to define unit variation. The set of institutions that defines the modern nation-state or any of its variations must be speci-fied. Most institutional research to date has concentrated on only one di-mension associated with states: internal institutional configurations. Even within that dimension, attention has been heavily concentrated on ad-vanced industrial democracies and representative institutions. Institutional analysis has been applied less frequently to other parts of the state appara-tus that span a wider array of states and have important implications for international relations. Military institutions, for example, particularly rela-tions between military bureaucracies and their political superiors, have been a historically important determinant of both state capabilities and po-

21. For a typology of such approaches, see Jepperson, Wendt, and Katzenstein 1996.

22. It does not appear to fit the norm-based account of Katzenstein (1996a), for ex-ample.

litical stability (Avant 1994). Movement from professional to conscript militaries (and back again) has been a source of political controversy and an institutional choice with external implications (Levi 1998a; Avant 2000).

Other dimensions that lie outside the internal ordering of the state and define the spectrum of units have received far less attention. Territoriality is often identified as a core institutional feature of the modern state. It is also a key dimension of unit variation: most political organizations are territorial in some sense but their territoriality differs from contemporary practices and interstate conventions. Cohen (1998) contrasts the Westphalian model of monetary geography—currency use matches state territories and their boundaries—with a far more complex portrait of transactional domains that span conventional boundaries. Territoriality defined as the coincidence of exclusive policy domains on a delimited territory has begun to unravel. Powerful states extend their policy domains well beyond their national boundaries through sanctions or agreement. Modeling the institutions of territoriality, which are central in defining state and unit variation, should become a central part of the institutionalist research agenda on the state.

Bridging both rational-choice and sociological institutionalism, unit environment appears and reappears as an exogenous and sometimes ad hoc feature in explanations of the state and its institutional profile. Avner Greif's narrative (1998) of the Genoese city-state awards a central but fluctuating role to external threat and intervention in establishing a self-enforcing political system. Finnemore (1996a) outlines a dominant role for the international normative environment in defining certain state institutions but also allows for an undefined level of local variation. The means by which the environment influences institutional development and variation requires clarification. Rationalist models (and conventional international relations) often rely on implicit notions of competition and selection. Sociological institutionalists typically adopt some combination of diffusion, socialization, and learning. The precise causal steps from environmental change to institutional evolution are too often omitted, however.

Treating the state and other units in world politics as composites of institutions has the attractive side benefit of providing international relations and comparative politics with a common vocabulary and methodology. The bright line between domestic and international politics disappears: nearly all politics becomes polyarchic, lying between pure anarchy and pure hierarchy.[23] This common institutional approach to states and other

23. As Milner notes, her use of polyarchy differs from the earlier (and widespread) use coined by Robert Dahl meaning democratic rule. A state's movement away from hierarchical organization in its politics is measured by the degree to which the preferences of key actors diverge, the level of power sharing among those actors, and the centralization of control over information (1997, 11, 1998).

political units has already enriched research on the European Union. The European Union is treated as a "highly developed political system" with a dense field of institutions that lacks both a state apparatus and high level of mass political participation (Hix 1999). Institutional analysis has often taken state institutions as fixed, defining the parameters of a game, and has then attempted to assess the policies that result from a particular institutional equilibrium. Any application of institutional analysis to the now-variable state or other units will require endogenizing state institutions, viewing them as a target of political calculation, actor strategies, and normative constitution.

Questioning the State: From Black Box to Pandora's Box?

The state in international relations has rapidly moved from ideal-typical constant to a variable that is subject to empirical investigation. The field of international relations has begun to investigate states rather than taking them for granted. This renewed interest has been driven by events—globalization, the collapse of cold war verities—and a convergence of different research streams—political economy, history, institutional analysis. The new agenda also marks the continuing and very slow motion breakdown of Eurocentrism in international relations.

The three research avenues described here bring different assumptions and different aims to this project, but their progress is also linked. Globalization or international economic integration has been one driver of unit variation over time. Although the rhetoric of globalization often proclaims the demise of the state, the realities of globalization raise research questions that chart far more modest outcomes. Political scientists have concentrated on the effects of globalization on policy autonomy and new political coalitions rather than state institutions. In assessing the effects of globalization on the state, bargaining among states and nonstate actors requires more accurate modeling. The outcome of such bargaining (or the anticipated reactions of governments to the demands of private actors) may produce a migration of some state functions to subnational actors or to regional or international institutions. Over time, such transfers could transform the existing institutional profile of the nation-state. The pattern of such transfers and their explanation provide a second avenue for investigating the influence of globalization on the state. A third means of transformation could also be examined: whether a globalized environment rewards or discourages particular institutional designs among states. Any of these approaches—bargaining outcomes, shifting levels of governance, or environmental selection of different institutional configurations—provides a more measured and accurate portrait of globalization's effects on the state.

Unit variation is the label that I have given to a research agenda that has more profound theoretical implications for conventional views of the state. The modern nation-state is simply one, temporarily successful contender amid a number of competitors over the course of history. Unit history has been extended to include the earliest civilizations and prestate societies. The ancestry and rivals of the sovereign territorial state are explored. The nation is disconnected from the state. And the empirical emptiness of the concept of nation or state is conceded for much of the world. The state as we knew it has not disappeared, but its central theoretical and historical position in international relations is undermined. This emergent actor agenda, in Cederman's phrase, has to date emphasized explanations for the emergence of particular types of units and the disappearance of others. In addition to those processes, the significance of such variation must also be assessed: have systems composed of different units exhibited different behaviors and outcomes? By means of which institutions—internal or interunit—were different units defined?

Finally, estimating the effects of globalization on the state and explaining larger patterns of unit variation require more precise unit definitions and a means of measuring variation. Institutional analysis may provide answers to these knotty problems of definition and measurement. However, current institutional research requires redirection in order to capture the scope of institutional changes raised by both globalization and unit variation. Its concentration on the contemporary industrialized democracies and their foreign policies should broaden to include a wider range of units and dimensions of variation. The dimensions of territoriality provide only one example of variation that could be illuminated by the application of institutional analysis. Recent research on the European Union demonstrates the potential of institutional analysis applied beyond the confines of the state.

Although this account has necessarily given a false coherence to an anarchic and effervescent research environment, several issues unite the old, the new, and the borrowed. If the now-open black box of the state is not to become a theoretical Pandora's box, theoretically informed taxonomies are required. One advances this recommendation cautiously in the field of international relations, where taxonomies with short half-lives have been particularly numerous. Nevertheless, a shared ability to identify and name the new subjects of investigation will be required.

Second, this research implies that sharp distinctions between domestic and international should be rejected. The perspective of unit variation confirms that what is a unit in one setting will be an environment in another. The old hard distinction between internal hierarchy and external anarchy, challenged by Milner, Lake, and others, has broken down theoretically and empirically. The warlords of Somalia are units in an anarchic setting within a (quasi-)state; European states inhabit an economic space and security community that is a unit in formation as well as a decidedly nonanarchic environment.

Finally, units can form the environment for other units and those environments vary as well. A blurring of the analytic distinction between domestic and international does not erase the lines between units and their environments. It is on this issue—the relative importance of the environment in defining unit identities and interests—that researchers divide. Rather than replicating old debates that treated this question by pronouncement, however, it would be better to view it as contingent and empirical. Careful definition of the environment, whether normative or material, and close investigation of the interaction between actors and that environment are required.

These challenges to the monolithic conception of the state in world politics could spell an end to its usefulness as a concept. From Nettl's "basic, irreducible unit," the state may become simply one combination of institutions, sharply bounded in time and space. Given the deep roots of the state in the study of international politics and its contemporary dominance as a political unit, it seems unlikely that the shorthand of the state will disappear. That shorthand should be deployed in a more tentative and precise way, however, recognizing that the state of today is not the state of the past or the future. Nor does the state's peculiar identity encompass all of the institutional possibilities in world politics.

Why Does It Matter?

Although the interaction of Mesopotamian empires or precolonial African states may offer intrinsic intellectual interest, skeptics may also question whether researching such historical exotica is a self-indulgence, diverting attention from critical contemporary issues. Certainly, rigorous scholarly attention to globalization can only clarify debates where misinformation and demagoguery are rife. Even the larger research agenda surrounding the state is very close to the headlines.[24] East Timor and Kosovo are international protectorates, a new or reinvented exercise of collective hierarchy, established after the fragmentation of two nation-states. Colombia is a state that has given political control over portions of its territory to armed insurgents. In sub-Saharan Africa the era of the quasi-state has collapsed in cross-border intervention and failed states. The research described here is not alone in questioning the state; the world contributes as well.

Clear diagnosis is not the only contribution that this research agenda can make, however. Already, those who wish to rebuild the old nation-state system and those who propose alternatives offer competing visions of the future. For much of the 1990s, an analogy from interstate to intrastate conflict dominated the discussion of ethnic conflict. Ethnic violence was traced to insecurity. The prescription for its end followed: reestablishing security within strong and ethnically homogeneous states. Partition became

24. The headlines in this case are drawn from *Foreign Affairs*, July–August 2000.

a solution of choice. Drawing on some of the theoretical innovations described here, David Laitin (1998a) has pointed out the low probability that nations (if they exist) can be aligned closely with states. Jeffrey Herbst (2000) questions whether state failure in Africa can be addressed successfully without radical changes in the terms of external support and an opening to institutional alternatives. Gidon Gottlieb proposes a "new space for nations" that is "not organized territorially into independent states" (Gottlieb 1993, 36). Their proposals reflect a first, provocative wave of prescription derived from this theoretical opening of the state in world politics.

Atul Kohli

State, Society, and Development[1]

How varying patterns of state authority emerge in developing countries and how state authority is in turn used to push these countries along a variety of developmental pathways are questions of enduring interest to scholars of comparative political development. Over the years these concerns have been addressed from a number of theoretical standpoints. Following World War II, and especially in the heyday of the cold war, liberal and radical scholars debated these issues under the rubric of modernization and dependency perspectives. Over the last two to three decades the best research in the subfield has instead been framed by what may be loosely labeled a state-society framework. Informed by this neo-Weberian standpoint, scholars have pursued a series of important questions: Why is it so difficult to create coherent state authority in the developing world? Where such state authority emerges, what are the origins and dynamics of revolutionary, authoritarian, and democratic regimes? How and why do states vary in their effectiveness in promoting social and economic development? In what follows I critically review some of the more recent important scholarly contributions aimed at unraveling these puzzles of intellectual and real-world significance.

After briefly identifying the defining elements of the state-society perspective, this review is organized in two main parts. The first part discusses research that seeks to explain the emergence of a variety of authority structures in the context of development, especially revolutionary regimes, bureaucratic authoritarian regimes, and democracies. The focus in the second part is on research that seeks to explain the impact of state structures and actions on the society and economy in developing countries. The

1. I would like to thank Jeffrey Herbst, Joel Migdal, and Deborah Yashar for their helpful suggestions on an outline of this essay; Sheri Berman, Jason Brownlee, Forrest Colburn, Peter Evans, James Mahoney, and two anonymous reviewers for their useful comments on an early draft; and Erik Kuhonta for his valuable research assistance.

84

essay concludes by briefly acknowledging some of the main criticisms of this research tradition, especially those developed by the more culturalist and rational-choice scholars, and by suggesting some useful future directions of research.

The general argument developed in this essay is that, when judged against such criteria as the capacity to generate cumulative and generalizable knowledge about important issues on the one hand and the ability to attract the interest of a range of senior and emerging scholars on the other hand, the state-society perspective represents a robust research tradition in the study of comparative political development. This is mainly because there is a good fit between what attracts scholars to this subfield and the state-society framework. Scholars of comparative political development generally pursue research on problems of real-world significance in one part of the world or another. Working within a state-society framework thus enables them to pursue theoretical issues at a middle level of generality without sacrificing either empirical specificity or relevance. While the resulting research generally clusters around problem areas, broadly shared assumptions and concepts also create a wider research community in which scholars can readily move from the study of one problem to another.

More specific arguments developed here focus less on paradigmatic issues and more on substantive debates in the study of comparative political development. Three interrelated themes that emerge during the review are notable at the outset. First, while the study of authoritarianism and democracy in developing countries is a lively research area, future research will benefit from being more genuinely comparative, especially across developing regions. It will additionally be important to situate the study of such processes of authority formation in their global context, both ideological and economic. Second, the study of authority structures will eventually need to move beyond the continuing categorization of regime types into democracies and authoritarians. While these are useful categories for some purposes, increasingly the variety within democracies will loom large. Moreover, it remains unclear whether democracies are good at facilitating such other-valued outcomes as economic growth and fair distribution. Other regime typologies—for example, predatory and developmental states that cut across the issue of democracy versus authoritarianism—may be as important for structuring research, especially if the focus is on issues of how state authority is used to promote or inhibit economic development. And third, the study of the state's role in economic development—again, a lively research area with important contributions—will benefit in the future by focusing as much on political as on bureaucratic variables and needs to be pushed toward asking where do differing state capacities to pursue development come from.

Prior to a full discussion, several caveats are also in order. First, I have for the most part avoided issues of the sociology of knowledge in this review essay. While these are of great interest, this is not the right place to worry

about, for example, how the end of the cold war might or ought to influence the comparative political study of developing countries. Second, the
criteria by which it was decided to review some bodies of literature and not
others, as well as to discuss some scholarly contributions in more detail
than others, has an element of arbitrariness. The main criteria for inclusion were scholarly contributions that build on each other and thus create
vibrant knowledge communities clustered around significant research
problems. Scholarly significance was also important in deciding what to include and what to exclude. In order to minimize unnecessary "canoniza-
tion," however, it is also important to state up front that my criteria for
inclusion were influenced by my ready familiarity with some literatures,
personal tastes, and my intellectual networks. Another way in which inclusion is somewhat arbitrary is that not all the scholars whose works are discussed may be happy to be included in a "club" that they neither helped
establish nor sought to join.

Third, while I pay some attention to paradigmatic battles, the focus below is on research and debates within a shared intellectual tradition. This
is a matter of intellectual taste. There are those who like to worry about
how to study a problem and there are those who study problems; I decidedly belong to the second group and hence my focus. While debates on
first principles are important, they also often rehearse well-defined positions rather than produce genuine give and take. No wonder paradigmatic
battles involve fewer intellectual issues and more political battles over the
control of departments, personnel issues, and the life of the profession.
And finally, among the criteria that I use for judging scholarship in this
review are the importance of the questions raised, the intellectual sophistication with which they were handled—including originality and generalizability—and their impact on future scholarship.

■ | The State-Society Perspective

The intellectual lineage of the state-society perspective can be readily
traced back to debates between Marx and Weber, in which, while taking
Marx seriously, Weber argued that political, social, and ideational life
could not be reduced to economic phenomena. Weber, of course, went on
to demonstrate how ideas may influence economic and political outcomes;
why authority and legitimacy structures varied, even within similar economic circumstances; and the autonomous significance of modern states
and bureaucracies. Evident in this Weberian dissent was a preference for
something less than an evolutionary and general theory of politics and
society on the one hand and a related strong claim that state and society
are analytically autonomous but mutually constitutive in the real world
on the other hand (Bendix 1962, 286–90). These early intellectual posi-

tions eventually influenced the emergence of what is discussed here as the state-society perspective.

After World War II, when the comparative political study of developing countries gained popularity worldwide but especially in North American universities, such Weberian modesty was lost in the grand ideological and theoretical debates involving liberal and Marxist scholars. Many social scientists, including political science scholars of development, embraced the "totalizing" vision of structural-functional sociology and hoped that modernization theories would gain a paradigmatic status.[2] An occasional dissent, evoking the earlier Weberian caution against grand theorizing could be heard but was lost in the forward march of general theory building (Bendix 1967, 1973; Rudolph and Rudolph 1967). The real opposition to modernization theory thus came from dependency scholars, who, with their Marxist sympathies, were equally committed to an alternative set of grand theories.[3]

A new generation of scholars in the 1980s sought to distance themselves from what had arguably become a dialogue of the deaf between modernization and dependency scholars. "Bringing the state back in" was an important salvo in this intellectual development (Stepan 1978; Evans, Rueschemeyer, and Skocpol 1985). The central claim was simple but powerful, namely, that state structures and actions often enjoy considerable autonomy from the underlying social structures and ought not to be treated as socially determined. A variety of scholars, in turn, found this theoretical stance congenial: those with Marxist sympathies who felt that "economic determinism in the last instance" was a formulation that could not solve most of the analytical anomalies faced by Marxism;[4] pluralist and other scholars of interest group politics who had noticed that state-structured interest groups—or corporatism—were significant determinants of political and economic outcomes (Schmitter 1974; Stepan 1978; P.J. Katzenstein 1985; Collier and Collier 1979); former modernization scholars who became dissatisfied with structural-functional political analysis;[5] and, of

2. Among numerous critical reviews of this body of literature, see Huntington 1971.

3. For reviews, see, among others, Palma 1978 and T. Smith 1979. Note that this generalizing tendency was more true of someone like Andre Gunder Frank than of, say, Fernando Henrique Cardoso, whose claims were less grand, almost Weberian in his insistence on history.

4. The Marxist scholars who sought to save Marxism from growing anomalies included Althusser 1969 and Poulantzas 1973. For a review of Marxist theories of the state, see Wright, D. M. Gold, and Lo 1975. Among state-society scholars who might have been sympathetic to Marxism but distanced themselves, were Theda Skocpol and Peter Evans. Also interesting here is the contrast between the early and later work of Guillermo O'Donnell.

5. This took some time in coming but eventually came. See Weiner 1991; Price 1991. Also notice Huntington 1968—an early dissenter—whose work was quite statist from the beginning.

course, Weberian comparativists who had all along resisted economic and social determinism of political life (Bendix 1964, 1978). A neo-Weberian consensus of sorts thus quickly emerged. Even when some scholars felt that statism was going too far in neglecting societal variables, this dissent was often friendly and within the broad state-society framework.[6] Numerous volumes employing a state-society framework thus emerged over the 1980s and the 1990s; arguably this framework became the preferred framework of most scholars working on the comparative politics of developing countries.[7]

Leaving aside this brief intellectual history sketch, how might one characterize the core theoretical elements around which the state-society perspective coheres? This characterization is not easy because the coherence, though real, is somewhat loose. There are few foundational texts. And the level of theoretical self-consciousness varies from study to study. Moreover, not everyone uses the same language: while many scholars use the categories of state and society, some prefer political elites and masses, others political elites and social classes, and yet others choose to break the macro concepts of the state and society into more specific components, such as leaders, ruling parties, regimes, and bureaucracies on the political side and into economic and noneconomic groups, upper and lower strata, organized and mobilized forces, or civil society on the social side. The results to the uninitiated may seem chaotic, but as we will see, they are not.

The first thing that distinguishes most scholars working in the state-society tradition is what they are not. They are not committed to working within and furthering research in one of the grand paradigms that seek to create very general theories and that compete for our attention. State-society scholars are thus neither Marxists (or dependency theorists) nor structural-functionalists (or modernization theorists) and, in terms of more recent debates, are often at odds with rational-choice scholars. While eschewing grand theory, most state-society scholars are very much social scientists, committed to generalizable knowledge—though often at a middle

6. See Migdal 1988 and Migdal, Kohli, and Shue 1994. Less friendly reaction along these lines may be Scott 1998.

7. An incomplete list of major book-length studies of comparative political development that employ a state-society framework would include the following: On **Africa**, see Herbst 2000 and 1990, Bratton and Van de Walle 1997, Young 1994, Price 1991, and Callaghy 1984. On **India**, see Weiner 1991, Rudolph and Rudolph 1987, and Kohli 1987. On **China**, see L. White 1998 and Shue 1988; an early precursor on China along these lines was Schurmann 1966. On **Latin America**, see Hagopian 1996, Collier and Collier 1991, Stepan 1978 and 1988, and Evans 1979. On **Northeast Asia**, see Woo-Cumings 1999, Woo 1991, Wade 1990, Amsden 1989, and C. A. Johnson 1982. On **Southeast Asia**, see Hutchcroft 1998, Doner 1991, and MacIntyre 1991. On the **Middle East**, see Waterbury 1983. For broadly comparative work, see Kohli forthcoming, Bermeo 2002, Collier 1999, Waldner 1999, Evans 1995, Waterbury 1993, Haggard 1990, Migdal 1988, and Skocpol 1979.

level, seeking to theorize not about all of politics but about more limited classes of political phenomena—and its empirical verification. This systematic commitment to seek causal explanations and to worry about their broader applicability also distinguishes the state-society scholars from those who seek to know what happened in specific empirical situations as an end in itself, as well as from scholars inspired by the literary turn in some of the social sciences that leads to a philosophical worry about causal explanation as a worthy end of scholarship.

More positively, state-society scholars generally share several important initial assumptions.[8] First, while state-society scholarship has emerged as a reaction to social and economic determinism, state-society scholars continue to share the key assumption of modern sociology, namely, that social reality is sui generis. Societies and other social formations, according to this well-known standpoint, develop characteristics that are independent of the individuals who compose these groups, that often outlast the individuals who may have helped create the groups, and that often socialize the next generation of individuals who become part of the groups. As a result, social reality needs to be studied directly, rather than as a summation of numerous individual actions. It ought not to be necessary to state this basic assertion of Sociology 101, but for the growing popularity of economic theories that treat the individual as a basic unit of analysis and rest their hopes on developing macro understandings by aggregating micro insights. Political science, including comparative political study of developing countries, has always built on neighboring social sciences, especially sociology and economics. It is thus important to note at the outset that most state-society scholars are closer to sociology: they build on the assumption of social reality as sui generis, take for granted that social and political reality has enduring and thus structural qualities, seek to study them in their own terms rather as an aggregation of numerous individual actions, and remain suspicious of the claim that one can develop macro understandings from numerous micro beginnings.

The second important initial assumption concerns the autonomy of the political within the social sphere. According to this theoretical position, political structures and processes, though influenced by societal dynamics, are not determined by them. Or to restate it more strongly in the original Weberian language, state and society represent two analytically autonomous arenas of legitimate coercion and associational life respectively, that mutually condition each other in the real world (Bendix 1962, 286–90). The implications of this simple but powerful assertion, in turn, are of far-reaching significance. Negatively, they suggest that socially reductionist theories of politics are false starts, thus cautioning against the

---

8. Following a well-established position in the philosophy of social science, one does not ask of such assumptions whether they are right but how useful they are as building blocks of knowledge.

utility of such grand social theorizing. More positively, this starting assumption opens up numerous avenues of research for political scientists and political sociologists interested in explaining political outcomes that are influenced in part by social forces and in part by political factors. It thus ought to be no surprise that numerous debates in the comparative political study of developing countries that we will visit below concern the relative explanatory weights of the role of states versus social classes, of political versus economic variables, and of elites versus masses.

A related third starting point for state-society scholars is a shared belief that ideas and institutions on the one hand and economic interests on the other hand cannot be reduced analytically to each other; instead, they mutually condition each other, and must both be taken into account for satisfactory comparative political analysis.[9] This initial assertion also has significant implications. For example, it follows that attempts to create materialist, or economic, theories of ideas and institutions are likely to be unsuccessful. Conversely, it is also the case that the tendency to view all interests as subjective constructs is an analytical blind alley. Instead of these more extreme positions, state-society scholars generally adopt more balanced assumptions: interests often have a subjective component, and given varying institutional configurations, there is always more than one path open for social actors to pursue their interests; and ideas and institutions that take root are often not at odds with the interests of the powerful in society.

And finally, state-society scholars tend to take history seriously. This seemingly banal assertion turns out on further reflection to be anything but that. Taking history seriously, of course, does not mean that all or even most state-society scholars undertake historically oriented research. Many scholars focus on recent developments and gather data, not from archives but via fieldwork. Taking history seriously suggests instead a shared belief that the past influences the present and, as a result, that satisfactory causal explanations must have a strong over-time component. This analytical standpoint follows in part from taking institutions seriously. As patterned beliefs and practices, institutions take time to root. Once rooted, institutions mold behavior. Political outcomes are thus partially path-dependent, influenced by institutions of an earlier origin, forcing state-society scholars to be sensitive to the impact of the past on the present.

Working at a middle level of theory and guided by such assumptions that state and society, as well as institutions and economic interests, mutually condition each other, has, of course, not led to the development of a single paradigmatic community but to the emergence of clusters of scholars with shared interests, who coalesce around specific research problems requiring explanation. This is because the main criteria for choosing a re-

9. I am indebted to Peter Evans for his help in clarifying this and the next general point in the discussion.

search problem for state-society scholars is not so much the utility of that research effort in building grand theory but the real-world importance of the problem. Theory for these scholars thus becomes a means for analyzing empirical puzzles deemed important, both by scholars and by members of the broader society. Generalizable insights that result from such research, in turn, set up future research aimed at confirming, challenging, or modifying these findings. State-society research on comparative political development has thus clustered around numerous significant questions that demand attention: Why do revolutions occur? Why is it so difficult to create viable states in some developing countries? Why have so many former authoritarian countries become democracies of late and what is their likely future? What types of states are capable of generating economic growth in the developing world? Under which conditions are states likely to do something to alleviate the worst of poverty and degradation so common in the developing world? The research I review here seeks to answer these and other significant questions. As noted already, I have organized the review in two parts: the first part focuses on the emergence of a variety of state structures in the developing world, and the second part reviews what we know about conditions of state efficacy for promoting development.

■ | Creating State Authority

Creating state authority that is coherent, enduring, and legitimate has always been a long drawn-out challenge, and it is no different in the developing world. Most of these states became states—or acquired a façade of a modern state—as a result of their encounter with colonialism. Among the characteristics of the European state system that Asia, Africa, and Latin America acquired, only the idea of a set boundary around a territory has proven to be resilient.[10] How stable governance ought to be organized within these boundaries, however, has often proven elusive. For example, Latin American countries emerged sovereign in the nineteenth century and have struggled ever since to discover authority structures that will endure, especially swinging back and forth between authoritarianism and democracy in the post–World War II period. Whether authoritarian or democratic, most regimes in Africa have retained strong elements of personalism and patrimonialism. By contrast, Asian countries have done somewhat better. The two giants, China and India, created revolutionary and democratic states respectively that have more or less endured over the past half-century. In the remaining Asian countries, however, from the Ko-

10. For one discussion of why even weak states, such as in sub-Saharan Africa, have continued to maintain territorial boundaries inherited from colonialism, see Jackson and Rosberg 1982.

reas to Indonesia or from Bangladesh to western Asia, authority structures have proven to be just as brittle as in the rest of the developing world, needing to be held together by force, only to be challenged periodically for their lack of legitimacy, and again facing problems of coherence. The resulting political drama of round after round of failed efforts at institutionalizing authority has excited scholarly imagination and generated a very large body of literature.

As I review the contributions of state-society scholars to this literature, it is important to note at the outset that many of these studies are responding to or are at least informed by prevailing arguments of an earlier vintage. One powerful argument that frames the subfield is that stable democracy—the most desired form of coherent, enduring, and legitimate state authority in the contemporary era—is a product of economic development. The original argument was, of course, put forward by Marx when he suggested that bourgeois democracy was a product of the advanced economic system created by the bourgeoisie, namely, capitalism. A more recent and influential restatement of this Marxist position was made by Barrington Moore, Jr. (1966), in his claim, "no bourgeoise, no democracy." Seymour Martin Lipset's widely cited modification of this Marxist argument (1959) expected all forms of economic development—whether capitalist or not—to lead to democracy, though the facilitating role of the middle class remained important in this argument as well. Whether in its Marxist or more liberal versions, this argument suggests that one should not expect stable democracy without an advanced economy. It can thus be argued that the failure to create coherent, enduring, and legitimate state authority in the developing world results from the economic condition they all share, namely, relatively low levels of economic development.

While many scholars have accepted this broad, framing argument, especially its validity at the two end points of low and advanced levels of economic development, just as many scholars have found it too general or the underlying theory not well specified or troubling in its inability to explain numerous departures from the norm, including the movements back and forth from authoritarianism to democracy. An early and also deeply influential such statement of dissent was Samuel Huntington's *Political Order in Changing Societies* (1968). Very much in the spirit of state-society framework insofar as it sought to highlight the autonomy of the political and the autonomy of institutions, Huntington proposed that economic development did not guarantee democracy. On the contrary, economic development mobilized groups and individuals out of their traditional social niches and made them available for new political commitments. If this process of social mobilization was not matched by a parallel process of deliberately crafting such political institutions as parties, the demand of social groups would exceed the state's political capacity for accommodation and response, leading to political chaos and decay. This argument was proposed in the middle of the 1960s. Since many developing countries were then experiencing political instability, the argument found growing empirical support and also came to be widely embraced.

These two arguments concerning the determinants of authority structures in the developing world, one emphasizing socioeconomic variables, and the other the salience of political institutions, constitute the master narrative of the subfield. Numerous state-society studies on the formation of authority structures that followed were framed by these debates. While a few scholars chose to study the emergence of revolutionary states, and a few more the issue of failed states, most scholars focused on the dynamics that might help explain the movement from authoritarianism to democracy and back. When building their explanatory edifice, some scholars explicitly went back to Moore, Lipset, or Huntington, but many simply assumed that a key theoretical puzzle was to assess the relative salience of interests versus institutions and of socioeconomic versus political variables, including, of course, how the two conditioned each other. The results constitute an exciting body of scholarship that tends to cluster around a specific research problem to be explained.

REVOLUTIONARY STATES

Studies of conditions under which major social revolutions occur and revolutionary states are established have a long and distinguished history. Historians have pored through the records of individual revolutions, political philosophers have worried about their desirability, and political and social analysts have sought to generalize about their causes and consequences. Both the French and Russian Revolutions led to numerous such ruminations. Following World War II, the revolution in China and other near-revolution-like conditions in the emerging developing world attracted the attention of a variety of scholars. Not surprisingly, these studies were informed by prevailing theoretical standpoints, namely, class analysis and interest group politics, and by structural-functional approaches, though psychological theories of revolutions also enjoyed their moment.[11] From the standpoint of this essay, a seminal contribution in the development of this literature was Theda Skocpol's *States and Social Revolutions* (1979). Prior to *States and Social Revolutions*, revolutions were understood mainly in terms of underlying socioeconomic (or psychological) determinants, whether those were class conflict, value disequilibrium, unmet demands of interest groups, or relative deprivation experienced by the masses.[12] On the basis of detailed historical studies of major revolutions, Skocpol turned

11. One good and ready guide to the large and relevant literature is Goldstone 1980.

12. For a quick review of these approaches, see Skocpol 1979, ch. 1, 5–14.

around this entire explanatory edifice; she argued instead that it was the prior weakening of state structures that enabled a variety of latent social conflicts and rebellions to coalesce into major social revolutions.

Skocpol's *States and Social Revolutions* has been reviewed extensively and like most major works it has attracted both admirers and critics.[13] There is no need here to go over this familiar ground. What is relevant here instead is the place of *States and Social Revolutions* in the development of the state-society literature, especially as it concerns developing countries. The first observation on this issue is that Skocpol was reacting to Barrington Moore's *Social Origins*. Moore had not only linked the emergence of capitalism to democracy but had also argued that cases of failed capitalism, especially where landowning elites failed to embrace commercial agriculture and became vulnerable to peasant revolts and even revolutions. Skocpol does not so much reject this argument—on the contrary, significant elements of it are embraced—as she modifies it by emphasizing the state's autonomous role. Her major contribution was to suggest that what all successful revolutions share is a prior weakening of the agrarian bureaucratic states. Under growing international pressures, some of these states fail to reform because of their dependence on landowning elites, crumble, and thus open up the political space for revolutionary forces. This argument fits well the three cases of France, Russia, and China that Skocpol discussed in detail and some other cases as well. Just as Weber had pluralized Marx's economic argument and made it much more broadly applicable and attractive—though by the same account, also less parsimonious—so Skocpol pluralized Moore, or made the analysis more multivariate, for the study of grand revolutions.

The second observation concerns the impact of *States and Social Revolutions*, both on the broader literature in comparative political development and on, more specifically, the future study of revolutions. The broader impact was considerable; *States and Social Revolutions* was one important stream among several that joined the flooding river that eventually became the state-society perspective. Its key general insight—leaving aside the heroes and villains of the story, as well as their political implications—was somewhat similar to that of Samuel Huntington in *Political Order*, namely, that political order results when state power is effectively grafted on top of social power. When for one reason or another this state power weakens or disintegrates, it then becomes possible to mobilize around inequalities of power in society with the hope of creating a new and revolutionary order. This general standpoint enabled Skocpol to argue effectively for the need to "bring the state back in," especially in an intellectual setting dominated by socioeconomic determinism.

The more specific impact of *States and Social Revolutions* on the fu-

---

13. See the references to the critiques of Skocpol's work and her responses in Skocpol 1994.

ture study of revolutions was even more significant. It essentially set the agenda for the next generation of scholars interested in revolutions in the developing world. Some scholars criticized it for ignoring leadership ideologies and built their own edifice (Colburn 1994). Others criticized it from a rational choice perspective, arguing either that Skocpol underestimated the strategic behavior of revolutionary leaders or that what was missing were the micro foundations of revolutionary behavior (DeNardo 1985; Taylor 1988). Especially relevant for the purposes of this essay, however, were the contributions of scholars who sought to extend the statist perspective to the study of revolutions in the developing world.

An important recent contribution in this domain is Jeff Goodwin's *No Other Way Out* (2001).[14] Goodwin seeks to explain comparatively all revolutionary movements—and a few successful revolutions—in the developing world during the cold war period. While focusing especially on Southeast Asia and Central America, he extends and modifies Skocpol's analysis to explain more recent revolutions and near-revolutions. Among the explanatory factors he emphasizes, two are central. First, revolutionary movements were generally a response to repressive, exclusionary authoritarian states that were relatively weak in the sense of being incapable of executing state authority, for example, personalistic dictatorships. Second, some of these states were especially vulnerable because they themselves helped create revolutionary movements that were able to further weaken these already weak states. While often persuasive, one wonders how Goodwin's analysis would have to be modified against cases from sub-Saharan Africa, where personalistic weak states have often led to inconclusive civil wars rather than to successful revolutions. Nevertheless, among the important implications of Goodwin's argument is that democratic and well-organized modern states may not be vulnerable to revolutions.

The literature on revolutions has clearly been additive. Instead of the earlier emphases on class inequalities or on the role of grand ideologies and legitimating value structures, recent scholarship suggests that the organization of state authority is the critical variable in understanding both whether revolutionary movements develop and whether they succeed. We know now, for example, that revolutions in the developing world do not seem to occur within states that are quite legitimate, for example, democracies, or within those which can organize repression effectively, for example, bureaucratic-authoritarian regimes. Instead, sites of revolution have been mainly highly illegitimate patrimonial regimes (as, for example, in Central America) or colonial regimes made ineffective due to special circumstances (as, for example, in Vietnam). The state's capacity to legitimate itself or to exercise legitimate coercion thus emerge as a key variable in understanding contemporary revolutions.

14. Another useful study which I chose not to discuss for reasons of space is Wickham-Crowley 1992.

In concluding this discussion on revolutionary states, it should be noted that this literature lost some of its vitality in the 1990s, especially among political scientists. The underlying reasons are not obvious. It may be because the prospects of more grand social revolutions appeared dim, and because some former revolutionary states like the Soviet Union collapsed and others like China and Vietnam metamorphosed into single-party authoritarian regimes with market economies. The idea that revolutions offer a shortcut to freer and better societies thus lost most of its elan in the late–twentieth century. While reinterpretation of past revolutions will continue to attract scholarly attention, comparative political development scholarship is more often moved by emerging real-world trends. An important analytical question that one is left with then is this: If the era of grand social revolutions is indeed over, why? What has changed in the global setting, in the organization of states, or in the patterns of social relations within states that would help explain this significant change? Following Skocpol, is it possible that the spread of the modern state—in lieu of agrarian bureaucracies, that is—with its enhanced bureaucratic and coercive capacities—even in democratic settings—has essentially closed off political spaces in which revolutionary challenges to the existing social order could be launched?

Bureaucratic Authoritarian States

Authoritarianism in the developing world comes in various forms. Monarchy in Saudi Arabia, personalistic rulers like Mobutu in Zaire, single-party rulers of Mexico, and military rulers like those who governed Brazil in the 1970s or Park Chung Hee of South Korea have all at one time or another been labeled authoritarian. Without a qualifier, authoritarianism is thus mainly a residual category—all regimes that are not democracies—and as such is too amorphous to be analytically useful. These regimes emerged in different circumstances, are (or were) organized differently, often rest(ed) on a variety of underlying social coalitions, and are (or were) more or less efficacious in promoting development. To develop generalizable knowledge about their origins and performance, therefore—knowledge that is not so general as to be totally uninteresting—scholars have often focused on subcategories of authoritarianism.

While a useful literature exists on both personal rule and on such other long-enduring authoritarian states as the "rentier states," the type of authoritarianism that has generated most theoretically informed debates is the bureaucratic-authoritarian regime.[15] Such regimes often came to

15. For one useful typology of authoritarian regimes, see Chehabi and Linz 1998. On personal rule—mostly in the African context—especially on neo-patrimonialism, see Clapham 1982. Also see Bienen and Van de Walle 1991. Notable contributions on the "rentier state" include Karl 1997 and Chaudhry 1997.

power after the breakdown of democratic experiments and resulted in the installation of authoritarian regimes run by bureaucrats—mainly military and technocratic elites—who promised orderly and rapid development. A number of such regimes came to power in the 1960s and 1970s, especially in Latin America but also in such other countries as South Korea, Indonesia, and Pakistan. The book that set the agenda for the study of these types of regimes was, of course, Guillermo O'Donnell's *Modernization and Bureaucratic-Authoritarianism* (1973).

O'Donnell's argument suggested that democracy in such South American countries as Brazil and Argentina was compatible in the 1950s with easy import substitution, a type of development model that rested on protected foreign corporations producing consumer goods for the rich elite of these countries. Once elite demand was saturated, however, this easy phase was exhausted, and what was needed next was deepening of industrialization, or a movement away from consumer goods to heavier industries. Capital and technological requirements for the latter were severe, requiring forceful intervention from the state to remove such bottlenecks as low rates of domestic savings, labor activism, inflation, and limited foreign investment. An authoritarian and interventionist state, led by a military and technocratic elite, thus became somewhat of a functional necessity, helping explain their rapid emergence in numerous middle-income countries that had undergone some industrialization but were struggling to forge ahead further.

This brilliant and highly suggestive political economy argument for authoritarianism demanded empirical scrutiny and indeed received it during the 1970s and the 1980s.[16] As one might expect, the scrutiny produced mixed results for the validity of the argument. Scholars with deep familiarity with significant individual countries like Brazil noted that numerous heavy industries were already in place prior to the 1964 military coup, and thus the functional need to deepen industrialization could not have been a major cause propelling authoritarianism (Serra 1979). Had O'Donnell and other Latin American scholars looked to a country like India, they would have also readily noticed the comfortable coexistence of democracy with heavy-industry-based import substitution. The deepening argument was thus found to be of questionable merit. By contrast, if O'Donnell's argument was understood more broadly to suggest that authoritarianism emerged as a way of coping with growing demands that fledgling democracies were unable to meet because of their political incapacity to remove a variety of bottlenecks—an argument that would be quite similar in spirit to the one proposed by Samuel Huntington in *Political Order* (1968)—then experiences of several Latin American countries provided supporting evidence.[17]

16. The most notable attempt was Collier 1979.

17. See Collier's conclusion in Collier 1979. Also see James Mahoney's very useful review of these materials (2000), which helped me formulate some of my thoughts.

This broader interpretation of course shifted the focus of analysis away from political economy concerns and toward more political factors, such as the role of growing polarization along class lines or elite-mass lines in precipitating military coups. Detailed analysis within Latin America led to the view that there were several patterns of authoritarianism, even within the region. Karen Remmer's more quantitative work (1989) disaggregated O'Donnell's hypothesis significantly, and David and Ruth Collier undertook comparative historical analysis in their majestic study, *Shaping the Political Arena* (1991), arguing that early patterns of labor incorporation had a significant long-term impact on party and regime dynamics. Since issues of breakdown of democracies go well beyond Latin America, scholars interested in such diverse middle-income countries as South Korea and Turkey also sought to extend O'Donnell's argument to make sense of authoritarianism in their respective parts of the world (Im 1987; Richards and Waterbury 1990).[18]

With the onset of the "third wave" of democracy, some of the interest in "why authoritarianism" may decline in the future but is not likely to go away. This is in part because past authoritarian arrangements continue to cast long shadows in many new democracies and in part because many of these new democracies remain vulnerable to future breakdowns. Moreover, reinterpreting the past is not only the domain of historians; more recent history continues to fascinate political scientists as well. Notice, for example, the important new book by Nancy Bermeo (2002). In this study Bermeo is troubled by a variety of past analyses of why democracies breakdown, especially Sartori's, but including Huntington's and O'Donnell's, that implicitly or explicitly implicate the popular sectors in such breakdowns. She thus undertakes a comparative analysis, first of interwar European cases and then in much greater detail of several Latin American cases from the 1960s, to examine the proposition that emergence of authoritarianism was preceded by mass disaffection and popular protest. On the basis of meticulous research, she documents with great care that such was not the case. She thus suggests that the threat of popular sectors has been exaggerated; installation of authoritarian regimes has to be understood instead in terms of ideologies and interests of the ruling elite.

It ought to be clear that O'Donnell's arguments about the origins of authoritarianism in the 1970s initiated an entire research program of studies that built on each other and have led to considerable cumulation of knowledge. As a result, we now know that the choice of the broad economic development strategy probably had little to do with the onset of authoritarianism, that the roots of military coups were more likely political, that these political patterns are probably influenced both by varying levels of economic development and by varying past political histories, but that

---

18. Another work—with earlier European cases as inspiration—that I have not discussed here was Linz and Stepan 1978.

in trying to understand this politics, one also ought not to exaggerate the role of popular protest. One is thus left with other political issues that still require further research: the roots of weak democratic institutions to begin with; the relative proclivity of military elites to intervene more readily in some periods than in others; the role of threat perception when authoritarian elites intervene, especially as this perception is influenced by prevailing ideologies; and the role of international factors. Future research on these and related issues will definitely benefit from more cross-regional research. Latin American materials have played a central and useful role in the development of this literature, but Latin American literature also suffers from an "almost Europe" regional bias. If one genuinely wants to understand the origins of more-bureaucratized authoritarian rule in developing countries, future research efforts ought to include such cases as South Korea and Turkey, as well as pursue such comparative questions as: Given two cases like India and Pakistan, with shared histories of British colonialism, why does Pakistan experience more frequent military coups than India?

Democratic States

The reemergence of democracy in a variety of developing countries over the 1980s gave rise to an enormous body of literature.[19] The central question motivating this research concerned the conditions of democracy in developing countries, especially factors that help democracies emerge but also conditions under which democracy might endure and flourish. Scholarly responses can be conveniently divided into those which emphasize socioeconomic variables, those which underline the significance of such political variables as leadership and institutions, and, of course, those which seek to provide synthetic accounts.

Relevant socioeconomic factors that may influence democratic processes can and have been conceptualized differently: some scholars think of them in terms of social classes, others in terms of levels of economic development, and yet others in terms of associational groups in civil society. Each of these conceptualizations has stimulated its own school of research. First, the focus on class analysis that Moore reintroduced to the study of comparative democracy has found a variety of expressions. The role of agrarian classes in the making of democracy, for example, was recently reemphasized in a fine study by Deborah Yashar (1997). Other scholars have pushed the argument in different directions. One important modification was the coauthored volume by Rueschmeyer, Stephens, and Stephens, *Capitalist Development and Democracy* (1992). On the basis

19. The literature is so large that an attempt at providing all the relevant citations would be foolhardy. For some recent reviews of this literature, see Shin 1994, Geddes 1996, and Mahoney 2000.

of a wide variety of quantitative and case materials, especially from historical European and Latin American cases, Rueschmeyer, Stephens, and Stephens emphasized the role of the working class in both broadening and deepening democracies. While commercialization of agriculture may remove some important antidemocratic forces from the historical scene, they suggest that the type of democracy preferred by capitalists is limited democracy. It takes workers in alliance with various other popular-sector actors to push for full suffrage and to give democracy some substantive depth.

Such a provocative argument was not likely to remain unchallenged, and it was not. Ruth Collier in a recent book (1999) takes issue with the Rueschmeyer-Stephens-Stephens thesis that workers are vanguards of democracy. While giving the working class its due, especially in contemporary Latin America, she undertakes detailed historical case studies to argue that Rueschmeyer, Stephens, and Stephens did not quite get it right; besides workers, critical forces that supported transitions to and consolidation of democracy were political, especially the roles of elites and parties. This argument is considerably less parsimonious than that of Moore, but by the same token, it also seems to better accommodate historical complexities and contingencies. A similar contingent tone is notable in Eva Bellin's recent important works (2000, forthcoming). She suggests that the roles of capitalists and of workers in promoting democracy in developing counties is contingent on concrete circumstances, especially their prior dependence on the authoritarian state.

Second, the old Lipset argument that economic development promotes democracy has experienced something of a comeback in recent decades. A number of scholars have noted that the correlation between higher levels of development and democracy continues to hold very well, and this some five decades after the original argument was proposed by Lipset (Diamond 1992; Lipset, Seong, and Torres 1993; Przeworski and Lemongi 1997; Przeworski, Alvarez, Cheibub, and Limongi 2000). However, what should one do with this correlation, especially in light of the fact that the original theory underlying the correlation was not very strong and that a variety of countries, at different levels of development, have recently started again to experiment with democracy? Are countries at low levels of development condemned to remain undemocratic? What is one to do with the Indian case, which may only consitutue an n of 1 but which with a billion people living democratically within it, throws up a substantial challenge to this view: Can India's experience not be replicated in a Nigeria? Why not?

Faced with both normative and analytical dilemmas, scholarly research has proceeded in several directions. Przeworski and Limongi (1997), for example, distinguish usefully between issues of transitions and survival; countries can transit to democracy at a variety of levels of development—because transitions depend on contingent factors, including leadership choices—but the chance that democracy will survive is a direct function of the level of economic development.[20] Diamond, Linz, and Lipset have organized three massive edited volumes which seek to preserve the core of the old Lipset argument but which also pluralize the argument enough to accommodate a wide range of cases.[21] And finally, Samuel Huntington (1991) has provided an evocative reformulation of the theme: while countries at low and high levels of development may indeed be associated with authoritarianism and democracy respectively, countries in the middle exist in a "zone of choice," where a number of identifiable factors can influence the nature of national authority structures.

And third, the Tocquevillian emphasis on associational life as a key ingredient of democratic life has also in recent years found renewed interest. The most important restatement of this position is, of course, Robert Putnam's historical study of Italy, *Making Democracy Work* (1993a). Putnam's well-known argument is that democracy in northern Italy functioned better than in the south because the north has for a long time enjoyed relatively dense associational life that promotes citizenship, civicness, and a sense of democratic efficacy. In the context of contemporary developing countries, similar arguments have been proposed for transitions, suggesting, for example, that civil society activism was an important ingredient pushing for democratic openings.[22] Moreover, the Putnam hypothesis relating the quality of democracy to the density of associational life has been modified to explain democratic deepening in specific cases and has given rise to a number of important research projects on developing countries.[23] Critics, of course, have hardly left this argument unchallenged. Aside from methodological issues, an important substantial criticism, for example, proposed by Sheri Berman (1997b) is that associational activism can just as easily be a source of breakdown of democracies as of their superior functioning; much depends on the quality of such institutions as political parties that mediate the relationship between demanding groups and the state.

This emphasis on political variables is also evident in a significant body of related literature. For example, several volumes that received quite a bit of attention sought to explain the relatively sudden transition to democracy in the 1980s, especially in Latin American countries (O'Don-

20. Przeworski (2001) has also recently undertaken the more ambitious task of building a theory that may help explain the correlation of wealth and democratic health.

21. See Diamond, Linz, and Lipset 1988. The first of the four volumes sets a general framework, the latter three deal with Africa, Asia, and Latin America respectively.

22. On Brazil, see, for example, Alvarez 1990.

23. See, for example, Varshney 2002. Also note that the Swedish International Development Agency financed a substantial project along these lines on India and South Africa. For early results, see Blomkvist et al. 2001.

nell, Schmitter, and Whitehead 1986a, b, c; O'Donnell and Schmitter 1986). Since some of the contributors to this volume had argued earlier that authoritarianism was rooted in structural factors, the sudden emergence of democracy posed a significant intellectual puzzle. The resolution, if it can be called that, was to emphasize the role of such voluntaristic variables as leadership. While it would be an oversimplification to suggest that, according to this literature, leaders can will democracy if and when they so wish, there is no doubt that the focus of this literature was on democracy from above. The argument ran that the transitions from authoritarianism to democracy often resulted from divisions among leaders, as a result of "pacts" among incumbent and opposition elites, or due to the changing cost-benefit calculus of the ruling elite. Numerous case studies, in turn, supported this general orientation.

It would be easy to criticize this literature as rather atheoretical, depending too heavily on voluntaristic acts of leaders for an explanation. And a number of authors did precisely that.[24] Others went on to develop their own explanations of transitions instead, emphasizing, for example, the role of economic crises.[25] While these criticisms and alternate explanations are valuable, three other observations need to be made. First, to the extent that leaders always encounter structural constraints and learn the limits of the possible through a process of trial and error, leadership actions are not only a voluntaristic variable. Second, the emphasis on the role of leaders originated from a deep understanding on part of scholars like O'Donnell that the shift from authoritarianism to democracy—though an important and normatively desirable change—was also a relatively limited change, especially if viewed from the standpoint of broader socioeconomic changes.[26] Put bluntly, transitions were not revolutions and did not involve any profound structural change in the social location of power. How much of a role should then be attributed to underlying structural variables? This leads to a third observation. The question of "why transitions," though important, is also a little too narrow to lead to theoretically interesting answers. The analytical focus ought to include what follows the transition, namely, the quality of governance offered within the new democracies.

A longer-term perspective on the building of new democracies naturally shifts attention away from leadership actions and toward more institutional concerns. This institutional literature on developing country democracies has gone in several directions. First, there is a growing realization that the authoritarian past casts a long shadow on new democracies. For example, powers of militaries do not vanish in new democracies, and if the authoritarian rulers were essentially personalistic, such as in many sub-

24. See, for example, Remmer 1991a.
25. See, for example, Haggard and Kaufman 1995.
26. See, for example, O'Donnell's subsequent essay (1994) and Kohli 1993.

Saharan African countries, new democracies are hardly able to transcend the problems of patrimonialism (Linz and Stepan 1996; Bratton and Van de Walle 1997). Second, a debate of sorts has emerged on whether a parliamentary or a presidential system of government is more suited to help new democracies stabilize.[27] This literature would benefit from a greater sensitivity to underlying issues of social power, though, to be fair, issues of ethnicity have received some attention (Horowitz 1985). And finally, the study of such exceptional cases as India, in which democracy has survived, provides a variety of insights into the role of institutions, not only in the transition to democracy but also in its consolidation and in the reemergence of problems of governability, when underlying institutions weaken (Kohli 1991, 2001).

Before concluding this section, a note should also be made of a couple of volumes that are distinguishable, not for accentuating one specific argument or another but for providing fairly balanced, synthetic accounts. One such important work is Samuel Huntington's *The Third Wave* (1991). Huntington in this volume seeks to develop a multivariate explanation for the "third wave" of democracy. The result is a study of considerable value for a general readership. Another important volume by Haggard and Kaufman (1995) is for a more-specialized audience but is also synthetic in ambition. It provides a balanced account of both transitions, especially emphasizing the role of economic crises that preceded them, and of the troubles faced by new democracies as they pursue a neoliberal economic agenda.

It again ought to be clear that the issue of democracy in the context of developing countries has given rise to a rich and complex state-society literature, the works of which often build on each other. In conclusion, one may thus ask, what has been learnt, and where should the literature go? First, the focus on leadership has proved to be a tad too narrow; it may be useful for understanding transitions to democracy—though even this has been challenged convincingly—but certainly needs to be broadened for issues of longer-term significance. Second, the study of consolidation of democracies is likely to be best framed by a simultaneous focus on socioeconomic and institutional factors on the one hand and to be best conducted in a broader, comparative context on the other hand. For example, the literature seems to suggest that more-advanced developing countries, with moderate inequalities and with well-organized political parties, may be in the best position to consolidate democracies.

The issue of what happens when one or more of these key ingredients are missing, ought to be investigated in a cross-regional context; scholars of Latin America, for example, often do not know much about what is happening in India or Africa, and vice versa, and are poorer for that neglect.

---

27. See Linz 1990a, the subsequent debate between Linz (1990a, b) and Horowitz (1990) on "Presidents vs. Parliaments," and Lijphart (1991, 1992).

And finally, the deepening of democracy—that is, of its embrace by the popular sectors—has not received much attention. Are new democracies strengthened or weakened by inclusionary politics and economics? How does globalization impact such classic dilemmas faced earlier by democracies that are by now well established? Answers to such questions also ought to be developed by cross-regional research that simultaneously focuses on the role of political institutions on the one hand and on the role of class and other forms of associational activities on the other hand.

■ | Using State Authority

States in most developing countries play a significant role in structuring their respective societies and economies. This "state-heavy" characteristic was in some cases inherited from a colonial past but for the most part was a product of ideas and interests of sovereign rulers, especially their perceptions concerning how to maintain order and to promote economic development. The sizable and interventionist states, in turn, have molded a variety of political and economic processes in the developing world, including interest group politics, patterns of class and ethnic cleavages, the nature of political institutions, and, of course, rates and patterns of economic growth. The analytical emphasis of state-society scholars on the "autonomy of the political" has brought this state's architectonic role into sharp relief, resulting in important new research over the last two decades. I first review the research that sheds light on the modes in which states structure the society and politics of developing countries; while individually insightful, these researches are often only loosely connected to each other. By contrast, the researches on the states' role in promoting or hindering economic growth that I review second build on each other more self-consciously and have generated an influential set of cumulative findings of real-world consequence.

How States Structure Society and Politics

A variety of factors give states and state elites some degree of autonomy from underlying social forces in developing countries: the capacity to define and pursue the national interest; the exercise of legitimate or not-so-legitimate coercion; the tendency of political ideas, organizations, and institutions to survive the initial forces that brought them into being; the weakness of organized social forces; and, of course, the needs of ruling elites to prolong their hold on power. Partially autonomous states, in turn, have often structured the nature of, and relations among, socioeconomic groups in developing countries, with long-term political significance. Examples of scholarly works that underline the fecundity of this perspective can be conveniently grouped into those that focus on how states have structured interest groups and institutions, ethnic politics, and distributional politics along class lines.

Two important books on Latin America, one by Alfred Stepan (1978) and the other by Ruth and David Collier (1991), demonstrate the state's impact on interest group politics, especially labor politics, and thus on the evolution of long-term political trends in the region. Among scholars of political development, Stepan was one of the earliest to emphasize the analytical autonomy of the state and to demonstrate the empirical utility of this standpoint. He suggested that Latin American states could be usefully categorized as more inclusionary or more exclusionary in their mode of labor incorporation. The nature of state-labor relations, in turn, was consequential for a variety of political trends. For example, he hypothesized that Mexico's relatively stable political evolution was based on inclusionary state-labor relations, whereas the more exclusionary model of Brazil generated political polarization and regime instability. Stepan of course also went on to examine a number of other statist hypotheses in greater detail against Peruvian materials.

David and Ruth Collier built on the type of framework suggested by Stepan and also emphasized the "autonomy of the political" as they compared and contrasted state-labor relations in the more-industrialized countries of Latin America. Their main categorization was similar to Stepan's but emphasized the distinction between state-controlled labor and labor mobilized and controlled by parties. If Brazil and Chile are examples of state corporatism, Argentina and Mexico are more cases of political parties' taking the lead on the labor question. Among their important arguments is the claim that party-led labor mobilization may invite reaction over the short run but is also likely to lead to longer-term integration of labor in the political system and thus to smoother political evolution. The impact of this important book by the two Colliers is already significant and is likely to grow over time as students are influenced by the general standpoint and digest the details. Aside from the framing importance of the concepts of path dependence and critical junctures—subjects best left for another discussion—the emphasis on the "autonomy of the political" was much needed in Latin American studies and is already bearing fruit. Notice, for example, a fine new book by Richard Snyder (2001) that demonstrates how neoliberal economic policies in Mexico have only created new needs for political management and thus given rise to a new form of statism in that country.

A similar statist standpoint informed my book on India, *Democracy and Discontent* (1990). In *Democracy and Discontent*, I argued that the weakening of such political institutions in India as the ruling national party had created an opening for personalistic and populist leaders to concentrate enormous powers, further deinstitutionalizing the polity, mobilizing demands that could not be readily met, and creating problems of governability. Unlike Huntington, however, a more explicit statist standpoint led me to suggest that political mobilization was more a product of elite initiatives and less of ongoing socioeconomic development and that deinstitutionalization also resulted more from the self-serving behavior of leaders and less from demands outpacing associational regrouping. Other younger scholars have followed up this argument, subjecting it to rigorous quantitative examination, confirming parts of the analysis but also questioning other parts, leading to important modification.[28]

A broadly comparative book that sought to analyze state capacities to achieve a variety of social goals in developing countries was Joel Migdal's *Strong Societies and Weak States* (1988). As the title suggests, Migdal argued that most states in developing countries were inefficacious and that the roots of this inefficacy lay in the presence of powerful social actors who managed to defy state edicts. Migdal's case materials in this influential book were mainly from sub-Saharan Africa and the Mideast, with the case of Israel's providing a check on the argument insofar as exceptional national security considerations there have helped create a much more efficacious state. From these inductive propositions, Migdal also argued for a broader analytical need to have a more-balanced state-society focus.

The focus on the state's structuring role has also influenced research on identity politics, including research on nationalism, race, and other forms of ethnic politics. A major contribution here was Benedict Anderson's *Imagined Communities* (1991 [1983]). In a subtle and brilliant book, Anderson persuades or provokes his readers less by rigorous hypothesis testing and more by his intuition and his historical and geographical sweep. If modern nationalism is understood as a social-psychological force that enables sizable human groupings to imagine themselves as communities that share and cherish important traits, Anderson's study provides nothing less than an analysis of the political and economic changes that undergirded the rise of modern nationalism. While he emphasizes a range of such factors, including such economic ones as the rise of capitalism and the related emergence of profit-oriented print technology, the state's role in constructing modern nationalism also looms large in his analysis. Thus, for example, roaming bureaucrats, traveling from place to place within specified political boundaries, became a source of national consciousness in Latin America, even prior to its emergence in western Europe. The use of such ruling instruments by states, including colonial states, as the census—needed to categorize citizens for a variety of tasks, including taxation—provoked individuals and communities to develop both national and subnational identities. And, of course, states that arrived late on the global scene, such as Asian and African states, undertook numerous deliberate state-led efforts to construct national identities, with more or less success.

Anderson's emphasis on the constructed nature of identities has inspired an enormous amount of research, especially by historians and an-

28. See, for example, Wilkinson 2001.

thropologists, who with their own epistemological assumptions are often less interested in causal generalizations than political scientists. The issue of how states construct identities, however, is important from a variety of standpoints and has hardly gone unnoticed by political scientists. A significant recent study, for example, is Anthony Marx's *Making Race and Nation* (1998). Marx undertakes a comparative analysis of Brazil, South Africa, and the United States around the issue of political determinants of racial stratification. South Africa for Marx provides a case at one extreme of legal racism, and Brazil with its more moderate social racism at the other end of the continuum, with the United States somewhere in between, though closer to South Africa. On the basis of a detailed historical analysis of each case, Marx explains these variations in racial patterns as a product of intraelite politics at an early stage of state building: the need of white elites to maintain unity and stability led them to legalize apartheid in South Africa, and by contrast, a moderately consensual and less-threatened elite created a more inclusive pattern of racial stratification in Brazil. This provocative macrohistorical hypothesis is likely to provoke future research that seeks to confirm these postulated relationships with reference to other cases or that challenges the proposed relationships while reinterpreting the same or other historical cases.

Another important study in this genre is Deborah Yashar's *Contesting Citizenship* (forthcoming). This is a detailed comparative analysis of the emergence of indigenous movements in Latin America, especially in Ecuador, Bolivia, and Peru. The study asks, why have indigenous movements emerged in Latin America in recent years and, within that frame, why are they more significant in cases like Ecuador and Bolivia but less significant in a case like Peru? The answer Yashar develops revolves around the changing role of the state in Latin America. The shift from corporatist to neoliberal arrangements has simultaneously reduced the autonomy and security of communities and enhanced their political spaces to organize dissent. Indigenous movements have emerged where this broader political change came to be combined with preexisting dense social interactions within indigenous communities. By contrast, where peasant networks were weak and national political opening was limited, indigenous movements have remained relatively insignificant.

Finally in this survey of recent research on the state's impact on the society and politics of developing countries, one may take note of some work on state's distributive role. In my 1987 book, *The State and Poverty in India*, I sought to analyze the conditions under which state intervention aimed at alleviating rural poverty in India succeeded or failed. On the basis of comparative regional materials within India, I identified the ideology and organization of the ruling parties on the one hand and the social base of the party's power on the other hand as the key variables that helped explain variations in redistributive outcomes: a well-organized social democratic party in power with a middle- and lower-class base, I argued, was most successful at prioritizing and pursuing antipoverty policies. This argument and research has subsequently been challenged, modified, or extended to other parts of the world by a number of other scholars.[29]

Besides India—the country with the largest number of poor people in the world—the other country around which state's distributive role has received considerable attention is the world's most unequal country, namely, Brazil. A recent study, for example, investigates the impact of democratization on equity (Weyland 1996).[30] Focusing on such specific policy areas as taxation and social security, Weyland analyzes why even democratic governments in Brazil have not been able to pursue policies that may benefit the lower classes. His answer focuses on organizational fragmentation in Brazil, including the absence of well-organized political parties that could aggregate the interests of the poor, as well as fragmentation within the state that weakens the capacity of state elites to push against the interest of dominant classes. Weyland thus continues an old but important insight that is worth reiterating, namely, that democratization does not necessarily translate into enhanced political power for the poor; the latter requires deliberate recrafting of political parties and of the state apparatus.

To sum up, these are just some examples of the type of research that has sought to demonstrate how states structure the society and politics of developing countries. While seemingly disparate—both by geographical and by topical focus—this research shares a theoretical unity insofar as the causal arrows here generally point from the state to society. Moreover, within more specific problem areas, such as corporatism, ethnic and race patterns, or welfare provision, researchers consciously build on each other's findings, debating and modifying existing propositions in the manner of "normal science." Some of this research would clearly benefit in the future by pursuing problems across regions. Nevertheless, the cumulative findings are already impressive. For example, we know by now that patterns of political inclusion or exclusion—whether along class or ethnic lines—were often structured by states themselves and often originated much earlier. Only comparative and historical research is likely to unearth such patterns and their causes and consequences. As another example, we also know that deliberate political attempts within the developing world to reduce inequalities or alleviate poverty have often been not very successful, hampered by political fragmentation, especially the absence of well-institutionalized left-of-center ruling parties. What role can states then play in redistributing a developing country's already scarce resources? While

29. For one direct challenge, see Mallick 1993. For a recent attempt to extend the argument see Harris 2001. For other modifications and extensions, see Ranade 1991, Kuhonta forthcoming, and Rani Tudor forthcoming. On related subjects, see Herring 1983, Echeverri-Gent 1993, and Heller 1999.

30. A study of related interest that finds elements of the Brazilian state more efficacious is Tendler 1997.

further research on this question is clearly important—especially in the context of countries with good economic growth and serious inequality—the discouraging record on this front has also contributed to a shift of focus away from the state as an agent of redistributions to the state as an agent of economic growth.

STATE AND ECONOMIC GROWTH

While sharing statist assumptions, the political economy literature on the state's role in promoting or hindering economic growth has developed in dialogue with the literature on economic development, especially the more policy-oriented literature. During the 1950s and the 1960s economic development was a robust subfield of economics that underlined the market imperfections prevailing in the developing world and often emphasized the positive role that the state could play in overcoming these imperfections.[31] Involved in their own disciplinary debates, political scientists unfortunately—and ironically—did not contribute to this literature; the positive role that states may play in promoting economic development thus remained undertheorized, and the conditions that may support such interventions poorly understood. A new generation of economists from the 1970s onward abandoned the old assumptions and prescriptions of development economics and increasingly came to embrace a neoclassical worldview that emphasized the proper functioning of self-regulating markets as the source of rapid growth and development. The recent statist literature that I now discuss has generally developed in reaction to this pro-market orthodoxy, shared by some scholars and practitioners of development.

The critique of development economics developed by neoclassical economists from 1970s onward began mainly as a critique of import substitution trading regimes and eventually by the 1990s became a full-blown critique of state intervention for development. It was initially proposed that tariffs (or quotas) and overvalued exchange rates that were often at the core of import substitution development strategies hurt economic growth because they misallocated resources, discouraged exports, and by the same token, limited much-needed imported technology. A more neutral trading regime, following the logic of comparative advantage, would instead lead to labor-intensive exports and higher growth rates. Large amounts of empirical materials were brought to bear on these arguments, especially the relatively high economic growth rates achieved by export-promoting East Asian countries on the one hand and the economic performance of import-substituting economies, sluggish in South Asia and Africa and crisis prone in Latin America on the other hand. The debt crisis of the 1980s not only gave urgency to this critique but also weakened the bargaining posi-

31. See, for example, Hirschman 1981.

tion of many developing countries vis-à-vis the developed countries to whom the debt was often owed. The external pressure to liberalize debt-ridden economies further focused attention on a variety of inefficiencies that could be attributed to interventionist states. These included bloated public sectors, government controls on economic activities, the urban bias of national pricing regimes, and numerous public subsidies; the resulting "Washington consensus" thus offered to all developing countries a more liberal model of development in place of the older model that depended heavily on *dirigism*.[32]

The statist response to this neoliberal critique involved a wide variety of social scientists and took several forms, especially a reinterpretation of East Asian success but also broader comparative analyses and quantitative studies. The basic message of this new research was that it was not the degree but the quality of state intervention that was of essence for understanding developmental outcomes; state intervention was not only compatible with but responsible for rapid economic growth in some parts of the developing world. A pioneering contribution in this context was Chalmers Johnson's formulation (1982) of the concept of the developmental state with reference to the state's positive role in Japan's rapid economic growth over the twentieth century. In a brilliant book that started out as a history of Japan's Ministry of Trade and Industry (MITI), Johnson ended up accomplishing nothing less than laying bare the political mechanisms that propelled the rapid industrialization of Japan.

In his interpretation of the Japanese model of development, Johnson (1982, conclusion) stressed the following: the high priority assigned by leaders to economic development as a national goal; a political system in which bureaucracy was dominant and staffed by a fairly small group of society's "best and the brightest"; a variety of "market-conforming" interventions by these bureaucrats that sought to mold the incentives of private producers; and finally, state-business cooperation, especially following World War II, that ensured that both state and business were able to pursue their core goals. Johnson was not very sure, and rightly so, as to whether this statist model of rapid economic growth—which differed from both laissez-faire capitalism and state socialism—could be readily emulated by other developing countries. What he was sure about, however, was that elements of this Japanese model were being practiced in other parts of rapidly growing East Asia, especially in South Korea and Taiwan, and that its success threw up an important intellectual challenge to certain Anglo-American liberal orthodoxies of how countries do and ought to develop economically (C. Johnson 1987, 1999).

32. See Williamson 1998. On import substitution versus export promotion, see Bhagwati 1986. On East Asia versus Latin America, see Sachs 1985. On urban bias, see Lipton 1977 and Bates 1981. On synthetic policy implications, see World Bank 1991.

This provocative formulation was not likely to remain unchallenged and was not.[33] For our purposes, however, what is important to note is that Johnson's study marked the beginning of a whole slew of studies—some of which were influenced by Johnson and others not—that similarly challenged the antistatist conclusions of neoliberal scholars. As one might expect, East Asian materials provided important case studies. The rapid economic growth of South Korea, for example, was interpreted as state driven in a number of important studies. The economists Il Sakong and Leeroy Jones (1980) provided an early overview that stressed the state's role in such areas as prioritizing economic development, supporting private entrepreneurs, and undertaking both indirect and direct interventions that were clearly associated with improved economic performance. Jung-en-Woo (1991) demonstrated how the state's control of finance in South Korea came to be used as a critical element of industrial policy that led to rapid industrialization. And the economist Alice Amsden (1989) provided the most ambitious revisionist interpretation that not only argued that the South Korean state deliberately got prices wrong so as to grow rapidly but also sought to provide an alternate theory of late development that emphasized the state's role in facilitating learning by doing within firms.

Empirical materials from Taiwan provided the core of a broad-based study of East Asian development by Robert Wade (1990). In this influential and widely read book, Wade demonstrates with meticulous care how a variety of such state interventions as selective protectionism, technology promotion, and deliberate export promotion came to be associated with Taiwan's rapid economic growth. He also generalizes from these specific materials to suggest the conditions under which states can lead rather than follow markets to higher rates and levels of production. If states in the rapid growth of East Asia constructively altered market incentives, managed conflict, reduced risks, and gave entrepreneurs direction, some economists are now also seeking to interpret these actions in terms of economic theory (Chang 1994). And yet other scholars have wondered to what extent these statist insights apply to such other Southeast Asian countries as Malaysia or Thailand (Felker 1998, Jomo et al. 1997).

If the economic success of East Asia has attracted a wide variety of statist analyses, the poor economic performance of numerous sub-Saharan African countries has also attracted similar analytical attention. Instead of arguing that poor economic performance is mainly a result of politically motivated distorted price regimes, scholars such as Richard Sandbrook (1985) argued persuasively that the problem lay deeper in poorly functioning states. Irrespective of the policy regime, state interventions in sub-Saharan Africa have been quickly personalized by Africa's neopatrimonial states, leading mainly to enrichment of ruling elites and their loyal follow-

---

33. For one of the numerous challenges by Japanese specialists, see Calder 1993. For a review of related debates, see C. Johnson 1999.

ers. Detailed country case studies have further unearthed the functioning of such neopatrimonial states that, instead of being developmental, readily turn predatory.[34] Crawford Young's majestic study (1994) traced the roots of such predatory states to the colonial experience, and Jeffrey Herbst (2000) proposed that exceptional demographic circumstances of sub-Saharan Africa have contributed to poor state formation. And if near-experimental evidence were needed in support of such arguments, it has been provided by widespread failure of structural adjustment policies in Africa. Pursued mostly at the behest of external donors, this new pro-market policy regime has failed to generate higher economic growth in most African countries. Whether in regard to individual countries or the continent as a whole, analysts studying this failure have concluded that deeper problems of ineffective states have made it difficult to pursue any developmental policy regime consistently.[35]

Besides subjecting the more extreme cases of developmental success and failure to statist analyses, a variety of more-mixed cases are also continuing to attract similar reinterpretations. While many Latin American elites as well as scholars of Latin America embraced neoliberalism in the aftermath of the debt crisis of the 1980s, not every one did. Barbara Stallings (1995), for example, provided a nuanced analysis of Latin America's post-1980 economic woes in terms of the limited capacity of states in the region to take advantage of the globalization of finance. Albert Fishlow (1990) also argued that the inability of many of the region's states to tax their populations contributes to low domestic savings rates, making them highly dependent on foreign investment for growth; as long as such investment is forthcoming the region grows, but when, for one reason or another, such investment dries up, growth declines, creating economic and political crises. Others have sought to reinterpret the high-growth experience of such significant countries as Brazil (from 1930 to 1980) in statist terms (Krieckhaus 2000), and yet others have juxtaposed the nature of states in Brazil and Mexico against East Asia with the aim of delineating how relative state capacity can be explained in terms of the characteristics of the bureaucracy (Schneider 1999). Outside of Latin America also, such mixed cases of Turkey and India have attracted statist analyses that wonder why these countries have not done as well as East Asia and provide answers in terms of the character and choices made by the state.[36]

Finally, more genuinely comparative, cross-regional studies have also sought to highlight the state's economic role in developing countries. An early such study was Stephan Haggard's *Pathways from the Periphery*

---

34. See, for example, Callaghy 1984.

35. See, for example, Lewis 1994 and Van de Walle 2001. For possible exceptions like Ghana, see Herbst 1993.

36. On Turkey, see Onis 1998. On India, see Herring 1999.

(1990). Haggard accepted the conclusion of many economists that export promotion was superior to import substitution as a development strategy but sought to underline that even export promotion strategies of East Asia were state driven, helping explain East Asia's superior performance vis-à-vis Latin America. More recently, John Waterbury (1993) undertook a comparative analysis of Mexico, Turkey, India, and Egypt around the issue of why states in such diverse countries opted for import substitution strategies, especially focused on the leading role of public enterprises. While Waterbury concludes that public enterprises in all his cases have not performed as their creators had hoped they would, he also suggests sympathetically that, given the interests and ideologies of developing country leaders, as well as their nascent private sectors following World War II, import substitution strategies may well have been a necessary stage in the evolution of state-market relations within these countries.

The most important recent work in this comparative genre is clearly Peter Evans's *Embedded Autonomy* (1995). This is a broad-based comparative analysis of the state's role in promoting industry—especially computer-related industries—in such countries as Korea, Brazil, and India. Evans seeks to explain why some states are more successful than others in industry promotion. His argument is both parsimonious and supported by detailed empirical materials. He argues that states that are most successful—developmental states—display the characteristic of embedded autonomy. The autonomy of bureaucracies lies in their being highly professional, that is, both skilled and not readily manipulated by a variety of personalistic interests. At the same time, however, these bureaucratized states are also well embedded in the social structure, especially insofar as cooperation between state and business elites is well institutionalized. State autonomy enables state elites to define and pursue developmental goals, and state embeddedness assures that this autonomous power is used in a manner consistent with the goals and interests of business. State-business alliances of this nature may have some unsavory characteristics but have proven to be highly instrumental in promoting rapid industrialization and economic growth in the developing world.

To sum up, this single country and comparative case study statist literature on economic growth has chipped away at the orthodoxy that getting prices right is the best way to promote economic growth in the developing world. Some quantitative work has also raised doubt about the empirical basis on which claims relating an open trade orientation to rapid economic growth rest.[37] The point here is not that this body of research is beyond criticism itself. The statist literature on economic growth can be criticized for having a weak underlying theory, for focusing too much on bureaucratic and not on political variables, and for not asking why some regions of the developing world have ended up with developmental states, and others

37. See, for example, Rodriguez and Rodrik 2001.

with predatory states.[38] Such criticisms are par for the course in any ongoing research endeavor; one set of contributions opens up paths for others to challenge, modify, and so push further the frontiers of knowledge.

More important, this statist body of research has already had considerable influence, even beyond the academy. For example, growing evidence that East Asian economic success was state driven, along with pressure from Japan to take account of this success, led the World Bank to commission its own study, *East Asian Miracle* (1993). While the Bank stopped well short of endorsing the role of state intervention and of industrial policy—and its selective use of evidence was suitably and widely criticized (Fishlow et al. 1994; Amsden 1994)—the study nevertheless went some distance in acknowledging the state's constructive role in East Asia. Similarly, the Bank in 1997 used its influential *World Development Report* to focus attention on the state's role in development. Once again, the bank's understanding of what the state ought to do in the process of development remains quite different than that entertained by many statist scholars. Nevertheless, by underlining the positive role that the state can play, the bank as an important signaling institution in policy and ideological debates on development signaled that its sharply pro-market and antistatist position was undergoing some modification.[39]

■ | Conclusion

This review of research on comparative political development that is informed by a state-society perspective has focused on some problem-oriented research programs. More specifically, I have discussed research that analyzes the origins and dynamics of revolutionary, authoritarian, and democratic states in the developing world on the one hand and how states mold the politics and economics of these countries on the other hand. Given the limitations of space and of the genre of a review essay that must touch on an entire subfield, the discussion has often been highly condensed and much has been left out. Numerous single country studies of merit have not been mentioned. I especially regret not discussing research on failed states, rentier states, and structural adjustment.[40] While good research exists on all of these issues, either it tends to be too policy oriented

38. I address some of these issues in much greater detail in my forthcoming book, *In Search of Development*.

39. Whether the financial crisis in East Asia in the late 1990s will fundamentally alter this new position remains to be seen. For one statist analysis of the financial crisis, see Wade 2000.

40. On the rentier state, see Bellin 1994, Chaudhry 1994, and Beblawi and Luciani 1987. On structural adjustment, see Haggard and Kaufman 1995. On failed states, especially in Africa, see Reno 1998 and Zartman 1995.

or the studies do not always build on each other, thus creating identifiable research programs that involve a substantial number of theoretically interested scholars. I also regret that the merits and shortcomings of individual contributions discussed here were not pursued in greater detail. Prior to concluding, therefore, I would like to take note of some general criticisms of the style of research discussed here, set them aside, and then suggest as an insider where some of this neo-Weberian research on developing countries should head in the future.

One broad criticism of state-society research, especially of the research that focuses more on state structures and actions, comes from scholars who are sensitive to local and cultural heterogeneity of developing country societies. Joel Migdal (2001), for example, chastises this body of research for assuming that states are all-knowing and all-powerful and for neglecting the variety of nonstate structures of power in society that foil state designs. James Scott (1998) has also recently and eloquently documented state-created developmental disasters, urging more respect for the local, both in developing practice and in our analytical lenses. I take these to be friendly and useful criticisms that ought to remind all state-oriented scholars not to mistake their analytical foci for some normative love of the state, as well as to balance their statist concerns in a more state-society direction.[41] A more extreme culturalist critique, however, that state and society are not useful distinctions because the boundaries between the two are horribly difficult to delineate mistakes analytical and empirical issues (Mitchell 1991). Of course, boundaries between states and society are diffuse in the real world, but one needs some prior analytical distinction to even make sense of that claim. The Weberian distinctions of state and society, that is, of arenas of legitimate coercion and of association, have served comparative scholars very well for quite some time; until and unless someone comes up with more powerful lenses, they remain useful distinctions for building a variety of theoretically informed empirical research.

A still harsher set of criticisms may be attributed to rational-choice scholars. Some of these are in the form of provocative polemics,[42] others are implicit in reviews of the subfield (Geddes 1991), and yet others can be heard in numerous professional conversations. Cumulatively they seem to suggest that state-society scholarship is atheoretical, methodologically flawed because it rests on too few cases, not rooted in microreasoning, and not social-scientific enough because knowledge within it does not accumulate. It would take me too far afield to consider such criticisms; for the present only a few brief responses must suffice.

First, the polemical claim that much of comparative politics scholar-

41. A collection edited by Migdal, Kohli, and Shue (1994) made precisely this argument in detail.

42. See, for example, Bates 1997a. As a response, see in the same issue, Johnson 1997.

ship, including scholarship in comparative political development, is dominated by atheoretical area studies can only be sustained by neglecting the
entire body of scholarship discussed here. All the studies discussed simultaneously contain specific empirical accounts and theoretical claims that are
of broader significance. Relatedly, the criticism that knowledge in comparative political development does not accumulate is also not sustainable in
light of the research reviewed. In each and every one of the five research
programs discussed, scholars have built on the work of each other, challenging and modifying existing claims, and so leading to newer findings
and insights.

The deeper issues at stake in the disagreements between rational-
choice and state-society scholars concern the level and type of theory
building that is appropriate for the study of comparative political development. Rational-choice scholars believe that a general theory of all politics,
including the politics of developing countries, is possible and desirable and
ought to be built on microeconomic reasoning. State-society scholars are
deeply skeptical of this starting position. They believe instead in middle-
range theory that is partly rooted in sociological assumptions and reasoning. Moreover, theory for state-society scholars is a means to understanding
real-world problems of significance, rather than an end in itself. They are
not content to wait till all the micropieces have been put together in a
macro–jigsaw puzzle that makes the whole and the parts of the world mutually intelligible. As a matter of fact, many of them simply do not believe
that this will ever happen. Given these fundamental disagreements, the
best one can hope for is an agreement to disagree.

None of these comments should be interpreted as if state-society research reviewed here is impervious to criticisms. Nearly every single contribution discussed could be subjected to a more-detailed scrutiny. That,
however, was not the purpose of this essay. The main purpose instead was
to chart the recent intellectual development in the subfield. I hope it is
clear to readers (especially readers who are not fundamentally hostile to
this type of scholarship) that the subfield is a vibrant one. State-society
scholarship in comparative political development tends to share some
broad neo-Weberian theoretical assumptions and often pursues research
problems of real-world significance, and knowledge within it tends to accumulate within problem-oriented research programs. Every field, however, has its blind spots and continuous effort ought to be made to improve
on its shortcomings. Outside criticisms of the subfield are telling us (who
work within the subfield) to avoid unnecessary reification of our analytical
categories on the one hand and to be more theoretically self-conscious and
rigorous in analyzing and documenting our claims on the other hand.
These criticisms ought to be taken to heart.

Even when viewed from the inside, state-society research on developing countries ought to move in some new directions in the future. I will
make two such suggestions as final concluding comments. First, state and

society are really nation-level concepts and thus create some blind spots to global influences. Scholars of developing countries are often well aware of international influences on national development trends; the literature on dependency even sought to make a paradigm of sorts out of such awareness. However, while rightly discarding the more economistic aspects of the dependency perspective, state-society scholars may have gone too far in embracing nation-level explanations. Whether reinterpreting colonial pasts or newer developments under conditions of increasing globalization, state-society scholars will need to create more open models in the future. Even outcomes like democracy, for example, cannot increasingly be debated mainly in terms of the impact of national economic and political determinants. International forces both stimulate democratization in the developing world and constrain its operation by limiting policy choices open to governments. The same is likely to be true of a variety of other political outcomes that grab scholarly attention.

Finally, far too much of state-society research has been structured around the regime typology of democracy and authoritarianism. Whatever the roots of this near-obsession—the role of liberal ideology cannot be underestimated—it does create some important blind spots. Authoritarianism is a residual category, too amorphous to be very useful analytically without further disaggregation. As more and more developing countries democratize, varieties of democracy will also need to be understood. While some such research is already underway, the concluding point that I wish to emphasize is at a deeper analytical level: a focus on democracy and its absence creates a bias toward understanding the distribution of power at the expense of how power may be aggregated and used constructively. Power, like wealth, has to exist before it can be distributed. In many developing countries, the need to create coherent and enduring state authority is more pressing than the issue of how to check and distribute this power. In other developing countries, where such modern states exist, both democracies and dictatorships are often powerless to pursue socioeconomic goals. Why? Research on such questions will be better structured around such typologies as developmental and predatory states rather than around democracy and authoritarianism. An important research task of the future will be to continue to theorize and to study empirically which types of national authority structures are capable of defining and pursuing developmental goals, and how readily such authority structures mesh with a democracy.

Jeffry Frieden and Lisa L. Martin

International Political Economy: Global and Domestic Interactions

International Political Economy (IPE) is a relatively new subdiscipline within political science. The first textbook in the area was published in 1977 (Spero 1977), and courses were not routinely offered until the middle 1980s. Even today, the boundaries of IPE are not always clear—the overlap with political economy research in comparative and American politics is especially great. We take the field to include all work for which international economic factors are an important cause or consequence. This ranges from the domestic politics of trade and exchange rate policy, through the politics of World Trade Organization (WTO) dispute settlements, to the impact of international flows of goods or capital on national political systems.

Despite imprecision about the definition of IPE, in the past twenty years the field has approached consensus on theories, methods, analytical frameworks, and important questions. This is not to say that scholars in IPE all agree with one another. However, disagreement today generally takes the form of contention among productive, theoretically and empirically motivated claims, rather than the paradigmatic clashes that earlier characterized IPE. Scholars typically see alternative approaches as complementary or applying under different, specifiable conditions. Other disagreements might be debates about the relative weights that we should attribute to alternative explanatory variables. These types of scholarly differences are the hallmark of a mature field of research that has moved from sweeping attempts at self-definition to formulating refutable analytical claims and evaluating their fit with empirical regularities.

This essay presents what we believe to be the consensus among political scientists with regard to the analysis of the politics of international economic relations. The review we present is not intended to be exhaustive. We do not, for example, attempt to include the work of scholars who challenge the positivist approach that is assumed here. We believe that this survey does reflect the principal focuses of North American scholarship, although it is not reflective of much European scholarship. Most publications in the principal U.S. journals of the profession and the subdiscipline, and most North American graduate training and research, are within the range of the theoretical and empirical topics and approaches presented here.

The most challenging questions in IPE have to do with the interaction of domestic and international factors as they affect economic policies and outcomes. Modeling interactive effects is complex, but there have been exciting research efforts in IPE along these lines. We begin with a survey of some of the more-promising efforts in this direction. It quickly becomes evident that many of the advances made in the study of domestic-international interaction would have been impossible without firm foundations in the analysis of domestic and of international factors in and of themselves. Indeed, recent work on the international-domestic research frontier builds heavily on progress made over the last couple of decades in the analysis of the domestic and international levels; and these analyses provide the essential building blocks for the current and future study of interaction.

The second section therefore turns to a discussion of the domestic politics of foreign economic policymaking. Here scholars typically begin with a picture of the principal economic interests at stake and their forms of organization, then investigate how these interests transit through institutions of national political economies that determine patterns of delegation and aggregation.

We follow with a discussion of the international level of analysis. This starts with strategic interaction among national states as they relate to one another in international economic affairs. It continues with a more-detailed analysis of the role that international institutions play in this interaction, with institutions as both cause and consequence of variation in these international economic relationships.

Throughout the paper, we call attention to empirical puzzles and outcomes that have received extensive attention in IPE, as well as some that have not received as much attention as we think they deserve. The research frontier for IPE is thus defined in terms of empirical puzzles as well as a theoretical agenda, although we do not cover more than a sample of the empirical work that has been done over past decades. One relatively well developed empirical subject area, from which we draw many of our illustrative examples, is international trade. Monetary relations have received somewhat less attention but are now the subject of substantial research efforts. Other areas, such as foreign direct investment, have been the subject of some scholarship in the past, but are now relatively neglected and are prominent candidates for modern analysis. Many of these substantive topics are relevant to ongoing debates about the causes and consequences of globalization for national and international political economies.

We also identify strands of research that are organized around general concepts, such as international cooperation or stability, rather than specific issue areas. Scholars have long been interested in such general questions as the sources of interstate conflict or collaboration. We do, however, note that some of this sort of scholarship on international interaction would benefit from the use of more-nuanced and measurable outcomes than cooperation. We also note that, despite a generally accepted theoretical architecture for their analysis, there has been strikingly little detailed empirical work on international economic institutions.

■ | Domestic-International Interaction

For decades, a principal challenge to students of international politics generally, and international political economy specifically, has been the need to take into account both the domestic political economy of foreign economic policy and the role of strategic interaction among nation-states and nonstate actors. While all scholars recognized the domestic and international levels as necessary building blocks of a more systematic and integrated analysis of international relations, the difficulties of this integration were just as evident. Recent models of domestic-international interaction have pushed IPE research forward along these lines in important ways, although of course much remains to be done. In this section, we present and discuss some of the frameworks that have been developed to guide the study of domestic-international interaction in IPE.

The core of the domestic-international connection is the impact of domestic institutions and interests on international interaction, and vice versa. Our ultimate goal is a simultaneous understanding of this mutual causation, recognizing feedback effects at both levels—a general equilibrium model, rather than a partial equilibrium one in which one level is held fixed while the other varies. Of course, endogenizing two such complicated levels is extremely complex, and progress has been made in small steps at best. Nonetheless, there have been some promising efforts at integration. Taken as a body of scholarship, they suggest the troubling yet exciting possibility that what we think we have learned from studies lodged solely at the domestic or international level may have to be revisited when we take interactive effects more seriously.

Like all of IPE, the interaction of domestic and international conditions can be analyzed in terms of three factors: interests, institutions, and information. The interests of economic and political actors are a driving force behind economic policy decisions, and scholars attempt to specify these interests with some precision. How interests are translated into outcomes depends on the strategic environment, especially institutions and information. Interests are aggregated through institutions, which also delegate responsibility for decision making to particular actors. The structure of information similarly influences bargaining and policy choice. All three of these factors—interests, institutions, and information—are important at the international and domestic levels, and domestic-international interaction can often be examined by looking in a more-focused way at these factors. For example, we might ask how domestic institutions affect available international information or how international institutions affect domestic interests. This more-disaggregated approach to the relationship between the national and the global helps us formulate arguments amenable to empirical evaluation.

One approach to domestic-international interaction looks directly at how the international economy affects domestic interests, institutions, and information in ways that then feed back to national policies.[1] The international economy might affect foreign national economic policymaking through two related channels. The first runs directly from the global economy to the preferences of national socioeconomic and political actors. In this variant, international economic trends directly affect the interests of domestic groups, leading them to move toward new policy preferences or to change their domestic political behavior. For example, the expansion of world trade can have a powerful impact on firms' or industries' trade policy preferences. New export opportunities can lead previously protectionist firms to turn toward free trade, as some argue was the case for U.S. manufacturers after World War II; alternatively, the opening of new export markets can lead free-trade firms to redouble their lobbying efforts. In a Stolper-Samuelson framework (for example, Rogowski 1989), the expansion of world trade strengthens owners of nationally abundant factors, such as labor in poor countries and capital in rich countries. Similarly, the state of international capital markets can have a big impact on the preferred policies of groups in potential borrowing countries: the prospects of access to thriving global financial markets can lead firms and sectors to champion national trade, monetary, or exchange rate policies they might not otherwise support. Again, all these involve a common causal mechanism: change in the international economic environment affects the policy preferences and behavior of domestic groups, and thus has an impact on national policymaking and foreign economic policies.

In addition to affecting domestic interests, the international economy might also affect domestic institutions, as by making a previously feasible policy difficult to sustain. For example, national capital controls are relatively easy to impose and enforce when the world's capital markets are dormant or barely active, as was the case until the middle 1970s. However, the explosion of international financial activity in the 1980s and 1990s made it

1. The essays in Keohane and Milner (1996) contain some recent examples; the tradition is closely related to early work on interdependence (for example, Cooper 1968; Keohane and Nye 1977), and also to dependency-influenced arguments about the effects of international markets on development.

extremely difficult for national governments, especially in the more finan-
cially developed industrial world, to sustain controls on cross-border investment. While this process reflected previous policy choice by some major
governments, it can be taken as the exogenous result of economic and
technological trends for most countries, and it dramatically altered the set
of policies feasible for governments to contemplate (Goodman and Pauly
1993; D. Andrews 1994). For example, Eichengreen (1996) argues that
movement toward Economic and Monetary Union (EMU) in Europe was
made inevitable by the increasing difficulties European nations had in sustaining capital controls that allowed them to run independent monetary
policies, and more generally that high capital mobility has forced most
countries to choose between irrevocably fixed and freely floating exchange
rates, eliminating the possibility of defending intermediate exchange rate
systems.

One variant of analysis of the impact of the international economy on
domestic institutions is about the effects of globalization on the prospects
for the social-democratic welfare state and similar social policies. For example, Rodrik (1997) has argued that economic integration has reduced
the ability of governments to tax capital, thus limiting the scope for government policies to deal with the social dislocations that globalization itself
creates. Others believe that these effects are less limiting, still allowing for
different national economic policy paths (Garrett 1998b). All these arguments share a common causal approach connecting the international and
domestic levels: globalization, understood as developments in international economic integration, alters the choices available to national governments; this in turn affects national policy (and, one could continue,
international outcomes).

While these perspectives look at the impact of international factors on
domestic interests and institutions, they can be turned around to look at
how the structure of international economic institutions alters the information available to and the policy incentives for some domestic actors. It has
been argued, for example, that this is the secret of the effectiveness of
WTO provisions allowing one country to retaliate for WTO-illegal policies
by another country by excluding some of the violator's exports. This will
lead exporters in the violator to lobby *domestically* against national trade
policies that might lead to such retaliation, even though, in the absence of
the prospects for retaliation, they would be indifferent (Goldstein and Martin 2000). For example, if country A obtains WTO permission to sanction
country B for its barriers to A's clothing exports, and country A then puts a
tariff on country B's grain exports to A, this will give B's grain farmers an incentive to lobby *within their own domestic political economy* for a reduction
in B's barriers to clothing imports. In fact, some scholars argue that one
important effect of international institutions is to change domestic informational and institutional conditions so as to permit such linkages among
domestic policies, mobilizing exporters against their own government's

trade protection. This line of thinking has been applied especially to the highly structured nature of interstate bargaining within the European Union, where cross-issue linkages are rife and often draw contending domestic interests into the political fray (L. Martin 2001). Here, too, the chain of causation goes from international institutions to domestic institutions, information, and interests, then to national foreign economic policies.

In all these approaches, international factors affect national policy by way of their direct effect on the domestic political economy. This effect may take place by restricting the set of feasible policies, by constraining domestic institutions, by altering domestic information, or by changing the preferred policies and behavior of domestic actors.

Another approach, not necessarily exclusive from the foregoing, posits that national governments stand between the domestic and international levels, intermediating between them in ways not reducible to one or the other level and in ways that bring interaction between the levels to the fore. A powerful metaphor for this view of national governments as mediating the domestic-international interaction is that of two-level games (Putnam 1988). Initial work on this problem had a very simple characterization of the relevant domestic institutions and interests. First, the central domestic institutional actor was assumed to be the "chief of government" (COG) or head negotiator, operating at both the domestic and international levels. Second, domestic interests were summarized in terms of the "win set," the set of all international deals that would be preferred to the status quo by domestic society. In fact, much research in the two-level games tradition concentrates on the determinants of the win set. Third, initial work assumed that the COG was a disinterested representative of the interests of his or her constituency. This assumption has often been dropped in work building on the metaphor, as the COG is allowed to have independent interests. Adding another set of interests leads to the identification of the "acceptability set," those international agreements that the COG finds preferable to the status quo. Any deal reached and implemented must lie within both the win set and the acceptability set.

The two-level game framework provides tools for thinking about domestic-international interaction. It also hints at more fully interactive analyses, inherent in what Robert Putnam called "reverberation" and what Jack Snyder called "synergy" (1993a). Synergy represents new possibilities that open up as the result of interaction between the domestic and international levels and might occur when negotiators are able to use international negotiations to create previously unattainable outcomes, thus enlarging their domestic win sets. Yet treatments of two-level games have not yet made much progress toward full interaction between the two levels.

Most work in this tradition has focused on how domestic interests, institutions, and information influence negotiation and cooperation on the international level. One promising avenue is to look at the impact of legislatures on the ability of governments to commit to international agreements (L. Martin 2000). In democracies, legislatures have the ability to block or frustrate the implementation of international commitments even if they do not require formal legislative approval. Therefore, agreements negotiated without legislative participation may lack credibility. Agreements gain credibility when the legislature has been involved in a structured, institutionalized manner in the negotiating process. One major reason has to do with considerations of uncertainty, as legislative participation reveals information to both its own government and others about which deals will be implemented. Evidence drawn from the United States and the EU demonstrates that the credibility of commitments rises with institutionalized legislative participation.

Other productive applications of the two-level games approach include work on trade bargaining that formalizes ideas about win sets and ratification, and treats uncertainty explicitly (Milner and Rosendorff 1997; Milner 1997). These models identify a president with preferences over the degree of trade liberalization and a legislature that must ratify any international agreement. They assume two countries; for simplicity, the domestic politics of the "foreign" state are not treated in as much detail as those of the "home" state. On the international level, a Nash bargaining solution specifies the outcome of negotiations. Analytical interest thus turns primarily to the effect of the ratification requirement in the home state. Here, two factors get the most attention: the interests of the legislature, particularly how its ideal point differs from that of the president, and the degree of uncertainty associated with international negotiations.

These models give rise to a rich set of conjectures about the conditions under which agreements will be reached and the distribution of benefits within these agreements. One of the important contributions of this work has been to identify the conditions under which the Schelling conjecture holds. This is the idea, present also in the two-level games metaphor, that negotiators can often benefit from having their hands tied. If a legislature must ratify an international agreement and if the legislature will only approve a narrow range of agreements, the negotiator can use this fact as bargaining leverage. Therefore, negotiators might see advantages in being bound by a legislature. Formal approaches show that this logic holds in some but not all circumstances. For example, when the legislature is too hawkish—it has little interest in trade liberalization, in contrast to the president—ratification requirements will undermine the prospects for any international deal.

Domestic informational conditions, in these models, have an important impact on international interaction. The work assumes that the legislature may not know precisely the content of a negotiated agreement, perhaps because legislators may not know just how any agreement will influence economic outcomes in their districts. The effect of such uncertainty on the prospects for international cooperation is complex.

"Endorsers" can come into the picture, experts or interest groups who send signals about whether they find the agreement acceptable. When such endorsers exist, uncertainty does not impede international cooperation; in fact, the prospects for cooperation may be better under these conditions than in the complete information game. Mansfield, Milner, and Rosendorff (2000) extend this framework to consider interaction between democracies and autocracies, where autocracies do not require legislative ratification. They find—perhaps consistent with the Schelling conjecture—that pairs of democracies have more success in lowering barriers to trade than pairs that match a democracy with an autocracy. Statistical work bears out this proposition.

An alternative approach to the formal analysis of how the informational setting affects domestic-international interaction considers domestic politics the source of uncertainty about international agreements (Downs and Rocke 1995). For example, when two countries sign a trade agreement, they are uncertain about the exact economic implications for domestic groups and about which domestic groups will be mobilized to apply political pressure in the face of unwelcome economic consequences. This implies that deeper cooperation—that which provides greater mutual benefits but also involves greater unilateral risks—requires more flexibility, or "imperfection," in agreements. Tightly binding agreements that do not allow states temporary breathing room in the face of unexpectedly high domestic costs will be unstable. Some room for maneuver, such as less-than-perfect enforcement of commitments, allows states to cooperate over the long term, even if they sometimes deviate temporarily from the strictures of the agreement.

Work on domestic-international interaction has made substantial progress over the past fifteen years. The two-level games project stimulated such work and provided a language for discussing the nature of interaction, and further work has developed the approach in very promising ways. Yet there is much to be done. At this point, the analysis of domestic-international interaction requires heroic assumptions and simplifications, such as to reduce domestic institutions to an executive and a legislature or to reduce domestic interests to a median voter. Future work will need to allow for more nuance and development, incorporating such other domestic institutions as political parties, courts, and central banks and a more-sophisticated treatment of domestic interests.[2] Models of domestic-international interaction will also need to address more issue areas than international trade, where they have been developed most successfully, perhaps because of the strong preexisting microfoundations. Despite the

2. Some progress along these lines has been made in the analysis-of-trade literature, where Grossman and Helpman (1995) provide microfoundations for both economic and political interests; politicians are assumed to be competing over campaign contributions from special interests.

continuing weaknesses and large agenda for the future, the analysis of domestic-international interaction has made substantial advances and holds
great promise. One reason this progress has been possible is that scholars
were able to build on well-developed domestic and international analyses,
specifically of the domestic politics of foreign economic policy and of international strategic interaction. Without these prior bodies of scholarship,
whatever the weakness of a focus restricted to the solely domestic or global
level, research progress on the *interrelationship* of the national and the international would have been impossible. It is to these two bodies of research that we now turn.

■ | The Domestic Political Economy of Foreign Economic Policy

Understanding how domestic and international factors interact to determine the politics of international economics requires a firm foundation in
theories both of domestic political economy and of international interaction. Most of the work in IPE has been directed toward providing these two
sets of building blocks. The first large area of IPE research examines national policies toward the international economy. This sometimes comes
close to the investigation of purely domestic factors about a policy that just
happens to involve foreigners. More commonly, the international connection itself plays an important part in the making of foreign economic policy. In any case our understanding of the domestic politics of international
economic policy requires careful analysis of the economic interests at stake
and of how they work their way through domestic political institutions.
Substantial work on both these aspects of the problem has greatly enhanced our understanding. This is especially true of trade policies, which
we use heavily as an example.

In this domestic analysis, we identify three analytical steps. First,
scholars specify the economic interests at stake. Second, they characterize the organization of these interests. Third, they investigate how these
interests are mediated through political institutions. In carrying out this
analysis, we can also differentiate between broad public policies and mass
interests—such issues as inflation, growth, and economic reform—on the
one hand and narrower policies and special interests—such issues as trade
protection, industrial subsidies, and sectoral regulations—on the other.

Economic Interests

Most IPE scholarship on foreign economic policymaking begins with an
explicit or implicit model in which politicians confront a combination of
pressures from concentrated interests and the broad public. This frame-

work and its emphasis on the demand side coming from self-interested socioeconomic actors has roots in three perspectives: the Stigler-Peltzman approach to the political economy of regulation; the analysis of rent-seeking, or directly unproductive behavior; and the analytical Marxism that applies neoclassical tools to traditionally Marxist concerns. In all these frameworks, governments weigh benefits to special interests against costs to the general public, as well as clashes among special interest groups, and different levels of concern over broad public goods. Variation in foreign economic policy is due, at least as a first cut, to differences in the character and intensity of the interest-group and public pressures, and to differences in the incentives of governments to respond to these pressures. Analysis of domestic interests can be structured along two dimensions: specifying the content of groups whose interests are at stake and specifying the organization of these interests.

An important starting point for domestic IPE is to ascertain the interests, or policy preferences, of groups both broad and narrow. This can be done inductively, by observation, interviews, surveys, and other empirical techniques to map the interests of the relevant populations. There has in fact been a great flowering of work along these lines recently, especially making sophisticated use of surveys of public opinion in the United States and western Europe. Scholars have used public opinion surveys to explore both interest-group and mass-public preferences about European integration in general (Dalton and Eichenberg 1993; Gabel 1998), about EMU in particular (Gabel 2001), and about trade policy (Scheve and Slaughter 2001a, b) in imaginative and instructive ways. These empirical investigations of individual, group, and mass public policy preferences are an important source of information.

Scholars have also deduced policy preferences on the basis of prior theories of how characteristics of particular groups will lead them to desire particular policies. One example of how this approach has been used with great effect is the study of trade policy. Here political scientists have had the raw material of trade theoretic conclusions from economists interested in the differential impact of trade policies, who have developed three models of the distributional effects of trade liberalization and protection. The first, the Stolper-Samuelson theorem, predicts that factors of production that are scarce in a country will benefit from trade protection, so that labor in capital-rich (developed) countries and capital in labor-rich (developing) countries should be protectionist. The Ricardo-Viner, or specific-factors, approach emphasizes comparative costs and asserts that factors of production specific to import-competing (exporting) industries will be protectionist (free trade). More recent developments look at scale economies, typically to argue that larger firms should prefer more-open trade.[3]

3. Alt and Gilligan 1994 surveys the first two; Milner and Yoffie 1989, Richardson 1990, and Chase forthcoming survey the latter, which is less developed.

There are other arenas in which theory helps us understand the expected interests of socioeconomic actors. Where economists have explored the distributional effects of foreign economic policies, political scientists can deduce the policy preferences of the affected interests. Sometimes there is only a short step from existing work in economics to these deductions, as in the analysis of immigration; at other times, it requires substantial extension and imagination, as in the analysis of foreign direct investment, currency policy, or financial regulation. And there are many issue areas in which there is little or no preexisting work to serve as a starting point for deriving groups' interests. Here scholars of IPE have developed original arguments about the impact, for example, of financial structure on currency policy preferences (Henning 1994) or of portfolio diversification on trade policy preferences (Schonhardt-Bailey 1991).

Just as scholars have deduced group interests from the distributional impact of targeted economic policies, they have also searched for theoretically grounded ways to specify mass interests over such broad areas as macroeconomic policy and the provision of public goods. One useful baseline is the simple idea that the public prefers those policies most likely to raise national income. This was in fact the unstated presumption of early studies of trade policy (notably Schattschneider 1935), based on the economic argument that free trade is the most efficient policy for any nation. In other areas, we can draw on efficiency and social welfare arguments to designate the purportedly most desirable policy—low inflation, effective countercyclical currency policy, social insurance against exogenous terms of trade shocks—and posit, at least as a first approximation, that these are the public will. Another possibility is to focus not on society as a whole but on the median voter and attempt to establish the expected policy preferences of such pivotal actors.[4] This is standard in studies of income redistribution, where it is common to assume that the net expected benefits of redistributive policies on the median voter will determine their electoral viability.[5] The generally applicable point is that if the median voter—more generally, the politically pivotal portion of the public—can, roughly speaking, be identified, it may also be possible to identify the policy preferences of this segment of the population.

The content of the foreign economic policy preferences of concentrated interests, mass publics, and pivotal actors is important, but politics involves a series of exchanges and exchange implies that socioeconomic and political actors are willing to trade off policy dimensions: firms that

4. While there are instances in which the median voter's interests are those which maximize social welfare, this is not always (and perhaps not usually) the case. The median voter, in other words, is not necessarily a representative agent of society; it is simply his or her pivotal position in the relevant political space that makes him or her crucial.

5. Meltzer and Richard 1981 is the classic source.

prefer both free immigration and free trade may compromise by forgoing the former to put together an effective coalition for the latter. Public opinion may be hostile to devaluation but even more hostile to the expenditure reductions and tax increases necessary to defend the exchange rate. For this reason, we need to know the relative intensities of actors' policy preferences, the weights groups and individuals place on their various policy goals.

The basic determinant of preference intensities is the size of the stakes. This may be a direct consequence of the amount of money transferred directly or indirectly or of the policy rents otherwise created. As with policy preferences themselves, scholars have also suggested some general characteristics of actors that affect their preference intensities. One such characteristic is the specificity of the actor's assets—physical or human capital, for example—to a particular use. The idea, drawn loosely from transaction-cost-based analysis, is that the more specific the asset the greater the actor's incentive to defend its value in its current use (Frieden 1991b; Alt and Alesina 1996). Firms with very specific investments will be more concerned to protect themselves from foreign competition; workers with specific skills will be more adamant about demanding social insurance to protect them against unemployment.

Although it is important to have a clear sense of the narrow and broad interests at stake, scholars also need a sense of the ways in which these interests are organized. One simple and powerful starting point is to distinguish between concentrated and diffuse interests, especially as most scholars have believed that concentrated interests are likely to dominate diffuse interests. This was the view, for example, of Schattschneider's pioneering study (1935) of the Smoot-Hawley tariff. Schattschneider assumed that concentrated protectionist industries would dominate the diffuse free-trade interests of disorganized consumers. The explanatory power of this general proposition has been confirmed in many contexts, as scholars find that mass publics or electorates often have little impact on policies whose effects are difficult to discern or technically complex.[6]

But simply distinguishing between concentrated and diffuse interests is not enough. For one thing, there are frequently conflicts of interest *among* concentrated interests. Many studies of trade policy, for example, have shown that antiprotectionist exporters, multinational corporations, and consuming firms can effectively counteract the influence of those who would like to restrict imports (Milner 1988; Destler and Odell 1987). Concentrated interests may also have intense views on general public policies.

6. The insight has been explored in much more detail since the publication of Olson 1965, which focused attention on such problems of collective action. In the realm of IPE, Gourevitch (1986), following on his influential 1977 article, found this bias in favor of concentrated groups to hold across many countries and time periods.

For example, while the simple concentrated-diffuse dichotomy might regard macroeconomic stabilization as a general interest policy of diffuse concern and opposition to stabilization as largely emanating from special interests, there are often concentrated groups with intense interests in broad stabilization policies. This might be the case of the financial sector, typically seen as strongly supportive of anti-inflationary policies despite their diffuse impact. Finally, despite the fact that policy is often biased in favor of special interests, there is no question that diffuse interests often have a powerful impact on policy. After all, politicians in democracies must be elected; most authoritarian regimes need support from at least portions of the mass public. And there is little doubt that mass publics do in fact, at times, have strong desires related to international economic policy, especially when it affects such prominent issues as inflation, unemployment, and taxation. Even where mass publics are not organized around such policy issues, there may well be incentives for political entrepreneurs to address these concerns. In other words, it is almost certainly untrue that debates over foreign economic policy always pit concentrated interests against the public or that the mass electorate is always bested by concentrated interests.[7]

In this context, it is important to note the ways in which groups, and even broad segments of the public, are organized, for this pattern of organization can have a powerful impact on policy. This is especially the case because individuals and firms often have crosscutting material interests, and similar economic agents can be organized into very different collectivities across countries; even within a single country, over time the organization of interests can change dramatically. An autoworker has at one and the same time economic interests associated with his industry, with a range of similarly constituted exporting or import-competing sectors, with the working class generally, with her or his region, and with her or his status as consumer. In addition, she or he may have strong partisan, ethnic, or other ideological commitments. It is perfectly plausible that in one setting, autoworkers will cohere and identify primarily with their industry, while in other settings they may divide in many different ways. Perhaps the most striking example of these differences is the tendency of workers in Japan to be organized along firm lines, in the United States along industrial lines, and in much of Europe along class lines.

Variation in the organization of economic interests has important implications for the making of policy. An obvious example is the difference

7. Gowa (1988) argued for such a position as applied to international trade and monetary policy, specifically that the former implicated specific interests much more than the latter and would therefore be more politicized. But the highly politicized nature of European monetary integration and currency problems in the developing world would seem to indicate the shortcomings of an approach based on such assumptions, perhaps because they misidentify the specific interests or underestimate the importance of mass publics.

between labor or management interests that are organized on sectoral as opposed to class lines. Where sectoral forms of association prevail, there is likely to be much more pressure for particularistic policies: trade protection, export subsidies, controls on or subsidies to foreign investment. Where class politics prevails, policies are less likely to focus on industry-specific benefits and more likely to involve concerns of broader interest to labor or capital as a whole. Scholars have long noted that northern European–style social democracies, with their densely organized and centralized labor movements, have tended to eschew trade protection in favor of class-based social insurance schemes, while countries with less of a tradition of class political organization (such as the United States and Japan) have tended to engage in more sectoral protection.[8] While this and other such relationships have been investigated with regard to the organization of labor, they also hold for the organization of business interests, which vary in similarly important ways among countries.

Scholars studying the domestic politics of foreign economic policy, then, pay considerable attention to the policy preferences of interest groups and of the broad public, to the intensity of these policy preferences, and to the organizational forms of these special and broad interests. This has been true in the analysis of international trade, financial regulation, currency policy, and foreign investment. The analysis of trade is probably the best developed of these literatures. We now have quite a nuanced understanding of which economic actors are most likely to demand protection or trade liberalization and under which circumstances. We have a preliminary sense of similar issues in international monetary policy, such as which actors are most likely to prefer fixed or flexible exchange rates. In areas such as financial regulation and foreign direct investment, our knowledge is more rudimentary, with some intriguing puzzles and preliminary analyses but only relatively sketchy theoretical and empirical work. The analysis of the content and organization of domestic interests promises to continue to make advances as it is extended to these underexplored empirical areas.

POLITICAL INSTITUTIONS

The interests, preference intensity, and organization of socioeconomic actors is only a starting point for the analysis of domestic constraints on foreign economic policy. These interests are mediated through domestic political institutions in ways that can fundamentally affect outcomes. This is especially true of the organization of the political system as it responds to political pressures.

8. Katzenstein 1985b is the classic statement. Some might argue that the small size of these countries dictated the form of interest aggregation. Whatever the direction of causation, there appears to be a strong correlation between the two.

Institutions perform two general functions: aggregation and delegation. Some institutions aggregate interests in ways that affect the ability of groups to organize and the weight they will have in the political process. Other institutions delegate decision-making authority to particular actors, similarly changing the weight of various interests in the political process. Still other forms of legislative and bureaucratic organization are best understood as delegating authority from one group of actors to another. In one way or another, electoral, legislative, and bureaucratic institutions serve to mediate the pressures brought to bear by organized interests and the general public and to transform them in ways that directly affect policymaking.

Electoral institutions matter to the making of foreign economic policy because they affect the transmission of societal interests to politicians. One impact is on the need for politicians to respond to policy-relevant concerns of the broad electorate: the more the electoral system reflects the preferences of the mass public (or median voter), the more policy has also to reflect these preferences. Some have hypothesized that systems of proportional representation, or more generally larger electoral districts, tend to reduce the impact of special interests and increase the electoral importance of the median voter. This would imply that such systems would be more likely to incline toward freer trade, and fewer sectoral benefits and subsidies, than first-past-the-post systems in which local or regional interests may be more powerfully represented.[9]

Different electoral systems may also affect the influence of special interest groups in ways other than local or regional particularism, such as when politicians rely heavily on private campaign contributions. Where election funding is entirely public, the scope for a direct contributions-based channel for the influence of interest groups is presumably more limited than in systems in which private contributions are very important. And as national electoral systems—or simply electoral environments—evolve over time, this can affect policy. For example, it has been argued that the increasing importance of urban middle-class voters in Japan facilitated the deregulation of the country's international financial institutions and put pressure on the government to allow the yen to appreciate (Rosenbluth 1993).

In addition to differences among countries' electoral systems, there are also differences in the electoral bases of different branches of government in a single country. This is not usually the case in unitary parliamentary systems, but in federalist systems or those with a division of powers, it is common for different levels or branches of government to be elected in different ways. Because it is uncommon for subnational units of a federal system to have a major role in foreign economic policy, the more important

9. Rogowski 1987b, McGillivray 1997, and Alt and Gilligan 1994 all present variants of these arguments, for which the evidence remains mixed.

differences in electoral institutions are among branches of government, such as different electoral institutions for two chambers of the legislature or for the legislature and the executive. Just as variation in district magnitude or proportionality may have a systematic impact on representation in comparative perspective, so will they affect the political incentives of, say, the upper and lower houses of the Japanese Diet or the U.S. Congress and president. The most common argument along these lines is indeed, as above, that smaller districts are more likely to reflect special interests, while upper chambers and executives are more concerned with broader or even national public opinion. This should tend to make the upper chambers and executives less favorable to trade protection, sectoral or regional subsidies and incentives, and other particularistic policies. The overall impact of these differences on policy depends, of course, on the legislative institutions by which policy is made and implemented.

Legislative organization, then, is a second important set of political institutions that affect foreign economic policymaking. The importance of agenda control, veto points, and other interactions among policymaking institutions is well established in the broader political science literature, and direct consideration of these factors has been drawn into analyses of the making of foreign economic policy as well. Where there are clear electoral differences among chambers or branches, it is important to determine the relative influence of the different units on policy. A constitutional structure, for example, that gives trade policy authority to the more localist legislature will produce different outcomes from one that delegates all trade policymaking to the executive. The areas in which different branches or chambers dominate; the constitutional status of international agreements and treaties; the order in which laws are designed, amended, vetoed, and approved—all these will affect policy.

The most-developed work on the impact of legislative institutions on foreign economic policy has to do with U.S. trade policy. One strand of scholarship asserts that Congress will be systematically more protectionist than the president, given the executive's national constituency. The disaster of the 1930 Smoot-Hawley tariff led policymakers to redesign trade policy institutions so that the president could, within carefully specified constraints, negotiate reciprocal trade agreements with other countries. This evolved into a system in which the executive essentially proposes trade policy to a legislature that can only make limited changes or none at all. This change in the institutional structure of U.S. trade policymaking is often given credit for the general liberalizing trend in U.S. trade policy (Haggard 1988; Bailey, Goldstein, and Weingast 1997).[10] More-differentiated analyses have extrapolated from the expected impact of this institutional structure to draw inferences about the effects of partisan control of Congress and the presidency on the outcome of trade policy.

10. But see Irwin and Kroszner 1999 and Hiscox 1999 for contending views.

Specifically, Lohmann and O'Halloran (1994) have argued that divided U.S. governments are likely to give rise to more protectionist policies than unified governments.

Even in unitary parliamentary systems, legislative institutions can be important. In the general political science literature, it has been argued that divided government in the U.S. system is analogous to minority government in parliamentary systems (Laver and Shepsle 1991). In similar ways, scholars have looked at the role of parties in parliamentary systems. One such approach focuses on the degree of party discipline, on the principle that a disciplined national party, like the U.S. president, is concerned about a national constituency. This leads to expectations that electoral and legislative institutions that lead to strong party discipline will typically deliver policies less in thrall to special interests, such as freer trade (McGillivray 1997). Another approach looks at the incentives to individual parties in multiparty governments, arguing that these differ from those faced by single-party majority governments. Where the government is made up of a coalition, it is difficult for voters to assign blame or credit to a particular party for government policy. This reduces the incentives for opportunistic partisan manipulation of foreign economic policy. One implication is that countries that typically have multiparty governments are more likely to adopt fixed exchange rates that prohibit the manipulation of currency values for partisan electoral purposes, or to put it differently, that single-party governments are more likely to choose adjustable exchange rates so that they can manipulate them for partisan electoral purposes (Bernhard and Leblang 1999).

The third sort of domestic political institutional variable commonly considered by IPE scholarship is *bureaucratic institutions*, especially patterns of delegation to bureaucratic and other agencies. The previously mentioned work on U.S. trade policy is about delegation from one elected body (Congress) to another (the president). In recent years, this delegation has become even more explicit, with the frequent use (or attempted use) of fast-track bargaining authority by the executive. Trade policy in the United States also involves a number of independent agencies, such as the International Trade Commission and the U.S. trade representative, with the potential authority to deal with trade policy issues ranging from allegations of dumping to other instances of unfair trade. The recent upsurge of interest in standards that relate to trade—environmental, labor, health and safety— has also led to the creation of delegated institutional mechanisms to deal with these issues, such as the independent agencies established under the auspices of the North Atlantic Free Trade Association (NAFTA). In the European Union, trade policymaking is delegated to the European Commission and, within this, to industry-specific groups that include representatives from many member states. Trade policy is not unique. International financial policy is typically handled by independent agencies with special responsibilities for national banking systems: central banks, national regulators, finance ministries.

The impact of delegation on the making of foreign economic policy is complex and controversial. Some scholars see independent agencies as particularly likely to be captured by special interests. Most scholars, however, regard independent bureaucratic entities from an explicit agent theoretic perspective in which the agency responds to the policy needs of politicians, albeit with some room for maneuver (slack). Often independent agencies are regarded as providing politicians a protective cushion from day-to-day or particularistic demands, while also ensuring their accountability to the public. The interplay of independence and accountability depends strongly on the issue area and on other characteristics of the political economy.

One well-developed literature is that on central bank independence, which typically begins with the assertion that independence can mitigate the time inconsistency of monetary policy.[11] Politicians can thus best respond to the policy preferences of the mass public (median voter) for low inflation by insulating the central bank from the temptation to alter monetary policy, within the boundaries of ultimate accountability to the political authorities. Central bank independence has also been drawn into analyses of international monetary policies. For example, it has been argued that governments in countries with independent central banks are less likely to engage in electorally motivated manipulations of exchange rates. A related argument has been made that governments that can commit credibly to low inflation with an independent central bank are less likely to need to fix their exchange rate in order to gain anti-inflationary credibility, so that central bank independence and fixed currencies are policy substitutes (Clark and Reichert 1998; Clark and Hallerberg 2000; Broz forthcoming). In all these cases, the relationships between political leaders and bureaucratic institutions have been drawn into the analysis of foreign economic policies.

As this discussion illustrates, there is a clear logic to the approach commonly used by scholars in the analysis of the domestic politics of foreign economic policy. In any given policy arena, we first specify the interests at play, drawing on observations of expressions of policy preferences or on established bodies of theory or on both. It is useful to distinguish between special and mass interests and between policies of primarily narrow or sectoral incidence and policies that broadly affect public welfare. We then look at the ways in which these interests are organized. Finally, we examine political institutions that determine the impact of organized and mass interests on policy through both aggregation and delegation. Elec-

11. Classic presentations can be found in Grilli, Masciandaro, and Tabellini 1991 and in Alesina and Summers 1993.

toral institutions affect the relationship among voters, interest groups, and politicians. Legislative institutions influence the ways in which politicians bargain toward policy outcomes. Bureaucratic institutions condition the ways in which policy is made and implemented, depending on the degree of autonomy delegated to bureaucratic agencies. Decades of scholarship in IPE demonstrate that this consensual method can provide convincing and ultimately revealing results.

This concatenation of methods has been applied successfully to the making of national policies toward international trade and finance, exchange rates, foreign investment, and other foreign economic policies. The literature on trade, particularly on the level of protection offered to various sectors, is especially well developed. That on international finance and exchange rates is moving forward rapidly, for example with detailed studies of the choice of exchange rate regimes and policy responses to market pressures on currencies. Foreign investment, both patterns of international investment flows and patterns of national policies toward foreign investment (regulation, control, international agreement), is a topic deserving of more and more-sophisticated study. In any case, the advances of this realm of IPE research have facilitated the systematic incorporation of domestic factors into a more integrated analysis of domestic-international interaction in the world's political economy.

■ | International Interaction

Along with the domestic politics of foreign economic policy, the second major building block of the larger IPE edifice is the analysis of strategic interaction at the international level. Scholars have developed theoretical and empirical approaches to the ways in which states relate to one another as they devise their international economic policies, and to the institutional forms that these international economic relations take. In this section we outline approaches to studying international interaction, illustrated with examples drawn from trade and monetary policies. In keeping with most U.S. research, the emphasis is on relations among states, rather than between states and such nonstate actors as multinational corporations or nongovernmental organizations. Many of the tools of analysis discussed here could, nonetheless, easily be adapted to these purposes.

Strategic Interaction among States

Scholars of IPE have long understood that the interactions of states in the international system influence economic policies and outcomes in crucial ways. For tractability, most arguments about strategic interaction take the characteristics of states as given, typically informed by the work on domestic political economy discussed above. Treating states as units—although not identical units—scholars ask how the constraints and opportunities offered by the international system and the processes of interaction with other states influence decisions and outcomes.[12]

The analysis of international interaction centrally involves three elements: the identification of state interests; the specification of the strategic setting; and the attention to the role of uncertainty, beliefs, and ideas in explaining policy choice.[13] Scholars typically strive to begin with a good understanding of state interests, the outcomes states desire. These interests are then placed within a strategic context that is largely determined by system characteristics. One important aspect of the strategic setting is the uncertainty on a particular issue (see Morrow 1999b), which makes state beliefs and how they change over time a central part of the analysis. While national interests are important to the analysis of international interaction, scholars are typically interested in identifying *patterns* of state interests and *variations* of interests across states and issues, rather than concentrating on individual states and actors within states. In other words, the goal is to come up with *general* patterns of state interests rather than particularistic, nationally specific ones. One approach is to build on the domestic analyses described above but to focus on commonalities among groups of countries. For example, patterns of interests can be characterized by specifying the degree of common interest among actors. Some studies of monetary cooperation during the interwar period suggest that changing perceptions of the degree of common interest were the primary determinant of international cooperation (Oye 1986a).[14] Even when a high degree of common interest exists, however, conflict about the distribution of gains from cooperation may intervene, even to the extent of delaying cooperation indefinitely (Fearon 1998a). In some settings, states may have no incentive to deviate from a cooperative outcome; in others, they may wish to renege if they can do so without punishment.

When states have a high degree of common interest, our attention is drawn to those factors that encourage or discourage realizing those common interests. These might be characteristics of the states themselves—for example, whether they have institutional structures that encourage living up to their commitments—or aspects of the international environment—for example, the costs of monitoring others' behavior. When the degree of common interest is low, in contrast, our attention turns to factors that influence outcomes in the presence of high levels of conflict. We might ask

12. For exposition of a framework similar to that outlined here, see Lake and Powell 1999a.

13. Information is, technically speaking, an aspect of the strategic setting. However, we isolate it as a third factor because of its importance.

14. Although other studies find more explanatory power in domestic economic interests and institutions; see Simmons 1994.

about first-mover advantages, the opportunity costs of using military force or holding out for a better deal, or the wherewithal of states to engage in coercive diplomacy.

A second approach is to look at how the position of nation-states in the international system affects their interests. That is, the focus is more outside in than inside out, asking how the international political or economic system shapes state goals. A simple starting point is to assume that all states want to maximize their economic welfare (although some combination of security and economic well-being is a common assumption as well). However, what policies allow a state to do so are heavily dependent on its position in the international political economy. Governments of large countries are more likely to be protectionist than governments of small countries, for example; the latter are likely to value exchange rate stability more highly than the latter.

Power differentials are often posited to affect state interests. Thus, a hegemonic state is said to have different interests in such issues as institutionalization, liberalization, and international cooperation than a weak state. For example, monetary coordination in Europe appears to be directly shaped by patterns of internationally determined interests. European countries most effectively coordinate their exchange rate and monetary policies when the United States acts in a manner that creates instability and negative externalities (Henning 1998). Thus, regional integration efforts in Europe have been most successful in the absence of hegemonic leadership (B. Cohen 1997). The long tradition of work in IPE that focuses on how patterns of interests depend on the distribution of power in the international system has developed from the initial presumption that a highly concentrated distribution of power led to preferences that facilitate cooperation (Kindleberger 1975; Krasner 1976). A second generation asked about the possibility of interests conducive to cooperation among small groups (Snidal 1985) and how the issues at stake influenced patterns of interests (Conybeare 1984; Gowa 1989). Recent work is even more careful about how the distribution of power influences interests, distinguishing among different types of players in the international system (Lake 1984) and considering the interaction of security and economic interests (Mansfield 1994). In one way or another, scholars interested in analyzing interstate interaction must begin with a clear (if simplified) picture of state interests, just as in domestic analysis.

Where the analysis of international interaction goes beyond domestic political economy is in its attention to the international political and economic strategic setting. By *strategic setting*, we mean the structure of interaction, the form of the game. How many states are involved in any particular negotiation or other mechanism of policy choice? Bilateral interactions create different constraints and opportunities than those involving a few states, which in turn differ from those involving large numbers of states. Can members of a "club" exclude outsiders, or is participation in the process of interaction open to all who wish to join? Are states interacting in a highly institutionalized environment or one with few rules constraining the nature of the interaction? These questions may lead us to examine implicit or explicit voting rules, such as whether unanimity is required or whether some version of majority rule prevails. For example, studies of debt restructuring suggest that relationships among lenders have a great deal of structure, creating a hierarchical pattern of interaction with the IMF and a few large banks at the top (Lipson 1986). This structure allows banks to overcome collective action problems to respond to debt crises. The international environment also influences the order in which issues will be considered or which issues will be considered or which issues will be linked to one another. Some other important aspects of the strategic environment include questions such as how much weight actors put on future relative to immediate outcomes, that is, the relevant discount factors. Studies of trade wars suggest that a long shadow of the future mitigates pressures for conflict (Conybeare 1986). We also care about the prospects for enforcing agreements. Roughly accurate answers to all these questions are necessary in the attempt to specify how international interaction matters for IPE.

One aspect of the strategic setting that is especially important is the nature of uncertainty. Strategies in an environment of complete information differ tremendously from those in which states are unsure of others' preferences or of the relationship between policies adopted and outcomes achieved. To simplify somewhat, two types of uncertainty are important for IPE: uncertainty about the preferences of others and uncertainty about causal relationships.[15]

States may only have estimates of the preferences of others. For example, they may not know the value another government attaches to the aggregate welfare of citizens as opposed to the particularistic welfare of special interests. They may not know how willing others are to sacrifice economic benefits for security concerns. Rationalist approaches assume that beliefs are updated in a systematic manner through the process of interaction, as information is revealed by the choices of other states and by the observed outcomes resulting from these choices.[16] States first develop strategies based on a best guess about others' preferences, taking into account that others will also make their best guesses, and perhaps bluff or otherwise misrepresent their true interests. As interaction progresses, states observe the choices and signals of others and update their beliefs (typically using Bayes' rule). They also attempt to manipulate information, some-

---

15. A related typology of beliefs can be found in Goldstein and Keohane 1993b; see especially Goldstein and Keohane 1993a.

16. Sociological approaches, which have been more common in the study of international security than in IPE and in European scholarship, posit other dynamics of belief change.

times having an incentive to obfuscate, at other times having an incentive to try to reveal their true preferences.

One of the more important tools in the analysis of beliefs and uncertainty is game theoretic investigation of signaling and reputation (see Morrow 1999b; Morrow 1994b; Kreps and Wilson 1982). In most settings, signals sent by states are most effective in changing the beliefs of others if these signals are costly. Otherwise, intended recipients are likely to dismiss signals as cheap talk. Analyses of some international monetary regimes sees them in this light, as commitment to a fixed exchange rate or a currency union involves a political cost that sends a signal about the intentions of governments (Giavazzi and Pagano 1988). However, in some circumstances even cheap talk can be an effective signal (Crawford and Sobel 1982). This occurs when states believe that they are likely to have a high degree of common interest and that they will be better off if they coordinate their actions rather than making independent choices. Alternative models of monetary regimes that see them as solving coordination problems rather than as commitment devices draw on this logic, identifying particular exchange rate systems as focal points (Frieden 1993; Broz 1997).

A second type of uncertainty in IPE is about the relationship between policies and outcomes, or causal relationships.[17] Some refer to this type of uncertainty as lack of precise knowledge about "the state of the world" (Goldstein and Keohane 1993a, 10). Examples of such uncertainty in IPE proliferate. Will fixed or flexible exchange rates improve investment flows and macroeconomic stability? What will be the costs of adjustment after conclusion of a trade-liberalizing agreement?

Where states are uncertain about the impact of their policies, prior beliefs again are central. Judith Goldstein's analysis of U.S. trade policy illustrates how the institutionalization of particular causal beliefs has structured the policymaking environment (Goldstein 1993). Uncertainty about the relationship between economic policies and outcomes, often called model uncertainty, can make efforts at monetary coordination counterproductive (Frankel and Rockett 1988; Iida 1990, 1999). While some authors refer to this type of uncertainty as states "not knowing their own interests," it is more fruitful to assume that states do know which outcomes they prefer, such as rapid economic growth, but are simply uncertain about which policies will get them closest to their goals.

In this setting, expert knowledge and learning are important. One common strategy in the face of causal uncertainty is to delegate some policymaking to experts, those with better knowledge about the relationship between policies and outcomes (Krehbiel 1991). This logic provides a way to ask about the influence of "epistemic communities" (Haas 1992) or "supranational entrepreneurs" (Moravcsik 1999). Another strategy is to

17. For theoretical discussions of causal knowledge, see Gilligan and Krehbiel 1989; Krehbiel 1991.

learn from observing the experience of others. Learning of this sort may account, for example, for diffusion of liberal economic policies in the last fifty years (Simmons and Elkins 2000).

The analysis of international interaction thus requires identifying the patterns of state interests, the strategic environment, and the nature of uncertainty and beliefs. With these factors in hand, analysts can go on to specify the strategies states will use. The interaction of state strategies, in turn, gives rise to equilibria, outcomes from which no state has an incentive to deviate. The goal of the analysis of international interaction is to identify equilibria, the circumstances under which they exist, and their characteristics in terms of aggregate welfare, the distribution of benefits and costs, and stability. Of course, completely and accurately taking all these steps is a mammoth undertaking, and one for which technology often fails us. Instead, most analysts isolate aspects of the problem, holding others constant or relegating them to the background, as in the examples summarized in this section.

The framework for understanding the impact of international interaction on IPE is well developed. It has been extended and applied in varied empirical contexts. However, substantial work remains to be done in this area to get a more precise sense of how international interaction matters for IPE. Greater attention to strategic interaction could inform empirical studies of the choice between trade competition and cooperation, including the choice to join and abide by trade agreements, the political problems associated with sovereign debt and its repayment, the logic behind currency unions and other exchange rate regimes, and the sources and implications of increased flows of foreign direct investment. One specific area in which such strategic interaction at the international level has assumed center stage is the study of international institutions and organizations, to which we now turn.

INTERNATIONAL INSTITUTIONS

Information, uncertainty, and beliefs are important explanatory variables in the analysis of international interaction. Some of the work summarized above refers indirectly to issues of uncertainty, for example, in asking whether policymakers share the same model of monetary policy or in emphasizing transaction costs. However, few of these studies directly address the degree of uncertainty or the role of beliefs in explaining patterns of cooperation, while uncertainty is central to the study of domestic-international interaction. A body of literature that has concentrated directly on informational issues is that on international institutions. The rationale for the existence and influence of institutions at the international level is driven almost entirely by informational considerations. In a world of complete information, according to most current arguments, states would not demand institutions and institutions would have no impact on outcomes. However, once we consider the myriad uncertainties that states confront, a potentially powerful role for institutions emerges.

The turn toward taking international institutions seriously can be traced to a collective project on international regimes (Krasner 1983) and to Robert Keohane's analysis of how institutions could facilitate the maintenance of patterns of cooperation "after hegemony" (1984). As Keohane's title suggests, much of the early work on institutions developed in reaction to the predictions of early hegemonic stability theory that international developed in reaction to the predictions of early hegemonic stability theory that international economic cooperation should plummet as U.S. power declined in the 1970s. However, in many areas of the international economy, cooperation appeared to be stable or to increase. At the same time, the international economy had become more highly institutionalized, and organizations such as the General Agreement on Tariffs and Trade (GATT) and the International Monetary Fund (IMF) had gained prominence. Perhaps these two trends were related, and international institutions accounted for the persistence of cooperation.

The modern analysis of international institutions begins with simple assumptions. As a first cut, states are treated as unitary actors; domestic politics have barely begun to be integrated into the models. These states are assumed to confront generic collective action problems. They may take the form of Prisoner's Dilemma–type games, where cooperation would benefit all, but each has an incentive to renege if it could do so undetected or without punishment. They may take the form of coordination or bargaining problems, where the difficulty is to choose a particular equilibrium in a situation in which the states disagree on which outcome they prefer (Martin 1992b). It is also possible for these problems to coexist; states may face a bargaining problem followed by an enforcement problem. In a world of no transaction costs, states could solve these dilemmas to reach Pareto-superior outcomes. However, actual problems of incomplete information, such as costs of bargaining and monitoring, can prevent their resolution, leaving all states worse off. International institutions can perform information provision functions that allow states to overcome collective action problems and therefore have an impact on patterns of behavior, even if these institutions do not regulate, enforce, or otherwise take on the characteristics associated with strong institutions on the domestic level.

This insight has led to a large body of theoretical and empirical literature on international institutions, both in IPE and international security (see Martin and Simmons 1998 for a review). Much of the empirical work has been plausibility probes—tests to see whether cases exist in which institutions perform the functions identified, and are associated with higher levels of international cooperation. Much of the early empirical work on institutions took the form of single case studies, and thus suffered from selection bias and difficulties in determining the causal impact of institutions. The latter is especially troubling in the study of institutions, since they are obviously endogenous: states choose and create institutions when they see a demand for them. Endogeneity makes the process of isolating the causal influence of institutions on outcomes difficult. One way in which this problem can be mitigated is to examine a large number of cases and to control for alternative explanations for both cooperative outcomes and the involvement of institutions. This has been done in the study of economic sanctions, for example, and institutions are found to have a substantively and statistically significant impact on levels of cooperation (Martin 1992a).

While theories of international institutions have grown more sophisticated over time, empirical work on the effect of institutions in IPE has been limited. It has been more evident in security issues (Duffield 1995; Wallander 1999) and environmental affairs (Keohane and Levy 1996). Recent years have not seen many focused studies of specific economic institutions. One obvious exception is the literature on the European Union. However, little of this literature adopts a particularly institutionalist perspective on the EU (despite the term *institutionalists* being tossed into some theoretical labels) or takes the factors identified as central to institutionalist theories seriously.[18] Application of institutionalist theories to economic institutions thus appears to offer another promising, highly productive avenue for existing research. Basic theoretical precepts are in place, but they need to be adapted to the complexities and context of specific institutions and issues.[19] The scope for careful empirical work is enormous. For example, Beth Simmons's study of the legalization of international monetary affairs combines the theoretical insights of institutionalism with careful empirical work to show that concerns of commitment and reputation help explain states' decisions to create and comply with the rules of the IMF (Simmons 2000).

One of the few sustained studies of a particular economic institution looks at the International Coffee Agreement (ICA) (Bates 1997). As with most international agreements relating to the regulation of the production of commodities, the ICA can be understood as a cartel. However, the history of the coffee agreement shows that the actions of intermediaries—the roasters—and major consumers—the United States—have a significant effect on the ability of producers to limit supplies and so keep prices high. The ability to maintain the cartel, and U.S. willingness to support it, depends on security and other political factors as much as economic considerations. From an institutionalist perspective, one of the most-interesting findings is that specific agreements reached within the ICA, for example, about the distribution of production quotas, were typically implemented

18. For one exception, see Andrew Moravcsik's work (1999) on the role of supranational entrepreneurs in the EU.

19. Economists have also begun to elaborate theories of international economic institutions. See Bagwell and Staiger 1999; Maggi 1999.

and had measurable effects on the price of coffee, indicating a causal impact of institutions on cooperation. One could imagine similar analyses being carried out on other commodity arrangements, integrating more systematically the variables identified by institutionalist theories.

Multilateral trade organizations have received more empirical attention than most economic institutions. Much of this attention has been focused on the dispute resolution mechanisms of GATT and WTO. The analytical framework for studying international institutions draws our attention to their ability to provide information about standards and state behavior. These functions enhance the value of having a reputation for living up to international agreements and allow decentralized enforcement of cooperative agreements to take place. The framework naturally leads us to focus on dispute resolution characteristics of institutions. Empirically, this work has been particularly interesting in the GATT and WTO context, as dispute resolution has been highly formalized (Goldstein and Martin 2000). Institutionalist analyses of GATT dispute resolution ask about the conditions under which states turn to GATT to resolve disputes (Busch 2000) and the factors that determine the outcome of GATT disputes (E. Reinhardt 1999). Outside GATT, James McCall Smith has explored the variation in formality of dispute settlement provisions in regional trade agreements (J. Smith 2000). Given the trend of other work on international cooperation discussed above, it is perhaps not surprising that empirical studies of GATT dispute resolution emphasize the importance of domestic factors, such as trade dependence and democracy, in determining outcomes. While our analytical framework begins with the simplifying assumption that states can be treated as unitary actors, it is inevitable that analysts begin to integrate domestic politics in a systematic manner into this framework. This move brings us back to our starting point, theories that concentrate on the interaction between domestic and international politics. But the development of such attempts to integrate domestic and international factors can now build on well-developed approaches to international strategic interaction.

In some ways, the empirical research agenda for international factors resembles that discussed above for domestic sources of policy. Work on trade issues is the most advanced, matched closely by that on monetary issues. However, empirical work at the international level differs in that much of it has been focused on broad concepts such as cooperation or stability. While useful, this focus has sometimes distracted from in-depth attention to specific issue areas and particular institutions. The potential for future research seems particularly promising, as we explore the functioning of specific economic institutions in much more detail and compare institutionalized interaction to interaction without the structuring effects of institutions. Doing so will, in part, require a turn away from broad synthesizing concepts to a focus on more concrete variation in state behavior, such as patterns of trade and investment flows and specific policy decisions. It will also allow us to feed this work back to the challenging attempt to integrate domestic and international analyses.

▪ Conclusions

The study of international political economy has made great advances in twenty-five years. After a period of internecine paradigmatic conflict, most scholars in the field have accepted a general, positivist approach to investigating issues in the politics of international economics. The subdiscipline has moved strongly in a direction in which new work builds self-consciously on, rather than firing broadsides against, existing work and in which abstract theoretical work complements empirical scholarship.

The study of IPE requires an understanding of how domestic and international factors interact, and this issue represents the current research frontier. However, understanding interaction requires solid building blocks on both the domestic and international levels. Thus, the investigation of an issue in IPE typically involves a series of interrelated and mutually complementary considerations. Scholars identify the socioeconomic interests at stake, how groups are organized, and how organized and general interests express themselves in the context of domestic electoral, legislative, and bureaucratic institutions. On this basis, other work focuses on the interaction of states at the international level, emphasizing especially the impact of the informational environment and the strategic setting on relations among states. The creation and operation of international institutions is a particularly important component of these international interactions.

While the general method of analysis is well established and widely accepted, this hardly means that IPE has exhausted its potential. In fact, it is surprising how narrow the range of analytical and empirical problems that existing scholarship has tackled in earnest is. Trade policy in the United States, the EMU in Europe, and a few international institutions have been studied in some detail; but almost every other area of IPE is wide open for investigation. It may be that a great deal of theoretical, analytical, and methodological brush needed to be cleared before scholars could give these issues as much attention as they warrant. If so, the academic study of IPE has virtually limitless opportunities to demonstrate the effectiveness and appropriateness of its theoretical and empirical tools.

We have identified both theoretical and empirical areas in need of further research. Theoretically, we see the most important frontier as the integration of the domestic and international levels of analysis. Some promising frameworks have been developed, but this work is in its infancy. We also see scope for applying existing frameworks to a wide variety of understudied empirical issues. Probably the best-studied area of IPE is trade, followed closely by monetary issues. Financial issues, including international investment of various types, receive little attention in the current literature. Likewise, theoretical work on international institutions has far outstripped the quantity and quality of empirical work. As international organizations such as the WTO, IMF, and potential investment agreements are the focus of sustained political attention and at the forefront of debates about globalization, applying the analytical tools of IPE more seriously to these institutions is likely to be both important and fruitful.

James E. Alt

Comparative Political Economy: Credibility, Accountability, and Institutions

Widespread fiscal difficulties in the late 1980s and the debate over the future of European fiscal and monetary policy in the 1990s produced a near consensus among scholars and practitioners that the design of political institutions matters for economic policy outcomes. Many believed that an independent central bank would produce credible low-inflation monetary policy (for instance, Grilli et al. 1991; Alesina and Summers 1993). This belief informed the design of the European Central Bank and institutional reform in several countries including Italy, New Zealand, and the United Kingdom. Others suggested that "transparent" fiscal institutions would enhance accountability and, if implemented, bring about desirable effects on policy outcomes like those required as conditions of participation in the European Monetary Union (von Hagen and Harden 1994; Alesina, Roubini, and Cohen 1997; Alesina and Perotti 1999). Concern for fiscal discipline also lay behind the extended campaign to enact a balanced budget constitutional amendment in the United States. The movement did not succeed but did encourage ongoing discussion about whether and how such laws affected policy (Poterba 1994; Alt and Lowry 1994; Lowry and Alt 2001), whether they could be statutory as well as constitutional (Inman 1999), and whether they increased economic volatility (Bayoumi and Eichengreen 1995; W. Crain 2000).

All these suggested institutional innovations in fiscal and monetary policy grew out of increasingly elaborate political-economic models of politicians responsible for economic outcomes' being accountable to and seeking reelection from an electorate that votes retrospectively. Out of these contributions comes an increased understanding of how markets and voters exercise their power to control politicians who hope to be seen as competent in carrying out policy. Principal-agent models that analyze the institutional design of incentives to act in certain ways and to reveal or conceal action and information dominate this literature. Lupia and McCubbins' model (1998) of delegation and voter information; Lohmann's analysis (1999) of information transmission in a complex economy;

Fearon's treatment (1999) of competence, moral hazard, and adverse selection in retrospective voting; and Ferejohn's explanation (1999) of the relationship between transparency and accountability all exemplify the new sophistication.

Frequently, the situations these newer models analyze involve the control of politicians by many actors (for instance, voters or market participants) engaged in strategic interaction. The literature is constantly dealing with multiplicity: multiple principals and agents, decentralized unions, governments of many parties. How many are they? How centralized or fragmented? How coordinated are their actions? Under what conditions of centralization, coordination, fragmentation, or numbers do we observe institutional effects on policy outcomes? Naturally enough, as a consequence, the results we review—estimates of systematic effects of institutional variations on outcomes—are also increasingly conditional and interactive.

Multiple actors responding to enforcement incentives can face coordination problems, in ways charted by Kreps (1990a). He shows how strategic communication in appropriate institutional settings can create "convergent expectations" that ameliorate the problem of coordinating enforcement strategies. In one way or another, this intuition grounds much of the modern, institutional political economy of monetary and fiscal policy. The first section provides an introduction, putting the more-specialized and policy-focused literatures in context. The second and third sections narrow the focus and describe respectively how, within institutional political economy, literatures have grown up around the key concepts of credibility in monetary policy and centralization and transparency in fiscal policy.[1] Both literatures reveal the interaction of economic theory and political analysis. This review deemphasizes the normative aspects of the literature and concentrates on the positive questions of how the institutions work and why, and what is the current state of empirical estimates of their effects.

In general, the results demonstrate the importance of relating policy outcomes to not only economic fundamentals but also the ideological or redistributive goals of political parties and interest groups and the institutional context in which policy is made. The final section sums up, relating transparency and credibility and highlighting how literatures on monetary and fiscal policy institutions have remained separate and how they might be brought together.

■ | The Political Economy of Institutions

Institutions affect behavior primarily by providing actors with greater or lesser degrees of certainty about the present and future behavior of other actors . . .

1. Even with that scope, this paper omits important material analyzing the extent of trade and the composition of the economy.

enforcement mechanisms for agreements, penalties for defection, and the like. The key point is that they affect individual action by altering [add: opportunities institutional actors have to affect] the expectations an actor has about the actions that others are likely to take in response to or simultaneously with his own actions. . . . From [a cultural] perspective, institutions provide moral or cognitive templates for interpretation or action. (Hall and Taylor 1996, 939)

Twenty-five years ago, political economy did not rate its own chapter in a multivolume *Handbook of Political Science* (Greenstein and Polsby 1975). The explosive growth of research since then now necessitates separate treatments that distinguish international from domestic political economy (as in this volume), as well as formal or rationalist from more historical approaches (as in the quotation above). Despite these distinctions, a frequent point of agreement is that these approaches view institutions as enabling communication, cooperation, or coordination in situations that involve multilateral enforcement of bargains. The coordinating function may not be viewed in exactly the same way, of course. To the rationalist, institutions provide information about others' incentives and menu of actions, while to the historian, they provide precedent and norms. But this is to a large extent the same thing described in two different ways.

The piece of political economy research reviewed below analyzes how the credibility of monetary institutions and transparency of fiscal institutions affect policy and outcomes like the inflation rate and scale or indebtedness of government. The central concept, institutions, refers to rules, procedures, norms, or conventions designed self-consciously to determine "who has the power to do what when." Political economy focuses on how political and economic institutions constrain, direct, and reflect individual behavior. It explains collective outcomes like production, resource allocation, and public policy in a unified way, stressing the political context in which market phenomena take place and using an economic approach, constrained maximizing and strategic behavior by self-interested agents. In sum, it emphasizes economic behavior in the political process and political behavior in the marketplace.

Institutions help individuals deal with certain fundamental problems of exchange, collective choice, and collective action. If there were no nonsimultaneous exchange, ex post opportunism would not be a concern. If information were fully and freely available, specialization and delegation would not produce agency costs. If nothing were ever chosen by vote, there would be no problem of cyclical instability. If there were no social dilemmas, problems of communication, cooperation, or coordination would seem less important. Instead, in the presence of these problems, institutions increase predictability, reduce uncertainty, or induce stability in human interactions.

A, perhaps the, comparative advantage of political science lies in studying self-consciously designed collective choices. Political scientists treat as a fact that choices are made in institutional contexts. That context, at least partly of human design, limits, constrains, channels, and determines *what* is available to choose, *how* choices from this feasible set are made, and *who* gets to make these choices. Relative to economics, a contribution of political science is to accord equal status to normative and positive questions, focusing *relatively* less on optimal arrangements and more on figuring out how things actually work.

Within the field, there is a sharp division between those who model institutions as rules, procedures, and choice *mechanisms* taken as preexisting and those who model institutions as rules, procedures, and choice mechanisms taken as equilibria in some underlying social game. Two contributions that take institutions as preexisting have been particularly influential: structure-induced equilibrium (see Shepsle and Weingast 1987)[2] and the Romer-Rosenthal setter model (H. Rosenthal 1990).[3] Others, like Schotter (1981) and Greif (1997), define institutions as equilibria in an underlying social game, emphasizing the *self-enforcing* characteristic and *coordinating* function of institutions. Models of such institutions focus on the conditions regarding common knowledge, shared information, and enforcement strategies that must be satisfied (Calvert 1995b).[4]

Suppose there were benefits to both rulers and ruled from private investments promoted by bargains limiting the wealth that the state can appropriate from citizens but that differences in timing and rates at which benefits accrue raise the risk of reneging or opportunism.[5] Suppose also that there is no independent third party with the power to compel the agreed performance.[6] Then such bargains will not be realized. Institutions

---

2. According to the structure-induced equilibrium approach, vetoes, gate-keeping, or agenda power arise in jurisdictions, specific domains of control like divisions in firms or specialized committees in legislatures, perhaps backed by further rules requiring self-restraint by other actors.

3. The setter model has more structure. It involves a proposer who offers a proposal in a defined sequence of moves, which results in the proposal's being subject to a take it or leave it choice, and a status quo, which is the reversion point if the choice is to leave it. This little sketch of political action turns out, like supply and demand curves, to help analysts make valuable predictions in institutionally complex situations.

4. The historical-institutional analysis of institutions governing exchange in the absence of a centralized legal system includes the game theoretic analysis of agency relations among medieval Mediterranean traders (Greif 1997) and the modern conception of political democracy as a commitment device (Masten 2000).

5. In the same way, politicians can gain from deals with each other, as when legislators trade votes in pursuit of the majorities necessary to enact legislation of benefit to their constituents, or parties bargain to form coalitions based on shared policy commitments.

6. Even if there were, it would be powerful enough to abrogate commitments and transgress the interests of others.

as equilibria can solve such *cooperation* problems by being self-enforcing, that is, by giving agents incentives to abide by the institutional rules. Such self-enforcing political bargains promote commitment, the assurance that when the time comes others will uphold their end of the bargain and encourage reluctant investors or legislators alike to take the risks and bear the costs necessary to achieve joint gains (North and Weingast 1989). Exactly such an institution is central to the analysis of credibility and monetary policy in the following section.

But suppose the self-enforcement of political bargains requires the threat of multilateral or collective action, whether violent, like some protests, or peaceful, like market responses. Suppose further that an individual can impose only a small sanction. Then deterrence of opportunism involves many participants, and would-be collective enforcers must settle on the definition of an infraction and find a way of communicating the occurrence of an infraction and the appropriate response to it (Masten 2000). These would-be enforcers face a problem of *coordination*, which institutions ameliorate by fostering focal points.

Kreps (1990a) shows how the coordination of beliefs offers an equilibrium strategy for dealing with unforeseen contingencies in repeated interactions. As Masten (2000) notes, "constitutions, legislative rules, and other widely shared norms or expectations about the allocation of decision authority may serve this coordination function." Hardin (1989) proposes that *written* constitutions hasten the process of convergence to shared conventions of behavior among individuals. He argues that "[contracts] are generally backed by external sanctions; constitutions are more nearly backed by . . . the difficulty of recoordinating on an alternative arrangement." While the literature is not as developed or clearly focused as in the case of monetary policy, the section after next makes central the coordinating role of institutions in fiscal policy.

■ | Monetary Policy: Central Banks, Labor Markets, and Parties

Twenty or even fifteen years ago, this review would have focused on the literature of whether monetary policy could be manipulated for electoral reasons, a literature that started from the stark question of whether Federal Reserve chairman Arthur Burns deliberately helped Nixon gain reelection. A quarter century after that event, Alesina, Roubini, and Cohen (1997) summed up a massive literature by saying, "Electoral monetary cycles occur frequently, but not always, and their size is small." Instead, for the past two decades, political economy research on monetary policy has been dominated by the time consistency problem. As Kydland and Prescott (1977) showed, policymakers with discretion to set monetary policy are tempted to expand the money supply in response to adverse shocks but the expectation of this temptation (typically among labor market participants) produces a positive inflation bias that could be avoided with a simple monetary rule. Barro and Gordon (1983) point out that unless policymakers are *credibly* committed to the rule, the basic problem remains.[7] The challenge for monetary policymakers is thus twofold: to establish institutions that resolve the time-consistency problem inherent in discretionary monetary policy and to find ways policymakers can commit credibly to those institutions.

Barro and Gordon (1983), Rogoff (1985), and others viewed the appointment of a relatively conservative, legally independent central banker as the best feasible solution to these problems, one which promises lower inflation at the same expected level of output, at the price of greater real fluctuation in the economy.[8] Keech (1995, ch. 8) provides an excellent review of a long list of measurement issues (like legal independence versus behavioral independence, the importance of appointment powers, the use of rules, and the relative priority of stabilization goals in practice) left in the background here.[9] Even so, examining the conjecture that there is an institution, the independent central bank, that "solves" the credibility problem (that is, gives policy that is ex post optimal and consistent with rational expectations) grounds more than a decade of serious comparative empirical work, much of it contributed by political scientists.

Early tests of the proposition, frequently by economists, showed that for a panel of Organization of Economic Cooperation and Development (OECD) countries, higher central bank independence did produce better inflation outcomes (Grilli et al. 1991; Cukierman et al. 1992; Alesina and Summers 1993). If anything, these empirical results were more positive

---

7. Without commitment, the monetary authority has incentives (from private information about its preferred inflation target) not to follow the "best" rule even if it announced it. Hence the rule is not necessarily credible even if announced, and announcing a noncredible rule is "pointless" (Persson and Tabellini 2000). The study of credibility, by contrast, is almost nonexistent in fiscal policy. Though credibility does occasionally appear in studies of debt and time-consistent capital taxation (Persson and Tabellini 2000, ch. 12) and fiscal stabilization and reform (Perotti 1999) it is not a major theme.

8. Retrospective mass voting cannot discipline the monetary authority. Appointing one whose preferences are for low inflation, so strong as to leave little doubt about intentions, and with the power to carry them out, provides a second-best solution under discretion. But is such an institution credible? That is, does the policymaker have incentives to behave in the appropriate way? Persson and Tabellini (2000, ch. 17) discuss the benefits of contracting for an inflation target.

9. Also neglected here is the comparison with central bank independence of alternative commitment technologies like fixed exchange rates (Clark forthcoming). Brief reviews of contractual and other approaches to the central bankers' political incentives can be found in Alesina, Roubini, and Cohen 1997, ch. 8, and Persson and Tabellini 2000, ch. 17.

about central bank independence than some theorists had claimed. Central bank independence was a free lunch, producing lower inflation (often by 2 percentage points or more) without even an increase in output variability. However, recent work has been less sanguine. For example, Campillo and Miron (1997) find that the inflation-fighting benefits of central bank independence are not robust to the inclusion of controls for debt, openness, political instability, or past experience with inflation, all of which might be expected to influence the demand for and ability to provide lower inflation. Generally, central bank independence has not been found to explain inflation performance outside the OECD countries (Cukierman et al. 1992; Campillo and Miron 1997; see also Maxfield 1997).

Nevertheless, there have been recent advances in pinning down the nominal and real effects of central bank independence. To a large extent, the progress has come from relaxing restrictive assumptions of earlier models by incorporating (ultimately strategic) interactions among an expanded set of institutional actors besides central banks. Labor market agents (and in particular the character of labor market organization) and partisan governments and legislatures play a prominent role in this literature. There is general agreement, for instance, that an independent central bank does reduce inflation but at some cost to employment; how much varies with labor market centralization in ways described below. Central bank independence should also moderate partisan cycles in inflation and growth, but compelling empirical evidence is elusive, for reasons that become clear below.

The simplest way to incorporate other agents is to consider how the central bank reacts to them, without making the interaction fully strategic. Franzese (1999) argues that as long as inflation results from some convex combination of the preferences of the bank and government, as Lohmann's description (1992) of a partially independent central bank would imply, the anti-inflationary benefit of central bank independence depends on all factors that might lead the government to inflate absent an independent bank. Therefore, if Left governments are expected to inflate more than Right governments, central bank independence should reduce inflation more given Left governance. Likewise, if greater union coverage puts upward pressure on wages or if coordinated wage bargaining produces wage restraint, central bank independence should be more beneficial where there is higher unionization but less helpful in lowering inflation where unions are well coordinated. Overall, Franzese shows for a panel of OECD countries that the impact of central bank independence is conditional on the inflationary pressure facing the bank, in the process finding much more precise estimates of the (conditional) anti-inflation benefit of central bank independence (especially in the face of shocks from abroad) than the preceding literature. Yet if central banks react to unions, and unions anticipate their reactions, a fully strategic model is needed to understand monetary policy.

Unions, Employers, and Monetary Policy

Fortunately, many recent papers consider how large unions might influence the setting of monetary policy by independent central banks. In Barro and Gordon's model, labor market actors have no wage-setting power and seek only to anticipate the level of inflation set by the monetary authority. But if labor market agents are not simply price takers, central banks must consider the behavior of wage-setting unions and employers when setting monetary policy. One important literature explores this proposition by combining insights gleaned from the study of corporatism with models of the behavior of independent central banks.

Students of corporatism have long argued that the structure and density of labor unions helps determine whether wage demands are militant or restrained. In the most influential study of corporatist institutions, Calmfors and Driffill (1988) argue that increasing the centralization of wage bargaining has two countervailing effects. First, unions' power to demand higher real wages increases, as labor from different unions becomes less substitutable (a competition effect). Second, as unions grow to encompass more consumers, the unions internalize the inflationary effects of real wage increases more (a strategic effect). Calmfors and Driffill argue that wage bargaining at the sectoral level is likely to unleash real wage pressure without the moderation that full encompassment would bring. Real wages, and thus inflation and unemployment, follow a hump-shaped curve over centralization of wage bargaining—either low- or high-centralization produces good outcomes, while moderate centralization can be disastrous.

Others have made parallel efforts to incorporate Calmfors and Driffill's insights into models of strategic interaction between wage-setting unions and inflation-setting central banks. There is broad agreement on the strategic problems. Labor unions want to coordinate wage restraint and central banks want credible inflation prevention. However, the newer models make qualitatively different predictions about inflation and unemployment, largely because they make different assumptions about the goals and organization of labor, its substitutability across industries and unions, and the elasticity of demand for labor.

The place to begin, according to Iversen (1998a, b, 1999), is with the wage setters. They must balance the desire for higher real wages with their fears of or dislike for (within-union and economywide) unemployment and (within-union) wage inequality. At the same time, they anticipate the central bank's reaction, which balances inflation against unemployment. Following Calmfors and Driffill, as the centralization of wage bargaining increases, so does a union's real wage setting power and also the inflation-cost of its own wages. Thus, if the central bank simply accommodates union wage demands (as Iversen supposes it will if the central bank lacks independence), the Calmfors-Driffill hump shape will result for both inflation and unemployment. However, with a nonaccommodating central bank (high central bank independence), the hump is inverted for unemployment and flattened (and lowered) for inflation. For low levels of centralization, inflation is lower, due to the independent central banks' solving the time consistency problem. Unemployment is unchanged, since money remains neutral (has no real effects) where unions are price takers.

For moderately centralized labor markets, Iversen argues, higher central bank independence leads to dramatic improvement in both inflation and unemployment, since the bank's credible threat discourages wage demands, solving the collective action problem posed by Calmfors and Driffill. Yet by contrast, for highly centralized economies, Iversen argues that high central bank independence may backfire. Encompassing unions in such economies face pressure from the median wage earner to maintain wage equality but find it difficult to achieve this by imposing wage compression (a *relative* lowering of wages) on their most productive workers. Employers are tempted to raise the wages of productive workers or sectors outside the bargaining agreement (a process known as wage drift). To reduce the effects of wage drift, unions may demand higher nominal wages across the board, accepting higher inflation as the price for wage equality. When conservative, independent central banks refuse to accommodate these demands, the consequence is higher unemployment.

Cukierman and Lippi (1999) also seek to incorporate the Calmfors and Driffill framework into a model of monetary policymaking. Specifically, Cukierman and Lippi assume that unions do not care about economywide unemployment or within-union wage inequality, that unions organize by craft rather than industry, and that labor is perfectly substitutable across industries but not unions. Accordingly, they show that while under most conditions central bank independence will lower inflation, the main impact of higher central bank independence on unemployment is to raise the curve Calmfors and Driffill described, producing worse outcomes generally and shifting its peak toward a higher level of centralization. So by changing assumptions, Cukierman and Lippi generate different predictions from Iversen. Organization by craft is common enough to justify their alternative treatment, but the assumption about substitutability is harder to accept.

Hall and Franzese (1998) take a different tack from both Iversen and Cukierman and Lippi. They argue that it is not centralization but *coordination* among bargaining units that matters for the strategic interaction of central banks and unions.[10] Effective coordination can achieve the same positive effects on inflation and unemployment as centralization by forcing the lead union to consider the inflationary consequences its demands would have if they were replicated throughout the economy. Where coordination is present, an independent central bank can further improve

10. They do not analyze the rationale (in the sense of the first section of this essay) for an institution that provides this coordination, however.

economic outcomes by credibly threatening to punish inflationary wage demands. However, absent labor market coordination, high central bank independence may raise unemployment. The central bank's threats to lower the money supply in response to wage demands are not credible, since in decentralized economies, any given union can discount the possibility that its actions will trigger monetary policy decisions. Unable to credibly threaten decentralized unions, a conservative central bank may preemptively tighten the money supply to undermine the ability of unions to demand higher wages in the first place—suggesting a potential real effect of central bank independence (Franzese, forthcoming).

Theoretical disagreements persist over the role of central bank independence in decentralized or uncoordinated labor markets and in highly centralized economies. Nevertheless, there is growing consensus that in moderately centralized or coordinated labor markets (which, after all, was for Calmfors and Driffill the worst case scenario), high central bank independence should produce lower inflation and lower unemployment. Despite the variety of specifications and measures (Iversen, Hall and Franzese, and Cukierman and Lippi all use different measures of labor market centralization or coordination, as well as different codings of central bank independence, with something to be said for each in every case), all the empirical work confirms the benefits of central bank independence (given moderate centralization or coordination of wage bargaining) for both inflation and unemployment. Where unions possess the ability to coordinate their wage demands but the temptation to defect for higher wages exists, conservative, autonomous central banks have proven a credible means of ensuring wage restraint.

Beyond this point, however, there remains considerable disagreement. In decentralized economies, Iversen does not find either real or nominal effects of central bank independence. Hall and Franzese find that central bank independence in those cases lowers inflation but raises unemployment. Cukierman and Lippi find that both unemployment and inflation are worse. There is no obvious explanation for this. At the same time, reassuringly for those who hope to see empirical evidence cumulate, in economies with highly centralized labor markets, most authors find modestly improved inflation under high central bank independence. But where Hall and Franzese, and Cukierman and Lippi observe a modest reduction in unemployment (for the latter, contrary to expectation), Iversen finds dramatically higher unemployment. While Iversen's measure of labor market centralization is less subjective and finer grained, a handful of outlier cases are probably crucial to the result for high centralization of wage bargaining. The damaging effects of public sector unions on wage restraint (Garrett and Way 1999) further complicate analysis of the high-centralization case. This may also underpin the relative failure of the high central bank independence–high centralization of wage bargaining combination (Franzese forthcoming). So while, broadly speaking, a lot of progress has been made in the last few years, divergent understandings and measures of central bank independence and centralization of wage bargaining still need to be reconciled in future research.

PARTIES AND MONETARY POLICY

So far the review has proceeded without mentioning political parties, as if the effects of parties were perfectly captured by either central bank independence or labor market centralization. However, reducing the problem of monetary policy to the interaction between unions and central banks leaves out partisan governments in at least three ways. Parties could have an independent role in the *institutional design* stage, by appointing central bankers and establishing the cost of overriding the bank. Parties could affect the monetary policy *decision* stage, by overriding central bank decisions.[11] Finally, governing parties could have independent effects in inflation and employment in *negotiations* with labor market agents, by making credible policy commitments in exchange for wage restraint.

INSTITUTIONAL DESIGN

Bernhard (1998) has argued that democracies with ideologically diverse coalition governments are more likely to adopt independent central banks, since backbenchers who do not share the ministers' policy preferences can use the central bank as an independent source of information to keep tabs on the cabinet's economic policies.[12] Bernhard supports his argument with panel data showing a tendency toward higher central bank independence in countries with center-left governments (intracoalition diversity) and federalism (regional diversity). While there has been little comparative work on the parties' role in the appointment process, some evidence from the United States shows that more conservative parties appoint more conservative central bankers (Chapell, Havrilesky, and McGregor 1993). At the least, the continuing partisan variation in appointments during a period of consistently high legal independence of the Federal Reserve has to raise concern about whether the comparative politics empirical work discussed above confounds central bank independence with central bank conser-

11. There is an extensive literature on how partisan preferences and institutions interact in a setter model framework in the setting of U.S. monetary policy. The most recent estimates (Morris 2000) are that each incremental point of "liberalism" (measured by ADA scores) of the "pivot" lowers the real federal funds rate by about seven basis points. That means roughly that the difference in interest rates attributable to say, the difference today between a moderate congressional Republican and Democrat, would be about two-tenths of a percentage point. Morris 2000 contains a complete bibliography of the relevant literature.

12. This is one point where the monetary policy literature borders on transparency, since the role of the independent central bank is to improve the monitoring of policy settings.

vatism. Put another way, analysis of the partisan origins of central bank appointments could be a worthwhile study for students of comparative monetary politics.

MONETARY POLICY DECISIONS

Independent central banks strike many observers as an obvious potential remedy for both opportunistic and partisan political cycles (Alesina, Roubini, and Cohen 1997; Waller 1992). Clark and Reichert (1998) provide some evidence that central bank independence does indeed moderate opportunistic behavior, but evidence for moderation of partisan cycles remains elusive. Lohmann (1998b) argues that decentralized appointment procedures for central bankers (as in the U.S. Federal Reserve Board, which combines executive appointments with privately selected board presidents) may be the best way to avoid opportunistic cycles, since centrally appointed bankers may behave opportunistically to improve their party's chance of reelection.

PARTISAN INTERVENTION IN LABOR NEGOTIATION

Lange and Garrett (1985) argue that partisan governments and labor market arrangements are complements. They believe the Right is better suited to a decentralized labor market while the Left does better in centralized labor markets, since it can credibly promise policy side payments for wage restraint. Right parties, and, presumably, conservative central bankers, may be unable to make such commitments, since neither depends on the votes of labor union members.

While Lange and Garrett initially found support for complementarity among parties and labor market institutions, in more recent work, Garrett (1998b) finds less evidence that a combination of Left governance and encompassing unions produces good economic outcomes. He finds no association between Left-encompassment and inflation and obtains significant results for growth and unemployment only for countries highly open to the international economy. Unfortunately, his results do not yet incorporate the more recent strategic analysis of interactions between the labor market and central banks, but this could certainly be combined with Lange and Garrett's earlier insights about parties.

OTHER INSTITUTIONS

Beyond unions and parties, a growing body of work argues that central banks will be more credibly independent where power is more divided, whether through separation of powers or through federalism. Lohmann (1998a) claims that German federalism may lie behind the legendary independence of the Bundesbank, since the Bundesrat allows the interests of the Lander to check the national government, protecting the central bank's legally independent status. Bernhard (1998) provides general empirical support for this proposition in a panel of OECD countries. However, while the finding of lower inflation rates in federal systems seems robust, Wibbels and Rodden (2001) show that the difference could result from decentralization of tax powers and the impact of borrowing costs, without reference to central bank independence.

Moser (1999a) generalizes the veto players argument, showing that where a central bank can be overriden only by the combined vetoes of separate policymakers (e.g., an executive and a legislature), central bank independence is more credible. It is also potentially more conservative, since the central bank can choose to accommodate the more conservative policymaker when necessary. And indeed, Moser finds that central bank independence more strongly reduces inflation in those OECD countries where bicameralism provides two potential vetoes on any change in central bank institutions. Still, while these early tests for association among separation of powers, federalism, central bank independence, and inflation give encouraging results, there is fairly high collinearity of these institutional variables across cases, not to mention the conspicuous presence of all of them in the United States and Germany. All this suggests that the analysis of their importance to monetary politics is still at an early stage.

■ | Fiscal Scale and Balance:
Fundamentals, Institutions, Parties

Both debt and spending levels have increased substantially across OECD countries since the mid-1970s. In large part as a response to the wide variation in fiscal policy settings and outcomes over the past thirty years, a vast literature, which has grown substantially over the past decade, examines fiscal policy decisions and outcomes. This literature has focused predominantly on *fiscal scale* (levels of spending and revenue) and *fiscal balance* (deficits, debt).[13] More than in the case of fiscal balance, the literature on fiscal scale has concentrated on the effects of institutions and politics, rather than explaining variation in the levels of taxing and spending (or indebtedness, in the case of balance) per se. Nevertheless, there are common elements in the explanations of both fiscal scale and balance. In particular, three types of factors affect fiscal policy outcomes: *fundamentals*, including economic variables and demographics; *institutions*, fiscal, political, and electoral; and *partisan politics*, the ideology of the incumbent.

Twenty years ago, a survey of explanations would have included each factor. Income growth and decline (Barro 1979), the level of income (e.g., Alt and Chrystal 1983) and its distribution (Meltzer and Richard 1981),

---

13. Keech 1995, ch. 7, provides an excellent discussion of a wide range of topics relevant to the analysis of fiscal policy.

the trade dependence of the economy (Cameron 1978), as well as the age structure of the population, exemplify the first. The number and geographical nature of legislators' constituencies (Weingast, Shepsle, and Johnsen 1981) is an example of the second, as is the hypothesis that some tax structures and electoral systems promote fiscal illusion (Buchanan and Wagner 1977). Some (Cameron 1978; Alt and Chrystal 1983) conjectured about parties and debt or the size of government. However, many of the conjectures seemed to have hit an empirical dead end by the early 1980s, and few contained any theoretical elements that could explain dynamics, growth, or change over time.

Since then, two approaches have dominated theoretical research on the fiscal effects of institutions. One examines policy as the outcome of a game involving *multiple principals and multiple agents*. What is central is both the multiplicity and also the agency problem, with opportunistic politicians who bargain over policy and rational voters who hold them accountable through retrospective voting (Persson and Tabellini 2000). In these models, institutions affect outcomes through two channels. First, the rules governing legislative bargaining and the nature of elections affect party competition directly. Through this competition the rules also affect fiscal policy. A fundamental question is, do the principals manage to play the agents off against each other or vice versa? Using this approach allows Persson and Tabellini to derive conjectures about conditions under which more decentralization can mean less corruption, when there will be a bigger electoral cycle and less transparency, when proportional systems produce more welfare–social security spending, and, if well-placed checks and balances allow voters to induce politicians to discipline each other, when presidential systems would produce a smaller size of total government spending.

The other approach treats (fiscal) institutions as a response to the *common pool resource* problem.[14] Its core intuition is that politicians spend more on their constituencies to the extent that they do not internalize the full costs of their spending and taxing decisions. Multiplicity matters again in this model. Competition between claimants on the budget generates a spending bias because each of n claimants internalizes only $1/n$ of the cost of financing an additional unit of spending (von Hagen and Harden 1995). More decision participants, more heterogeneity among them, more spillovers, all exacerbate the problem. The intuition is that reducing the number of decision makers or centralizing the budgetary process lowers spending.

This section first reviews fiscal scale and then fiscal balance. It examines the fiscal performance of both OECD countries and the U.S. states. Unsurprisingly, largely because of substantial institutional differences, the

---

14. This approach goes back to Weingast, Shepsle, and Johnsen 1981 and even earlier.

literatures on OECD countries and the U.S. states have grown independently, with separate concepts and explanations. Disappointingly, little can be said with great confidence about the determinants of fiscal scale and balance. Fundamentals matter but leave much unexplained. In terms of the residual variation, effects of politics and institutions are not yet well understood. The effect (particularly) on fiscal balance of centralization and transparency of fiscal institutions is clear, but endogeneity remains a concern. Do transparent institutions produce good performance, or does good performance lead to institutions that give voters a better look?

Fiscal Scale[15]

FUNDAMENTALS

A long tradition links spending levels to fundamentals. According to Wagner's law, public spending rises with per capita income (Mueller 1989). Franzese (1998a) provides recent supporting empirical evidence for this. Other economic variables like growth or unemployment also affect spending. In general, positive economic events reduce spending in the short term while negative events like an increase in unemployment trigger either discretionary or automatic spending increases. Economic variables explain much of the variation in spending.

The relationship between external trade and the level of spending is less clear. Cameron (1978) identified a positive relationship between trade and spending. In subsequent empirical work, Garrett (forthcoming) reports that although open economies have higher levels of public spending, recent increases in trade have led to slower growth in public spending. Garrett and Mitchell (2001) find a negative relationship between openness and spending, a finding partly confirmed by Rodrik (1998) in a smaller sample of countries. Rodrik also claims that measures of external risk (for instance, volatility in the terms of trade) have a larger effect than trade itself. He finds that public spending increases as external risk increases. So increases in globalization may have slight contractionary effects on public spending.

Public spending also should respond to demographic variables, most notably characteristics of the income distribution and of the voting population. According to Meltzer and Richard (1981), there should be a positive relationship between transfer spending and both the skew of the income distribution, since with a right-skewed income distribution typical of industrial societies, the median voter would have an income less than the mean. Building on this, Franzese (1998a) shows that if an increase in the distance between the income of the actual median *voter* and average income in-

---

15. The voluminous, earlier public choice literature on the growth and size of government is not discussed here. See D. Mueller 1989 for a useful summary.

creases transfers, then increased voter participation also has a positive effect on the scale of government (see also Hicks and Swank 1992).

Indeed, there is plenty of survey evidence that lower-income individuals prefer more redistribution. Hence, it is a little paradoxical that more unequal societies do not on the whole redistribute more than more egalitarian ones. There could be measurement problems here, but Moene and Wallerstein (2001) offer a partial resolution by distinguishing between transfers as welfare and transfers as insurance for the temporarily unemployed. This result is more consistent with Rodrik's (above). Iversen and Soskice (2001) offer more support, showing how job insurance policy preferences depend on individuals' views of their immobility, or the difficulty they would have securing an equally good job if they were to become unemployed.

EFFECTS OF BUDGET INSTITUTIONS

There are scattered empirical findings, reflecting the fact that empirical research on the effects of political and fiscal institutions has been directed more toward explaining variation in fiscal balance than scale. Von Hagen (1992) provides some evidence that decentralized budget processes lead to higher levels of spending. Similarly, Kontopoulos and Perotti (1999) find a strong relationship between the number of spending ministers and spending growth. In terms of the U.S. evidence, Rueben (1995) shows that tax limitation laws are associated with slower growth in both spending and revenue. Balanced budget laws also seem to reduce spending growth (Poterba 1996; Bohn and Inman 1996). In general, models that predict a spending bias make stronger predictions than when they are used in the case of deficits.

In a recent paper, Ferejohn (1999) provides a theoretical analysis of transparency. He argues that increasing transparency facilitates voter control and monitoring of elected representatives, inducing greater executive effort which, in turn, increases voter confidence and the willingness of voters to spend resources through the public budgets, leading to an increase in the scale of government. Budget process transparency means commitment to nonarbitrary language (for example, generally accepted accounting principles), independent auditing and verification, and more information and more justification in fewer documents. Using a variety of measures published by the National Association of State Budget Offices (1995, 1999) and the National Conference of State Legislatures (1998), Alt, Lassen, and Skilling (2002) show that the expected links between transparency, executive job performance, and fiscal scale appear in the U.S. states.

EFFECTS OF POLITICAL AND ELECTORAL INSTITUTIONS

In an imaginative application of common-pool theory, Baqir (1999), following Weingast, Shepsle, and Johnsen (1981), shows that a greater number of districts (seats) on city councils predicts higher spending, even after controls for ethnic heterogeneity, other sorts of dispersion and spillovers, and electoral system characteristics. For similar reasons, political institutions that fragment decision making across branches of government (for example, divided government or minority government) are thought to increase spending, because each agent internalizes less of the costs of their spending decisions. However, there is little direct empirical evidence on this point, and, as documented in the U.S. states, divided government may in fact make attaining desired spending levels more difficult.

Other electoral institutions also seem to matter. For example, Persson and Tabellini (1999) predict that proportional systems of voting lead to higher spending. Milesi-Ferretti et al. (preliminary work, 1999) and Kontopoulos (1997) provide supportive evidence for OECD countries and Stein, Talvi, and Grisanti (1999) provide related evidence in Latin American countries. Franzese (1998a) finds a positive relationship between the frequency of the electoral cycle and transfer spending. Further, Pampel and Williamson (1989) link spending growth to electoral competition.

PARTISAN POLITICS

Here, the intuition linking the ideological complexion of the government to fiscal scale or the size of government is clear. Left governments are more likely than Right governments to want or to target a high level of spending. Moreover, in addition to examining straight ideological complexion, the existence of social democracy, Christian democracy, and corporatist institutions (for instance, union power or collective bargaining) is predicted to lead to increased spending.

Clear results exist with respect to the U.S. states. Alt and Lowry (1994) and Besley and Case (1995) find that Democrats have a higher target spending level. Alt and Lowry (2000) confirm this. Nevertheless, in OECD countries, although early cross-sectional studies (Cameron 1978; Roubini and Sachs 1989a, b) found a positive relationship between Left governments and the fiscal scale, recent work is empirically less conclusive, according to a recent survey by Blais, Blake, and Dion (1993, 1996). For example, in a well-known paper, Hicks and Swank (1992) find that Left governments spend more, but their results are not robust. When Beck and Katz (1995) reestimate using more rigorous methods, they find coefficients that are not significant. Franzese (1998a) confirms that the partisan effect is not significant although it moves in the expected direction. Similarly, Garrett (forthcoming) does not find a significant partisan effect, although he notes that countries with more frequent Left governments are associated with higher spending. Perhaps in spite of work showing clearly that parties have different preferences, as Garrett (1998b) notes, "government spending is driven far more by the business cycle and demography than by political conditions."

Blais, Blake, and Dion conclude that "the partisan composition of government makes a difference, though a small one" (1993, 57). More pertinently, they find that, on average over all results, if a government of the Left has been in control for ten years, spending will be 5 percentage points higher than if a government of the Right had been in control. Amazingly enough, that is almost exactly the same steady-state magnitude of difference found by Alt and Lowry (2000) for the difference between Democratic and Republican parties in the U.S. states. So there is some empirical convergence here, even if confidence in individual results is not strong.

Fiscal Balance

Apart from fundamentals, even before the 1980s, theoretical models showed how political and institutional factors like fiscal illusion and geographically dispersed interests could affect fiscal balance (surpluses and deficits). An excellent review of newer developments (Alesina, Roubini, and Cohen 1997) adds four types, including models of debt as a strategic variable (Alesina and Tabellini 1990; Tabellini and Alesina 1990; Persson and Svensson 1989), intergenerational redistribution (Tabellini 1991), distributional conflict (Alesina and Drazen 1991), and fiscal institutions (von Hagen 1992). Nevertheless, the empirical literature lagged behind these theoretical developments, and even after ten years of empirical research, some of these theoretical models still lack empirical support. Indeed, until Franzese 1998b there were few direct tests of these models.

Rather, since Roubini and Sachs 1989a, b, the empirical literature focused more on measuring the effects of (exogenous) political institutions on fiscal performance. A stronger consensus has emerged that institutions have a real effect on fiscal balance. Three classes of institutions in particular seem to be important: fiscal institutions (the presence of a centralized budgetary process, balanced budget laws), political institutions (coalition government, divided government), and electoral institutions (electoral system, political stability).[16]

FUNDAMENTALS

The normative benchmark for explaining variation in the fiscal balance is the tax-smoothing model (Barro 1979; Lucas and Stokey 1983), where deficits result from temporary variations in the economic environment. Franzese (1998b) lists the economic controls that should be included in a test of the model—unemployment, real growth, interest rates, the terms of trade, and the openness of the economy—and finds that these variables all

16. Despite some very strong prior beliefs, the consensus seems to be that there is no systematic effect of the size of government on measures of economic performance (Slemrod 1995). A large macroeconomic literature examines the effect of fiscal balance on economic growth or performance, surveyed by Bernheim (1989) and Barro (1989).

have a substantively large, and statistically significant, effect on fiscal balance in the expected way. Increases in growth and the terms of trade improve fiscal balance, while increased unemployment, interest rates, and openness worsen the fiscal balance.[17] Overall, Franzese (1998b) estimates that fundamental factors explain about 43 percent of the variation in debt accumulation in postwar OECD countries. Since this leaves a good deal of variation in debt accumulation unexplained, models incorporating political and institutional factors have been developed to explain the remaining variation.

BUDGET PROCESS INSTITUTIONS

The spending bias from fragmentation or the common-pool problem does not easily generalize into a deficit bias (Alesina and Perotti 1996; Kontopoulos and Perotti 1999) since the increased spending can be financed by taxation (Weingast, Shepsle, and Johnsen 1981). There is one dynamic common-pool resource model in which fragmented budgetary decision making leads to a deficit bias (Velasco 1997), but the results are sensitive to functional form and general statements cannot always be made (Kontopoulos and Perotti 1999). Like others following Roubini and Sachs, Kontopoulos and Perotti appeal to the intuition that governments with fragmented decision-making structures will face greater problems reacting to negative shocks, but concerns remain with this conceptual framework.[18]

Nevertheless, Poterba and von Hagen (1999) conclude that findings that the budgetary decision-making process has a large and significant effect on fiscal performance are robust. Fiscal institutions respond to the deficit and spending bias caused by the common-pool resource problem (von Hagen and Harden 1995; Velasco 1997). Establishing a centralized budgetary decision-making process (for example, creating a dominant role for the minister of finance or establishing negotiated fiscal targets) is an appropriate response to this problem, as it better internalizes the common-pool costs associated with multiple ministries. Evidence in von Hagen 1992, 1998, von Hagen and Harden 1994, 1995, Hallerberg and von Hagen 1997, and de Haan et al. 1999 strongly supports this position for

17. High interest rates produce higher costs of servicing debt, dominating the effect of low interest rates in producing a good time to borrow. Debt can also smooth out longer-term changes like that associated with an aging of the population. However, such demographic variables do not seem to have much explanatory power for variation in debt accumulation.

18. The relationship of fiscal policy and output volatility has also been examined. One stylized fact to emerge is that many fiscal policy settings are pro-cyclical, so fiscal policy can lead to more rather than less volatile output. This pro-cyclicality is frequently associated with weak or fragmented political and fiscal institutions. This is particularly true in developing countries (Gavin and Perotti 1997; Talvi and Vegh 2000) but is also the case in OECD countries (Lane 1999; Fiorito 1997).

OECD countries. Stein, Talvi, and Grisanti 1999 and Alesina and Perotti 1999 do the same for Latin American countries. Kontopoulos and Perotti 1999 shows that fragmented decision making caused by a high number of spending ministers is associated with higher spending and deficits in OECD countries (with each extra minister producing perhaps an extra 1/6 percentage point of growth).[19]

In the United States there is more concern with the effect of balanced budget laws. Bohn and Inman (1996) show that tight balanced budget rules reduce deficits, and maybe also spending growth. Poterba (1994) and Alt and Lowry (1994) show that there is a more rapid fiscal tightening in response to an unexpected deficit in states where there are tight rules. Poterba (1996) surveys this literature and concludes that the empirical evidence shows that "tightly drawn anti-deficit rules, especially when coupled with limits on government borrowing, reduce state deficits and affect spending and borrowing levels as well," so states with tighter requirements generate superior fiscal performance. Data on relative state bond yields shows that balanced budget laws affect the risk premium charged on debt issued by these states. Lowry and Alt (2001) show how a balanced budget law found in about half the U.S. states improves the ability of market investors to learn about policy from noisy signals. However, these laws may also increase output volatility (Bayoumi and Eichengreen 1995; Crain 2000).

In a similar way, the transparency of institutions affects the cost of monitoring and assessing performance and thus the potential for agency problems. It is widely believed that fiscal transparency has a large and positive effect on fiscal balance. Indeed, Alesina, Roubini, and Cohen assert that "hierarchical-transparent procedures have positive effects on fiscal discipline" (1997, 240). Alesina and Perotti claim that "a lack of transparency makes fiscal discipline and expenditure control harder to achieve" (1996, 403) and Poterba and von Hagen write that "higher levels of transparency are associated with lower budget deficits" (1999, 2). According to the IMF, "transparency in government operations is widely regarded as an important precondition for macroeconomic fiscal sustainability, good governance, and overall fiscal rectitude" (Kopits and Craig 1998, 1). Indeed, both the IMF and the OECD are currently developing codes of best practice for fiscal transparency.

However, the case connecting institutional transparency and fiscal

19. Fiscal rules have also been examined recently, largely motivated by the provisions in the Maastricht Treaty. There is little evidence that these rules have a substantial effect in OECD countries (Kopits and Symansky 1998), though the consensus is that fiscal rules will lead to more volatile output (Bayoumi and Eichengreen 1995). Centralized budgetary processes also seem to lead to better consumption smoothing in the economy, and reduce the pro-cyclicality of fiscal policy (Arreaza et al. 1999).

policy outcomes is far from compelling, more often asserted rather than empirically established. Von Hagen (1992) and de Haan et al. (1999) show a very weak link between some measures of fiscal transparency in European countries and fiscal performance. Alt, Lasssen, and Skilling (2001) show that OECD countries with more transparent budget processes accumulate less debt over time. Alesina and Perotti (1999) argue that transparency has a positive effect on fiscal performance in Latin American countries but use very indirect measures of transparency. However, many remain convinced of the importance of fiscal transparency, justifying further analysis.

Even less analytical attention has been paid to why particular (centralized, transparent) fiscal institutions are established than to why countries have independent central banks, creating problems in estimating the effects of fiscal institutions (Poterba 1996; Alesina and Perotti 1996). These institutions do emerge endogenously in accounts of budgetary reform in the United States (Kiewiet and McCubbins 1991; Stewart 1989). Recent attempts to understand and explain systematically the origins of variation in fiscal institutions (Hallerberg and von Hagen 1997; Strauch and von Hagen 1999) leave much to be done. Indeed, Poterba and von Hagen identify the endogeneity of budget rules as "the single most important issue for further work" (1999, 12).

POLITICAL AND ELECTORAL INSTITUTIONS

Tsebelis (1999) models how more veto players lead to greater policy inertia or stability. Others propose that fragmented decision making leads to worse fiscal performance rather than inertia. Thus, Persson and Tabellini surveying the literature, claim that "debt and deficits appear to be correlated with specific political and institutional features; debts have typically been accumulated by countries ruled by coalition governments and/or unstable governments" (2000, 345). Of course, if stability or inertia means not responding to shocks, resulting in debt accumulation, these approaches are not at all inconsistent.

Indeed, Roubini and Sachs (1989a, b) found that coalition and minority governments generated worse fiscal performance, accumulating more debt. However, this finding has been challenged subsequently. Edin and Ohlsson (1991) found that poor fiscal performance was associated with minority governments rather than coalition governments. De Haan and Sturm (1994, 1997) and Borrelli and Royed (1995) find that neither of these results is robust. More recently, Kontopoulos and Perotti (1999) find a weak relationship between the number of coalition parties and fiscal performance. In bad economic times, having more parties in the governing coalition slows the government's response to shocks (see also Alesina and Perotti 1996). Alesina, Perotti, and Tavares (1998) find that coalition and minority governments are equally likely to tighten fiscal policy, although these governments seem to find fiscal tightening difficult to sustain.[20]

In U.S. states, Alt and Lowry (2000) provide evidence that divided government makes it more difficult for each party to adjust to its desired level of spending. Alt and Lowry (1994) and Poterba (1996) find that U.S. states with divided government take longer to respond to budget imbalances due to economic shocks. McCubbins (1991) attributes U.S. federal deficits in the 1980s to divided government, but Alt and Stewart (1990) do not identify a consistent relationship between divided government and fiscal balance in the United States over the last 130 years. Despite the wealth of findings, a reasonable person would not yet be convinced that a systematic relationship exists between fragmented political institutions and fiscal performance.

Electoral process characteristics also influence fiscal balance. (Ignore for now the connections between the electoral system and coalition or divided government.) Polarized political parties facing electoral uncertainty were identified as an important determinant of fiscal balance: the more likely a party was to be replaced by one with very different priorities, the more incentive it had to tie the hands of its successor by increasing borrowing (Alesina and Tabellini 1990; Tabellini and Alesina 1990). However, despite the continued popularity of the theory, this model has found little empirical support (Franzese 1998b).

However, some evidence associates political instability with worse fiscal performance. Grilli et al. (1991), Franzese (1998b), Roubini and Sachs (1989a), and de Haan and Sturm (1994) report that debt is positively related to the number of changes of government and the frequency of elections in OECD countries. Further, Alesina, Roubini, and Cohen (1997) report some evidence of a small systematic fiscal loosening prior to elections. Edwards and Tabellini (1991) and Roubini (1991) show that more frequent government turnover is associated with slightly worsened fiscal performance in developing countries. Kontopoulos (1997) also finds that elections that are more competitive generate higher spending levels and deficits. This result appears stronger in countries with more proportional electoral systems.

PARTISAN POLITICS

There is no clear theoretical prediction about the relationship between partisan policy preferences and fiscal balance. Lowry, Alt, and Ferree

---

20. Examining the macroeconomic effects of fiscal tightening, the key finding is that many recent fiscal adjustments have had an expansionary effect on the economy, particularly those implemented at high debt levels, those which focus the adjustment on spending cuts, and those which occur in bad times (Giavazzi and Pagano 1990, 1996; McDermott and Westcott 1996; Alesina, Perotti, and Tavares 1998; Alesina and Ardagna 1999; Perotti 1999).

(1998) show that U.S. voters have clear expectations that different parties will provide different fiscal scale but no expectation of partisan differences in fiscal balance. Alesina, Roubini, and Cohen (1997) find no relationship between the ideological complexion of the incumbent and fiscal performance. Franzese (1998b) finds very small partisan effects on balance. Intuitively, Left parties might accumulate debt, as they want to spend more and may be more reluctant to tighten fiscal policy. However, from even casual observation, Belgium, Italy, and Japan, dominated by Right parties, have the three highest debt levels in the OECD.[21] Most empirical studies contain some measure of ideological complexion of government, and no systematic effect has been detected.[22] While the consensus seems to be that partisan effects do not explain patterns of debt accumulation, there is some suggestion that polarization has a negative effect on fiscal performance, and this may be more important than the ideological complexion of the government per se.

■ | Summary

What is the state of the discipline? First of all, we're in a new world. Standard textbooks in macroeconomics will include formal models of politics and political variables in macromodels. Examples include the extensive treatment of institutions and parties in Persson and Tabellini (2000) and interest group behavior in Grossman and Helpman (forthcoming) among others. Not only that but there is also the simple fact that the empirical work on monetary and fiscal policy to date—much of it done by political scientists—shows that things political scientists know and care a lot about, like parties and institutions, really matter for policy outcomes.

Monetary institutions are designed to resolve intertemporal coordination problems (time inconsistency) with minimal distributive implications. Because monetary policy is less distributive in nature than fiscal policy, there may be fewer disagreements among groups on the optimal policy outcome.[23] Therefore, central bank independence (depoliticizing the process) seems like an appealing way to solve the intertemporal coordination problem. But that is only a part of the question of why monetary institutions take the form they do.

21. An exception is the model of Persson and Svensson (1989), where parties differ over the scale of government, in which left-wing parties should run a surplus, right-wing parties run a deficit. Direct tests of this model have not found empirical support.

22. Results are not robust and in fact vary according to the countries included and the sample period.

23. Still, partisan differences do exist with respect to the trade-off between unemployment and inflation.

The banker's concern for preserving a reputation as a means to attain credibility is a driving force in the model of central bank behavior. But is there more credibility in some settings than others? Why? Are there alternative commitment devices that would give as much credibility? With what other costs and benefits? Opportunistic policy settings could also be avoided by contracting, as well as by making policy decisions subject to multiple veto players. The latter, though, could lead to more uncertainty about the inflation level, so inflationary expectations might not come down as quickly, and so raise the costs of disinflation. Also, multiple veto players does not resolve the issue of who *proposes* the optimal rate, solved in the case of central bank independence by *assuming* the central banker is a conservative.

In the case of fiscal institutions, two types of coordination concern us. One, between members of the governing party or coalition, enables them to balance the budget across the cycle and reduces the spending bias (intratemporal coordination). The other is between competing political parties that alternate in office through time (intertemporal coordination). Absent coordination, more debt accumulates and spending growth is higher and more volatile.

Credibility is less able to solve these fiscal coordination problems. A brief thought experiment reveals why. In ways analogous to a central bank's announcing an inflation target, state governors (often by law) announce a target deficit when filing the budget. At that point, private actors form an expectation of what, given their information at that time, they think the deficit will be. The bank's credibility is measured by how close inflation expectations are to the announcement (Faust and Svensson 2000), and governors are more credible the less the difference between their announcement and private expectations of fiscal balance at the time the announcement is made. In monetary policy, labor supply and thus income growth depend on these expectations. In fiscal policy, a balanced budget law allows markets and governors to coordinate on and communicate a standard for responsible conduct, lowering interest rates on state debt (Lowry and Alt 2001). This may be the only quantity in an economic model that depends on the credibility of the governor's announcement, so reputation and credibility are smaller issues here.[24]

So more transparency seems like a good thing to have, and indeed it probably usually is. In general, transparency better allows agents to understand whether deviations from expectations are the result of opportunism or stochastic shocks, a central concern in models of accountability. But where should we look for transparency? Some place it at the level of the political system, arguing that democracy is by its nature more transparent

---

24. This is probably also why no one finds that laws requiring the *announcement* of a balanced budget have any effect. Instead the outturn is what is observed and judged by markets and voters.

than autocracy. Others look at the regime level, as if transparency were a variable characteristic of a political system. Transparency might reside in a system's propensity to generate complex, multiparty governments or the extent to which it diffuses power across branches of government, or government and opposition. These things of course also vary over time within individual systems. And transparency can be found in the characteristics of individual institutions like budget processes, where the commitment to nonarbitrary language, availability of independent verification, and presence of more information and justification in (other things equal) fewer documents increase the ability to detect what is going on. This is not far-fetched: the OECD and IMF cross-nationally and various organizations within countries now routinely survey and publish such information.

As a concluding note, while credibility and transparency seem like complements, in fact increasing transparency too far undoes credibility, that is, reduces the extent to which the concern to maintain a reputation can give policymakers incentives to behave in socially desirable ways. The logic of this is that while more transparency, like the desire for credibility, can induce greater effort from an agent, at the limit knowing too perfectly what an agent's preferences are undoes the agent's ability to induce a response (Faust and Svensson 2000). In some partisan models of political economy, voters are *sure* of the redistributive motives of politicians (Alesina and Rosenthal 1995), so policymakers who redistribute ex post cannot achieve best credible outcomes (Besley and Pande 1998). Trade-offs like these will inform attempts to further endogenize monetary and fiscal institutions—an important direction of research in the next few years.

James D. Morrow

International Conflict: Assessing the Democratic Peace and Offense-Defense Theory

International relations saw four main movements during the decade of the 1990s. First, game theory attracted attention as a way to study the microfoundations of the field (cf. Powell, this volume). Second, interest in statistical methods revived in both international political economy and conflict. Third, the constructivist movement challenged the questions, approaches, and results of the mainstream. Fourth, the end of the cold war led to new problems for study and a shift in focus away from great power rivalry. The first three of these trends created methodological ferment, which fortunately bubbled forth with less acrimony than in past decades (cf. Knorr and Rosenau 1969 for a view of the 1960s). However, the field has not reconciled this ferment into a commonly accepted approach for using these methods. This essay reviews progress in three areas: game theoretic microfoundations, the democratic peace, and offense-defense theory. Each of these areas has predominantly used one of three methods: formal models, large-*n* statistical studies, and case studies, respectively. This essay goes beyond reviewing each of these areas to discuss how the three methods can be combined fruitfully, which none of these areas has fully done to date.

Because this essay reviews only three literatures, albeit three central literatures in conflict in the last decade, it cannot do justice to the diversity of topics and approaches studied. I refer interested readers to reviews on the following topics: the causes of war (Levy 1998), deterrence (Huth 1999), alliances (Morrow 2000), arms races (Glaser 2000a), civil-military relations (Feaver 1999), internal war (David 1997), and psychological approaches (Rosati 2000).

This essay complements David Laitin's review in this volume of comparative politics, which focuses on the contributions of formal models, large-*n* studies, and case studies to that field. I begin with the microfoundations of conflict as developed in game theoretic models. The democratic peace has been driven by large-*n* studies, and case studies have been central to the study of the effects of the offense-defense balance. I review each of those literatures in order. I conclude with some general comments on how the three methods complement one another and the proper roles for each in the study of international conflict. I use the three literatures to illustrate the concluding argument.

■ | Bargaining and the Microfoundations of Conflict

Systemic theories attempt to explain international conflict as a consequence of the properties of the international system. Microfoundations address the actor-level processes that underlie such systemic theories. During the 1990s, noncooperative game theory took ideas about how images enter into bargaining first stated by Jervis (1970) to study the microfoundations of international conflict (e.g., Fearon 1995b; Morrow 1989; Powell 1999).

This analysis focuses on the origin of crises and their escalation to war. Crises force states to bargain over issues, such as division of territory. They arise because a state makes demands for changes in the status quo. Events outside the control of any government, border skirmishes for instance, can provide an opportunity for a state to press demands, but the key is that a state chooses to use a random event in this way. Crises are purposive acts by states seeking to change the status quo.[1] Implicit in such demands is the possibility that the crisis might escalate to war if the initiator of the crisis does not receive sufficient concessions. War occurs when one side uses violence and the other resists violently; the bargaining over the issues in dispute has failed. War then requires choices by both sides to fight. Further, either side could avoid war by offering sufficient concessions to convince the other to settle for peaceful change in the status quo. Unlike some arguments where a state seeks war and would not accept any settlement (e.g., Lebow 1981, 23–40), this view asserts there always exists some settlement that a side would accept short of war. Further, the focus on the origin and escalation of crises matches the most-used data collections on international conflict, the Correlates of War and the International Conflict Behavior projects.

This approach does not address why states have conflicts of interest. It assumes that such conflicts exist and then examines when those conflicts of interest lead to crises and war. This assumption of conflict of interest is common across other current approaches to international conflict. Much earlier literatures tried to explain the basis of conflicts of interest in individuals (cf. Waltz 1959 for a critique of such arguments), but those approaches have generally been dropped.[2] Constructivists hold out the hope of explaining how conflicts of interest arise and can disappear, but their ar-

1. Huth (1996) studies when territorial conflicts burst into crises and when they are resolved by negotiations.

2. Mercer 1995 is a recent attempt to explain why groups have conflicts of interest drawing on psychology.

guments explain why actors can manage conflicts rather than why conflicts of interest disappear (see Wendt 1999 on cultures of anarchy). After all, conflicts of interest are common in domestic politics as well as international politics; violent conflict is not.

The central question in this work is why the parties fight when there are peaceful settlements that both would prefer to conflict. Conflict is costly in material terms for nations and personal terms for leaders (Bueno de Mesquita and Siverson 1995). The issues in a dispute can generally be resolved through a number of possible settlements. The contending sides disagree about the desirability of these possible settlements. Imagine a conflict over a piece of territory. Each side in the dispute would like to control all the territory, and each views controlling more territory as better. There are many ways to divide the territory, and given that war is costly for both sides, there are probably many divisions of the territory that both would prefer to war. Why then do states go to war?

To avoid war, the contending states need to agree on a specific settlement. These negotiations create a dilemma for both sides. Each side would like to use the threat of conflict to convince the other to agree to a deal more favorable to its interests. If a state knew exactly the best deal it could extract from the other short of war, it would make that demand on the threat of going to war. The other would accept the deal rather than fight. However, the other side's minimal acceptable deal depends on the value it places on fighting a war; a value that combines how important the stakes are to it, its judgment about its chances on the battlefield, and how it assesses the likely costs of a war. All of these are known only to that state; they are, in the language of game theory, its private information. The state making the demand cannot know any of these three, although it certainly has some beliefs about each. It cannot be certain which demand will extract the best possible settlement for itself, and asking for too much leads to war. The dilemma rests between asking for too little and demanding too much.

The dilemma of uncertainty extends further to how the target responds to a demand. A state making a threat has the incentive to exaggerate its threats. The side receiving a demand must judge the credibility of the threat. Because the recipient tries to judge how willing the threatening state is to go to war, the latter may be able to benefit by exaggerating its resolve to fight. If successful, the target of its threat may grant more than is necessary to conciliate the threatener. However, the target understands the threatener's incentive to overstate its willingness to fight when making a demand. It should discount the signals of resolve that the threatener makes with its demand, reducing the credibility of the threat in its eyes and the chance that it will grant sufficient concessions to dissuade the threatening state from war. The dilemma produced by private information about resolve leads to excessive demands and overly aggressive actions and to the tendency to downplay the seriousness of the other side's demands and demonstrations of resolve. Both of these effects increase the chance that the sides will fail to reach an agreement to settle their differences short of war.

Costly signals help to transmit a party's resolve to the other side. When one side is uncertain about the other side's resolve, the former may be convinced if the latter takes an action that only resolute types are willing to take. If the irresolute types are unwilling to take that action, then observing the action is sufficient for the observer to conclude that the acting state is resolute. The costs of sending the signal prevent the irresolute types from taking the same action as the resolute types.

Costly signals, however, cannot solve the problem of uncertainty in all cases. First, there cannot be perfect signals of resolve. Imagine that there was an action that always convinced the receiver that the sender was resolute and so the receiver should grant the demands of the sender to avoid war. Then every type of sender would like to send that signal, regardless of its resolve, because it would gain its ends peacefully. However, the receiver should not believe that the sender is resolute after receiving the perfect signal precisely because the sender would always want to send it regardless of its resolve. Perfect signals of resolve are contradictory by their very nature. Second, although war is costly, the costs of conflict cannot be the sole source of signaling costs. Otherwise, actions in a crisis would be costly only when they triggered war. But then why would any party ever choose to go to war? War would be costly, and there would still be the prospect of a peaceful settlement short of war. Some costs outside of just war must exist in order that at least one state prefers going to war instead of continuing to bargain. Fearon (1994a) solves this problem with audience costs that build throughout the crisis, with a domestic audience's imposing a cost on the party that backs down to avoid war. A side might then choose to fight to avoid having to pay audience costs even though it saw settlements it preferred to war.[3]

War could occur because there is no settlement that both sides prefer to war. Fearon (1995b) discusses two reasons why this could occur, commitment problems and indivisibility of issues. A commitment problem occurs when one side has an incentive to renege in the future on any agreement.[4] The other side is unwilling to settle short of war because it knows the first side will break the deal in the future. Indivisibility of issues could prevent the existence of a division of the stakes that both sides would prefer to war.

I see these arguments as reasons why conflicts cannot be resolved rather than why they begin. We know that a peaceful status quo outcome

3. The audience cost argument clarifies earlier lines of argument about reputation by Snyder and Diesing (1977). Alastair Smith (1998) explains why domestic audiences would be willing to impose costs on their leader after the crisis.

4. R. Harrison Wagner has promoted the idea of commitment problems as a source of war; see Wagner 1994.

exists before a crisis. If either of these problems cause war in a situation, such a stable status quo cannot exist by definition. Otherwise, both sides could avoid war by agreeing on the status quo ex ante. These causes of conflict are important when a crisis arises from a shock which eliminates the possibility of returning to the status quo. For example, the dissolution of Yugoslavia into separate republics foreclosed the possibility of returning to the status quo. Majority groups could not commit to protecting ethnic minorities, leading minorities to see war as preferable to any peaceful settlement in the same state as the majority (Fearon 1994c).

Commitment and indivisibility of issues can explain why some violent conflicts are extremely difficult to end. Once the status quo is no longer possible, the sides may not be able to find a solution under which both are willing to live in peace. I see both of these problems as central to the explanation of protracted conflict, particularly civil wars (Walter 1997).

These arguments on the microfoundations of international conflict provide four central lessons for studying war. First, war is not predictable in the sense that the outcome of individual cases can be known in advance (Gartzke 1999). Private information compounded by incentives to misrepresent that information and to disregard signals about it is the primary reason for war. The elements of private information about resolve that drive an individual dispute to war cannot be determined by others prior to the onset of war; they are subjective judgments about the likely outcome on the battlefield and how important the stakes are to an actor. The best predictions we can hope for are probabilities of war and lesser conflict.

Second, we may be able to predict variation in the likelihood of war across sets of dyads or international systems. The probability of war in a crisis may vary systematically because the availability of costly signals varies across dyads. Those dyads with more costly signals or a richer menu of such signals may have a lower probability of war than other dyads (Morrow 1999a).

Third, the factors that make war more likely in a dyad also make a crisis less likely (Fearon 1994b). One of the costs of initiating a crisis is the chance that it will escalate to war. If the parties can anticipate the magnitude of that chance, then coercive diplomacy becomes less attractive as the risk of war rises.

Fourth, ex post measures of resolve, such as actions taken in a crisis, should predict the outcome of a crisis better than ex ante measures, such as the balance of capabilities before the crisis (Fearon 1994b). Actions taken in a crisis include the effects of private information as revealed by those actions during the crisis, while precrisis acts reflect only the observable factors and judgments about the other side's private information.

Although these microfoundations focus on the origin and escalation of crises, their principles can be applied to security policies before crises break out. A state's perception of its security depends on what motivations it believes that other states have. Discerning the motivations of other states through foreign policy short of crises is the problem of uncertainty central to the microfoundations of conflict. Arming and seeking allies not only increase a state's capabilities; they also signal its willingness to use force to defend or change the status quo, depending on the state's goals.[5] The difficulty of determining whether preparation for war is aggressive or defensive is central to the security dilemma, the fount of offense-defense theory.

The development of game theoretic microfoundations has primarily proceeded through formal modeling. The empirical tests of these arguments are large-n studies because the hypotheses concern variation across many cases; case studies are less suitable because unobservable factors drive the outcome of individual cases. Some examples of large-n tests are Bueno de Mesquita and Lalman 1992, Fearon 1994b, and Eyerman and Hart 1996.

▪ | The Democratic Peace

The democratic peace is the observation that pairs of democracies are much less likely to go to war than dyads that include at least one other type of system (Rummel 1983; Doyle 1986b, Bremer 1992; Maoz and Russett 1993; Russett 1993). After extensive debate as to the truth of this empirical regularity, there appears to be consensus on this proposition. However, such consensus does not exist on the explanation of this regularity. This section examines first how the field arrived at a consensus that the regularity exists and then the debate on the significance and meaning of the democratic peace.[6]

The idea that democracy is conducive to peace goes back at least as far as Kant (1795). Showing that democratic dyads are more peaceful than other types of dyads requires clear definitions of war and democracy and the idea to look at democratic dyads. The proposition that democracies are more peaceful than other types of states does not appear to be true (however, see Ray 1995; Rousseau et al. 1996; Benoit 1996). Even if democracies are less likely to engage in war than other types of states, the effect of a democratic dyad is much greater than simply doubling the pacifying effect of democracy. The puzzle is why democratic dyads are unusually peaceful when democracies are not.

Before examining the theories proposed to explain this regularity, I discuss its establishment as stylized fact. Early efforts (Small and Singer 1976)

5. Glaser 1992, 1997, Kydd 1997a, and Morrow 1993, 1994a, 2000 are attempts to use arguments from game theoretic microfoundations to analyze security policy.

6. The literature on the democratic peace is huge, and there is no way I can do justice to all the contributions for and against that proposition in my brief review here. Ray 1998 is an excellent review essay on the topic and can lead the reader through the literature in detail.

were inconclusive largely because the lack of a clear definition of democracy made a full large-n study on dyads that went to war and dyads that did not extremely difficult. The first general effort (Rummel 1983) covered the period 1976 to 1980 because of its coding of democracy was limited to that period, opening up that study to the criticism that it could not be extended beyond that limited sample. Doyle's work (1986b) relied on his own coding of liberal republics (following Kant) rather than democracy. The precise definition of democracy is critical because there are a number of borderline cases, such as the War of 1812 and the Spanish-American War (cf. Ray 1995). The strength of the relationship varies with how these cases are coded. Not surprisingly, those who wish to discredit the democratic peace tend to include those cases as wars between democracies, while the proponents exclude them.

These coding arguments (including another about exactly which states went to war with each other in general wars) also played the role of focusing the discussion on which characteristics of democracy lead to the peaceful nature of pairs of democracies. This evidence could be quite valuable in distinguishing among possible explanations of the regularity.

There were questions whether the relationship was a statistical artifact. Spiro (1994) pointed out that individual years of a particular dyad were not statistically independent of one another and examined the data year by year in an attempt to show the relationship existed only because the proponents compounded essentially the same observations over and over. However, this test pushed the interdependence argument too far; alternative tests (Maoz 1998; Beck and Tucker 1996) showed that the relationship still held even when interdependence of dyadic observations over time was considered in the analysis.

Green et al. (2001) argued that the democratic peace is spurious because the statistical analysis lumps together many dyads that have other unobserved characteristics than joint democracy. They show that the statistical effect of a democratic dyad on the initiation of disputes becomes statistically insignificant when each dyad is allowed to have its own baseline rate of conflict.[7] However, the democratic peace contends that democratic dyads as a group are essentially different from other dyads; Green et al. fail to test whether the set of base rates of conflict for democratic dyads are different from other dyads. They argue that you should not assume that democratic dyads operate the same as other dyads; yet this is precisely the empirical claim of the democratic peace. Democratic dyads are different.

Explaining the regularity required more than establishing that it existed. Early in this literature, two broad explanations—the norms argument and the constraint argument—were proposed. The norms argument contended that leaders in democracies were used to dealing with their oppo-

---

7. For the statistically knowledgeable, Green at al. (2001) run a fixed effects model which includes a constant for every dyad over time.

nents in ways that recognized the legitimacy of their positions and demands through cooperative solutions, such as compromise and open electoral campaigning. When democracies faced one another, their leaders extended their common norms of limited, rule-bound competition to find peaceful solutions to their international disputes, such as through the use of conflict resolution techniques (Dixon 1994). On the other hand, democracies understand that nondemocratic opponents will not abide by such norms, and so democracies must rely on the tactics of power politics in their disputes with nondemocracies (Maoz and Russett 1993).

The constraints explanation begins with the observation that democratic leaders must gain the ascent of others throughout the government in order to go to war. Between democracies, the dual effect of these constraints is such that war is unlikely. Between a democracy and an autocracy, the autocracy may attempt to use the constrained nature of the democracy to take advantage of it in a crisis, making both sides more belligerent and war more likely (Morgan and Campbell 1991). Further, the public character of a democracy makes it easier for others to perceive how the constraints will affect its behavior in a crisis (Bueno de Mesquita and Lalman 1992).

These initial arguments suffer from several problems as explanations of the democratic peace. First, the two arguments are almost two sides of the same coin rather than competing explanations. Leaders in the norms argument learn the ways of limited competition because they operate within a system that places constraints on what they can do. Those constraints operate only because the politicians within a democratic system agree to abide by the constitutional rules of the system. Systems do differ in the constraints they place on their leaders and in the extent to which they rely on normative rather than formal constraints on power (think of the differences in the democracies of Great Britain and the United States). Some have tried to use these differences to support one or the other argument (notably Maoz and Russett 1993), but essentially, these two arguments may not be separable.

Second, neither argument develops its microfoundations in detail (the exception here is Bueno de Mesquita and Lalman 1992). The norms argument asserts that crisis bargaining between democracies will be different than "normal" power politics. However, that assertion hardly moves beyond the original observation that democratic dyads are much less likely to go to war than other dyads. Further, the norms argument does not seem to account for the "autocratic peace"—the observation that autocratic dyads are less likely to go to war than autocratic-democratic dyads (Beck and Tucker 1998).[8] If democracies do not fight one another but are as likely to go to war generally as other types of states, then the chance of war in a mixed dyad must be higher than in an autocratic dyad.

8. Honor among tyrants, perhaps?

Case studies might be able to unravel this problem, except that neither the norms argument nor the constraints argument is well-enough developed to support the detailed predictions that could be tested with case studies. Maoz (1998, 10–13) is correct to take Layne's (1994) case studies to task as a contradiction of the normative argument. Layne's failure to find that democracy did not appear as a factor in the decisions of states in crises is irrelevant. The norms argument contends only that the pattern of negotiations and calculations is different in democratic dyads than others. Owen's case studies (1994) supporting the democratic peace as a liberal peace approach a tautology; he defines liberals as those who do not want to fight other states that are liberal, and then if the liberals make enough noise, the liberal democracy does not go to war. It is hard to see how this argument advances hypotheses beyond those in the original empirical regularity. Again, the norms and constraint arguments do not provide the range of testable hypotheses that a case study could profitably test.

One explanation of the democratic peace is that there is nothing to explain. Farber and Gowa (1995; Gowa 1999) argue that the democratic peace is limited to the post–World War II period and that shared interests among democracies during that period accounts for their lack of conflict. In short, there is a regularity that needs no novel explanation. They present evidence that when the period from 1815 to 1980 is broken into the pre–World War I, interwar, and postwar eras, the rate of militarized disputes and wars between democracies is statistically significantly lower than the rate in other dyads only during the postwar period. They then argue that the common interests induced by bipolarity account for the relative peace among the democracies in the cold war era.

Their argument is less than convincing. First, the lack of statistical significance requires the separation of the pre-1914 and interwar periods. When these two are combined, the escalation rate of disputes to war in democratic dyads—the central concern of the democratic peace—is significantly less than for other dyads (also see Maoz 1998, 31–38; Thompson and Tucker 1997). Second, the microfoundations that I described earlier in this paper suggest that less chance of escalation may lead to a higher rate of disputes because the risk of war is less. The rate of militarized disputes in democratic dyads may be irrelevant to the democratic peace. Third, the interest argument poses a chicken-or-egg problem; do states have shared interests because of their common regimes, or common regimes because of their shared interests? For example, would Italy have remained in the Western bloc if it had gone Communist in the late 1940s? Fourth, if shared interests produced by bipolarity sustained the peace in the democratic world, why did they fail to do so in the Communist world where the Soviet Union invaded its ally Hungary in 1956, fought with China in the late 1960s, and intervened militarily in its other allies repeatedly (Ray 1998, 38)?

Fifth and finally, Farber and Gowa (1995) never provide an indicator of common interests that would allow us to see if democracy has an independent effect after controlling for interests. The advocates of the democratic peace did the hard work of arriving at a consensus of how to measure democracy for empirical tests; the proponents of interests now need to develop indicators of interests and show empirical results that those indicators are consistent with their arguments about how interests operate. On this point, Green et al. (2001) argue that their baseline rates of conflict in a dyad reflect shared interests, but that argument assumes that state interests change less often than government type. They present no evidence for their claim.

Three approaches have attempted to develop explanations of the democratic peace and test them against evidence. The first examines possible causes of peace related to democracy that supplement the democratic peace. Oneal and Russett (1997) contend that the democratic peace should be thought of as the liberal peace, where trade plays a large role in creating peace among nations. They examine the cold war years and find that joint democracy and higher trade flows are related to a lower frequency of disputes.

This approach is promising, yet it suffers from several important limitations. First, as noted above for the argument that interests cause the democratic peace, microfoundations suggest that lowering the risk of war should raise the chance of a dispute. Evidence that the rate of disputes is lower in democratic dyads may or may not be consistent with a democratic peace. Second, the microfoundations of the argument that higher trade flows help to produce peace are unclear (Morrow 1999a). The common argument that states with healthy trading relations will avoid war with each other out of the fear of losing the trade misses the point that what makes one state less willing to fight, and so more willing to make concessions, should raise the demands of the other side. I am not claiming that trade has no effect on how conflict prone a dyad is, only that the theory behind that argument is incomplete at this time. Third, it may be that we observe that dyads with large trade flows are also peaceful because the anticipation of peaceful relations encourages trade (Pollins 1989; Reuveny and Kang 1996). Further research could answer these questions and advance the standing of this explanation for the democratic peace.

The second approach turns to the microfoundations of conflict to develop a theory of why democratic dyads should be more peaceful and then tests the implications. Building on a suggestion in Fearon's discussion (1994a) of audience costs; Schultz (1998, 1999, 2001) examines how the role of a lawful opposition increases the ability of a democracy to signal its resolve during a crisis. The opposition presumably has a better understanding of the government's resolve than the opposing state does. It also has the incentive to exploit the crisis for its own political gain should the crisis end in an undesirable outcome—war or major concessions—for the state. Then the actions of the opposition serve as a signal for the resolve of the government. When the government is highly resolved, the opposition will support the government because there is little chance of political gain and a great chance of partisan loss from opposing the government's stance. When the government is weakly resolved but pursues a strong stand in the crisis anyway, the opposition should oppose the government's actions in the crisis in the hope of gaining politically. The prospect of this opposition disciplines the government, leading it to settle those crises quickly. In a democratic dyad, this improved signaling by both parties makes a peaceful settlement of a dispute much more likely than other types of dyads.

Schultz (1999, 2001) tests this argument using both large-n tests and case studies. The theory provides detailed predictions both of what statistical patterns we should expect in the data and what actions and responses we should expect in the case studies. The theory provides the hypotheses that structure both types of empirical work, and the combination of both reinforces our confidence that the theory is supported by the evidence.

A third approach to explaining the democratic peace looks at broader patterns of behavior by democracies in conflicts (Bueno de Mesquita et al. 1999). Democracies are more likely to win the war they fight than autocracies are (Lake 1992); in wars between democracies and autocracies, the democracies initiate the war more often than the autocracies (Bennett and Stam 1998); and democracies that initiate wars suffer lower costs than autocracies that initiate wars (Siverson 1995). Bueno de Mesquita et al. (1999) observe that democratic leaders are less secure in office than autocratic leaders and that losing wars or fighting costly wars increases the risk of replacement to leaders (Bueno de Mesquita and Siverson 1995). They propose a model of removal from office tied to crisis and possible war to examine how decisions in a crisis vary with the institutions that select and remove leaders from office. Democratic leaders select when they go to war more carefully than autocratic leaders, requiring a greater chance of winning before they are willing to fight. Further, democratic leaders commit more resources to the war effort than other leaders (Reiter and Stam 1998). That model explains all these regularities and proposes additional regularities supported by the evidence, such as the willingness of democratic leaders to engage in low-cost conflict. Here the theory ties together a set of observed regularities into a consistent whole and proposes novel regularities.

These three candidate explanations of the democratic peace are not mutually exclusive. All three could be operating as part of the complete explanation. Certainly the signaling properties of an opposition and the selection and effort effects of more tenuous leader tenure seem closely related and compatible within a more general theory. Both rely on the same microfoundations. Searching for more hypotheses that can be tested against both large-*n* data sets and case studies should be the next direction in efforts to explain the democratic peace.

■ | Offense-Defense Theory

Offense-defense theory derives from the idea that war and conflict are more likely when it is relatively easy to conquer territory (Jervis 1978). When the offense is advantaged, states will be more aggressive in their designs because the prospect of conquest is easier and they will be more militaristic in their security strategies because the threat of being conquered is greater. The broadest statement can be found in Van Evera (1999) where the offense-defense balance is claimed to make just about every dimension of security affairs, from alliances to arms races to diplomacy, more belligerent and difficult to resolve short of war.

Technology and military organization are the two main sources of the offense-defense balance. Although there is some disagreement about exactly how weaponry and organization combine to create advantages for the offense or defense, mobility is thought to favor the offense, while firepower favors the defense. Sometimes, geography and the force-to-space ratio is included in the offense-defense balance. These additions move the concept from being a characteristic of the international system to one of dyads. A state's probability of victory in a war depends on many factors in addition to the offense-defense balance. The balance of capabilities and support from third parties, at a minimum, also affect which side wins a war (Glaser and Kaufmann 1998; Lynn-Jones 1995).

The idea that ease of conquest leads to war is attractive in the abstract. It moves beyond structural realism to produce a theory where the security dilemma is a variable to be explained, rather than a constant. The argument can be extended to explain the tightness of alliances (Christensen and Snyder 1990), the likelihood of competition versus cooperation in international politics (Glaser 1992, 1994–95), and nuclear strategy (Glaser 1990). Formal models can reflect the offense-defense balance and show that increasing offensive advantages produce higher levels of armaments (Powell 1993).[9] Offense-defense theory can lead to novel hypotheses and added theoretical sophistication beyond structural realism.

Specifying the offense-defense balance as a concept has proven difficult. Levy (1984) pointed out that the concept was used to mean at least four different things. Efforts centered on refining the concept. The most careful effort to date is Glaser and Kaufmann (1998) who begin by assessing the margin of force each side needs to win a war in the dyad as an at-

---

9. However, also see O'Neill 1990 where increasing the advantage to the offense either decreases the chance of war or has no effect on it.

tacker and as a defender, holding the other side's forces fixed. The product of these margins defines the offense-defense balance that a state faces against another particular state; is it easier for the state in question to build offense or defense to defeat the other in a war?[10]

The measurement of the offense-defense balance has proven problematic. At times, some proponents of the theory appear to judge perceptions of the balance solely by whether an actor thought the attacker would win a war (Christensen 1997, 74, 78–80, 91–92), even though the theory clearly recognizes that more than the balance determines which side wins a war. Glaser and Kaufmann's proposed measurement (1998) of the balance depends on net assessments. Net assessments implicitly assume that analysts can judge which side will win a war from a given military balance. However, if the outcomes of war were predictable, then the sides would not have to fight; the loser would surrender the stakes to avoid the costs of war (Wagner 2000). Instead, war is inherently unpredictable, and different analysts may not arrive at net assessments, and hence judgments of the balance, that are even close to one another.[11]

Another problem for measurement of the balance is that states can influence it through the militaries they choose to construct. Van Evera (1999) says the offense was advantaged during the period from 1792 to 1815 and the defense was advantaged from 1815 on.[12] Neither technology nor the possibilities for military organization changed when the Napoleonic Wars ended in 1815. All the ways Napoleon and revolutionary France before him created mass armies capable of offensive campaigns were as available after Waterloo as they were before. However, the monarchs of Europe chose to build small, professional armies instead of the large, citizen armies they built from 1813 to 1815 to defeat Napoleon. This difference resulted from an implicit agreement among monarchs that the suppression of liberal revolution was more important than building a powerful army for interstate warfare. As Best (1986, 204–6) argues, militaries during the Restoration were professional because monarchs thought their

10. This directional balance will differ for the states in a dyad whenever geography or technology creates an advantage for one side (Glaser and Kaufmann 1998, 58).

11. The use of net assessments may arise from the extensive study of nuclear strategy in strategic studies. Net assessment is much easier to perform for a strategic nuclear war, and it is more likely to achieve some consensus on an assessment. The factors that produce risk are much less likely to have any effect on the outcome of a nuclear war. Indeed, it may be the certainty of judging that strategic nuclear war will be a disaster that provides its deterrent power.

12. Van Evera (1999) takes the endogeneity of the offense-defense balance very far, claiming that the balance is a cause of itself as states adopt more offensive means as the offensive becomes advantaged. Glaser and Kaufmann (1998) reject this full endogeneity, I think correctly for the purpose of their theory, because, otherwise, something else determines that balance, and we cannot think of the offense-defense balance as a primitive concept.

most likely targets were their own populations. Is the offense-defense balance a fundamental concept if it can be changed so dramatically through
national policy (Shimshoni 1990–91)?

The two World Wars are central to the development of the theory.
World War I is commonly thought of as a war where the defense was dominant because of the roles of the machine gun and artillery. World War II is
seen as an era where the offense was dominant as the introduction of the
tank and ground support aircraft led to mobile warfare, making it possible
to conquer large amounts of territory quickly. However, most leaders before each of those wars perceived the balance in the opposite way; they
thought that attacking armies would sweep to victory in 1914 and that the
war in 1939 would lead to another stalemate in the trenches (J. L. Snyder
1984). The difference between the actual and perceived balances could
pose major problems for testing the theory. Proponents may be able to shift
whether the actual or perceived balance is critical across cases to eliminate
cases that contradict the theory.

The paradigmatic cases of the World Wars pose a puzzle for the
theory. Offensive dominance is claimed to make war more likely, yet the
perceived dominance of defense helped to lead to World War II. Offense-
defense theorists argue that perceived dominance of the offense before
World War I led to tight alliances and overly aggressive war plans that
caused the Austro-Serbian crisis after the assassination of the archduke to
escalate into a general war (J. L. Snyder 1984; Van Evera 1984). In contrast, the British and French perception that the defense was stronger in
the 1930s discouraged them from taking the steps that might have deterred
Hitler from attacking Poland. Indeed, Hitler drew back from the brink on
August 26, 1939, when he first realized the possibility that Britain and
France would go to war if he attacked Poland. Here the dominance of defense helped to trigger the German-Polish war that spread to a general war
in Europe. Hitler's belief that Britain and France would not go to war for
Poland increased his willingness to attack Poland. Indeed, his belief was
correct; Britain and France did nothing to aid Poland against the German
onslaught (Christensen and Snyder 1990; Van Evera 1999, 151–56). Together, the two World Wars suggest that either offense dominance or defense dominance can play a key role in the outbreak of general war.

Offense-defense theorists respond to this observation in two ways, both
about why perceived defense dominance should not be thought of as a
cause of World War II. First, Hitler believed that the offense was advantaged, and so was willing to go to war even if Britain and France were
likely to go to war over Poland. Second, Hitler's quest for domination in
Europe was the central cause of World War II independent of the offense-
defense balance. Even if France and Britain had not gone to war after the
German invasion of Poland, Germany would have gone to war with them
later in any case.

In response, one could argue counterfactually that World War I would have occurred even if state leaders held the belief that the defense was advantaged (cf. Trachtenberg 1991, 63, 71). Austria would have gone to war with Serbia in 1914, anticipating that a major power can defeat a minor power regardless of the offense-defense balance. Russia would then face the same decision between war and watching Serbia be crushed by Austria that it faced in 1914. Had Russia intervened, the Great Powers would then have faced the same chain of intervention decisions as in the actual July crisis. Would Germany allow Austria to fight Russia alone? If it intervened, would France stay on the sidelines in the war between Russia and Serbia on one side and Austria and Germany on the other? If France did remain neutral at the outbreak of war, could the Germans trust the French to stay on the sidelines? The one decision for war that we could all agree would not have happened immediately would be the British intervention into the war. The German invasion of Belgium was key in rallying the cabinet in favor of intervention, and Belgium would not have been invaded in a defensive German war plan (Ferguson 1999, 158–66).

It is difficult to see how such lines of historical and counterfactual argument can resolve the status of offense-defense theory. Trachtenberg (1991) provides detailed historical evidence that preemption played little role in the 1914 crisis contrary to the received story from offense-defense theory. The counterfactual arguments depend closely on the theory held; if one believes that offense-defense theory is true, then the judgment that World War I would not have occurred if the defense was broadly believed to be advantaged is straightforward. However, other theories lead to different counterfactual conclusions. We need to look elsewhere to test the validity of offense-defense theory.

The examination of additional cases to test the theory requires an assessment of the balance. Measures that are easier to collect than the net assessment procedure that Glaser and Kaufmann propose would assist in examining additional cases. Morrow (1993) used war plans to assess the perceived offense-defense balance as offense dominant during the 1860s. War plans should reflect leaders' perceptions of whether the offense is advantaged. There are, of course, some difficulties in using war plans as a general indicator of the perceived balance: (1) detailed war plans become necessary only with the onset of mass mobilization in the mid–nineteenth century, (2) war plans are typically offensive in nature, perhaps to gain first-strike advantages, and (3) war plans reflect strategic considerations beyond the offense-defense balance, such as power asymmetries, state goals, and alliances (Sagan 1986).

Such indicators of the offense-defense balance would be useful to conduct large-n tests of the hypotheses of the theory. The theory purports to be general across time and space, and it would be useful to know whether the set of cases to which the theory applies is limited. Such limits could help us identify underlying but unidentified conditions that are necessary for the theory. However, most empirical examinations of the theory are limited to the two World Wars or else make judgments about the offense-defense balance that are not reproducible (Quester 1977; Van Evera 1999).[13]

An example may clarify the advantages of testing the theory on cases beyond the usual set. Christensen and Snyder (1990) extend the logic of offense-defense theory to account for the tightness of alliances under multipolarity. Their argument is that perceived offense dominance leads to tight alliances and the rapid spread of small conflicts into general war, while perceived advantages for the defense lead to loose alliances that undermine deterrence of powers seeking to dominate the system. World War I corresponds to the first case, and World War II to the second. Morrow (1993) points out that the 1860s contradict this argument. Offense was believed to be advantaged by national leaders, yet France and Austria failed to coordinate their policies to stop the unification of Germany under Prussia. Christensen (1997) responded by modifying the theory so that it only holds when all sides perceive a general threat to the status quo; this he claims did not exist during the 1860s. This modification of the theory seems reasonable and consistent with its arguments. However, the three cases now examined require support either for novel predictions in the details of the case or in cases not yet used in the construction of the revised theory. Without such novel tests of the revised theory, the theory has no empirical support independent of the cases used in its construction.

A careful examination of the logic of inference may clarify the issue here. Table 1a depicts how the two cases considered by Christensen and Snyder (1990) fit their argument. The argument claims that alliances will be overly tight when the offense is advantaged and fail to be tight enough to deter a state seeking hegemony when the defense is advantaged. Each of the World Wars is placed in the relevant cell of Table 1a, and the evidence conforms to their hypothesis; all cases should fall on the main diagonal of the table. Table 1b presents Morrow's addition (1993) of the 1860s. It is a discordant case according to the original hypothesis. Table 1c presents the revised theory, which constructs a more elaborate hypothesis by differentiating those cases, such as the 1860s, where states did not believe that any state sought hegemony. Again, the hypothesized pattern of cases on the diagonal returns in the upper portion of Table 1c as the revised theory predicts.

The lack of additional cases undermines our confidence in the generality of the hypothesis. The period 1688 to 1714 when a large coalition formed to stop the expansion of France under Louis XIV would be a useful case to consider. Defense was advantaged during this period; it was an era of siege warfare (Van Evera 1999, 171). There was no question that France posed a threat to the system in the eyes of other states. According to the theory then, we should find loose alliances that failed to deter Louis XIV. Two general wars did occur during this period; however, according to one general history,

13. A notable exception is Hopf 1991.

TABLE 1A. CASES TESTING CHRISTENSEN AND SNYDER'S ARGUMENT: FIRST CUT

| | ALLIANCE BEHAVIOR | |
PERCEIVED ADVANTAGE	CHAIN GANGING	BUCK-PASSING
OFFENSE ADVANTAGE	World War I	
DEFENSE ADVANTAGE		World War II

TABLE 1B. CASES TESTING CHRISTENSEN AND SNYDER'S ARGUMENT: ADDING THE 1860s

| | ALLIANCE BEHAVIOR | |
PERCEIVED ADVANTAGE	CHAIN GANGING	BUCK-PASSING
OFFENSE ADVANTAGE	World War I	The 1860s
DEFENSE ADVANTAGE		World War II

> She [France] faced a fairly solid coalition of states who had all been bullied by Louis over the last two decades and who were to manage to stick together through this war and that of the Spanish Succession until the ascendancy of France was destroyed. (McKay and Scott 1983, 45)

Closer examination of these wars might show that the coalition was not strong or that the perceived advantage was with the offense. It could be that the Nine Years' War from 1688 to 1697 fits the theory because Louis XIV did not realize that the coalition would form to oppose him, although France anticipated that the War of Spanish Succession would be a general war.

Examination of such additional cases would assist the development of the theory in two ways. One, proponents would be forced to provide clearer operational definitions of the independent and dependent variables, which would enhance the commonality of understanding of these concepts. Although I have focused on the measurement of the offense-defense balance, there are also questions about whether the theory seeks to explain all wars or only the largest, most significant wars (cf. Van Evera 1999, 1 for the latter claim). Two, the theory would be tested on novel evi-

TABLE 1C. CASES TESTING CHRISTENSEN AND SNYDER'S ARGUMENT: CHRISTENSEN'S REVISION

When States Perceive a State Seeking Hegemony

PERCEIVED ADVANTAGE	ALLIANCE BEHAVIOR	
	CHAIN GANGING	BUCK-PASSING
OFFENSE ADVANTAGE	World War I	
DEFENSE ADVANTAGE		World War II

When States Do Not Perceive a State Seeking Hegemony

PERCEIVED ADVANTAGE	ALLIANCE BEHAVIOR	
	CHAIN GANGING	BUCK-PASSING
OFFENSE ADVANTAGE		The 1860s
DEFENSE ADVANTAGE		

dence, cases not used in the development of the theory to date. Should the theory be revised again in response to these cases, the proponents would need to seek out unexamined cases or novel hypotheses to demonstrate that the newly revised theory explained something beyond the evidence used in its construction.

Fearon (1995a) provides a piece of general evidence that is a puzzle for offense-defense theory. The period from 1648 to 1789 is generally considered to be dominated by defense, while offense was favored from 1815 to 1913. The theory concludes that war should be more common in the latter period than the former. The opposite is true, however. War and great power war are much more common from 1648 to 1789 than from 1815 to 1913 according to Levy's data (1983). A revised version of the theory might be able to account for this pattern, but a comparison of a large number of cases gives rise to this puzzle.

A revision of the theory could begin by looking at some unstated premises of the theory. Fearon (1995a) points out that offensive advantages increase the variance of war outcomes—a higher chance of all-out victory or crushing defeat. If state leaders are risk-averse, then increasing the variance of outcomes makes war less attractive to them, holding the mean outcome constant. Implicitly then, offense-defense theory focuses on the unusual leaders who are not risk-averse and so do not lower their value for war as the variance of outcomes rises. This assumption may be reasonable given the expressed desire to explain large wars if we believe that large wars are triggered by unusual risk takers like Hitler.

If this argument is correct, offense-defense theory would not attempt to explain the large number of wars that are fought for limited ends. In many wars, neither side seeks to conquer the other. For instance, Ethiopia and Eritrea went to war over some border territory. The threat of total defeat led Eritrea to settle their dispute on grounds favorable to Ethiopia, but Ethiopia did not pursue its military advantage to conquer Eritrea.

Defensive advantages should make limited wars more likely. Such wars often occur in territorial disputes where one state seizes the territory in dispute to present the other side with a fait accompli (Huth 1996). Because such preemptive moves are not opposed by substantial force initially, the offense-defense balance is irrelevant for the success of the initial blow. On the other hand, defensive advantages increase the ability to hold the seized territory afterward; this forces the target to choose between accepting the fait accompli and fighting a long and bloody war as Ethiopia and Eritrea did. Fait accompli is an attractive tactic under such conditions.

Such limited wars may trigger general wars or turn into long, bloody conflicts on their own. The rapid expansion of World War I overshadows its origin as a war between Austria and Serbia; World War II began with the German-Polish War. The Iraq-Iran War was a war over limited territorial ends that proved difficult to end even after massive loss of life. General wars are not generally sought by either side; wars begun with limited intentions can trigger them.

Work connecting game theoretic microfoundations and offense-defense theory is in its infancy. Glaser (1997, 178–81, 183–85; also see Kydd 1997a) argues that offensive advantages complicate signaling of intentions, although he does not show how such advantages lead all types to adopt military policies that send the same signal. The ability to distinguish offensive and defensive capabilities, rather than just offense dominance, is central to his argument about spirals of mistrust. States could infer the motivation behind a rival's military buildup if offensive and defensive weapons are different. It could be argued that offensive advantages reduce the range of bargains that both sides would accept short of war, and so increase the difficulty of reaching a settlement short of war. Offensive advantages also could create a commitment problem where the greater attractiveness of attacking leads neither side to trust the other to honor a deal in the future. How the offense-defense balance affects the efficacy of costly signals should be explored further.

The expectations of state leaders about the likely course of fighting clearly affect their choices about whether and when to go to war. Offense-defense theory correctly emphasizes the role of such expectations in the initiation of war. Further, proponents of that theory can present detailed cases where they claim the offense-defense balance operates as the theory claims it does. However, strategic responses to expectations about the likely course of a war may not be as straightforward as the theory assumes. Offensive advantages may make war less likely in some situations, while defensive advantages increase the risk of war in others. Reaching a consensus on the general pattern here requires the examination of a wider range of cases, through novel cases as well as large-*n* comparisons.

■ | Three Methods and the Three Literatures

Game theoretic microfoundations, the democratic peace, and the offense-defense balance provide a comparison of the state of methodology for the study of international conflict as each line has drawn heavily on one of formal models, large-*n* studies, and case studies. Microfoundations as a research program uses models to elaborate arguments about conflict. The democratic peace as a research program has been primarily empirical using large-*n* studies. Offense-defense theory has been driven by case studies. All would benefit from greater integration of all three methods. This section presents my views of how formal models, large-*n* studies, and case studies should be integrated and illustrates my argument with the three research programs.

Science develops a common understanding of how and why the phenomena in question occurs; methodology addresses how shared scientific understanding can be created. Research methods seek to render research results open for skeptical questioning with the object of reaching consensus as to whether observations accord with theory. Methodology is not about how one arrives at insights about politics; it is about how one demonstrates scientifically to others that one's insights are true. This is not to say that reaching a shared agreement is easy, only that methods try to make such agreement possible.

Formal models, large-*n* studies, and case studies each have a distinctive contribution to the creation of a shared scientific understanding of international conflict. Formal models provide a way to open up the logic of a theory to close examination. Elaboration of a theory is critical to determine what conclusions follow from the theory, and so what hypotheses test the theory. Both large-*n* and case studies can be used to test the hypotheses of a theory, although each has particular advantages. A common view is that large-*n* studies deal more effectively with questions of external validity— whether we can generalize the results from the cases studied to others— while case studies are stronger on internal validity—whether the causal process is operating in the cases studied (Campbell and Stanley 1966). I agree with this view but wish to expand on the complementary role of large-*n* and case studies and the proper form of each.[14]

Large-*n* studies provide us with confidence that a general pattern predicted by a theory appears across a number of cases. Such patterns can be novel facts in the sense of being unknown before their documentation. The democratic peace exemplifies a novel pattern found through statistical analysis. The range of patterns that we can examine, however, is limited to variables that can be quantified across a large number of cases. Small and Singer's (1976) inability to find the democratic peace rests in part on the lack of a clear definition of democracy when they did their research. Although regimes involved in each war could be coded without difficulty, the regimes of the large number of dyads that remained at peace in a given year could not be coded without great effort. Consequently, it was difficult to determine whether the lack of wars between democracies resulted only from the rarity of war and democracy historically. Measuring variables typically involves a compromise between the accuracy of a measure and its ease of collection across a large number of cases. Often we must settle for indicators which we believe are correlated with a variable even though they include substantial measurement error. For example, war plans could be used as a measure of the offense-defense balance because they depend in part on that balance as perceived by the governments making those plans. Still, many factors other than the offense-defense balance enter into a state's war plans, and war plans include error in their measurement of that balance.

Case studies, in contrast, allow the collection of more precise information about variables in hypotheses. By focusing on a single case, a researcher has the ability to collect and assess information in much greater depth than is possible across a large number of cases. The focus on a single case also allows us to test hypotheses that could not be tested in a large-*n* study because of the lack of information on many other cases. The range of hypotheses drawn from one theory that can be tested by detailed study of a case is the source of the belief that case studies assess the causal process better than large-*n* studies. Still, case studies present issues in the measurement of variables. Case studies are often presented as narrative rather than explicit tests of hypotheses; this presentation can obscure what values the variables take on the case according to the researcher. This obscurity hinders the ability of readers to judge those values against the case material and determine whether the case supports or contradicts the hypotheses. Judgments of the perceived offense-defense balance from statements about which side was likely to win the war is an example of this problem. Explicit judgments about variables also aids the effort to test the same hypotheses

14. Huth 1988 provides an excellent example of the complementary role of large-*n* and case studies.

on different cases. Researchers can transfer the principles behind the judgments to assess the variables on other cases.

All empirical work faces the question of whether the hypotheses follow from the theory being tested. In international relations (and political science more generally), our theories rarely make definite predictions about individual cases or classes of events. They may represent only part of the full causation of individual cases or may apply only to a limited range of cases, or the underlying concepts may be unobservable and so empirical assessments of them may be only partial and prone to error. Then any test of a single event is rarely decisive for or against any theory. The proponents of a theory contradicted by a single test or the opponents of a theory supported by such a test can appeal to other plausible causes to account for the observation in that test. Further, such critical tests are often difficult in our field because we share general knowledge of the historical record that we use for testing. Novel facts are hard to find in our field, although archival work or the search for statistical patterns may uncover them.

Research on game theoretic microfoundations may be able to assist with this issue. The unpredictability of individual events is a central conclusion of such work, and it forces the search elsewhere for testable hypotheses. With this point in mind, I turn to the implications of microfoundations for empirical work with either large-n or case studies.

First and foremost, it is critical to examine variation across and within cases, rather than to try to predict the outcome of individual cases. Private information plays a large role in determining the outcome of a crisis, and private information is not knowable to others in full by its very nature. Our theoretical expectations then cannot extend to the prediction of individual cases. We may be able to predict variation across sets of cases though. These theoretical expectations can confront evidence in a test. Some sets of dyads may be more likely to go to war than others.

The unpredictability of individual cases favors large-n analyses where probabilities of conflict can be estimated more reliably than from a small number of cases. These studies attempt to identify which sorts of cases are more likely to undergo a crisis and escalate to war. The statistics of such studies are complicated by the role of private information. Decisions to initiate and escalate disputes cannot be seen as independent (Reed 2000), and what we can determine about private information from actions in a crisis are limited by how we measure those actions (Smith 1999). Large-n studies also face the well-known problems of constructing indicators of concepts that can be collected across a large number of cases and of defining the relevant scope of cases that are believed to be comparable.

The unpredictability of individual cases does not rule out the use of case studies, but the focus of case studies should be shifted to examining variation within cases. If private information does drive behavior in crises, its values are fixed within an individual crisis, and its specific value should produce a consistent pattern of behavior. The testable prediction is that certain sets of behavior should be found together in individual crises. Case studies allow us to delve more deeply into detailed patterns of behavior in a crisis.[15] This focus on patterns of behavior differs from the typical focus on explaining the events of the case.

This search for patterns, however, is possible only if the theory being tested is capable of making predictions about detailed patterns of behavior in a crisis. Some theories, such as Waltz's version (1979) of neorealism, explicitly state that they cannot predict actions in a crisis. Others make such predictions based on implicit theories of how the judgments of states can be understood from the internal acts of a government, such as memoranda. Such implicit theories should be made explicit so they are open to scrutiny. Because case studies seek to exploit the detail of the case to increase both the effective observations available for a test and the range of hypotheses tested (Campbell 1975; King et al. 1994, 217–28), it is critical to have clear and explicit expectations about the hypotheses to be tested in advance of conducting the study. Otherwise, the theory can be adapted to fit the details of the case, rather than the details testing the theory.

Second, the indeterminacy of individual crises limits what we can expect from our theories of conflict (Gartzke 1999). Theories that purport to predict when wars will occur hold out the prospect of solving the problem of war if we can eliminate the conditions that such theories identify as the complete causes of a war. Unfortunately, such theories cannot exist given the microfoundations elaborated above. The occurrence of war is necessarily unpredictable both to the parties involved and to us as observers.[16]

Theories with probabilistic predictions can still be used for policy analysis. Beyond predicting the risk of war in a situation, the chances of war could be manipulated using the theory as a guide. However, the risk of war could not be eliminated, and reductions in the risk of war would be accompanied by undesirable countereffects. For instance, the advent of nuclear weapons may have reduced the chance of war while raising the consequences of war should it occur. The total expected risk, probability times consequences, might not have changed greatly, but its form had. Such changes in the form of the risk might be welcomed by all parties even if the total expected risk had not changed.

Third, case studies may allow us to delve into ex post information about the private information in cases more thoroughly than large-*n* studies can. This added detail contains both benefits and dangers. One danger is the belief that such studies can explain the onset of conflict because the fit of a theory to the data is better when ex post information is used. The

15. The Behavioral Correlates of War data set, collected by Russell Leng, could also be used for such studies.

16. Kuran (1991) provides a similar argument about the unpredictability of revolutions.

better fit may also lead some to believe that case studies necessarily provide better tests than large-*n* studies. Instead, each type of test has a different role that complements the other. Ex post information about both sides' resolve may allow further tests on the pattern of behavior to be expected in a particular conflict. Still, events in a crisis do not reveal the complete value of private information, and so we should not overestimate what we can learn about it from the events of a crisis (Smith [1999] presents statistical methods for dealing with this issue in large-*n* studies).

The two empirical research programs reviewed here reflect the microfoundational point that war is predictable only in a probabilistic sense across dyads and seek to explain variation in the probability of war across dyads. The two research programs have taken different approaches to dealing with the issues raised in testing a probabilistic theory. Tests of the democratic peace have compared large numbers of cases to look for the variation in probability; tests of offense-defense theory have searched for many different behaviors that should be found together in particular cases according to the theory.

Both could benefit from use of the other empirical approach. The democratic peace is now moving toward several candidate explanations with microfoundations that could be examined with cases to support detailed predictions from those explanations. Offense-defense theory should be moving toward addressing a wider range of cases in the hope of pinning down the concepts empirically and theoretically as well as testing the theory beyond the cases from which it was drawn.

Of the two research programs, the democratic peace has done a better job of creating a consensus about its terms and the evidence for its claims. There are shared definitions of democracy and war that allow for comparisons of different research projects in the program. Offense-defense theory has built consensus among its proponents primarily about its application to and explanation of particular cases. Unfortunately, those understandings may not translate to other cases yet to be studied.

Offense-defense theory has paid greater attention to theory than the democratic peace. The early efforts to explain the democratic peace rarely advanced to the stage where the candidate theories made novel predictions beyond the existing empirical results. Offense-defense theory, on the other hand, has clear expectations for the cases, provided that the concepts of that theory could be assessed empirically.

The democratic peace has faced more challenges that its empirical regularities could have alternative explanations. The empirical cases of offense-defense theory have not faced that challenge often but should. Offense-defense theory predicts that aggressive behaviors—such as arms races, fait accompli tactics, tight alliances, and military secrecy—should be found together. But so do other explanations, such as those about the underlying motivations of states. If states can shift the offense-defense balance greatly by how they build their militaries, the argument that underlying motivations cause both these aggressive behaviors and the offense-defense balance could be compelling. Again, moving away from the explanation of individual cases could help resolve this issue. Within an individual case, it is easy to find alternative explanations for particular actions; across a large number of cases, it is hard to find any one of those alternative explanations supported frequently.

Science is about the creation of a shared understanding of why events occur across the scientific community. Scientific understanding requires a logically sound theory that is supported by empirical tests of the observable consequences of theory. Such understanding takes a great deal of work, both theoretical and empirical, to create. I only hope the next decade's research into international conflict will be as fruitful as the last decade's.

Stephen M. Walt

The Enduring Relevance of the Realist Tradition[1]

Writing in the 1983 edition of this volume, Robert Keohane declared that " 'Political Realism' has constituted the principal tradition for the analysis of international relations in Europe and its offshoots in the New World." Noting that attacks on realism were a frequent occurrence throughout its lengthy reign, Keohane also observed that "the very focus of these critiques seem only to reconfirm the centrality of Realist thinking in the international political thought of the West" (1983, 503).[2]

Realist theories are still widely criticized, but the realist tradition has yet to be supplanted by an alternative perspective with similar range or explanatory power. Although critics were quick to announce the obsolescence of realist theory in the wake of the cold war (Kegley 1993, 1995; Kratochwil 1993; Rosecrance and Stein 1993; Lebow 1994; Koslowski and Kratochwil 1994; Vasquez 1997), the real world has paid scant attention to these academic obituaries. Major powers remain acutely sensitive to the distribution of power, are wary of developments that might leave them vulnerable, and still strive to enhance their positions at the expense of potential rivals. Although states do cooperate in a variety of ways, they continue to guard their autonomy jealously and find extensive collaboration difficult to sustain. Military force remains a depressingly constant feature of political life, and events such as the 1991 Persian Gulf War, the Rwandan genocide, the Bosnian conflict, and the simmering rivalry between India and

1. I thank Stephen Brooks, Mlada Bukovansky, Dale Copeland, Michael Desch, Colin Elman, Miriam Elman, Markus Fischer, Charles Glaser, Keir Lieber, Sean Lynn-Jones, Michael Mastanduno, John Mearsheimer, Steven Miller, John Ruggie, Jack Snyder, Randall Schweller, Josh Spero, Allan Stam, Marc Trachtenberg, William Wohlforth, Christine Wohlforth, and the editors for valuable comments on earlier drafts of this essay.

2. This view was recently echoed by Michael Mastanduno: "Realism is now both the dominant paradigm in the study of international relations and the most challenged" (1999, 139).

Pakistan remind us that insecurity and the struggle for survival are still important elements of the human condition.[3]

Thus, the realist tradition remains the single most important approach for understanding international politics. It identifies and explains the central *problematique* in the field of international relations and sheds considerable light on a diverse array of important international phenomena.[4] As a result, no serious scholar can safely disregard its arguments and implications. Even prominent critics of realist theory acknowledge its central place in the discipline, and many of its arguments are echoed by scholars who are not normally regarded as "realists."

The realist tradition has a distinguished lineage, and it includes the works of Thucydides, Niccolo Machiavelli, Thomas Hobbes, Friedrich Meinecke, E. H. Carr, Hans Morgenthau, and others. In the field of international relations, Kenneth Waltz's *Theory of International Politics* (1979) has been the central point of departure for over two decades. Accordingly, this chapter examines the main developments in realist thought since *Theory of International Politics* was published. Realism remains a creative and relevant research enterprise, and scholars working in the realist tradition continue to make important advances. Their efforts in recent years have helped refine the basic logic of the theory, broadened its range of application, and explored its implications for the future. Debates within the realist tradition and between realism and its intellectual rivals have spurred theoretical progress throughout the field of international relations, and realist theories continue to provide important insights into the basic nature of international politics.

The remainder of this essay is organized as follows. The first section defines the realist tradition and proposes two criteria for judging its theoretical progress. The next section examines competing versions of realist theory, focusing on the recent debates between the neorealist, defensive, offensive, and "neo-classical" variants. The third section explores how different realist theories have illuminated a number of central issues in the field. The last section turns to the current research agenda: what questions remain unresolved, and what lines of inquiry are likely to yield new theoretical progress? The essay concludes with further reflections on the place of realist theories within international relations.

3. These conflicts include both internal and international wars, and the realist tradition has much to say about both subjects.

4. For example, realist theories offer cogent explanations for the rarity of regional hegemony, the sensitivity of states to shifts in the balance of power, the formation of spheres of influence, the barriers to extensive cooperation between states, and the tendency of states to imitate each other. Realist theory does not provide the only explanation(s) for these (and other) phenomena, but it does provide a set of arguments that one cannot easily dismiss.

▪ | What is the Realist Tradition?

Scholars often refer to different theoretical traditions as "isms" (e.g., Marx-*ism*, Keynesian*ism*, behavior*ism*, liberal*ism*, etc.) and then use these labels to identify (or pigeonhole) individual scholars. Although such labels provide a convenient shorthand, this tendency has unfortunate consequences and ought to be resisted. Although social scientists often have strong personal attachments to particular worldviews, a social science theory is not a religious movement like Catholicism, Protestantism, or Buddhism. Rather, a theory is simply an intellectual tool that we use to help make sense of the world around us. Scholars do not sign a loyalty oath when they work within a particular theoretical tradition, and no methodological laws are broken when a scholar draws on more than one theoretical tradition when seeking to explain some particular phenomena.[5] Although such paradigmatic distinctions can be useful, treating them as orthodoxies that require individual loyalty and using them to label individual scholars fosters unnecessary discord between rival traditions and does little to enhance our collective understanding of world politics. In general, our attention should focus on the theories themselves, rather than on the individual scholars who create or employ them.

In this essay I have tried (albeit with only partial success) to avoid the labels of "realism" and "realists" and relied instead on the term *realist tradition*. The theories emerging from the realist tradition provide a set of tools that can be employed by anyone who finds them useful, but scholars who use realist theories may also employ other theories when working on problems where realist theory is incomplete or inappropriate.

There is no single realist theory, of course, just as there is no single theory of social networks, evolution, or neoclassical economics. Rather, the realist tradition encompasses a family of related arguments sharing certain common assumptions and premises.[6] Realist theories seek to explain politics as it *really* is, as opposed to normative theories that offer prescriptions for how politics *ought* to be. The realist tradition also tends to emphasize the continuity of historical experience and is skeptical of efforts to transcend the competitive nature of political life.

Applied to international politics, theories in the realist family share the view that the international system is anarchic (meaning that there is no central authority that can govern world affairs or protect different states from each other). Realist theories have focused primarily on states, be-

5. We can also distinguish between efforts to refine or develop a particular theory (i.e., by clarifying its logic or extending its explanatory range) and efforts to use one or more theories to explain a specific historical process or recurring phenomena.

6. For recent efforts to define the realist paradigm, see Frankel 1996; Keohane 1983; Walt 1992, 1997a, 1998; James 1995; Gilpin 1986, 1996; Grieco 1990, 1997; Brooks 1997; Van Evera 1999; and Donnelly 2000. Alternative conceptions include Kegley 1995 and Legro and Moravcsik 1999.

cause states have been the most prominent social groups in recent world history, but realist theories have also been applied to a variety of nonstate actors as well. Realist theories generally assume that states seek to survive and that they pursue their ends in a more or less rational manner, although different theorists vary in their strength of their commitment to this premise.

The central conclusion of all realist theories—what might be termed the realist *problematique* —is that *the existence of several states in anarchy renders the security of each one problematic and encourages them to compete with each other for power or security.* Realist theories see the insecurity of states (or groups) as *the* central problem in international relations, and they portray international politics as a self-help system where states must provide security for themselves because no one else will.[7] Thus, the realist tradition places power at the center of political life: it sees the acquisition and management of power as the main issue that political actors face. It also takes a fairly pessimistic view of the human condition, emphasizing the recurring elements of tragedy rather than the hard-won instances of progress.

This conception of international politics is widely accepted, even among scholars who do not usually think of themselves as realists. For example, much of the recent formal work in international relations assumes that states are independent actors in anarchy, generally seeking to maximize their chances for survival subject to various exogenous constraints (see Powell 1990, 1999; Lake and Powell 1999b; Fearon 1994a, 1995b; Kydd 1997a, b). The extensive literature on power transitions also shares many assumptions with the realist tradition, although scholars working in this subfield disagree on whether their theories are realist (DiCicco and Levy 1999). Similarly, the rationalist approach to international institutions (sometimes termed neoliberal institutionalism) adopts most of the core premises of realist theory and has yet to escape its intellectual orbit (see Keohane 1984, 14, 67; Mearsheimer 1994–95, 430–32; Keohane and Martin 2002; Waltz 2000a, 24–25). Even scholars working in different research traditions sometimes acknowledge the historical association between anarchy and competition, while maintaining that other factors (e.g., democracy, norms, shared understandings and discursive practices, etc.) can help states overcome these incentives (Wendt 1999; Ruggie 1996, 1998). By identifying the core problem of international politics—the insecurity and competition induced by the existence of independent states in anarchy—

7. Legro and Moravcsik offer a different conception of realism's core premises, but few scholars working in the realist tradition would endorse it. In their version of realist theory, states have "fixed and uniformly conflictual preferences." This view thus treats a key *conclusion* of realist theory (i.e., the occurrence of conflict) as an assumption (1999, 13–16). In fact, one of the important advances in contemporary realist theory has been to show that conflict can arise even if state preferences are not initially at odds.

the realist tradition has set the terms of debate even for those thinkers who do not accept its generally pessimistic conclusions.

In short, the basic elements of the realist tradition are akin to the theory of universal gravitation. On earth, gravity is a force that heavier-than-air objects must overcome in order to fly. One can think of several ways to overcome this force (aircraft, balloons, rockets, etc.), but the fact that gravity can be countered does not mean it has ceased to exist or that knowledge of its role is not essential for designing a workable flying machine. As we shall see, a number of realist theories suggest ways that states can try to mitigate the incentives for competition, but virtually all of them recognize how hard it is to eliminate them completely.

CRITERIA FOR EVALUATION

The utility of a research tradition may be judged by two basic criteria. The first criterion is *explanatory power*: do theories drawn from this research tradition tell us useful things about political events in the real world? Does the theory help us understand phenomena that are both widely prevalent and important? Political science is an empirical enterprise, and the ultimate value of any analytical approach lies in its capacity to explain important aspects of the real world of politics.[8]

A second criterion is *internal fertility*: is a given research tradition able to refine its theoretical claims, while expanding (or in some cases, bounding) the range of phenomena to which they apply?[9] Is it able to answer critical objections and explain specific anomalies without losing its theoretical

---

8. Stephen Van Evera argues that explanatory power can be judged by the percentage of variance explained by the independent variable(s), the range of topics covered by the theory, and the prevalence of the phenomena being explained (1997, ch. 1).

9. Social scientists often invoke Imre Lakatos's "methodology of scientific research programmes" (1970), when assessing different research traditions, but they rarely recognize its limitations. Lakatos argues that the key criterion for choosing theories is "excess empirical content," but he never explains how one measures this elusive trait and historians of science have found it difficult to apply his approach to the real world of scientific practice. Lakatos also warns that research traditions "degenerate" when scholars employ ad hoc amendments to account for anomalies (while failing to anticipate "new facts"), but working scientists routinely (and correctly) embrace ad hoc assumptions in the conduct of normal science. Moreover, accusations that a research program is degenerating are difficult to establish because a single progressive advance can redeem a lengthy series of failures. To show that a research tradition is degenerating, therefore, one would have to show that *none* of it contains new insights. Given the many problems with Lakatos's criteria, it is not surprising that his schema is often used as a cudgel with which to bash whatever research tradition a particular critic happens to dislike (see Laudan 1977; Suppe 1977; McCloskey 1994; Walt 1997a). It is equally unsurprising that advocates of different theoretical traditions generally believe that their own enterprise meets Lakatos's criteria (Elman and Elman 2002).

coherence? Are theories based on the research tradition able to illuminate new topics or provide novel insights into past events? Do theories drawn from the particular tradition help identify the flaws in alternative approaches and suggest ways that they might be repaired?

Judged by these criteria, the realist tradition remains an important and lively arena of scholarly inquiry. To see why this is so, let us now consider some of the most important recent developments.

■ | The Varieties of Contemporary Realist Theory

The Neorealist Foundation

Contemporary realist theory begins with Kenneth Waltz's landmark *Theory of International Politics*. In this book, Waltz sought to place realist thought on a firmer social scientific foundation (Waltz 1979, 1991). Drawing on the philosophy of science, neoclassical microeconomics, and systems theory, Waltz developed an extremely parsimonious theory of the international system that sought to explain enduring regularities in international behavior across wide ranges of time and space. Waltz conceived of the international system as an anarchic order composed of states which sought "at a minimum, to survive" and argued that this condition created a "self-help" system in which competition was rife, cooperation difficult, and balances of power tended to form. This positional picture also suggested that bipolar structures would be less war prone than multipolar orders and that low levels of interdependence were more conducive to peace.

Waltz's most fundamental contribution was his emphasis on the international system as an active and autonomous causal force. For earlier realist thinkers, such as E. H. Carr (1946) or Hans J. Morgenthau (1946, 1948), international anarchy was a permissive condition that allowed human aggressiveness to express itself. Conflict occurred because humans craved power or because certain states had revisionist goals, and because there was no central authority to stop them from pursuing these ambitions.

For Waltz, however, the anarchic international system was an active force that "shaped and shoved" the states that made up the system.[10] The condition of anarchy forced all states to worry about their security and compelled them to take active measures to obtain it. Because systemic effects were present, one could not explain international outcomes by looking solely at the characteristics of states or even their underlying preferences. Rather, Waltz argued that "state behavior varies more with differences of power than with difference in ideology, in internal structure of

10. In Waltz's words: "Each state arrives at policies and decides on actions according to its own internal processes, but its decisions are shaped by the very presence of other states as well as by interactions with them" (1979, 65; 1986, 343).

property relations or in governmental form" (1986, 329). Being placed within an anarchic order encouraged states with different internal characteristics to act in similar ways; by the same logic, states with similar characteristics would behave quite differently if they were placed in a different external environment. These systemic pressures encouraged national leaders to emulate successful behavior by other states, and states that failed to compete effectively were more likely to be eliminated from the system. For Waltz, the pressures of competition in an anarchic realm explained why states tended to balance power, why efforts to increase one's own power might be self-defeating, and why bipolar systems were more stable than multipolar ones.

By locating the sources of insecurity in the characteristics of the system rather than in human nature, Waltz's conception encouraged efforts to mitigate the competitive pressures he identified. If conflict were ultimately due to human nature (as Morgenthau believed), then efforts to create a more peaceful world were doomed to fail. But if conflict arose from the circumstances in which states were placed, then *in theory* one could identify especially dangerous conditions and fashion appropriate policies to mitigate them. One could be "realistic" in appraising the obstacles while recognizing that there was more room for improvement than earlier realists had recognized.[11]

Theory of International Politics sparked an enormous reaction, much of it critical. Because anarchy was a constant and changes in polarity occurred only rarely, critics argued neorealist theory was unable to explain international change (Ruggie 1983; Buzan, Jones, and Little 1993) and could provide only general predictions about state behavior (Keohane 1983). Other commentators complained that theory was historically inaccurate (Schroeder 1994a) or accused Waltz of helping to legitimate a dangerous discourse of power politics, thereby contributing to the very problems the theory purported to explain (Ashley 1984). And a number of writers observed that neorealism did not provide detailed policy guidance, because its core variable—polarity—was difficult (if not impossible) for states to manipulate (Van Evera 1999).

Finally, a number of scholars noted that Waltz's theory was underspecified. As Randall Schweller has emphasized, if we accept Waltz's assumptions that the system is anarchic and all states merely seek to survive, then there is no need for them to worry about each other and no reason for conflict to arise. In order for competition to occur, the theory must allow for

---

11. Morgenthau, Carr, and other earlier realist scholars did offer various prescriptions for peace. Indeed, as Marc Trachtenberg (2001) observes, many scholars working in the realist tradition see the world as highly competitive yet advocate policies of moderation. This irony reflects their sense that in a dangerous world, excessive ambition and ideological zeal can place even powerful states at risk. By freeing realist thought from a pessimistic focus on human nature, however, neorealism offered a more optimistic basis for action.

the possibility that at least one state will try to alter the status quo. Yet in part because he systematically excluded unit-level elements, Waltz's neorealist theory did not explain how this might occur (Schweller 1996; see also Milner 1991; Wendt 1999).[12] Similarly, some of Waltz's other predictions (such as the propensity for states to balance power or the peaceful nature of bipolar systems) were not strictly deducible from his premises in the absence of additional information about the preferences of states and the structure of their interactions (Wagner 1993; Powell 1999).

These various critiques share a common theme, namely, that Waltz's purely structural theory was too parsimonious, unable to account for a number of important issues, and prone to indeterminate (or incorrect) predictions. Not surprisingly, therefore, much of the subsequent work within the realist tradition has sought to build on Waltz's important insights while enriching his spare depiction of the international system.

Recent realist research is also less parsimonious because it has placed greater emphasis on empirical testing. Like Carr and Morgenthau, Waltz illustrated his arguments with apt examples but did not test them with systematic empirical evidence. By contrast, most of the subsequent research in the realist tradition has relied on a broader base of quantitative or qualitative evidence. This increased attention to empirical testing is consistent with realism's long-standing emphasis on studying politics as it really is and has helped subsequent scholars enrich Waltz's stark conception.

DEFENSIVE REALISM

A central development in contemporary realist theory has been the emergence and refinement of defensive realism (Jervis 1978; Van Evera 1984, 1985, 1999; Walt 1989; Snyder 1991; Glaser 1994–95; Lynn-Jones 1995; Taliaferro 2000–01). Defensive realism accepts the basic idea that international anarchy forces states to worry about their security as well as Waltz's claim that states generally balance against especially strong or aggressive powers.

Defensive realism then makes an important revision to Waltz's purely structural theory. Waltz defined different international systems solely in terms of the gross distribution of power (i.e., bipolar or multipolar) and omitted other aspects of the physical and military environment of states. By contrast, defensive realists focus on the "fine-grained structure of power" (Van Evera 1999) and emphasize how geography and technology combine

---

12. As discussed below, Schweller's critique is not as damning as it appears. History offers no example of a great power that was a pure security seeker, so it makes sense for great powers to act as if other states had at least some revisionist aims. More importantly, a world of pure security-seeking states would still be prone to competition, either because each state could not be sure that the other states were benign or because none could guarantee not to become aggressive in the future (Jervis 1976, 62; Copeland 2000b, 199–200; Mearsheimer 2001).

to affect the security of states. In particular, defensive realism relies on the crucial concept of the *offense-defense balance,* generally defined as the relative ease or difficulty of conquest (Quester 1977; Jervis 1978; Van Evera 1984, 1999; Glaser and Kaufmann 1998). Acknowledging that anarchy encourages states to worry about security; defensive realists nonetheless assert that the offense-defense balance determines the *intensity* of security competition between states. When technology, geography, and so on, make conquest easy, states are less secure, cooperation is more difficult, and competition and war will be more intense, frequent, and extensive.

This amendment leads to two additional theoretical claims. First, defensive realism argues that most states can enhance their security by adopting defensive military postures, especially when the offense-defense balance favors the defending side. Under these conditions, a defensive military posture allows states to protect their own territory without threatening others and to do so in the most cost-effective way. Moreover, adopting a defensive posture enables status quo states to signal their peaceful inclinations (Jervis 1978; Glaser 1994–95; Kydd 1997a, b). Thus, defensive realism suggests that states can make probabilistic judgments about other states' intentions and that status quo powers can use this knowledge to dampen the competitive pressures inherent in anarchy.

Second, in part because they believe that states are strongly inclined to balance aggressive powers, defensive realists argue that expansion is usually difficult and rarely profitable. Nationalism and the emergence of postindustrial "information" economies make it difficult to exploit conquered territories (especially in the modern era): this means that the gains from conquest are not cumulative and usually subject to diminishing returns (Van Evera 1990–91; Kaysen 1990; Brooks 1999). Expansion may yield strategic benefits under certain conditions, but defensive realism believes such circumstances will be rare. Thus, defensive realists generally endorse policies designed to preserve the status quo and see ambitious attempts to expand as self-defeating anomalies that are inconsistent with rational statecraft and probably the product of some sort of domestic political pathology.[13] These claims are buttressed by ambitious attempts to test the theory through careful empirical studies (Snyder 1991; Van Evera 1999).

Defensive realism has not gone unchallenged, of course. Critics charge that the concept of the offense-defense balance incorporates virtually any factor that could conceivably affect the outcome of a war, raising doubts about whether it is possible to design military postures that will have the predicted effects (Levy 1984; Shimshoni 1990–91; Lynn-Jones 1995; Betts 1999; Lieber 2000). By attacking a core concept in defensive

---

13. These two claims—that status quo states can signal benign intentions and the relative difficulty of conquest—reinforce each other. If conquest is hard, then states do not need to assume the worst about other states' intentions and can rely on less than perfect evidence about them.

realism, these critiques also cast doubt on its key prescriptions. If states cannot measure the offense-defense balance or distinguish between offensive and defensive capabilities, then security-seeking states cannot escape the security dilemma and cannot signal their peaceful intentions in a convincing manner. Other scholars have challenged the claim that expansionist behavior is generally unprofitable, either by suggesting that the gains from conquest are greater than defensive realists maintain or by emphasizing the barriers that impede the formation of strong balancing coalitions (Liberman 1996a; Mearsheimer 2001; Kaufman 1992). And as defensive realists have sometimes conceded, relatively few great powers seem to have acted in the manner the theory recommends. Although this is not a fatal shortcoming, it does not increase confidence in the explanatory power of their arguments.[14]

Offensive Realism

The strongest challenge to the defensive variant of realist theory has come from other scholars within the realist tradition. This group—sometimes termed offensive realists—has offered both a sharp critique of the defensive realist position and proposed a more rigorously systemic account of the competitive nature of international politics.

Offensive realism challenges its defensive cousin on several grounds.[15] Waltz and the defensive realists begin by assuming that all states seek to survive. But as noted, it is not clear why conflict will occur unless at least one of the states in the system has some other reason to overturn the status quo. Defensive realism reinforces this status quo bias by arguing that conquest is usually difficult; this implies that rational states will rarely be inclined to expand.

To overcome this puzzle, offensive realism emphasizes the inability of states to gauge one another's intentions with 100 percent confidence. Even if states could judge current intentions accurately, they cannot be sure that intentions will not become more aggressive in the future. Because states cannot know what others might do, they have a powerful incentive to increase their own power so as to be ready for a challenge if it does emerge. Moreover, states are probably aware that other states face the same problem; this means that other states will be tempted to increase their own power as well. Thus, states are driven to compete for power because they

14. Defensive realists would respond by noting that those states that ignored the theory's implications (e.g., Wilhelmine and Nazi Germany, Imperial Japan, and possibly the former Soviet Union) tended to suffer especially grave foreign policy reverses.

15. The summary in these paragraphs is based on Mearsheimer 2001, but elements of these arguments can also be found in Spykman 1942, Wight 1979, Gilpin 1981; Schweller 1994; Labs 1997; Zakaria 1998; and Copeland 2000a.

are uncertain about the intentions of others and because they know that others may be driven to compete for power by similar fears. Even a world made up of status quo powers might still exhibit high levels of competitive behavior, simply because none of these powers could be certain what other states would do in the future.

Several implications follow. First, where Waltz and the defensive realists argue that states should not try to maximize power (for fear of provoking a hostile coalition), offensive realists suggest that all major powers are constantly looking for opportunities to improve their relative power position. Second, defensive realists see balancing as the preferred tendency for most states, while offensive realism predicts that states will normally choose to pass the buck rather than shoulder the burdens of balancing themselves. Given a choice, great powers try to get other states to do the fighting and dying necessary to prevent a hegemon from emerging. Balancing is the fall-back option when buckpassing fails, but great powers will prefer to let other states fight while they remain safely on the sidelines. Third, the temptation to pass the buck explains why efforts to balance an aggressor are often inefficient; this is one reason why offensive realists believe that opportunities to expand are more common than defensive realists do. Fourth, offensive realists also believe that the gains from expansion are usually cumulative; for them, conquest often pays. Taken together, these claims imply that great powers will compete more vigorously, because all face similar temptations and all recognize the danger of falling behind. Even states that might otherwise be content with the status quo will be inclined to try to alter it in their own favor, because if they don't, some other state is likely to try to seize the moment and shift it against them.

Thus, offensive realism sees anarchy as an even more powerful disposing force than Waltz's neorealist theory did. Where Waltz argued that the fear that others will balance discourages attempts to maximize power (1979, 127), offensive realists argue that power maximization is precisely what the system encourages. Most importantly, the desire to acquire more power does not occur because humans are driven by a lust for power (as Morgenthau suggested) or because certain regimes are driven by nonsecurity motives such as an expansionist ideology. Rather, states strive to increase their power even if their only goal is to preserve their independence, because the stronger a state is, the more likely it is to survive the vicissitudes of international life.

These incentives do not imply that the great powers are constantly at war, however. Rather, offensive realism sees great powers as opportunistic aggressors; it implies that states look for opportunities to increase their power at acceptable cost and risk (Mearsheimer 1994–95; 2001; Labs 1997; Zakaria 1998). Indeed, the system encourages states to be *prudent* expansionists; because all great powers are in competition with each other, they must try to gain more power only when circumstances are favorable.

Given this conception of the international environment and its consequences, offensive realism predicts that security competition (and the danger of war) will be greatest in multipolar systems, because states will be more inclined to pass the buck and efforts to expand are less likely to face rapid and effective opposition.[16] Opportunities for expansion will also increase when power is unevenly distributed among the major powers, because this allows the strongest state(s) to gain more power at the expense of the weaker states. Thus, security competition will be most intense when the system is multipolar and the distribution of power is heavily skewed. Indeed, when a major power becomes strong enough to make a plausible bid for regional hegemony—as Napoleonic France, Wilhelmine and Nazi Germany, and Imperial Japan did—offensive realism predicts the outbreak of a hegemonic war.[17] Although each of these attempts ultimately failed, supporters of the theory argue that each of these aggressors had a plausible "theory of victory" and came close to success. Unlike their defensive counterparts, therefore, offensive realists do not need to invoke domestic variables in order to explain even highly expansionist behavior (Copeland 1996a, 2000a; Mearsheimer 2001).

Although advocates of offensive realism have also marshaled considerable historical evidence to support their case, it is hardly immune from criticism. First, the claim that states will try to increase their power whenever circumstances are favorable is difficult to falsify; if competition is intense and great powers are actively seeking to expand, then offensive realists will see this as supporting the theory. But if competition is mild, then they are likely to argue that conditions for expansion were not attractive. The theory is not tautological, but a proper test requires an independent measure of the costs and risks of expansion.[18]

Second, as its advocates admit, the theory faces a number of historical anomalies, including Germany's failure to launch a hegemonic war in 1905 or the U.S. failure to exploit its economic superiority and nuclear monopoly during the early cold war.[19] More generally, offensive realism has

16. Multipolarity also increases the risk of entrapment whereby states are dragged into a war by the fear that their allies will be defeated or will defect if they do not come to their aid (Snyder 1984; Christensen and Snyder 1990).

17. According to Dale Copeland (1996a, 2000a), whose work combines elements of both offensive and defensive realism, such a conflict is especially likely when the leading state is strong enough to make a plausible bid for hegemony and also believes that its relative power will decline sharply in the future. Copeland also argues that preventive wars are more likely in bipolar systems, at least under certain conditions.

18. For a preliminary attempt to provide such a test, see Mearsheimer 2001, ch. 9.

19. Russia's defeat in the Russo-Japanese war gave Germany a window of opportunity, but Germany's leaders chose not to exploit it. Similarly, although U.S. policymakers debated the possibility of preventive war during the early cold war, they ultimately declined to use the U.S. nuclear advantage to deny the Soviets an analogous capability or to extract other concessions (Trachtenberg 1991, ch. 3).

trouble explaining why the leading power would ever permit another state to catch up (at the very least, it should work very hard to prevent it). Proponents of the theory tend to portray the international system as a realm where intense competition is endemic, but great powers sometimes try to moderate the level of competition and may succeed in doing so temporarily (Trachtenberg 2001; Schroeder 1994b). In general, in fact, offensive realism understates the risks of relentless competition and underestimates the possibility that states could increase their security by agreeing (either formally or tacitly) not to compete in certain ways. Although offensive realism allows for such arrangements so long as they leave the balance of power unchanged, the theory cannot account for such behavior and suggests it will be quite rare.

Despite these limitations, offensive realism offers a powerful systemic account of key aspects of international behavior, including the sensitivity of states to relative position or the widespread tendency for war aims to escalate. It also avoids defensive realism's ambiguity on whether expansion is desirable and its reliance on contested concepts like the offense-defense balance.

Reconciling Offensive and Defensive Realism?

Offensive and defensive realism are rival theories within the same broad family. They emphasize different assumptions, employ different causal logics and reach different conclusions. Offensive realism assumes states cannot discern intentions with any confidence (thereby encouraging worst-case planning); defensive realism suggests that they can (and do) under a fairly wide range of conditions (Brooks 1997). Offensive realism argues that the system forces all states to compete for power; defensive realism believes these structural imperatives are much weaker and traces aggressive behavior to various domestic pathologies operating within an anarchic setting. Thus, offensive realism is more pessimistic about the prospects for moderating international competition, while defensive realism believes that proper strategic policies can reduce (though not eliminate) the insecurity inherent in anarchy.

Despite these clear differences, the gap between these two strands of realist theory may not be as large as it first appears. Defensive realists recognize that states can sometimes increase their security by expanding, and they invoke unit-level variables only to explain exaggerated security fears or consistently self-defeating aggression. Similarly, offensive realists admit that *excessive* expansion can leave a state worse off. Both defensive and offensive realists recognize that the efficiency of balancing behavior can vary, and agree that inefficient balancing can make opportunistic aggression more attractive. Offensive realists reject the concept of an offense-defense balance, but John Mearsheimer (who has produced the most careful and detailed explication of offensive realism to date) uses a key element of this concept—geography—to explain why no state can aspire to global hegemony.[20] These similarities reveal that there is more overlap between the two strands of thought than either group has recognized.

Indeed, the differences between offensive and defensive realists may depend less on conceptual disagreements than on differing assessments of empirical conditions, which in turn shape the interpretation of specific historical cases. As already noted, defensive realists generally believe that balancing tendencies, defensive military advantages, and the power of nationalist resistance combine to make conquest difficult and generally unprofitable. As a result, they see Germany's decision for war in 1914 or Japan's policy of expansion in the 1930s as a departure from realist behavior that must be explained in some other way (Snyder 1991; Van Evera 1999; Kydd 1997a). By contrast, advocates of offensive realism believe that conquest is often profitable and argue that military and diplomatic conditions before World Wars I and II facilitated the German and Japanese attempts to establish regional hegemony. Thus, the question of which theory is more accurate depends not on the deductive rigor of the two alternatives but on which theory best fits the historical record.

Neoclassical Realist Theory

Some critics of neorealism have suggested that Waltz's quest for parsimony and scientific rigor sacrificed the practical wisdom found in the work of Thucydides, E. H. Carr, and Hans J. Morgenthau (Ashley 1984). In this spirit, a number of scholars have proposed a new synthesis that some commentators have termed neoclassical realism (Rose 1998). Like other realist theories, the neoclassical variant sees the system as anarchic, emphasizes the importance of relative power, and highlights the importance of security in the face of rival centers of power. But where Waltz insisted that his theory was not a theory of foreign policy, the neoclassical strand of realist theory pays less attention to explaining the properties of the system as a whole and focuses primarily on explaining specific foreign policy decisions.

As Rose (1998) has noted, neoclassical realists believe "there is no immediate or perfect transmission belt linking material capabilities to foreign policy behavior." Neoclassical realists acknowledge the role of relative power, but they believe that power is impossible to measure precisely and frequently misunderstood. Accordingly, any attempt to analyze foreign policy must also consider how power was perceived by the decision makers.

20. Mearsheimer stresses the difficulty of projecting power over large bodies of water. This constraint—which is a form of defensive advantage—explains why states can establish hegemony within a region (as the United States has done in the Western hemisphere) but not over the entire world. In theory, technological developments might eventually overcome the "stopping power of water" and permit one state to establish global hegemony. Defensive realists would regard this as a shift in the offense-defense balance (Mearsheimer 2001, ch. 4).

As the "neoclassical" label implies, this perspective is in some ways a return to the earlier views of Thucydides, Machiavelli, Carr, and Morgenthau, where anarchy is a permissive condition rather than an independent causal force. Because there is no overarching authority to control what states do, unit-level forces within states can affect the choices they make. Power is the underlying variable in the neoclassical version of realist theory, but the causal logic of the theory places domestic politics as an intervening variable between the distribution of power and foreign policy behavior. At the same time, neoclassical realists also believe there are clear limits to these domestic effects. Over time, shifts in the balance of power will constrain state behavior, and leaders or regimes whose strategic vision is clouded will pay a price for their lack of clear sight.

Thus, neoclassical realism seeks to combine the main elements of structural theory with an empirically grounded sensitivity to the calculations that real-world decision makers face. This perspective has produced a number of important historical analyses that combine a concern for shifting balances of power with particular attention to the ways that national leaders interpreted and reacted to it. Thus, Randall Schweller (1998) has offered a novel explanation for World War II, arguing that a tripolar distribution of power facilitated Hitler's revisionist aims, and Fareed Zakaria (1998) argues that the U.S. rise to world power was delayed (though not prevented) by the absence of a strong state apparatus. William Wohlforth (1993) suggests that disagreements about the true balance of power shaped U.S. and U.S.S.R. conduct throughout the cold war, and Thomas J. Christensen (1996) argues that Sino-U.S. hostility in the early cold war was rooted in anarchy but exacerbated by each side's efforts to mobilize domestic support. Similarly, Daniel Byman and Kenneth Pollack (2001) have recently called for renewed attention to the ambitions and personalities of particular leaders in order to explain why certain states chose highly aggressive foreign policies.

Because neoclassical realism eschews a monocausal focus on either domestic or systemic variables, it is especially well suited to the construction of historical narratives.[21] Unfortunately, this open-minded eclecticism is also its chief limitation. Neoclassical realism tends to incorporate domestic variables in an ad hoc manner, and its proponents have yet to identify when these variables will exert greater or lesser effects. Furthermore, neoclassical realism relies almost entirely on theoretical arguments developed by others and has yet to offer a distinct set of explanatory hypotheses of its own. Thus, where neorealism sacrificed precision in order to gain parsimony and generality, neoclassical realism has given up generality and predictive power in an attempt to gain descriptive accuracy and policy relevance.

21. Several neoclassical works have been criticized on purely historical grounds; see Lynn-Jones 1998.

■ | ## The Vitality of Contemporary Realist Theory

In addition to various efforts to refine or restate the core premises of realist theory, much of the recent work in the realist tradition seeks to explain particular empirical puzzles and to engage in critical debate with alternative approaches. Some of these efforts have also led to important theoretical refinements, and these works reaffirm the continued vitality of realist thought.

ALLIANCE THEORY

Given the central role that alliances play in the operation of a balance of power system (Morgenthau 1959), it is not surprising that recent realist research has devoted considerable attention to exploring the dynamics by which alliances are formed and their effects on subsequent state behavior. Building on Waltz's claim that great powers tended to balance against the strongest state or coalition rather than "bandwagon" with it, subsequent research argued that states were in fact more likely to balance against *threats* (Walt 1987, 1988). Threats were conceived as a function of power, geographic proximity, offensive capabilities, and perceived intentions, and this revision helped explain a number of empirical anomalies in Waltz's theory.[22] This line of research also explained why especially weak or isolated states might be somewhat more inclined to "bandwagon" than the major powers were. Balance of threat theory has been challenged by several critics (Kaufman 1992; Labs 1992; Brand 1994; Barnett and Levy 1991; Vasquez 1997), but it also received support from a number of empirical studies (Garnham 1991; Priess 1996; Mastanduno 1999; Walt 1992).

Perhaps the most ambitious extension of realist theory in the realm of alliances is Glenn Snyder's *Alliance Politics* (1997), which adds a series of systemic variables to Waltz's structural theory in order to explain different patterns of alliance behavior.[23] The resulting theory is not as parsimonious as Waltz's, but what is gained is a more detailed set of predictions than a purely structural theory can provide. Other research on alliances has ex-

22. For instance, balance of threat theory explained the relative lack of balancing against the United States both during and after the cold war, and the size of the coalition that defeated Iraq during the 1991 Gulf War (Walt 1987; Garnham 1991).

23. Specifically, Snyder adds relationships (patterns of alignment, interest, capability and interdependence), interactions (the processes by which relationships are translated into outcomes), and structural modifiers (military technology and institutions) to define a variety of international systems whose dynamics he then deduces. In essence, Snyder takes variables Waltz consigned to the unit-level and restores them to the systemic level, arguing that they are qualities of the system as a whole rather than merely properties of the units. His work is clearly realist in orientation, as revealed by his statement that "strategic interests are largely derived from the structure of the international system and the alignments that form within it" (1998, 23).

plored the relative importance of internal versus external threats (David 1991), the tendency for revisionist states to prefer "bandwagoning" to balancing (Schweller 1994), the twin dangers of abandonment and entrapment (G. Snyder 1984), the impact of perceptions and military technology on alliance cohesion (Christensen and Snyder 1990; Christensen 1997), the stability of different alliance patterns (Mueller 1995), and the future of contemporary alliance commitments (Mearsheimer 1990; Layne 1993; Hellman and Wolf 1993; Walt 1997b, 1998, 1998–99).

REALIST THEORIES OF INTERNATIONAL POLITICAL ECONOMY

Realist theory has also made major contributions to the study of international political economy. In general, realist scholarship in this area emphasizes the central role that power plays in shaping the calculations of states, and it highlights how the possibility of conflict and war can shape state behavior in a variety of nonmilitary realms (Kirshner 1999). As a result, recent realist scholarship has provided a useful counterpoint to theories that neglect or bracket these elements.

An obvious contribution was Joseph Grieco's seminal work on relative gains and international cooperation (Grieco 1988, 1990; Gowa 1986). Responding to the liberal argument that international institutions could enhance the prospects for cooperation by providing information and reducing the risk of cheating, Grieco showed that institutionalist theory had overlooked the central role of power. In particular, liberal institutionalism had underestimated the obstacles to cooperation by ignoring the issue of how the gains were distributed. Because the fear of war and the desire for national autonomy makes states sensitive to the balance of power, they will be wary of cooperative arrangements that might leave others significantly better off over time. The point was not that cooperation was impossible (especially when security concerns were low), only that institutionalist theory had portrayed it as easier than it really was.

Grieco's work launched a vigorous debate, and a careful reading shows that most of his critics ultimately confirmed or conceded his basic point.[24] As the leading institutionalist, Robert Keohane, later acknowledged, Grieco "made a significant contribution by focusing attention on the issue

---

24. For example, Duncan Snidal used a formal model to show that the importance of relative gains declined as the number of powers increased, but his results depend on the assumption of equal returns to scale from any act of cooperation. As he notes, "unequal gains diminish the incentives of one side to cooperate . . . for both absolute and relative gains reasons." In this model, in short, relative gains do not impede cooperation because there were by definition no gaps in gains. Snidal justified this assumption by saying that any gaps that did arise could be corrected through side payments, but this point (which was also noted by Grieco) essentially means that states can cooperate if they can cooperate in dividing up the gains. Compare Snidal 1991, 717, n. 29; and Grieco 1990, 233–34.

of relative gains, a subject that had been underemphasized, especially by liberal or neo-liberal commentators on the world economy" (1993, 283).[25] Having conceded the theoretical issue at hand, the central question is largely empirical: how often (and how extensively) has a concern for relative gains led states to forgo mutually beneficial agreements?[26] Although the realist position received additional support from several empirical studies (Krasner 1991; Mastanduno 1991; Matthews 1996; Nayar 1995), these efforts should not be regarded as definitive.[27]

Scholars working within the realist tradition have offered a host of other studies within the subfield of political economy. In *Allies, Adversaries, and International Trade* (1994), Joanne Gowa shows how the bipolar distribution of power during the cold war encouraged the expansion of economic interdependence among the OECD states (see also Mastanduno 1999, 1991). Institutions and values played important supporting roles but were less important than the shared objective of opposing the Soviet Union. More recently, Lloyd Gruber's *Ruling the World: Power Politics and the Rise of Supranational Institutions* (1999) showed how powerful states can force weaker powers to accept second-best outcomes by threatening to "go it alone." Gruber's analysis (which was backed by an exemplary set of case studies) thus challenged the widespread belief that

---

Similarly, Robert Powell (1991) has constructed a formal model showing that relative gains do not impede cooperation when the costs of warfare discourage the use of force. This result is consistent with Grieco's claim that cooperation was easier when a state's sensitivity to relative gains was low (i.e., because it was relatively secure). Because Powell assumes states have identical preferences, his formulation is more consistent with realist theory than Grieco's. But the underlying principle — that the fear of war makes states sensitive to relative gains and discourages cooperation — is identical.

25. Keohane qualified this concession by arguing that Snidal's and Powell's work had significantly diluted the force of Grieco's critique. But as discussed in the previous footnote, Powell's and Snidal's analyses are consistent with Grieco's central theoretical claim.

26. As Jervis (1999) notes: "the greatest deficiency in the absolute/relative gains literature is that it has remained largely at the level of theory and prescription, with much less attention paid to when decision makers *do* in fact exhibit relative gains concerns" (47, n. 14; see also Liberman 1996b).

27. Efforts to test competing liberal and realist theories of cooperation face serious methodological and interpretive hurdles. Liberal theorists can point to cooperation among the OECD countries as evidence that institutions have facilitated mutually beneficial arrangements; realists respond by noting that the conditions they regard as conducive to cooperation were also present. More generally, both liberal and realist theories identify obstacles to cooperation and recognize that states will sometimes fail to make mutually beneficial deals, but realists believe that the obstacles are larger and that the number and scope of actual agreements will be smaller. But as Kirshner notes, "distinguishing between these subsets in practice is extremely difficult, to the point that it raises serious questions regarding the tractability of such endeavors" (1999, 83; see also Downs, Rocke, and Barsoom 1996).

international institutions are inherently fair and Pareto improved and corrected the tendency for scholars of political economy to downplay or disregard the central role of power.

Realist theory has also returned to the familiar question of economic interdependence. These works include efforts to explain the limited effectiveness of economic sanctions (Pape 1997), as well as several related studies showing how expectations about the future affect the relationship between economic interdependence and international conflict. Although the specific variables in these models are different, the underlying logic of these works is quite similar. Specifically, both the potential impact of economic sanctions and the pacifying effects of international interdependence depend on each side's expectations about the future benefits of continued economic interchange. Sanctions exert the greatest coercive impact when they threaten a valuable long-term relationship, precisely because they threaten an anticipated stream of long-term benefits. By contrast, threatening or imposing sanctions has little effect when the relationship is modest or believed to be evanescent (Drezner 1999–2000, 1999, 1997). By a similar logic, the expectation that if war is avoided, high levels of trade will continue increases the expected costs of conflict and thus provides an additional incentive to remain at peace. If states fear that trade may be disrupted (whether by war or by some other cause), however, then interdependence is a source of vulnerability and states are more likely to use force to gain control of the resources they need (Copeland 1996b, 1999–2000; Liberman 1999–2000). In both theories, in short, expectations of the future drive present-day policy decisions.

Scholarship in the realist tradition continues to remind us that international economic relations shape, but are also shaped by, the political structure of international relations. From this perspective, the growth of international trade, communications, and currency transactions (often lumped under the heading of globalization) has been underwritten by U.S. military power and backed by an extensive array of alliance commitments and regulatory arrangements (Gilpin 1976; Waltz 2000b; Kapstein 1994).[28] The realist perspective also provides a different account of the spread of neoliberal practices in Latin America, eastern Europe, and elsewhere. Instead of seeing this process simply as the triumph of economic efficiency over elite rent seeking, a realist account would also emphasize the desire to emulate U.S. practices in the wake of its cold war victory and the use of U.S. power to encourage these decisions (Sterling-Folker 1997; Wade 1992).

28. As Joseph Nye (1995, 90–91) has commented, "It has become fashionable to say that the world after the Cold War has moved beyond the age of power politics to the age of geoeconomics. Such cliches reflect narrow analysis. Politics and economics are connected. International economic systems rest upon international political order." Nye's views are especially interesting insofar as his scholarly work is liberal in orientation and frequently critical of realist theories.

New Insights on New Issues

One sign of the continued fertility of realist theory has been its ability to illuminate new topics that were not addressed in earlier realist scholarship. Shortly after *Theory of International Politics* was published, for example, Barry Posen (1984) used a combination of realist theory and organization theory in a prizewinning account of the sources of military doctrine. Scholars working in the realist tradition have also developed theories to explain important elements of domestic politics. For example, Avery Goldstein (1991) used Waltz's neorealist theory to explain coalition formation in the Chinese Communist Party, and Michael Desch (1996, 1999) argued that more dangerous international environments led to the formation of stronger state bureaucracies and more tranquil civil-military relations. Other scholars have developed realist theories explaining the relationship between revolution and war (Walt 1996; Conge 1996), and the spread of military innovation (Posen 1993a; Resende-Santos 1996; Goldman and Andres 1999).

Realist theory has also made a central contribution to the burgeoning literature on ethnic conflict. In particular, Barry Posen's seminal article "The Security Dilemma and Ethnic Conflict" (1993b) showed that key elements of realist theory could explain why certain multiethnic societies were especially prone to conflict in the event that the central government collapsed. Posen's basic insight has been echoed by a number of subsequent writers (Lake and Rothchild 1996; Fearon 1998b; Rose 2000), and expanded or modified in several other works (Kaufmann 1996, 1998). Although these works vary in a number of respects, each takes as its starting point the idea that the collapse of central authority within a state can place different ethnic groups in a "state of nature" analogous to the anarchic international system. These conditions do not make ethnic war inevitable (for the same reasons that states are not always engaged in war), but they do make it more likely. When violence does break out, moreover, efforts to end the fighting are likely to fail in the absence of external guarantees that can ameliorate the insecurity the contending parties are likely to face (Walter 1997).

Realist Theory and International History

Realist theory has also informed a number of important interpretations of past historic events. Markus Fischer (1992) has argued that relations among the heterogeneous political units of feudal Europe exhibited the competitive dynamics that realist theory predicts (i.e., alliances, security competition, war, etc.) despite the ideology of Christian universalism that infused the period. Fischer's work thus challenged the constructivist claim that a transformation in norms, identities, or the structure of property rights can overcome the competitive tendencies of an anarchic political order. It also suggested that realist theory could be fruitfully applied to the premodern era (see also Hall and Kratochwil 1993; Fischer 1993).

Scholars working in the realist tradition have offered powerful new interpretations of the Concert of Europe. The Concert is often invoked as a case that shows how shared identities and institutionalized norms can dampen the level of great power competition (Schroeder 1994b), but Korina Kagan (1997–98) and Matthew Rendell (2000), in separate treatments, present a powerful challenge to this view. Although there was no great power war between 1815 and 1850, Kagan and Rendell argue that shared identities and common norms did little to encourage restrained behavior. Instead, as Kagan observes, "the great powers played the game very hard indeed, and not according to Concert rules. Rather than mutual consideration, mutual mistrust and exploitation were the name of the game. The chief source of restraint was countervailing force" (1997–98, p. 54). By showing that realist theory can account for an episode long regarded as a paradigmatic case of great power cooperation, these analyses both reaffirm the value of the realist tradition and cast doubt on several prominent alternatives.

Realist theory has also shaped a number of recent studies of the cold war. In separate works, historians Melvyn Leffler (1992) and Marc Trachtenberg (1999) showed how security considerations—and especially a concern for relative power—drove U.S. (and European) calculations during the early years of the cold war. Similarly, Mark Sheetz's study of NATO's early history presents a striking confirmation of realist logic and a challenge to the claim that international institutions can help states overcome significant security fears. Although the United States repeatedly tried to create arrangements (such as the European Defense Community) that would enable it to withdraw its troops, these efforts failed because "regimes and institutions were not able to overcome the logic of anarchy or ameliorate the security dilemma in the absence of American power" (1999, 6–7). Realist theory receives further support in recent studies of U.S. policy toward the former Soviet bloc, which demonstrate that the United States was far more offensively minded than previously believed (Mitrovich 2000; Grose 2000).

Finally, several recent works suggest that the realist tradition may tell us more about the end of the cold war than any of its theoretical rivals. In particular, the work of William Wohlforth and his collaborators (Wohlforth 1994–95; Schweller and Wohlforth 2000; Brooks and Wohlforth 2000–01) shows that the cold war ended because Soviet power was eroding rapidly and because Soviet leaders saw few alternatives to capitulation.[29] Far from disconfirming realist theory, in fact, the end of the cold war is consistent with its emphasis on material power and its view of the international sys-

---

29. For a series of Soviet statements acknowledging that they could no longer afford to compete with the West, see Brooks and Wohlforth, 2000–01, 46–47.

tem as inherently competitive. Among other things, the United States did not respond to the Soviet Union's repeated concessions by reducing the pressure or offering compensating concessions in return. Instead, as realist theory predicts, the United States steadily increased its demands as the Soviet Union's position grew weaker, and proceeded to exploit its victory when the Soviet Union finally collapsed.[30]

These examples demonstrate that realist theory continues to illuminate important historical events and processes. It is hardly the only way to think about the past (even for those who are solely interested in foreign policy), and some international developments are inconsistent with realist premises and require an alternative perspective (for an important example, see Kaufmann and Pape 1999). Yet the studies discussed in this section remind us that abandoning the realist tradition would deprive us of a powerful tool for grasping much of international history, thereby impoverishing the interpretation of the past and distorting our understanding of the present.

THE POST–COLD WAR WORLD

The realist tradition has long been concerned with contemporary events, and a number of scholars have used realist theory to analyze contemporary world politics and to forecast its future course. Although most of these writers reject the optimism that characterized the immediate aftermath of the cold war, their predictions have been quite diverse. According to John Mearsheimer, the lack of a great power rival is eroding the U.S. commitment to Europe and will eventually rekindle security competition within Europe itself (Mearsheimer 1990, 2001). Other writers agree that NATO is likely to erode now that there is no external threat to hold it together (Walt 1997b, 1998–99), but some believe that the separate European states are more likely to draw together in order to balance the United States (Waltz 2000a). In separate treatments, Waltz and Christopher Layne predicted that a combination of "imperial overstretch" and external balancing would undermine the preeminent position of the United States and hasten a return to multipolarity (Waltz 1993; Layne 1993). This view has been countered by William Wohlforth (1990), who argues that U.S. preponderance is now so large as to deter a hegemonic challenge or even a serious effort to balance it (see also Joffe 1995). Wohlforth's article is an important theoretical advance, insofar as it applies Waltz's structural approach to a new configuration of power (unipolarity) and suggests that bandwagoning rather than balancing is the expected behavior in such a realm. Aaron Friedberg and Denny Roy have used realist theory to predict emerging se-

---

30. When Mikhail Gorbachev complained that "U.S. policy is one of extorting more and more concessions," U.S. secretary of state George Shultz replied, "I'm weeping for you" (quoted in Wohlforth 1994–95, 121).

curity competition in Asia (Friedberg 1993–94; Roy 1994), and several other scholars have used realist arguments to explain why Japan may be abandoning its antimilitarist political culture and shifting to a policy of "reluctant realism" (Twomey 2000). Michael Mastanduno has provided a similar appraisal for the United States, arguing that its foreign policies since 1991 are largely consistent with realist balance of threat theory (Mastanduno 1999).

These views share the common belief that much of contemporary world politics is still characterized by a concern for security and power. The precise forecasts differ, however, because different authors invoke different realist theories and employ different parameter values when analyzing contemporary events. Thus, Mearsheimer anticipates renewed competition in Europe because he believes that European integration will not overcome the durable power of nationalism and that the absence of a hegemonic rival in Europe has removed the need for U.S. protection and will soon produce a U.S. withdrawal. Waltz disagrees, largely because he thinks Europe is more likely to unify in opposition to U.S. dominance. Both anticipate renewed competition, but they disagree about the identity of the units that will be competing. Similarly, Wohlforth's optimism rests not only on a theoretical refinement of existing structural arguments but also on a careful assessment of global power trends. He recognizes the *potential* for renewed competition should the United States withdraw but believes that this is precisely why the United States should (and will) remain engaged (see also Art 1996a).[31]

CRITIQUES OF ALTERNATIVE APPROACHES

Just as E. H. Carr once offered a trenchant critique of earlier idealist approaches to international relations, contemporary scholars have used realist theory to challenge a number of alternative perspectives. These efforts include important critiques of institutionalist theory (Grieco 1990; Krasner 1991; Mearsheimer 1994–95; Schweller and Priess 1997; Waltz 2000a) and the recent wave of cultural approaches in security studies (Desch 1998). Not surprisingly, scholars working in the realist tradition have also challenged the so-called democratic peace hypothesis on a variety of grounds. In particular, realist critics have suggested that the absence of war between democratic states is a statistical artifact, valid only for the post-1945 period, or better explained by the distribution of power or some other

---

31. To an extent, this debate rests on different assessments of the effects of U.S. engagement on the overall probability that the United States would have to fight a major war. Disengagement might increase the overall danger of war but makes it less likely that the United States would be immediately involved. Engagement lowers the overall risk of war but makes U.S. involvement virtually certain if war does come.

factor (Spiro 1994; Layne 1994; Rousseau and Mueller 1995; Elman 1997; Farber and Gowa 1995; Gowa 1999).[32]

These various exchanges were often quite sharp, in part because some participants appeared to view the competition between rival approaches in purely zero-sum terms.[33] Reasonable people can differ in their assessments of these debates, but each of these critiques raised important questions about these different nonrealist approaches and forced advocates of these perspectives either to refine their theories, qualify their claims, or search for additional empirical support.[34] Just as criticisms of different realist theories have helped their proponents rethink and refine their positions, these realist critiques helped the field as a whole become more rigorous and sophisticated.

SUMMARY

This survey of recent realist scholarship suggests that it meets the two criteria for theoretical progress identified earlier. First, realist theory continues to shed useful light on a diverse array of important contemporary phenomena. It is not the only useful way to think about alliance relations, ethnic conflict, international cooperation, international political economy, security competition, and so on, but our understanding of these (and other) phenomena would surely be impoverished (if not grossly distorted) were the insights of the realist tradition neglected.

Second, realist theory remains theoretically fertile. The family of realist theories has become more diverse, and as the debate between offensive and defensive realism shows, debates within realism have clarified competing causal logics and identified key sources of disagreement. Realist theory has also moved into new subject areas and offered a host of new hypotheses on more familiar subjects. Realist theory has also answered the charge that it was better at identifying the sources of conflict than suggesting sol-

32. Donald P. Green, Soo Yeon Kim, and David H. Yoon have recently offered an important methodological critique of much of the democratic peace literature, see Green, Kim, and Yoon 2001 (and the various responses to them).

33. Thus, Theo Farrell (1999, 168) likened realism to a sinking ship, and Bruce Russett predicted that "the theoretical edifice of realism will collapse" if the democratic peace hypothesis is confirmed (1995, 164). More reasonably, Ze'ev Maoz pointed out that the democratic peace research program had also generated "considerable empirical support for nation- and dyadic-level propositions derived from realist perspectives" and suggested that "the realist and liberal perspectives on world politics may complement each other quite well" (1997, 193).

34. In a recent survey, Keohane and Martin (2002) acknowledge Mearsheimer's charge that institutions were largely epiphenomenal, and thus have little *independent* effect on state behavior. In particular, they admit that "institutional theory has not yet responded very well to this fundamental challenge." See also Maoz 1997, 192–93.

utions, and scholars working within this tradition have offered several practical remedies based on their theoretical insights.

These achievements also show that recent claims that realism is degenerating are mistaken (Vasquez 1997; Legro and Moravcsik 1999). This charge rests on the observation that different realists have advanced competing arguments on a variety of subjects and that some scholars have combined structural and unit-level arguments when analyzing particular international phenomena. With respect to the first point, condemning a research tradition because it contains competing hypotheses would require us to toss out virtually every body of theory in the social sciences (Walt 1997a, 932). More importantly, disagreements between different realist theories are an important source of theoretical progress, just as they are for other approaches to international relations. When different realist theories generate different predictions, therefore, it is more properly seen as a sign of theoretical vigor than evidence of degeneration.

Similarly, the fact that some scholars invoke unit-level variables in conjunction with realist theory is hardly persuasive evidence of degeneration, especially when realist theory helps explain why other unit-level variables are needed. In his version of defensive realism, for example, Jack Snyder (1991) uses domestic variables to explain *excessive* expansion (i.e., expansion where the costs exceed the benefits). Snyder explicitly acknowledges that states in anarchy can sometimes increase their security by expanding and that the constant concern for security empowers those who may have other reasons for advocating expansionist policies (1991, 8). Snyder uses domestic politics to explain deviations (i.e., *over*expansion) from this realist baseline. It is a theory of domestic politics, to be sure, but realist theory identifies both why a unit-level explanation is needed and why certain groups (e.g., the military) enjoy privileged positions within policymaking circles.[35] Finally, realist logic also explains why these states suffered from their failed attempts to expand (i.e., they were defeated by defensive coalitions brought into being by their expansionist behavior).

My own work on alliance formation emphasizes the role of power (and especially military power) in a manner consistent with realist logic. If the power of other states were not a major concern, national leaders would not bother to form alliances at all. States look for allies in order to balance the power of other states, and that search intensifies when other states appear to have malign intentions. Balance of threat theory also predicts that domestic variables (e.g., ideology) will have larger effects when structural

---

35. Both Snyder (1991) and Stephen Van Evera (1984) emphasize the role of military organizations in shaping foreign policy behavior, but a pure theory of domestic politics would have trouble explaining why states would create military organizations in the first place. By emphasizing the need for states to protect themselves in an anarchic setting, however, the realist tradition can account for this nearly universal tendency quite easily.

elements (i.e., the distribution of power, the ease of conquest, etc.) are muted or indeterminate. Thus, a state facing two neighbors of equal capability will look to domestic factors when gauging which is more dangerous, and a state that is objectively very secure will be more heavily influenced by its own domestic constraints and freer to indulge ideological or other preferences. To say that these arguments are not "realist" is peculiar, at the very least.[36]

Indeed, as Jennifer Sterling-Folker has argued, realist theories are especially well suited to the incorporation of unit-level variables in a causally consistent manner. At the most fundamental level, realist theories focus on the impact of the external environment on state behavior. *How* states try to respond to these environmental pressures will also be affected by domestic factors, however, and which level dominates is ultimately an empirical issue. In the real world, governments try to reconcile external *and* internal pressures, and there is no degeneration when scholars invoke both types of explanation (Sterling-Folker 1997).

The bottom line is that realist theory is alive and well. It remains relevant, rigorous, and theoretically fecund. Not every realist work survives the crucible of academic scrutiny (which is as it should be), but scholarship grounded in realist theory continues to provide important insights into key elements of world politics.

Like any theoretical tradition, of course, the realist family contains gaps, disagreements, and unresolved puzzles. Although one can never be sure how a theoretical enterprise will evolve in the future, the next section identifies several especially promising areas for future research.

■ | A Research Agenda for the Realist Tradition

CONCEIVING AND MEASURING POWER

The concept of power is central to realist theory, yet there is still little agreement on how it should be conceived and measured. We still lack a firm conceptual foundation on which to base valid measures of national power, although several recent works have made considerable progress on this problem (cf. Wohlforth 1993, 1999; Copeland 2000a; Mearsheimer 2001; Schweller 1998). Identifying appropriate criteria for measuring national power is especially difficult because the relevant components have undoubtedly changed over time. Population, GNP, military spending, and coal and steel production may have been valid indicators in the past, but

36. Other examples of scholars combining realist and nonrealist variables in a causally consistent manner include Posen 1984, Christensen and Snyder 1990, and Snyder 1998. Waltz also recognized that structural theories could be supplemented by theories of domestic politics (see Waltz 1986, 331).

what indicators can capture the declining role of smokestack industries or the growing importance of information technology (Brooks 1999; for a preliminary effort, see Tellis et al. 2000)?

More valid measures of power would aid efforts to test different predictions derived from realist theory and would also help resolve the debate between offensive and defensive realists on the profitability of conquest. Similarly, although defensive realists argue for greater attention to the "fine-grained structure of power" (and especially on the so-called offense-defense balance), they have yet to provide a simple and compelling way to measure it (for initial attempts, see Glaser and Kaufmann 1998; Van Evera 1999; Lynn-Jones 1995).

Finally, realist theory generally implies that power should be broadly (though not perfectly) fungible across issue areas. If this is the case, then we should observe great powers using their diverse capabilities (e.g., military power) to extract concessions in otherwise unrelated areas. Although there have been a few intriguing efforts along these lines (e.g., Spiro 1998; Art 1996b; Stein 1980), the topic of fungibility of power and the possibility of issue linkage remain underexplored by realists and nonrealists alike.

THE IMPACT OF INFORMATION

As offensive realists have recently clarified, the pessimism that pervades much of realist theory reflects the uncertainty that pervades most of international political life. States are insecure in part because there is no central authority to protect them from each other, because they do not know how the balance of power will evolve, and because they cannot be sure what other states are going to do.

It follows that realist theory ought to be interested in factors or developments that affect the quality of information available to states. Thus, recent research on revolutions suggested that these events increased the risk of war in part by reducing each side's ability to calculate the balance of power and to estimate the likelihood of revolutionary contagion (Walt 1996). And as noted earlier, several defensive realists have argued that states can signal benign intentions by making specific military policy decisions (i.e., adopting a defensive military posture), thereby reducing an opponent's uncertainty and leaving both sides more secure than before (Glaser 1994–95; Kydd 1997a, b). Similarly, the rationalist approach to international institutions argues that institutions facilitate cooperation by providing information to states, thereby reducing the fear that others will cheat (Keohane 1984).[37] Other scholars suggest that states can use past be-

---

37. Thus, the rationalist approach to institutions is a subset of the realist family rather than a distinct alternative. Its contribution to our understanding of world politics depends on whether the effects of institutions are large or small. As noted earlier (n. 27), however, measuring the independent impact of institutions is not easy.

havior or domestic characteristics to make probabilistic judgments about a state's future conduct (Fearon 1994a; Shultz 1999), although the reliability of these inferences remains contested (Mercer 1996; Copeland 1997; Huth 1997; Hopf 1994).

Testing Causal Mechanisms

Social science in the United States places a premium on theoretical novelty and undervalues careful empirical testing. This tendency is unfortunate, as it encourages faddishness and divorces scholars even further from the real world. Moreover, debates within the realist family and between supporters of realist theory and those of its various rivals should not be resolved by asking who can muster the flashiest abstract argument; rather, we should ask which explanation best fits the facts. Determining which theory (or approach) is most useful is an empirical question, and rendering such judgements usually requires careful historical evaluation of the specific causal mechanisms identified in each theory.

Thus, an important part of the research agenda should be an effort to conduct more systematic and fine-grained tests of key realist predictions. One obvious way to do this is to investigate whether the motivations of key decision makers are consistent with the expectations of different theories. It matters what states do, but it also matters *why* they do it.

To take an obvious example, offensive and defensive realism offer contrasting predictions about the goals of national leaders and the policies they are likely to favor. Offensive realists predict that leaders will be constantly concerned about the balance of power and actively searching for opportunities to improve their position. They should also be relatively disinterested in gauging other states' intentions and inclined to assume the worst because they cannot be sure that others are not (or will not become) malevolent. By the same logic, they will expend little effort signaling their own commitment to the status quo (save as an effort to hoodwink rivals). By contrast, defensive realists predict that great powers will often look for ways to stabilize the status quo and will devote considerable effort to distinguishing status quo and revisionist powers. An obvious way to test these competing theories, therefore, is to examine the conduct of great powers and especially the perceptions and motivations of key leaders. Earlier realist scholarship has made a start on some of these questions but can hardly be considered definitive.

Much the same prescription applies to the realm of political economy. Prior work has clarified the conceptual disputes between realist and nonrealist approaches to interdependence, cooperation, and institutions; what is needed now are more careful efforts to evaluate these claims empirically. One especially promising strategy is to compare competing predictions about the motivations of key actors, rather than simply counting the number of institutionalized agreements or trying to devise unbiased measures of cooperation. When states refrain from cooperating, for example, is it because they were worried that others would cheat or concerned that others might reap disproportionate gains? When states negotiate new cooperative arrangements, do the terms reveal a sensitivity to the distribution of gains or is the bulk of the effort focused on developing appropriate verification measures? If realist theory is correct to highlight the problem of relative gains, then we should be able to find clear cases where states refrained from pursuing mutually beneficial deals because one (or both) parties were worried about the effects of the arrangement on the long-term balance of power.[38] If scholars working in the realist tradition hope to bolster their critiques of various institutionalist arguments, showing that states have acted in a realist manner *and for realist reasons* would obviously strengthen their case.[39]

MAPPING THE POST–COLD WAR WORLD

As discussed earlier in this essay, a number of scholars have used realist theory to describe the current era of world politics and to predict its future course. Efforts to update these forecasts—and to identify why some predictions were not borne out—should be part of the future research agenda. Is Mearsheimer correct in anticipating a gradual U.S. retrenchment and the reemergence of great power security competition? If not, why not? Will other major powers combine to check the threat of U.S. preponderance—as Waltz has predicted—or is Wohlforth correct in predicting that the unipolar world of U.S. preponderance will prevent significant great power conflict for a generation or more? Will the rise of China trigger balancing behavior in Asia and an intensifying Sino-U.S. rivalry (as most realist theories would predict), or will economic interdependence, democratization, and expanded membership in international institutions integrate China into the society of nations and prevent another familiar cycle of great power competition?

Efforts to map contemporary world politics should also address the phenomenon of globalization. The rapid expansion of international trade, finance, and communications, along with the increased prominence of various nongovernmental organizations, have led some observers to foresee a new international order in which states are eventually supplanted by some new form of global governance (see Ohmae 1995; Mathews 1997; Reinicke 1998). At the very least, apostles of globalization believe that states will be increasingly bound by the impersonal power of the market-

38. The obvious example here is CoCom, which limited Western economic cooperation with the former Soviet bloc (Mastanduno 1992). For contrasting empirical assessments, see Matthews 1996 and Liberman 1996b.

39. For other predictions about the post–cold war international political economy, see Kirshner 1999.

place and will find their freedom of action constrained to a far greater extent (Friedman 1999; Strange 1996).

Realist theory casts a different light on these claims. First, the current situation is not unprecedented: although it does have certain novel features (such as the size of global currency transactions and the plummeting cost of communications), current levels of interdependence are roughly equal to the first decade of the twentieth century. The term *globalization* is also something of a misnomer, given that the phenomenon is largely confined to the advanced industrial countries of Europe, North America, and Asia and has had relatively little impact elsewhere.[40]

Second, realist theory suggests that the real question is not whether globalization will vanquish the state (which shows no signs of withering away anyway) but rather how it will affect the relative power of different states. Just as some countries raced ahead following the industrial revolution in the nineteenth century, some contemporary states will compete more effectively in global markets and exploit new information technologies more readily than others. Instead of creating a more homogeneous world, in short, globalization is more likely to exacerbate global inequalities and alter the hierarchy of power among states. The realist tradition also warns that such a trend could be dangerous, because large shifts in power usually foster insecurity, competition, and a heightened risk of war (Copeland 2000a; Gilpin 1981).

Finally, realist theory has long emphasized the interrelationship of politics and economics; close economic ties normally depend on stable political relations (Gilpin 1976, 2000; Buzan 1984). For the past fifty years, the United States has provided a political order that has nurtured the growth of world trade and made it possible to create novel institutions like the European Union. If that political stability were to evaporate, however, the globalization process could easily unravel. When considering the post–cold war order, in short, the realist tradition offers a valuable corrective to the belief that economics is trumping politics (Waltz 2000b).[41]

BUILDING A BETTER MICROFOUNDATION

The microfoundations of the realist tradition are not as firm as one might wish. The treatment of states as unitary rational actors is both widely accepted and problematic, and the claim that states (or leaders) place a premium on survival can be challenged as well. Thus, one obvious way to broaden and strengthen realist theory would be to develop more persuasive microfoundations for its generally gloomy expectations.

40. See Hirst and Thompson 1999, Waltz 2000b, and Gilpin 2000, 24–25.

41. Even an ardent globalizer like Thomas Friedman understands that the current order rests on a particular structure of political and military power. In his pithy phrase, "without America on duty, there will be no America Online" (1999, 376).

One possibility is evolutionary biology, as recently argued by Bradley Thayer (2000). According to Thayer, an evolutionary perspective can explain why humans establish hierarchies of dominance, are readily indoctrinated, and quickly draw distinctions between members of their own group and outsiders. He suggests that these insights can explain competition and war without invoking anarchy as an independent causal force. This line of inquiry is in its early stages and should be viewed with some skepticism, but it could provide a set of underlying assumptions that would buttress the realist worldview.

Jonathan Mercer (1995) proposes a different answer to the same problem, arguing that social identity theory explains the tendency for individual humans to form strong group loyalties, and thus to favor measures that will favor their own group over others. Although the jury is still out, these perspectives offer firmer grounds for the realist claim that states can be thought of as unitary, self-interested actors.

REALISM AND DOMESTIC POLITICS

The realist tradition has focused primarily on international politics, but it is in fact a broader approach to political life that is potentially relevant to other questions. Realist theory has made important contributions to the study of ethnic conflict *within* states, and some scholars have also made analogies to other quasi-anarchic realms (such as gang warfare in inner cities). In the future, scholars should look for other arenas that realist theory has tended to neglect.

One topic—arguably neglected since Thomas Hobbes—is the origins of the state system itself. Ashley Tellis (1995–96) points out that realist theory simply assumes the existence of states-as-actors without explaining why states arose in the first place. Although Tellis does not provide such a theory himself, his comments remind us that Hobbes and other early realists saw the creation of the state as a solution to the incessant warfare that confronted individuals in the (anarchic) state of nature. A realist approach to state formation would emphasize the imposition of sovereign authority in order to mobilize power and create security for ruler and ruled alike, as opposed to approaches that regard the state as a voluntary contract between sovereign and subject or between free and equal citizens. Similarly, Michael Desch's recent work on the international sources of domestic cohesion and civil-military cooperation suggests that external constraints may play a larger role in domestic politics than previously recognized (Desch 1996, 1999).

FOREIGN POLICY

Realist theory can also be used to develop more sophisticated theories of foreign policy. Although Waltz maintains that neorealism is a theory of international politics rather than a theory of foreign policy (cf. Elman 1996c; Waltz 1996), few scholars seem to have been persuaded by this argument (Fearon 1998c; Mearsheimer 2001). If the insecurity of anarchy constrains the states in the system, then surely it affects some of their subsequent behavior. There seems to be little reason for realist theory to confine itself to explaining the systemic properties of particular orders, and most scholars working in the realist tradition (including Waltz) have used their theoretical understanding to make foreign policy recommendations (e.g., Walt 1989; Layne 1997; Art 1998–99).

International Law

A final possibility is international law. Until recently, scholarship linking international relations and international law has generally been dominated by liberal or constructivist approaches. This tendency is unsurprising, given that realist theory tends to downplay the role of norms and rules while these rival traditions place a high premium on them. But there is still a place for a realist approach to this subject, highlighting the dominant role of major powers, their ability to evade legal constraints when they feel it is necessary, and the tendency for customary law to reflect the interests of states rather than any exogenous set of normative standards.[42]

■ | Conclusion

International relations is an eclectic and contentious discipline. As I have argued elsewhere, its intellectual and methodological diversity is a desirable quality, because global political processes are unlikely to be captured by a single intellectual or methodological approach (Walt 1998, 1999). Moreover, the coexistence of different research traditions encourages a fruitful competition between them, forcing each approach to confront anomalies, refine its explanatory logic, and conduct more robust empirical tests.

Unfortunately, the clash of competing ideas can also lead to intolerance and intellectual imperialism.[43] Given the many contributions that

42. For initial attempts along the lines suggested here, see Goldsmith and Posner 1999, 2000 and Alvarez 2001.

43. It is tempting to apply realist theory to the academic world, which can be viewed as a quasi-anarchic realm in which scholars compete for power, prestige, and other scarce resources (e.g., grants, awards, positions for their students, etc.). As in international politics, scholars often form alliances to advance these interests and may try to increase their own power by attacking other approaches. Thus the structure of academic politics explains why scholars who reject the substantive conclusions of realist theory often behave in a remarkably realist fashion.

the realist tradition has made (and continues to make) to our understanding of world politics, it is still striking to observe the hostility it provokes. As Robert Gilpin gloomily observed a few years ago, "nobody loves a political realist," and especially not in the liberal United States (Gilpin 1996; Shimko 1992; Jervis 1998). This hostility is evident in the harsh rhetoric that critics of realist theory sometimes employ, as well as the speed with which they declared a venerable research tradition dead in the immediate aftermath of the cold war.[44]

More recent events confirm that realism remains strikingly relevant. The United States and its allies have fought three wars in the past ten years, at least one of them (the 1990–91 Persian Gulf War) motivated by balance of power considerations. Bill Clinton may have claimed that the "cynical calculus of power politics" was obsolete, but his policies as president demonstrated an abiding appreciation for the realities of power. Clinton soon discovered that invoking the United Nations was not a viable substitute for a foreign policy, engaged in humanitarian intervention and peacekeeping operations with great reluctance, and promoted narrow U.S. interests in bilateral trade negotiations. The United States took advantage of Russia's weakness to expand NATO up to the Russian border, pressured the post-Soviet republics into giving up their nuclear arsenals, and reaffirmed its security ties in Asia in preparation for a future competition with China. Clinton also showed an ample willingness to use force (against Iraq, Sudan, Afghanistan, and Serbia) even in the absence of authorization from the U.N. Security Council. The United States also rejected a global ban on land mines and the creation of an international criminal court, for fear that these agreements would place unacceptable constraints on U.S. freedom of action.

The new administration of George W. Bush shows no sign of reversing these tendencies, and key Bush advisers have openly proclaimed their commitment to realist principles. Bush's decision to abandon the 1972 Anti-Ballistic Missile Treaty illustrates the tendency for great powers to seek superiority over future rivals, and the forceful U.S. response to the terrorist attacks of September 11, 2001, reminds us that great powers pay scant attention to diplomatic niceties when their own security is threatened.[45] Realist theory tells us that powerful states are likely to act in this way (especially when they face few immediate constraints), and it also cor-

---

44. Manifestations of intolerance include John Vasquez's explicit attempt to discourage continued funding for realist research (1997, 899), Bahman Fozouni's suggestion that scholars examine "why for the past several decades the discipline of international politics remained mesmerized by a false theory" (1995, 508), and Stanley Hoffmann's declaration that "realism is utter nonsense today" (Friedman 1993). See also Farrell 1999 and Ashley 1984.

45. Among other things, U.S. leaders have minimized allied participation in order to keep a free hand to wage war as they wished, declared that the United States does not need authorization from the United Nations in order to use force, and used a combination of threats and bribes to gain support from countries such as Pakistan.

rectly predicts that other states (including some close U.S. allies) will be alarmed by U.S. unilateralism and become eager to find ways to limit it.

No matter where one looks, in fact, one sees additional signs of realism's enduring relevance. In Africa, anarchy and insecurity combine to trigger reciprocal massacres in Rwanda and Burundi. In the Middle East, the peace process between Israel and the Palestinians founders over each side's unwillingness to accommodate the other's security concerns.[46] In South Asia, India and Pakistan acquire nuclear weapons, partly due to fear of China (in India's case) and partly out of fear of each other. Japan is shedding its pacifist veneer, and already maintains a borderline nuclear capability as a hedge against the removal of the U.S. security umbrella (Green 2001; Mack 1997; Harrison 1996). Even in Europe, where the construction of a "pluralist security community" is most advanced, influential elites warn of a "renationalization" of foreign policy should the United States withdraw (Art 1996a; Bertram 1995). Thus, in an era where some commentators believe power politics is irrelevant, the United States continues to keep roughly 200,000 troops in Europe and Asia, largely to prevent the outbreak of renewed security competition there.

These developments suggest that efforts to excommunicate realist theory are doomed to fail. Barring a fundamental transformation in the basic nature of world politics, the realist *problematique* will continue to influence the behavior of states. Major powers will continue to compete, the shadow of organized violence will continue to loom large in their calculations, and competition between and within states will sometimes spill over into open warfare. Although efforts to promote cooperation through the development of shared norms and institutions will be made and will sometimes succeed, these efforts are unlikely to overcome the fundamental problems identified by the realist perspective. As a result, students and scholars will always be drawn back to the realist tradition, if only to understand the full nature of the challenge that humankind faces.

Realist theory is far from perfect, of course, and this inventory of recent accomplishments cannot obscure its limitations. Many realist theories are not as precise as one would like, the realist family does not address a number of important topics (such as the growing global commitment to human rights), and it cannot account for many aspects of international change. The core concept of power is not well conceptualized, key hypotheses are untested, and variations within the realist family have proliferated faster than they have been resolved. Given these problems, it would be fair to conclude that the realist tradition is the *worst* approach to the study of world politics—except for all the others.

---

46. From a realist perspective, the central problem between Israel and the Palestinians is simple. A viable Palestinian state could be a potential long-term threat to Israel's security; this means that an agreement that would be acceptable to the Palestinians is hard for Israel to accept, and vice versa.

2 |

Democracy, Justice, and Their Institutions

Utilizing thin criteria, the *World Bank Development Report* for 1997 reported that "[i]n 1974 only thirty-nine countries—one in every four worldwide—were independent democracies. Today, 117 countries—nearly two of every three—use open elections to choose their leaders." Concern about the scope and nature of democracy, especially about its relationship with liberalism, and about its stability have been central to political science, especially American political science, since its inception. The essays in this part that consider these issues confront enduring problems of democracy, justice, and heterogeneity and delve into the institutional components of democracy, ranging from legislatures to the organization of civil society.

Ian Shapiro discusses "The State of Democratic Theory." He begins with an examination of the main contending views of democratic purposes, those which involve the search for a common good and those which attend to the legitimate management of power relations. He argues that the latter understanding of the enterprise makes better sense but that it is compatible with an appropriately stripped down view of the former. His attention then shifts to mechanisms for advancing democracy. Starting with the debates among Schumpeter and his critics, he argues that wholesale rejections of Schumpeterian democracy are unpersuasive, concluding that the more fruitful path is to explore ways to make competitive democracy work better, expand its reach beyond governmental institutions, and supplement it with other institutional devices. This leads him to a consideration of the literature on the extent to which electoral systems can operate as engineering devices to promote competitive democracy in societies usually thought antithetical to it. He concludes that there is no good reason to suppose any society inherently incapable of democracy but argues for an incremental approach given the dearth of reliable knowledge about the adaptability of politicized identities to the requirements of competitive democracy. Existing scholarship reveals that we do know something about the economic preconditions for viable democracy. But we are mainly in the dark, he insists, about the cultural and institutional factors that influence democracy's viability, and too little is known about which democratic institutional arrangements are best. If Schumpeterian democracy needs supplementing, then questions arise: Who should do the supplementing and what should it be? Because there are no perfect decision rules, a purely procedural scheme like competitive majority rule can produce self-defeating results. Partly for this reason, some democratic theorists argue for theories of substantive democracy against which the results of procedures can be evaluated. Shapiro notes, however, that we confront a proliferation of such theories, yet lack a compelling way to choose among them. To deal with this conundrum, he argues that the best course is for courts or other second-guessing institutions to play a reactive, escape-valve role to limit the perverse consequences of democratic procedures.

"Justice" by Jeremy Waldron inquires about the present state of discussion in legal and political theory. By "justice," he means social or distributive justice; that is, the evaluation of social policy and institutional arrangements on the basis of the way they affect the distribution of scarce resources and opportunities among individuals in society. He claims that the term "justice" does not take in the whole of liberal political philosophy, and argues that recent theoretical discussions ostensibly about justice have tended to drift away from that subject and become meditations on political morality in general or public reason in a multicultural society. This has left a significant gap in our philosophical discussion of issues about wealth, poverty, and distribution, a gap that economic theorists who are relatively uninterested in distributive issues have not been slow to fill. If political philosophy in the 1970s and early 1980s was dominated by a fierce and focused debate about social justice occasioned by the publication of John Rawls's first book in 1971, the past ten years or so have seen a blurring of that focus under the influence of Rawls's later work, and a diversion of the fierce energies that A Theory of Justice aroused into a safer and less consequential discussion of the nature of political argument in a multicultural society. He argues for a return to concerns with social justice, especially given the growing global concerns with poverty and inequality.

Romand Coles's "Pluralization and Radical Democracy: Recent Developments in Critical Theory and Postmodernism" illuminates some of the most important debates and developments in recent critical theory and postmodernism. These types of theories are diverse in their philosophical perspectives, subject matters, styles of theorizing, political implications, and sometimes even the conversations of which they understand themselves to be a part. Coles briefly orients the discussion around some of the critiques of political liberalism that have emerged from theorists associated with these positions. He addresses several of the philosophical differences and political stakes between Habermasian critical theory and various postmodernisms, showing that a wide range of positions exists within each theoretical school and noting that some of the most promising work emerges by drawing on insights from both critical theory and postmodernism. Central to this essay is a cluster of questions concerning the nature and scope of democratic dialogue and power; the way theorists interpret the role of bodily affect, disposition, and perception in democratic engagement; and the way responses to the former are entwined with theorists' approaches to political questions concerning practices of rights, coalition politics, order, responsibility, and our relation to political institutions. The essay's discussion moves from political liberalism to critical theory to postmodernism. Coles maintains that this order should not be taken to suggest the endorsement of an uncomplicated linear progression of value from one to the next.

From these more abstract, theoretical debates, we turn to an examination of the literature on a variety of political institutions in democracies. Gerald Gamm and John Huber examine research on one of the fundamental institutions of democracy, "Legislatures as Political Institutions: Beyond the Contemporary Congress." They argue that for the bulk of political scientists today, the study of legislatures is the study of the U.S. Congress. Although this generalization fairly approximates the contemporary field, this was not the state of the discipline at the turn of the last century. Their paper's main objective is to understand the implications for legislative studies of the dominance of work on the contemporary Congress. The most obvious ramification is the extent to which congressional scholarship has served as a model of positivist, rigorous, scientific research for the more general study of legislatures, and the extent to which congressional scholarship has sustained the discipline's interest in institutions during an era otherwise dominated by behavioral work.

They also contend that the breadth of research on Congress—drawing on participant observation, roll-call analyses, interviews, rational-choice theory, and even history—has demonstrated the importance of embracing multiple approaches to analysis. But the primacy of congressional research has also exacted costs, primarily in biases that are created in the types of questions scholars pose and in the types of answers they provide to these questions. Important avenues for legislative research, for example, include efforts to explain the choice of institutional arrangements or to analyze the impact of institutions on the behavior of individuals, other political institutions, or policy. Gamm and Huber conclude by arguing that recent research happily has begun to move beyond some of the biases inherent in a Congress-centered approach.

Turning to the developing world, "The Great Transformation in the Study of Politics in Developing Countries" by Barbara Geddes looks at the impact of democratization. She argues that students of developing countries in the year 2000 were like geographers in 1520: the known world began changing about 25 years before, and we are still trying to figure it out. Just as most observers were explaining the fragility of democracy in developing countries, democratization began its recent global sweep. In a second equally unexpected development, many governments began to abandon state interventionist economic policies in favor of greater market orientation. These events have led to a reevaluation of the theoretical underpinnings of the study of comparative development, affecting what we consider worthy of study, the set of stylized facts we accept as more-or-less true, our basic understanding of the economics of development, the theoretical approaches we use to explain politics, and the research methods we favor. She claims that these events may interact with changes in the methods of studying these developing countries to produce mutually reinforcing progress in our understanding of political and economic development.

Kathleen Thelen examines a key relationship for democracy in "The Political Economy of Business and Labor in the Developed Democracies." She underscores a central development in the literature that has driven a broad reorientation in the study of labor, social democracy, and the welfare state by directing attention to the contribution of employer interests and strategies in shaping the political economy of labor in the advanced industrial countries. Thelen explores the distinctive strengths and weaknesses of two distinct strands in this new literature, claiming that neither can stand alone and that insights generated by each are incomplete, even misleading, to the extent that scholars fail to incorporate the insights of the other. More broadly, she illustrates the explanatory power of an historical-institutional framework by underscoring the weaknesses of research strategies that emphasize one component—the historical or the institutional—to the neglect of the other.

Ian Shapiro

The State of Democratic Theory

My aim here is to assess the current state of democratic theory. Such an undertaking needs a yardstick, two of which suggest themselves. One is normative, implied when we ask how persuasive the theories are that seek to justify democracy as a system of government. The other is explanatory, prompted by asking how successful the theories are that try to account for the dynamics of democratic systems. Normative and explanatory theories of democracy grow out of literatures that proceed, for the most part, on separate tracks, largely uninformed by one another. This is unfortunate, partly because speculation about what ought to be is likely to be more useful when informed by relevant knowledge of what is and what is feasible, and partly because explanatory theory too easily becomes banal and method driven when isolated from the pressing normative concerns that have fueled worldwide interest in democracy in recent decades. Accordingly, I take an integrative tack, focusing on what we should expect of democracy and on how those expectations might best be realized in practice.

Sharpening this focus, one inevitably confronts dissensus on both issues. The present essay is organized around these disagreements. I begin with a discussion of the main contending views of democratic purposes, those involving the search for a common good and those that attend to the legitimate management of power relations. I make the case that the latter understanding of the enterprise makes better sense but that it is compatible with an appropriately stripped down view of the former. In the second section, my attention shifts to mechanisms for advancing democracy. I start with the debates among Schumpeter and his critics, dividing the latter into two groups: those who think his competitive democracy desirable but insufficient and those who think it undesirable. I find wholesale rejections of Schumpeterianism to be unpersuasive, concluding that the more fruitful path is to explore ways to make competitive democracy work better, expand its reach beyond governmentalist institutions, and supplement it with other institutional devices. This leads to a consideration of the literature on the extent to which electoral systems can operate as engineering devices to promote competitive democracy in societies usually thought antithetical to it in the third section. Here I conclude there is no good reason to suppose any society inherently incapable of democracy, but I argue for an incremental approach given the dearth of reliable knowledge about the adaptability of politicized identities to the requirements of competitive democracy.

Even if democracy might in principle operate anywhere, it becomes plain from the literature on its durability, examined in the fourth section, that this does not mean democracy is easily instituted, or, once installed, destined to survive. These, too, are subjects about which empirically well supported generalizations are hard to come by. As with the literatures on democratic purposes and electoral engineering, the literatures on getting and keeping democracy prompt the thought that the state of democratic theory is a bit like the State of Wyoming: large, windy, and mainly empty. The sprawling scholarship reveals that we do know something about the economic preconditions for viable democracy, but, notwithstanding the confident assertions of various commentators, we are mainly in the dark about the cultural and institutional factors that influence democracy's viability. Prudence suggests that although it is wise to try to inculcate support for democracy among those who operate it, it is far from clear how important this is or how to achieve it.

If Schumpeterian democracy needs supplementation, the questions arise: who should do the supplementing and what should it be? Debates about these issues are taken up next. Because there are no perfect decision rules, a purely procedural scheme like competitive majority rule can produce self-defeating results. Most obviously, majorities can use their power to undermine democratic freedoms by abolishing opposition, undermining future political competition. But democratic procedures can have perverse consequences in a host of subtler ways as well. Partly for this reason, some democratic theorists argue for theories of substantive democracy against which the results of procedures can be evaluated. As I note in the fifth section, however, we confront a proliferation of substantive theories, yet lack a compelling way to choose among them. As a result, I agree with those who propose a middle-ground approach, in which courts or other second-guessing institutions should play a reactive, escape-valve role in limiting the perverse consequences of democratic procedures. This is followed by a discussion of alternative ways for courts to behave in democratic systems, leading to the conclusion that their legitimacy will likely vary with the degree to which they act in democracy-sustaining ways.

■ | Conflicting Views of Democratic Purposes

The idea that democracy does or should converge on the common good finds its locus classicus in Rousseau's *Social Contract*, and in particular in his contention that decision procedures should converge on a general will that embodies the common good. Rousseau (1968, [1762] 72) famously, if vaguely, characterized this by saying that we start with "the sum of individual desires," subtract "the plusses and minuses which cancel each other out," then "the sum of the difference is the general will." Attempts to make sense of this formulation have spawned two literatures: an aggregative one, geared to finding out just how we are supposed to do the relevant math, and a deliberative one, concerned with getting people to converge on the common good where this is understood more robustly than totting up exogenously fixed preferences.

Aggregative Versus Deliberative Conceptions of the Common Good

Much twentieth-century literature on aggregation has focused on the difficulties of achieving it coherently. Its proponents accept that the goal of democratic decision procedures should be to discover something like a general will, referred to in the modern idiom as a social welfare function. Following Arrow (1951), they often notice that even moderate disagreement frustrates its discovery and conclude that democracy is impossible as a result. The possibility of voting cycles (results moving among outcomes depending on the order of voting) means that any given outcome may be an artifact of the decision procedure or who controls the agenda, not anything that might meaningfully be identified as the popular will. The result has been a large technical literature about the relative merits of different decision rules as aggregative procedures, and the constraints that must be imposed on preferences to avoid the possibility of cyclical majorities. These literatures have been the subject of many reviews and will not be discussed here.[1] Suffice it to note that if the purpose of democracy is to arrive at social welfare functions, in many circumstances this may be elusive.[2]

The deliberative view is concerned with transforming preferences

---

1. The most comprehensive and accessible, if somewhat dated, review is Mueller 1989, ch. 6. See also Shapiro 1996, ch. 2 and Przeworski 1999.

2. Here we should distinguish the observation that cyclical preferences in the population make outcomes of democratic decision rules *arbitrary*, in the sense that had things been voted on in a different order some other proposal would have won, from the claim that they are *manipulable*, in the sense that some agenda setter determines the result. Despite the claims of some commentators to the contrary, there is little evidence of successful manipulation of this kind in democratic polities (see Green and Shapiro 1994, ch. 7; Mackie 2000). This distinction matters because there may be reasons for according legitimacy to results that are arbitrary but not manipulated, in the relevant senses, from the perspective of the power management view discussed below. It should, however, be noted that even the claim that results are arbitrary depends on the proposition that cyclical preferences are likely in large populations. For a contrarian argument, see Tangian 2000 17, 337–65.

rather than aggregating them. It is not really Rousseauist (Rousseau had no faith in deliberation as a useful political device). However, it owes something to his injunction that people should not vote their individual preferences but rather their perceptions of what is good for the society as a whole.[3] The goal is to move us "beyond adversary democracy" (Mansbridge 1980). Deliberative remedies are put forward in response to various maladies that are perceived as pervading contemporary democracy. Poor quality of decision making, sound-bite politics, low levels of participation, declining legitimacy of government, and ignorant citizens are among the more frequently mentioned. The idea is that if we can get away from the soap opera of electoral one-upmanship, more thoughtful and effective political choices will result.[4] Deliberative forums can range from town meetings, to designated deliberation times, to citizen juries and "deliberative polls"—randomly selected groups who become better informed about particular issues and render decisions as to what should be done (Fishkin 1991). On some accounts such entities should inform existing processes, on others they should replace them en route to instituting a more robust participatory politics. The unifying impulse motivating these proposals is that people will modify their perceptions of what society should do in the course of discussing this with others. The point of democratic participation is more to manufacture the common good than to discover it on this account.[5] The assumption is that if people talk for long enough in the right circumstances, they will agree more often and this is a good thing.

Both propositions can be challenged. Deliberation can bring differences to the surface, widening divisions rather than narrowing them. This is what Marxists hoped would result from consciousness-raising: it would lead workers to discover their interests to be irreconcilably at odds with those of employers, assisting in the transformation of the proletariat from a class in itself to a revolutionary class for itself. In the event, these hopes proved naive. The general point remains, however, that there is no obvious reason to think deliberation will bring people together, even if they hope it will and want it to. A couple with a distant but not-collapsing marriage might begin therapy with a mutual commitment to settling long-standing differences and learning to accommodate one another better on matters

3. For Rousseau, voting was a means of disciplining private interest by getting people to focus on what is best for society as a whole. As he put it: "When a law is proposed in the people's assembly, what is asked of them is not precisely whether they approve the proposition or reject it, but whether it is in conformity with the general will which is theirs; each, by casting his vote, gives an opinion on this question" (1968, [1762] 153).

4. For one influential argument, see Gutmann and Thompson 1996. For criticism, see Macedo 1999.

5. Indeed, deliberative theorists sometimes write as if the activity of searching for the common good is itself the common good. See Shapiro 1996, ch. 4 for discussion.

that cannot be resolved. Once honest exchange gets underway, however, they might unearth new irreconcilable differences, with the effect that the relationship worsens and perhaps even falls apart in acrimony. Deliberation can reasonably be expected to shed light on human interaction, but this may reveal hidden differences as well as hidden possibilities for convergence. It all depends on what the underlying interests, values, and preferences at stake are.[6]

Even when agreement is achievable through deliberation, it is not always desirable. People may not want to settle some disagreements. They may derive satisfaction from differentiating themselves from one another, as contemporary theorists of difference suppose. Alternatively, they may perceive consensus as leading to mediocrity, as Mill and Tocqueville worried. It is the competition of ideas—argument rather than deliberation—that such theorists thought vital to liberty, and, as I observe below, institutional analogs of this thought lie at the core of many contemporary democratic commitments. Suffice it to conclude here that deliberation need not lead to agreement, and when it does this may not be advantageous.

Managing Power Relations

The deliberative view is also criticized on the grounds that its goal of fostering agreement rests on overly sanguine assumptions about power. One person's consensus is another's hegemony, and although uncoerced agreement may be feasible in some ideal world or "speech situation" (Habermas 1979, 1984), in the actual world power relations suffuse virtually all human interaction. The most trenchant versions of this critique, most recently associated with Michel Foucault (1972, 1977, 1980) but with progenitors as different as Plato, Hobbes, Marx, Mosca, and Michels, can be taken to imply that democratic control of power relations is impossible: power relations evolve, displacing one another over time, but they are never eliminated. Collective life remains power and domination all the way down.[7]

The ubiquitous view overreaches in two respects: by failing to discriminate among different ways in which power is exercised and by equating the valid observation that power suffuses all collective life with the implausible claim that all collective life is reducible to power relations. To recognize power as ubiquitous is not to concede that all power is alike or that some ways of living with it might not be better than others. And to say that power relations suffuse activities as various as workplace, family, and church is not to deny that things go on in all these areas other than exer-

6. See Sunstein 2000 for a discussion of empirical conditions under which deliberation leads to a divergence rather than a convergence of opinion.

7. See Laclau and Mouffe 1985 and Hayward 2000 for illustrations and discussions of this view.

cises of power. Producing goods and services may often, and perhaps inevitably, involve power relations, as may pursuing intimacy, affection, education, and spiritual fulfillment. But these activities are not themselves power relations.

Important challenges for democratic theorists revolve around devising mechanisms to govern the power dimensions of human interaction as well as possible, while minimizing interference with the other activities in which people engage. Rather than see democracy as a device for discovering or manufacturing the common good, democracy can be understood as a device for managing the power dimensions of activities people engage in as they pursue their own—individual or shared—conceptions of the good. Democracy is a subordinate or conditioning good on this account, and the creative challenge is to find ways to structure power relations democratically while limiting interference with the superordinate goods people pursue.

At a minimum this involves making decision making more inclusive of those who are affected by the results and creating avenues for meaningful—if loyal—opposition by those who are adversely affected by prevailing decisions. Because there are no perfect decision rules, a degree of imposition attaches to all collective decisions. Those who lose may reasonably aspire, therefore, to achieve a different result in the future. This suggests that opposition rights are important for democratic politics independently of the value of inclusive participation, though they have been relatively underattended to by democratic theorists.[8] To the extent that this commitment rests on an idea of the common good, it is perhaps best characterized as Machiavelli did when he identified it as that which those with an interest in avoiding domination share in common.[9]

Conceiving of democracy as a system for structuring power relations offers several advantages. First, it poses normative questions about democracy in a "compared to what?" framework, since democracy is now judged not by the either/or question whether it produces social welfare functions or leads to agreement but rather by how well it enables people to manage power relations measured by the yardsticks of promoting inclusive participation and minimizing domination. By its terms this is a comparative question. Second, the power-centered approach invites us to avoid another kind of binary thinking—about democracy itself. Ways of managing power relations can be more or less democratic. On this conception, relevant questions concern how much democracy is possible or desirable in a given

8. Exceptions are Dahl (1971), Burt (1992), Shapiro (1999), Schiffrin (1999), and Pettit (2000).

9. See his consideration in *The Discourses* of the Roman argument that the common people should be made the guardians of freedom because, unlike the aristocracy whose desire is to dominate, their desire is not to be dominated (1970, 1: 5 [c. 1517]).

situation. Particularly when democratizing power relations comes at a price in terms of other goods, these are important questions to ask. It is one of the singular contributions of Dahl's idea of polyarchy that it turns questions about democracy into more-or-less questions rather than whether-or-not questions.[10] Third, the power-centered approach brings the normative literature on democratic theory into confrontation with the empirical political science literature on democracy. Democratic theorists have often paid too little attention to this literature, giving their speculations a less than worldly quality and leading most others to ignore them as a result.

Even when theorists take up the first two questions, inattention to empirical practice can mar the results. For instance, Buchanan and Tullock (1990) answer the "how much democracy?" question by noting that its benefits must be traded off against other valuable ways of spending one's time. Requiring high levels of agreement enables people to protect their interests, they say, but this takes time that could be spent on other activities. So they come up with a sliding scale: the more important an issue to you, the more likely you are to preserve a veto power by insisting on unanimity rule or something close to it. For things that matter less, however, it will make better sense to run the risk that you will lose on any given vote, accept majority rule, and reduce decision-making costs. Democracy is thus best suited to issues of moderate importance on their account. Issues of high importance should be insulated from democracy, while issues of low importance might best be delegated to administrators. Yet Buchanan and Tullock assume, without adducing any evidence, that it is the standard panoply of libertarian protections that people most value, so it is these that are to be insulated from change by supermajorities or even unanimity rule. If we query that assumption, their substantive claims are all thrown into doubt.

The costs of failing to attend to actual politics run deeper, as can be seen if we focus more carefully on the "compared to what?" question. Even if we knew what people regard as the most important questions (which includes the heroic assumption that they all agree on this), why assume that they would want to insulate these from democracy by insisting on supermajorities or unanimity rule? This can only make sense if we start, as Buchanan and Tullock do, from the fiction of no collective action in a pre-

10. Dahl identifies eight elements that measure the degree to which the conditions of polarchy are met. These eight conditions deal with four periods: voting, where votes by members of the political system must have equal weight, and the choice with the most individual votes wins; prevoting, where members have equal chances of presenting alternatives and information about alternatives; postvoting, where those leaders or policies that won the vote displace those with less votes and the orders of elected officials are followed; and the interelection period, where decisions are subordinate to those made during elections, for example, an interim senator will be replaced by the senator who wins the next election (1956, 71–76, 84–89).

political condition, and then ask what decision rule people would choose in order to minimize the likelihood that their preferences would be frustrated in the future to the extent that they agree to depart from that condition. But, as Barry (1990), Rae (1975), and others have noted, if we jettison this unrealism there is no reason to regard unanimity rule as the appropriate default option, since it privileges the status quo.[11] In the real world of ongoing politics, if I assume that I am as likely to oppose a given policy as to support it regardless of whether or not it is the status quo, then majority rule or something close to it is the logical rule to prefer. At a minimum, we would want to know who benefits from, and who is harmed by, the status quo, before rendering a judgment on the desirability of privileging it against change.[12]

The "compared to what?" perspective suggests a more realistic question: not "whether-or-not collective action?" but rather "what sort of collective action?" That is, we consider the power dimensions of different collective action regimes vis-à-vis one another. Perhaps due to their proclivity for thinking in social contract idiom, libertarian commentators often write as if not having collective action is a coherent option in societies that nonetheless have private property, enforcement of contracts, and the standard panoply of negative freedoms. As Holmes and Sunstein (1999) have recently reminded us, however, these are costly institutions that stand in need of effective collective enforcement. The libertarian constitutional scheme is a collective action regime maintained by the state, and disproportionately financed by implicit taxes on those who would prefer an alternative regime.

The literature on deliberative democracy is likewise vulnerable. Apart from the conceptual difficulties already mentioned, inattention to "compared to what?" questions often makes deliberation look better than it should. For instance, advocates of deliberative democracy such as Gutmann and Thompson (1996) and Ackerman and Fishkin (2000) argue for the merits of deliberation by pointing out how little of it there is in contemporary politics dominated by superficial television campaigns and political advertising. But sound-bite politics and media driven campaigns may well result principally from the powerful American antipathy toward publicly financed elections and the concomitant influence of private money in politics. This would presumably remain in a world of expanded deliberative institutions, given the Supreme Court's 1976 decision that reg-

11. See Barry 1990, Rae 1969, 40–56, and M. Taylor 1969, 228–31. When the number of voters is odd, the optimal decision rule is majority rule, n over 2, plus ½; when n is even, the optimal decision rule is either majority rule (n over 2 plus 1) or majority rule minus 1 (simply n over 2). Generally see Mueller 1989, 96–111.

12. Even if we accept the contractualist metaphor the logic of Buchanan and Tullock's defense of unanimity rule can be shown to break down once time and externalities are taken into account (see Rae 1975, 1270–94).

ulating political expenditures is an unconstitutional interference with free speech.[13]

Any credible defense of deliberative democracy in the U.S. context would have to show how deliberative institutions would be any less corrupted by those with the resources to control agendas and bias decision making than existing institutions are and that it would merit its cost. Consider, for instance, the proposal for a "deliberation day," to be held a week before national elections, in which everyone would be paid $150 to show up at their local school or community center to deliberate. According to its proponents (Ackerman and Fishkin 2000; 29) this would cost $15 billion a year in public funds, not to mention the indirect costs to the economy. It is hard to see what benefit would result from so vast an expenditure once candidates have been selected, platforms chosen, interest groups deployed, and campaign funds spent. By contrast, $15 billion a year spent to support fledgling third parties or publicly financed elections might attenuate many of the pathologies that lead people to call for more deliberation.[14]

A fourth advantage of the power-centered approach is that it offers a tractable perspective on long-standing conundrums about the relations between democracy and citizenship. Democratic theory is often said to be impotent when confronted with questions about its own scope. It depends on a decision rule, usually some variant of majority rule, but this assumes that the question "majority of whom?" has been settled. If this is not done democratically, however, in what sense are the results that flow from democratic decision making genuinely democratic? Thus Shapiro and Hacker-Cordón observe that "a chicken-and-egg problem lurks at democracy's core. Questions relating to boundaries and membership seem in an important sense prior to democratic decision-making, yet paradoxically they cry out for democratic resolution" (1999b, 1).

If democracy is about managing power relations, it becomes unnecessary to think of questions about citizenship as different from questions about any other superordinate good that is conditioned by democratic con-

13. In *Buckley v. Valeo* 424 U.S. 1 (1976) the Court held, inter alia, that although Congress may regulate financial contributions to political parties or candidates, it cannot otherwise regulate private expenditures on political speech. The Court has since allowed some minor constraints on corporate expenditures in *Austin v. Michigan State Chamber of Commerce*, 110 S.Ct. 1391 (1990), but for all practical purposes the *Buckley* rule makes it impossible to limit privately funded political advertising.

14. Ackerman and Fishkin insist that "it is a big mistake to view the annualized cost of $15 billion through the lens of standard cost-benefit analysis" on the grounds that its "large" benefits "cannot be reckoned on the same scale as other elements in the cost-benefit equation" (2000, 29). Even if we were to concede that the benefits could coherently be declared to be large at the same time as they are said to be incommensurable with their costs, their claim ignores the point stressed here: that its benefits surely should be weighed against other ways in which such a sum could be spent to enhance U.S. democracy.

straints. The claim to a democratic say in collective decisions, whether or not one is a citizen, appropriately rests on the causal principle of having a pertinent affected interest. The rallying cry of the American revolutionaries, after all, was "No taxation without representation!" not "No taxation without citizenship!" There might be good reasons for restricting citizenship, but this does not mean that noncitizens should be denied rights to vote on matters that affect their pertinent interests, as when a decision is taken to deny the children of illegal aliens access to the California public schools[15] or when "guest workers" in foreign countries claim a say in the laws that govern them (see Barbieri 1998). The causally based view has been invoked in a number of recent arguments aimed at decentering citizenship as decisive in determining rights of democratic participation, and replacing it with systems of overlapping jurisdiction in which different groups are sovereign over different classes of decisions, as is occuring in the governance of the European Union. The operative thought here is that the appropriate demos should be settled decision by decision, not people by people.[16]

Difficulties are, of course, bound to arise in settling conflicting claims about whose pertinent interests are affected by a given decision. Controversial as this might often be, arguments about who has a legitimate claim to citizenship are scarcely less so (see R. Smith 1997). Moreover, there is instructive experience with arguments about affected interests in other arenas. In dealing with tort actions, for instance, courts develop rules for deciding who should have standing to sue, for sorting genuine from frivolous claims, and for distinguishing weaker from stronger allegations to have been adversely affected by an action. The comparison illustrates that institutional mechanisms can be developed to assess and manage conflicting claims about how pertinent interests are affected. They may be imperfect mechanisms, but they should be evaluated by reference to the other imperfect mechanisms of collective decision making that actually prevail in the world, not by comparison with an ideal that prevails nowhere.[17]

■ | Schumpeterian Competition

The most influential twentieth-century approach to the democratic management of power relations is Schumpeter's argument (1942) in *Capitalism*,

15. This was passed as Proposition 187 by a majority of 59 to 41 percent in a California ballot initiative in November 1994 and subsequently struck down in federal court as violating the constitutional right to education regardless of immigration status and because immigration law is a federal rather than a state matter.

16. See Pogge 1994b, Antholis 1993, and Wendt 1994. For other arguments that decisions about membership should not be seen as anterior to democratic decision making, see Shapiro and Hacker-Cordón 1999b, esp. chs. 6, 10, 12, 15.

17. For elaboration and defense of his claim, see Shapiro 1999, 31–39.

Socialism and Democracy. It reduces to a double claim: (1) that structured competition for power is preferable both to Hobbesian anarchy and to the power monopoly that Hobbes saw as the logical response to it and (2) that the choices among anarchy, monopoly, and competition are the only meaningful possibilities. Both of Schumpeter's claims were innovative, and, although they have drawn heavy critical fire, neither has been driven from the field.

ADVANTAGES AND LIMITATIONS OF STRUCTURED COMPETITION

Schumpeter's view is often said to be conservative. There is substance to this, but focusing too quickly on it obscures the radical dimensions of his argument. He was radical first in seeing an alternative to the idea that Western political theorists had taken over more or less self-consciously from Hobbes: that power is a natural monopoly. Conventional liberals, Marxists, and elite theorists all held variants of this view. On the surface republicans took a more complex view that power is divisible and can be controlled by competition among the political branches. However, as Dahl (1956, 30–32) showed long ago, Madison's account was long on rhetoric— "ambition will be made to counteract ambition"—(Hamilton, Madison, Jay 1966 [1788], 160) and short on explaining how such mechanisms would actually work. *The Federalist* solution was mainly a matter of engineering institutional sclerosis to make all government action difficult and so protect the interests of landed elites. In this it was not qualitatively different from standard liberal justifications of bicameralism, strong constitutionalism, and other types of institutional veto that have often been put forward to limit democracy (see Riker 1982, 13: 101–16; Riker and Weingast 1988; Holmes 1995).

Schumpeter's account was a radical departure in that he thought that rather than succumb to power (Hobbes) or hem it in (all these others), it could be controlled by being turned into an object of electoral competition. The authors of *The Federalist* had distinguished incentives from constraints in the pursuit of power; Schumpeter actually delivered on an incentives-based account.[18] Whereas constraints are geared to limiting politicians' power via rules (such as separation of powers or other constitutional limitations), incentives link what politicians find strategically beneficial to the demands of competitive politics.

18. Thus in *Federalist No. 48* Madison insists that "mere demarcation on parchment of the constitutional limits of the several departments, is not a sufficient guard against those encroachments which lead to a tyrannical concentration of all the powers in the same hands." Such "exterior provisions" are inadequate and must be supplemented, as he elaborates in *Federalist No. 51*, by giving "those who administer each department the necessary constitutional means *and personal motives* to resist encroachments of the others" (Hamilton, Madison, Jay 1966 [1788], 150–51, 159–60, emphasis added).

Once parties are modeled on firms trying to maximize votes as analogs of profits, then leaders can be seen as disciplined by the demands of competition. Attempts by Downs (1957) and others to turn this into a predictive theory of electoral competition have been less than successful (see Green and Shapiro 1994, ch. 7), but as a normative theory Schumpeter's account broke new ground. From his perspective, the value of competition is twofold: it disciplines leaders with the threat of losing power in the same way that firms are disciplined by the threat of bankruptcy, and it gives would-be leaders the incentive to be responsive to more voters than their competitors are. The—always problematic—theory of representative government is thus replaced by a political analog of consumer sovereignty.

Schumpeterian democracy is often denoted "minimal" for one of two reasons: its exclusive focus is on (usually national) political institutions narrowly defined, and Schumpeter's definition of democracy is by reference to competition for power. However, nothing inherent in Schumpeter's reasoning thus limits it. To say that social arrangements other than national political institutions should be democratized is not to deny that Schumpeterian tools might be useful in that endeavor, as Shapiro (1999, chs. 4–7) has illustrated. Nor is it to assert that national political institutions could not benefit from Schumpeterian reform even if other reforms might also be deemed necessary. Notice, too, that even in Schumpeter's formulation the sense in which competitive democracy is minimal can be exaggerated. The competitive requirement has been read by modern Schumpeterians like Huntington (1991) to mean that a polity is not democratic unless governments have at least twice given up power following electoral defeat, which would arguably have ruled out the United States until 1840, Japan and India for much of the twentieth century, and most of the so-called third wave democracies in the ex-Communist countries and sub-Saharan Africa. Minimal, in short, does not mean negligible.

Conceding this, it is less than clear that electoral competition is much of a disciplinary system given the high rates at which incumbents are often reelected (see Lowenstein 1995, 653–67). But again there is the response: compared to what? The discipline of the electoral constraint might seem modest when compared to an ideal that prevails nowhere, but achieving it would be a substantial gain for the billions who live in countries where it is lacking (see Przeworski 1999, 43–50).

The sense in which Schumpeterianism produces responsive government is also constrained. In theory at least, the standard Left criticism of markets—that they reward those with greater resources—does not apply. One-person, one-vote is a resource equalizer that is widely seen as a nonnegotiable requirement of democracy, despite occasional defenses of markets in votes on efficiency or intensity grounds (see Buchanan and Tullock 1962, 125–26, 132–42). The difficulty in practice is that, particularly in the United States, politicians compete in the first instance for campaign contributions and only secondarily for votes. Perhaps there would be decisive voter support for confiscatory taxes on estates worth over $10 million, but no party proposes this. Indeed, in June 2000 the U.S. Congress gave strong bipartisan support to a bill that would abolish the existing estate tax—paid by only the wealthiest 2½ percent of Americans.[19] It seems likely that politicians avoid taxing the wealthy for fear of the funds that would be channeled to their electoral opponents if they sought to do so. Empirical study of such claims is inherently difficult, but it seems reasonable to suppose that the proposals politicians offer are heavily shaped by the agendas of campaign contributors; why else would they contribute? Add to this the fact that the small number of major parties means that what we really get is oligopolistic competition, and it becomes clear that the sense in which parties are as attentive to voters as firms in competitive markets are to consumers is highly attenuated.

These powerful objections are aimed not at the idea of political competition but rather at the ways in which the system is imperfectly competitive. Disproportionate power of campaign contributors could be reduced (proposals for reform abound),[20] and reforms could be instituted to increase the number of parties, facilitating more competition. Indeed, it is remarkable that public interest litigants, activists, and political commentators (not to mention political theorists) do not argue for attempts to use antitrust laws to attack the existing duopoly. If competition for power is the life blood of democracy, then the search for bipartisan consensus (and the ideal of deliberative agreement that lies behind it) is really anticompetitive collusion in restraint of democracy. Why is it that people do not challenge legislation that has bipartisan backing or other forms of bipartisan agreement on *these* grounds? It is far from clear that there are fewer meritorious reasons to break up the Democratic and Republican Parties than there are to break up AT&T and Microsoft.[21]

There are legal obstacles to antitrust action against political parties but also untested legal possibilities. For instance, the Supreme Court's Noerr-Pennington doctrine rules out applying antitrust laws to "valid governmental action, as opposed to private action."[22] But this does not speak to activities by political parties. Moreover, although the Sherman Act has

19. The Death Tax Elimination Act of 2000, or House Resolution 519, was passed by a vote of 279 to 136 on 9 June 2000. The Senate voted for it by 59 to 39 on 14 July 2000—Bastille Day! It was subsequently vetoed by President Clinton. However the estate tax was subsequently reduced and slated for repeal in 2009 as part of President George Bush's comprehensive tax cut enacted in 2001.

20. See Ackerman 1993 and Ayres 2000 for examples.

21. The Progressives did advance a version of this critique (see Epstein 1986, 17–71). The lone voice in the contemporary literature seems to be Wittman's (1973).

22. *Eastern R.R. President's Conf. v. Noerr Motor Freight*, 365 U.S. 127 (1961), 136.

generally been held not to apply to noneconomic entities such as labor unions, exceptions are made when a conspiracy is alleged between such an entity and a business to injure the interests of another business or when the agreement sought does not encompass a "legitimate union interest."[23] Analogously, activities by political parties might not be exempted if they allied with corporate contributors to promote anticompetitive practices or could otherwise be shown to be seeking agreements with one another which went beyond "legitimate party interests."

The constitutional obstacles to applying antitrust principles to politics are rooted in the right of petition and the "ability of the people to make their wishes known to their representatives."[24] But the rationale for this type of political exemption does not go to forms of collusion that undermine the process of free political expression itself, which parties engage in by maintaining prohibitive costs to entry, agreeing to exclude minor parties from political debates, and related practices. Because the Sherman Act has been held to apply only to business combinations[25] and to organizations that have commercial objectives,[26] antitrust regulation of such behavior might require additional lawmaking. It is hard, for obvious reasons, to envision legislators enacting such laws, but it is less difficult to think of political antitrust measures being adopted as a result of ballot initiatives.

Arguments about the merits of party proliferation (usually to be achieved via proportional representation) are sometimes advanced on the quite different ground that this would lead to fairer (read: more representative) outcomes. Notice that such arguments can be oversold. Proportional representation may lead to more representative electoral outcomes by offering voters a broader array of parties, but it need not lead to more representative governments. Frequently we see this in Israel when small extremist parties needed for any viable governing coalition exert disproportionate influence on government policy, leading to highly unrepresentative government. Nonetheless, trying to ensure that the parties competing with one another are more representative of the electorate is a challenge that can in principle be taken up within the Schumpeterian framework, and

23. *Connell Constr. Co. v. Plumbers & Steamfitters Local Union No. 100*, 483 F. 2d 1154, 1164 (5th Cir. App. 1973); see also *Local Union No. 189, Amalgamated Meat Cutters v. Jewel Tea Co.*, 381 U.S. 676.

24. *Noerr*, 356 U.S. 137, 138. Thus the court rejected a claim by the State of Missouri that the National Organization of Women had violated the Sherman Act by organizing a conference boycott in states that had not ratified the Equal Rights Amendment, holding that the participants were engaging in legitimate forms of political organizing rather than undermining commercial competitors (*Missouri v. National Organization of Women, Inc.*, 467 F. Supp. 289, 304 [1979], cert. denied 449 U.S. 842 [1980]).

25. *Parker v. Brown* 317 U.S. 341, 351 (1943).

26. *Klor's Inc. v. Broadway-Hale Stores, Inc.*, 359 U.S. 213 n. 7, and *Apex Hosiery Co. v. Leader*, 310 U.S. 469, 493 n. 5.

there is some reason to think that, on average, proportional representation leads to policies that are closer to the preferences of the median voter than does competitive alternation in power (see Rae 1967, 1995; Powell 2000).

ALTERNATIVES TO SCHUMPETERIANISM?

Pressed sufficiently far, however, the emphasis on representativeness turns into a rejection of the competitive ideal. This becomes evident if we suppose that a government could represent all interests optimally[27] and ask who the opposition would then represent? Sometimes the implicit ideal of those who emphasize representativeness is agreement: if all groups are fairly represented, then they can negotiate an outcome that all can accept, making opposition politics unnecessary. This fallacious reasoning has already been explored in my discussion of Buchanan and Tullock; it need not detain us here.

A different defense of proportionality and consensus democracy rests on the belief that disagreements in some societies are so profound that promoting competitive politics amounts to pouring gasoline on conflictual fire. Proponents of this view generally have ethnically and racially divided societies in mind, and they think of the relevant identities as both primordialist and overdetermining: given for all time and more important than all other matters. Unless there are enough crosscutting cleavages of interest to institutionalize uncertainty about future outcomes, losers have no reason for allegiance to the system. Minorities will expect to lose on every issue.[28] When elections amount to an ethnic or racial census, minorities would do better to reach for their guns, try to secede, or otherwise defect from the political process (see Shapiro 1996, chs. 4, 7).

Such thinking gives rise to consociationalism. Its injunction is to devise systems of minority vetoes or other mechanisms to force leaders of different groups to work out a modus vivendi and govern as a "cartel of elites" (Lijphart 1969, 213–15, 222). Here the appeal to consensus is not based on

---

27. Achieving such optimality is elusive in practice, as the architects of the McGovern-Frazier reforms to achieve pure proportionality within the Democratic Party learned when it became apparent that there are more pertinent interests than could be represented proportionately (see Ranney 1975). It may also be elusive in theory (see Rae et al. 1981).

28. If A is opposed to B on issue 1, but knows that in the future he is likely to be allied with B in opposition to C on issue 2, then A has an incentive to moderate his present conflict with B as much as possible and cultivate her as a future ally. If, on the other hand, A and B know that they are likely to be on opposite sides of the fence on every issue, then there are no incentives favoring moderation, and if one of them calculates that he will always be in the minority, he has no self-interested reason to be committed to a democratic order. The pluralists generalized this, arguing that only when cleavages are pluralistic or crosscutting will a democratic order be stable (see Miller 1993, 734–47).

fairness but rather on avoiding civil war. If the primordialists are right, competitive democracy is impossible in such circumstances and consociational accommodation is the best we can hope for. If they are wrong, however, their remedy might sustain—or even produce—the malady to which it is alleged to respond.[29] Perhaps consociational arrangements (such as those embodied in the Dayton accords in the Yugoslavian conflict) are required to end ethnic civil wars, but this does not mean they supply a viable basis for democracy. Critics of primordialism are quick to emphasize that consociational institutions can manufacture or exacerbate ethnic division. In their view, ethnic, racial, and other group-based antipathies are neither natural nor necessary. Politicized divisions might have developed differently than they have, and they can change (see Vail 1989). These writers seldom get into the technicalities of how they believe this might be accomplished, but they think it plausible to suppose that politicized identities could develop that differ radically from those presently prevailing in the world. In particular, people might come to accept, perhaps even celebrate, differences that today are sources of mutual hatred (see Jung 2000, ch. 9).

Conceding that politicized identities change and are socially constructed does not, however, generate the conclusion that they are infinitely malleable. It does not even entail that those identities that might not have been mobilized politically but nonetheless have been can subsequently be demobilized. This is more than the problem of getting the toothpaste back into the tube. The extent to which things are alterable may not vary with the degree to which they are socially constructed at all. Many features of the natural world, ranging from the temperature of our bath water to the genetic structure of our beings, can be altered by conscious human design. Socially constructed phenomena, by contrast, often defy all efforts at conscious human control. Markets are human constructions, yet we may be unable to regulate them so as to operate at full employment without inflation for long periods of time. Ethnic hatred might concededly be learned behavior and hence by its terms socially constructed, yet we may have no idea how to prevent its being reproduced in the next generation. Proponents of social constructionism leap too quickly from that idea to the assumption of alterability; at best the two are contingently related.

An intermediate and more plausible account might run as follows. Human beings are shaped by context and circumstance, but they are also constrained by their inherited constitutions. These constitutions may themselves evolve, but at a given time and place they limit the possibilities of social reconstruction. Human psychology is always malleable but never infinitely so, and certain ways of shaping it are likely to be more effective

29. As Courtney Jung and I have argued is the case in regard to South Africa (see Jung and Shapiro 1995; Shapiro and Jung 1996). More generally, Horowitz (2000) points out that consociationalism has been singularly unsuccessful as a device for managing ethnic conflict.

than others in any given situation. The interesting questions concern what the limits to this malleability are and which forms of social reconstruction are likely to be more satisfying and effective than others. The difficulty for democratic institutional designers is that these are empirical questions about which there is not much accumulated knowledge in the social sciences. As a result, it seems wise to work at the margins and to think about institutional redesign rather than tabula rasa design. Identities are fixed to some—usually unknown—degree, but they also adapt to circumstances, incentives, and institutional rules. The goal should be to reshape such constraints, where possible, so that at the margins identities evolve in ways that are more, rather than less, hospitable to democratic politics. From this perspective the critique of consociationalism is that, to the degree that politicized identities are malleable, it tends to reproduce the wrong ones.

▪ | Electoral Incentives and Multiplying Cleavages

Electoral systems are potential instruments for undermining ethnic conflict in the service of promoting competitive politics, but, given what has just been said, it is unclear how effective they can be. Assuming opinion to be at least partly mobilized and shaped from above, a logical place to start is the incentives facing candidates for office. In a Schumpeterian spirit the goal should be to avoid encouraging aspiring leaders to foment group-based hatred as they seek power. From this perspective we can array electoral systems on an ethnic engineering continuum, ranging from *reactive* systems that cater to ethnic difference, through *reflective* systems that are neutral with respect to existing preferences, to *proactive* systems that seek to alter them in ways that promote competitive democracy (see figure 1).

Secession and partition anchor the continuum's reactive pole. Next to it come apartheid and consociationalism (the former imposed by the stronger party, the latter sanctified by some kind of elite agreement), where the aspiration is to achieve functional partition within a unified polity. Further along are systems that engineer around ethnic differences to produce diversity in legislatures, as is the case with gerrymandering to create majority minority districts in the American South. These reactive responses all take ethnic difference as given, hoping to work around it. Toward the center of the continuum we come to reflective responses: those that are sensitive to ethnic difference but neutral in the sense of being biased neither in favor of it nor against it. The various cumulative voting schemes discussed by Lani Guinier's fit this description.[30] Here the principle is to give each

30. For Guinier's proposals, see Guinier 1991, 1077–154, 1994a, 109–37). On the battle over her confirmation as assistant attorney general for civil rights, which she lost for her advocacy of this scheme, see Guinier 1994b. Her fate suggests a criterion, in addition to representative fairness, for evaluating proposed decision rules: whether they can be widely understood and perceived as democratic.

Figure I | Ethnic Engineering Continuum

Reactive — Reflective — Proactive

Secession/Partition · Apartheid · Consociationalism · Seat pooling · Maj/min district gerrymandering · Cumulative voting · Geo. distrib. requirements · Weighted choices w/ethnic parties · Poona pact voter as many votes as there are seats. If a state is to have eight congressional representatives, every voter gets eight votes that can be cast however they wish: all for one candidate or spread among several. If there are intense ethnic preferences, members of a particular group can cast all eight votes for "their" representative; if not, not. Unlike racial gerrymandering and consociationalism, reflective schemes respond to ethnic preferences without doing anything to produce or reinforce them. As a result, they avoid the critique of reactive systems that they promote balkanization. Yet by the same token cumulative voting does nothing to ameliorate or undermine potentially polarizing forms of aspirational difference where these are present.

For engineered responses aimed at reducing such conflicts, we move to the proactive part of the continuum: arrangements that supply would-be leaders with incentives to avoid mobilizing support in ways that exacerbate cultural competition and to devise, instead, ideologies that can appeal across the divisions of relevant groups. Hence Donald Horowitz's contention that, when group-based antipathies are strong, electoral systems are needed that give elites incentives to compete for votes among politicized groups other than their own, and so promote accommodation rather than exclusionary politics (1991, 155, 1985). He describes a successful example of this kind from Malaysia, in which Malay and Chinese politicians were forced to rely in part on votes delivered by politicians belonging to the other ethnic group. The votes would not have been forthcoming "unless leaders could portray the candidates as moderate on issues of concern to the group that was delivering its votes across ethnic lines." In such situations, which Horowitz identifies as having operated for considerable periods (and then failed) in countries as different as Lebanon, Sri Lanka, and Nigeria, compromises at the top of a coalition are reinforced by electoral incentives at the bottom (Horowitz 1985, 154–55).

Another possible device is geographical distribution requirements, such as the Nigerian formula for presidential elections employed in 1979 and 1983, in which the winning candidate had to get both the largest number of votes and at least 25 percent of the vote in two-thirds of the then-nineteen states of the Nigerian Federation. This type of system would not work in countries like South Africa, however, given the territorial dispersion of politicized groups. In such circumstances, the two most-promising candidates are proportional representation, utilizing the single transferable vote system, and an alternative vote rule, listing more than one ordered preference but declaring elected only candidates who receive a majority, rather than a plurality, of votes. Both systems require politicians to cater to voters' choices other than their first preferences, assuming heterogeneous constituencies, so that the politicians' incentives work in the appropriate moderating directions. This will be further accentuated by the alternative vote system, assuming that parties proliferate (Horowitz 1985, 184, 166, 187–96). In many circumstances such vote-pooling systems are more likely to achieve interethnic political cooperation than consociational arrangements or systems, whether first past the post or proportional, that merely require seat pooling by politicians in coalition governments. As reactive systems, they do nothing to moderate group antipathies. On the contrary, they give politicians incentives to maximize their ex ante bargaining position by increasing what economists might describe as their group's reservation price for cooperation.

Proactive incentives to avoid appealing to intergroup antipathies will not always work. Parties might proliferate within politicized groups in ways that undermine this dimension of the logic behind weighted vote schemes.[31] Moreover, some of the worst of what often (misleadingly) gets labeled interethnic violence is actually intraethnic violence that results when different parties seek to mobilize support from the same ethnic group. Much of the South African violence that erupted in the eastern part of the country after 1984 resulted when the United Democratic Front (representing the then illegal African National Congress [ANC]) was formed and challenged Inkatha Freedom Party (IFP) support among Zulus there, and some of the worst violence among white nationalists resulted from comparable competition for the white nationalist vote. There are limits to the degree that intraethnic competition of this sort can be ameliorated by weighted vote mechanisms. If parties have incentives to mobilize support in more than one ethnic constituency, they should avoid campaigning as ethnic parties any more than they have to. In practice, however, parties like the IFP—whose raison d'être is ethnic—may have little scope to campaign on any other basis. Accordingly, they may resist—perhaps violently—any inroads into their "traditional" sources of support. They can only play a zero-sum ethnic game.

When relying on the logic of cross-group mobilization does not lead to ethnic accommodation, it may be possible to move further along the continuum and become more explicitly proactive, as in the 1931 Poona Pact in India. It requires that Untouchables be the representative in 148 designated constituencies, a number corresponding roughly to their proportion in the population (Van Parijs 1996, 111–12). This both ensures that the specified number of Untouchables become parliamentary representatives and gives aspirants for office an incentive to seek support from all sectors of heterogeneous constituencies, not merely "their own" ethnic group. (Untouchables are not prohibited from running elsewhere, but, as geographically dispersed minorities in all constituencies, they are seldom elected.[32]) Attractive as such solutions can be in some circumstances, they involve manifestly paternalistic institutional design that is unlikely to win legitimacy unless there is widespread acknowledgment that a minority has been

31. For elaboration of these and related difficulties confronting Horowitz's proposals, see Shapiro 1993, 145–7.

32. In 1996 they occupied 3 out of a total of 400 (Van Parijs 1996, 112).

unjustly treated over a long time and that it will not otherwise be represented.[33] Even then, such proposals will likely be attacked on many of the same grounds as are reverse discrimination and affirmative action. They can also be expected to provoke the charge, if from a different ideological quarter, that those competing for the designated minority spots will lack the incentive to represent the relevant minority interests. Rather, the temptation will be to try to outperform the competition as Uncle Toms.

The further institutional designers try to move along the continuum toward explicit proactive systems that force integration in exclusionary and racist societies, the more they will learn about how much redesign of ethnic antipathy is feasible in them. At present the only statement that can be made with much confidence is that there is no particular reason to think any society inherently incapable of Schumpeterian electoral competition. As the Indian and Japanese examples underscore, even societies with profoundly inegalitarian cultures and undemocratic histories have adapted to the demands of democratic politics in ways that many would have insisted was impossible before the fact. South Africa may turn out to be another such case in the making, though the jury must remain out until ANC hegemony faces a serious challenge.

▪ | Democracy's Durability

This is not to say that competitive democracy is easily established or, once established, easily sustained. Generations of scholars have theorized about the conditions that give rise to democracy. Tocqueville (1966 [1832]) alleged it to be the product of egalitarian mores. Seymour Martin Lipsett contends it is a by-product of modernization (1959, 69–105). For Barrington Moore the critical factor is the emergence of a bourgeoisie (1966, 413–32), while Rueschemeyer, Stephens, and Stephens (1992) argue that the presence of an organized working class is decisive. It now seems clear that there is no single path to democracy and, therefore, no generalization to be had about which conditions give rise to democratic transitions. Democracy can result from decades of gradual evolution (Britain and the United States), imitation (India), cascades (much of Eastern Europe in 1989), collapses (Russia after 1991), imposition from above (Spain and Brazil), revolutions (Portugal and Argentina), negotiated settlements (Poland, Bolivia, Nicaragua, and South Africa), or external imposition (Japan and West Germany) (see Przeworski 1991, ch. 1; Huntington 1991, ch. 1; Shapiro 1996, ch. 4). Perhaps there are other possibilities. No matter how democracies come into being, however, it may be that they are more

---

33. According to Nagel, a comparable solution operates with respect to four seats reserved for New Zealand's Maoris, who are also geographically dispersed (1993, 11).

likely to survive and thrive in some circumstances than others. Here the literature takes three tacks: institutional, economic, and cultural.

The institutional literature grows out of Linz's contention (1978, 1994) that parliamentary systems are more stable than presidential ones. He argued that presidential systems tend toward polarization both in the political culture and between presidents and congress, which they lack the institutional mechanisms to alleviate. Parliamentary systems, by contrast, were said to be more stable and better able to deal with leadership crises. Linz's view has been challenged by Shugart and Carey, who differentiate among more and less stable presidentialisms (1992, ch. 3), and Mainwaring and Shugart, who suggest that weak or "reactive" presidential systems, such as that in the United States, can be as stable as parliamentary ones (1997a, 12–55). Subsequent scholarship suggests that the arrangements that matter most may have less to do with whether or not presidentialism and more to do with other institutional features. For instance, a substantial presence of the presidential party in the assembly, favorable conditions for coalition politics, and centralized executive authority in the government may contribute more to stability than parliamentary institutional arrangements. This may account, in Latin America for example, for the differences between the more stable and governable countries like Argentina, Chile, Colombia, and Uruguay and less stable ones such as Ecuador, Peru, and contemporary Venezuela (see Foweraker 1998, 665–70; Cheibub and Limongi 2000).

The state of the art in the economic literature is Przeworski et al. 2000, ch. 2, which explores the impact of economic development on the stability of democratic regimes. The authors find that although economic development does not predict the installation of democracy, there is a strong relationship between economic development (in particular the level of per capita income) and the survival of democratic regimes. Democracies appear never to die in wealthy countries, whereas democracies in poor countries are fragile, exceedingly so when per capita incomes fall below $2,000 (1975 dollars). When per capita income falls below this threshold, democracies have a one in ten chance of collapsing within a year. Between per capita incomes of $2,001 and $5,000 this ratio falls to one in sixteen. Above $6,055 annual per capita income, democracies, once established, appear to last indefinitely. Moreover, poor democracies are more likely to survive when governments succeed in generating development and avoiding economic crises (Przeworski et al. 2000, 106–17).

The cultural literature is more difficult to pin down. In some countries governments stage coups rather than give up power when they are voted out of office, yet no defeated U.S. president contemplates sending the tanks down Pennsylvania Avenue. Pressed for an explanation, many appeal to beliefs, ideology, or some other cultural variable. Intuitively plausible as this might be, it is hard to study systematically, partly because people mean so many different things by culture and partly because cultural explanations tend to be residual explanations.

Huntington contends that commitment to democratic values on the part of political elites is necessary for democracy to endure (1991, 36–7). This plausible conjecture may help explain the (otherwise puzzling) endurance of Indian democracy against the odds. Indian elites were often trained in Oxford and Cambridge during the colonial period, and may have imbibed commitments to democracy from the English. It was not true, by contrast, of African political elites; this perhaps has something to do with why democracies did not generally survive in British ex-colonies there. Perhaps institutional variables account for the difference, however. The British engaged in direct rule in India, whereas indirect rule through local surrogates was the African norm (see Mamdani 1996). As the successful installation of democracy in Japan and the Federal Republic of Germany after World War II might suggest, democracy can be imposed on countries where it has no successful track record so long as there is direct control until democratic institutions take root. Detracting from this account and again suggesting the importance of culture and beliefs is the U.S. example, where democracy survived despite British reliance on indirect rule. Institutional, cultural, economic, and other variables probably all play their parts. Unfortunately, the available data does not lend itself to the kind of large-n multivariate analysis which would be required to get a systematic grip on their relative importance.

As a conceptual matter, commentators in the rational choice tradition have contended that worrying about the democratic commitments of citizens is either unnecessary or pointless in a democracy. For instance, Przeworski defines a democracy as a system of spontaneous or self-reinforcing compliance that operates successfully only when self-interested players who fail to get their way calculate that it is to their advantage to accept defeat and wait for the next chance to prevail within the rules, rather than destroy the system. When the system works, normative commitments to democracy, while sometimes present, are "not necessary to generate compliance with democratic outcomes" (1991, 19–34). The strategic calculation, by anyone who has the power to destroy the system that it is in their interest not to do so is sufficient, and likely necessary as well, for the system to survive. Otherwise the "commitment problem," as game theorists since Thomas Schelling (1960) have labeled it, cannot be solved. If Przeworski is right, trying to induce normative commitments to democracy in elites is a waste of time. In the circumstances where they are needed to prevent breakdown they will probably not produce that result, and, where breakdown does not threaten, they are redundant. Just as incentives matter more than constraints in this scheme, they also matter more than culture and beliefs.

Przeworski himself notes the existence of a counterexample to his discussion of necessity, however, and there appear to be other instances where groups whose instrumental interests are harmed by democratic processes have nonetheless supported them (see Shapiro 1996, ch. 4). In subsequent work, Przeworski has acknowledged that to date there has not been a theoretical solution to the commitment problem that relies exclusively on self-interested spontaneous compliance (1999, 25–31). As an empirical matter, this logic would leave unexplained the compliance of many political losers who have no reasonable prospect of winning in the future. Jimmy Carter and George Bush are two recent U.S. illustrations, but this practice goes back two centuries in the United States to John Adams's acquiescence in his defeat by Jefferson and the Republican Party in 1800.[34]

It is, in any case, too simple to say that a certain structure of preferences (such as one that the pluralists referred to as a system of crosscutting cleavages) will lead to self-sustaining democratic institutions while others will not. Preferences are not primordial givens; they are shaped, partly by education and acculturation and partly in response to institutional arrangements as we have seen. As a result, it seems wise to try to structure things so that people will reflect on their goals from the standpoint of the reasonable demands of others and be prepared to modify the ways in which they pursue them so as not to undermine democracy. This means that losers must come to accept the legitimacy of present defeats and sometimes even try to play constructive roles in implementing policies they oppose, while winners should appreciate the wisdom of not exploiting every dimension of their present strategic advantage. They should see the wisdom of tolerating—even valuing—continuing opposition, even if this limits the degree to which their goals can be maximized in a given situation. In short, it is prudent to assume that if democracy is to survive, people will have to be persuaded to value it for more than its short-term instrumental benefits.[35]

Another strand of scholarship on the role of culture in democratic stability focuses on mass rather than elite beliefs. Some research suggests that mass beliefs about democracy may play a role in its durability, but the effect does not seem to be strong and it operates in conjunction with numerous other variables.[36] There is also literature, centered on Putnam (1993a,

34. Hardin describes Adams's acceptance of defeat as "perhaps the most important single action by anyone under the U.S. Constitution in its first decades . . . that made the nascent American democracy meaningful in a way that must be at the core of any sensible definition of democracy" (1999, 136).

35. This suggests that Wollheim's paradox (which turns on the possibility of tension between what an individual wants and how he ought to view that preference in the event that he does not prevail through procedures of democratic decision that he accepts as legitimate [1962, 77–87]) should be thought of more as a problem of political socialization than as a philosophical paradox.

36. An empirical study suggesting that no single variable is decisive is Berg-Schlosser and De Meur 1994, 253–80. For an analysis suggesting that some aspects of political culture matter more than others for sustaining democracy, see Muller and Seligson 1994, 635–52.

1993b, 2000), which attends to mass political culture in a different way. Here the suggestion is not that mass beliefs *about democracy* are important but rather that it is membership and, above all, trust in local associations that makes democracy durable over the long haul. Putnam's thesis grew out of a study of Italy in which he argued that effective government and institutional success were contingent on the vitality of the civic community. Putnam found that those regions of Italy that had an ongoing tradition of civic engagement also had a higher level of institutional success than those regions without civic participation, despite exhibiting identical institutional structures.

For civic engagement to flourish, community members have to trust in the reciprocity of those around them and have the ability and resources to utilize social networks. Putnam deployed the term *generalized reciprocity* to connote a social understanding that one's efforts to participate and protect the common good will be reciprocated by others, known or unknown. However, Putnam distinguished two different types of networks: horizontal, the organization of individuals of equal status and resources, and vertical, the organization that brings together those of unequal status in relations of dependence or hierarchy. It is horizontal networks, which usually emerge from community participation, that he held to be critical in generating the social capital needed for institutional success. Indeed, vertical networks, for example, the Catholic Church, feudal landholdings, and clientalism, cannot cultivate the social trust he deemed essential, because the inferior and superior will experience different outcomes from the same moment of cooperation (Putnam 1993a, 173–75). On Putnam's account, horizontal civic participation, like an upward spiral, brings about the greater trust, networks, and norms that make generalized reciprocity, and hence institutional success, possible.

In a like spirit, Putnam (2000) argues that in the contemporary United States the erosion of local community participation undermines democratic participation and with it stability and governability. In the first 65 years of the twentieth century, participation in political groups, formal social clubs, and informal clubs like bowling leagues or bridge clubs was steadily increasing. After the mid-1960s, however, it began to decline. Putnam charts and then seeks to explain this waning tradition of community socializing and political participation, blaming it on numerous factors ranging from suburbanization to the mass media, particularly television, as well as demographic changes: as the older and involved generation dies out, the younger generations of baby boomers and generation Xers do not fill in the ranks in social, political, or philanthropic organizations. Nor are they interested in the informal social networks enjoyed by the older generation. The result, on Putnam's telling, is atrophy of the social networks that support the generalized reciprocity that is essential to effective democratic institutions.

Suggestive as this might be, Putnam's argument has drawn heavy critical fire, both from historians of Italy and students of contemporary U.S.

democracy (see Goldberg 1996; Sabetti 1996; Levi 1996; Gobetti 1996; Ladd 1999, 25–119). As a theoretical matter, it is difficult to see why strong local attachments and trust within local civic groups should be expected to translate into trust of democratic political institutions. Rousseau argued long ago allegiance to "sectional societies" is more likely to undermine than reinforce commitment to the collective good (1968 [1762] 150ff). Levi makes a similar point in relation to Putnam: we might more plausibly expect intensive trust in local civic associations to breed distrust of government rather than trust, as it does among militia groups for example (1996, 45–56). A possible line of response might be that it is large publicly committed civic institutions that are important for democracy, but it is hard to differentiate the Boy Scouts from the Hitler Youth on that count. At present, as with the literature on the allegedly deleterious effects of "divided societies," it is difficult to see a compelling case, conceptual or empirical, that low levels of civic trust are subversive of democracy.

■ | Supplementing Schumpeterianism

Although few today would endorse the idea of single party democracy, many democratic theorists are uncomfortable with the reduction of democratic politics to the procedures of competitive pluralism. Sometimes this is motivated by the recognition, since Arrow (1951), that there are no perfect procedural decision rules. Sometimes it flows from the view that democracy involves multiple commitments that can conflict. The question then becomes: what additional necessary conditions should be required? Here the challenge revolves around the reality that a substantive standard seems needed to decide when procedures have failed or relevant conflicts have occurred and to determine what would count as an adequate supplement or remedy. Yet there are as many theories of substantive democracy as there are substantive democratic theorists, and it seems unlikely that any one will win the philosophical high ground.[37] This suggests either an arbitrary choice among them, or the resort once more to procedures, and so a chicken-and-egg problem.

Some have responded to this conundrum by trying to work out a middle ground between procedural and substantive views, developing quasi-substantive constraints on democratic procedures. For instance, Burt (1992) contends that democracy involves foundational commitments to both majority rule and nondomination, with the ever-present potential for conflict when majorities make decisions that lead to domination. Judicial review is warranted when such conflicts arise, he argues, and courts should not conduct it in ways that assume they know how the conflict should be resolved.

37. See Ely 1980, Beitz 1988, and Habermas 1994 for examples. For further discussion of this point, see Shapiro 1996, ch. 2.

Rather they should declare that the domination that has emerged from the democratic process is unacceptable and insist that the parties try anew to find an accommodation. Thus in contrast to what many have seen as the altogether too timid approach taken by the U.S. Supreme Court in the school desegregation cases of the 1950s and after, on Burt's view the Court took the right stand. In *Brown v. Board of Education* (347 U.S. 483 [1954]) the justices declared the doctrine of separate but equal to be an unconstitutional violation of equal protection, but they did not describe schooling conditions that would be acceptable. Rather, they turned the problem back to southern state legislatures, requiring them to fashion acceptable remedies themselves.[38] These remedies came before the court as a result of subsequent litigation, were evaluated when they did, and were often found to be wanting (Burt 1992, 271–310). But the Court avoided designing the remedy itself, and thus the charge that it was usurping the legislative function.

Ruth Ginsburg has made a powerful case that when courts move beyond a reactive role, they undermine their legitimacy in a democracy. Although she thinks that it is sometimes necessary for the court to step ahead of the political process to achieve reforms that the Constitution requires, if it gets too far ahead it can produce a backlash and provoke charges that it is overreaching its appropriate place in a democratic constitutional order (1993, 30–38).[39] She and Burt both think that the sort of approach adopted by Justice Harry Blackmun in *Roe v. Wade* (410 U.S. 113 [1973]) exemplifies this danger. In contrast to the *Brown* approach, in *Roe* the Court did a good deal more than strike down a Texas abortion statute. The majority opinion laid out a detailed test to determine the conditions under which any abortion statute could be expected to pass muster. In effect, Justice Blackmun authored a federal abortion statute of his own. As Ginsburg put it, the Court "invited no dialogue with legislators. Instead, it seemed entirely to remove the ball from the legislators' court" by wiping out virtually every form of abortion regulation then in existence (1993, 32).

On the Ginsburg-Burt view, the sweeping holding in *Roe* diminished the Court's democratic legitimacy at the same time as it polarized opinion about abortion and put paid to various schemes to liberalize abortion laws that were underway in different states. Between 1967 and 1973 statutes were passed in nineteen states liberalizing the permissible grounds for abortion. Many feminists had been dissatisfied with the pace and extent of this reform. This is why they mounted the campaign that resulted in *Roe*. Burt concedes that in 1973 it was "not clear whether the recently enacted state laws signified the beginning of a national trend toward abolishing all abortion restrictions or even whether in the so-called liberalized states, the

---

38. *Brown v. Board of Education II* 349 U.S. 294 (1955).

39. See also "Nomination of Ruth Bader Ginsburg to be an Associate Justice of the United States Supreme Court: Report Together with Additional Views," Executive Report, 103-6-93-1, U.S. Senate 1993.

new enactments would significantly increase access to abortion for any-one." Nonetheless, he points out that "the abortion issue was openly, avidly, controverted in a substantial number of public forums, and unlike the regimen extant as recently as 1967, it was no longer clear who was winning the battle" (Burt 1992, 348). Following the *Brown* model, the Court might have struck down the Texas abortion statute in *Roe* and re-manded the matter for further action in the Texas state legislature, thereby setting limits on what legislatures might do in the matter of regulating abortion without involving the Court directly in designing that regulation. This would have left space for democratic resolution of the conflict, ensur-ing the survival of the right to abortion while at the same time preserving the legitimacy of the Court's role in a democracy (Burt 1992, 349–52).[40]

A comparable view is developed by Shapiro (1999), who argues for suspicion of hierarchical outcomes on the grounds that they limit the ca-pacity for effective opposition which democracy requires. Hierarchies are often legitimate, and when they are created in democratic ways, they have a particularly strong claim on our allegiance. Yet hierarchies have propen-sities to atrophy into systems of domination, necessitating institutional con-straints that shift burdens of proof to those who would defend them. Sometimes the appropriate policing mechanisms are courts, conceived on the Ginsburg-Burt model, sometimes they are other second-guessing insti-tutions. Whatever the mechanism, the goal is to give participants in a dem-ocratic order incentives to find ways to pursue their goals that maximize inclusive participation in decision making at the same time as they mini-mize domination. As with the Ginsburg-Burt view, there is no presumption that a third-party institutional designer knows what the right answer should be. Rather, the thought is to try to structure things so that the players them-selves will have incentives to discover, even invent, ways to avoid perverse consequences of democratic procedures and to minimize the tensions be-tween democracy and the pursuit of other goods.

Some will find this too minimal a role for courts in protecting impor-tant freedoms, plumping instead for a liberal constitutionalism that con-strains democracy rather than this democratic constitutionalism that seeks only to make it operate more effectively (see Rawls 1971; Ackerman 1980; Dworkin 1986). At least since Tocqueville's time it has been common to

---

40. The Ginsburg-Burt approach was eventually adopted by the Supreme Court in *Planned Parenthood of Pennsylvania v. Casey*, 112 S.Ct. 2791 (1992). By affirming the existence of a woman's fundamental constitutional right to an abortion, recog-nizing the legitimacy of the state's interest in potential life, and insisting that states may not pursue the vindication of that interest in a manner that is unduly burden-some to women, the Court set some basic parameters within which legislatures must fashion abortion regulations. This approach was reaffirmed in *Stenberg v. Carhart*, 120 S.Ct. 2597 (2000), when the Court held that a Nebraska statute out-lawing partial birth abortions imposes an undue burden on women. These issues are taken up further in the editor's introduction to Shapiro 2001.

worry that democracy is a threat to political freedom. But, as Dahl (2002, ch. 4) has recently reminded us, Tocqueville was wrong. In the century and a half since he wrote, political freedoms have turned out to be safer in democracies than in nondemocracies by a considerable margin. Almost half a century earlier Dahl had registered skepticism that, even within democracies, constitutional courts could be shown to have a positive effect on the degree to which individual freedoms are respected (1956, 105–12). Subsequent scholarship has shown his skepticism to be well founded (see Dahl 1989, 188–92; Tushnet 1999; Hirschl 1999). Indeed, there are reasons for thinking that the popularity of independent courts in new democracies may have more in common with the popularity of independent banks than with the protection of individual freedoms. They can operate as devices to signal foreign investors and international economic institutions that the capacity of elected officials to engage in redistributive policies or interfere with property rights will be limited. That is, they may be devices for limiting domestic political opposition to unpopular policies by taking them off the table (Hirschl 2000).

From a different quarter it might be objected that the middle-ground views I have surveyed are in fact implicitly substantive. If courts or other second-guessing agencies intervene in the results of democratic procedures declaring them to be unacceptable on democratic grounds, there must be a theory of substantive democracy, however implicit, by reference to which such judgments are rendered. Embracing this conclusion involves too quick a dismissal of the potential for middle-ground views. Their motivating intuition is that people can reasonably find things unacceptable even when they cannot articulate an account of what would be acceptable. During the 1970s in South Africa many people had no doubt that apartheid violated essential principles of democratic governance, but few—if any—of them could have spelled out a consistent theory of democratic representation or even said how they would resolve the various conundrums about representation that have arisen in the post-apartheid South Africa. They were against domination in Machiavelli's sense mentioned in the first section, even if they could not have explained what they favored. This is dramatic but not atypical; in many ways human beings are reactive adaptive creatures. They reject what is unacceptable and shy away from what fails, assuming that it must be possible to come up with something better. Often this is more of a regulative ideal than an implicit theory, and sometimes the hope will prove vain. But not always. The middle-ground views rest on the supposition that often enough human ingenuity can rise to the challenge thrown up by the failures of democratic procedures and that loading the dice to facilitate that outcome is a better democratic solution than the going alternatives.[41]

41. A different variant of the middle-ground views is put forward by Pettit (1997, 2000).

■ | **Concluding Comments**

It is conventional, though partly misleading, to distinguish power management views of democratic purposes from those geared to the search for a
common good. Aggregative and deliberative views of the common good
run into serious difficulties as we saw in the first section, where I argued
that the alternative focus on democracy as a means for legitimate management of power relations offers distinct advantages. This does, however, rest
on a conception of the common good, if a comparatively thin or subordinate one. I paraphrased Machiavelli by suggesting that it embodies what
those with an interest in avoiding domination share in common. It requires
rights both of inclusive participation and of loyal opposition: freedom to
participate in decisions that affect you and to oppose and try to change outcomes you reject by working through the system.

My discussion of the best means for securing democratic rights of participation and opposition was organized around an examination of the critics and defenders of Schumpeterian democracy in the second section.
There I argued that the Schumpeterian conception is flawed for two reasons: democratic polities are often not competitive in ways that the model
assumes and Schumpeterian's exclusive focus on governmental institutions
is unsatisfying given the ubiquity of power relations in other realms of social life. Powerful as these criticisms are, I suggested that the appropriate
response is not to reject the Schumpeterian ideal outright but rather to
find ways of making politics more genuinely competitive and of extending
democratic constraints to nongovernmentalist arenas of collective action.
The dangers of rejecting the idea of political competition were seen in my
discussion of consociationalism: it can lead to a self-fulfilling prophecy that
democracy is impossible or to an embrace of the implausible proposition
that institutionalized consensus is an appropriate vehicle for democracy. I
did not discuss the extension of democracy into nongovernmental domains
of social life, a subject I have explored extensively elsewhere (see Shapiro
1999).

If there is no good reason to assume democracy is impossible in some
parts of the world, this does not mean it is possible in all circumstances, as
I noted. Entrenched antipathies might be difficult to overcome in the relevant ways, dictators might have vicelike grips on power, or other factors
might make democratic innovation unlikely. Yet transitions to democracy
can occur in improbable settings (most recently Nigeria in 1999–2000),
and, when they do occur, this can be by one of a several possible routes.
More consequential is whether democracy, no matter how instituted, is
likely to survive. On this there is surprisingly little accumulated knowledge
in political science. The absence of severe poverty and the presence of economic growth seem to help, but the literatures on which institutional and
cultural factors are more or less conducive to democratic political stability
remain very much works in progress.

In the last section I turned to the critique of Schumpeterianism that, as a purely procedural view, it can generate perverse results. Obvious instances are when majorities vote to disenfranchise minorities or otherwise render their opposition ineffective. Responding to the weakness of pure proceduralism with theories of substantive democracy creates difficulties of its own, the most striking's being the need to choose among them without resort once more to proceduralism. However, I suggested that a fertile area of democratic theory is being developed by a group of quasi-substantive theorists who are attending to institutional devices geared to limiting democracy's propensity to produce outcomes at variance with its constitutive ethos. I focused particularly on their accounts of the appropriate role for constitutional courts. Unlike liberal constitutionalists, for whom such courts exist to protect liberal values from the vicissitudes of democratic politics, theorists in this group argue that we should limit courts to protecting democracy from itself. Intervention is legitimate only when the democratic process threatens to break down or when acting on the democratic imperative undermines another.[42] Even then, on these views, if courts are to build and maintain their legitimacy in democracies, they should always intervene in democracy-sustaining ways.

42. One example that suggests itself from the discussion of oligopolistic competition and collusion in the second section would be for U.S. courts to entertain public interest antitrust actions against political parties.

JEREMY WALDRON

Justice

What is the present state of discussion in legal and political theory so far as the topic of justice is concerned? By *justice*, I mean social or distributive justice: the evaluation of social policy and institutional arrangements on the basis of the way they affect the distribution of scarce resources and opportunities among individuals in society. It will be quite important to my argument in this chapter that the term *justice* does not take in the whole of liberal political philosophy. One point that I shall emphasize is that recent theoretical discussions ostensibly about justice have tended to drift away from that subject and become meditations on political morality generally, or public reason in a multicultural society. This has left a significant gap in our philosophical discussion of issues about wealth, poverty, and distribution, a gap that economic theorists who are relatively uninterested in distributive issues have not been slow to fill.

If political philosophy in the 1970s and early 1980s was dominated by a fierce and focused debate about social justice occasioned by the publication of John Rawls's first book (1971), the past ten years or so have seen a blurring of that focus under the influence of Rawls's later work (1980, 1985, 1996), and a diversion of the fierce energies that A *Theory of Justice* aroused into a safer and less consequential discussion of the nature of political argument in a multicultural society.

Social justice is about equality, property, need, desert, and opportunity. It is about structures that govern people's access in society to the main sources of well-being: wealth, income, employment, education, enterprise, health care, and so on. The debate inspired by A *Theory of Justice* raged around such propositions as:

> Social and economic inequalities are to be arranged so that they are . . . to the greatest benefit of the least advantaged. (Rawls 1971, 83)

[U]ndeserved inequalities call for redress; and since inequalities of birth and natural endowment are undeserved, these inequalities are somehow to be compensated for. (Rawls 1971, 100)

[T]he difference principle represents, in effect, an agreement to regard the distribution of natural talents as a common asset. (Rawls 1971, 101)

From Rawls's critics, these positions elicited equally robust responses: "Taxation of earnings from labor is on a par with forced labor" (Nozick 1974, 169), "[D]istributionist theories cannot be theories of justice" (Mack 1976, 145), and " 'Social justice' can be given a meaning only in a directed or 'command' economy" (Hayek 1976, 62). Great progress was made in the analytic understanding of these and related issues. The role of maximin, the logic of historical entitlement, the relation between desert and respect for persons, the currency of equality (resources, well-being, capabilities), the argument for Rawls's "difference principle" over radical equality claims (on the one hand) and over claims of need (on the other), the relation between justice and liberty—these were just a few of the topics whose discussion flourished in the decade or so following the appearance of Rawls's magisterial book. Some of that discussion was focused on particular questions of policy—the defense (or critique) of welfare rights, for example, or redistributive taxation or the discussion of affirmative action.

From a theoretical point of view, however, the most encouraging feature of the discussion initiated by Rawls was the elaboration of various model-theoretic devices—the original position, the veil of ignorance, the notion of lexical priority (as opposed to a priority expressed through the metaphor of weight), and the distinctions between pure, perfect, and imperfect procedural justice—not to mention the revival and more rigorous use of existing theoretical constructs like the difference between classical and average utilitarianism, the distinction between the right and the good, and the idea of a Lockean proviso. All of this meant that when philosophers of justice turned their attention to issues of public policy, they were able, in some cases at least, to offer a distinctive contribution qua philosophers. They did not simply convert the new normative spirit in political theory into an opportunity for political advocacy.

That's where we were in the 1970s and 1980s. And some of that discussion persists: certainly, the theoretical apparatus that was introduced in Rawls's conception (and in the debates surrounding it) has become a permanent part of the theoretical landscape. It is not beyond question; nothing in our theoretical landscape, however venerable, is beyond question. But as far as one can tell, this model-theoretic apparatus is the most enduring part of Rawls's legacy, even if the particular claims that Rawls embodied in that framework are opposed or rejected by many theorists.[1]

Something happened, however, in the late 1980s to turn the mainstream of liberal discussion away from the hard detail of issues about

1. Indeed theoretical interest in the use of these tools may have been heightened by the recent publication of Rawls's article-length writings (Rawls 1999a) and of a restatement (Rawls 2001) of the main themes of Rawls 1971.

justice. John Rawls (especially in Rawls 1996) continued to contribute powerful model-theoretic ideas—overlapping consensus, for example, and the burdens of judgment—but the debate they evoked was no longer oriented specifically to issues of social justice. Beginning with his John Dewey Lectures at Columbia, Rawls began paying particular attention to the issue of how one might argue politically in a society whose members held disparate and opposed ethical, philosophic, and religious conceptions.[2] Indeed, he seemed to be rejecting a universalist approach in favor of one that was connected with the particular difficulties faced by our own society:

> [W]e are not trying to find a conception of justice suitable for all societies regardless of their particular social or historical circumstance. . . . We look to ourselves and to our future and reflect upon our disputes since, let's say, the Declaration of Independence. How far the conclusions we reach are of interest in a wider context is a separate question. (1980, 518–19)

This makes it sound as though a theory of justice is expected to capture only the particularity of U.S. thought and practice. It resonated with a theme emphasized by Walzer (1983): that a well-ordered society is a society true to its own understandings; or, if it is to be reproached as unjust, it is to be reproached as having fallen away from values that already have a purchase in the life and practice of its members. Critics quickly established of course that the Walzerian position would work only if one could identify and privilege a set of understandings relevant to justice that could be construed definitely as "ours" for the purpose of this sort of reflection on what it would mean for "our" society to be well ordered. And arguably that condition is not given (see Dworkin 1985a).

A well-ordered society is defined in Rawlsian theory as one in which citizens can justify their shared arrangements to one another (Rawls 1971, 453 ff.). But most people live in multicultural societies whose members hold a variety of beliefs about the building blocks of social justification—things like autonomy, God, human nature, relations between the sexes, the importance of reason, and the meaning of life. So what if a pious Muslim asks a secular materialist to justify (say) the toleration of pornography? What vocabulary should they use in the ensuing discussion? Or what if an economist asks a Catholic theologian to justify antieuthanasia laws? What sort of dialogue or conversation would certify a society like this as well ordered? It is no good saying, "Well, put them behind the veil of ignorance, and see what they come up with." The veil of ignorance is itself a way of modeling ideas about fairness, and the problem posed by pluralism is that

2. This had been raised also in earlier discussions about liberal neutrality in Dworkin 1978 and in Ackerman 1980.

fairness may be understood quite differently (or may not figure prominently at all) in various traditions.

In his second book, *Political Liberalism*, Rawls (1996) insisted that
public justifications in a well-ordered society must in some sense stand
above or apart from the religious, cultural, and philosophical issues that divide the citizens. A person does not show another the requisite respect if he
responds to requests for justification in terms that he knows the other cannot accept. So a Left liberal like me may not say, for example, to a Social
Darwinian that even the feeblest person is entitled to our compassion because he is created in the image of God. I must find some way of putting
my point about equality that can be affirmed even by people who do not
share my religious convictions. The principles of justice, the assumptions
(like basic equality) that they rest on, and the model-theoretic conceptions
(such as the original position) that we use to elaborate them—all these
must be made intelligible to and must be capable of commanding the allegiance of people whose deepest convictions are not reflected in their own
terms in the content of social justification.

I do not intend to examine in detail the ideas like overlapping consensus, public reason, and political liberalism, which Rawls uses to answer this
challenge. This is not because they are unimportant; it is rather because
they are not specific to the issue of justice (which is what I am commissioned to study in this chapter). Since 1980 much of what Rawls has written and much of what is most hotly debated in his work, though presented
under the label "justice," is in fact general political philosophy—dealing
either with general metatheoretical questions about objectivity, universalism, discourse ethics, and the need for shared frameworks or—when he
deigns to descend to first-level concerns—with issues about toleration, constitutionalism, democracy, and civil rights, rather than with issues specific
to social justice (the issues that dominated the first wave of discussion generated by Rawls 1971) such as distribution, desert, needs, opportunities,
and markets, and the rival claims of equality, fairness, and economic efficiency. Of course the detailed elaboration of Rawls's political liberalism is
not irrelevant to justice (and I shall say something in a moment about its
specific applicability in that regard); but most of his discussion since 1980
has proceeded on a much more general front.[3]

Something similar may be said, too, about the debate between liberals
and communitarians that was sparked by Michael Sandel's critique (1982)
of Rawls's book. Though Sandel's work was initially focused quite closely
on the detail of Rawls 1971, it did raise much more general issues about social and ethical ontology, issues whose discussion has taken us into fertile
and fascinating territory—but territory miles away from the site of contesta-

---

3. This is true also of discussions between Rawls and Jurgen Habermas, and their
respective disciples (see Habermas 1998a; Rawls 1995).

tion about social justice, where the claims of the Rawlsian liberals and the Sandelian communitarians were initially staked.

This tendency of discussions of justice to open up into much broader philosophical discussions has been well known since Aristotle's time. Not only is "justice . . . often thought to be the greatest of virtues," said Aristotle, but "proverbially 'in justice is every virtue comprehended' " —or, at least, every virtue that relates to one's dealings with other people. Still, Aristotle said, it is also worth "investigating . . . the justice which is a *part* of virtue," that is specifically those fairness-related virtues which have to do with the regulation of "graspingness," the regulation of people's tendency to grab what is more than their share under various conditions and circumstances (1954, 106–12).

Admittedly, it was an important thesis of Rawls's first book that social justice, even in the narrower of the two senses that Aristotle distinguished, is to be understood in relation to the impact on individuals of the whole basic structure of social institutions taken as a single scheme, so that one cannot reach a verdict about the justice of (say) the taxation system, without considering its relation to the welfare system, the education system, and the system of liberties that enables individuals to make something of the resources and opportunities assigned to them (1971, 7). That meant that even a discussion dedicated specifically to social justice would have to consider issues like the nature and priority of liberty and the relation between justice and the constitution. And so reflecting on how to argue about justice would involve reflecting on how to argue about these topics as well.

Even so, it does not follow that social justice is merely a matter of reflecting on the way to argue about basic liberties. Even under Rawls 1996, a discussion of social justice should still involve an attempt to grapple with detailed issues about economy, equality, efficiency, opportunity and fairness under the specific constraints of political liberalism. And, in my view, *that* is what people working within the present Rawlsian paradigm seem to be neglecting: they are much more interested in discussing the constraints of political liberalism itself—and the troubling issues that are most immediately raised as we attempt to elaborate those constraints (e.g., issues about religious freedom, cultural accommodation, and so on)—than in pursuing the discussion of social justice under those auspices.

I don't underestimate the difficulty of dealing with social justice issues within the framework of political liberalism. These are not issues that can be dealt with by a strategy of vagueness or evasion—putting about a set of anodyne formulas that mean all things to all people. A theory of social justice has hard, critical work to do, on Rawls's original account: it has to settle complex questions about freedom, equality, and opportunity, and it has to hold its own against rival conceptions (against Nozick 1974, for example, or against utilitarian or efficiency-based approaches). If there is a fault in Rawls's later work, it is a tendency to lose sight of the difficulty of the social and economic argumentation in A *Theory of Justice*. The actual examples of overlapping consensus for a pluralist society provided in *Political Liberalism* are laughably easy by comparison. Both Kantians and non-Kantians might favor democracy, Rawls says; and both Christians and secularists may well oppose slavery (Rawls 1996, 122–25). The hard part comes when we try to establish an overlapping consensus among (say) Christian fundamentalists, Hindus, secular humanists, scientific determinists, and members of the dot-com generation on the definition of *equal opportunity*, the use of economic incentives, and the distinction between liberty and the worth of liberty.

Just to give a taste of the difficulty, consider the problem of the relevance of desert to basic social entitlement. This was central in social justice discussions in the 1970s and 1980s, and various approaches to it informed people's views about market success, the problem of the undeserving poor, and so on. Now, it was not hard to see that insistence on a strong theory of desert might mean that a theory of justice would have to buy into social and religious controversies about virtue (cf. Dworkin 1978, 138; Hayek 1976, 73 ff.). But it was much more difficult to know what to *do* with that point or what would be a fair or a neutral way to move on from it. Does one simply reject desert in this sphere (and the whole view of the person that goes with desert), or does one try to develop a thin theory of desert or to modify the assumptions, for example, about freedom and background responsibility for character, that deserving is sometimes thought to presuppose? Can we imagine an overlapping consensus on problems like *that* between (say) the Protestant work ethic, the notion of apostolic poverty, and ideas of the fundamental solidarity of community?

It is easy to despair of answering questions like this under the conditions that Rawls's later work has emphasized. It would be a pity, however, if Rawls's followers were to abandon his most challenging theorems on social justice simply because they do not fit the template of "public reason" which he has now made central to his theory (Rawls 1993, 212 ff.). Certainly, it would be a shame to do so without considering what becomes of the primacy of justice in a liberal theory if we are forced to admit that some liberal values (like toleration and basic liberties) can be elaborated in overlapping consensus while others (like economic equality) cannot.

I should add that issues about desert and social justice have not been wholly neglected in the most recent discussion. In a recent book, David Miller has argued (against the claims made in Rawls 1971) that we do possess "a coherent concept of desert that is sufficiently independent of our existing institutions for it to serve as a critical weapon in the armory of social justice," and Miller insists that theories of social justice would lose touch with popular opinion if they pretended to ignore it (1999, 155). Samuel Scheffler also observes that liberal political philosophy has often been viewed as carelessly repudiating ordinary beliefs about the responsibility of the individual for his or her own actions in relation to social justice (1992,

299; cf. Rawls 1971, 103–4). "The widespread reluctance among political philosophers to defend a robust notion of preinstitutional desert" is traceable, Scheffler suggests, to the assumption of a naturalistic worldview, which alone seems (to liberals, certainly not to their opponents) to stand above the ferment of religious and cultural controversy between various worldviews in a pluralistic society (1992, 309). It seems we cannot take desert and responsibility as seriously as ordinary intuitions require without abandoning this stance of philosophical neutrality. Scheffler offers no comfortable solution to this difficulty, but his willingness to raise it represents an important mapping of the concerns of political liberalism onto issues specific to social justice.

While Miller and Scheffler confront questions about the neutrality of the terms in which society evaluates distributions, other theorists have asked about the terms in which individuals state their own preferences and conceive of their own interests, so far as issues of justice are concerned. The work of Amartya Sen (1982) and Ronald Dworkin (1981a, 1981b, 2000) on equality invites us to consider what it would be to treat as equals, for the purposes of justice, persons with quite different sorts of aims and aspirations for their lives. One person may be willing to put up with a great deal of pain for the sake of some athletic achievement; another may be an aesthete with exquisitely expensive tastes. Is there a neutral metric of justice or equality under whose auspices we can define a fair distribution of resources to these individuals?

Equality of utility seems unfair to the athlete, who values something other than happiness and freedom from pain; but equality of wealth or income seems unfair to the person with expensive tastes, who may get much less satisfaction than others from a given stock of resources. Again, one individual may prefer a life of leisure, another a prudent and productive life. Or one individual prefers working communally with others, while another prefers a small holding of his own. Is there a fair basis on which we can say what all these people are entitled to ab initio (let alone in the context of an ongoing scheme of social and economic cooperation)? Dworkin has developed an interesting set of model theoretic devices—an initial auction of resources, packaged in different ways, and a hypothetical insurance market to deal with issues of choice and affliction—as a basis for thinking through such questions under fairly challenging assumptions about the incommensurability of individuals' aims and circumstances (1981a).[4]

Philippe Van Parijs (1995) has attempted to do something similar for

---

4. In the preface to Dworkin 2000, there is an indication that Dworkin intends to develop the philosophical basis of his 1981 and 1981a more systematically in a book. But as it stands, Dworkin 2000 is not such a systematic exposition. In the meantime, Rakowski 1991 is the major book-length elaboration of a position like Dworkin's.

our discussion of freedom; his book *Real Freedom for All* argues that a free society is required to offer a basic income to everyone, irrespective of what they propose to do with it or how they intend to live. Of course, no society does this or does it directly, and most people's sustenance is not predicated on any such starting point. Nevertheless Van Parijs argues that the distinctions we do draw between individuals for the purposes of assessing justice and entitlements—the distinction for example between the idle and the productive—have no legitimacy unless they presuppose such an initial distribution or are conditioned by what such a presupposition would distributively entail. Without that condition a claim that the lazy are not entitled to subsistence would have to presuppose the rest of us have the right to pick and choose who we exclude from the resources available in society, and that, Van Parijs (1995) argues, is indefensible.

The works just referred to exhibit exactly the virtues that are called for but not displayed in Rawls's later work. They address problems associated with the diversity and incommensurability of people's comprehensive conceptions of what makes life worth living. But they do so without losing sight of the central issues of justice. By contrast, recent work ostensibly on justice by Brian Barry, which also pays specific attention to the problem of developing a theory in a way that is fair or impartial to rival religious, cultural, and philosophical conceptions, is almost completely schematic so far as the detail of social justice is concerned. Barry has produced two volumes of a projected three (or perhaps four) volume *Treatise on Social Justice.* The first volume (1989b) developed a most valuable contrast between theories of justice that proceed from the premise that justice must be to everyone's advantage and theories of justice that see no need for such a premise. The second volume (1995) was supposed to set out the implications of Barry's own view—a view of the latter type—for the distribution of benefits and burdens in a society (1989b, xiii). It turns out, however, that most of Barry 1995 is devoted to an exploration of what it would mean for a theory of justice to be impartial as between rival conceptions of the good, and that largely schematic discussion is illustrated by examples (e.g., about constitutional guarantees of religious freedom) drawn from outside the specific area of social justice. Let me say again that I don't for a moment doubt the importance of discussions like this (or that of Scanlon 1998, with which Barry has great sympathy). The issue of how to argue and justify normative positions in political philosophy in a pluralistic society is massively important. But though that discussion is a necessary preliminary for theorizing about social justice, it is not itself a substitute for it. And one worries a little when one sees the task of detailed argumentation about justice being indefinitely postponed.

How much of this has to do with changes in political circumstances? There can be no doubt that the changes of the 1980s and 1990s have put liberal egalitarianism on the defensive. It is less clear, what effect this has had on discussions of justice in academic political philosophy. F. A. Hayek once wrote:

> I have come to feel strongly that the greatest service I can still render to my fellow men would be that I could make the speakers and writers among them thoroughly ashamed ever again to employ the term "social justice." (1976, 97)

But the disconnect between Hayek's endeavors and mainstream political philosophy was shown by the fact of his laboring under the impression that he and John Rawls were in general agreement on these matters.[5] At any rate, the political success of Hayekian and other New Right ideas certainly has not stifled discussions of social justice (though it may have contributed somewhat to the embarrassed postponement of detailed discussion that I was complaining about at the end of the previous section).

The events of 1989 to 1991 have perhaps made it harder to sustain straight-faced worries about whether liberal justice can be made appealing to the followers of Karl Marx. People don't spend as much time these days as they used to pretending that there is an important and troubling line of argument (as opposed to a few throwaway lines) in pamphlets like *The Critique of the Gotha Program* (Marx 1977 [1875]) which modern theories of justice need to address, nor do they invest the energy as they used to invest (certainly in the Britain of my acquaintance in the late 1970s and 1980s) in the thankless task of trying to convince Marxists that liberal work on justice should not be dismissed as just another bourgeois trick (cf. Husami 1978; Buchanan 1982).

Perhaps what the new political mood *has* produced is a philosophical environment in which it is easier for philosophers to pose tough questions about the motivation to be just and about the basis of the demand that each of us should submit the prosperity of our families to the demands of social justice. Such questions no longer require us to imagine a Thrasymachus breaking into our discussion from the outside like a wild beast (Plato 1995, 16). Instead we can ask quite calmly, as Thomas Nagel (1991) has asked in an influential book, whether there is not a level of sacrifice that it is unreasonable for the state to impose upon the well-off, for the benefit of the poor, in the interests of justice. Is there not a standpoint, Nagel asks—the standpoint of one's personal concerns and affections— from which the egalitarian demands of impartial justice can be made to

---

5. Cf. Hayek 1976, xiii. "Though the first impression of readers may be different, Rawls's statement which I quote later in this volume (1976, 100) seems to me to show that we agree on what is to me the essential point." The quoted passage from Rawls to which he refers (and with which he agrees) specifies the design of the basic structure as the important problem of justice. See also the discussion of this in Waldron 1993a, 29–31.

seem unreasonable? And if they do seem unreasonable from the personal point of view of, say, a prosperous middle-class American, isn't that an important fact that moral and political philosophy must reckon with, rather than just a sordid clash between justice and amoral self-interest (in which of course justice *ought* to prevail?) Doesn't it require us to rethink our conceptions of justice from the beginning, and to call in question our initial sense of what justice is entitled to demand?

Of course, the issue of how demanding morality may reasonably be is a hardy perennial (see, e.g., Scheffler 1982): it has flared up in recent years in debates about yuppie ethics (cf. Baron 1987; H. Shue 1988) initiated, for example, by the consequentialist rigorism of Shelly Kagan's book *The Limits of Morality* (1989) and by some provocations published in the popular press by Peter Singer (1999). But its direct application to claims about justice—and the shameless assumption that justice may have to yield to the demands by some of us for a good life, even if such a life is not available to all—does seem a remarkable feature of the recent philosophical debate.

The demandingness of justice is an issue that the Rawlsians had hoped to finesse, by a combination of strategies. First, Rawls had argued in *A Theory of Justice* that the two principles of justice as fairness, applying as they did to the basic structure of society, did not make any particular demands on individuals, except that they accept and support the basic structure of just institutions (1971, 6–10, 73–78, 93–101). Within that structure, individuals were conceived as free to act from self-interested or partial motivations if they wanted to. However, this thesis has been heavily attacked in recent work by G. A. Cohen (1997, 2000). Cohen argues that "justice requires an ethos governing daily choice which goes beyond one of obedience to just rules" (2000, 136), for, as Okin (1989) and others have argued, the basic structure cannot be understood as something independent of what people do in their daily lives. Just institutions cannot therefore be expected to survive in the face of powerful popular sentiment about the unreasonableness of the demands of justice on individual lives.

Rawls had also attempted to finesse the point by presenting his theory of justice as a conception which works in the interests of everyone: "In justice as fairness society is interpreted as a cooperative venture for mutual advantage" (1971, 84) He said that "everyone may expect to improve his situation if all comply with these principles, at least in comparison with what his prospects would be in the absence of any agreement" (1971, 296). Brian Barry has done political philosophy a major service by dissecting and refuting this claim. He shows that Rawls makes no more than a half-hearted effort to argue for a mutual advantage interpretation, that is, to show that there are none who might do better for themselves in a situation where no one observed Rawlsian principles than in a situation where everyone did (1989b, 71–74, 241–54). The most Rawls can show is that the difference principle does not worsen anyone's prospects relative to a baseline of simple equality. But simple equality is not what we have at present; and Rawls fails to show—he does not even try to show, nor could he show—that the readers of his book (let alone those who are too busy managing their wealth to bother with books about justice) would do as well as they are doing at the moment, if his two principles were to be put into effect. In response to an imagined complaint from a well-endowed person who would have less (than he has at present) under the difference principle, Rawls writes:

> It is clear that the well-being of each depends on a scheme of social coopera-tion without which no one could have a satisfactory life. . . . The difference principle . . . seems to be a fair basis on which those better endowed, or more fortunate in their social circumstances, could expect others to collaborate with them when some workable arrangement is a necessary condition of the good of all. (1971, 103)

But this is just a gesture. It is not argued for; Barry shows that there is no basis in Rawls's model for arguing for it; and the logic of the original posi-tion is against it, inasmuch as that conception requires each party to bar-gain without any awareness of what he could hope to achieve for himself by trusting to his own force or cunning.[6]

Let me add that this is not a point *against* Rawls: a mutual advantage condition on theories of justice is quite implausible, if the baseline from which advantage is to be calculated refers to existing holdings in the world. It's just a point about truth in advertising. But it does mean that the Rawl-sian enterprise has to face up to the problems posed by the gulf between justice and the partial interests of individuals.

Many of these themes play out in complex and difficult forms in the dis-cussion of global justice. In 1971, Rawls had assumed that theoretical dis-cussions of social justice could be confined, for the time being, to the case of "the basic structure of society conceived for the time being as a closed system isolated from other societies" (8). But obviously there are issues that require us to loosen this restriction. The framework for international trade and the global economy, the existence of borders and immigration restric-tions, and the regulation of transnational environmental effects—all these raise questions of justice that cannot be properly addressed within the con-fines of Rawls's assumption. There is now a growing body of work about global justice (see, e.g., Barry 1989a; Pogge 1994b). Some of it attempts to develop and apply the Rawlsian framework to this wider context (cf. Pogge

6. Barry has also done sterling work in regard to some confused claims made about the relation between justice and mutual advantage by David Gauthier, in behalf of his theory of justice in Gauthier 1986 (see Gauthier 1998, 120 ff.; Barry 1998, 218–24).

1989); others pursue the subject more directly (e.g., Jones 1999). Perhaps not surprisingly, in view of our discussion in section 1, John Rawls's ostensible contribution (1999a) to this discussion is mostly not about global justice at all but about liberal approaches to international relations and human rights issues.

Much elementary work remains to be done in this area. First, theorists of global justice need to address the question of the extent to which talk about justice presupposes an agency or an institution (like the state) capable of doing justice. If it does, then the application of global justice theory is confined either to the work of global institutions or to those aspects of particular countries' institutions—like their immigration policies, trade preferences, environmental regulations, and so on—which have an extra-territorial impact. I suspect it is a mistake to confine the discussion in this way. In 1976, F. A. Hayek tried to convince us that we could not talk about the justice or injustice of market outcomes because these outcomes are not "the result of a deliberate allocation" by the state (64). We were not convinced: though we accepted that the use of an evaluative concept like justice must be restricted to arrangements that were in some sense subject to human control, we did not accept that its use was restricted to outcomes that were deliberately contrived, let alone those that were deliberately contrived by the state or a statelike institution (see Plant 1984, 3–5).

Well, the same applies in the global context. Certainly the disparity of access that people in different countries have to natural resources and to established frameworks of economic interaction is not a natural fact (like the weather); and even if it were, it is not a natural fact that humans can do nothing about (nothing to make it better, nothing to make it worse). Even accepting that it is an inadvertent resultant of millions of human decisions, we are required nevertheless to assess it at the bar of justice, because those decisions *could* be regulated within frameworks that are different from those within which they are currently regulated. There are also things that large numbers of people in the world could do to change the way they are regulated, despite the fact that there is no world government. So there is a question to be answered about the justice of our persisting with the current framework (or with its present trajectory of change).

These points are important in combating a tendency to think about global justice in terms of what distinct societies, whose members happen to be endowed with different levels of wealth and resources, owe to one another. The image that is sometimes used is that of two island societies, which have only recently become aware of each others's existence, and one is much poorer than the other: do the residents of the wealthier island owe anything to the residents of the poorer island if the former managed to secure their greater wealth without any interaction with the latter (cf. Nozick 1974, 185–86)? But that is nothing like the situation in the real world. First of all, there have been in fact millennia of interaction between peoples and of movement of peoples back and forth across the face of the earth. Second, the main obstacles to poor people's access to resources such as minerals, fertile land, water, and so on, are human made (border fences, immigration control, etc.), not natural.

Once there is a physical possibility that that a person (or a whole people), P, might use a given resource, then the claim that that resource belongs rightfully to A and that A is entitled to exclude P, must be defended in a way that takes proper account of P's interests. It is not enough for A to show that her claim is defensible vis-à-vis the interests of her immediate neighbors B and C. Once P appears on the horizon, A's claim must be defensible to P as well. Otherwise there is no legitimacy to A's claim that P ought to leave her holding alone, and nothing but force or lies to back it up. From this point of view, it is not *global* justice theory that requires special justification. What requires special justification is the restriction of the scope of a theory of justice to the members of a particular society; and even if such justifications can be made out, they are likely to imply that any claims established by such restricted theorizing are purely pro tem or in personam, holding only between the individuals whose interests have been considered, without prejudice to the interests or claims of outsiders.

The point can be stated even more starkly with regard to borders and immigration controls, whose effect is to exclude outsiders not so much from access to natural resources as from participation in the established local or national economy in a given territory. Morally, it is quite inappropriate to concoct a defense of the justice of immigration controls with reference only to the interests of people on one side of the fence. Such controls have an impact on would-be migrants as well as existing residents of the country of immigration, and an assessment of their justice requires an assessment and comparison of those impacts (Carens 1995b). This is not a matter of taste, with cosmopolitans swinging one way, and communitarians the other. It is a matter of the elementary logic of justice, and its neglect I think—even in academic debates about immigration—bears witness once again to the fact, which we discussed in the previous section, that the primacy of justice (over, say, self-interest or national interest) is no longer uncontested.

Turning now from the clash between justice and particular interest to issues within the theory of justice itself, there has been an intriguing fallout from the events of the past ten years: a resuscitation of what amounts to a conception of justice based on aggregate utility.

This is not what one would have expected from the debates of the 1970s. One might have thought that the triumph of markets and capitalism after 1989 would have produced by the end of the century an owl of Minerva taking flight in Nozickian garb. It was, after all, Nozick 1974 that sharpened the debate about justice, rights, private property, and equality in the 1970s, taking the arguments of the Right from the repetition of tired, spittle-laden slogans about liberty into the realm of systematic and analytically respectable accounts of self-ownership and historical entitlement. For those of us on the Left, it was Robert Nozick (rather than, say, F. A. Hayek or James Buchanan) who undermined our confidence in simple formulas of equality and who convinced us—for example, through the famous Wilt Chamberlain example—that "no end-state principle or distributional patterned principle of justice can be continuously realized without contin-uous interference with people's lives" (1974, 160–64).

But Nozick did his work almost too well to be much use to the tri-umphant Right after 1989. He argued honorably. He was never prepared to say that his historical entitlement critique of equality amounted to a de-fense of existing market institutions, nor was he willing to pretend that a Lockean defense of property of the kind he outlined could go any distance toward legitimizing contemporary disparities of wealth in (say) the United States. On the contrary he thought it undeniable that contemporary hold-ings would be condemned as unjust by any remotely plausible conception of historical entitlement. (The point of the argument in Chapters 7 and 8 of Nozick 1974 was that egalitarians were condemning the existing distri-bution for the wrong reason—for example, simply as unequal—rather than on account of the violence, fraud, expropriation, ethnic cleansing, state corruption, and so on, involved in the history of most significant holdings of property in the United States.) Once actual historical injustice was es-tablished, then the burden fell on the part of his conception dealing with the rectification of injustice. And for Nozick, it was an open question whether the actual operation of (say) Rawls's difference principle might not approximate the operation of a plausible process for rectifying historic in-justice. That, he said, would involve addressing some quite difficult ques-tions about time, counterfactuals, and second-best principles:[7]

> These issues are very complex and are best left to a full treatment of the prin-ciple of rectification. In the absence of such a treatment applied to a particu-lar society, one *cannot* use the analysis and theory presented here to condemn any particular scheme of transfer payments, unless it is clear that no consider-ations of rectification of injustice could apply to justify it. (1974, 231; Nozick's emphasis)

This was not the sort of thing defenders of free markets and opponents of welfare wanted to hear in the 1990s.

Instead what interested them was the consequentialist defense of mar-ket institutions. Whatever the case with Lockean entitlement (and who re-ally wanted to open *that* can of worms?), market structures operating on a set of holdings simply accepted as given (or, by some other stratagem, put largely beyond question) showed themselves able to generate immense prosperity for a surprisingly broad sector of society. Thinking people of

7. I attempted to grapple with some of these conundrums in Waldron 1992.

course knew that inequality would escalate if market economics was given its head; but they reckoned that so long as the general atmosphere of consumer prosperity buoyed most people's hopes, those who sounded alarms about a greater and greater amount of wealth and power being concentrated in fewer and fewer hands could be made to sound like spoilsports (or Soviet-era dinosaurs).

In relation to this pragmatic dismissal of distributive concerns, the Rawlsians and Nozickians might in principle make common cause. Both denied that this implicit utilitarianism treated individuals with the right sort of respect; both rejected the proposition that prosperity for most could justify poverty for a few (cf. Rawls 1971, 19 ff; Nozick 1974, 33). Both were prepared to argue that the implicit utilitarianism of the market-based approach was an inappropriate ground for thinking about justice.

They would have had their work cut out, of course. Utilitarians did not simply lie down in the face of the original Rawlsian critique. Early respondents to *A Theory of Justice* took the argument back to Rawls, maintaining that the best bet for parties in Rawls's original position would be the principle of average utility and that Rawls's argument in favor of a maximin approach was simply not convincing (Harsanyi 1975). Others insisted that the philosophical critique of utilitarianism was founded on a misapprehension about the utilitarian conception of the place of rules in moral life and that the critique underestimated the resources of *indirect utilitarianism* (Hare 1981). Still others denied the aspersion cast on utilitarianism by Rawls (1971, 26–27) and others, that it failed to take seriously the distinction between persons:

> [S]ince there is no fact of "separateness" that anyone has overlooked, no delusion that a group of persons is one super-person, the protest that utilitarians overlook separateness amounts to no more than the claim that one ought not to transfer the model of intrapersonal trades to interpersonal trades. It is an expression of one view about equal respect, and so not a reason for choosing it. (Griffin 1986, 169–70)

In the philosophical study of justice, the worry about utilitarianism was always that it seemed insufficiently interested in distributive issues: its interest seemed to be riveted in the aggregate or average bottom line of the social distribution, not the matrix of distributive outcomes for individuals. But the eye to the aggregate or average outcome need not be the result of lack of concern about distributive matters; on the contrary, there is always some aggregate element even in the most individualized theory of justice. Thus, in the passage from which my last quotation was drawn, the moral philosopher James Griffin made the following point:

> [M]erging people's interests into a single moral judgment by maximizing them *is* a distributive principle. It is a view, right or wrong, about when sacri-

ficing one person for another is justified. It is just a modern muddle to contrast sharply distributive and aggregative principles, as if an aggregative principle could not also be fully deliberately distributive. . . . Similarly, no plausible principle of distribution—think, for instance, of Rawls's Difference Principle —could be purely distributive, without some maximizing tendency, as if reducing everyone to the same level of misery could satisfy it. Every plausible principle of equality is based on the thought that everyone matters and matters equally, and to stress only the formal features of distribution is to recall the *equally* but to forget the *matters*. Even a principle of a minimum acceptable level of welfare has, if not a maximizing, at least a quantitative element. And the principle of utility, too, represents another conception of the distribution that equal respect for persons requires. (1986, 168–69, Griffin's emphasis)

Something like the Griffin approach—that is, careful presentation and defense of utilitarianism as a *fair* and *just* basis for making hard choices between individual utilities in society—is evident, too, in contractarian defenses of average utilitarianism.[8]

Unfortunately, however, very few utilitarians have devoted this level of care to the distributive issue. And Griffin himself acknowledges that where aggregative measures are actually used—for example, in economic analysis—the casual blurring or sidelining of the distributive issue is often quite striking: "It crops up commonly in regarding, as economists often do, an aggregative principle as a principle of 'efficiency' and other principles as ones of fairness" (Griffin 1986, 168). Thus it is often hard to tell whether those who defend the operation of a market economy as efficient, for example, intend that to be an evaluation of its justice (or an evaluation responsive to concerns about its justice).

Casual confusions of this kind are particularly evident in what has become known as the "economic analysis of law" (EAL). I want to spend some time with this approach, because as things stand it represents one of the most powerful tools used in the academy to deflect intellectual interest from distributive issues.

We may begin with the article of faith, accepted uncritically by most economists, that interpersonal comparisons of utility are meaningless and that accordingly neither economists nor any other social scientists could pronounce (on welfarist grounds) either for or against policy proposals that involve balancing costs to some against benefits to others. When this began to be accepted in the early decades of the twentieth century, its impact on debates about social justice was mainly to discredit the traditional utilitarian argument for equality of income, based on the diminishing marginal

---

8. Here I am thinking of the argument in Harsanyi 1975. But I also have in mind the case for the selection of utilitarian principles in the original position, sympathetically presented (but later argued against) in Rawls 1971, 161 ff., in a section Rawls entitles "The Reasoning Leading to the Principle of Average Utility."

utility of money; see Cooter and Rappoport 1984, for a superb account. Inevitably, however, policy scientists became restless under the force of the implied principle of restraint—"No comment on any policy proposals other than Pareto-improvements"—and various strategies were evolved for evaluating proposals that seemed likely to leave some people in society worse off. One strategy was to ask whether the winners (under a policy that involved costs as well as benefits) might gain enough to be able to compensate the losers (by the latter's own lights) and still be better off. This was the famous Kaldor-Hicks criterion (see Coleman 1992, 167), which promised to certify almost anything a classical utilitarian would approve of as a (potential) Pareto improvement.

As far as anyone can tell, this (or something like it) is the evaluative notion appealed to in modern law-and-economics discussions of wealth-maximization.[9] The EAL is committed to the principle that disputed rights and resources should be allocated to those who value them most. This after all is what voluntary market transactions do. When I buy your peach for a dollar, I lose a dollar and you lose a peach; but I gain something I value more highly than my dollar and you gain something you value more highly than your peach. Thus the transaction increases the amount of human value accruing from the possession and use of peaches (and dollars) on both sides (cf. Posner 2001, 98).

Consider now a more complicated transaction. Imagine that your peach trees are dying because the water you might use to irrigate them is being used instead by my factory. And suppose that with this water my factory produces more for me than your orchard produces for you; indeed, it produces so much more for me that I could pay you all you might earn from an irrigated orchard and still have plenty left over for myself. Obviously, then, the amount of human value accruing from the use of this water is greater if it is used in my factory than in your orchard. And that would be the market outcome, at least in an ideal world: if I had a legal right to the water, you would not be able to offer me enough to divert it to your orchard; and if you had the legal right to the water, I would be able to buy that right from you and use it in my factory. Value would be maximized in either case. The only additional real-world question is: how costly will the process of bargaining be, and how much of the net gain will be eaten up in lawyers' fees, negotiating time, and the costs of drawing up the appropriate contracts or conveyances? According to the EAL, the law should be such that the process is as costless as possible. In the example we are considering, in which the facts about relative profitability are known, an initial legal assignment of the water right to the factory owner will minimize the time and trouble of transacting. So if a court ever faces the ques-

9. Certainly, it is the version appealed to in Richard Posner's canonical account (1980, 487). Here I follow the analyses of Coleman 1982 and Dworkin 1995.

tion about where the water right should be assigned, *that* should be the basis on which it answers the question.

Now, patently, this question, "What can the law do to facilitate market outcomes?"—asked in this way—does not address issues of distributive justice. And one would have thought that those issues were important in our example. After all, it makes a huge difference to the individual wealth and well-being of the respective parties (under the efficient outcome) where the water right is initially located. If it is initially located with the orchardist, then even though the factory owner eventually gets the water, the orchardist will end up with at least as much money as he would have received from his irrigated crop; but if (as the model suggests) the court assigns the water right initially to the factory owner, then the orchardist will end up with nothing, or nothing but the value of parched land and dead trees. True, the factory owner will have enough from her profits to compensate the orchardist. But it is no part of the wealth maximization model that this compensation should actually be paid. Any insistence that it should be paid is at best a distraction, according to EAL, and at worst a recipe for multiplying transaction costs.

This carelessness about distributive outcomes has two sources: the so-called Coase theorem, foundational to EAL, which states that the initial assignment of entitlements—and a fortiori distributive outcomes which are just a function of initial entitlements—is irrelevant to the maximization of wealth (Coase 1960), and the assimilation of a Kaldor-Hicks improvement to a Pareto improvement. Both points should be the focus of criticism. First, the initial distribution of entitlements makes no difference to the pursuit of efficient outcomes even if it is fallacious to infer that efficiency *ought* to be pursued without regard to the distribution of entitlements. (And note that the fallacy obtains even in a world of costless transactions.) The initial (and the eventual) allocation of entitlements may matter for reasons that have nothing to do with efficiency; it may matter for reasons of justice.

Second, the legal imposition of a Kaldor-Hicks improvement (as between the orchardist and the factory owner) has none of the normative respectability of a Pareto improvement (e.g., as between the person with the peach and the person with the dollar). When we bypass the need for a voluntary transaction in the imposition of a Kaldor-Hicks improvement, we are not *in any way* honoring the preferences of the losing party. Hypothetically, the orchardist might prefer a certain sum *c* of compensation to keeping his right to the water; but if *c* is not actually to be paid, then the orchardist has no relevant preference at all (except to keep the water right) and that is not honored in the least by transferring the right to someone who would pay *c* if he had to but does not. To oppose a Kaldor-Hicks imposition in the name of justice is therefore not to oppose justice to human welfare, nor is it to oppose justice to people's revealed preferences, nor is it to oppose justice to a scheme that makes everyone better off. It is rather to insist on the importance of respecting actual individuals with their actual preferences in the actual world; and it is to oppose the imposition on individuals of actual losses for which nothing but hypothetical compensation is envisaged.

All this was pointed out decades ago (Coleman 1982). But the leading advocate of wealth maximization, Richard Posner, has evidently failed to learn the lesson. In his recent writing, he is willing to concede that distributive issues like inequality may pose certain costs of their own—for example, in social stability—which the advocate of wealth maximization would do well to take into account (2001, 102). But this is not a way of taking distributive issues seriously: such issues are important in themselves, and important in regard to respect for individual persons. They are not just something to be factored into a sort of aggregative social pragmatism.

A somewhat different line that economic scholars take is to say that if issues of distributive justice and equality are important, they should be handled by the legislature and should not contaminate the economic reasoning of courts. This is a spectacularly ill-conceived response. It is not an accident or a nuisance that distributive issues often arise in lawsuits. Even people who agree cheerfully about what counts as an improvement may disagree bitterly and even violently about how the benefits of any given improvement should be distributed. And it is typical (some would say definitive) of lawsuits that they embody such questions. Plaintiffs and defendants are not like public interest lobbyists in a legislature, putting forward rival solutions in the name of efficiency to some problem of common concern. They are desperately concerned precisely with the distributive features of a given solution, because their individual lives, fortunes, and liberty may hang in the balance.

Recent jurisprudence has emphasized that parties come to court not as lobbyists with various bright ideas for legal reform and clarification but—at least in their own eyes—as right bearers: each party thinks she is *entitled* to the outcome for which she is rooting. Ronald Dworkin has made much of that in his legal theory (1977, 82 ff.); but subsequent discussion has oriented the point mainly to what Dworkin says about right answers: each party thinks the law already justifies the outcome he seeks, and Dworkin believes jurisprudence should attempt to make sense of that thought. But the same point may also be oriented toward the distributive issue: plaintiffs and defendants approach litigation in the spirit that nothing matters more than the distributive question of who (in particular) ends up with what.[10] I don't just mean they are greedy and self-interested. For each

---

10. I think this is what Dworkin is getting at with his distinction between legal principles and legal policies: when a legal principle is at stake in litigation, the distributive issue between plaintiff and defendant is an instance of something that goes to the very heart of the justification of the provision in question (1977, 90–100).

of them, their position is a matter of what is legally right: plaintiff insists that he, in particular, is legally entitled to some benefit or resource or compensation, and defendant insists that he is not. To say that courts should try and finesse the distributive issue is to ignore the fact that which way a certain benefit goes on the distributional matrix is, almost invariably, what the lawsuit is exactly about.

The very best economic analysis in law concedes all this, and acknowledges too that legal issues cannot be solved without a basis of thinking about utility that takes distributive issues seriously. Thus a recent and important long article by Louis Kaplow and Steven Shavell called "Fairness Versus Welfare" says that legal analysis requires a social welfare function affording some defensible basis for aggregating welfare across individuals, and that fundamental conceptions of justice are appropriately deployed in designing and critiquing such a function (2001, 985–89). The principles of fairness that they criticize are not to be identified with such conceptions but rather with moralistic ideas that are independent of welfare judgements, even those that already take distributive considerations appropriately into account (Kaplow and Shavell 2001, 989). Indeed, they cite Rawls 1971 as a source of insight on the fundamental question of distribution, and they in common with others among the more scrupulous practitioners of the EAL acknowledge that in any sensible division of intellectual labor, philosophy will be assigned frontline responsibility for developing these conceptions. Now, whether that is intended sincerely or not by the economists, and whether they intend—as Kaplow and Shavell actually do—to take notice of what emerges from the philosophical discussion of justice is an open question. Mostly it has been my aim in this essay to emphasize the importance of that assignment, so far as the theorizing about justice is concerned. The economists are not going to develop theories of just distribution; at best they will expect the political philosophers to do it. So if political philosophers do not give their attention to this topic (because they would rather discuss more fashionable topics like public reason in a pluralist society), there is a danger that nobody will and the economists will be able to wander off happily confirmed in their suspicion that there is, after all, nothing—or nothing rigorous—to be said on this subject.

ROMAND COLES

Pluralization and Radical Democracy: Recent Developments in Critical Theory and Postmodernism

■ | Introduction[1]

This essay aims to illuminate some of the most important debates and developments in recent critical theory and postmodernism. These theories are highly diverse in their philosophical perspectives, subject matters, theoretical styles, and political implications. I initiate my discussion with critiques of political liberalism in the hope of soliciting readers who are relatively unfamiliar with this body of theory (as well as those immersed in it) to enter into reflections and dialogues they might otherwise avoid.[2] I begin with Habermasian criticisms, as these diverge least from many themes in political liberalism. From there, the perspectives discussed increasingly deepen and broaden the terrain of contestation, and the focus shifts to the philosophical differences and political stakes between critical theory and various postmodernisms. Central questions concern the nature and scope of democratic dialogue and power; the way theorists interpret the role of bodily affect, disposition, and perception in democratic engagement; the interpretation of important sites, objects, and practices of power and radical democratic contestation; and how responses to the questions are en-

---

1. I wish to thank Jane Bennett, Kimberley Curtis, Bonnie Honig, Ira Katznelson, and an anonymous reviewer for their helpful comments on and criticisms of earlier drafts of this essay; and Tania Roy and Matt Diamond for their vital research assistance.

2. I do not wish to suggest that responding to political liberalism has been the central focus of critical theory and postmodernism. The latter have sought to expand our sense of the terrain of politics and possibilities for action through various engagements that have often had much more to do with exploring directions suggested by Foucault, Derrida, Adorno, Butler, Deleuze and Guattari, Arendt, Heidegger, Nietzsche, and others, in the face of ongoing political struggles concerning race, gender, sexuality, ecology, economic equality, postcoloniality, radical democratic community power, technology, prisons, nationalism, education, identity, coalition, and so forth.

twined with approaches to rights, coalition politics, order, responsibility, and political institutions. Surveying a range of positions, I suggest that some of the most promising work draws on insights from—as well as tensions between—both critical theory and postmodernism.

One of the most important contributions of many of the works at hand is to elaborate, in numerous ways and across many domains, more receptive and generous modes of dialogical political contestation than one finds in most liberal theory. The textual strategy that follows seeks to embody these insights. If much of the theorizing under discussion is often blithely dismissed or ignored by other perspectives, we must resist the impulse to return the favor.

In what follows, I pursue fewer dialogues in more depth, rather than try to cover exhaustively but thinly the vast terrain invoked by the terms *critical theory* and *postmodernism*. There are costs of omission that accompany this strategy, but it is, I think, the most promising way to enact the substantive insights suggested. My claim is that the most compelling insights are emerging precisely in the *tensions* between different positions. These only come to light through patient explorations that disclose the complexities of blindness and insight in the contestations that follow. While both critical theory and postmodernism have made great advances in recent years, the engagements between them have often had the character of ships passing in the night—or polemic. If it is at the agonal intersections between them that one finds what is most promising, the only way to elaborate this insight is by dwelling at these points with a care that might have some power to persuade those not already convinced. The mode of this dwelling is as important as the sites themselves. By enacting an alternative practice of engagement, one might not only discern things missed by more constrained optics, but also possibly shed another kind of light on both certain persistent weaknesses in some of the perspectives at hand and more hopeful paths.

■ | Political Liberalism and Its Limits

Liberalism has many faces.[3] Yet the mode of liberalism that has the greatest constructive influence on political theory, and the mode which others feel most compelled to critically address, is political liberalism as articulated foremost by John Rawls (1996). At the heart of Rawlsian liberalism is a notion of reciprocity rooted in the idea of society as a system of cooperation between free and equal citizens. Political life thus construed is to be

3. There are numerous contemporary exponents of liberalism whose theorizing has been forged partly through engagements with critical theory and postmodernism. Among the most remarkable, one would have to include Flathman (1992, 1998), Kateb (1992), and Moon (1993).

guided and limited by conceptions of freedom, equality, and fairness that constitute a "public reason" presiding over constitutional questions and all matters concerning fundamental questions of justice. Such reason requires that citizens keep their moral, theological, and philosophical differences out of political life when basic matters are at stake, unless "in due course public reasons, given by a reasonable political conception, are sufficient to support whatever the comprehensive doctrines are introduced to support" (Rawls 1996, li–lii). Public reason's directions and limitations "provide the *common currency* of discussion and a deeper basis for explaining the meaning and implications of the principles and policies each group endorses" (1996, 165, my emphasis). Formulating deliberation as exchange of agreed on terms of linguistic currency, Gutmann and Thompson write: "the primary job of reciprocity is to regulate public reason, the terms in which citizens justify to one another their claims regarding all other goods." The good given and received is that we all make claims on terms that we can accept in principle (1996, 55).

If, in decades past, the common currency of public reason was given more transcendental grounding, since the 1980s, political liberalism has increasingly understood itself as the expression of the deepest commitments of the tradition of liberal democratic societies. Political liberalism seeks to avoid aggressive articulations of historical contingency and irony (like Rorty 1989), proclaiming instead a neutrality toward such philosophical worldviews. Yet the teleological story Rawls (1996) now tells of the emergence of political liberalism—from a modus vivendi among those warring over comprehensive doctrines to a constitutional consensus to a deepening "overlapping consensus"—is replete with contingencies of power and worldviews.

That said, political liberalism understands itself as the deepest expression of this tradition and claims to articulate the terms that ought to singularly ground political legitimacy. Political liberals acknowledge reasonable pluralism within the political liberal family. Yet all who lie beyond this family—from libertarians to Arendtian radical democrats to those religious traditions that understand themselves politically—are, insofar as they enter the contestations of political life in ways that exceed the limits defined by political liberalism, making claims that are morally (not legally) illegitimate from the Rawlsian position.

Accompanying this constraint on difference in the public sphere is a rather restrained affirmation of broad-based political engagement. Many political liberals now urge that "forums for deliberation should abound" (Gutmann and Thompson 1996, 37; Fishkin 1991), within the limits of public reason. Yet much political liberalism is infused with the proceduralism that Rawls articulates when he writes that the advantage of the least well-off (articulated by the difference principle) should be inscribed in public law and not apply "to particular transactions of distribution, nor to decisions of individuals and associations, but rather to the institutional background against which these transactions and decisions take place" (1996, 283). Secure in the knowledge that elsewhere in the social system the necessary corrections to preserve justice are being made: "individuals and associations are then left free to advance their ends more effectively within the framework of the basic structure" (269).

While political liberal negotiations of the balance between proceduralism and deliberative forums vary, their affirmations of deliberation are generally framed in terms of sites of political discussion designed to inform the determination and administration of proper policies. Rarely does one find discussions of possible transfigurations of everyday political, social, and economic life that might increase political dialogue and engagement or much support for contemporary social movements that often enact such engagements. Civil society is conceived more as a site for nurturing support and consultation than as a location of pluralizing insurgent mobilizations that cultivate social forces aimed at transforming the practices and mores of liberal polities.

■ | Critical Theory Contestations

To make this assignment manageable, I limit my present discussion of critical theory to those theories associated with the Frankfurt School.[4] I first trace the account of critical theory given by Jurgen Habermas, its leading contemporary figure. Then I work through its difficulties and increasingly discuss those who draw on early critical theory to engage themes proximate to some of those discussed in the following section on postmodernism.

In the dominant Habermasian account (e.g., Habermas 1987; Benhabib 1986; Honneth 1991), critical theory begins in the 1930s with the efforts of Theodor Adorno, Max Horkheimer, Herbert Marcuse, and Walter Benjamin to challenge an "instrumental reason" that banishes reflection on human ends and focuses exclusively on the rationality of efficient means. Entwined with instrumentality is the systematic organization of politics, society, and the culture industry in ways that integrate humans and nonhuman nature into a totality of ever-increased productivity that disproportionately empowers the few and assimilates virtually everyone into a one-dimensional society.

According to Habermas, these theorists so exaggerated their criticism that they undermined their foundations and misapprehended modern political, social, and ethical developments. Reducing rationality to instrumental reason, they missed how enlightenment theory and political practice *also* unleashed a "communicative rationality" that pointed toward a more just and defensible order of things. Entangled in nihilism, Adorno lost sight of hopeful developments in modernity, like universalist ethics,

4. For overviews of the Frankfurt School, see Jay (1973) and Held (1980).

constitutional democratic politics, and democratic social movements. While Habermas criticizes the "colonization" of these developments by market and bureaucratic systems, he argues that this colonization has not eroded the foundations of communicative rationality or overridden their contemporary sociological and political manifestations.

Habermasians engage political liberalism on four related fronts. They challenge Rawlsians on:

The question of normative foundations

The static and reifying implications of these foundations

The extent to which differences are normatively precluded in political discourse

Political liberalism's limited understanding of democratic practices

Questions concerning normative foundations are central to the engagement between Habermas and Rawls (Rawls 1996; Habermas 1998a; see also Baynes 1992; Chambers 1996). Initially, Habermas (1990) criticized Rawlsian liberalism for grounding its normative position in monological subjectivity and enlightened self-interest. Morality thus founded is implicated in modes of self-assertion that ultimately undermine universalist goals and harbors ahistorical assumptions that block critical reflection on how power is inscribed in definitions of need, the good, and subjectivity itself. For Habermas, selves originate in and are sustained through communicative action. Moral theory seeking to secure the best aspects of enlightenment deontological universalism—while jettisoning the worst—should ground itself in the communicative structures and pragmatic presuppositions of everyday lifeworld interaction.

Habermas argues that Rawls's political turn toward a hermeneutic position claiming to express the intuitions of a liberal democratic tradition still harbors some of the old problems and introduces new ones. Habermas discerns static tendencies, as the original position still frames the pursuit of the universal in an overly "monological fashion" by "imposing a common perspective on the parties . . . . through informational constraints . . . [that] neutralize the multiplicity of particular interpretive perspectives from the outset. [In contrast] discourse ethics . . . views the moral point of view as embodied in an intersubjective praxis . . . which enjoins . . . an idealizing *enlargement* of . . . interpretive perspectives," through "mutual criticism of the appropriateness of the languages in terms of which situations and needs are interpreted. In the course of *successively* undertaken abstractions, the core of generalizable interests can then emerge step by step" (1998a, 57–58).

For Habermasians, normative philosophy should be oriented toward clarifying the "demanding presuppositions of the 'public use of reason' " and argumentative practice (1998a, 59). The "principle of universalization (U)," presupposed in everyday communication, states: "*All* affected can accept the consequences and the side effects its *general* observance can be anticipated to have for the satisfaction of *everyone's* interests. . . ." (1990, 65). This position frames all substantive claims in a manner that solicits the discursive participation of all affected to determine or revise their validity. It "does not bracket the pluralism of . . . worldviews at the outset" (1998a, 59) but rather "includes the other" insofar as "needs and wants are interpreted in light of cultural values," in a process where worldviews must be engaged and criticized in actual public discourses in light of (U) (1990, 76–78). Habermas maintains the deontological priority of justice over the good but argues that the former is substantively discernable only as the visions of the latter are openly employed and filtered through rational discourses.

Habermas argues that with Rawls's hermeneutical turn toward the liberal democratic tradition, "practical reason is robbed of its moral core and is deflated to a reasonableness that becomes dependent on moral truths justified otherwise" (1998a, 82–83). Rawls's liberal intuitions both rely for their moral force on "a lucky convergence" of particular doctrines, and simultaneously exclude these doctrines when they overstep the limits of liberal intuitions as Rawls discerns them. This combination of reliance and exclusion leads to a moral deficit that manifests itself in a paucity of potentially context transcending arguments that can be offered when the "neutralizing" dimensions of political liberalism face the "others" who exceed the boundaries Rawls ascribes to the democratic tradition. Rawls's may be closer to Rorty's contingency than he intends.

Habermas's quasi-transcendental discourse ethics and his foregrounding of actual participation and "the inclusion of the other" have important political implications. In contrast both to liberal models of democracy based exclusively on affirmations of formal rights, and communitarian models focused on the material conditions and public autonomy required for freedom, discourse democracy focuses on a "*proceduralist understanding of law* that is centered on the procedural conditions of the democratic process" (1998b, 18, 1996; Rosenfeld and Arato 1998). Popular sovereignty and human rights are seen as "co-original," "complimentary," and "nourished from the same root." Habermas seeks to ensure private rights *and* public autonomy by emphasizing "a public of citizens who participate in political communication in order to articulate their wants and needs, to give voice to their violated interests, and . . . to clarify and settle the contested standards and criteria according to which equals are treated equally and unequals treated unequally" (1998b, 244).

Habermasian visions of the public sphere have shifted away from an earlier embrace of a radically democratic socialist totality, and most critical theorists now argue that state bureaucracies and market systems "can no longer be transformed democratically from within . . . without damaging their proper systemic logic and therewith their ability to function" and coordinate action in an immensely complex society (Habermas 1992, 444;

Cohen and Arato 1994; Rosenfeld and Arato 1998). Hence, instead of subjecting states and markets to direct radical democratic governance, a "separation of powers" is necessary, in which state, economy, and a heterogeneous civil society are each granted a degree of autonomy. The task of radical democracy is to "erect a democratic dam" against state and economic colonization of the lifeworld and to make these systems more responsive to the communicatively generated guidance of the practically oriented demands of the lifeworld.

During the 1980s, Habermas stressed the irreducibly conflictual dimensions of the relationship between civil society and states and market systems. Systems figure primarily as colonizing powers that public spheres must endlessly resist and attempt to sensitize to the demands of the lifeworld. More recently, critical theorists tend to identify more particular conflicts (rather than a general theory of conflict) and emphasize that democratic steering is an efficacious (and therefore legitimacy-bestowing) aspect of modern societies, especially during times of crisis.

Discursive democracy involves the delicate interplay between informal public spheres (associations, social movements, etc.) and formal publics (representative institutions). The former provide a "context of discovery" which, free of procedural regulations, is far more "wild" and "unrestricted," ranging "more widely and expressively" (Habermas 1996, 307–8). Here struggles around need, recognition, and identity can be pursued over broader and more uncertain terrain. Gradually, these struggles can gain attention and "be taken up by responsible political authorities, put on the parliamentary agenda, discussed, and if need be, worked into legislative proposals and binding decisions" (Habermas 1996, 314). In Habermas's view, the flows of communication and influence are often one directional, such that informal public spheres are eclipsed and distorted by political economic power. Yet in times of crisis these flows can and do change direction in ways that allow the informal realms of civil society to become increasingly influential. Concerning issues like feminism, ecology, poverty, and the arms race, informal public spheres have shown they can have considerable influence on national political discussion and policy. Though often weak and discontinuous, this influence illustrates that discursive democracy is not just an ideal, but an ideal with significant efficacy in the practices of constitutional democracies. In marked contrast to political liberalism, the insurgent aspect of informal public spheres plays an elemental role in the ongoing practice and development of democracy.[5]

In contrast to more radical democratic formulations, however, these public spheres are repeatedly urged to exercise "intelligent self-restraint" and "leave intact the modes of operation internal to functional systems and other highly organized spheres of action" (Habermas 1996, 372); they must

5. For provocative discussions of these issues, see the wide range of analyses in Bohman and Rehg (1997).

limit themselves to "mild forms of indirect steering" (Habermas 1998b, 19). The best that democratic citizens can do is seek to enhance their capacities for such steering through policies and practices that aim—along with every development of state protections of private rights and every extension of state powers to provide entitlements requisite for public autonomy—to enhance the capacities of "*affected parties themselves* to conduct public discourses" in civil society (24).

Just as Habermasian democracy is more insurgent and contestatory than political liberalism but less so than many articulations of radical democracy, it occupies a middle ground concerning questions of difference and democracy. Though Habermas criticizes political liberalism for excessively limiting the pluralism of worldviews, he himself is not immune to this charge. As Rawls argues, Habermas's "immodest quasi-transcendental position aims to be too comprehensive," offering "a general account of meaning, reference, and truth or validity both for theoretical reason and for several forms of practical reason." All religious and metaphysical views in excess of the Habermasian account thus appear to "lack any logical force of their own" and often criticized summarily "without taking much time to argue against them in detail; rather, he lays them aside—or occasionally dismisses them" (1996, 376–78). Brian Shaw, a sympathetic critic, traces Habermas's "regrettable mixture of indifference and contempt for religious belief" (1999, 634) and suggests that religious discourses cut across and disrupt Habermas's overly tidy Kantian distinctions between truth, morality, and aesthetic modes of validity.

Once again, the deepest philosophical moves have important political implications. Habermas comprehends modernity in part as a process of "pluralization of the lifeworld." In this context, the best way to reduce potential conflicts is through universalistic law and deontological discourse that limits the political influence of ethical visions of the good through an ongoing testing process that evaluates their general acceptability in light of (U) (Habermas 1998a, 42). The (U) is said to act like "a knife that makes razor-sharp cuts between evaluative statements and strictly normative ones, between the good and the just" (Habermas 1990, 104).

But how sharp is this razor and how does it work? If value orientations are "enlisted" for their descriptions, information, and interpretations in normative discourses, are they not inextricable from the normative claims that result? Discourses aimed at universalization would put pressure on particular visions of the good, but the latter would always profoundly influence and pressure the former as well, so the logics and meanings of justice and visions of the good would never be entirely separable. If this is true, then we should expect that normative discourses will not always facilitate consensual resolutions to conflicts among those of different traditions and worldviews (Coles 1997; McCarthy 1998; Bernstein 1998; Moon 1995). Moral claims would not necessarily rise above conflicts over the good but rather often remain deeply entangled with them. Given Habermasian expectations for the consensual effects of normative discourse, Rawls seems right when he charges: "Habermas's description of the procedure of reasoning and argument . . . is . . . incomplete. It is not clear what forms of argument may be used, yet these importantly determine the outcome. Are we to think . . . that each person's interest [and evaluations] are to be given equal consideration? What are the relevant interests? Or are all interests to be counted?" (1996, 430). If Habermas and others have flagged the impositional and unreciprocal aspects of Rawlsian public reason, Rawls in turn identifies a certain formalistic deficit in the Habermasian alternative.

While Habermas's position has moved in directions that are more inclusive of the other, significant problems remain. In Habermas's hands, the deontological razor, however illusory it may be, cuts into the world in a manner that radically privileges the position of "normative discourse" in relation to the pluralistic worldviews it claims to engage. As Bernstein argues, it does so by means of the "violently distortive fiction" that ethical traditions develop exclusively with an eye to the realization of their own particularist goods and values. This fiction distorts, because many traditions are oriented equally toward "universalistic demands and obligations." Maintaining the sharp separation *elevates* discourse morality above all modes of evaluative theory and practice, by denying *both* the historical entanglements of all universalistic claims *and* the transcendence of many traditionalist positions (Bernstein 1998, 301, 1993; Shaw 1999; see also Butler 1996, 2000). He rhetorically *lowers* traditionalist and other evaluative positions by casting their horizons in terms that are radically particularist, thereby conjuring them as inherently oblivious and violent toward their others unless enrolled in and limited by the strivings of discourse ethics. In question is not Habermas's claim that traditions encroach on each other, sometimes violently. Rather it is whether discourse ethics is as free from this encroachment as Habermas claims and whether traditions are as inherently devoid of potent and distinct resources for transcending their limits, listening to the claims of others, and so forth, as Habermas suggests. Insofar as neither argument proves to be true, we are faced with different contending historical projections of the universal that would have to engage in dialogue and negotiation with one another with less probability of consensual resolution—but also less deaf oblivion—than critical theory would generally have us believe.

To better address these difficulties, Benhabib "emphasizes and even radicalizes those aspects of a discourse ethic which are universalistic without being rationalistic, which seek understanding among human beings while considering the consensus of all to be a counterfactual illusion, and which are sensitive to differences of identity, needs and modes of reasoning. . . ." (Benhabib 1992, 8). Attentive to context and "concrete others," she seeks to bring universals and particulars into creative tension with one another in ways that more intelligently transfigure the boundaries between the good and the just, and public and private (1986, 1992).

Though Benhabib's writing is often rich, synthetic, and probing, perhaps her proximity to Habermas's paradigm leaves her at times more enmeshed in some of his problems than she wishes to be. Hence, in response to I.M. Young's suggestion (1997) that "greeting, storytelling, and rhetoric" ought to be given a more prominent place in theories of public dialogue, Benhabib writes: they "cannot become the public language of institutions and legislatures in a democracy for the following reason: to attain legitimacy, democratic institutions require the articulation of the bases of their actions and policies in discursive language that appeals to commonly shared and accepted public reasons. . . . Young's attempt to transform the language of the rule of law into a more partial, affective, and situated mode of communication would have the consequence of inducing arbitrariness," as rhetoric sways without reason, and stories remain local and sometimes inaccessible to others, and so on (1996b, 83).

At the moment, I am less concerned with Young's position (which is more nuanced than Benhabib would suggest) than Benhabib's response. This is because what one witnesses, perhaps, is that when pushed, a certain set of fundamental Habermasian orientations tend to reassert themselves and overdetermine the response, inspite of Benhabib's insightful efforts to open them in hopeful directions. Hence, while Benhabib writes toward engagements that would recognize people as having a "concrete history, identity, and affective-emotional constitution" (1992, 159), she quickly rejects narrative and affect—at least in the political discourses within decision-making institutions—when it is shown how these frequently introduce problematic contingencies and nonidentity into political discourse. Perhaps positions more capable of sustaining the sensitivities for which Benhabib calls would stand at a greater distance from the Habermasian paradigm that significantly engenders them?

Habermas's own rhetoric appears to play no small role in pushing toward a different star than those that often guide Benhabib's promising efforts. Accompanying his more rhetorical than reasoned rendering of visions of the good and his rhetorically exaggerated sense of capacity of discourse ethics to disentangle critical theory from both, many of Habermas's texts engender an insistent and sometimes almost singular striving for consensus (Coles 1992b). Consensual striving is often rhetorically disclosed in association with terms like *restore* and *reach*, which tend to shift our attention away from questioning the damages that might *also* be *imposed* in the *forging* of many moral and political agreements. In this light, ongoing agon related to strong commitments to particular modes of seeing and doing is summarily shunned. Tarrying between nonidentical positions is seen merely as a barrier to "carrying on the world's business." And criticizing the idea that the purpose, legitimacy, and function of ethicopolitical discourse is wholly related to the *achievement* of universalizable norms in the midst of political conflict is seen as inching toward treason.

Nowhere is this clearer than in the recent encounter between Habermas and one of his most loyal interpreters, Thomas McCarthy (1998), who presents a sharp set of arguments about the entwinement of the good and the just, similar to those presented above. He concludes that, given the messy historicity of normative claims, sometimes consensus will be forged, yet sometimes disagreement will appear to be intractable. Many questions may not even ideally have "one right answer." Thus he questions Habermas's overly "cognitive" and "consensus-seeking" understanding of political discourse and legitimacy. Beyond a minimal consensus concerning "the basic rights and principles of the democratic constitutional state . . . we would need an account of democratic public life that is decidedly less centered on rational consensus than [Habermas's] is" (1998, 125–26). McCarthy remains a strong proponent of discursive democracy, yet suggests that the advantages of the latter should be framed less in terms of the movement toward consensus—though these advantages do sometimes occur, can be important, and should be sought—and more in terms of the role discourse democracy plays in establishing and maintaining relations that are free from violence. In combination, discourse and majority decision making facilitate cooperative action even when there is disagreement, by inscribing the tentativeness of human understanding and relations in practices that allow minorities an open space to contest majority decisions and possibly persuade people to change policy. Beyond these practical benefits, discourse democracy has cognitive benefits, even when these exceed the framework of "movements toward consensus." In pluralistic societies, the benefits of discursive contestation often consist in weeding out errors and ideology. Moreover, such practices can help us discover and cultivate "mutual accommodation," "respect," "tolerance," and "reasonable disagreement." McCarthy notes there are tensions between these advantages and theories of dialogue supposing the ultimate existence of one right answer to most normative questions. Interestingly, however, Habermas can hear in McCarthy's arguments only an "anti-universalism" that slides dangerously and in spite of itself toward Carl Schmitt's decisionism (1998c). Habermas (1987) has made these claims repeatedly about postmodernists and early critical theorists, but when he levels them at McCarthy, questions arise about how the possibilities, hopes, and fears engendered by the Habermasian rhetorical disclosure of the world might tend to contribute to a significant deafness precisely in the name of a particular rendering of inclusion.

Bernstein argues, relatedly, that *in addition to* the procedural side of democracy, emphasized by Habermas, democratic practices capable of resisting the "garbage in, garbage out" phenomena require a richly developed ethos of dispositions, including "a *willingness* to listen," "*respecting* the views of minorities," and the "*courage* to change one's mind" (1998, 291; see also 1993). With MacIntyre, Bernstein accents these "internal goods" of democratic practices.

Wellmer (1991, 1998) further develops these themes. Greatly influenced by the theory of communicative action, Wellmer seeks to avoid Habermas's "objectivist misreadings" (which overemphasize an imaginary consensus end point) and embraces instead a "weak localizing" interpretation that emphasizes a dialogical openness and movement beyond limits that resist constraints of power and dogma, while recognizing that we are—as finite beings within a particular horizon—always constrained by history, contingency, and an "obscurity and opacity [that] are continually being renewed." Dialogue pluralizes and further opens horizons as often as it brings about convergence and fusion. Truth appears partially at best, and our ability to grasp it is forever having to prove itself anew in the movement of dialogue, practices, and applications that confirm it or call it into question. What is "striking" about our "ability to understand" is "its orientation toward the future" (Wellmer 1998, 234).

Habermas (and those closest to him) agree, but there is a difference. Habermas's embrace of a fallibilism that will "not rule out" the possibility of new transforming experiences is far too weak for Wellmer. Greatly informed by Adorno's sense of the "traces of contingency, opaqueness, and violence in linguistic meaning" and social life (1998, 233), Wellmer calls us beyond fallibilism to urge that cultivating radical receptivity and greater capacities for engaging the uncanniness of the future is crucial for the pursuit of truth, freedom, and justice. Wellmer pushes dialogical ethics and politics in fascinating directions that seek to resist the "compulsion to identify," by constructing constellations and "syntheses that will provide new stimuli for communication" and a "logic of 'nonreifying' argumentation." In the midst of a world structured around often odious modes of power, the capacities of finite beings for radical dialogue and pluralizing democratic politics requires repeated provocations that help open us to that which is defined as "the meaningless, the taboo, the socially excluded and heterogeneous aspects of their experience" (1998, 167).

Wellmer argues that these closures are very often anchored and perpetuated at the affective level. Hence Adorno's aesthetic theory becomes a particularly important site for cultivating our capacities for more generous engagements with excluded heterogeneity. The sublime in art is, from an "energetic" standpoint, "shocking"; it bursts into our interior space and "generates a tremor, a vertigo, loosening the confines of the experiencing ego" (163). It aids the paradoxical work—so important to a more generous democratic politics—of communicating the uncommunicable, and thereby allows us dialogically to experiment with modes of seeing, being, and becoming that have been marginalized and condemned. One could think here of modes of sexuality; abnormal ways of reflecting, carrying one's body, or expressing oneself in public; public presencing of religious corporate bodies and practices; spiritual celebrations; shocking personal and collective modes of registering socially unacknowledged suffering; radical solidarities with "illegal aliens"; taboo relationships toward death and dying; and wildly sympathetic relationships with nonhuman beings—for starters.

Wellmer argues not that democratic politics should be replaced by aesthetics but rather that, because power works significantly at levels other than that of linguistic communication, democratic discourses and struggles must *also* and importantly experiment with modes of expression and receptivity better able to engage these levels. We must bring them partly to the surface, expose them from new vantage points of vision and feeling that loosen the virtually automatic sway they often exercise on us, and open them to critical reflection and modification (1998, 167, 163).

In the United States, a resurgence of interest in Adorno parallels and extends many of these ideas. Rather than a theorist of nihilistic aesthetic subjectivism, Adorno emerges as a theorist with major insights for a dialogical democratic ethic and politics of a more "receptive generosity" (Coles 1997), which resists closures in Habermasian critical theory through unending engagements with that which remains nonidentical—beyond the limits of the dominant orders (Dallmayr 1992; Morris 2001; Phelan 1993; Schoolman 2001). In the more philosophical and ethical registers, what distinguishes such theories is an accent on the epistemological and ethical centrality of cultivating responsiveness to nonidentity, the importance of engaging aesthetic and affective sensibilities in these efforts, and an understanding of democratic dialogue and engagement that is more affirmative of agonism, paradox, and contingency.

For Adorno, all identities—concepts, selves, groups, communities, nations—fail to exhaust the materiality that they both emerge from and seek to make coherent and intelligible. Nonidentical remainders are engendered ever-anew in our efforts to grasp and give form to selves, communities, and the world. Adorno's point is not that all our efforts here are for naught or that they all inevitably share the same degree of blindness and violence. We can do better or worse—epistemologically and ethically—as we negotiate questions of identity. Yet even under the best conditions, Adorno suggests, we can never entirely leave blindness and damage behind us—and this truth grows in magnitude the more we attempt to deny it. The upshot of this insight of "negative dialectics" is that the most hopeful dialogical practices are those suspended between the tensional pulls of reconciliation between self and others and an intransigent resistance to all claims that pure reconciliation does or even can exist; those suspended between efforts toward consensus and ongoing incitements toward agonistic dissent. Both harmony and agon, when taken as primary ethical and political aims, tend to engender blindness and damage toward others—the former by concealing the damages of its claims to and yearnings for reconciliation, the latter by blinding itself to and sometimes fostering the violence that becomes visible through our yearnings for reconciliation (Coles 1997). Like many of Adorno's oppositions, the poles of this tension that might enliven more generous and receptive political dialogue, "keep faith with their own substance through their opposites" (1973, 15) and they "are linked by criticizing one another not by compromising" (61). This insight—this tension-dwelling—holds significant promise for moving beyond the mutually deaf oppositions that have become entrenched in encounters between some consensualist critical theorists and some agonal postmodernists.

In terms of political economy, the directions initiated by more difference-affirming critical theorists are often entwined with challenges to the dichotomous character of Habermas's "lifeworld system" paradigm, and they tend toward more radical democratic and insurgent efforts to transform state power and markets.[6] As the costs of overemphasizing consensus come to light, so too do the weaknesses of overvaluing coordination in administrative and economic life. The claim is not that these are not crucial aims but rather that they must be situated, pursued, and limited in relation with other aspirations that cultivate democratic capacities and practices for dialogically elaborating modes of cooperation *and* ongoing possibilities for people on the undersides of power to contest these modes in radical democratic fashion. These efforts are also pursued by post-Marxists informed by themes of contingency, pluralization, and agon developed by numerous critical theorists and postmodernists.[7]

▪ | Pluralizing and Radicalizing the Democratic Responsibility

Proximate themes are explored by numerous theorists frequently associated with postmodernism. Postmodernism is a highly contested concept, and many who are labeled *postmodern* resist the term. In fact, within political theory in the 1990s, *postmodern* perhaps coheres most in its frequent function as a term of dismissal.[8] In the hands of many of its critics, postmodernism names a knot of noxious themes: nihilism, anarchy, singular obsessions with difference, myopic identity politics, deconstruction re-

6. For a sample of more radically democratic arguments in this vein, see McCarthy 1991, ch. 6, Forbath 1998, and Coles 1997.

7. For example, Bowles and Gintis (1986), Laclau and Mouffe (1985), Reinhardt (1997), and Corlett (1998). Post-Marxist theorists such as these draw significantly on postmodern themes in the context of working through the theoretical and practical problems of western Marxism. Laclau and Mouffe have been especially influential during the past decade.

8. For liberal critiques of postmodernism, see Spragens 2000 and Moon 1993. For Straussian criticism, see Rosen 1987 and Zuckert 1996. For communitarian criticism, see Taylor 1984. MacIntyre (1990) criticizes from the vantage point of "tradition." Moderate "New Left" criticism finds expression in Todd Gitlin 1995 and Rorty 1998.

duced to destruction, genealogy reduced to war, anti-Enlightenment, antiuniversalism, and the abolition of normative foundations.

What is remarkable (but often unremarked), is that if you round up a list of usual postmodern suspects—say, Judith Butler, William Connolly, Iris Young, Jacques Derrida, Michael Shapiro, and Shane Phelan—for all their important differences, none will ascribe to this knot, and most recognize it as a noose and have repeatedly resisted it.

To provoke some distance from these dismissive stereotypes, consider first the nuances articulated by a few writers concerning their relationship to different aspects of modernity. Foucault writes of enlightenment as "a form of reflection within which I have tried to work" (1986, 96) and a dialogical "critique and permanent creation of ourselves in our autonomy" (1984, 44). Derrida writes: "It is a logic, logic itself, that I do not wish to criticize here. I would even be ready to subscribe to it, but with one hand only, for I keep another to write or look for something else, perhaps outside Europe" (1992, 69). He articulates and provocatively explores the tensional mixture of debt and genealogical suspicion in relation to dominant understandings of democracy, universalism, consensus, and numerous other themes and practices. Connolly argues: "We need new improvisations today, those that rework rather than eliminate secular, liberal practices of majority rule, minorities, progress, dissent, rights, sympathy, tolerance, and creative dissidence" (1999, 96). Far from being an antiuniversalist, Judith Butler writes that "the task that cultural difference sets for us is that articulation of universality through a difficult labor of translation" not governed by the a priori assumption that "a Kantian can be found in every culture" (1996, 52).

These positions express what Derrida calls a "double contradictory law"—the idea that justice, ethics, and promising democratic practice, call us to work within the difficult tensions of a double obligation: that of dialectically extending the most compelling moments of the inheritances of reason and justice *and* that of cultivating a more radical receptivity toward that which has been marginalized, excluded, colonized, or never imagined by these inheritances—or perhaps that which hasn't yet emerged. The blindness and violence that accompany our finitude make *both* of these efforts necessary. Our judgement is likely best—or least bad—when developed in the tensions between the orientations of the best practices so far and the cultivation of a radical yearning to receptively engage challenges from other perspectives, practices, and struggles.

This double relationship is not a weakening of some purportedly more radical position that would wholly reject "modernity" in the name of "the new." As Derrida says, thinking of the political disasters of the twentieth century, "we know the 'new' only too well." Often what happens under this name is "the worst" (1992, 18). We need to dialectically protect and extend within any historical legacy those institutions, practices, and knowledges that prepare us to engage others receptively and to resist the worst. But we know too, he suggests, of the endlessly renewed processes and pressures within our logos and order that exclude and wage war against others, otherness, and other possibilities *as such* in the name of fending off "the worst." Hence, we must cultivate a stance that would dispose us toward a radical receptivity that "anticipates the unanticipatable." Ethical-political positions that would resist evil and participate in opening a more generous future would be those that cultivate judgement and will in the midst of the tensions of this double contradictory law (Derrida 1992, 1994; Critchley 1992, 1998; Beardsworth 1996).

Connolly's writing exemplifies the kind of rich political theory that emerges from a "bivalent tension" (1999, 71) and offers a sense of how such theorizing often moves back and forth between ontological, affective, ethical, and political registers. Deeply informed by Foucault's genealogies of power, Connolly develops genealogies of the territorial politics of the nation-state, the drug and culture wars, capital punishment, the functioning of the secular in contemporary liberalism, and constructions of race. Yet he is powerfully aware that genealogy's strategies of disclosure, detachment, and escape from hitherto invisible modes of power, while crucial, are insufficient for political theory. It is also necessary to cultivate one's ethical and political commitments.

The work of projecting a "generous ethical sensibility grounded in appreciation of the fugitive abundance of being" (1995, xiii) is tacit in Connolly's writing in 1991 and becomes increasingly central in his writings in 1995 and 1999. With a retrospective glance, Connolly argues both that all political orders have been implicated in substantial blindness and unacknowledged violence and that many of those people and modes of being which were excluded have struggled against these confines in ways that eventually enacted freer and more just and democratic possibilities for coexistence. Hence he prospectively wagers that current and future orders do and will similarly harbor unacknowledged exclusions; many of these excluded modes of being and becoming will likely harbor transformative possibilities for justice, freedom, and flourishing that exceed the terms and practices that currently legitimate their exclusion; and working against the grain of the closures we all almost certainly harbor in varying degrees toward peoples and modes of being that challenge the orders with which we identify, we would do well to cultivate a more radical "critical responsiveness" toward others and still inchoate otherness within and around us.

Connolly's stance is both indebted to prevalent liberal democratic theory and very critical of it.[9] On the one hand, Rawlsians are "superb at acknowledging the justice of newly acknowledged claims and constituencies once the politics of becoming has carried their voices within range of [their] hearing" (1999, 68). The political liberal "moral code" of justice, including aspects of its conceptions of liberty, equality, reciprocity, tolerance, rights,

9. For a related critique, see Honig 1993.

democratic cooperation, and distribution, is often important in contemporary efforts to protect, inform, and empower movements for justice among diverse currently recognized groups. Yet while it is "indispensable to social regulation, judgment, and coordination, it is also too crude, blunt, and blind an authority to carry out these functions sensitively . . . particularly when new and surprising modes of suffering are encountered" (59).

Contemporary pluralism comes up far short due to the way it assumes the posture of a privileged and relatively static and definitive code. First, Connolly claims, it often blindly and dogmatically resists newly emergent struggles to register hitherto excluded groups and ways of being (e.g., illegal aliens, nonhuman beings, future unborn generations, and those who would bring "doctrines" into the struggles of public life to contest political liberalism). Second, even when it finally acknowledges the legitimacy of claims brought forth by some social movements, it tends to assimilate these claims to its own categories, remaining obstinately deaf to and unchanged by the challenges posed to its formulations. Many struggles around sexuality, for example, don't simply aim at inclusion in the current definitions of reciprocity and personhood but seek also to transform them, as they foreground and "challenge the visceral experience of exclusive sensual naturalness upon which heterosexual identity had been based . . . and "elevate a new dimension of being into the rubric of personhood itself" (68).

These challenges would involve not only changes in heterosexual identity but also—by drawing to the fore the visceral, affective, and pre- and unconscious dimensions of people's response to the world—challenge the cognitive rationalist assumptions that underpin many liberal (and Habermasian) formulations of just deliberative exchange, reciprocity, tolerance, and fairness. Transformations in these terms might, then, radically alter the understandings, sensibilities, and practices with which we aim at justice. Dialogues and struggles around justice would thus often have to engage in a micropolitics that seeks to transfigure the affective registers of our lives and social order. These alterations around specific relations like race and sexuality could cumulatively enhance our capacities for broader engagements in a more generous "politics of becoming" that stretches strenuously beyond itself to hear and be transfigured by others who are— and by otherness that is—barely audible to us.

Numerous theorists influenced by various strands of postmodernism develop related lines of analysis. Drawing on Levinas and Derrida, Michael Shapiro (1997) develops an "ethics of encountering otherness," in the context of his efforts to unmap the "violent cartographies" of colonial encounters. These structures of visibility and invisibility—and related practices—remain powerful today, he argues, and they are perpetuated by the nation-state-oriented geopolitical map of "security studies" that conceals the extensive violence toward peoples excluded from this map. Iris Young (1997) develops an ethics of communication through the lens of "asymmetrical reciprocity," in which listening and questioning come to play prominent roles in helping us live more generously in the midst of deep differences and the deafness of myriad social practices.

Melissa Orlie (1994) draws on Nietzsche and Arendt to cultivate a political perspectivism that incorporates a plurality of embodied views in order more thoughtfully to respond to the will to power that necessarily attends our embeddedness in the world. Stephen White (1991), drawing on critical theory and postmodernism, articulates a notion of responsibility that negotiates between a responsibility to act and a responsibility to otherness. Through a Levinasian reading of Derrida, Simon Critchley (1992, 1998) cultivates an ethics that accents the blindness and violence enmeshed in even the best ethicopolitical projects.

Jane Bennett (1996) challenges the way aesthetics has been marginalized from many central modern "code only" ethics and argues that Foucault's aesthetics of the self is integral to enhancing "the range of possibility in perception, enactment, and responsiveness to others." Bennett shares the aim of an ethics more responsive to otherness, but she is wary of efforts like Critchley's that she thinks overly accent the importance of "disenchantment." She (2001) argues for an ethical sensibility that cultivates "enchantment" as crucial to inspiring and fashioning care for otherness.

Resonating with some recent critical theory informed by Adorno, these theorists argue that the conditions and practices of democracy and justice hinge vitally on our ability to respond to others beyond our horizons of clear vision and comfort. And this in turn requires arts of the self and micropolitical engagements aimed at transfiguring how we perceive and affectively respond to the world. Struggles played out on these registers then interact with macropolitical economic struggles concerning, for example, family law, medical benefits, agricultural practices, redistributive programs, immigration policy, urban design, environmental practices, relations of production, military practices, and health care.

Despite many commonalities, there are important differences among these theorists on numerous fronts, such as how much constructive ethical and political work is desirable, how to strike the balance between opening and structure, the degrees to which they accent the tragic and the playful, the ways they emphasize learning and struggle in democratic contestation, and their proximity and distance to different modes of everyday politics. Rather than sketch many differences, I explore in some depth differences between Connolly and Young to offer a sense of some of these stakes.[10]

10. Among the developments in recent critical theory I omit in order to work more carefully with less, of particular importance is the scholarship on Hannah Arendt. Much of this work engages debates proximate to those above. Hence, one finds Benhabib's more consensual reading (1996a), Honig's agonistic Arendt (1993), Villa's agonistic accent (1996) tempered by Arendt's reading of Kant's theory of judgement. Numerous contributions in Honig 1993 explore tensions around difference, bringing Arendt to bear on issues of gender, sexuality, race, and so forth

In an effort to bolster a "politics of difference," Young (1990) very insightfully explores ways in which power functions at the affective level. On her reading, explicit racism, homophobia, ableism, and other modes of power that earlier operated in conscious and visible forms have significantly receded, as "conscious acceptance" has increasingly gained sway in many public spheres. At the same time, however, "unconscious aversions" remain deeply lodged and in some cases intensify, in manners that often mark, degrade, and devalue numerous groups.

Drawing on Julia Kristeva (1977) and others, Young argues compellingly that the formation of identity is entwined with "abjection," which produces and maintains the border that separates and defines it. "Abjection is the feeling of loathing and disgust that the subject has in encountering certain matter, images, and fantasies" (1990, 143)—that cross or threaten the borders by which selves and associated groups emerge and are sustained. These threats illuminate the contingency, arbitrariness, and always compromised existence of borders—the radical proximity of the dangerousness just on the other side of the vulnerable edge that is the condition of one's identity.

Young argues that abjection is historically linked to group differences and structural power. However, "even if abjection is a result of any subject's construction, nothing in the subject's formation makes group loathing necessary" (1990, 145). Once fabricated, group abjection becomes an insidious force undergirding social relations (influencing our sense of attractiveness, intelligence, competence, maturity, respectability, and thereby influencing hiring, promotion, voting, racial profiling, punishment, etc.). Yet its link with groups and power may be severed or at least greatly attenuated, by working to acknowledge heterogeneity within the groups with which one identifies and by working in a variety of settings to transform the unconscious aversions between groups. Young "does not wish formally to regulate" aesthetic and affective expression and judgement, "because the dangers to liberty are too great. . . . The injunction to 'be just' in such matters amounts to no more and no less than a call to bring these phenomena of practical consciousness and unconsciousness under discussion, that is, to *politicize* them . . . fostering politicized cultural discussion, and making forums and media available for alternative cultural experiment and play." Yet, depending on what she means when she refers to "a kind of social therapy" and "consciousness raising" (1990, 152–53), a host of questions begin to emerge—including those from Foucaultians concerned about the modes of power lodged in many forms of therapy.

These questions are linked to others concerning institutions and prac-

---

Questions of democracy and civil society are explored in Issac 1998; themes of narrative and politics in post-Archimedian times in Disch 1994; the relation between ontology, aesthetics, and ethics in Arendt's thought as an alternative to the enclave politics of late modernity in Curtis 1999.

tices of pluralization and coalition. Young has tended to focus on a politics of coalition structured around various kinds of institutional modes of group representation, caucuses of oppressed groups, reserved seats, group veto power, and so on. More often than Connolly, she accents themes of constructive political and social organization. He too affirms social movements and coalition politics, but he tends to gesture, with the Deleuzean term *assemblages* (Deleuze and Guatarri 1987), toward looser, more multiplicitous, and perhaps more dynamic sets of alliances, saying less about institutional forms and requisites. One should not exaggerate these differences; and neither is deaf to the concerns of the other (contrary to their exchange in Young 1992 and Connolly 1993). Yet they are not insignificant. I suspect that Connolly eschews "therapy" and avoids endorsing some of the above mentioned institutions of group representation in part because his work emphasizes themes that accent questions concerning the ways some such institutions might reify groups and pose a barrier to future possibilities of critical responsiveness, by concentrating power around some insurgent relational groupings at the expense of others. To gain deeper insight into the political differences and further illustrate how the work in each different register has implications for the others, we must return to Young's and Connolly's thoughts on identity and exclusion.

As Stephen White (2000) reminds us, there are no seamless arguments from these ontological-ethical reflections to very particular political practices and institutions. There are only tendential workings to and fro between questions and concerns that emerge at the various registers of political theory and political practice. Yet the political differences at hand are, I suspect, partly prefigured by the philosophical reflections under discussion. For Young, abjection may be unavoidable in selves, but it is not necessarily linked to groups. While group-oriented abjection is central now, she accents a political horizon of the coexistence of differences beyond exclusion. There would still be opacity, ambiguity, and distance, but group relations would not, for the most part, be implicated in power and marginalization. Her ethical-ontological reflections foreground the idea that group differences are "often compatible and might enrich everyone's understanding when they are expressed" and deemphasize the likely reemergence of "othering" (1990, 189).

For Connolly, however, while difference beyond exclusion is an important *point* in the constellation of his ethical-political yearnings, his horizon is constituted by the *tension* between this idea and a sense that significant exclusionary compulsions will continue to accompany every (including group) identity. This latter sense is rooted in interpretations of history, the precariousness of the human condition, and resurgent drives to security. It suggests that identities, which are always significantly related to social relations and power-laden recognitions among groups, will endlessly tend to (re)engender pressures toward marginalization, abjection, blindness, and unacknowledged violence.

We can and should resist these tendencies through multiple ethical and political practices; and coexistence can be less violent, richer, and ethically transformative. Yet these possibilities wane when we cease to attend to the tragic dimension that always likely accompanies them. Negative dialectics, receptive generosity, and critical responsiveness solicit a vigilant and ever-renewed witness not only (with Young) to the rich possibilities beyond each relational identity but also to the seemingly ever-renewed energies of exclusion (which Young downplays). Having suggested these connections, it is important to note that they are indeterminate and malleable, as evidenced by Young's recent shifts (2000, ch. 4)—in the face of empirical criticisms—toward more "fluid" and "pluralizing" modes of group representation.

Shifting the angle of interrogation, the danger risked by genealogical positions like Connolly's is that their suspicions concerning power lurking in all relational identities and practices, as well as their (related) yearning for a futural and inchoate responsiveness, might tend to inhibit the development of needed constructive theorizing concerning political mobilizations, practices, and institutions. Since the mid-1990s, Connolly and several of the other theorists are moving in directions that articulate the tensions between dialectical construction and genealogical responsiveness in promising ways. But these developments in critical theory and postmodernism are still very young, and the difficult work of entwining genealogy and construction is just beginning to emerge. The extent to which what currently seems promising might also generate significant barriers to needed developments remains to be tested in coming efforts at theoretical articulation and ethical-political practice. Constructively, Young (2000) is making increasingly incisive contributions to questions of representation and institutional design. This is especially true in her most recent discussions of local participation, region governance structures, and multidimensional global democracy, where possibilities for democratic "inclusion" are explored in a manner that is both radically transformative and institutionally specific.

■ | Politics of the Double Gesture between Critical Theory and Postmodernism

Further light is shed on the political promise of the ontological-ethical "double contradictory law" or "bivalent tension," by interrogating the contestation between two theorists who are simultaneously very insightful and limited by some of the dangers that reside in Habermasian critical theory and genealogy. Kenneth Baynes, a Habermasian, criticizes Wendy Brown, a radical democratic genealogist, for constructing what he believes is a critique of rights that concludes "that the language of rights is likely to do more harm than good, that rights codify and reinscribe the very powers they were designed to confront, and thus that radicals and progressives should think twice before including rights within their emancipatory projects" (2000, 451). Baynes thinks Brown's skepticism toward rights continues Marx's critique of how (particularly proprietary) rights can depoliticize and naturalize material inequalities and conflicts of civil society, construct an illusion of liberty, equality, and community in the state, and ideologically disguise the complicity between state and capitalist power. Moreover, inspired by Foucault, Brown argues that contemporary rights discourses often "converge with the disciplinary production of identities seeking them": rights become "disciplinary modalities of power producing the very subjects whose rights become a method of administering them" (2000, 118).

Baynes's alternative account (1992), drawing on Habermas and LeFort, emphasizes how democratic practices and rights are cogenerative and "mutually suppose one another." The paradoxes surrounding rights are part of a constructive dialectic of deepening and broadening democratization. By creating "new modes of access to the public sphere," by recognizing, protecting, and sometimes even soliciting myriad associational possibilities, and by continually "outrunning themselves" such that each right creates a basis for new rights—rights enhance freedom, equality, and practices of *discursive democracy* engaged in interpreting their scope, meaning, application, and so on.

Brown claims that Baynes misreads her. She offers not a totalizing critique of rights but rather a critique articulated specifically in relation to the politics of identity and injury. Baynes ignores the strong dialectical twist in Brown's argument that rights "may be most effective to the degree that they remain empty of specific content . . . articulate a political universal that, as an ideal or a vision, operates as a critique of status quo inequalities and hence as an incitement to address those inequalities politically rather than legally" (2000, 469). Driven by the Habermasian underestimation of both the extent to which power operates through the production of subjects and the need for a politics that contests these productions,[11] Baynes's positive dialectic "soothes" modern "anxieties about critique," but it marginalizes the genealogical investigations and democratic struggles that might empower more emancipatory democratic projects. Democracy gets reduced to the "agenda of elected officials."

Ships passing in the night. Brown is less dismissive and more dialectical than Baynes suggests, and Baynes is more cognizant of power and political contestations beyond parliamentary discourse than Brown recognizes. More importantly, their projects—and critical theory and genealogy more generally—might mutually inform each other far more than they do. Brown's genealogies might radicalize the critical theorists' democracy-rights dialectic in ways that more explicitly and reflectively address the pol-

11. For this argument, see also Cruikshank 1999 and Dumm 1987.

itics of subject formation and the ways some articulations of rights risk undesirable complicities with it. Genealogies of power and complicity might move critical theorists toward more robust contestations of often-unrecognized modes of power in civil society (including markets). In turn, this radicalized dialectic might enhance Brown's political critique in manners that are more specific, complex, and nuanced concerning the mobile relations between "empty" and "specified" rights in contemporary struggles, which often contain many of the dynamic, broadening, and politicizing impulses suggested by Baynes, even as they often harbor dangers suggested by Brown.

I am *not* suggesting that the dialectical critical theory and genealogy can or ought simply merge. They cannot and ought not. Each performs works of affirmation and critique that should remain irreducible to the other. Genealogy must strive beyond the constraints of even the most radical dialectic. And dialectical theory, to develop affirmative energy and direction, requires more explicit horizons.

Yet mutual irreducibility need not mean dismissive deafness. Might not Baynes's one-sidedness be entwined with a faith in humans' capacities for a highly consensual and rational communicative dialectic that leads him often to avoid—and become anxious in the face of—some of the deepest considerations of power, blindness, and contingency that might call this faith into question? Might not Brown's equally resolute, maybe even anxious, avoidance of some of Baynes's insights be engendered by a tacit faith in a genealogical vision that too singularly identifies human freedom with incessant unmasking and too often perceives the identities of selves, groups, and practices through a lens that reduces them too much to an effect of disciplinary power?

Alternative ontological-ethical articulations of a bivalent sensibility and double obligation might better prefigure the work of an analogous double gesture in more directly political registers: a progressive politics that develops *both* textured critical dialectical ideals and institutions *and* a genealogical and deconstructive responsiveness that exceeds these ideals and exposes them to their limits. Presently, this might imply the development of a radical dialectic of rights and democracy *and* genealogical inquiries into their limits and insidious complicities with power. Each pole should be transfiguratively informed, invigorated, and chastened by the other. Careful judgment is enhanced by these discrepant impulses and the lively paradoxes, tensions, and partial mediations between them. Theorists will weight and mediate these poles and tensions differently, and therefore the agon between critical theorists and radical democratic genealogists will continue. But it would be more edifying if each side listened to and worked more with insights cultivated by the other.

Is this a kind of "reflective equilibrium" (Rawls 1971) for radicals, between discourse ethics and genealogy, such that the movement to and fro between different levels of inquiry gradually adjusts each so that they might form a coherent framework? Efforts to interrogate incoherence *are* an indispensable *part* of political theory. Yet the double gestures under discussion, including the reciprocal adjustments and interrogations between double gestures at different registers of theorizing, exceed this singular imperative. Instead, the aim should be to figure each register of inquiry and the relations between them so that they *also* solicit a certain *disequilibrium* that enlivens our judgment in the midst of essential but conflictive impulses and insights. Moreover, instead of aiming exclusively to formulate a position that is *defensible* (*defensive*), the disequilibriums of the double gesture are constructed, in no small part, in order to enhance our receptive capacities and our vulnerability to other voices. The ethical vice of unreflective deafness is the congenital defect of every imagined equilibrium.

The political promises of these double gestures are apparent in considerations of democracy above, beneath, and across the boundaries of the nation-state. Habermas has recently argued that the protection of individuals requires the protection of their culturally specific "intersubjective life contexts." This implies giving serious attention to the demands of minority cultures within states for political autonomy, rights, and benefits. Above the state, he theorizes postnational civil societies "composed of interest groups, nongovernmental organizations, and citizen initiatives and movements" that address transnational problems and generate shared political cultures, in relation to which institutions of regional integration and associated political parties are beginning to develop (1998a, 153).

He formulates provocative institutional designs for "cosmopolitan democracy" that might, prodded along by social movements, move beyond the fetishization of state and interstate relations. Hence, for example, he advocates a second chamber in the U.N. General Assembly, in which "peoples would be represented . . . not by their governments but by directly elected representatives. Countries that refuse to permit deputies to be elected by democratic procedures (giving special consideration to their national minorities) could be represented in the interim by nongovernmental organizations appointed by the World Parliament itself as the representatives of oppressed populations" (1998a, 187). He argues for a World Court that can initiate prosecutions and is no longer restricted to considering relations between states. Young's (2000) vision of multidimensional and multilayered democratic "global regulatory regimes" adds an important set of tasks to this general agenda. Habermas senses the limits of proposals framed in analogy to national constitutions, and calls for "more institutional imagination" (2000, 188).

Recent works by genealogists such as Michael Shapiro (1997), who relentlessly exposes and works beyond "violent cartographies" of our statist political imaginations, and Bonnie Honig's explorations (2001) of the relationships between democracy and foreigners, might significantly spur institutional and noninstitutional imaginations. Searching for democratic practices that might better resist xenophobia, Honig explores the idea of the "*taking* foreigner": "an honorific democratic practice—that of demanding or, better yet, simply enacting the redistribution of those powers, rights, and privileges that define a community and order it hierarchically. Here the iconic taking foreigner puts foreignness to work on behalf of democracy by modeling forms of agency that are transgressive, but (and therefore) possessed of potentially inaugural powers. Carried by agencies of foreignness, this revalued taking stretches the boundaries of citizenship and seems to call for a rethinking of democracy as also a cosmopolitan and not just a nation-centered set of solidarities, practices, and institutions" (2001, 8). Note how this might complicate the borders of minority as well as majority cultures.

Such analyses might stretch the imagination further beyond the limits of sovereignty than Habermas has yet to venture. In combination with insights by Tully (1995), whose discussion of constitutionalism is informed by indigenous peoples, common law, postmodernism, and feminism, we might be drawn to explore dissipations and pluralizations of sovereignty that work with and beyond liberal democratic developments. Liberals like Pogge (1994b) and Kuper (2000), parallel to Habermas, argue that vertically dispersed powers of sovereignty in nested territorial units can better accommodate various allegiances and facilitate the exercise and protection of person's liberal rights. Beyond Pogge, however, Kuper suggests that liberals supplement territorial conceptions with the further dispersal of sovereignty horizontally according to functional requirements and tasks (see also Dryzek 1990, 1996). "Our practical task is to gradually pluralize the global basic structure by creating a variety of forms of democratically responsive, semiautonomous legal authority. . . ." (Kuper 2000, 666).

More genealogical cosmopolitanism(s) (in conjunction with some of the best postcolonial theorizing [Mignolo 2000]), by accenting the importance of vulnerability and responsiveness toward others and otherness within and beyond the democratically institutionalized matrix of groups, scales, and issues, might further disperse and push democratic theory and practice in ways that further register the *dissonant dynamic* (and thus *temporal*) struggles and suppressed solidarities within any "now," no matter how territorially, culturally, and functionally variegated its structure may be. In a sense, even Kuper's functional dispersion remains too territorial/sovereign, insofar as it projects a relatively static spatial matrix onto the realm of "issue areas." He takes the territorial model and simply turns it at a right angle to imagine horizontally as well as vertically dispersed structures of sovereignty. This is crucial and has much to offer.

Yet his spatial metaphors may reinforce too great a drive toward consolidation and integration in institutional designs. A more receptive generosity and agonistic democracy seeks often to question (and sometimes to resist) this, in part by rearticulating a more dynamic and less structured democratic situation that is perhaps better evoked by a nonlinear and tensional democratic *temporality* among beings and events moving and struggling according to many distinct and often dissonant drummers (Tully 1995). These temporalities variously overlap, reinforce, encroach on, and resist one another, such that even under the best conditions at any moment, the negotiations, agreements, institutions, and directions that are forged will likely fail to respond well to many questions, peoples, and admirable alternative possibilities. The aim is to infuse the presence of all theories and practices with a sense of absence. As Derrida puts it, "*What is proper to a culture is to not be identical to itself.* There is no cultural identity without this difference *with itself*" (1992, 14).

Democratic practices inflected by the best in deconstruction approach this temporal dispersion and suppression in each moment, culture, and institution as a solicitation, against whatever odds, to reopen their structures of present responsiveness to fresh negotiations with those clamoring within and beyond the problematic constraints, productions, and gates which have arisen. They seek not only to maximize responsiveness in institutional designs (though they contribute to this too, by repeatedly rendering unresponsiveness more visible) but also to cultivate a capacious sense for, and yearning to receptively engage, those to whom our responsiveness has as yet failed to engage. More concretely, this means expanding our capacities to form and engage groups, movements, and nascent practices that cut across and seek to radically reform (or sometimes even abolish) the jurisdictional "spaces" of established institutions. It means enhancing our capacities to affirm that democracy is in no small way the dynamic messy coexistence of practices and institutional spaces that contest as well as complement one another.

Yet how might this ethos articulate itself in relation to institutional designs? In addition to "inclusion," toward what constructive democratic practices might social movements, indigenous peoples, marginalized traditions, and emergent groupings aim in order to enhance capacities for responsiveness to alterity? How might various constituencies aim to intensify the transfigurative exposure of institutions to that which lies beyond their limit? Let me briefly suggest three possibilities that begin to emerge when we begin to think and act in the tensions between critical theory and genealogy.

First, we might aim to design practices that seek to make people situated in dominant institutions experience these institutions and themselves as being "otherness to be included," rather than fortifying an unquestioned sense that they and these institutions unproblematically occupy the central position of "the includers." Consider public hearings, for example. The most usual formats for inclusion provide an opportunity for individuals and associations to listen to officials and provide comments in settings designed and presided over by representatives of the institution involved. Struggles from more genealogical perspectives, or "border thinking" perspectives emerging in numerous postcolonial sites (Mignolo 2000), might seek to transform institutions in ways that required representative bodies regularly to attend public meetings designed by and presided over by the most-marginalized groups in those groups' chosen public spaces. This is prefigured by the meetings currently conducted by grassroots urban coalitions associated with the Industrial Areas Foundation, where public officials meet the social movement on its terms, times, and terrain. What if such practices of engagement between governing institutions and the least well-off were required at regular intervals, so that, for example, representative bodies had to meet with indigenous peoples in places, times, and modes chosen by the latter?

Second, we might aim to design variegated institutions in ways that have more space for tensions between different jurisdictions, scales, groups, and issue regimes to be given a hearing and negotiated. This would render more indeterminate the partial sovereignties and inside/outside boundaries of institutions, in ways that would provide more openings for groups relatively disempowered by given institutional jurisdictions to gain voice and power. Instead of imagining variegated institutions as nested within an overly (neo-Hegelian) systematic framework where domains are clearly demarcated and each layer fits neatly within limits governed by layers higher up, sites might be designed where more interactive powers might emerge. Young's design, wherein "regional government sets a framework for inter-local negotiation, conflict resolution, and cooperation whose issues are on the local, as well as regional, public agenda" (2000, 234), provides an example that might kindle our imaginations of other interinstitutional relations that facilitate engagements between public bodies that are not included in one another.

Third, in conjunction with engagements stemming from sensibilities and practices like those sketched above, institutions might be designed in ways that enhance their capacities *in relation to the capacities of others* for ongoing dynamic transfiguration in response to those whom they disempower at any given point in time. The ever-challenging and essentially translucent aim here is to orient this process of transformation in ways that secure rights and practices of currently established freedom and justice to protect against the bad, while opening them to changes that increase their responsiveness and accountability to those they poorly address.

These modes and institutions of responsiveness may sometimes pose serious threats to smooth coordination. But responsiveness may also often disclose unwonted solidarities that can enhance coordination. In any case, smooth coordination may not always be the most ethical or politically desirable goal. It certainly is *not* when it comes at the expense of justice; and justice and responsiveness are tightly entwined. What the most promising theorists under discussion seek to cultivate, above all else, are our democratic capacities to be more receptive and generous in relation to the *questions* concerning the damages and suppressed possibilities typically concealed by the dominant paradigms of political inquiry.

Gerald Gamm and John Huber

Legislatures as Political Institutions: Beyond the Contemporary Congress[1]

For the bulk of political scientists today, the study of legislatures is the study of the U.S. Congress. Other legislatures do exist, of course. The U.S. states have legislatures. The U.S. cities have legislatures. National, provincial, and local governments throughout the world have parliaments, representative assemblies, and legislatures. Even Europe—and, on rare occasions, the world assembled as the United Nations—has a legislature. But the scholarly world of legislative studies is, overwhelmingly, a world that studies the U.S. Congress. And the study of Congress tends to be the study of the postwar House of Representatives.

Although this generalization fairly approximates the contemporary field, it was not the state of the discipline at the turn of the last century. In that earlier time, when the study of legislatures similarly flourished and enjoyed comparably high stature within the broader discipline, scholars studied various national legislatures. Moreover, studies of Congress were bicameral, historical, and grounded in comparisons with other nations as well as the U.S. states. Wilson (1885) and Lowell (1902) examined the U.S. Congress through the prism of the British House of Commons, and Lowell analyzed data that extended back to the time of the Civil War. Follett (1896) and Fuller (1909) studied the House Speakership by examining its historical development, and each scholar compared the office to antecedents in Britain and the American colonies. Similarly, McConachie (1898), Alexander (1916), and Harlow (1917), in their studies of rules and legislative organization, collected their evidence from state legislatures, other countries, and congressional history.

This paper attempts to assess the state of legislative studies in our own

1. The first draft of this paper was presented at the Annual Meeting of the American Political Science Association, August 31–September 2, 2000, Washington, D.C. We are grateful for helpful comments from Alison Alter, Randy Calvert, John Carey, Gary Cox, Daniel Diermeier, Barbara Geddes, Ira Katznelson, Gerhard Loewenberg, Helen Milner, Paul Pierson, and Ken Shepsle. We are also grateful to Joel Andersen for his assistance in surveying the journal literature.

time. Unlike many such essays, however, our primary purpose is neither to provide a comprehensive review of the vast literature nor to summarize all recent advances and debates in the field. This daunting task has been admirably accomplished by others, either in broad surveys or in more-focused essays on particular areas of legislative research.[2] Instead, the main objective of this essay is to understand the implications for legislative studies of the dominance of work on the contemporary Congress. The most obvious implication, we believe, is the extent to which congressional scholarship has served as a model of positivist, rigorous, scientific research for the more general study of legislatures—and the extent to which congressional scholarship has sustained the discipline's interest in institutions during an era otherwise dominated by behavioral work. Also, we contend, the breadth of research on Congress—drawing on participant observation, roll call analyses, interviews, rational-choice theory, and even history—has demonstrated the importance of embracing multiple approaches to analysis.

But the primacy of congressional research has also exacted costs, primarily in biases that are created in the types of questions scholars pose and in the types of answers they provide to these questions. Important avenues for legislative research, for example, include efforts to explain the choice of institutional arrangements or to analyze the impact of institutions on the behavior of individuals, other political institutions, or policy. Although research on Congress has often promoted these goals, we believe it has also frustrated them. In this essay, we discuss how this has occurred and how recent research has begun to move beyond some of the biases inherent in a Congress-centered approach.

■ | The Dominance of Congress in Legislative Studies

Legislative scholars have for some time pointed to the fact that the modern study of legislatures has become inexplicably intertwined with the study of the U.S. Congress. Thus Mezey argues that "most of the legislative literature is firmly rooted in time and place, and for much of the subfield the place is Washington, D.C." (1993, 356). He argues that this leaves legislative research "theoretically impoverished" (357), identifying a need for more comparative work. In Hedlund's 1983 review essay on the organizational attributes of legislatures, he finds that the overwhelming emphasis is

2. For an excellent overview of the literature, see Mezey 1993. *Legislative Studies Quarterly* has recently been publishing a series of useful survey articles, such as Rasch 2000; S. S. Smith 2000, and Hibbing 1999. These and other essays are collected in the volume edited by Loewenberg, Squire, and Kiewiet (forthcoming). For reviews of the positive theory of congressional institutions, see Shepsle and Weingast 1995. For a review of much of the literature on the European Union, see Moser 1999b.

on Congress and he calls for increased research on subnational and foreign legislatures (358). And when *Legislative Studies Quarterly* was launched in 1976, Malcolm Jewell, in the Editor's Introduction, complained that "the growing wealth of information and analysis about the U.S. Congress has not been matched by comparable studies of U.S. state legislatures" (1976, 2). Consequently, a central reason for the creation of this journal was to encourage research on assemblies other than Congress.

Despite these calls for change, recent history shows a field that remains firmly rooted in the study of Congress. One way to see this dominance empirically is to look at the recipients of prizes that are given in the field of legislative studies. Since 1988, when it established the Fenno Prize and the Congressional Quarterly Press Award, the Legislative Studies Section of the American Political Science Association has awarded prizes to nine books and to ten papers, designating them the best work of their kind in "legislative studies." Without exception, every one of these nineteen books and papers has been about the U.S. Congress—and, laying aside formal theory, Congress only.[3]

Indeed, this Congress can itself be a rather narrow creature. In the world of legislative studies, Congress tends to be a one-house legislature that came into existence in 1947. Of the nine books that have won the Fenno Prize, just one emphasizes the Senate (Sinclair 1989) and none draws extensively on pre-1947 history. The ten award-winning papers include just two Senate papers and one historical paper. The field of legislative studies is anchored firmly in the study of the postwar House of Representatives.

The history of these two awards neatly summarizes the dominance of congressional research in the modern study of legislatures. Examining all the articles published over the last few years in the *American Political Science Review, American Journal of Political Science,* and *Journal of Politics,* we identified a total of 110 empirical articles on legislatures (not including another 23 articles that presented formal models of legislatures without significant empirical content).[4] Of these 110 articles, 94 were solely about a U.S. legislature. Just 16 of these articles incorporated a legislature outside the United States—and even some of these 16 included Congress in their analysis. Of the 94 U.S. articles, 71 looked only at Congress, and 55 looked only at the contemporary Congress. (Surprisingly, at least to us, the journal literature contained more articles on U.S. states—23—than on all non-U.S. legislatures combined.)

Legislative Studies Quarterly demonstrates a similar bias toward Congress. Of 87 articles published since 1995 (not including 8 formal models),

3. For a list of award winners, see www.apsanet.org/about/sections/pastwinners/section3.cfm.

4. For this analysis, we looked at the *American Political Science Review* since 1993 and the two other journals since 1996.

65 looked only at the United States.[5] Of the 65 U.S. articles, 39 examined the contemporary Congress, 4 drew on congressional history, and 22 analyzed state legislatures. The remaining 22 articles were either cross-national or focused solely on a non-U.S. legislature. Although less pronounced than the bias demonstrated in the awards presented by the Legislative Studies Section and in the first-tier general journals, the publication record of *Legislative Studies Quarterly* confirms the dominance of congressional scholarship in legislative studies. Even in this journal, established in part to emphasize the study of legislatures other than the U.S. Congress, fully half of all scholarship is devoted to this single national legislature.

■ | The Evolution of Modern Legislative Studies

The modern study of legislatures traces its roots to the post–World War II era. In the 1950s and 1960s, even as the behavioral revolution transformed our understanding of voting behavior, several political scientists worked to develop a parallel body of scientific work on institutions. While some scholars studied the presidency, the courts, local governments, bureaucracies, or non-U.S. institutions, the largest body of work focused on the U.S. Congress. Between 1957 and 1961, White published *Citadel* (1957), Truman published *The Congressional Party* (1959), Matthews published his article on Senate folkways (1959) as well as *U.S. Senators and Their World* (1960), and Huitt published his three seminal articles on Senate norms and leadership in the *American Political Science Review* (1957, 1961a, b). This literature was surprisingly cohesive. Apart from Truman 1959, all of it described and analyzed the postwar Senate, all of it emphasized the centrality of norms to the Senate, and all of it drew on sociological theory.

The emphasis on the Senate proved to be short lived. With the important exception of Ripley (1969a, b), legislative scholars in the 1960s and 1970s turned their attention to the House of Representatives. In his 1962 article and in *The Power of the Purse* (1966), Fenno examined the internal operation of the House Appropriations Committee. In this work, with its focus on norms and its sociological framework, Fenno was clearly influenced by the earlier Senate studies. Fenno's research on the House occurred within a rich scholarly context. A major set of scholars in the 1960s and 1970s—including Ripley (1967), Jones (1970), Manley (1970), and Peabody (1976)—also analyzed the postwar Congress, with special attention to the House.

Although emphasizing the contemporary Congress, most of this work was infused with an appreciation for history. Indeed, a surprising number

5. Joel Andersen collected these data from *Legislative Studies Quarterly*. We are grateful to him for his research assistance.

of articles and monographs published in these years emphasized historical change or reconstructed an episode or norm from the congressional past. Much of this work was by historians—such as Galloway (1962), Donald (1965), Rothman (1966), Livermore (1966), Silbey (1967), Patterson (1967), Merrill and Merrill (1971), and Benedict (1973)—produced in an age when historians still valued the study of elite political institutions. But political scientists also produced a significant scholarship in congressional history—including Jones (1968), Abram and Cooper (1968), Cooper (1962, 1970), D. Price (1971, 1975, 1977), Polsby (1968), Polsby, Gallaher, and Rundquist (1969), Ripley (1969a), and D. W. Brady (1972, 1973), Brady and Althoff (1974), and Cooper and Brady (1981a, b).

Legislative scholars in this era were self-conscious in their aspirations to develop a positivist study of the field. Thus Fenno situated himself among scholars whose "main thrust is descriptive rather than reformist" (1966, xvii). And Huitt and Peabody, in characterizing the landmark Study of Congress project, insisted that "reform is not the target of this research project." Rather, they hoped that the various books produced by this project would simply "tell interested people as much as possible about how Congress works" (Ripley 1969a, v–vi). Through the 1970s, this positivist mission was pursued through a scholarship that was thickly descriptive and often grounded in the tools of sociology. Fenno (1962) and Polsby (1968), exemplars of this literature, explicitly grounded their studies in social theory and organization theory.

Two books, Fenno's *Congressmen in Committees* (1973) and Mayhew's *Congress: The Electoral Connection* (1974b), marked a major reorientation in the study of Congress. Together, Fenno and Mayhew demonstrated the effectiveness of studying Congress with an approach that borrowed more from economics than from sociology, an approach drawn from the growing field of rational-choice theory. "How to study legislative behavior is a question that does not yield a consensual answer among political scientists," Mayhew (1974b, 1, 5) wrote in the introduction to his book. "Mostly through personal experience on Capitol Hill, I have become convinced that scrutiny of purposive behavior offers the best route to an understanding of legislatures—or at least of the United States Congress." Fenno, in a long footnote, recognized that his new emphasis on "goal seeking by the members" represented a sharp break from his earlier work, where he drew on "the literature created by people studying social systems" (1973, xvii n. 1). Famously, Fenno argued that legislators were driven by one of three major goals: "re-election, influence within the House, and good public policy" (1). Mayhew, of course, argued that the reelection goal was itself sufficient to explain the broad contours of member behavior.[6]

6. Mayhew looked beyond the reelection goal, though, in explaining the internal organization of Congress. Leaders and prospective leaders are also motivated by institutional prestige and power, according to Mayhew (1974b, 145–46).

In the late 1970s and 1980s, growing numbers of rational-choice theorists examined questions relating to legislative organization. But their work, often technical and abstract, remained inaccessible to many students of actual legislatures. At the same time, congressional scholars increasingly followed Fenno's and Mayhew's models of study, analyzing the implications of rational, individual actors, rather than describing the workings of collective social systems. Shepsle and Weingast (1987), explicitly utilizing the tools of rational-choice theory to address a central question in congressional organization, demonstrated the extent to which work in formal theory had converged with work on Congress.

Although they were writing during the heyday of congressional reform, when the basic institutions of Congress were undergoing historic change, scholars generally described a Congress dominated by strong, autonomous committees, where party leadership was irrelevant. With the advantage of hindsight, we can see that this depiction was quickly becoming anachronistic in the 1970s. Yet this was Mayhew's classic depiction of the institution in his 1974 book, where he emphasized the centrality of committees and noted that parties "are more useful for what they are not than for what they are" (1974b, 97). Six years before, in his article on the "institutionalization" of the House, Polsby (1968) had described an institution that was fully mature. Fenno's work (1973) on the committee system began with assumptions about legislator goals, which were pursued against a fixed institutional setting. And Fenno's exploration (1978) of "home style," where he analyzed the behavior of members in their districts, took the institutional environment as a given. A decade later, Shepsle and Weingast (1987) were still navigating this same institutional world.

In 1989 Shepsle acknowledged that this "textbook Congress"—the Congress of weak party leaders and strong committee chairs—had begun to come apart in the 1960s, though its image had continued to linger in scholarship for many years after. Many scholars, of course, had recognized the change as it was occurring. Analyzing the majoritarian revolt against Rules Committee chair Howard W. Smith in the early 1960s, Jones (1968) called attention to an early skirmish in the battle for reform. Many congressional scholars described the reforms as they were implemented in the 1970s, and others began to assess the impact of institutional change on legislators' actions. Sinclair (1989), Smith (1989), Rohde (1991), and Aldrich (1995) all compared the congressional worlds before and after reform to explain changes in member behavior. They sought also to explain why the institution had changed. A similar body of scholarship emerged after Republicans gained control of the House and Senate in 1995. In a short essay, Fenno (1997) examined why House Republicans experienced problems in governing when they moved into the majority. And, in a fascinating study of a southern congressional district that he had originally visited in the early 1970s, Fenno (2000) demonstrated how changes in the media and legislative careers affect a member's district style.

The transformation of the House and Senate in the 1970s and 1990s forced scholars to recognize that the institution was not static, that stylized facts were plastic. Changes in the institution itself led to changes in scholarship, as Rohde (1991) and Cox and McCubbins (1993) developed new theories to account for the prominence of parties in congressional decision making. As congressional scholars reckoned with the historic shifts of the late twentieth century, historical scholarship attracted new interest. Poole and Rosenthal's sweeping 1997 study of ideological shifts in Congress is grounded in an exhaustive study of roll call votes, and their database has become a rich mine for other scholars.

But most scholarship on the Congress has remained ahistorical. Affected more by the rational-choice revolution than by any revolution in subcommittee rights, closed rules, or filibusters, most congressional scholars have continued to study short periods of time in which the institution itself could be held constant. The study of Congress has become increasingly scientific, with the generation of explicit propositions to test, the creation of new data sets for testing these propositions, and the utilization of sophisticated methods to adjudicate substantive debates. We see this, to take one example, in studies of individual and committee preferences, where scholars have developed an impressive array of arguments about how to use (or not use) roll call voting data to measure preferences. We also see it in studies of legislative procedures, the relative influence of parties and exogenous preferences in shaping voting behavior, and the impact of partisanship on leadership and elections.

For some, the upshot of this evolution is that congressional studies have become too specialized. Mezey, for instance, objects that with "each article on each topic, the questions seem to get narrower, the issues more arcane, and findings less relevant to all but the small group of scholars pursuing that specific line of research" (1993, 356). For others, of course, this narrowness is the hallmark of a mature subfield engaged in rigorous normal science. From this perspective, the narrowness of many research projects is inevitable if one really wants to be able to distinguish with confidence the validity of competing empirical claims.

It seems odd in some ways that mature normal science would emerge primarily through the study of a single legislature. After all, if the applicability of legislative theories is limited to a specific legislative arena (e.g., the House) during specific periods (e.g., the postwar period), then it seems doubtful that these theories can be deemed in any sense general. But it is precisely the goal of a mature normal science to produce general theories that are not sharply constrained by time or space. This is the concern that dominates Mezey's review of legislative studies. He points out that "one can no more have a theory of legislatures that applies only to the United States Congress than a theory of relativity that applies only to Chicago" (1993, 357). He thus argues for increased comparative and historical work that will generate theories that in fact apply across political systems or across time.

Regardless of how one evaluates the costs and benefits of mature normal science, the evolution of congressional studies stands in sharp contrast to legislative research on other countries, which clung to a much older approach. Until the 1980s, students of non-U.S. legislatures typically worked on developing typologies of parliaments according to the various roles and functions that parliaments played across political systems and on coding individual parliaments according to where they fit in the various typologies. Work in this tradition was typically motivated by the normative question of whether "parliament matters"—that is, whether the "institution of parliament" influences the outcome of the legislative process.

This focus on parliamentary functions went back at least as far as Bagehot (1966 [1867]), who argued famously that the English Parliament's purpose is not to influence policy but rather to elect the executive, keep it informed about constituent interests, and keep the public informed about public policy.[7] Since Bagehot, a similar functionalist orientation often dominated comparative research on legislatures. Numerous efforts have been made, for example, to refine and improve the typologies of parliamentary roles (e.g., Blondel 1973; Wahlke et al. 1962; Packenham 1970; Polsby 1975; Mezey 1979; Sisson 1973) or to describe parliamentary structures in efforts to define such roles (e.g., Lees and Shaw 1979).

This mode of comparative legislative research still prospers. Recent work has attempted to sort out how and under what circumstances various parliaments play significant roles in policymaking (e.g., Olson and Mezey 1991; Arter 1984; Damgaard 1992; Liebert and Cotta 1990; Norton 1993). There has also been considerable effort to understand how members of parliaments perceive their own roles (e.g., Cain, Ferejohn, and Fiorina 1987; Searing 1994; Park 1988).

One notable feature of almost all of the typological research cited above is the absence of testable, causal arguments.[8] Instead, the research has a highly descriptive quality, with the primary goal being to interpret the actual role that legislatures or legislators are playing in different political systems. Mezey goes so far as to argue that this body of research has "yielded nothing in the way of testable propositions that would help to explain the differences and similarities in legislative performance that we observe cross-nationally" (1993, 351). Perhaps it is in this regard that the congressional literature stands in such sharp contrast to other legislative research. And this may help explain why so many of the prizes and publications in leading journals are devoted to works that aim explicitly to develop

---

7. The famous work by Jennings (1957) makes a similar argument.

8. The obvious exception is some of the work on individual roles, where efforts are made to deduce specific factors that affect individual perceptions of their roles (e.g., Searing 1994; Cain, Ferejohn, and Fiorina 1987).

original theoretical arguments or test such arguments in a sophisticated way.

▪ | Borrowing Arguments: The Impact of Congress on Comparative Studies

By this standard, considerable progress has been made in the comparative study of legislatures over the last ten years. In particular, the rigorous mode of congressional research, where causal arguments about legislative behavior are derived and tested, has changed legislative research on other countries by altering not only the basic methodology of research but also the types of questions that are posed and the types of answers that are offered. Perhaps most notably, following the development of the spatial model in studies of American politics, many comparative studies have moved away from their earlier functionalist orientation and toward an effort to develop and test causal arguments about legislative organization and behavior. Theoretical arguments originally developed in the study of Congress have been borrowed by scholars studying other political systems.

The distributive politics theory in the Congress literature, for example, has led to a series of arguments about the agenda power of committees and the composition of committees (e.g., review essays in Shepsle and Weingast's 1995 edited volume). Drawing on this same basic theoretical framework, Laver and Shepsle (1990, 1996) develop and test an original argument about how ministerial portfolios are allocated in parliamentary democracies. Their theory leads us to expect that the policy preferences of ministers will influence in predictable ways the types of portfolios that ministers receive during government formation. Similarly, Huber (1992, 1996a) draws partially on distributive theory to argue that the "package vote" in France is used to preserve agreements across political parties in the governing majority on distributive issues.

Issues of proposal and veto power within the House have also been central in the Congress literature. This type of theoretical work, which draws on a framework originally developed in Romer and Rosenthal 1978 (see the review in Rosenthal 1990), examines how the distribution of proposal and veto power in the policymaking process influences political behavior and policy outcomes. Research on Congress has applied this approach in a variety of contexts, including the use of restrictive amendment procedures (e.g., Krehbiel 1991; Dion and Huber 1996), the institutional origins of committee power (Shepsle and Weingast 1987), the use of executive vetos (Cameron 2000), and the impact of divided government on policy change (e.g., Krehbiel 1998; Howell et al. 2000).

Recently, this approach to legislative theorizing has been applied in a variety of contexts outside the Congress. Tsebelis (1995, 1999) utilizes the framework to develop and test the argument that as the number of partisan and institutional veto players increases in a political system, the propensity for major policy changes will decrease.[9] A related "veto players" argument is developed by Bawn (1999b), who shows that spending levels in different German ministries are influenced by the level of conflict across parties in coalitions and between the Bundestag and the Bundesrat. The framework has also been used by Tsebelis (1994), Moser (1997), Steunenberg (1994), and Crombez (1996) to develop theoretical debates about the circumstances under which the European Parliament can influence policies in the European Union. Huber (1996b) uses the framework to argue that the existence of a confidence procedure in parliamentary democracies gives prime ministers proposal power and relegates assemblies to veto players, which is the opposite of what we find in many presidential systems, where legislatures propose and presidents veto. Rasch (2000) draws on the framework to study strategic voting behavior in parliamentary settings. Vanberg (1998) uses the framework to examine the ability of the parliamentary minority to use threats of constitutional review of legislation to extract policy concessions. And Baldez and Carey (1999) invoke the framework to argue that the rules for budgeting in Chile have a systematic impact on spending levels.

The Baron and Ferejohn bargaining models (e.g., 1989a, b), originally developed to study legislative procedure in the U.S. Congress, have also been imported by scholars studying noncongressional settings. In the Baron and Ferejohn framework, bargaining outcomes are shaped in large part by the preferences legislative actors have to reach agreement quickly rather than slowly (i.e., legislative actors discount the utility of future payments). This framework allows them to argue, for example, that closed amendment rules can be more efficient than open amendment rules because they facilitate quicker agreement. This same insight has been adopted in the comparative context by Tsebelis and Money (1995, 1997), who study bicameralism. They argue that the power of the upper houses in a political system will often depend on their powers of delay. Upper houses can use such power to extract concessions from lower houses (and cabinets), which may have superior agenda power but also often prefer quick action that is made possible only by the acquiescence of the upper house. Similarly, Baron (1993) uses the framework to study the type of outcomes that should emerge from coalition bargaining processes, and Baron (1998) uses the framework to study cabinet bargaining after coalition formation is complete.

Principal-agent theory represents another area where theoretical efforts to explain behavior in the U.S. Congress have been imported by oth-

9. See also Tsebelis 1994 on the European parliament, Bawn 1999b on bicameral bargaining in Germany, and Heller 1997 on budget politics in Italy.

ers. Kiewiet and McCubbins (1991) were the first to develop this framework to study Congress, arguing (among other things) that institutional structures allow congressional control over budget outcomes and that committee assignments and committee behavior are largely controlled by political parties. This same framework was adopted by Ramseyer and Rosenbluth (1993), whose use of the principal-agent framework to reinterpret Japanese legislative politics has clear antecedents in the application of principal-agent theory to the study of Congress. More recently, it has been used by Strom (2000) to interpret the chain of delegation in parliamentary systems for voters to bureaucrats. And the principal-agent framework has played a central role in Steunenberg's work on delegation in the European Union (Steunenberg 1994).

We find, then, over the past ten years an impressive and growing list of examples where a Congress-centered theoretical approach has been exported, with positive results, to the study of other settings. To be sure, it remains a small subset of legislative studies. But it nonetheless represents a dramatic change over what came before. In evaluating the body of comparative scholarship that borrows from congressional insights, we offer several observations.

First, many of the applications of congressional research do not occur in studies of legislatures only. Scholars of other systems may have previously dismissed the relevance of congressional theories because legislatures in other systems often seem to play a peripheral role in the policy process. But many scholars drawing on congressional theories have applied them not to parliaments but to cabinets in parliamentary systems. In our view, this extension of Congress-centered theory to the study of cabinets does not remove the research from the domain of legislative studies. On the contrary, since Bagehot, scholars have recognized that the cabinet is in many respects a supercommittee of the legislature and that activity in the cabinet thus lies squarely in the legislative domain. It is therefore quite natural to view the politics of cabinet government as "legislative politics" in parliamentary systems.

Second, none of these examples is characterized by an automatic and unaltered application of congressional approaches to another setting. Instead, each of these studies of non-U.S. settings makes modifications and theoretical extensions to the ideas first published in the congressional literature, resulting in arguments that are tailored to their new applications. That said, these studies have a theoretical lineage that can be traced back to the study of Congress. Methodologically, these studies share with previous congressional scholarship a preoccupation with developing empirically refutable claims about legislative behavior. In this respect, those who have borrowed from Congress are clearly making it possible to advance beyond the limitations of previous typological research in non-U.S. settings.

Third, the influence of congressional research in other settings has two dimensions. One is simply that we now have impressive new theories of "other places." The Ramseyer and Rosenbluth study of Japan, for example, turns on its head the conventional wisdom about the power of the Japanese bureaucracy. Tsebelis and Money draw attention to what were previously dismissed as irrelevant upper chambers. Bawn gives us evidence of when the Bundesrat shapes policy outcomes in Germany. Laver and Shepsle provide us with a clear deductive theory about how coalitions distribute agenda control. And the numerous papers on the European Parliament have clearly enriched our understanding of how policy is made in the European Union. These are but a few examples of how using a framework born in the study of Congress has helped us to understand other times and places.

The second dimension concerns the generality of our theories. Since this research has revealed that many of the theoretical arguments developed with an eye toward Congress are not parochial in their ultimate scope, it is now possible to draw connections between phenomena traditionally viewed as quite distinct. We can now see connections between the dynamics of committee assignments in Congress and the assignment of portfolios in parliamentary systems. The research cited above also demonstrates similarities between policymaking during coalition government in parliamentary systems and policymaking during divided government in the United States. The roles played by political parties in solving agency problems have many similarities in Japan and the United States. And the importance of agenda procedures for facilitating distributive agreements is similar in France and the United States.

Fourth, the rational-choice approach to research on the contemporary Congress has had an indirect effect on our understanding of legislative institutions in other settings. One of the main benefits of the congressional mode of research is that it requires scholars to examine carefully the subtle details of institutional design, focusing in particular on agenda institutions—the rules for making and approving policy proposals. When this analytic approach has been exported to other settings, scholars have often discovered that information about relevant institutional details has never been collected. Consequently, the export of the Congress mode of research to other settings has forced scholars to undertake theoretically informed empirical research on the nature of legislative institutions. In attempting to study portfolio distribution, for example, Laver and Shepsle could not use existing research to identify the agenda powers of cabinet ministers, a deficiency in the existing literature that they responded to with their 1994 edited volume. The chapters in Döring 1995b provide an array of institutional data, the collection of which was motivated almost entirely by theoretical frameworks developed in studies of Congress. And the chapters in Strom, Müeller, and Bergman (forthcoming) typescript provide a carefully collected new data set on the institutional arrangements that govern coalition formation and dissolution.

Finally, it is worth noting that while studies of Congress have exercised considerable influence on the study of other legislatures, the study of other legislatures has had almost no discernible impact on studies of Congress. Probably the only significant exception relates to Cox and McCubbins's *Legislative Leviathan* (1993), concerning the role of party in the House of Representatives. Many of the theoretical ideas in that work about the incentives of individual representatives to delegate authority to party leaders were first developed in Cox's *The Efficient Secret* (1987), a study of the emergence of party discipline in the British House of Commons in the nineteenth century.

■ | Research Biases

Research on Congress has clearly enriched legislative studies over the last decade, through its impact on how other assemblies have been studied. But this influence has brought with it some clear biases in how legislative scholars pose and address research questions. Most important, congressional scholarship has tended to emphasize the individual behavior of legislators, rather than policy outcomes.

This emphasis on individual behavior has theoretical roots. As Mayhew (1974b) and rational-choice scholars have emphasized, legislators can be examined as autonomous reelection seekers, acting independently of party organizations. Individual legislators, especially in the U.S. context, can be held personally accountable by voters. But empirical, rather than theoretical, considerations probably explain the overwhelming emphasis by congressional scholars on individual behavior. In contrast to comparative studies of multiple legislatures, studies of the contemporary Congress tend to be studies in which the institution is held constant and dramatic changes in policy outcomes are rare. What varies most in a single legislature is the behavior of individuals, and the availability of roll call and electoral data facilitate this research bias. Comparative scholars, in contrast, can more easily study aggregate outcomes across legislatures than individual behavior within legislatures.

Logically, of course, we could imagine comparative studies of individual behavior or studies of the contemporary Congress that emphasize policy outcomes. Both literatures exist. Regulatory policy, budget policy, and pork-barrel politics have all been extensively studied by congressional scholars. But, as we report below, research on policy outcomes represents a small part of the work on Congress. Overwhelmingly, current congressional research focuses on individual action.

Given the dominance of congressional literature, the entire subfield of legislative studies is shaped by a perspective that emphasizes the individual. There are striking differences between those studies which focus on Congress and those which focus on other settings. More generally, we argue, scholarship on any single legislature is fundamentally different from scholarship that is either cross-sectional or longitudinal in design. Historical and comparative studies of legislatures allow scholars to ask questions about the design and impact of institutions that cannot be examined in studies of the contemporary Congress, where the institutional context is exogenous. In historical and comparative scholarship, institutional variation could be internal to the legislature—such as variation between legislatures in degrees of professionalism, in rules, or in the nature of committee systems—or the variation could be external to the legislature—including differences between separation-of-powers and parliamentary systems, or variation in electoral rules. In research on the contemporary Congress, in contrast, institutions are generally held constant.

Surveying recent literature published in the three leading journals, we found that work on the contemporary Congress is dominated by studies of individual behavior. Some form of individual behavior was the dependent variable in 33 of the 55 articles on the contemporary Congress that we identified in recent issues of *APSR*, *AJPS*, and *JOP*. Voting behavior is by far the most common dependent variable in the literature. Recent efforts to explain and characterize patterns of roll call voting include, for example, Box-Steffensmeier, Arnold, and Zorn 1997, Herrick, Moore, and Hibbing 1994, Fett 1994, Krehbiel 2000, Rothenberg and Sanders 2000, Hero and Tolbert 1995, Norton 1999, Hutchings 1999, Gartzke and Wrighton 1998, Vega and Firestone 1995, Grofman, Griffin, and Berry 1995, Overby and Cosgrove 1996, Clucas 1997, Maltzman 1998, Bailey and Brady 1998, Hood and Morris 1998, Swers 1998, Forgette and Sala 1999, Groseclose, Levitt, and Snyder 1999, Snyder and Groseclose 2000, Hager and Talbert 2000, and Nokken 2000. Congressional scholars analyze many other forms of individual behavior as well—including the decision to retire (e.g., Kiewiet and Zeng 1993; A. Gerber 1996; Moore and Hibbing 1998; Hall and van Houweling 1995; Groseclose and Krehbiel 1994), the decision to cosponsor bills (Kessler and Krehbiel 1996; Krehbiel 1995; Schiller 1995), the decision to discharge bills from committee (Kessler and Krehbiel 1996; Binder, Lawrence, and Maltzman 1999; Krehbiel 1995, 1999), the decision to hold hearings (Diermeier and Feddersen 2000), the behavior of party leaders (Sinclair 1999), and a vast amount of research on the behavior of legislators in committees.

In addition to studies of individual behavior, another large body of congressional research examines the internal organization of legislatures, accounting for another ten articles in our sample. Research on the composition and role of committees (including debates regarding the relationship of committees to the floor and tests for committee outliers), legislative procedures, and agenda-setting powers all fall into this category.

Literature on other single literatures—including research on a single state legislature or a single non-U.S. national legislature—share the biases of literature on the contemporary Congress. Of twelve articles that discuss a single legislature (not including articles on Congress), three examine individual behavior and another three examine legislative organization. Thus Kathlene (1994) examines gender differences in legislator behavior at hearings, using data from Colorado; Ames (1995a) studies voting in Brazil; Hamm and Harmel (1993) examine the role of the Speaker in Texas; O'Brien and Luehrmann (1998) study institutionalization in China; and Remington and Smith (1998b) analyze organizational features of the Russian Duma.

Policy outcomes, which are only rarely examined in the context of Congress, are much more prevalent in comparative studies of legislatures. Of the 55 articles on the contemporary Congress, just four analyze policy outcomes, including Lee (1998, 2000), Carsey and Rundquist (1999), and Jones, True, and Baumgartner (1997). However, cross-state and cross-national projects often seek to explain differences in budget levels, welfare priorities, public goods programs, and the independence of central banks and judiciaries. Of the 27 cross-legislative studies in our sample, 14 focus on policy outcomes. Among studies of state legislatures, this includes Alt and Lowry 1994 and Abney and Lauth 1997, which analyze budgetary issues; Skocpol et al. 1993, which examines the origins of mothers' pensions; and M. A. Smith 1997, which investigates the policy consequences of partisan turnover. Although less common than in cross-legislative contexts, historical work on Congress also raises important policy questions, including studies of divided government in the United States (e.g., Cameron 2000; Mayhew 1991; Edwards, Barrett, and Peake 1997; Binder 1999; Coleman 1999), the adoption of constitutional amendments and the admission of U.S. states (e.g., Stewart and Weingast 1992; King and Ellis 1996; Crook and Hibbing 1997; Wirls 1999), and the policy implications of electoral realignments (e.g., Sinclair 1977, 1978, 1982; Brady 1985, 1988). Only rarely do comparative studies of legislatures emphasize individual behavior or questions of internal organization.

■ | **The Standard Template for Congressional Research on Institutions**

Within the rational-choice, institutionalist framework that is central to research on the contemporary Congress, the template for the development of new theoretical arguments about legislatures is easily recognizable. Scholars make assumptions about the goals, abilities, and information of the relevant participants (usually members of Congress and the individuals with whom these members interact, such as bureaucrats, the president, voters, or interest groups). They might assume, for example, that members are motivated by their policy preferences, by the desire for reelection, or by the desire for internal advancement within Congress. Scholars will also define the relevant institutional context. They might care, for example, about the relevant rules for setting an agenda, about special prerogatives of committees, or about the prerogatives of particular members holding leadership positions. Finally, they will derive testable hypotheses about how strategic politicians will behave given their preferences and the institutional context.

Charles Cameron's study (2000) of the presidential veto is an excellent recent example of this mode of theorizing. Cameron wants to understand how bargaining between the U.S. president and Congress unfolds given that Congress can propose bills, the president can veto them, and supermajorities can override a veto. He therefore develops a signaling model that makes straightforward assumptions about how the institutional details of the U.S. presidential veto and the congressional power to override the veto interact to structure bargaining between the president and Congress. He also makes assumptions about preferences and information, assuming that the participants care about policy outcomes. Finally, Cameron develops hypotheses about when vetoes should occur and about the nature of policy outcomes under various configurations of preferences.

Of particular interest to Cameron is the impact of divided government on bargaining. He finds that the probability of vetoes and veto threats is relatively high during divided government on important bills. More important, his theory predicts and his evidence confirms that policy is more moderate during divided government than during unified government. The analytic and empirical rigor of the work, along with the substantive contributions it makes to our understanding of policy outcomes, makes this recent book a path-breaking study of executive-legislative relations in the United States and a model for legislative scholarship generally.

There is a great deal of influential work on Congress that proceeds in similar fashion. Like Cameron, some of this research develops an explicit formal model, but much of it does not. All such studies, however, have in common that they examine strategic legislative behavior where the institutional setting is fixed. Prominent examples in the last ten years of books on Congress in this mode include Epstein and O'Halloran 1999, Krehbiel 1991, 1998, Bianco 1994, Kiewiet and McCubbins 1991, Cox and McCubbins 1993, Shipan 1997, Schiller 2000, and R. L. Hall 1996.

Beyond congressional studies, a similar approach has often been adopted. Examples include Huber 1996a on France, Londregan 2000 on Chile, Remington and Smith 1998b on Russia, and Ramseyer and Rosenbluth 1993 on Japan. And though Laver and Shepsle's study (1996) of portfolio distribution and Tsebelis and Money's study (1997) of bicameralism are cross-national in scope, their mode of theorizing follows the lead of congressional scholars in holding the institutional setting constant.

Holding the institutional setting fixed creates some significant advantages for scholars and is crucial for answering certain types of important questions. Cameron's book, for example, helps us to understand how divided government affects legislative behavior and policy outcomes in the United States. The other research cited above has a similar theoretical foundation, with the goal being to explain variation that exists in behavior and outcomes within a fixed institutional setting. Legislative theories of this sort are not only admirable in their analytic elegance and empirical rigor; they are also obviously substantively important. It is, after all, interesting to understand the factors that influence variation in policy outcomes within the U.S. government.

It is also the case, however, that when institutions are treated as constants, it is impossible to explore effectively several important issues about legislative institutions. The first concerns the origin of legislative structure. The second concerns the impact of institutions on individual behavior and legislative outputs. In what follows, we describe the nature of the biases created in our understanding of these two issues, and we discuss recent efforts to avoid these biases by generating theories where the institutional context varies.

■ | Origins of Legislative Institutions

Research on the contemporary Congress does offer interesting theories of institutional *origins*. In this vein, scholars make claims about fundamental problems that legislators must address. They then develop and test theoretical claims about how the problem is resolved when particular institutional arrangements exist. If the tests support the theory, then there is an implicit or explicit claim that the institutions exist to solve the particular problem — or that the legislature has organized itself in a particular way in response to the problem. The problem with this approach is that theories developed in this fashion, however plausible they might be, have a functionalist flavor that renders them essentially untestable as arguments about why legislators organize themselves in the ways that they do.

The example of delegation to committees helps to clarify how the Congress literature develops theories of institutional origins, and where the drawbacks lie with respect to this mode of theorizing. Scholars have widely recognized that committees often receive special privileges. Majorities in legislatures, for example, often give special agenda control to committees, to take but one example. But why would a majority give up power to a minority in the legislature? What are the origins of these institutional arrangements?

One prominent answer to this question is the informational theory developed chiefly by Gilligan and Krehbiel (1987, 1989) and Krehbiel (1991). Their argument is simple and compelling. They assume that an informational problem exists: legislative majorities do not always know which policy will achieve the desired outcome when a new issue arises. Majorities therefore need expertise, which is costly. Who in the legislature will be willing to pay these costs, and what will induce such members to share their information? The answer in informational theories involves commitment to committees. If a majority grants special procedural prerogatives, such as restrictive amendment procedures, to committee members, then committee members can often be induced to pay the costs of specialization (because their policy proposals will be privileged in floor voting). These procedural protections also make it possible for the committee members to share their information with the floor (because the procedural protections make it difficult for the floor to turn around and use the information against the committee members). Thus, by committing to give up certain rights to a minority, the majority can benefit. This is particularly true when the committee membership is itself controlled by members of the floor. The informational theory is rich with empirical predictions about such things as committee composition and the utilization of restrictive procedures. In his book, Krehbiel (1991) tests many of these predictions and, finding support, argues for an informational perspective on legislative organization.

This mode of argument about institutional origins is hardly unique to the informational perspective. In fact, almost any research on Congress—or on any other single legislature—that speaks to the question of why legislatures are organized the way they are takes a similar tack. According to the distributive approach, to take another example, procedural advantages are also given to committees as commitment devices. But the starting assumption of this perspective is not an informational problem but rather a distributive one—majority rule decision making on more than one issue at a time is inherently unstable (because no policy exists that is preferred by a majority to all other policies). Special privileges for committees are therefore created to solve the problem of majority rule instability and to make possible log rolls or other distributive agreements (e.g., Shepsle 1979; Shepsle and Weingast 1981; Weingast and Marshall 1988; Baron and Ferejohn 1989a). Distributive theories thus argue for a distributive perspective on legislative organization.

Partisan explanations for committee deference, like the other two approaches, have tended to take the institutional context for granted. In arguing that parties constitute a form of "legislative cartel," Cox and McCubbins (1993) suggest that individual legislators have depended on party organization throughout the postwar era and that the continuities in this arrangement overwhelm any changes. Indeed, a central argument in their book is the contention that the seniority system, even in its heyday, never constituted a genuine alternative to partisan decision making in the House. Rohde (1991), in proposing the concept of "conditional party government," makes the case that the influence of party organization on individual behavior waxes and wanes with party homogeneity. In developing this argument, Rohde explicitly contrasts the textbook Congress of the 1950s and 1960s with the postreform Congress. Yet, Rohde (and, in recent work, Aldrich and Rohde 2001) builds his general model out of the material of a single legislature, in this case the majoritarian House.

This mode of theorizing is not limited to the general study of organizational forms. It is also used to explain the choice of specific institutions in specific places at specific moments. In their historical study of institutional creation by the English parliament following the Glorious Revolution, North and Weingast (1989) argue that parliamentary institutions were designed largely in response to commitment problems faced by members of Parliament themselves. At this particular historical juncture, Parliament had substantial control over the design of new legislative and executive institutions, and they could have decimated the crown's power. But this did not occur. Instead, Parliament—fearing its own inability to constrain itself from creating pork-barrel projects, and thus fearing its own inability to secure the rights of property holders (who would be taxed to pay for such projects)—designed institutions that allowed the crown to propose spending while Parliament could approve it. This form of institutional commitment, North and Weingast argue, not only prevented Parliament from abusing its own powers but also insured the crown with considerable income—enough to go to war with France from 1689 to 1697.

In arguments about institutional origins of this form, as in many functionalist arguments, the consequence of the institutional form is said to be its cause (Stinchcombe 1968). Informational theory argues that delegation to committees exists because it solves informational problems. Distributive theory argues that delegation to committees exists to solve distributive problems. Partisan theory argues that delegation to committees occurs to cement the dominance of party leaders over legislative affairs. And, in a different context, North and Weingast argue that delegation of limited powers to the crown occurred after the Glorious Revolution to solve a commitment problem faced by members of Parliament. These theories about institutional origins differ in an important way from many functionalist arguments in sociology because they posit a clear and explicit microfoundation for behavior and choice. But, like sociological functionalism, the theories, as theories of institutional origins, are largely untestable.

In research that focuses on a single case—usually the postwar U.S. Congress, but, as we indicate, also in arenas like the seventeenth-century English Parliament—the central cause of the institutional arrangements being studied does not vary. Distributive theories, for example, assume that distributive problems exist, while informational theories assume that policy uncertainty exists. Therefore, the theories do not attempt to explain how legislative organization varies as a function of these problems.

There are clear advantages to this approach. These theories focus on problems that are so fundamental to legislative politics that it is unlikely the problems would be irrelevant to institutional design in any political system. Indeed, the rigorous and sustained treatment of competing explanations for committee deference represent perhaps the most significant contributions to legislative studies in the last twenty years. Because the research questions are tightly focused and because the institutional context is held constant, questions of committee deference in Congress have forced scholars to build their cases with ever-increasing theoretical, analytical, and empirical rigor.

On the other hand, there are drawbacks associated with theorizing about institutional origins in this way. First, there is clearly variation across political systems as well as over time in the United States regarding the form and degree of delegation to committees—variation that obviously cannot be explained by variation in distributive conflict or the need for information. Do legislatures that do not delegate substantial autonomy to committee, as in many parliamentary systems, fail to solve their distributive and informational problems? Are distributive and informational problems nonexistent in such countries? Second, delegation to committees does not represent the only way to address these problems. Diermeier (1995), for example, makes a compelling case that seniority systems can encourage specialization. Laver and Shepsle (1990, 1996) and Austen-Smith and Banks (1990) describe the ways that cabinet institutions solve distributive problems in parliamentary systems, and Huber (1996a, b) describes the role of confidence motions in this context. Thus, it seems doubtful that informational or distributive problems are a sufficient condition for observing delegation to committees.

Finally, careful historical research on the choice of particular institutions often reveals the unintended consequences that result from the selection of particular organizational forms. In Cooper's (1970) study of committee origins in Congress, he discovers a strong bias by Jeffersonian Republicans against standing committees. Imbued with an ethos that demanded chamberwide discussion of any issue, Republicans preferred to do their work in the committee of the whole and restricted committees to the work of writing legislation that the larger body had discussed. Yet, as Cooper shows, these same Republicans ultimately turned to committees, first as bulwarks against executive encroachment and later as agents to perform work that the executive was leaving undone. Binder (1997) shows, too, the extent to which short-term calculations override long-term goals. The suppression of minority rights, which distinguishes the House from the Senate, arose not from any overarching plan or ideology but from transient partisan considerations. And the triumph of unlimited debate in the Senate, Binder contends, is the logical consequence of an obscure early decision to remove the "previous question" rule from the Senate's rules. Understanding institutional origins, in short, requires recognizing the contingency and circumstances of decisions. Path dependence often overwhelms rational choice. This insight, gleaned from history, can often be neglected in an approach to institutional origins that draws data only from a single contemporary legislature.

Unlike the great body of research on the modern Congress, comparative and historical legislative studies provide a means for enriching legislative theories of institutional origins by allowing for a wider variety of theoretical explanation. In particular, these studies permit the development of theories where the broad institutional setting influences the legislative institutions that are chosen, with different settings leading to different institutional arrangements. Proceeding this way, the institutional arrangements in a particular chamber, such as the structure of a committee system, are not viewed as functionalist solutions to universal problems (like the need for information or the need to make collective decisions in multidimensional policy spaces). Instead, they are viewed as optimal solutions to the unique political setting in which the legislators find themselves. And this approach to theorizing about the origin of legislative institutions—unlike arguments drawn from the contemporary Congress or rooted in path-dependent historical accounts—has the additional advantage of being directly testable. If such theories are correct, then legislative institutions should vary in systematic ways across systems according to the institutional arrangements in that system.

A good example of this approach to legislative theory building comes from a recent formal model developed by Diermeier and Myerson (1999), who address a question central to the development of informational and distributive theory: Why should legislative chambers delegate special prerogatives to a minority of their members, as they do when they create strong committees or the need for supermajorities? Although the question is similar to that in previous studies of Congress, the theoretical approach is quite different because it is explicitly comparative. Instead of posing a problem that might be viewed as largely universal to legislative decision making, they develop a bargaining model that examines the broader institutional context in which legislators find themselves.

Diermeier and Myerson begin with the assumption that there is variation across political systems in the extent to which a particular legislative chamber must bargain with other political actors before new legislation can be adopted. Some countries, for example, have bicameral legislatures, both of which must agree on a bill before it can become law. And some countries have a separation of executive and legislative powers, with executive approval of legislative proposals necessary before these proposals can take effect. Diermeier and Myerson want to understand how variation in the political context of this sort affects incentives for a legislative chamber to create "hurdle factors"—institutional arrangements within the legislative chamber that create additional hurdles that must be passed before a proposal can be approved by that chamber. As noted, examples of hurdles include strong committees with agenda power. In such a chamber, the committee must approve a bill before the floor can consider it.

The main claim of their theory is straightforward. The more that the broad institutional context requires a chamber to bargain with other institutional actors outside the chamber (like presidents or another chamber), the more incentives that chamber will have to create internal hurdles. This is true because such internal hurdles give the chamber more leverage in its negotiations with outside actors. If a president, for example, must satisfy only one actor in a chamber (such as the median member, or a strong leader to whom all power is delegated), he will be able to extract more concessions than if he has to satisfy multiple agents in the chamber (such as the floor majority and a strong committee with gatekeeping power).

Diermeier and Myerson's model thus demonstrates how a comparative approach enriches theorizing about the origin of legislative institutions. From the perspective of their theory, the legislative institutions in the U.S. Congress, which give substantial power to minorities within each chamber, are due not to a need for information, to resolve distributive conflict, or to ensure partisan control over outcomes. Rather, they are a function of the considerable division of power that exists in the American political system. Their general argument, it is useful to underline, is directly testable by looking at how the number of hurdle factors in legislatures is related to the number of institutional actors that must agree on policy change. Though to our knowledge the argument has not been tested directly, Diermeier and Myerson note that their main empirical claim is consistent with the stylized fact that committees are stronger in presidential than parliamentary systems (e.g., Lees and Shaw 1979). The significance of their model comes in its powerful assertion that the most basic rules of the game—in this case, U.S. checks and balances—matter more to committee strength than any of the features examined through the perspective afforded by any study of the contemporary Congress alone.

Other recent scholarship has developed theories of institutional origins using the comparative approach. Compared to Diermeier and Myerson's formal model, much of this research is less explicit with respect to theory but has the advantage of containing an empirical component. Carey and Shugart's 1998 edited volume on decree authority, for example, examines incentives to create and utilize institutional arrangements that permit executives to perform legislative functions. They consider both the creation of *constitutional decree authority*, where the constitution delineates situations where the executive can make law by decree, independent of legislative action, and *legislative decree authority*, where the assembly votes laws that delegate authority to the executive to make laws by decree. In the coeditors' theoretical and empirical chapters (Carey and Shugart 1998a, b), they argue that constitutions will be more likely to include constitutional decree authority if the individual expected to control the executive is responsible for making the constitutions, if it is easy for legislators to change the constitutions, and if a strong veto does not exist. It is useful to note that consistent with the comparative approach, none of these hypotheses about institutional origins could be tested in a single country study. Carey and Shugart also argue that delegated decree authority will be most likely to occur when a strong veto exists, the issue is urgent, the judiciary is independent of the executive, and a legislative majority supports the executive. Some of these arguments could be tested within a single country—and are by various authors who contribute country studies to the edited volume—but other arguments are explicitly comparative, such as the features of the judicial system and the nature of the executive veto, and thus cannot be tested in a single country (because the relevant explanatory variables are constant within a system). These hypotheses are tested by Carey and Shugart (1998b) by compiling cross-national information from their case studies.

We have discussed these two examples in some detail to illustrate the types of arguments that can emerge about institutional origins from a comparative perspective. But there are many other recent works that exist in this vein. Some of these are empirical and focus on non-U.S. settings. Cox, Rosenbluth, and Thies (2000), for example, show that institutional variation that exists between the upper- and lower-house electoral rules in Japan affect the propensity of Japanese deputies to join party factions. Huber (2000) shows that incentives of parliamentary majorities to create automatic budgeting procedures are influenced by the level of cabinet turnover. And Bernhard (1998) shows that incentives of legislative majorities to delegate fiscal policymaking to independent central banks is influenced by the committee structure in the legislature.

Other arguments in this vein are abstract formal models. Diermeier and Feddersen (1998) show that the level of party discipline within a legislature should be influenced by the nature of legislative-executive relations. Carruba and Volden (2000) develop a model where the voting rule in a legislature should vary with the size of the legislature. Laver (1999) argues that party unity will be a function of the institutional features of coalition agreements in parliamentary systems, as well as how institutions affect the cost of losing office. And Diermeier (1995) develops a model where decisions for legislators to specialize are influenced by expected rates of turnover in the legislature.

Similar arguments have been developed in the American politics literature, often using historical or cross-state data to provide variation. Cox and Katz (1999) argue that the redistricting plans adopted by state legislative majorities are influenced by whether there are partisan or bipartisan institutional arrangements governing the redistricting process. In another context, Hamm and Harmel (1993) argue that the way that the minority organizes itself in the Texas assembly depends on the size of the minority.

Not surprisingly, historical work has played a central role in investigating the origins of legislative institutions. Some historical studies focus on short periods of time. Although they cannot offer a comparative perspective on the effects of institutional change, such studies do provide insights into the historical roots of modern institutions as well as fresh laboratories for testing legislative theories. Thus Gamm and Shepsle (1989), Jenkins

(1998), and Canon and Stewart (2001) have all contributed to debates regarding the origin of standing committees by examining their development in Congress in the early nineteenth century. Jillson and Wilson (1994) study how the structure of the Continental Congress frustrated effective decision making in the 1770s. Katz and Sala (1996) argue that the introduction of the Australian ballot influenced the creation of committee property rights in the U.S. House of Representatives. Other scholars—King and Ellis (1996), Crook and Hibbing (1997), Wirls (1999)—have scrutinized the adoption of the Seventeenth Amendment, which established direct election of senators, analyzing the conditions that lead legislators to change their own institutions. And Theriault (2001) examined the Pendleton Act and other legislation that shifted the incentive structure for career-seeking legislators. Skowronek (1982), Skocpol (1992), Sanders (1999), James (2000), and Carpenter (2001), in their excellent studies of U.S. national policy in the late nineteenth and early twentieth centuries, all demonstrate the relevance of Congress to broad political changes.

Other historical work, which examines longer periods of time, can analyze the sources of institutional change or the consequences of new institutions for individual behavior. Cooper and Brady (1981a), in their study of congressional leadership, provide an important early model for this work. This form of scholarship also includes studies of the congressional reforms of the 1970s, including changes in floor activity and committee structure. It includes Schickler's (2001) major new study of institutional innovation in Congress as well as the landmark books by Binder (1997) and Dion (1997), which examine the circumstances under which a legislature changes its rules to limit minority rights. Binder and Smith (1997), in their study of the filibuster, also contribute to the literature on institutional change. Stewart (1989) examines how individual preferences shaped the reorganization of budget politics in the House between 1865 and 1921. Swift (1996) addresses the early transformation of the Senate into a meaningful legislative body. And Gamm and Smith (2000, forthcoming a, b), in reconstructing the emergence of Senate party leadership through the nineteenth and twentieth centuries, find that short-term partisan concerns contribute to long-standing shifts in party organization.

The advantage of comparative and longitudinal analysis is clear. In examining legislatures through a cross-sectional or historical lens, scholars can discern how institutions emerge and change. They can do this because comparative and historical analysis affords variance in institutional forms. Taking advantage of this variance is not straightforward. In comparative work, the difficulty comes in controlling for the array of structural features that may differentiate national legislatures. But the difficulty may be even greater in historical work, even in work that examines long stretches of time. To the extent that the U.S. Congress has changed radically over time, so has the rest of the political system—which makes the nineteenth-century Congress as foreign as the Bundestag to students of the contemporary Congress. But, in other respects, institutional variance is quite limited in historical studies. Compared to variations between foreign legislatures, the basic outlines of U.S. congressional organization have changed little since the early nineteenth century, when the Speaker emerged as a party leader and standing committees assumed a leading role in the legislative process.

But this problem is most pronounced in studies of the contemporary Congress, where scholars generally hold the institutional context fixed. The irony, of course, is that scholars studying the contemporary Congress have contributed more than any other set of legislative scholars to our understanding of the importance of rules, agendas, committees, and leadership. Any serious student of legislatures properly cuts their teeth on Fenno, Mayhew, and all their progeny. All we suggest is the continued need to extend the analytical rigor and positivist orientation of this work to arenas where the institutional context is not fixed. While such research venues clearly present their own thorny difficulties of conceptualization and measurement, the recent literature also shows that they open avenues for understanding the origins of legislative institutions that are closed in studies of the contemporary Congress.

▪ | Institutions and Their Impact

A second limitation associated with congressional research concerns the development of theories about the *impact* of organizational structure. A central objective of legislative studies is not only to examine the origins of institutions but also to analyze their effect on individual behavior. As in the study of institutional genesis, the bulk of research on the modern Congress holds the institutional context fixed, and thus provides very little insight into this important issue. After all, when institutional arrangements do not vary in one's research, it is impossible to make testable claims about how these arrangements affect behavior.

Research on the contemporary Congress has provided a wealth of impressive institutional theory, but the theories have been of a particular type, with important implications for where we find the biggest holes in our theories of how legislative institutions influence behavior. In particular, rather than developing theories of how, for example, institution x affects some output y, we have a preponderance of theories of the form: *given* institution x exists, how does some other variable z affect y? Cameron's book (2000) on legislative-executive relations, for example, cannot offer insights into how the veto affects legislative bargaining outcomes because there is no variation in the existence of the veto in American national politics. Instead, Cameron's work asks: Given the particular institutional features of the veto, how do variables like divided government and the importance of legislation affect legislative bargaining outcomes? Similarly, Laver and Shepsle (1996) ask: Given the institutional arrangements that shape government policymaking in cabinets, how do the spatial preferences of political parties affect the allocation of portfolios? And research on committee assignments in Congress asks how the spatial preferences of individual members affect their assignment to committees, given the agenda institutions that exist in Congress—or, in R. L. Hall's 1996 study, the ways in which legislators participate in Congress, taking for granted the particular rules and institutions of the contemporary House.

In all of these influential studies, since the institutional setting is fixed, it does not and cannot serve as an explanatory variable. A vast body of research on the contemporary Congress has this characteristic. In demonstrating the power and elegance of a theory grounded in the idea that legislators are single-minded seekers of reelection, Mayhew (1974b) took for granted the institutional world of the textbook Congress. This Congress was crucial to Mayhew's argument, since the committee system and the weakness of party reinforced the individuality of career-minded legislators. Despite the centrality of this institution to Mayhew's argument, the demise of the textbook Congress did nothing to shake the influence of Mayhew's theory of legislator behavior. On the contrary, legislative scholarship continues to build on Mayhew's insight and approach.

Since the institutional context is fixed in most Congress research, we obviously do not gain direct insights from congressional studies about how the presence or absence of particular institutions affects the behavior of individual legislators. Instead, we typically develop and test arguments that focus on factors outside the legislative institution itself. Overby and Cosgrove (1996), for example, emphasize the impact of majority-minority districts on voting behavior in the House. Maltzman and Sigelman (1996), in their analysis of one-minute speeches, focus on policy and electoral goals of individual members as their independent variables. In other studies of member behavior, Alan Gerber (1996) emphasizes race and Kiewiet and Zeng (1993) emphasize age as predictors for retirements; Moscardelli, Haspel, and Wike (1998) emphasize ideology and Bailey and Brady (1998) emphasize constituency characteristics as predictors of votes; Cox and Magar (1999) emphasize majority status as a predictor of PAC contributions; Kessler and Krehbiel (1996) argue that individual attributes like an individual's tenure in the House, electoral vulnerability, and individual preferences affect decisions to cosponsor bills; Box-Steffensmeier, Arnold, and Zorn (1997) argue that voting behavior is a function of a representative's constituency characteristics, interest group links, their institutional position within the legislature, party affiliation, and ideology; Rothenberg and Sanders (2000) examine how voting is affected by individual and consituency characteristics, as well as the individual's intention to resign at the next election; and Schiller (1995) looks at how individual characteristics, including an individual's positions within the Senate, affect cosponsorship strategies.

The same bias in the nature of explanatory variables exists in the handful of Congress studies that examine outputs, like policy outcomes. Perhaps the most well developed variable in this context is preference conflict within legislative settings. Thus the literature on divided government, an excellent example of research that focuses on policy, examines how preference conflicts (i.e., divided government) affect policy outcomes (Cameron 2000; Mayhew 1991), the form of delegation to agencies (Epstein and O'Halloran 1999), the approval of presidential appointments (McCarty and Razaghian 1999), and the incidence of budgetary conflict (Clarke 1998).

Historical and comparative approaches, in contrast, have the potential to pose questions of the form: "How does institutional arrangement x affect legislative behavior or output y?" Such research has a fairly long tradition in studies of parliamentary government, one rooted in research on cabinet formation and dissolution. Strom (1984, 1990), for example, argues that particular legislative institutions (related primarily to committee systems) affect the propensity of minority governments to form. Strom, Budge, and Laver (1994) examine how legislative institutions affect coalition formation more generally, and de Winter (1995) examines how the government's control of the agenda affects the duration of coalition formation processes. Other scholars have examined legislative outputs in non-U.S. settings. Baldez and Carey (1999), for example, examine how rules for making budgets affect budget deficits in Latin America, Thies's (1998) comparison of Japan and the United States examines how committee structures affect the pace of policy change, Huber (1998) examines how turnover in the cabinet affects health care cost containment, and Döring (1995a) examines how the government's control of the agenda affects legislative outputs. Morgenstern (2000) examines how variation in electoral laws affect voting unity in legislatures. And, in a recent formal model, McCarty (2000) explores how variation in a president's veto power affects distributive politics.

Much of the best work in this tradition is on the U.S. states. Thus Francis and Kenny (1997) analyze the impact of term limits on legislative tenure, Abney and Lauth (1997) examine the effect of the line-item veto on budget restraint, and Fiorina (1994) and Squire (1998) investigate the impact of legislative professionalization. Finally, Elisabeth Gerber (1996, 1999) examines the impact of citizen initiatives on policy outcomes. Each of these works helps us to understand how the institutional context in which legislators find themselves affects the choices that legislatures make.

▪ | Discussion

Legislative studies is one of the oldest and liveliest subfields in political science. In the late nineteenth century, early leaders of the discipline—from

Wilson to Bryce to Lowell—regarded legislatures as the central political institutions in a democratic regime. Early scholarship was normative and reformist. Wilson, for example, wrote about Congress in part to propose that the U.S. national legislature model itself more after the British House of Commons, with vigorous debates that educated the public. Normative concerns have never disappeared entirely: the scholarly obsession with Congress is surely due in part to a broad affection and respect for the institution.

But since the renaissance of legislative studies in the 1950s and 1960s, the field has shifted its focus. Scholarship on legislatures is judged today primarily by its contributions to science and theory, less on its relevance to reform efforts. The consequence is a subfield that has yielded a massive theoretical and empirical literature with all the hallmarks of mature normal science. This has led to some of the liveliest debates in the discipline. It has also supported a broad range of research methods and offered leadership in the development of new theoretical and methodological tools. In our view, it is indisputable that the rigor now characterizing the study of foreign legislatures and U.S. state legislatures is due primarily to the continuing debates and literature on Congress. Thus, by the measure of its influence on legislative studies specifically and the study of political science generally, congressional scholarship has been a remarkable success.

A central argument of this paper, however, is that the predominance of Congress carries with it some clear costs. One obvious drawback is that the more we study the contemporary Congress to the exclusion of other legislatures, the more we know about one specific legislature and the less we gain in our understanding of other specific legislatures and of the nature of legislatures generally. Sound theories of legislatures depend on careful studies of an array of institutions. This problem, of course, can be remedied (and is being remedied) by simply studying other legislatures.

Another drawback is less evident. As we argue, the emphasis on Congress—especially studies that focus on specific periods when the institutional context does not change—leads scholars to pose different questions and offer different theories than can be developed from a comparative or historical perspective. We have focused in particular on how the "Congress template" makes it virtually impossible to develop and test theories of the origins of institutions or theories about how the presence of particular institutional arrangements affects behavior and choice.

The bias of most existing legislative research away from these types of institutional questions is not simply an issue for arcane debates among social scientists. The bias also limits the ability of political scientists to address some of the central normative concerns of the present. In particular, as the recent wave of democratization has occurred, there has been a crucial need for answers to questions about institutional design. Institutional engineers across a wide range of countries and political settings want to know, "What type of institutional arrangements should we adopt in our legislatures, and what will be the consequences of adopting them?" Even debates in the U.S. Congress over campaign finance reform, term limits, and rules reforms would benefit from comparative research. Legislative scholars have discovered themselves ill equipped to answer these questions because we lack well-developed theories of legislative institutions that have been devised and tested across time and space.

In our view, then, it is not just the natural progression of normal science but, more importantly, the very real needs of practitioners around the world that are orienting the research frontier of legislative studies today toward questions that comparativists of all sorts tend to ask—questions that investigate the origins of institutions and the impact of institutions on behavior. Legislative studies is thus poised to enter an extraordinarily fruitful marriage of positive method with normative concerns, one that will solidify the scientific quality of research, while making it possible to influence the design of the democratic institutional arrangements around the world.

BARBARA GEDDES

The Great Transformation
in the Study of Politics
in Developing Countries

Students of developing countries in the year 2000 were like geographers in 1520: the known world had begun changing about 25 years earlier, and we were still trying to figure it out. Just when most eyes were focused on explaining the rise of authoritarianism in developing countries, democratization began its current sweep through much of the world. More human beings currently live under democratic governance than at any previous time in recorded history. In a second equally unexpected development, many governments began to abandon state interventionist economic policies in favor of greater market orientation. On top of everything else, the Soviet empire collapsed and, with it, the only coherent competitor to capitalist economic organization. Though scholars greeted most of these changes with delight, few predicted them (cf. Fleron and Hoffman 1993; Remmer 1995; Kalyvas 1999).[1]

These real world events have led to a wholesale reevaluation of the theoretical underpinnings of the study of comparative development. This reevaluation has affected what we consider worthy of study, the set of stylized facts we accept as more or less true, our basic understanding of the economics of development, the theoretical approaches we use to explain politics, and the research methods we favor. The study of developing countries has changed almost as much during the last 25 years as the world we study.

In this essay I have three goals: to describe the political and economic transitions that have taken place, to note the effects these changes have

1. A number of scholars analyzed the fragilities and contradictions within one or another kind of authoritarianism. See, for example, O'Donnell 1978, 1979 for analyses of the potentially destabilizing tensions between alliance partners within bureaucratic-authoritarian regimes. See Kalyvas 1999 for a summary of the many descriptions of the weaknesses and dysfunctional aspects of communist regimes. No one to my knowledge, however, expected or predicted the sweep of democratization and economic reform across much of the developing world that we have witnessed.

had on theories and methods used in the study of developing countries, and to review some of the most important recent research on politics and political economy in developing countries. I shall not try to provide a comprehensive review of new work but instead to highlight interesting examples of what I consider some of the most promising directions for new research.

▪ | Then and Now: Transitions

At the beginning of 1974, identified by Huntington (1991) as the start of the "third wave" of democratization, dictatorships of one kind or another governed 82 countries.[2] Only 19 dictatorships still survived at the end of 2000. During these years, 95 authoritarian regimes disintegrated (some countries endured more than one dictatorship during the period). These transitions have resulted in 54 surviving democracies, some quite flawed but many stable and broadly competitive; 13 democracies that lasted only a short time before being overthrown in their turn; and 45 new authoritarian regimes, 17 of which lasted into the new millennium.

When authoritarian governments ruled most developing countries, few political scientists interested in these countries paid much attention to the development of theories of democratic politics. Most focused instead on other questions and debated different theoretical arguments. Although some scholars attempted to extend corporatist or pluralist concepts to authoritarian settings, most focused their attention on explaining the transition to authoritarianism, the relationships between authoritarian governments and elite economic interests, and the link between international economic forces and third world authoritarianism.[3] Those interested in developing countries thus paid little attention to the new theories being developed for the study of democratic politics in the United States and Western Europe. The behavioralist "revolution" bypassed most of those working on developing and Communist countries for the simple reason that the primary forms of evidence used by behavioralists, survey and voting data, simply did not exist. Few in the field saw the relevance of rational-choice theorization of party and legislative politics in settings in which

2. Figures here and elsewhere are drawn from a data set collected by the author that includes all authoritarian regimes except monarchies lasting three years or more, in existence at any time since 1946, in countries with a million or more inhabitants. See Geddes 1999b for more details about the data set.

3. See Stepan 1978, Schmitter 1973, and various essays in Malloy 1977, for efforts to use the corporatist framework to illuminate the relationship between authoritarian governments and major interest groups, especially labor. See especially Skilling 1966, Skilling and Griffiths 1971, and Hough 1974 for the extension and adaptation of interest group theories to explain intragovernment conflict over policy choice in the Soviet Union.

parties, if they existed, faced no competition and legislatures, if they existed, rubber-stamped decisions made elsewhere.[4]

Instead, many of those interested in developing countries focused their attention on a prior and arguably more urgent question, explaining the democratic breakdowns that had occurred in numerous places during the sixties and seventies. Authoritarianism and political inequality were blamed on the effects of international capitalism (Cardoso 1973a; Evans 1979). Transitions to authoritarianism in some of the more industrialized developing countries were attributed to the need to accumulate capital more rapidly as countries industrialized. In one of the most influential arguments, O'Donnell (1973) reasoned that as dependent countries moved from the early stage of industrialization, when products were simple and capital needs modest, to a more advanced stage, when more intense capital accumulation would be required in order to produce more sophisticated products, conflict would intensify between owners and workers. Governments would face a trade-off between acceding to workers' demands and pursuing rapid growth. They would no longer be able to do both at once. As this conflict intensified, upper- and middle-class citizens would withdraw their support for democratic politics, thus producing an elective affinity between authoritarianism and advancing industrialization. In other words, although economic development is generally expected to increase the likelihood of democracy, it was argued that in late-developing countries it would have the opposite effect.[5]

As democratization has spread, students of developing and ex-Communist countries have not rejected old ideas but rather have simply put them aside like clothes that don't fit any more. The old arguments did not aim to explain many of the subjects that now seem interesting, such as the evolution of party systems in new democracies, the development of new legislative institutions, public opinion and voting behavior in new democracies, judicial reform and other efforts to initiate the rule of law, or the effect of political institutions in a multitude of policy domains. So many analysts have turned away from them in order to embrace the theories available in mainstream political science as the bases for explaining politics in new democracies. The research being done by these analysts

---

4. There are some obvious and extremely well-known exceptions to this statement, including Robert Bates, David Laitin, and Samuel Popkin, but they are exceptions. The barrage of criticism to which especially Popkin (1979) and Bates (1981) were subjected is an indication of how out of step they were with dominant ideas at the time.

5. While most developing countries remained authoritarian, political scientists interested in them read a literature not read by other political scientists, engaged in theoretical debates not followed by others in the profession, and believed arguments inconsistent with the standard theories and stylized facts of most of the discipline. See Hagopian 2000 for a useful review of the literature on political development.

contributes to the general political science literature on these subjects. Among these scholars, the state, conceived as an actor, has receded in theoretical importance, as analysis focuses on the institutionally structured choice processes of politicians whose actions determine what the state does. We now focus on the effects of particular political institutions on state decision making, trying to explain policy decisions, choice of leadership, and institutional change, rather than treating the state as a black box, unitary actor, or embodiment of elite interests.[6]

As the same kinds of subjects become politically important and available for study in developing and developed countries, the training of graduate students focuses less on building specific country expertise and more on tools and theories considered of general use. When the study of developing countries first began to attract substantial numbers of political scientists during the fifties, very little reliable information about the countries was available in libraries or databases. A norm developed that each graduate student should spend at least a year doing research in one country, since such immersion was the only way to acquire reasonably accurate information about how politics and other things in the country really worked. As added benefits, most who thus immersed themselves acquired fluency in the language, made lasting friends in the academic community, and developed an understanding and appreciation of the arguments and theories current among intellectuals in the country. This type of research can be thought of as a vast fact-finding mission conducted by numerous independent scholars, many of whom published books with names like *Politics and Policy in Country X, 1964–73*. These studies remain the best, sometimes the only, easily accessible sources of information about many events in developing countries.

This research strategy, though probably necessary in the circumstances, hindered theory testing. Scholars who had to invest very heavily in language training and fieldwork simply did not know enough about enough other countries to subject knowledge claims to rigorous reality checks. Moreover, the kinds of public data archives that would have allowed empirical tests of arguments in the absence of deep individual knowledge did not exist. As more and better quality data have become publicly available from a much larger number of countries, however, training norms have begun to change. Intensive fieldwork remains a necessary component of research in the comparative field, but we now recognize the usefulness of combining country-specific expertise with training in the use of tools for testing arguments and enough knowledge about the rest of the

6. In the field of international relations, where it often makes sense to treat states as unitary actors, the state continues to be a central concept. It also remains an important concept in sociology. Political scientists, however, tend to disaggregate the state into its constituent decision-making components when trying to explain particular domestic outcomes.

world to give the analyst perspective. Area specialists are gradually assimilating into the mainstream of political science.

Then and Now: Economic Development

From the end of World War II until 1980, developing countries grew robustly on average. Except for those in sub-Saharan Africa, developing countries achieved more rapid growth on average than industrialized countries. Nevertheless, the income gap between rich and poor countries increased, large numbers of people remained desperately poor, and most developing countries suffered recurrent economic crises and bouts of severe inflation.[7]

Because students of developing areas have always focused as much on economic development as on more narrowly political outcomes, ideas current among economists have always influenced us. For several decades after World War II, a special branch of economics, development economics, was devoted to the study of the economies of industrializing countries. It was never a major branch of the economics discipline, but it shaped the views of most political scientists studying developing countries. This subfield of economics stressed the limited or unequal benefits of international trade, market failures, and uneven development (e.g., Hirschman 1958; Nurkse 1961; Fishlow 1978). Development economists generally supported state intervention in developing economies to overcome market failures and quicken the pace of industrialization.[8] The subfield tended to be less technical than other branches of economics; this made it more accessible to intellectuals from other disciplines.

A more radical challenge to neoclassical economics, the structuralist school that arose in Latin America, also influenced political scientists working on developing countries. I spell out the structuralist interpretation here in more detail than might seem warranted so that readers unfamiliar with this set of ideas can contrast them with the current orthodoxy and thus understand just how great the intellectual shift has been.

7. To understand this widening gap, one must think through the arithmetic. If a rich country has a GDP equal to $10,000 per person and is growing at 2 percent per year, at the end of the year its GDP per person will be $10,200. If a poor country has a GDP equal to $1,000 per person and is growing at 10 percent per year, at the end of the year it will have a GDP of $1,100 per person. The gap at the beginning of the year is $9,000, but the gap at the end of the year is $9,100, even though the poor country is growing five times as fast in per capita terms. Thus an increasing income gap does not imply slow growth by the poorer country.

8. See Deepak Lal 1997 for a detailed discussion and critique of the theoretical ideas central to development economics and a review of the evidence inconsistent with these ideas.

Central to the structuralist critique of neoclassical economics is the claim that the distribution of the gains from trade between developed and developing economies disadvantages the developing (Prébisch 1950; Singer 1950; Myrdahl 1958). Inflation, a worsening problem in developing countries from the late forties to the eighties, stems largely from two phenomena, according to structuralists: reliance on the export of primary products to earn foreign exchange and the persistence of a dual economy, that is, stark differences in development between urban and rural areas. Reliance on primary product exports, according to the structuralists, causes inflation and balance of payments problems both because of deteriorating terms of trade and because primary products experience very wide and rapid international price swings. Structuralists blame the persistence of these problems, despite rapid industrial growth, on the prevalence of foreign corporations in their economies (Sunkel 1973; Cardoso 1973a, 146–48).

In short, structuralists developed a plausible and logically coherent argument that attributed development problems to the consequences of integration into the international capitalist economy and to exploitation by foreign economic and political interests. Dependency theory, which dominated much academic thinking about development during the sixties and seventies, relied on the structuralist critique of neoclassical economics for economic theory and interpretations. Dependency theorists hypothesized two broad causes of economic difficulties: impersonal economic forces arising from the dependent country's position in the international economy and the influence of transnational corporations and their domestic allies' pursuit of their own interests in opposition to national interests (e.g., dos Santos 1970; Frank 1967, 1970; Cardoso 1973b; Brown 1963; Baran 1957; Evans 1979, 19–38; Leys 1974, 8–18).

Structuralist economic theories provided a well-developed set of arguments about why some of the stylized facts of economics apparently did not hold in industrializing countries: although investment normally causes growth, foreign investment, it was claimed, did not; or, if it did, the growth was uneven and caused distorted development. Although trade normally benefits all parties, developing countries, it was claimed, get a smaller share of the gains from trade than do the more advanced countries; although the gap between rich and poor has narrowed in most countries as they have developed, it was claimed that in late-developing countries industrialization increased inequality. These ideas influenced policymakers in developing countries as well as academics studying them.

Ideas about the causes of development difficulties have changed in response to the "inconvenient facts" observers have had to confront during the last 25 years.[9] Beginning sometime between the late seventies and late

9. Max Weber's term (1958).

eighties, growth faltered in nearly all developing countries outside of Asia.[10] Inflation worsened, in some countries reaching astonishing heights. As governments struggled to respond to the crises of the eighties, the policies proposed by structuralist economists worsened conditions where they were tried (Rodrik 1994, 81–82). Although the greatly increased cost of international borrowing after the second oil shock in 1978–79 precipitated the crises, it was twenty years of state interventionist economic policies that had left developing countries so utterly vulnerable to a rise in world interest rates.

Initially, policymakers in most developing countries, as well as the academics who advised and studied them, railed against the high interest rates and resisted interpretations that put some of the blame for the economic crisis on the shoulders of developing country policies. Over a period of about ten years, however, the neoclassical explanation of the crisis was gradually accepted. This explanation placed the blame for economic difficulties on the import-substitution industrialization (ISI) policies most developing countries had pursued from the fifties through the seventies. As Rodrik (1992) has noted, it is not protectionism, which we usually think of as the hallmark of ISI, that led to the unsustainable deficits characteristic of the ISI strategy but rather the other policies typically bundled with protectionism.[11] In most countries, the development strategies initiated to foment industrialization had made use of overvalued exchange rates to shift resources out of the export sector (dominated by agriculture and mining) and into the manufacturing sector. Over the years, overvalued exchange rates had the unintended consequence of discouraging exports and artificially cheapening, and thus encouraging, imports (except of products protected by tariffs). Recurrent and worsening balance of payments crises resulted. Some countries, notably, Argentina under Perón and several African countries, used an even blunter instrument, marketing boards, to capture the surplus generated by agricultural exports. Farmers were required to sell to marketing boards at below market prices, and the government reaped the profits gained from its position as monopoly middleman. These profits were then used for state investment and subsidies to private manufacturing firms. Needless to say, marketing boards also discouraged legal exports.

Industrialization strategies also led to increasing budget deficits in most countries as governments built infrastructure, invested in basic industries, and hired masses of public employees both to staff these enterprises and to reward political supporters but failed to raise taxes to pay for it all. Budget deficits led to recurrent problems with inflation. Potential investors

10. Most Asian developing countries managed their economies with remarkable success until 1997.

11. See Rodriguez and Rodrik 2001 for a review of the evidence on the effects of trade liberalization.

faced with repeated bouts of inflation and unpredictable policy interventions showed a distressing tendency to put their money elsewhere.

The budget and trade deficits generated by the policy strategy were sustainable for a remarkably long time because of inflows of foreign capital, in the form of investment, debt, and aid. When the excess capital in the hands of oil exporters after the first oil shock in the midseventies caused the price of money, that is, the interest rate, to drop in the midseventies, nearly all developing countries borrowed heavily. Had the interest rate remained low, they probably could have repaid their loans, but it did not. After the second oil shock, when developed countries raised their own interest rates in order to reduce domestic demand for oil, developing countries suddenly found themselves in an untenable situation. Most continued borrowing more and more at higher rates to cover the interest payments coming due during the first couple of years, but then Mexico declared itself unable to meet its obligations in 1982 and the debt crisis began. Suddenly, most lending to developing countries stopped. Countries that had relied on inflows of foreign capital to sustain the import-substitution industrialization policy strategy for as much as twenty-five years could no longer do so.

■ | Academic and Policy Responses to the Real World

Governments in most countries initially resisted the policy prescriptions of neoclassical economists. They tried various heterodox policy packages, but these invariably worsened inflation. Meanwhile, Chile, which had made the transition to market-oriented economic policies during the seventies under the repressive auspices of General Augusto Pinochet, although initially blasted by the debt crisis like the rest of the developing world, recovered very quickly. By 1985, Chile's economy had resumed steady growth. Chile was the most unambiguous example of successful market-oriented policies but not the only one. Taiwan, South Korea, and Singapore had grown very rapidly following market-friendly policy strategies for a decade or two prior to the debt crisis. Their experience was frequently cited by those advocating market-oriented policies as evidence of the success of this strategy (e.g., Little 1979; Lal 1997), but other analysts saw them as cases of successful state intervention (Amsden 1989; Wade 1990; Haggard 1990), and consequently their experience was not taken as definitive evidence in favor of orthodox policies. Two former basket cases, Bolivia beginning in 1985 and Ghana beginning in 1983, also began to make modest economic progress under market-oriented reforms, as did a few other infrequently studied small countries. By the late eighties, the evidence was piling up.

The so-called Washington consensus has grown out of the contrast between experiences with heterodox policy packages proposed by economists influenced by the ideas of the structuralist school and experiences with more market-oriented policies (cf. Rodrik 1994). This is not to say that the market-oriented policy package has been successful everywhere it has been tried or that it has benefited everyone in the countries that have adopted it. It has done neither. But it is the only policy strategy that has been successful in any respect, and thus has been accepted, in the same spirit in which Winston Churchill embraced democracy, as a bad system but better than all the others.

With the disastrous economic failure of both the state-socialist economies and most of the developing mixed economies during the eighties and early nineties, development economics has all but disappeared as a special branch of economics with its own distinctive set of arguments and ideas, as has the structuralist school. Writing about developing and ex-communist economies is now dominated by the ideas of mainstream neoclassical economics, as is the advice given their policymakers by economists (e.g., Sachs 1986, 1993; Sachs, Tornell, and Velasco 1995; Dornbusch 1992; Rodrik 1992, 1994, 1996; Aslund 1995). Although some think the pendulum has swung too far in the direction of unfettered markets, scarcely any observers of developing countries have sustained the uncritical attitudes toward state intervention in the economy that once prevailed. Where once slow, distorted, and unequal growth were attributed to the machinations of self-interested dominant classes and the exploitation inherent in the international division of labor, now these problems are rather routinely viewed as unforeseen consequences of state interventionist development policies. In short, where once structuralists, dependencistas, and those influenced by them relied on a set of distinctive ideas for understanding obstacles to development in late industrializers, now we explain slow growth in developing countries using the same set of ideas about fiscal responsibility, a predictable policy environment, secure property rights, and investment in human capital that would explain it anywhere else.

The wide acceptance that standard economic theories apply with as much force in developing countries as elsewhere has of course entailed the abandonment of the ideas associated with dependency theory and the structuralist school in economics. Observers clung for a decade or two longer to certain unexamined ideas about the costs and benefits of economic reform to different groups, but these also are now being abandoned. Nearly all political scientists who wrote about market-oriented reform during the eighties and early nineties, before very much experience with reform had accumulated, emphasized the unpopularity of reform, especially with the organized working class and urban popular sector (e.g., Haggard and Kaufman 1992, 1995; Przeworski 1991). Since the reforms were expected to be unpopular, many in the early nineties still believed that authoritarian governments could best initiate them. If democratization had occurred before economic reform, then the most-promising political situation for initiating reforms, it was implicitly argued, would be that which most closely resembled authoritarianism, a strong insulated executive unconstrained by the legislature (Haggard 1990; Haggard and Kaufman 1995).

Analysts were led astray by a failure to anticipate the high costs of failure to reform and the broad popularity of reforms that brought down very high inflation. It took a long time to correct this misunderstanding. Reforms under repressive governments in Chile and Mexico were examined repeatedly; the radical reform in newly democratic Bolivia got less attention. Almost no one checked to see whether politicians who initiated market-oriented reforms were really more likely to be defeated at the polls, as analysts expected.[12] It took a surprisingly long time for most observers to notice that the most democratic East European countries (Poland, Hungary, the Czech Republic, Slovenia) reformed their economies the fastest. As evidence of the progress of economic reform in various countries has trickled in, however, these last vestiges of the belief that different theoretical laws rule political and economic processes in developing countries are being undermined.

As mainstream theories have become widely accepted, methodologies associated with neoclassical economics and the subfield of American politics in political science have also become more common in the study of both politics and economics in developing countries. We are seeing a move away from the kind of small-n inductive studies that had previously been standard. Deductive arguments play a larger role in explanations, as political scientists increasingly draw insights from work by economists. As more political scientists have come to accept basic economic arguments about the causes of growth, fruitful interactions between economic theories and political scientists' real-world knowledge have become more frequent.

Large-n quantitative studies of the causes of growth, coups, democracy, and other "big questions" have also become more persuasive (e.g., Barro 1991, 1997; Londregan and Poole 1990, 1996; Przeworski et al. 2000). Although quantitative studies have their own set of characteristic weaknesses (the old "garbage in, garbage out" problem), recent ones have taken a big stride forward from what was once the standard practice, drawing general conclusions from the repeated observation of a few well-known cases while ignoring the rest.

These intellectual transitions have followed the real-world transitions to democracy and markets in various regions. Economic reforms have been undertaken, though by no means completed, in nearly every country in the world, and the study of economic development, like policymaking,

---

12. Notable exceptions are Joan Nelson (1992) who gathered information on a number of less-studied smaller countries that challenged the standard ideas and Carlos Gervasoni (1999), who showed that the initiators of economic reforms in Latin America were more likely to be elected.

is now dominated by standard economic ideas. Changes in the study of politics have occurred more slowly and discontinuously. In the regions of the world in which democratization has gone furthest, Latin America and eastern Europe, young area specialists are most fully assimilated to mainstream disciplinary norms, not only with regard to the theoretical shoulders on which they stand, but also with regard to the quantitative and formal methodologies they use. Democratization is more recent and much less thorough in Africa and Asia, and scholarship on these areas has moved less fully into the mainstream. Scholarship on the Middle East remains more isolated from many of the currents of contemporary political science, just as rulers of these countries have resisted being swept up by the "third wave."[13] Theories drawn from the mainstream can be adapted to authoritarian contexts, but data limitations still constrain what can be done.

■ | The Study of Developing Countries
    in the Next Decade

The real-world transformation during the last twenty-five years has placed three main subjects on the research agenda for scholars who work on developing and ex-Communist countries: democratic politics in situations of institutional flux and fluid political loyalties, the politics of economic policy making in partly reformed economies, and the politics of ethnic mobilization.[14] The second is an obvious descendant of earlier work on economic policymaking. The first and third have come to the forefront of the agenda as a result of the transformations. Several very influential scholars began working on ethnic politics well before it came to the top of the field's agenda (e.g., Young 1976; Horowitz 1985; Laitin 1986), but as ethnicity has become a political flashpoint in ever more regions of the world, the topic has moved from the margins of research on developing countries to the center. The study of democratic politics had an even more marginal place in comparative development than ethnicity prior to the eighties. Even though there were a number of long-lived democracies among developing countries before the "third wave," the study of politics in them was

13. There are of course some impressive exceptions in Middle East scholarship, for example, Lust-Okar 2001, Lust-Okar and Jamal 1999 and Posusney 2001. And a number of younger scholars are making efforts to rejoin the broader political science community.

14. I include ex-Communist countries in the developing country category here. Before the collapse of Communism, there may have been a good reason to treat them as a separate category, but that reason no longer exists. Currently, even the most developed parts of eastern Europe are going through the same processes and facing many of the same problems as developing countries in Latin America and Asia. It therefore seems to make theoretical sense to lump them in this category, at least for now.

left to country specialists. Mainstream theories of comparative development did not include systematic analyses of democratic political processes.

These three issues are now at the top of the agenda. I shall make no attempt at a comprehensive review here. Instead, I want to highlight types and examples of work I consider especially promising.

POLITICS IN NEW DEMOCRACIES

The institutionalist approach to posttransition politics simply takes the transitions as given, thus bypassing the cul-de-sac of unresolvable arguments about consolidation, and seeks to analyze current political processes. This work borrows and, where needed, revises theories used originally for explaining U.S. and West European democratic politics. One of the advantages of this approach is that it avoids the value-laden arguments about what consolidated democracy should be and how far some competitive but flawed real political systems deviate from whichever definition is chosen. Instead, analysts draw expectations about the effects of particular political practices from theories developed in the study of democratic politics elsewhere; if outcomes in new democracies differ from expectations, existing theories must be modified. This more-detailed and theoretically informed examination of political processes results in a more accurate assessment of exactly how and why the differences affect outcomes, if they do.

Standard theories of democratic politics begin with the assumption that citizens vote, if they do, for candidates they expect to favor the policies and provide the individual benefits and services most advantageous to themselves. Politicians are assumed to seek the continuation and enhancement of their political careers.[15] Democracy gives those who seek political careers an incentive to respond to the citizen interests that will help to keep them in office. The institutionalist approach to the study of politics examines the effects of formal institutions and rules on the strategic behavior of citizens as they pursue their goal of improving their own welfare and politicians as they pursue their goal of remaining in office. Institutions affect whom citizens will seriously consider voting for, which citizens politicians will be most responsive to, what kind of campaign strategies politicians will choose, how many parties will develop, how disciplined the parties will be, whether politicians and parties will focus on offering policy goods or individual services and benefits, whether effective legislative institutions will arise, whether gridlock will develop between the president and the legislature, how strong the status quo bias in policy will be, and, many believe, the likelihood that democracy will survive.

Perhaps the best-known finding associated with this approach is that

---

15. Some authors add sincere policy preferences to the set of primary goals sought by politicians, but none leave out the goal of continuing in office (see Aldrich and Rohde 2001; Ames 1987).

two-party systems tend to arise in countries with first-past-the-post electoral systems. In such systems, citizens are reluctant to waste their votes on small parties that have almost no chance of being elected, and politicians, knowing that citizens feel this way, are reluctant to waste their efforts forming new parties or running as third party candidates. This finding (Duverger's law) and some others about the effects of features of the electoral system on the party system have been well established by West Europeanists.

The effects of other democratic institutional variations, however, are less well understood. Of special salience in developing countries are a number of issues mostly irrelevant in western Europe and hence not yet much studied: the effects of institutional legacies imposed by outgoing authoritarian governments; the search for the institutional contributors to the perpetuation of high levels of personalism, clientelism, and corruption in open competitive democratic systems; and the need to build a theoretical understanding of presidentialism, both the effect of institutional variations in presidential powers on presidential-legislative bargaining over policy, and the effect of institutional variations in the way presidents are elected on the development of party systems.

During transitions to democracy, the outgoing authoritarian government often tries to negotiate or impose conditions that will protect its members and allies from future prosecution and from disadvantageous policy changes. Many, for example, have granted themselves amnesties for human rights violations. A number have also tried to tinker with the electoral rules in order to prevent future electoral victories by parties they distrust. The Alianza Popular Revolucionaria Americana (APRA) party in Peru, for example, was outlawed most of the time from the thirties to the midsixties, and the Peronist Party in Argentina was not allowed to compete in elections most of the time from 1958 to 1974. As O'Donnell (1973) has shown, simply outlawing popular parties is an unsuccessful institutional manipulation almost guaranteed to backfire. Most of the institutional manipulations initiated by authoritarian governments are similarly unsophisticated and have little long-term significance because new democratic governments have strong incentives to change them. The Pinochet government in Chile, however, imposed a number of mutually reinforcing institutional changes that have proved difficult to change. Some of these have had long-lasting effects, and understanding these effects accurately is necessary in order to understand contemporary politics in Chile.

Among the institutional legacies of the Pinochet dictatorship in Chile is a proportional electoral system with district magnitude equal to 2. The Pinochet government initiated this revision of the traditional high-magnitude Chilean electoral system for the explicit purpose of reducing party fragmentation and advantaging the second-largest party in the political system, which was expected to be conservative. Much ink has been spilled over the limits on representation and competition, and thus on the full realization of democracy, entailed in this institutional manipulation.

Most observers expected it to change what had been a vibrant multiparty system with a left, right, and center much like that in France into a much more centrist system in which left-leaning citizens would have no representation (e.g., Scully 1994; Rabkin 1996; Guzmán 1993). Some of the effects of the new system are easy to observe: as expected, conservative parties, the second-largest bloc, are overrepresented in the legislature; although the number of parties has not declined as expected, they have coalesced into two stable blocs offering joint lists so as not to let competition among them defeat their own side.

The effect of the new system on the representation of underlying citizen opinion, however, is not easy to observe with the naked eye. To figure it out requires a spatial model of politics borrowed from mainstream political science. By modeling Chile's system, open-list proportional representation with district magnitude equal to 2, Magar, Rosenblum, and Samuels (1998) are able to show that in districts with a low probability that either bloc will win both seats (that is, about 80 percent of the districts), candidates will cluster at the median of each bloc, not the district median. In other words, the system actually creates incentives for the election of candidates somewhat spread out in the ideological space, not clustered at the center as most observers had expected. Both left and right citizen opinion is represented in congress. We now have a much more accurate understanding of the effect of this particular legacy of authoritarianism on the representation of citizen interests.

The Magar et al. study (1998) exemplifies a strong trend in the study of politics in new democracies. Analysts use theories and models developed in the study of politics in established democracies to figure out the effects of the particular features of new democratic systems that have not been fully understood by more casual observers. New democracies are experimenting with many institutional innovations. Scholars trying to figure out the effects of these innovations rely on the same theories that have structured our understanding of democratic politics in the older democracies for decades, adapting them to new conditions as needed. Empirical testing of arguments is becoming standard. With such sturdy theoretical shoulders to stand on, progress in working out the effects of electoral rules on Latin American and East European party systems, campaign strategies, and legislative behavior has been quite rapid.

Scholars writing about numerous different countries have produced an impressive body of literature on the effects of the institutional variation in new democracies, in the process adding considerably to preexisting literature.[16] Most new democracies have presidential or semipresidential systems. Presidential elections create centripetal incentives in party systems in the same way that single-member legislative districts do.[17] Where legisla-

16. For a very useful summary, see Carey 1998.

17. But see Filippov, Ordeshook, and Shvetsova 1999 for a more nuanced view.

tors are elected by proportional representation, as they are in most new democracies, the electoral system is pulled in both directions, toward a two-party centrism by presidential elections and toward more ideologically dispersed multipartism by PR legislative elections.

Work on the Latin American presidential systems has discovered that rules that affect the size of presidential coattails determine which pull is stronger. Where presidential and legislative elections occur at the same time, presidential coattails are strong and parties that cannot compete for the presidency often fade away; two-party systems tend to emerge. Where elections for different offices occur on different schedules, parties that have no hope of winning presidential elections can nevertheless continue to do well in legislative and municipal elections, and thus survive (Shugart 1995; Shugart and Carey 1992). Presidential runoffs also appear to encourage the persistence of small parties. Rather than forming preelection coalitions, small parties enter the first round in order to establish their bargaining power as coalition partners for the second round. Moreover, legislative elections occur at the same time as the first round of the presidential election (if they are concurrent), which means that small parties run in them as well. For these reasons, party fragmentation tends to be greater in countries with presidential runoffs.[18] In parliamentary systems, district magnitude has the greatest effect on party fragmentation, but in presidential systems, district magnitude has less effect than run-offs and concurrent election schedules (Jones 1995).

The effects of a number of electoral rules have been pretty thoroughly worked out. These include, besides the effect of presidential runoffs and different election schedules on party fragmentation noted above: the effect of preference voting, term limits, and running multiple lists under the same party label on party discipline in the legislature and candidate campaign strategies (e.g., Ames 1995a, 1995b, 2001; Carey 1996; Taylor 1992; Archer and Shugart 1997; Cox and Shugart 1995; Morgenstern 1999). These are the nuts and bolts of democratic politics, and a great deal of progress has been made in figuring them out. With the institutional basics understood, it then becomes possible to estimate the effects of important societal characteristics such as ethnic heterogeneity with reasonable confidence (Ordeshook and Shvetsova 1994).

In some new democracies, parties seem to be ideologically incoherent, legislative decision making is obstructed by disorganization, legislative and interbranch alliances are held together by pork rather than shared policy goals, and campaigns focus on the distribution of individual gifts in-

---

18. There has been some controversy over the effects of runoffs, but the balance of the evidence at this point supports the claim that they encourage party fragmentation. It is very hard to disentangle this question empirically because runoffs have generally been initiated in countries with fragmented party systems, so it is hard to judge whether the runoffs are cause or effect.

stead of policy promises. Other new democracies, however, function much as long-established European democracies do; parties are ideologically cohesive and disciplined, interbranch relations depend on party loyalties, and campaigns focus on party programs rather than individual candidates. Political systems of the first type are sometimes called candidate centered, and those of the second type, party centered. Explaining these differences ranks high on the research agenda for institutionalists.

Some progress has been made in identifying the political institutions that perpetuate candidate-centered systems. Most has been written about electoral rules that result in intraparty competition. These include the open list in PR systems, in which citizens may vote for individual candidates and list order is determined by the number of votes received; *sublemas*, multiple lists run under the same party label; and the single nontransferable vote, in which parties field multiple candidates in multimember districts, citizens vote for one individual candidate, and seats are awarded on the basis of votes to individual candidates. Carey and Shugart (1995) have suggested that four features of ballot structure and rules that guide the translation of votes into seats determine where political systems fall on the continuum between candidate and party centered. Other observers have noted the additional influence of governors' deleterious effects on national party discipline in federal systems (Samuels forthcoming; Mainwaring 1997) and the importance of noninstitutional factors such as the preferences of the very poor and uneducated for immediate individual goods rather than promises of poorly understood policy changes that may never materialize (Desposato 2001).

The first steps have also been taken toward figuring out some more complex institutional issues. Scholars are beginning to build an understanding of presidential powers and the relationship between presidents and legislatures. These studies begin from the premise that the probability of democratic breakdown is increased by conflict between the president and the legislature.[19] Scholars have explored two factors that might contribute to potential conflict or stalemate. The first is divided or minority government. Conflict or stalemate is obviously less likely if the president's party has a majority in the legislature, so analysts pursuing this line of thought emphasize the electoral rules that increase fragmentation in the party system, which in turn increases the likelihood of minority presidents.

The second involves the president's constitutional powers to set the legislative agenda, veto legislation, and issue decrees, that is, the president's power to pursue his own agenda even without legislative support. The implicit idea here is that stalemate is less likely if the president can do much of what he wants without legislative support. Carey and Shugart (1998a)

---

19. Although it is widely believed that minority presidents and divided government increase the likelihood of democratic breakdown, Cheibub (2002) shows that they have no effect on democratic survival.

have proposed an index to measure these presidential powers, though they have not shown what effects they have. A recent discussion of presidential powers by Mainwaring and Shugart (1997a) attempts to combine the constitutional powers emphasized by Carey and Shugart in other work with what they call partisan powers, meaning essentially the amount of support the president has in the legislature. This addition brings the notion of presidential powers closer to what we think of intuitively as strong presidents. At this point, these arguments have not gone very far either in terms of theorization of the relationship between presidents and legislatures or in terms of showing clear empirical effects of different arrangements. I have not yet seen spatial models and the veto players argument used to elucidate these arguments in a systematic way, but since this is an obvious thing to do, I am sure it will be done.[20]

Legislatures in developing and ex-Communist presidential systems have traditionally received much less attention than presidents because analysts have considered them less influential. Legislatures are beginning to be taken more seriously, however, and some pathbreaking work has recently appeared. John Londregan's (2000) study of the Chilean Senate is the first to offer an in-depth analysis of legislative committees in a contemporary Latin American legislature.[21] Tom Remington and Steve Smith (1995; 1998a, b) have done a series of studies that draw on the literature on the U.S. Congress to analyze the Russian Duma and its relationship to the president. Legislative studies are on the research frontier for those working on new democracies.

The work noted above focuses on the effects of political institutions, but such analyses always lead back to the prior question: What caused the institutions in the first place? The period of transition has been a good time to investigate this question because a large number of countries have chosen new democratic institutions or modified old ones. Scholars analyzing these choices have shown that in both Latin America and eastern Europe new political institutions have been chosen to further the electoral interests of those who served on the roundtables, legislatures, and constituent assemblies that picked them (e.g., Frye 1997; Remington and Smith 1996;

---

20. Spatial models and veto players arguments have been used to explain specific processes in specific countries. For example, Lisa Baldez and John Carey (1999) model the Chilean budget process using a veto players model. But no one working on developing countries has used these tools to work out the full logic of how agenda setting, decrees, and vetoes, all of which vary quite a bit in detail among countries, work.

21. Ames (1987) analyzes the role of committees in the Brazilian Chamber of Deputies between 1946 and 1964. Several other scholars studied legislatures in various countries during the seventies (Agor 1971; Hoskin, Leal, and Kline 1976; Packenham 1970), but contemporary studies drawing on the very sophisticated U.S. congressional literature have barely begun to appear.

Colomer 1997; Geddes 1995, 1996; Benoit and Schiemann 2001; Luong 2000; Bernhard 1997).

The convergence to mainstream theories and methodologies for analyzing politics in democratic developing countries is occurring because a very large body of theory on democratic politics exists, and those who are making use of it can see that it gives them leverage for understanding a good deal of what is going on. Like any other innovation, it is spreading because it helps users to do what they want to do, which is to explain various aspects of democratic politics. Once the countries that analysts were interested in democratized and politics became more orderly and transparent, useful theories were available for understanding them. Voting behavior could be observed and analyzed, and it became possible to do surveys.[22] Democratization opened up niches for certain kinds of work, and scholars, many of them young and well trained, moved into them.

THE STUDY OF ECONOMIC POLICY AND DEVELOPMENT

In the study of economic policy and development, economists (e.g., Alesina and Drazen 1991; Fernandez and Rodrik 1991; Rodriguez and Rodrik 2001; Aslund 1995; Barro 1997) lately have done much of the most influential work. Let me single out just one that has changed the way I think about the politics of economic reform. Dani Rodrik (1994) models the effect of trade liberalization on welfare. He shows that only during periods of high inflation and deep crisis do the welfare benefits of trade reform outweigh its redistributive effects. This is a clear and concise explanation for one of the repeated findings to arise in inductive studies of reform efforts: reforms that bring down very high inflation face little opposition, even if they also impose costs on some groups, and the politicians who initiate them tend to be reelected. Examples include the radical Menem reforms in Argentina, where inflation had reached about 3,000 percent before the initiation of liberalization; the equally radical reforms initiated in Bolivia in 1985, where inflation had risen to about 40,000 percent (the finance minister in charge during reforms was later elected president); the Fujimori reforms in Peru, where inflation had topped out at about 7,500 percent; and the more moderate reforms that brought inflation down from about 2,000 percent in Brazil in 1995 (where, as in Bolivia, the finance minister credited with initiating the reforms was later elected president).[23]

I discuss this article because it has the characteristics one would hope

22. See Fleron 1996 for a review of much of the recent work on public opinion in ex-Communist countries.

23. Inflation figures from the International Monetary Fund, *International Financial Statistics Yearbook*, 1999, 127.

to find in a model. It is clear and easy to understand. It provides a persuasive, theoretically grounded explanation for a set of observations many who study economic reform had noticed. We already knew in a loose kind of way that when things got really bad people who might otherwise have been expected to oppose reform would support it. Various ad hoc reasons for this have been suggested, but Rodrik's argument is at once connected logically to a strong body of economic theory and entirely plausible. Once I had read it, I put this aspect of reform onto the very small shelf where I store phenomena successfully explained.

Political scientists doing exciting work on economic policy have tended to draw basic insights from Douglass North (1981, 1985, 1989a, b, 1990), who attributes the persistence of economically inefficient institutions to their usefulness to rulers. This perspective helps explain the initiation and persistence of obviously dysfunctional laws and institutions. It can be extended to explain a great deal of behavior in the incompletely reformed economies characteristic of developing and ex-Communist countries (e.g., Frye 2000; Shleifer and Vishny 1998). Resistance to completing reforms in Russia comes, as shown by Hellman (1998), from those who have grown rich from partial reforms and their allies in government, not from those hurt by reforms. One of the reasons corruption is hard to end is that it funds political campaigns and raises the incomes of officials and politicians (Shleifer and Vishny 1993; Geddes 1999a). State ownership of enterprises that could be more efficiently run by private owners allows politicians to reward supporters with jobs, postpone politically dangerous mass layoffs, and supply subsidized fuel and raw materials to favored private firms. The politicians and officials who can trade these resources for political support tend to obstruct privatization (Geddes 1999a).

One of the legacies of authoritarianism in many developing and all ex-Communist countries is an overcentralization of decision making, useful to rulers for maintaining control but economically inefficient. As countries democratized, subnational levels of government in many gained control of more decision-making and revenue-extracting power than they had had before. The World Bank and other international agencies and nongovernmental organizations supported the impulse toward decentralization, believing it would contribute to more participatory politics and also more efficient allocation of scarce resources. A substantial body of theory in economics and political science supported these beliefs (e.g., Tiebout 1956; Weingast 1995). Brazilianists and Russian specialists, however, not to mention Yugoslav specialists, tend to take a much more jaundiced view of decentralism and federalism (Mainwaring 1997; Samuels forthcoming; Pleština 1992; Treisman 2000a, b; Andrews and Stoner-Weiss 1995; Ordeshook 1996). The debate about whether federalism is good or bad in general probably cannot be resolved. Instead, it seems far more fruitful to try to figure out how it works in different contexts and issue areas.

Dan Treisman's (1999b; see also Shleifer and Treisman 2000) analysis of the effects of Russian federalism on taxation and the initiation of economic reforms takes some important steps toward doing this. Using the intuitions provided by common-pool models, Treisman argues that revenue sharing creates incentives for provincial political leaders to shirk collecting taxes and to collude with firm managers to hide resources. Since the amount of revenue provinces get is not tied to the amount they collect, provincial leaders have no reason to put effort into tax collection. In fact, they can keep more revenues at home, either for their personal use or to spend responding to constituents' needs, if they collude with businesspeople to underreport their assets and then split the taxes saved.

Treisman's argument explains why Russian tax revenues have fallen, which in turn explains a good deal about the inability of the central government to pursue a coherent reform policy and provide an adequate social safety net. The argument will not generalize to all federal systems because the details of revenue collection and sharing differ across systems, and the consequences would in any case be less pernicious in countries in which the provincial populations see themselves as less different and feel less alienated from the center than in Russia (Treisman 1999a). Jones, Sanguinetti, and Tommasi (2000) use a similar model for analyzing the Argentine federal system, thus demonstrating the usefulness of the approach beyond the specifics of the Russian case.

THE POLITICIZATION OF ETHNICITY

The central theoretical difficulty for scholars who seek to understand the politicization of ethnicity is that ethnic identity is changeable and malleable, as are the interests and attitudes any particular identity implies. This means that the interesting questions have to do with how, when, and why people identify with one of their ethnic options rather than another, perceive their grievances as caused by their ethnicity, feel threatened by other ethnic groups, and decide which among their options for action and inaction to pursue in order to protect themselves or improve their situation (Brubaker 1992 and 1996; Marx 1998). In the face of this analytically difficult substantive problem, observers have noted that ethnic identity is constructed, and described ways it has been constructed in various settings. This work has forced the old idea of ethnic identity as built on unchanging primordial loyalties into the dustbin of history. Explaining how, when, and why ethnicity is constructed dominates the current research agenda for students of ethnic politics.

Questions dealing with ethnicity and identity have been addressed from many different intellectual perspectives. I focus here on those that seek to explain the political consequences of ethnic identity: primarily, political mobilization, peaceful coexistence, violence, assimilation, and secession. Most of the time people with differing ethnic identities live side by side peacefully whether they feel hate, fear, envy, contempt, admiration, or liking for each other. Explanations for the kinds of mobilization, violence, and attempts to secede that call ethnicity to our attention have to explain what causes the usual state of peaceful coexistence to break down (Fearon and Laitin 1996, 2000).

Even though people feel ethnic loyalties intensely and can be motivated by them to incredible and seemingly irrational acts of heroism or cruelty, scholars have successfully used systematic arguments to explain some behavior motivated by ethnicity. Several authors have suggested arguments for why political entrepreneurs mobilize support within ethnic groups, rather than, for example, economic interest groups (Bates 1983; Laitin 1995). Fearon (1998c) has shown that the inability of new states to credibly commit to protecting the future rights of a minority can make it rational for the minority to fight to secede, even though both groups would have been better off if the commitment could have been made and violence avoided. Posner's study (1998) of the choice among options in Zambians' ethnic repertoires shows the same kind of instrumental reaction to circumstances. He shows that voters preferred candidates from their own (small) tribes when their choices were limited to district-level candidates all from the same party. In multiparty elections, however, both before and after the single-party interlude, voters chose candidates from their (larger) linguistic groups without regard for tribe within a linguistic group. In other words, if tribal candidates could win, voters preferred them, but when a broader support base was needed in order to win elections, voters' loyalties moved up to the next higher level in the hierarchy of potential identities, language group.

David Laitin's wise book (1998a) about Russians stranded in non-Russian republics after the collapse of the Soviet Union stands out in the current literature on ethnicity. Laitin uses a tipping model to gain insight into the choices of individuals about whether to learn the titular language. The tipping model illuminates the contingent nature of decisions about whether to assimilate, fight, or flee. Tipping models help us to understand sudden mass changes in behavior, such as the transition from quiescence to mass mobilization during the collapse of Communism in Romania and East Germany (cf. Przeworski 1986).[24] Laitin also explains the behavior of potential ethnic leaders. He links the strategies of potential nationalist elites to the availability of career opportunities at the center of a multiethnic state to explain their decisions about whether to mobilize ethnic opposition to the center. These arguments, in interaction with information about the economic and demographic context in the various post-Soviet republics, explain why Russians in Estonia are learning Estonian and trying to assimilate while Russians in Kazakhstan refuse to learn Kazakh and keep their suitcases packed.

---

24. Lohmann (1994) suggests an alternative way of thinking about the popular mobilization in East Germany and other similar phenomena.

Laitin's rationalist arguments are embedded in a very thorough empirical investigation into how real people perceive their situations in four ex-Soviet nations. Arguments in the book are supported by survey research, in-depth observation and interviews with a small number of families, and content analysis of newspapers. The result of these multiple forms of evidence is an extremely persuasive interpretation of events.

Laitin's work shows that although people feel ethnic loyalties deeply, they also respond rationally to the situations they face in everyday life as they define and redefine their ethnic identities. In my judgment, this book exemplifies the best work currently being done on ethnicity, in that it uses some of the tools provided by economic models to help understand otherwise puzzling or seemingly irrational actions and that it also explores in depth and detail how people perceive their situations. Several different kinds of empirical detail support the arguments and interpretations made in the book.

Although the study of the effects of ethnicity remains very diverse and research methods within the field remain quite contested, here too we see that models drawn from economics are being used in some of the most influential studies, and rigorous tests of arguments in at least a few.

▪ | Methodological Convergence

Changes have begun in the way students of developing countries do research, propose knowledge claims, and decide whether to believe the knowledge claims proposed by others. The changes have occurred in at least three important areas: our response to economic models of politics; the quality, amount, and availability of data relevant to the interests of scholars working on developing countries, along with our level of statistical skills; and standards for what constitutes persuasive evidence. The second two are related but not as closely as might at first appear.

The implications of the simplest economic models, such as the collective action problem, seem to have percolated throughout the comparative field. Where once analysts working in the tradition of comparative historical sociology might have been accused of failing to understand the implications of the logic of collective action, that is no longer true (cf. Thelen 1999). Most economic models have much narrower potential areas of application, of course, but that is not the only reason they have spread less far. Many comparativists find abstract models that so grossly simplify reality intellectually uncongenial. Nevertheless, the models are spreading and becoming more influential because they are levers and pulleys for the imagination. Just as you can lift more with a lever than with your bare hands, you can sometimes figure out more about a situation if you have a few simple models to apply to it than if you have to rely only on your untutored intuitions.

It may be useful to divide models into two categories: those, like the collective action problem, which lay out a logic that applies to and may illuminate many situations and those which aim to explain a particular real-world outcome. Besides the collective action problem, the first category contains a number of other logical explications of simple interactions among individuals, such as tipping games, chicken, battle-of-the-sexes, Arrow's paradox, and divide-the-dollar. These models are not in themselves falsifiable; they are logical constructions that may or may not be useful for interpreting particular situations. The common-pool logic used by Treisman to help explain tax problems in Russia is an example of the usefulness of this kind of model, as is the tipping model used by Laitin to illuminate sudden changes in language acquisition.

The second category contains the many models that purport to explain specific patterns of outcomes and are thus, in principle if not always in practice, falsifiable. Like other arguments, they can be right or wrong, and they need to be supported by evidence to be persuasive. Because they are simple, logically consistent, and based on explicit assumptions, they can sometimes illuminate a relationship that had not been obvious before. Such is the case with the Rodrik (1994) model of the relationship between high inflation and the effects of trade liberalization on citizen welfare described above. It adds crispness and clarity to the explanation of an empirical regularity many observers had noticed. We would not, however, take it seriously if it did not conform to empirical evidence.

Both kinds of models are being incorporated into studies by comparativists. The first kind has been used as a central analytic tool in explanations of civil-military relations (Hunter 1997), administrative reform (Geddes 1994), peasant rebellion (Popkin 1979), authoritarian breakdown (Geddes 1999b), and regime transition (Colomer 1995; Przeworski 1992). These kinds of models also play a subsidiary role in a very large number of studies. Collective action problems, for example, explain why peasants fail to organize effectively in Bates' study (1981) of African agricultural policy and why concentrated industries get more of what they want in the Latin American policy process in Frieden's study (1991a) of the effects of the debt crisis.

The second kind of model has the same status as any other proposed argument; we should believe it if evidence supports it. Most of our understanding of the effects of different kinds of economic policies now derives from economic models of the second kind, whether we have individually read them or not.

In discussing the increasing use of economic models by scholars interested in developing countries, I do not mean to suggest that they have become standard or commonplace. They have simply become more common and familiar than they used to be, and I think many of us rely on them for our understanding of some subjects even without being aware of the source of our insights.[25]

Large-n studies have also begun to play a greater role in the comparative development field as data have improved in quality, relevance, and accessibility. Quantitative studies can be used both to test theories and for inductive explorations. I will deal with theory testing below when I discuss standards of evidence. Here I focus on quantitative studies with an inductive thrust. At one end of the continuum from inductive to theory testing are broad quantitative studies that seek to discover the causes of some outcome by trying out indicators of as many potential causes as possible in statistical models. All inductive studies are guided to a considerable extent by the theories and speculations available in the literature, but at the most inductive end of the continuum analysts appear quite theoretically agnostic and eclectic; they throw everything they can think of into a regression or some other statistical model and see what patterns seem to emerge. Some recent large-n studies of growth and effective governance have these characteristics (e.g., Acemoglu, Johnson, and Robinson 2000; LaPorta et al. 1999), as do some studies of why coups occur (Londregan and Poole 1990, 1996) and what causes democracy (Barro 1999).

Other studies, which fall between the inductive and theory-testing ends of the continuum, aim to find out if some particular potential cause really has the effects that have been suggested. Michael Ross's study (forthcoming) of the effect of oil and other natural resources on the likelihood of authoritarian government is a good example of this kind of work. It shows that reliance on oil exports increases the probability of authoritarian government; the finding is persuasive because Ross shows that it does not depend on any particular measurement or specification decision. Another such study is Bienen, Londregan, and van de Walle's (1995) of the effect of ethnic heterogeneity on leadership turnover in Africa. They show that ethnic heterogeneity does not increase the fragility of African governments. Gasiorowski and Power (1998) use a large-n study to test the argument that parliamentary systems are more stable than presidential, and find that among developing countries, they are not.

None of these studies tests a particular theory, although in all cases more than one causal mechanism connecting purported cause and effect has been suggested in the literature. Instead, these studies aim to establish whether a correlation suggested in the literature really exists between a particular potential cause and an outcome, while remaining somewhat agnostic about why the correlation might exist. These studies occupy a midpoint on the induction-theory-testing continuum because they confirm (or fail to confirm) empirical regularities without trying to confirm particular theo-

---

25. See Levi 2000 for an insightful and much more thorough review of the use of economic models in the comparative field than is possible here.

retical explanations of the empirical regularity. Where they fail to confirm a hypothesized relationship, as in the Gasiorowski and Power and Bienen, Londregan, and van de Walle studies, the results cast doubt on all the arguments that have suggested that such a relationship should be expected to exist. Where the analyst shows that the relationship does indeed exist, however, the task of explaining why it exists remains on the research agenda. These kinds of large-n studies have become much more important in the field of comparative development as a means of discovering and confirming empirical regularities, but they should not be interpreted as statistical expressions of theories. They are empirical investigations—like case studies but more rigorous and structured. Once patterns have been established empirically, theories can be proposed to account for them. Then the implications of the theories can themselves be tested.

Large-n studies had a bad reputation among comparativists for a long time because of the poor quality of most of the data available and because of the feeling that most of the quantitative work being done was mechanistic and insensitive to the real meaning of the indicators thrown into regressions. These issues remain challenges with which those doing large-n cross-national studies must contend. Some of the data sets available off the shelf have well-known and obvious flaws that should, but do not always, give analysts pause when they decide to use them. Sometimes cases are left out of analyses that the reader suspects would overturn results if included. Sometimes model specifications determine results. Many large-n studies are unpersuasive because we suspect that if the author had included other cases or a different time period, had specified the model more appropriately, or had used an unbiased indicator for some variable, the results would have been different (see Levine and Renelt 1992). The best large-n studies do add to our store of knowledge, however, and I think everyone in the field nowadays accepts this.

What counts as adequate evidence to support an argument and, more broadly, the importance of systematic empirical confirmation of arguments remain contested in the comparative development field. On the side influenced by the political science mainstream, it is expected that arguments will be tested using observations chosen in ways that do not bias results, that measurements and classifications of key concepts will be explicit, that the author's argument will be confronted with rival arguments in the literature, and that some means will be found for holding constant other factors known to affect the relationship of interest but not themselves considered interesting. These conditions can be met through the thoughtful use of statistics, but quantitative methods are neither necessary nor sufficient to achieve them. Careful qualitative research designs can also do so. Those who disagree with these mainstream-influenced methodological norms either do not see their scholarly task as including the systematic presentation of evidence or show evidence that, however otherwise convincing, fails to conform to one or more of the expectations listed above.

The line dividing the two sides on this issue crosscuts the main cleavage between more traditional comparativists and those who borrow models from economics and theories from the study of American politics. Those who question the constraints imposed by the norms of evidence that characterize much of the rest of political science include historical institutionalists and comparative historical sociologists, on the one side, and economic modelers in both economics and political science, on the other.

Historical institutionalists and comparative historical sociologists (e.g., Rueschemeyer, Stephens, and Stephens 1992; Yashar 1997; Collier and Collier 1991) place a high value on the importance of supporting evidence.[26] Their studies usually describe with great care the processes and interactions leading up to the event or change of interest. Among practitioners, these descriptions are considered solid evidence, especially useful for illuminating causal processes and sequences. Many historical institutionalists see conventional norms about case selection and the number of observations needed to test arguments as limiting their ability to focus on the processes and mechanisms central to understanding. They defend several methodological strategies that many nonpractitioners see as undermining the logic of inference: selection of cases on the basis of outcomes (Collier and Mahoney 1996), the use of small-n research designs without regard for the number of causes being examined (Mahoney 2000b), and the idea that path-dependent processes cannot be explained by standard causal models (Abbott 1988; Mahoney 2000a).

The disagreement about research norms that separates historical institutionalists and comparative historical sociologists from those more influenced by the political science mainstream is often articulated as a disagreement about the value of small-n versus large-n research designs (e.g., Lieberson 1991), but number of cases is not the only, and possibly not the most important, issue.[27] A small-n study in which the cases are chosen to reduce the likelihood of introducing bias, concepts are defined in concrete ways that leave the classification of cases unproblematic, and rival arguments are taken seriously can be much more persuasive than a large-n study using a truncated sample and indicators that fail to capture the meaning of concepts or turn rival arguments into strawmen. If, however,

26. For exemplars of the historical-institutional approach, see those cited in Thelen 1999 and Thelen and Steinmo 1992.

27. See Mahoney 2000b for a careful elucidation and defense of small-n research designs, especially in comparative historical sociology. It is noteworthy, however, that the methods Mahoney suggests would be most useful for increasing the persuasiveness of small-n research strategies, the method of concomitant variation (i.e., ordinal measurement of enough cases so that simple statistical tests can be carried out) and pattern matching (the testing of implications of the argument at a lower level of analysis), both increase the n. The number of observations (n) used in any particular test of an argument need not be the same as the number of ordinary language cases, often countries, that are the main focus of a study.

small-n studies claim to test arguments using evidence that comes from the same cases from which the arguments were induced, use unclear criteria for classifying into categories, and ignore rival arguments or turn them into strawmen, then many will find them unpersuasive.

In contrast to historical institutionalists, modelers, whether in economics or political science, often seem to reject the idea that arguments need to be confirmed empirically. Arguments are frequently published with just a couple of glancing references to real-world events to supply plausibility. And there is a substantial group of consumers of these arguments who seem to find economic models so inherently plausible that they need no empirical confirmation. There are of course some models that are so fruitful in terms of the jolt they give the imagination that empirical confirmation has little or nothing to do with their value. Most models, however, are simply arguments written down in mathematical form. The producers and consumers of these models often seem to find them persuasive without empirical confirmation, but, as with the evidentiary standards of historical institutionalists, those from outside often do not.[28]

Usually these two groups have little to do with each other, but Bates et al. (1998) seem to be trying to bridge the gap by embedding economic models in careful descriptions of events under the rubric of "analytic narratives." Bates et al. do not of course reject testing arguments, but they do downplay its importance. They note that many economic models cannot be tested directly but give little attention to the possibility or desirability of testing the implications of arguments that cannot themselves be tested. Instead, they suggest that narratives demonstrating how models work in one or a few particular instances supply persuasive evidence of the usefulness of the models for explaining outcomes.

In other parts of the comparative development field, however, standards about what constitutes persuasive evidence are slowly converging to the mainstream. In the study of democratic political processes, more and more arguments are being tested carefully. Barry Ames (1987, 2001) deserves special mention as an exemplar and forerunner of this trend. Early work on the effects of political institutions, including my own, tended to be supported by rather spotty evidence, and much still does (e.g., Shugart 1998; Mainwaring and Shugart 1997b). Analysts have gradually begun to produce more empirically thorough support for their arguments, however. Mark Jones' investigation (1995) of the institutional causes of party fragmentation and minority government in Latin America, John Carey's analysis (1996) of the effects of term limits, and John Londregan's analysis (2000) of the Chilean Senate are good examples in the Latin Americanist

---

28. Green and Shapiro (1994) have articulated the best-known critique. Even though many of their specific claims are incorrect, they have identified a central weakness of rational choice (of which economic models are a subset): that many arguments are not tested empirically.

field. Remington and Smith's studies (1995, 1998b) of the Russian Duma set a high standard for research on ex-Communist countries.

In the study of economic development, there is something of a bifurcation between models and empirical work. Many of the models have not been tested, and many of the empirical studies do not seek to test particular models. Greater interaction between models and data remains on the research agenda in studies of the causes of economic policymaking and growth. Data are readily available for testing many of the models of economic policy and growth, however, and the study of economic development by political scientists seems to be moving rather rapidly in the direction of using large-n studies both to explore relationships and to test arguments.

Most empirical work on identity and ethnicity has been descriptive or interpretive, while most models and rational-choice arguments have not been supported by systematic arrays of evidence. This situation is beginning to change, however, as demonstrated in the work by Laitin (1998a) and Posner (1998) described above.

■ | Conclusion

As substantial parts of the developing and ex-Communist world have converged on the political and economic systems previously characteristic only of the most industrialized countries, the academic field of comparative development has begun to converge on the theories and methodologies originally developed to study the politics of those same industrialized countries. The standard arguments of neoclassical economics have replaced structuralist and dependency-influenced explanations of development and growth. The study of political processes in new democracies has blossomed, fertilized by theories and methods previously honed in the study of the older democracies. Approaches to the study of ethnicity remain eclectic, but a few scholars in this area too have begun collecting systematic data and making use of economic models as analytic tools.

This convergence is uneven and incomplete, depending on the degree of real-world convergence in the region being studied. This unevenness is especially notable for those whose research focuses on politics. For analysts interested in Latin America, eastern Europe, and democratic developing countries in other parts of the world, the sudden access to a set of fruitful and well-developed theories and methodologies has opened up exciting research frontiers in multiple areas, and high quality new research is pouring out. Understanding is growing rapidly about how new democratic institutions are chosen and changed; the effects of new democratic political institutions on emerging party systems, legislative behavior, and bargaining between the executive and the legislature; and what shapes the opinions and voting behavior of citizens in new democracies.

The intellectual situation for those interested in areas that have not democratized, however, seems to me more difficult. They can adopt the fruitful approaches of the mainstream, and a few have done so (e.g., Manion 1996a, b; Lust-Okar 2001), but they cannot stand on the shoulders of several decades of democratic theory in the way others can. Moreover, their access to good quality data remains limited. Fewer scholars are now studying the kinds of governments they study, and the scarcity of useful theories of day-to-day authoritarian politics remains as severe as ever, perhaps more so, as many observers impressed by the spread of democracy seem to have forgotten that many of the world's people still live under autocracy.

KATHLEEN THELEN

The Political Economy
of Business and Labor
in the Developed Democracies[1]

■ | Introduction

The past decade has witnessed important innovations in the study of the
political economy of business and labor in the developed democracies. For
many years the literature in this area was organized around the concept
of democratic corporatism. This concept was closely associated with a few
northern European countries that seemed to provide a model of how
strong and encompassing unions—backed up by labor-sympathetic governments—could mold political-economic institutions to sustain a highly
successful social-democratic variant of capitalism that featured low unemployment, universalistic welfare benefits, and an egalitarian income distribution. However, the concept also served as the key point of reference
within a general analytic framework for the study of labor across the developed democracies.

Beginning in the 1980s, changes in the political and economic context brought new strains to labor relations across the advanced industrial
world. More turbulent international markets and a resurgence of neoliberal ideology complicated politics as usual in the classic democratic-
corporatist countries, but more importantly in the present context, these
developments also revealed important shortcomings in the analytic framework that had developed around the concept of corporatism. The literature
in this area had yielded important insights by drawing attention to the way

1. I thank James Alt, David Collier, Chris Howell, John Huber, Ira Katznelson,
Cathie Jo Martin, Helen Milner, Paul Pierson, Jonas Pontusson, Theda Skocpol,
David Soskice, Sven Steinmo, and Peter Swenson for comments.

371

that institutional arrangements mediated common international pressures faced by the advanced industrial countries in the 1970s and early 1980s. Yet the framework seemed singularly ill suited to understanding the *dynamics of change* in these political economies in subsequent decades, when the nature of the problems they faced shifted and the institutions themselves were part of what was getting renegotiated.

This chapter assesses the state of the discipline in the political economy of business and labor in the developed democracies. It does so by addressing a key development in the literature that has reoriented the study of labor, social democracy, and the welfare state—prompting a reinterpretation of the results of a great deal of previous work while setting important agendas for the future as well. Whereas the traditional corporatism literature had focused most of its attention on *labor* (the structure and strategies of unions), a newer body of work has redirected our attention to the contribution of *employer* interests and strategies in shaping the political economy of labor in the developed democracies.

The literature that "brings capital back in" (Swenson 1991) comes in two broad variants. One highly influential stream emphasizes the role of employers as crucial partners in *cross-class coalitions* that preside over the genesis and then contribute to the reproduction of key political-economic institutions, including but not limited to wage-bargaining institutions. This body of work takes issue with the corporatism literature's almost exclusive focus on union organization and strength as the most important constitutive force in shaping institutional and political outcomes. It focuses instead on employer interests—and especially on conflicts of interest among capitalists—in terms of preferred political and institutional outcomes. In this literature, cross-class alliances that bring together segments of capital and of labor are what generate and sustain key institutional outcomes and policies.

A second literature, which emerged at about the same time, similarly drew attention to the role of employers but, in this case, employers were brought back in through the concept of *employer coordination*. Like the first, the second literature rejects the corporatism literature's heavy emphasis on the strength and organization of labor, but in this case replaces that with an analysis of cross-national differences in the capacity of employers to coordinate among themselves. Here again, the focus is on employer interests. However, in this body of work the interests of firms in their relations with labor flow from their embeddedness in a broader set of interlocking institutional arenas that define and sustain distinctive trajectories of capitalist development, or "varieties of capitalism" (Hall and Soskice 2001b).

These two perspectives are almost always treated as complementary, and in many ways they are. Both have certainly played an enormous role in reorienting labor scholarship in such a way as to highlight the constitutive power of employers and employer organizations in shaping political-economic institutions and outcomes. Each perspective has its own following, and there are a number of scholars who are producing excellent work at the intersection of the two. However, on closer examination we can see that the central analytic tools that anchor each of these approaches—in the first case, the notion of cross-class coalitions and in the second case, the notion of employer coordination—represent very different kinds of variables. The literature on cross-class coalitions draws attention to the *political settlement* on which institutions rest and emphasizes how, at critical moments in history, dominant players in the political economy forge institutions that further their material interests (see also Zysman 1983). By contrast, the literature on varieties of capitalism understands institutions in terms of the *coordinating functions* they perform and emphasizes how different institutional configurations drive firm preferences rather than the other way around.

This chapter explores the contributions—and the distinctive strengths and weaknesses—of these two strands of the literature. I argue that neither perspective can stand alone and indeed, that the insights generated by each one are incomplete and even misleading to the extent that scholars fail to situate these within a framework that incorporates the insights of the other. The coalitional perspective emphasizes agency and politics (winners and losers), but it often downplays or fails to problematize the role of institutions in influencing which kinds of coalitions emerge and prevail. The second perspective, by contrast, emphasizes the role of institutions in shaping employer preferences, but its emphasis on the functional contributions of particular institutions to firm strategies often obscures the *political* foundations on which these institutions rest and which lie behind their reproduction.

Viewed from the vantage point of the broader methodological themes running through this volume, the argument elaborated in the pages below illustrates the explanatory power of an historical-institutional framework (Hall and Taylor 1996; Pierson and Skocpol this volume; Thelen 1999; Thelen and Steinmo 1992). It does so by underscoring the weaknesses of research strategies that emphasize one component—the historical or the institutional—to the neglect of the other. Specifically, the literature on cross-class coalitions—while often appropriately *historical* (especially in the sense of situating employer strategies within a particular historical context)—is frequently insufficiently *institutional* in the sense of taking account of how employer preferences themselves have been molded by features of the political-institutional environment. Conversely, the literature on varieties of capitalism is deeply attuned to the impact of *institutions*—indeed the whole perspective is organized around understanding the way that institutional arrangements shape firm strategies and preferences—but insufficiently *historical* in the way that it conceives of these institutions and neglectful of the political (as opposed to efficiency-based) dynamics behind their reproduction.

Moreover, both perspectives have been criticized by some for "bend-ing the stick too far in the opposite direction," that is, overemphasizing the role of employers and losing sight of traditional class (as opposed to cross-class) conflicts and distributional struggles (see, esp. Iversen and Pontusson 2000, 31; Pontusson 2000; Howell 2001). My thesis here is that a successful synthesis of these two perspectives hinges on the self-conscious incorporation of a stronger temporal dimension into the analysis (cf. Pierson and Skocpol, this volume). As soon as we do this, class conflict and the constitutive power of labor are brought back out of the shadows. Sustained attention to the way in which policy feedback sets the context within which successive contests over particular innovations are fought will reveal how the strength of unions and the influence of their political allies shape both the kinds of employers that labor unions face and the interests and coalitions they are likely to pursue.

The chapter proceeds in four steps. First, I address the literature on democratic corporatism from the 1970s and early 1980s, and demonstrate how recent developments—both theoretical and empirical—pose a challenge to some of the analytic conventions on which that literature was based. Second, I look at some of the scholarship that has reoriented the debate on labor politics by reinserting employer interests and show how each of the two strands of thought sketched out above has provided insights into developments in industrial and labor relations over the last decades that appeared anomalous against the backdrop of the previous corporatism literature. Third, I make the case for a synthetic framework that blends together the emphasis on agency and power that is more fully elaborated in coalitional analyses with the logic of alternative institutional frameworks that figures so prominently in the second, varieties of capitalism, perspective. I use two brief empirical examples to illustrate the analytic leverage that can be gained through an historical-institutional approach that incorporates insights from both literatures. A fourth section concludes.

■ | The Democratic Corporatism Literature

In the 1970s and early 1980s the study of labor in the developed democracies was dominated by the literature on democratic corporatism.[2] This term was used to refer to a situation in which highly organized business and labor associations were incorporated into policymaking networks, thus facilitating negotiated trade-offs across various economic and social policies. Corporatism in this sense applied best to a rather narrow set of mostly northern European countries that were characterized by centralized labor movements linked to strong social democratic parties. The convention was

2. For an extended discussion and critique see Thelen 1994, on which this section draws.

to think of corporatist arrangements as having been put in place by strong labor movements,[3] and many analysts took the degree of labor's centralization as a basis for measuring the "degree of corporatism" across the whole range of advanced industrial societies (Cameron 1984; Schmitter 1981; Wilensky 1976). The "most corporatist" countries were characterized by highly developed welfare states, centralized and egalitarian wage bargaining institutions, and strong labor participation in managing economic and industrial adjustment processes. The "least corporatist" countries, by contrast, were characterized by less developed and less egalitarian welfare states, high levels of inequality, and contentious and largely counterproductive relations between unions and employers in the face of adjustment pressures.

A large literature analyzed the structure and logic of corporatist decision making and examined the link between such arrangements and positive economic performance in the 1970s and 1980s (e.g., Cameron 1984; Crepaz 1992; Moene and Wallerstein 1999). However, starting in the 1980s, traditional bargaining and welfare state institutions throughout the advanced industrial world came under increasing stress due to new fiscal constraints and heightened competitive pressures associated with globalization. These trends shifted the focus of labor scholarship from the past successes of corporatist arrangements to contemporary strains and the reconfiguration of industrial relations and other labor institutions (A. Martin 2000; Pontusson and Swenson 1996).

However, contemporary trends fit very uneasily within the traditional corporatist framework. Centralized wage bargaining in some—but not all—of the classic corporatist countries has been undergoing profound change (Lange, Wallerstein, and Golden 1995). Meanwhile, traditionally noncorporatist countries such as Spain and Italy have seen a *recentralization* of bargaining (Locke and Baccaro 1996; Perez 2000; Regini 1997; Regini and Regalia 1997; Royo 2000). The old taken-for-granted link between bargaining centralization and labor strength seems curiously out of sync with these developments. Strong labor movements in countries like Sweden have been unable to defend centralized bargaining arrangements, while concertation has been emerging in countries where the corporatism literature would tell us that unions were too weak and fragmented to force it (Perez 2000, 441).

These developments seemed vexing within the traditional corporatism framework, and together, they revealed two broad problems with the analytic conventions that underpinned labor scholarship based on that framework. First, much of the traditional literature on corporatism systematically ignored the constitutive role of employers and employers' organizations in forging and sustaining the institutional arrangements governing labor poli-

3. An exception is Katzenstein (1985).

tics.[4] Recent work has shown that employer coordination is at least as important as the centralization of unions in achieving many of the economic outcomes associated with corporatism (C. J. Martin 2000; Soskice 1991). Moreover, and as events in Sweden and Denmark in the 1980s forcefully demonstrated, the fate of corporatist arrangements hinges crucially on employer strategies: where employers are intent on decentralization, even the strongest labor movements cannot resist.

Second, the corporatism literature of the 1970s and 1980s tended to focus a great deal of attention on wage bargaining and to view collective bargaining institutions in relative isolation from other related institutional spheres. Although corporatist bargaining was concerned with negotiating *policy* trade-offs involving (for example) monetary and social policies, the *institutional* interconnections that linked wage bargaining to other political-economic arenas—including financial institutions, vocational education and training institutions, and welfare state institutions—went largely unexplored.[5]

By contrast, a good deal of the contemporary labor literature is precisely concerned with examining the interactions between various institutional realms, with the interface between financial institutions and collective bargaining structures figuring especially prominently.[6] Related, but not identical to this, is a growing concern with the broad issue of *institutional complementarities*, which goes beyond the question of how policies generated in one arena (e.g., by central banks) affect choices and strategies in other arenas (e.g., collective bargaining). Studies of institutional complementarities, both historical and contemporary, explore the ways in which the existence of certain kinds of institutions in one realm (e.g., industrial relations) may promote the development of complementary institutions in other realms (e.g., vocational training or welfare state institutions) (Ebbinghaus and Manow 2001; Hall and Soskice 2001a; Huber and Stephens 2001; Streeck 2001; Swenson forthcoming).

A number of recent works have challenged the analytic foundations of the traditional literature. The two strands of theorizing discussed below move in important ways beyond the conventions associated with the classic model of democratic corporatism, and each of them contributes key elements for an

---

4. It is symptomatic that almost all rankings of degrees of corporatism were based on the organizational characteristics of the labor movement (e.g., Cameron 1984; Schmitter 1981).

5. However, Wolfgang Streeck was already dealing with these issues in work that ran mostly parallel to that taking place within the dominant corporatism framework. His contributions will be discussed subsequently, as they played a major role in the reorientation of labor scholarship generally.

6. See, for example, Hall 1994; the contributions by Franzese and Hall and Iversen in Iversen, Pontusson, and Soskice 2000; Soskice 1990b; Soskice 1997; and Soskice and Iversen 1998.

alternative analytic framework for understanding the political economy of advanced capitalism. The next two sections sketch out those features of the literatures under review that constitute important building blocks in such a framework: the role of employers in cross-class coalitions, and the institutional framework within which employer preferences emerge and are articulated.

▪ | Employers in Cross-Class Coalitions

As noted above, the conventional wisdom held that corporatism was fundamentally a product of labor strength, as highly centralized union confederations were able to use their political and market power to "push back" capital and institutionalize a prominent role for labor in the political economy. However, when in the 1980s employers in some countries turned their sights on corporatist bargaining institutions, it suddenly became clear that these arrangements had always rested on the active or tacit support of capital.

Peter Swenson's work has been enormously important in highlighting employers' constitutive, not passive, role in the genesis of centralized bargaining institutions in Sweden, which was long considered the paradigmatic case of corporatism and labor strength (see also Fulcher 1991). Swenson's work took issue with conventional accounts of the origins of the Swedish model, highlighting how some employers, acting in their own interest, actively orchestrated the centralization of bargaining that became the basis for labor's strength and incorporation into corporatist institutions in the postwar period (Swenson 1989). Building on work by Carpenter (1972), Ulman (1955), and others (Bowman 1985; Jackson 1984), Swenson underscored how under certain market conditions employers may find it to their advantage to promote unions and to invest them with considerable power in regulating labor markets.[7]

Swenson's work also invokes the notion of cross-class coalitions developed by Gourevitch and others, and uses it in a nuanced way.[8] Whereas a

7. Bowman showed that employers often actively promote union regulation in sectors characterized by fierce product-market competition. He works out a general argument in game theoretic terms, and illustrates it with the example of the bituminous coal industry in the United States at the turn of the last century. In this case, employers promoted unionization and collective bargaining as a means for controlling competition among themselves by standardizing labor costs, and they went so far as to endorse and support strikes by the union to bring defectors back into line (Bowman 1985, 58–59).

8. Gourevitch's analysis (1986) of the construction of various political economies is organized around the concept of cross-class coalitions, and the general idea is employed in some classics in political economy such as Polanyi 1944. More recent applications include Luebbert 1991 and Rogowski 1987a. I thank Peter Swenson for assistance in tracing the roots of the concept.

good deal of traditional labor research treated the centralization of bargaining in Sweden as the result of maneuvering between labor and capital as "blocs," Swenson's analysis traced the process back to a cross-class alliance between employers in industries exposed to international competition and workers in low-pay sectors. In a first phase of centralization (the consolidation of the union confederation over industry-level unions in the 1930s and 1940s), the metalworkers' union joined forces with metal employers to rein in their colleagues in higher-pay sectors (for example, construction) that were sheltered from international competition. In a second phase, which ushered in centralized wage bargaining in the 1950s, "metalworkers fell out of the coalition but were pressured into acquiescence with a combination of lockout threats by employers and threats of government intervention by Social Democrats" (Swenson 1989, 228). For Denmark, too, Swenson argued that organized employers "wanted and aggressively promoted the centralization of industrial relations" (1991, 515), and "coerced" unions into this. In both cases, employers not unions are seen as the driving force behind centralization, though they achieved their ends by seeking and promoting strategic alliances with segments of the working class who had their own reasons for going along. In both cases as well, the innovators were powerfully abetted by Social Democratic Parties that intervened at crucial junctures in ways that shored up the alliance for centralization at the expense of its opponents on both sides of the class divide (Swenson 1991, 525–26).

In the meantime, a large and growing body of scholarship has revisited historically crucial turning points in the development of particular political economies, with an eye toward identifying the role played by employers in the genesis of institutions and policies that have traditionally been seen as the product of labor strength. Philip Manow, for example, has produced a reinterpretation of the genesis of Modell Deutschland that specifically rests on an analysis of cross-class alliances (Manow 2000). Manow examines the so-called Bremen Agreement of 1956 that first established in Germany the now-familiar system of coordinated industry-level bargaining under the leadership of the metalworkers' union. Whereas the centralization of bargaining in Sweden reflected a cross-class alliance across sectors, Manow's analysis of Germany points to an intraindustry deal within the metalworking sector between export-oriented and domestically oriented firms. The deal was consolidated in part by a trade-off that exchanged a system of wage distribution preferred by large firms in heavy industry for welfare policies that allowed employers in export-oriented manufacturing to adjust employment to sudden shifts in demand (Manow 2000).

In a similar vein, Isabela Mares has written a fascinating account of the genesis of unemployment insurance systems in France and Germany in the pre- and interwar period (Mares 2000). Mares rejects labor-centered explanations of the origins of unemployment insurance, particularly their neglect of the interests of employers and their role in political outcomes.

As she puts it, "Without investigating empirically the preferences of firms, most studies *assume* that employers were opposed to the introduction of all social policies and infer that the introduction of any social policy reflects the victory of trade unions and their political allies over a business community forced into retreat" (Mares 2000, 226). In the case of Germany, Mares finds evidence of significant conflicts of interest between small and large firms with respect to preferred outcomes. Large firms in intensely competitive and volatile markets vigorously resisted the introduction of a union-run Ghent system. However, they supported a contributory insurance system over the existing means-tested (flat-rate) one as the best way to off-load the costs of unemployment and to preserve the investment they had made in their workers' skills.

Mares follows the lead of Swenson not just in highlighting the role of employers in these outcomes, but specifically in highlighting the strategic alliances that produced them. Where she breaks with Swenson is in her account of the process through which the relevant alliance was forged. Swenson sees cross-class coalitions as coming together, frequently though not necessarily always, on the basis of a "prestrategic convergence of interests of unions and employers for a particular social or labor market policy" (Mares 2000, 228). Mares contrasts her own view with this, arguing that her strategic alliances come together *during negotiations,* and are often facilitated by policy entrepreneurs who help to produce compromises that represent the second-best preferences of key actors.

IMPLICATIONS FOR CONTEMPORARY LABOR POLITICS

Although many of the theoretical innovations associated with cross-class coalitional analysis were rooted in detailed historical analyses of particular countries, the insights these studies have yielded have been extremely useful for making sense of recent broad trends in labor politics. The last two decades have been characterized by heightened pressures for flexibility in industrial relations institutions across the advanced industrial world, but the results have varied cross-nationally. Convergence theories predicting a uniform slide into deregulation have not been borne out (Berger and Dore 1996; Boyer and Hollingsworth 1997; Ferner and Hyman 1998; Wallerstein, Golden, and Lange 1997; Zysman 1996). But theories that attributed the resilience of traditional bargaining institutions in some countries to successful union defense do not provide much purchase, either, on observed cross-national patterns of stability and change (e.g. H. Katz 1993; Turner 1998). The evaporation of employer support for traditional bargaining arrangements has precipitated their breakdown in some strong-labor countries (including Sweden), while employers' continued willingness to negotiate compromises within existing institutions in other cases (e.g., Germany) has contributed to greater resiliency despite overall lower labor strength.

The search for explanations for these anomalous developments in contemporary industrial relations institutions has been very much guided by insights gleaned from the literature on cross-class alliances surveyed above. Iversen (1996), for example, argues that bargaining decentralization in Sweden and Denmark was a product of a cross-class realignment, set in motion by employers in export-oriented sectors. These firms relied on skilled labor and found themselves constrained by union solidaristic wage policies that narrowed wage differentials, especially those between skilled and unskilled workers (see also Pontusson and Swenson 1996). Firms in such industries led the drive for decentralization and they were abetted in their project by skilled workers who had also come to resent wage policies that benefited unskilled (also public sector) workers (Garrett and Way 2000; Mahon 1991).

Employers' interests also figure prominently in a number of studies that explain the opposite phenomenon—the resurgence of centralized bargaining in traditionally weak-labor–noncorporatist countries such as Italy, Spain, and Portugal. Perez, for example, argues that renewed concertation in Italy and Spain is in no way a function of labor strength; rather, bargaining centralization in both countries was orchestrated by employers and facilitated by governments that provided incentives that brought labor on board (Perez 2000). Richard Locke and Lucio Baccaro's analysis of industrial relations reforms in Italy in the 1990s similarly cites employer interests and conflicts within labor as decisive to ultimate outcomes. Specifically, export-oriented employers in Italy were a driving force behind the move toward industry-level bargaining, accompanied by changes in the rules for shop-floor representation that strengthened the so-called most representative unions against growing challenges by new and often more militant local organizations (Locke and Baccaro 1996, 20, 24).

Contributions and Correctives

The literature on cross-class coalitions has made an enormous contribution to the study of labor politics in advanced capitalism and many of the core insights that it has produced appear to have become internalized by labor scholars on a broad scale. The convention of viewing cross-national differences in wage bargaining, welfare-state, and other institutions to variation in the strength and centralization of unions has by and large been replaced by a concern with uncovering the role that employers have played in generating and sustaining such institutions.

Ongoing work has also revealed some gaps and blind spots, however. A good deal of the early work in this vein was organized around a refutation of a particularly strong version of the power resource model that saw centralized bargaining and other institutions associated with social democracy and corporatism as the product of labor strength. With this as the foil, it is perhaps not surprising that many analyses have been devoted to uncovering the heretofore-unappreciated contribution of (segments of) capital to such outcomes. However, many of them have paid scant attention to the *political-institutional* sources of divergent employer interests, and they have also failed to explore the structural configurations that privilege the emergence and triumph of some cross-class alliances over others.

Coalitional analyses provide an important corrective to studies that simply assume that outcomes and policies that benefit labor must have been opposed by employers (see especially Mares 2000, 226). Through intensive archival research, labor scholars have found that many putatively prolabor institutional and policy innovations were congruent with the interests of at least some segments of capital. However, as Hacker and Pierson (2000) have pointed out, establishing that business interests drove these developments requires more than demonstrating that ultimate outcomes were congruent with business interests (the old truism that correlation does not establish causation). In fact, Hacker and Pierson argue that it even requires more than documenting that employers voiced their support for particular policies, for employers may merely have been selecting the least bad from a menu of options not of their own choosing.

Invoking insights from studies of agenda setting, Hacker and Pierson point out that the crucial issue in most situations is not the final choice between particular policy options but rather the prior question of whose preferred range of options form the choice set from which actors are allowed to select. The example they offer responds to revisionist accounts of the history of the U.S. welfare state: "Scholars have spent countless hours in archives trying to chart the behind-the-scenes role of business leaders in the formulation of the Social Security Act—all the while skipping over the obvious point that *the overwhelming majority of employers would have preferred no legislation at all*" (2000, 12, Hacker and Pierson's emphasis).[9] This argument resonates with an important insight from the work of institutional sociologists such as Dobbin (1994) who argue that in order to understand cross-national differences in outcomes, it is necessary to pay attention not just to a particular decision node (even the final one) but rather to the *range of options* that are entertained in the first place, which are often completely different cross-nationally.

The coalitional approach also focuses a great deal of attention on the winning coalition and often glides over the institutional factors that shape the kinds of coalitions that are likely to emerge and prevail. As Iversen and

---

9. This same point comes out in Fulcher's analysis (1991) of the centralization of bargaining in Sweden. In that case, employers' choice of confederal bargaining took place in a context where unified and centralized industry-level unions existed and where therefore decentralized bargaining would have left individual firms confronting powerful unions on their own—a much worse scenario.

Pontusson point out, "some other alliance is always possible, and there is always some uncertainty about the prospects of success and the actual payoffs of any particular alliance" (Iversen and Pontusson 2000, 32). For example, in the analysis of bargaining centralization in Denmark and Sweden, Swenson demonstrates without a doubt that some segments of capital were in on the winning coalition. But what is not really problematized in any sustained way is the prior question of why the interests of some capitalists prevailed over others in internal organizational struggles, that is, how it came to be that peak employer associations brought their full weight—including massive lockouts—to bear on behalf of the centralizers and against the opponents of centralization, who were members of the same associations. Swenson writes of "dominant" employer groups, but the source of their dominance is not established apart from the fact that they ultimately prevailed.

It may be that a certain indeterminacy is inherent in cross-class coalitional approaches. After all, there is no point in undertaking a coalitional analysis unless the outcome could have been different had that coalition not prevailed. This indeterminacy has been addressed by some of the more recent work, which stresses the role of policy entrepreneurs or state reformers in brokering the coalitions that tip the outcomes in one direction or another. We see this in Mares's analysis of unemployment insurance in Weimar Germany, where political entrepreneurs were key players in forging a coalition based on the second-best preferences of some unions and employers associations. In Swenson's analysis (1997) of the United States, too, policy entrepreneurs are crucial actors in "arranging the alliance" between segments of labor and capital around social policy legislation in the New Deal. The argument is that policy reformers acted on signals sent by prominent capitalists (that they would accept and indeed in some ways welcome certain forms of social insurance) and proceeded to craft legislation around these firms' interest in policies aimed at eliminating cutthroat competition and stabilizing consumer demand.

Emphasizing the role of policy entrepreneurs or reformers in many ways simply reinforces the idea that very different outcomes were possible, and indeed some of these analyses explicitly embrace a highly contingent view of key choice points. Such a perspective thus places a great deal of emphasis on agency, sometimes quite appropriately. However, in doing so, these formulations tend to obscure the *broader institutional arrangements* within which these agents are maneuvering and which often bias outcomes at various junctures by rendering certain coalitions more likely than others or by magnifying the voices of some segments of labor and capital over those of others. This is where the second literature noted above comes in.

▪ | Varieties of Capitalism: Bringing Institutions Back In

At around the same time that these authors were analyzing the role of cross-class alliances in the origins of corporatism in the centralized systems of northern Europe, another strand of research was emerging which also took issue with the labor centeredness of the corporatism literature. This body of work also brought capital back in, though on somewhat different terms from the coalitional analyses surveyed above. Some of the key works are by David Soskice, and the central variable that emerged from his work was that of employer coordination. Beginning with several important articles in the early 1990s, Soskice argued that the capacity of employers to co-ordinate among themselves—not labor strength and centralization—was the key to understanding the macroeconomic outcomes traditionally associated with corporatism. Soskice's original reinterpretation of corporatism did not so much reject the corporatism literature of the 1970s as it did suggest that this model no longer captured the key elements behind economic success in the context of more volatile international markets since the 1980s (Soskice 1990a, 171).

In this and subsequent work, Soskice developed a general theoretical framework for understanding divergent trajectories and degrees of success in what he called "coordinated" versus "noncoordinated" (or "liberal") market economies.[10] The core of the distinction goes back to differences in the capacity of employers to coordinate among themselves in order to create the conditions that can both secure wage restraint and encourage firm-based innovation and adaptation to rapidly changing markets. In an important article in 1990, Soskice (1990b) offered a critique of the influential Calmfors-Driffill model that had associated positive economic outcomes with either highly centralized or very decentralized wage-setting institutions. A major part of Soskice's critique of the Calmfors-Driffill model involved the reclassification of a number of countries (including Switzerland, Japan, Germany, the Netherlands, and parts of Italy) where the level of union centralization did not accurately reflect the degree of wage coordination that *employers* were able to achieve (sometimes informally) in these economies (1990b, 42). In a way, Soskice substituted the concept of employer coordination for the corporatism literature's emphasis on union centralization. He argued that when countries were correctly classified—according to levels of business co-ordination not union centralization—the coordinated systems actually still enjoyed a comparative advantage over uncoordinated market economies in both wage restraint and innovation (1990a, 191).

10. The nomenclature has gone through several iterations, but despite some changes in labels, the countries understood to belong to each of these broad types have remained the same. Thus, coordinated market economies include Norway, Sweden, Japan, Germany, Switzerland, and Austria, while noncoordinated, or liberal, market economies comprise the Anglo-Saxon countries—Britain, the United States, Ireland, Canada, and Australia.

Importantly for present purposes, Soskice views employer interests with respect to wage bargaining and other labor relations institutions (works councils, for example) in terms of the embeddedness of firms within a broader cluster of political economic institutions including financial institutions, bank-industry linkages, vocational training systems, and more recently, welfare state institutions (see also Ebbinghaus and Manow 2001). He stresses strong complementarities among the various institutions that make up each of the two types of political economy (esp. 1999, 109). Thus, for Soskice, coordinated market economies are characterized by institutions that: (1) ensure companies long-term financing, (2) assign unions a role in maintaining cooperative industrial relations within the company and in coordinated wage bargaining across companies, (3) encourage serious investments on the part of companies in initial vocational training for youth, and (4) sustain cooperation across companies in the development of technology and in standard setting (1999, 106–7). Uncoordinated market economies, by contrast, feature (1) financial systems based on short-term financing but also high risk taking, (2) more deregulated labor markets and more adversarial industrial relations, (3) education and training systems that emphasize general education over strong initial vocational training, and (4) limited coordination (indeed, intense market competition) among companies in areas such as research and development and standard setting (110).

In the early versions of the framework, the comparisons between the two types of economies were mostly invidious (the idea being that the former produced superior economic performance). However, more recent work with Peter Hall has fleshed out the alternative logic (including strengths as well as weaknesses) of the liberal or uncoordinated model. What emerges is a picture in which different institutional configurations generate firm strategies based on differences in comparative institutional advantage. Thus, "the institutional frameworks of liberal market economies [such as the United States and Britain] provide companies with better capacities for radical innovation, while those of coordinated market economies [e.g., Germany, Japan] provide superior capacities for incremental innovation" (Hall and Soskice 2001b, 41). As a result, each is associated with specialization in the production of a different set of goods.

Soskice's original formulations were very much influenced by a larger literature—much of it more sociological in orientation—that drew similar distinctions between what Wolfgang Streeck calls liberal and socially embedded political economies (Streeck and Yamamura forthcoming).[11] An

11. In fact, a great deal of contemporary theorizing in this vein can be traced back to Streeck's pioneering work on the German model of diversified quality production (especially Streeck 1991). In that body of work, Streeck challenged neoclassical economic theory by showing how social institutions that systematically interfered with the free play of market forces could produce a distinctive type of capitalism, and one that can in fact be uniquely successful in the marketplace.

important volume by Boyer and Hollingsworth (1997) also pointed to distinctive national "social systems of production" that are defined by a set of complementary and mutually reinforcing institutional arrangements that together support different types of firm strategies in international markets. In fact, this whole line of thought was popularized in a book by a French businessperson and economist, Michel Albert (1993), who draws a distinction between what he calls the Anglo-Saxon and the Rhineland versions of capitalism.

All of these works share a great deal in common. The core institutional features they point to are nearly indistinguishable. The countries they place in each of the two polar categories (however labeled) are also virtually identical (with Germany anchoring the coordinated market economies and the United States cited as the paradigmatic liberal market economy). All of these scholars also have trouble sorting countries such as France that seem not to fit either ideal type very well. What distinguishes Soskice's version of the argument, however, (and this is the reason I focus on it in the present context) is his emphasis on employer coordination as *the* key and defining feature that separates the two types of systems (1999, especially 126, 130).

In Soskice's version, economies based on different capacities for business coordination support distinctive types of firm strategies in the market, and employer preferences in terms of labor relations institutions flow from the contribution that these institutions can be expected to make to these strategies. Thus, for example, employers in coordinated market economies support centralized wage-setting institutions as a means to control competition among themselves in labor markets (reduce poaching) and protect firm investments in worker skills. Similarly, strong works councils come out in this literature as important mechanisms to encourage long-term and trustful relations between workers and employers, which is important for the success of firm strategies based on flexibility and high-quality production. As with the literature discussed above, this emphasis thus puts an entirely different spin on institutions that we typically associate with labor strength.

Implications for Contemporary Labor Politics

The varieties of capitalism approach has provided important insights into trajectories of change within and divergence across countries in wage bargaining and other institutions of crucial importance to labor politics. Hall and Soskice (2001a), especially, have argued that globalization pressures are if anything likely to enhance differences between the two types of economies rather than drive convergence. Because firms in the two types of systems are invested in different types of strategies, they and their governments will want to strengthen the particular mechanisms on which their comparative national advantage is based. This means that firms in liberal market economies such as the United States will have an interest in intensifying market pressures (deregulation), while those in coordinated market economies such as Germany will seek to retain previously built coordinating capacities in the face of new challenges. Although these systems are not invincible, they thus represent self-reinforcing equilibria.

This perspective finds strong corroboration in the conclusions drawn by two important recent volumes that embrace as an organizing theme the broad distinction between liberal and coordinated market economies developed by Soskice (Iversen, Pontusson, and Soskice 2000; Kitschelt et al. 1999). Synthetic chapters in each book—drawing on the combined research of the contributors—paint strikingly similar pictures of overall trajectories of change. The editors of both volumes conclude that recent developments point toward convergence within and divergence between coordinated and liberal market economies along a number of important dimensions (Iversen and Pontusson 2000, 3; Kitschelt et al. 1999, 444). If one looks specifically at wage bargaining institutions, the results are very similar (Thelen 2001). In liberal market economies such as the United States and the United Kingdom, the trend in industrial relations institutions has been strongly deregulatory—including the collapse of multiemployer or pattern bargaining, and an overall decline in the number of workers covered by collective agreements of any sort. These changes have been more dramatic in the United Kingdom than in the United States (given previously higher levels of unionism in Britain), but the dominant trends in both have been toward an escape from all forms of union regulation or, where this is impossible or impractical, a strong preference for dealing with unions that are cut off from national-level bargaining structures and strategies.

The trajectory of change in industrial relations institutions in the coordinated market economies has been quite different, although here too there have been substantial strains and, in some cases, important institutional reconfigurations. The breakdown of peak-level confederal bargaining in Sweden has received the most attention, but contrary to some of the more breathless predictions from the early 1980s of a slide into full deregulation, wage bargaining has reequilibrated at a level that very much resembles the German model of coordinated, multiindustrial negotiations (and led by the export sector which now negotiates more or less as a bloc). The changes in Italian bargaining structures, described above, move in the same direction—not toward deregulation but toward coordinated industry-led bargaining—albeit from a rather different starting point. Similarly, in Germany, employers' continuing interest in a high degree of coordination has played a role in shoring up traditional bargaining arrangements there, despite high unemployment and lower union membership than in the traditionally corporatist countries (Thelen 2000b).[12]

12. This entire argument, along with a survey of developments in wage bargaining institutions across a range of countries, is developed in Thelen 2001.

The results of more detailed case studies, moreover, seem to confirm that the broad patterns that we observe cross-nationally do in fact fit the logic of the overall argument. It does appear that the stability of relatively centralized bargaining in some countries is not simply a function of successful union defense against employer efforts to deregulate labor relations but goes back in some large measure to employers' own continuing interest in these institutions. The high premium that employers still place on coordination goes back partly (as before) to an interest in wage restraint, but it is also related to the extreme vulnerability of employers to industrial strife. If anything, this vulnerability has grown in recent years, as competition in international markets now increasingly depends on the ability of a firm to deliver at high quality and on a just-in-time basis (Thelen and Kume 1999; Thelen and van Wijnbergen 2000).

CONTRIBUTIONS AND CORRECTIVES

It seems clear that there is much to be gained from analyzing labor relations as one important subsystem within a broader institutional configuration that is sustained at least in part by the coordinating capacity of employers. The question is, is anything lost? Soskice's view of institutions has a distinctly utilitarian cast, and emphasizes how institutions solve various collective action problems in ways that redound to the benefit of all—in this case, of all firms.[13] Thus, for example, in the coordinated market economies, strong unions and centralized bargaining are characterized mostly as resources for (and not so much constraints on) firms that need to control labor costs, secure workers with suitable skills, and maintain cooperative relations with their workforce (e.g., Soskice 1996, 4–9). The kinds of corporate strategies that firms pursue in such political economies "require" industrial relations systems that equalize wages by skill levels (to discourage poaching), link bargaining across industries (to ensure wage restraint), and give workers incentives to maintain a high degree of flexibility on the shop floor (Soskice 1996, 1999).

What is obscured, however, in characterizations of labor institutions based on their functional or efficiency effects are the questions of power and political conflict that drove the development of these institutions in the first place, and the political settlement on which they are premised. This becomes clear if we juxtapose Streeck's and Soskice's different perspectives on institutions such as centralized bargaining and strong works councils. In Streeck's view, such institutions were manifestations of labor strength, and their existence, in his felicitous formulation, both "forced and facilitated" a shift toward firm strategies based on high quality, high skill, and high value-added production. Soskice's formulations, by contrast,

---

13. In this, Soskice's view shares similarities with a broader rational-choice literature on institutions (e.g., Weingast 1998; Weingast and Marshall 1988).

tend to deemphasize the power (constraint) side of institutions and to emphasize employer interests over union strength as the key to the existence and reproduction of such arrangements.

As the literature surveyed above shows, however, institutional arrangements governing relations between workers and employers are the product of political struggles in which there are winners and losers on both sides of the class divide.[14] To be fair, it should be noted that Soskice is not concerned with the *origins* of the institutions which characterize coordinated market economies and which distinguish them from liberal market economies but rather with the kinds of incentives that they present to firms as they adapt to currently changing market conditions. However, if it is true that institutions reflect political settlements, then the reproduction of those institutions cannot rest solely on the functional contribution they make to firm strategies. It must rest also, at least in part, on the reproduction of the political settlement on which they are founded. Since firms within a single national political economy participate in different segments of the international market (which may reward or punish different types and levels of coordination and where competitive conditions change over time), shifts in the international context should constantly introduce new tensions into even the most stable arrangements.

More generally, the fact that firms need particular kinds of institutional supports for certain kinds of strategies does not mean that they will get them. Solutions to various coordinating problems do not just need to be found, they have to prevail politically. In this regard, what is most striking about the rational-choice literature on coordination and collective action is that most of it rejects the straight utilitarian logic that is the backbone of the varieties of capitalism framework (see, especially, Bates 1988a). Instead, scholars in this framework have begun to invoke explicitly various cultural and political variables (Bates, de Figueiredo, and Weingast 1998; Greif 1998; Levi 1998a; Ostrom 1999).

Moreover, as an empirical matter we know that there are significant tensions at work behind many of the institutions around which the varieties of capitalism literature is organized. But these tensions are difficult to analyze within that framework, which tends to build from a stylized, composite picture of employer interests. In this literature, employer coordination is a national-level—and more or less binary—variable; this is to say that countries are coded as either *having* or *lacking* institutions to facilitate

14. I should note that more recent collaboration with Peter Hall goes beyond previous formulations that focus exclusively on efficiency effects to emphasize how institutions also facilitate deliberation (Hall and Soskice 2001, 11–12). This is important, for as Hall and Soskice note, strategic interactions often take the form of multilevel games in which there is no single, unique equilibrium and in which the capacity to achieve cooperation depends on the quality of deliberative institutions. The capacity for deliberation is clearly important, but it is not the same thing as power, which is what I want to stress here.

nonmarket coordination. From this coding then flow different (though again highly aggregated) notions of employer interest—in the case of coordinated market economies, an interest in maintaining coordination and, in the case of liberal market economies, an interest in further deregulation.

However, as the coalitional perspective emphasizes, different segments of capital have different interests, and conflicts among them are likely to be constantly activated by changing international conditions. In an ideal-typical free market, institutions that outlive their functions would be abandoned, and firms whose interests are no longer well served by the dominant institutions might just disappear. However, in the world of politics, firms, sectors, and established institutional interests will likely put up a fight. Only by disaggregating employer interests will we be able to analyze the political struggles among them and, in so doing, gain insights into the kinds of forces that can undermine as well as stabilize preexisting arrangements, for example, as the preferences of key coalition members regarding optimal institutions change in response to new market challenges (Pontusson and Swenson 1996) or as exogenous changes empower new actors whose stake in the old system is more tenuous or even nonexistent (Iversen 1996).

My point for the varieties of capitalism literature, then, is the mirror image of the point about coaliational analysis. The varieties of capitalism literature are extremely powerful and persuasive in laying out the institutional logic within which employers conceive of their interests and formulate their strategies. However, the weakness of the approach is that it tends to portray these institutions in an ahistorical way, neglecting especially the question of the political as opposed to the utilitarian or market logic on which these institutions rest. Among other things, an emphasis on the political settlement and coalitional alignments behind these institutions will yield insights into the (cross-nationally different) *fault lines* that we can expect to emerge in different systems in the context of putatively common international strains.

■ | Toward a Synthesis of Cross-Class Alliances and Varieties of Capitalism

The discussion above already foreshadows my conclusion, which is that each of the two perspectives I have outlined—one emphasizing political maneuvering and cross-class coalitions, the other focusing on institutional logics and developmental trajectories—works best when brought into closer dialogue with the other. From the political coalitionists we can take the important insight that the institutional arrangements that make up a political economy, including industrial relations and welfare state institutions, represent and rest on a particular alignment of interests and therefore balance of power within and across classes in capitalist societies. From the institutionalists we take the idea that these institutions cannot be reconfigured at will, not least because they are linked into broader configurations that influence the kinds of interests and strategies that both labor and employers are likely to pursue.

However, beyond simply plucking the best insights from each, the synthesis I have in mind brings these elements together in the context of an historical-institutional framework that incorporates a strong temporal dimension (Pierson and Skocpol, this volume). The coalitional perspective, while appropriately historical (especially in the sense of contextualizing the interests and preferences of key actors), is frequently insufficiently attentive to the institutional constraints under which these interests are formulated and pursued. Conversely, the varieties of capitalism literature, while deeply attuned to the impact of institutions, is often insufficiently historical and in particular strangely silent both on the political origins of these institutions and on the political processes through which they are reproduced (but also sometimes reconfigured) over time.

Explicit attention to institutional legacies and policy feedback can address both weaknesses by clarifying the ways in which interests and institutions interact over time (Skocpol 1992; Weir 1992b). Such a perspective, moreover, brings the constitutive role of labor and of partisan politics—which tend to recede into the background in both literatures—back into clear focus. Situating individual moments of innovation in a broader temporal and institutional framework will reveal, namely, that the choice sets that employers face at any given moment are profoundly conditioned by the historically evolved position and power (or weakness) of organized labor and its political allies.

To illustrate these points, I offer two brief empirical examples, one coming out of the literature on welfare state development, the other from the literature on trends in collective bargaining institutions. Both examples incorporate core insights from the literature surveyed above that "brings capital back in," but they situate employer interests and strategies within a broader framework that captures the impact of policy and institutional legacies that otherwise often escape notice. Both of them serve as a corrective to coalitional analyses that zero in on specific choice points but often miss the structural features that define the key actors and the strategic options they face, and to varieties-of-capitalism analyses that tend to emphasize the economic logic of particular institutional arrangements but neglect the political coalitions and dynamics on which they are based. Both examples illuminate important elements of path dependence in the genesis and evolution of key institutions that mediate relations between labor and capital in advanced industrial societies.

PATH DEPENDENCE IN THE EVOLUTION
OF THE WELFARE STATE

Recent work on the development of the welfare state in several advanced industrial countries has benefited from insights generated by the literatures discussed above. Work in this area is more likely than before to highlight the role of employer interests in the genesis of social policies that were conventionally associated with labor strength.[15] To stay with a familiar example, Swenson provides striking archival evidence that shows that Swedish employers in the early 1950s—far from opposing universalistic welfare policies—actively supported them (though they were careful to let labor take the credit) (Swenson forthcoming). Swenson shows how policies such as comprehensive health insurance and generous sick pay provided solutions to specific pathologies that had developed in the Swedish labor market as a consequence of centralized bargaining arrangements. Specifically, centralization brought with it both wage restraint and wage compression, which in turn caused labor market scarcity, especially in times of buoyant demand and growth. In such a context, firms had turned to other measures—generous plant-based social benefits—to attract and retain scarce labor, thus unleashing "unhealthy" competition among firms that existing institutions (governing wages) were unable to control. Universal welfare policies in the 1950s restabilized centralized labor market governance by dampening the resulting escalation of plant-based policies.

Swenson correctly asserts that these policies cannot be seen as a product of labor power *against* employers if employers themselves had their own reasons for embracing them, and this serves as a powerful corrective to much of the received wisdom. However, if we situate events in Sweden in the 1950s in a broader institutional and temporal framework, what is equally striking is all the options that employers might have much preferred but that never made it to the agenda. This is the gist of an alternative account offered by Evelyne Huber and John D. Stephens (2001), which is premised not on a rejection of the coalitional perspective so much as its incorporation into a framework that places what Pierson and Skocpol (this volume) refer to as "period effects" and "temporal boundary conditions" at the center of the analysis.[16]

15. Although, as C. Martin (1995) has pointed out, this work harks back in some ways to a previous body of scholarship in the corporate liberal tradition that examined business support for social initiatives as functional to the long-term interests of capital (e.g., Kolko 1977; Weinstein 1968).

16. To be clear, I think that Swenson and Huber and Stephens would not have much to disagree about when it comes to the interpretation of particular policy episodes. The difference, rather, is in what each type of analysis highlights. Swenson's theory clearly emphasizes employer interests or preferences, while Huber and Stephens are concerned with the broad structural factors that shape these preferences both cross-nationally and over time. Swenson alludes to the way in which

In their study of welfare state development across the advanced industrial world—an analysis that blends quantitative analysis of eighteen developed democracies with qualitative case studies stretching over several decades within individual countries—Huber and Stephens draw attention to the impact of broad structural conditions that shape the goals and strategies of key actors (here, especially, of employers). Analyses based on single country cases or on smaller slices of time, they argue, will often privilege agency and choice in their explanations of policy outcomes, because the structural constraints remain in the background, "unchanging and therefore invisible" (2001, 8–9). In such cases, "researchers are likely to attribute more causal importance to the preferences and strategies of [specific] actors than warranted, or at least they lose sight of the way in which the constraints of the larger power distribution and the institutional context shape the preferences and strategies of these actors to begin with" (33). In short, and as Cathie Jo Martin's work has also demonstrated, beyond pointing to the role of employers, the key is to understand the *sources* of business preferences, and addressing this issue requires attention not just to a firm's market environment but to the political landscape employers face as well (C. J. Martin 1999, 2000).

The political-coalitional approach discussed above is sometimes presented as an alternative to institutional analysis, which—it is argued—does not take interests seriously enough.[17] However, Huber and Stephens' analysis reminds us of the ways in which these interests are themselves mediated by broad structural factors (they emphasize state structure, the party political landscape, and market structures) within which contests among competing societal interests are played out (also C. J. Martin 1999). The welfare discussion in Sweden in the 1950s unfolded in a context in which a number of institutions were already in place, including centralized bargaining and strong and encompassing unions backed up by a Social Democratic party that had been in power continuously for the previous twenty years. Under these conditions, options that were very much on the agenda elsewhere—e.g., based on internal labor markets and strong company-based career ladders, as prevailed in the United States and Japan—were simply no longer viable in Sweden (Huber and Stephens 2001, 29–30). In other words, and as the varieties of capitalism perspective would underscore, what Swedish employers wanted in the 1950s was very much shaped by the kinds of strategies that these firms were (by that time) pursuing and that were supported by a number of complementary institutions that made

---

employer strategies are influenced by "established organizational practice, or economic, cultural, political and legal conditions" (Swenson forthcoming), but these are not issues that he pursues at a theoretical level (as Huber and Stephens do).

17. This is the approach, for example, of Swenson's critique of Skocpol (in Swenson forthcoming).

certain courses of action more feasible and took others off the agenda entirely.

This example represents a classic case of path dependence (Pierson 2000a), in which the effects of previous turning points become virtually invisible as once-viable alternative developmental trajectories grow increasingly remote over time. Huber and Stephens articulate at a more general level the way in which the legacies of past policies shape the goals, expectations, and preferences of key actors, and specifically in this case, employer strategies in welfare state development. Among the four mechanisms they cite, two stand out as particularly important. First, structural conditions affect the *range of options* that are available to employers in different countries and at different junctures. As pointed out above, if we focus very narrowly on the expressed policy preferences of key actors over alternatives A and B in a given debate, we may miss the much more important fact that X, Y, and Z are not on the menu at all (Hacker 2000; Hacker and Pierson 2000). Huber and Stephens' strategy for recovering the impact of these structural variables relies on counterfactual reasoning backed up by over-time analysis and comparisons between countries in which market conditions were broadly similar but state or partisan structures were markedly different.

Second, and at a deeper level, past policies affect what Huber and Stephens call the *distribution of preferences* by which they mean the universe of actors who are around to express their interests in the context of particular (later) policy debates. This is a point that I associate very closely with the work by Wolfgang Streeck mentioned above (1997, esp. 199), and one that Huber and Stephens invoke and deploy in a new way. The basic point is that "national frameworks of social policy contribute to distinctive competitive environments in which some types of employer activities are rewarded and others are not—and in which some types of firms survive and others do not" (Hacker and Pierson 2000, 15). In the case of Sweden, decades of centralized bargaining, wage compression, and social democratic hegemony set in motion changes that, over time, completely reconfigured the political-economic and industrial landscape. These factors "progressively eliminated low-wage sectors and thus eliminated one source of opposition, low-wage employers, to the further pursuit of [a high-wage, high-social-wage] path" (Huber and Stephens 2001, 30). Here we have a good illustration of Pierson and Skocpol's argument that policies often produce distinctive sets of winners and losers, and in at least some cases the losers in one round may simply not survive to fight the next (Pierson and Skocpol this volume).

In sum, although coalitional accounts are sometimes framed as alternatives to institutional analyses, it seems much more fruitful to think of them as natural complements. Capitalist interests are clearly important, but the *source and distribution* of these interests must be sought, as the institutionalists would argue, in the logic of the structural framework in which they find themselves. Moreover, once we situate employer interests within a broader temporal and institutional framework, the constitutive power of labor reemerges from the shadows. Attending to the ways in which the political and economic organization of labor shapes the strategic context employers confront is a necessary antidote to some of the more breathless claims about business interests in the construction of industrial relations and welfare state institutions. Despite the now widely acknowledged role of employers, broad cross-national research continues to show that a well-organized and politically connected labor movement is the sine qua non of strong and strongly egalitarian welfare states and other outcomes associated with democratic corporatism (Bradley et al. 2001; Hicks 1999).[18]

THE POLITICS OF COORDINATION: STABILITY AND CHANGE IN INDUSTRIAL RELATIONS INSTITUTIONS

Just as coalitional analyses are incomplete unless embedded in an analysis of features of the institutional context that shape the interests, strategies, and alliance opportunities of the key actors, so too would the varieties of capitalism literature benefit from more sustained attention to the *political processes and dynamics* that sustain but also sometimes disrupt the institutional arrangements to which they have so usefully drawn attention. To my mind, this is nowhere more important than in that literature's treatment of the singularly important notion of employer coordination. Much of the literature in this area treats such coordination as a condition that some countries exhibit and others lack, when in reality coordination is a political process, and an outcome that often has to be actively sustained and nurtured. While the varieties of capitalism literature has given us powerful tools for understanding differences in the logic of firm strategies in coordinated versus noncoordinated market economies, the use of employer coordination as a more or less binary, national-level variable and the language of equilibrium tend to blend out important aspects of the political settlement on which such coordination is based in individual countries.

Recent changes in wage bargaining can serve to illustrate. As noted above, collective bargaining institutions in the coordinated market economies have seen significant changes over the past twenty years. While these changes have often fallen short of a complete breakdown of coordination, they have often resulted in important changes in the character and level of coordination. This can be enormously important, for as Iversen and Pontusson (2000) point it, it matters a great deal to many (especially distribu-

18. Swank's work (2001a, b) attributes differences in the resilience of the welfare state in the face of globalization to the differing capacities of its main constituencies, of which labor is not the only one but the most consistent.

tional) outcomes whether employer coordination is achieved at the national level (as in Sweden in the 1970s) or at the industry level (as in Germany) or through more informal relations between large firms (as in
Japan). To make sense of many of the recent changes in collective bargaining institutions in the advanced industrial countries requires that we pay attention to the political processes through which coordination is forged,
maintained, and also sometimes renegotiated.

This point can be made clear with reference to the German system of
industrial relations, which most cross-national studies have coded as a
paragon of stability (e.g., Wallerstein and Golden 1997) and continued
functionality. Consistent with the logic of the varieties of capitalism literature, the resiliency of traditional bargaining institutions in Germany in the
face of many new strains since the 1980s rests in some large measure on
employers' continuing interest in wage restraint and labor peace (Thelen
2000b; Thelen and Kume 1999). These are two outcomes that the German
system has in the past generated with some consistency and with which, apparently, many German employers seem to be quite unwilling to part.

However, beneath the veneer of formal stability and continued coordination, there are substantial changes afoot. Without going into all the details, a growing chasm has been developing among employers who are
differently situated both within the traditional collective bargaining system
and in the market.[19] There is a sizable core of firms which remain deeply
committed to the current system of coordinated multiemployer bargaining
and which are willing (and able) to pay almost any price to preserve social
peace. But this group exists alongside other firms (less powerful within the
employers associations) which have been pressing for reforms within the
traditional structures and which, in the absence of such reforms, have—individually—simply been opting out of the system altogether.

As in the previous case of welfare state institutions, attention to the
feedback effects of previous policies and arrangements is critical for understanding the current situation, for in Germany the *very same forces* that are
shoring up centralized bargaining institutions in the short run appear to be
undermining these structures in the long run. Specifically, the German
system traditionally rested on a particular kind of accommodation between
the country's large export firms and its sizable sector of small- and medium-
sized enterprises. The core of the deal was one in which the large firms
typically bore the burden of industrial conflict in order to secure moderate
wage settlements that small firms could afford—and which typically did
not come close to exhausting the ability of large firms to pay. In the last
twenty years changes in international markets have disrupted this basic
deal, as the core firms in the German system—locked as they are into
strategies based on high quality and reliability which render them ex-

19. For a complete analysis, see Thelen and Kume 1999 and Thelen and van
Wijnbergen 2000.

tremely vulnerable to industrial strife—have become increasingly conflict averse. This situation has led to a series of industry settlements in recent years that come much closer than ever before to exhausting the ability of the strongest firms to pay, thus prompting a hemorrhaging of the employers association, as weaker firms opt out of the industry-level contracts altogether. The effects of such bargaining rounds feed back in deeply paradoxical ways—stabilizing the system in a formal sense (by allowing the unions to defeat demands by some employers for formal decentralization), while at the very same time undermining the deeper foundations on which it rests (because central bargains cover a shrinking number of firms).

The point of this story in the present context is to underscore the fact that employer coordination is a dynamic political outcome and that it is not necessarily self-sustaining. The varieties of capitalism literature tends to attribute the stability of institutional arrangements in coordinated market economies like Germany to the benefits of coordination (to employers generally) and the ability of leaders of business associations to recognize, protect, and nurture them (Soskice 1999). But the German case makes clear that the feedback effects generated by these institutional arrangements interact with changes in the external environment in ways that introduce new strains (or render old ones salient in a new way). As the coalitional perspective underscores, these arrangements rest on a particular balance of power within key employer associations and between these and unions. The continued viability of the institutions is not just a question of their efficiency effects but also the reproduction of the political settlement on which they are based. Thus, against the sometimes somewhat functionalist tint to some of the varieties of capitalism literature, it seems clear that there is nothing to guarantee that German employers will succeed in reconstituting their organizations on the basis of a new coalition or internal balance of power, despite the fact that their failure to do so might well be against their individual and collective interests.

This brings us, again, back to the issue of union power. The German industrial relations system has been invoked in the varieties of capitalism literature as a prime example of the importance of employer coordination (*rather than* union strength) to centralized bargaining arrangements. German unions have always organized a much smaller percentage of the national workforce than the classic corporatist countries of northern Europe.[20] However, what has compensated for the relative weakness of German unions in the past is a very high degree of organization on the employer side (Katzenstein 1987; Thelen 1991, ch. 1).[21]

20. At its peak, unionization in Germany was around 35 percent, a far cry from Sweden's 80+ percent organization rate, for example.

21. Since contracts signed by Germany's employer associations are binding on all member firms, a very large majority of German workers have traditionally been covered by union contracts despite modest unionization levels.

Contemporary developments in Germany now reveal the extent to which employer coordination cannot substitute for and in many ways depends on union strength and organization. One of the problems today stems from the fact that union presence is concentrated in precisely those core firms which are willing and able to pay a high premium for labor peace. One sees in Germany today the outlines of an emerging alternative cross-class coalition based on alliances of labor and capital within the large-firm sector but potentially increasingly delinked from small- and medium-sized firms. In fact, more intense cooperation between unions and employers within the large-firm sector appears to be contributing to a perverse dynamic that itself undermines the very institutions that both are trying to preserve (Thelen and Kume 1999, especially 498). Whatever the ultimate outcome in Germany, the general theoretical point is the same. Employer coordination does not just happen; it has to be managed and sometimes renegotiated in the face of new challenges. Moreover, it seems that in the German case employer coordination cannot substitute for union strength; it may be more precise to say that the former depends crucially on the latter.

▪ | Conclusion

The conclusions of this paper are familiar even if they bear repeated emphasis. As always, the analysis of institutions and of political dynamics go hand in hand. Cross-class coalitional analysis makes most sense when the political processes that lead to the success of particular coalitions over others are situated within a broader institutional and temporal context that takes account of the way institutions forged at one juncture create constituencies, facilitate the articulation of some interests, disarticulate other groups, and affect how various actors view their own interests, also in relation to others. These are the kinds of factors that are often difficult to capture if one focuses narrowly on particular policy episodes. Yet the impact of the broader structural variables is in fact often decisive at these junctures, making some coalitions and some courses of action seem more reasonable, or more possible, than others.

Conversely, however, the kinds of institutional arrangements to which the varieties of capitalism literature has directed our attention must be seen not so much as static or self-reinforcing characteristics of different political-economic systems but as the outcome of past and also ongoing political processes. In particular, the institutions that generate and sustain a high degree of coordination among employers in the coordinated market economies, I have suggested, do not sustain themselves; employer coordination has to be nurtured and, occasionally, even renegotiated entirely. To point to the functions of institutions is not enough, for in order to persist institutional and other outcomes have to prevail not just on efficiency grounds but in the political arena as well.

3 | Citizenship, Identity, and Political Participation

This part focuses on considerations of such vexing questions as the contours of citizenship in a globalized world and the differences between identity politics and traditional interest politics. Issues concerning participation and political behavior are placed in the company of questions about identity and the social construction of behavior. In so doing, all the subfield lines are crossed, for the issues raised here are central to political theory; challenge American, comparative, and international politics; and invoke methods as diverse as behaviorism, rational choice, and constructivism.

In "Political Theory and Political Membership in a Changing World," Seyla Benhabib examines the development of Anglo-American political theory in the 1990s with a special focus on studies of citizenship. Under contemporary conditions of globalization, she argues, the modern nation-state system, characterized by the domestic world of territorially bounded politics and the external world of foreign, military, and diplomatic relations is undergoing profound structural transformations. The four main purposes of the modern state—territorial dominion, administrative control, cultural hegemony, and democratic legitimacy—have all been weakened by these changes. What, she then asks, are the appropriate principles of political membership defining access and entitlement to citizenship for liberal democracies under the current conditions of the "deterritorialization of politics"? Focusing on normative citizenship theories as well as key institutional developments, she claims that liberal democracies are built on an internal paradox: the right to self-determination, including the right to control and police one's borders and access to them, and universalist rights claims which individuals are entitled to in virtue of being moral persons, not as citizens of a particular polity. Immigration, naturalization, and asylum and refugee policies are caught between these contradictory demands.

Kay Schlozman's assessment in "Citizen Participation in the United

States: What Do We Know? Why Do We Care?" notes that because research on participation has been connected so tightly to the development of the sample survey, only in the last half-century has it emerged as a field of inquiry for American political science. The past decade has witnessed important intellectual advances from work that grounds empirical research in the fundamental concerns of democratic theory to ask questions such as why do people take part, why are aggregate rates of participation changing, and what difference does it make? One important focus is on individual differences in activity. Multivariate empirical analysis makes clear that the origins of political participation are complex. However, the importance of mobilization through political, nonpolitical, and personal channels shows that the characteristics of individuals intersect with contextual factors in generating participation. Researchers have investigated a variety of aspects of the political environment including electoral laws and regulations and the nature of campaigns and candidates along with such social factors as the nature of the community and the nonpolitical institutions with which individuals are affiliated.

Explaining the decline in political participation in recent decades, a different intellectual enterprise from accounting for participation itself, defines another important part of this research program. Not only have voting and other forms of political activity waned since the 1960s, but participation in community organizations and clubs and in religious, voluntary and charitable activities and informal socializing have ebbed as well. The decay in voluntary activity is surprising because the increase in educational attainment over the second half of the twentieth century would have led us to expect the reverse. To explain these important puzzles, we need longitudinal, preferably panel surveys containing a rich battery of items and samples large enough to include ample cases of individuals who engage in such rare political acts as attending a political protest or making a large contribution. Unfortunately, it now seems unlikely that the resources for such work will become available.

Nancy Burns attends to another issue of identity politics in "Gender: Public Opinion and Political Action," arguing that we are at a tremendous turning point. We have conceptualizations, methodological tools, cumulative knowledge, and a vast set of new questions to answer. And we have at hand one other immensely valuable resource, the theoretical and methodological work in other subfields and disciplines, work that can be reconfigured and combined to illuminate the role of gender. Burns examines critical issues concerning conceptual developments and method (studying categories in an individualistic discipline), issues that have often characterized the contributions gender scholars have made to political science (linking life spaces), and issues that will and should drive the future study of gender and politics (building truly comparative analyses). The core point of her examples is to encourage serious interdisciplinary borrowing wherever it offers theoretical or empirical guidance.

Michael Dawson and Cathy Cohen assay "Problems in the Study of the Politics of Race." Lamenting the unevenness of our knowledge and the fragmentation that afflicts the study of race and politics, they urge fresh attention be paid to specific processes that produce different patterns of racialization at different times and in different circumstances. In promoting attention to the theoretical foundations of empirical research in this area, Dawson and Cohen suggest the value of linking studies of race to other bases of ascription, such as gender and sexuality, and advance a program of research linking normative and positive dimensions. This large project, they insist, should not be limited by the tendency of political science to borrow heavily from economics but should also be informed by scholarship in sociology, psychology, gender studies, and history. Key themes in a reinvigorated approach to race would include the terms of relations among nonwhite groups, the role of ideology and attitudes, state-based racial categorization, and the changing dynamics of immigration. Their overall goal is to reduce the level of parochialism they believe to be a characteristic of current scholarship in the field within political science.

Morris Fiorina examines how old theories face new realities in "Parties, Participation, and Representation in the United States." By some familiar indicators U.S. democracy is in an unhealthy state. Trust in government has dropped precipitously since midcentury. Political participation in particular and civic engagement in general are down from midcentury levels. Yet according to two venerable lines of democratic theory—participatory theory and responsible parties theory—the operation of U.S. democracy today is superior to what it was at midcentury. Fiorina suggests that this puzzle can be explained by noting that American politics today is less representative of mainstream sentiments than it was at midcentury. One important reason is that the personal material rewards for participating in politics have greatly declined in importance, leaving ideological incentives to fill the void. Almost by definition, ideologically motivated participators are extreme participators, reshaping parties and increasing polarization. Thus, centrist citizens turn away from a politics they see as unnecessarily conflictual, excessively symbolic, and focused on peripheral issues.

Amy Gutmann offers an assessment of identity versus interest politics in "Identity and Democracy: A Synthetic Perspective." The ever-growing attention to group identities and identity groups in normative political theory parallels their salience in contemporary democratic politics. Groups of individuals bound together by a given shared social identity based on nationality, ethnicity, gender, color, class, physical disability, or political ideology make political claims that range from exempting themselves from disproportionately burdensome laws to exercising sovereignty.

A growing and wide-ranging scholarship on group identity and associational freedom in nonideal democracies suggests that "Who should decide what and how in democratic politics?" cannot be answered without taking more notice of the political role of group identities and civic associations. The scholarship on identity and democracy is internally divided over whether voluntary or involuntary group identities generally operate for the better or the worse in democratic politics. What Gutmann calls the school of culture emphasizes the essential contribution that cultural groups make to the lives of individuals in providing a sense of secure belonging and a set of scripts that give meaning to individual lives. The school of culture therefore warns against treating the ideal of the free and equal person as if actual individuals could be conceived independently of any and all cultural contexts. By contrast, the school of choice emphasizes the value of individual freedom from involuntary groups, the freedom to criticize and revise culturally given identities, and a correlative right of free association. The school of choice therefore issues precisely the opposite warning from the school of culture: do not treat cultural groups as if they were primordial, sovereign authorities over individuals who should be accorded the civic standing of free and equal persons in democratic societies. This essay develops a humanist synthesis that avoids the temptation, on the one hand, to elevate cultural groups over the individual and, on the other hand, to conceive of individuals free from socially given identities. A humanist synthesis integrates considerations of culture and choice and attends to the dynamic interplay between group identities and democratic politics.

Randall Calvert attempts to stretch boundaries in "Identity, Expression, and Rational-Choice Theory." Political scientists usually see identification and expression as cultural or psychological processes, either basic to human motivation or deriving immediately from some form of built-in human orientation toward social groups, and thus irreconcilable with sharply instrumental and strategic accounts of human behavior. Nevertheless, rational-choice theorists have attempted with increasing frequency to bridge the theoretical gap between identity and expression, on the one hand, and strategic rational action, on the other. Calvert summarizes these efforts and assesses the contribution they have made toward our understanding of identity and expression. The survey focuses on three connected phenomena which either currently are or during some earlier era were viewed by political scientists as primarily identity expressive and irrational: voting participation, partisanship and ideology, and ethnic politics and violence.

Thomas Risse also seeks a convergence in paradigms in his essay on "Constructivism and International Institutions: Toward Conversations across Paradigms." As a theoretical approach, institutionalism can be differentiated from other approaches in international relations in terms of the substantive claim that institutions matter, that is, that they exert clearly identifiable and independent effects on political life. The various institutionalisms can then be distinguished according to which types of effects they ascribe to political and other institutions. Institutions might constrain behavior, but they might also influence preferences or even constitute identities. Rationalist institutionalism follows a "logic of consequentialism." In contrast, constructivist insights in the study of international institutions focus on a "logic of appropriateness" in terms of rule-guided behavior and the enactment of cultural scripts, on the one hand, and a "logic of arguing" emphasizing deliberative and communicative processes, on the other. Risse's essay emphasizes insights that social constructivism brings to the study of international institutions. Yet, rationalist and constructivist institutionalisms do not constitute either/or propositions, he shows, but complement each other to a considerable extent. He thus issues a plea for theoretical synthesis and for conversations across paradigms rather than continued trench warfare. He also mounts an appeal for problem- rather than paradigm-driven research on international institutions.

Seyla Benhabib

Political Theory and Political Membership in a Changing World

■ | Political Theory in the 1990s: The Return of the Real[1]

In his lucid overview of the development of political theory in the 1980s, William Galston expressed the hope that in the future theorists would "try harder to take real political controversies as their point of departure and to attend to the terms in which these debates are conducted. There should be less top-down theorizing or, to put it another way, more of an effort to employ the method of reflective equilibrium—judgment of abstract principles in light of concrete realities, not just vice-versa—that Rawlsians often preach but seldom practice" (1993, 41). Writing shortly after Mikhail Gorbachev's resignation as president of the Soviet Union, Galston urged his theorist colleagues to focus more carefully on actual historical developments and political conflicts, without, nevertheless, giving up the critical and normative functions of conceptual elucidation, institutional design, and assessment.

Much political theory in the 1990s was motivated by similar considerations. As the decade progressed, the big inter- and intraparadigmatic struggles between theoretical approaches, such as postmodernism, critical social theory, feminism, deconstruction, neopragmatism, critical legal studies, on the one hand, and the more empirical and positivistic approaches, on the

1. I have discussed these issues with many colleagues in different contexts. My thanks go to the editors of the volume, Ira Katznelson and Helen Milner, for their superb counsel and guidance. Thanks also to Amy Gutmann and Ian Shapiro for their extensive remarks on an earlier draft of this paper and to Carolin Emcke, Veit Bader, James Sleeper, Morris Kaplan, Peter Shuck, Glyn Morgan, Pratap Mehta, Jean Cohen, Nancy Fraser, Nadia Urbanati, Jennifer Nedelsky, and Melissa Williams for their comments during the delivery of some or other version of these thoughts at Columbia University, University of Toronto, University of Amsterdam, Harvard University, and New School University. Finally, I am grateful to my research assistant Annie Stilz for providing valuable editorial and substantive suggestions throughout.

other, gave way to a postparadigmatic peace. Not only were there signs of theoretical exhaustion, generated in part by the all-too-rigid separation of paradigms which had characterized earlier debates (see Benhabib, Butler, et al. 1995), but under the weight of historical developments, theorists across disciplines felt compelled to account for those differences which really made a difference. The civil war in the former Yugoslavia, ethnic cleansing, mass murders, mass rape, and the dislocation of several million people in the heart of Europe confronted theorists of "difference" with the moral and political obligation of stating clearly which forms of ethnic, cultural, linguistic, and sexual difference were worthy of our moral and political support and why.

The civil war in Yugoslavia was the bloodiest and most tragic, but certainly not the only, scenario that followed the fall of Communism in eastern and central Europe. To the early democratic triumphs of the Solidarity movement in Poland in the previous decade were added the democratization movements in countries like Hungary, the Czech Republic, eastern Germany and the Baltic states. As political scientists developed models for studying transitions to post-Communist regime types, political theorists reflected on "the revolutions in Europe" (Laclau 1990) from the perspective of the resurgence of democracy, social movements, civil society, and citizens' activism (Cohen and Arato 1992; Isaac 1998). The transformations of regimes in these countries contributed to the revival of one of the most ancient and honorable preoccupations for students of politics, namely, the study and design of constitutions (Elster 1993; 1996; 1998). The challenges of advising and designing constitutional transitions not only in eastern and central Europe, but in the newly liberated South Africa as well, put on the map some of the fundamentals of political regimes, such as majoritarianism, parliamentarianism, the role of the courts vis-à-vis elected bodies, the formulation of bills of rights, and their status within constitutional systems.

As the pace of history quickened after the fall of Communism in eastern and central Europe and the Soviet Union in 1989, not only in Europe but all around the globe, a paradoxical development made itself felt. On the one hand, global integration in the spheres of economics, armament, finance, communication, information, and tourism proceeded with a dizzying pace; on the other hand, cultural, ethnic, linguistic, religious separatisms, and demands for regional and local autonomy increased worldwide. Thus European integration under the aegis of the European Union was accompanied by intensified Basque separatist aspirations in Spain; continuing bloodshed among Catholics and Protestants in Northern Ireland; regionalist right-wing resurgencies in Italy through the agitation of the Northern League; and the emergence of Islamic fundamentalism as a political force not only in the Middle East but among immigrant and guest worker communities in Europe as well. Reflecting on the paradoxical logic of integration and disintegration,

Benjamin Barber coined the memorable phrase, "Jihad vs. McWorld" (Barber 1995).

Perhaps no other movement for cultural and political autonomy has affected the core of liberal democratic theory as much as the Mouvement Québécois. Building on the status of the province of Quebec as heir to one of the three founding nations of the state of Canada—the Anglophone, the Francophone, and the "First Nations"—the Mouvement Québécois brought Canada to the brink of a constitutional crisis. This state of affairs generated intense and creative soul-searching among many Canadian political theorists among them, Charles Taylor (1993, 1994), William Kymlicka (1995b, c), James Tully (1995), Joe Carens (1995a, 2000), and Ronald Beiner (1995). Under the impact of the Canadian crisis, the relations between group identity and liberal democracy, between liberalism and culture, and between multiculturalism and democratic citizenship were placed on the agenda of political studies throughout the 1990s.

Whether through its own internal logic of development or through the call of history, political philosophy in the 1990s has produced post- and multiparadigmatic works that are characterized by a greater degree of engagement with actual social and historical developments. Counterfactual thought experiments and rarefied examples, typical of analytical moral philosophy, have given way to a more serious engagement with institutions and constitutions, with social movements and cultural trends.

In the following, I would like to examine these broad trends by analyzing a cluster of concepts that are central to the study of politics from a normative and institutional point of view: the nation-state, citizenship, and political membership in liberal democracies. By focusing on what is at times referred to as the field of citizenship studies, I want to illustrate as well as contribute to the further development of a normative political theory that is historically situated and institutionally informed.

■ | The Deterritorialization of Politics

The modern nation-state in the West, in the course of its development from the sixteenth to the nineteenth centuries, struggled to attain four goals: territorial dominion, administrative control, collective cultural identity, and political legitimacy through increased democratic participation. There is widespread consensus that these four functions of the state—territorial dominion, administrative control, cultural hegemony, and democratic legitimacy—are all undergoing profound transformations. The modern nation-state system, characterized by the innerworld of territorially bounded politics and the outerworld of foreign military and diplomatic relations—in short the state-centric system of the nineteenth and early twentieth centuries—is, if not at an end, at a minimum undergoing a deep re-configuration.[2] James N. Rosenau captures these changes in brief and dramatic terms: "The international system is less commanding, but it is still powerful. States are changing, but they are not disappearing. State sovereignty has been eroded, but it is still vigorously asserted. Governments are weaker, but they can still throw their weight around. At certain times publics are more demanding, but at other times they are more pliable. Borders still keep out intruders, but they are also more porous" (1997, 4). Arguing that these contemporary developments present a qualitatively altered stage in the development of the world political system, David Held and his colleagues have introduced the phrase the "deterritorialization of politics, rule and governance" to capture these changes (1999, 32).

Globalization brings with it the embedding of the administrative-material functions of the state in an increasingly volatile context which far exceeds its capacities to influence decisions and outcomes. The nation-state is on the one hand too small to deal with the economic, ecological, immunological, and informational problems created by a more interdependent environment; on the other hand, it is too large to contain the as-

2. States, of course, can be nation-states, multinational states, and multinational federations. These categories are sociological as well as juridical. On the one hand, they refer to the composition of the population defined as citizens and residents of a state within a given territory; on the other hand, they refer to the legal and juridical representation and status of different peoples as they coexist with one another. For example, most European states, like France, Germany, Italy, Greece, and Sweden are nation-states, both sociologically and juridically, even if their populations are becoming increasingly multicultural. The United States, on the other hand, is sociologically a multinational and multicultural society, but legally, it is a nation-state, for arguably, with the exception of Native Americans, Guam and the territories of Puerto Rico (which has commonwealth status), no ethnic and national group retains territorial rights, and even the first three groups have only partial internal and juridical autonomy over their designated territories. Canada, Belgium, and contemporary Spain are multinational and multicultural states which are straddling the borderline between a federation and a nation-state. The province of Quebec enjoys the status of "asymmetrical federalism": Quebec has certain linguistic, educational, and social autonomy rights which set it apart from other provinces of the Canadian federation. Belgium is linguistically as well as administratively sectioned into different communities of French, Flemish, and German enclaves; the province of Cataluña in Spain enjoys considerable linguistic, administrative, and social autonomy.

Throughout this first section of the paper, I will use the term *state* to cover these multiple formations and will only resort to the locution of the nation-state when I am calling attention to the sociological as well as legal-juridical status of the political unit. From the standpoint of a theory of political membership, the changing nature of some contemporary states, as they face the challenges of increased multicultural and multinational autonomy demands, suggests new understandings of citizenship, as well as raises fundamental puzzles about immigration policy: Who determines immigration policies and entry conditions, and at which administrative and juridical levels—the city, the province, the state, or the federation?

pirations of identity-driven social and regionalist movements. Under these conditions, *territoriality* is fast becoming an anachronistic delimitation of material functions and cultural identities. As a global economy undermines the power of nation-states to define redistributive policies and to achieve economic justice at home, alternative sources of cultural hegemony are provided by the inter- and transnationalization of culture, the movement of peoples across porous state borders, and the rise of global media. *Democratic legitimacy* now has to be attained in nation-states where the "we" of "we, the people" is increasingly frayed and amorphous. The crises of redistributionist politics affect solidarity across social classes, while the rise of multiculturalist- and identity-politics-driven movements fragment the "we" and render its boundaries fluid and porous. Who are "we"? Along with the weakening of democratic sources of legitimacy through the decline of the redistributive role of the state, collective cultural identities are growing increasingly volatile and fragmented.

The changing character of the nation-state has implications for the theory and practice of citizenship. Citizenship in the modern world has meant membership in a bounded political community which was either a nation-state, a multinational state, or a federation of states. The political regime of territorially bounded sovereignty, exercised through formal, rational administrative procedures and dependent on the democratic will formation of a more or less culturally homogeneous group of people, can only function by defining, circumscribing, and controlling citizenship. The citizen is the individual who has membership rights to reside within a territory, who is subject to the state's administrative jurisdiction, and who is also, ideally, a member of the democratic sovereign in the name of whom laws are issued and administration is exercised. Following Max Weber, we may say that this unity of residency, administrative subjection, democratic participation, and cultural membership constitutes the "ideal typical" model of citizenship in the modern nation-state of the West (see Weber 1978 [1956], 901–26). The influence of this model, whether or not it adequately corresponds to local conditions, extends far beyond the West: modernizing nations in Africa, the Middle East, and Asia, which entered the process of state formation at later points than their West European counterparts, copied this model wherever they came into existence as well.

What is the status of citizenship today, in a world of increasingly deterritorialized politics? As a normative category as well as institutional practice, which has so far defined political membership in the state-centric world, how is citizenship being reconfigured under contemporary conditions? How has the fraying of the four functions of the state—territoriality, administrative control, cultural identity, and democratic legitimacy—affected the theory and practice of citizenship?

This contribution examines debates around citizenship and political membership of the last decades, primarily in political theory but with an eye to political sociology and comparative politics as well. My question is:

What should be the normative principles of democratic membership in a world of increasingly deterritorialized politics? If consequences of the new global constellation are the more fluid movement of peoples across borders and the formation of multiple political allegiances that escape the boundaries of national citizenship, what would be appropriate principles of political membership in this deterritorialized system? Political membership is one aspect of the theory of citizenship, albeit a crucial one. It concerns the institutional processes of access to and acquisition of the status of citizenship. It deals with the principles and institutions of incorporating aliens and strangers, immigrants and newcomers, refugees and asylum seekers into existing polities.

■ | Citizenship Theories, Past and Present

The practice and institution of citizenship can be disaggregated into three components: collective identity, privileges of political membership, and social rights and claims. While political theorists tend to focus on the privileges of political membership, social scientists and social historians have been more interested in the formation of collective identities and the evolution of rights and claims associated with the status of citizenship.

COLLECTIVE IDENTITY

Citizenship entails membership in a political entity which shares certain linguistic, cultural, ethnic, and religious commonalities and which can be distinguished from similar political entities. The precise form of such an entity, whether it is a multinational empire or a national republic, a commonwealth or a federation, varies historically. Viewed analytically, however, the concepts of citizenship, in the sense of being a member of a political community, and of nationality, in the sense of being a member of a particular linguistic, ethnic, religious, and cultural group, are to be distinguished from one another. Political communities need not be composed of nationally and ethnically homogeneous groups. Historically this was just as little the case in the multinational and multiethnic Hapsburg and Ottoman Empires as it is the case today in the United States, Canada, Australia, and New Zealand.

PRIVILEGES OF MEMBERSHIP

The oldest meaning of citizenship is that of the privileges and burdens of self-governance. For the ancient Greeks, a *politos* is a member of the *polis*, one who can be called to military sevice as well as jury duty and who must pay taxes and serve in the *Ecclesia* ("Assembly") in his capacity as member of his *Demei* (family clan) at least one month of the year. The link between the city and the citizen is retained in the etymology of *civitas* and *citoyenne* on the one hand and *Burgher* and *Burgh* on the other.

Citizenship confers on its holders the right of political participation, the right to hold certain offices and perform certain tasks, and the right to deliberate and decide on certain questions. Aristotle wrote in the *Politics:*

> The state is a compound made of citizens; and this compels us to consider who should properly be called a citizen and what a citizen really is. The nature of citizenship, like that of the state, is a question which is often disputed: there is no general agreement on a single definition: the man who is a citizen in a democracy is often not one in an "oligarchy." (1941 ed., 1247b–75a)

In making the identity of the citizen dependent on the type of political regime, Aristotle is emphasizing the contingent nature of this concept. It is not nature, but the city and its conventions, the *nomoi,* that create the citizen. Yet precisely in Aristotle's work we also see how this insight into the socially constituted aspect of citizenship goes hand in hand with an exclusionary vision of the psychosexual attributes of citizenship. Even if it is regime types that determine who a citizen is, in Aristotle's view, only some are "by nature fit" to exercise the virtues of citizenship; others are not. Slaves, women, and non-Greeks in general are excluded from the statutory privileges of membership, but this exclusion is considered rational insofar as these individuals do not seem to possess the virtues of mind, body, and character essential to citizenship. This tension between the social constitution of the citizen and the psychosexual characteristics that the ideal citizen ought to possess accompanies struggles over the meaning of citizenship down to our own days. Struggles over whether women should have the vote, whether non-White and noncolonial peoples are capable of self-rule, or whether a gay person can hold certain kinds of public office illustrate the tension between the social and the naturalistic dimensions of citizenship (see Kerber 1997; Landes 1988; Scott 1988).

SOCIAL RIGHTS AND BENEFITS

The view that citizenship can be understood as a status that gives one the right to the possession of a certain bundle of entitlements, benefits as well as obligations, derives from T. H. Marshall (1950). Marshall's catalogue of civil, political, and social rights is based on the cumulative logic of struggles for expanding democracy in the nineteenth and early–twentieth centuries. Civil rights arise with the birth of the absolutist state, and in their earliest and most basic form they entail the rights to the protection of life, liberty, and property; the right to freedom of conscience; and certain associational rights, like those of contract and marriage.

Political rights in the narrow sense refer to the rights of self-determination, to hold and run for office, to enjoy freedom of speech and opinion, and to establish political and nonpolitical associations, including a free press and free institutions of science and culture. Social rights are last in Marshall's catalogue, because they have been achieved historically through the struggles of workers', women's, and other social movements of the last two centuries. Social rights involve the right to form trade unions as well as other professional and trade associations; health care rights; unemployment compensation; old age pensions; and child care, housing, and educational subsidies. These social rights vary widely across countries and depend on the social class compromises prevalent in any given welfare state democracy (Soysal 1994).

The primary focus of citizenship studies in political philosophy has been, until very recently, on the privileges of membership. Largely under the influence of the liberal-communitarian controversy (see Avineri and De-Shalit 1992), the theory and practice of citizenship was examined from the standpoint of one predominant theme: In light of divergent conceptions of liberal justice and the human good, how should we think of the virtues and obligations of citizenship? Should citizens view themselves as moral persons with multiple and competing allegiances, as liberals enjoin them to? Or should citizenship be viewed as a "thick moral identity" that is constitutive of who we are as individuals in some deep sense, as communitarians enjoin? This literature on the virtues and duties of citizenship was largely removed from the historical and social analysis of the transformations of institutions and practices of citizenship (see Sandel 1982; Macedo 1990; Galston 1991).

In their critique of liberalism, or to use Michael Sandel's felicitous phrase, of "the procedural republic," communitarians are indebted to Hannah Arendt's political philosophy (Sandel 1996, 26–27 ff.). Particularly in *On Revolution*, Arendt (1963) argued that there was an ambivalence at the heart of the U.S. Republic. The famous principles of the Declaration of Independence sanctified life, liberty, and the pursuit of happiness. Yet as debates among the framers of the Constitution showed, from the beginning the pursuit of happiness was ambivalent between an individualistic vision of the good life, spent in the accumulation of material goods and the joys of private pursuits, and a public happiness, which could only be attained in the pursuit of common good with others, in acting and deliberating together. Sandel (1996) followed Arendt in believing that, in the course of U.S. history, the first meaning of happiness triumphed over the second, thus eclipsing the virtues of engaged and political citizenship.

As political theorists debated the identity and virtues of the citizen, a new literature on the evolution and changing logics of citizenship was produced largely by political sociologists and sociological historians (see Brubacker 1992; Tilly 1990, 1992; Hobsbawm 1992; Soysal 1994; Bauboeck 1994; Bader 1995, 1997). Retrieving some of T. H. Marshall's classical analysis (1950) on citizenship and social class, this recent litera-

ture highlighted the need to ground our conceptions of citizenship historically as well as sociologically.

Two books, however, marked a new departure within political philosophy for citizenship studies, and each in its own way attempted to integrate
historical-sociological with normative insights: Judith Shklar's *American
Citizenship: The Quest for Inclusion* (1991) and Ronald Beiner's edited volume, *Theorizing Citizenship* (1995).

In her three Tanner lectures, collected in *American Citizenship*, Judith
Shklar focuses on the contradictions at the heart of U.S. conceptions of citizenship. The ideals of equality and social standing are fundamental to
U.S. citizenship. Social standing means that one is free to earn one's livelihood and to become one's own master through work (Shklar 1991, 3 ff., 64
ff.). Yet the reality of black chattel slavery, which existed in the U.S. Republic from birth until after the Civil War, left its indelible marks on the
country and compromised this ideal. The tension between the ideal of
equality and the reality of slavery was transformed in future years into a
continuing persistence of racism, inequality, poverty, and class differentials
at the heart of the Republic.

Unique to Shklar's analysis was the insistence that the U.S. ideal of citizenship and one's status as a wage earner were deeply implicated in one
another. Arguing against those like Jean-Jacques Rousseau and Thomas Jefferson, who would ground citizens' virtues in agrarian communities of self-
ownership, Shklar claimed that the capacity to earn one's living through
one's efforts was more quintessentially American than these other visions.
Wage earners were not "wage slaves," as Marx erroneously argued, and as
none other than true slaves themselves would have claimed. Wage earning
required independence and skill, self-reliance and the ability to cooperate
with others in civil society and the economy. And these ideals harmonized
well with the U.S. conception of liberty as self-discovery (Shklar 1991, 71
ff.). Using the U.S. case as an example, Shklar gave the concept of citizenship a nonantiquarian and definitely modernist mooring. Not the martial
virtues of war and courage, nor even the political virtues of deliberation
and persuasion, but rather, the social virtues of self-reliance through cooperation came to the fore in her account.

Ronald Beiner's volume (1995) of collected essays bears an affinity
with Judith Shklar's in that, contrary to backward-looking jeremiads about
the decline of citizenship, both are committed to thinking through the
paradoxes of citizenship in the modern world. Beiner begins the volume
with observations relating to several historical events: the fall of Communism in east-central Europe and the Soviet Union, the growth of the European Union into a political-administrative entity, and the rise of identity
politics and multicultural movements, all of which challenge nation-states
from within. Beiner argued that these historical changes make it necessary
to rethink citizenship in the modern world. In the post-Communist period,
new nation-states emerged in areas which had been strongly multicultural

and multinational societies. Minority cultural rights became an issue for the Germans in the Baltic States; the Hungarians in Rumania; the Russian-speaking minority in Lithuania, Latvia, and Estonia; and the Roma Gypsies in Hungary, the Czech and Slovak republics, and Rumania. While the new post-Communist states were struggling with the dilemmas of wanting to recreate homogeneous nation-states in contexts that were hardly hospitable to them, throughout the 1990s some Western states like Canada struggled with multiculturalist movements (like those of the Québécois and the First Nations) which were demanding greater linguistic and regional autonomy. Citizenship and national membership stood in a tenuous relationship to one another. The contributors to the Beiner volume examined various aspects of the history and institution of citizenship along these lines.

The Shklar and Beiner volumes, in addition to anchoring the virtues and privileges of citizenship in the realities of the modern world, signaled a new realism and institutional perspective on the part of political theorists who analyzed this concept. Shklar's work, however, did not question the boundaries of political communities from a normative perspective. While it could be argued that the U.S. ideal of citizenship through social standing was particularly hospitable to immigrants, who after all joined this republic as wage earners first and citizens second, Shklar did not pursue this line. Shklar's reticence is characteristic of the field, in which political membership as a topic has been ignored. This observation is confirmed by the concluding essay in the Beiner volume by Will Kymlicka and Wayne Norman on "Return of the Citizen: A Survey of Recent Work on Citizenship Theory" (1995, 283–322). Noting the explosion of interest in the concept of citizenship among political theorists, Kymlicka and Norman state in a footnote that they will not deal with immigration and naturalization (310). Instead, the survey focuses on the responsibilities and virtues of citizenship, on citizenship and the welfare state, and differentiated citizenship in multicultural societies.

In *Theorizing Citizenship*, Joe Carens's contribution (1995a) alone, under the title "Aliens and Citizens: The Case for Open Borders," inquired whether the territories of nation-states were justifiable from a moral point of view and questioned the state-centric assumptions which had hitherto governed international relations as well as political theory.

▪ | Political Membership in Liberal Democracies

Surprisingly, political membership was rarely considered an important aspect of domestic and international theories of justice. The one prominent exception here is Michael Walzer's work. In *Spheres of Justice*, published in 1983, Walzer pointed out that membership is the first social good that needed to be distributed, in that the distribution of all other goods, like income and positions, benefits and opportunities, depended on individuals' being recognized as members of a polity who are then entitled to such benefits. Yet ten years later in *Political Liberalism*, John Rawls would still argue that, "The first is that we have assumed that a democratic society, like any political society, is to be viewed as a complete and closed social system. It is complete in that it is self-sufficient and has a place for all the main purposes of human life. It is also closed . . . in that entry into it is only by birth and exit from it is only by death. . . . For the moment we leave aside entirely relations with other societies and postpone all questions of justice between peoples until a conception of justice for a well-ordered society is on hand. Thus, we are not seen as *joining society at the age of reason, as we might join an association, but as being born into a society where we will lead a complete life*" (1996 [1993], 41; my emphasis).

Even if Rawls meant to use the model of a closed society as a counterfactual fiction, as a convenient thought experiment in reasoning about justice, by not making conditions of entry and exit into the political community a central aspect of a liberal-democratic theory of justice, he assumed that the state-centric model of nations with fairly closed and well-guarded borders would continue to govern our thinking in international relations. This became amply clear in *The Law of Peoples*: "An important role of a people's government, however arbitrary a society's boundaries may appear from a historical point of view, is to be the representative and effective agent of a people as they take responsibility for their territory and its environmental integrity, as well as for the size of their population" (Rawls 1999a, 38–39). He adds in a note: "This remark implies that a people has at least a qualified right to limit immigration. I leave aside what these qualifications might be. . . . Another reason for limiting immigration is to protect a people's political culture and its constitutional principles" (39). But marginal though "the qualified right to limit immigration" may appear in articulating a "law of peoples," it is not so. Transnational migrations and the constitutional and policy issues suggested by the movement of peoples across borders are central to interstate relations. It is not so much Rawls's claim that there "must be boundaries of some kind" (39), which is problematical, but rather his disregard of the rights and claims of others as they relate to and affect the identity of the liberal democratic polity. In not articulating explicit conditions of entry and exit into liberal democracies, Rawls is misconstruing the nature of membership in them. From a philosophical point of view, these issues bring to the fore the constitutive dilemma between sovereign self-determination claims, on the one hand, and universal human rights principles, on the other.

Despite the widespread neglect of questions of political membership in mainstream political theory, three directions of thought have recently crystallized among defenders of *deterritorialized citizenship*, advocates of *cosmopolitical citizenship,* and *civic republican skeptics* who warn of the decline of citizenship in the wake of these developments.

James Rosenau and Yasemin Soysal see the rise and spread of a new human rights regime, despite all its pitfalls and hypocrisies worldwide, as heralding a new political consciousness and new forms of political membership. The nation-state is waning; the line between human rights and citizens' rights is being eroded. New modalities of deterritorialized citizenship are emerging. Especially within the European Union, argues Soysal (1994), national identities and allegiances are being scrambled rapidly, and it would be hypocritical to want to make "good Germans" out of Turks when contemporary Germans themselves are hardly sure what their own collective identity consists of. Multicultural enclaves in large cities everywhere in the world are harbingers of the new faces of a citizenship which is no longer based on exclusive attachments to a particular land, history, and tradition.

Advocates of open borders and cosmopolitical citizenship, like Joe Carens and Martha Nussbaum, align themselves with the Kantian legacy of a world republic in order to articulate the transformative potentials of the present. Radical universalists argue that, from a moral point of view, national borders are arbitrary and that the only morally consistent universalist position would be one of open borders. Joe Carens (1995a), for example, uses the device of the Rawlsian "veil of ignorance," against the intentions of Rawls himself, to think through principles of justice from the standpoint of the refugee, the immigrant, and the asylum seeker. Are the borders within which we happen to be born and the documents to which we are entitled any less arbitrary from a moral point of view than other characteristics like skin color, gender, and genetic makeup with which we are endowed? Carens's answer is no. From a moral point of view, the borders which circumscribe our birth and the papers to which we are entitled are arbitrary, since their distribution among individuals do not follow any clear criteria of moral achievement and moral compensation. Citizenship status and privileges, which are simply based on territorially defined birthright, are no less arbitrary than one's skin color or other genetic endowments. Therefore, claims Carens, liberal democracies should practice policies that are as compatible as possible with the vision of a world without borders.

Cosmopolitical citizenship, as advocated by Martha Nussbaum (1997a), entails not so much a political practice but a moral attitude of not placing the affairs and concerns of one's immediate community ahead of those of others who may be strangers to us, residing in faraway worlds. In Nussbaum's version, cosmopolitanism is a universalist ethic that denies the claims on us of what is known in moral theory as special obligations. These are obligations that emerge out of our situatedness in concrete human communities of descent or sympathy, genealogy, or affiliation. Nussbaum denies that patriotism, which she considers a privileged commitment to a specific territorially bounded national community, constitutes such a special obligation. Patriotism does not trump "the love of humanity" and should not lead us to ignore the needs of others with whom we share neither culture nor descent, neither history nor genealogy.

Even if we concede that such a cosmopolitical moral attitude has many arguments to recommend it in many circumstances, it is unclear what political, as opposed to moral, practices cosmopolitical citizenship would assume and which institutions, if any, would correspond to this mind-set. It is also interesting to note that this was not the meaning of cosmopolitanism for Kant (see Benhabib 2001).

Unlike the cosmopolitans, the defenders of republican citizenship, like Michael Walzer (1983), Michael Sandel (1996), and David Jacobson (1997), see in the waning of the nation-state the decline of citizenship, whether under the impact of the rise of international human rights norms or through the spread of attitudes of cosmopolitical detachment. Citizenship entails membership in a bounded community. The right to the determination of the boundaries as well as identity of this community are fundamental to democracy; therefore, the argument goes, economic and political globalization threaten to undermine citizenship.

In an elegant passage which has been extensively quoted, Walzer writes:

> To tear down the walls of the state is not, as Sidgwick worriedly suggested, to create a world without walls, but rather to create a thousand petty fortresses. The fortress, too, could be torn down: all that is necessary is a global state sufficiently powerful to overwhelm the local communities. . . . The distinctiveness of cultures and groups depends upon closure and, without it, cannot be conceived as a stable feature of human life. If this distinctiveness is a value, as most people (though some of them are global pluralists, and others only local loyalists) seem to believe, then closure must be permitted somewhere. At some level of political organization, something like the sovereign state must take shape and claim the authority to make its own admissions policy, to control and sometimes restrain the flow of immigrants. (1983, 39)

There is a quick slide in Walzer's argumentation from "the value of the distinctiveness of cultures and groups" to the need for closure and to the justification for "something like the sovereign state" to control boundaries and set admissions policy. Walzer does not differentiate the methodological fiction of a unitary "cultural community" from the actual institutional polity. A democratic polity with pluralist traditions consists of many cultural groups and subgroups, many cultural traditions and countertraditions; furthermore the national culture itself is formed by the contested multiplicity of many traditions, narratives, and historical appropriations.

Equally significantly, Walzer does not distinguish among principles of *cultural integration* and principles of *political integration*. Cultural communities are built around their members' adherence to values, norms, and traditions which bear a prescriptive value for their identity, in that failure to comply with them affects their own as well as others' understanding of membership and belonging. Though there is always contestation and innovation around such cultural definitions and narratives, what does it mean to be an observant but a nonorthodox Jew? What does it mean to be a modern Moslem woman? What does it mean to be a prochoice Catholic? Cultural traditions consist of such narratives of interpretation and reinterpretation, appropriation and subversion. In fact, the more alive a cultural tradition, the more contestation there will be about its core elements. Walzer invokes throughout much of his work, not only in *Spheres of Justice*, a "we." This "we" suggests an identity without conflict, a unity without "fissure." It is a convenient methodological fiction, but its consequences for political argument can be invidious.

Political integration refers to those practices and rules, constitutional traditions and institutional habits, which bring individuals together to form a functioning political community. This functioning has a twofold dimension: not only must it be possible to run the economy, the state, and its administrative apparatus, but there must also be a dimension of belief in the legitimacy of the major institutions of societies in doing so.

Principles of political integration are necessarily more abstract and more generalizable than principles of cultural identity. Modern states presuppose a plurality of competing as well as coexisting worldviews; in the modern state, political life is just one sphere of existence among many others with claims on us, and the disjunction between personal identities and allegiances and public choices and involvements is constitutive of the freedom of citizens in liberal democracies. Of course, there will be some variation across existing political communities as to the constituents of such political integration: the typology of civic and ethnic nationalisms indicates such a range. Nonetheless, in liberal democracies *conceptions of human and citizens' rights, constitutional traditions as well as democratic practices of election and representation* are the core normative elements of political integration. It is to them that citizens as well as foreigners, nationals as well as resident aliens, have to show respect and loyalty, and not to the vagaries of this or that cultural tradition.[3]

---

3. Arguably, in some of his later writings, most notably in *What it Means to Be an American,* Walzer emphasizes the "twinned values of a singular citizenship and a radically pluralist society" (1992, 17). The pluralist argument does not consider cultural homogeneity to be essential for a stable polity but does require strong political socialization and adherence to common political values. This position does draw the distinction between *cultural and political integration,* suggested above; nonetheless, the conceptual problem as to how the obligation of an existing polity to accept immigrants and refugees is to be understood, remains the dividing line between my position and that of Walzer. Walzer's contextualism does not change in his later writings. See *On Toleration* (1997) and my critique in Benhabib, *Kulturelle Vielfalt und demokratische Gleichheit.* 1999b, 75.

■ | Membership and the Paradox of Democratic
          Sovereignty

Inevitably, these attempts to suggest new modalities of political membership in a globalized world have been vague. The institutional and normative practices that would accompany deterritorialized and cosmopolitan
citizenship have not been articulated. More significantly, all approaches
are avoiding or skirting a paradox, namely, that of democratic legitimacy.
Advocates of deterritorialized and cosmopolitical citizenship hardly face
this paradox. Defenders of civic republicanism, by contrast, refuse to acknowledge that there is a paradox at all, in that they collapse the boundaries between the ethical and the democratic communities or between
cultural and political integration.

  Liberal democratic rule in modernity means that all members of a sovereign body are to be respected as bearers of human rights and that the
consociates of this sovereign freely associate with one another to establish a
regime of self-governance under which each is to be considered both author of the laws and subject to them. Since Rousseau, however, we know
that the will of the democratic people may be legitimate but unjust, unan-
imous but unwise. "The will of all" and "the general will" may not correspond either in theory or in practice. Democratic rule and the claims of
justice may contradict one another.

  Yet this paradox of democratic legitimacy has a corollary which has
been little noted: Every act of self-legislation is also an act of self-
constitution.[4] "We, the people" who agree to bind ourselves by these laws,
are also defining ourselves as a "we" in the very act of self-legislation. It is
not only the general laws of self-government which are articulated in this
process; the community that binds itself by these laws, defines itself by
drawing boundaries as well, and these boundaries are territorial as well as

---

4. In her response to an earlier version of this paper, Amy Gutmann questioned
whether there was a genuine paradox here, as opposed to a conceptual tension, ambivalence, unclarity, and the like. I would insist that the foundations of all liberal
democratic republics are paradoxical, in that they are based on an affirmation of
two principles which necessarily, and not just accidentally, pull in different directions. These are the principles of universal human rights on the one hand and of
democratic sovereignty, requiring closure and exclusivity, on the other. The recurrence within liberal democratic thought and practice of the question of the nation,
and attempts to reconcile nationalism and liberalism are a confirmation of the
depth and intractability of this problem. The nation permits closure by making belonging dependent on birth right or, in some rare cases of civic nationalism, like
the French and the American, on acculturation and political socialization. However, whether belonging can or should be defined in such terms, and the tension
between such more- or less-closed definitions of belonging and universalist human
right principles remain unresolved. I follow Hannah Arendt in her trenchant analysis of these paradoxes; and like her, I do believe that more or less just and democratic institutional and political solutions to these paradoxes are possible. See
Arendt 1957 and Benhabib 1999a, b, and 2001 for further discussion.

civic. The will of the democratic sovereign extends only over the territory which is under its power; democracies require borders. At the same time that the sovereign defines itself territorially, it defines itself in civic terms: full members of the sovereign body are distinguished from those who "fall under its protection" but who do not enjoy "full membership rights." Women and slaves, non-Christians, and members of nonwhite races as well as servants and propertyless white males have historically been excluded from membership in the sovereign body. They were, in Kant's famous words, "mere auxilliaries to the commonwealth" (1996 [1797], 92).

Furthermore, as was the case with the American and French Revolutions, "we, the people" empowers itself as the sovereign in the name of truths held to be universal and self-evident, namely that "all men are created equal and endowed by their creator with inalienable rights." Thus the democratic sovereign draws its legitimacy not merely from its act of constitution but, equally significantly, from the conformity of this act to universal principles of human rights that are in some sense said to antedate the will of the sovereign and in accordance with which the sovereign undertakes to bind itself. "We, the people" refers to a particular human community, circumscribed in space and time, sharing a particular culture, history, and legacy; yet this people establishes itself as a democratic body by acting in the name of the "universal" (Ackerman 1991). This tension between universal human rights claims and particularistic cultural and national identities is constitutive of democratic legitimacy. Modern democracies act in the name of universal principles which are then circumscribed within a particular civic community. This is the "Janus face of the modern nation," in the words of Juergen Habermas (1998a, 115).

Let me stress that the urgency of articulating principles of political membership in the global era does not arise in the first place from an increase in migration figures. In absolute numbers, the middle of the nineteenth century and the interwar period in Europe (1919 to 1939) involved larger masses of population moving across continents than has been the case in Europe since World War II (Sassen 1999). Rather, this urgency arises in the first place due to shifts in interstate relations through the emergence of an international regime of human rights, and in Europe in particular, through the emergence of the European Union (EU). The political and legal transformations brought about by the EU are creating economic, constitutional, and legal quagmires in this domain (see Benhabib 1999a). Within the European context, three developments are of particular note:

1. The acquisition by citizens of member states of the EU of a European pass and European citizenship.
2. The increasing discrepancy between the rights of EU citizens who reside in countries other than their countries of origin and third-country nationals who are residents of EU member countries but

who are not European citizens. While EU citizens can vote, run for, and hold office in local elections as well as in elections for the European parliaments, third-country nationals cannot do so.

3. The agreements of Schengen and Dublin which liberalized border controls among the signatory countries (Belgium, the Netherlands, Luxembourg, France, and Germany in 1990, signed in Schengen; they were joined by Italy, Portugal, Spain, Sweden, and Finland subsequently), also intended to homogenize asylum and refugee-granting practices across the EU states.

Taken together, these three factors have created large discrepancies among the legal status of European Union citizens and foreigners, whether born on the soil of the country in question or not. There are no uniform naturalization procedures across the EU countries. Furthermore, in the wake of the Schengen and Dublin agreements, there has been a sharpening of admission requirements to refugee and asylee status throughout the EU. Whether or not these sharpened practices are still compliant with the requirements of the Geneva Convention remains an open question (Neuman 1993).

Other factors contributing to the salience of questions pertaining to political membership are: changing patterns of migratory flows and of sending and absorption models, mainly caused by the geopolitics of the world's labor markets; the large numbers of refugees and displaced peoples created through civil wars, ethnic and tribal conflict, and border reconfigurations, in short, through the decay and transfiguration of the nation-state structures in many parts of the world like Africa, the Middle East, as well as the Balkans and eastern-central Asia.

As Saskia Sassen notes, "labor migrations are embedded in larger social, economic, and political structures, and . . . they are consequently bounded in geography, duration, and size. There is a geopolitics of migration and there is the fact that migrations are part of systems: both set parameters for migrations" (1999, 155). Such migrations are now global phenomena. There are seasonal as well as long-term migrations from all over the Mediterranean basin countries, not only to northern Europe but also to the oil-rich countries of the Gulf region; likewise, the strong economic performance of Southeast Asian countries have created migratory flows to those countries from as far away as Australia and Germany.

With reference to patterns of immigration within and outside Europe, Rainer Bauboeck has recently observed:

On the one hand, immigrants who settle in a destination country for good may still keep the citizenship of the sending society and travel there regularly so that the sending country rightly regards them as having retained strong ties to their origins. . . . Temporary migrants, on the other hand, often find it difficult to return and to reintegrate. Some migrants become permanent residents in destination countries without being accepted as immigrants and without regarding themselves as such; others develop patterns of frequent movement between different countries in none of which they establish themselves permanently. . . . International migration transnationalizes both sending and receiving societies by extending relevant forms of membership beyond the boundaries of territories and of citizenship (1998, 26).

Add to these trends and currents, the figures concerning refugees and displaced persons.[5] According to the World Refugee Survey, released by the U.S. Committee for Refugees, in 1999 7 million people fled their homes, bringing the world total of refugees and internally displaced people to 35 million.[6] The main reason for this increase is internal conflict: border redrawings (Adzerbaijan and Armenia, Eritrea and Ethiopia); separatist aspirations (Chechnya); civil war as in Colombia, East Timor, Sierra Leone, and Angola; ethnic and tribal wars as in Bosnia, Kosovo, Indonesia, and Sri Lanka; and forced resettlement of populations, as in the case of the Kurdish population in the southeast of Turkey. "In 1993 and 1994 alone, internal conflicts worldwide forced an estimated 10,000 persons a day to flee their homes and either cross borders or become displaced persons inside their own countries" (Cohen and Deng 1998, 3).

These factors then—shifts in interstate relations, the patterned geopolitics of labor market migrations, the transnationalization of immigration as a result of changes in sending and absorption patterns, and the increased flow of refugees and displaced persons—all suggest that the question of political membership in the global era is a central aspect of the deterritorialization of politics. Contemporary liberal democracies will have to articulate institutional practices as well as normative principles to deal with this new reality, while remaining true to the paradoxical dualism of universal human rights principles and democratic sovereignty.[7]

5. The distinction between refugees and displaced persons is not a strict one; the same group of individuals can have either status, depending on whether they remain within the jurisdiction of their own governments. According to a Brookings Institution report on displaced persons, "Those who were forced from their homes for the same reasons as refugees but who remained under the jurisdiction of their own governments were excluded from international protections: their own governments were expected to provide for their well-being and security" (Cohen and Deng 1998, 2).

6. "Washington File. USCR World Refugee Statistics." *http://www.amb-usa.fr/ washfile/Wednesday/ 310.htm.*

7. "States the world over consistently have exhibited great reluctance to decide which persons will, and which will not, be admitted to their territory, and given a right to settle there. . . . States insist that they will undertake no binding obligations to grant rights of permanent settlement to persons arriving at their borders, and that each nation has the sovereign right to determine for itself which persons are

■ | Future Questions and Research Agendas

Disaggregation of Rights Claims

The irony of current citizenship and immigration practices in most liberal democracies in the world, including the United States, is that whereas social rights and benefits (like unemployment compensation, retirement benefits, some form of health insurance, and in some cases educational and housing subsidies) are granted to citizens as well as legal aliens and residents, the transition to political rights and the privileges of membership remains blocked or is made extremely difficult (see Benhabib 1999a, 720 ff.). Once again, political practice is changing slowly but surely. In Denmark as well as Sweden, foreigners, that is, third-country nationals, can participate in local and regional elections and be candidates for them. In Norway, Finland, and Holland, these rights are granted at the local but not regional levels. Similar attempts in Berlin, Hamburg, and Schleswig-Hollstein to grant local election rights to those foreigners who have resided in Germany for more than five years have been declared unconstitutional by the German Constitutional Court (Weiler 1995). What we are beginning to see is a disaggregation effect, through which the constituents of citizenship like collective identity, political membership, and social rights and benefits are being taken apart from each other (see Cohen 2000). One can have one set of rights and claims without the other: one can have political rights without being a national, as in the case of the EU; more commonly, though, one has social rights and benefits, in virtue of being a foreign worker, without either sharing in the same collective identity or having the privileges of political membership. The danger in this situation is that of permanent alienage, namely, the creation of a group in society that partakes of property rights and civil society without having access to political membership.

These changing institutional practices confront political theorists with questions as to why or how citizenship status ought to be granted or withheld from foreigners and resident aliens of liberal democratic states. Are citizenship practices constituent of a liberal theory of democratic and international justice? Or are these policy matters and institutional arrangements to be left to the discretion of individual states?[8] I want to suggest that the transition from membership in the institutions of a nation's civil society

---

acceptable for such admission" (Patricia Hyndman, "Refugees under International Law with a Reference to the Concept of Asylum," *Australian Law Journal* 60, no. 3 [March 1986]: 153, 154).

8. I thank Professor Brian Barry for having brought this question to my attention during a discussion of my paper at the APSA meetings held in Washington, DC, on August 31, 2000.

to political membership should not be blocked and that this is properly a matter of justice. Liberal democratic states can only block such transitions of status, insofar as they misunderstand and misconstrue their own dual normative commitments to respecting universal human rights on the one hand and being self-determining entities on the other. The transition from civil to political citizenship, I would argue, is a human right. Denying citizenship to foreigners and asylees, refugees and foreign laborers, who have resided in our midst for a certain period of time and who have fulfilled certain conditions, would be a denial of their human right to membership.[9]

Contemporary societies are complex, fragmented, and contradictory structures. In such societies human conduct and interactions assume many and diverse forms. We are just as authentically members of a family, of a neighborhood, of a religious community, or of a social movement, as we are citizens of a national or multinational state or a federation. While the modern democratic state remains a possible structural expression of democratic self-determination, the complexity of our social lives integrates us into associations that lie above and below the level of the nation-state. These associations mediate the manner in which we relate to the state. If we stop viewing the state as the privileged apex of a form of collective identity, but instead view it as a "union of unions" (Wilhelm von Humboldt), then citizenship should also be understood as a form of collective identity that is mediated in and through the institutions of civil society.

The increasing analytical as well as institutional separation of the three dimensions constitutive of citizenship—collective identity, political membership, and social rights and entitlements—suggests the need to rethink the identity and virtues of citizens from a normative point of view. In virtue of what do we establish our claim to exercise political rights? What abilities and competencies must we show to participate in and run for local elections? Increasingly, it is what one does and less who one is, in terms of one's origin, which will and should determine these claims.[10] Applied to

9. I have explored the philosophical aspects of the "right to have rights" with reference to Arendt's political philosophy in my Baruch de Spinoza lectures, *Transformations of Citizenship: Dilemmas of the Nation-State in the Era of Globalization* (Benhabib 2001).

10. I do not hereby mean to imply that all citizenship rights should be based on nonascriptive characteristics. The acquisition of residency and citizenship rights through family lineage and family unification procedures is based on ascriptive and nonvoluntary characteristics of persons. As long as the acquisition of residency and citizenship are possible through other than familial bonds as well, I see no problem in recognizing the special status of family claims. The argument here would be that rights which accrue to individuals insofar as they are family members reflect the logic of the modern state, in that the state relates to its citizens not just as political members but also as private persons in civil society and the family.

the case of contemporary Europe, this means very concretely: if an Italian or a Portuguese national can take up residence in Paris, Hamburg, or London and run for office as well as vote in local elections in those countries after about six months, what is the justification for denying similar rights to a Turkish or Croatian national, to a Pakistani, or to an Algerian who has resided in these countries, participated in the economy and civil society of these countries, and is a member of a trade union, religious group, school board, or neighborhood association? The liberal-democratic state is a "union of unions"; while the virtues and abilities that make an individual a good neighbor, a reliable coworker, or an honest businessperson may not be immediately transferrable to the virtues and abilities required by political citizenship, it is just not the case that there is an ontological divide between them.

How then can we formulate just conditions of political membership? What may we expect future citizens to know and to demonstrate competence in? Is it reasonable to impose language proficiency requirements on them? What about a test of civic knowledge, which demonstrates some acquaintanceship with the history and constitutional essentials of a country? And what do we do about the fact that most individuals who have citizenship by birthright may themselves be quite incompetent in one or the other respect in which we require newcomers to demonstrate proficiency? While civic republican thinkers may *inflate* the conditions of transition to citizenship to compensate for their own frustrated ideals of responsible and engaged citizenship, liberal thinkers may be inclined to *deflate* citizenship and reduce it to economic partnership alone.[11] A theory of just political membership will have to navigate some middle course between these alternatives.

I am not suggesting that first admittance should automatically lead to full membership—the logical consequence of an "open borders" position. Rather, I am urging porous borders, which permit transition from first admittance to civil and then political membership along a continuum of transparent, publicly articulated, and constitutionally consistent conditions (see also Bader 1997). Because human rights principles and sovereignty claims are the two pillars of the liberal democratic state, practices of political incorporation must respect the fluidity of the boundaries between citizen and aliens, nationals and foreigners. If there is a fundamental human

---

11. There have been attempts to develop an economic and narrowly utilitarian approach to citizenship and immigration policy (see Gary Becker "An Open Door for Immigrants—the Auction," *Wall Street Journal*, 14 October 1992, A14). Although self-interest considerations play a large role in determining immigration and labor market policies, they alone cannot define adequately the *nature of liberal democratic membership*. These theories tend to view the political association as some glorified insurance or shareholder company, thus eliding any philosophical characterization of the identity of the democratic polity. But political membership is not only about interests; it is about identity. It is not only about exit; it is about voice.

right to exit,[12] there must also be a fundamental human right to entry, though not necessarily to admittance. While admittance does not guarantee membership, it does entail the human right to know how and why one can or cannot be a member, whether or not one will be granted refugee status or permanent residency and on what grounds. The actions of the liberal democratic state should be consistent, transparent, and publicly accountable in their treatment of foreigners as well as citizens. In articulating such conditions, the liberal democratic state must treat the other(s), the foreigner and the stranger, in accordance with internationally recognized norms of human respect and dignity.

SITE OF CITIZENSHIP: LOCAL, GLOBAL, OR NATIONAL?

In a world of increasingly deterritorialized politics who should make decisions about citizenship rights and the transition from civil to political membership? My arguments in this essay have sought to expose the paradoxical and dual logic of liberal democracies, which are caught between human rights claims and self-determination assertions. Yet I have assumed that the state system, more or less as we know it, is the site for entry into and exercise of membership. Isn't there a contradiction here? Indeed, the dilemmas and issues posed by political membership send us to the heart of the tensions within the state-centric world system. As long as citizenship status is tied to membership within a territorially bounded and sovereign state, such states will remain the sites for entry into as well as access to membership.

A brief look at most international airports of the world, such as New York, London, Frankfurt, Paris, Amsterdam, Tokyo, and Mexico City, makes this amply clear: lines are always formed to distinguish citizens, that is, valid passport holders, from others who may be tourists or strangers, returning migrant workers, or noncitizen family members. Those who seek asylum and refugee status are segregated from passengers waiting in these other lines. In some cases, they are not even permitted to board their respective carriers; in other cases, when they reach their desired land of refuge via legal air travel or, if they are lucky enough, that is, not to perish on the high seas or in transport trucks, they are taken into immediate custody by government and customs officials. Their status at the moment of entry into a country without appropriate papers is not very different than that of a criminal: they are *les san papiers*, "those without papers." To be without papers in the state-centric world is a form of civil death. These practices often escape the sight of the democratic citizenry in the name of whom and for the protection of whom they are exercised. But should such

12. Although the U.N. Charter does not recognize a human right to immigrate, to deny this right to citizens is compatible neither with human rights to liberty of movement nor with the self-understanding of liberal democracies.

decisions be in the hands of border patrols and customs officials alone? What is the responsibility that democratic citizens owe to strangers and foreigners?

Two developments counteract these tendencies toward the increased policing of national borders: practices of dual citizenship and of city or regional citizenship. Dual citizenship, although rejected by many nation-states and kept as a jealously guarded secret by many others, reflects the multiple, overlapping and fluid identities of citizens under contemporary conditions. Worldwide, the number of individuals who count more than one language group, more than one ethnicity, ancestry, or race, as their own is increasing; yet our institutional practices do not respect and recognize the complexities of our cultural identities. The institution of dual citizenship admits to the potential disjunction between a common national identity and citizenship; but dual citizenship creates the specter of conflicting alliances and thus threatens the order of territorially bounded states. In the recent debates which preceded the reform of German citizenship law, over whether or not to permit birthright citizenship to children of foreigners, the specter of a war between Germany and the Turkish Republic, which is the principal sender country for the guest workers resident in Germany, was frequently raised. It was conveniently forgotten that Turkey has been a staunch ally of the West since the 1950s and is, along with Germany, a member of NATO, thus making it highly unlikely that these two countries would go to war against each other. As multilateral treaties and organizations like the Organization for Security and Cooperation in Europe, the European Union, and even the North American Free Trade Association (NAFTA) increase in number, the practice of dual citizenship will become more salient and harder to avoid.

New sites of citizenship are also emerging at thresholds and spaces which lie below as well as across the boundaries of nation-states. Countries like Switzerland practice cantonal citizenship: access to national citizenship is mediated through membership in and acceptance by the individual cantons. Likewise, there are developments in the cities of Amsterdam, Hamburg, and Bremen (despite the ruling of the German Supreme Court against them in the case of the latter two) to grant citizenship status to foreigners who have resided in these municipalities for a certain period of time. Amsterdam, for example, grants its foreign residents the right to vote as well as run for office in local elections after five years. Of course, the conundrum of individuals who may have municipal citizenship but whose application for national citizenship may be denied will have to be faced by these countries in the near future.

At what level then should entry and acceptance decisions be made— the national, the regional, or the local? We are witnessing indeed a "dispersal of sovereignty" (Sandel 1996, 345 ff.), downward and upward, but away from the nation-state. As political and economic devolution leads cities and regions to increase in economic importance (Sassen 1991,

1996), thus increasing the lateral dispersal of sovereignty, a more vertical dispersal of sovereignty through increased integration into multinational, transnational, and global organizations and institutions is also taking place (Held et al. 1999). Illustrating these paradoxical trends, within the European Union for example, while there are attempts to formulate a uniform refugee and asylum policy to be determined at the level of the European Council of Ministers, there are also attempts at formulating local and municipal conditions of citizenship.

POLITICAL MEMBERSHIP, IDENTITY, AND DIFFERENCE

One of the most intensely debated aspects of democratic theory and practice in the last decades has been the question of "difference." How do gender, culture, ethnic and "racial" differences among the citizenry affect the equal value of citizenship for all in liberal democracies (Benhabib 1996b)? Do the legal and political institutions, which claim impartiality and neutrality, serve the interests of all in equal measure? Or are claims to impartiality ideological smoke screens, behind which the dominant subjectivity of one small group among the citizenry is hidden, namely that of white, Anglo-Saxon and usually propertied males (Young 1989, 1990)? Are democratic representative institutions and the public sphere of current regimes so configured as to accomodate the subjectivity of individuals of diverse colors, cultures, and gender? How can democracies be reformed such as to accomodate difference (Phillips 1991, 1993, 1995; Young 2000)?

In this contribution I have not considered issues of difference as they would affect membership and citizenship practices. However, a disproportionate number of the world's population that is seeking entry and admission into liberal democracies come from usually nonwhite and non-Christian third world countries like India, Bangladesh, Afghanistan, Pakistan, China, Thailand, Vietnam, Cambodia, the Phillipines, Burundi, Rwanda, Algiers, Morocco, and so on. Women and children are those whose legal status of membership is most precarious. In most cases, in virtue of not having access to the labor markets, women and children can only become immigrants through family unification law. Immigration can increase their vulnerability by making them dependent on the authority of the male at home, not only for their living but also for their legal and civil status. However, in other markets where female labor is more coveted than that of male—the international "nanny connection," the manufacture of textiles and clothing apparel, some segments of the electronic industry—female migration can also lead to increased independence and financial and civil self-sufficiency for women. Citizenship studies in the coming decades will have to focus on the empirical as well as normative aspects of practices of political membership as they are interlaced with gender, cultural, ethnic, and "racial" differences (see "Hypatia" 1997, 1998).

The rapidly growing literature on multiculturalism (see Taylor 1994;

Kymlicka 1995b; Tully 1995) also has implications for membership and citizenship practices. As liberal democracies become more diverse and fractured within, as the unitary ideal of citizenship is challenged within the borders of these territories, it becomes more difficult to know exactly what to expect of newcomers and how to integrate them into the receiving societies. Ronald Beiner quotes Jean-Marie Colombani, the editor of *Le Monde:* "Just when we need a strong sense of nationhood to help integrate and absorb a new generation of immigrants, with different races and religions, the French are asked to transfer their allegiance to some vague European idea. This contradiction is feeding an identity crisis and undermining trust in our political leadership."[13] Caught between the pull of the European Union on the one hand and the demands for multiculturalism on the other, European nations in particular have become quite insecure about their integration and absorption policies.

A more confident note that "citizenship in diverse societies" or "group differentiated citizenship rights" need not lead to the decline of citizenship and to illiberal immigration practices is sounded by Canadian political theorists Will Kymlicka and Wayne Norman (2000) and Joe Carens (2000). Both are committed to reconciling strong multiculturalist visions with the basic principles of liberal democracies. Kymlicka, however, draws a strong distinction between the rights of immigrants in liberal democracies and the rights of indigenous peoples, who possess a "societal culture" (1995b, 80). Immigrants' claims to equal access to societal culture can be met, in his view, by enabling them to integrate into "mainstream cultures" (114). In addition to providing language training, argues Kymlicka, liberal democracies should permit special Sabbath and Sunday closing laws and special dietary regimes and dress codes for immigrant groups. Special representation rights, territorial concessions, or distinctive language rights are not to be granted to immigrants; in Kymlicka's scheme they are reserved for indigenous peoples and national minorities.

Carens argues that the asymmetry on which Kymlicka bases this differentiation collapses, for his concept of societal culture is fundamentally flawed (2000, 56). It undermines, in Carens's view, the claims to cultural rights for immigrants; it weakens the claims of smaller, more vulnerable minorities; it homogenizes culture and propagates a kind of monoculturalism (56; for a similar critique of Kymlicka, see Benhabib 2001). Whereas it is unclear what admission and integration policies—except for language instruction—would follow from Kymlicka's model, Carens claims that a "commitment to liberal democratic principles sets limits to the range of morally permissible policies. There are some things that no liberal democratic state may legitimately do and other things every liberal democratic state is obliged to do" (2000, 108). To demand some proof of linguistic competency is permissible, but to forcibly assimilate immigrant groups by

13. Cited in the *Washington Post,* 21 March 1989, A32, and in Beiner 1995, 20.

totally banishing their languages from the public to the private realms is not. Likewise, to deny immigrants entry on the basis of their color, creed, ethnicity, and religious beliefs would contradict human rights and the constitutional commitments of liberal democracies.[14]

Theories of multicultural democracy then, would not lead one to embrace a wholly different set of criteria for admission and entry than would other versions of liberal democratic theories. Rather, the distinctive accent of multicultural democratic theories would be in how they conceptualize the transition to political membership. Given that language and special representation rights, and even some form of territorial autonomy, are granted certain minority groups by multicultural theorists, what would be the basis for denying them to immigrants? Indeed, what constitutes the litmus test for political membership in societies with "diverse citizenship" (Kymlicka 2000)? Wouldn't there be a natural tendency in such societies toward the devolution of admissions and naturalization policies from the state and federal level to provincial and regional governments, as is currently the case with the province of Quebec in Canada, for example, which sets its own immigration and naturalization criteria? Would such processes of devolution be good for newcomers and outsiders? Would they be compatible with the universalist commitments of liberal democracies or would they lead to the resurgence of local particularisms and exclusivist ideologies?

CITIZENSHIP IN THE UNITED STATES: A MODEL FOR THE REST?

The institution and practices of U.S. citizenship pose a special dilemma for citizenship theorists: on the one hand, with the possible exception of

---

14. The most challenging philosophical issue confronting us in developing a just theory of democratic membership in the global era is to give substance to universalist human right claims, while respecting the right of democratic polities to set some reasonable and fair limitations on their immigration policies. The Geneva Convention of 1951 pertaining to the Status of Refugees and Asylees stipulates that the right to be granted refuge from persecution on the basis of one's race, color, creed, and political activities is a universal human right of the individual. This right of refuge also entails the right of "non-refoulement," that is, that refugees should not be returned to their countries of origin, even when their claim to asylum has been denied if doing so would endanger their life and liberty. Hence in extraditing refugees, signatories to the Geneva Convention must prove that they are being granted safe haven in third countries.

Given this status of international law, how can we define universal human rights in terms that both respect differences among various constitutional and legal traditions and set constraints on these traditions and practices? This puzzle about reconciling generality and diversity in the formulation of human rights assumes a particularly acute form in immigration, refuge, and asylum disputes, in that these practices bring to light most clearly the contradictions and frailties of the international system of nation-states.

Canada, no other major country in the world has been built around the integration, absorption, and naturalization of millions of immigrants, refugees, and asylees from the entire world. In many respects, the transition from civil to political membership that I advocate parallels most closely the U.S. practice of granting permanent residency to foreigners who meet certain requirements, thus enabling their transition from permanent residency to citizenship within three to five years. For the hundreds of thousands of permanent residents who become U.S. citizens every year, this is a process that requires proof of language competence; proof of residency for three consecutive years, beginning from the date of acquisition of permanent resident status; proof of financial independence or employment status (proof that the foreigner who is becoming a citizen will not be a burden on the state's welfare system); and demonstration of civic competence through a brief exam by an Immigration and Naturalization Service official. In many ways, and with the arguable exception of demonstration of financial status which itself permits different interpretations, these practices provide an idealized model of citizenship through consent and civil membership. Add to this the fact that any child born on U.S. territory automatically acquires U.S. citizenship, the United States presents itself as the total counterpart to ideologies of *jus sanguinis* ("citizenship by parental genealogy"). Nevertheless, even the practices of U.S. citizenship are riddled through with contradictions, inconsistencies, exclusions, and arbitrary classifications. Viewed against the evidence of history, the liberal democratic ideal of political membership by consent appears as a chimera.

In his impressive study, *Civic Ideals: Conflicting Visions of Citizenship in U.S. History*, Rogers Smith (1997) argues that "through most of U.S. history, lawmakers pervasively and unapologetically structured U.S. citizenship in terms of illiberal and undemocratic racial, ethnic, and gender hierarchies, for reasons rooted in basic, enduring imperatives of political life" (1). Singling out the struggle between the liberal, individualist, and civic republican traditions that have dominated U.S. political thought and practices since its inception, Smith nonetheless contends that liberalizing and democratizing changes have been often accompanied by the resurgence of inegalitarian ideologies and institutions. Such resurgences, more often than not, resulted in exclusionary practices which are at the core of the first nation in modern political history to base itself on the principles of popular consent through rightful association. Smith points out that "when restrictions on voting rights, naturalization, and immigration are taken into account, it turns out that for over 80 percent of U.S. history, American laws declared most people in the world legally ineligible to become full U.S. citizens solely because of their race, original nationality, or gender. For at least two-thirds of American history, the majority of the domestic adult population was also ineligible for full citizenship for the same reasons"

(1997, 15). Far from being a model, in Smith's account, U.S. citizenship turns into an example to be avoided.[15]

Smith sees these ideological inconsistencies and contradictory and exclusivist practices to be driven by the imperatives of elites to offer myths of civic identity and foster a sense of peoplehood. From a normative point of view, however, his observations raise the question whether liberal democracies should permit any kind of closure at all. We are dealing with two kinds of exclusion here. On the one hand, there is the exclusion of those who have been denied legal personhood and political citizenship, namely black chattel slaves, until after the Civil War (1865) and the passage of the Fourteenth Amendment. Women, who were not granted full suffrage in the United States until 1920, were nonetheless citizens. On the other hand, we find immigration and naturalization laws pertaining to everything from the voting status of foreign residents to the military obligations of foreigners, immigrants, and fortune seekers, who have flocked to the United States in the last two and a half centuries.

While conceding that the first two kinds of exclusion constitute blatant injustices and historical wrongs, one has to ask whether Smith's account heeds the distinction between *justice claims* in a liberal democratic understanding of membership and *policy matters* which should be left to the discretion of the lawmakers. Throughout much of its history, the United States's immigration and naturalization practices have been governed by quotas not only pertaining to race and gender but also to nationality, ethnic origin, and even religion. It is interesting that for Smith these quota-based exclusions cannot be regarded as the prerogative of a political sovereign. In fact, Smith extends the same liberal, universalist nondiscrimination clauses to citizens and strangers, members and residents alike. If Michael Walzer and John Rawls err by stressing the sovereign right of collectivities to determine immigration and naturalization policies—without spelling out the constraints which ought to guide such policies—Smith errs by eliminating the tension between universal rights and sovereignty claims altogether.

---

15. With the passage of the Immigration and National Acts Amendments of 1965 (*U.S. Statutes at Large* 79 [1965]: 911), discriminatory immigration clauses which had all but prevented immigrants from Asia and other third world countries to come to the United States were declared illegal. Prior to 1965, U.S. law had consistently restricted non-European immigration. A 1790 federal law limited citizenship privileges to whites; blacks (including slaves and free blacks) and Chinese immigrants who came to the United States to work in the 1840s were not accorded citizenship rights. In the 1920s national origin laws were passed that expressly gave preference to established European groups, while barring Japanese immigration entirely. Since 1965 these patterns have radically changed: In 1992, 29 percent of immigrants came from Asia and 44 percent came from Latin America and the Caribbean (see D. L. Coleman 1996, 1120–21, n. 149).

What, if any kind of closure then, becomes justifiable in liberal democracies? Smith's answer would be: none based on ascriptive characteristics of individuals, including not only race and gender but nationality, ethnicity, linguistic, and religious background as well. I agree with this claim. Citizenship, immigration and naturalization practices ought to be governed by standards of universal human rights that individuals are entitled to by virtue of being human. But policies which are *governed* by these principles may not be *determined* by them. As Carens puts it: "There are some things that no liberal democratic state may legitimately do and other things that every liberal democratic state is obliged to do" (2000, 108). Where do we draw the line? This is a question that Smith's book urgently raises but does not answer.

■ | Conclusion

As trends toward the deterritorialization of politics continue, as changes in absorption and immigration patterns hold apace, as the numbers of refugees and displaced persons rises, and as new political regimes like the EU in Europe emerge, political membership will remain one of the most-pressing theoretical and practical problems for liberal democracies for the next half-century. Liberal democracies, which are caught between human rights claims and sovereignty assertions, will have to examine their immigration, absorption, and naturalization policies in the light of these dual commitments. Immigration law has rarely left the domain of administrative regulation; it has rarely been discussed as an aspect of constitutional tradition and interpretation (see Neuman 1996). Under the impact of social and political changes, this state of affairs is changing in Europe as well as the United States. We can expect that in the next couple of decades, significant constitutional issues will emerge in the wake of the deterritorialization of politics. A new political constellation will demand new political answers. I have suggested in this contribution that the most compelling answers to these problems will require not only normative theory but a hybrid mode that draws on historical-institutional analysis, as well as comparative politics and jurisprudence.

Kay Lehman Schlozman

Citizen Participation in America: What Do We Know? Why Do We Care?[1]

Citizen participation goes to the heart of democracy. In fact, it is difficult to imagine democracy on a national scale without the right of citizens to take part freely in politics. Through their political participation, citizens seek to control who will hold public office and to influence what policy-makers do when they govern. When they take part politically, citizens communicate information about their preferences and needs and generate pressure on public officials to respond. Concern about the participation of American citizens as an object of systematic investigation by political scientists dates back at least as far as Harold Gosnell's pathbreaking work, *Getting Out the Vote* (1927). However, because research on participation is connected so tightly to the development of the sample survey, only in the last half-century has it emerged as a field of inquiry for American political science. The past decade has witnessed important intellectual advances from work that grounds empirical research in the fundamental concerns of democratic theory. This chapter reviews that literature and asks: What is participation and why do we care about it? Why do people take part? How can we explain the decline in aggregate rates of participation? What does the tyranny of the sample survey imply for participation research?[2]

Many, though by no means all, Americans are active in politics. Roughly half of American adults will cast a ballot in a presidential election,

1. This essay draws heavily from what I have learned about political participation from Henry E. Brady, Nancy Burns, and Sidney Verba and from our jointly authored work. I am fortunate, indeed, to have benefited from their brains, their wisdom, and their friendship in the course of a long research collaboration. I am grateful to Henry, Nancy, Sidney—and to Jan Leighley and Robert Y. Shapiro—for helpful comments.

2. A number of helpful sources contain general discussions of political participation. Among them are Milbrath and Goel 1977, Bennett and Bennett 1986, Leighley 1995, Brady 1999, and Conway 2000. These sources provide extensive references to earlier works and thus are an important supplement to the emphasis in this chapter on research published over the past decade.

but fewer than one-tenth will campaign for any candidate. In any year, roughly one in three will get in touch with a public official, one in six will work informally with others in the neighborhood or community to solve a local problem, and fewer than one in twenty will attend a protest or march. About half belong to an organization that takes stands in politics. It is widely known that the United States lags behind other democracies in electoral turnout, a regularity that is explained by a number of factors: the fact that voter registration is left to the initiative of the individual in the United States, the scheduling of elections on Tuesdays, the possibility of divided government, the number of elections and the length of the electoral ballot, the absence of polarization between the parties, the weakness of the parties as mobilizers of citizens, and the way that turnout is measured.[3] However, what is true for voting is not true for all kinds of political participation. When it comes to other forms of political activity—for example, contacting public officials, working in electoral campaigns, or getting involved in their communities—rates of participation in America compare very favorably with those in other democracies.[4]

■ | Mapping the Terrain: The Boundaries of Voluntary Political Activity

"Voluntary political participation" refers simply to activity that has the intent or effect of influencing government action, either directly by affecting the making or implementation of public policy or indirectly by influencing the selection of people who make those policies. Citizens in American democracy who wish to have an impact have a variety of participatory options. They can communicate their concerns and opinions directly to policymakers, or they can seek to affect policy indirectly by influencing electoral outcomes. They can donate their time or their money. They can use conventional techniques or protest tactics. They can work locally or nationally, with others or on their own, in an informal effort or in the context of a formal organization.[5]

Each of the three defining components of the domain of behavior known as "voluntary political activity" has porous, ill-defined borders. First, with respect to the *political* nature of this domain of endeavor, it is essential to recognize that the distinction between political and nonpolitical ac-

3. For summaries of these arguments and extensive citations, see Teixeira 1992, 9–18; Dalton 1996, 43–47; and Lijphart 1997.

4. See Verba, Schlozman, and Brady 1995, 69–70; Dalton 1996, ch. 3; and Putnam 2000, p. 31.

5. For an extremely useful guide to the various kinds of participatory acts, the technical problems in measuring participation, and the available data sources, see Brady 1999.

tivity is by no means clear, and voluntary activity in both the religious and secular domains outside of politics intersects with politics in many ways. For one thing, participation in these spheres is in many ways a politicizing experience. Those who engage in voluntary activity outside politics may develop organizational and communications skills that are transferrable to politics; they may make social contacts and, thus, become part of networks through which requests for participation in politics are mediated; and they may be exposed to political cues and messages, as when a minister gives a sermon on a political topic or when organization members chat informally about politics at a meeting.

Furthermore, the institutions that provide a context for nonpolitical voluntary participation have a complex relationship to politics and public purposes. For example, churches and, especially, nonprofit organizations undertake many activities—ranging from aiding the homeless to funding cancer research to supporting the symphony—that are also undertaken by governments here and abroad.[6] Moreover, many voluntary associations and even churches get involved directly in politics, and their attempts at influencing policy outcomes constitute a crucial source of input about citizen views and preferences. Support of an organization that takes stands on public issues, even passive support or support motivated by concerns other than government influence, represents a form of political activity. For many citizens it may be the main form of political participation, albeit often at second hand.

Activity that is *voluntary* is not obligatory and receives, if any pay at all, only token financial compensation. Nevertheless, the boundary between choice and coercion is indistinct. When a request for participation is accompanied by leverage—for example, when it comes from the boss—the boundary of the voluntary may be breached. Similarly, the distinction between voluntary activity and paid work is not always clear. It is possible to serve private economic purposes through social and political activism. Many people seek to do well while doing good, undertaking voluntary activity for which they receive no compensation—for example, in their churches, in charities, in politics—in order to make contacts or otherwise enhance their jobs or careers or to pursue policy goals that have consequences for their pocketbooks.

Finally, with respect to *activity*, it is sometimes difficult to distinguish the point at which actually doing politics shades into being attentive to politics. Thus, working for a mayoral candidate or attending a pro-life march are clearly political acts, but what about following political events in the news or watching public affairs programs on television? Similarly ambiguous is the status of communication about political issues—political discus-

6. Indeed, the sharing of functions among a variety of private, nonprofit, and public institutions is one of the hallmarks of the peculiar American political economy. On this theme, see the essays in Wuthnow 1991.

sions among friends, letters to the editor of a newspaper, calls to radio talk shows—in which the target audience is not a public official.

The fuzziness of the borders that surround the domain of voluntary political activity implies that, no matter how sophisticated the conceptualization of this terrain, what really matters are the actual measures. Many studies of political participation focus exclusively on what is, at least with respect to national politics in any modern democracy, the single most important political act: the vote. Although its decisive role in the choice of governing elites renders the vote as the first among equals of forms of democratic participation, the vote is in many ways distinctive among participatory acts. Because voting is, by far, the most common form of political activity and because the principle of one-person, one-vote implies that the vote cannot be multiplied in volume, voters are, in the aggregate, more representative of the public than are other groups of participants. Furthermore, the constellation of participatory factors that explain voting is different from that for other political activities: attitudes such as political interest figure more importantly and civic skills less importantly in the explanation. In addition, the rewards attendant to voting are sui generis: voting provides more in the way of civic gratifications such as the sense of having done one's duty and less in the way of material or social benefits. For these reasons, it is a mistake to use voting as a surrogate for the entire array of kinds of political activity.[7]

■ | Why Does Democratic Participation Matter?

Discussions about democratic participation—and civic engagement more generally—are ordinarily conducted as if the reasons why we care about it are self-evident. Rather than make such presumptions, it seems appropriate to make explicit why political participation matters. When we bother to ask, we see that there are three broad categories of reasons for caring about levels of political activity: the creation of community and the cultivation of democratic virtues, the development of the capacities of the individual, and the equal protection of interests in public life.[8]

7. On the ways that voting is unique among political activities, see Verba, Schlozman, and Brady 1995.

8. This discussion of the various reasons for concern about participation, which draws heavily on Schlozman, Verba, and Brady 1999, ch. 12, makes no claims to being either novel or definitive. There are a number of helpful discussions—which vary in the rubrics used to categorize the salutary consequences of civic involvement—about why we care about civic engagement. Among them are Mansbridge 1980, ch. 17; Parry, Moyser, and Day 1992, ch. 1; Putnam 1993a; Skocpol 1996; Newton 1997; Edwards and Foley 1997; and Putnam 2000, esp. sec. 4. For empirical results based on experimental data, see Morrell 1999. For philosophically informed analyses of the consequences of associational life, see Rosenblum 1998b and M. E. Warren 1998, 2001.

First, political participation—and voluntary activity more generally—have implications for community and democracy. The heirs to Tocqueville who make this argument stress several themes. When people work together voluntarily—whether for political or nonpolitical ends—democratic orientations and skills are fostered: social trust,[9] norms of reciprocity and cooperation, and the capacity to transcend narrow points of view and conceptualize the common good.[10] Thus, when there is a vigorous sector of voluntary involvement—and the strong associational foundation that underlies it—it becomes easier for communities and for democratic nations to engage in joint activity and to produce public goods. Communities characterized by high levels of voluntary activity are in many ways better places to live: the schools are better, crime rates are lower, and tax evasion is less common.[11] Moreover, a vital arena of voluntary activity between individual and state protects citizens from overweening state power and preserves freedom. Those who are concerned about declining rates of civic participation in the United States emphasize these multiple beneficial consequences for politics and society.

The other two reasons for concern about levels of political participation shift our attention from social to individual benefits. Not only does the community gain when citizens take part but, as John Stuart Mill pointed out, individuals grow and learn through their activity. Political participation builds individual capacities in several ways: those who take part learn about community and society, they develop civic skills that can be carried throughout their lives, and they can come to have a greater appreciation of the needs and interests of others and of society as a whole.[12]

The third rationale for concern about civic engagement, one that has particular relevance for political scientists, acknowledges the conflicting interests of individuals and groups and focuses on equal protection of interests. This perspective draws nourishment from Madison's fundamental

9. This perspective clearly draws from James S. Coleman's concept (1988) of social capital. For an informative essay on the relationship between social capital and social and economic outcomes, see Jackman and Miller 1998.

10. Many commentators point out that the inevitable result of collective action is not necessarily to foster community and democracy. Some groups—for example, militias—hardly promote democratic values. Moreover, organizations of like-minded individuals beget conflict as well as cooperation. See, for example, the arguments and references contained in Foley and Edwards 1997; Berman 1997b; Fiorina 1999a; Rosenblum 1998b, 1999; and Putnam 2000, ch. 22. For a more general discussion of the criticisms of participatory democracy, see Berry, Portney, and Thomson 1993, chs. 1, 8, 9.

11. For elaboration of this theme, see Putnam 2000, sec. 4.

12. See, for example, Bachrach 1967, Pateman 1970, and Parry 1972. For empirical evidence supporting this point of view, see Berry, Portney, and Thomson 1993 ch. 11.

insight in *Federalist* No. 10 that differences of opinion are sown in the nature of humankind, especially in the unequal acquisition of property. Through the medium of political participation, citizens communicate information about their preferences and needs for government action and generate pressure on public officials to heed what they hear. Of course, we know that public officials act for many reasons only one of which is their assessment of what the public wants and needs. And policymakers have ways other than the medium of citizen participation of learning what citizens want and need from the government. Nonetheless, what public officials hear clearly influences what they do. Therefore, so long as citizens differ in their opinions and interests, the level playing field of democracy requires that we take seriously the fact that citizens differ in their capacity, and desire, to take part politically. The democratic principle of one-person, one-vote is the most obvious manifestation of the link between voluntary participation and equal protection of interests. However, for forms of voluntary political participation beyond the vote—for example, writing letters to public officials, attending protests, or making political contributions—there is no such mandated equality of participatory input.

The questions raised by an emphasis on equal protection of interests are somewhat different from those raised by a focus on the nurturance of community and democracy or the development of the individual. First, the cooperative voluntary activity that promotes community and democracy or fosters individual faculties need not be explicitly political. Indeed, some versions of the neo-Tocquevillian argument about community and democracy focus explicitly on voluntary activity in the zone between state and market. In contrast, when equal protection of interests is at stake, the voluntary activity that counts is necessarily political. Furthermore, when it is a matter of the cultivation of democratic habits or the education of individuals, the aggregate quantity of civic engagement is critical. When we move from a conception of congruent community interests to one of clashing individual and group interests and, thus, to a concern with equal protection of interests, questions of representation come to the fore. What matters is not only the amount of civic activity but its distribution, not just how many people take part but who they are.

■ | Why Do Individuals Participate?

An important item on the agenda of concerns for students of political participation is to explain individual differences in activity. Multivariate analysis makes clear that the origins of political participation are complex and that different kinds of political participatory acts require different explanatory models.[13] Many factors enter into an explanation of why individuals choose to take part in politics. In their accounting of the mainsprings of participation, the Civic Voluntarism Model, Verba, Schlozman, and Brady (1995) group the variety of characteristics that predispose an individual to be politically active into three sets: resources, orientations to politics, and recruitment. In other words, in their construction, individuals are more likely to take part when they can, when they want to, and when they are asked.

When individuals command the *resources* that make it possible to do so, they are more likely to participate. Important among these resources are the civic skills—those organizational and communications capacities that make it easier to get involved and that enhance an individual's effectiveness as a participant—that are acquired throughout the life cycle during childhood beginning at home and in school and later on, during adulthood, on the job, at church, in nonpolitical organizations, and in politics itself.[14] Another crucial resource is money to make contributions to campaigns and other political causes. Available time would also seem to be an essential resource for political activity. Interestingly, when other participatory factors are taken into consideration, however, the number of hours left over after accounting for time devoted to school, paid work, and the care of home and children has no impact on participation, and the busy are as politically active as the leisured.[15]

In addition, several psychological *orientations* facilitate political activity. All else equal, individuals are more likely to participate if they are politically informed, interested, and efficacious, that is, if they know and care about politics and if they think that their participation would make a difference. Although political efficacy has generated particular attention among participation scholars, knowledge about politics is equally strongly related to participation, and interest in and attentiveness to politics are even more tightly connected to political activity. As would be expected, those who identify with a political party also have higher rates of participation, especially in electoral politics.[16] The strong relationships between

13. The discussion in this section and the remainder of the paper is implicitly multivariate. That is, unless explicitly stated to the contrary, the reader can assume that assertions about the various attributes that are associated with participation imply that other factors have been taken into account. Thus, there is an implied "all other things equal" in every sentence that describes empirical findings from research into political participation.

14. Respondents in the Citizen Participation Study were asked whether they had undertaken such activities as giving a presentation or speech or chairing a meeting in various nonpolitical venues. For discussion of the measurement of civic skills and their role in political participation, see Verba, Schlozman, and Brady 1995, ch. 11.

15. See Verba, Schlozman, and Brady 1995, chs. 12–13.

16. There is a great deal of variation in the ways that these psychological orientations to politics are measured. Further variation is introduced by the differences in

these political orientations and political participation raise questions of causal order. Does, for example, political interest raise political activity or does taking part in politics cultivate political interest?[17]

It is not simply general political predispositions that figure among the factors associated with participation. After all, political participation is about politics; thus the content of political preferences matters as well. Those who have intense issue commitments—for example, those who take a strong pro-life or pro-choice position on abortion—are, not surprisingly, more politically active.[18] The relationship of group consciousness to political activity is more problematic. Of course, the Marxian concept of group consciousness—the belief that group members have common problems requiring joint political action—originally grew out of class analysis. However, contemporary discussions of group consciousness are more likely to focus on a sense of political solidarity and shared political fate that is anchored in race, ethnicity, or gender. In contrast to the results for other politically relevant orientations, the findings about the participatory consequences of group consciousness have been decidedly mixed.[19]

The catalyst for political participation is *recruitment*: those who have the wherewithal and the desire to take part into politics are more likely to

---

the ways that individual measures are combined into scales. For descriptions of the various measures, discussions of their use in the literature, and extensive data, see the essays by Reef and Knoke (political alienation and efficacy, ch. 7), Citrin and Muste (political trust, ch. 8), Price (political information, ch. 10), and Weisberg (partisanship, ch. 12) in Robinson, Shaver, and Wrightsman 1999, as well as Abramson 1983; Bennett 1986; Iyengar 1990; Zaller 1992; and Delli Carpini and Keeter 1996. The summary works on participation mentioned earlier are also extremely helpful: Milbrath and Goel 1977, Bennett and Bennett 1986, Leighley 1995, and Conway 2000.

17. On this issue see the discussion by Leighley (1995), who points out the shortcomings of cross-sectional survey data for dealing with these issues. For an empirical analysis that seeks to address the problems of uncertain causality and finds support for the impact of political orientations on participation, see Verba, Schlozman, and Brady 1995, 350–355.

18. See Verba, Schlozman, and Brady 1995, ch. 14.

19. In their analysis of the roots of participation among African Americans, Verba and Nie (1972) demonstrated links between group consciousness and political participation. The findings about the impact of group consciousness on activity in subsequent analyses are not especially consistent (see, for example, Schlozman and Verba 1979, ch. 10; Shingles 1981; Miller, Gurin, Gurin, and Malanchuk 1981; Klein 1984, 136; Tate 1991; Tolleson Rinehart 1992; Ardrey 1994; Wilcox 1997; Leighley and Vedlitz 1999; as well as the discussions in Walton 1985; Flammang 1997, 116–19). One regularity underlying what would seem to be discrepant results is that an association between group consciousness and political activity is more likely to emerge in studies conducted during the 1960s and 1970s—when the temperature of U.S. politics was elevated—than in studies based on data collected later. In their 1990 data, Burns, Schlozman, and Verba (2001, chs. 10–11) find that group consciousness does not generate participation but, instead, channels partici-

do so if they are asked. Systematic inquiries confirm the well-known role of parties in mobilizing turnout and electoral activity.[20] Rosenstone and Hansen (1993, ch. 6) emphasize the extent to which it is not simply the characteristics of individuals but the operations of mobilizing institutions that determine participation and make a more general argument about the implications for participation of the attempts at political mobilization that come at the behest of politically motivated strategic elites—not only party activists but also those who run electoral campaigns or lead political organizations or movements. Beyond the efforts of political elites, processes of recruitment to citizen participation inhere in day-to day life outside of politics: requests for political activity may also come from those we know —relatives, friends, neighbors, workmates, fellow organization or church members—as well as from the managers, leaders, and staff of nonpolitical institutions. No matter whether the request comes in a mass mailing, through a phone call, or over the backyard fence, those who seek to get others involved choose as their targets people who would be likely to participate if asked. Thus, while the request may generate activity, those who are asked tend to have characteristics that make them inclined to take part.[21]

The various factors that shape participation are not equally relevant for various participatory acts. For example, strength of partisanship has a more substantial effect on voting than on getting involved in a community problem-solving effort; income is much more strongly related to campaign giving—and, in particular, to the size of the gift—than to protesting; civic skills matter more for time-based political activities such as contacting a

---

pation. That is, group consciousness does not act as an independent participatory factor for African Americans, Latinos, and women. However, if active, group-conscious members of all three groups are more likely to participate on issues having relevance to group identities.

20. Recent studies demonstrating that the participatory payoff of party efforts at mobilizing citizens include Southwell 1991; Huckfeldt and Sprague 1992; Wielhouwer and Lockerbie 1994; Huckfeldt and Sprague 1995, ch. 12; and Wielhouwer 1999. On the basis of a randomized field experiment, Gerber and Green (2000a, b) show the impact of nonpartisan get-out-the-vote messages. When delivered through personal canvassing, the consequences for participation of these mobilizing messages were substantial. In contrast, telephone calls with similar messages made no difference.

21. On informal processes of recruitment to citizen activity as well as the significance of institutionally based mobilization efforts by employers and leaders of nonpolitical organizations or religious institutions, see Verba, Schlozman, and Brady 1995, chs. 5, 13. On group-specific processes of political mobilization for racial and ethnic minorities, see Leighley 2001. For analysis of the attempts by rational recruiters to locate potential activists and discussion of the problems of causal direction raised by these processes of targeting, see Brady, Schlozman, and Verba 1999. Rosenstone and Hansen make a parallel argument with respect to the attempts by political parties to mobilize likely and sympathetic voters (1993, 166–69).

public official than for voting; and so on.[22] Hence, in generalizing about the roots of political activity it is important to bear in mind the differential relevance of various participatory factors for different political acts.

THE ENDURANCE OF THE SES MODEL

It is common to deride the Socio-Economic Status (SES) model of participation—which stresses the strong association between political activity and an individual's income, occupation, and, especially, education—as simplistic, apolitical, and atheoretical.[23] Yet, the SES model, which is fundamental to such pathbreaking analyses of political activity as Verba and Nie's *Participation in America* (1972) and Wolfinger and Rosenstone's *Who Votes?* (1980), shows no signs of early demise. Its endurance can be attributed in part to its considerable empirical power in predicting political participation. In contrast to other variables often discussed as being central to the understanding of participation—for example, characteristics of political and social context—in any multivariate analysis, socioeconomic status is invariably positively associated with political activity.[24] Even critics of the SES model never fail to include socioeconomic variables in their analyses when they probe the consequences for participation of such political variables as registration laws or the competitiveness of elections.

Moreover, recent scholarship has begun to address its theoretical deficiencies by elaborating the causal links between political activity and high levels of income, occupation, and education. Verba, Schlozman, and Brady (1995, ch. 15) make headway in explaining how the components of socioeconomic status function to produce participation and demonstrate why education is so central to this process. Not only does education have a direct impact on political activity, but more importantly, education has indirect effects through its consequences for the acquisition of nearly every other participatory factor. The well-educated earn higher incomes on the job; are more likely to develop civic skills at work, in organizations, and, to a lesser extent, in church; are more likely to receive requests for political activity; and are more politically interested and knowledgeable.[25] Nie,

22. See Verba, Schlozman, and Brady 1995, 356–64.

23. See Leighley 1995, 183–88, for a trenchant summary of the criticisms of the SES model.

24. While the positive association between SES and political participation seems to obtain across democracies, researchers have made clear that voter abstention in nondemocratic systems may have a very different meaning and, thus, very different demographic contours. Brady and Kaplan (forthcoming) find no relationship between education and voting in Estonia during the 1980s and argue that "the act of voting during the Soviet era was not about political choice and representation, but a ritual in which the better educated may have chosen to abstain."

25. For a summary of how education operates to raise turnout, see Jackson 1995.

Junn, and Stehlik-Barry (1996) address the puzzling discontinuity between the fact that, within any cross-sectional sample, high-SES individuals are the most politically active and the fact that rising levels of education with-in the public have not produced commensurate returns in participation. They stress the primacy of relative rather than absolute education. According to their analysis, what matters for political activity is the positional advantage accruing to those who are well educated relative to their age cohort rather than any particular level of educational attainment. Thus, they construe educational attainment more as a sorting mechanism that allocates "scarce social and political ranks that place citizens either closer to or further from the center of critical social and political networks" (6). In particular, they demonstrate the relationship between educational level and what they call "network centrality," being personally acquainted with or known to people in important positions in local or national politics and the media (ch. 3).

The strength of the relationship between political participation and such indicators of community attachment as home ownership and length of residence in the community poses an analogous problem but has received less attention from scholars. Like SES, community attachment is consistently a powerful predictor of activity, especially on the local level. Unlike SES, we know relatively little about why. Until we establish *how* community attachment operates to facilitate participation—by creating a stake in community outcomes, by making it easier to know how and where to take part, by increasing political interest and knowledge, by placing individuals in networks of mobilization, all in ways not measured by surveys—researchers will probably continue to include it, without much theoretical justification, in their multivariate analyses, where it will figure significantly in the explanation of activity.

■ | From Whom Do Public Officials Hear?

The processes by which people come to take part imply that, taken together, activists are not representative of the American public and, thus, that public officials are disproportionately likely to hear from people with certain politically relevant characteristics. Participatory input is stratified not only by socioeconomic status but also by race or ethnicity, by gender, and by age. In terms of overall participation, Anglo-Whites are more politically active than are African Americans and, especially, Latinos. Men are more politically active than women. And the middle-aged are more politically active than are young adults or the elderly.[26]

26. These regularities are not completely consistent across particular acts. African Americans are not underrepresented among protesters, women are not underrepresented among voters, and the young are not underrepresented among campaigners.

Cataloguing the groups that are under- or overrepresented among activists does not, however, constitute a causal explanation. It is essential to understand what it is about being, say, Anglo-White or male that leads to higher levels of participation. In most cases, group differences can be explained in terms of disparities in participatory factors just discussed. Once group differences in participatory resources—in particular, education and income—are taken into account, the disparities in participation among Anglo-Whites, African Americans, and Latinos disappear.[27] Similarly, once the differences between men and women in resources and such political orientations as political interest, information, and efficacy are controlled, the gender gap in political activity closes.[28]

The deficit in activity of the young is more difficult to explain. It is commonly asserted that the younger citizens are less likely to take part because they have not yet settled down. According to this story, once they acquire the roles and responsibilities of adulthood—full-time jobs, families, and mortgages—they will become more active.[29] However, with other factors taken into account, these adult roles and responsibilities do not have an independent impact on participation. Rather any association between political activity and marriage, jobs, or parenthood is a function of differences in resources, recruitment, and political orientations related to various adult statuses.[30] That is, under certain circumstances, adult roles are associated with enhanced levels of participatory factors, but it is the resources, recruitment, and orientations, not the adult statuses, that matter

---

27. See Verba and Nie 1972, Verba, Schlozman, Brady, and Nie 1993, Verba, Schlozman, and Brady 1995, and Leighley and Vedlitz 1999. For descriptive data about participatory differences among various Latino nationality groups, see de la Garza et al. 1992, ch. 8.

28. See, Burns, Schlozman, and Verba 2001, ch. 10.

There is also the possibility that the process works differently for different demographic subgroups. That is, group differences in political participation could result not from group differences in participatory endowments (in other words, in the *levels* of participatory factors) but from group differences in the participatory payoff from participatory factors (the *effects* of participatory factors). Burns, Schlozman, and Verba (2001) make the most systematic investigation of this possibility and find that the gender disparity in activity results almost entirely from men's advantage with respect to a variety of participatory factors and not from gender differences in the efficacy of these factors in producing participation. This approach seems to have greater potential for understanding participatory differences among racial and ethnic groups. See, for example, Hritzuk and Park 2000 and Leighley 2001.

29. See, for example, Verba and Nie 1972, ch. 9.

30. On the indirect effects of marriage and children on political activity and on how those effects are different for men and women, see Burns, Schlozman, and Verba 2001, ch. 12. On the processes of convergence that render members of a couple more like one another politically during the early years of marriage, see Stoker and Jennings 1995.

for activity.[31] Nonetheless, in contrast to the circumstance for gender or race, differences in participatory endowments among age groups do not fully explain the gap in participation between the young and their elders. Indeed, the unexplained difference in activity between those in their twenties and those in their forties is actually larger than the initial disparity between African Americans and whites or between women and men.[32]

Memberships in demographic groups may not be the key to the causal understanding of political activity. They are, however, absolutely fundamental to politics.[33] Thus, understanding the origins of group differences in participation does not put the matter to rest. Knowing, for example, that disparities in participation among Latinos, African Americans, and Anglo-Whites stem not from race or ethnicity per se but from group differences in participatory factors, most of which are rooted in class differences, does not obviate the fact that policymakers are hearing less from African Americans or, especially, Latinos. These are groups with distinctive political preferences and participatory agendas: they differ in their opinions on public matters and, when they are active, they are concerned with a different mix of issues. Hence, it makes a difference with respect to equal protection of interests if participatory messages to policymakers underrepresent input from African Americans and Latinos. That the sources of these group differences in activity lie in characteristics other than race or ethnicity does not vitiate the political significance of disparities in participation.[34]

31. This paragraph draws from Schlozman, Brady, Verba, and Erkulwater 2001. They show that the relationship between the assumption of adult roles and political participation is complex. In general, full-time work enhances such participatory factors as income and work-based civic skills and recruitment. However, young adults who take on the adult responsibilities of full-time jobs and children in their late teens or early twenties are actually less politically active than those who stay in school and delay parenthood and full-time work until they are somewhat older. Moreover, the participatory consequences of parenthood—which are indirect rather than direct—differ for men and women. Parenthood pushes fathers into the work force; having toddlers keeps mothers home with attendant consequence for the acquisition of work-based participatory factors and, thus, for political participation.

Strate, Parrish, Elder, and Ford (1989) focus on the central role of "civic competence" (a composite of political attentiveness, media use, and political knowledge) in their analysis of age-related effects with respect to voting.

32. Green and Shachar's finding (2000) that voting in one election increases the probability of voting in subsequent ones lends credence to the notion that one possible answer to the puzzle of life-cycle differences in political activity lies in the independent impact of habit.

33. The discussion in this and the following paragraphs draws heavily from Verba, Schlozman, and Brady 1995, ch. 7.

34. Nor does it obviate the importance of the question of why there are such enduring and pronounced socioeconomic differences among groups defined by their race or ethnicity. Class differences along racial or ethnic lines reflect the legacy of historical and social processes that have everything to do with racial or ethnic status.

The same logic obtains for participatory differences rooted in groups defined by gender, class, age, or such politically relevant characteristics as dependence on government benefits. When the messages to public officials are skewed, then the democratic norm of equal responsiveness to all is potentially compromised. Although the politics of policy outcomes hinge on many factors, only one of which is what policymakers hear from citizens, it is hardly surprising that Medicare benefits for the elderly generate more political attention than Medicaid benefits for the poor, that student loan programs have taken a much bigger budgetary hit than have veterans' benefits, or that the voices of public aid recipients were barely audible in the controversy over welfare reform.[35]

These considerations force us to rethink somewhat the important argument made by Wolfinger and Rosenstone (1980, ch. 6) about the political consequences of the demographic skew in the electorate. Wolfinger and Rosenstone demonstrate that, although the electorate is not demographically representative of the public at large, voters do not differ from nonvoters in their partisan leanings or their opinions on policy matters as expressed in surveys, a finding that obtains for other forms of political activity as well.[36] However, political participants, including voters, can be distinguished from inactives in ways that are of great political significance: although similar in their attitudes, they are distinctive in their personal circumstances and dependence on government benefits, in their priorities for government action, and in what they say when they get involved. These disparities are exacerbated when we move from the most common political act, voting, to acts that are more difficult, convey more information, and can be multiplied in their volume. Thus, the demographic stratification of activist publics is of potential political consequence.[37]

35. For evidence comparing the rates of political participation of recipients of means-tested and non-means-tested government benefits and demonstrating how much lower the former are than the latter, see Verba, Schlozman, and Brady 1995, 217–19. On the complexities of participatory representation and how actual or anticipated political participation might influence public officials, see Verba, Schlozman, and Brady 1995, ch. 6.

36. In their discussion of turnout, Gant and Lyons (1993) make an argument similar to Wolfinger and Rosenstone's. For additional perspectives, see Bennett and Resnick 1990; Teixeira 1992, 101–4; and Lijphart 1997.

37. We have seen that, when it comes to demographic characteristics, there is widespread agreement on the nature of the demographic biases that differentiate voters from nonvoters but controversy over the meaning of those findings. With respect to partisanship, the situation is inverted. If either party is favored by low or high turnout, the political implications are quite clear. However, there is no consensus as to whether variations in turnout systematically help one party or the other. For differing views, see the controversy between Radcliff (1994, 1995) and Erikson (1995a, b), as well as Nagel and McNulty 1996, 2000.

▪ | Beyond the Individual: Contextual Effects

The scholarly inquiries that have made the past ten years a decade of progress in participation research are based on the results of sample surveys. Survey-based scholarship has been legitimately criticized as unduly individualistic—ignoring the impact of the political and social contexts in which individuals are embedded.[38] To overcome the implicit individualism of the sample survey, participation researchers have attached additional information—gathered either in surveys or from archival sources—about political and social context to individual records and have used aggregate data analysis to connect political and social characteristics to levels of turnout within political jurisdictions.

Substantial cross-national variations in electoral turnout make clear that the propensity to go to the polls is not simply a function of the attributes of individuals and suggest that we must pay attention to the participatory consequences of electoral laws and arrangements. Using the states as laboratories, a large number of studies consider a variety of electoral reforms designed to raise turnout by making it easier to vote.[39] A number of these electoral reforms have been shown to have a positive impact on turnout: among them, easing restrictions on casting absentee ballots, permitting mail-in ballots, and, not surprisingly, compulsory voting.[40]

The extent to which registration requirements act as a deterrent to turnout has long been a focus of concern not only among scholars (see, in particular, Wolfinger and Rosenstone [1980]; Powell [1986]) but also among policymakers. In fact, it was the impetus behind the National Voter Registration Act of 1993. The National Voter Registration Act contains several provisions designed to lower barriers to registration: registration by mail; restrictions on the purging of voter registration lists; agency-based

---

38. For discussion of the need for contextual analysis and summary of the literature to that point, see Books and Prysby 1988; for discussion of the nature of contextual effects and the difficulties in studying them, see Huckfeldt and Sprague 1995, chs. 1–2. Huckfeldt and Sprague have a more-limited and more precise concept of contextual effects than the rather general sense in which they are discussed here.

39. One potential source of discrepancy among the studies cited below is the decision whether to concentrate just on turnout or to model registration and turnout as separate processes, or to model candidate choice as part of the turnout process. For discussion and citations, see, among others, Jackson 1996, Timpone 1998, Brown, Jackson, and Wright 1999, and Lacy and Burden 1999.

40. On absentee eligibility, see Oliver 1996. Oliver makes clear that reducing the hurdles to absentee voting is not sufficient on its own but is effective only in combination with efforts by parties to mobilize voters. On all-mail elections, see Southwell and Burchett (2000), and on compulsory voting, see Franklin 1999. Oliver and Wolfinger (1999) consider another possible deterrent to voter registration, the fact that in some states jury lists are constructed from registered voters, and find no evidence that jury aversion depresses voter registration. On compulsory voting and its possibly unconstitutional status in the United States, see Lijphart 1997, 8–11.

registration at public assistance and unemployment compensation offices; and, most notably, the "motor voter" provision for registration at state motor vehicle bureaus. The numerous studies assessing these and other measures aimed at easing registration requirements suggest that provisions for motor voter and agency registration, as well as extensions of the registration period closer to the election, including same-day registration, all raise voter registration while provisions for mail registration and restrictions on purging have no impact.[41] There is, however, less agreement about the magnitude of the changes occasioned by these reforms.[42] Furthermore, the findings are quite inconsistent when it comes to the representational impact; that is, whether liberalizing registration requirements alters the composition of the electorate with respect either to partisanship or to the demographic characteristics, in particular, the race and SES, of voters.[43]

Less permanent aspects of the political context also have potential consequences for participation. Scholars have investigated a number of hypotheses about how characteristics of electoral contests influence turnout: visible elections, close elections, and high levels of campaign spending would all be expected to elevate turnout, and divisive primary seasons and negative campaigning would be expected to depress turnout. Unfortunately, beyond the well-known regularity that turnout is higher when there is a presidential contest at the top of the ticket, empirical inquiries reach no consensus on how these attributes of elections affect the propensity to go to the polls.[44] Another contextual factor with possible implications for

41. Teixiera (1992), Mitchell and Wlezien (1995), Rhine (1995), Knack (1995), Knack and White (1998), and Martinez and Hill (1999) all consider several of these reforms together. Franklin and Grier (1997) concentrate on motor voter. Highton (1997) focuses on same-day registration. A number of analysts point out that, because states require the renewal of driver's licenses only at several-year intervals, the effects of motor voter provisions would not be expected to be immediate. Knack (1995, 809) discusses the necessity of paying attention to the ways that particular reforms interact. Thus, the absence of effect from mail-in registration may reflect that, if coupled with more powerful programs like motor voter or same-day registration, mail-in registration becomes less needed.

42. Part of the issue is whether higher rates of registration translate into higher rates of turnout. Modeling registration and voting as separate selection processes makes clear that the less-motivated voters who were deterred from registering by high barriers may be less likely actually to vote if their registration results from the lowering of the registration hurdle. On this logic, see Knack 1995, Timpone 1998, and Martinez and Hill 1999.

43. With respect to whether facilitating registration ameliorates the socioeconomic bias in the electorate, see the conflicting findings in Nagler 1991, Highton 1997, Timpone 1998, and Martinez and Hill 1999.

44. As mentioned, inconsistent results of multivariate analyses may reflect decisions about how to model the processes. Furthermore, Leighley and Nagler (1992b) confirm Wolfinger and Rosenstone's model and underscore the importance of individual-level characteristics in explaining voting. Jackson (1996) finds

participation is the way citizens respond to the characteristics of political elites. Having attractive choices on the ballot seems to raise participation.[45] Furthermore, for African Americans and women, the presence of fellow group members in the political environment—running for or holding visible public office—is ordinarily but not always associated with higher levels of political activity, often by virtue of its effect on political interest, political knowledge, or some other participatory orientation.[46]

---

that, although personal factors are important as predictors of turnout within the electorate, campaign factors gain explanatory power as predictors of turnout when the analysis is confined to explaining turnout among the registered. While senatorial and gubernatorial elections on the ballot seem to enhance turnout, there is disagreement as to whether the effect obtains only in off-years (Jackson 1999) or in presidential years as well (Boyd 1989). Although Nownes (1992) and Hogan (1999) find no effect for either a history of competitiveness or the closeness of the election, Cox and Munger (1989) and Franklin and Hirczy de Miño (1998) confirm earlier studies showing that turnout rises in close elections. Cox and Munger argue that the relationship between closeness and turnout reflects not the calculations of rational voters who bother to go to the polls only when their vote would have the possibility of making a difference but rather the calculations of strategic elites who spend more and engage in enhanced mobilization efforts when the election is expected to be close.

Related to the concern with closeness is the finding in Franklin and Hirczy de Miño 1998 that divided government at the national level is negatively associated with turnout. Contrary to the common wisdom and results in Cox and Munger 1989 and Hogan 1999 that show a positive impact on turnout from campaign spending, Southwell (1991) finds a negative association between spending and turnout. Since voter mobilization efforts that might accompany higher spending are not measured, the causal mechanism linking spending and turnout is not clear. Boyd (1989) finds that primary contests depress turnout; in contrast, Stone, Atkeson, and Rapoport (1992) find that any demobilizing effect from the divisiveness of primaries is more than offset by the mobilizing effect of nomination campaigns. Kahn and Kenney (1999) and Wattenberg and Brians (1999) contest the finding in Ansolabehere, Iyengar, Simon, and Valentino 1994 that negative campaign advertising depresses turnout. Finally, Norrander (1991) finds that although political characteristics of the campaign have some effect on the likelihood of voting in presidential primaries, the two most powerful variables are characteristics of individuals: age and interest in politics.

45. Southwell (1991) demonstrates that negative evaluations of candidates are associated with abstention in Senate elections. Lacy and Burden (1999) show that the presence of Perot on the ballot in 1992 raised turnout by nearly 3 percent beyond what it would have been had there been no third-party option.

46. For African Americans, Bobo and Gilliam (1990), Tate (1991, 1993, ch. 5), Gilliam (1996), and Gilliam and Kaufmann (1998) find an impact on psychological engagement with politics or political activity of having African Americans on the ballot or in office, but Gay (1998) does not. For women, Hansen (1997), Sapiro and Conover (1997), Kahn and Kenney (1999), and Burns, Schlozman, and Verba (2001) all find a positive relationship between a gender-integrated political environment and the orientations to politics associated with activity. On the basis of much more limited data, Koch (1997) does not.

Researchers have also considered the implications of other aspects of the nature of the community, including its political culture, racial diversity, and size.[47] Although most of these studies focus exclusively on the vote as a form of political activity, J. Eric Oliver (2000, 2001) considers a variety of kinds of participation and leads us to rethink much of what we thought we knew about the consequences of suburbanization for civic life. His analysis shows that, taking other factors including the characteristics of individuals into consideration, with increases in the size, affluence and economic homogeneity of municipalities comes a decline in rates of participation.[48] Often, Oliver is able to nail down the causal process behind the contextual effect. For example, those who dwell in large cities are less likely to be mobilized by friends and neighbors—a result of the fact that they are less likely to know and to interact with their neighbors.

INDIVIDUALS IN INSTITUTIONAL CONTEXT

The relevant environment for political participation is not confined to the jurisdictions in which individuals live. A crucial component of the analysis of individual political participation is the role of the nonpolitical institutions of everyday life—the workplace, religious institutions, voluntary associations—in generating participation. These nonpolitical institutions operate in several ways to facilitate a variety of kinds of political activity, not just voting.[49] Sometimes the mobilization is, to use Leighley's (1996) term, *intentional:* employers, clergy, and organization leaders and their

47. Adopting Daniel Elazar's well-known categories, King (1994) demonstrates that a "moralistic" political culture in which democracy is valued and citizens are understood to have a responsibility to take part is associated with higher levels of turnout. Schlichting, Tuckel, and Maisel (1998) and Hill and Leighley (1999) find a relationship between racial homogeneity and turnout. However, Brace, Handley, Niemi, and Stanley (1995) find that the creation of majority-minority districts does not necessarily result in higher levels of turnout.

Hill and Leighley (1994) bring analogous considerations to a concern with the socioeconomic representativeness of state electorate and find that the determinants of the turnout and the class representation of a state's electorate are different. The mobilization variables that have an impact on turnout (for example, the restrictiveness of registration) are not related to the extent to which the SES composition of a state's electorate reflects the SES composition of a state. Instead, the representativeness of states' electorates is positively associated with the level of per capita income and negatively associated with the ethnic heterogeneity of the population.

For an ethnographic approach to the patterns of Latino politics in five large cities, see de la Garza, Menchaca, and De Sipio 1994.

48. In contrast, Alesina and La Ferrara (2000) find economic (and racial and ethnic) heterogeneity to be negatively associated with a different kind of involvement, membership in organizations.

49. On this theme, see Verba and Nie 1972, ch. 11; Peterson 1992; Verba, Schlozman, and Brady 1995, pt. 3; Calhoun-Brown 1996; Leighley 1996; Harris 1999; Greenberg 2000; Radcliff and Davis 2000; and Burns, Schlozman, and Verba 2001.

staff may take political stands in the name of the institution and ask those affiliated with the institution to take political action, either as part of an effort to further institutional ends or as part of a generalized campaign to boost turnout or political activity. Often, the participatory consequences emerge as a by-product of institutional functioning: the interactions that occur when people come together in institutions build social capital, deepening trust and democratic values, and develop the informal social networks in which political discussions take place and through which requests for participation are mediated; furthermore, activity in these nonpolitical contexts enhances civic skills, the organizational and communications skills so useful in the political sphere.

In certain ways, these institutions are fungible with respect to political participation. An individual can acquire civic skills as an officer of the Elks or on the religious instruction committee at church, can receive requests for political activity from workmates or from fellow organization members, and so on. However, in fundamental ways, these institutions are not interchangeable.[50] Reflecting processes of differential selection into institutions and differential treatment within institutions, nonpolitical institutions differ in terms of the extensiveness of the participatory factors they provide and the way those participatory factors are distributed. For example, the workplace is a rich source of civic skills, but work-based civic skills flow disproportionately to those with high levels of education and jobs that require expertise. In contrast, although internally hierarchical, religious institutions distribute civic skills in a much less stratified manner than places of employment do. Furthermore, there are substantial differences among institutions when it comes to the political messages that accompany institutionally driven political activity. When a church makes institutionally based attempts to mobilize the flock for political action, the policy matter at stake is likely to be quite different from that embraced by a labor union. Thus, the processes by which individuals come to be affiliated with institutions and gain participatory factors within institutions have implications for who takes part and what they say.

THE PUBLIC PROMOTION OF PARTICIPATION

Ordinarily, we think of participation as emerging from below, spontaneously or in response to the efforts of strategic elites. However, there is an important top-down element as well: governments act in many ways to invite citizen participation. While the efforts of federal bureaucracies to organize constituencies ranging from farmers to veterans are a staple in the analysis of organized interests, this theme receives less attention among

50. For an analysis demonstrating the singular importance of nonpolitical organizations in generating political activity, and a critique of Verba, Schlozman, and Brady, see Ayala 2000.

scholars of citizen participation.[51] An exception is Berry, Portney, and Thomson's analysis (1993) of five cities in which urban governments have experimented with participatory democracy—citywide systems of promoting neighborhood associations and giving them authority in local decision making. On the basis of their systematic evaluation of the implications of this kind of strong democracy, Berry, Portney, and Thomson deliver a mixed but positive verdict. Neighborhood-based participation does give citizens a real voice in governance. The neighborhood groups involved are seen as responsive to their constituents and effective in influencing policy (189). Furthermore, these arrangements seem to promote democratic values such as an increased sense of community and governmental legitimacy (chs. 9–10). Nevertheless, they seem not to generate greater participation. Rates of overall participation in the five cities are "unexceptional" when compared with other cities that share their characteristics (81). While these arrangements do not overcome the class bias characteristic of participation in the United States, neither do they exacerbate SES stratification.

■ | The Decline in Democratic Participation

Michael Schudson's sprawling history (1998) of civic life in the United States reminds us that the possibilities and expectations for citizen participation have been transformed several times throughout American history. Recent decades have witnessed a decline in political participation. Explaining that decline, a different intellectual enterprise from explaining participation itself, is another important item on the agenda of participation scholars. The well-known erosion in voting turnout that began after the recent high in 1960 was the first, and most immediately visible, manifestation of a more general trend. The decay in turnout is surprising because, for two sets of reasons, we might have expected turnout to have risen over the period. First, the educational attainment of the public rose substantially in the second half of the twentieth century. Second, a variety of procedural reforms including, for example, reductions in residency requirements and, most recently, motor voter provisions have made it easier to register and vote.

Why, despite these forces that would have been expected to boost turnout, has turnout ebbed? Ruy Teixeira's answer (1992, ch. 2) to the puzzle first posed by Richard Brody (1978) focuses on a variety of potential causes, most of which involve the changing characteristics of the individuals within the electorate.[52] He discusses aggregate changes in a number of

51. See, for example, Walker 1991.
52. See also Cassel and Luskin 1988.

political orientations. He dismisses one common assumption, that increasing cynicism is responsible for decreasing turnout by showing that, while the public is, indeed, more politically cynical, cynicism has no independent effect on turnout.[53] Thus, we cannot explain the decline in turnout in terms of increased cynicism. However, the erosion both in citizens' perception that the government is responsive and in their sense that their votes matter does help to explain changes in turnout. In addition, although the causal mechanisms are not always spelled out in detail, the decline in social connectedness—as measured by the diminishing rate of marriage and lower rates of church attendance—and the changing age structure of the population that occurred as the baby boom generation entered the electorate also explain the falloff in turnout. Furthermore, the erosion in political connectedness—the decline in strong partisan identifications, in newspaper reading, and in campaign interest—helps to account for changes in turnout. Finally, one structural factor, the increase in the frequency of elections and the complexity of ballots, contributes to the erosion of turnout.

Others have elaborated this explanation. Rosenstone and Hansen (1993, ch. 7) emphasize changes in the characteristics of the system in addition to changes in the characteristics of individuals. They stress, in particular, the consequences of the decline in voter mobilization by parties and social movements.[54] Miller and Shanks (1996, ch. 5) focus on the distinctive characteristics and behaviors of recent entrants into the electorate. They demonstrate that the post–New Deal generations that came of age after 1968 are less party identified and less socially connected than their elders, tendencies that would themselves contribute to the decline in turnout. Moreover, the non-party-identified and socially disconnected members of post–New Deal generations are substantially less likely to go to the polls than members of older generations with similar characteristics.[55]

The decline in voting is part of a more general erosion in voluntary ac-

53. This conclusion is supported by Nownes 1992.

54. This line of reasoning has proven controversial. In their discussion of the origins of the decline in turnout, Abramson, Aldrich, and Rohde (1999, 85) point out that the decline in contacts from political parties has not tracked the decline in turnout very well. In fact, even though turnout was falling, party contacts rose during the first part of the 1960s and rose again in the 1990s. (Rosenstone and Hansen's data end in 1988.) Gerber and Green (2000b) suggest a resolution to the inconsistency. Their experiment in New Haven demonstrates the relative effectiveness of personal canvassing compared to direct mail and phone calls as a means of mobilizing voters. Thus, while parties may be reaching a larger share of the electorate, they are using less personal—and, thus, less effective—methods.

55. Lyons and Alexander (2000) connect the concern with party contacting to the generational analysis. They show that younger cohorts are less affected by party contacts.

tivity since the 1960s. Rosenstone and Hansen (1993, ch. 3) use the frequencies from the Roper Social and Political Trends data, a two-decade series of polls that included a large battery of participation items, to establish that the decrease in electoral turnout is not an isolated political phenomenon. Rather it is part of a decrease in all forms of political activity that is related to structural changes in American political politics, in particular, the weakening of party efforts to mobilize voters. The decline in other forms of political activity is not, however, as steep as for voting turnout. In fact, for a few kinds of political participation, in particular, making electoral contributions, the volume of activity has increased. What this means is that there has been a transformation in the mix of participatory activities. The widely discussed decline of American political parties and the reinvigoration of interest groups, coupled with the nationalization and professionalization of both sets of institutions, have redefined the role of the citizen activist as, increasingly, a writer of letters and checks.

Furthermore, broadening our purview beyond conventional understandings of what constitutes political participation introduces further ambiguity. Joe Soss (2000) argues that applying for and receiving government welfare benefits can be construed as a form of political participation, analogous to other forms of political action. Because many who are eligible for government benefits do not become claimants, applying for welfare is—like many modes of political activity—a voluntary act that is undertaken in search of selective, material benefits and that involves political learning and the cultivation of political orientations. The number of clients of means-tested and non-means-tested government programs has varied substantially over the past half-century but does not track the secular decline in voting. Similarly, going to court can be interpreted as a form of political participation—in essence, the judicial analogue to particularized contacting. That is, individuals who file suit use public auspices to gain benefits, usually from other private parties. One of the hallmarks of recent decades is Americans' increased litigiousness. While these forms of public involvement for which there has been no obvious decline have consequences for individuals' ability to protect their interests, their implications for the creation of social capital and for individual learning are less clear.

With his resonant metaphor of *Bowling Alone*, Robert D. Putnam (2000) recast the conversation by placing the decline in voter turnout and other forms of political activity in the context of an overall erosion in civic engagement and social activity. Not only have voting and other forms of political activity waned since the 1960s, but participation in community organizations and clubs; religious, voluntary, and charitable activity; and informal socializing have ebbed as well. Thus, Americans are less likely not only to vote or get involved in a campaign but also to belong to the PTA, to attend church, or to go on picnics or give dinner parties. Although they are more likely to watch sports on television, they are less likely actually to do sports.[56] Concomitant to these trends is a decline in social trust.[57]

In his search for the sources of the decline in civic engagement, Putnam (2000, sec. 3) examines a large number of possibilities. A number of social trends—for example, the transformation of family life in the United States, White flight from racial integration in the aftermath of the successes of the civil rights movement, big government, and the entry of women into the workforce—turn out not to have the expected impact in diminishing civic engagement.[58] Pressures of time and money as well as suburbanization, sprawl, and commuting do contribute to the decline of civic engagement although the effect is less substantial than is sometimes assumed. The major culprits are the effects of electronic media, especially television, in privatizing leisure and the replacement of the long civic generation by the much less engaged baby boomers and generation Xers.[59]

What are the implications of the decline in political participation for matters of participatory representation? As fewer voices are heard, has there been any change in whose voices are heard? With respect to voting, there is no consensus as to whether the decline in turnout has come disproportionately from those at the bottom of the SES hierarchy and, thus, has exacerbated the demographic bias of the electorate.[60] In their study of the

56. Putnam's first exposition (1995) of his thesis generated a great deal of discussion and considerable criticism. In the eventual book-length version, Putnam not only corrects some errors and takes heed of points made by his critics but also marshals additional evidence in support of his contention that civic engagement is declining. An extended—though not especially compelling—rebuttal can be found in Ladd 1999.

57. The relationship between participation and social trust represents another example in which the causal direction is uncertain. Brehm and Rahn (1997) demonstrate that, while participation and interpersonal trust are reciprocally causal, participation is an even stronger cause of social trust than vice versa.

58. In his nuanced discussion, Putnam (2000, 277–79) makes clear that the various aspects of civic engagement are not inextricably bundled. Thus, instability in family structure is probably associated with decreasing religious attendance and participation in youth-related activities, though not with other aspects of civic decline. Similarly, women's increased workforce participation has affected social connectedness much more than the more public forms of involvement (194–203). In fact, Burns, Schlozman, and Verba (2001, chs. 8, 10, 12) demonstrate not only that women with full-time jobs are more politically active than those at home full-time but that work itself provides participatory factors.

59. These two factors interact. The impact of television is especially pronounced for members of these younger generations.

60. For differing points of view, contrast Rosenstone and Hansen (1993, 241–45) with Leighley and Nagler (1992a) and Shields and Goidel (1997). Shields and Goidel (2000) find no change in the SES stratification of campaign donors over the period. Since, unlike voters who are limited to a single ballot, donors can vary how much they give, Shields and Goidel's findings might have been different if their data had contained measures of the size of the contribution.

consequences for political stratification of the overall decline in various modes of political activity, Brady, Schlozman, Verba, and Elms (2002) find that the socioeconomic bias in political participation fluctuated somewhat in the two decades separating the early 1970s and early 1990s, but was more or less the same at the end of the period as at the beginning.

In contrast to the stability in the socioeconomic stratification of political participation is the changing ideological composition of activist publics. Survey data confirm the impression gleaned from journalistic accounts, that citizen politics in the United States has become more polarized. Putnam finds that the decline in civic engagement has been especially pronounced within the large, and growing, sector of the public that describes its political views as moderate, thus producing a circumstance such that political activists are drawn disproportionately from the ranks of those at both ends of the political spectrum (2000, 342). Furthermore, Berry (1999, ch. 7) links the rise of citizens' groups of the left to what he calls "liberalism transformed": these national-level organizations that are active in Washington politics often entail only a checkbook commitment from members and alter the focus of representation from class-based economic concerns anchored in unions to postmaterialist issues like political reform, consumer protection, and environmental preservation.

In contrast to Putnam's emphasis on the decline in civic engagement and Berry's analysis of the eclipse of the representation of the economic concerns of the working class and the poor, are sociological studies in the tradition of Harry Boyte's *The Backyard Revolution* (1980) that consider local activity that builds the civic capacities of ordinary citizens. These studies tend to be ethnographic rather than survey-based and descriptive rather than causal. In addition, they tend to concentrate on the left end of the political spectrum. For example, even when they consider faith-based organizing, they tend to focus not on grassroots religious activity in the name of conservative social concerns but on initiatives on behalf of a progressive agenda. Recent examples include Mark R. Warren's study (2001) of the Alinsky-style Texas Industrial Areas Foundation and Carmen Sirianni and Lewis Friedland's investigation (2001) of "community renewal" on a national basis.

■ | The Tyranny of the Sample Survey in Participation Research: Past and Future

As I assembled my half of the reading list for my department's graduate field seminar in American politics a few months ago, I faced almost an embarrassment of riches when it came to the proposed session on political participation. As I hope this essay has made clear, during the past decade scholars of participation have produced a large quantity of important research, including a number of first-rate books.[61] The bulk of this research partakes of several characteristics that make it at once both quite contemporary and rather old-fashioned. Most of the studies reviewed here are relentlessly empirical: they use quantitative evidence, usually the results of national sample surveys, and sophisticated statistical techniques to consider causal questions. They generate methodological controversies about such matters as the choice of specific statistical methods, the correct specification of the model, and problems of causal direction. Yet, even when they seem unduly narrow, the questions posed are anchored in such enduring issues of democratic theory as the cultivation of democratic values, legitimacy, and equality.

The emergence of systematic study of political participation is tied inextricably with the development of the sample survey, and to a certain extent the research progress in the recent past reflects the availability of new data sources.[62] None of the data sets available to participation researchers is perfect. The discipline's principal source of longitudinal data about the political commitments, characteristics, and behaviors of the American public, the American National Election Studies (ANES), is an invaluable archive. It contains excellent measures of a variety of kinds of electoral participation, but because it is tied to biennial elections, it contains only intermittent measures of nonelectoral political participation. Thus, the ANES is of limited utility to those interested in political activity construed more broadly. In fact, the availability of the ANES, with its electoral focus, may help to explain why so much of the participation research since Verba and Nie's agenda-setting work (1972) appeared has focused exclusively on the vote as a form of citizen activity. Within the existing framework of participation research, progress could be made on a number of the central intellectual problems discussed here—for example, matters of causal direction or distinctions among various kinds of participation—if only better data were available. What is needed are longitudinal, preferably panel, surveys containing a rich battery of items and samples large enough to include ample cases of individuals who engage in such rare political acts as attending a political protest or making a large contribution.[63] Since the

61. For the record, the book that I chose to teach for the session on political participation has neither my name nor that of any of my research collaborators on the cover.

62. These include, most notably, the Citizen Participation Study, the Roper Social and Political Trends data, and the DDB Needham Life Style surveys.

63. Although panel surveys would allow us to trace the participatory histories of individuals and to explain much more fully changes in individual political activity, panel studies have the disadvantage that attrition is relatively high and those who cannot be found in later waves are unlikely to be a random sample of initial members of the sample.

ANES is currently threatened by budget cuts from the National Science Foundation, it is extremely unlikely that the resources for such a study would become available.

Sample surveys are in many ways the appropriate instrument for research on political participation from the standpoint of both social science method and democratic theory: they not only provide a reasonably accurate baseline view of the American public but permit the assessment of the extent to which the norm of political equality is violated by politically relevant differences between participants and the public at large.[64] Nevertheless, surveys also have serious limitations. Surveys are justifiably criticized for failing to capture the historical and social context in which respondents' view are embedded. In addition, even when the questionnaire is long and the questions are well formulated, surveys cannot capture the rich texture of individuals' thinking and experiences. Thus, data from surveys gain greater resonance when supplemented by less superficial—but also less systematic—evidence gleaned from other sources: longer, open-ended interviews; participant observation; historical analysis; the media; or popular culture. If incorporated into research on participation, such qualitative sources not only would yield a deeper and more-rounded picture of the complexity of social life but would supply hypotheses worth testing, generating the questions we want to answer more systematically.[65]

At the same time that this has been a productive period for participation research that adheres to a certain framework, this research is limited by the fact that it seems somewhat divorced from other developments in the social sciences. Perhaps most surprising is the relative paucity of references to the dominant perspective in the certain fields within the discipline, rational choice. In what now seems to be the distant past, Anthony Downs (1957, chs. 3, 14) and Mancur Olson Jr. (1965) posed a formidable challenge to democratic theory by positing the irrationality of voting and collective action on behalf of shared political objectives.[66] Of course, the rational-choice perspective is hardly completely absent. Studies often use the language of costs and benefits as a way of exploring the compensatory benefits—whether material or, to an extent not always recognized by the

---

64. On this issue, see Verba 1996.

65. Recent examples of this kind of work include M. E. Warren 2001 and Sirianni and Friedland 2001.

66. Whiteley 1995 contains an extended discussion of the rational choice challenge to political participation and the theoretical failures of rational choice in accounting for participation as well as extensive citations to the literature. For additional discussion and empirical evidence about the benefits attendant to various kinds of participation, see Schlozman, Verba, and Brady 1995. For an assessment that seeks to specify the circumstances under which rational choice approaches are helpful in understanding political activity, see Verba, Schlozman, and Brady 2000.

stronger advocates of the rational-choice perspective, intangible—and the magnitude of the costs.[67] By and large, however, there seems to be tacit agreement with John Aldrich's observation that voting is "the major example of the failure of rational choice theory" (1993, 247) and an implicit assumption that rational-choice approaches are more productive for other political science problems, such as the behavior of legislators. In short, researchers seem to go about the business of seeking to understand political participation with much less concern about the free-rider problem than might have been expected.

Another surprise is the absence of intersection between research on participation and research on social movements.[68] On superficial examination, these two literatures seem quite separate. Cross-references in either direction are infrequent. The vocabulary is different. While participation scholars (by and large, political scientists) seek causal explanation and agonize over the choice of statistical method and the specification of the model, scholars of social movements (in the main, sociologists) are oriented to the construction of theory and obsess over matters of definition and categorization. Most importantly, the dependent variables tend to differ: students of political participation seek to explain individual behaviors, students of social movements to account for collective events.

Nevertheless, there is a great deal of substantive overlap. Contrary to what might be expected, research on political participation takes social structure seriously and research on social movements investigates the opportunities offered and constraints imposed by political institutions and processes. This overlap implies that these two sets of scholars have much to learn from one another. For example, the literature on participation tends to give short shrift to the role of deeply held political convictions in animating political activity; the emphasis in the social movement literature on "framing"—in particular, the processes by which politically relevant iden-

67. Examples include Uhlaner 1989, Morton 1991, and Teixeira 1992. Note that self-interested motives should not be equated with a rational-choice perspective. Green and Cowden (1992) find that White parents whose children were being bused were more likely to take part in antibusing protests, an action that involves self-interested objectives but would be considered irrational from the perspective of the free-rider problem—unless a particular individual is so well known or influential that he or she could make a difference by acting alone.

Empirical studies do not always substantiate the rational-choice perspective. For example, Oliver and Wolfinger (1999) adduce data to test the assumption that individuals make the rational choice to avoid registering to vote so as to avoid jury duty and find that the assumption does not hold up empirically.

68. The literature on social movements is very extensive and deserves a bibliographical essay of its own. As an introduction, see the helpful essays and references to the literature in two edited volumes: Morris and Mueller 1992 and McAdam, McCarthy, and Zald 1996, esp. Introduction and chs. 1, 2, 6, 11. A few recent works include Meyer and Staggenborg 1996, McCarthy and Wolfson 1996, Minkoff 1997, Tarrow 1998, and Cress and Snow 2000.

tities are constructed and definitions of collective interest emerge and are transformed—is a useful corrective. Reciprocally, social movement research pays scant attention to the way that what Sidney Tarrow (1998) calls the "contentious politics" of social movement activity relates to the ordinary participation that links citizens to policymakers on a day-to-day basis.[69] In the American context, the boundaries between contentious and mainstream politics are quite indistinct, and social movement activists often realize policy gains by using very conventional forms of involvement such as going to court. Furthermore, the rejection of sample surveys as unduly individualistic can lead social movement researchers to erroneous inferences. Although it is intrinsic to the understanding of social movement activity that it, by posing a challenge to authorities, is the "weapon of the weak," systematic evidence from surveys shows that the poor are underrepresented among protesters—although to a lesser extent than they are underrepresented among other kinds of activists.[70]

Similarly, historians and political scientists in the American political development tradition sometimes take up matters surrounding political participation. Alexander Keyssar's history (2000) of suffrage is an outstanding example.[71] However, there seems to be relatively little cross-fertilization between historically-oriented and survey-based studies of political activity.

Most serious is the failure of contemporary scholarship on participation to connect with inquiries that ask one of the most fundamental questions in political science, "Who governs?" The black box that has foiled students of organized interests for so long—the difficulty of making systematic assessments of the relative importance of various factors in influencing public outcomes—challenges participation researchers as well. It is easy to adduce evidence from anecdotes and case studies to demonstrate that citizen input through the medium of participation is one, though only one, among many factors that have an impact on policy. An exception to the absence of investigation into the policy consequences of citizen participation is Andrea Campbell's forthcoming study of the links between activity by senior citizens and policy on Social Security. Although her findings are not politically counterintuitive, she is able to demonstrate with systematic evidence that threats to Social Security produced upsurges in activity by se-

---

69. In light of its emphasis on matters of definition, it is especially puzzling that the social movement literature never elaborates the relationship between social movement organizations (SMOs) and the larger category of interest groups.

70. See Verba, Schlozman, and Brady 1995, 190–91.

71. Examples by political scientists might include historical studies of women's participation in party politics by Andersen (1996) and Freeman (2000) and work by Skocpol (1999) and Skocpol, Ganz, and Munson (2000) on the history of voluntary associations.

nior citizens and policy response by Congress.[72] In the aggregate, however, we know far too little that is systematic about the way that participatory messages are received and interpreted and the circumstances under which they make a difference.

Finally, perhaps political science's most consistently thoughtful student of democracy, Robert A. Dahl (1994), challenges us to think in fundamentally new ways about citizen participation in a democracy. He traces how the movement from the direct, or assembly, democracy of the Athenian city state to the representative democracy of the nation state recast the role of the citizen activist. We are now in the midst of a similarly fundamental transformation associated with internationalization and the creation of transnational institutions. He poses the question of whether democracy can adapt to this transformation and whether there will be a place for meaningful citizen participation in a transnational system. Or are citizen activity in its current incarnation, and the possibilities for democratic renewal and accountability that accompany it, about to be changed profoundly in an increasingly global world?

---

72. Other inquiries that have attempted to link political participation to policy outputs include those by Hill, Leighley, and Hinton-Andersson (1995) (as corrected in Ringquist, Hill, Leighley, and Hinton-Andersson 1997), who show that the mobilization of lower-class voters in a state is related to the generosity of state welfare benefits, and Fording (1997), who shows that, where coupled with electoral power, political violence can bring policy benefits in the form of increased welfare benefits.

Nancy Burns

Gender: Public Opinion and Political Action[1]

In 1983, when Marianne Githens discussed the state of the gender and politics field she wrote of the "mass of conflicting data and interpretations" and yearned for political science to look at gender and politics with clearer eyes (1983, 489). In 1993, when Susan Carroll and Linda Zerilli (1993) turned to assess the field, they were cautiously optimistic, pointing to the tremendous growth in the field, to the ways in which feminist theory and more empirically based work were drawing on each other, and to the challenges remaining with respect to central conceptual categories in the field. In this review, I take up this topic again and conclude that we are at a tremendous turning point. We have conceptualizations, methodological tools, cumulative knowledge, and a vast set of new questions to answer. And we have at hand one other immensely valuable resource—the theoretical and methodological work in other subfields and other disciplines, work that we can reconfigure and put to our own purposes.

I center my attention here on the literatures on American political behavior and public opinion—broadly conceived—at the mass and elite levels. In the first pages of the review, I worry about critical issues of conceptual development and method, issues that have often characterized the contributions gender scholars have made to political science, issues that will, I suspect, drive the future study of gender and politics. The first of these issues is preoccupied with studying categories in an individualistic discipline, the second, with linking life spaces, and the third, with building truly comparative analyses. The last pages of this review turn to specific literatures—on social movements, participation, public opinion, and elite

1. The article has benefited tremendously from suggestions and criticisms from Michael Dawson, Ira Katznelson, Mary Katzenstein, Claire Jean Kim, Donald Kinder, Helen Milner, Rebecca Morton, Karen Orren, Pam Trotman Reid, Kay Lehman Schlozman, Abigail Stewart, and the participants in the Conference on the State of the Discipline; from Anna Maria Ortiz's research assistance; from Barb Opal's help obtaining publications; and from years of conversations with Donald Kinder, Kay Lehman Schlozman, and Sidney Verba.

politics—and offer a guide to these literatures, set against the backdrop of these three defining concerns.

Throughout, I make suggestions about where the field might turn next. In making these suggestions, I point to literatures in other subfields and literatures in other disciplines as sources of theoretical guidance. At heart, I'm a social scientist. So I turn to literatures that offer theoretical lenses conducive to my social science bent or literatures that develop empirical portraits of gender in action, that is, to history, anthropology, philosophy, psychology, sociology, and economics. Other scholars writing this review might find their theoretical inspiration in other fields than these, and so might substitute literature for anthropology, architecture for sociology, or biology for economics. I suspect, though, that even with these substitutions, there would be significant overlap in the places we'd go for inspiration. In the end, the point of my examples is to encourage serious interdisciplinary borrowing wherever it offers theoretical or empirical guidance. And while I draw especially heavily from my list of seven disciplines, others might develop a different and equally compelling list.

■ | Conceptualization and Method: The Problem of Categories in an Individualistic Discipline

I start this review at the beginning: What do we mean by gender? From relatively early empirical efforts to untangle gender from data, scholars have been sure that gender is a multifaceted life experience, with many pieces, growing out of the complicated ways humans make people's—women's *and* men's—sex matter in a range of unlikely settings. But scholars have had access to different data and have been concerned with speaking to different theoretical traditions. What sometimes have looked like differences in the definition of gender have tended to be differences in measurement and data and method, instead. To take one example, nearly twenty years ago, Sapiro (1983) argued that gender is a constellation of life experiences; and her analyses centered on comparing the consequences of particular constellations in women's lives. Though today we might have more detailed data about the content of life experiences, Sapiro's approach is not tremendously different from the Giddens-inspired one (1984), combining structure and choice, constraint and agency, scholars are more likely to employ today. More recent accounts sound quite similar to Sapiro's conceptualization: to Nicholson's mind, for example, gender operates as a "network of characteristics" (1994, 100–1), or to Deaux and LaFrance, it is "a repository of possibilities from which situations select" (1998, 807). Gender is a repertoire of mechanisms that provide social interpretations of sex, that enable sex to structure people's lives. Gender is a set of ways in which people and institutions make sex matter. Gender is a principle of social organization. Gender is a hierarchy.[2]

Gender is not a property of individuals. It is a property of groups (Jackman 1994). Part of the theoretical and empirical difficulty of undertaking analyses of gender comes in trying to figure out which are the right groups for any particular inquiry, in trying to see how some women or some men share particular manifestations of gender, that is, how they share experiences with particular elements of the repertoire of mechanisms through which people and institutions make sex matter. Scholars have wanted to know where, when, how, and for whom sex is made to matter and what the consequences are for politics of this mattering. This is a difficult question to answer, largely because gender scholars in political science often have two valuable and competing goals. They want to devise theory and method to study categories—properties of groups—in a discipline taken with individualism. They want to understand how the category, woman or man, comes to matter in individuals' lives.

One standard approach has been to adopt gender as a rather content-free dichotomous variable dropped into a regression, on the idea that that will offer evidence about whether, by chance, gender matters.[3] This approach uses a particular definition of the right groups for all inquiries. This kind of analysis, used mostly outside the field of gender and politics, assumes that the right groups are all women and all men, that whatever gender is, it happens to differentiate the average woman from the average man. It ignores variation within the category, variation in the ways in which sex comes to matter for women and for men. *Perhaps* there are experiences that all women share; that they are rapable comes to mind. And *perhaps* there are experiences that all men share. Catherine MacKinnon (1987) relies on precisely this distinction between women's and men's location in the hierarchy of sexual access to generate a compelling analysis of how gender matters in some parts of the law.[4] The power of her analysis is most evident in some domains, such as the law relating to sexual harassment or domestic violence. But it would be odd to apply her analysis to all dependent variables we might investigate with respect to gender.

To get the gender result right—to see properly how gender matters—

2. As Stevens says of categories like these, "race always entails race-ism, just as much as gender differences always entail sexed forms of domination and that class entails exploitation" (1999, 173). MacKinnon makes the same point: gender, she says is "a question of power, specifically of male supremacy and female subordination . . . at root a question of hierarchy" (1987, 40).

3. For one helpful criticism of this approach, see Achen 1992. See, as well, the discussion in Barth 1969 about the importance of investigating continuous boundary maintenance in the face of categories that are ostensibly dichotomous.

4. Jackman (1994) relies on this distinction as well to motivate her analysis of the creation and maintenance of gender hierarchy.

we have to figure out whether the things that differentiate all, or almost all, women from all, or almost all, men are the things that drive the social and psychological processes relevant to the dependent variable at hand. Often those who take gender as a dichotomous variable fail to take this first step. In the end, with the clear exception of analyses like MacKinnon's (1987) and Jackman's (1994), this particular solution to the problem of categories in an individualistic discipline has not been very satisfactory. It relies on an odd melding of individualism and essentialism. And, again with notable exceptions, it generates results that can't tell us much about gender because these analyses are usually not tied to processes or mechanisms through which we make people's sex matter.

The analytic problem of gender is complicated in two ways. First off, because gender is a property of groups and because any group composing half the population is especially heterogeneous, the processes or mechanisms through which sex comes to matter will almost always operate on some women and some men, not all women and all men. That is, these processes will have some specificity. The second complication comes from the intimacy between women and men and the extent to which women and men share social locations. These aspects of social organization mean that while gender is sometimes carried out through overt coercion—discrimination and violence—and sometimes through more subtle forms of social pressure, it is also often carried out through the complicity of women. As Nancy Hirschmann puts it, "women [sometimes] seem to choose what they are in fact restricted to" (1996, 52). Roberta Sigel (1996) calls this "accommodation." Mary Jackman (1994) sees this as a consequence of the paternalism through which gender is maintained. These features of gender make gender harder on analysts than some other relatively bounded categories. Unlike race—wrapped up as it is with striking spatial segregation—average differences between women and men are rarely "divides" (Kinder and Winter 2001), and thus the wedding of an undifferentiated category to an individualistic enterprise makes less sense in the study of gender than it does in the study of some other bounded categories.[5]

Theorists have been working to devise ways to think about categories—like gender—that sometimes matter in people's lives, categories that sometimes unite some people, categories that matter to different people for different reasons, categories that, despite their lack of regularity and dependability, profoundly and persistently structure people's lives (Haslanger 2000; Wingrove 1999; I. M. Young 1994). At the same time, scholars who focus on intersectionality—that is, on the overlap between categories like gender and race—have spent their time on the other side of this issue (Crenshaw 1992; Higginbotham 1992; hooks 1984; Kim 1999; Nakano Glenn 1992; Stoler 1996), on the sometimes imperialistic reach of gender, race, and ethnicity, on the ways in which a focus on gender alone

5. "Bounded" is how Tilly (1998a) describes categories like gender and race.

erases systematic distinctions of race and a focus on race alone obliterates gender. In so doing, these scholars of intersectionality have highlighted the struggle to include categories and the hierarchies they represent in analyses of individuals. They have focused especially on one aspect of categorical specificity—on who is in the relevant category. And they have paid somewhat less attention to the places and dependent variables where this more specific category plays a role. And sometimes scholars have simply traded one category—women or African Americans—for another—African American women—without seeking to build an accommodation between categories and individuals. It is surely true that there are differences between some African American women and some white women, but it is also surely true that some of the pieces of the hierarchy of gender pay precious little attention to the differences between these two groups. We want accounts that specify when categories matter, which categories matter, and for whom they matter (Burns, Schlozman, and Verba 2001).

Gender scholars need categories—be they comprehensive or somewhat more circumscribed. Otherwise, we risk "morselizing" (to borrow Robert Lane's word) experience and missing the systematic and common ways categories like gender or race work in a range of different settings, for a range of different people. Categories are what we study. Of course, we need theory and method suited to accommodate categories to the analysis of individuals. And that accommodation has come when we have connected categories to processes and mechanisms, thereby noticing *and organizing for our analyses* the tremendous heterogeneity within categories. There is much more to do on this problem of categories, theoretically and empirically. We will succeed to the extent that we tie the ways we use categories to specific parts of the repertoire through which sex comes to matter in women's and men's lives.

This problem of categories makes trouble for empirical analyses. It turns out that it can be hard to see the property of a group in individual data. And it is especially hard to see the complicated residues of gender when our data have come from individuals at a single point in time. This is partly to do with the special nature of gender as a category, with the social organization that keeps gender from generating a divide. Attending to these two things together—the place of categories in individual-level analysis and the social organization of gender—requires sophisticated methodological tools. But only recently have we been able to train these sophisticated tools on the problem of understanding the difference gender makes in political life. By contrast, in some other fields, in some other surprising fields like econometrics, scholars have built quite good careers developing methods to untangle the ways gender interacts with economic institutions like the workplace (Heckman 1979; Heckman and Willis 1977; for a political application of these tools, see Schlozman, Burns, and Verba 1999). In these other fields, studying gender has meant developing new tools of quantitative analysis that notice the ways gender links social spaces, that allow for the heterogeneity in the category. In political science, we haven't done quite as much of this as we should have. We have not worked to devise new quantitative approaches that cross the divide between category and individual with the same zeal that we've applied to developing qualitative approaches to studying gender. But we are starting to remedy this, starting to figure out how to craft or reconfigure quantitative tools to allow us to see the residues gender leaves in our data. As a consequence, armed with new methodological tools, scholars are having more luck linking sophisticated conceptions of gender with individual-level data.

I hope we hone methodological tools that center on two features of gender. The first: because of the social organization of gender, it is much easier to see as it cumulates in people's lives than it is to see in a cross-section. Despite that, we have rarely used analyses of panel data to untangle gender from data.[6] Scholars less committed to methodological individualism and more comfortable with categories than most political scientists turn to aggregate analysis to solve this problem (Jackman 1994; Tilly 1998a). These aggregate analyses can sometimes offer a clear view of the cumulation of inequality, and they can do this with cross-sectional data. But we are individualistic political scientists, after all, and so we will have to devise different strategies, starting perhaps with a larger investment in panel analysis.

And the second: while gender does, of course, happen in politics, gender operates in *most* social institutions, and, as a consequence, much of the action is often offstage, *in* the variables we use to explain political outcomes and not in the coefficients in our models (for efforts to develop an analytic method to address the issue, see Burns, Schlozman, and Verba 2001; Sapiro and Conover 1997; and, for an excellent conversation on just this point, talk to Sue Carroll). This has important consequences. First, gender has already done much of its work when, for example, it gives people levels of education or engagement with religion and not politics. Second, gender scholars have often pointed to the links gender builds between public lives and private ones, frequently aiming to sort out the implications of the way we organize our private lives for power in public spaces (Blair and Henry 1981; Burns, Schlozman, and Verba 2001; Carroll 1989; Gurin 1987; M. M. Lee 1976; McGlen 1980; Okin 1989; Sapiro 1983; Stoper 1977). They have insisted that we notice the relevance of outcomes in domains outside of politics for political thought and action.[7] And they have said we should go farther than that: we should examine the details of social processes outside of politics and work out the implications of those processes for political analysis. Because gender comes to matter in almost

6. For important, early exceptions to this claim, see Andersen 1975 and Andersen and Cook 1985.

7. Again, MacKinnon makes this point especially clearly: she says that men "get preferred because society advantages them before they get into court" (1987, 35).

all social institutions in one way or another, it builds a special kind of linkage across these institutions. As scholars, political scientists have developed a special talent for ignoring these linkages. We have an unfortunate habit of attending to the coefficients in our models and not to the levels of the variables with which our respondents come to our equations, a practice that—in its rush to individualism, in the ways it erases the consequences of categorical treatment—can make gender invisible. Of course, we may want categories to organize our individual-level analyses by making us focus on categorical differences in coefficients; but if categorical treatment happens to individuals outside of politics, we may be even more interested in categorical differences in the levels of variables in our models. In addition, perhaps because of the widespread reliance on gender as a content-free dichotomous variable, political scientists are used to the idea that gender can be captured in a single coefficient. Usually, however, it can't be: when gender is in coefficients, it is often in a *pattern* of coefficients. (Think, for example, about how to see the role gender plays in access to the workforce: one important part of that would be in the pattern of coefficients on children and marriage for women compared with those same coefficients for men.) Gender scholars—and scholars interested in the residues of hierarchical categories in general—must push political science to new practices.

In my discussion to this point, I have assumed the value of comparative study. The field has recently and profitably turned in that direction. Gender scholarship has often run on implicit comparisons between different groups of women or between women and men, but it has made advances more recently by taking advantage of the explicit comparative leverage that comes from developing theoretical claims about gender in men's lives or working class women's lives or African American women's lives. These claims have been successful when they have turned on the particular mechanisms that make sex matter and when they have been comparative. This expansion of comparative possibilities has made a tremendous difference to work on gender in a range of subfields—American political development (see, for example, Mettler 1998; Skocpol 1992), public opinion (Conover 1988; Sigel 1996), legislative turnover (Blair and Henry 1981; Carroll 1989) and participation (Burns, Schlozman, and Verba 2001). Political scientists, like scholars in other disciplines, have often studied men, but they have rarely studied men with an eye to the ways in which gender shapes men's thoughts and actions (for excellent exceptions, see J. Adams 1996; Bederman 1995). In contrast with other disciplines, political science has been slow to take up the comparative leverage on gender offered by different groups of women. We must expand our commitment to comparative study—of hierarchies and of intersectionality—to understand how, for all its variability, gender is a systematic social force.

To my mind, the issues I have outlined in these first pages characterize the field and outline its possibility for growth. Some pieces will likely endure—the variability of gender, its location in a constellation of life experiences, and the focus on interlocking life spaces. Some pieces present challenges to new generations of scholars—to think more creatively about the place of categories in an individualistic discipline like political science, to devise better methods for seeing gender in individual-level and often cross-sectional data, and to develop the theoretical tools for more comparative work on gender. The likely next step for political science, the postinstitutional step, will be to develop a rich account of the interaction between institutions and individuals, to draw more forcefully than modern institutional analysis has on the psychological and sociological foundations of thought and action, and to place those richer accounts of thought and action in the context of the increasingly strong work on institutions themselves. Gender scholars, who must deal repeatedly with gender in a range of settings for a range of people, should be in front of this new political science.

The field is in a remarkable position, with the foundations laid for a tremendous range of interesting research, without being overtilled, and with a deep supply of theoretical tools. The field is especially fortunate. It is coming of age precisely when the comparative possibilities of gender scholarship—possibilities grounded in the study of comparative hierarchies and in the comparative study of intersectionality—are exploding.

■ | Citizens and Elites, Action and Opinion

With this overview in hand, I turn my attention to the questions, approaches, and evidence from the literatures in American politics on social movements, public opinion, participation, candidates, and policymakers. In almost all of these literatures, explanatory tastes have been driven, in part, by the field's desire for an account of gender that can contend with heterogeneity.

Of course, as in any field, gender scholars have also been guided by explanations that depend partly on the explanatory turn in vogue at the time, and most recently, that explanatory turn has centered on institutions. Early work focused on the roots of gender in childhood and centered its attention on socialization within the family (Greenstein 1965; Hess and Torney 1968; Iglitzin 1974; Orum, Cohen, Grassmuck, and Orum 1977). As early as the mid-1970s (in Andersen's [1975] and Welch's [1977] seminal articles), we tried to locate gender away from childhood socialization and within adult life. Initially and not surprisingly, the impulse in this turn to adulthood was to focus on roles and role expectations within the family and the workplace. More recently, we've maintained our concern with institutions, but we have drawn our theoretical inspiration less from Parsons and more from a pragmatic interest in the details of adult institutions (once again, with a focus on the family and the workplace). And we increasingly nod to theoretical traditions in other fields, traditions that develop the case for the connection between gender and institutional life. Surely, in the not too distant future, we will integrate more fully theoretical approaches to institutions and institutional life developed in other fields into our scholarship—organization theory (Powell and DiMaggio 1991), gender theory like Eagly's (1987) in psychology, for example. Our theoretical impulses value constraint—as opposed to gender as a set of choices freely made—and contingency—as opposed, perhaps, to essentialism—in a way that is consistent with the theoretical turn to institutions in other fields.

Chances are high that we will return to things we have abandoned. Childhood surely *is* part of the story of the variability of gender. Our worry about explanations rooted in childhood socialization was that these explanations neglected contingency and variability. In early accounts of childhood socialization, there seemed to be one way for little boys, one way for little girls. But this problem is not inherent in explanations rooted in childhood. Work in the last ten years in psychology and political science provides gender scholars the tools to reconsider socialization to politics in a more contingent and variable way (in psychology, the work of Eccles [1994] and her colleagues focuses on the mechanisms of gender socialization; in sociology, see Thorne 1993 on childhood play; and in political science, Jennings and Stoker 1999 and Jennings, Stoker, and Bowers 1999 provide the empirical lens for a reconsideration of the roots of gender variability in childhood).

The Contours of Institutional Analysis

WHAT WE HAVE DONE

In their recent institutional turn, gender scholars have had several analytic goals in mind. Sometimes, they've been interested in understanding how gender is conceptualized within an institutional space and in sorting out the consequences of that conceptualization (Epstein 1988; Skocpol 1992; Orloff 1996). In so inquiring, they have followed Goffman's fascination with the ways humans can make gender relevant in almost any setting. And they have followed his outline for institutional analysis. As Goffman put it, "It is not, then, the social consequences of innate sex differences that must be explained, but the way in which these differences were (and are) put forward as a warrant for our social arrangements, and, most important of all, the way in which the institutional workings of society ensured that this accounting would seem sound" (1977, 302).

Other times, scholars have been interested in whether the rules of conduct in an institution define and enable women's fights for standing and power. M. F. Katzenstein (1998) offers an account along these lines. In her story of efforts to change two conservative institutions—the military and the Catholic Church—from within, military women and women in the Catholic Church faced different rules of conduct. Military women had access to the judicial system; they thus had ready-made routes and forms for contestation. These activists won regularly, but their victories were on small issues suited to available legal arguments. Such routes didn't exist in the Catholic Church. So women in the Catholic Church had to make their own way; their way was persuasion, discursive politics, an effort to change the basic ideas church members held about gender. In Harvey's account (1998), the institutions were political parties, but the story wasn't much different. The incentives offered up by politics shaped the strategies party leaders, leaders of women's groups, and members of Congress pursued immediately following Woman Suffrage.

Scholars have also looked at whether any different voice women might use depends on the positions of power they hold within institutions. While these arguments have been developed extensively in other disciplines (Eagly 1987; Kanter 1977), versions of them are starting to appear in political science. Sigel, for one, says that institutional constraints, "rather than women's preferences or skills, explain most of the ways that women's behavior differs from that of men" (1996, 16). Okin, too, draws on this perspective. She says, for example, "Once we admit the idea that significant differences between women and men are *created by* the existing division of labour within the family, we begin to see the depth and the extent of the social construction of gender" (1998, 127). To some extent, work that argues that women's arguments depend on the opportunities presented them fits here as well (Katzenstein 1998; Reingold 2000), as does the linguistic analysis offered by Kathlene (1994).

WHAT WE HAVE LEFT UNDONE

Mostly outside of political science, scholars have been interested in the sex segregation of institutions, and they've been especially engaged with the possibility that sex segregation and role differentiation anchor ends of a continuum. Jackman, for example, argues that when sex segregation of institutions disappears, we get role differentiation between hierarchical groups: hierarchy is regularly and predictably managed and maintained through separation of one sort or another, that is, through spatial segregation or role differentiation (Jackman 1994). Others have been interested in the consequences of sex-segregated social life for women's economic and political opportunities more broadly (Smith-Lovin and McPherson 1991). This scholarship draws on increasingly sophisticated ideas about social networks (Granovetter 1973; McAdam and Paulsen 1993). And, as Ridgeway and Smith-Lovin point out, "The picture that emerges from the research about social networks is one in which women seldom meet men in status-equal, role-similar interactions" (1999, 195). We've seen mere traces of this important work in political science. Huckfeldt and Sprague (1995) look especially at political discussion among husbands and wives. Stoker and Jennings (1995) examine the joint political activity of husbands and wives. Sapiro (1983) considers the determinants of the size of women's social networks. And Burns, Schlozman, and Verba (2001) explore the consequences of sex-segregated organizations for women's and men's skill development.

One other important line of work, mostly outside of political science, has explored the extent to which men and women "do gender" in a particular domain. To what extent do women and men play out their ideas of appropriate gender roles within a domain? To what extent are they accountable to gender? This interactional approach (put forward most forcefully by West and Zimmerman [1987]) builds on the models developed by Goffman (1959, 1977) and focuses more on the connections between our own ideas and our actions than on any sort of external constraint that might shape behavior. In psychology and sociology, scholars have focused on where our gender role beliefs come from, on the specific, gendered socialization processes that encourage children to value certain pursuits and to code those pursuits as male or female (Eccles 1994; Thorne 1993). In political science, scholars have worked with related ideas, though the connection to the interactional school has been tenuous. In particular, scholars have differentiated women with respect to their views of women's proper roles, and they have argued that the beliefs that work to keep women at home also influence the kinds of political involvements in which women engage (Clark and Clark 1986; Gurin 1987; Klatch 1987; Luker 1984; Mansbridge 1986; Mathews and DeHart 1992; Sapiro 1983; Tolleson Rinehart 1992).

We have work to do to round out our current fascination with institutional analysis. I hope that as scholars pursue this line of inquiry, they build tighter links to other disciplines and to institutional analysis (in addition to the literature on American political development, where the linkages are already strong) in other fields in political science. I hope as well that we use the lens gender provides us to develop new ways of thinking about institutions.

The Literature

SOCIAL MOVEMENTS

I turn away, now, from conceptual and explanatory issues that concern the field as a whole, and to specific literatures. I start with the literature on social movements because it is perhaps the most conceptually rich of those I examine here, and many of the ideas developed in this literature could be interestingly and profitably combined with the work on citizen and elite behavior I will turn to next. Among the literatures I examine here, this one is the most distant from methodological individualism, and so its successes—like the successes in the study of gender and social policy—have come largely without having to contend with the problem of categories.

What have scholars found in this literature? To start, they have shown that women's movements, like most social movements, depend heavily on indigenous—preexisting, sex segregated—organizations and networks. We have seen this over and over again: in Jo Freeman's pathbreaking work (1975) on the networks that enabled the modern women's movement; in Nancy Cott's book (1977) on the ways in which women used the skills and arguments they developed within religious institutions to move to public work on social reform; in Jane Mansbridge's arguments (1986) about the mobilizing advantages of anti–Equal Rights Amendment (ERA) forces compared with pro-ERA activists; Mathews and DeHart's engrossing account (1992) of the whole range of networks on which anti-ERA activists could draw. Of course, this reliance on indigenous organizations is a general result about social movements (McAdam 1982). What is perhaps especially interesting is the repeated reliance on an institutional space in which women have been especially active (though not always especially honored): religious institutions.

Organizers have been quite creative: they have drawn on religious institutions to craft a wide range of women's movements. Women seem to have only fleeting opportunities—like those Freeman (1975) outlines—to draw on other kinds of indigenous institutions. Women's movements that haven't been able to rely, for the long term, on the grassroots support provided through indigenous institutions have sometimes ended up relying on a small group of activists, for good or ill (Mansbridge 1986). Of course, other social movements—movements not focused on gender—that rely on indigenous organizations often end up reproducing the gender hierarchies within those organizations (see, for example, C. J. Cohen's discussion [1999] of gay and lesbian activists' efforts to be heard in modern African American politics and Payne's investigation [1995] of women's activism within the early, rural Civil Rights movement). There are hints in this literature about what might be special about women's indigenous institutions, about the difficulty—striking in comparison with race—of finding a segregated space in which to build consciousness and resources.

In the past, women seemed able to turn arguments others made to limit their roles to their own purposes, exploiting those arguments to open up more spaces for political power. Women's abilities to do this were enhanced because, historically, accounts of gender—unlike accounts of some other group-based hierarchies—were especially nuanced and well developed in political life (for the strongest elaboration of this argument, comparing the possibilities of this strategy for women, Blacks, the working class, and Jews, see Herzog 1998; for other important versions of this account, see Cott 1977; Bederman 1995).

In addition to subverting arguments others make to limit their roles, women have also been able to use small grants of power or standing within institutions to push for change. They have used the space others have given them or they have taken for themselves in elite institutions in creative ways. Harrison (1988) writes of the ways in which women developed strategies to ensure policies to aid women reached the federal agenda and to ensure the appointment of women in the federal bureaucracy. Katzenstein (1998) tells of strategies women developed to change conservative institutions from within. Freeman (2000) describes the approaches women invested in traditional party politics devised to make a space for power inside American political parties. And Andersen (1996) points to the changes wrought in the practice of electoral politics from the political incorporation of women. These works provide the grounding for new questions gender scholars could ask: Compared with other kinds of hierarchies, does gender make for an odd kind of integration into these spaces? If the focus were race and not gender, how would the story change? Does intimacy provide access? Does essentialism make it easy to keep some forms of institutional segregation alive?

Scholars believe that the sometimes surprising places where feminists find themselves make for a diffuse and potentially resilient movement (Boles 1994; Costain 1992; Katzenstein 1998). This has been true even inside American political parties, where women were active and influential well before women had the right to vote (Andersen 1996; Cott 1990; Edwards 1997; Freeman 2000; Harrison 1988; Harvey 1998; Higginbotham 1990). Their insider strategies often changed the relationship of the parties to political issues (like the ERA; see Harrison 1988; Freeman 1987), and these strategies almost always increased the representation of women in federal bureaucracies.

Consciousness has been an undependable resource for politics. While scholars have fine-tuned their measures of gender consciousness over time from Gurin's seminal work (1985) on gender consciousness through Tolleson Rinehart's important effort (1992) to tease ideology out of the measure of gender consciousness and Wong's efforts (1998) to compare measures of closeness to a range of different groups, scholars have had trouble demonstrating the impact of consciousness.[8] In recent years especially, they have had an easier time demonstrating that consciousness relates to policy preferences than to political action (Conover 1988; Conover and Sapiro 1993). While consciousness may channel political action (Burns, Schlozman, and Verba 2001), it has been only unreliably connected to political participation since the early 1980s. Many scholars—using a range of measures differing in the details—find that the power of gender consciousness to generate action has waned over the last thirty years. In the 1970s, women's

8. Of course, consciousness has a long history in the study of race and class (for a discussion, see, for example, Elster 1985; Schlozman and Verba 1979; Verba and Nie 1972).

consciousness seemed to encourage political participation among women (Hansen, Franz, and Netemeyer-Mays 1976; Conway, Steuernagel, and Ahern 1997, 88–91; Miller, Gurin, Gurin, and Malanchuk 1981; Klein 1984, 136; Tolleson Rinehart 1992, 134–139). Since then, no. And, when scholars have compared the power of Black consciousness with the power of gender consciousness to generate activism, they have gotten different results, sometimes finding that Black consciousness is especially important (Wilcox [1997], who found that gender consciousness did not make a difference) and sometimes not (Ardrey 1994). But Sigel (1996, 127) offers hope that scholars will pay more attention to the priority that members of a disadvantaged group give to their group membership. She argues that when scholars move to incorporate priority into their traditional measures of group consciousness, they will see much more clearly the role of group consciousness in shaping a range of outcomes. In a related fashion, I. M. Young (1994) suggests we look for mechanisms that trigger consciousness, that U.S. women may not wear their consciousness on their sleeves (see, as well, Tolleson Rinehart 1992; Sapiro and Conover 1997). Dawson (2001) develops promising new tools for examining Black feminist consciousness. Work in psychology has continued to refine measures of gender consciousness (Henderson-King and Stewart 1994) and offers guidance here as well. It would be helpful to understand more thoroughly whether gender consciousness takes a different form than race consciousness. What trouble does intimacy make for conceptions of linked fate?

The existing work on consciousness and the changing results over time—changes that seem more connected with the year the data were collected than with the method employed by the researcher—suggest a dynamic account of consciousness, one that links elite mobilization to mass participation and that draws more heavily on notions of political opportunity (Tarrow 1994; see Sapiro and Conover 1997). We have important beginnings of this argument in Costain 1992, Conover and Gray 1983, Klein 1984, and Katzenstein and Mueller 1987. One could go even farther to develop a rich account of the incentives and actions of elites and their consequences for citizen behavior, perhaps along the lines of Rosenstone and Hansen (1993) or Kollman (1998). Harvey (1998) does some of this, but, though she alludes to citizen behavior, her work and her evidence are concentrated at the elite level.

Gender identity is clearly at home in, comfortably articulated with, a whole range of social movements. Of course, Goffman could have told us that. Gender-identified women are at home in the Klan and can develop a perfectly sensible account of why women's values belong in the Klan (Blee 1991) (*and* they use surprising indigenous institutions like the Quaker Church to develop the base for Klan organizing). Because women sometimes buy into hierarchical accounts of gender, through the cooptation Jackman (1994) describes or the accommodation Sigel (1996) points to, this malleability—this fit of gender identity with many different kinds of movements—is perhaps not surprising (Tolleson Rinehart's work [1992] to pull ideology from gender identity moves in exactly this direction). As a consequence of this malleability, elites have been able to exploit gender identity for their own ends, in the ways Harvey (1998) suggests, as a kind of campaign slogan parties learned how to use, or in the ways Bonk (1988) points to, in which women are seen by politicians as a kind of infinitely re-describable, recombinable, redividable group.

Women's marginal political space has sometimes provided the impetus for expanding Americans' political repertoire (Tilly 1986). Flexner (1975) describes women's successful work to modernize lobbying strategies in order to win Woman Suffrage. Charles Payne (1995) tells of the ways in which women were shunned as public spokespersons for the Civil Rights movement but, in the face of these barriers, used their skills to develop new, tremendously successful, grassroots strategies for the movement. Katzenstein (1998) takes up this topic as well and arrives at an account of discursive strategies of women in the Catholic Church. Kollman discusses the ways groups like the National Organization for Women (NOW) have tried to shape public opinion, hoping that "Public legitimacy for policies [NOW proposes] . . . will follow the group's activities rather than precede them" (1998, 108). Freedman (1999) analyses the consequences of the campaigns pro-choice and pro-life groups wage, in Freedman's words, to "manipulate ambivalence," that is, to build legitimacy for their side among those who don't yet know their own minds. And Dawson (2001) provides evidence of the emerging payoffs to the discursive strategies Black feminists are pursuing within the academy.

The work on gender and social movements has explored—powerfully—the ways in which women have and haven't been able to rely on social movements to create political change, the special forms women's activism has taken, the special strategies women's activism has employed, and why. The picture that emerges from this literature taken as a whole is of the creative potential embedded in the just-marginal position of women with respect to the political system. This literature can do more, now, to develop accounts of comparative hierarchies within and across social movements, to think about the comparative study of intersectionality, to ask what exactly is special about gender.

PUBLIC OPINION

The literature on gender and public opinion has been consumed—more than the literature on social movements—by a focus on difference. The best work has looked at difference in the context of theoretical accounts of women, men, and gender taken together. Though it's been closer to the individualistic core of the discipline, this literature has only just started to struggle with the tension between individuals and categories.

Scholars have carefully mapped the terrain on which there is a gender gap in opinion on political issues (Frankovic 1982; Goertzel 1983; Klein

1985; Shapiro and Mahajan 1986; Conover 1988; Kenski 1988; Miller 1988; Welch and Sigelman 1989; Bendyna and Lake 1994; Conway, Steuernagel, and Ahern 1997; Norris 1985; on local political issues, Schumaker and Burns 1988; Burns and Schumaker 1987). For the past two decades, women have been more Democratic than men. And they've consistently supported welfare policies and opposed international aggression and the use of violence somewhat more than men. At the local level, men have been more supportive of economic growth, and women more supportive of public welfare and neighborhood protection, though the differences are larger among policymakers and activists than among citizens (Schumaker and Burns 1988, 1080). The places where there has been no gap are less surprising in light of the work of Tolleson Rinehart (1992) and Sigel (1996) demonstrating the tremendous variability in women's views of their own roles: there have been no aggregate differences of opinion on abortion, women's rights, or the Equal Rights Amendment (Craig and O'Brien 1993; Ladd and Bowman 1997). Scholars—worried that the literature has gotten caught up in an essentialized account of gender—have emphasized that, where there are differences, "they are certainly not large enough to warrant making the kinds of sweeping statements differentiating women and men that have long been part of stereotype" (Conover and Sapiro 1993, 1095).

We know something as well about the ways in which women and men prioritize issues. Recent work has begun to explore women's and men's political priorities (Paolino 1995; Kaufmann and Petrocik 1999; Sapiro and Conover 1997; Dolan 1998), sometimes looking at the connections between salience and vote choice in general and sometimes exploring the link between support for women candidates and salience. In the general models, it seems as if women and men do sometimes find different issues salient when they make political choices, though the results are still murky. The most-intriguing result is that "women are considerably less likely than men to cast egocentric economic votes, but are as likely, or perhaps more so, to cast sociotropic economic votes" (Welch and Hibbing 1992, 197). The results are clearer when the focus is on support for women candidates; women sometimes weight issues such as parental leave and their own views on feminism more heavily in these vote choices (Paolino 1995; Dolan 1998), though there is more work to do here to develop a richer theoretical account (see the important beginnings to do just that in Huddy and Terkildsen 1993). Results from the participation literature also suggest that women and men may sometimes prioritize issues somewhat differently. When scholars ask people about the issues on which they participate, they find that, while the bundles of issues on which women and men participate are remarkably similar, there are a few issues on which women are more active than men—education and abortion—and a few on which men are more active than women—taxes and foreign policy (Schlozman, Burns, Verba, and Donohue 1995). Interestingly, women's greater activism on abortion (in data taken in 1990) comes from women opposed to abortion. In addition, disadvantaged women much more than disadvantaged men are active on issues of basic human needs and crime and drugs (Burns, Schlozman, and Verba 2001). And, scholars suggest, gender conscious women's participation *is* different from other women's in its focus on gender-related issues (Burns, Schlozman, and Verba 2001). In one other way, scholars have looked at the differences between women and men in terms of political priorities; they have compared how thought-out, how elaborated, women's and men's views are about political and social issues surrounding gender. What they have found is that men seem much less engaged with the topic of gender than are women (Sigel 1996).

What are the roots of these differences in opinion? What conceptual tools have we used to think about this question? The classic piece on this topic is Luker's compelling portrait (1984) of the worldviews of pro-choice and pro-life activists. Luker developed an argument about the opinion ingredients (Kinder and Sanders 1996) of abortion views. To her mind, views on abortion are intimately tied with "beliefs about the roles of the sexes, about the meaning of parenthood, and about human nature" (1984, 158; see, too, the accounts in Mathews and DeHart 1990; Mansbridge 1986; and Klatch 1987). Scholars have built on the foundation Luker provided to think about other forms of gender-based opinion ingredients, and they have asked whether men's and women's opinions are similarly structured. They have explored group differences in the links between feminism and ideas about motherhood, comparing groups of African American women activists with groups of white women activists and finding that some African American women activists are more comfortable with putting motherhood at the center of their feminism than are some white women activists (Polatnick 1996). They have explored the possibility that maternal thinking might offer special guidance to opinion (Ruddick 1989). With the data available, it looks like the answer is no (Sapiro and Conover 1997). They have investigated the possibility that women with feminist or gender consciousness might be more supportive of the Democratic Party, abortion rights, women's rights, or the ERA and more opposed to violence; in general, the answer here seems to be yes (Carroll 1988; Conover 1988; Sapiro and Conover 1997; Tolleson Rinehart 1992). They have begun to explore the possibility that context itself can make feminist consciousness more relevant for individual-level opinion for some people some times (Sapiro and Conover 1997). Some scholars have focused on men's social welfare attitudes and the extent to which it is those attitudes which generate much of the gender gap in partisan identification and vote choice (Kaufmann and Petrocik 1999). By building accounts based on heterogeneity and its link to specific processes, this part of the public opinion literature has begun to offer hints about how to work out an accommodation with individualism.

There have been more fleeting efforts to examine the other side of this question, the consequences of *sexism* as opposed to gender consciousness for public opinion. There are hints of this in Tolleson Rinehart's examination (1992) of the consequences of traditional views on gender for policy views and more than hints in Sanbonmatsu's effort (2000) to measure gender stereotypes and to assess their consequences for vote choice. Jackman (1994) offers one of the few accounts of the ways aspects of sexism shape public opinion. Her aggregate-level analysis, combined with the increasingly rich psychological literature on varieties of sexism (see the helpful review in Deaux and LaFrance 1998), provides the foundation for exploring this issue at the individual level. Jackman (1994) makes a strong claim that sexism in the United States is carried out more through paternalism than through coercion and hostility; Sigel's (1996) data on women's accommodation to inequality provides some supporting evidence. Using aggregate analysis, Jackman (1994) argues that, even among men, sexism is not much about hostility. In psychology and at the individual level, the story looks more complicated (see, especially, Glick and Fiske 1996). This emerging—and extremely promising—part of the literature would do well to look at the ways scholars have studied racism and public opinion.

The literature on gender and public opinion has tremendous potential for growth, as scholars take up the comparative study of hierarchies, drawing lessons from and developing comparisons with the rich and varied ways scholars have explored the connections between racial thought and public opinion and as scholars spend more time in literatures in other fields—like psychology—where scholars have developed a wide range of theoretical tools to use to think about thinking about gender. These other fields offer mechanisms that political scientists can use to think systematically about the variability of gender.

PARTICIPATION AND CIVIC ENGAGEMENT

The literature on gender and participation, too, has focused on difference, on the gap between women and men. However, the literature has been less centered on charting the terrain of difference and more concerned with explaining the gap. As a consequence, this literature has grappled more often with variability among women and men.

With respect to political participation, scholarly analyses of gender and political activity have reported small but persistent sex differences in overall levels of political activity. This small gender gap in participation is, it seems, narrower in the United States than in other countries (Christy 1987; Verba, Nie, Kim, and Shabad 1978). Scholars have been developing a mostly structural story of constraint, located in institutions outside of politics.

Scholars have offered four major explanations for women's slightly lower levels of political participation in the United States—all centered on the heterogeneous but systematic ways gender structures individual lives. First, scholars have suggested that the difference is a consequence of resource disparities between women and men. Earlier work focused on in-

come and education (Welch 1977); later work looked at a wider array of resources, ranging from institutionally acquired skills to free time to the control of money at home (Burns, Schlozman, and Verba 1997, 2001).
Second, scholars thought that women might participate at lower levels
than men because marriage, motherhood, and homemaking socialize
women out of politics (Andersen 1975; Jennings and Niemi 1981; Sapiro
1983; Welch 1977). Third, scholars have asked whether childhood socialization depresses women's political involvement (Welch 1977). Finally,
scholars have examined the role of perspectives on gender roles as a cause
of political activity; this explanation is often linked to adult or childhood
socialization (Clark and Clark 1986; Sapiro 1983; Tolleson Rinehart
1992).

The cumulative results of the investigations of these hypotheses have
been mixed. Women's employment mattered in the earlier investigations
(Andersen 1975; Welch 1977); it seemed to matter less or have mixed effects in later investigations (Beckwith 1986; Jennings and Niemi 1981;
Tolleson Rinehart 1992). Education has almost always helped women;
however, the gender-based education differential has been persistently narrowing (Welch 1977). At times ideology mattered, with liberal, less traditional, or more gender conscious women participating at higher levels
(Andersen 1975; Clark and Clark 1986; Sapiro 1983; Tolleson Rinehart
1992). Under some conditions, women's roles have influenced their political involvements (Clark and Clark 1986; Jennings and Niemi 1981; Sapiro
1983).

Early scholars yearned for data on the details of institutional experiences, especially for details about the workplace, in order to move farther
from the dichotomy of gender and toward a differentiated view of the
processes that come to make sex matter (Andersen and Cook 1985, 622).
These scholars built a field by creatively and opportunistically making do
with the data available on employment, housewife status, parenthood,
marriage, education, beliefs about women's place, and gender consciousness to test complex theoretical ideas about the relationship between gender and political participation. With the advent of data sets containing
much more detail on experiences in the workplace and in the family,
scholars have been able to broaden their investigations to examine more
fully the mechanisms that link gender with political involvement (Burns,
Schlozman, and Verba 2001). They have been able to ask, in more detail,
whether and how inequality at home shapes political participation. They
found that division of labor doesn't seem to matter directly. For women,
what does seem to matter is participating in the process of decision making
within the family, and for men, what matters, alas, is being in control at
home (Burns, Schlozman, and Verba 1997, 2001).

In the end, the current account on the table is one of small cumulative differences in resources growing out of a host of institutions, in childhood and in adulthood. Women have access to lower levels of education

and income. But they are also tremendously disadvantaged—and men are tremendously advantaged—by the ways gender links the home and the workplace, putting men in and keeping more than a few women out of the workplace. The workplace goes further than that to disadvantage women; in particular, workplaces allocate their benefits—money, politically relevant skills, and mobilization—on the basis of gender. Marital status and children do not have a direct impact on political participation in the cross-section, but they do have an indirect effect. For women, the indirect effect comes largely from the ways large-scale division of labor at home keeps some women with small children out of the workforce. For men, the indirect effects come from advantages to men, advantages that come from the ways children encourage men's workforce *and* religious participation. The story has come to center on the way gender links institutions and on the centrality of gender to institutions outside of politics. And in so doing, this literature has moved to an accommodation with categorical analysis.

That the roots of political life should rest, in part, in nonpolitical civic life comes as no surprise. Women have, of course, been involved in nonpolitical civic life for a very long time. And their movement between civic spaces has been well documented in the literature (Cott 1977; Davis 1981; Giddings 1984; Greenberg 2001; Harris 1999; Lerner 1979; Scott 1984). These nonpolitical civic spaces have often provided the skills and mobilization to bring women (and men) to politics (Tate 1991, 1994; Harris 1999; Walton 1985).

With all of this work, puzzles remain. The first is that of women's low psychological involvement with politics. Evidence of these lower levels of psychological involvement with politics is all around us (Andersen 1975; Baxter and Lansing 1983; Beckwith 1986; Bennett and Bennett 1989; Delli Carpini and Keeter 1993, 1996; Rapoport 1982, 1985; Sapiro 1983; Soule and McGrath 1977; Tolleson Rinehart 1992). The most successful recent efforts to understand women's lower levels of political engagement have turned to look at politics itself, at the paucity of elite women in politics, especially. Through both longitudinal and cross-sectional analyses, these efforts have suggested that the presence of women in visible political positions engages women citizens (Verba, Burns, and Schlozman 1997; Burns, Schlozman, and Verba 2001; Hansen 1997; Sapiro and Conover 1997). McDermott (1997) makes a compelling case for the role candidate gender plays in low-information elections, demonstrating the power candidate gender has in shaping vote choice when citizens know little about a candidate. And Huddy and Terkildsen (1993) explore the traits and issue competencies that women and men have in mind when faced with cues from candidate gender; their work suggests that traits—such as compassion and trustworthiness—might be at the center of people's interpretation of gender in the electoral context (see, too, Kahn 1992). Stenner (2001) goes farther than this to show that women confronted with strong female candidates gain self-esteem and self-confidence. This self-esteem and confi-

dence lead to an increase in their political knowledge and interest. In Stenner's experiments, men experience exactly the opposite outcome when
faced with strong women candidates: they tune out. Work by Kahn suggests
that the media has historically covered women candidates less well than
men candidates (Kahn 1994a) and that this difference in coverage may
make women candidates seem less viable (Kahn 1992, 1994a).

This line of work offers increasingly tight linkages to the psychological
literatures that can provide guidance about the mechanisms that might enable women candidates to engage women (and possibly disengage men)
with the political system, mechanisms that move the literature to a clearer
view of contingency and variability. In addition, because the gap in engagement appears to open well before women and men are settled into
adulthood, we'll want to turn back to consider childhood. With the theoretical tools I mentioned earlier, we can develop a contingent account of
gender and childhood socialization to politics.

Another puzzle centers on the comparative study of gender and political action. There is very little work developing the theoretical and empirical bases for a comparative and intersectional account of women's and
men's participation. Consider, for example, Asian-American women's political participation. As Junn has pointed out using aggregate analysis, basic
resource-based models of the constraints on political action—models focusing on education and income—seem to do a poor job of accounting for
Asian-American women's levels of political activity (Junn 1997). Consider,
as well, the work of scholars studying Arab-American women's political action (Lin and Jamal 1998), demonstrating the consequences of the organization of Arab-American interest groups for women's and men's political
action. There are hints about how a fully comparative analysis would go:
building on the emerging literature on African American women's and
Latinas' political activity (Ardrey 1994; Baxter and Lansing 1983; Fulenwider 1981; Hardy-Fanta 1993; Harmon-Martin 1994; Welch and Secret
1981), Burns, Schlozman, and Verba (2001) suggest that the constraints
many African American women and Latinas face are located in the institutions outside of politics. Inequality, they suggest, accumulates for these
women almost everywhere, in almost every institution, sometimes along
lines of gender (treating most women in these groups in more or less similar ways), sometimes along the lines of race or ethnicity, always along the
lines of class, and sometimes in inventive combinations. The one clear exception to this story comes from the participatory benefits religious institutions provide to African American women's political action. Payne's work
(1995) on the early, rural Civil Rights Movement also has things to offer
here: pointing (as do Lin and Jamal 1998) to the incentive structures embedded in social organization, to the central role of surprising networks,
and to the problem for African American women's activism that arises
when actors outside the movement assume that women can't be leaders
and go in search of African American men to speak for the movement.

Scholars in this literature have started to build the links between individuals and institutions, to build accounts of structure and agency together. And the task for scholars, now, is to develop an account of these linkages in a way that takes better account of comparative hierarchies and comparative intersectionality. This will be easier to do the more scholars ground their analyses in the mechanisms and processes offered up by other disciplines.

CANDIDATES

The literature on candidates for political office has been focused largely on the disadvantages women face in the electoral process, and as a consequence has remained focused on the contours of the aggregate differences between women and men.

Women have taken different paths to political office than men, paths that are more likely to travel through voluntary organizations or teaching careers than through law offices or businesses (Burrell 1994; Carroll 1985; Duerst-Lahti 1998; Gertzog 1995; Kirkpatrick 1974), though there are hints that this may be changing (Dolan and Ford 1997). And, historically, women ran for their first political office later in life than did men (Stoper 1977); recent analyses suggest that this practice continues (Burrell 1994). Early on, scholars redirected concern away from women's choices and focused on problems at the level of the political system. They found that women's lower levels of recruitment to office had to do less with whether there were pools of eligible women and much more to do with the strategies parties pursued to recruit candidates. Where parties used male networks for recruiting, not surprisingly, they found male candidates (Rule 1981). Carroll (1985) broadened this system-level examination considerably to find the problems women had with access to campaign money, incumbency, and the rareness of open seats. Burrell's recent work (1994) examines House candidates and worries, especially, about the numbers (low, to her mind) of women choosing to run for political office. She finds that political parties, more recently, have been especially welcoming of women candidates, that the gap in fundraising has closed and perhaps reversed, with women candidates in the 1990s often receiving more money than their male counterparts. But, as Burrell points out, "Money is still a problem since so few women have been able to run as incumbents" (1994, 128).

In a promising line of work, scholars have looked at another feature of the electoral system, multimember districts. They found that these districts were especially good for black and Anglo-white women's recruitment and election (Carroll 1985; Rule 1990, 1992). When scholars looked cross-nationally, however, the results were not nearly as crisp as in examinations that had focussed solely on the United States (Welch and Studlar 1990). At the local level, things remain murky as well. Some scholarship points to the very different structural features underlying African American men's and women's election to local office, focusing especially on the advantages district-based elections give to men and not to women (Karnig and Welch 1979; see, too, Welch and Herrick 1992). MacManus and Bullock (1989), however, could find only fleeting influences of electoral structure on election of women to office. Scholars usually find that women have an easier time getting access when the office is less desirable (Diamond 1977; Welch and Karnig 1979).[9] In the end, as Carroll put it, "Barriers in the political opportunity structure affect the recruitment of women candidates, reduce their probability of winning election, and constrain their future officeholding aspirations" (1985, 157). Given the growth in the literatures on such topics outside of the subfield, it may be time to revisit this question, with new ideas about the mechanisms through which these institutions operate.

POLICYMAKERS

Scholars in this literature have been especially interested in two questions: whether women change legislative processes and whether women face discrimination in legislatures.

How much do the differences between women and men rest in the institutional spaces and positions of power in which they find themselves? Fowlkes, Perkins, and Tolleson Rinehart took up this question in 1979 in their investigation of motivation and roles among party activists:

> [We] encourage a closer and more general examination of the political structures in which men and women operate. The actual mechanisms by which party context affects organizational orientations and behavior are yet to be determined. The parties may attract people of different backgrounds and expectations, or the organizational setting and its political environment may mold and shape party recruits. (1979, 780)

While studies have continued to find some differences in political ambition and expectations (Kirkpatrick 1976; Constantini and Bell 1981; Jennings and Farah 1981) and differences in goals (with women somewhat more interested in problem solving than in conflict) (Constantini and Craik 1977; Kirkpatrick 1974), scholars are increasingly likely to consider the intersection of context and gender, and increasingly likely to locate explanations away from women's and men's choices and in the institutional spaces in which women and men find themselves.

Women policymakers often have different policy priorities than men (Thomas 1994; Kelly, Saint-Germain, and Horn 1991; Welch and Thomas 1991; Mandel and Dodson 1992; Mezey 1994; Rosenthal 1998; Saint-Germain 1989; Schumaker and Burns 1988). Sometimes women understand the causes and consequences of problems differently than men

9. For a helpful review of this literature, see Darcy, Welch, and Clark 1994.

(Kathlene 1995a). And women often consider one of their jobs to be representing women (Burrell 1994; Tamerius 1995; Thomas 1991; Bratton and Haynie 1999). In creative combinations of theory on gender with theory on legislatures, Thomas and Welch (1991) find that women state legislators prioritize bills on children and family more than men and that they are "proudest of [the] advance of women's issues" (1991, 452) and Tamerius (1995) finds that women legislators act on their priorities: they give more speeches on feminist concerns, cosponsor more feminist legislation, and sponsor more feminist legislation than their male counterparts. Jennings suggests that African American women mayors pay more attention to issues of basic human need than other mayors (Jennings 1991).

Women's sometimes distinctive priorities are easier for women to enact when there are other women in office and where there is a women's caucus to provide continuing organization and support (Thomas 1991). Norton (1995) points out that these priorities are also easier to enact when women hold positions of power on the appropriate committees and subcommittees. Schumaker and Burns suggest that structural biases in local government—especially the overwhelming structural push for economic development—mean that, at the local level, the preferences of women policymakers and activists are much less likely to win than those of men, and their analyses suggest that "the participation of more women, greater depth of involvement by women, and greater involvement in stronger groups by women does not significantly increase the impact of women on the resolution of community issues" (1988, 1091). Flammang (1987), too, finds that, at the local level, perhaps because of the structural features Schumaker and Burns identify, women in positions of power have trouble turning their priorities into policy. Bratton and Haynie (1999) find that, at the state level, bills introduced by women in state legislatures are as likely to pass as those introduced by men.

Scholars have paid attention to other features of the claim that institutional position conditions political voice. Reingold (1996, 2000) finds that women and men use quite similar legislative strategies to get their jobs done; she suggests that, as much organization theory would argue, institutional norms dominate any individual differences in opinions or goals. Interestingly, Schlozman (1990) and Nownes and Freeman (1998) find exactly the same pattern when they compare women and men lobbyists: they use indistinguishable strategies, though their priorities are different. Harvey (1998) applies this insight to postsuffrage gender politics. Harvey's account suggested that postsuffrage women activists were less committed to a particular brand of politics than they were to winning (Harvey 1998). In the end, this work suggests we attend even more systematically to the institutional space in which women and men policymakers operate—to the details of the institutions of legislatures and city councils and bureaucracies and to the sometimes structural limitations on levels of government. In the most inventive effort I know of to do just this, Mettler points to the structural limits on women's policy successes that grew out of the New Deal, "as programs geared toward men became nationally administered programs and those aimed toward women retained state-level authority. What emerges as truly exceptional about the construction of the welfare state in the New Deal, then, is that citizens became divided by gender between two different sovereignties that govern in very different ways" (1998, 19).[10]

Scholars have also investigated whether gender shows up in interactions to undercut women's authority, after women have gained access to institutions, after they've gained positions of power. This sort of investigation suggests a form of gender that's more free floating, less tied to particular institutions or positions of power. When Kathlene (1994, 1995b) examined interactions in twelve state legislative committee hearings, she found that women in positions of leadership used different styles than men did, and, especially when women were in positions of leadership, men reacted in verbally aggressive ways. She argued that, at least in these legislative committees, access and position didn't translate into equal power for women (Kathlene 1994). Examining the 1990 hearings on the nomination of David Souter to the Supreme Court, Mattei (1998) found that men interrupted witnesses who were women more often than they interrupted men, questioned women more on issues of fact, and challenged women's claims more often than they challenged men's. The differences in effect on policy, then, may be in more subtle details of policy than scholars have examined thus far.

These literatures on candidates and policymakers have made important advances in recent years. There are new places to take these literatures. They could be more fully integrated with the innovative work coming out now on gender and political parties (Wolbrecht 2000). They could be linked more tightly to the formal literatures on electoral systems. They could be tied, even more than they already have been, to work on mass politics and to work on interest group networks. These literatures should be a valuable site for building the link between theories about institutions and theories about individuals.

■ | Conclusion

With this review in hand, what are my hopes for the future? That gender scholars within political science become more self-conscious about the systematic ways gender as a social category, as a principle of social organization, is different from other principles of social organization. That gender scholars push farther to develop methodological tools to carry their rich understandings of gender to individual-level data, where the tension be-

10. For a different account of the interaction between federalism and gender, see Skocpol 1992.

tween categories and the discipline of political science is acute. That gender scholars take advantage of the gains from explicit comparative analysis among women and men, groups of women, groups of men, always. And that political science take lessons from gender scholars about interlocking life spaces, about where to look for the residues of hierarchy in individual-level data, about the care with which one should treat choices and constraints, about political repertoires, and much more.

To return to an earlier theme, the field is in an enormously promising position, with theory, data, method, cumulative knowledge, and questions in hand. We are at a kind of beginning, I think, with much of the crucial struggle for legitimacy—and the discursive work that required—behind us. Work on gender in other disciplines—history and psychology and sociology come to mind—moved perhaps more quickly past the struggle for legitimacy. These fields have tools and approaches we could put to good use in ours. We've started to do that. There's more to do. And there always will be. Work on the complicated and subtle implications of gender in peoples' lives, in public life, and in institutional life requires serious interdisciplinarity.

MICHAEL C. DAWSON AND CATHY COHEN

Problems in the Study of the Politics of Race

■ | Introduction

The study of the impact of race *on* politics is overdue for reinvigoration. While contributions to our understanding of racial politics continue to be made, some important lines of research have become stagnant. For example, daily we learn more about the racial attitudes, voting patterns, and policy opinions of whites and African Americans in particular. Often left unexplored, however, in such analyses are the differences in opinion and behavior that exist within groups. Furthermore, we have little understanding of how such differences map onto the politics of communities, not just the individual acts of people within certain socially imposed groupings but the ways in which those acts are read collectively as manifesting some community consciousness, identity, and politics.

Part of the reason for our unequal levels of information regarding racial politics in the United States is political science's excessive reliance on the discipline of economics as a source of methodological and theoretical inspiration as well as our constant emphasis on the individual level of analysis. This dependence has led to the emergence of dominant methodological approaches in political science, rooted in the use of economic modeling and the individual as the unit of analysis. These problems are exacerbated by the high degree of fragmentation found within the study of racial politics. The fragmentation is found along a variety of fissures. One fissure is between both positive and normative theory on one hand and empirical studies on the other. Thus, rarely are we confronted with work on race and politics that engages important normative theories and concepts like justice, equality, or democracy through a lens informed by careful empirical work. Another fissure corresponds to the race of researchers. Political scientists of different races largely pursue different research agendas and often different methodological approaches as well. The absence of significant comparative studies—except the relatively small number of studies that compare whites and African Americans—across racial and ethnic groups and across historical periods means that we loose the superior insight that is likely to be garnered from studies that are explicitly comparative at least in their theoretical perspective if not in each empirical research endeavor.

Our task is to address fragmentation and other problems that afflict the field of race and politics. We emphasize the need for a firm theoretical foundation on which to conduct empirical research as well as research directions we believe to be promising. One central theme that extends throughout this essay is the need to understand the process of racialization and racial orderings throughout history and from the perspective of different racial and ethnic groups. More often than not political science seems oblivious to the different methods, times, and reasons groups become racialized subjects. Further, the dynamic trajectory of racial ordering and its consequences for not only policy areas such as immigration but also the evolution of state operations and orientations seems noticeably absent from our analyses. Exploring the historical and specific processes of racialization should provide greater insight into such staples of political science inquiry as electoral realignment, public opinion shifts, and interest group proliferation.

Another focus of our analysis will be on the need to reinvigorate the study of race and politics by highlighting the intersections of race with other "ascriptively" based social cleavages. Sociology, for example, has long profited from the study of race and class. William Julius Wilson's work for all the controversy it has sparked over the past two decades has been enormously influential in shaping the research agenda of a significant portion of the social sciences. This influence is in no small part due to his focus on the intersection of race and class in American politics and society. Both the *Declining Significance of Race* (1980) and *The Truly Disadvantaged* (1987) had the intersection of race and class as their central problem. Similarly, legal theorists such as Kimberle Crenshaw (1990) owe the power of their work in part to their rigorous focus on the importance of the intersection of race and gender. Within political science, Cathy Cohen's work (1999) similarly draws its authority from its probing of the intersection of race and sexuality in her study of the politics of AIDS in black communities. We believe that the study of race and politics must move toward greater investigation of the intersections of forms of subordination as well as the intersection of the concerns of political science with those of the other social sciences.

We begin this essay with a brief overview of a theoretical framework for understanding racial dynamics within the United States, that of racial ordering. We follow that discussion with a cursory examination of some of the major areas of contributions that continue to be made in the study of race and politics. Several problems in both theoretical and empirical research will then be discussed. The main emphasis, however, will be on working through several examples of areas of research that might help revitalize the research agenda in race and politics. Finally, we argue that forging a strong link between normative and positive political theory and empirical studies of race will be critical to reinvigorating the study of race. To keep the discussion manageable, we limit our discussion to research in the United States though one of the more vigorous areas of current research is the comparative study of race and politics.

■ | Theoretical and Empirical Problems in the Study of Race

Theoretical Problems

This essay was originally titled "Ascription and Social Changes," which is of course both too vague and too massive. We initially decided on the title because so much of the literature dealing with the process of racialization and categorization in the United States has centered on how people of color have been ascribed behaviors and attributes meant to justify their secondary position. A close examination of the literature dealing with race and politics, especially that originating from political scientists, however, suggests that far from examining the social processes that racialize, categorize, and constrain the life opportunities of different groupings of people in this country, largely people of color, most of this work has focused on individual manifestations of political differences that correlate with visible and self-identified racial differences.[1] Most of this literature takes racial categories as a given as well as the resulting ordering of occupants within these hierachcical categories. Ignored are the historical and social contexts through which the complicated processes of racialization and categorization utilized in this country have developed and evolved.

Webster's defines *ascription* as:

1. The act of ascribing: attribution 2. Arbitrary placement in a particular social status (Webster's New Collegiate Dictionary, 9th ed., 109)

The benefit of using ascription, as defined by Webster, as a central concept to describe the process of racial classification in the United States is that it allows us to underscore the social processes or construction of racial categories. Furthermore, the inclusion of *arbitrary* in the definition, which is not to be confused with random, reminds us of the willed placement of groups within categories and for reasons having little or nothing to

1. One work that explicitly undertakes a massive study of race and other forms of ascription in American political development is Rogers Smith's 1997 *Civic Ideals: Conflicting Visions of Citizenship in American History.*

do with biology. This seems to be a fact that political science has forgotten, hidden perniciously by excessive focus on the individual as the unit of analysis to the exclusion of all other candidates. Most social scientists and biologists reject biological deterministic explanations of racial classification, recognizing racial classifications or orderings as the clear product of social processes. From this perspective, emphasis is placed on the actions of elites and segments of the state in creating, imposing, and justifying racial and ethnic orderings meant to privilege and protect those with power. This process of classification is, of course, a dynamic one, where categories expand and subdivide over the years with a changing political economy.

Thus, to better understand the process of racial classification and its consequences for politics in this country, political scientists and other scholars must move away from individualist models where respondents and their political views and actions are examined or counted independent of the historical and social context in which their racial and ethnic identities are given meaning. Similarly, we must move away from models where the aggregate of individuals within an out-group, such as the percentage of African Americans, is plugged into the equation as the experience of the entire group or the threat posed to other groups. Without any attention to the historical and current context of these interactions or phenomena we may be severely misinterpreting the meaning of the data. Instead, we must utilize frameworks that acknowledge the processes of racialization and categorization that are embedded in social interactions where groups are assigned places within changing social structures. These structures are tightly rooted in but not completely defined by the political economy. This theoretical conception of race as produced by and part of social, political, and economic structures will enable political scientists to better understand key phenomena such as preference formation and perceptions of individual and group interests.

There are, of course, many competing definitions of social processes and social systems that might be employed for an analysis of racialization and racial categorization. One that we believe to be helpful is that of William Sewell (1992). For Sewell a social structure, and there are many that comprise our lived experience, is defined by a distribution of material resources and an associated schema. Labor markets, for example, fit Sewell's definition of a social structure. Labor markets hierarchically distribute jobs and wages (among other things) across industries, firms, regions, individuals, and social groups. On the schema side, labor markets are associated with normative behaviors and roles which must be abided by if one wants to participate, statuses which vary across occupations, expectations of appropriate levels of certification or credentials for a given location within the market, and other scripts which signal and communicate appropriate interactions and actions. Our contention is that the best way to understand racial groups, particularly as differentiated from ethnic groups, is that the former are associated with a social structure where race is the organizing principle for distribution of material and psychological resources as well as a racial schema which assigns roles, scripts, behaviors, expectations, stereotypes, and normative evaluations based on citizens' racial assignment. One key aspect of racial structure in the United States, we and others contend, is that it contains a racial hierarchy that orders not only status and honor but distributions of life chances as well. In short, there is a racial order within the United States that structures and is structured by not only American society but also American politics, political institutions, and the state.

Tom Holt argues, in his book *The Problem of Race in the 21st Century* (2000), that racial orders must be understood within their historical context. Holt divides the history of the United States into three periods, each characterized by a modal organization of the nation's political economy. Fairly typically he divides U.S. history into three modal periods; pre-Fordist, Fordist, and post-Fordist. During the pre-Fordist period, slavery and its immediate aftermath, marked by Reconstruction, forged the dynamics and structural logic of the racial order. Jim Crow racism, where blacks were partly integrated into the bottom of the industrial economy but were neither full participants in either the polity or civil society, predominated during most of the Fordist era.[2] It was also during this era that Holt identifies organized industrial manufacturing as the central dynamic motor and organizing principle within the economy. A much more complicated racial dynamic has evolved alongside the service and high-tech centered economy of the post-Fordist era according to Holt.

Holt argues that while the "tropes" of racial ideology are fairly constant, the "repertoire of practices" varies over historical periods. In other words, two phenomena stay fairly constant. First, the ordering of the racial structure has remained relatively impervious to change with the twin anchors of whites on top and blacks at or near the bottom remaining constant throughout all three periods. The contestation in the middle has been about who does not get lumped with blacks. For example, middle-class blacks, immigrants of Asian and Latino/a descent, as well as various central and southern Europeans and Irish, have all gone to great lengths to distance themselves from either blacks in general or poor or working class blacks specifically during different historical periods. Claire Kim describes this process as the "minorization of immigrants" (2000, 36).

Second, just as the main contours of the racial order have remained

2. Some works which outline the racial ordering of various types of good within the United States up to and including life chances are Farley and Allen's *Color Line* (1989) and Oliver and Shapiro's *Race and Wealth* (1995). Many other works document these differences across a wide range of domains. For example, enormous racial differences continue in the twenty-first century in health outcomes, wealth, labor market participation, and perceived status, just to name a few categories.

constant so too have the stereotypes associated with African Americans. Some of the main features of this demonized imagery include blacks being stereotyped generally as lazy, dependent on the state, less intelligent, and prone toward criminality. While black men are constructed as dangerous and rapacious and black women are construed as lewd and domineering. What has changed across historical epochs argues Holt have been the racial practices used by the state and its citizenry to maintain the racial order. Thus, fundamental to understanding the racial social structure in the United States is recognizing the consistency and resiliency of this structuring framework. So while the practices for managing racialized subjects evolve, the general ordering and justification remains largely unmoved, in particular for those African Americans on the bottom. Racialization, thus, comes to have a near totalizing effect on the lived experience of African Americans, intersecting and transforming all other identities and social locations. One important implication argues Holt is that "Racism colonizes other categories and concepts—like economic rationality and justice and notions of values and entitlement" (2000, 76). Higginbotham's exhortation to feminist historians a decade earlier to beware how race "colonizes" other categories is equally applicable to political scientists who study race:

> Feminist scholars, especially those of African-American women's history, must accept the challenge to bring race more prominently into theories and analyses of power. The explication of race entails three interrelated strategies, separated here merely for the sake of analysis. First of all, we must define the construction and "technologies" of race as well as those of gender and sexuality. Second, we must expose the role of race as a metalanguage by calling attention to its powerful, all-encompassing effect on the construction and representation of other social and power relations, namely, gender, class, and sexuality. Third, we must recognize race as providing site of dialogic exchange and contestation, since race has constituted a discursive tool for both oppression and liberation. (1992, 252)

We must remember that when Holt and Higginbotham write of the colonizing effect of race, there is also an inherent recognition of the ways in which race interacts with other categories of social organization such as gender, class, and sexuality to produce different racialized experiences for members of the same racial and ethnic group. This claim by Holt and Higginbotham about the colonizing or totalizing effects of racialization and racism leads to several important questions, at least two of which are particularly significant for political science. First, is he right? Has the ordering and tropes of racial groups remained relatively constant over time, creating a fairly permanent and resistant social structure? And second, if he is even partially right, what are the implications for theoretical and empirical research in political science? Will such a social structure be the means through which an ordering of preferences, lived experience, and consciousness is formed and shaped for those of different racial and ethnic categories? While sociologists, historians, and economists may have more to say about the empirical validity of Holt's claims than political scientists, the latter certainly have a significant amount to contribute to the second set of investigations.

If Holt is right, and the evidence political scientists provide could well prove important, then political preference formation should not only be racialized but be fundamentally anchored in racial considerations. If Holt is right, we should observe racially distinguishable outcomes produced by the institutions of the state. If Holt is right, we should see individuals perceive self-interest in racial terms. If Holt is right, empirical democratic theorists and students of American political development should observe, as do political theorists such as Judith Shklar and Rogers Smith as well as historians such as Eric Arnesen, (white) "American" conceptualizations of citizenship being tied and created in opposition to the civic, economic, social, and public categories or spheres understood as blacks. As Shklar, Smith, Arnesen, and Toni Morrison have argued, white American citizenship has been defined as being not black (Arnesen 1994; Morrison 1992; Shklar 1991, 1998). Clearly just observing (even many) sets of phenomena consistent with Holt's account is not sufficient; one also needs to show the patterns are not caused by factors outside of Holt's theory as well as demonstrate the causal mechanisms within Holt's theory. But this is work that political scientists should be well equipped to pursue.

Beyond the experience of African Americans, attention to racialized social structures should also inform our understanding of the political behavior of other racial and ethnic groups. For example, as intimated above, the idea of a racial order also helps to explain how long-standing racial and ethnic groups as well as new immigrants are integrated into the polity. The work of Claire Kim in political science and ethnic studies and that of Mary Waters in sociology both illuminate how the racial order strongly overwhelms ethnic identity. Waters (1999) uses the idea, first introduced by Merton, of a master status. A master status is one which trumps and, to use Holt's term, colonizes, other status identities. West Indian immigrants, for example, lose advantages gained from their ethnic backgrounds as they are racialized as African American. In contexts where they are constructed as being in close proximity to African Americans, they are consigned to the same segregated neighborhoods, face the same market discrimination (although at least in the labor market not to the same degree as native born African Americans), and otherwise have a subordinate status forced on them by the U.S. racial order (Waters 1999).

Kim, however, reminds us that racial orders are dynamic. They are moving, changing, adapting processes; thus she uses the term "racial ordering." She continues, "What is still missing in [the race and politics] literature is recognition of how all groups both native-born and immigrant —get constructed as 'races' and positioned in the racial order in a way that shapes each one's distinctive set of opportunities, constraints, and resources on an ongoing basis" (2000, 38). As the work of many young scholars of race and politics have demonstrated, racial orders give meaning to identities and through the process of racialization forge group identities that are themselves a source of political preferences and loyalties (Wong 2001; Rogers 2000).

For example, we already know that perceptions of racial interest powerfully shape individual preferences (Dawson 1994), but we are only learning the extent to which different racial and ethnic groups process, discuss, and engage in politics in significantly group-structured ways. The work of Sanders (1995) and Harris-Lacewell (1999) shows how group membership, internal norms of interaction, and perceptions of others' group affiliations strongly structure political discourse. Indeed, separate racial groups might have different meanings attached to the same political concepts and events. Different racial groups may very well also have different rules (or "grammars") for interpreting how political and social phenomena are processed and understood (Dawson 2001). When meanings and interpretations of politics are unstable across racial groups, the foundation for meaningful political communication is undermined.

Beyond largely empirical understandings of racialized politics, Iris Young (2000), assuming that racial groups exist within a hierarchical social structure, argues that we need a theory of the politics of groups that is relational, that takes into consideration the power disparities between groups. Such disparities in power and the attendant outcomes might explain many whites' resistance to changes in the racial status quo, since they perceive racial policies, thought to be truly egalitarian by blacks, as harming their (largely unspoken) racial group interests (Dawson 1997; Huddy and Feldman 2001; Voss 2001). Thus, the theoretical lens of a historicized racial order allows us to explain the claim made by Paul Peterson in his book *City Limits*—as well as a wealth of empirical findings documenting—of white resistance to racially egalitarian policies:

> . . . whites see even black allocation demands as redistributive in nature. What benefits blacks is perceived as damaging white interests—*and thus it does*. Token integration of community institutions is perceived by whites as the first step in an inevitable process of total racial change, and in what becomes a self-fulfilling prophecy whites stop using that community resource. The result is that minority group demands are often redistributive and therefore beyond the capacity of the local officials to grant. (1981, 159, my emphasis)

Such observations are extremely consistent with the hypotheses that racial orders foster individual perceptions of group and self-interest as well as group and individual identities. It is an example of the interaction between social structure and identity. In this case a racial order, one could hypothesize, helps to determine and solidify one's primary (for political purposes) group identity, one's perception of self-interest, and therefore, one's political preferences. No matter how much one might detest the normative implications of this process as personified in the Peterson quote, allowing the possibility that not just race but also racial ordering is at the center of one's incorporation into and understanding of politics will at the very least allow us to have a fresh perspective on much of American politics. Thus, if we are willing to accept even a part of the proposition that racialization and racial ordering produces distinctive world political views among racial and ethnic groups, then we should also be exploring to what degree this type of process also structures policy preferences, candidate positions, the character of American social movements, domestic political alliances, and electoral choice, to name a few areas demanding our investigation.

The possible existence of racial orders should have profound consequences for the conduct of empirical and theoretical research within political science (additional treatments of the importance of the concept of a racial order can be found in Bobo's and Dawson's essays in Sears et al. 2000 and Dawson 2001). Unfortunately that is not the case, and indeed research on race enjoys less status in this field than in any other discipline in the social sciences with the probable exception of economics. Often missing from the study of race as pursued in political science, is any commentary on the larger moral debates such as those contemplating what makes a good polity and how best to use our empirical and theoretical knowledge to move the country in the direction of expansive democracy. One consequence of not having the study of race more central in political science is the failure not only to fully contribute to these debates but also to examine some of the most interesting intellectual problems of our time. Fortunately, some are standing on the margins and engaging such questions.

Contributions in the area of race and politics have traditionally been made in three areas. The first and the dominant form of contribution has been in the analyses of racial politics. This area of research has primarily focused on white racial attitudes on one hand and the attitudes and political behaviors of various racial minorities on the other. The second area of significant contribution has been pursued by scholars interested in the effect that race has on public policy development and implementation. A major question of interrogation for these researchers has been the mechanisms through which concern with race has limited the ability of public policy to redress racial inequality. Examples of work in this area include research on the politics of school desegregation, racial redistricting, and the distribution of urban services. Third, and closely related to the second major strand of research, has been the study of race and state in the United States and other polities. One strand of this research has focused on the role of the politics of race in American political development. Recent work in this area includes the texts of Gwendolyn Mink (1995), Michael Brown (1999), and Rogers Smith (1997). To varying degrees, each work provides an important corrective to an area which has been largely understudied by leading scholars of American political development for the past two decades despite the centrality of race within American political, social, economic, and cultural history. We take two approaches in sketching possible avenues for channeling research in race and politics. First, we sketch some lessons that might be learned from other disciplines. Second, we make some suggestions about key areas for continued or new study in the field. In both cases our comments are meant to be taken as suggestive and not nearly exhaustive of all the exciting possibilities for research.

▪ | What Other Disciplines Offer the Study of Race and Politics

Exciting avenues for addressing some of the theoretical and empirical problems within the study of the politics of race can be found by exploring the frontiers of racial research and theorizing in the other social sciences. The best work in the area of race and politics is often characterized not only by a strong combination of theoretical and empirical analyses but also by an attentiveness to work outside of the discipline. Racial politics are embedded within a social order, have a long history central to the histories of polities such as the United States and South Africa, often involve conflict over the distribution of material resources, and have complicated psychological roots. Cross-disciplinary awareness is fundamental to moving the research agenda forward. Below we explore several examples from psychology, sociology, economics, and gender studies and show their relevance for research in political science. The following examples are meant to be merely suggestive and not exhaustive of the possibilities either within or across disciplines.

PSYCHOLOGY

As Nobel Prize winner Herbert Simon (1985) suggested, political science has as much to learn from psychology as from economics. One critical area of interest to political scientists is that of preference formation. What roles institutions, early socialization, political context, and political (or organizational) culture play in shaping preferences that have often been treated as exogenous is a hot topic within both political science and economics. One example of where studies in psychology can be useful is found in the work of neural social psychologist John Cacioppo on how the "affect system" affects racial prejudice. Cacioppo and his colleagues have been testing how the affective system, a neurophysiological system designed to "differentiate hostile from hospitable stimuli and to respond accordingly," operates on a different level than the human cognitive structure (Cacioppo and Berntson

2001, 96). The dual system leads to the phenomenon of "being of two minds at once" (102). Primates' affective systems are trained by stimuli at an early age to categorize associations between events and objects into likes and dislikes. Homogenous communities make it likely that outsiders or minorities become associated with negative stimuli since there is less of a range of stimuli in the environment. This might particularly be the case if, as Gilliam and Iyengar (2000) show, minorities in the United States are systematically and discriminatorily associated with crime as portrayed through dominant media and news sources. Thus it is quite possible that white Americans, for example, due to early childhood socialization by the media, hold egalitarian beliefs on the cognitive level but are also prone to act in a discriminatory fashion in a variety of other domains as a result of the social neurological conditioning of their affective system. The implications from this work for the fields of political science, public policy, and the law are numerous. From a pure research standpoint it suggests that the feud between Kinder and Sniderman about whether a new form of racism or principled conservatism best explains white ambivalence about racially egalitarian policies may be even more miscast than many of us believe. Indeed, if Cacioppo's research findings are replicated, then it is likely that we would have to entertain the proposition that under some conditions the *same individuals* act as egalitarians and under others as racists without being cognitively aware of their different behaviors.

The legal and policy ramifications are also significant. A prima facie case can be made, in contravention to recent appellate court decisions, for diversity in educational and other institutions as having a positive effect in and of its own right. Clearly, in terms of affective learning, racially and ethnically diverse living and learning experiences are important for young children. Similarly, if Cacioppo's findings hold, there would be pressure on various media sources, particularly television, to show more diverse groups on screen, rejecting stereotyping in entertainment and news and presenting instead more positive minority images. All of these implications are of importance to both policy and political science.

Cacioppo and his colleagues could be wrong. This program of research is still the subject of significant debate within the field of social psychology. Further, even if this program receives further empirical verification, those concerned with the normative debate over race in this country would have to be prepared to confront those who would misuse the research to claim that any attempts to set policy to address racial divisions are doomed to failure since these divisions are "biologically based." As in many other areas of racial inquiry, getting the research "right" does *not* end the obligations of scholars to society.

We have seen that there are alternative explanations for the discrepancy in egalitarian and tolerant attitudes on one hand and hostility to some policies on the other. In the end whether Cacioppo's research, that of Michael Neblo (2000), the already well established research programs in

political science, or some other candidate proves to have the best explanation for the discrepancy between Kinder's and Sniderman's research is in
one sense immaterial. For our purposes here, what is important is the possibility that by either drawing on the relevant research outside of political
science or adopting new methodological approaches within the field, we
can move beyond the largely moribund if still acrimonious debates of the
past decade.

ECONOMICS

The critique of political scientists over reliance on economics is not meant
to suggest that those of us in political science who study processes of racialization, categorization, and its political consequences do not have much to
learn from economics research. The point, instead, is to express concern
over the excessive reliance on economics as a source of methodological innovation and rigor to the exclusion of all other disciplines and forms of investigation. Economists have historically if quietly also made major
contributions to studying race in the context of the American political
economy. A series of studies a few decades ago probed the relationship between economic outcomes and government antidiscriminatory policies
(Landes 1968 and Heckman and Payner 1989 are two examples of this type
of work). More recently economists, some of whom have appointments in
political science departments, have explored the political economy of race
in ways that are important for political scientists to incorporate into their
own research. Alesina, Baqir, and Easterly (1999), for example, have recently researched the degree to which the homogeneity of local political
jurisdictions affect the size and scope with which local electorates are willing to support through taxes the provision of public goods. Not surprisingly, they find that the more homogenous local U.S. communities are, the
more likely they are to support both a broad range and generous level of
support of public goods. These findings, while buttressing the hopes of local activists attempting to expand the arena of public goods, raise serious
concerns both for those who are interested in using state policy to redress
social inequalities and for normative political theorists concerned with
widening the bonds of obligations between citizens.

Scholars based in business schools have also been conducting research of interest to students of race and politics. One key area is the degree to which the information technology revolution is contributing to the
balkanization of American civil society (Alstyne and Brynjolfsson 1997).
They model the conditions under which the expansion of multiple forms
of electronic communication channels leads either to a more unified and
diverse set of associations for members of a society or to more tightly knit
and less diverse networks. The essential question they ask is whether the
networks of cyberspace are more or less likely to lead to further balkanization of the polity. The implications for both normative and empirical stud-

ies of race are clear. Studies by researchers such as Harris-Lacewell (1999) and Sanders (1995) on racial attitudes demonstrate homogenous, tightly linked groups and networks are more likely to produce not only more extreme political views but also more-polarized political communities as well. Similarly, those concerned with democratic deliberation, the minimization of ethnic and other intergroup violence, and political and racial tolerance would all be concerned that the opening of cyberspace may very well lead to more, not less, balkanization of polities. All of these areas of concern are of great importance as we attempt to refashion an inclusive and egalitarian U.S. democratic praxis. Unfortunately, the political consequences of the information technology revolution on racial politics in arenas ranging from political mobilization, extremist politics, and democratic deliberation remains largely unexplored.

Sociology

Beyond psychology and economics many of the other social science disciplines also have the potential to inform and help improve the work of political scientists who study race and politics. Sociologists, for example, have long focused on the importance of groups, organizations, and networks as key analytical units. To the degree that we want to understand levels of analyses other than the individual, we might borrow from our colleagues and recapture a sociological imagination. For example, political theorists such as Young have found it useful to draw on social theorists and sociologists such as Giddens when theorizing about democracy, inclusion, social structure, and oppression. Social theorists and sociologists such as Paul Gilroy (2000) have begun to imagine a civil society and politics that are not framed by racial classifications. Political theorists, we suspect, would have much to say about the normative implications of Gilroy's conception of the good society as well as the likelihood of such polities coming into existence within the current political milieu. More traditionally, sociologists continue to pioneer the study of the intersection of race with other social defining characteristics such as class. Patillo-McCoy (1999) and Collins (1997), for example, conducted studies of the political implications and causes of the dynamics of class formation within the African American community. As with the work on racial attitudes, a healthy exchange between sociologists and political science in this field could substantially enrich the larger enterprise of studying of race and politics.

History

Historians such as Robin Kelley (1990, 1994) have taken concepts like infrapolitics from political science and then used them in historical investigations of black politics in ways that help us expand our conception of political action. Historians of race have also conducted numerous studies which suggest that both the scope of political action and the ideological range of political action within the United States is much greater than we have thought in the recent past (see Sanchez 1993; Kelley 1990; Foner 1980, 1984a, 1988 for just a few examples). Both Sanchez's examination of Chicano politics in the first half of the twentieth century as well as Kelley's examination of black political movements during the same period suggest a wider range of mass ideological influence than normally given credence within studies of the United States.

The work of Barbara Ransby (1996) and Evelyn Higginbotham (1992) has expanded our understanding of political leadership and the indigenous institutions used in movement formation. Similarly, historians like Barbara Savage (1999) have explored the use of cultural institutions like the media, in her case radio broadcasts, as a means of influencing public opinion on race during World War II. Greater attention to these works and others might produce a tighter grounding of public opinion work in both sociological and historical research about the nature and evolution of racial hierarchies within the United States and help improve the study of race and politics (Dawson 2000). Finally, theorists of deliberation and democracy will also find very rich materials in historical studies of the politics of race. One need only examine the Reconstruction period—arguably one of the most democratic eras in U.S. history—to begin such an investigation.

GENDER STUDIES

The work of scholars within gender studies has been very important for the study of the politics of race. Scholarship produced by black feminists, for example, suggests several research avenues of interest for those who study the politics of social cleavages and specifically the politics of race. Theorists such as critical legal theorist Kimberle Crenshaw and sociologist Patricia Hill Collins have for several years examined the implications of the intersections of different social orders such as race, gender, and class. Crenshaw (1990) argues that the intersection of race and gender creates a special legal position for black women, which cannot merely be explained by adding the benefits and liabilities of an individual's race and gender. Collins (1998), using a similar mode of analysis, argues that distinctive political and social identities and worldviews, found in particular among women of color, are the product of the intersections of race with other social cleavages. The work of these feminist theories has empirical implications that are testable by political scientists. Recent public opinion work shows that support for a black feminist political agenda is strongest among black women who feel positively linked to others on the basis of both race and gender. High levels of support for a black feminist political agenda are often evident among respondents who have such a dual linkage. Support lessens among those who feel linked solely on the basis of race and is even less evident among those who feel linked solely on the basis of gender (Dawson 2001). Finally, feminist perspectives on what gets classified as normal or objective as well as public and private could also serve as useful models for critiquing scholarship on the politics of race.

The argument made here is not that we need to import wholesale the studies of race found in allied disciplines but that *exchange* between political science and these disciplines can greatly improve our research agendas. If, for example, we tied studies of the influence of the media and racial segregation on racial attitudes to Cacioppo's findings, we begin to have a firmer grasp of why racial attitudes so strongly affect politics. If we add our understanding of the psychological origins of racial attitudes to the dynamics of the structural effects provided by phenomena such as cyberbalkanization and residential segregation, we begin perhaps to build a more fully specified model that combines individual-level psychological mechanisms with structural constraints. This statement is, of course, highly speculative and possibly wrong, but the basic point is that a more robust research agenda for the politics of race will draw on political and social theory, psychology, economics, and sociology as well as the other allied disciplines.

Finally, while we have focused on the benefits to be gained by an exchange of ideas and methods across social science disciplines, there is a new generation of scholars, often coming out of newly appointed graduate degree granting programs and departments like those in African American studies, ethnic studies, and women and gender, who have an interdisciplinary focus and intellectual commitment. These researchers have been trained to explore and engage questions, theories, and methods across not only social science disciplines but also fields in the humanities. Their breadth of knowledge is expansive with a seemingly unlimited possibility of intellectual exchange. The only possible drawback to a truly interdisciplinary approach may be limits in the depth of expertise. For many it takes great time commitment and investment in just one discipline to become knowledgeable of the literature, normative frameworks, and methodological approaches. The question, of course, is can this new generation of scholars flourish within these parameters for success. Only with time will we be able to assess if an academy structured around disciplinary specialization will make interdisciplinary scholarship cost prohibitive, especially as the tenure clock in many universities continues to tick at a faster pace.

■ | Toward an Expanded Race and Politics Research Agenda

There are several areas in the research of race and politics that could benefit from more attention from political science. Luckily, some in the field have already started to create new paths of investigation and inquiry. Below we provide a brief exploration of some of the more interesting areas of research in the study of race and politics. Generally, we highlight one book or article to epitomize the type of innovative scholarship we have called for throughout this essay. In no way is the following meant to define the state of the field. Instead, this is a very limited attempt to highlight what research has already been initiated and what is possible.

THE INTERSECTION OF RACE WITH OTHER SOCIAL CLEAVAGES

One promising way to study the politics of race and other social cleavages is to theoretically and empirically analyze the political consequences of the intersection of different social orders. Cathy Cohen's work (1999), as we already suggested, is one example of combining theoretical and empirical agendas through the political analyses of the intersection of race and sexuality. The work of sociologists and feminist theorists increasingly suggests that it is important for students of racial politics to pay attention to social difference and power disparities within subordinate racial groups (C. Cohen 1999; Patillo-McCoy 1999). Only with a more-complicated understanding of the multiple sites of power can we represent the complex nature of race and politics in the twenty-first century.

CONFLICT AND COOPERATION BETWEEN NONWHITE RACIAL GROUPS

Another means of importance in the study of race and politics is the analysis of the conflict between subordinate groups. The Los Angeles riots sparked a wave of research that utilized approaches ranging from the historical to game theoretic on the dynamics of cooperation and conflict between racial minorities. Much of this work has largely been focused on what has been perceived as the relatively low level of cooperation and relatively high level of conflict between blacks and Korean Americans. One exemplary piece of scholarship from this mode is Claire Kim's *Bitter Fruit*. Kim explores both the areas of conflict and cooperation that existed between blacks and Koreans in Brooklyn during the Red Apple boycott. Unfortunately, while scholars are beginning to explore the areas of conflict and cooperation between blacks and Koreans and other minority groups like Latinos, there is even less work analyzing the political interactions between a wider range of racial groups. Thus, there is obviously much room and need for additional work in this realm. This is also an area ripe for the combination of ethnographic research, historical research, and statistical or formal modeling (Freer 1999).

Moving beyond the Black-White Paradigm

It is important for those who study race and politics to move beyond the traditional black-white paradigm and for researchers in the largely racially fragmented camps to start building a more-unified research agenda. There are questions of race important across racial and ethnic groups that must be addressed by many of us. For example, how are political parties being reshaped after being structured around the politics of black and white cleavages since before the Civil War? How will alliance formation change, and how will racial identities and perceptions of racial group issues shift as the racial order within the United States goes through its most massive restructuring since the immigration of central, eastern, and southern Europeans in the late nineteenth and early–twentieth centuries? Interestingly, research on these issues is often being pioneered by political scientists who have joint appointments in either ethnic studies or specific identity base programs and departments like African American studies and who are drawing on the rich research traditions of these fields. Pei-te Lien and her colleagues around the country are one such example of researchers pioneering the investigation of Asian American political behavior while critically drawing on, revising, and extending research that has it roots in turn in African American and Latino/a studies.[3]

Ideology and the Politics of Race

What role does ideology play in the politics of race? Parallel research by a number of researchers who have used the National Black Politics Study, 1993–1994, including Dawson (2001) and Harris-Lacewell (1999), find that ideology has been and continues to be a powerful influence in shaping individual opinion, black social movements, and black politics more generally. Scholars whose work is rooted in the study of other racial and ethnic groups will be well positioned to answer such questions as: How do racial and other ideologies shape the politics of race more generally? To what degree will ideological meanings shift across the multiple divides of the United States' new racial terrain?

---

3. See Chang's volume (2001) for an excellent set of essays that covers several issues within Asian American politics. The September 2001 issue of *PS* (a journal of the American Political Science Association) includes several short essays on the contours of minority politics from the standpoint of Asian American politics. Also we are seeing more conference panels dedicated to Asian American politics in addition to the panels on Latino/a and black politics. Still tremendously understudied and of low visibility is work on Native American politics.

INVIGORATING THE STUDY OF (WHITE) RACIAL ATTITUDES

Too often when political scientists talk about race and politics, they are referring solely to the study of white racial attitudes. An enormously important and fruitful area of research, the problem has come from conflating research on white attitudes with the study of race and politics. Be that as it may, it remains one of the most critical areas of engagement. Most effort by political scientists has been focused on explaining the discrepancy between relatively tolerant and egalitarian attitudes of whites and the robust lack of white support for racially egalitarian public policies (see Sears, Sidanius, and Bobo 2000 for a good presentation of the state of the art in this realm). Central to this strand of research has been the protracted and often vituperative debate between Sears, Kinder, and their colleagues on the one hand and Sniderman and his colleagues on the other (each of the main protagonists' most recent position is represented in Sears, Sidanius, and Bobo 2000). A powerful alternative to these dual explanations comes from outside of political science. Sociologist Larry Bobo and social psychologist Jim Sidanius both argue that group threat and conflict, in other words, perceptions of racial groups' interests, drive white racial policy preferences (their most current thinking is also represented in Sears, Sidanius, and Bobo 2000). Unfortunately their work remains to be fully engaged by political scientists. A consensus among neutral observers is that racial considerations play the major role in shaping white attitudes but that politics is not unimportant (Dawson 2000).

A new generation of researchers is incrementally taking the study of white racial attitudes into productive new areas. Neblo (2000), for example, uses methodological innovations to suggest that the reason that the three different explanations for white attitudes on racial targeted programs can best be explained by realizing that different segments of the white populace systematically behave as principled conservatives, symbolic racists, or racial partisans. One of the most fruitful areas of new research is the study of media effects in racial politics. Gilliam and Iyengar (2000) have persuasively demonstrated the effect that the "action news" format of local television news has in perpetuating devastating stereotypes that associate black and Latino men with crime. Gilens's work (1999) shows the effect that broadcast and print media have in both racializing and driving negative white attitudes toward means-tested social welfare programs. Oliver and Mendelberg (2000) show how certain types of segregated neighborhood environments reinforce white racial hostility. Their work is notable because it brings back into discussion the intersection between class and race in white racial attitude formation—a question that has long interested students of black racial attitudes.

On the other hand, an area that has been relatively ignored by political scientists has been the persistence of the pernicious racial stereotypes that seem all too prevalent in the U.S. populace. The leading work on stereotypes and how they affect racial politics has been conducted by sociologists (see Bobo and Kluegel 1997 for one excellent example). Racial stereotypes provide one possible candidate for the mechanisms which underlie the findings that those such as Oliver, Mendelberg, and Gilens describe (Bobo 1988, 2000). There is also comparatively little research comparing attitudes across racial groups. One of the more ambitious attempts to compare black and white racial attitudes can be found in *Divided by Color* (Kinder and Sanders 1996) though it still pays much more attention to white attitudes. The lack of comparison across groups is in large part due to the racial divide within the political science research community (Dawson and Wilson 1991; Dawson 2000).

Collecting Appropriate Data for Studying the United States' Complex Racial Terrain

For a number of years researchers interested in conducting public opinion or elections studies of people of color have labored under the handicap of using the American National Election Studies or the General Social Survey. Neither important study is designed to provide adequate coverage of minority communities or the survey instrumentation necessary for probing the political beliefs and behaviors of communities with their own significantly distinct political histories and outlooks.

This situation has begun to be remedied. There is a two-decade-old tradition of survey research that focuses on the political behavior, racial group consciousness, and political attitudes of African Americans that grows out of the research program of James Jackson of the University of Michigan (Gurin et al. 1989; K. Tate 1993; Dawson 1994a). This data collection agenda continues as Katherine Tate conducted a 1996 follow up to the 1984 and 1988 National Black Election Studies. Bobo and Dawson conducted a 2000 pre/postelections study that focused on the electoral politics of race. Dawson and Brown conducted the 1993–1994 National Black Politics Study which while not an election study, built on the Michigan studies although its focus on political ideology and the politics of black theology marked a radical departure from the Michigan tradition.

This set of studies (and a few similar data sets such as the 1995 *Washington Post*, Kaiser Family Foundation, Harvard University Racial Study) represents the preferred data collections for microlevel work on African American public opinion and political behavior. Some like the Michigan studies provide rich data on African Americans. Others like the *Post*, Kaiser, and Harvard racial study and the Bobo and Dawson 2000 election study provide rich opportunities for the comparative study of racial attitudes at the microlevel (the 1995 *Post* study is particularly valuable since it has very rich content and oversamples of blacks, Asian Americans and Latino/as). All represent substantial improvement over the standard practice of relying on the General Social Survey, or even worse, the American National Election Studies which while historically important and critical for studies in their domains, are ill suited for the study of the politics of race.

While the collection of data on African Americans has the most robust tradition, important work has also been done in collecting appropriate microlevel data for the study of the country's Latino/a population and more recently the Asian American population as well. The studies mentioned above conducted by Pei-te Lien and her colleagues, the Pilot National Asian American Political Surveys (PNAAPS), are providing rich data for the analyses of Asian American politics. According to Wong (2001), "PNAAPS is the first multi-city, multi-ethnic, multi-lingual survey of Asian Americans' political attitudes and behavior." This massive enterprise entailed using an interviewer pool that covered several different languages as well as innovative sample designs. Like black and Latino/a survey work, this study necessitated confronting tough methodological problems such as sample design. Like work in Latino politics (and increasingly black politics), this study demanded multilingual capability. Many of these issues were confronted systematically in the pioneering work of Rodolfo de la Garza, Angelo Falcon, F. Chris Garcia, and John A. Garcia in their Latino National Political Survey of 1989–1990. This study has laid the foundation for much of the modeling of Latino/a beliefs and behavior over the past decade.

Finally, new methodological approaches need to be developed given the increasing difficulties with survey work and the inherent limitations of the social survey as a research tool. For example, Melissa Harris-Lacewell (1999) has conducted a series of innovative experimental studies which focus on changes in black ideological discourse by conducting experiments in natural environments as well as collecting public opinion data in settings such as barber and beauty shops which are sites of much "black talk." Taeku Lee (1997) read several thousand letters to the president about racial conflict in the United States to get a feel for the dynamics of opinion formation on race during the Truman through Nixon administrations. He then used this data in conjunction with sophisticated statistical modeling to make a strong contribution in both the race and politics and public opinion fields. More innovative studies like those cited can only help continue the reinvigoration of the field.

THE DYNAMICS OF IMMIGRATION PATTERNS AND THE POLITICS OF RACE

Changing immigration patterns have profoundly restructured the contours of American politics and the politics of race. Party politics, the politics of urban areas, public opinion, and so on, are all being reshaped by this phenomenon. How do these changes shape the way we conduct the study of the politics of race and our previous paradigms, models, and findings? Scholars such as Garcia-Bedolla (1999), Wong (2001), and Jones-Correa (1998) are exploring the internal dynamics of political socialization and in-corporation within and across immigrant communities. Both authors bring to our attention the dynamic process of immigrant political incorporation, the internal community-based discourse around politics, and the differ-ences in both consciousness and political action evident when researchers take generation, class, gender, and region into account. These scholars and others like DeSipio and De La Garza (1998) also remind us that immigra-tion patterns impact public opinion and institutional mobilization like that expected of political parties in past years.

Racial Politics, the New Economy, and the Information Technology Revolution

The information technology revolution and the new economy are critical areas within which to study the rapidly changing dynamics of the interac-tion of race, public policy, and distributive justice. How are these tech-nologies distinctively affecting the development of different racial and ethnic communities? Are these new forums for interaction fostering new or unique political ideologies, replacing previous methods and tools of mobi-lization and exacerbating those involved in the deliberative process and those who are not? Can new interactive media and cyberspaces be seen as a new agora? Or as discussed, will the outcome of these technologies be "cyberbalkanization" and even more politically polarized communities? What are the political implications in terms of resources, mobilization, and racial conflict of the digital divide? What should be the state response to very large private corporations deciding which communities get wired for broadband access along racial lines even if the decision-making logic is claimed to be nonracial?

Do the new technologies, using Habermas's distinction, merely strengthen the ability of corporate and government elites to foster mass opinion, or do they provide a new mechanism by which critical public spheres can exercise their ability to regulate the state? Anthropologists are leading the way in showing how cybercommunities are leading to an un-settling of traditional racial identities as well as fostering what had previ-ously been perceived as relatively marginal political ideologies such as libertarianism. In the field of political science, no one seems to be publicly pursuing research in this area. No doubt our research is not exhaustive and there are those currently engaged in such work. In the meantime, until such research receives a public viewing, we encourage those concerned with race and politics to consider the area of information technology as ripe with possibilities.

SEEING AS A RACIALIZED STATE

How do state policies such as the census and assigning goods based on racial criteria shape racial formation, conflict, and cooperation? How do state policies encourage/discourage racial mobilization and countermobilization? In turn how do racial conflict and politics shape the state itself? Studies of Brazil, the United States, and other polities by several pioneering political scientists are beginning to transform our understanding of the relationships between race, state, and civil society (Nobles 2000; Hanchard 1994). Other scholars such as Lieberman (1998), Mink (1995), R .M. Smith (1997), and M. K. Brown (1999) have pushed us to consider the ways in which issues of race have shaped state policy as well as the designation of citizen. Research that explores the construction and evolution of the state as a racialized entity with interests to preserve and advance will do much to invigorate the study of institutions and American political development in political science.

The work of Canon (1999) and Frymer (1999) continues the tradition of looking at national political institutions from the standpoint of race and politics. This is a critical tradition that should be embraced by political scientists. While there is a relatively robust literature on redistricting and race, the field of minority politics pioneered the study of race and political institutions. Hanes Walton Jr.'s entire corpus looks at institutions ranging from the political parties to the bureaucracy from the standpoint of black politics (see 1972 and 1988 for just two of many examples). Walters (1988) does the same for the study of the presidency.

Generally, Americans have most interaction with the local level of the federal system, and that is where the fiercest racial conflict occurs. There is a vast literature on local minority politics. Two strands can only suggest the richness of the literature. Dahl (1961), Pinderhughes (1987), and Hero (1992) all examine U.S. pluralism through the lens of ethnic and racial politics. Reed is perhaps the most prolific, insightful, and acerbic of the scholars who use local racial politics as a lens through which to examine American democracy (1999). Local courts have been examined both from the standpoint of race and crime (Rose and McClain 1990) and as a vehicle for bringing about egalitarian local social policy (Hochschild 1984). Many other topics such as political mobilization have been fruitfully explored through the lens of local racial politics.

Again, these are just a few of several research areas that could open up new territory for the study of race and politics. As we suggested earlier, the work mentioned is not exhaustive of what is currently being pursued in the field of race and politics. Instead the examples mentioned are illustrative of the many ways scholars are trying to expand our understanding of race and politics, its origins, its implications, and its solutions for overcoming fragmentation and stagnation within the field of politics and race as well as the discipline of political science.

■ | Conclusion

Strong contributions to the study of race and politics continue to be made. To reinvigorate the study of race and politics though, we need to broaden our horizons along several dimensions. One way forward is to reforge links between positive and normative theory on the one hand and empirical studies on the other. Another is by seriously thinking about ascription and social cleavages from the standpoint of social structure. Linked to this is the need to focus on the study of groups as groups and not merely as aggregations of individuals. The suggestion here is that the payoff from such analyses will yield a better understanding of the constraints that racial groups put on individual preference formation than can currently be found. Beyond political science, there is a wide range of work being pursued in the other social sciences which can greatly enrich the study of the politics of race in political science. Becoming more familiar with these literatures will enable us to ask new questions and bring new perspectives to old debates. Finally, we reiterate once again the importance of probing the intersections of race with other ascriptive social cleavages. Failure to do so increases the probability that research on race in political science will remain relatively parochial.

Morris P. Fiorina

Parties, Participation, and Representation in America: Old Theories Face New Realities[1]

■ | Introduction

Theory and reality interact continuously. Reality shapes theories, but theories in turn shape understandings of reality. Theory generally trails reality in their ongoing interaction. Theorists construct new models and modify old ones on recognition that the political world has changed; consequently, revised understandings arise after new realities have arrived—and sometimes departed. This paper argues that important components of traditional democratic theory now lag the realities of contemporary American democracy. Thus, what we teach our students about parties and representation is outdated, a reflection of conditions that prevailed from the mid-nineteenth to the mid-twentieth century, not the realities they see around them.

My arguments takes off from several developments that many observers view as indicators of serious problems in American democracy. These include the near-half-century decline in the public's regard for government and politics, the similarly long-term decline in voting turnout and other forms of political participation, and the more general long-term decline in civic engagement and social capital that is currently the subject of much academic and popular discussion. While scholars have invested considerable time and energy describing and dissecting these developments, my interest here is different. According to two major lines of argument about how to improve American democracy, the condition of American democracy today should be judged superior to its condition at midcentury, but the aforementioned developments seem inconsistent with that judgment. This paper considers possible explanations for this gap between scholarly theory and popular perceptions, and argues that ordinary citizens are correct: empirical developments have left us teaching theories whose fit with reality has diminished.

1. I wish to thank Bonnie Honig, David Mayhew, Helen Milner, Margaret Weir, and an anonymous referee for helpful comments on earlier drafts of this article.

511

The Condition of American Democracy 1: Declining Trust and Rising Cynicism

By various time series compiled by various survey research organizations, cynicism about government is up, confidence and trust in leaders and institutions are down. Figure 1 provides some familiar illustrations. I will not belabor these well-known trends but briefly note that a number of caveats apply to them. First, while there is a common tendency to decry trends like these, plausible arguments to the contrary exist. For purposes of this discussion, however, a normative stance is not required. The simple empirical proposition that evaluations of government are lower now than four decades ago is the issue. Second, while there also is a natural tendency to assume that the more positive evaluations of government measured shortly after midcentury are the norm and the less positive contemporary levels are the aberration, that too is a questionable assumption. American history has had its ups and downs, and one suspects that trust in government might have been low at various other times—during the late-nineteenth-century period of industrial warfare, for example. Whether Americans in 1960 were historically typical or abnormally trusting can not be determined from this data, but again, the simple empirical decline from midcentury is the issue here..

Figure 1 | Trust and Faith in the National Government Are Down

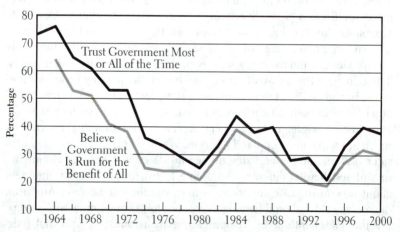

Source: American National Election Studies.
Data on the 1958 and 1986 responses to the second question do not exist.

Third, confidence in leaders and institutions outside the political sphere has fallen as well (Lipset and Schneider 1983). As social scientists we need to keep this development in mind. Generalization is our stock in trade, and purely political explanations do not speak to the broader decline. Still, confidence in all leaders and all institutions has not fallen at the same rate or to the same levels, and confidence in some has recovered.[2] Thus, variation is present, so that arguments that apply principally to politics but somewhat to other spheres as well have some explanatory potential. The argument presented below has that characteristic.

A broad phenomenon like deteriorating evaluations of government obviously has many causes (Nye, Zelikow, and King 1997, pt. 2; Chanley, Rudolph, and Rahn 2001). To some extent, leaders no doubt have earned the distrust of the citizenry: Vietnam and civil disorder in the late 1960s; Watergate, stagflation, and the Iranian hostage crisis in the 1970s; out-of-control deficits and Iran-Contra in the 1980s; Bill Clinton in the 1990s. Perhaps the negative evaluations held by Americans are no more than a natural reaction to a long litany of abuses of office and the seeming incompetence of officeholders. Other observers emphasize the economy—the end of the postwar expansion and the arrival of the inflationary era in the early 1970s shook confidence in the government's ability to maintain prosperity, and their confidence did recover a bit during the Reagan boom and again during the Clinton prosperity. Some scholars look beyond such objective events and trends to perceptions, in particular to perceptions shaped by the media, especially TV. With their characteristic negativity and pursuit of scandal, the media make Americans believe that government is less competent and leaders less trustworthy even though the reality may not have changed.[3] It is highly probable that all these and other developments contribute to the trends detailed in figure 1. The arguments offered below are intended as additions, not alternatives.

THE CONDITION OF AMERICAN DEMOCRACY 2: THE DECLINE OF POLITICAL PARTICIPATION

For several decades academic and popular commentators have bemoaned the decline of voting turnout in the United States. From a modern high in 1960, presidential turnout fell every election until 1992, when the Perot challenge generated a 5 percent surge (Figure 2). That rise was temporary, however, as turnout fell below the symbolically significant 50 percent mark in 1996 and rose only to a little below the 1992 level in 2000, despite what one overenthusiastic reporter (Von Drehle 2000, 1) characterized as "the largest voter mobilization effort in history." Congressional turnout also has declined over the past generation, although a bit more erratically (see fig-

2. Confidence in the executive branch fluctuates but does not show much, if any, trend. Similarly, confidence in the courts has not fallen. Confidence in the military has increased.

3. This is the "videomalaise" thesis, generally attributed to Robinson (1976). See also Sabato 1991.

ure 2). Numerous observers are at least partly sympathetic with Benjamin Barber's verdict on these trends: "In a country where voting is the primary expression of citizenship, the refusal to vote signals the bankruptcy of democracy" (1984, xiii).

Not everyone is so enamored of the value of voting, but other forms of participation have declined as well (Rosenstone and Hansen 1993, ch. 3). Political participation takes time and energy, of course, and contemporary Americans are overworked according to some scholars (Schorr 1991). But the fall in participation appears to be less a consequence of competing demands and more a reflection of a fall in psychological engagement. Delli Carpini and Keeter (1996, ch. 3) report that despite a vastly more educated public and an explosion of information broadcast over the airwaves, contemporary Americans know at most as much as those of a generation ago. Why? In part because they don't care: popular interest in government and public affairs has declined by about 20 percent since the 1970s (Putnam 2000, 36).

Again, there are numerous disagreements about the description, explanation, and implications of these trends. McDonald and Popkin (2000), for example, criticize the way the Census Bureau calculates turnout, arguing that if measured properly, turnout does not show a steady decline since 1960 as much as a sharp drop in 1972 to a lower level that persists to this day. Some are more sanguine about the effects of lower turnout than those who share Barber's views. Numerous scholars have puzzled over the respective sizes of institutional, demographic, and psychological contributions to declining participation (e.g., Rosenstone and Hansen 1993; Teixeira 1992). Clearly, however, only a few curmudgeons regard the low

Figure 2 | Turnout in the United States Has Declined since 1960

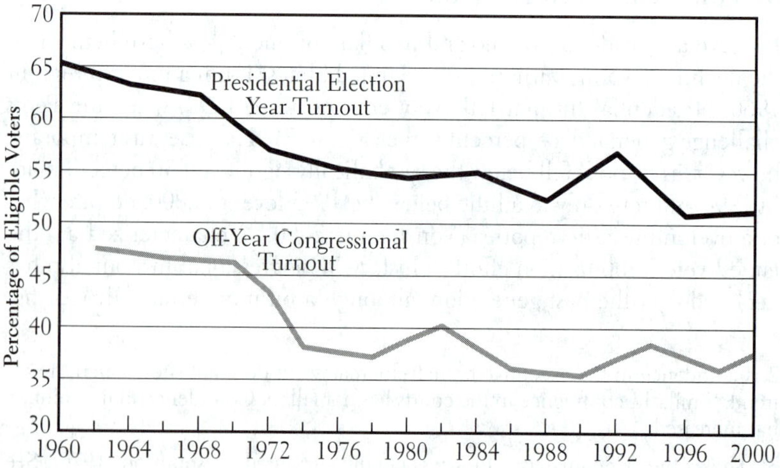

Source: Federal Election Commission.

political participation levels that exist today as a healthy feature of democracy.[4]

Some observers have argued that political participation is not so much in decline as in a process of transformation. Specifically, people vote less, go to fewer political meetings, and forgo buttons and bumper stickers because they feel that their time and energy can be better spent in activities other than classic forms of electoral participation. Instead, they join and contribute to groups that influence communities and government, they volunteer their time, and they support nonprofit groups and organizations that increasingly take on public functions (Ladd 1999). That optimistic argument is challenged by the third development.

THE CONDITION OF AMERICAN DEMOCRACY 3: THE DECLINE IN CIVIC ENGAGEMENT

The associated concepts of civil society, civic engagement, and social capital have received an enormous amount of attention during the past decade. *Civic engagement* refers to the voluntary activities of people in their communities, workplaces, churches, and other social contexts. Such activities can be highly political, entirely nonpolitical, and anything in between. Civic engagement occurs in *civil society:* "those forms of communal and associational life which are organized neither by the self-interest of the market nor by the coercive potential of the state" (Wolfe 1997, 9). In classical political theory a strong civil society is a bulwark of democracy (Tocqueville 1966).

Within democracies civic engagement is thought to contribute to a healthier, more peaceful, more prosperous society by generating what James Coleman (1988) called *social capital,* an intangible resource analogous to physical or financial capital. Social capital consists in the first place of information networks that pass useful knowledge from one member of society to another. In the second place social capital consists of expectations and obligations that minimize conflicts and lubricate social relations. In the third place, social capital consists of norms that specify obligations and punish transgressions thereof.

In the eyes of its proponents, civic engagement generates social capital. Norms will be effective only if individuals recognize their existence. But individuals will not recognize their obligations if they do not know them. And such critical information will not be passed on if individuals do not communicate in the first place. Civic engagement brings people together; interacting enables them to communicate their preferences and expectations, and working together builds bonds of trust and mutual obligation. Thus, societies with high levels of civic engagement will be societies that can draw on extensive reserves of social capital.

4. George Will (1986) probably comes closest.

Contrary to what Ladd and others have argued, Putnam (2000) shows that civic engagement in the United States has declined. Political, civic, and religious participation, philanthropy, social contacts—all are down from earlier decades. While numerous critics have quarreled with various parts of these arguments, analyses, and data, Putnam's arguments strike a responsive chord in many lay people as well as scholars. In particular, they look back fondly on an era when presidential turnout exceeded 60 percent, when partisans enthusiastically pinned on campaign buttons, when every (i.e., all three) TV channel provided gavel-to-gavel coverage of the presidential nominating conventions, when people trusted their government and each other, and when government and society seemed in some general sense better.

The argument that civic engagement and social capital have declined partly incorporates the previous two arguments. Relative to Americans of midcentury, citizens today are not as closely connected with each other and because they interact less now, they trust each other and government less now, and this will lead to still lower participation in the future. Would a negative dynamic like this have been predicted by midcentury political scientists? On the contrary, there is good reason to believe that such a development would have surprised them.

■ | Improving American Democracy

By my reading there are two major strains of argument about how American democracy can be improved. The first underlies the long-standing populist tradition and the more recent participatory movement of the 1960s. In a nutshell, if democracy is government by the people, then American democracy can be improved by empowering citizens and opening up established structures and processes. The second argument has enjoyed more support within the academy than in the popular arena. First exposited around the turn of the century by Woodrow Wilson and others, it holds that U.S. institutions diminish the effectiveness of democratic government. The way to overcome these institutional impediments and make American democracy more effective is to strengthen parties (Ranney 1954). Let us consider these in turn.

IMPROVING AMERICAN DEMOCRACY 1: OPEN IT UP

The participatory argument received a very sympathetic hearing in the late–twentieth century, a hearing that translated into practice. For a long generation, reformers (joined by others seeking political advantage) have diligently stripped away the insulation around political institutions and processes, leaving them more open to popular participation and pressure.

TABLE 1. CHANGES IN AMERICAN POLITICS SINCE 1960

Presidential nominating process

Candidate-centered politics

Open meetings

Recorded votes

Expanded rules of standing

Enhanced judicial review

Open bureaucracy

Intervenors

Maximum feasible participation

Proliferation of local bodies

Advocacy explosion

Proliferation of polls

New technologies

Propositions

Table 1 lists some of the changes that have taken place since the 1950s, indeed, most of them since the mid-1960s, when confidence in government began to decline.

Some of the changes are widely recognized, but others are less so. Among the former, changes in the presidential nomination process are the best-known example. Until the mid-1960s stereotypical nomination politics consisted of party bosses choosing nominees in "smoke-filled rooms." Party leaders ignored Estes Kefauver's 1952 primary victories, and they were impressed by John Kennedy's critical 1960 primary victories only as demonstrations that he could carry Protestant states. As late as 1968 Hubert Humphrey won the Democratic nomination without entering a single primary. But Goldwater's "amateurs" upset the Republican establishment in 1964, and when McGovern's new politics activists did the same on the Democratic side in 1972, the new era was firmly in place (Ceaser 1979; Polsby 1983).

Meanwhile, the decline of local party organizations, the weakening of citizen party identifications, the advent of television campaigning, and other factors contributed to a broader change—the development of candidate-centered politics. The most notable (and most studied) example was in the congressional arena where the personal advantage of incumbency surged in the late 1960s (Mayhew 1974a; Gelman and King 1990). But more generally, the old order in which a single party organization or an encompassing interest group delivered the vote for a larger set of candidates associated with it was replaced by a new order in which each individual candidate built a personal organization and communicated directly with supporters. Two-step flows, opinion leaders, and related concepts from the voting literature of the 1940s and 1950s (Berelson, Lazarsfeld, and McPhee 1954) largely disappeared from the voting literature of the 1970s and 1980s, as the influence of intermediaries in the electoral process declined.

Changes in arenas other than the electoral are less widely recognized but also significant. The movement toward "government in the sunshine" resulted in changes in the internal processes of governing institutions. In Congress, for example, the early 1970s saw the opening of many committee meetings to the public, and a movement away from anonymous voting procedures in favor of putting everything on the record. Many scholars have pondered the consequences of congressional decentralization in the 1970s (e.g., Dodd and Schott 1979); fewer have reflected on the consequences of making the activities of its members so much more visible. Movement in this direction occurred all through American democracy as open meetings and agendas published in advance increasingly became the norm.

At roughly the same time it became easier to get one's day in court. The Supreme Court expanded doctrines of standing, enlarging the class of interests entitled to a hearing in the courts (R. Stewart 1975). Similarly, new congressional statutes expanded standing. Congress and the courts worked in tandem to open up the bureaucracy. Congress mandated new procedures that enabled interested constituencies to learn about agency proposals and participate in agency decision processes, and the courts reinforced these requirements and became increasingly aggressive about judicial review. Congress even subsidized nongovernmental intervenors in some cases. The end result of these changes is an administrative process that is far more visible and open to public participation than was the case in 1950.

At the local level, the watchwords of the Great Society were "maximum feasible participation" (Greenstone and Peterson 1973). Old structures were bypassed in favor of new ones that empowered new groups. Local bodies of all sorts proliferated (Burns 1994). And most of these were subject to the kind of open government requirements mentioned above. The days when many smaller cities and towns were run by mayors and councilors fronting for a few big business interests are long gone (Ehrenhalt 1991).

Changes such as these are on the supply side of politics—the people and processes that supply public policy outputs are more exposed to popular influence today than a generation ago. But there have been important changes on the demand side as well. Most obvious is the "advocacy explosion"—the proliferation of interest groups documented by Scholzman and Tierney (1986), J. L. Walker (1991), and others. In the 1950s a small number of large sectoral interest groups worked with party and institutional leaders. Today a plethora of smaller particularistic interest groups lobby everyone—often working indirectly through the grassroots—and help to finance the campaigns that grow ever more expensive.

Another demand-side change is the increasing information available to politicians. Not only do constituents have more information about what politicians do, politicians have much more information about what constituents think (Geer 1996). Younger scholars today may not appreciate how recently the widespread use of polling came to American politics. But John Brehm's (1993) striking tabulation (figure 3) shows the polling explosion—beginning, of course, in the 1960s.

Figure 3 | From Rare to Everyday: Media Coverage of Poll Results

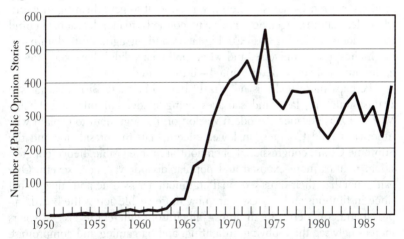

Source: John Brehm, *The Phantom Respondents* (Ann Arbor: University of Michigan Press, 1993); 4.
Note: Figure shows the number of stories cited under "public opinion" in the *New York Times*. According to John Brehm the cited public opinion stories "by and large report poll results, and only rarely reflections on public opinion in the broader sense."

Polling is just the most prominent example of a set of new technologies that provide more direct links between politicians and voters. Letters and postcards were supplanted by long distance telephone, WATS by fax, and fax by e-mail and the Internet. A citizen who so desires may easily contact his or her representative in seconds, a far cry from the 1950s, when the time and effort to write a letter were required. Most attention to these developments has focused on the enhanced ability of members to reach constituents, but the new technologies are two way: elected officials find it easier to reach constituents, but the reverse holds as well.

Finally, to an increasing extent, citizens and groups now dispense with leaders and representative institutions altogether. The past generation has seen growth in the use of the procedures of direct democracy—the initiative, referendum, and recall.[5] Many decry this trend (e.g., Broder 2000), but the point here is simply that for better or for worse, it is another example of how popular pressure can increasingly make itself felt in the governmental arena.

The preceding list is partial, to be sure, but I think it sufficient to make the general point. During the past generation American political institutions and processes have become increasingly permeable to popular participation and increasingly subject to popular pressure. How ironic, then, that Americans so dislike what reformers have wrought. Americans liked their government better, trusted their leaders more, voted in higher numbers, and in general participated more in public life when party bosses chose nominees in smoke-filled rooms, when several dozen old men (mostly southerners) ran Congress, when it was difficult to get a hearing in court, when legislatures, agencies, and city councils made decisions behind closed doors, when big business, big labor, and big agriculture dominated the interest group universe, and when politicians didn't have the tools to figure out what constituents wanted—if they cared.

Perhaps there really is no puzzle here. Long ago Bismarck advised against watching laws and sausages being made. Hibbing and Theiss-Morse (1995) advance a modern version of that argument to explain why Americans hold Congress in lower esteem than the presidency and the Supreme Court: congressional operations are more visible, hence congressional politics more exposed and popular disapproval more severe. One can generalize their cross-sectional argument across time and suggest that since institutions and processes are now more visible across the board, approval and confidence in all drops—albeit from different levels—as voters increasingly see the lobbying, infighting, and bargaining and compromise that politics entails. This argument probably explains some of the irony noted above, but I doubt that it is the whole story. Before adding to it however, let us consider the second strain of argument about the improvement of American democracy.

Improving American Democracy 2: Strengthen the Parties

Another line of argument about democratic reform locates the deficiencies in American democracy in a different place. Especially within the acad-

5. After bottoming out in the 1960s, use of the initiative surged, although five states account for more than half of all initiatives. See "A Century of Citizen Lawmaking," http://www.iandrinstitute.org.

emy, critics have seen the problem less as one of limited participation in government than as one of control of government. Federalism, the separation of powers, checks and balances—the fundamental institutions of the United States operate to hinder coherent action and obscure responsibility for government action. Making the popular will (if it can be said to exist) known through participation is not enough; the popular will must be focused. What is needed is a means of imposing coherence on government action, of centralizing the authority that institutions decentralize. According to various scholars over the decades, that means strong or responsible political parties.

As noted above, the case for strong parties was advanced at the turn of the century. It has regularly been elaborated since, most prominently in the 1950 report of the American Political Science Association's Committee on Political Parties, "Toward a More Responsible Two-Party System." In the 1970s numerous articles and books decried the party decomposition then apparent (e.g., Burnham 1970, ch. 5; Broder 1971), and a Committee for Party Renewal even was established in the mid-1970s (Mileur 1991). In 1995 there was a palpable sense of excitement among American politics scholars when the House Republicans behaved much like the responsible party that we had read about in our textbooks.

Everett Ladd (1992) undoubtedly was correct in noting that support for strong parties to some degree reflects a preference for activist government. Wilson was arguing for a party that would enable a strong president to impose his leadership. The APSA committee did its work during the heyday of the New Deal public philosophy. And most recently, concerns over the state of the parties resurged during the energy crisis and stagflation of the 1970s, both of which seemed to require some major, coordinated government response.

Still, not only statists see the value of responsible parties. For many scholars the electoral accountability provided by cohesive parties was a more important consideration than the programmatic efficiency they would provide. Without the collective responsibility provided by parties, members of Congress could escape responsibility for the policies advocated by their activists and presidential candidates, and they had every reason to hang their presidents out to dry when the going got tough (Fiorina 1980). Ending this electoral irresponsibility—which reached its apogee with a more or less continuous state of divided government—was clearly a concern of modern supporters of strong parties.

Like advocates of participatory democracy, supporters of strong parties have gotten much of what they advocated over the course of the past three or four decades. The APSA report is far more often cited than read, but those who read it typically report a response of the following sort: "Gee, a lot of what those guys wanted actually has happened." Professors Baer and Bositis (1993) have done the profession a great service by carefully reading the report and judging the extent to which its numerous recommendations have been adopted. I hope they will forgive me for reducing their 40-page assessment into the crude tabulation in Table 2.

TABLE 2. APSA REPORT AFTER 40 YEARS

FATE OF PROPOSAL	DEMOCRATS	REPUBLICANS	SYSTEM
Full implementation	13	6	5
Partial implementation	7	5	5
De facto movement	8	9	5
No change	3	10	3
Negative movement	2	3	2

Source: Grossly adapted from Denise Baer and David Bositis, *Politics and Linkage in a Democratic Society* (Englewood Cliffs, NJ: Prentice-Hall, 1993), Appendix.

Some of the APSA committee's recommendations applied to the internal processes of the parties, and others to the larger system. The recommendations range from minor (reducing the number of convention delegates) to major (making congressional committee chairs responsible to the parties). Some of the proposals never had a chance (abolition of the Electoral College), while some of the proposals were fairly easy to implement (party conferences). But even granting these problems in adding up successes and failures, on the whole the crude tabulation in table 2 strongly suggests that the committee was quite successful. The Democrats, fittingly, have adopted 28 of 33 proposals; the more conservative Republicans have gone along with 20 of the 33, and 15 of the 20 recommendations for the larger system have been implemented at least to some degree. Nelson Polsby (2000) has quipped that the committee "sought both to rewrite the U.S. Constitution and to reform human nature." Against odds like that they seem to have done rather well.

And therein lies a second irony! Some of the best political science minds of the 1930s and 1940s proposed a plan to improve American democracy. Whether as a direct result of the power of their case or not, much of that plan has been implemented. But the result is not what the APSA committee might have anticipated. Current generations of Americans blessed with to-day's more responsible parties like and trust their government much less and participate less in politics than their predecessors who were afflicted with the unreformed, less responsible parties of midcentury. Here again, a venerable set of arguments about how to improve American democracy seems incon-sistent with the judgments of the people who live under it.

▪ | Explaining the Gaps between Theory and Reality

These broad inconsistencies between theories and data raise three logical possibilities. The first is that both general theories are individually valid, but when implemented together, they offset or produce some kind of negative interaction. An example might be the charge of some critics that the APSA report was schizophrenic: on the one hand it called for centralization, but on the other hand it doffed its hat in the direction of the participatory tradi-tion by calling for more grassroots involvement. Perhaps the two simply are impossible to reconcile. Getting more popular involvement prevented party reforms from achieving the desired end of enhancing coherence and disci-pline. Thus, neither theory is invalid, but democratic theorists failed to work out how they would operate if implemented simultaneously.

Another possibility is that both theories are valid, even operating si-multaneously, and would have contributed to a healthier democracy had not some overlooked or unanticipated third factor overriden the positive ef-fects of both theories. Again, the media provide the obvious example of such an explanatory villain. Had television never been invented, perhaps Americans today would participate more and like and trust their govern-ment more than Americans of 1960, as suggested by both democratic re-form traditions. I don't believe this, but it is a possibility.

A third possibility is that one theory is right and the other one wrong, and the harmful consequences of the wrong theory more than offset the beneficial consequences of the correct one. The arguments (e.g., Crozier, Huntington, and Watanuki, 1975) about the overload of democratic sys-tems that were offered in the 1970s provide an example. According to such arguments the participatory movements of the 1960s delegitimated politi-cal authority and overwhelmed gatekeeper institutions. As a result, democ-racies were in crisis, overloaded with popular demands that exceeded their aggregative capacities. Thus, party theorists could be right, but the gains produced by party reforms were overwhelmed because the participatory theorists were so wrong.[6]

6. I have not been able to think of a symmetrical argument, where the participa-tory theorists are correct but the party theorists so wrong that the validity of the par-ticipatory argument is not apparent.

And there is a final possibility, namely, that both theories are faulty. That is the position I will argue in the rest of this paper. My contention is not that party and participatory theorists had it wrong from the beginning but rather that important implicit assumptions underlying both theories have been undermined by the evolution of American democracy. The consequence is that both theories are inaccurate now, whatever their merits fifty years ago.

THE PROBLEM WITH PARTY THEORY

Party theory assumes fealty to a set of basic party principles. As Polsby (2000) notes, "Parties should make promises and stand by their promises and risk the loss of elections if they fail to deliver on their promises." While agreeing with that characterization I believe that most supporters of strong parties implicitly added the qualification "but not if the risk is too large or too long term." In other words, party theorists accept the idea of popular sovereignty and in consequence the notion that real-world parties are and will remain Downsian: they will appeal to the broad mass of the electorate in an attempt to win elections (A. Downs 1957). To be sure, parties have different constituencies and generally support somewhat different policies, but when important interests are at stake—namely, control of government, especially long-term control of government—they will rise above their principles in order to win. This reasoning underlies the standard model of party competition in which parties converge to the position of the median voter in the electorate. To political scientists of the 1950s—the era of "me too," "not a dime's worth of difference" politics—the Downsian assumption must have looked all too true.

A second subsidiary assumption also was widely held: the issues that would dominate American politics in the modern world were issues of foreign policy, the national economy, and the welfare state.[7] Given the United States's position as the undisputed leader of the free world, international engagement was a given. Only the means to consensually held foreign policy and national defense ends were in dispute. Similarly, except for a few "reactionaries," everyone recognized the necessity for some government role in maintaining economic stability and social welfare; the questions were how much and what instruments to use—issues that lent themselves to compromise. "Half a loaf is better than none" was the outlook of the members of Congress described by 1950s scholars. In particular, the committee on political parties worked during the one generation in American history when the kind of divisive social issues that reemerged in the 1960s were dormant. Such issues were an important part of American politics in earlier eras as political historians have shown, but the parties of

---

7. As Baer and Bositis note, the APSA report was relatively silent on the issue of race (1993, 205).

earlier eras generally attempted to suppress such issues and were capable of doing so (Kleppner 1979).

In sum, the general viewpoint of 1950s party scholars was that parties would differ but they still would position themselves well within the mainstream of public opinion. Moreover, their differences would not be so severe as to produce deadlock. Competition between two responsible parties would produce reasonably representative government.

Things seem different today. The new reality that is not yet sufficiently incorporated in our accounts is that between 1960 and 1990 the trade-offs parties made between policies and votes shifted in the direction of policies.[8] In 1964 worldly wise political scientists chuckled at the Goldwaterite slogan "I'd rather be right than president" but in the ensuing decades such sentiments became quite widespread—especially among Democrats in the 1970s and 1980s, then again among Republicans in the 1990s. Close observers (e.g., Sundquist 1981, 371) maintain that in Congress, at least, members coming into the institution in the 1970s were more policy oriented than those they replaced. The traditional party organizations selected candidates on the basis of party loyalty and service—and electability if the district was marginal—but as the traditional parties declined, a newer generation of candidates increasingly was recruited by or at least supported by social movements and interest groups. Even if they are not personally more policy committed, newer members are more dependent on activist constituencies who compose their personal organizations and fund their campaigns.

Party activists, of course, are a large part of the story. They always have had a point of view, and even in the 1950s their points of view on many issues were quite distinct from the mass public, as documented by McCloskey, Hoffman, and O'Hara (1960). But activists are far more distinct today. As figure 4 shows, the ideological distance between Democratic and Republican activists has grown steadily in the past three decades. More anecdotally, when asked about his priorities the incoming chair of the California Republican Party replied that "killing our babies is the issue of the century . . . cutting taxes or any other issue pales in comparison."[9] Whatever happened to "maximizing the number of Republicans elected," the response that state chairs like Ray Bliss no doubt would have offered in the mid-1960s?[10]

If I am correct in arguing that today's parties and candidates are more

8. I am referring here to general theories about parties and representation. The developers of specialized formal theories of electoral competition have been quite active in constructing models in which parties and candidates differentiate themselves. For a survey, see Fiorina 1999c.

9. John McCarthy quoted in Marinucci 2000.

10. Longtime state chair of Ohio, Bliss was named Republican national chairman after the Goldwater debacle. He was generally considered to be organizationally gifted.

Figure 4 | Party Activists Have Grown More Extreme

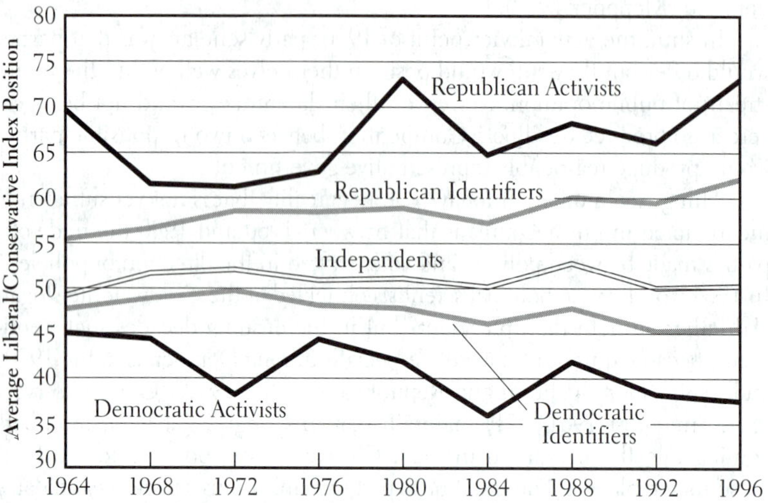

Source: ANES 1948–1996 Cumulative Data File.

Notes: Activists are defined as respondents who engaged in three or more campaign activities as coded in vcf0723. Learners are coded as partisans. The Liberal/Conservative Index (vcf0801) measures a respondent's relative thermometer ratings of "Liberals" and "Conservatives." It is calculated by subtracting the Liberal Thermometer score from 97 and averaging the result with the Conservative Thermometer score. Cases are weighted by vcf0009.

ideological and committed to specific policies, then the answer to why party reforms have not produced greater citizen happiness with government is apparent: citizens don't like principled parties—especially when party positions are far from the center of public opinion. A generation of research has shown that the mass public is generally moderate in its views and takes a nonideological, pragmatic approach to issues (Kinder and Sears 1985). Moreover, for most people politics is a peripheral concern. Why should they be positively disposed toward a public arena overrun by activists and candidates whose outlook is just the opposite?

The Problem with Participatory Theory

The problem with participatory arguments is related to that just proposed. Those who put their faith in expanded participation assume that the desire to participate is widely distributed; thus, opening government doors will lead to a more representative democracy. Unfortunately, the reverse appears to be true. Contrary to the presumptions of political theorists, participation is not a natural act; it is an unnatural act. Left to their own devices ordinary people generally will devote little by way of time and resources to politics. Participation today is the province of those who feel strongly about an issue or candidate, either because they have particularly extreme views or because they are directly affected in a way that others are not and this tends to make them hold particularly extreme views.

It is striking how little political scientists really know about political participation. Take as the state of the art Verba, Schlozman, and Brady's *Voice and Equality* (1995). This magesterial study greatly adds to the stock of knowledge about political participation, but it impresses as much for what it indicates about what we don't know, a remark in no way intended as critical. Verba, Schlozman, and Brady flip the standard question and ask, "Why *don't* people participate?" Their answer is threefold: because people can't—they don't have the resources, because people don't want to—they don't have the motivation, and because no one asked—they weren't mobilized. They propose a resource mobilization account of participation that enables them to bring virtually every known correlate of participation into a coherent empirical analysis.[11] As summary Tables 3 and 4 illustrate, however, the results are sobering.

TABLE 3. VERBA, SCHLOZMAN, AND BRADY EXPLANATION OF KINDS OF PARTICIPATION

	R^2
Time-based acts	.23
Voting	.38
Contributions	.13
Political Discussion	.42

Source: Adapted from Verba, Schlozman, and Brady 1995, Table 12.7.
Independent variables: education, vocabulary, family income, job level, nonpolitical organization, religious attendance, civic skills, political interest, political information, political efficacy, partisan strength, citizenship.

If we were to analyze the vote choices of these same respondents, our models would produce R^2 and pseudo-R^2 in the .7 range—with a far smaller number of right-hand side variables. But elaborate models of participation yield R^2s that are much smaller (table 3). And when we turn to participation in specific issue domains and add still more right-hand side

11. This comment is not meant as criticism, only as a statement of fact. Verba, Schlozman, and Brady's resource mobilization framework provides a broad theoretical umbrella that subsumes all the standard correlates of participation, as well as numerous nonstandard ones.

Table 4. Verba, Schlozman, and Brady
Explanation of Focus of Participation

	R^2
Activity on basic human needs	.03
Activity on education	.09
Activity on abortion	.08

Source: Adapted from Verba, Schlozman, and Brady 1995, Tables 14.2, 14.4.
Independent variables: education, income, job variables, organization variables, church variables, political interest, self-interest (e.g., receipt of means-tested benefits/school age children), and abortion attitudes.

variables (mainly personal interest or impact), the models yield R^2s less than .1 (table 4). The simple facts are that many people who have the resources don't expend them, many people who have the motivation don't act on it, and many people who are asked refuse—and we are not very good at picking out the small minority who are different.

I think the missing explanatory variable is motivation. Verba, Schlozman, and Brady include motivation in two ways, one general and one specific. General motivations are tapped by the standard concepts of efficacy and duty, but their results suggest that most people who are efficacious and dutiful nevertheless are not going to sit through a three-hour city council meeting or spend their Saturday afternoon at a caucus. Specific motivations are tapped by measures of self-interest or personal impact, but their results indicate that people who appear to have a direct interest nevertheless are not motivated to pursue it. Having observed participators in recent years, I have concluded that the principle factor motivating them is that they care deeply about the subject of their participation, although why they do often escapes me. They are intense, and their intensity leads to their participation.

Social psychologists and political scientists long have understood that extremity is the handmaiden of intensity (Allport and Hartman 1925; Cantril 1946). Common discourse recognizes that close relationship by the absence of pairings like "rabid moderate" or "wishy-washy extremist." Intensely held views generally are extreme views—relative to the issue and the population—and these are the views that are most common among political participators.

Consider the abortion issue. As figure 5 suggests, Americans have relatively settled and generally qualified views on legal abortion. They favor it overwhelmingly in what are considered traumatic circumstances and express significant reservations when the reasons seem less dire. In particular,

Figure 5 | Popular Attitudes toward Legal Abortion since *Roe v. Wade* (1973)

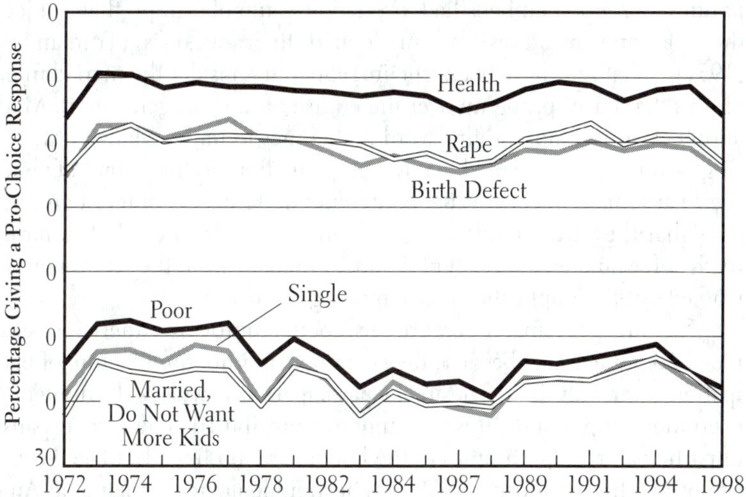

Source: Calculated by the authors from the General Social Survey 1972–1998 Cumulative Data File.

Note: Respondents who answered "don't know" are included in the calculation.

anyone who has delved into public opinion on this subject knows that only tiny minorities would support forfeiting the life of a mother on the one hand or destroying a healthy eight-month fetus on the other. Yet the political debate is defined by those minorities. In the Democratic primaries Al Gore was attacked from the left because as a Tennessee congressman he suggested that a fetus might be more than a clump of tissue, and in the Republican primaries John McCain was attacked from the right because he favored legal abortion in cases of rape, incest, or birth defects. In fact, these two candidates bracketed the positions held by 80 percent of the American people (see figure 5). The abortion issue could have been compromised in a way acceptable to the great mass of the American people thirty years ago, but it has not because of the implacable views of those active in the politics of the issue.[12] Tellingly, in some European democracies, where participatory theories have never been so popular, the abortion issue was generally settled long ago with much less conflict than surrounds the issue in the United States.

Abortion is all too typical of the issues and the debate that the advo-

12. Some colleagues disagree, suggesting that the courts polarized the issue to begin with and have helped keep it polarized. I concede this point in part, but note that in *Webster* and *Casey*, the courts have moved toward compromises that Congress seems unable to achieve.

cacy explosion has brought to American politics. Fifty years ago pluralist scholars argued that interest groups exercised a moderating influence on politics. Group members had overlapping memberships that subjected them to cross-pressures and moderated their outlooks (Truman 1971 [1951]). That may have been true in 1950, but consider the myriad interest groups that have sprung up over the course of the past generation. Moderation certainly is not the first word that comes to mind. Many of them are single-issue groups devoted to advancing an all-or-nothing point of view on their particular concern. What contemporary scholar of interest groups argues that they are a moderating influence? In this case scholars have already reformulated a branch of democratic theory, but they have not as yet worked out the implications for larger arguments.

In sum, participatory arguments about improving American democracy have gone astray because they overlook an important feature of participation. Not only is the desire to participate not widely distributed, but even more importantly, it is not randomly distributed. The great expansion of participatory opportunities in the last generation has advantaged extremists of all stripes (Fiorina 1999a). The nonideological, pragmatic Americans mentioned above sit at home while extremists participate—whatever the issue: presidential politics, sex education, land use, leash laws, and so on. Another reason contemporary Americans do not like government or want to participate in political processes is because the people who populate the public arena are not like them.

■ | Why Have Underlying Assumptions Become
         Less Accurate?

Why would today's party activists and elected officials weigh policy concerns more heavily vis-à-vis electoral considerations than their counterparts of earlier generations? I suggest a very simple hypothesis: the *personal* material rewards linked directly to political participation have greatly diminished. The material rewards allocated by government, of course, have *not* diminished. Insurance companies, teachers' unions, agribusiness, and myriad other interests stand to gain or lose huge amounts from government actions, as suggested by the large sums of money they contribute to campaigns and expend on lobbying. What I am arguing is that the personal material rewards to political activism are less today than for much of our history before the mid–twentieth century. Table 5 lists some of the reasons for the declining importance of material incentives.

Civil service, of course, is the oldest and most widely recognized means of removing material incentives from politics. Accounts of nineteenth-century politics attribute staggering patronage resources to the parties—tens of thousands of jobs in large states like Pennsylvania and New

TABLE 5. REMOVAL OF MATERIAL INCENTIVES FOR POLITICAL PARTICIPATION

Civil service

Public-sector unionization

Conflict of interest laws

Universalistic policies/Entitlements

Changes in political culture

Media (junkyard dogs)

York.[13] And not only were the patronage recipients themselves subject to political mobilization, the party organizations appropriated portions of their paychecks and pressed them into service to mobilize others. But for more than a century both reformers and elected officials have extended protection from arbitrary control of public employment, for different reasons to be sure and with predictable consequences. If the toll collectors on the eastern state turnpikes today knew they would lose their jobs if the governor lost the next election, their levels of political participation no doubt would be much higher. But extension of civil service had been going on for three-quarters of a century when the shift toward a hypothesized more ideological basis for political participation began, so it may not play a major role in the current public discontent.

Public-sector unionization has much the same impact as civil service protection, although it is much more recent. True, public employees vote at higher rates than others, but the more relevant question is whether they participate at rates as high as they would if their jobs were subject to the decisions of political leaders.[14] Recently I had occasion to review tapes made twenty-five years ago when I conducted interviews in two congressional districts for an earlier project. In one interview a county chair in a state then undergoing unionization opined that this would kill off the patronage system in his state. He said that the parties had managed to work with civil service, but unionization would be the death knell for the patronage system. In retrospect, we can see that unionization would diminish the ability of parties and public officials to mobilize public-sector workers and their families. If the members of the American Federation of State, County, and Municipal Employees, the National Education Association, and other public-sector unions depended not on their unions for economic gains but on the decisions of public officials in the country's 86,000 jurisdictions,

13. Keller cites estimates that in New York State one in every eight voters was a federal, state, or local officeholder (1977, 239).

14. On turnout of public employees, see Wolfinger and Rosenstone 1980, 94–101.

their levels of political engagement no doubt would be higher than at present. This is a subject that deserves more systematic study.

Not only was politics a primary source of jobs at one time, but it was a primary means to personal advancement through what was charmingly referred to as "honest graft" (Riordan 1963, 4). Whom you knew in politics might be the key to a contract, a tip, or some other means of turning a profit. Thus, it paid—literally—to participate in politics and government, with predictable results, positive and negative. But modern politics is much "cleaner." Rather than a commonly held goal, in many cases conflict of interest is now a crime. And if you can't personally profit from participation, fewer people will participate.

Just as jobs are no longer bestowed at the pleasure of party and elected officials, neither are policy outputs. If your neighborhood's garbage collection or snow removal depends on its turnout rate, turnout will be higher ceteris paribus, than if such services are automatic, a matter of right. Scholars have long recognized the negative impact of government-provided social welfare on the urban machines. This is only a special case of a broader phenomenon. When people feel that public benefits depend directly on their personal actions or those of their close associates, they will be more engaged than when those benefits accrue as a matter of law or right. The modern movement toward universalism and entitlements is a movement that encourages free riding on the political engagement of others—with predictable consequences.

The decline of old-fashioned parties organized around material rewards is associated with a change in campaign style. Labor-intensive campaigns staffed by public-sector workers have given way to the modern hi-tech campaign staffed by professionals. The transformation has gone along with a sharp rise in the costs of campaigns, in large part driven by the costs of television. Corporations and other interest groups contribute for instrumental reasons now as they always have, but it is likely that the basis for individual campaign contributions has shifted. In the older party era, patronage workers often were dunned a portion of their salaries, recipients of contracts were assessed a portion of their contracts, favor recipients were asked to reciprocate, and so forth. Such "contributions" were the price of a job or other material government benefit. Today, many fewer people are subject to such material pressures. Instead, individuals voluntarily contribute to political campaigns on the basis of the causes they believe in. And, what evidence we have suggests that contributors, like those who participate in other ways, are more extreme in their views (Brown, Powell, and Wilcox 1995).

Each of the aforementioned changes probably reflects gradual changes in the political culture, an admittedly amorphous but undoubtedly significant factor in diminishing the personal material rewards of political participation. As Mayhew notes, in what he calls "traditional party organization" (TPO) states, the parties rely on material rather than purposive incentives (1986, 20), to use Wilson's typology (1973).[15] In TPO states the public sector is viewed as a large employment bureau.[16] The cost of government is regarded as a benefit in part, since government spending provides jobs (Weingast, Shepsle, and Johnsen 1981). And part of the exchange is the expectation that those benefited will participate in politics when the party calls on them. A younger, better-educated population that thinks of the public sector as something that should provide efficient services at minimum cost is in conflict with the older party culture, and this newer subculture is historically ascendant, of course.

Finally, changes in media values and practices help to drive out personal material rewards as a reason for political activity. Scandal is a staple of the "junkyard dog" media. The media ferret out and publicize instances of conflict of interest, honest graft, and favoritism. Even where old-time temptations still exist, the potential costs of succumbing to temptation may deter the potential sinner. Moreover, the media analyze motives and speculate on the presence of ulterior ones ("Never assume a good motive if a bad one is available"). The only participants who can demonstrate credibility are those who can show that their political stands harm their personal material interests.

If we remove material reasons for participation, why would people participate? Well, there is the altruistic desire to serve one's fellow human beings. I don't think it's overly cynical to suggest that this is not a major factor in explaining political participation, although for some people, it is indeed the explanation. At any rate I can see no obvious reason why this motivation should have become more or less common in recent decades.

A second incentive would be the desire for visibility and adulation, a "love of fame" as Hamilton puts it in *Federalist No. 72*. No doubt this is why some people go into politics, but again, there is no obvious reason why this motivation should be more or less important for political participation today. Indeed, with the growth of the entertainment industry, there probably are more avenues outside politics for publicity seekers and exhibitionists now than in earlier periods of history.

A third reason people participate is in response to what Wilson calls "solidary" incentives (1973, ch. 3). People want to belong to a group, to interact with others whom they like, to affirm symbols and allegiances, and so forth. Historians argue that such incentives have been extremely important stimuli for political participation in the American past (McGerr 1986). Clearly they are much less important today, but again, it seems unlikely that their erosion plays a major role in explaining popular disaffection now

15. Of course, material incentives also are important in states not categorized as TPO. Massachusetts is a good example.

16. I cannot back up this claim with survey data, but I grew up in Pennsylvania and have lived in New York and Massachusetts, and this is certainly my impression of attitudes prevailing in the older subcultures of those states.

because they had greatly diminished in importance at least a generation before the present discontent began.[17]

As the material incentives for political participation declined, it seems likely that ideological incentives took up most of the slack. More than in most of our history, participation today reflects a desire to impose one's view of a better world on the rest of society. Most people today participate because they really do want to save the whales, outlaw abortion, stop global warming, get government off our backs, or achieve some one of a plethora of other ends.[18] And while many people share such goals, the people who participate will be those who feel most intensely about them and whose points of view are most one sided. Again, the reemergence of social issues in the 1960s and afterward—racial, ethnic, religious, cultural—reinforces these trends. Because such issues deeply implicate values, the resulting preferences are intensely held.

In sum, the replacement of material incentives by purposive ones, combined with the growing importance of social issues has transformed political participation in the United States. People who went to meetings or worked in campaigns because their jobs depended on it were different from people who now do so out of ideological zeal. In particular, people who participated because it paid to do so probably were a reasonable cross-section of the electorate, certainly a more representative sample than self-selected participants activated by a cause. Moreover, with real economic benefits at stake, materially motivated participants naturally would be concerned to keep the benefits flowing; this gave them a strong incentive to represent the opinions of the electorate whose decisions controlled the flow. Theories of parties and representation implicitly based on such premises will generate different conclusions—positive and normative—than will theories based on today's realities: parties and participants more extreme in their viewpoints, more reluctant to compromise their positions, and more willing to sacrifice electoral victory for principles.

■ | ### Consequences of Displacing Material by Ideological Incentives

If the preceding broad arguments are correct, then a number of conclusions about contemporary politics follow naturally. The most obvious is that politics has become more conflictual. If participants hold more ex-

17. As indicated in the subtitle of McGerr's work *The American North, 1865–1928* (1986). McGerr argues that the advertising approach began to replace the mobilization approach about the turn of the century.

18. True, many activists make their living running or working for such organizations. The fact remains, however, that they do not run or work for just any organization. Their ideological preferences point them toward certain issue areas.

treme positions, feel more intensely about their positions, and have little to lose materially by deepening and prolonging controversy, then conflict will be more common.[19] Indeed, in politics today prolonging and deepening controversy may advance one's cause by generating publicity and contributions. Of course, nostalgia always is a danger when thinking about long-term change. Certainly, politics in the 1960s was conflictual, to note the obvious objection. But that was a decade of abnormal politics, as suggested by the tag sometimes applied to it, "the time of troubles." Politics then was about war and race, about young Americans dying and African Americans being denied the most basic rights and privileges. Today, participants go to the mat over leaf blowers, leash laws, and salamanders.

Normal politics today is more conflictual also because of a second characteristic: it is more symbolic. The importance of positions vis-à-vis outcomes has increased. Participants struggle mightily over statements, labels, and gestures that are unlikely to have any real impact. This is a natural consequence of the increased importance of ideological incentives.[20] If I participate because of the rightness of my cause, then opposition is illegitimate. Society must be forced to recognize my cause whether anything tangible follows from that or not. The resurgence of social issues and the rise of what often is called identity politics have reinforced this tendency. Did it really matter whether George W. Bush chose a pro-choice or pro-life running mate? Whether students said a prayer before a high school football game? Whether gays are permitted to marry or whether their relationships receive some alternative but equivalent legal status? Whether Jews can string twine between telephone polls to create symbolic eruvs?[21] To the participants involved in debates like these the answer is a resounding yes! But to millions of uninvolved Americans observing the cross fire, the answer more likely is not really.

A third consequence of the displacement of material incentives by ideological ones is that politics becomes less relevant to the needs and concerns of the mass of Americans. One can understand the frustrations of old-line social democrats who complain that Democratic candidates today devote much energy to identity politics, gun control, abortion, and other issues of critical importance to their constituency groups, while failing to invest comparable energy in advocating a flattening of the income distribution, improving education, and making medical care available to all.[22]

19. As suggested by the classic quip attributed to Wallace Sayres, "the reason academic fights are so vicious is that there is so little at stake."

20. Jane Mansbridge makes this point in the specific case of the women's movement (1986, especially ch. 10).

21. An Eruv is an enclave where the strict restrictions on Sabbath behavior are loosened.

22. Ralph Nader's charge that the Democrats have become lackeys of "corporate America" seems to contradict the argument made in this paper. That is, Nader complains that the Democrats and Republicans differ insignificantly on economic

The preceding characteristics of contemporary politics reinforce the long-standing advantage of the status quo in American politics. A federal system with a separation of powers and a wide array of checks and balances makes it difficult to act, as the proponents of strong parties recognized. The changes in participation discussed above enhance that long-standing generalization. If participants take more extreme positions on issues and focus primarily on issues that do not engage the mass of the American people, they are unlikely to mobilize stable popular majorities that can overcome the usual inertia of the system.

That lack of success in turn suggests two tendencies that are concerns from a democratic theory standpoint. The first is that participants will attempt to escape from electoral politics. If you cannot mobilize majorities behind your point of view, then find a nonmajoritarian arena in which to fight. The courts are the obvious alternative. Develop a legal strategy that results in unelected judges imposing an outcome that elected officials would not (Melnick 1994). If you can criminalize or otherwise delegitimate the actions of your opponents (Ginsburg and Shefter 1990), so much the better. But the courts are not the only alternative. Persuade the president to act unilaterally (Moe and Howell 1999) or have legislators insert a "stealth rider" in a must-pass appropriations or omnibus bill. Such strategies are not at all new, of course, but modern developments make them relatively more attractive than mobilizing majorities and winning elections.

Finally, we come full circle. Not only do the characteristics of contemporary politics tempt elites to leave the electoral arena, they push ordinary people to do so too, indeed, to leave politics altogether. If politics has fallen into the hands of people who take it altogether more seriously than you do, who froth about issues that seem to you peripheral, who advocate policies that strike you as extreme, who demonize their opponents, and who reject reasonable compromises and if, as a consequence, nothing seems to happen very quickly other than judges tossing an occasional bombshell, then why in the world would you devote your valuable and limited time and energy to politics?

In recent decades turnout in U.S. elections has declined, and commentators were disappointed in 2000 when despite intense voter mobiliza-

---

issues, a charge that, if true, appears to be at odds with my argument that the parties have become more polarized. An alternative interpretation is that many of today's Democratic activists and officeholders are not very concerned with traditional economic issues. By muting their positions on those issues, they can raise the corporate cash to win elections and attempt to implement social policies that they care intensely about. For example, late in the 2000 campaign, feminist and gay-lesbian groups attacked Nader for his supposed indifference to their issues (Marinucci and Simon 2000). For his part, Nader claimed that Gore and Bush differed only in how fast their knees hit the ground when the corporations called. Evidently, the two sides differed on the issues they viewed as important.

Figure 6 | Turnout Has Declined Primarily Among Less Partisan Americans (Presidential Elections)

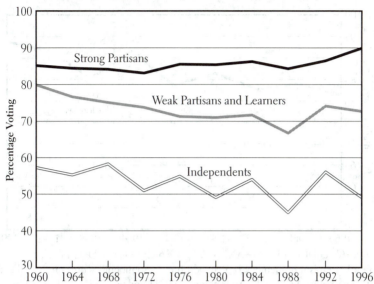

Source: Calculated using the ANES 1948–1996 Cumulative Data File.
Notes: Apoliticals are coded as Independents. Cases are weighted by vcf0009.

tion efforts, turnout barely exceeded 50 percent. One of the features of the turnout decline that has not been adequately recognized is that it largely reflects the nonparticipation of moderates. As traced in figure 6, strong partisans report turnout rates as high as ever. Increased nonvoting among weak identifiers, independent leaners, and independents is the source of the turnout decline. On the one hand that observation is not new; we have long known that declining partisanship was a contributor to the turnout decline (e.g., Abramson and Aldrich 1982). But we have not thought about the implications, namely, as indicated in figure 7, a hollowing out of the electorate as moderates participate at lower rates than the extremes. Over the long term this development may encourage candidates to adopt narrow mobilization strategies—appeals to one's base, in preference to centrist strategies designed to win over the median voter (Fiorina 1999c). The fact that centrist pressures seem strongest at the presidential level, where turnout runs around 50 percent than in, say, off-year House elections, where turnout runs around 35 percent suggests that a strategic switch may be rational (to the candidates) somewhere in that range.

The reason that the Hibbing and Theiss-Morse explanation for the present discontent strikes me as incomplete is that it misplaces the blame for that discontent. Reminiscent of Jimmy Carter's "malaise" speech (Nelson 1999, 211–18), Hibbing and Theiss-Morse lay the blame for disaffection with government squarely on citizens themselves. We are distrusting

Figure 7 | Turnout Has Declined Primarily Among Moderates (Presidential Elections)

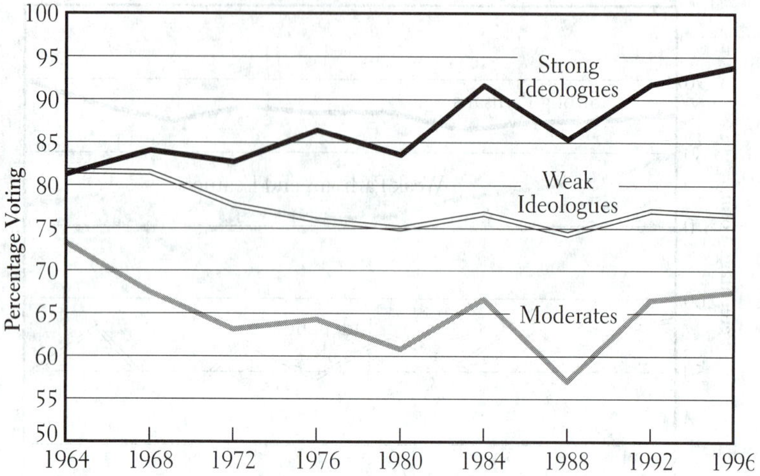

Source: Calculated using the ANES 1948–1996 Cumulative Data File.

Notes: Extremism of ideology is recoded from a respondent's scores on the Liberal and Conservative Feeling Thermometers (vcf0211 and vcf0212).

To maintain consistency with the NES coding prior to 1970, respondents who answered "Don't know" to either feeling thermometer are coded as 50 on that feeling thermometer. Using these recoded thermometers, a modified version of the Liberal/Conservative index is constructed following the procedure used to construct vcf0801.

Finally, the modified Liberal/Conservative Index is recoded into categories of ideological extremism. Codes 0–24 and 75–97 are recoded as Strong Ideologues, 25–48 and 50–74 as Weak Ideologues, and 49 as Moderates. Cases are weighted by vcf0009.

and cynical because at base we don't like fundamental features of democratic politics. We regard interest groups as wicked, we don't like conflict, and we don't like the bargaining and compromise necessary to settle conflicts. To Hibbing and Theiss-Morse, such attitudes betray naivete about democratic politics. Maybe so. But there is a difference between giving interest groups a fair hearing and allowing selfish and self-righteous groups to dominate the political debate. There is a difference between reasoned disagreement and adolescent temper tantrums and name-calling. And there is a difference between compromises among public officials who disagree in good faith and last-minute logrolls by gridlocked partisans at summits. I am not nearly as sure as Hibbing and Theiss-Morse that the American people should bear the entire blame for their discontent.

▪ | Academic and Practical Implications

If the preceding account is persuasive, the question remains, what can be done about it? I am not optimistic that much can be done about the developments described above. Americans are not about to legalize conflict of interest, outlaw public-sector unions, and bring back the spoils system — and they probably would not like the resulting politics any better. That purposive incentives have become more important motivators of political activity is a reality that is not likely to change. The first order of business is to update our theories of representation and electoral competition to take account of these new conditions so that we do not inadvertently lead people astray.

For example, the Supreme Court recently overturned the California blanket primary as an unconstitutional infringement on the party's freedom of association.[23] My impression is that most political scientists applauded the court's decision, but this approval partly reflects an outdated, positive view of the role of parties in a democracy. In reaching its decision, the Court ruled that the state interests claimed by blanket primary supporters were not sufficiently compelling to outweigh the First Amendment rights of the parties. Reading the opinion one cannot help but wonder whether the court's judgement about the balance was influenced by a generally positive view of parties' role in a democracy, a view promulgated by generations of political scientists.[24]

Imagine, for example, that the California plaintiffs had been the kind of corrupt old-style machines that provoked the Progressive movement. Would the Court have been equally solicitous of their associational rights? Perhaps not. The Court's judgment about whether an organization's rights of free expression outweigh the state's claim that it is furthering a compelling interest undoubtedly reflects in some part the justices' views of the value the organization contributes to society. If today's parties contribute less value to American democracy than the textbook portrait of midcentury depicts, we need to make that clear.[25]

As for practical rather than intellectual suggestions, the only one I can offer is analogous to the old hair-of-the-dog remedy for hangovers. Given that we cannot go backward, we need to go farther down the road the populist tradition marks out. If the expansion of participatory opportunities has generated unrepresentative participators, the obvious solution is to increase participation so as to make it more representative by diluting the extreme

23. *California Democratic Party v. Jones*, 530 U.S. 1 (2000).

24. The majority opinion even paraphrases Schattschneider's comment that democracy is "unimaginable without parties" (*Ibid.*, 6).

25. This is not a brief for the specific form of the California blanket primary. As Justice Scalia suggests, a nonpartisan blanket primary could deliver the same benefits, in theory, and it would pass constitutional muster.

voices that dominate contemporary politics. The problem is not that the doors to the public arena have been opened, but that they have not yet been opened so wide that people simply cannot avoid walking through them. Thus, while some contemporary theorists have the general idea right—more participation—their specific recommendations point in precisely the wrong direction. The answer is not, for example, strong democracy, where meetings and deliberation are expanded (Barber 1984). That sort of trend has helped to put us in the present situation. Barring a sudden transformation in human nature, or failing that, the sudden disappearance of TV, the Internet, and other forms of entertainment, the requirements of strong democracy will only decrease participation and make politics less representative.[26]

On the contrary, much more thin democracy is what we need. Given a world in which time is scarce and recreational opportunities are plentiful, the best hope is to proliferate very low cost participatory opportunities, so that majorities can easily weigh in against unrepresentative minorities.[27] For example, we should be open to the burgeoning discussion, however nonsensical it seems at times, about electronic town halls and digital democracy; there may be some promise amidst all the hype. Participatory theorists may decry proposals like these as still further departures from ideal democracy, but we do not live in an ideal world.

I conclude with two extended caveats. First, this essay obviously reflects a majoritarian point of view.[28] In *Federalist No. 10* Madison discounted the likelihood of minority tyranny because by definition minorities would be outweighed by majorities. The argument is persuasive when one considers minorities that are attempting to change the status quo. As an empirical matter, out-of-the-mainstream proposals advocated by various minorities typically are killed somewhere in the process. Thus, minorities often are frustrated. But Madison's argument is less persuasive when one considers minorities that are resisting changes in the status quo. The intricate system Madison and his colleagues devised advantages minorities who resist change; they need only control one veto point in the process. Thus, developments in the past half-century or so have reinforced the system's bias against change, increasing the costs of government and

26. The analogy is to Oscar Wilde's oft-quoted observation that the problem with socialism is that it requires too many evenings.

27. Lijphart's recent call (1997) for compulsory voting is relevant here, although politically infeasible. Compulsory voting is a way of making *nonparticipation* costly.

28. It should go without saying that I am in no way advocating muzzling minority points of view. The question is not whether minorities should have every opportunity to present their cases and persuade majorities. The question is whether procedural and institutional changes should give them influence disproportionate to their numbers.

delaying the decisions of government, and consequently frustrating majorities. In sum, contemporary politics typically frustrates *both* minorities and majorities.

Second, it is possible that nothing much can be done about the present condition because, practically speaking, we already live in the best of all possible worlds. That is, while my argument suggests that today's parties are more a part of the problem than the solution, it may still be the case that they are the best alternative available to a modern democracy, an argument that has been made many times. Various political scientists have made the case that political vacuums are no more long lived than natural ones. If parties do not organize politics, politics will be organized by narrower personal factions and special interest groups.[29] A politics dominated by today's narrow interest groups unconstrained by the larger encompassing forces that parties provide may be even less attractive than a politics dominated by polarized, policy-oriented parties. If Americans in large numbers cannot be induced to participate in politics at least at the level of voting, then the parties as presently constituted still may be the best available alternative, even if they are less a force for representative government than they have been in the past.

I hope that such a lesser-of-other-evils conclusion is simply the product of my limited imagination. The problem, of course, is that living with the least of various evils might not be stable. The ultimate result may be that feared by those who are troubled by the trends discussed in the first section of this paper—a turn away from a public sector that has lost the confidence and support of the citizenry and a turn away from public life that has taken on unattractive features. While we may be entering a new era in which citizens of democracies the world over claim to want less centralized, less intrusive government, there is no good evidence that they want government to do less rather than more (Clark 2000). But in the present context it is hard to see how public officials can consider the myriad demands of citizens without increasing the level of popular frustration as well.

29. On factional politics see, of course, Key 1949, esp. ch. 14. On parties versus interest groups, see Schattschneider 1942, esp. ch. 8.

Amy Gutmann

Identity and Democracy: A Synthetic Perspective

The ever-growing attention to group identities and identity groups in normative political theory parallels their saliency in contemporary democratic
politics. Groups of individuals bound together by a shared social identity
such as nationality, ethnicity, gender, color, class, physical disability, or political ideology make political claims that range from exempting themselves from disproportionately burdensome laws to exercising sovereignty.
A large literature has developed over the past three decades centering
around the claims of identity groups in democratic politics, often beginning with the premise that individual identities are socially constructed
(rather than essentialist) and then pursuing the political implications of social construction. The idea of the social construction of identity is so open
ended, however, that it has no political implications, leaving us with the
question of whether the use of identity in political analysis is at all meaningful (Brubaker and Cooper 2000).

What is identity group politics? Is it reducible to interest group politics? Are there any political implications of a shared group identity, for example, for exemption from otherwise valid laws or for group rights? Critics
of identity group politics often contrast it to the free association of individuals. Free association is thought to enable people to develop their identities
as they see fit, not as any group determines for them. Yet associational freedom permits group exclusivity, and exclusions based on ascriptive group
identity perpetuate a negative identity group politics, which leaves many
people—simply by virtue of their group identity—with less than equal freedom, opportunity, and civic standing. Should democratic governments
therefore constrain civic associations not to discriminate against people on
the basis of their group identities?

A growing and wide-ranging scholarship on group identity and associational freedom in nonideal democracies addresses this question. It suggests that "Who should decide what and how in democratic politics?"
cannot be answered without taking more notice of the political role of
group identities and civic associations in nonideal contexts than ideal theo-

ries of justice ever do (Rawls 1971, 1999b; Carens 2000). In every existing nonideal democracy, individuals identify themselves and are identified by others, especially for public purposes, with voluntary and involuntary groups defined by social markers such as nationality, ethnicity, gender, race, age, disability, and political ideology. Even if none of these group identities—nor all of them taken together—completely defines any individual, group identities both constrain and liberate individuals, depending on the identity, the individual, and the context (Appiah 1996, 97–99). Group identities also play a central role in democratic politics, for better and for worse, because most individuals can be politically influential only in groups and some groups are far more justice friendly than others.

The scholarship on identity and democracy is internally divided over whether voluntary or involuntary group identities generally operate for the better or the worse in democratic politics. The "school of culture" emphasizes the essential contribution that cultural groups make to the lives of individuals in providing a sense of secure belonging and a set of scripts that give meaning to individual lives. The school of culture therefore warns against treating the ideal of the free and equal person as if actual individuals could be conceived independently of any and all cultural contexts. By contrast, the "school of choice" emphasizes the value of individual freedom from involuntary groups, the freedom to criticize and revise culturally given identities, and a correlative right of free association. The school of choice therefore issues precisely the opposite warning from the school of culture: Do not treat cultural groups as if they were primordial, sovereign authorities over individuals who should be accorded the civic standing of free and equal persons in democratic societies.

In this essay, I propose a synthesis that avoids the temptation, on the one hand, to elevate cultural groups over the individual, and, on the other hand, to conceive of individuals free from socially given identities. I build this synthesis on the insights offered by the schools of culture and choice at their strongest, and I therefore criticize those claims that rest on a conception of democratic societies as mere aggregations of either comprehensive cultural groups or free and equal individuals. A synthetic perspective situates the humanist ideals of freedom, opportunity, and civic equality for all persons within nonideal democratic contexts and, by so doing, offers a perspective on identity politics that is absent from ideal theories of justice. In the context of a society still suffering from a legacy of racial and gender discrimination, for example, racial minorities and women often have no better political alternative than to engage in collective action with the aid of identity groups and the aim of achieving greater civic equality and justice. For members of subordinated groups to eschew all identity associations would be counterproductive to justice. Yet not all identity groups are justice friendly, and therefore a synthetic perspective needs to distinguish among different kinds of ascriptive identity politics. Without the National Association for the Advancement of Colored People (NAACP), for example, African Americans would be worse off than they are today, whereas without the Klu Klux Klan (KKK) they would be better off, yet both are ascriptively based associations. To tell African Americans that they should not identify as a group for the purposes of democratic politics is to tell them to ignore both history and contemporary reality; to tell them that they should only identify as an ascriptive group would be similarly misleading.

Many commentators on identity politics condemn it without qualification while many others uncritically applaud it. To understand and evaluate different kinds of identity groups and how they function in nonideal democratic contexts, I begin by recognizing the irreducible tension between individual freedom and the shaping of individual identities and democratic politics by groups. When we recognize this irreducible tension, we are in a better position to understand the relationship among group identities, democratic politics, and the ideals of individual freedom, opportunity, and civic equality. The first section asks what identity groups are, and what is the relationship between identity and interest group politics. Can identity group politics be reduced to interest group politics? Is interest group politics, as commentators suggest, "an inherent part of the governing process of a democracy" while identity group politics "is antithetical to the basic principle of one indivisible nation" (Connerly 1997)? The next two sections examine two opposing schools of thought on the role of group identity in democratic politics: the schools of culture and of choice. The final section develops the implications of a more synthetic perspective by revisiting the divisive issue of group rights and by raising the question of how missing identities might alter democratic landscapes.

■ | Identifying Identity Group and Interest Group Politics

An identity group, as the name suggests, is bound up with who people are, not merely with what they want. The distinctive and defining feature of an identity group is the identification of its members as a certain kind of person, and therefore its members' mutual identification with people of that kind, where the kind is a consequential social category (Fearon 1999). This mutual identification around a social category is independent of—yet also clearly compatible with—the pursuit of instrumental ends by the group. When a group of people who mutually identify around a social category act in politics on the basis of a group identity—whether for the sake of gaining recognition for the group or furthering the interests of the group—they are part of identity group politics.

Identities and therefore identity groups are socially constructed. To say this, however, is not to say much more than that genes and physiognomies do not determine our social identities. "People are limited by, but they are

not prisoners of, their genes, their physiognomies, and their histories in settling on their own identities. And if powerful social forces motivate identity
exploration—as they seem to do in our age—it is the constructivist face of
identity that seems the more real" (Laitin 1998a, 21). Almost everything
that informs our social identities—such as race, gender (as distinct from biological sex), ethnicity, and nationality—can be called social constructions. To say that racial, gender, ethnic, and national identities are social
constructions is not to say that they are any easier to change than our genetic inheritance or physiognomy. Most African Americans, women, and
deaf people cannot "pass" for white, men, or hearing individuals; they can
reinterpret these ascriptive identities but they cannot give them up. For
some people, ethnic identities that are connected to a native language may
be somewhat easier to change, by a decision to speak a second language
and give up certain customary ways of acting, but even an ethnic identity
can be difficult to alter except by generational change.

Yet many people do change their ascriptive identities over time, sometimes quite deliberately and strategically. The social construction of identity is most evident when identities are "constructed and reconstructed
as social opportunities change" (Laitin 1998a, 20). To account for such
change, especially among ethnic minorities, political scientists propose a
rational-choice theory about the social construction of identity. A rational-
choice theory posits that people retain or change their social identities according to what best satisfies their interests, and what best satisfies their
interests depends in turn on the payoffs people predict from the alternate
identities that are available to them. According to rational-choice theory, in
any given social context, people choose the available identity that they predict will best serve their interests. When identity change is possible, on this
theory, it is interest driven. Even ascriptive identity, when it is not simply a
social given, is one among many tools in the arsenal of interest-based politics. But this does not mean that identity politics is reducible to interest
politics; what it means is that identities and interests interact, and the two
kinds of politics work together. Both need to be understood for what each
contributes to understanding politics.

A rational-choice theory that admits all kinds of actions as interest
based (by positing interests that conform to all the revealed preferences of
people) is a hollow shell into which all actions can be fit and said to conform to its premise: people act in ways that reveal (and therefore reflect)
their interests. Actions reveal people's preferences, and their interests are
said to be their revealed preferences. All political action can be placed
within such a rational-choice framework before it is analyzed. Used as an
unfalsifiable framework of analysis, a rational-choice theory cannot claim
that identity politics is reducible to interest group politics in any substantively meaningful sense. If we stipulate that all human behavior is interest
driven, then *everything* is reducible to interest group politics, but not in a
way that informs our understanding of how democratic politics works. To

say that human behavior is interest driven is to say nothing, for example, to understand actions that reflect group identification or moral commitment on the part of people and those that reflect nothing more than a self-welfare goal. The most plausible alternative to reducing all identity politics to interest politics does not deny that changes in identity are interest driven. Nor does it claim that identity politics conflicts with a politics based on interests. Rather it suggests that identities inform people's interests. Because identity often informs interest, identity cannot be *reduced* to interest. Interests do not always, or even generally, precede identity in a way that would permit an insightful observer to explain people's behavior by their prior interests, without knowing their identities.

How then is an identity group analytically different from an interest group? The ideal type of interest group organizes around a shared instrumental interest of individuals (Olson 1971). The ideal type of identity group organizes around mutual identification among its members. In political practice, most organized groups are both identity and interest groups. Members are drawn to the group because of their mutual identification and because they share an instrumental interest pursued by the group. David Truman subsumes identity and interest groups, and everything Madison called a "faction," into his definition of interest groups: "any group that . . . makes certain claims upon other groups . . . for the establishment, maintenance or enhancement of forms of behavior that are implied by the[ir] shared attitudes" (1971, 33). More analytical definitions of identity and interest groups that are not so broad as to verge on being meaningless are preferable.

The defining features of identity and interest groups—the mutual identification of people with one another, on the one hand, and the seeking together of a shared instrumental goal, on the other—are often mutually reinforcing. Most identity groups pursue instrumental interests of their members and thereby encourage more people to see their identities as bound up with a group. Many interest groups encourage people to join by orienting themselves around some mutual identification that is broader than the specific interests that they are pursuing at any given time. Some interest group theorists call these solidary incentives (Cigler and Loomis 1995, 9). The greater the role that identity plays in attracting and retaining members, the more a group is an interest group. The greater the role that the pursuit of shared instrumental interests plays in attracting and retaining members, the more a group is an interest group. Most groups that act in democratic politics are a combination of both, and for two good reasons. First, people's identification with one another influences their sense of what they want, and people's sense of what they want influences with whom they identify. Second, individuals who identify with others are better able to organize politically, and organized groups can be far more politically effective than an equal number of unallied citizens (Moe 1980). This observation provides the single most salient answer to the question of why group identity matters so much in democratic politics. Group identification—whether it be around gender, race, religion, sexual orientation, ethnicity, nationality, age, disability, or ideology—provides no less "real" a set of reasons for people to organize politically than purely material incentives. As important, the two kinds of reasons—identity and interest—are often mutually reinforcing.

Once we recognize the reality of identity group politics and its interaction with interest group politics, along with its social construction, we avoid reification, which is the single most common charge of academic critics who suggest that analyzing identity politics as a real phenomenon entails approving of " 'groupness' itself " (Brubaker and Cooper 2000, 31). Quite the contrary, we are now in a better position to consider two serious challenges that identity politics presents in democratic politics. First, illiberal identity groups erect obstacles to the civic equality of some members, often women and disadvantaged minorities, who do not want to choose between their cultural group identity and their recognition as equal citizens. Must members of illiberal cultural groups be forced to choose? Second, voluntary groups claim the right to associate as their members see fit and therefore the right to exclude those they deem unfit for membership. Should civic associations that prejudicially exclude people associated with historically disadvantaged identity groups be permitted to discriminate even at the cost of civic equality, equal liberty or opportunity for those who are excluded? In examining how the schools of culture and choice address these challenges, I develop a more synthetic perspective on identity and democracy, which is consistent with furthering the ideals of civic equality, basic liberty, and opportunity for all persons, regardless of their group identities.

▪ | The School of Culture: Questioning Claims about Comprehensiveness

A societal culture, or culture for short, as Will Kymlicka (1995b) describes it, typically consists of a common language, history, institutions of socialization, range of occupations, lifestyles, and customs.[1] As commonly understood by the school of culture, culture is not a "continuously contested,

1. See Kymlicka 1995a, 18. What Kymlicka calls a societal culture, Joseph Raz and Avishai Margalit call a pervasive culture. A pervasive culture "defines or marks a variety of forms or styles of life, types of activity, occupation, pursuit, and relationship. With national groups we expect to find national cuisines, distinctive architectural styles, a common language, distinctive literary and artistic traditions, national music, customs, dress, ceremonies and holidays, etc. None of these is necessary." People who share—or come close to sharing—a pervasive culture and whose "identity is determined at least in part by their culture" are "serious candidates for the right to self-determination" in the account offered by Margalit and Raz (1994, 114).

imagined and reimagined melange" of disparate influences (Tully 1995, 11; Waldron 1995, 105–8). Rather it is a coherent set that both informs and limits what it is feasible for people to be and to imagine.[2] Culture provides a constraining context for meaningful choice, and an "anchor for self-identification and the safety of effortless, secure belonging" (Margalit and Raz 1994, 114).

The societal cultures of modern democratic societies not only inform and structure people's choices; they also shape people's desires and needs for social recognition. The "politics of recognition" refers to the modern need for individual identities to be politically recognized. People in modern society, Charles Taylor famously argues, following Rousseau and Hegel, "can flourish only to the extent that [they] are recognized. Each consciousness seeks recognition in another, and this is not a sign of a lack of virtue" (1994, 50). Axel Honneth, another theorist of culture, agrees with Taylor that people have basic rights to living freely, and freedom means not being imposed on by an external authority. Honneth also argues, without any obvious ambivalence, that people need to be politically recognized by government for their deepest particularity (1996, 1995, 255–56).

There is, as Taylor realizes, an unresolved anomaly in the politics of recognition. People want to be recognized not only as generically human but also as culturally distinctive, and this places seemingly impossible demands on democratic governments that contain more than a single distinctive culture within them. A democratic politics of recognition needs both to respect deep cultural differences—by way of some group rights—and also protect the basic rights of individuals that include free speech, press, religion, suffrage, political participation, equal protection, and due process (Taylor 1994, 59–60). The group rights must leave room for protecting basic individual rights, and vice versa. A defensible balance of respect for individual and group rights makes it possible for every person—whether associated with a majority or minority culture—to be treated as a civic equal.

Why, theorists of choice ask, are group rights needed at all? Why can't individual rights suffice for recognizing people as civic equals with various cultural identities? If everyone living within the territorial boundaries of a democracy identified equally with the dominant societal culture and was treated as a civic equal by it, then individual rights would suffice. Individual rights are problematic because of a contingent fact about every modern democratic society: not every person identifies equally or is treated as a civic equal by the dominant societal culture. The problem cannot be resolved by finding a neutral societal culture, because there is no such thing.

---

2. "Familiarity with a culture determines the boundaries of the imaginable. Sharing in a culture, being part of it, determines the limits of the feasible" (Margalit and Raz 1994, 119).

A neutral societal culture would not even be desirable, were it possible. People reasonably—and passionately—want to be reciprocally recognized in their cultural particularity, not only as (culturally naked) human beings. They want to feel at home in their society, not like foreign visitors. The bias of a societal culture solves this problem but creates another: it disadvantages some people relative to others and unfairly so because the disadvantage accrues on the basis of ascriptive characteristics, not by virtue of anything the person has voluntarily done. The more systematic and severe the disadvantages that accrue to individuals whose identities are tied to a different culture, the less able democracies are to secure basic liberty, opportunity, and equal respect for all their citizens by a uniform set of individual rights.

How can a societal culture unfairly advantage or disadvantage different groups? Most democratic societies today contain subordinate identity groups whose members are identified with a different culture from the dominant one. Because the dominant culture is public, it affects the life chances of everyone who inhabits the society. Government conducts its business, public schools teach, and the mass media broadcast in the dominant language and in conformity with a culturally distinctive calendar. Family law conforms to the dominant culture. Established business enterprises and civic associations favor people who identify with the dominant culture. Distance from the dominant culture carries with it economic, educational, and social disadvantages, which originate not in voluntary choices but in inherited identities. At the same time, democracies publicly profess their commitment—deeply rooted in democratic thought (although persistently violated in practice)—that individuals should not be disadvantaged by unchosen attributes, such as an ascriptive group identity.

The problem is most acute with regard to what Kymlicka calls a "national minority," a group like the Québécois who have their own societal culture but who live within a larger democracy (1995b, 10–12). But the problem also applies to members of any ascriptive group who are disadvantaged by the societal culture of a democracy where they settled in order to live a minimally decent life rather than because they considered it the best of several good choices. Immigration cannot be considered voluntary settlement so as to impose disadvantages as if by the immigrants' consent. The distinctive political claim of the school of culture is that in the absence of any special measures, members of societal cultures will have unequal freedom and opportunity. To make matters worse, a democratic government's failure to consider special measures is also reasonably perceived as disrespectful of their identities. The school of culture therefore defends some special rights for members of otherwise disadvantaged cultural groups.

Group rights present a prospect and a problem for democracy. The prospect is that some group rights may be able to provide a legitimate means—in addition to individual rights and popular rule—to pursue justice for members of groups who are otherwise unfairly disadvantaged.

Group rights that exempt members of some groups from public policies that impose unfair burdens and special aid to overcome the unfair disadvantages illustrate this prospect. The problem is that other group rights may violate basic individual rights. Group rights that limit the basic rights of individuals in order to protect an endangered cultural practice or to defend absolute sovereignty for the cultural group illustrate this problem. The challenge is therefore to distinguish between legitimate and illegitimate group rights (Levy 1997; Lukes 1997; Williams 1998).

The country that is the theoretical home of group rights offers a good example of the defensibility of special exemptions from laws that impose unfair burdens on members of an identity group (because of their group identity). Such special exemptions are meaningfully considered a kind of group right, since they apply to individuals only by virtue of their group identity.[3] In 1990, the Royal Canadian Mounted Police decided to exempt a group from a long-standing rule. They exempted Sikhs from wearing the wide-brimmed hat that has long been part of their required uniform. The exemption made it possible for Sikhs to join the Mounties without giving up their identity as Sikhs. One might consider this decision innocuous—the rule is far from earthshaking in its significance—but it is quite typical of many rules that have raised public controversies over group rights. The Mounties' decision met with six years of protests, beginning with a petition to parliament signed by 210,000 Canadians and demonstrations displaying antiturban badges and anti-Sikh slogans and ending with an appeal in 1996 to the Canadian Supreme Court, which refused to hear the challenge (Winsor 1996).

The Mounties' example illustrates two important but often neglected points: (1) no controversial claim about identity is needed to defend exempting members of a group even from some rules that reflect no intent to discriminate; and (2) some group rights can provide effective ways of respecting individual rights, which classical liberal defenders of individual rights have neglected but need not oppose. On a Lockean liberal argument, the government is not required to exempt minorities from facially neutral laws that unequally burden their religious beliefs, but neither is it prohibited from doing so as long as the exemption does not violate someone else's rights.[4] A crucial feature of this exemption is that it lifts unfair burdens (borne by members of a group through no fault of their own) and

---

3. Some liberals deny that these kinds of special exemptions are group rights because they want to reserve the idea of group rights for rights that have no liberal justification. But to define all group rights as illiberal and therefore unjustified obscures the substantive agreement that is possible in cases like that of the Sikh Mounties.

4. I examine competing interpretations of Locke's view on facially neutral laws and religious believers in Gutmann 2000, 127–64. For a contrasting view, see McConnell 2000, 90–110.

does not violate any individual rights. By contrast, other group rights—which liberals must oppose—violate basic individual rights. No democratic perspective that takes the interests of individuals seriously can defend cultural practices that violate basic individual rights, whether of members or nonmembers of a cultural group.[5] Because the moral value of the group derives from the way it supports the interests of individuals over time, maintaining a customary practice of the group at the expense of the basic liberties and opportunities of individuals is morally indefensible (Blake 2000).[6]

When a group demands the right of self-governance over its customary legal practices, and those practices include extensive discrimination in family law against the basic rights of some of its members (often women and children), its demands are suspect to the extent that the larger society would otherwise protect those rights. The group may still have extensive rights of self-government, but self-governing rights—like all rights—can and should be limited by competing rights. Even when groups cannot have extensive rights of self-government, they may be justifiably guaranteed representation within a legislature that would otherwise routinely pass discriminatory legislation against the group, which the courts would uphold or refuse to review. Guaranteed representation for a group is more problematic the less internally democratic the group is and the more its members must give up other freedoms for their votes to be counted as part of the group. Two critical points emerge that call for a far more nuanced view of group rights than is typically offered: (1) group rights of self-government and representation are not all or nothing, and (2) group rights should be assessed on the basis of how well they protect the basic interests—including the basic rights—of individuals compared to the available institutional alternatives.

Why do theorists of culture argue as if group rights of self-government are all or nothing? A starting premise of the school of culture is that societal cultures *partly* determine the identity of their members and provide a secure sense of belonging. The authority of a group to govern itself is thought to follow from the idea that the self-governing group represents the societal culture to which its members belong. But this idea presumes that

5. See, for example, a doctor's description of the practice of clitoridectomy on young girls, which is sometimes misrepresented as analogous to male circumcision, Dreifus 2000, F7.

6. The aesthetic value of cultural practices is a different issue, which I cannot address in this essay. Charles Taylor attributes to individuals an interest in their culture surviving over time, since people want to be assured that their descendants will share the same culture as they do. This raises the difficult question of what the basic interests (and therefore the basic rights) of individuals are and how they should be determined (Taylor 1994, 51–73); and for a sense of how heated the debate over culture can be, see David Bromwich, Michael Walzer, and Taylor in *Dissent* (1995, 89–106).

a single societal culture is comprehensive in constituting people's identities, which no major theorist of culture explicitly defends (because it is apparently indefensible). When a single culture is assumed to constitute the shared identity of members of a minority group, it is easy to conclude that any degree of government by the larger society—even when in defense of the basic rights of women, half the members of the minority group—constitutes imposition by a "foreign" power. This conclusion is doubly misleading because it assumes what it sets out to argue and its assumption is indefensible. The assumption is that a single societal culture so comprehensively constitutes the identities of individuals as to justify granting the group comprehensive sovereign authority to rule its "own" members even at the price of violating their basic rights.

Grant that some cultures are far more comprehensive than others in shaping people's lives, and it is still not credible to assume that one and only one societal culture exclusively encompasses the cultural identities of citizens of contemporary democracies.[7] When this assumption is applied to Native American women, for example, the effect is to force women (but not men) to choose between membership in their Native American tribe and equal democratic citizenship. Theorists of culture analogize intervention by a democratic government to vindicate the rights of Native American women with foreign intervention into the affairs of another country (Kymlicka 1995a, 167). Kymlicka recognizes that the Santa Clara Pueblo wrongly violated women's rights, but he defends its authority to do so on grounds that no country has any right to intervene in the affairs of another country in order to vindicate the rights of women.

The problem with this perspective is that it assumes without argument that the analogy with foreign countries supports the case for nonintervention. But should a national government be assumed to have such comprehensive sovereign authority that it may violate individual rights even if an established legal tribunal could prevent it from so doing without any violence? If not, then even when no established tribunal exists, political theorists should explore the case for establishing one. A nationalism—whether writ large or small—that unnecessarily authorizes the systematic violation of individual rights is not a nationalism worthy of defense. Theorists of culture like Kymlicka who agree that cultures derive their moral value from aiding individuals, not vice versa, have the resources to correct their own tendency to grant more sovereign authority to minority cultures than they would grant a similarly oppressive majority culture when peaceful ways of overcoming the oppression are available.

Other theorists of culture take a relativist view about what oppression entails; they argue that the cultural identity of people determines what

---

7. To consider the single societal culture of a pluralistic democracy to be the aggregate of all the cultures within it would simply further confuse matters and "prove" the case by a misleading definition.

counts as oppression. Many of the group rights that are prominently defended in contemporary politics—and also in political theory—threaten to perpetuate the subordination of half the world's population, namely women. The cultural relativist view is that the cultural identity of women comes attached to these practices, which are not identified as oppressive because this interpretation is itself identified as foreign to the indigenous practice. To try to obliterate the practices is viewed as tantamount to trying to obliterate these women, to do away with their cultural identities, with who they are. The relativizing move here allows a cultural identity to go morally imperial and lets it block any vindication of the basic rights of women. On this analysis, cultural identity precludes the vindication of women's equal rights with men, but this preclusion is as much of an imposed theoretical construct as any. A cultural identity is assumed—although never actually shown—to comprehend the entirety of a person's identity, and a cultural identity is allowed to become morally imperial and therefore to deny basic rights to women. Group rights to enforce child marriage, forced marriage, polygamy (or, more accurately, polygyny), clitoridectomy, discriminatory divorce, unequal schooling of girls and boys, and unequal property rights threaten the basic rights of women in a way that no argument from cultural identity alone has ever been able to overcome.[8] Is there any reason that the dominant members of cultural groups should be granted the right to restrict the basic rights of women?

A school within the school of culture explicitly defends a broad cultural right within liberal democracies to restrict the basic rights of women. Avishai Margalit and Moshe Halbertal argue that, "Protecting cultures out of the human right to culture may take the form of an obligation [of liberal democratic governments] to support cultures that flout the rights of the individual in a liberal society" (1994, 491). This defense of the right to culture therefore goes so far as to claim that liberal democracies have an obligation to support cultures in their midst that flout the rights of women, among other individuals. Ultra-Orthodox Jewish culture in Israel, according to this argument, must be supported by the state in its totality, which includes flouting the rights of women in schooling, divorce law, and inheritance, and respecting Ultra-Orthodox men as the guardians of the authoritative rules of a publicly supported cultural community (493). One individual right is treated as independent of any particular culture and that is the right to exit a cultural community.[9] This is the right that undermines the rule of cultural relativism. If individual identities are so comprehen-

8. For an extended discussion, see Okin, Moller, et al. 1999, Nussbaum and Glover 1994, and Nussbaum 1997b.

9. The right of exit to a free market society is also the only right of individuals recognized by Chandran Kukathas who defends the right of minority groups—no matter how illiberal—to be left alone (1992, 105–39). For a critique of Kukathas on the right of exit, see Kymlicka, 1995a, 190, 234–35, n. 18.

sively tied to a particular culture, then theorists of culture cannot consistently defend even this minimalist right of individuals to exit an oppressive community. If individual identities are not so comprehensively tied to a particular culture, then far more than a right to exit is needed to protect the basic interests of individuals in living the lives of free and equal citizens in the context of a multicultural democratic society.

The failure of the "no more than a right to exit" argument offers a sobering reminder of the dangers of tying individual identity far too comprehensively to a single societal culture. Margalit and Halbertal begin by claiming that each particular culture creates a person's "personality identity." They then claim that "every person has an overriding interest in his personality identity—that is, in preserving his way of life and the traits that are central identity components for him and the other members of his cultural group" (505). If we accept this *overriding* interest of individuals, no theoretical room remains for an *individual right* to exit. Rights protect basic interests of individuals. An individual cannot have a basic interest in freeing herself from her personality identity *if her basic (and overriding) interest is defined as preserving her personality identity.* But this logic of course begs the crucial question: Is there any good reason to assume that the basic and overriding interest of all women lies in preserving their personality identity as defined by the other members of their cultural group?[10]

The basic tenets of the view that an individual's *overriding* interest lies in preserving the entirety of her personality identity, where that identity is given by her culture, are misleading. Many women (and men also, of course) reasonably think that they do not have a basic interest in preserving the cultural identity that has been imposed on them. They also reasonably doubt that a culture creates—rather than influences—the entirety of their "personality identity." Some women reasonably think that their particular cultural community unjustifiably subordinates them to men and discriminates against them by denying them basic liberties and opportunities available to men. They are thereby denied the equal civic and political standing that is due them. As long as *any* woman reasonably thinks this, the "right to culture" argument fails as a defense of the authority of a cultural community to preserve itself by denying women their basic liberty and opportunity rights and their status as civic equals. (The same argument applies to any person; the example of women is so striking because the violations of their

---

10. One might revise the perspective to say that a person has an overriding interest only in her personality identity as she defines it, not as defined by other members of her cultural group. This starting point would support many more culturally independent rights of individuals than the right to exit. Individuals would then have a right to resist having a cultural group impose laws and rules on them that violate their personality identities. But this is not the view of personality identity that Margalit and Halbertal defend. Their view does not permit any clear distinction between what is important to the individual and the group of which she is a member.

rights are at once so conspicuous and so commonly excused or even justified on cultural grounds.)

Why isn't the formal right of exit an adequate antidote to granting cultural groups the authority to treat their members in illiberal ways? Once
theorists of culture defend a right to exit from cultural groups, they are implicitly acknowledging the value of individual consent and respect for persons. They then cannot consistently justify subordinating individuals in
cultural groups that deprive them of the necessary conditions for making the right to exit effective. A formal right of exit can be an adequate
antidote to illiberal ways in which truly voluntary associations treat
their members. But groups that represent societal cultures—by the very
premises of theorists of culture—are not voluntary associations. When
quasi-comprehensive cultural groups violate rights with the support of
democratic governments, they greatly reduce the basic liberties and opportunities that their members would otherwise have to live a life of their own
choosing either inside or outside the community. An Ultra-Orthodox
woman in Israel is not educated to support herself or her children outside
of the Ultra-Orthodox community. She is not taught the legitimacy of
questioning her tightly circumscribed place in the Ultra-Orthodox community. To claim that she has an overriding interest in preserving a culturally imposed personality identity is to claim that her overriding interest is to
subordinate her life to a comprehensive set of laws over which she has no
say in interpreting or altering.[11] This is not a claim that anyone can make
authoritatively on her behalf.

There is thus a paradox in claiming the subordination of women is justified because their overriding interest lies in being subordinated. For anyone to know that this is the case, women, like men, must be given equal
freedom to decide the kinds of lives they want to live within the range of
the possible.[12] Denying them the freedom in the first place cannot validate
the claim that they do not really want or need this freedom. No theoretical
argument can justify the subordination of women within cultures that deny
them any basic rights other than a formal right of exit. For women to have
the effective right to assess whether they want to remain within a cultural
group that subordinates them or to exit that group, a democratic society
must secure them an effective right to exit, an education for equal citizenship in the larger society, and other basic rights as well. An effective right to
exit means at minimum being able to exit and still support oneself and
one's children. Securing women these rights means not ceding cultural
groups within a democracy the authority to control schooling and family
law so as to effectively deny women the same basic liberties and opportuni-

11. This premise is also another example of a general conflation of what a person's
identity is and what that person ought to do. For a critique of this conflation, see
Hardin 1995, 6–10.

12. John Stuart Mill was the first to point this out (1975, 451–56).

ties as men. Democratic states may need to tolerate some violations of basic rights when political intervention would make matters worse, but a pragmatic argument of this kind denies any obligation on the part of a democratic state to support cultural groups at the expense of violating the basic rights of individuals.

Taken at its strongest, the school of culture recognizes that there is no group right to subordinate individuals to a societal culture by violating their basic rights. At its weakest, it erects indefensible obstacles to vindicating the basic rights of members and nonmembers of cultural groups. Even if the societal culture of the Israeli Ultra-Orthodox Jewish community were self-contained for members of that community, its effects on nonmembers would still be morally and politically relevant. The politics of cultural minorities rarely can be isolated from a broader politics, which to extend the Israeli example, profoundly affects the liberty and opportunity of Palestinians, Israeli Arabs, and non-Orthodox Israeli Jews.

The politics of cultural identity groups also shapes the identities of future generations in ways that the school of culture assumes to be legitimate extensions of a group right to self-determination. Cultural groups within democratic societies are an intricately interdependent part of the larger society. They must be able to interact politically and often economically as well with people outside their groups, and people outside their groups with them. This interdependence, moreover, affects the liberty, opportunity, and civic standing of both outsiders and insiders to these groups since each depends on the other to ensure the equal protection of rights. If some members of cultural groups identify only with a single group, it is therefore not because the comprehensive conditions of their lives are independent of the larger society. (Ultra-Orthodox Jews in Israel depend heavily on support from the rest of society for their schools, police protection, and national security.) Members of cultural groups also influence the larger politics of democratic societies as much as many other citizens, sometimes even more so (as the Israeli example also illustrates.) Members of distinctive cultural groups are also often more dependent on the larger society to support their distinctive cultures. This is not an argument against the dependency of cultural groups or their influence on the larger society. Quite the contrary, it is an argument against a politics or political theory that posits the comprehensiveness of societal cultures and therefore depends on denying the interdependence of cultures and cultural communities within democratic societies.

■ | **The School of Choice: Questioning the Conditions of Voluntariness**

The basic premise of the school of choice is the freedom of individuals to identify and live as they like, not as anyone else determines. The mark of a free person is "living as one likes, associating on one's own terms, engaging in voluntary relationships of all sorts, finding or trying to find pleasure in them, and also finding in them opportunities for many kinds of experience" (Kateb 1998, 37–39). Free people tolerate "being regulated only with deep constitutional regret."[13] They need to be politically recognized not for their particular group identities but rather as bearers of equal rights.[14] Among these rights are those that protect equal citizenship and freedom of association (Kateb 1994, 1998).

The freedom of individuals is limited by socialization and social context, and the school of choice at its strongest recognizes this. Cultural identities are imposed by socialization. I did not choose to be a Jewish-American woman conceived in India and born in the United States to a German-Jewish refugee father and Jewish-American mother. This causally determined cultural identity (scientists may soon be able to add a detailed description of my genetic determination) is compatible with my freedom to identify as something more than a Jewish-American woman (with determinate genetic markers). I could also choose to identify as *other* than what I am identified as, but not without a far greater struggle than were I born *other*. Although I in fact identify as a Jewish-American woman, I also identify as more than that, and more than the aggregation of all my ascriptive identities put together. It is of course quite possible that my freedom to identify as something more than my ascriptive identities is causally determined by the interaction between genetic capacities and social context. But this kind of causal determination is compatible with the value that the school of choice places on freedom of association.

The value of free association depends not on whether human identity is independent of causality but rather on whether individuals are accorded the freedom within a democratic context to identify *as they themselves see fit, not as government—or a similarly powerful agent in society—determines for them*. This freedom in turn depends on whether individuals are free to enter and exit associations at their own will, rather than someone else's. Herein lie prospects and problems for the school of choice, and for anyone who values freedom of association as a legitimate source of identity formation and affirmation. Free association can create a democratic culture of voluntary associations that are appropriate sites for recognizing a wide range of group identities. Voluntary associations, precisely because they are voluntary, are places where a democratic *culture* of recognition as distinct from a *politics* of recognition can flourish. A democratic culture is com-

13. For his more general critique of a politics of recognition, see Kateb 1994, 511–37.

14. Axel Honneth, a theorist of culture, diverges from theorists of choice on this precise point. Although Honneth agrees that freedom means not being imposed on by an external authority, he argues that people need to be politically recognized by government for their deepest particularity (Honneth 1995, 255–56, 1996).

posed of many uncoordinated sites of recognition consisting of voluntary associations where people identify with one another in a multitude of ways.

An uncoordinated landscape of voluntary associations is also a realm of many misrecognitions. Associations that prejudicially exclude people on the basis of their race, gender, ethnicity, and other ascriptive characteristics are a source of negative identity politics. Negative identity politics poses a challenge to theorists of choice who claim that unregulated freedom of association liberates people from the social typecasting of their identities and lives. Unregulated civic associations in the United States simplistically stereotyped women and men; homosexuals and heterosexuals; Christians, Jews, and Muslims; African Americans and whites; and many more social categories of people. Before examining the challenge that this organized prejudice presents for the school of choice, we should also appreciate what theorists of choice view as the virtue in tolerating misrecognition. Any culture that is free to be changed by the (necessarily imperfect) people whose lives it shapes is also bound to mischaracterize and misunderstand people. Some degree of misrecognition—not every degree or the degree of the status quo—is a price worth paying for freedom of association and for the recognition that people are more than what public recognition in any society of human beings makes possible. This sometimes painful realization is perhaps the hardest won insight of human freedom and the school of thought that prizes freedom above all else.

Freedom of association still carries with it the prospect that all people can be publicly (but not authoritatively) recognized for some of their particularities if they so desire. To be publicly recognized in all of one's particularity, friendship and love would become public projects. This is the politics of recognition taken to its logical extreme. Love is not love that strives to make itself public in all its particularities; it is at best the public manifestation of love, which is a pale packaged imitation (as television talk shows all too vividly reveal). A civic society that strives without pathology to satisfy the desire for public recognition cannot aspire to create a public culture of authenticity. Only people themselves, acting freely through their associational choices, can recognize each other for who they are, and even then only imperfectly.

Yet some misrecognitions are troubling on the grounds of freedom itself; they reflect the failure of a democratic society to secure the conditions under which members of unjustly subordinated groups have as much effective freedom as their peers. The school of choice cannot avoid confronting the question of the social conditions under which some people are prevented from affirming their identities through their associational choices. Conditions of exit out of associations and entry into them are critical to assessing whether they support individual freedom. Let's begin with the issue of exit since it is the more straightforward. Voluntary associations can be so called only if people who choose to join them are not compelled to remain members (Barry 2001, 155–93). It is almost as simple as this:

Voluntary associations cannot prevent their members from leaving and still be considered voluntary or the basis of free affirmation of identity by individuals. Democratic governments therefore must guarantee that all people be effectively free to exit any association that they are permitted to enter.

Under what conditions do individuals have an effective right of exit?[15] This question is not easy to answer in some cases because the freedom to enter an association that demands great commitment over time is prima facie part of what freedom of association includes. This is especially evident when we consider the freedom of identity formation that civic associations at their best can protect. Religious associations, to take a central set of examples, may be attractive to many people precisely because they make quasi-comprehensive demands on their identity and therefore not only on their lives today but also into the future. But freedom of religious association includes the right of individuals to change their religious association at will. A democratic government therefore must protect individuals against those associations that effectively deprive their members of those conditions that make the right to exit effective. One of those conditions is economic independence, which is missing when the price of exiting a civic association is to be bereft of any property (*Hofer v. Hofer*, S.C.R. 958–92 [1970]). How high can barriers to exit be and still be legitimate? From the perspective of choice, barriers to exiting an association are more suspect to the extent that they resemble the barriers to exiting a society, which cannot be considered a voluntary association precisely because the barriers to exiting are so high (for most people). Although drawing precise lines between legitimate and illegitimate barriers to exit will be difficult, the school of choice supplies the grounds for saying that freedom of association is absolutely incompatible with preventing people who want to exit a group from so doing.

The school of choice also needs to address the issue of blocked entry. Although freedom of association entails the freedom of groups to prevent some people who want to join them from doing so, the right to exclude is not absolute. To insist that associations include everyone who wants to join would violate their members' freedom to associate as they so choose. But to insist on their unlimited freedom to exclude women and negatively stereotyped minorities on prejudicial grounds entails limiting the effective freedom of women and minorities, preventing them from associating and identifying as they wish.[16] If exclusions were more or less random, falling

15. See Rosenblum 1998a, 101ff; Kymlicka 1995a, 234, n. 18. My discussion of the school of choice refers more generally to Rosenblum's book, which is the most comprehensive statement to date of the relationship between identity, associational freedom, and democracy by a theorist of choice.

16. Of course they can form another group with people who want to associate with them, but this is their second-best scenario. The same also holds for the people who are excluding them: if forced to include, the excluders can leave the association and form a new one.

on everyone more or less equally, and having no other significant civic effects, then absolute freedom of association might not be problematic from
a democratic perspective. Equal freedom and civic equality could still prevail. But the discriminatory policies of civic associations are problematic
when they deprive individuals associated with historically disadvantaged
identity groups of valuable civic opportunities through no fault of their
own. Accompanying this problem is another, less-commonly noted one,
which directly challenges the claim that unregulated freedom of association supports the free public affirmation of individual identity. Prejudicial
exclusions of women and negatively stereotyped minorities from equal
membership in civic associations are yet another public expression of the
involuntary typecasting of identity to which the school of choice stands
opposed.

The same perspective of choice that affirms the right of free association also opposes the involuntary typecasting of individual identities, for
the same reasons and on the same grounds. Civic associations contribute
to a negative identity politics when they exclude entire groups based on
their ascriptive identities or relegate them to second-class membership.
The question therefore arises: What limits may be placed by democratic
governments on which civic associations not to exclude people on the basis of their race, gender, or other involuntary identities? Not all exclusions
from all associations are equal from the perspective of choice. Legal imposition of membership on expressive associations—such as churches and advocacy groups—would undermine their expressive purpose. Membership
impositions on intimate associations of family and friendship would undermine the very meaning of intimacy. A blanket imposition of liberal democratic norms on all associations would violate the most basic freedoms of
expression and intimate association, and therefore are consistently opposed
by theorists of choice.

Associations that provide public goods and are not primarily expressive
or intimate do not need to discriminate to carry out their primary purposes.
A strong case can be made for opening up their prejudicially blocked
entries on grounds of freedom, opportunity, and civic equality. When
pre-judicial exclusion contributes to treating women and disadvantaged
minorities as second-class citizens on any of these grounds (freedom,
opportunity, or civic equality), then nondiscrimination laws are in order
(Rosenblum 1998b, 158–90). They can help equalize the effective freedom and opportunity of women and minorities, express their civic status as
equals, and thereby also support their equal ability to identify as they wish
through association.

When do exclusions from civic associations reinforce second-class citizenship? The school of choice is divided over particular cases because the
idea of second-class citizenship is not self-interpreting and room remains
for reasonable disagreement. All can agree that to require all associations to
be nondiscriminatory would place unjustifiable limits on the freedom of

individuals to express themselves and pursue their particular identities by free association. All can also agree that to exempt all civic associations would place an unjustifiable burden on members of groups who are systematically discriminated against in society, effectively eviscerating their equal freedom to identify as they see fit rather than as dominant groups in society typecast them. Second-class membership does not automatically entail second-class citizenship, but when the two are mutually reinforcing, the school of choice can defend opening up prejudicially blocked entries to civic associations through the enforcement of nondiscrimination laws.[17]

▪ | Toward a Humanist Synthesis: Revisiting Group Rights and Considering Missing Identities

Group rights divide the two schools of thought, but far less than either tends to recognize. The school of choice explicitly rejects group rights. But some group rights, as we have seen with the Sikh exemption from Mounties policy, support rather than impede the equal freedom and opportunity of individuals. Theorists of choice can defend group rights that at their moral foundation do not inhere in groups but rather inhere in individuals because of their group identity. Theorists of choice can therefore view some group exemptions as a way of fairly applying various individual rights, such as religious freedom. Theorists of culture can view the same exemptions as a way of respecting cultural differences, which cannot be understood purely on an individual level or as simply a manifestation of individual freedom. The two schools therefore can converge in political substance even if they continue to dispute in political theory what counts as a group right. When we leave the terminological dispute behind and instead synthesize the insights of the two schools, we can see that both perspectives, taken at their strongest, depend on valuing individual freedom in the context of cultural differences that are not themselves simply a matter of individual choice. We also see that both perspectives tend to neglect the critical role that democratic processes, institutions, and ideals play in selecting and mobilizing some group identities rather than others.

As long as people are free agents, cultures cannot be completely comprehensive in constituting their identities, and as long as societies socialize people in particular ways, they cannot be completely voluntaristic agents in creating their identities. Democratic processes and institutions add an important set of variables and values into any perspective that accepts the irreducible tension between individual and group. This synthesis raises a series of critical questions for further research, which are both empirical and normative in nature. What group identities get selected by democratic

17. As Nancy Rosenblum argues (1998a, 172–76).

citizens for political action, and why? What role do democratic processes and institutions play in making organization and mobilization of some group identities more or less likely? How do different democratic structures of governance affect the mobilization and effectiveness of subordinated minorities? Under different democratic conditions, what exemptions from facially neutral laws are permissible or even necessary? What identities are unfairly disadvantaged by different democratic processes and institutions, and how can group rights or exemptions help address different degrees and types of unfairness? What are the alternatives to group rights or exemptions?

Turning the normative tables, we also need to ask: When are group rights nothing more than an unjustifiable assertion of the power of a group over its members (or over outsiders to the group)? When is identity politics not even a second best in nonideal democracies because broad-based issue networks are more effective in moving in the direction of greater justice? Synthesizing the two sets of questions, we can ask: What broad-based issue networks are mobilized independently or in cooperation with identity groups, why, and to what effect for the liberty, opportunity, and civic equality of persons?

As these questions indicate, a synthetic perspective is not morally neutral and does not therefore claim to resolve all differences between the two schools of thought, which are partly attributable to conflicting weights given to the value of cultural belonging and individual freedom. A synthetic perspective defends the idea that individual freedom is always exercised within social constraints but those constraints are not a static given; the constraints can change over time with the exercise of individual freedom of association, and this freedom in turn depends on interaction with governmental processes and institutions to be fully effective. A synthetic perspective therefore not only criticizes some undefended moves of both schools from their starting premises, it also merges the remaining (moral and empirical) insights into a more nuanced and dynamic view of the relationship between group identity, democracy, and individual freedom and civic equality. More moderate members of both schools move in the direction of this synthesis. Taylor, for example, defends only those group rights which do not threaten the basic freedom and opportunity of individuals, and Rosenblum defends only those prejudicial exclusions from voluntary associations which do not threaten the civic equality of members of unfairly disadvantaged groups. Taken at their strongest, both schools converge in defending the basic freedom, opportunity, and civic equality of all persons (Kymlicka 1995b; Taylor 1994; Kateb 1998; Rosenblum 1998b). A synthetic perspective that draws on an ideal of realizing basic freedom, opportunity, and civic equality for all persons can be called humanist, because at its most fundamental level it treats all persons—regardless of their group identity—with equal concern.

The two schools of thought are at their weakest from a humanist perspective when they neglect these values. The school of culture is at its weakest therefore when it falls back on the authority of cultural groups over their members, as if a self-contained societal culture constitutes the identity of its members with a corresponding claim to sovereign nationhood. Even limited democratic governance by the larger society in defense of individual rights then becomes equivalent to foreign intervention into the affairs of a self-determining nation. The school of choice at its weakest neglects political rights of equal citizenship, which are among the basic rights of individuals that can only be exercised in groups. Equal rights of citizenship fail to be respected when more-powerful governments routinely intervene in the affairs of less-powerful governments without due regard for the equal political as well as civic rights of all persons. The basic rights of equal citizenship can be exercised by individuals only in self-governing groups, and the sovereignty of all self-governing groups (not only the least powerful) must be limited to make room for recognition of basic civil as well as political rights (Habermas 1998a, 129–53, 203–36, 239–64; Rawls 1971, 228–30, 1996, 334–71, 381–96).

When they avoid some characteristic missteps from their basic premises, both schools can agree that the purpose of rights—whether individual or group—is to protect the basic interests and respect the dignity of individuals as civic equals. Group rights can meaningfully refer to those rights which protect those basic interests of individuals which are (voluntarily or involuntarily) attached to a particular group identity. The interests ultimately to be served by group rights are therefore *individual* interests. A synthetic perspective avoids conflating the identity of a community with that of the individuals who are part of that community, but it also refuses to isolate individuals from their social contexts, to reduce their interests to self-welfare (as opposed to an interest in or commitment to the well-being of others), or to assume that facially neutral laws suffice to protect the basic rights and civic equality of individuals. Democratic governments therefore need to take into account particular group identities and exempt some citizens because of their group identities from some facially neutral policies. At the same time, they must not grant groups rights—or assume group rights themselves—that threaten the basic liberty, opportunity, or civic equality of persons.

Beyond the issue of group rights, other implications of a humanist synthesis are worth exploring in far greater detail than is possible here. What I call the challenge of missing identities follows from recognizing the dynamic interaction between individual freedom, group identity, and democratic institutions and ideals. In brief, the challenge is to consider the humanist group identities that are missing from democratic politics, or relatively underrepresented, whose addition would help move democracies in the direction of greater justice. If group identities change over time in the interaction between civil society and democratic politics, people committed to humanist values can ill afford to ignore the challenge of missing identities. The groundwork for the challenge is laid in the following provisional conclusions from our previous analysis:

- People are greater than any single culture can comprehend or any sovereign authority can represent.

- There is no principle or even presumption against cultural or group change (Clifford 1988, 338). Such changes do not necessarily entail moral loss (or even cultural loss, except by tautology). Overcoming the negative stereotyping of the group identities of women and unjustly subordinated minorities, for example, would be a moral gain from a humanist perspective, and possibly a cultural gain as well.

- Democratic governments may facilitate identity change over time for the better or worse. Citizens should be effectively free to interpret, revise, and reject the group identities into which they are socialized, partly through the procedural mechanisms of democratic governance.

- Absolute sovereignty claims of cultural groups in violation of basic rights along with prejudicial exclusions from powerful civic associations are among the injustices that call on the collective capacity of democratic citizens to vindicate their rights to equal liberty, opportunity, and civic equality.

- Because collective action in democratic politics is a condition for moving in the direction of greater justice, justice-friendly groups are indispensable, and one way of building them is on the basis of a shared humanist identity, which partially constitutes the self-conception of people who mutually identify with the cause of decreasing injustice and defending the basic rights of individuals.

The challenge of missing identities is neglected in ways that remind us of the missteps taken by the school of culture when it restricts identity change to what national sovereignty over subordinated individuals makes possible. The charge of discrimination against women brought by Julia Martinez, a member of the Santa Clara Pueblo tribe and U.S. citizen, illustrates the challenge of missing identities. The Pueblo tribal council had refused to vindicate Martinez's right to equal protection under the Indian Civil Rights Act of 1968 (ICRA), which says that "no Indian tribe in exercising powers of self-government shall . . . deny to any person within its jurisdiction the equal protection of its laws."[18] A 1939 law, approved by the tribe and U.S. federal government, excludes intermarrying women and their children but not intermarrying men and their children from the tribe and therefore from the rights to hold tribal property, vote in tribal elections, hold tribal office, and claim welfare benefits that are tied to tribal

18. *U.S. Code*, vol. 25, sec. 1302 (8).

membership. The Pueblo's quasi-sovereign status was the basis on which the U.S. Supreme Court concluded that the tribe had the authority to violate the equal protection of women. Only Justice Byron White, in dissent, disputed the connection between being a quasi-sovereign nation and having the authority to violate basic rights. Did Julia Martinez not have a basic right to be treated as a civic equal to her Pueblo male counterpart? No one arguing the *Martinez* case challenged her basic right to civic equality. What they challenged was her standing as a U.S. citizen to vindicate her basic right despite the legitimacy of the ICRA that explicitly grants her equal protection.

Why assume that the Pueblo has the sovereign authority to violate the equal rights of women? It cannot be because the Pueblo are in fact sovereign over their own laws, since they are not. As we argued above, it cannot be because societal cultures are self-contained and therefore have absolute sovereignty rights over their members. The factual premise of self-containment is faulty and, even if true, the conclusion of absolute sovereignty is a non-sequitur. The Martinez case vivifies the lack of self-containment of societal cultures. The 1939 General Allotment Act that codified unequal citizenship rights for Pueblo women and men, far from being indigenous to the Pueblo, required the approval of the U.S. government at the time and "seems to have been supported, if not influenced and encouraged, by the traditions of the United States" (Resnik 1989, 725). It is therefore fitting to ask: "Why is it seen as a matter of cultural survival when men guarantee exclusive access to Indian women as a requirement of tribal membership, but when an Indian woman attempts to claim that her family is an Indian family, to choose who to make a family with, it's called a threat to cultural survival" (MacKinnon 1987, 67)?

The challenge of changing identities is to search for ways in which democratic processes and institutions can aid unjustly subordinated individuals in vindicating their basic rights, rather than taking established identities for granted. Justice White's dissent in the *Martinez* case illustrates one way in which Pueblo women could have been aided in their just cause of changing unequal membership rules in an ascriptive group. White argued that the Court should require the tribal government itself to revise the membership rules in a way that respects the equal rights of women. In so doing, with the urging of many Pueblo women whose identities had already come into conflict with their tribal authorities, the Court would have contributed to changing identities in the direction of greater justice as had Congress when it passed the ICRA. Instead the Court helped to further entrench the dominant group identities that established the discriminatory law in the first place.

As the Martinez case illustrates, rather than taking group identities as static, a humanist synthesis attends to the dynamic interaction between political institutions and group identities. Taking the interaction between democracy and identity seriously means not assuming that the best way of defending our cherished values is to repress challenges to them, rather than to find ways of bringing those who disagree with us into a more equal and potentially constructive relationship (Hollinger 1995, 84–85). An illustrative case in point is the French government's policy of permitting Muslim men to immigrate with their multiple wives. Feminists have criticized the policy for being too permissive on the issue of polygamy and ignoring "the burdens that this practice imposes on women and the warnings disseminated by women from the relevant cultures" (Okin et al. 1999, 9–10). Polygyny (which permits men but not women to have multiple spouses) puts important values of gender equality at risk.

But it does not follow that a democratic government should close its borders to polygynous men and women from cultures where the practice is legal. A morally and politically relevant question is how alternative public policies are likely to affect the equal freedom of polygynous women and their female children over time. Prohibiting their entry into France would almost certainly have made matters considerably worse from the perspective of those Muslim women and their female children who want to find a way of moving toward a condition of more equal freedom. An immigration policy that admits polygynous Muslims and then gives women the effective freedom to exit from their marriages, providing a social support system for them and their children, takes the interplay of identity and democracy seriously by recognizing democracy's potential to change identities for the better.

The converse of the capacity of democratic politics to influence group identities over time is the capacity of group identities to influence democratic politics over time. Democratic society can benefit from the addition of some group identities that are now missing or relatively underrepresented. The presence of some missing identities would push democracy in the direction of greater justice. Many critics of identity politics are chagrined at the "the decline of species-centered discourse" (Hollinger 1995, 66). But a reversal of the decline of a certain discourse alone—however welcome—would not make nearly as much political difference as an increase in humanist group identities and associations in democratic politics. Democratic politics needs people who identify as humanists for political purposes and are therefore prepared to act collectively and consistently with humanist discourse. Many organizations already reflect the willingness and ability of individuals to rally around a humanist identity and cause, rather than a narrower identity politics.

Facing up to the challenge of missing identities requires a recognition of the dependency of democratic politics and justice on humanistic associations, and their dependency in turn on various kinds of mutual identification among people, not only around a group identity but also around a humanistic ideology. The NAACP, National Organization for Women (NOW), the American and International Red Cross, Doctors of the World, and the United Nations Association—to name just a few—support and reflect justice-friendly group identities. From the perspective of mobilizing more people to identify, organize, and act together within democratic politics in justice-friendly ways, one problem with most of these organizations is that they are what Robert Putnam calls "tertiary" rather than "secondary": most people participate only by credit card (Putnam 2000, 52). The vast majority of humanists never meet together for the sake of mobilizing, demonstrating, bargaining, lobbying, or campaigning for just causes.

There are important exceptions worth noting however. Members of the U.N. Association, a genuine federation, meet together to pursue humanistic causes. For humanists to have a greater impact in democratic politics, they need to create more secondary associations that succeed in bringing people together in politically effective ways. Humanists consistently oppose identity politics that exacerbates injustices against groups, but otherwise have no reason to be critical of people for publicly identifying and associating with others on particularistic grounds. Humanists themselves can be politically most effective when their mutual identification is strong and their organization for political purposes correspondingly more efficient and effective.

By attending to the matter of missing identities, we highlight a largely unrecognized bias of the identity politics of our time, which parallels the bias of the earlier pluralistic politics (Connolly 1969). Both critics and defenders of identity politics tend to neglect problems arising from the underrepresentation of some identities and interests in a democratic politics that is unavoidably driven by demands of identity and interest groups of many kinds. In democratic politics, people are most influential in groups. Theorists therefore need to think about the ways in which a politics that necessarily depends on groups can work to better secure liberty and opportunity for all individuals, not only for the more powerful groups or for the more powerful members of less powerful groups. The relationship between group identity and democratic politics, I have argued, is more complex than blanket critiques and defenses of identity politics suggest. I also have argued that despite their strikingly different starting premises, theorists of culture and choice can converge on consequential political conclusions if they avoid some characteristic missteps from their starting premises and develop a more synthetic perspective. I have presented the broad outlines of a humanist synthesis that integrates considerations of culture and choice and attends to the dynamic interplay between group identities and democratic politics. Political theorists ignore the potential for changing identities at the peril of assuming that individuals must endure existing injustices that are now protected by oppressive groups, discriminatory associations, and tyrannical governments. These injustices can be overcome only by collective human agency, not by cultural complacency or political inaction.

RANDALL CALVERT

Identity, Expression, and Rational-Choice Theory

■ | Introduction

Self-identification with social groups or moral principles, and the expression of identification through behavior, abound in politics. Political scientists discern identification and expressive action at every level of political interaction, ranging from the actions of individual voters to the policies of governments in international relations. Most prominently, identification with partisan, ideological, or social objects has served as the raw material for some of the classic analyses of electoral politics in democracies. Ethnic identification plays a central role in the study of democratic transitions and of the politics of developing nations generally.

Political scientists usually see identification and expression as cultural or psychological processes, either basic to human motivation or deriving immediately from some form of built-in human orientation toward social groups.[1] Such processes are often regarded as irreconcilable with rational-choice accounts of human behavior. Nevertheless, rational-choice theorists have attempted to bring their approach to bear on these phenomena, in order to take advantage of the theory's analytical tools and its portability across different political settings. In some cases, rational-choice theorists have been hostile to identity and expressive processes, seeking to explain them away as epiphenomenal or illusory.

Not all rational choice applications have taken this approach, however. Occasionally and with increasing frequency, some have attempted to bridge the theoretical gap between identity and expression, on the one hand, and strategic rational action, on the other, taking the phenomena seriously and contributing toward the examination of their effects or their

---

1. The foundational works in psychology on identity include Erikson 1968, Billig and Tajfel 1973, and Tajfel and Turner 1986. Invocations of the idea of group identification to explain phenomena in political science go back at least to Campbell et al. (1976 [1960], ch. 12).

foundations. My purpose in this survey is to summarize these efforts and to assess the contribution they have made toward our understanding of identity and expression. I do this by focusing on studies of three connected phenomena which either are or were viewed by political scientists as primarily identity-expressive and irrational: voting participation, partisanship and ideology, and ethnic politics and ethnic violence. These three areas have been the main locus of rational-choice work on identity and expression.[2] Moreover, this combination of topics provides, I believe, a compelling illustration of the breadth of applicability of these rational-choice models, their interconnections, and the real nature of their limitations.

▪ | Overview

Rational-choice efforts to address identity and expression fall into three categories, which first appeared in the following chronological order: (1) analyses in which choice phenomena replace identity and expressive phenomena, essentially denying their importance; (2) analyses that take identity and expressive motivations as given features of individual preference and examining their effects in rational-choice terms; and (3) analyses that construct more foundational rational-choice models of social interaction and use them to examine the nature and effects of identity and expressive phenomena that occur within social interaction. This survey concentrates purely on the latter two categories. However, it is helpful to begin by briefly tracing the development of all three approaches.

Early rational-choice analyses, concentrating on the politics of developed democracies, attempted to supplant the focus on identity and expression by describing them in entirely alternative terms. For example, Downs's "economic" analysis (1957) of democracy combined a purely instrumental, self-interest model of political action with the need for low-cost information, producing a theory in which partisanship and ideology served simply as rules of thumb carrying no inherent significance as phenomena of identification. Although appealing in some respects, this theory quickly became entangled in a paradox of its own making, the so-called paradox of not voting. Olson's logic of collective action (1965) emphasized selfish maximization and mutual monitoring, at the expense of sociological concepts of groups, roles, and norms, to account for collective action. But al-

2. However, this survey does not venture into the literature on laboratory experimentation, where both psychological and various choice theoretic approaches have been the basis for examinations of group-related phenomena. The experimental literature, where it has touched on rational-choice ideas, has been primarily concerned to debunk rational-choice theories; however, little experimental work has yet been undertaken applying rational-choice models to group identity phenomena in the sophisticated fashion treated in the empirical studies I survey here.

though Olson was surely correct about the existence of barriers to the representation of large-group interests in a democracy, there are nonetheless prominent examples of large-scale collective action for which by-product or selective-incentive explanations seem unsatisfying unless sociological phenomena are invoked. Moreover, survey and interview studies seem at times to portray group, partisan, and ideological attachments as being so unexamined, so ingrained or having so little policy content that neither an advantage-calculating nor even a rule-of-thumb explanation seems to do them justice.

Subsequent theorists of collective action discerned solidary and expressive basic motivations in the context of rational participation (Salisbury 1969; Moe 1980). Although this formulation seems merely to substitute the language of utility for psychological motivations, applications of this approach in the study of voting participation most clearly indicate what a rational-choice analysis can add to the recognition of such nonmaterial benefits. The next section examines several such studies in detail, explaining in what sense these models exhibit scientific progress in the sense of Lakatos (1978).

It also examines a recent attempt by Overbye (1995) to place voting participation in a broader context of interaction among rational actors, in which participation has communicative or reputational value in addition to its political effect. In other words, politically expressive behavior is motivated by instrumental considerations outside the political arena, so that the model is, potentially, a productive complement to direct psychological theories of expression. This complementarity yields the major overall argument of this survey: rational-choice models do not contradict the existence of identity and expression; far from being incompatible with traditional psychological and cultural approaches to identity, rational-choice models, properly formulated, can be a valuable addition to social science's tools for studying those phenomena.

Building on Overbye's social notion of rationally expressive behavior, the third section turns to the related but wider topics of partisanship and ideology. Expressive and classical instrumental explanations alike have invoked ideology and partisanship as criteria by which voters choose among candidates. Yet, unlike mere voting choices, partisanship and ideology are identification phenomena. I summarize two approaches to these topics—one a formal and mathematical model, the other a primarily historical and empirical study that explicates a clear rational-choice foundation—that, like Overbye, approach ideology and partisanship as explicitly group-related phenomena that may emerge from strategic interaction among rational actors.

The following section turns to the seemingly different politics of ethnic, as opposed to civic or partisan, identity. Voting participation and partisanship are phenomena of a stable and developed system of political institutions. Even ideology, insofar as it operates on or through a system of political choice among candidates or policies, is mostly found in this more institutionalized setting (even if the ideology aims at radical change in those institutions). On the other hand, the most dramatic manifestations of ethnic identity occur in settings of unstable or transitional political institutions. Rational-choice treatments of ethnic politics divide into the same two classes as the recent analyses of identity and expression in voting. Those in the first class take ethnic-related preferences or beliefs for granted and use standard game-theoretic methods to examine how strategic decision making leads to interesting phenomena of ethnic politics. Those in the second class begin with models of interaction among rational actors and derive a theory about the basic nature of ethnic identification. Here again, the literature I survey consists of a mixture of formal rational-choice models and informal analyses on a firm rational-choice basis.

The final section offers some overall conclusions about the use of rational-choice models for examining identity and expressive phenomena. It also offers some summary comments concerning the wide range of uses to which rational-choice theories may be productively put and the real limitations of such theories, which, I argue, are quite distinct from the limitations usually enunciated.

■ | Expressive and Instrumental Voting

Butler and Stokes (1969) distinguished instrumental and expressive motivations for voting. As they noted, rational-choice theorists have also wrestled with this distinction. Downs (1957) originated the formal rational-choice approach in which voting was purely instrumental. This model implies that, if voting were the least bit costly, turnout would be approximately zero. Riker and Ordeshook (1968) formulated a generalization of Downs's model that included a noninstrumental benefit of simply participating in the election, independently of the voter's choice and of the election outcome, which they dubbed the "citizen duty" motivation. This section examines several models that have attempted to deal more generally with the idea of expressive voting using a rational-choice framework.

THE IMPLICATIONS OF EXPRESSIVE CHOICE

Fiorina looks beyond the simple notion of citizen duty, noting that "One may vote to express solidarity with one's class or peer group, to affirm a psychic allegiance to a party, or simply to enjoy the satisfaction of having performed one's civic duty" (1976, 393). Using a model including expressive motivations both independent of and dependent on the voting choice, Fiorina theoretically derives unanticipated effects and finds empirical evidence for them. For example, the model implies (in hypothesis 8) that a voter whose candidate evaluations differ from her party ID is more likely to defect from the party if she believes the election to be close than if she expects a wide election margin. Fiorina's data bear out this and other similar predictions. This indicates that the voter treats expression as an argument in the utility function, some of whose other arguments are instrumental. Fiorina also finds that "expressive factors probably dominate instrumental factors as an explanation of turnout" (410).

Fiorina's theoretical account of expressive voting is fully compatible with previous social-psychological accounts, although he eschews any discussion of internal mental processes (such as dissonance reduction or need for approval) that might underlie the expressive motive. On the other hand, Fiorina's formal approach adds a significant achievement to previous discussions of the expressive vote: his comparative statics analysis yields specific predictions not otherwise available and not previously anticipated. These results ought to hold true regardless of the mental mechanism underlying expressive motives. Of course, any assertion that a voter votes for candidate X because he is motivated to express his preferences for candidate X runs the distinct risk of being merely tautological. Fiorina's approach, however, is clearly progressive, in the sense of Lakatos (1978), generating "excess empirical content" in the form of the new, corroborated predictions. Fiorina's work, however, does not in any sense argue for the greater reality of a rational choice or social-psychological picture of human action. Rather, the gain is of a more modest, inductive nature: if voter behavior is partly expressive, then certain other, unanticipated properties of voter behavior follow from that. These properties may themselves have important political implications.

RATIONAL EXPRESSIVE VOTING WITH PSYCHOLOGICAL ROOTS

Schuessler also addresses directly the possibility that voters may be rationally motivated by expressive in addition to instrumental concerns. Unlike Fiorina, he gives this expressive motivation an explicit psychological gloss in terms of identity: for expressive voters, "voting is a means to express political beliefs and preferences and, in doing so, to establish or reaffirm their own political identity" (2000, 88). The expressive value of an act, according to Schuessler, depends on who else also does it, how many do it, and who does not do it. This gives rise to an interdependence among the choices of expressively motivated voters that is closely analogous to equilibrium reasoning in game theory; to explain the dynamics of voter support of parties or candidates, Schuessler employs a Schelling-style (1978) diagrammatic analysis of the symmetric, n-player, two-strategy game played by voters for whom the expressive value of the vote depends solely on how many others vote the same way. The implications of this model depend, of course, on the particular shape of the payoff curves in those Schelling diagrams, that is, on the precise way in which expressive benefits depend on the numbers of people also engaging in the same expressive behavior and the numbers doing otherwise or doing nothing.[3]

Apart from the additional, specific assumptions he examines about the psychological motivations of voters, that is, the source and nature of the expressive benefits they experience, Schuessler's account is very much in the same vein as that of Fiorina (1976). The additional assumptions could provide additional scientific progress in the same sense. The rather loose theoretical basis of those additional assumptions gives little a priori reason to believe those new predictions will be borne out, but this is a matter to be resolved empirically.

SOCIALLY INSTRUMENTAL EXPRESSIVE VOTING

Fiorina (1976) and Schuessler (2000) posit basic preferences that are expressive in nature. Overbye (1995), in contrast, offers a mechanism *underlying* the expressive motivation of voters that is itself derived from a rational-choice approach—in fact, can even be derived from a so-called thin rational-choice account that posits instrumental, material self-interest at the root of all motivation. In effect, Overbye reformulates expressive voting into a species of instrumental voting. He suggests that

> voting may be regarded as a rational investment decision: not an investment in a particular electoral outcome, but in a type of reputation which the individual is interested in maintaining when carrying out his/her everyday activities. This solution not only solves the paradox [of participation], but may also provide a bridge between adherents of the public choice paradigm and scholars who advocate 'sociological' approaches to political behaviour. (1995, 369)

Overbye's approach "opens up the possibility of accounting for social phenomena such as 'group identity' . . . while staying firmly within a public choice (economic man) framework" (385).

An approach like Overbye's offers the potential for further scientific progress over Fiorina's and Schuessler's theories. In addition to positing an instrumental foundation for expressive benefits, Overbye also recommends a specific theoretical approach, namely the use of asymmetric-information games. Specifically, he suggests a game in which an agent (namely, whatever voter we are considering at the moment) has information not in the possession of her principals (namely, all the other players), such as the true utility function of the agent. Overbye is especially interested in a model in which each agent may have preferences that either do or do not incline

---

3. Additional assumptions about the effects of uncertainty and of negative campaigning on expressive value lead Schuessler to further predictions concerning how voting and turnout react to those factors. These assumptions are motivated by psychological claims.

him to be honest and cooperative in his general dealings with others.[4] In a game theoretic equilibrium, any action taken by the agent generally allows the principals to get a better idea of the agent's preferences; the agent therefore has an incentive to maintain a reputation of honesty and cooperation. For example, a merchant's willingness to vote for an extreme conservative party may be taken by potential working-class customers as an indicator that the merchant might try to cheat them in business dealings. For the posited behavior to constitute a game theoretic equilibrium, the parameters of the game (payoffs, discount factors, etc.) must obey certain conditions, generating specific predictions about empirical behavior. This is the potential source for excess empirical content.

Although Overbye suggests this asymmetric-information approach, equally useful would be a repeated-game approach in which reputable political behavior results in trust or in continued cooperation from one's fellow citizens in later, nonpolitical circumstances. Most of what Overbye says about the workings of his principal-agent formulation applies equally well to such a repeated-game model, with the intermediate goal of building reputation replaced by that of maintaining cooperation. As in Overbye's analysis, the requirements for equilibrium in a repeated game would place constraints on payoffs and discounting, generating predictions through the analysis of comparative statics.

Overbye's analysis aims, as does Fiorina's, at an improved explanation of the conditions under which citizens will vote, and also at an analysis of how they will vote, under various circumstances. The foundation of the expressive motivation in Overbye's analysis is the rather stylized story about reputation value; presumably, then, a more substantial account of the processes that generate this reputation value could provide a richer set of predictions linking those processes to voting behavior. For example, if (to take Overbye's motivating story literally) a reputation for honest or public-regarding behavior enabled a merchant to sell more goods at an increased price, then we might relate the characteristics of the market for those goods to the individual's voting behavior. But it is easy to imagine an analogous, more general account of social interaction in which one's voting behavior might have an impact on one's trustworthiness or reputation for good interactions and in which reputation engenders behavior in an agent's principals that benefits the agent.

Expression, in the world sketched by Overbye, occurs in the sending of a signal concerning one's true preferences or intentions. The sort of extended social model I have described would also generate a natural model

---

4. The honest, cooperative agent might have altruistic preferences, in which case the model is not one of pure self-interest; or, in a setting of repeated interaction, she might have a high discount factor or a poor ability to discern opportunities to cheat, in which case the model could work even with purely self-interested motives.

of group identification. To identify with a group would mean to share and express expectations with members of that group that prescribe how specified forms of other-regarding behavior will be rewarded—the values of the group. Individuals outside the group would not be expected to proffer or to reward such behavior in dealings with members of the in-group. In a given society, relations across groups might be uncooperative or cooperative, and the patterns of these underlying relations might determine the way electoral politics reflect group membership.

▪ | Ideology and Partisanship

In Butler and Stokes's account (1969), the voter's expressive motivation to go the polls and vote for a given *party* (in the British context) is due to the voter's psychological identification with that party. This is exactly the definition given by Campbell, Converse, Miller, and Stokes (1976 [1960], 121) for their conception of party identification, which determines a voter's long-term tendency (in the U.S. context) to choose candidates having one party label or the other. Elsewhere, political scientists have described voters' long-term tendencies in terms of ideology, a general way of making sense of the political world that tells the voter, based on minimal information, what position to favor on a given policy or what parties or candidates to favor in elections.[5] In some settings, ideology, like partisanship, can be seen as an identity-expressive phenomenon, in which members of a group share a common ideology thought compatible with the interests of the group. Typically such an ideology goes beyond merely specifying the group's interest, also providing a program of political action that all members of the group will support, even though alternative organized courses of action might equally well serve those interests. In short, as Bawn (1999a) has nicely put it, ideology provides a blueprint around which a group maintains a political coalition.

Rational-choice analysts have given considerable attention to specifying alternative models of partisanship and ideology. They have usually treated the phenomena as classically instrumental, information-economizing strategies; the first subsection below examines exemplars of such work. The second and third subsections turn to more recent research, which portrays the phenomena as being based in rational behavior in a context of repeated interaction in a group, contributing to the maintenance of political coalitions. These social interaction models of partisanship and ideology are closely analogous to Overbye's model of voting participation, as described above. In each, members of a group, playing a sequential game, use an equilibrium strategy profile in which they adhere

5. See, for example, Downs 1957 and Enelow and Hinich 1982.

to the prescriptions of a particular party or ideology in their voting. This game and this equilibrium involve all sorts of activity beyond voting in the current election, but as a by-product of its more general activities, the group produces coalition maintenance, which happens to be a collective good for them.

Ideology and Partisanship as Decision-Making Aids

In reaction to the view of party identification as a social-psychological phenomenon, Fiorina (1977) proposes a contrary, rational-choice viewpoint. He portrays party identification as a purely decision theoretic phenomenon, a "running total" of an individual voter's previous experiences under conditions in which politicians' party labels serve as consistent, if imperfect, guides to their likely actions in office. In Fiorina's description, this running total serves as a cue to voters about how to evaluate candidates. In the absence of any additional, specific information about a particular candidate, the record of that party's previous candidates provides a cue. (For related models of party ID as a decision-making aid in voting, see Jackson 1975 and Zechman 1979.)

In Downs's approach (1957), voters are unable (rationally unwilling, actually) to learn the implications of every policy position of every candidate, relying instead on ideology to summarize these implications cheaply if somewhat inaccurately. This approach is elaborated and clarified by Hinich and his coauthors (Hinich and Pollard 1981; Enelow and Hinich 1982), who portray ideology as the projection of multidimensional policy positions onto a one-dimensional ideological scale and explore the theoretical implications and empirical manifestations of this method of voting. Both the Fiorina-type models of party ID and the Hinich-type models of ideology carry numerous implications for patterns of voting behavior and of party and ideological change, which have been subjected with considerable success to statistical testing based on survey data, part of a lively literature on voter learning and the mutual effects of candidate preferences and party and ideological preferences.[6]

A Social Game Theoretic Model of Ideology

Recently, rational-choice analysts have returned to the question of the nature of partisanship and ideology, because the simple decision theoretic interpretations seem to miss a social component important to the genesis and effects of those phenomena. The game theoretic literature on electoral competition generated a corresponding theoretical anomaly: Myerson and Weber are the first to have pointed out the fact that any electoral system presents participants with an enormous coordination problem, a problem

---

6. See, for example, Shively 1979 and Franklin and Jackson 1983.

to which partisanship or ideology might be the solutions (1993, 112–13). Cox (1997) exploits this insight with enormously productive results concerning the nature of multiple-party electoral systems. These authors see the structure of party membership as the accomplishment of a coordination equilibrium, in which groups or individuals having varying but related interests manage to stick together as a coalition over a number of different issues and elections, and thus to achieve some of the goals they have in common. Aldrich (1995) employs the same view of party in his theoretical and empirical study of the development and nature of the U.S. party system.

But how are these coordination solutions realized in the electorate? Bawn (1999a) addresses this question by taking a somewhat broader game theoretic look at the problem of defining and maintaining a coalition in a setting where preferences vary both across voters and over time. Her model is central to the set of approaches I review in this paper, concerning both electoral and ethnic politics. In effect, she formalizes the repeated-game version of the model envisioned by Overbye (1995) as well as by the other authors to be examined subsequently. Bawn focuses on the phenomenon of ideology rather than party membership, but in fact everything that she, Aldrich, Cox, or Myerson and Weber say can be applied equally well to both phenomena. The common features of party and ideology to which all these models appeal is that voters are able to commonly categorize candidates in terms of the candidates' party labels or ideological affinities, and those labels or affinities in turn indicate the policies those candidates will pursue once in office.

Specifically, Bawn defines ideology as "an enduring system of beliefs, prescribing what action to take in a variety of political circumstances" (1999a, 305). Really, the term is "a catch-all to refer to all opinions and preferences that arise from anything other than a direct personal stake in the issue" (304). Both here and in her summary statement that "Ideologies create preferences by defining coalitions" (304), she uses the term *preferences* in a nonstandard way. But her general theoretical apparatus is identical to that used by the other instrumental-rationality theorists reviewed here: *basic* preferences concern the policy outcomes of elections; these basic preferences, together with information about candidates and about the expected behavior of other voters, produces a *derived* preference ordering over candidates, according to which the voter chooses. It is these derived preferences that are created by ideology in Bawn's model.

Bawn portrays a system of successive voting decisions, treated by voters as an indefinitely repeated game, and derives various contingent-strategy equilibria in which patterns of ideological, as opposed to self-interested, voting are maintained. In her "Game of Politics," in each period t, there is an opportunity to provide a benefit B to one of three players designated at random. One other randomly chosen player would bear a cost C_t to provide that benefit, drawn from a uniform distribution on $[0, 2B]$. To participate in the decision, each player has to bear a participation cost $v < B$; a participant may vote for or against acquiring the benefit for the designated player. The benefit is provided only if it receives the support of a majority of the players casting votes. Bawn examines both stagewise equilibria and various repeated-game equilibria, of which the latter incorporate contingent strategies where a player supports benefits for another as long as the other player behaves analogously. The analysis illustrates how each equilibrium possesses or lacks properties such as efficiency, commitment (requiring some players to sometimes act against their short-term interest), individualism (whether the required action depends on properties of some predesignated group, such as net benefit to a fixed subset of players), hierarchy (unevenness of treatment within the implicit coalition), and exclusion (whether some players are excluded from ever receiving benefits). Bawn also goes on to examine a prior "Game of Ideologies" in which the players choose among different ideologies.

Thus the theory "proposes that all ideologies have interest at their core, but that interest is mediated by the social and political environment. What makes a system of beliefs 'enduring' is that *its members do better in the long run by following the ideology's prescriptions than they would by deviating, given the actions of others*" (306, Bawn's emphasis). The overall approach derives, as Bawn points out, partly from those of Calvert (1995a) on the theory of institutions as repeated-game equilibria and Kreps (1990a) on viewing culture in terms of coordination.

Bawn's model describes an ideology simply as the set of prescribed actions in an equilibrium strategy profile for the repeated game; it portrays no sets of principles, beliefs, or values resembling those on which a real-world ideology is usually based. Yet her ideologies are indeed intended to represent such real-world ideologies. One should think of the ideological principles of the real world as the description of the class of benefits or benefit-cost combinations in favor of which the subscriber is expected to vote. In any real-life context, identities are attached to the players, and the benefits result from certain government actions; an ideology describes who the beneficiaries are to be (labor, owners of property, the small family farmer) and what sort of benefit they are to be granted. An ideology that can be described clearly in such terms can be adhered to, and monitored, by its subscribers, in the required way, while a complex and ambiguous description will be more difficult to implement.

Considerations such as these bring us back to the coordination problem with which Myerson and Weber and Cox are concerned. Bawn's model conceptually subsumes theirs: her repeated game of voting has multiple cooperative equilibria, and no ideology is implemented unless a sufficient number of players share expectations about the prescribed strategies. The choice among these amounts to solving a coordination problem, and Bawn's "Game of Ideologies" simply represents one mechanism by which it might be solved. Which equilibrium the players eventually coordinate on determines which ideology they (or a subset of them) follow. In precisely the sense of Schelling (1960), this is the role of the principles, values, and statements of belief that define real-life ideologies: to create focal points in the game of choosing ideology.[7]

Bawn's conception of ideology is social in the sense that, unlike the information-economizing models of Fiorina and Hinich, it cannot be described as a solely individual-level phenomenon. Rather, ideology depends on the existence of shared understandings and expectations among members of a group. The model is easily extended to provide an even more broadly socially based conceptualization of ideology or partisan identification. Both the "Game of Politics" and the "Game of Ideologies" are entirely concerned with political choices. Ideology is enforced by political rewards and the threat of political repercussions. However, an alternative model incorporating broader forms of social interaction, where only a subset of iterations of the game involve political choices, would work in exactly the same way. In that case, the model would portray a social basis for ideology, with enforcement based on social rewards such as interpersonal cooperation and on threats of social repercussions such as noncooperation or shunning. This is the direct route to formalizing not only Overbye's suggestion that expressive voting is rooted in instrumentalism but also Harvey's suggestion (1998) about the basis for partisan attachments, to which I now turn.

PARTY IDENTIFICATION IN A GAME THEORETIC SOCIAL SETTING

Harvey's goal in *Votes without Leverage* (1998) is to explain the pattern of policy responsiveness toward women's concerns in the United States during the eventful middle half of the twentieth century. Immediately before and especially just after the suffrage amendment, women's organizations were a powerful lobbying group, and issues broadly identified as women's concerns received considerable attention in new federal programs. This ended abruptly in the late 1920s, and never resumed until the 1970s. Harvey argues that several common explanations for this pattern fail, either because they fail to explain other obvious related phenomena or because they call, inappropriately in her view, on special features of women to explain politics concerning women. Instead, Harvey advances a more parsimonious explanation via a theory of electoral coalitions involving rational choice and strategic politicians.

Harvey espouses a view of party that, like Bawn's model of ideology, is the product of both rational choice and social construction. Rational voters

---

7. This application of focal points is brought partially into the theory by Kreps (1990a).

participate in a broader social game of which politics is a part and in which the formation of parties and the manifestation of party voting are equilibrium phenomena. She motivates this in rational-choice terms, by connecting voting choices to other aspects of social exchange (1998, 33–38), in terms sufficiently general to be applied even to purely self-interested individuals. By voting as prescribed by the norms of one's group, one can enjoy the benefits of cooperative relations with members of the group in other, nonpolitical settings.[8] "When members of some group follow the cues of other group members in order to avail themselves of the resulting benefit of cheaply purchased social acceptance, we can say that they *identify* with that group" (35, Bawn's emphasis). Because partisan participation is rewarded or punished by social groups, Harvey reasons that the larger the number of group members engaging in a particular form of participation, the greater the individual benefit (through social exchange) to each of them. This conclusion matches that of Schuessler (2000), whose work Harvey cites, and she adopts the same analytical tool to generate propositions about the success of women's lobbying efforts: Schelling-style games (1978) that demonstrate a tipping point, a threshold level of adherence to a particular voting pattern, above which other voters want to join the pattern and below which the current participants begin to drop out.[9] The pattern in this case is a willingness of women generally to vote for or against candidates depending on whether they support or oppose the issues promoted by women's groups such as the League of Women Voters, at that time an active lobbying force, rather than voting based on other issues or on established party labels. This situation, Harvey points out, presents a coordination problem to be addressed by political entrepreneurs. Her full

8. Harvey addresses the objection that the use of the secret ballot would make group norms on voting choice impossible to monitor and hence unenforceable. One could, after all, simply lie if asked how one voted. "Lying bears risks, however; one may have a 'tell' that alerts others to the fact that one is lying, or one may simply be tripped up by objective evidence contradicting one's story. . . . Lying to a group, if one is caught, can have serious negative consequences" (1998, 37). In an instrumental-voter account such as Harvey's, moreover, the only reason to vote contrary to one's group's norm is if one is trying simultaneously to satisfy the conflicting norm of another group. Reporting one's vote differently to members of different groups sets up the conditions for discovery.

9. A rough spot in Harvey's argument here, as in Schuessler's, is that there is no inherent reason to believe mere numbers should *generate* solidary selective benefits. The level of such benefits will depend just as much, for example, on the density and importance of relationships with those other participants, and perhaps a larger group necessarily means more marginal relationships. On the other hand, it is easy to imagine circumstances where the larger-numbers benefit would work as posited here. When Laitin (1998a) applies the same technique to the analysis of language adoption, as described below, there is a more solid reason for supposing that the more fellow group members adopting the language, the higher the benefit to each individual of doing so.

substantive account is too detailed to present here, but in the end the political parties, for reasons made coherent by the theory, gain the upper hand over women's groups in mobilizing women voters, and women's policy concerns are submerged in the orthogonal issue concerns of the parties. This pattern changes only with the general weakening of the parties as a force for voter mobilization in the late 1960s.

Even this cursory account of Harvey's substantive analysis demonstrates, however, how her appeal to a game theoretic, social-interaction-based theory of partisanship was made necessary by the substantive problem she wanted to explain. A decision theoretic account of party voting could not explain the phenomena she observed. But, Harvey argues in effect, a group identification or other psychological account, based on the special attributes of women as a group and on social attitudes toward women, is also not a promising explanatory tactic. If followed in the study of other, similar political phenomena, this tactic would result in the accumulation of a collection of special-purpose accounts explaining the political fortunes of each social group in terms of the special properties of that group. While this approach might generate additional predictions about that group, it would have little to offer to predict the fortunes of any new, as yet unexamined group. Harvey's ambition is to assemble an explanatory apparatus that can be used not only to explain other aspects of the fortunes of women in politics and society but also to explain the fortunes of any group in politics.

CONCLUSION

The political importance of partisanship and ideology comes down to their effects on people's political choices. But whereas expressive theories of voting are primarily concerned with the participation decision—a fairly straightforward collective action problem—voting choice, aside from the participation problem, is a more complicated matter. Even in the myopic, single-election setting, if there are multiple candidates or if we look at the whole process of winnowing down to two candidates, voters face a serious problem of coordination. Current rational-choice theory is weak on how coordination is achieved, but it can at least clarify conditions under which it can occur and what the results can look like. Bawn's model of ideology does exactly this. Regarding Bawn's model as the formalization of Harvey's social exchange basis for partisanship, one gets some idea of the potential power of this approach for understanding historical phenomena of democratic politics.

With this demonstration in mind, I turn to the critical application of rational choice to the identity-expressive politics of ethnic conflict. Many of the same theoretical techniques, as well as some new ones, have been brought to this task; moreover, the above models of partisanship and ideology offer an excellent guide as to how to formalize some even broader,

more powerful theoretical ideas put forward by rational-choice students of
ethnic politics.

■ | Ethnic Politics

Voting choice, voting participation, and partisanship all occur in an institutionalized political setting, in which stable rules define a game where
voters make their decisions and ultimately affect the state of the world. The
most critical setting for ethnic politics and ethnic conflict, however, is in
unstable and transitional polities, where the political rules of the game are
essentially up for grabs. M. Taylor's (1976) repeated interaction approach
to cooperation in communities first provided a basic method for thinking
about rational behavior in such contexts; subsequent work by Ullman-
Margalit (1977), Hardin (1982), and especially Sugden (1986), explored
further the notion of social norms as game theoretic equilibrium phenomena. Harvey's (1998) account of partisanship and Bawn's (1999a) game theoretic model of the role of electoral ideology exploit this approach and
suggest how one might examine other forms of group-oriented political behavior in a less-structured political context, provided that there is sufficient
social structure: individuals must be able to anticipate possible future interactions with relevant other individuals or to draw inferences for the present
from a relevant history of interactions. Making one or both of these assumptions, rational-choice theorists have taken two approaches to the
study of ethnic politics in unstable or transitional polities, corresponding to
the approaches used in the models of electoral behavior surveyed above. In
the first approach, analysts overlay strategic gaming on a fixed background
of ethnic identities and cultural meanings. In the second, they suggest
more foundational models of identity and expression based on principles of
instrumental rationality and social interaction.

Rational Ethnic Violence in a Cultural Context

The analyses in the first category follow a common pattern: positing some
initial, low level of ethnic identities and suspicions available for political
exploitation, they attribute outbreaks of ethnic violence to self-reinforcing
fears in a setting of uncertainty or inability to commit. Each study attributes ethnic violence to the stoking of ethnic suspicions by political leaders
or other special political circumstances. Their accomplishment is to identify a partial alternative to the "ancient hatreds" hypothesis of ethnic violence. They argue that ethnic violence is not inevitable but occurs under
specified and perhaps preventable circumstances.

Fearon (1998b) presents one such analysis, in which a majority and a
minority group may either resort to violent conflict or peacefully enjoy

some division of the gains from staying together.[10] The problem is whether they will succeed in arriving amicably at a sharing arrangement. The specific puzzle: Serbs and Croats in Krajina overwhelmingly opposed ethnic divisions as late as 1990; but when Croatia declared independence in 1991, the region immediately erupted into ethnic warfare with, Fearon says, broad participation in at least some localities. Does such a sudden change of feelings indicate the fragility of peace between neighboring ethnic groups?

Under normal conditions, the majority (who, in the most threatening case, control government as a unified team) should offer the minority at least enough benefits to make it not worthwhile to secede, including any cost of violent rebellion. Both sides can be better off staying together. But under certain circumstances, there is a problem of commitment that causes a prospective new minority *always* to pursue resistance and secession. The problem arises because, once a newly ascendant majority group has consolidated control over the state apparatus, it will be better able to resist a secession attempt and hence can keep the minority with a smaller offer. The rational strategy for the minority, then, is always to attempt secession before the majority has consolidated power, assuming that, as consolidation makes secession increasingly hard, the minority's share will keep getting smaller.

The special setting in which this sequence of events can happen is as follows: before the majority group gained control of the government, the two groups have been part of some larger jurisdiction in which their majority-minority status was reversed or in which neither had controlled the government. Moreover, following their secession from the previous jurisdiction, the new majority is for some reason unable or unwilling to commit to ceding a measure of governmental control to the minority.[11] This, Fearon says, was the situation in Krajina and in a few other areas, and it is only in those areas that Fearon says we should worry about inevitable, "explosive" ethnic wars erupting.[12]

Fearon's simple extensive-game model is imposed on a situation in which ethnic identities and competition are already clearly defined and in which they dominate the prospective politics of the new country. If alter-

10. If there were no such gains, he points out, the two groups should split up by mutual agreement. Of course, this assumes there is a geographic basis for such a split.

11. Fearon does not state this second condition as part of the circumstances for ethnic conflict, but it is a maintained feature of his model. Without this condition, the commitment problem could be solved constitutionally in the new government.

12. Of course, Fearon has presented only one mechanism by which ethnic conflict can occur; if one fears widespread recurrences of such conflict, one will probably not be comforted until other such mechanisms can be shown not to exist or can be subjected to analyses with similar results.

native coalitions of subgroups were possible or if the distribution of the gains were not so strictly constant sum, then there would be other ways out besides secession. So we might say that Fearon, rather than examining the game theory of ethnic identity, is studying the strategic rationality of its expression through secessionism and ethnic violence. In his account, such expression is the result of preferences and rational fears concerning the division of resources; but the existence of those preferences and the basis of those fears is taken as given.

Similarly, Bates, deFigueiredo, and Weingast (1998) present a model of strategic interaction in political transitions and ethnic politics, in a setting in which the intergroup rivalries and tensions (and the groups' behavior as unitary actors for purposes of analysis) are taken as given. They examine two illustrative cases: democratic transition in Zambia and ethnic warfare between Serbs and Croats, first in non-rational-choice terms involving deployment of symbols and exploitation of cultural attitudes (such as ethnic hatreds), and then in terms of strategic actions. In both cases, an election is the climactic event: the culmination of President Kenneth Kaunda's reelection campaign in Zambia (not primarily an episode of ethnic politics), and the electoral fortunes of the Slobodan Milosevic government in Serbian-controlled Yugoslavia. The strategic analysis of each case is based on one- and two-dimensional spatial models in which the location of a pivotal voter—the pivotal member of the Zambian urban lower class and the pivotal Serb, respectively—is at issue.

In both models there is uncertainty, whose resolution or exacerbation drives the observed political cataclysms. President Kaunda and his opponents in Zambia are uncertain about the location of the pivotal voter, and the pivotal Serbian voter is uncertain about true Croat intentions and hence about what level of ethnic solidarity she should support. Symbolic actions affect beliefs about these true values, causing an effective change in the location (or perceived location) of the pivot, bringing about the abrupt changes that were observed: the unexpected defeat of Kaunda at the polls despite his one-party rule and the relatively sudden outbreak of ethnic warfare in Croatia.

These models make no attempt to portray the underlying nature of ethnic attachments, symbols, or policy preferences. Rather, taking those cultural features for granted, they explore the strategic situation, which involves the deployment of symbols that play on existing cultural attitudes. Ethnic fears are taken as given, although at too low a level at the outset to provoke ethnic warfare; rather than expressing ethnic identity, the Serb-Croat conflict consisted of the rational actions of people whose initially mild fears were exploited by politicians, invoking cultural symbols strategically, with disastrously self-reinforcing effects.

In a related analysis applied to the Krajina conflict and to the Hutu-Tutsi conflagration in Rwanda, de Figueiredo and Weingast (1999) examine in more detail the theory of belief formation in the presence of incomplete information. When negotiations between the Milosevic and Franjo Tudjman governments break down, Serbs can observe that fact but cannot observe whether the failure is due to evil intentions on the part of Croats or to sabotage by Milosevic in an effort to stoke ethnic unrest and thus maintain his own political power. The algebra of Bayesian updating is such that, as long as both interpretations are thought possible, the failure of negotiations increases the Serbs' estimate of the probability that the Croats have evil intentions. Thus even if Serbs are fully rational and realize there is a good chance that Milosevic is corrupt, Milosevic can still be successful in strengthening his position, increasing Serb fears by sabotaging negotiations himself. In this model, rational learning by rational actors still leaves room for corrupt politicians to play the ethnic card. For their part, strategic corrupt politicians can be expected to appreciate and take advantage of this opportunity, yielding a conclusion rather more pessimistic than that of Fearon (1998b), especially if we imagine Tudjman following the same strategy on the other side.

This adverse arithmetic works, however, only if the danger posed by underestimating the evil intentions of (enough) Croats is thought by (enough) Serbs to be higher than the danger of underestimating Milosevic's corruption. Once again, then, we are looking at a model in which ethnic identities and suspicions are assumed preexisting, and the analysis deals only with the mechanism by which those identities and suspicions become expressed in ethnic violence perpetrated, not in reluctant obedience to a corrupt dictator but with apparent enthusiasm in certain quarters of the population. These rational-choice analyses differ only in degree from primordialist explanations of ethnic conflict: although the rational-choice models posit initially insufficient levels of competition and suspicion to motivate violence, the inexorable workings of politics stokes that competition and suspicion until a war results.

RATIONAL-CHOICE EXPLANATIONS OF ETHNIC IDENTIFICATION

Another set of studies takes on more fundamentally the task of replacing identity and expressive motivations as explanatory primitives with an underlying model of rational, ultimately instrumental choice. The approach to community and social norms developed by M. Taylor (1976), Ullman-Margalit (1977), Hardin (1982), and Sugden (1986) reaches its most extensive use thus far in analyzing ethnic identity and ethnic politics in the work of David Laitin and Russell Hardin.

THE CHOICE OF ETHNIC IDENTITY

Laitin's *Hegemony and Culture* (1986) is the first, among these rational choice social theories, to take on the idea of culture as distinct from mere social norms and to treat culture as an equilibrium phenomenon involving strategy and choice and analyze it from a rational-choice standpoint. In this study of the failure of Nigeria to erupt into Christian-against-Muslim religious warfare as a result of disagreements over the writing of their 1976 constitution, Laitin writes that culture has two faces. "Culture orders political priorities" due to shared values, while also "shared cultural identities facilitate collective action" due to the ease of communication (1986, 11). Culture involves deeply held shared values, but cultural identities and meanings can be and are strategically manipulated. One must address both faces of culture in order to understand the politics of culture or the role of culture in politics. This Laitin does in examining the development, in particular, of the Yoruba ethnic group a few decades earlier and how it wielded political power and, among other things, prevented any breakdown of Nigerian society along religious lines in the 1970s. An ethnicity had been created, not, to be sure, out of whole cloth but certainly in response to political expediencies. Once created, ethnicity provided a political resource that could be applied toward various political ends.

Laitin's later work takes on issues of individual identity more directly. *Identity in Formation* (Laitin 1998a) examines choices and attitudes of ethnic Russians and members of the local nationality in the fourteen former Soviet republics, via survey analyses, ethnographic work, "discourse analysis" of local newspaper discussions, and elite interviews. These choices involve language, residency, and citizenship; attitudes are those toward own and other ethnic groups and toward ethnicity in general.

For his definition of identity, Laitin adopts that of the psychoanalyst E. H. Erikson (1968). "Erikson sees 'identity formation [as] a process . . . by which the individual judges himself in the light of what he perceives to be the way in which others judge him in comparison to themselves and to a typology significant to them; while he judges their way of judging him in the light of how he perceives himself in comparison to them and to types that have become relevant to him' " (1998a, 20).[13] Laitin studies Russians who now find themselves a minority group in each former Soviet republic and who are faced with choices about whether to try to assimilate to the larger society or maintain a separate identity. Similar to Schuessler (2000) and Harvey (1998), Laitin diagrams a Schelling-style (1978) n-player 2-action symmetric game to analyze situations of identity choice. He concludes that "assimilation cascades" are most likely when assimilation offers economic advantage, does not unduly harm one's in-group status, and results in acceptance by the out-group (1998a, 28–29). Along with his empirical analysis, Laitin uses this approach to produce a number of specific and counterintuitive predictions concerning the future course of Russian assimilation into the dominant cultures of the former Soviet Republics.

13. Note the resemblance of this definition to the infinite-regress-resolving tools and mutual knowledge features central to Bayesian Nash equilibrium.

For Laitin, the specifics of an ethnic culture are products of equilibrium among that culture's members. Laitin does not commit himself to a particular view of the nature of basic preference that causes people to value their culture's particular art, language, mythology, and so on, but indicates much of that value should be explained by the material advantages of easy communication and cooperation among members who share those cultural ideas. Certainly Laitin infers that ethnicity and culture become objective realities because they are equilibrium phenomena and that changing conditions, such as the abrupt political change in the former Soviet Union, can disrupt the equilibrium and force predictable changes at the individual level. Interested primarily in the choice of language, Laitin does not venture to explain the roles of more purely symbolic features of a culture; once in place, they may indeed facilitate communication, but why was the whole repertoire of mythologies and religious rituals created in the first place? Although this question is beyond the scope of Laitin's work, it does, as we will see, receive direct treatment in Hardin's.

In an important companion to the nonformal analyses of Laitin (1986, 1998a), Fearon and Laitin (1996) specify rigorously the form of a game and equilibrium that might characterize one aspect of interethnic cooperation (that is, peaceful coexistence) in the presence of real ethnic division. They point out that interethnic cooperation is, contrary to much commentary, the rule and interethnic conflict the exception across the world. So the puzzle is to find a model of ethnic interaction that could account for the simultaneous existence of both patterns of behavior. To this end, they employ a model of 2-player repeated prisoner's dilemma games with random matching among the members of two "ethnic groups." To represent the interaction patterns among ethnic communities, Fearon and Laitin assume that members of one group are unable to distinguish among individual members of the other (for purposes of cooperation or retaliation). Nevertheless, the authors find, cooperation can be maintained through various equilibria in which deviations from an interethnically cooperative path of play are enforced by each group against in-group members, regardless of which members of the out-group their deviations are committed against. Thus there are equilibria supporting both cooperation and conflict between the groups, and shifts in the game's parameters could bring about transitions from one type to the other.[14] Although the model presents an account of interethnic cooperation, as in Laitin's other studies, it is not intended to explain the origin of the emotional, symbolic, or ritualistic aspects of intraethnic relations, although clearly these may be part of the mechanisms by which intraethnic cooperation occurs.

14. Nothing in the model predicts the relative prevalence of ethnic cooperation and ethnic conflict under the conditions when both are possible; equilibrium conflict is always possible.

THE BASIS OF ETHNIC IDENTITY

Hardin's theoretical treatment of ethnicity in *One for All* (1995) focuses more directly on such symbolic features of ethnic cultures, as well as on the advantages that ethnic identity presents for material gain through co-operation and coordination. Methodologically, Hardin's explicit intention is to determine the maximum explanatory power that self-interest and rational choice could have:

> In this study, I propose to go as far as possible with a rational choice ac-count of the reputedly primordial, moral, and irrational phenomena of ethnic and nationalist identification and action. . . . [I]f we can rely on the actors' knowledge to determine what it is rational for them to do, we may often find apparently group-oriented action intelligible without the mystification of pri-mordialism and without strong claims of moralism either. . . . Throughout this book I use the term 'rational' to mean to have narrowly self-interested inten-tions. (1995, 16–17, 46)

For Hardin as for Laitin, the central feature of identification is the identi-fier's willingness to take action because of the group that, individually and at least myopically, is bad for the identifier. And for Hardin, as for Laitin, people do not merely *have* identity; they also accrue, obtain, or even choose it, and an important task for the theorist is to explain how they do so.

Hardin sees social interaction as consisting of a variety of cooperation and coordination problems occurring all the time among subsets of indi-viduals, in which people interact most frequently with fellow members of certain ethnic or other groupings. This interaction offers opportunities for mutual gain through cooperation or exchange, such as those explored by Overbye, Bawn, and Laitin. Power in cooperative relationships depends, among other things, on the control of resources. Coordination offers op-portunities to accomplish things as an organized group that smaller groups, less-organized groups, or individuals could never accomplish. Hardin does not explore the role of coordination in selecting among equilibria in re-peated cooperation problems, although neither does he force a distinction between the two situations.[15] He does, however, see coordination as overall the more important of the two processes in understanding what lies behind ethnic identification. Power in coordination relationships involves the abil-ity to direct the concerted behavior of numerous people, which need not (but may often) require resources.

Consistent with the cases Laitin explores, Hardin emphasizes the cen-tral role of politics, not as a result or as a medium but as a basic causative ingredient of ethnic conflict. When one group coordinates on a pattern of internally cooperative behavior, this coordination can be used as a political

---

15. However, the way that cooperation problems generate coordination problems was a major topic in Hardin's earlier book, *Collective Action* (1982, chs. 10–15).

resource to gain economic advantage for group members. By and large, this advantage would come at the expense of other groups in the same country or economy, so they have good reason to fear and oppose one another's political efforts on their group's behalf. Each group wants to control political positions ("positional goods," Hardin calls them) so it can control the allocation of material goods ("distributional goods") such as subsidies, resources, and language regulations. Cooperation within an ethnic group can be self-reinforcing, since the political achievement of benefits for the group can provide the group's political leaders with stronger selective incentives to dole out. These benefits also make the threat of exclusion from the group more persuasive as a means of enforcing cooperation.

Ethnic identification is an equilibrium that requires members to contribute to the group's collective action. Typically, it also requires that each member engage in symbolic expression indicating that he or she upholds the prescribed behaviors and requires that members follow prescribed ways of interacting with others to facilitate pairwise and small-group cooperation. In some cases, the ethnic identification equilibrium prescribes withholding of cooperation from, and even participation in hostilities against, members of other ethnic groups.

Standard accounts of ethnic relations emphasize the emotional, moral, and habitual aspects of ethnic identification, and Hardin confronts this issue directly. "Explanations of ethnic conflict often invoke emotions. Unfortunately, explaining ethnic conflict as emotional may not be explaining it at all or may be explaining only aspects of it given that it happens. The part we most need to explain is why the behavior happens, why such behavior is ethnically oriented. And we need to explain why one group falls into conflict with another" (1995, 56). Hardin thus distinguishes between the internal, mental processes by which particular instances of ethnically related behavior may be accompanied, and the underlying, long-run pressures to adopt or maintain ethnic identifications. Similarly, he disputes the claim made by Elster (1989b) and others that norms are distinguished from rational behavior in that normative behavior is not outcome oriented. Hardin argues at length that this distinction cannot be maintained, appealing to the information-economizing function of habits and to the tendency of people to treat behavioral rules consequentially at some times and habitually at others. Although, as Hardin admits, people may sometimes intentionally violate their private interests, the rational-choice incentives he describes are the major eventual influences on the course of ethnicity and ethnic politics. This is the major conclusion of both Hardin's theoretical and Laitin's empirical analyses.

CONCLUSION: THE POLITICAL BASIS OF ETHNIC CONFLICT

Laitin and Hardin, like Overbye and Harvey, ultimately attribute identity to the benefits from in-group cooperation in life generally and in politics in particular. Sometimes too, Hardin emphasizes, there is a benefit from organizing for political competition against another group. This motivation plays an important, implicit role in Harvey's account of partisanship as well. There is thus, in Hardin's and Harvey's accounts, an essential *political* component to ethnic and partisan conflict. Such conflict is not, at root, a result of psychological identifications and basic expressive motivations but rather a result of the opportunities available to an appropriately organized group to pursue benefits through political means. Ethnic conflict has primarily political rather than social-psychological roots. It is maintained, however, by social as well as political means.

■ | Discussion: A Complementary Approach to Identity and Expression

The rational-choice treatments of identity and expression surveyed perform two kinds of analysis. First, they derive predictions and explanations, not otherwise obvious, that follow from an initial *assumption* that identity and expression are basic motivations. This is the contribution of Fiorina and of Schuessler on voting participation and voting choice and of Fearon and of Bates, deFigueiredo, and Weingast on ethnic conflict. More fundamentally, however, the other rational-choice studies explore the connections between expression and instrumentality to derive and apply new theories of the basic nature—and thence of the emergence, maintenance, and change—of identity and expression.

This survey indicates that rational choice and identity-expression, although often seen as mutually exclusive analytical and theoretical alternatives, may in many instances be complementary and mutually clarifying approaches. Rational-choice models are especially good for clarifying the role of individual actions in patterns of group identity and expressive behavior and for generating hypotheses about that role. On the other hand, there are important questions about identity and expression that rational-choice theory, even extended in the ways surveyed in this paper, is unable to address. Those questions depend on other approaches to resolve multiple equilibrium puzzles, for example, and to clarify the values that guide social coordination. Moreover, rational-choice theories of identity and expression, at least thus far, have depended on strong common-knowledge conditions that, while useful tools for answering some questions, are completely inappropriate for others.

After reviewing the major themes and accomplishments of the rational-choice literature on identity and expression, this final section turns to the distinction between the supposed and the real limitations of those theories.

RATIONAL CHOICE IN THE NARROWLY POLITICAL VERSUS SOCIAL CONTEXT

The work of Overbye, Bawn, Harvey, Laitin, and Hardin exemplifies the deconstruction, as Hardin (1995, 18) puts it, of identity-expressive behavior in terms of instrumental rationality. Each of these authors portrays actions that appear symbolic or expressive when viewed as purely political phenomena as being instrumental in a wider social sense. Political actors are also social actors. They associate with other social actors in repeated encounters throughout their lives; they interact with members of specific social groups more often than with nonmembers of those groups. In these repeated interactions, certain behavior is prescribed by social norms: forms of everyday cooperation, as well as symbolic acts that indicate one's membership in the group and intention of adhering to its norms in the future. At a social level, we can see these actions as instrumental; certainly they have an impact on the individual's well being, and they are subject to change over time even if, at any given moment, the actors behave out of habit or simple principle rather than out of calculation. Stable patterns of social behavior, in short, resemble equilibria in repeated games. There is much to be gained by using that approach, among others, to analyze them.

PARTICIPATION AND PARTISANSHIP AS SOCIAL STRUCTURE

This is most simply illustrated in voting participation. A norm requiring members to participate in, and be minimally informed about, the electoral process may be reinforced by the implicit threat of reduced status and hence reduced cooperation from other group members. In that case, instrumental social behavior appears, from a purely political standpoint, to be expressive behavior. Similarly, in some social groups there is an expectation not just that members will vote but that they will vote for candidates of a certain party or candidates who adhere to certain ideological principles. In Bawn's model of ideology, for example, sanctions take the particular form of a conditional exchange of mutual political support. Extended as I suggested to the context of repeated social and not just political interaction, her model can produce political behavior that appears expressive or altruistic when viewed from a purely political perspective but may be purely instrumental when seen in its wider social perspective.

It bears emphasizing that this approach does not involve any comparison between so-called thick and thin rational choice (see, e.g., Ferejohn 1991). Rather, the difference between the purely political approach in which a voter cannot be seen as rationally, selfishly instrumental, and the broader social approach in which she can, is that the latter approach draws no artificial boundary around the narrow political setting in formulating an explanation of voter behavior. There is nothing about rational-choice theory, thick or thin, that should lead us to ignore nonpolitical consequences of the voting act. There is obviously nothing that should lead us to ignore the reactions of other participants in a game theoretic picture of life that, after all, includes nonpolitical as well as political actions and events.[16]

THE INSTRUMENTAL FOUNDATIONS OF ETHNIC POLITICS

The main tenets of this whole view, as applied to ethnic politics, include the following: Ethnic identification is socially constructed, in the sense of mutual equilibrium expectations in a setting of multiple equilibria. Within the resulting constraints, identification or its intensity is partially subject to choice by the individual.[17] Expressing one's ethnic identification consists of (1) undertaking action that is individually costly but demanded by the group, usually (but not necessarily) a collective good for the group, or (2) producing symbolic expression that indicates one's identification.[18]

Ethnic identification and its forms of expression change over time and respond to the strategic manipulation of politicians and to changes in economic and demographic conditions. Thus, under the right conditions, ethnic violence can be perpetrated through the efforts of political leaders striving cynically to gain or hold office. And under the right conditions, ethnic conflict can be suppressed or eliminated by the action of politicians seeking to maintain democracy, peace, and economic development. Hence there is a politics of ethnicity central to the configuration of ethnic identities and the occurences of ethnic violence.

As with electoral politics, the acts contributing to ethnic politics and ethnic conflict depend in many respects on how people respond to incentives. Although these responses may not be instantaneous or perfect, they are constantly present; they are cumulative; under certain circumstances they may take the form of tipping phenonema; and they accumulate rapidly. To understand the danger of ethnic conflict and democratic failure

16. The same idea applies immediately to studies of political participation other than voting that appeal in broadly rational-choice terms to solidary and expressive benefits motivating collective action. Such analyses include Salisbury 1969, Wilson 1973, and Moe 1980, as well as more recent game theoretic work concentrating on information transmission and coordination among participants whose motivation includes some fundamentally noninstrumental component, such as Kuran's "internal payoffs" (1991, 18).

17. Individuals' *claims* about their motivations (whether in survey responses or natural communication) are poor evidence as to whether that motivation is expressive or instrumental. Any ethnic-identity equilibrium is likely to include the behavioral prescription that one should deny that ascriptive group members, especially including oneself, have any choice in the matter. In the settings modeled in this paper, an individual motivated by social-instrumental concerns might feel required to profess true attachment to the group, and hence claim expressive motivation. On the other hand, an expressively motivated individual might justify his or her actions in instrumental terms.

18. On the rational-choice theory of symbolic expression generally, see Chwe 2001.

and the opportunities of democratic consolidation and social toleration, we need to understand these individual choice effects.

ON THE DISTINCTION BETWEEN INSTRUMENTAL AND EXPRESSIVE ACTION

Political scientists, especially those studying voting and elections, have traditionally partitioned political acts into two categories: instrumental and expressive. Attitudes and actions connected with ethnic politics are often posed as examples of inherently expressive action, not understandable in instrumental terms. In view of the approach outlined in this essay, it seems that we need instead to distinguish three such categories, obscuring the expressive-instrumental distinction. First, there is policy-oriented, instrumental action: the actions of the Downsian voter and of the ethnically tolerant citizen who seeks the benefits of ethnic peace. Second, there are the actions of the socially oblivious expressive voter: heedless of policy consequences *or* of community reputation, this voter casts her vote or acts out her ethnic heritage purely out of a compulsion to express her feelings or preferences or self-image. But, as with art, expression is not mere solipsism. Rather, it relates to the understandings of other individuals; it occurs and has meaning in a social context. This suggests a third category of political action: the actions of the socially influenced, instrumental actor who votes in accordance with the expectations of her social group or mistreats out-group members in the way expected by in-group members, *in response* (in social-psychological terms) to the expectations of the group or *in order* (in rational-choice terms) to continue to enjoy the benefits of membership in the group. Such instrumental expression elides the original distinction entirely.

ABILITIES AND DISABILITIES OF RATIONAL CHOICE

The attempts surveyed here to model identity and expressive phenomena using rational-choice tools offer some important examples of what rational-choice theories can and cannot do. The theory is well adapted for some tasks often said to be beyond its purview, but it has limitations, probably inherent, that have seldom been noted by its critics. Rational choice's parsimony and portability, its ability to generate clear hypotheses from clear assumptions, and, of course, its full accounting of individual incentives makes it, at least at present, an indispensable part of the analytical arsenal of social science as a discipline. Yet it requires supplementation in order to give a full accounting of identity and expressive phenomena, as well as other features of social life.[19]

19. In view of a common misconception, I emphasize that it is not the object of rational-choice theorizing to show that human beings are rational maximizers of utility. Rationality is a simplifying assumption, and therefore is by definition false. It is nonsense to speak of "falsifying rational-choice theory." The assumption's justification must lie in its usefulness as compared with other available methods of theorizing. (One might, of course, falsify *a* rational-choice theory.)

SOCIAL BEHAVIOR OF RATIONAL ACTORS

Rational-choice theories rest on individual information and individual preferences. It is natural to suspect such theories of being inapplicable to inherently *social* processes, and many critics have expressed that suspicion.[20] However, the repeated-interaction models of game theory offer a representation of truly social phenomena that can be surprisingly nuanced, by focusing on the role of shared expectations. Moreover, the issue of other-regarding behavior is central to social theory, and seems, on the surface, to contradict the self-regarding nature of rational choice.[21] But every one of the rational-choice identity models cited—Overbye, Bawn, Hardin, Harvey, and Laitin—would generate considerable identity and expressive behavior (and could equally well generate other forms of cooperative behavior) even if the basic preferences of individuals were purely selfish and material. Of course, this does not prove that human motivation is selfish. It demonstrates, however, that the fact of other-regarding behavior is perfectly compatible with motivations that are selfish and material, but strategic. The point of modeling socially oriented behavior by the indirect mechanism of equilibrium cooperation in games, rather than by simply making the straightforward assumption of altruistic motivations, is to take advantage of the fact that the selfish-motivations approach generates cooperation under some conditions but not others and offers predictions about when cooperation is possible and when it must disappear. Simple altruism or identity expression hypotheses fail this basic test.

GENUINE LIMITATIONS ON RATIONAL-CHOICE THEORIES OF
IDENTITY AND EXPRESSION

This is not to say that a more-sophisticated non-self-interest or expression model could not ultimately generate superior hypotheses. Several substantial criticisms of self-interest models use the methods of classical rational choice and the related tools of evolutionary game theory to show how motivations contrary to self-interest could emerge and persist in an evolutionary setting.[22] These evolutionary models provide powerful tools for ap-

20. Accordingly Granovetter (1985) and Sen (1978), among many others, have argued that rational-choice theories present an inherently "undersocialized" model of human behavior; Elster (1989b) distinguishes between the instrumental behavior of rational actors and the norm-driven behavior of people in societies; C. Taylor (1971) argues that some goods and some motivations are "irreducibly social" and cannot be viewed in terms of individual preferences and decisions.

21. Many critiques of rational-choice and self-interest theories have looked at some instance of systematically other-regarding behavior and drawn the incorrect implication that individual motivation must therefore be inherently other regarding. This syllogism is made especially clear, for example, by Monroe (1996) and by most of the authors represented in Mansbridge (1990).

22. See, for example, Hamilton 1963, 1964 on kinship altruism, Frank 1988 on nonselfish behaviors, Boyd and Richerson 1985 on the conditions for true group

propriate alternative accounts of selfless-seeming social behavior. It is not hard to imagine how a similar evolutionary account of group identity behavior, or perhaps even true expressive motivations, might be constructed. However, thus far such models (with the notable exception of kinship altruism models) only portray very broad, generalized tendencies toward altruism, revenge seeking, aggression, or other general traits. As such, they offer little insight into the many instances where people act unselfishly, refrain from seeking revenge, or behave passively. Important work remains to be done in specifying the boundaries of selfishly rational and unselfish or irrational behavior from an evolutionary standpoint. In the meantime, game theoretic models offer a basis for the sometimes-yes, sometimes-no answer to "Will humans cooperate?" and related questions.

By allowing the possibility of a wide variety of group-oriented behavior, as well as selfish behavior, game theoretic models reflect anthropology's theme of "biological unity but social diversity." However, game theory (and rational choice generally) does little to specify anything about the form or content of norms or culture. To put it another way, game theory shows how various equilibrium patterns of cooperation could be maintained but says little about which of several equilibria will emerge. It expresses well the general nature of coordination, but it says little about exactly how coordination will be achieved.[23] This is a fundamental limitation of game theory as an analytical tool for social theory. Even given a perfect game theoretic model of some social or political interaction, to know how individuals will behave would also require empirical study or additional theoretical structure. Overbye and Bawn only show that systematic participation and ideology could be maintained in a setting of recurring interaction. They offer little guidance as to what patterns of behavior *will* arise, given initial conditions. Hardin and especially Harvey and Laitin use this sort of thinking in combination with historical, ethnographic, survey, and other empirical techniques to analyze real instances of group identity and expressive behavior. Such a combination of techniques is ultimately indispensable. Game theory proposes how observed phenomena might fit together, and thereby offers some predictions about other phenomena to look for and about how exogenous changes can sometimes require some sort of behavioral shift (such as when a falling discount factor renders repeated-game cooperation impossible). It seldom can offer any deterministic prediction of exactly what society will look like following an exogenous or policy change.

Game theory models, and by extension rational-choice models of other types, have a second and more fundamental limitation: they assume

---

selection for altruism, and Basu 1996 on the general difference between fitness and utility in the hawk-dove game.

23. For game theoretic treatments that nicely characterize this problem, see Fudenberg and Maskin 1986 on multiple equilibria in repeated games and games of asymmetric information and Crawford and Haller 1990 on coordination.

that, beyond perhaps some carefully specified and limited layer of incomplete information, all players are equally aware of what game they are playing. When a relevant social situation occurs, all participants unambiguously recognize it as an iteration or stage of a particular game, subject to a predetermined set of equilibrium expectations. Among the papers surveyed here, all the ones that use repeated-interaction reasoning to portray identity or expression, whether formally or informally, rely heavily on this assumption. Instances of voting choice or of intraethnic interaction are universally seen as such by all the participants, and all agree on what, if any, expression of identity is prescribed by existing norms.

In real life, however, any new political or social situation may be subject to a variety of interpretations fitting it into a variety of different equilibrium patterns. Every rational actor in every instance must ask herself: Of what repeated interaction is this new situation an iteration? In this sense, each such situation presents a *new* equilibrium selection, or coordination, problem for political actors to solve, not simply a new instance of a solved problem. Real political actors, faced with such situations, engage in argument, interpretation, and deliberation aimed at influencing the outcomes of those coordination problems.[24] This is the point at which political actors or social agitators can influence behavior. For example, ethnic violence can be created if it is successfully advertised by people who will benefit from it, such as ethnic political leaders or people who hope to gain some economic good through conflict. Or, ethnic conflict can be avoided if cooler heads prevail. And in either case, the outcome of the current situation affects future situations by providing a relevant precedent that may serve subsequently as a focal point or as rhetorical ammunition. This is an important mechanism by which group identity is created and ethnic conflict promoted or retarded.

Current choice theoretic tools are thus ill suited, at present, to deal with some very basic features of political life. Efforts at influencing interpretations are surely informed by strategic thinking, but seen in the context of solving new coordination problems, they occur outside any established equilibrium in the classic sense. Hermeneutical efforts such as discourse analysis seem to be the only tools presently available to address these processes, but as far as I am aware, these carry no systematic methods for the analysis of individual strategy.[25] Eventually, an effective analysis of identity and expression in politics will depend on our making some connection between, if not indeed a coherent synthesis of, rational choice and such interpretive methods.

24. For a discussion of the theoretical issues that arise, from a rational-choice standpoint, due to this ambiguity, see Calvert and Johnson 1999.

25. Indeed, the seminal approach of Habermas (1984) begins with a fundamental distinction between "communicative and strategic action." On the use of discourse analysis for general purposes of empirical political research, see, for example, Dryzek and Berejikian 1993.

Thomas Risse

Constructivism and International Institutions: Toward Conversations across Paradigms[1]

■ | Introduction

Institutionalism as a theoretical approach can be differentiated from other approaches in international relations in terms of the substantive claim that institutions matter, that is, that they exert clearly identifiable and independent effects on political life. The various institutionalisms can then be distinguished according to which type of effects they ascribe to political and other institutions (see Hall and Taylor 1996; Aspinwall and Schneider 2000; Keohane 1989). Institutions might constrain behavior, but they might also influence preferences or even constitute identities. Rationalist institutionalism follows a logic of consequentialism. In contrast, constructivist insights in the study of international institutions focus on a logic of appropriateness in terms of rule-guided behavior and the enactment of cultural scripts, on the one hand, and a logic of arguing emphasizing deliberative and communicative processes, on the other.

This essay emphasizes insights which social constructivism brings to the study of international institutions. Yet, rationalist and constructivist institutionalisms do not constitute either-or propositions but complement each other to a considerable extent. In this sense then, the essay is a plea for conversations across paradigms rather than continued trench warfare. It is also an appeal for problem- rather than paradigm-driven research on international institutions. There are enough empirical puzzles in the real world to be tackled to keep us busy for the years to come.

The essay starts with clarifying metatheoretical assumptions behind ra-

1. For critical and very helpful comments on the draft, I thank Tanja Börzel, Ron Jepperson, Ira Katznelson, Bob Keohane, Helen Milner, Kathryn Sikkink, and an anonymous reviewer.

tionalist and constructivist institutionalisms. I then concentrate on substantive issues in the life cycle of international institutions, in particular the emergence and change of international norms and institutions, on the one hand, and their impact on (domestic) political life in terms of rule compliance, on the other. I conclude with remarks on the complementarity as well as the remaining differences between rationalist and constructivist institutionalisms.

■ | Institutionalism and International Relations: Theoretical Departures

Rationalism and Constructivism: What's the Difference?

There is considerable confusion on what precisely is at stake in recent controversies between rational choice and social constructivism (for a thorough discussion see Fearon and Wendt 2002). First, neither rational choice nor constructivism represents a *substantive* theory of international relations on the same level as, say, realism, liberalism, Marxism, or the various institutionalisms. While most realists and Marxists subscribe to a rationalist ontology, neither liberal theorizing about domestic politics and international relations nor arguments about the impact of international institutions are confined to either rational choice or constructivism. Rational choice and constructivism are metatheoretical approaches to the study of social reality rather than substantive theories of international relations.

Second, some have argued that constructivists use interpretive or historical methods based on a postpositivist epistemology, while rational choice sticks to (neo-) positivism using formal modeling or large-n quantitative studies as their preferred methods. This claim is difficult to sustain. Rationalist and constructivist scholars use quantitative as well as qualitative methods (for large-n studies informed by a constructivist ontology see the Stanford school of sociological institutionalism, e.g., Boli and Thomas 1998, 1999; for formal modeling work using interpretive methods see Bates, Greif, Levi, Rosenthal, and Weingast 1998). The main controversies on methodological and epistemological questions are increasingly taking place within constructivism itself (see, e.g., Adler 1997; Price and Reus-Smit 1998; Hollis and Smith 1990; Laffey and Weldes 1997; Milliken 1999; Wiener 2001) as well as between the latter and various postmodern approaches (Walker 1993; Der Derian 1995; Albert 1994). Debates within constructivism center around the questions of to what extent conventional methodologies focusing on causal explanations are suitable to understand intersubjective meanings, what distinguishes causal from constitutive explanations, and to what degree we can strive for middle-range theories and generalizations across time and space. The debate between constructivism and postmodernist thinking concerns more fundamentally the possibility of making truth claims and of being able to adjudicate among competing claims. The following discussion brackets the debate on methodological and epistemological questions, because I want to concentrate on the substantive contribution of constructivist approaches to our understanding of international institutions.

Finally, it is misleading to claim that rational choice inherently assumes that humans are self-interested egoists striving to achieve material gains, while actors hold altruistic preferences informed by moral values and ideas in constructivist accounts. Rational actors can be power maximizers, need satisficers, or altruists. Many ideational accounts are compatible with an instrumentally rational logic of action. Principled and causal beliefs, even collective identities (see Calvert's contribution to this volume; also Fearon and Laitin 2000; Goldstein and Keohane 1993), can enter the utility functions of actors, affect cost-benefit calculations, and influence strategic interactions themselves.

So, what then is the difference between rational choice and constructivism (see also Fearon and Wendt 2002; Adler 2002)? First, rational choice is based on methodological individualism according to which "[t]he elementary unit of social life is the individual human action" (Elster 1989a, 13). In contrast, constructivists insist that human agents do not exist independently from their social environment and its collectively shared systems of meanings (culture in a broad sense). The fundamental insight of the structure-agency debate is not only that social structures and agents are mutually codetermined. The crucial point is that social constructivists insist on the mutual *constitutiveness* of (social) structures and agents (Adler 1997, 324–25; Wendt 1999, ch. 4). The social environment in which we find ourselves, defines ("constitutes") who we are, our identities as social beings. At the same time, human agency creates, reproduces, and changes culture through our daily practices. In sum, social constructivism occupies a—sometimes uneasy—ontological middleground between individualism and structuralism by claiming that there are properties of structures and of agents which cannot be collapsed into each other.

Second, it follows that constructivism points to the *constitutive* role of social structures including norms instead of just concentrating on the causal effects of the social environment on actors (Onuf 1989; Kratochwil 1989; Wendt 1999). Many social norms not only regulate behavior, they also constitute the identity of actors. The norm of sovereignty not only regulates the interactions of states in international affairs, it also defines what a state *is* in the first place. Human rights norms not only protect citizens from state intervention; they also (and increasingly) define what it means to be a civilized state in the modern international community. Constructivists concentrate on the social identities of actors in order to account for their interests (e.g., Wendt 1999, esp. ch. 7; Lapid and Kratochwil 1996a; R. Hall 1999; Conin 1999; Reus-Smit 1997; various contributions in Katzenstein 1996b). Constructivism insists that collective norms and understandings define the basic rules of the game in which they find themselves in their interactions (Wendt 1999, 25, 287; Kratochwil 1989, 26). This does not mean that constitutive norms cannot be violated or never change. But the argument implies that we cannot even describe the properties of social agents without reference to the social structure in which they are embedded. I will comment below on the consequences of this insight for the study of international institutions.

Another useful way to distinguish between rational choice and social constructivism concerns the emphasis on different logics of social action and interaction or on different rationalities.[2] Rational choice emphasizes instrumental rationality, while constructivism focusses on rule-guided behavior, on the one hand, and communicative rationality, on the other.

Three Rationalities: The Logics of Consequentialism, Appropriateness, and Arguing

A driver stops at a red light located in a dark forest at three o'clock at night. Three interpretations describe what happened. According to the first story, the driver notices the red light, looks around, and checks whether another vehicle is approaching or whether a police car is somewhere hidden behind the trees. Since she is risk-averse, she stops. According to the second account, the driver stops, because this is what one ought to do in front of a red light. A third story claims that the driver faces a conflictual situation. On the one hand, she would like to get home as soon as possible, because a sick child is waiting for her. On the other hand, she knows that running a red light violates a social rule and if everybody did that . . . As a result of this reasoning process, she stops.

Each story emphasizes a different logic of social action (see Risse 2000, 2–7, for the following). The first account follows a logic of consequentialism (March and Olsen 1989, 1998) which is the domain of rational choice. Agents enact given identities and interests and try to realize their preferences through strategic behavior. The goal of action is to maximize or to optimize one's interests and preferences.

The second account emphasizes a logic of appropriateness: "Human actors are imagined to follow rules that associate particular identities to particular situations, approaching individual opportunities for action by assessing similarities between current identities and choice dilemmas and

---

2. It has become common in U.S.-dominated political science to reserve the term *rationality* for rational choice. This has led some scholars to mistakenly assume that social constructivism somehow deals with the "irrational" aspects of political life. Instead, rationality should not be confined to strategic-instrumental behavior.

more general concepts of self and situations" (March and Olsen 1998, 951). Rule-guided behavior differs from strategic and instrumental behavior in that actors try to do the right thing rather than maximize, or optimize, their given preferences. The driver in the second story does not calculate her interests or preferences but simply stops at the red light, because this is what society expects from her in such a situation, as she learned twenty years ago during her driving lessons. The logic of appropriateness entails that actors try to figure out the appropriate rule in a given social situation. Normative rationality implies constitutive effects of social norms and institutions, since these rules not only regulate behavior, that is, have causal effects, but also define social identities ("good citizens stop at red lights"). Normative rationality also entails socialization effects. A Martian would drive right through, because he does not know the rule. Norm-guided behavior requires at least knowledge of the rule and some internalization of the knowledge.

Most of the controversy between rational choice and constructivism has focussed on the relationship between the logic of consequentialism and the logic of appropriateness, at least in North American international relations. This debate has overlooked that constructivism actually encompasses at least two modes of social interaction. In many social situations, actors regularly comply with norms which they have internalized and which they take for granted. In the second story, the driver did not even think about whether to stop at the red light. While strategic behavior is explicitly goal oriented and intentional, the "taken for grantedness" of norm-regulated behavior implies that enacting the norm does not need to be a conscious process. In this case, the social structure of norms exerts its effects on actors almost directly, since actors know what is expected of them and what constitutes appropriate behavior. The logic of appropriateness does not imply that actors approve of the social norms, only that they know about and have internalized them. This version of a logic of appropriateness, which is rather widespread in the constructivist literature, emphasizes structure over agency.

But March and Olsen (1989, 1998) also mention rule-guided behavior as a conscious process whereby actors have to figure out the situation in which they act, apply the appropriate norm, or choose among conflicting rules. In the third story, the driver is faced with two conflicting norms of appropriateness. One ought to stop at a red light, even at three at night. But parents also are supposed to look after a sick child. The internalization of norms does not help in this situation. Strategic calculation does not help, either, when actors are confronted with conflicting norms and preferences are unclear. The more the norms are conflicting or contested, the less the logic of the situation can be captured by the statement "good people do X" but by "what does 'good' mean in this situation?" or even "what is the right thing to do?" But how do actors adjudicate which norm applies? They reason (even if this deliberation takes place in one person's head, as in the third story). Social constructivism not only encompasses the logic of appropriateness, but also a logic of truth seeking or arguing. Arguing implies that actors try to challenge the validity claims inherent in any causal or normative statement and to seek a communicative consensus about their understanding of a situation as well as justifications for the principles and norms guiding their action. Argumentative rationality means that the participants in a discourse are open to be persuaded by the better argument and that relationships of power and social hierarchies recede in the background (Habermas 1981; Müller 1994; Checkel 2001; Risse 2000). Argumentative and deliberative behavior is as goal oriented as strategic interactions; however, the goal is not to attain one's fixed preferences but to seek a reasoned consensus. As Keohane (2001, 10) put it, persuasion "involves changing people's choices of alternatives independently of their calculations about the strategies of other players". Actors' interests, preferences, and perceptions of the situation are no longer fixed but subject to discursive challenges. Where argumentative rationality prevails, actors do not seek to maximize or to satisfy their given interests and preferences but to challenge and to justify the validity claims inherent in them—*and* are prepared to change their views of the world or even their interests in light of the better argument. In other words, argumentative and discursive processes challenge the truth claims which are inherent in identities, interests, and norms.

What distinguishes the three logics of action identified here? While I took an agency-centered perspective to introduce the three logics, this should not be confused with methodological individualism identified with rational choice. The logic of appropriateness in particular makes no sense, unless we assume constitutive effects of social structures and norms on social agents. If taken to the extremes, this version of social constructivism becomes overly structuralist. Actors are reduced to social automatons enacting rules or overly socialized agents who deeply believe in the validity of social norms.

As a result, a constructivist account that takes the mutual constitutiveness of structures and agency seriously, encompasses not only rule-guided behavior but also a mode of social interaction that allows to challenge the norms and rules themselves, thereby "bringing agency back in." I suggest, therefore, that an emphasis on arguing represents a more agency centered version of constructivism. Challenging truth claims and the validity of norms and rules constitutes a possibility for actors to change these social structures through a reasoned consensus rather than simply reproducing them. Still, argumentative rationality presupposes intersubjectivity, that is, once again, the embeddedness of actors in a social environment.

While the emphasis on agency in the logic of arguing brings this mode of interaction closer to rational choice, it represents a different form of agency. Instrumentally rational actors know what they want and try to realize their interests and preferences in light of their knowledge of other actors' interests and preferences. Thus, they strategize, bargain, or signal in social interactions. They might recalculate their strategies in light of the other actors' responses, but the purpose of the action remains to optimize or maximize one's expected utilities. In arguing mode, however, actors' preferences, interests, and even identities are endogenized insofar as they are subject to challenges and counterchallenges. Actors following a logic of argumentative rationality engage in truth-seeking behavior and strive to achieve a reasoned consensus. In contrast to consequentialism, truth-seeking behavior brackets one's interests or preferences.

Of course, all three logics of social action represent ideal types. In reality, they often mix and it is hard to identify the dominant logic. In the story of the driver in front of the red light, for example, the observable behavior is consistent with each of the three accounts. More important, real actors often behave according to several logics of social action. In bargaining situations, for example, instrumentally rational actors routinely use arguments in order to convince *others* that their interests and preferences in fact can be justified in terms of the common good. But even strategic arguing or rhetorical action (Schimmelfennig 1997, 2000) requires that actors follow the rules of argumentative rationality. Instrumentally rational actors have to give reasons for the validity of their preferences if they want to persuade others. Of course, these reasons can then be challenged by other speakers in the public sphere. If speakers want to remain credible in such discussions, they must reply with another round of reasoning, while bargaining threats or promises are considered inappropriate. Thus, instrumentally rational speakers tend to entrap themselves in the logic of argumentative rationality, even if they had no intention to enter a true dialogue to begin with (Risse 1999).

There are also many social situations in which the logic of consequentialism and the logic of appropriateness mix. If we assume that social approval constitutes a basic desire of human beings, following rules of appropriate behavior enters the utility functions of instrumentally rational actors. At this point, the difference between the first and the second accounts of the driver's motives might become minute and rational choice could then model under which conditions the desire for social approval trumps more narrowly selfish interests, and vice versa. Of course, constructivists would point out that the desire for social approval as basic human interest is ultimately irreconcilable with methodological individualism, since it inherently constitutes human beings as *social animals* embedded in society. In other words, the logic of appropriateness would enter cost-benefit calculations of utility-maximizing actors by defining in the first place what constitutes costs and what constitutes benefits. Moreover, the imagery of human action adopted here is still one of a calculating machine whereas constructivists would emphasize the "taken for grantedness" of social rules and obligations. Ultimately, however, the difference between the two metatheoretical approaches is one of emphasis on a continuum of social action rather than a sharp and easily discernible distinction.

Constructivism and the Study of International Institutions

Let me now turn to the constructivist approach to the study of international institutions. Before proceeding, we need to define some crucial terms. There are at least as many definitions of (international) institutions as there are theoretical perspectives. In the following, I use the term *international institution* in the sense of *relatively stable collections of communicative practices and rules defining appropriate behavior for specific groups of actors in specific situations of international life*. This definition follows and amends March and Olsen (1998, 308) which goes beyond the widespread understanding of international institutions as patterned rules structures (e.g., Keohane 1989, 3) by including communicative practices, while leaving the question of rule-consistent behavior outside the definition.

Following the conventions in institutionalist research, *international regimes* would then be those institutional arrangements that meet the explicit-rules test. One should not restrict the concept of international regimes to agreements among *states*, but include "private" international regimes (Cutler, Haufler, and Porter 1999). Finally, international *organizations*—both interstate and nongovernmental—are international institutions with a "street address," that is, with specific role assignments to individuals and groups and with the capacity to act independently (Rittberger 1994).

The original regime definition distinguished between principles, norms, rules, and decision-making procedures with increasing degrees of specificity from the first to the last (Krasner 1983, 2). In the meantime, norms and rules are used almost interchangeably in the literature. There is general agreement that norms are "standards of appropriate behavior for actors with a given identity" (Jepperson, Wendt, and Katzenstein 1996, 54). In other words, there is an inherent intersubjective quality to norms: "We only know what is appropriate by reference to the judgements of a community or a society" (Finnemore and Sikkink 1998, 252; see also Kratochwil and Ruggie 1986). If norms are standards of appropriate behavior in the sense of "Good people do X," rules specify these norms and apply them to particular situations as "specific prescriptions or proscriptions for action" (Krasner 1983, 2). They usually take the form of "Do X in order to get Y" (Fearon 1997). Social norms and rules are shared by a collectivity, while principled beliefs can be held by individuals. Of course, this immediately raises the question of when a norm becomes a norm rather than individual beliefs about right or wrong. Communicative practices are key to the definition of when principled beliefs become collectively shared norms.

I now proceed by specifying further how constructivism approaches the study of international institutions in contrast to rational choice. Following a logic of consequentialism, *neoliberal institutionalism* or rationalist regime analysis has convincingly shown against various versions of realism that "cooperation under anarchy" is possible and that narrowly self-interested actors can achieve stable and enduring cooperation and overcome collective action dilemmas (Keohane 1984, 1989; Oye 1986a; Zürn 1992; see Martin and Simmons 1998). The main point was to establish that we do not have to assume altruistic interests or the presence of a hegemonic power with vastly superior resources to explain international cooperation. Rationalist institutionalism employs a rather "thin" understanding of institutional effects. They are mostly confined to influencing the *behavior* and policies (preferences over strategies) of actors, while the underlying interests (preferences over outcomes) or identities remain outside and are exogenized. The principal imagery in this understanding of international institutions is one of constraining behavior by affecting cost-benefit calculations of actors and their strategies.

Beginning in the mid-1980s, rationalist institutionalism came under attack from the emerging constructivist thinking in international relations. This literature originated intellectually from the so-called Grotian tradition and notions of an international society of states as a social context in which governments operate (see, e.g., the English school in international relations theory, Bull 1977). These scholars shared the institutionalist mantra that international cooperation matters but disagreed with rational choice on metatheoretical assumptions. As Ruggie and Kratochwil pointed out, the "emphasis on convergent expectations as the constitutive basis of regimes gives regimes an inescapable intersubjective quality. It follows that we *know* regimes by their principled and shared understandings of desirable and acceptable forms of social behavior. Hence, the ontology of regimes rests upon a strong element of intersubjectivity" (Kratochwil and Ruggie 1986, 764). In other words, they argued that the logic of appropriateness is inescapable when theorizing about international institutions.

Constructivist institutionalism then adopts a "thick" understanding of international institutions as social structures deeply embedding actors such as states. International institutions matter not only in terms of constraining and regulating actors' behavior and strategies. They also constitute these actors in the sense that they define their identities and interests. Corporate actors such as nation-states do not even exist outside social structures and institutions such as sovereignty. Institutions provide the social norms and rules enabling social interaction in the international realm in the first place. An emerging empirical literature inspired by constructivist reasoning focusses on such constitutive institutions in international life. Constructivists emphasize, for example, the mutually constitutive relationship between states as agents and sovereignty as a constitutive norm of the international system: "States define the meaning of sovereignty through their engagement in practices of mutual recognition, practices that define both themselves and each other. At the same time, the mutual recognition of claims of sovereignty is an important element in the definition of the state itself" (Biersteker 2002, 57; Biersteker and Weber 1996). Hall adds to this a study of the transformation of collective identities from territorially based to nation-based sovereignty as constitutive principles of the nineteenth- and twentieth-century international system (R. Hall 1999). Following Wendt's famous dictum that "anarchy is what states make of it" (Wendt 1992), constructivist institutionalists have looked at broad institutional arrangements that are based on a collective identity of its members, in particular security communities (Adler and Barnett 1998; Cronin 1999; also Reus-Smit 1997). This and other work does not focus on specific international regimes but on constitutive norms and arrangements in international life providing actors such as states with a knowledge structure of appropriate behavior which enables their interactions in the first place.

Constructivist institutionalism has so far interpreted the logic of appropriateness in two ways to provide an account of how international norms acquire their "taken for grantedness." The first account emphasizes socialization processes. Actors including corporate actors and organizations become acquainted with new international norms through processes of social learning as a result of which they acquire new interests and identities. When they accept the validity of the norms and their policy prescriptions as binding, they have internalized them in a socialization process (Finnemore and Sikkink 1998, 902; Checkel 1999). In the more extreme versions of this argument, actors have to actively endorse the new norms and to believe in the validity of its prescriptive status to make the norm binding.

In contrast, sociological institutionalism as understood by Meyer and his colleagues (e.g., Meyer, Boli, and Thomas 1987; Meyer et al. 1997) emphasizes institutions as providing cultural scripts and downplays the autonomy of individual actors. Nation-states are seen as "embedded in a world polity and culture, and the common cultural contents and trends of these states are sought" (Jepperson 2000, 4). Actors follow these scripts and take them for granted as social facts, because they know about them, not necessarily because they believe in them. If socialization plays a role at all, it is about acquiring social knowledge rather than about endorsing the validity of social norms.

What does the logic of arguing add to these understandings of international institutions? First, arguing and persuasion provide micromechanisms for socialization and social learning, irrespective of whether this learning is about acquiring new social knowledge and skills or about getting socialized in the validity of an international norm. Second, an emphasis on arguing sheds light on processes of norm change. Third, a focus on deliberative processes improves our understandings of institutional effects. Institutions do not just reduce transaction costs or provide rules of appropriate behavior. They also serve as discourse arenas enabling deliberative processes geared toward problem solving. They do so by establishing relationships of trust among actors which are deemed crucial for processes of communicative persuasion and consensus seeking. In Habermasian terms, institutions provide a "common lifeworld," a common set of references and of experiences to which actors can relate in their communicative interactions.

Toward Conversations between Rationalist and Constructivist Institutionalisms

International institutions as constraining actors' behavior, as constituting interests and identities, or as discourse arenas for problem solving—are these three images incompatible and mutually exclusive? Here, we need to distinguish the analytical from the empirical level. Analytically speaking, strategic-instrumental behavior, rule following out of a logic of appropriateness, and arguing in terms of challenging truth claims need to be kept separate, since they emphasize different logics of action and interaction. On the empirical level, however, things start to blur. Actors in the real world regularly apply the different logics in their behavior. We also find many institutionalist arguments in the literature which combine elements of the three social logics. This holds true for historical institutionalism (and its varieties; see contribution by Pierson and Skocpol) and for actor-centered institutionalism (Scharpf 1997). The question then becomes *which* social logic of interaction is likely to prevail in which situation and under what conditions. Following March and Olsen, a clear logic should dominate an unclear one (1998, 952–53). The more uncertain actors' preferences are, the more we would expect movement from the logic of consequentialism to arguing and rule-guided behavior. Moreover, one logic of action might incorporate another under certain circumstances. Strategic constructions or rhetorical action, for example, follow an instrumentally rational logic, but are embedded in and validated by the logics of appropriateness and of arguing. Finally, the different logics might follow each other sequentially. For example, tough distributional bargaining is only possible if a prior consensus has been established through a reasoning process concerning the definition of the situation and rules of fairness ("common knowledge" assumption in noncooperative game theory).

The institutionalist literature has evolved to the point where similar empirical anomalies are theorized by different institutional theories which should lead to conversations across metatheoretical commitments. Let me discuss three examples. First, both rationalist and sociological versions of institutionalism theorize about path-dependent processes. Pierson explains why particular institutional solutions are often unpredictable and why political institutions are locked in despite growing inefficiency. Increasing return processes are self-reinforcing, because "the relative benefits of the current activity compared with other possible options increase over time" and the "costs of exit . . . rise" (Pierson 2000a, 252). Pierson's starting point is rational, utility-maximizing actors, but institutional structures increasingly affect and narrow down their range of choices, irrespective of the efficiency of institutional solutions. Thus, he criticizes functionalist accounts of institution building and the assumption that institutions are created to serve some particular purpose. Even if they did originally, they might survive for quite some time because of positive feedback loops and self-reinforcing processes.

It remains unclear, how far away this argument is from the "taken for grantedness" of social norms emphasized by sociological institutionalism. As DiMaggio and Powell put it, "sociologists concur with rational-choice scholars that technical interdependence and physical sunk costs are partly responsible for institutional inertia. But these are not the only, or the most important, factors. Institutionalized arrangements are reproduced because individuals often cannot even conceive of appropriate alternatives . . ." (DiMaggio and Powell 1991a, 10–11). This sociological account of path-dependent processes emphasizes that institutions embody cultural understandings and scripts which actors reproduce in their daily practices and thereby transmit to other actors. Both accounts of path-dependent processes emphasize "inefficient histories" (March and Olsen 1998, 957–58) in the sense that institutions survive irrespective of whether they serve some useful and functional purpose. The two accounts differ, however, with regard to the causal mechanisms by which path-dependent processes are kept moving. Sociological institutionalism emphasizes cultural understandings and the "taken for grantedness" of social norms, while the more rationalist version of historical institutionalism focuses on sunk costs and, thus, implies that institutional solutions affect the cost-benefit calculations of actors. We need a conversation between the two interpretations in order to figure out more precisely where they differ. Moreover, we also need empirical indicators which differentiate between the two accounts. Last but not least, both accounts emphasize continuity and, if taken to the extremes, institutional determinism at the expense of institutional change and conflict.

The second example concerns the difference between the "taken for grantedness" of social norms or the enactment of cultural scripts, on the one hand, and arguments about "bounded rationality" (Simon 1982; review in Odell forthcoming), on the other. "People act not on the basis of objective reality but on the basis of perceived reality and of assumed cause-and-effect relationships operating in the world they perceive" (Scharpf 1997, 19). Scharpf's actor-centered institutionalism takes care of cognitions including orientations toward socially appropriate behavior. If we add to this that meaning structures may be shared intersubjectively and that people may deliberate about the appropriate course of action under given circumstances, we enter the logics of appropriateness and of arguing and, thus, of social constructivism, as discussed above. If the "boundedness" of bounded rationality has to do with collectively shared meaning structures, that is, is a property of social structure in which actors are embedded, a conversation with constructivism should be possible. Unfortunately, as Odell points out, most empirical work on the international political economy pays some lip service to bounded rationality and incomplete information but then proceeds with limiting utility functions to narrowly defined selfish interests under complete information (Odell forthcoming). At the same time, constructivists who take the mutual constitutiveness of structure and agency seriously, need to theorize choice situations, unless their actors become so structurally determined that they do nothing but enact social scripts and cultural norms (on this point, see Finnemore 1996b; Checkel 1998). At the end of the day, the difference between constructivists, emphasizing social structure and the inherent intersubjective quality of norms, and rationalists, accepting the inherent boundedness of rationality, might be overstated *if* the latter agree that the limitations on unrestricted rationality stem not only from limited capacities of individuals to process information but also from their embeddedness in a society and social culture.

The last example concerns the controversy about causal versus constitutive effects of political institutions. Rationalist institutionalism starts with the constraining effects of institutions on actors' choices and focuses on the regulatory impact of institutions. Institutions can also effect actors' strategies or policies to achieve certain goals (preferences over strategies, see Calvert's contribution).[3] We enter the realm of constitutive effects, the more we assume that institutions influence actors' interests (preferences over outcomes) and identities. It is here where many authors see the main dividing line between rationalist institutionalism, on the one hand, and historical, sociological, or constructivist institutionalism, on the other (Thelen and Steinmo 1992, 8; DiMaggio and Powell 1991a, 9). If this is true, a nice division of labor between the two institutionalisms could emerge. Constructivists would be in charge of explaining actors' preferences, while rationalist approaches would explain how agents act on the basis of these preferences. Introducing the logic of arguing already makes clear that things are not that simple and that there is an alternative to the rational choice logic of agency. Arguing assumes a mode of interaction where preferences are no longer fixed but subject to challenges and coun-

---

3. It is often very difficult to decide which preferences over strategies are in contrast to more deep seated interests (preferences over outcomes). Ultimate desires such as survival, welfare, or love do not get us very far in explaining the strategies or behavior that actors might choose to achieve them. See Powell's contribution in this volume on this point.

terchallenges and where the action orientation is no longer to attain one's own interests but to reach a reasoned consensus. More important, the logic of appropriateness implies that social institutions not only constitute actors' identities and interests but also affect their behavior enacting these identities.

Yet, it is hard empirically to differentiate between the regulatory and the constitutive effects of social norms. As Tannenwald points out, most social norms both regulate and constitute (1999, 437). Human rights, for example, regulate the behavior of governments toward their citizens, but they also define what it means to be a member in good standing of international society rather than a pariah state. But how do we know constitutive effects when we see them? Constructivist scholarship has not developed far toward an accepted methodology of how to discern constitutive effects of social norms. In particular, there is sometimes a tendency to overestimate the constitutive effects of norms. If everything constitutes, nothing does. Does the rule to drive on the right side of the street in the United States and in continental Europe "constitute" actors, or does it simply regulate traffic? Moreover, measuring rule-consistent behavior as such does not get us far, because it does not differentiate between regulatory and constitutive effects. Krasner's argument (1999) about sovereignty as "organized hypocrisy" is based on a strong "decoupling" of states' paying lip service to sovereignty as constitutive for the international system and of their behavior violating the norm. This implies that we need to take a closer look at communicative practices in order to discern whether social norms constitute actors or merely regulate their behavior. The more actors refer to the norms when defining and describing who they are and the more outsiders to the community also describe it in those terms, the more these self-descriptions are shared by the wider community to which the actors refer and the more we have probably found constitutive norms.

In sum, rationalist and constructivist approaches do not seem to be that far apart. There is ample room for conversations across theoretical and seemingly insurmountable paradigmatic boundaries. This becomes even more obvious when we look at empirical contributions to the study of international institutions.

■ | Explaining the Emergence of International Institutions

The starting puzzle of rationalist institutionalism in international relations has been to explain why and under what conditions instrumentally rational actors (mostly states) holding egoistic and at least partly conflicting preferences nevertheless cooperate (overviews in Martin and Simmons 1998; Hasenclever, Mayer, and Rittberger 1997, ch. 3). International regime analysis took off in the United States and elsewhere during the early 1980s and quickly became a major field of application for noncooperative game theory specifying the conditions under which coordination and collaboration were possible to produce public goods or to avoid mutually undesired outcomes (e.g., Oye 1986a; Stein 1990; Hasenclever, Mayer, and Rittberger 1997; Zürn 1992).

In the meantime, constructivist institutionalism emerged and has developed into a "clear reflective research program" (Keohane 1989, 173). We can now distinguish two accounts from sociological or constructivist institutionalism on the emergence of international institutions. The first emphasizes preexisting social structures, be they domestic or international, and uses an imagery of institutional imitation and diffusion, while the second is more agency centered and uses an imagery of entrepreneurship and persuasion.

On the more structuralist side, the Stanford school of sociological institutionalism has probably done most to advance an empirical research program that systematically shows the emergence of an international social structure or world culture which has deeply affected national practices from science and education to social security (survey in Jepperson 2000). Why is it that elementary school curricula around the world feature mathematics even in countries that lack teachers with the adequate knowledge? Meyer and his colleagues view this and other phenomena as an ongoing process of modernity and rationalization whereby Western cultural standards diffuse on a worldwide scale and serve as scripts to be downloaded in domestic institutions (Thomas et al. 1987; Boli and Thomas 1998; Meyer et al. 1997). The dispersal of these cultural values works through mimetic imitation and through incorporation of environmental structures, that is, the incremental and unintended adaptation by which organizations map environmental features into their own structures (see DiMaggio and Powell 1991b). This account strictly employs the logic of appropriateness whereby it is irrelevant whether the rules actually serve some functional or useful purpose ("inefficient history"; see March and Olsen 1998, 314–15). Less structuralist, Finnemore explored in more detail how international organizations such as the U.N. Educational, Scientific, and Cultural Organization, the International Red Cross, and the World Bank serve as agents of norm change shaping state interests and preferences in various issue areas of international relations (Finnemore 1996a).

This and other work shows that new international institutions are rarely created from scratch but are usually embedded in or evolve from previous institutional arrangements. Price demonstrated, for example, that the norm against the use of chemical weapons emerged out of a particular and rather restrictive provision of the 1899 Hague Declaration, which was later broadened in various international agreements (Price 1997). New norms and new institutional arrangements need to resonate with preexisting rules and arrangements in order to survive. The evolution and embeddedness of new norms from and in existing institutions must not relate to the international system; they can also refer to domestic rules and institutions. Klotz showed, for example, that the international norm against apartheid originated from U.S. civil rights struggles leading to the domestic institutionalization of the norm of racial equality (Klotz 1995). Tannenwald's argument about the (informal) norm of no first use of nuclear weapons parallels Price's claim about the chemical weapons taboo, but the origins of the norm can be found in the U.S. domestic context and were internationalized later (Tannenwald 1999). Risse-Kappen argued that the transatlantic security community with distinctive rules of consultation represents an externalization of the domestic norms of mutual respect which characterize liberal democracies and, thus, the domestic structures of the members of the community (Risse-Kappen 1995).

This research mostly uses a backward-looking design whereby newly emerging norms are traced back to their origins in preexisting institutions (Scharpf 1997, 26). Post hoc historical accounts of the origins of new norms are fairly common in this literature. While rationalist institutionalism brackets actors' preferences and, thus, leaves the origins of mixed-motive games unexplained, constructivists' emphasis on the endogeneity of interests has often produced narratives with little generalizability. Constructivist work has only started to develop testable propositions about under which conditions new norms and institutions emerge out of which preexisting arrangements. To do so, we need to bring agency back into the picture.

Agency-centered work from a constructivist perspective typically focuses on "moral entrepreneurship" (Nadelmann 1990), in particular norm-promoting agents such as domestic public interest groups, epistemic communities, or transnational advocacy networks. Epistemic communities are networks of actors with an authoritative claim to knowledge and a normative agenda (Haas 1992). The literature on epistemic communities emphasizes cognitive processes such as learning (Adler and Haas 1992). Haas and others argue that such knowledge-based communities are the more influential, the higher the uncertainty about cause-and-effect relationships in the particular issue area among policymakers, the higher the consensus among the scientists involved, and the more scientific advice is institutionalized in the policymaking process.

Transnational advocacy networks are those relevant actors working internationally on an issue, who are bound together by shared values, a common discourse, and dense exchanges of information and services (Keck and Sikkink 1998). While epistemic communities are knowledge based, the primary characteristic of advocacy networks are shared principled beliefs. Typical examples include global networks in the human rights areas, women's rights groups, or networks and International Non-Governmental Organizations (INGOs) in the environmental sector. Keck and Sikkink argued that advocacy networks effect norm creation processes in various stages of international policymaking, such as issue creation and agenda setting, and that they influence discursive positions of states and international organizations, institutional procedures, and policy change (Keck and Sikkink 1998, 25). Empirical research in such diverse issue areas as human rights, environment, and international security (see, e.g., Keck and Sikkink 1998; Price 1998; Princen and Finger 1994; overview in Risse 2002) has singled out the agenda setting phase as particularly conducive for the impact of advocacy networks but also prenegotiations when national governments try to figure out their position in multilateral negotiations. Nonstate actors are less likely to influence actual negotiating processes, unless they are directly represented at the bargaining table, as is increasingly the case in many international governance institutions (O'Brien et al. 2000). This research has identified the following conditions under which transnational networks are likely to have an impact on international norm creation:

- Network characteristics such as density, material resources, and organizational capacities but also ideational resources such as moral authority combined with legitimate claims to knowledge

- Characteristics of the campaign targets, such as their vulnerability to both material and normative pressures

- Characteristics of the institutional environment (both domestic and international) in which the advocacy networks operate and which determine both their access to political actors and their ability to form winning coalitions

While these conditions determine which norm-promoting agents are successful or fail, empirical work in this area often suffers from a selection bias. We know mostly about cases in which advocacy networks and epistemic communities were able to influence state preferences and international negotiations. We know far less about failed campaigns.

Most recently, agency-centered constructivism has started developing complex models of international norm creation and institutional change combining all three logics of social action specified above. Take the norm life cycle model developed by Finnemore and Sikkink. During the phase of norm emergence, norm entrepreneurs typically link the rules they advocate to preexisting consensual norms or challenge the existing rules of *appropriateness* (1998, 254–65). By framing and reframing issues, however, they engage in strategic constructions and, thus, act according to the logic of *consequentialism*. The successful use of these strategic constructions largely depends on their ability to change the views and sometimes even interests of their targets or of some third-party audiences. Since transnational advocacy networks usually do not command material resources, their strategic constructions need to be persuasive. In other words, the logic of *arguing* enters the scene here. The ultimate success of strategic constructions depends on their persuasiveness with an audience and, thus, the "power of the better arguments." Once a sufficient number of (materially and ideationally) powerful actors have become convinced of the validity of the new norm, it reaches prescriptive status in international society and, thus, defines the new logic of appropriateness. At this point, a "norm cascade" sets in. This model provides an example of combining the three logics of action proposed by rational choice and constructivism in a time sequence. The logic of consequentialism prevails when norm entrepreneurs challenge an existing logic of appropriateness. Yet, they must make a persuasive case in order to convince others of the validity of the promoted norms. Here, the logic of arguing takes over. Once the tipping point of a norms cascade is reached, we (re-) enter the realm of rule-guided behavior. This example represents a sequential mode of combining the three logics of action.

Another example of combining the different logics of social action in a theoretically sophisticated way is Oran R. Young's work (1994, 1997) on "institutional bargaining." Young is as concerned as constructivists about insufficient attention to the supply side of international institution building. His starting point is boundedly rational actors who are uncertain about the strategies available to them and their interaction partners as well as about how possible bargaining outcomes satisfy their preferences. Under these conditions, "integrative bargaining" geared toward common problem solving rather than distributing fixed payoffs is necessary to achieve a cooperative solution (O. R. Young 1994, 126–27). Young then discusses several factors promoting integrative bargaining such as the availability of equitable solutions or the presence of entrepreneurial, structural, or intellectual leadership (on the latter, see O. R. Young 1991). Young's work represents an example of how a clear logic dominates an unclear one (March and Olsen 1998, 952). Under conditions of uncertainty, rule-guided behavior and communicative rationality prevail over the logic of consequentialism.

In sum then, we can observe an emerging convergence in the study of norm creation and international institutionalization processes toward complex models that combine the various logics of social action. Yet, the challenge ahead for constructivist work on the emergence of international institutions is to specify more clearly the conditions under which new principled ideas and new knowledge become consensual by "catching fire" among a variety of actors. Why is it that some strategic constructions, or "issue frames," work and are persuasive, while others don't? "Cultural fit," or norms resonance, is too broad a concept to provide analytical leverage. So far, constructivist institutionalism has not made much progress compared to the social movement literature which also failed to provide testable hypotheses on the conditions of successful framing (e.g., McAdam, McCarthy, and Zald 1996). If one wants to avoid the rationalist fallback

position that new ideas resonate, because they fit with some given instrumental interests of actors, constructivist scholarship needs to make progress
on the persuasiveness of arguments. To put it in terms of the logic of arguing: What counts for a better argument? Properties of the speaker, for example, her credibility, legitimate authority, or knowledge, as the literature
on epistemic communities claims (Adler and Haas 1992)? Properties of the
argument itself, for example, universal claims to general human values versus appeals to narrowminded self-interests? Yet, ethnic identity constructions and appeals to ethnic nationalism and hatred have been successful
enough during the twentieth century to challenge this liberal optimism,
unless the scope conditions are specified.

▪ | Exploring Compliance with International Norms: An Emerging Research Area

Most work on international institutions has focused on explaining the
emergence of new international norms and regimes. Institutions and
norms were found to matter when states and other actors cooperated to
create them and changed their communicative practices accordingly. The
question of rule-consistent behavior, of rule compliance and regime effectiveness has been side-stepped for quite a while. There might have been an
implicit rationalist and functionalist bias here: If governments go through
tough and sometimes costly bargaining processes to establish international
institutions in the first place, why would they ignore the agreed-on norms
and rules afterwards?

Before I discuss the emerging literature on compliance, some definitional clarifications are in order (see Börzel and Risse 2002; Raustiala and
Slaughter 2002). One should distinguish among the implementation of,
compliance with, and effectiveness of international norms and rules. *Effectiveness* concerns the impact of a given international institution in terms of
problem solving or achieving its policy objectives. *Implementation* means
the process of putting international rules into legal and administrative practice, that is, incorporating them into domestic law, providing administrative
infrastructure and resources necessary to put the rule into practice, and instituting effective monitoring and enforcement mechanisms, both internationally and domestically. *Compliance*, as understood here, incorporates
the implementation process but does not necessarily imply effectiveness in
terms of problem solving. Compliance means rule-consistent behavior,
that is, a "state of conformity or identity between an actor's behavior and a
specified rule" (Raustiala and Slaughter 2002, 3).

Irrespective of the particular theoretical approach, most authors agree
on the starting condition for compliance problems. The more inconvenient the international rules, that is, the higher the material and ideational

costs required for ensuring rule-consistent behavior, the greater the compliance problems are likely to become. In other words, some degree of misfit between the international rules, on the one hand, and the domestic policies, problem-solving approaches, institutions, or collective identities, on the other hand, determines the degree of compliance problems in the first place (see, e.g., Breitmeier and Wolf 1995, 347–48; Börzel 2001; Underdal 1998, 12; Cortell and Davis 2000; Checkel 1997, 2001). The two institutionalisms differ as to how they conceptualize "misfit" and what hypotheses they develop to explain compliance with inconvenient rules.

Rationalist institutionalism faces a puzzle concerning compliance. Assuming perfect information, rational actors who behave strategically and anticipate the consequences of their action should not face compliance problems in the first place. If they decide to cooperate to solve some collective action problems or coordinate behavior, the costs of complying with inconvenient rules should have entered their utility functions to begin with. This is why neorealists argued that powerful states would only agree to those norms and rules with which they can comply rather effortlessly (Downs, Rocke, and Barsoom 1996). This includes setting up international or domestic monitoring and enforcement mechanisms to ensure rule compliance of smaller states and to take care of free riders. Under conditions of complete information, compliance problems for powerful states might arise in cases of "incomplete contracting," that is, if the international rules are less clear or the international monitoring and enforcement mechanisms are less stringent (Abbott et al. 2000; Raustiala and Slaughter 2002). This leads to the hypothesis in the legalization literature that compliance with inconvenient international norms is likely to be higher, the more specific the rules and the more effective the monitoring mechanisms are (Abbott et al. 2000; Legro 1996).

If we relax the assumption of complete information, even powerful states are likely to face compliance problems. Under conditions of bounded rationality, compliance problems might occur because of "involuntary defection." The managed compliance perspective argues, for example, that states are generally willing to abide by the rules but lack action capacities and resources of the administrative and political system (Chayes and Chayes Handler 1995). International institutions are supposed to prevent involuntary defection through technical and financial support and capacity building. But involuntary defection might also occur, because national governments are unable to foresee the domestic consequences of international arrangements (Zürn 1997). Domestic—private or public—actors may try to override or subvert an international agreement against their own government (cf. the nonratification of the comprehensive test ban agreement by the U.S. Senate). Two accounts can be distinguished. The first refers to domestic institutional features such as the number of veto players in a given polity (Tsebelis 1995), or the autonomy of the national government vis-à-vis society. The second focuses on domestic societal interests. International institutions lead to a redistribution of power capacities among the relevant actors in a political, social, or economic system (Milner 1988; Rogowski 1989). The more domestic actors are empowered by international norms and rule structures and the more this differential empowerment changes domestic winning coalitions, the more we would expect increasing compliance and institutional change. In sum, rationalist institutionalism emphasizes enforcement, legalization, capacity building, and the redistribution of domestic resources as the main remedies for dealing with compliance problems.

Constructivist or sociological institutionalism focuses on quite different processes, since it conceptualizes the compliance problem differently. However, noncompliance with international norms and rules should be as puzzling for constructivists as it is for rationalists, once the logic of appropriateness kicks in. Cultural isomorphism predicts a "compliance pull" of international norms (Franck 1990), the more these norms have acquired consensual status as standards of appropriate and legitimate behavior in international society. In other words, once the "norm cascade" sets in and a critical mass of states subscribes to the new rules (Finnemore and Sikkink 1998), compliance should improve. Judging from the empirical record, however, there does not seem to be a straight line from collective identification with international institutions to rule-consistent behavior. When states ratify international treaties, they do not automatically implement the rules, let alone comply with them, as a strict understanding of the logic of appropriateness would suggest (Liese 2001).

Constructivists offer the following accounts for the compliance puzzle. First, sociologists point to decoupling whereby behavior does not conform to institutional norms and rules in which actors are embedded. According to Meyer and Rowen, "decoupling enables organizations to maintain standardized, legitimating, formal structures while their activities vary in response to practical considerations" (1991, 58). In other words, we need to distinguish between the prescriptive status of an international norm and rule-consistent behavior. Even fully implemented international rules might not lead to the desired behavioral change of the rule targets. Even if every elementary school curriculum around the world contains mathematics and calculus, this by no means implies that elementary school instructors actually teach mathematics everywhere. A study on international human rights regimes found little correlation between increasing ratification of international treaties and improvement of human rights (Keith 1999). In the case of the European Union, transposition of its law into domestic legislation is extremely high at roughly the 95 percent level on average, but if we move further down the road of implementation, compliance varies (Börzel and Risse 2002).

Decoupling does not seem to be a universal condition; it varies tremendously. Unfortunately, sociological institutionalism of the Stanford school variety is of limited help in accounting for this variation. This

school is so much concerned with demonstrating the structural homogeneity of corporate actors including states in the contemporary world
system that it has little to offer about the degrees of decoupling. However, emphasis on decoupling challenges the neofunctionalist version of
rationalist institutionalism which often brackets rule-consistent behavior
assuming that legal implementation suffices to ensure the latter.

Constructivists have also used the "cultural misfit" proposition mentioned above to specifically account for variation in norm implementation
and rule compliance and the differential diffusion of norms into domestic
practices. According to the "resonance hypothesis," new international
norms are more likely to be implemented domestically and ultimately
complied with, the more they are compatible with preexisting domestic
norms or collective understandings and identities embedded in a social
and political culture (Ulbert 1997; Checkel 1997; Cortell and Davis
2000). The greater the misfit between international rules and regulations
and domestic rules and procedures, the more difficult rule compliance becomes. The resonance hypothesis has generated quite substantial empirical research across various issue areas of international life including
citizenship norms, environmental rules, and international trade (overview
in Cortell and Davis 2000).

But it is also problematic, for three reasons. First, change agents and
norm entrepreneurs are in the business of strategic constructions. In other
words, they deliberately make international norms and rules "resonate"
with preexisting domestic norms and collective understandings. Second, if
resonance with domestic norms explains the emergence of new international norms (see above), observed noncompliance cannot result from
"cultural misfit" but must be explained differently. Finally, a complete
match between the international norms and the domestic culture is not
particularly interesting, since it should result in automatic compliance. In
other words, a certain degree of cultural misfit or incompatibility is necessary to ascribe causal weight to international norms. I suggest, therefore, to
treat the "cultural misfit" proposition as the starting condition for compliance problems from a constructivist perspective (see also Börzel 2001).
While rationalist institutionalists would conceptualize the problem of inconvenient rules as one of raising (material and ideational) costs, constructivists would emphasize the lack of resonance with domestic norms and
collective understandings including identities.

Thus, cultural misfit can only be a starting point for dealing with compliance questions from a constructivist perspective. It might account for
differential rates of decoupling, but it does not offer a positive explanation
for compliance despite inconvenient rules. Once again, we need to leave
overly structuralist accounts and bring agency back in. Agency-centered
constructivism would emphasize the logic of arguing and see compliance
with international norms and rules as a fundamentally intersubjective and
interpretative process (see Kratochwil 1989). No matter how robust and

how precise international regulations are, there is always room for interpretation. As a result, persuasion rather than enforcement or capacity building becomes the dominant mechanism to ensure rule compliance (Checkel 2001). But what makes a norm persuasive? At this point, constructivist institutionalists and legal scholars emphasizing the legitimacy of a rule have much in common (Franck 1990; Koh 1997; Hurd 1999; Joerges and Neyer 1997). As legal scholars point out, the perceived legitimacy of a norm increases compliance. Legitimacy is not a given or simply the result of a particular procedure of rule generation but is linked to democratic participation and deliberation in the negotiating process leading to the norm in the first place. The more those concerned by a norm participate in the process of norm generation and the more they perceive the rules as fair and just, the greater the likelihood of rule-consistent behavior (Dworkin 1986; Franck 1995; for an empirical evaluation, see Zürn and Joerges forthcoming).

Legal scholars also emphasize processes of norm interpretation by which actors deliberate about the meaning of certain rules. Even the most specific rules need to be interpreted and applied to concrete circumstances. Actors often disagree about the meaning of a rule and how to apply it. The logic of arguing kicks in again, even if actors—governments accused of norm violation and their accusers alike—behave instrumentally and strategically (Schimmelfennig 1997). Such argumentative processes resemble court proceedings even if they are carried out in front of a public international audience rather than specific courts or (international) commissions monitoring compliance (for evidence in the human rights area, see Risse 1999). The point is that accusers and defendants have to accept a common legal basis and to give reasons for their opinions if they want to persuade an audience. We can extrapolate from this that compliance with international rules should increase, the more discourse arenas exist allowing for such processes of legal internalization. These can be domestic or international courts but also international organizations or commissions monitoring compliance with international treaties. Thus, constructivists agree with rationalists that international monitoring mechanisms are important for improving rule compliance, but for different reasons. The emphasis is on discourse arenas enabling argumentative processes rather than simply the provision of information about rule compliance.

Rule compliance and implementation then constitute a socialization process during which actors—governmental, transnational, and societal—gradually became acquainted with international norms as a result of which they assume their "taken for grantedness" and become habitualized practices. The emphasis is on the constitutive effects of international norms in shaping the interests and identities of actors. These scholars then focus on learning processes, on institutional emulation, and arguing. Checkel specifies several conditions under which social learning understood as the change of preferences and the socialization into new rules occur (Checkel

2001). These conditions refer mostly to the institutional environment in which learning processes take place (dense interactions among participants, insulation from political pressures, shared professional background) but also to external factors (crises or policy failures).

Empirical work on socialization from a constructivist perspective has just begun. As a result, there is not yet sufficient empirical evidence to evaluate the propositions about arguing stated above. Moreover, there is a tendency among scholars focusing on socialization to overemphasize norm internalization. Socialization was meant to provide a microfoundation for processes of norm diffusion which sociological institutionalism of the Stanford school variety has bracketed (on this point, see Checkel 1999). Yet, we do not need to assume that each individual actor has to deeply internalize an international norm and to believe in its validity in order to comply with it. Institutionalized practices, organizational routines, and standard operating procedures can do the trick independently of individual convictions. In these cases, socialization simply means getting acquainted with the rules and the ensuing role expectations and acquiring the knowledge to enact them.

More recently, scholars have developed complex models of rule compliance which integrate the three logics of social action. In the human rights area, for example, Risse, Ropp, and Sikkink (1999) have developed a five-stage "spiral model" to specify the conditions under which international human rights norms are implemented and complied with in the domestic practices of mainly third world states. This model specifies the dominant actors to move the process from one phase to the next as well as the dominant mode of interaction. It builds on the "boomerang pattern" of interaction suggested by Keck and Sikkink where domestic nongovernmental organizations bypass their state and search out international allies in transnational advocacy networks to bring pressure to bear on their government in order to enforce compliance with international law (1998, 12–14). During early phases of the spiral model, transnational advocacy networks are the dominant actors moving the process further; interactions between these networks and norm-violating governments largely follow instrumental rationality. When later stages are reached, the domestic opposition gradually takes over and the social logic changes from instrumental to argumentative rationality and processes of persuasion. The more human rights norms achieve prescriptive status in the domestic context, the more the logic of appropriateness and institutionalization/habitualization processes dominate.

Theory-guided empirical work on compliance with international norms and institutions has not yet moved much beyond the stage of plausibility probes. The recent move toward integrative models suggests, however, that movements across the boundaries of the two institutionalisms are necessary and possible: For example, constructivist work has identified shaming as a powerful mechanism by which states can be brought into compliance with international norms (e.g., Klotz 1995; Liese 2001). However, shaming involves all three logics of social interaction. It is part of an argumentative process by which governments or a wider audience are meant to be persuaded to change their preferences. Its success then depends on the logic of arguing. But the shaming agents such as INGOs or other norm-promoting agents use it as strategic constructions to blame a rule-violating government. Thus, they follow a logic of consequentialism. At the same time, those being shamed must accept the underlying norm as a legitimate standard of appropriateness for shaming to be successful. Thus, shaming connotes a process in which all three logics of action are at play and arguing and instrumental rationality as a strategic construction are embedded in the logic of appropriateness. In contrast, the spiral model of human rights change adopts a sequential view of how the different logics relate to each other.

Finally, some of the pathways to compliance identified by rationalist as compared to constructivist-sociological institutionalism can be treated as functionally equivalent. A high degree of legitimacy of international norms or their internalization into the domestic political systems might compensate for a lack of enforcement mechanisms. In the absence of societal reform coalitions whose resources could have been strengthened by international norms, norm entrepreneurs might introduce discursive processes of persuasion in order to increase compliance.

In sum, work on compliance suggests fruitful combinations of the various logics of social action identified by the two institutionalisms. Sometimes, the pathways and mechanisms suggested are mutually exclusive. Persuasion and enforcement through sanctions hardly go together. Yet, managed compliance through capacity building and increasing the legitimacy of international norms through a more participatory and deliberative process of norm creation can well be combined. Norm entrepreneurship using strategic constructions to shame states into compliance closely resembles a mechanism by which international institutions provide ideational resources to societal reform coalitions to further their goals.

▪ | So What?

The survey of the recent literature documents that both rationalist and constructivist-sociological approaches to the study of international institutions are by now well-established research programs in the field of international relations and have yielded significant theoretical and empirical insights. Both approaches have gone well beyond the rather trivial insight that "institutions matter" and have developed testable propositions on the conditions under which international norms and rule structures emerge and gain their prescriptive status, and domestic compliance with these norms and rules is to be expected. Moreover, rationalist and constructivist institutionalisms have begun to specify the causal mechanisms that lead to institutional change and explain norm compliance, such as two-level games, the differential empowerment of domestic actors, moral and political entrepreneurship, persuasion, learning, other socialization processes, and so on.

Yet, as I tried to show, rationalism and constructivism identify different logics of social action. Rational-choice approaches emphasize a logic of instrumental rationality and of consequentialism and are self-consciously agency centered. In contrast, constructivism can be divided in more structuralist accounts focusing on the logic of appropriateness and rule following and on more agency-centered concepts concentrating on argumentative rationality and persuasion. On a metatheoretical level, these three logics are quite distinct and, I claim, cannot be collapsed into each other. Yet, the "games real actors play" (Scharpf 1997) consist of various combinations of the different logics which actors have at their disposal. Problem-driven scholars who strive to explain some puzzles in the real world better make sure that their theories are open enough to allow for incorporating different logics of action.

Thus, at the beginning of the new century, scholars are beginning to leave their paradigmatic trenches and start talking across metatheoretical divides. In fact, the most-interesting institutionalist work is no longer to be found among the metatheoretical purists, be they rationalists or constructivists. Rather, as I tried to show, innovative work today combines the different logics of social action and demonstrates how different causal pathways using bargaining, arguing, or rule-following mechanisms complement each other in various ways. I find this the most-promising avenue for future institutionalist work in international relations. Scholars increasingly accept the notion that social reality cannot be reduced to one single logic of action and that, therefore, an approach such as rational choice which emphasizes the logic of consequentialism simply will not do. Some of these conceptualizations (such as the norm "life cycle") follow a sequential rationale and specify which logic dominates in which phase of norm creation or implementation. The different logics of action might also be embedded into each other. Strategic constructions or framing processes follow the logic of consequentialism but are embedded in collective understandings of appropriateness and require arguing geared toward a reasoned consensus in order to be successful. Last but not least, some theoretical concepts such as path dependence or bounded rationality are currently used by both metatheoretical camps which should again inspire conversations across paradigms.

While work across metatheoretical boundaries is only beginning, it has dramatic consequences for our practical knowledge of international politics. First, an understanding of international negotiations that incorporates both arguing and bargaining can lead to improved diplomatic processes in many international negotiations, providing tools to overcome deadlock situations. Second, if we conceive of world politics as an international society of states based on collective understandings of what constitutes appropriate behavior, we will come to different policy prescriptions than if we conceived it as balance of power politics. It makes a big difference in the contemporary discussions about humanitarian interventions, for example, whether we consider a country's "supreme national interest" as solely concerned with immediate survival as a state or whether we extend this view toward the preservation of a community of states bound by basic rules of appropriate behavior. Such a broader view of the national interest does not solve the complicated trade-offs, but it alters the frame of reference. Third, the sociological institutionalist emphasis on decoupling between the prescriptive status of norms and rule-consistent behavior should alert us that implementation of international norms in domestic law is a necessary but not sufficient step toward rule compliance. Last but not least, if we view international institutions as discourse arenas, this should have important consequences for institutional design, particularly in light of the emerging public-private partnerships in international governance (Reinicke 1998; O'Brien et al. 2000). These examples suggest that the debates between rationalists and constructivists are not just controversies in the intellectual ivory tower but have implications for the conduct of world politics.

4 | Studying Politics

This part examines some of the tools that political scientists use to make their truth claims. Two themes are prominent: the diversity of approaches that spans the subfields, and the strength of the claims that link methods to substantive areas of interest. Attention to the microfoundations of institutions as well as to choice and strategic interaction partner easily with rational-choice theory, while a focus on large processes and slow development conduces to a more sociological and historical approach to institutionalism. These essays contain many suggestions for moving across boundaries in order to use multiple methods.

David Laitin's "Comparative Politics: The State of the Subdiscipline" is a case in point. He issues a call for a multimethodological approach. As a distinct subdiscipline, comparative politics is defined both by substantive and methodological criteria. Substantively, research in comparative politics seeks to account for the variation in outcomes among political units on consequential questions that have been posed in political theory. Methodologically, an earlier consensus about the comparative method differentiated it from the statistical and case study methods and emphasized the isolation of key variables through the use of strategic controls. Today, Laitin argues, a new consensus is on the horizon, one that emphasizes a tripartite methodology, including statistics, formalization, and narrative. All three methods involve a constant interaction between theory and data (and thus are all theoretic) but with different emphases. In the first component of the tripartite method, cross-sectional or diachronic data are employed to find statistical regularities across a large number of similar units. The second component of the tripartite method is formalization. Formal modeling, in providing an internally consistent logic that accounts for the stipulated relationships among abstract variables, assures us that our causal stories are coherent and noncontradictory. The observable implications of our formal models, once they are derived, invite statistical test. The third component is narrative. Comparativists examine real (and virtual) cases to trace historically and theorize empirically the translation of values on independent variables to values on dependent variables. If statistics addresses questions of propensities, narratives address questions of process.

To be sure, the tripartite subdiscipline reported in this paper is only emerging. To illustrate the progress in the comparative politics discipline over the past decade, Laitin examines work on three consequential political outcomes, each of which is connected to perennial concerns in political theory and posseses political relevance today: democracy, civil war, and forms of capitalism. For each outcome, he reports on the progress coming from research based on each component of the tripartite methodology, while noting missed opportunities for advances because of inattention across the methodological divides. The aim of this essay is to advance the view that even with a focus on the big dependent variables, cumulative findings can be developed if done in the context of the tripartite methodology.

Barry Weingast focuses on key developments in "Rational-Choice Institutionalism." From pluralistic premises noting that no approach dominates the study of institutions, he explains the comparative advantages of the rational-choice perspective in covering three categories of questions: the effects of institutions, the necessity of institutions, and the endogenous choice of particular institutions, including their long-term durability and survival. Rooted in the economic theory of the firm, economic history, and positive political theory, this approach possesses distinctive features in providing microfoundations for institutional analysis. Methodologically, treating institutions as humanly devised constraints translates into studying how institutions constrain the sequence of interaction among the actors, the choices available to particular actors, the structure of information and hence beliefs of the actors, and the payoffs to individuals and groups.

The rational-choice approach to institutions divides into two separate levels of analysis. In the first, analysts study the effects of institutions, treating them as exogenous; in the second, treating them as endogenous, they study why institutions take particular forms, why they are needed, and why they survive. In combination, these approaches provide both a method for analyzing the effects of institutions and social and political interaction and a means for understanding the long-term evolution and survival of particular institutional forms. The study of endogenous institutions yields a distinctive theory about their stability, form, and survival. In contrast to approaches that take institutions as given, this approach allows scholars to study how actors attempt to affect the institutions themselves as conditions change. This approach potentially provides the microfoundations for macropolitical phenomena such as revolutions and critical elections. Explicit models of discontinuous political change, Weingast concludes, provide an exciting new set of applications of rational-choice theory.

Paul Pierson and Theda Skocpol assess the trajectory of "Historical

Institutionalism in Contemporary Political Science." Contemporary political scientists are familiar with leading examples of historical institutionalist
research without necessarily realizing that they exemplify a coherent genre
that analyzes organizational configurations where others look at particular
settings in isolation; and they pay attention to critical junctures and long-
term processes where others may look only at slices of time or short-term
maneuvers. Researching important issues in this way, historical institutionalists, they argue, make visible and understandable the overarching contexts and interacting processes that shape and reshape states, politics, and
public policymaking. Despite the great variety of their studies, historical institutionalists commonly employ distinctive and complementary strategies
for framing research and developing explanations. Three important features especially characterize historical institutional scholarship. Practition-
aers address big, substantive questions that are inherently of interest to
broad publics as well as to fellow scholars. They take time seriously, specifying sequences and tracing transformations and processes of varying scale
and temporality, and they analyze macrocontexts and hypothesize about
the combined effects of institutions and processes rather than examining
just one institution or process at a time. Pierson and Skocpol show both
how historical institutionalism is experiencing a bold new phase of
methodological development and how its focus on substance and its theoretical eclecticism open the way for fruitful cross-fertilization with sister research traditions.

Karen Orren and Stephen Skowronek evaluate recent research on the
United States in the genre of historical institutionalism in their essay "The
Study of American Political Development." Situating American Political
Development in relation to recent intellectual trends in the study of political history, social theory, and rational choice, they argue that its growing
influence reflects a more general reconsideration of the temporalities of
governance and a recognition that theory building requires more careful
attention to the distinctive ways in which politics changes over time. Their
paper marks the field's departure in recent years from the assumptions of
consensus theory and from realignment theory's scheme of periodization.
Orren and Skowronek then distinguish three concurrent lines of inquiry
into how institutions affect political change over time and conclude with a
sketch of emergent conceptions of history and their implications for theory
building.

Robert Powell's "Game Theory, International Relations Theory, and
the Hobbesian Stylization" argues that strategic interaction is at the center
of much of the work that has been done in international relations since at
least the end of World War II and claims that one very important approach
to understanding this interaction abstracts away from many of the details of
international politics and foreign policy to focus on the strategic logic of a
simple, stylized model of the international system. Game theory, in turn, is

a central tool for analyzing strategic interaction. Not surprisingly, then, international relations theorists have tried at various times over the last half-century to use game theory to advance their understanding of these problems. Powell thus asks what game theory offers international relations theory, inquires about the extent to which what game theory has to offer is needed, and surveys some of the effects on international relations theory that come with adopting a more game theoretic approach. Above all, Powell emphasizes that game theory is not a theory of international relations but a research tool. Its use entails costs and benefits; however, he argues, after a review of some of the major debates in the field, that its benefits outweigh its costs. Formalization forces basic mechanisms underlying all political interaction to the fore and thereby facilitates a more-integrated approach to the study of politics more generally and international politics in particular.

Charles Cameron and Rebecca Morton advocate merging formal theory and empirical methods in "Formal Theory Meets Data" to fashion a new genre of political studies. First discussing what they mean by a formal model and the general relationships between models and empirical analysis, they contend that empirical analysis based on nonformal theorizing has advantages and disadvantages: it allows a researcher to be open to new and unexpected patterns in the data, but it also means that the researcher may miss important causal factors by using goodness of fit and statistical significance as his only judges as to the success of his analysis. They hold that formal theory provides empirical analysis with a guide that can help a researcher uncover causal factors by suggesting which variables should be measured and the expected functional form of the relationships between the variables in the empirical estimation. However, empirical analysis based on formal models is not easy. Working with a formal model as the basis for devising the empirical model means that the researcher must confront difficult questions about the relationship between the two. They show how researchers either work with empirical models that are inspired by the formal model or directly derive the empirical model from the formal model, using "structural" estimation techniques. And they indicate how researchers handle randomness when they undertake empirical analysis of formal models either by using experimental analysis and thus reducing the causes of randomness through experimental design control or by directly incorporating the randomness within the structure of the formal model.

In "Reclaiming the Experimental Tradition in Political Science," Donald Green and Alan Gerber argue for a different approach to the study of politics than the previous authors, one that is now gaining ground in cognate fields, including economics. They claim that the tradition of field experimentation has been largely forgotten in political science, having been supplanted by other methodologies. Nevertheless, field experimentation remains a powerful method for drawing inferences about cause and effect, often more so than the observational studies and lab experiments that currently dominate empirical research. And they contend that field experimentation based on randomized interventions is more valuable and feasible than political scientists typically suppose. While perhaps most feasible in stable domestic contexts, they see no inherent reason why other areas of politics cannot usefully appropriate such experimental methods.

David D. Laitin

Comparative Politics: The State of the Subdiscipline[1]

Comparative politics is a distinct subdiscipline of political science, defined by both substantive and methodological criteria. Substantively, research in comparative politics seeks to account for the variation in outcomes among political units on consequential questions that have been posed in political theory. Comparative politics research places these outcomes on dimensions and seeks to account for the placement of political units on these dimensions. It then seeks to account for differences in placement along these dimensions among political units and for the same political unit in different time periods.

Methodologically, an earlier consensus about the comparative method differentiated it from the statistical and case-study methods, and it emphasized through the use of strategic controls the isolation of key variables. Beholden to the discussions of J. S. Mill, comparativists worked out the implications of using the method of similarity, or the method of difference, to capture the workings of independent variables.[2] Today, a new consensus is on the horizon, one that emphasizes a tripartite methodology, including statistics, formalization, and narrative.[3] All three methods involve a constant interaction between theory and data (and thus are all theoretic), but with different emphases.

In the first component of the tripartite method, cross-sectional or diachronic data are employed to find statistical regularities across a large

1. The author would like to thank Kanchan Chandra, Peter Gourevitch, Donald Green, Peter Katzenstein, Ira Katznelson, Peter Lange, Lisa Martin, Helen Milner, and Gerald Munck, all of whom commented on earlier versions of this essay. Mary-Lee Kimber provided research assistance for it.

2. The classic statements on the comparative method, by Eckstein, by Lijphart, by Przeworski and Teune, by David Collier, and by Skocpol and Somers are all cited and neatly developed in Lichbach and Zuckerman 1997b.

3. My identification of a tripartite methodology takes a step beyond the approach advocated in Bates et al. 1998, in which formalization and narrative are highlighted but statistical work is largely ignored.

number of similar units. Whereas statistical techniques were once seen as alternatives to the comparative method, they are increasingly seen as an important element in that method but only one step toward explanation.

The second component of the tripartite method is formalization. Formal modeling, in providing an internally consistent logic that accounts for the stipulated relationships among abstract variables, assures us that our causal stories are coherent and noncontradictory. The observable implications of our formal models, once they are derived, invite statistical test. These exercises in comparative statics have set new methodological challenges in comparative politics.[4]

The third component in the tripartite methodology is narrative. Comparativists examine real (and virtual[5]) cases to trace historically and theorize empirically the translation of values on independent variables onto values on dependent variables. If statistics addresses questions of propensities, narratives address questions of process. Narratives are helpful in suggesting how statistical anomalies arising from contradictory results in cross-sectional and diachronic analyses can be resolved. Furthermore, narratives provide reliable information on the measurement of key variables. Also, in juxtaposing theory to cases, as comparative narratives demand, methods of similarity and difference are especially useful in making sense of cases that are off the regression line. These "Millian" exercises have the potential to discover formerly omitted variables that, once plugged into statistical analyses, alter previous findings.

To be sure, the tripartite subdiscipline reported in this paper is only emerging, and it has hardly been noticed by leading practitioners. Indeed, the editor of *Comparative Political Studies* wrote in the introduction to a special issue devoted to the organization of the field that comparativists have a commitment to "explanatory accuracy" that accounts for a "fragmented discipline" (Caporaso 2000, 699–700). Caporaso's judgment is correct, and the subdiscipline has paid a cost for not taking full advantage of the emergent consensus. As this paper will show, opportunities for advance have been missed because of the field's fragmentation. Thus, in identifying an *emergent* subdiscipline, this review plays the Leninist role of pushing history.

The dependent variables that engage the attention of the comparative politics subdiscipline are not timelessly and unambiguously arranged, like the unanswered conundrums that drive mathematicians. There are two crucial differences between the questions that drive political scientists and those that drive mathematicians. In comparative politics, questions are chosen because they have vital interest for the world we live in. Questions

4. On testing the observable implications of our models, see Geddes 1991. On the challenges of testing formal models statistically, see Alt and Alesina 1996.

5. See Lustick 2000 for the use of virtual data to study the construction of ethnic identities.

concerning democratization were prominent on the agenda of comparative politics for the past decade in large part because they were on the agenda of citizens, politicians, and the informed public around the world. Comparativists will drop old questions, not because they are solved but because new questions have pushed their way onto the political agenda. And so, in the wake of events of September 11, 2001, Hobbesian questions of making the world safe from terror may supplant Lockean questions of making the world open to freedom on the comparative field's agenda. Choice of the dependent variable cannot be separated from the goals, interests, and generational perspectives of researchers. Reviews of progress in comparative politics by different reviewers or written in different periods will therefore highlight different dependent variables.[6]

Also, questions comparativists ask about outcomes continually get specified anew, as the way we ask our questions about political outcomes changes over time. In the Hobbesian period, civil war meant the collapse of monarchy; in today's world, it increasingly means rebellions fought in the name of an ethnic group against state authority. While there may well be explanatory factors that cross eras and types of civil wars, small respecifications of a dependent variable can have large repercussions concerning the significance of independent variables. Concerning democracy, Moore (1966) was attentive to the protection of individual liberties. Today, some democratic theorists are attentive to the protection of property rights. These different foci imply different dimensions, although both could use "degree of democratic consolidation" to name their variable. Researchers' values can not so subtly influence the specification of a dependent variable with implications for the explanatory power of different independent variables. The downside of this incentive to respecify problems given changing concerns within the research community is that questions in comparative politics never get satisfactorily solved, as on the brink of discovery they get specified in a new way, opening up new lines of inquiry.

In light of this tendency toward fragmentation through multiple specifications of the big dependent variables, are there better ways to organize the field? My attempt to create a consensus is not the only alternative. Lichbach and Zuckerman's work (1997a) reflects a widespread belief that the field is divided by a set of paradigmatic approaches—structural, cultural and rational choice—each with its own insights. Alternatively, many remain indebted to Samuel Beer's teachings to focus on the relative power of three independent variables: interests, ideas, and institutions. There are several advantages to the establishment of coherence based on indepen-

---

6. My predecessor for this decadal review, Rogowski (1993), made no mention of comparative democracies as on the agenda. See Shin 1994, 138, n. 9, for the tide of publications on democracy that followed on the heels of Rogowski's review. Of the three dependent variables singled out for attention in my review, only one (forms of capitalism) received serious attention by Rogowski.

dent variables. First, it is surely the case that some independent variables are causal for more than one dependent variable, and the focus on dependent variables tends to ignore the broader implications of changes in powerful independent variables. For example, many comparativists (e.g., Collier and Collier 1991), focus on the independent affects of "world historical time" and its implications for a variety of political outcomes. The cumulative impact of this variable is missed when each study isolates a single dependent variable. Indeed, this review, with its focus on three dependent variables, gives no treatment to critical junctures in world historical time as an independent variable. Second, the focus on big dependent variables can be intractable. We may never be able to answer the question "What causes democracy?" but we can make considerable progress if we ask instead, "What is the effect of economic growth on the survival chances of democracy?" (Geddes 1991). Third, since compelling explanatory variables are few and attractive dependent variables are many, it is easier to keep a catalogue of cumulative findings if the field is organized by independent variables.

Nonetheless, the identification of competing approaches or alternative explanatory variables is, in my judgment, the wrong way to go in developing a discipline. Doing so focuses attention on the explanatory limits of a particular method or a favored variable rather than the degree to which we collectively in comparative politics have accounted for variations on important outcomes. We would not be interested in learning about the effect of x on y unless we cared about the value of y. True, the specification of big dependent variables in comparative politics induces some fragmentation. But the thrust of this paper is to show that even with a focus on the big dependent variables, fragmentation can be contained, and cumulative findings developed if done in the context of the tripartite methodology.

To illustrate the progress in the comparative politics discipline over the past decade, I shall examine work on three consequential political outcomes, each of which is connected to perennial concerns in political theory. But each has political relevance in our age with a corresponding high level of attention in comparative research. The three outcomes are democracy, civil war, and forms of capitalism. For each outcome, I will report on the progress coming from research based on each component of the tripartite methodology. I will also report on the missed opportunities for advances because of inattention across the methodological divides.

▪ | Democracy

Comparative studies of democracy and its alternatives have focused on the factors that differentiate democratic countries from nondemocratic ones. Here I will begin with studies in the tradition of Lipset (1959), relying primarily on statistical analysis. I then examine new studies, in the tradition of Moore (1966), relying principally on historical narratives and the patterns uncovered by these narratives. Finally, I discuss recent formal models of democratization.

STATISTICS

What distinguishes democracies from nondemocracies? This is a question that begs for statistical analysis. Przeworski et al. (2000) have made a fundamental contribution to comparative politics in compiling a data set that enables them to provide fresh answers to this age-old question.[7] Their data are consistent with Lipset's finding (1959) that there is a strong relationship between economic development and democracy. But Lipset's data did not allow him to distinguish two possible reasons for this correlation. Are democracies the result of modernization? Or do democracies survive more successfully once a certain level of economic growth is attained? Meanwhile, poor democracies fall into dictatorship. In this scenario, democracy tends to survive if a country is modern, but democracy itself may arise randomly, exogenous to the level of economic development.

Przeworski et al. provide powerful evidence that modernization is not the cause of democracy. They collected data from 141 countries annually from 1950 through 1990 and coded them dichotomously as to whether they were democracies. Their metric, the probability of a transition to democracy, shows "dictatorships survived for years in countries that were wealthy by comparative standards . . . conversely, many dictatorships fell in countries with low income levels"[8] (2000, 94).

Meanwhile, their data show that if "the causal power of economic development in bringing down dictatorships appears paltry . . . per capita income has a strong impact on the survival of democracies" (98). In fact, over $7,000 in per capita income brings a zero probability of the collapse

7. There is no consensus on the specification of the dependent variable. Collier and Levitsky (1997) demonstrate that in political science there are nearly as many types of democracy as there are studies of it. Those working in the Moore tradition (1966) face the challenge that the master specified the dimension of democracy to dictatorship in an ad hoc way, differently for each country studied. Przeworski et al.'s minimalist specification (2000) is in the Schumpeterian tradition (1942). O'Donnell, in the tradition of Dahl (1956, Appendix), presses for a maximalist specification, as he sees no real democracy unless the informal workings of institutions squelch particularism (1997, 46). Bollen (1993) and Coppedge and Reinicke (1990) have used techniques such as factor analysis to arrive at an underlying dimension of democracy richer than Schumpeter's. Schaffer (1998) argues for a varied specification that is more sensitive to local cultural meanings. Clearly our findings on democratic outcomes are affected by these specification choices, and progress on explaining democratic outcomes will continue on multiple paths given these varied specifications.

8. The findings held up with exploratory uses of scaled democracy scores.

of a democracy, where there is a 12 percent chance if income per capita is less than $1,000. The collapse of Argentina's democracy at $6,055 is the highest in the data set. O'Donnell (1978) used the Argentina case to challenge Lipset, but he did this, according to Przeworski et al., by examining a "distant outlier." Three of the four transitions to authoritarianism at per capita incomes of greater than $4,000 occurred in Argentina, and the fourth in Uruguay (Przeworski et al. 2000, 90–98). Przeworski et al. correctly predict 77.5 percent of the 4,126 annual observations merely by knowing per capita income. Furthermore, they find, democracies survive more successfully under conditions of economic growth, whereas dictatorship fail equally under conditions of economic growth and conditions of economic decline.[9]

What about political culture? Lipset (1994), while acknowledging the importance of economic prosperity, insists that legitimacy, the key to the sustenance of democracy, requires a supportive political culture. Diamond (1999b) too insists on the importance of regime legitimacy and a political culture that favors democratic institutions. Survey research, he points out, shows that people condition their support of democracy less on economic conditions and more on the institutional workings of the political system.[10] The corruption of the regime, the behavior of parliamentarians, and the responsiveness of elected representatives all play important roles in assuring legitimization. The key criterion for legitimization is that all significant political actors believe that democracy is appropriate for their society, and all significant political competitors believe that democracy is "the only game in town." Although Diamond acknowledges that economic performance plays a role in all regressions, "many more political variables than economic ones have significant effects" on survey support for democracy (quotes from 65, 193). The strongest advocate of the political culture foundation for democracy is Inglehart who claims "that over half of the variance (in a sample of European or run-by-European states) in the persistence of democratic institutions can be attributed to the effects of political culture alone" (1990, 41).

Statistical respecifications of Inglehart's data by Muller and Seligson (1994) (who also enhance the scope of those data with material from Latin America) show that for most elements of the civic culture package, Inglehart had the causal arrows going in the wrong direction. With changes in the level of democracy across decades as their dependent variable, Muller and Seligson show that interpersonal trust is not an explanation for democ-

9. But see Remmer's findings (1991b). Through a statistical analysis of voter volatility in Latin America, she attacks those who see economic crisis as the death knell for democracies. Przeworski et al. predict correctly in Latin America on the basis of GDP per capita alone, and for them, the economic crises of the 1980s were not consequential. Nonetheless, Remmer's findings merit further testing.

10. Here Diamond (1999b, ch. 5) relies on data from Rose, Mishler, and Haerpfer 1998 and Shin and McDonough 1999.

racy but a result of having experienced a long period of democratic rule. The only variable in the civic culture package that holds up as having independent causal influence on democracy is that of the population favoring moderate reform (over revolutionary change or the suppression of reform).

While not testing political culture, Przeworski et al. (2000) examine other factors besides economic level and growth. Once economic controls are added, however, duration of democracy is not significant. Nor do cultural factors, such as the majority religion, seem to have much explanatory power. Knowing the degree of ethnic fractionalization, which many scholars have seen as an added hurdle for democratic consolidation, adds almost nothing to the predictive power of their hazard model. Educational levels, however, do add predictive power, independent of economic levels.

The one powerful noneconomic predictor of democratic longevity is parliamentary institutions, which are less subject to collapse than presidential democracies. To be sure, parliamentary regimes are more likely in rich countries and presidential regimes were especially prevalent in Latin America. But controlling for wealth and region, parliamentary regimes still survive significantly longer than do presidential regimes.

Przeworski et al. (2000) have set a new standard in research differentiating democratic from nondemocratic regimes. Yet much remains to be done. For one, political system variables have been insufficiently specified to be used in statistical analyses. The presidential-parliamentary dichotomy is especially worrisome, inasmuch as nearly 10 percent of the cases are coded as mixed and there are theoretical reasons, as I discuss in the formal models section, to believe that the finding in favor of parliamentarism may be biased by missing some underlying variable explaining regime choice.

Second, Przeworski et al. (2000) have ignored several opportunities to challenge their economic variables with a variety of institutional ones that are prevalent in the democracy literature. Political system variables tell us little about the capacity of democratic states to protect property rights, secure a rule of law, and administer laws without corruption. Linz and Stepan (1996) give conceptual foundations for newly reconstituted institutional variables. Treisman (2000a) has begun to use data on comparative corruption in a way that can be appropriated by democratic theory. Also ignored is the institutional power of the military. Not only state institutions should be considered, but societal ones as well. Przeworski et al. have no indicators for the strength or density of civil society. In light of the gaggle of books and papers that purport to show the importance of civil society for the consolidation of democracy (in addition to those I've reviewed so far, see Putnam 1993a; Schmitter 1997), it is a surprise that they did not collect systematic data (even if they would need to impute for missing years) on this factor. That Przeworski et al. (2000) do not have well-designed tests for political and societal institutions, in order to see if they alter the coefficients of the economic variables, is an invitation for new research.

Third, Przeworski et al.'s (2000) cross-sectional findings are nearly impossible to interpret causally. What are the mechanisms that undermine poor democracies or sustain rich ones? It seems impossible to narrate the progression of events from democracy to dictatorship or reverse in terms of variables such as per capita income. Here is where the other two prongs of the tripartite methodology come into play. Comparativists need to formalize the discovered relationships, and they need to get down to narrative to see if actors in the real world of democracy are conditioning their behavior on the factors that the formal models highlight.

NARRATIVES

What pushes some countries at specific historical periods into democracy? How do fledgling democracies persevere when they face crises? These are questions that require sensitivity to change over time and lend themselves better to narrative rather than statistical analysis. To be sure, Przeworski et al.'s data allow for some diachronic analysis. But these data do not tell us who precisely is doing the acting and where these people fit into the social spectrum. In the past decade, very much in the Moore tradition, research on the historical role of social classes in the making and unmaking of democracy has addressed these questions, and here I will review the studies of Luebbert (1991), Rueschemeyer, Stephens, and Stephens (1992), and Ruth Collier (1999).[11]

Luebbert examined the maintenance of democratic institutions under the challenging conditions of the interwar depression. Like Moore, he found the key to democratic strength in the interwar period to be in the middle classes. But he demonstrated that the so-called marriage of iron and rye was not, as Moore argued, the source of fascism. In fact, Luebbert showed, rural support for fascism did not require a landed elite. In Germany, Spain, and Italy, rural support for fascism was found mainly in areas in which the family peasantry rather than the landed elites predominated. Only in southern Italy was there a landed elite that could deliver votes, and they (ironically) sided with the liberals (concerned more for patronage than with class conflict). Their support for fascism came only after Mussolini attained power.

Liberal democracy survived in those countries where the middle classes were not divided by religion, language, region, or urban-rural differences. A united middle class was not afraid of workers, who were, without much struggle, incorporated into the electoral system. Workers gained in dignity what they lost in income, and were not responsive to radical unionist programs. Meanwhile, liberal hegemony failed where preindustrial

---

11. For a review of critical commentaries on Moore's classic, see Weiner 1976. On recent empirical tests of the hypotheses, see Valenzuela 2000 and Mahoney 2000a.

cleavages divided the middle classes. Divided among themselves, the middle classes were afraid to ally with the workers, compelling them to build trade unions for protection. Under these conditions, the workers needed an electoral alliance to defeat the middle classes. When they successfully allied with the middle peasantry or family farmers, social democracy was the result. However, whenever socialists sought to organize the agrarian proletariat in politics, the family peasantry was pushed into an alliance with the middle class, which became a fascist alliance. Thus, one of the bitter historical ironies: where interwar working-class leaders committed themselves to social justice through taking up the cause of the rural workers, they forced a coalition of middle classes and family peasants, and this was the route to fascism.

Not only Luebbert but many others in the Moore tradition give far more attention to the independent role of the working class, which is a factor that plays only a small role in Moore's alliance patterns. Rueschemeyer, Stephens, and Stephens, in their comprehensive historical treatment of western Europe, Latin America, and the Caribbean, cannot find empirical support for Moore's principal claim in regard to the bourgeoisie. *Pace* Moore, Rueschemeyer et al. find that the middle classes, after their inclusion into the power framework, are ambivalent toward democracy. Therefore, it takes the working class (which, unlike peasants, can organize themselves politically) to affect the true balance of power (where no social group can establish hegemony over the others) upon which democracy rests. But in the end, the authors amend their generalization about working class power as the key to democracy. Only under conditions where a party system can effectively protect the interests of the upper classes, they find, will these classes accommodate to the pro-democratic pressures of the working classes.[12]

Collier (1999) also seeks to delineate the role of the working classes in democratization. Examining cases from both the nineteenth and late–twentieth centuries, and from Latin America as well as western Europe, she finds several distinct paths toward democracy. By looking at seven

---

12. Their original supposition, going into the study, was that the working class was the "most consistently pro-democratic force," except where it was mobilized by a charismatic but authoritarian leader or a hegemonic party linked to the state apparatus. This point makes little sense theoretically. The middle classes only wanted to include themselves and no one below them. This is the same with the working class. Neither was more democratic. It is just that the working class was lower on the totem pole, and once they were included, the vast majority of the population had voting rights. The equation of a particular group's or class's outward commitment to the ideology of democracy with the attribution of causality to that group or class in explaining democratic outcomes is common, especially in the case study literature. See, e.g., Hsiao and Koo, 1997. The key question for democracy is not a group's or class's desire to undermine autocrats, but the probability that a group or class coalition in power will leave power should an out-group win an election. On this point, see Przeworski 1991, ch. 1.

distinct patterns of democratic initiation, she finds that labor plays at least some role in four of those patterns. Her narratives provide plausible evidence of labor's role in democratization across historical periods. But there is a methodological problem with this argument, foreshadowed by the Rueschemeyer et al. recognition (1992) of the need to protect the interests of the upper classes if democracy is to be successfully implemented. Collier only examines labor mobilization in the initiation of successful democracies. If she had coded labor mobilization for every year, she might have found that the higher the mobilization, the lower probability of democratic initiation. This is a real selection bias problem. It could be the case—profoundly undermining the Collier thesis—that the stronger labor shows itself, the more reluctant the right is to accept a democratic constitution. A more complete data set could determine whether Collier's thesis holds, or its opposite.

The historical expositions that accompany studies in the Moore tradition, from nondemocracy to democracy, as well as the reverse, provide a rich narrative complement to the cross-sectional studies. And as is usually the case, the implications of the cross-section and the narrative findings are in some tension with one another. As Rueschemeyer et al. (1992) point out, regional comparisons allow for a large set of sequences under different contexts that can all lead to democracy. Therefore "the similarity of the correlation between development and democracy in different contexts is fortuitous . . . the only underlying homogeneity is the overall balance of power between classes and between civil society and the state. While this is enough to produce the correlation between development and democracy observed in the statistical studies, the same balance of power between pro- and antidemocratic actors can be produced in a large number of ways" (Rueschemeyer et al. 1992, 284).

These historical comparisons are impressively detailed. There has been some cumulating of knowledge. We now have considerable historical evidence that it is the weakening of labor-dependent landed elites rather than the rise of an industrial bourgeoisie that opens the path to democratic politics (Mahoney 2000a). Yet the proliferation of paths and sequences reduces one's confidence in the generality of the findings in any study (Munck 2001a). Either the studies are historically circumscribed, with the authors' being unwilling to make projections about countries in different eras or different areas (as with the case of Luebbert), or the studies are so broad as to lead to a congeries of possibilities and little way of knowing which of many paths will be followed by a case not already in the data set (Collier 1999, Rueschemeyer et al. 1992). Rueschemeyer et al. intimate that better statistical models would include regional dummies, as the patterns seem to be regionally specific. Collier (1999), however, shows that similar patterns can cross regions but not eras. Compelling statistical work, in large part due to the degrees of freedom problem with an immense number of intervening variables, has not kept up with this narrative tradition. To be sure, Dahl (1971) set the standard in hypothesizing multiple paths yet still subjecting his cases to statistical analysis. Ragin (1987) offered an innovative approach to perform statistical analyses of complex sets of hypotheses with multiple paths such as Moore's theory, but there have only been rare and inconclusive tests relying on his techniques (e.g., Grassi 1999). Vanhanen (1997) has run large-*n* statistical tests of democracy that include proxies for Moore's variables (power balance in society). But data on the distribution of societal power hardly provide an historical mechanism that accounts for democratization. Research that is sensitive to the findings in the grand narrative tradition yet keyed into the cross-sectional findings in the statistical tradition remains on the agenda.

Linz and Stepan's work is in the narrative tradition, but they look less at class structure and examine instead the role of institutions. While they acknowledge that high GDP is favorable to democracy (consistent with Przeworski et al. as well as with Moore), they insist that this fact "does not tell us much about *when, how,* and *if* a transition will take place and be successfully completed . . . economic trends in themselves are less important than is the perception of alternatives, system blame, and the legitimacy beliefs of significant segments of the population or major institutional actors" (1996, 77). To support this point, and relying on a comparison of the Netherlands and Germany in the 1930s, Linz and Stepan show that the economic decline was equal in both countries but only in the latter there were strong groups able to articulate blame for the economic crisis (77). Earlier (1990a and 1990b), Linz emphasized the importance of political institutions (favoring parliamentary over presidential systems) and with Stepan (1992) the sequencing of elections (favoring a sequence from central elections to regional ones).

In their monumental comparison of transitions and consolidation in southern Europe, South America and post-Communist Europe, Linz and Stepan (1996) point to five necessary conditions for the survival of democracy, which include a vibrant civil society, an autonomous political society, the rule of law, a usable state, and a set of rules, norms, institutions and regulations that undergird an economic society. Furthermore, there are seven independent variables (each with a range of values, most often nominal) that help predict successful consolidation. They include the relationship of state to nation, the type of prior regime, the leadership base of the prior regime, the pattern of the transition to democracy, the legitimacy of major institutional actors, and the environment in which the democratic constitution was drafted.[13] The degree of freedom problem for the testing of these ideas statistically is, however, immense.

---

13. Before laying out their five necessary conditions and seven independent variables, Linz and Stepan warn their readers, "We will not restrict ourselves to the procrustean bed of this framework. The specificities of history are also important" (1996, xiv).

Until there are more parsimonious narrative models and better-specified variables in narrative accounts, ones that can be coded for cases outside the domain of cases in which the pattern was originally found, the narrative-based approach will not challenge sufficiently findings relying on the statistical approach. But both the statistical and narrative approaches have set new problems for the third element of the tripartite methodology, that is, formal models.

FORMAL MODELS

Formal models have been offered to explain the occurrence of democratic transitions and the creation of stable democratic outcomes. In the early 1980s, the project on transitions from authoritarian rule, edited by O'Donnell, Schmitter, and Whitehead (1986a), set as a premise of the project that democratization was less a product of long-term macro conditions and more of a project of short-term contingent bargains by elements of the political class that had a range of options. This premise set the research program for formal models of the transition period. In one of the latest versions, there are six different categories of actor (radicals and moderates among hard-line rulers, soft-line rulers, and the opposition), each with a different preference ordering among democracy, nondemocracy, and reform (Colomer 2000, ch. 2). Colomer finds three routes to democracy on the basis of an analysis of strategic games among these players. Furthermore, two chapters of narrative illustrate these routes in the Soviet Union and Poland. This formalization of democratic transitions has its illuminating moments, for example, in showing how Gorbachev had no utility-increasing move when confronted by the putschists in August 1991. But there are problems with this approach as well. Consistent with Woodruff's critique (2000) of this genre of modeling, the sociology setting up Colomer's games (e.g., in explaining why a certain set of the six actors was present or not in a particular case) carried far more weight in accounting for the outcomes than the equilibrium analysis itself.[14] But second, and consistent with my tripartite framework, there is no attempt to see if the observable implications of the formal analysis can be put to any form of statistical test. No regularities in the world were systematically accounted for.

Formal democratic theory in the past decade has focused less on transitions and more on the microdynamics of democratic stability. Przeworski (1991) has addressed the problem of why actors out of power might choose not to rebel against democratically elected rulers. Weingast (1997) has ad-

14. Colomer diverges systematically from predictions based on Nash equilibria. It is unclear whether he is using a Nash refinement or a solution concept that ignores Nash. He appeals to efficient equilibria that are Pareto superior to the Nash equilibrium without providing a general solution concept of why these outcomes are likely to be reached.

dressed the problem of why democratically elected rulers might choose not to confiscate property rights (including voting rights) from their enemies— to assure longevity of rule—and thereby undermine the democratic system. Whereas Przeworski asks the conditions under which democracy is immune from revolution from below, Weingast asks the conditions under which democracy is immune from revolution from above.

The theoretical literature remains, however, disconnected from the empirical regularities discussed earlier. The statistical relationship between per capita income and democracy is not accounted for in these models. If this is a robust empirical finding, then our theoretical models should have a parameter for per capita income such that the democratic equilibrium is more unstable to the extent that the parameter goes down in value.

Nor have formal models of democracy shown why some institutional forms are more conducive to democracy than others. What is it about parliamentary rule that makes it more stable than presidential? The dichotomous variable of parliamentary versus presidential hardly captures theoretical intuitions about institutional stability (Shugart and Carey 1992). Does presidentialism allow for the election of nonrepresentative candidates (Linz and Valenzuela 1994; Powell 2000)? Cox shows that this depends on how well voters can coordinate and how strategic they are (1997, 233). Perhaps presidentialism, associated with a two-party system, denies minorities outlets to modulate majorities, outlets that are available to them in the Proportional Representation (PR) systems associated with parliamentary rule? But minorities in two-party systems play a role in pre-election coalition building; meanwhile minorities in PR systems play a role in postelection cabinet building. Neither system is inherently more compatible with minority representation.[15]

Perhaps (in a surmise by Przeworski, personal communication) the key to the difference is that at times of deadlock between the head of state and the parliament, in a parliamentary regime there will be a vote of no confidence, and the possibility of a new government that can address the deadlock anew. Meanwhile the legislature in a presidential system has no way of compelling the head of state to step down. If the deadlock is particularly severe, the president (or the military) has an incentive to declare a constitutional crisis and disregard democratic institutions. One problem with this idea is that early elections in parliamentary regimes rarely affect the seat allocation of the parties, and thus this is hardly a method to overcome interparty deadlock. However, it may be the case that the threat of new elections creates incentives for compromise while the actual calling for elections (due to rare cases where parties have different assessments of their relative electoral strength) reflects the failure of compromise. We would thus ob-

15. These issues are addressed theoretically by Taagepera and Shugart (1989), who set up the terms for a debate that remains lively, most notably in the pages of *Electoral Studies*.

serve no changes in seat strength after such elections, but the threat of such elections could still induce compromise. A formal model focusing on the existence of this threat might show Przeworski's surmise to be correct.

There are alternatives still that could be modeled. Perhaps the answer to parliamentary longevity lies elsewhere still and is to be found by analyzing the endogenous selection of institutions, as suggested in Geddes's empirical analysis (1996) of Latin America and eastern Europe? Londregan (2000) suggests that key differences may be in more microlevel institutions, such as legislative committees. Finally, the answer may turn on whether the parliamentary-presidential dichotomy is hiding some underlying variable, such as the number of "veto points" (Tsebelis 1995), or whether the system is an integrated or bargaining one (Niou and Ordeshook 1997). Whichever is chosen, it would need to be linked to a theoretical argument telling us precisely what it is about each type of system that influences regime longevity. Accounting for the relative success of parliamentary regimes or finding the reason why this success is a robust statistical finding remains a challenge to formalists.

A final gap in the formal literature on democracy is that it ignores insights coming from the class bargaining literature. Modelers might ask, in a system with workers, a middle class, two classes of peasants, and a landed class, under what conditions will working-class mobilization yield democracy? Luebbert's approach, which finds that the bourgeoisie and workers can reach a class compromise under certain conditions, is consistent with a model developed by Przeworski and Wallerstein (1982). But this cannot be the only democratic equilibrium, and formal theorists should be modeling the patterns identified by scholars in the Moore tradition to check for equilibrium possibilities.[16]

The past decade of comparative research on democracy has been a rich one empirically, both statistically and in the exploration of historical and contemporary cases. Formal modeling of democratic transitions and consolidation is making initial inroads. But as the last few points should make evident, the great gap is in the interstices between the methods. Comparativists relying on each of the three methods have been insufficiently reflexive on the advances in their counterparts to ask new questions of data, to model statistically recurrent processes, and to adjust the focus of narrative to variables that come out as important in statistical and formal studies.

16. A more radical approach is suggested by Gourevitch (1998). He points out that Moore's core insight is to find the root of political conflict to be in the axes of cleavage. Since microregulation has replaced macroeconomic policy among the advanced industrial countries as the foundation for core cleavages, Gourevitch finds it unlikely that battles among social classes will impinge on political institutions. The fragmented specialized issues of microregulation, however, will begin to carve their way into political coalitions, conflict, and institutions. If Gourevitch is correct, the Moore tradition should find its way into the microanalytic game theoretic approach that has long been considered its rival.

■ | Order

Since the end of World War II, Hobbesian fears of disorder informed the subfield of international relations, but students of comparative politics could forget Hobbes and ask the Lasswellian questions (1936) of who gets what, when, and how? To be sure, comparativists studied revolutions, but mostly as historical phenomena (Skocpol 1979; Goldstone 1991).

Events in the late 1980s brought Hobbes back into the center of comparative politics. The states of the "second world" collapsed. Several states in the third world, mostly in Africa and Asia, collapsed as well. And an unnoticed trend since the end of World War II became quite clear, begging for explanation. This trend is the decrease in the probability of interstate war and the increase in the probability of civil war. Furthermore, civil wars were increasing in number in large part because they were in many cases interminable, whereas interstate wars have been far more likely to end in a negotiated settlement. With the dependent variable respecified as the ability of a state to withstand collapse, or ethnic and other forms of insurgency, the number of cases facilitated statistical analysis. Data sets such as the Minorities at Risk (MAR) and State Failure allowed comparativists to sort out statistically polities that were more or less subject to rebellion (Gurr 2000; Collier and Hoeffler 2000; Fearon and Laitin 1999). In a complementary effort, formal models seek to identify the causal mechanisms that might be driving the statistical findings. Because the breakdown of order was in many cases caused by insurgents acting in the name of ethnic/national groups, many of the theoretical advances build on the seminal work of Horowitz (1985), whose focus was on ethnic conflict in general. The latest case-based narrative research relies on formal models (Kalyvas forthcoming) and statistical methods (Varshney 2002) and can potentially elucidate the workings of the formally derived mechanisms.

STATISTICS

In standard comparative politics treatments of revolution, it was argued that the number was too few to allow for standard statistical methods. Skocpol (1979) relied on critical comparisons, and Goldstone (1991) on a Boolean schema developed by Ragin (1987). The J curve (Davies 1972) and resource mobilization (Tilly 1978) hypotheses lent themselves to statistical tests, but most tests of these theories have been in the historical narrative tradition.[17]

Ted Gurr's Minorities at Risk and State Failure teams, in their books, articles, and accompanying data sets, rely primarily on the statistical method.

---

17. Statistical work on the sources of order (because it did not address the great revolutions), and here I refer to the work of Hibbs (1973), tended to get lost in comparative research on revolution.

Gurr (1993) reports on a data project that involved extensive coding on demographic, cultural, social, military, economic, and political variables for 233 "politicized communal groups" from 93 countries in all the world's regions. To be included, groups must either have experienced discrimination or have taken political action in support of collective interests. This data set has been criticized for several problems, probably the most severe being that the cases were chosen on the dependent variable, thereby leaving out many groups which, for lack of mobilization, were not seen as being at risk. In response, and in an attempt to improve the data, the Gurr team has worked with the research community to help correct many of the problems.

What do the data show? Gurr claims that level of group grievances and strength of the group's sense of identity are the most important independent variables (1993, 123–138). Yet, oddly, this reported finding had no statistical support. The wider research community (second-generation users of the MAR data) finds otherwise. Fearon and Laitin (1999) report that the level of GDP per capita in the country (a variable they added to the data set) is the most robust predictor of rebellion. Toft (1998) reports that the geographical concentration of groups in historic territories is a powerful predictor of rebellion. Saideman (2001) reports that foreign support is important for rebellion, and this foreign support is more likely to be forthcoming if the group borders on a country that is dominated by their ethnic kin. Meanwhile, no study controlling for GDP and geographic concentration has shown that level of economic, cultural, or political grievances can differentiate cases of high rebellion from cases with low or no rebellion. In fact Laitin (2000) reports that degrees of language grievance have no relationship at all to rebellion and that in some specifications, there is a weak negative relationship, showing lower levels of rebellion the greater the grievances over language policy.

The second-generation findings from the MAR data set are in accord with many of the central findings from the State Failure Task Force (Esty et al. 1995, 1998). Unlike MAR, the State Failure data set uses country/year as its unit of analysis, and the dependent variable is state failure, a concept that includes revolutionary and ethnic wars, mass killings, and disruptive regime changes. The robust explanatory variables include living standards in the country (measured by infant mortality), level of trade openness, and level of democracy (where "partial" and "recent" democracies are most likely to suffer failure). Consistent with the nonfindings on grievances by second-generation MAR analysts, the State Failure Task Force finds (almost) no support in their statistical models for the hypothesis that ethnic discrimination or domination generates state failure.

NARRATIVES

Case studies of the breakdown of legitimate domination are a growth industry. Here I will review two of the ways in which the dimension of disorder has been analyzed: explaining the collapse of state authority and explaining the eruption of ethnic violence and civil war.

The collapse of the Soviet state—given the wide acceptance in political science that Samuel Huntington (1966) got it right, that is, that Leninist systems might be inept in providing many public goods but could produce order—came as a shock to political scientists, even those who were specialists in Soviet studies. On the causes of the Soviet collapse, area specialists have been divided: Suny (1993) sees it as caused by the emergence of national consciousnesses, seeded by the Soviet state, that could not be contained by that state; similarly Beissinger (2001) sees it as due to the tides of nationalist mobilization that undermined the regime's ability to maintain order; Roeder (1993) sees it as inherent in the sclerotic institutional arrangement of Leninist states, where selected officials had powerful incentives not to innovate; Hough (1997) sees it as caused by the loss of will by the Soviet intelligentsia (and incredibly self-destructive policies by Gorbachev) to lead what was sure to be an extremely difficult political and economic transition; and Solnick (1998) sees it in the loss of confidence by agents of the state in the ability and will of the Soviet leadership to exert domination over government and society, and therefore these agents grabbed as much property as they were able, to ensure themselves a livelihood should the state collapse. As it was rational for any agent to steal from the state, it was rational for all to do so, and thus there was a cascade that emasculated the resources of the Soviet state.

Lohmann's discussion (1994) of informational cascades and the breakdown of the East German regime has a similar dynamic. The lesson these narratives provide for theory is the equilibrium aspects of what once was called institutionalization. Seeing political order as an equilibrium compels us to analyze it in terms of coordinated expectations; suggesting that even highly institutionalized polities, given informational cascades of possible breakdown, can unravel at breakneck speeds.

State collapse in Africa has also generated a significant narrative corpus. Despite a cogent literature elaborating on the weaknesses of the precolonial (Herbst 2000) and the postcolonial African states (Callaghy 1987; Migdal 1988; M.C. Young 1994), professional practice within political science has too long continued to give state officials and state policies priority in its analyses. But with publication by Bayart (1993), Mamdani (1996), and Reno (1995), a radical shift occurred. In Reno's image the "shadow state"—the set of informal networks of state officials, ethnic chiefs, members of secret societies, local thugs, foreign governments, international firms, and independent traders—exerts domination over countries in near-total disregard for the apparatus that claims a seat in the United Nations. The shadow state constitutes political authority; the formal state, that is, the bureaucratic apparatus that negotiates with foreign governments and makes commitments to international agencies, is a ruse. Shadow state networks can topple formal states, and the costs of sustaining a rebellion are low. Foreign patrons, such as Colonel Mohammar Qaddafi, who has been willing to supply training and weapons to support a gaggle of local insurgencies, are a resource of immense importance in organizing a rebellion. Another resource is international aid from NGOs that comes in response to the collapse of the state. This aid is confiscated and deployed by rebels with the same ruthless energy as smuggled diamonds. Ethnic ties are another resource, useful for recruiting armed bands of supporters by local tyrants, but these ties are of far less use in many cases (e.g., Bazenguissa-Ganga 1999) than is often portrayed in accounts that are based more on justifications of the rebellion by rebel leaders than on actual observance of the exploitation of resources by rebels.

Ellis (1999) offers a compelling narrative of state collapse in Liberia. In this shocking yet clear-headed exposition, readers learn of insurgents eating the hearts of their enemies, castrating civilians and keeping the excised organs as trophies. In these dramas, rebels rely on renditions of traditional magic as a resource to sustain domination. Ellis argues that the colonial state was only a thin layer covering indigenous systems of rule. This state dissipated because with the end of the cold war, there were no patrons interested in propping it up. Once dissipated, unconstrained contests for power, in which memories of traditional practices played a powerful role in insurgent strategies, reduced states into anarchy. Ellis's is hardly the last word in accounting for the collapse of the colonial state, in Liberia, in Sierra Leone, in Somalia, in the Congo (Brazzaville), in the Congo (Kinshasa), and in Cambodia, but it is inconceivable that a satisfactory theory of state breakdown will be written that is not informed by the narrative corpus in which Ellis's is a model.

The narrative mode is not limited to a fascination with state collapse. The seminal work of Adam (1971) showed the importance of tracing carefully the mechanics of bureaucratic order especially under conditions where regimes lack legitimacy. Scott (1990) keeps an ethnographer's ear to the ground in order to hear the "hidden transcripts" of resistance, ones that challenge but also reify political order. Wedeen (1999) examines the cult of former Syrian President Hafiz al-Asad, where he was portrayed as a master in all arenas of human action, from diplomacy to pharmacy. Why, Wedeen asks, would a regime spend scarce resources on a cult whose rituals of obedience are transparently phony? Indeed, most Syrians did not believe the cult's claims. The book concludes that Asad's cult operated as a disciplinary device, generating a politics of public dissimulation in which citizens made believe they revered their leader. By inundating daily life with regime discourse, Wedeen argues, the cultists enforced obedience and induced complicity. This study does not rule out other explanations for Asad's success in fostering complicity. Nor does it assess the magnitude of the discourse affect. Nonetheless Wedeen's narrative, which includes cartoons, jokes, and other forms of everyday complicity, illustrates how discourse strategies can be employed as explanatory variables.

As to narratives of ethnically based violence, the most compelling narratives have been provided by Brass (1997) from research in north India. He investigates a range of local incidents, some of which blow up into ugly riots and become classified as "communal violence" in standard accounts. Brass reports on a class of actors known as riot professionals who have an interest in turning everyday forms of local violence into a large-scale communal riot. These professionals may be politicians who need the violence to solidify their voting blocs (as confirmed by Wilkinson 1998); alternatively, they may be entrepreneurs who gain profit from the looting that riots promote. Once an incident catches the attention of riot professionals, they seek to activate the masses, who can use the violence to loot for themselves or to settle scores with local enemies. Kalyvas's microscopic study (forthcoming) of a region in the Greek civil war similarly finds a powerful alliance between urban ideologues who had macroagendas such as Communism and village actors who had local scores to settle and were willing to denounce neighbors as enemies of the occupying army in order to justify murdering them. These ethnographic studies of violence show that the solidarity between leadership and killers in civil war cannot be explained simply by preexisting solidarities. These solidarities must be accounted for in their own right. Furthermore, both the Brass and Kalyvas narratives make clear that ethnically based and ideologically based civil wars may have quite similar dynamics. The separation of ethnic war from civil war as objects of study (as suggested by Kaufmann 1996) seems not to be a useful one.

Comparative case studies complement ethnographies in the narrative tradition. Bunce (1999) compares the dismemberment of the Soviet Union, Yugoslavia, and Czechoslovakia with the goal of differentiating the violent case (Yugoslavia) from those that split apart with minimal violence. She identifies two factors of importance: the interests of the military and whether the dominant national group had its own institutions under the ancien régime. Since there were no unique Russian or Czech institutions in the Communist period, post-Communist leaders of these republics were compelled to minimize tensions between them and those republics that had their own institutional apparatuses. This minimized the level of violence. The Serbs had their own institutions under the ancien régime, and with a military that had a strong interest in maintaining the federation, violence ensued. Varshney (2002) compares the few Indian cities that have had significant communal violence with comparable cities (in terms of demographics, history, and region) where violence has been minimal. He finds that preexisting patterns of civic engagement, where Muslims and Hindus belonged to labor unions, political parties, or business associations, helped cauterize communal conflict before an ugly incident could serve as a spark for violence.

FORMAL MODELS

International relations modelers began addressing the violence that ensued after the collapse of the Soviet Union and the Yugoslav Federation. Posen (1993b)—in a quasi-formal realist model—recognized the internationality situation as quite familiar: anarchic. Relying on a security dilemma framework, he explains cases of violence on the basis of such factors as a national group's overestimation of the weakness of state authority, and the window of opportunity that chaos held for the fulfillment of long-term goals. Walter and Snyder (1999) edited a volume where security dilemma ideas were applied to cases in Africa and Asia as well. However, Fearon (1998b) discounts the mechanism of the security dilemma and hypothesizes that under conditions of newly gained independence, the ruling faction (or ethnic group) was unable—even if it wanted to—to commit to the future well-being of losing factions (or minority ethnic groups). Under such conditions, minorities would have an incentive to rebel early, rather than wait to see if the cheap talk of the ruling group was honest, because to wait so long would mean having a much lower chance of winning in a rebellion.

These international relations models assume that ethnic groups were sufficiently self-organized as to act like states, as unitary actors. The apparent rapid rise of ethnic consciousness and groupness, however, requires some explanation. Kuran (1998) suggests that levels of group solidarity have a cascade or tipping quality to them. If you have some weak ties to an ethnic identification, and an increasing number of people similarly situated begin to wear ethnic clothes, perform ethnic rituals, learn historic languages, and portray themselves as members of that ethnic group, the greater the pressure will be on you to follow suit. Depending on people's hidden preferences for ethnic attachment, it is possible to move from complete demobilization to near-total mobilization in a rather short period. Jack L. Snyder (1993b) identifies a clear signal that sets off a cascade—the weakening of the state. This signal increases demand for protection from one's national group.

Insurgencies, however, are not always the result of state failure; they arise under stable conditions as well. Thus the need for a theory to account for rebellion in light of the failure of the standard grievance models to differentiate countries susceptible to rebellion from those that are not. Collier and Hoeffler (2000) model rebellion as the apex of organized crime. Rebels don't extort from shopkeepers as do mafias, but they control the export of primary produce. Leaders of rebellions therefore need a sufficient number of followers in order to challenge the state military forces at the various choke points in the sale or export of primary products. Subject to the availability of primary products, recruitable looters, and a weak army of the state, rebellions will prosper. Fearon and Laitin (1999) develop a model of insurgency (also opposed to a grievance model) where young men choose whether to join the legitimate economy or to join a rebellion;

meanwhile the state decides how many resources to put into counterinsurgency. These two simple models, though differently constructed, help explain why country-level GNP (worse job opportunities for youths, and lower predicted levels of counterinsurgency spending), availability of primary products, and group concentration of population (especially if concentrated in mountainous zones) are better predictors of rebellion than variables that measure cultural differences or group grievances.

As with democracy, the interesting gaps in the literature on order are the missed opportunities that lie between the different methods. While formal work on the question of the breakdown of order and the rise of civil wars within states has been developing rapidly, it has not kept pace with the cross-sectional and narrative reports. Findings from state failure, for example, linking state failure to low levels of trade openness, have not been formalized. Nor has the failure in statistical models to find any relationship between grievances, discrimination, and inequality and rebellion received adequate formal treatment. Most glaringly, the narratives have portrayed consequential players (e.g., riot professionals) and have shown high levels of intragroup and interstate fragmentation, but formal modelers haven't specified the implications of wars between moderates and radicals among insurgents, or between armies and presidents within states.[18]

Formal modelers who work on signaling and "cheap talk" have not sought to wrestle with the narrative evidence of discourse regimes sustaining political order. The greater the attention to the origins of order and the details of disorder, the more powerful will be our future models. Missed opportunities exist in the other direction as well. Too many narrativists, for example, focus on the ethnic bases of civil wars without paying attention to statistical results showing ethnic difference to be inconsequential in predicting civil war. Brilliant expositions of communal violence (such as Brass 1997 and Varshney 2002) are presented as if formalization would provide no further insight. Yet more attention to the strategy space of rioters may help determine the conditions under which riot professionals will do their professional thing. The comparative literature on order is advancing on all three methodological fronts, but there is insufficient cross-fertilization, which limits solid cumulative gains.

■ | Forms of Capitalism

As Rogowski (1993) highlighted in the previous decadal review of comparative politics, the political economy of the advanced industrial states is a research program of considerable energy and growth.[19] Historical

18. The exception is DeNardo (1985) who models intrarebel dynamics.

19. For an insider's guide through this extensive literature, see P. Hall 1999.

institutionalists set the research agenda.[20] In the classic text of the period (Katzenstein 1978), political strategies among OECD states in adjustment to the collapse of the Bretton Woods system and to the oil shocks constituted the dependent variable. The independent variable was country institutions that were themselves a product of distinct historical trajectories. The institutional capacities and interests of ministries of finance, central banks, commercial banks, and labor unions set limits to and provided opportunities to respond to the economic challenges. Historical institutionalists envisaged a continuum of different types of capitalism, ranging from strong states relative to society (associated with mercantilist political strategies) to strong societies relative to state institutions (associated with liberal political strategies).

Comparative political economy did not coordinate on a single dependent variable for collective analysis. In different studies, economic growth, economic stability, wage equality, redistribution, the social groups paying most heavily for the costs of readjustment, and political strategy were featured on the left side of the field's equations. But in the 1970s there was an implicit and by the 1990s an explicit sense that these outcomes formed into coherent packages which Esping-Andersen (1990) called the different "worlds" of capitalism: liberalism, corporatism, and a third form, associated with Christian Democracy, that presents a unique package of high equality and low taxes, and by so doing, sacrifices growth (Swenson 1989; Iversen and Wren 1998). To be sure, much analysis in this field has specified relationships within each world. But the glue that holds this field together is the question of what caused and what sustains the different worlds of capitalism (Gourevitch 1978).

STATISTICS

"Forms of capitalism" is a vaguely specified dependent variable, and its values are nominal. This suited the historical institutionalists, who were more interested in coherent narratives than high r^2s.[21] But the turbulence of the field was a more formidable problem for variable specification than was any methodological resistance by the historical institutionalists. Consider the problematic of the field a decade ago, as seen by Rogowski (1993), whose dependent variable was "comparative economic growth": "Among

20. Gerschenkron 1962 is the seminal work. For a comprehensive account of historical institutionalism as used in comparative political economy, see Thelen and Steinmo 1992.

21. To be sure, there is a long tradition of statistically based research (much of it done in Europe, but Hibbs 1977 reflects research on both sides of the Atlantic) that revealed stability in the institutional patterns elaborated by the historical institutionalists, with a wide variety of policy outcomes conditioned on the type of capitalism for each Organization of Economic Cooperation and Development (OECD) country.

the economically advanced nations, the continuing Japanese 'miracle' and the quite respectable growth of the continental European economies [that] contrasted sharply with the dismal record of the U.S. and the U.K." (1993, 431). A variety of theories was offered. Hall (1986), for example, sought to account for Britain's long economic decline on the basis of a theory of the interaction of institutions and economic ideas. Others stressed the combination of institutions and interests. However, a decade later the countries were reversed in growth records, and explanations for economic decline had to account for Japan's long recession rather than the United States's. Explanatory models are difficult to nail down when the world economy has been changing so rapidly that it is hard to place political units on any important dimension and to have confidence that the relative values for those political units would stay sufficiently stable as to allow for a community of scholars to account for the variance.

Despite these modeling difficulties, available data on Organizational Economic Cooperation and Development (OECD) states encouraged statistical analysis. Some (such as inflation) were produced and standardized by governments themselves; others, such as indicators of corporatism (Schmitter and Lehmbruch 1979) or central bank independence, required careful construction by the scholarly community; others still, like union concentration, were built from virtual scratch by the scholarly community (for a preliminary analysis of a new data set, see Wallerstein, Golden, and Lange 1997). Using these data, comparativists moved beyond issues of response to economic crisis to other variables on the left side of their expressions: explaining the trade-off on inflation versus unemployment; explaining the level of trade openness; and explaining variation in wage equality (Iversen and Wren 1998).

Much work in this tradition puts forms of capitalism on the independent variable side of the expression. Social democracy is shown to be associated (in contrast to free market liberalism) with a larger government sector, greater equality, public investment in task-specific technical skills, growth advantages in some sectors, and a comparative advantage in the face of economic shocks (Cameron 1978; Hibbs 1977; Garrett and Lange 1986; Garrett 1998b).

Back to forms of capitalism as a dependent variable, perhaps the most hotly debated issue in the study of the comparative political economy of the advanced industrial states is in assessing the impact of globalization. Some see differences weakening. Rodrik (1998) foresees common demands for widespread growth in government spending, especially welfare spending, as a form of insurance against the shock of job loss and social dislocations in the face of globalization, at the terrible cost of losing all mobile capital. Scharpf (1991) and Lambert (2000) see globalization undermining the welfare state in even solidly corporatist governments. Garrett (1998a) is far more optimistic about democratic corporatism and sees it as a best response to the forces of globalization, cushioning market dislocations and providing lucrative investment sites for mobile capital. Iversen and Cusack (2000) challenge this consensus, and argue that the effects of globalization are weak, in comparison to technological changes in production. To the extent that those who see the forces of globalization to be strong, we should expect increasing convergence of structure and strategy of OECD states; to the extent the Iversen-Cusack position is correct, we should expect variations in economic growth, in growth of the welfare state, and in wage equality, depending on technological profiles of state economies.

FORMAL MODELS

Historical institutionalists did not model the patterns that they had discovered in the 1970s. As a result, there were important gaps to be filled. Questions obvious to theorists, such as why there wasn't convergence toward the institutional patterns that were most efficient, did not get addressed. Why, for example, if Britain lacked the political institutions to control the City, could it not construct them to enhance political effectiveness (Blank 1978)? Historical institutionalists did not have a well-worked-out answer to what maintained institutional patterns over time. More important, historical institutionalists emphasized the interaction between politics and economics but did not incorporate this insight into testable models. In the past decade some progress has been made along these lines.

Hall and Soskice, in specifying historical institutions as equilibria, have begun to connect findings of the historical institutionalists with those of the statistical analysts. "Political economists," they write, "have always been interested in the differences in the economic and political institutions that occur across countries. . . . [C]omparative political economy revolves around the conceptual frameworks used to understand institutional variation across nations" (2001a, 1). Relying on endogenous growth theory, which would have us predict that different national rates of growth are conditioned by the institutional structure of the national economy, Hall and Soskice focus on comparative institutions. Since institutions affect the character of technological progress and rates of economic growth, understanding institutions as equilibria plays a direct role in explaining growth.[22]

The Hall-Soskice approach is based on the new economics of organization, with the firm as the fundamental unit in a capitalist economy adjusting to exogenous shocks. In the model, firms reduce risk by making commitments to their workers and to other firms, and this occurs in several spheres: bargaining over wages and working conditions; securing a skilled labor force; getting finance; coordinating with other firms, e.g., on standard setting; and getting employees to act as agents of the firm. Strategies

---

22. This move, to see the political foundation of modern markets, was foreshadowed by Ruggie's notion (1983) of "embedded liberalism."

to resolve these commitment-coordination problems are conditioned on the national institutional environment. The "national political economies" (2001a, 8) form the principal units of variation, as "we emphasize variations in corporate strategy evident at the national level. We think this is justified by the fact that so many of the institutional factors conditioning the behavior of firms remain nation-specific" (16). The principal dimension on the dependent variable is nations in which "firms coordinate their activities primarily via hierarchies and competitive market arrangements" (liberal market economies, or LMEs) and those in which "firms depend more heavily on non-market relationships to coordinate their endeavors with other actors and to construct their core competencies" (coordinated market economies, or CMEs) (8). The LMEs are Coasian; that is, firms keep arms length from other firms and engage in formal contracting. The CMEs have much incomplete contracting, widespread sharing of private information, and more collaborative interfirm relations. In equilibrium, LME firms should invest in switchable assets that have value if turned to another purpose; CME firms should be more willing to invest in asset specificity, which depends on the active cooperation of others. The separate components of these political economies are complementary, in the sense that high returns from one component entail high returns for another component in the system. So CME firms that give long-term employment contracts profit when they are in a financial system that doesn't punish short-term losses. Complementarity explains the clustering among the solutions to the commitment problems across the spheres of risk.

The model makes predictions in regard to the exogenous shock of globalization. The microeconomists' assumption of pressures to liberalize everywhere, they argue, is based on the (wrong) view that the key to profitability is lower labor costs; this is true for LMEs but not CMEs. Thus the hypothesis is that under globalization, CME firms might relocate in LME countries in order to get access to the radical innovations, while LME firms might move some activities to CME settings to secure quality control and publicly provided skills for labor. (Here they would make a different prediction from Garrett 1998a, who sees the CMEs as having a superior equilibrium in the face of globalization). A second hypothesis is that conflict between labor and capital in the face of globalization will be low in CMEs, where capital and labor often line up in support of existing regulatory regimes (and where labor unions will remain strong), but high in LMEs, where business is pushing hard for deregulation of labor markets (and where labor unions will weaken). The social cleavages that result will therefore be different in the two political economies.

The Hall-Soskice approach takes account of many of the cross-sectional findings in the comparative political economy field, most importantly the apparent stability of social democracy under a wide range of challenges, but also of the intercorrelations of high government spending, social welfare provisions, and union density that come together as a package. However, once you endogenize politics and economics, new forms of statistical testing (as suggested in Alt and Alesina 1996) are in order and remain on the agenda. This approach also takes into account the principal framework of the early historical institutionalists, who took for granted the equilibrium properties of the different forms of capitalism. It makes sense of why we should expect some degree of cross-national variation in effects of the apparently homogenizing force of globalization. (For a complementary theoretical account of why we should expect greater heterogeneity as a result of globalization, see Rogowski 1998.) And finally, it presents a compelling alternative to price theory, which sees institutions as constraints to efficiency but not as sets of equilibria that are dynamically stable. However, as we will see in the next section, the findings in formal theory diverge somewhat from a new generation of narratives in historical institutionalism.

Narratives

From the 1970s, debates within the historical institutionalist research program have been on the causal factors (sectoral balances, timing of industrialization, level of social partnership among classes, and land/labor/capital ratios) explaining the emergence of the different worlds of capitalism. Because of the methodological orientation of the historical institutionalists, the literature they produced was rich in narrative, where case studies (Zysman 1977) and comparisons (Katzenstein 1985; Gourevitch 1986) were the dominant mode. Even Rogowski's strongly theoretical treatise (1989)—where land/labor/capital ratios explained political coalitions—contained historically based narratives elaborating the theory with real-world cases.

The historical institutionalists have continued to write empirically dense narratives that speak directly to the dependent variables that have defined statistical and formal research, but their impact on the practice of statistical and formal modelers has been limited. Consider Katzenstein (1984, 1985). He sought to explain how political stability in the small European states could be maintained under conditions of enormous economic flexibility. The answer was in corporatist governance. He identified two subtypes of the democratic corporatist form of capitalism, liberal and social. Like many of the historical institutionalists, he provided an historical account for these patterns, highly influenced by the structural factor of smallness making these states "takers" rather than "makers" of international rules. What distinguished the first volume (Katzenstein 1984), however, was the careful sectoral analyses in Austria (the social corporatist example) and Switzerland (the liberal corporatist example). In these narratives, the ideology of social partnership coming from a common sense of vulnerability plays an important role in sustaining countrywide institutions (1985, 87–89). This ideological variable is hard to specify for more general explanations, but it should have paved the way for future cross-sectional and theoretical work that encompassed this factor (as well as other variables identified in the narratives), as a test of the magnitude of their impact on sustaining historical institutions. In general the fuzzy variables that attracted the historical institutionalists as consequential rarely find their way in cross-sectional statistical research or in formal theories of the market.

In the 1990s, with questions turning toward the breakdown of institutional differences, Berger and Dore (1996), having observed industrial processes in Japan and Europe, were convinced that national political economies would retain their institutional integrity. In a commissioned set of narrative studies, their intuitions were in large part confirmed, as were those of the historical institutionalists in regard to the oil shocks. National institutions were retaining their historic peculiarities in the face of globalization. Thelen and Kume (1999) find similarly in regard to labor policy in Germany and Japan. It is notable that these studies have not compelled those who have emphasized the homogenizing impact of globalization to figure out why, at least in the short run, the world isn't conforming to their predictions.

Now consider Pierson (1994). He uses the narrative mode in comparing the dismantling of the welfare state under Thatcher and Reagan. By examining two of what Hall and Soskice call LMEs, one would have predicted that under conservative governments, there would have been significant retrenchment. Pierson finds, instead, grand goals but very limited success. Seeking to explain the failures to cut back programs conservative leaders considered inefficient and evil, Pierson finds institutional structure to be of limited power. For example, consider the institutional variable of veto points. The numerous veto points in the U.S. system as compared to the few such points in the U.K. system would lead to the prediction that given the same goals, Thatcher would be more successful than Reagan. Wrong. Reagan, on the margin, was more successful. Pierson finds, instead, that the relative success of programs to survive the conservative onslaught could be explained by the very features of the programs being dismantled. He calls this policy feedback. This variable would not be easy to explore statistically, since every policy has many dimensions of policy feedback, some allowing for easy dismantling, others blocking any change. Consequently, there is no simple value of policy insulation for social programs. Pierson suggests that, "a more promising strategy is to develop middle-range theories that acknowledge both the complexity of feedback and its context-specific qualities" (1994, 171).

But two more concrete proposals suggest themselves. Given the differences the cross-sectional and theoretical literatures find between LMEs and CMEs, Pierson's study should be replicated across this divide to see if policy feedback is consequentially important in the same way in two different political economies. The Hall-Soskice portrayal of LMEs suggests that they would be far more capable of dismantling welfare state programs (and their theory would predict that by holding steady against the welfare state,

Reagan and Thatcher effectively held back its predicted development given growth in GDP).[23] But Pierson's study suggests an alternative—that it isn't institutional structure but the policy complexities of welfare state benefits that make them resistant to exogenous shocks. Pierson (1996) examines four cases that do cross the CME/LME divide (Sweden and Germany are added) and finds in contrast to the Hall-Soskice portrayal, there is no clear evidence of CME relative success in sustaining the welfare state.

Second, Pierson's list of programmatic criteria should be organized in a way to allow exploratory statistical tests on policy feedback. In Pierson (1996), data on relative retrenchment are presented cross-nationally but no attempt is made to capture policy feedback (and a set of other proposed independent variables, 176–78) with cross-national data. (More progress is made in Myles and Pierson 2001.) Narrative uncovered a plausible variable to explain crucial outcomes in political economy; this variable requires attention in the formal and cross-sectional domains.[24]

Still to be assimilated by scholars in the comparative political economy field, Herrigel (1996) in his examination of German industrialization finds that the notion of a national economy with its peculiar institutions to be a sham. Close examination shows that there has long been two intersecting German institutional frameworks, each with its own internal logic. The implication of Herrigel's research is that future cross-sectional studies are making a grave error to the extent that they use OECD tapes that rely on country-level trends. To be sure, if central bank independence or monetary policy is the key independent variable, this may present no problem. But if variables such as Katzenstein's (density of social networks) are being tested, Herrigel's work demands that we disaggregate our economic data to the lowest administrative level. To develop such data (though OECD is beginning to collect some data at the level of region) would be an enormous enterprise. But if the variables pointed to by Katzenstein and Herrigel are seen to be consequential, there can be no alternative than to seek major funding for far more disaggregated economic data than OECD supplies the research community for free.

The theoretically informed narratives of the historical institutionalists present several clear challenges and opportunities to the statistical and formal models in comparative political economy. The overall research program remains vibrant; it lacks only the sense of challenge to reconcile inconsistent findings across the tripartite methodology.

23. Pierson does not perform general equilibrium tests of his model. This may help to explain why he believed that the massive budget deficits incurred by Reagan would long endure and help conservative successors, arguing fiscal necessity, to dismantle other parts of the welfare state.

24. Given Lambert 2000, we see that dismantling the welfare state (in Australia) is not as formidable a task as Pierson's book suggests. This variation can easily be taken advantage of in cross-sectional work.

■ | **Conclusion**

This review has identified a potential coherence in the comparative politics subdiscipline. The hope here has been to present not only coherence but also a frame within which most comparativists will be able to fit their contributions and the contributions of colleagues whose work they most admire. To be sure, not all dependent variables of consequence have been treated herein and not all possible specifications of the dependent variables have been discussed. Nor have consequential independent variables in the classical tradition, such as class structure, political culture, or the socioeconomic status of the population, gotten their own sections. They were brought into the analysis to the extent that theorizing in the past decade linked them to the three dependent variables that received attention here.

Nor still have the big "isms" that dominate many debates received special attention. But the independent variables these isms privilege have gotten attention, whether they were discourse regimes (postmodernism) or country GDP (modernization theory). Unhooked from their isms, these variables can be assessed as to the magnitude of their effect and their interaction effects with variables from other isms.[25] To be sure, many comparativists have bet their careers on the power of independent variables (often associated with a particular paradigmatic school) to explain a range of outcomes. Others have focused on important changes in parameter values that should affect all past explanations. But comparativists who are engaged in these scholarly endeavors should have no trouble in placing their work in the framework provided herein. Moreover, if they cannot link key independent variables or parameters to consequential outcomes, they should reduce their confidence in the importance of the factors that they are analyzing.

Finally, while this review has not highlighted the substantive progress in our subdiscipline, major findings on each of the dependent variables demand summary. High GDP per capita helps explain the consolidation of democracy but not its initiation. Cultural differences and group grievances have no explanatory power in regard to rebellion. Meanwhile, country-level data such as per capita GDP, population size, terrain, and economic growth are better able to explain civil wars. Each form of capitalism constitutes a robust equilibrium and is far less subject to homogenizing effects that one might predict in looking at globalization and the revolution in electronics. (If this last perspective is correct, my successor writing the re-

---

25. Those who organize the field by paradigm would segregate Wedeen's book, discussed in the section on order, in a postmodernism ghetto. However, by taking a standard postmodern variable—regime of discourse—and showing its role in accounting for order, this review seeks to incorporate postmodern insights into the standard comparative corpus, alongside explanatory models coming from other isms.

view of comparative politics for the next decade will not have a section on the causes of the demise of social democracy.)

The central concern here has been in the organization of research for the comparative field. My argument is not that all comparativists should have highly cultivated statistical, formal, and narrative skills. But, it would be a great loss to comparative politics if only one of these skill sets were to define the subfield. My fear is a Chomsky-like revolution in comparative politics, where the formal theorists drive the field workers out of the subdiscipline. An equal fear is if the field workers put up barricades separating themselves from the findings in the formal and statistical worlds. Utopia is in the social organization of physics. In that discipline, there is a division of labor between the experimentalists and theorists, and a pervasive sense of mutual hostility between the camps. But the difference is that in physics, it is unimaginable that the experimentalists would ignore the implications of the most recent theoretical findings, if only to blow them out of the water. Meanwhile, theorists grudgingly seek to account for empirical realities that experimentalists report.

Methodologically, this review argues that in comparative politics, interdependence across the tripartite methodological divide, with grudging toleration built on mutual suspicion of practitioners across the divide, is a key to scientific progress. Despite the occasional portrayal of a Manichean world of qualtoids versus quantoids, this review shows specks of evidence that a common focus is emerging. Comparativists are finding that in a division of disciplinary labor, they need to satisfy two audiences. First, they must demonstrate that their work meets standards within their own methodological community. But second, they ought to feel challenged, even threatened, by advances by scholars within the other two methodological traditions and feel pressure to adjust or delimit their claims in light of findings in those traditions.

This hoped for interdependence is far more promise than reality. The promise is common focus on consequential dependent variables and a joint attempt to address variance across polities on these variables, by scholars working within three methodological approaches. Those scholars who see this as a reflexive and interdependent division of labor—and not as a war among paradigms—will be remaking the comparative method.

Barry R. Weingast

Rational-Choice Institutionalism[1]

■ | Introduction

Political science has witnessed a revolution in the study of institutions. As Hall and Taylor (1996) emphasize, three approaches predominate: the sociological (March and Olsen 1989), historical institutionalism (Evans, Rueschemeyer, and Skocpol 1985; Thelen 1999), and rational-choice approaches to political institutions (North 1990; Riker 1982). An impressive aspect of this revolution is that no approach dominates. Each perspective has its comparative advantages.

The purpose of this essay is to explain the comparative advantages of the rational-choice perspective. Rational-choice theory provides a distinctive set of approaches to the study of institutions. It covers three categories of questions: the effects of institutions; why institutions are necessary at all; and the endogenous choice of particular institutions, including their long-term durability and survival. Rooted in the economic theory of the firm (Coase 1934, 1960; Milgrom and Roberts 1991; Williamson 1985, 1996), economic history (North 1981, 1990), and positive political theory (Hinich and Munger 1997; Riker 1982; Shepsle and Bonchek 1997), this approach provides a systematic treatment of institutions. Although it has much in common with other approaches to institutions, rational-choice theory has its distinctive features, most importantly, providing the microfoundations of institutional analysis. Applications range across all political and social problems, from the effects of the major political institutions of the developed West (such as legislatures, courts, elections, and bureaucracies) to more recent studies of developing countries (for example, ethnic conflict, international security, equilibrium traps that prevent development, and democratic stability).

1. The author gratefully acknowledges helpful conversations from Randy Calvert, Rui de Figueiredo, John Huber, James Morrow, Theda Skocpol, and Kathy Thelan.

Rational-choice scholars model institutions as "humanly devised constraints" on action (North 1990). Methodologically, this definition translates into studying how institutions constrain the sequence of interaction among the actors, the choices available to particular actors, the structure of information and hence beliefs of the actors, and the payoffs to individuals and groups.

The rational-choice approach to institutions divides into two separate levels of analysis (Shepsle 1986). In the first, analysts study the effects of institutions. In the second, analysts study why institutions take particular forms, why they are needed, and why they survive. The first approach takes institutions as exogenous; the second as endogenous. Moreover, the first level of analysis is clearly antecedent to the second: A choice theoretic approach to institutions requires that individuals have expectations about the effects of institutions. As this level naturally arose first, it is far more developed than the second.

The second level of analysis, in turn, takes the study of institutions to a deeper level. In combination, these approaches provide both a method for analyzing the effects of institutions and social and political interaction and a means for understanding the long-term evolution and survival of particular institutional forms. The study of endogenous institutions yields a distinctive theory about their stability, form, and survival. In contrast to approaches that take institutions as given, this approach allows scholars to study how actors attempt to affect the institutions as conditions change.

This approach potentially provides the microfoundations for macro–political phenomena such as revolutions and critical elections (see, e.g., North and Thomas 1972; North 1981; Stewart and Weingast 1992; Poole and Rosenthal 1997; Riker 1982, ch. 9; Weingast 1998a). Until recently, macro–historical phenomena remained largely the domain of historical institutionalists. Although applications of rational-choice theory are relatively new to these questions, its approach provides links with microbehavior, potentially affording a new methodology for comparison across cases. Explicit models of discontinuous political change provide an exciting new set of applications of rational-choice theory.

This essay begins with the study of the effects of institutions, then takes up the question of why institutions are needed at all, and ends by considering the endogenous choice and survival of institutions.

■ | The Effects of Institutions

Rational-choice approaches begin with a set of individuals, assumed to have a well-defined set of preferences. This first approach takes institutions as exogenous. Institutions affect individual interaction and choice in a variety of ways: institutions constrain individual choices, how individuals interact, their information and beliefs, and their payoffs.

Institutional Sources of the Balance of Power between the Executive and the Legislature

The relative powers of the executive and the legislature vary considerably across nations. Presidents in many Latin American countries, such as Argentina and Mexico, are sufficiently powerful relative to their legislatures that these systems are often referred by the appellation *presidentialismo*. The U.S. Congress, in contrast, is one of the most powerful legislatures in the world. Prime ministers in most European parliamentary systems are agents of the majority party (or ruling coalition) without electoral independence of the legislature. These differences reflect a host of institutional details about legislative-executive relations. One of the hallmarks of rational-choice analysis is the demonstration of how microlevel details imply macropolitical differences. This subsection provides a comparative framework for showing how various powers and institutional details affect both the legislative-executive balance of power and policy choice.

UNITED STATES

We begin with the context of the United States, where these techniques were first developed. Although the president can propose legislation, only a member of Congress can officially introduce it into Congress. If legislation is brought to the floor, it is typically considered under an "open rule" where any and all amendments are allowed. The executive holds veto power.[2]

To keep the discussion manageable, we consider a single policy dimension, which might be considered a left-right political dimension or a more specific policy issue, such as degree of protection of the environment or the size of the budget for the armed services. The model represents the executive and members of the legislature as having preferences over the policy dimension. The president and each legislator are assumed to have an *ideal policy* that they prefer over all others and to prefer policies closer to their ideal to those further away. The model also distinguishes a particular policy Q, called the status quo. This represents the policy that will remain in effect if no action is taken. We label the executive's ideal policy E and the legislative median's ideal L.

Figure 1 | Executive, Legislature, and Status Quo

2. For simplicity, this analysis ignores the complication of a veto override; it can be easily incorporated (see Brady and Volden 1997; Cameron 2000; Krehbiel 1998).

Consider the scenario in figure 1, where the status quo Q is on the left. The executive's ideal policy, E, is a bit more to the right, while the median legislator prefers policy L considerably more to the right.

If the legislature were free to chose policy without considering the president, it would introduce legislation and, given the open rule, produce a policy L on the right. Yet legislators must take the president's veto into account.[3] To see the efects of the veto power, consider the set of policies that the executive prefers to the status quo, namely, all policies between Q and $E(Q)$ (see figure 2).

Figure 2 | The Effect of a Presidential Veto

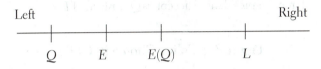

Left   Right

Q E $E(Q)$ L

If the legislature presents the president with legislation to the right of $E(Q)$, the president will exercise his veto, yielding the status quo. Although the congressional median prefers all policies to the right of Q over Q, only those policies preferred to Q by the president will become legislation. The best the median in Congress can do is pass legislation equal to $E(Q)$. In this configuration of preferences, the presidential veto constrains congressional policymaking.

Of course, the executive veto is not always constraining. This can easily be seen by supposing that the positions of the legislative median and the executive were reversed in the figure. Following Kiewiet and McCubbins (1987, 1991), this discussion shows that the president's veto power is asymmetric. For example, if the above policy issue represents budgetary issues, the analysis shows that the president's veto constrains budgetary decisionmaking only when the president wants a lower budget than Congress. When the president wants more than Congress, the veto is not credible, so Congress can ignore the president's interests.[4]

STRONG PRESIDENTIAL SYSTEMS IN LATIN AMERICA

Among modern legislatures, the U.S. Congress is unusually powerful. In contrast, the strong presidential systems of Latin America typically grant the president greater powers over the legislature than in the United States. As Londregan (2000) suggests for Chile, these systems can be modeled as

3. Cameron (2000) provides the best analysis of presidential veto power and its effects on the legislative process. See also Kiewiet and McCubbins (1987), Matthews (1989), and McCarty and Poole (1995).

4. The basic model abstracts from a range of important legislative, executive, and bureaucratic institutions that may be incorporated into the model.

granting the president the power to present the legislature with a take-it-or-leave-it choice over policy.[5]

To emphasize the analysis's comparative dimension, I use the same policy configurations of preferences and status quo as used in the analysis of the United States. In the first scenario (figure 3), the president's ability to present the legislature with a take-it-or-leave-it choice allows the president to obtain his ideal policy E. Although the legislature might threaten not to pass the president proposal of E unless the president moves his proposal closer to L, this threat is not credible. Vetoing E results in the status quo, which makes a majority in the legislature worse off. Thus, in this political environment, the president can force the legislature to accept his ideal policy. In contrast, the U.S. Congress's greater ability to amend legislation allows it to force the president to accept $E(Q)$ instead of E.

Figure 3 | Policy Choice in Chile

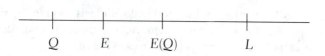

In the second scenario (figure 4), the Chilean president must consider the legislature's veto. To succeed, the president's proposal must make the median legislature better off than the status quo. Hence we consider $L(Q)$, the policy such that L prefers all policies between Q and $L(Q)$ to Q. The median legislator, and hence a majority in the legislature, will accept any of these policies. The president can take advantage of his take-it-or-leave-it powers by presenting the legislature with the policy among this set which he most prefers. In this scenario, the best the executive can do is $L(Q)$.

Figure 4 | The Effect of Legislative Veto in Chile

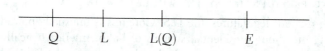

5. Among the many powers listed by Londregan for the case of Chile are: (1) the president can impose time limits in which constitutional legislation must be passed or rejected; (2) constitutional provisions "contain powerful veto provisions that allow the president to have the last word in the legislative debate by introducing amendments along with his or her veto, amendments which must be voted up or down without further change by the Congress"; and (3) as with most Latin American legislatures, Chile's is understaffed and lacks infrastructure to help it fight the president (2000, 66).

Here too, the rules advantage Latin American presidents over the U.S. president. Whereas the U.S. Congress can force the president to accept L, the weaker powers of the Chilean congress allow the president to obtain $L(Q)$ instead of L.

The Chilean constitution contains some critical features designed by the dictator Augusto Pinochet and his supporters to limit the policy flexibility of the democratic governments after the return to democracy. One of the most important of these features is the creation of a set of institutional senators appointed by the president and various enclaves. Pinochet's preferred party could not gain an electoral majority in the presidential election or a majority in the Chamber of Deputies or the Senate. The creation of a set of institutional senators, initially appointed by Pinochet and his faction, allowed his party to maintain a majority in the Senate for many years. This constitution-induced Senate majority thus institutionalized divided government in Chile, and along with it a veto for the opposition on the right against the center-left coalition, the *Concertación*, which typically controls the presidency and the lower chamber.

To show the effect of this constitutional detail on Chilean policy choice, we derive a comparative statics result, showing executive-legislative choice with and without this rule. First, consider the legislature without the institutional senators, which I will call unconstrained democracy. These rules allow the *Concertación* to control the presidency and the congress. Although the election is likely to produce some differences among the medians in the two chambers and the president, these will all be members of the *Concertación*, so for simplicity I ignore these (relatively small) differences. The rules of unconstrained democracy yield a situation with the status quo on the right created under the Pinochet regime and both chambers of the legislature's favored policy located at L and the president's favored policy located at C on the left:

Figure 5 | Postauthoritarian Political Environment In Chile without Institutional Senators

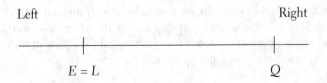

Left   Right

$E = L$ Q

Given congress's legislative powers, the president will introduce legislation of his ideal policy E, and the congress will accept this (see figure 5). Of course, this degree of policy change is a disaster from the perspective of Pinochet and his supporters because it grants the new government the ability to alter the fundamental issues Pinochet and his supporters sought to protect, such as the economic system and the absence of sanctions for human rights violations under the dictatorship.

Institutional senators affect Chilean policy choice by affording the opposition a veto over policy. As in figure 5, the president's preferred policy and the median preferred policy C in the Chamber of Deputies are located on the left. The institutional senators imply that the median preferred policy S in the Senate is held by a member of the opposition party, who prefers to maintain the status quo (see figure 6).

Figure 6 | Postauthoritarian Political Environment in Chile with Institutional Senators

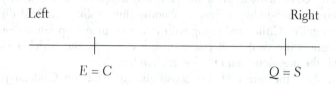

Because the constitution creates divided government, the opposition on the right holds the power to veto major changes. Institutional senators produce a major effect on public policymaking. As figure 6 suggests, the degree of policy movement available to the ruling *Concertación* depends on the location of the Senate median. Some issues, such as human rights, appear just like figure 6, allowing the ruling coalition no flexibility. On other issues, such as labor and education, some institutional senators have more moderate preferences. This implies a median senator having a preferred policy between Q and P, allowing the ruling coalition to change policy.[6]

PARLIAMENTARY SYSTEMS

Space constrains my ability to analyze parliamentary systems at the same level of detail using the same framework. Parliamentary systems without an independent executive produce different policy outcomes than presidential systems. Because the prime minister is an agent of the majority party or ruling coalition, her preferences tend to be closely aligned with the party median. These settings can be analyzed using the same framework, for example, by assuming in a Westminster system that the prime minister's preferences correspond to the party median's position.

6. Londregan's theory and empirical analysis allow us to guage Pinochet's success in rigging the system to preserve the status quo after the period of democratization. The creation of the institutional senators greatly constrains the democratic government's ability to alter the status quo. On policies with a consensus among members of the opposition on the right, the institutional senators allow the Senate to preserve the status quo.

The Role of the Courts: Expanding Civil Rights

The above discussion left policy abstract. To show the power of these models to yield new and surprising conclusions, I turn to the evolution of an important policy area in the United States, expanding the meaning of civil rights legislation.

The landmark Civil Rights Act of 1964 represented a dramatic departure in the status quo, forcing southern states to end their system of apartheid suppressing African Americans. Beginning in the early 1970s, a series of court cases expanded the meaning of this act.[7] In brief, the Civil Rights Act was an antidiscrimination law, requiring equal opportunity for all individuals regardless of race, creed, or gender. Several critical court decisions in the 1970s expanded the meaning of the act to include a degree of affirmative action.

A major puzzle is why a conservative Supreme Court under Chief Justice Warren Burger expanded civil rights. Surely the conservative majority on the Court preferred the status quo to this outcome.

Eskridge (1992b) suggests that the answer to this puzzle lies in the interaction of Congress and the courts. On constitutional issues, the Supreme Court is just that—supreme. To overrule a Supreme Court constitutional decision, the country must amend the Constitution. As amendments are difficult to pass, the Supreme Court controls constitutional interpretation. In other areas, the Supreme Court's authority is less supreme. On statutory decisions—decisions to interpret the meaning of legislation—the Court does not have the last word: elected officials can overturn a judicial decision interpreting legislation by passing new legislation.

Eskridge argues that the conservative Court acted strategically, forestalling an even larger change in the scope of the law through legislation. His argument draws on an additional piece of theory from the pivotal politics model (Brady and Volden 1997; Krehbiel 1998), the "filibuster pivot." Although based on a seemingly small detail from the Senate, this institution proves critical for legislation in the United States. The Senate allows a minority of senators to defeat a bill by "filibustering," continuing the debate to prevent a measure from coming up for a vote. The Senate can end a filibuster only by a supramajority vote.

To pass the 1964 legislation required defeating a filibuster by southern Democrats. To do so required obtaining the support of two-thirds of the Senate. The effect of the filibuster is to require that legislation not just make a simple majority better off than the status quo, but two-thirds of the Senate.[8]

---

7. Notably, *Duke Power* (1971) and *United States Steelworkers v. Weber* (1979).

8. The rule has since been altered to require sixty of one hundred senators instead of sixty-seven.

The following policy setting reveals the effect of the filibuster:

Figure 7 | The Filibuster Pivot

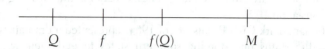

In figure 7, Q is the status quo policy, f is the ideal policy of the filibuster pivot, and M is the median legislator's ideal policy. The filibuster pivot prefers all policies between Q and $f(Q)$ to Q. Any policy outside of the range makes the pivot worse off. If the Senate tries to pass the median legislator's preferred policy M, senators on the left will filibuster, and the majority favoring M will not be able to defeat the filibuster.

The main result of the pivotal politics model in this context is that the majority can move policy from Q toward M as far as $f(Q)$ but no further. Moreover, $f(Q)$ is the equilibrium policy choice that will result under an open rule amendment process. Much of the drama in the passage of the 1964 act concerned the parliamentary maneuvers to defeat the filibuster.[9]

To understand the transformation of civil rights by a conservative Supreme Court in the 1970s, consider the following policy setting:

Figure 8 | Civil Rights Policy

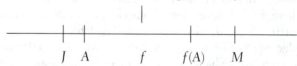

The set of policy alternatives represents the degree of federal support for civil rights, J represents the ideal policy of the conservative Supreme Court majority, A represents the policy enacted by the 1964 act, f is the ideal policy of the filibuster pivot (a conservative Republican), and M is the median senator's ideal policy (see figure 8). As before, the filibuster pivot prefers all policies between A and $f(A)$.

The critical feature of the new political environment of the 1970s is that the median in Congress was far more liberal than the median in the 1964 Congress that passed the Civil Rights Act. Eskridge argues that the more liberal Congress would undoubtedly pass new civil rights legislation moving policy from A to $f(A)$.

In this setting, the Supreme Court acted first to preserve as much of the status quo as possible. By acting first, the Supreme Court moved policy

---

9. See, e.g., Eskridge and Frickey (1988), Graham (1990), and Whalen and Whalen (1985). Rodriguez and Weingast (1995) provide a model and evidence from the perspective developed here.

from A to f. This move precluded any further move by Congress: Because any policy change from f toward M would make the filibuster pivot worse off, no legislation was possible.

This model has several implications. First, it shows the power of the model in specific policy settings to give new answers to important political puzzles.[10] Second, it shows the strategic role of the courts in the United States policymaking process.

VARIANTS

Rational-choice models studying the effects of institutions represent a light industry in political science: there are simply too many variants to mention. Among the topics receiving considerable attention are:

1. Models of cabinet formation and parliamentary systems (see, e.g., Austen-Smith and Banks 1988; Baron 1993; Laver and Shepsle 1996; Moser 2000; Tsebelis 1994)

2. The recent gridlock/pivotal politics model in U.S. politics, that looks more closely at legislative details (Brady and Volden 1997; Krehbiel 1998)

3. The delegation of policymaking authority to the bureaucracy (Fiorina 1981; Epstein and O'Halloran 1999; McCubbins and Schwartz 1984; Moe 1989; Weingast and Moran 1983)

4. Elections (see, e.g., Bawn 1993; Cox 1999)

5. The role of information and uncertainty in politics (see, e.g., Gilligan and Krehbiel 1990; Austen-Smith and Riker 1987; Austen-Smith and Banks 1996; Krehbiel 1991)

6. Constitutional choice (Colomer 1995, ch 6; Hardin 1989; Przeworski 1991; and Riker 1986, chs. 4, 8).

▪ | Why Do Institutions Exist?

The previous discussion took institutions as given and studied their effects. This is by far the dominant mode of analysis in all three brands of institutional analysis. Works of this type, however, beg the question of why institutions are necessary at all. Why can't a society or group do without them?

---

10. Rational-choice theorists have applied analyses of this type in hundreds of contexts. In addition to the cites for the courts in no. 7, see Brady and Volden (1997, ch. 2), on the minimum wage; Ferejohn and Shipan (1989) on telecommunications policy; Riker (1986, ch. 11), on federal aid to education; Weingast and Moran (1983) on regulation by the Federal Trade Commission; and Weingast (1984) on the Securities Exchange Commission.

The purpose of this section and the next is to study a range of rational-choice models that explain why institutions exist and why they take the specific form they do. In brief, the answer is parties often need institutions to help capture gains from cooperation. In the absence of institutions, individuals often face a social dilemma, that is, a situation where their behavior makes all worse off. The prisoner's dilemma is the classic social dilemma, though there are many others (see, e.g., Elster 1989b). In this section, I use a variant of the prisoner's dilemma derived from Milgrom, North, and Weingast's (1990) model of the "Law Merchant." This model demonstrates why institutions are necessary for human interaction in complex societies.

Consider a group of individuals who face gains from cooperation. These gains may be economic gains from exchange or social gains from cooperation, say, to produce social peace and prosperity. The problem is that members of the society face various types of incentive problems where many or all individuals have short-term temptations not to cooperate. The prisoner's dilemma and coordination dilemmas illustrate this problem. Moreover many individuals are vulnerable to the action of others. Prior to the rise of the nation states, farmers were vulnerable to roving bandits who would expropriate the fruits of their labors. Similarly, once firms have made significant sunk investments, say in a water delivery system, citizens are tempted to force them to provide the water at unremunerative prices. Finally, individuals may fail to cooperate because they cannot agree on a distribution of the gains from cooperation.

Appropriately configured institutions restructure incentives so that individuals have an incentive to cooperate. Moreover, because incentive problems differ greatly across environments, the types of institutions necessary to mitigate these problems also varies. The essence of institutions is to enforce mutually beneficial exchange and cooperation. Oliver Williamson summarizes this logic:

> Transactions that are subject to ex post opportunism will benefit if appropriate safeguards can be devised ex ante. Rather than reply to opportunism in kind, therefore, the wise [bargaining party] is one who seeks both to give and receive "credible commitments." Incentives may be realigned, and/or superior governance structures within which to organize transactions may be devised (1985, 48–49).

Studying the limitations of the familiar repeated prisoner's dilemma reveals the logic of this approach to institutions. The well-known "folk theorem" in game theory, popularized in political science in the context of the prisoner's dilemma by Axelrod (1984) and Taylor (1976), shows that although players have a short-run temptation to cheat, they have long-run incentives to cooperate.

Consider the following prisoner's dilemma.

	C	D
C	1, 1	−1, 2
D	2, −1	0, 0

Clearly, both players are better off cooperating (C) than defecting (D), since each receives 1 from mutual cooperation and 0 from mutual defection. Yet each player is better off defecting: if the row player chooses to cooperate, column receives 1 from cooperation and 2 from defection; if row defects, column receives −1 from cooperation and 0 from defection. If both players follow their short-run incentives to defect, they are both worse off, since mutual defection implies the absence of cooperation.

A different result occurs, however, if the players interact over time. When this game is repeated, and assuming that the players do not discount the future too heavily, they can sustain cooperation. In repeated play, players' choices today reflect not only their payoffs today but how they anticipate that their opponents will react to their behavior. Typically players use trigger strategies, such as, "I'll cooperate with the other player as long as she cooperates, but if ever she defects, I will follow this defection in kind."

An opponent's trigger strategy alters a player's incentives. By tying behavior today with (negative) consequences tomorrow, trigger strategies alter the trade-off between defection and cooperation. An opponent's trigger strategy presents a player with the following choice: cooperate today, which yields cooperation in this and every future period. Defect today, which yields a short-term gain but which causes mutual defection in all future periods.

This analysis yields the following payoffs:

Cooperating forever yields payoffs that are a series of 1s, discounted by δ for each period:

$$1 + \delta 1 + \delta^2 1 + \delta^3 1 + \ldots = 1/(1 - \delta)$$

Defecting today and facing mutual defection thereafter yields:

$$2 + \delta 0 + \delta^2 0 + \delta^3 0 + \ldots = 2$$

For δ sufficiently large, each player will prefer cooperation. The calculation above implies that as long as $\delta > \frac{1}{2}$, the players will cooperate.

This discussion illustrates an important feature of rational-choice institutionalism: cooperation must be *self-enforcing* in the sense that all players in society have incentives to cooperate.

Several stringent assumptions prevent this model from being a general model of social interaction. Its conclusions are wildly optimistic, implying that it cannot explain a range of common breakdowns in cooperation, such as wars, ethnic conflict, government and private opportunism, and other systematic failures to capture gains from cooperation.

The model's flaws derive from its simplicity. Two assumptions implicit in the standard prisoner's dilemma model, both concerning defection, limit its wide applicability to the world. Everything is public in the prisoner's dilemma. First, it is obvious what actions constitute defection; there is a profound absence of moral ambiguity and an inexplicable degree of social consensus about how to cooperate. Second, defection is observable in the sense that anyone who defects is immediately known.

As Greif, Milgrom, and Weingast (1994) and Milgrom, North, and Weingast (1990) show, the failure of either assumption plagues the logic of cooperation described above. First, consider moral ambiguity or a lack of consensus about what constitutes cooperation. In contrast to the prisoner's dilemma, people often have fundamental disagreements about what is best for society. For two reasons, multiple ways to cooperate hinder the ability of a society to cooperate. First, individuals must somehow coordinate on the particular way to cooperate; disagreement often leads to cooperation failure (see Weingast 1997). Second, people often disagree about the best way to cooperate in part because of distributional effects. Some means of organizing society benefit one set of individuals at the expense of others, while another means of cooperation yields the opposite result. In this setting, cooperation may fail in part because the parties fight about which mode of cooperation to implement.

The second assumption causes cooperation to fail in a different way. Consider a large group of actors—whether individuals in a society or nations in the world system. In each round of play, the actors are paired and they interact through a prisoner's dilemma. Yet they do not always interact as pairs sufficiently frequently to sustain cooperation. Axelrod and Keohane (1985) show that in this setting cooperation can nonetheless be sustained if the players use generalized trigger strategies in which all players punish another player's defection, regardless of whether they were the target of that defection. Axelrod and Keohane set their analysis in the international system, where different states must decide whether to honor bilateral treaties with one another. As the players interact, each has an incentive to honor the treaty when defection is punished by the entire community.

Sustaining cooperation in this environment clearly depends on the assumption that defection is observable, that is, known by all members of the community, not just the target of the defection. Yet this rules out a host of problems common to bilateral relationships. Often the interaction in a bilateral relationship is private. Outsiders to the relationship have no way of knowing what really took place. Instead, they typically observe a dispute in which both players present internally consistent accounts of how the other defected.

The following example reveals the problems raised by the lack of observable defection. In the 1970s, the United States claimed that Japanese firms were unfairly dumping television sets on the U.S. market, selling them below costs. The Japanese argued that they were not dumping. Instead, they could sell their televisions at costs below those of the U.S. manufacturers because Japanese firms were more efficient producers and thus had much lower costs. Both claims are plausible; yet both cannot be simultaneously true. So who is right? Were the Japanese dumping? Or was the United States opportunistically claiming the Japanese were dumping?

The inability of outsiders to tell what really happened hinders their ability to punish defection. When community enforcement is required to police defection, some defections may go unpunished because the community cannot verify whether a defection in fact took place. This in turn gives rise to a type of opportunism: if some defections cannot be observed, opportunistic players can masquerade their subterfuge qua defection in a plausible rationale that the other defected. Put simply, in the face of these two problems, cooperation cannot be sustained.

The failure of cooperation in the face of uncertainty about who defected, in turn, provides the rationale for institutions. Consider the problem with observing defection. The law merchant model shows how institutions can help resolve problems that arise when defection is not observable (Milgrom, North, and Weingast 1990). The context is the rise of trade during medieval Europe prior to the development of the modern state with a formal legal system extending over its territory. At this time, merchants found that resolving disputes was a major problem. Because defection was hard to detect, sustaining faithful cooperation and exchange was difficult.

Over time, a system of private law judges emerged, whereby some merchants specialized in resolving merchants' disputes and became known as law merchants. A body of precedents and rules evolved for resolving disputes. These principles enabled the law merchant to resolve a range of problems among merchants.

But how did a legal system without appeal to sanctions by the state work? Put another way, why did merchants abide by the law merchant's judgements?

The answer is that the law merchant as an institution complemented the incentives of repeat play to make cooperation self-enforcing where decentralized interaction (as described above) led to failure of cooperation. By investigating disputes and declaring which merchants had defected, the law merchant made cooperation self-enforcing where only defection could be sustained without this institution. The law merchant institution did this in two ways. First, the law merchant's ruling provided an observable signal to the community announcing whether cooperation or defection had taken place. By publicizing defection, the law merchant's judgment could be used to trigger punishment.

Second, this system had two cost advantages over punishment through trigger strategies. First, in a decentralized system envisioned by Axelrod and Keohane, every player must know the full history of every other player. In contrast, the law merchant system requires only that the players find out which players have judgments against them by the law merchant. Second, trigger strategies require that, in the future, other merchants forgo the benefits of trade with the errant merchant. Creating law, even without the force of the state, provided another alternative: as part of the a judgment against a merchant, the latter was asked to make the plaintiff whole, that is, to pay a fine. Of course, the absence of a nation-state implied that the law merchant could not put the merchant in jail or force him to pay a fine. Yet the law merchant system provided an incentive for the errant merchant to make good on judgments against him: by making the plaintiff whole, the errant merchant could prevent the community from initiating its trigger strategy against him. Because outstanding judgments implied punishment by the community, merchants had incentives to make good on their fines.

The role of institutions in the law merchant system complements the incentives of repeat play. Because defection is unobserved, repeat play alone à la the prisoners' dilemma without institutions cannot sustain cooperation. Adding the law merchant to the system, however, changes the consequences of defection and helps the community police defection. Institutions are thus critical to creating the self-enforcing conditions for mutual cooperation.

This latter conclusion is a general result of rational-choice institutionalism. Institutions arise in part to help create the conditions for self-enforcing cooperation in an environment where there are gains from cooperation but also incentive problems that hinder a community's ability to maintain cooperation.

This model applies to a range of problems. The U.S.-Japan dumping example suggests an explanation for one purpose of the General Agreement on Tariffs and Trade and its successor organization, the World Trade Organization, which help govern international trade. These organizations have no independent force of law in the sense that they have no means of coercing member states to obey their rules. Yet they do have the means of investigating disputes among members and coordinating punishments when judgments are made against particular countries. The law merchant approach provides a model of how this works; that is, how the international institutions help sustain self-enforcing trade agreements even when these institutions have no independent ability to punish its member states.

Calvert (1995a) applies this approach to the study of Congress. A range of possibilities exist. One is that this model helps explain one of the roles played by the congressional leadership: they help police exchange among members. In this setting, many exchanges are bilateral or among small groups and are negotiated in private. They are thus not readily visible to others. As with the law merchant model, outsiders to the exchange cannot easily observe defection; instead, they observe a dispute, typically accompanied by two plausible but contradictory accounts in which each party blames the other. Outsiders have no way of knowing what happened. Because other members of Congress have strong incentives to police defection, they need institutions to help resolve such disputes. The leadership has long been recognized for helping put together deals.

■ | Endogenous Institutions

Having suggested why institutions exist, I now turn to a more in-depth investigation of endogenous aspects of institutions: when will institutions matter and why do they take particular forms instead of others? An important concept throughout this study is credible commitments, self-enforcing incentives provided by institutions for relevant actors to behave in a certain manner.

AN ENDOGENOUS MODEL OF THE INDEPENDENT JUDICIARY

Although nearly all countries have judicial systems, these vary enormously in their independence and authority. In some countries, courts are an independent branch of government capable of overruling decisions by government officials, while in others they are subservient to politics. What determines the degree of independence of the courts? Clearly many factors matter (see, e.g., Shapiro 1981). In this subsection, I review how rational-choice theorists address this question for democracies, emphasizing its comparative implications.

The spatial models of the separation of powers in the previous section took the powers of the various institutional actors as given. This subsection adds a court to address the question of judicial independence. Clearly, the power of the judiciary varies considerably among systems. Although political scientists have characterized these differences well, what they have done less well is explain them. There is a tendency to assume that the independence of the judiciary is a characteristic inherent in the judiciary itself, such as the norms of judges. In this section we show instead that the power of the judiciary depends critically on the relationship between the judiciary and the other branches of government.

Consider a presidential system with a legislature independent of the president. Courts nominally have the power to interpret legislation, that is, the power to alter the legislation's meaning and hence policy. In what follows, I draw on a range of now standard models in the application known in the legal literature as positive political theory and the law.[11] The approach begins with the one-dimension spatial model and the policy preferences of three actors, the executive's (E), the Congress's (C), and the courts' (J), with the status quo policy (Q). Consider a typical political configuration (see figure 9).

Figure 9 | The Role of Courts in Interpreting Statutes

Notice that every policy between E and C is legislative equilibrium: Any bill preferred by one makes the other worse off, so no legislation can pass. But these status quos are not necessarily equilibria when we allow the judiciary to interpret the meaning of the law. When asked to judge the law and given their preferences and the latitude afforded them by virtue of their role as interpreters, the courts will move policy from Q to their ideal point J.

Of course, the courts' ability to influence legislation depends on the political configuration. For example, suppose that the court's ideal is outside the interval between E and C (to the right of C in figure 10).

Figure 10 | Constraints on an Extremist Court

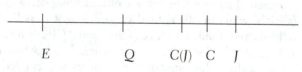

If the court attempts to implement its ideal policy J, it will fail. Because the policy J is outside the range of E and C, both Congress and the president are better off moving policy back between their ideals, specifically, inside the region between $C(J)$ and C.

These examples illustrate a general result: in a separation of powers system, the range of discretion and hence independence afforded the courts is a function of the differences between the elected branches. The narrower the range of policies between the branches, the lower judicial discretion. This can be seen using figure 11, a variant of figure 10. In this

---

11. Marks (1988) provided the pioneering work. See also Epstein and Knight (1999), Eskridge and Ferejohn (1992), Eskridge (1992), Farber and Frickey (1992), Levy and Spiller (1994), McCubbins, Noll, and Weingast (1987, 1989), and Cohen and Spitzer (1994).

Figure 11 | Courts Facing Elected Officials
with Very Different Preferences

political setting, J holds the same relation to E as in the first figure, but C is much closer to E, perhaps representing united government in which the same party holds the presidency and a majority in Congress. If the courts attempt to implement their ideal policy J, they will fail. Both the executive and Congress prefer all points between their ideal policies to J. The best the court can do is to implement policy C. This approach shows how judicial independence depends on the political environment.

This perspective yields a range of comparative implications about the independent authority of courts. In political environments where the legislature is subordinate to the president, the latitude of courts is small, so they cannot exert much political independence or authority. In the strong presidential systems of Latin America, for example Argentina or Mexico, the courts typically exercise relatively little independent authority. Yet, as Chavez (2000) shows, the perspective explains the vicissitudes of judicial independence in Argentina since democratization. When government is divided (at least one branch held by the opposition), courts have more latitude. Thus, the courts were relatively independent during the Alfonsin presidency in the 1980s, when the opposite party held one chamber of the legislature. In contrast, the dramatic pliancy of the courts through most of President Carlos Saúl Menem's term in the early 1990s reflected his party's hold of united government. The emergence of a more independent judiciary at the end of Menem's term occurred when he too faced divided government.[12]

This perspective also explains aspects of Chile's judicial independence (Chavez 2000; Levy and Spiller 1994; Londregan 2000). In the postauthoritarian era, Chile has been characterized by both a strong presidency and divided government. As noted above, the system is rigged so that the opposition holds a working majority in the Senate through the institutional senators. As the model predicts, Chile also has an independent judiciary (also initially rigged to a degree to favor Pinochet's interests).

Barros (2000) describes the emergence of a degree of judicial independence during Chile's authoritarian period. Although the range of judicial independence was relatively small in comparison to that in the democratic era, Barros shows that it was nonnegligible after 1980 and grew

12. Chavez (2000) also shows that this logic applies to judicial independence across Argentina's provinces.

over time. Judicial independence arose in part because the branches of the armed services had no mechanism for coordinating their activities. This problem emerged in the first days of the coup, when two different branches issued conflicting curfew decrees. In the 1980s, the courts began to rule on constitutional issues. Although the courts' latitude was relatively small, the regime's preference for a referee allowed the courts to emerge as an interpreter.

The history of the judicial independence in the United States also fits the model. Consider first the partisan era of the first 150 years of the republic. Prior to World War II, the typical pattern was for one party to dominate electoral institutions and the courts: the Federalists prior to 1800, the Jeffersonian and Jacksonian Democrats until 1860; the Republicans until 1930; and the Democrats until the end of World War II. For example, in the seventy years between 1860 and 1930, the Republicans held united government in half the Congresses, while the Democrats held united government in only four.[13] Except for some crucial appointments during the Wilson presidency, the Republicans dominated appointments to the courts during this era.

This pattern has not held during the post–World War II era, in which divided government and swings between the parties have been common. Although Franklin Roosevelt managed to create a Democratic Supreme Court, neither party has dominated appointments to the courts since World War II.

The model explains the varying degree of judicial independence. During the partisan era, courts were instruments of the ruling party and exhibited relatively little independence on statutory issues. In contrast, the courts have been most independent since World War II, having become a major interpreter of legislation and a champion for a host of new rights.

Since World War II, swings between the two parties have been the norm. Although each party has held united government for short periods (e.g., the Democrats for 1961–1968, 1977–1980, 1993–1994; the Republicans for 1953–1954); this is often followed by periods of divided government, particularly with a Republican president and a Democratic Congress or a divided Congress (1955–1960, 1969–1976, 1981–1992). No party has been able to dominate appointments to the Supreme Court.

The substantial political and constitutional differences between the Democrats and the Republicans has granted the Supreme Court considerable discretion. Per predictions of the model, the post–World War II era has had one of the most independent Supreme Courts, one involved in creating a host of new rights and intervening in many policy areas. Although every major Supreme Court decision has been met with elected of-

13. Although divided government was the norm between 1874 and 1896, the Democrats rarely held the Senate or the presidency. This allowed the Republicans to dominate judicial appointments even during these years.

ficials who have decried it, nearly all have also had elected officials who have at supported it. The absence of sustained united government implies the Court has had the political discretion to exercise its authority in many areas.

Similarly, the above perspective explains the two big confrontations between the courts and the elected branches, the first in the late 1860s during Reconstruction and the second in the 1930s during the New Deal. Although these cases differ significantly, in both partisan and ideological change afforded a confrontation between a determined set of elected officials and a judiciary of very different persuasion. In both cases, the Supreme Court suddenly faced a united government with very different preferences, much like that in figure 11. Without any political officials to protect them, they capitulated.

DEMOCRATIC CONSOLIDATION QUA SELF-ENFORCING DEMOCRACY

One of the most exciting topics in comparative politics concerns the question of long-term democratic stability or consolidation. Linz and Stepan (1996, 5) argue that consolidation occurs when democracy is the "only game in town," that is, when no significant groups advocate violating the constitutional rules. Further, constitutionally, citizens and politicians "become habituated to the fact that political conflict will be resolved according to the established norms and that violations of these norms are likely to be both ineffective and costly" (see also Burton, Gunther, and Higley 1992; Diamond 1999a).

Although scholars are clear on the definition of consolidation, there is no consensus on the conditions that produce it. In this section, I review recent rational-choice contributions to the topic, which provide a critical advance to our understanding of the conditions that produce democratic consolidation.[14]

I (Weingast forthcoming) begin by restating the definition of democratic consolidation as requiring three conditions: (1) No significant group out of power advocates the use of force to secede or capture the government. (2) Those in power respect the constitutional rules; in particular, they do not use their power to transgress the rights of their opponents. (3) Citizens are willing to defend the constitutional rules by withdrawing their support from leaders and groups who advocate violating the rules.

Stated in this manner, democratic consolidation is centrally concerned with incentives: consolidation requires that democracy is self-enforcing in the sense that all actors have incentives to adhere to the rules.

---

14. The discussion draws on the work of Colomer (1995), Fearon (2000), Przeworski (1991, 2001), and Weingast (1997, forthcoming).

Because consolidation is centrally concerned with incentives, rational choice theory provides a necessary input into understanding this question.

The relevance of this approach is demonstrated by considering what I call the "Przeworski moment" (Przeworski 1991, ch. 2): a party in power has just lost an election but retains power until the date of legal transition: Why would it ever give up power? Democratic consolidation clearly necessitates that this party do so. Because the Przeworski moment is a time when many democracies fail, it is not obvious why parties in power adhere to the rules. Przeworski provides the abstract answer: it must be in the interests of those in power to do so.

In what follows, I provide two principles relevant for this question and then summarize two results about the conditions that produce democratic consolidation. The first principle concerns the *rationality of fear* model (de Figueiredo and Weingast 1997). The concept of the rationality of fear is based on the premise that, when citizens or groups are threatened, they take steps to defend themselves. Suppose that a threat involves a certain probability of becoming a reality. The main result is that, the larger the magnitude of the stakes, the lower the probability triggering defensive action. For very large threats—for example, those concerning people's lives and livelihoods—the probability triggering defensive reaction can be quite low, such as one in ten.

The rationality of fear model implies discontinuous political change. When citizens' perceptions of a threat is just below the probability threshold triggering their reaction, they continue to honor the rules. Suppose that an event occurs that increases the probability of the threat; then the probability rises above the threshold. Per the model, the threatened citizens suddenly defect from the regime as a means of protecting themselves. This principle shows why situations involving high stakes can be so explosive: first, the probabilies triggering support for extraconstitutional action, such as violence, can be quite low; second, when the probability of the threat nears the threshold, small increases in the perception of the threat can trigger action.

The second principle follows from an observation of Przeworksi (1991, ch. 2): all successful constitutions limit the stakes of politics. The reason is easily seen in the context of the first principle. When constitutions limit the stakes of politics in ways valued by most citizens, the citizens are far less likely to resort to extraconstitutional means to defend themselves. Constitutional limits that protect what citizens value imply that they are less likely to experience threats that cause them to support defections from the regime.

This argument implies a selection effect: democracies that limit the stakes of political competition are more likely to survive. When democratically elected governments threaten what some citizens consider their fundamental rights, they support leaders who will defend them. Democracies with constitutions that place constraints on government valued by citizens are more likely to survive because they are less likely to threaten their citizens.[15]

This mechanism has dozens of applications. For example, consider Chile in the early 1970s. Many on the political right felt their economic rights threatened by Allende's government, leading them to support the military (see, e.g., Valenzuela 1978). Similarly, during the Second Republic in Spain, many agrarian landholders, the church, and industrialists felt threatened by the regime, leading them to support Francisco Franco (Agüero 1995; Alexander 2002). In the United States, large numbers of Southerners felt threatened by the newly elected Republicans in 1860 (see, e.g., Weingast 1998). In each case, a sufficiently large group of citizens supported extraconstitutional action that a civil war or coup ensued.

In short, the relevance of the rationality of fear model for democratic consolidation is this: constitutions that limit the stakes of power are more likely to survive.

I now suggest how these principles interact, and add three additional results about democratic consolidation. The first result concerns the particular institutions of democratic governance. It is remarkable that students of democratic consolidation typically ignore how the constitution works, in particular, the ways in which the institutions of governance interact with democratic stability.[16] A critical aspect of these institutions follows from the second principle above: constitutional institutions often help lower the stakes of politics by creating self-enforcing limits on politics or by creating procedural limits on democratic decision making that reduce the set of feasible choices of elected officials. Put another way, constitutions that impose widely accepted substantive and procedural limits on the government lower the stakes of competitive elections and thus make it more likely that democracy will survive.

Democratic stability in the United States in the early–nineteenth century illustrates this conclusion. From the beginning of the republic, Southerners worried about the safety of their "property" and their "peculiar institutions," that is, slavery. A necessary condition for them to have remained in the Union was that Northerners provided a credible commit-

15. This argument suggests an explanation for the selection effect finding of Przeworski et al. (2000), that richer democracies are far more likely to remain democratic than poorer ones. The reason is that sustaining a vibrant economy requires secure property rights, which in turn require limits on government. In other words, economies that grow satisfy the second principle above noted in Przeworski (1991), and therefore make democracies more likely to survive.

16. Students of pacts often note that they restrict government decision making (e.g., O'Donnell and Schmitter 1986) but rarely study how or why these work. Although some scholars have studied effects of different election mechanisms (e.g., Linz and Stepan 1996), this is separate from studying the effects of different institutions of governance and public choice. An important exception in this literature is Ordeshook's study (1996) of Russia.

ment to honor Southern rights in slaves (see Weingast 1998). Several mechanisms of the Constitution contributed to this. First, federalism helped devolve many issues, such as property rights and slavery, to the states, outside the purview of the national government. Second, the separation of powers of the national government also limited the scope of democratic policymaking at the national level. Beyond these institutions, however, Southerners required an additional limit. From nearly the beginning of the republic and made explicit in the Missouri Compromise of 1820, a critical aspect of U.S. democratic stability was sectional balance—the notion that both sections would have equal representation and hence veto power in the U.S. Senate. Veto power implied that Southerners could veto any attempt by Northerners to use the national government to attack slavery. Moreover, it is clear that this power was necessary. With some frequency, Northerners used their majority in the House of Representatives to pass several antislavery initiatives. Further, the coming of the Civil War is wrapped up with the demise of section balance in the 1850s (Weingast 1998).

The second result concerns pacts, agreements often between previously warring groups that modify or specify the rules of the political game. Pacts have long been recognized in the literature as critical to democratization and democratic consolidation (see, e.g., Burton, Gunther, and Higley 1992; O'Donnell and Schmitter 1986). The literature is far less successful at explaining why some pacts succeed while others fail. Rational-choice approaches provide an answer: successful pacts must be self-enforcing; that is, they must provide the parties to the pact with incentives to abide by the pact's provisions. How does this work?

Weingast (forthcoming) provides four conditions for self-enforcing pacts. First, the pact must create (or be imbedded in a context that has already created) a set of rules and rights, that is, substantive and procedural limits on the state. Second, the parties agreeing to the pact must believe that they are better off under the pact than without it. If this condition fails for one of the parties, that party will be better off without the pact, so the pact will fail. Third, each party agrees to change its behavior in exchange for the others' simultaneously doing so. Fourth, the parties to the pact must be willing to defend the parts of the pact benefiting the others against transgressions by political leaders. This occurs when each party anticipates that its rights will be defended by the others: that each party is better off under the agreement than not and that if ever one party fails to protect the rights of others, the others will fail to come to its rescue. Put another way, the pact becomes self-enforcing when all parties are better off under the pact and when all realize that unilateral defection from the pact implies that the others will also defect, destroying the pact.

Because there is no external authority to police the democratic rules, these rules must be self-enforcing. Rational-choice institutionalism thus provides important additions to the literature on democratic stability and consolidation.

RATIONAL-CHOICE MODELS OF ETHNIC CONFLICT

The study of ethnic conflict has become a light industry within political science and sociology. A range of approaches have emerged. Perhaps one of the best works on this topic is Horowitz 1985. Horowitz discusses "severely divided societies" in Asia, Africa, and the Caribbean, arguing that ethnic identity elsewhere is different. In the west, "there is an important overarching level of identity. . . . A survey of Switzerland that tapped levels of identity found that, in spite of ethnic differences, about half of all respondents identified themselves as Swiss" (1985, 17–18). This view takes the degree of ethnic conflict as exogenous.

Rational choice provides a different perspective, suggesting that the degree of ethnic and related forms of conflict is endogenous. In particular, this conflict depends in part on whether there exist political institutions that adequately protect groups from being taken advantage of. Adequate protection is modeled in terms of credible commitment (Fearon 1994c; Fearon and Laitin 1996; de Figueiredo and Weingast 1997). In societies where institutions provide credible commitments against ethnic conflict, ethnic identity becomes only one of many bases of group formation and interaction. Moreover, these institutions allow the emergence of many cross-cutting cleavages. In these societies, ethnicity is only one of many bases for the formation of individual identity. In contrast, in societies without adequate institutional protection against ethnic violence, coalitions become based largely or solely on ethnicity, as does identity. Horowitz's observation about the Swiss is thus not an exogenous difference that separates the west from the areas he studies but part of the phenomena to be explained.

In what follows, I draw on Fearon's model (1994c) to suggest the importance of credible commitments and the emergence of ethnic conflict in their absence. A fundamental puzzle about ethnic conflict concerns why it occurs given that it is so costly, and typically for both sides.[17] One answer is that ethnic conflict is simply irrational; the participants are sufficiently emotionally involved in mutual hatreds that their decisions are not rational. Most approaches now reject this view. Nonetheless, these approaches fail to answer this fundamental puzzle.

Fearon provides a creative new insight into this question. Consider a society with a majority group M and a minority group m. Facing the possibility of conflict, the two groups have the opportunity to fight or to bargain for a peaceful solution. Both groups have access to arms.

The minority moves first and must decide whether to fight now or to bargain with the majority and accept some accommodation (see figure 12).

---

17. I call this the *economic puzzle* about ethnic conflict in "Constructing Trust" (Weingast 1998); the *political puzzle* of ethnic conflict concerns how to explain the timing of the outbreak of ethnic conflict, whether among groups that have never experienced such conflict or ones that do so after long periods of peace.

A bargain is assumed to involve a division of the social surplus. For simplicity, the total surplus is normalized to 1, so that a decision about its division is simply a proportion x going to the minority and $1 - x$ retained by the majority. As part of the peace bargain, the minority agrees to disarm. If the minority decides to fight, then with probability p_1 the minority wins and captures all the surplus. With probability $1 - p_1$, it loses, and the majority retains all the social surplus. Fighting costs the minority and majority c and C respectively. Total social surplus when the groups cooperate is 1; and when they fight, $1 - (c + C)$.

Figure 12 | Ethnic Conflict as the Absence of Credible Commitment

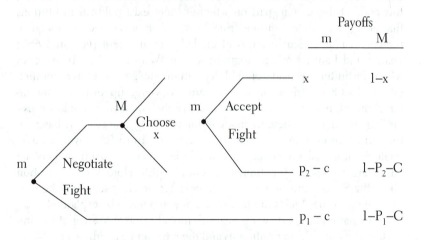

If the minority accepts the bargain, it lays down its arms. The majority then decides whether to honor the bargain, and if not, what proportion x of the surplus to give to the minority. The minority must then decide whether to acquiesce and accept x or to fight. If it fights, the minority wins with probability p_2. As before the costs of fighting are c and C respectively. Because accepting the bargain involves the minority's laying down its arms, the probability of winning if the minority then fights is lower than if it decides to fight at the beginning; that is, $p_2 < p_1$.

Payoffs from this interaction are modeled as follows: If the minority decides to fight at the beginning, then with probability p_1, the minority wins the payoff of 1 and with probability $1 - p_1$, it loses and receives nothing. Regardless of whether it wins, the minority must pay the cost of fighting. Thus, the minority's expected payoffs are $p_1 * 1 + (1 - p_1) * 0 - c = p_1 - c$. Similarly, the majority's expected payoffs are: with probability $1 - p_1$, the majority wins the social surplus and with probability p_1, it loses and receives none of the surplus; in both cases it must pay the costs C of war. Thus, the majority's expected payoffs are $p_1 * 0 + (1 - p_1) * 1 - C = 1 - p_1 - C$.

If instead the minority decides to bargain with the majority, it receives an offer of x from the majority. If it decides to accept this, its payoff is x and the game ends. If it decides to fight, then as before, its payoffs are $p_2 * 1 + (1 - p_2) * 0 - c = p_2 - c$. For the majority, its payoffs are x if the minority accepts the majority's proposal. If instead, the minority rejects this proposal, then its payoffs are $p_2 * 0 + (1 - p_2) * 1 - C = 1 - p_2 - C$.

To solve this game for the payoffs and behavior, we work backward through the game tree, first considering the minority's decision assuming it at first decided to bargain with the majority. At this last decision node (in the upper right of the figure 12), the minority will acquiesce if and only if $x \geq p_2 - c$. We then move back a step to calculate the majority's decision about x. Because it wants to maximize its portion of the surplus, and knowing the minority's decision rule about whether to fight, the majority will choose x so that the minority just barely prefers not to fight; that is, it will set $x = p_2 - c$.

Knowing the majority's decision about the allocation of the surplus, the minority can make its decision at the first node (on the left of the figure 12). If it decides to bargain, then, regardless of what the majority promises it initially, once it lays down its arms, the majority will give it only $x = p_2 - c$. If it decides to fight now, it receives $p_1 - c$. Because $p_2 < p_1$, the minority prefers to fight now rather than to accept a bargain.

The real problem in this interaction is the inability for the majority to credibly commit to treating the minority honorably. Both sides would be better off if they could avoid fighting; fighting imposes (often quite large) costs on both. Thus, were they able to bargain credibly, they could save the costs $c + C$ of ethnic conflict. Yet once the minority acquiesces, the majority can take advantage of it. Knowing this, the minority prefers to fight rather than bargain. In the absence of institutions credibly protecting the minority, the majority cannot prevent itself from behaving opportunistically and taking advantage of the minority.

Fearon's analysis does not address the question of timing: if this mechanism was always present in Yugoslavia, why did Yugoslavia not self-destruct during the previous forty years? And if it was not present during the previous years, why did it appear in the late 1980s and early 1990s? The answer is that the institutions of the *ancien Yugoslav regime* protected against this in several ways: they created a balance of ethnic groups, with Croats and Slovenians balancing Serbs; they created institutions that decentralized much decision making in ways that both made the central state and granted each of these ethnic groups a set of resources under their control; and finally, Marshall Tito, as head of the regime, steadfastly punished any attempt to make ethnic appeals. These institutions helped construct the basis for trust among ethnic groups, making ethnic peace self-enforcing.[18]

18. Burg (1983) describes these institutions in greater detail, and Weingast (1998) provides an argument about why they were self-enforcing in "Constructing Trust".

The *ancien regime* broke down in the mid-1980s for several reasons. For example, the fall of the Soviet Union and changes in Europe gave the Slovenians and Croats hope they might defect and join Europe. Further, after Tito's death, Yugoslav leaders had no interest to—or could no longer—restrain ethnic appeals. Once Slovenia defected from Yugoslavia, these institutional changes set the stage for the mechanism identified by Fearon, which applied in two ways within Yugoslavia: first, with the larger Serbian group's potentially taking advantage of the Croats; and within Croatia, the Croatian majority's taking advantage of the Serb minority.

GREIF'S MODEL OF THE PODESTA IN THE RISE OF GENOA

Greif (1998, forthcoming) has studied the rise of medieval Italy in a variety of contexts. An especially interesting idea concerns the role of political institutions in the trading rivalry of Genoa and Pisa.[19] In the early years of the rivalry, Genoese merchants fell behind those from Pisa, in part because the two main clans spent too many resources fighting one another instead of cooperating in their competition with rival Pisa. Greif explains how, although Genoese merchants had a collective interest in cooperation to compete with their rivals, their incentives led them instead to fight one another.

After many years of falling behind Pisa, Genoese merchants adapted an institution from elsewhere in Northern Italy, called the Podesta, to suit their needs. The Podesta was a foreigner whom Genoa invited to be mayor. They endowed him with some resources but not so many that he could vanquish either clan.

The Genoese hoped that the Podesta would help solve their internal feuds so that they could focus their energy and resources on competing with Pisa. To this end, they charged the Podesta with the following behavior: If either clan attacked the other, the Podesta was to side with the defender. Although the resources granted the Podesta were small relative to those of the clans, they were big enough so that the Podesta plus one of the clans implied a large advantage over the other clan. (Because the two clans were relatively evenly matched, these conditions were not hard to meet.)

For our purposes, the principal question is how did the institution of the Podesta make cooperation among the clans self-enforcing? Why not side with one of the clans instead and, subjugate the other clan and divide its resources?

Greif's analysis answers this question by analyzing the incentives facing the Podesta. The Podesta's primary interest is to maximize personal power, influence, and wealth. Consider the Podesta's incentives to side with the defender when one clan attacks the other. If the Podesta joined a coalition with the attacking clan to subjugate the other, then nothing protects the

19. This subsection discusses only one aspect of Greif's especially rich approach.

Podesta once the other clan is subjugated. The succeeding clan will then have no use for the Podesta and will simply get rid of it. If, on the other hand, the Podesta sides with the defender, the coalition is likely to succeed and the Podesta will continue in his position of prestige and power. Following the charge is thus better for the Podesta than the alternatives.

Greif also discusses the larger implications of his model for the problem of the political foundations of economic development. Genoa's political institutions formed a necessary part of the successful economic development. Without an institution that helped Genoese merchants cooperate and focus their energy on competition with Pisan merchants, the Genoese merchants could not cooperate with each other. The institution of the Podesta allowed them to cooperate and, in the long run, gain the upper hand over Pisa.

CRITICAL JUNCTURES IN THE AMERICAN REVOLUTION

Paralleling the literature, this essay has thus far concentrated on rational-choice institutionalism, only occasionally referencing other perspectives. Although political science draws on several rich approaches to institutions, there has been far too little cross-fertilization among these approaches. In this subsection, I provide a rational-choice interpretation for a concept originating in historical institutionalism—the notion of critical junctures or points of dramatic, irreversible, and discontinuous change (Collier and Collier 1991; Pierson and Skocpol 2002). According to Collier and Collier, these are "major watersheds in political life . . . [which] establish certain directions of change and foreclose others in a way that shapes politics for years to come" (1991, 27).[20]

What mechanisms underlie a critical juncture? Why do they happen only sometimes, and why at a particular moment? I address these questions in the context of Rakove, Rutten, and Weingast's (2000) and Schofield's (1999) discussion of the American Revolution.[21]

Historians of the American Revolution emphasize the role of ideas (Bailyn 1967; Greene 1986; Rakove 1996; Reid 1995): the Americans and the British fought because of fundamental disagreements over the nature of the constitution, the structure of the empire, and the mechanisms protecting liberty in the colonies. As Wood suggests, "If the origin of the American Revolution lay not in the usual passions and interests of men, wherein did it lay? . . . Never before in history had a people achieved a 'revolution by reasoning' alone. . . . The Revolution was thus essentially intellectual and declaratory" (1966, 162–63).

20. Katznelson (2000) opens his paper with the critical juncture in which Eve hands Adam the apple.

21. Elsewhere, I provide a model of the mechanism underlying the critical juncture leading to the U.S. Civil War (Weingast 1998).

The Americans, drawing on the constitutional ideas surrounding the English Glorious Revolution of 1688, emphasized the role of precedent: practices enshrined for a generation or more attained constitutional status. With respect to the empire, they argued that it had a federal structure (though they didn't use that term): sovereignty was divided, with the British having control over the empirewide issues of security and trade and the Americans having control over their local affairs, including religious and social regulation, taxation, and the structure of economic and political rights. This system had evolved over the 100 years prior to the revolutionary crisis (1763–1776) and had thus, by the Americans' reasoning, attained constitutional status. This view implied that the British lacked authority to regulate or otherwise control domestic colonial affairs.

The British, in contrast, had begun to evolve different ideas of their constitution, which attained its mature form in the nineteenth century. They argued that the British Parliament had supreme authority in Britain and the empire, including the power to interpret and alter the constitution. The British also believed that the structure of empire was a matter of policy choice, not the constitution. After the Seven Years' War (1756–1763), the British began to exercise their powers, including the imposition of relatively modest domestic taxes on the American colonies.

For our purposes, the actors in American colonial politics can be divided three groups: at one end of the political spectrum stood the small group of radicals seeking immediate remedial action, in the middle was a large group of moderates, and at the other end of the spectrum stood the loyalists. The moderates were politically pivotal: if they remained loyal to the British, revolution had no hope; if they joined the radicals, a revolution would ensue.

The radicals reacted strongly to the new British policies, arguing that the British actions represented a major change in precedent that if unchallenged would allow the British to Intervene in all domestic affairs. For them, this signaled that the British were no longer a benign and remote presence. The radicals' rhetorical argument about precedent was clever: by suggesting this small tax could imply much larger changes, they argued that the British action threatened American liberty. If the British could impose domestic rulings here, they could do so for any policy, including religion, economic regulation, or slavery.

Initially most Americans disagreed with the radicals and did not believe that this minor tax signaled a major change in the British view toward America. Yet a decade later, the moderates had come to side with the radicals to support fighting the British. How did this occur? I argue that a critical juncture took place.

To model this, Rakove, Rutten, and Weingast (2000) draw on the rationality of fear concept discussed above (de Figueiredo and Weingast 1997). The new idea proposed by the radicals was that the British had become a malign presence bent on taking away American liberty. This meant the possibility of significant new taxes, limits on religious freedom, and significant new economic regulatory restrictions. In short, American lives and livelihoods were at stake. Initially most moderates thought the likelihood that the radicals were right was quite low. Rakove-Rutten-Weingast model this by assuming that the moderates had beliefs about the probability P that the radicals were right; implying that with probability $1 - P$, the radicals were wrong, that the British were not malign, and that the status quo would by and large prevail.

As noted above, the rationality of fear mechanism implies several results relevant for this context. First, there exists a threshold probability P^* such that, if American moderates believe that the likelihood of the new idea exceeds P^*, then they would change sides and fight the British. Second, the larger the stakes, the lower is P^*. The high stakes of the crisis implied that P^* was likely to be significantly closer to 0 than to 1.

Rakove-Rutten-Weingast model the initial situation, in which most Americans did not believe the radicals, by assuming that the moderates' belief of the probability P that the radicals were right was too low (i.e., $P < P^*$). The critical juncture occurred because over time events occurred that changed the moderates' beliefs. Explicit in the radicals' view of the world was that the British would significantly alter the structure of American liberty, which depended on the colonial assemblies. In every colony, these assemblies established the laws that protected American liberty.

At several points during the revolutionary controversy, the British decided to show a strong hand to the Americans. When New York refused to agree to quarter British troops in 1766, the British passed the New York Suspending Act, which rendered all acts of the New York Assembly void until it voted funds for troops. A few years later, in 1773, following the Boston merchants' protest of the new duties on tea—known as the Boston Tea Party—the British reacted even more strongly with what became known in America as the Intolerable Acts: they disbanded the Massachusetts Assembly, imposed marshal law, and closed the port of Boston.

To the surprise of most Americans, the British had acted just as the radicals predicted: they had taken away the heart of the institutions protecting American liberty—the colonial assembly. Regardless of British intentions, it became clear to the majority of Americans that the British were no longer a benign, remote presence. British behavior raised most Americans' beliefs about the probability P that the radicals were right. When these beliefs became larger than the critical threshold P^*, the moderates came to support the revolution.

This model has several implications. First, it shows how politics can exhibit discontinuous change: Americans supported the status quo as long as P remained lower than the critical threshold P^*. Once P rose sufficiently so that it was above the threshold, however, Americans suddenly reacted to defend themselves. Second, this model provides a mechanism for why this critical juncture—the point of no return—occurred. Per the rationality of fear model, Americans came to fear the British and acted to defend themselves. It shows how and why the political cleavage underlying the revolutionary crisis changed so as to support a revolution and forever alter American politics. Third, the model suggests the microfoundations of macropolitical, indeed revolutionary, change. Finally, this exercise reveals the complementarity of rational-choice institutionalism and historical institutionalism. It began with a concept devised by historical institutionalists but not by rational-choice institutionalists, and then showed how rational-choice models can incorporate this notion.

Conclusions

I close the two sections on why institutions are needed and endogenous institutions with four observations. First, the approach shows that, to survive, institutions must be self-enforcing in the sense that relevant actors have incentives to abide by them. Democratic consolidation requires that members of a society adhere to a list of rules: those in power must abide by the results of elections; those out of power must refrain from the use of force to seize the government. The law merchant rules are effective because merchants have an incentive to abide by his rulings. Only in some political environments do political officials have an incentive to adhere to judicial constraints. And to keep peace among the clans, the Podesta must have the appropriate incentives.

Second, many important political phenomena reflect the breakdown of institutions, such as the emergence of ethnic conflict following the destruction of the institutions that promoted trust, including incentives against ethnic conflict. Similarly, the American Revolution occurred when the institutions protecting American liberties changed following the Seven Years' War, and Americans had incentives to defect from the empire.

Third, the rational-choice approach emphasizes the mechanisms explaining why institutions have particular effects and why they survive. Extensive literatures have long existed on each of the endogenous institutions (or their breakdown) surveyed here—the law merchant, the independent judiciary, democratic stability, ethnic conflict, and the American Revolution. The comparative advantage of the rational-choice approach is to add a focus on the mechanisms that promote stability or breakdown.

Fourth, the approach demonstrates that a critical reason for institutions is to support cooperation. As is well known, in many environments repeat play alone is sufficient to support cooperation. Yet the law merchant model shows how in complex environments this is not true and that institutions help make cooperation self-enforcing.

▪ | Conclusions

Three approaches to institutions contribute to modern political science, and each makes valuable contributions (Hall and Taylor 1996). The purpose of this paper is to survey rational-choice institutionalism. The paper divides institutional analysis into two separate modes.

The first mode of institutional analysis takes institutions as given and studies their effects. This is by far the dominant form of institutional analysis in all three approaches. This paper surveyed two sets of analyses studying the effects of institutions. The first studied the interaction of the legislature and executive. This discussion illustrated a hallmark of rational-choice institutionalism: the demonstration that seemingly small differences in institutional details often have macropolitical effects. This application emphasized the institutional sources of political differences across types of democratic systems. The second application provided a new explanation for the judicial expansion of civil rights in the United States. The analysis revealed the strategic behavior of the courts, in this case, a conservative Supreme Court expanding civil rights legislation in an effort to forestall a more far reaching revision by the Congress.

The second mode of institutional analysis studies institutions as the endogenous variable, attempting to provide explanations for why particular institutions exist, evolve, and survive. Although the less developed of the two modes of rational-choice institutional analysis, it has larger power in the long run. This paper develops these ideas in two ways. First, it provides an analysis of why institutions exist. Developed in the context of the institutions underpinning the rise of trade in medieval Europe, this analysis showed that in some contexts, the incentives of repeated play are sufficient to enforce long-term social cooperation. The prisoners' dilemma is the best-known example. Yet in more complex environments, repeat play alone fails to provide for long-term cooperation. The analysis shows that, in some contexts, institutions evolve to alter incentives so that cooperative behavior becomes self-enforcing. Put another way, a fundamental aspect of institutions is that they provide the means for the enforcement of cooperation.

The medieval law merchant, for example, issued rulings in disputes among merchants prior to the rise of the nation-state and thus without any means to enforce its judgments. This institution nonetheless proved critical for maintaining cooperation and exchange among merchants because it helped identify defectors. The inability to ascertain who defected implies not only that defection goes unpunished but that opportunistic players exploit this inability. By providing a mechanism for publicizing defectors, the law merchants' rulings provided vital information to the community, enabling it to maintain cooperation.

Second, the essay turned to a series of applications of the approach that explain the evolution of particular types of institutions. The first application provided a segue from the discussion that took institutions as exogenous. That discussion studied the conditions for an independent judiciary capable of placing constraints on elected officials. It applied the conditions for an independent judiciary to a range of democratic systems. The second application raised the issue of democratic consolidation, that is, the conditions for long-term democratic stability. This discussion showed that incentives are fundamental to democratic consolidation and suggested a range of conditions providing for self-enforcing democracy. The third application concerned ethnic conflict. This discussion showed that a fundamental aspect of this type of conflict is the absence of credible commitments to protect the rights of minorities. The fourth application studied the institutions of cooperation in medieval Genoa.

I conclude this survey with three observations about the value of the rational-choice approach. First the discussion on the effect of institutions shows how rational-choice institutionalism helps integrate the study of American politics into the larger study of comparative politics. The research such as that reported in this essay takes an important step toward that goal for institutions in democratic societies.

Second, rational-choice theory provides a variety of mechanisms that afford predictions of discontinuous change. A large range of questions in political science involve sudden change—the emergence of ethnic conflict, wars, the transition to or the failure of democracy, revolutions, major policy swings within particular countries. The various mechanisms of discontinuous change thus hold promise for new insights into these phenomena. An interesting implication of this development is that rational-choice theory has begun to discuss macropolitical phenomena, events that were once largely the domain of historical institutionalism.

Finally, let me touch on a few issues at the frontiers of rational-choice institutionalism. First, endogenous emergence, choice, and survival of institutions are likely to be major topics of the next decade. Second, choice theorists of many stripes have begun an impressive set of investigations into the limits of rationality in combination with the means of extending the theory to cover these more general circumstances. These include Elster (1999) on emotions and Knight and North (1997) on cognitive science, not to mention one of the first provided by Kahneman and Tversky (1978). Third, rational-choice theorists have long included the study of uncertainty and incomplete information in their analysis. The far-reaching results in those areas of study suggest that we have yet to see the full implications and power of these tools. Finally, an important frontier for the discipline, increasingly the subject of research, is the integration of rational-choice institutionalism with other forms of institutional analysis, particularly historical institutionalism. The discussion here about critical junctures in the American Revolution suggests the plausibility of this goal.

Paul Pierson and Theda Skocpol

Historical Institutionalism in Contemporary Political Science

Like the character in Moliere's play who spoke prose all his life without knowing it, contemporary political scientists are familiar with leading examples of historical institutionalist research without necessarily realizing that they exemplify a coherent genre—much as do works in the other two major research approaches practiced in empirical political science, survey-based behavioralism and rational-choice modeling. Historical institutionalists analyze organizational and institutional configurations where others look at particular settings in isolation; and they pay attention to critical junctures and long-term processes where others look only at slices of time or short-term maneuvers. Researching important issues in this way, historical institutionalists make visible and understandable the overarching contexts and interacting processes that shape and reshape states, politics, and public policymaking.

Stephen Skowronek's *The Politics Presidents Make* (1993), for example, reveals recurrent cycles in the nature and success of presidential leadership throughout U.S. history. Another long-term study in American politics, John Mark Hansen's *Gaining Access: Congress and the Farm Lobby, 1919–1981* (1991), develops a model of interest group interaction with government and uses it to explain the emergence, persistence, and ultimate eclipse of the political influence of national farmers' associations. Ranging across nations as well as time, Peter A. Hall's 1986 book *Governing the Economy: The Politics of State Intervention in Britain and France* explains how institutions and organizations intersect to shape not just the policies of governments but also the strategies and alliances of interest groups and public intellectuals. Painting on even grander canvases, *Shaping the Political Arena: Critical Junctures, the Labor Movement, and Regime Dynamics in Latin America* by Ruth Berins Collier and David Collier (1991) and *Birth of the Leviathan: Building States and Regimes in Early Modern Europe* by Thomas Ertman (1997) explain regime dynamics and the varied formations of modern national states. In the study of international relations, *Activists Beyond Borders* by Margaret Keck and Kathryn

Sikkink (1998) analyzes the historical roots and contemporary proliferation of transnational advocacy networks, while Judith Goldstein's *Ideas, Interests, and American Trade Policy* (1993) shows how the institutionalization of policy ideas at an earlier juncture had lasting consequences for subsequent U.S. trade measures.

These are but a few of many possible citations, for historical institutionalist studies have cumulated to provide wide-ranging as well as causally precise understandings of such important matters as transitions to democracy,[1] the emergence and demise of authoritarian regimes,[2] the intersection of domestic and international politics,[3] the origins and development of welfare states,[4] social identities in politics,[5] the political dynamics of gender rights,[6] the development of economic regimes,[7] and the causes and consequences of social movements and revolutions.[8]

Obviously, studies using historical-institutionalist strategies of analysis vary in many important ways. Some are explicitly comparative, while others analyze trends within just one macrocontext. Some offer suggestive interpretations (e.g., Hart 1994), while others develop explicit models framed in general terms (e.g., Hansen 1991; Luong 2002). Some historical-institutionalist studies draw extensively from primary sources (e.g., Gamm 1999), while others synthesize findings from secondary publications (e.g., Skocpol 1979; Downing 1992). And some deploy arguments about strate-

1. See, for example, Anderson 1999; Baloyra 1987; Bratton and Van de Walle 1997; Diamond 1999b; Downing 1992; Gould 1999; Haggard and Kaufman 1995; Rueschemeyer, Stephens, and Stephens 1992; and Yashar 1997. A comprehensive review of hypothesis testing and cumulative theoretical development in this field appears in Mahoney 2002.

2. Examples include Chehabi and Linz 1998; Doyle 1986a; Ekiert 1996; Im 1987; Mahoney 2001; and Snyder 1998. For further review of the literature, see Mahoney 2002.

3. Examples include Friedberg 2000, Gourevitch 1986, Ikenberry 2001, Katzenstein 1978, Krasner 1978, Simmons 1993, and Sparrow 1996.

4. See Esping-Andersen 1990, Flora and Heidenheimer 1981, Hacker 1998, Hicks 1999, Howard 1997, Huber and Stephens 2001, Immergut 1992, Maioni 1998, Pierson 1994, Skocpol 1992, and Steinmo 1996. The striking cumulation of knowledge in this field is reviewed in Amenta 2002 and Pierson 2000d.

5. Examples include Anderson 1991, Hattam 1993, Katznelson and Zolberg 1986, Kryder 2000, Lustick 1993, Marx 1998, Varshney 2001, and Vogel 1978.

6. Examples include Charrad 2001; Htun forthcoming; Jenson 1986; Mettler 1998; and O'Connor, Orloff, and Shaver 1999.

7. For key examples from a wide-ranging literature, see Karl 1997, Richards and Waterbury 1990, Soskice 1999, Streeck 1992, Thelen 1993, 1994, and Zysman 1994.

8. Important examples include Banaszak 1996; Goldstone 1991; Goodwin 2001; McAdam 1982; McAdam, Tarrow, and Tilly 2001; Skocpol 1979; Tarrow 1998; and Wickham-Crowley 1992.

gic choice and the impact of the rules of the game (e.g., Immergut 1992; Pierson 1994), while others adopt culturalist modes of explanation (e.g., Anderson 1991; Hattam 1993). Any vibrant tradition of research encompasses variety and flourishes through internal debates, and historical institutionalism is certainly no exception. In another context, we could elaborate differences among works with historical-institutionalist features—defending our own choices within these debates.

But we have a different goal for this chapter. Despite variety on many key dimensions, historical institutionalists commonly employ distinctive and complementary strategies for framing research and developing explanations. What historical institutionalists broadly share becomes apparent when we juxtapose their ways of asking questions and seeking answers—their research strategy—to the strategies normally used by behavioralists and rational-choice modelers. Without denying variety within major approaches, this essay aims to make distinctive core strategies visible, so that we can see the advantages and limits of historical institutionalism compared to the other research approaches extensively used in empirical political science.

We characterize historical institutionalism and other leading approaches in empirical political science on the basis of "elective affinities" shared in practice by many scholars who do each style of work. We are not saying that everyone in each camp marches to the same tune. And we recognize that many scholars blend styles of research in highly creative ways (as we will suggest in the conclusion to this chapter, "boundary crossers" are often among the most creative scholars in our discipline). Practitioners of major approaches nevertheless share ways of posing questions and developing explanations—giving historical institutionalism, behavioralism, and rational-choice modeling characteristic features, strengths, and weaknesses. Operating as if we were anthropologists documenting the folkways of neighboring and comingled clans, we explore how historical institutionalists, compared to their cousins doing behavioralism or rational choice, regularly go about defining research agendas and developing explanations.

Three important features characterize historical-institutional scholarship in contemporary political science.[9] Historical institutionalists *address big, substantive questions that are inherently of interest to broad publics as well as to fellow scholars.* To develop explanatory arguments about important outcomes or puzzles, historical institutionalists *take time seriously,* specifying sequences and tracing transformations and processes of varying

---

9. Although we discuss historical institutionalism as one of three major research tendencies in contemporary political science, we readily acknowledge that the relevant literatures also include contributions from "comparative historical" political sociologists. This is hardly surprising. Leading approaches in the social sciences invariably bring scholars together across disciplinary boundaries; and political scientists of every persuasion have long shared theories and methods with their cousins in sociology and economics.

scale and temporality. Historical institutionalists likewise *analyze macro contexts and hypothesize about the combined effects of institutions and processes* rather than examining just one institution or process at a time. Taken together, these three features—substantive agendas, temporal arguments, and attention to contexts and configurations—add up to a recognizable historical-institutional approach that makes powerful contributions to our discipline's understandings of government, politics, and public policies.

To explain how this approach works and make the case for its fruitfulness, we discuss in turn each of the three aspects of historical-institutionalist scholarship, pausing at appropriate points to explore advantages or limitations compared to strategies used by other families of political scientists. We focus on what creative communities of scholars actually do, paying less attention to what they or others say they do (or claim they should do). At the end of the chapter, we step back to consider some of the broadest issues of empirical research method and strategies of knowledge cumulation: Can historical institutionalists really develop valid arguments from case studies and small-*n* comparisons? How scientifically fruitful are research agendas driven by substantive questions rather than the elaboration of a theory or techniques? And what are the prospects for combining the strengths of historical-institutional analysis with advances in strategic modeling or statistically sophisticated survey research? Historical institutionalism is experiencing a bold new phase of methodological development, yet its focus on substance and its theoretical eclecticism simultaneously open the way for fruitful cross-fertilization with the best of sister research traditions.

■ | Big Questions and Real-World Puzzles

Despite the disparate phenomena they investigate, historical institutionalists formulate their research programs in recognizable and distinctive ways. A historical-institutionalist scholar usually starts by asking about varied, historically situated outcomes of broad interest—perhaps posing a puzzle about why something important happened, or did not happen, or asking why certain structures or patterns take shape in some times and places but not others. Why have revolutions occurred in some times and places but not others? How did the U.S. state develop its specific pattern of institutional features? Why have welfare states emerged and developed along various paths? Why have some countries become stable democracies, while others have not? Under what circumstances do ethnic identities become prominent in national or international politics? The focus is on explaining variations in important or surprising patterns, events, or arrangements— rather than on accounting for human behavior without regard to context or modeling very general processes presumed to apply at all times and places.

Proceeding through a constant movement back and forth among cases, questions, and theories, historical-institutionalist scholars immerse themselves in historical instances not only to test previously formulated hypotheses but also to come up with fruitful new puzzles. The problems that interest historical institutionalists often come from identifying heretofore unexplained real-world variations—or from realizing that empirical patterns run counter to received academic or popular wisdom. For example, several recent studies of the development of U.S. social policies started with the observation that standard treatments of the United States as a lagging and ungenerous welfare state miss extensive systems of private social provision encouraged by public subsidies and regulations. Building from this insight, scholars such as Howard (1997), Gottschalk (2000), and Hacker (forthcoming) have developed broader and richer causal accounts of the development of U.S. policy. Similarly, scholars looking into the global evolution of rights for women noted that breakthroughs often occurred under surprising political circumstances, for example, under militaristic or authoritarian regimes. Such observations soon inspired more extensive and nuanced comparative-historical studies (e.g., Charrad 2001; Htun forthcoming; Jenson 1986) highlighting the impact of various state-building sequences, institutional contexts, and political coalitions on movements for women's rights.

From the points of view of academic marketing and disciplinary recognition, there may be drawbacks to the substantively focused and puzzle-driven nature of historical-institutionalist research. Contributions tend to be clustered in somewhat separate topical literatures and scattered across subfields dealing with different eras or regions of the world. But there are also telling advantages to research focused on big, important substantive problems, including studies that start by trying to resolve anomalies not previously noticed or explained. Social science must ultimately be judged, claims Lewis Coser, "on the basis of the substantive enlightenment . . . it is able to supply about the social structures in which we are enmeshed and which largely condition the course of our lives" (1975, 698). Historical institutionalists are mindful of this supreme test. Grappling as they are with such matters as social movements, the development of the modern state, the rise and fall of civic engagement in democracies, the origins and dynamics of political economies, regime transformations, and patterns of public policies, historical institutionalists avoid academic navel gazing. Grappling with pressing puzzles, historical institutionalists address real-world questions of interest to educated publics and university students—not to mention topics that appeal to book publishers.

Within political science itself, it is also worth noting, historical institutionalists bridge many divides, including the gulf that sometimes separates normative theorists from empirical researchers. Normative dilemmas are frequently apparent in the phenomena explored by historical institutionalists, whose studies thus contribute empirical substance to debates raging among political theorists. What is more, research agendas shaped by historical institutionalists may draw considerable interest from formal theorists and behavioralists. The literature on the development of modern welfare states exemplifies multiple forms of bridging. Normative concerns about equality, democracy, and liberty are frankly acknowledged and explored in this literature. And because research invariably focuses on major, real-world developments and dilemmas—as historical institutionalists prefer—choice theorists and survey researchers have been drawn into academic dialogues remarkably free of sterile paradigm disputes. Theoretical and methodological dialogues have been highly fruitful, and particular studies often combine modes of analysis (see the literature reviews in Amenta 2002; Pierson 2000d). With historical institutionalists playing a central role, the entire research community has used a full range of methods and research designs to develop ever sharper and broader explanations—and richer normative understandings—of the origins and dynamics of national systems of economic regulation and social provision. Everyone seems to realize that theoretical eclecticism, multiple analytic techniques, and a broad comparative and historical purview works best.

■ | Tracing Historical Processes

Historical institutionalists may ask big questions and bridge divides within and beyond academia, but how do they go about developing explanations? We have already alluded to what is perhaps the most distinctive feature of this approach: Whether particular works use comparisons or analyze various aspects of one theoretically justified case, historical institutionalists take history seriously, as something much more than a set of facts located in the past. To understand an interesting outcome or set of arrangements usually means to analyze processes over a substantial stretch of years, maybe even many decades or centuries. Scholars working in this tradition have developed compelling methodological and theoretical justifications for historically grounded investigations, by which they mean investigations that look not just at the past but at *processes over time*.

Some reasons for taking history seriously concern methodology and are already recognized (if not always practiced) by political scientists of many persuasions. Extending the time frame of social inquiry obviously widens the range of experience available for examination. This simultaneously makes more data available and generates greater variation in outcomes. Such widening of the empirical terrain is especially important for political scientists, because many matters of great interest—especially macrophenomena such as revolutions, state building, democratization, the construction of welfare states—occur relatively infrequently, or only partially, within any particular slice of time. Historically informed investigation also sensitizes investigators to temporal boundary conditions or period effects, with respect to claims about causal relationships. By examining a wider range of historical settings, an analyst can consider the possibility that supposedly universal effects in fact only hold under particular circumstances.

Historical investigations can also contribute to causal inference. Because theoretically grounded assertions of causal relationships imply temporal relationships among variables (either that one precedes the other or that both happen at essentially the same time), examining historical sequences is extremely useful for testing such assertions (Rueschemeyer and Stephens 1997; Mahoney 2000b). Optimally, assertions of causality should be borne out not just by a correlation between two variables but also by a theoretical account showing why this linkage should exist and by evidence suggesting support for the theorized linkage. Although social research does not always achieve this ideal, efforts to systematically trace social processes can make an essential contribution to the rigorous assessment of claims about social causation (Bennett and George 1997; Hall 2002). Here the relatively small number of cases in many historical institutional studies can become an advantage, allowing for exactly the sorts of detailed examinations of *processes* needed to evaluate claims about causal mechanisms.

Important as these general methodological advantages are, historical institutionalists are also pushing beyond them to *theorize about historical dimensions of causation*. As we are about to see, historical institutionalists have recently begun to underline the theoretical power of their *dynamic* approach to social change and politics. Without the kind of attentiveness to temporally specified process that is a distinctive hallmark of historical-institutionalist scholarship, important outcomes may go unobserved, causal relationships may be misunderstood, and valuable hypotheses may never receive consideration.

PATH DEPENDENCE, SEQUENCES, AND CONJUNCTURES

A central example of why history may be causally critical involves claims about *path dependence* that are common in historical institutionalist scholarship (see, e.g., Collier and Collier 1991; Ertman 1997; Hacker 1998; Shefter 1977; Huber and Stephens 2001). *Path dependence* can be a faddish term, lacking clear meaning, but in most historical-institutionalist scholarship, it refers to the dynamics of self-reinforcing or positive feedback processes in a political system (Pierson 2000a; cf. Mahoney 2000b). A clear logic is involved in such path-dependent processes: Outcomes at a critical juncture trigger feedback mechanisms that reinforce the recurrence of a particular pattern into the future. Such processes have very interesting characteristics. They can be highly influenced by relatively modest perturbations at early stages. Once actors have ventured far down a particular path, however, they are likely to find it very difficult to reverse course. Political alternatives that were once quite plausible may become irretrievably lost. Thus, events or processes occurring during and immediately following critical junctures emerge as crucial.

There are strong theoretical grounds for believing that self-reinforcing processes are prevalent in political life. Once established, patterns of political mobilization, the institutional rules of the game, and even citizens' basic ways of thinking about the political world will often generate self-reinforcing dynamics. In addition to drawing our attention toward critical junctures or formative moments, arguments about path dependence can thus help us to understand the powerful inertial "stickiness" that characterizes many aspects of political development. These arguments can also reinvigorate the analysis of power in social relations, by showing how inequalities of power, perhaps modest initially, are reinforced and can become deeply embedded in organizations, institutions, and dominant modes of political understanding. Path-dependence arguments also provide a useful and powerful corrective against tendencies to assume functionalist explanations for important social and political outcomes. Perhaps most important, an appreciation of the prevalence of path dependence forces attentiveness to the temporal dimensions of political processes. It highlights the role of what Arthur Stinchcombe (1968) has termed historical causation in which dynamics triggered by an event or process at one point in time reproduce themselves, even in the absence of the recurrence of the original event or process.

An appreciation of increasing returns dynamics is one important justification for the focus on issues of *timing and sequencing* that constitutes a second important theoretical rationale for examining historical processes. In path-dependent processes, the order of events may make a fundamental difference. Historical institutionalists tracing broad patterns of political development across a number of countries often argue that the timing and sequence of particular events or processes can matter a great deal (Anderson 1986; Gerschenkron 1962; Kurth 1979; Shefter 1977; Ertman 1997). In Ertman's analysis of European regime formation, for example, it is the sequence of two processes—the expansion of literacy and the onset of military competition—that is crucial to paths of state building. The prevalence of literacy powerfully affected the bargaining position of those who would collect state revenues. Where countries faced intense military challenges prior to the era when literacy became widespread, the character of the state's fiscal apparatus was likely to be very different than when the order of these two processes was reversed. Crucially, because of path-dependent effects these differences were long lasting; that is to say, a country's bureaucratic structures, established at an early juncture, did not simply adjust once literacy rates rose to a higher level.

Jacob Hacker's study (2002) of the development of U.S. social policy presents a second compelling example of this kind of argument. Hacker explores the distinctive paths of development of public versus private, employer-based systems of health care and pension provision in the United States over the past century. Although both policy sectors have roughly equal mixes of public and private spending, they developed along fundamentally different lines. In health care, public interventions have served as supplements or compensations added to a prior set of institutions featuring private provision. By contrast, in pensions, a public core system of retirement provision developed first, with private arrangements playing a supplementary or complementary role. Through processes of policy feedback, these different sequences of public and private intervention generated quite different interest group environments, shifting both the policy preferences and political resources of crucial actors like employers. Moreover, the different patterns of development produced very different distributional outcomes, profoundly shaping the contours of contemporary political struggles over social provision. Any scholar who merely discusses these contemporary struggles without awareness of the history that shaped the terrain of preferences and actors will miss much of central causal relevance to explaining politics and policymaking today.

Waldner's study (1999) of state building and economic performance in late-developing countries rests on a similar claim. He contrasts Syria and Turkey, where state building and mass incorporation occurred simultaneously, with Korea and Taiwan, where greater elite consensus allowed state building to precede mass incorporation. In the latter cases, state elites were able to institutionalize structures that facilitated long-term economic development before the challenges of bargaining with nonelites had to be confronted. In the former cases, patterns of state building were fundamentally altered by the immediate need to win support from broader social groups. Thus Waldner identifies two distinctive paths of late state development, generated by different sequences of state building and incorporation.

Like these arguments of Ertman, Hacker, and Waldner, most propositions historical institutionalists offer about the causal impact of sequences are grounded in claims about self-reinforcing or positive feedback processes (Pierson 2000c). Relative timing, or sequence, matters because self-reinforcing processes, playing out over time in political and social life, transform the consequences of later developments. Path-dependent arguments about self-reinforcement explain why and when sequencing can matter. Increasing returns processes occurring during particular periods generate irreversibilities, essentially removing certain options from the subsequent menu of political possibilities.

Although many path-dependent arguments stress the institutionalization of particular configurations that subsequently prove difficult to dislodge, the focus on sequencing illuminates how arguments about path-dependent processes can be incorporated into explanations of political change as well as political inertia. For instance, path-dependent processes may operate to institutionalize specific political arrangements that ultimately prove vulnerable to some displacing event or process emerging at a later stage in political development (Collier and Collier 1991; Luebbert 1991). The Colliers' work on labor incorporation in Latin America provides an excellent example. In some of their cases, labor was excluded from political participation at a critical juncture, and positive feedback led to the institutionalization of regimes where organized labor had little access to political influence. Over time, however, key changes in social and economic life made it impossible to maintain these systems of labor exclusion. Eventually, organized labor had to be incorporated. When this took place at a later stage of political development, however, it necessarily occurred on quite different terms and with different consequences than was true for countries experiencing early incorporation. The key point is that options available for early incorporators were not available for late incorporators.

It is highly instructive to contrast these arguments about path-dependent sequences with arguments rational-choice theorists have made about sequences within highly institutionalized settings (Shepsle 1986). Working from Arrow's impossibility theorem, which suggests the prospect of endless cycling in many collective-choice situations, rational-choice theorists have argued persuasively that institutional arrangements governing agenda control and decision-making procedures can produce stable outcomes. By demonstrating the crucial role of sequencing as choices are made, these arguments rest on the equivalent of a path-dependent mechanism: Steps in a sequence are irreversible because institutional rules cause forgone alternatives in early rounds to be dropped from the range of possible later options (as, for example, in committee voting rules that require a sequence of binary choices, with losers eliminated). By showing how such irreversibilities can be generated in a wide variety of social contexts, however, it is possible to expand this crucial finding to a far broader range of social phenomena than those covered by the rational-choice literature stemming from Arrow's work. In comparative historical analyses, analogous arguments are often applied to large-scale social changes such as democratization (Collier and Collier 1991; Collier 1999), industrialization (Gerschenkron 1962; Kurth 1979), state building (Ertman 1997; Shefter 1977), or welfare state development (Huber and Stephens 2001). Sequencing matters not only for collective choices within legislatures but also potentially for *any* sociopolitical process where self-reinforcement means that forsaken alternatives become increasingly unreachable with the passage of time.

Historical institutionalists also employ timing and sequence arguments to highlight *conjunctures*—interaction effects between distinct causal sequences that become joined at particular points in time (Aminzade 1992; Orren and Skowronek 1994; Sewell 1996). The ability to identify and explore such conjunctures is a major advantage of the more macroscopic inclinations of historical institutionalism. For example,

Skowronek's account (1993) of U.S. presidential leadership emphasizes the interaction of slowly developing modern institutional capacities and the particular position of an individual president within the sequential rise and decline of a dominant political coalition. The explanatory power of Skowronek's analysis therefore derives from highlighting the intersection of long-term developments with recurrent political cycles. Other historical institutional accounts have focused on the political effects produced when separately unfolding processes conjoin. Thus Ertman (1997) stresses links between military competition and developing social capacities for bureaucratic governance, Shefter (1977) analyzes the interaction of state building and party formation, and Skocpol (1979) attributes social revolutionary outbreaks to conjunctures of domestic and international conflicts. These analysts focus on distinct sociopolitical processes that become linked in different and causally crucial ways depending on relative timing. The causal centrality of such conjunctures, it should be stressed, would never be noted by analyses investigating or theorizing about single processes in isolation.

SLOW-MOVING CAUSAL PROCESSES

Another theoretical justification for focusing on historical process is to draw attention to lengthy, large-scale, but often very slow moving social processes (Pierson 2002). Historical institutionalists seek to be attentive to the unfolding of both causal processes and important political outcomes over extended periods of time. Most political scientists are strongly predisposed to focus on aspects of causal processes and outcomes that unfold very rapidly. Yet many things in the social world take a long time to happen. Some causal processes and outcomes occur slowly because they are incremental; it simply takes a long time for them to add up to anything. Changes in pension systems, for example, are not fully translated into levels of public spending for a half-century or more. A second possibility is the presence of threshold effects; many social processes may have little significance until they attain a critical mass, which may then trigger major change (McAdam 1982; Goldstone 1991; Baumgartner and Jones 1993). Alternatively, slow-moving processes may involve transformations that are probabilistic during any particular period and therefore several periods may be necessary before the transformation occurs. Under such circumstances, the social outcome of interest may not take place until well after the appearance of key causal factors. Particularly when it focuses on macroscopic processes, historical-institutionalist research is often primarily interested in such structural preconditions for particular outcomes, rather than the specific timing of those outcomes (Collier 1999; Moore 1966; Rueschemeyer, Stephens, and Stephens 1992). When either structural causes or threshold effects are at work, analysts adopting a short time frame are likely to focus erroneously on the more idiosyncratic or precipitating factors that trigger outcomes. Because some crucial social conditions may change only slowly, analysts studying a narrow time frame will be strongly inclined to take them as fixed and therefore irrelevant to their causal accounts (Rueschemeyer, Stephens, and Stephens 1992; Kitschelt 1991).

Another possibility is that causal processes involve chains with several links, which require some time to work themselves out. To the extent that causal chains of this sort are at work, analyses must frame their studies on a broad time scale. Collier and Collier's influential work on labor incorporation in Latin America presents arguments of this kind, in which the ultimate outcomes of interest reflect a sequence of key developments over extended periods of time (Collier and Collier 1991). Indeed, this type of claim about long-term, multistage causal processes is often invoked in work on state building (Flora 1999a, b) or democratization (Luebbert 1991; Collier 1999).

Swank (2001a) offers an instructive recent example. In assessing the impact of political institutions on welfare state retrenchment, he criticizes the view that fragmented institutions will limit cutbacks by increasing the number of veto points available to defenders of the status quo. Swank argues that this is true as far as it goes but notes that the long-term, indirect effects of institutional fragmentation run largely in the other direction. Not only does institutional fragmentation limit the initial expansion of the welfare state, but it also reinforces social heterogeneity, inhibits the growth of encompassing interest groups, and weakens cultural commitments to universalist social policies. All of these long-term effects strengthen the welfare state's opponents and weaken its advocates. Thus many of the most important effects of institutional fragmentation work themselves out only indirectly and over extended periods of time. Ahistorical analyses typically seek to consider the effects of institutions while holding constant other variables, but these variables are in part the long-term consequences of institutional structures. Ahistorical investigations are therefore likely to systematically misread the impact of institutional structures on the politics of the welfare state.

Analysts who fail to be attentive to these slow-moving dimensions of social life may ignore potentially powerful hypotheses. They are particularly likely to miss the role of many sociological variables, like demography (Goldstone 1991), literacy (Ertman 1997), or technology (Kurth 1979), as well as the impact of other slowly building pressures such as international military competition and fiscal overload (Skocpol 1979). Their explanations may focus on triggering or precipitating factors rather than deeper causes (Kitschelt 1991). Perhaps most fundamental of all, they may fail to even identify some important questions about politics because the relevant outcomes happen too slowly and are therefore simply off their radar screens.

HISTORY AS PROCESS, NOT JUST ILLUSTRATION

In the ways we have just surveyed, theoretical attentiveness to historical processes represents a formidable comparative advantage of historical institutionalism, especially since this attentiveness is linked to macroscopic analysis focusing on institutions and organizations in addition to aggregates of people. Most research in the behavioral tradition uses surveys that offer a snapshot in time. And even when surveys are repeated to offer a longitudinal series, it is rare indeed for behavioral analysts to consider changing institutional contexts, critical conjunctures, or path-dependent large-scale processes as causally relevant to the changing modes of individual behavior they probe. There are exceptions, certainly, such as Carmines and Stimson's dissection of the processes by which race became a transforming issue in U.S. partisan politics, or Putnam's consideration of the impact of World War II and other watershed historical events on "life course" developments for late-twentieth-century U.S. adults (Carmines and Stimson 1989; Putnam 2000). But for the most part, survey analysis relies on one-time data about attitudes and self-reported behaviors to explore individual-level hypotheses about mass patterns. Change over time often enters the discussion only speculatively, as when a researcher reports differences between working women and housewives at a moment in time, and then go on to speculate that the changing proportions of such persons in the population may signify a continuous social change.

To be sure, some rational-choice scholars have turned to historical case studies in recent years. But most of the analytic advantages we have outlined are absent in this work, because the past enters only in a highly restricted sense, as what might be termed illustrative history, the mining of the historical record for outcomes that can be "explained" by particular rational-choice models. Previously established models may be applied in interesting ways to examples in the past (cf. Bates et al. 1998), but the tools of game theory turn out to be poorly suited to analyzing conjunctures or exploring slow-moving macroprocesses. Rational-choice theory faces considerable difficulties in moving from the micro- to the meso- or macrolevels of analysis that are typically featured in works that analyze processes over long stretches of time (Elster 2000; Munck 2001b). Rational choice's reliance on theory-driven agendas and on the identification of empirical terrain favorable for its preferred methods leads relentlessly back to an emphasis on the micro. And the results of game theory quickly become indeterminate or unmanageably complex as one increases the number of actors involved (indeed, in game theory the problem of indeterminacy is often rife even at the microlevel). The fact that many macroprocesses take considerable time to play out presents a further difficulty, since game theory generally requires that all the relevant actors, preferences, and payoffs be established and fixed simultaneously at the beginning of a game. In short, there are real obstacles in rational-choice theory to serious consideration of many key aspects of historical processes.[10]

■ | Analyzing Institutions in Context

Historical institutionalism is characterized by the second part of its label as well as the first. But what does *institutionalism* mean for this family of scholars? We can say of much political science today what Richard Nixon once said of Keynesianism: We are all institutionalists now. In political science today many scholars analyze how institutions influence political behavior and shape processes ranging from legislative decision making to social movements (Hall and Taylor 1996). As Thelen (1999) has ably elaborated, both rational-choice institutionalists and historical institutionalists presume that organizationally embodied routines play a crucial role in allocating resources and structuring the incentives, options, and constraints faced by political participants. In this sense, institutionalism is indeed a broadly shared approach in contemporary political science.

But even though institutionalists of different stripes have converged on some complementary questions and findings (Thelen 1999, 372–81), important differences remain. Rational-choice scholars tend to focus on rules of the game that provide equilibrium "solutions" to collective action dilemmas. Historical institutionalists, meanwhile, probe uneasy balances of power and resources, and see institutions as the developing products of struggle among unequal actors. Rational-choice scholars often focus on one set of rules at a time. Historical institutionalists, by contrast, typically do meso- or macrolevel analyses that examine multiple institutions in interaction, operating in, and influenced by, broader contexts. They pay close attention to ways in which multiple institutional realms and processes intersect with one another, often creating unintended openings for actors who trigger changes. Historical institutionalists investigate the rise and decline of institutions over time, probing the origins, impact, and stability or instability of specific institutions as well as broader institutional configurations. Sometimes the principal goal is to explain the institutional arrangements themselves, at other times to use variables referring to institutional configurations to explain other outcomes of interest.

10. Even where rational-choice theory seems better equipped, it has made very limited moves in this direction. For instance, despite Douglas North's important work (1990) on path dependence, his strong focus on historical process has been largely ignored by rational-choice theorists (for partial exceptions, see Aldrich 1994; Harvey 1998).

INSTITUTIONAL EFFECTS

Much research in historical institutionalism adopts a mesolevel focus, concentrating, for example, on policy developments in a particular issue area (e.g., Hacker 1998; Immergut 1992; Weir 1992b) or changes in organizational fields (e.g., Skocpol, Ganz, and Munson 2000). Historical institutionalists may also tackle the most macrolevel developments, such as modernizing intellectual transformations (Wuthnow 1989) or state formation (e.g., Anderson 1986; Doyle 1986a; Tilly 1975; Downing 1992; Ertman 1997; Skowronek 1982). In either case, analyses tend to highlight and explore causes operating at the interorganizational or interinstitutional level. Certainly, historical institutionalists accept the principle that causes should ultimately be consistent with plausible accounts of individual motivation and behavior (Little 1991). But they also believe that the patterns of resources and relationships in which individuals find themselves have powerful channeling and delimiting effects and that many of these effects are expressed through the conjoint impact of multiple institutions. As Ronald Jepperson puts it, these processes occurring "within and between institutions . . . are of course produced via the behavior of people, but . . . the causal linkages involved in these collective processes are far removed from the aggregation of simple social behavior" (2001, 5–6). So historical institutionalists aim to make those patterns visible and trace their causal impacts.

Historical institutionalists rarely focus on a single institutional or organizational site of contestation, as rational choice scholars often do. There is a strong tendency to doubt the power of many claims about institutional effects that rest solely on an analysis of that institution in isolation. Research on U.S. policy development, for instance, typically focuses on the interplay among multiple organizational actors in multiple institutional settings (Baumgartner and Jones 1993; Skocpol 1992; Weir 1992a). Melnick's analysis (1994) of the "rights revolution" that has fueled regulatory expansion in the United States provides a good example. Tracing this revolution through multiple venues and over an extended stretch of time, he demonstrates that it must be understood as the result of an interaction between the courts and Congress, with newly emergent citizens' organizations playing a crucial role in coupling these distinct institutional sites. Advocates of policy activism in the federal courts and congressional committees have, through interplay between the two branches, been able to advance their agendas beyond what a majority in Congress would have been likely to produce on its own.

Similarly, recent work in both comparative political economy (Kitschelt, Lange, Marks, and Stephens 1999; Hall and Soskice 2001) and social policy (Esping-Andersen 1990; Huber and Stephens 2001) has focused on how *configurations* of policies, formal institutions, and organizational structures generate distinctive welfare state regimes or varieties of capitalism that operate in fundamentally different manners. Outcomes are generated not by some universal operating principles characteristic of a given type of actor or realm of activity but by intersections of organized practices (such as labor markets, firm structures, or crucial policy arrangements). These practices will often have originated at different times and then formed configurations that advantage key actors (such as employer associations and labor unions). These actors, in turn, will generally work to maintain the configuration with only incremental adjustments even when economic, cultural, and geopolitical circumstances shift.

Institutional Development

Issues of long-term institutional development are also central to historical institutional research agendas (Thelen 1999). Historical institutionalists are typically suspicious of functional explanations, in which institutional outcomes are explained by their consequences. In such functional accounts, institutions develop because of their capacity to solve certain collective problems. The implicit or explicit claim is that rational actors produced these outcomes in order to solve these problems.

As suggested above, concern with issues of institutional development within historical institutionalism is strongly linked to theorizing about the causal relevance or origins, sequences, and temporal processes. Functional accounts of institutions seem most plausible when investigations take a one-time snapshot, because long-term effects and inconsistent "layers" of institutional development (see Schickler 2001) are not so readily noticed in such studies. In most cases, synchronic analysts simply probe an extant institution to uncover benefits for particular actors. Analysts then infer that these benefits explain the institution, implying that the actors who are presently advantaged (or their forebears) created the institution to produce the benefits. This is a plausible hypothesis, but it is only a hypothesis and over-time investigation of institutional origins and dynamics often does not bear out such lines of reasoning.

By examining issues of institutional origins and change over an extended time frame, historical institutionalists have been able to highlight a number of potential problems for functional accounts (see Thelen 1993, 1994, 1999; Pierson 2000b for relevant findings and arguments). Functional interpretations of politics are often suspect because of the sizable temporal gap between actors' actions and the long-term consequences of those actions. Political actors, facing the pressures of the immediate or skeptical about their capacity to engineer long-term effects, may pay limited attention to the long run. Thus the long-term effects of institutional choices, which are frequently the most profound and interesting ones, should often be seen as the *by-products* of social processes rather than the realization ("congealed preferences" as Riker put it) of actors' goals.

A second issue concerns unintended consequences. Even where

actors may be greatly concerned about the future in their efforts to design institutions, they operate in settings of tremendous complexity. As a consequence, they will often make mistakes. Thus institutions may not be functional even in a context of far-sighted actors, because they do not operate as intended. Although widely acknowledged to be significant in actual politics, political scientists often treat unintended consequences as an error term or simply ignore them by failing to investigate institutions over time. In cross-sectional studies of institutions, the issue of unintended consequences vanishes from view, since either the long-term consequences of institutional choices or the original factors generating the institutional choice will be outside the scope of the analysis. By contrast, historical institutionalists examining institutional development often stress the surprising long-term consequences of earlier political choices and conflicts (Anderson 1986; Luebbert 1991; Skocpol 1992; Thelen 1999, 2002).

Historical institutionalists, finally, emphasize the ways in which institutions are remade over time (Thelen 1999, 2002). Because of strong path-dependent effects, institutions are not easily scrapped when conditions change. Instead, institutions will often have a highly "layered" quality (Schickler 2001; Stark and Bruszt 1998). New initiatives are introduced to address contemporary demands, but they add to rather than replace preexisting institutional forms. Alternatively, old institutions may persist but be turned to different uses by newly ascendant groups. In either case, the original choices are likely to figure heavily in the current functioning of the institution. Thus institutions will rarely look like optimal solutions to present collective action problems.

Clearly, attentiveness to history and the investigation of meso- or macrolevel institutional configurations are highly complementary strategies of analysis. Tracing politics through time is very helpful for identifying the boundary conditions for particular theoretical claims. Even more significant, the emphasis historical institutionalists place on conjunctures and sequencing draws attention to the temporal connections among social processes, and highlights the importance of meso- or macrolevel analysis of institutional configurations. Furthermore, while path-dependent or increasing returns processes can play out at a microlevel (e.g., in the way individuals develop and reinforce particular mental maps of the social world), they are often most significant at the meso- or macrolevel. Particular sets of institutions and organizations are often mutually reinforcing or complementary—the presence of each enhances tendencies for the development of others—in a manner that can be seen as a kind of coevolutionary or selection process playing out over considerable stretches of time. A good example is the recent research in comparative political economy focusing on varieties of capitalism (Hall and Soskice 2001b; Estevez-Abe, Iversen, and Soskice 1999; Soskice 1999). This work stresses how different political economies have developed along quite different lines because of the coevolution of mutually reinforcing institutional and organizational structures. Patterns of firm organization, systems of interest intermediation and key social and economic policy structures contain institutional complementarities that place national political economies on distinct, path-dependent courses of development.

One can also see the advantages of a combined focus on institutions and temporal processes in the development of extensive historical institutionalist work on *policy feedbacks* (Heclo 1974; Weir and Skocpol 1985; Pierson 1993). Many of the works cited here emphasize that government policies establish some of the most important structuring rules of modern societies. The specific design of policies can have an enormous effect on the resources and strategies subsequently available to political actors—indeed, in many contexts, policies can be as important as formal political institutions in shaping political processes and outcomes (Esping-Andersen 1990; Skocpol 1992; Weir 1992a; Pierson 1994; Huber and Stephens 2001; Campbell forthcoming; Hacker 2002). The success of this line of argument demonstrates very clearly how the particular vantage points encouraged by different analytical strategies can either highlight or obscure important aspects of social reality. Because rational-choice scholarship is so focused on the pursuit of broad generalizations, it has concentrated almost entirely on recurrent, carefully delimited *formal* institutions such as legislatures or central banks.

Only a few rational-choice scholars (such as Bates 1988b) focus on the state overall and highlight the ulterior effects of state policies. In formal institutional accounts, policies are usually treated as dependent variables, with their further political consequences through feedbacks falling beyond the scope of analysis, either because these consequences are seen as too idiosyncratic or because analysis of policy feedbacks would require attentiveness to processes unfolding over time. But this omission will not do, because the expanding activities of states—and the policy feedbacks flowing from them—have been a central fact of modern life. Fortunately, state expansion and policy feedbacks have been at the center of historical-institutionalist analyses, even as these phenomena have largely vanished off the radar screen of the more universalist studies of formal institutions. The distinctive foci and contributions of rational-choice and historical-institutionalist work on institutions thus provide a clear demonstration of the advantages of pluralist political science, employing multiple strategies of inquiry. Without competitive pluralism in social science theorizing and research, important issues can too readily fall off the agenda of scholarship.

CAUSAL CONFIGURATIONS AND CONTEXT EFFECTS

The strong emphasis on interaction effects in historical institutionalism reflects some core working assumptions about how most sociopolitical processes operate. Analysts are strongly affected by their basic presumptions about how social processes work; and they tend to frame their problems, generate hypotheses, and employ methods of analysis and research designs that fit such presumptions (Abbott 1988; Hall 2002). Behavioralists, for example, are happy to use statistical techniques to analyze data from as many "cases" as possible—often data from surveys of thousands of individuals—because they are prepared to assume that very general variables operating independently of one another come together to account for the patterns of behavior they are trying to explain. Historical institutionalists, by contrast, assume that operative variables may not be independent of each other at all. When it comes to analyzing the origins and impact of institutions, causally important variables are often bundled together in the real world; and there may be alternative causal paths to similar outcomes (Ragin 1987; Shalev 1998). Historical institutionalists tend to suspect from the get-go that causal variables of interest will be strongly influenced by overarching cultural, institutional, or epochal contexts. This is not a matter of getting mired in thick description. As Andrew Abbott puts it: "Context has two senses. . . . The strict sense . . . denotes those things that environ and thereby define a thing of interest. The loose sense simply denotes detail. The acute reader will note that these correspond nicely to the two judgments of the scientific worth of contextual information. If decontextualization is merely the removal of excess detail, then it's a fine thing, scientifically. If, on the other hand, it is the removal of defining locational information, it is a scientific disaster" (1997, n. 10). Because historical institutionalists share the latter set of expectations, researchers in this tradition tend to move up from single institutions to broader contexts—*they look at forests as well as trees.* And they almost always seek to discover and explicate the impact of configurations of organizations and institutions on outcomes of interest (Katznelson 1997).

In addition to presuming—and concentrating attention on—causal configurations conceptualized at the organizational and institutional level, there is another way in which historical institutionalists highlight interaction effects. They often do this by pointing to overarching contexts—types of regimes, eras, regions, and cultures—that place bounds around the theorizing being done in any given study. Historical institutionalists rarely aim to write about all of humankind through all of global history. Scan the titles of major historical-institutionalist works, for example, and you will often find the proper names of regions of the world or the beginning and ending dates of the specific period that the argument is to cover. This is not done because historical institutionalists in political science are trying to be historians; they do not aspire to just tell stories about a time and place. Nor are dates given only to describe critical junctures when a change occurs that the analyst seeks to explain (e.g., Clemens 1997; Skowronek 1982). Beyond such an obvious use of dates and place, historical institutionalists often set limits to the applicability of their causal arguments, arguing in theoretically explicit ways why variables appear and combine in characteristic ways in one era but might not exist or combine in the same way in other eras.

For example, in his book about the growth (or not) and success or failure of guerrilla-led revolutionary movements, Timothy Wickham-Crowley (1992) develops a rigorous causal analysis and suggests (in his conclusion) that his model links up with theoretical explanations of revolutions in many regions and eras. But Wickham-Crowley carefully bounds his own argument, restricting it to Latin America since 1956. In analytical terms, he explains that specific developments and events created background conditions to generate many guerrilla movements with similar aims and methods, thus setting the stage for the variables he explores to account for movement growth and success or failure. In the end, Wickham-Crowley's careful delineation—and explanation—of the overarching context within which his variable-based analysis applies reinforces its theoretical power. As we move to other continents and periods, we can ask about changes that might influence the variables in play and the likely relationships among them.

Another way in which historical-institutionalist works highlight overarching contexts is by deliberately juxtaposing two or more contexts, to show how variable configurations already analyzed (across multiple cases) may play out in new ways when the overarching context changes. In the revolutions literature, Goodwin (2001) does this by, first, developing explanations for revolutionary successes and failures within Central America and East Asia, and then highlighting the somewhat different actors and conditions that come into play within each region. Addressing a very different problem—Pierson (1994) identifies variables about institutions and established policy characteristics that can explain why British and U.S. conservative politicians succeeded or failed with attempted cutbacks in a number of social policy areas. Yet he also steps back and stresses that the key causal relationships governing policy determination are quite different in the recent period of austerity than they were when welfare states were greatly expanded.

Scholars in other major political science traditions are often much less attentive to overarching contexts than historical institutionalists, in part because they prefer to focus on individual-level behavior or microprocesses but also because they are reluctant to write like historians. Ironically, the result can be less theoretically powerful work. Behaviorialists happily rely on types of data only available at one point in time or just for short time spans but do not necessarily think through what that means. As a result, significant overarching contexts can go unnoticed, unconceptualized. For example, behavioralists sometimes fail to notice that very similar individual-level patterns—joining more or fewer voluntary organizations, voting at different rates—can end up having very different meanings, depending on the kinds of organizations or institutions that predominate in a given nation or era. Theories invoked in behavioralist studies can end up being profoundly underspecified.

Rational-choice scholars, meanwhile, often write as if the models they present were infinitely generalizeable, even as they smuggle all kinds of institutional, cultural, and epochal specifics into their empirical operationalizations. This may seem an optimal way of arguing; isn't social science supposed to generalize? But, in practice, this kind of approach means that we leave important variables implicit and we fail to see how changing background conditions might cause the same variables to play out in very different ways. Again, the preference of rational-choice theorists for examining microsettings strongly reinforces this tendency.

■ | Research Strategies and the Accumulation of Knowledge

Tackling big, real-world questions; tracing processes through time; and analyzing institutional configurations and contexts—these are the features that define historical institutionalism as a major strategy of research in contemporary political science. We have stressed the comparative advantages these approaches afford to all who would better understand government and politics. But we must also acknowledge the claims of critics who dismiss historical institutionalism as a valid approach to doing cumulative social science. Critics of historical institutionalism sometimes pen manifestos announcing that case studies and small-*n* comparisons cannot generate valid knowledge, because cases are not randomly selected and there may not be enough statistical degrees of freedom to test all conceivable hypotheses rigorously (cf. Geddes 1990; Goldthorpe 1991; Lieberson 1991). Statistical methodologists (such as King, Keohane, and Verba 1994) also worry that the historical-institutionalist proclivity for tackling significant issues predisposes them toward "selection on the dependent variable," that is, choosing cases where a phenomenon of interest has occurred, while ignoring the instances where it has not occurred.

Historical institutionalist books and articles are sometimes denounced in ways such as these one at a time, in isolation from one another—an approach that surely would be laughed out of court if applied to isolated works in any other tradition. In all research traditions, individual works build on one another, often extending lines of analysis, retesting arguments, and correcting for earlier limitations. The real issue is whether historical institutionalists in general have headed up blind alleys, because their studies, considered collectively as well as individually, are improperly designed. This is not the place for an exhaustive review of the profusion of recent methodological reflections in this genre, but the major signposts on the road can be mentioned.

Methodological challenges have, in our view, been good for historical institutionalism. Not only have these critiques been testimony to the visibility and intellectual impact of the studies they have dissected. Challenges have had a bracing impact, prompting historical institutionalists to spell out their metatheoretical presumptions and sharpen rationales and tools for doing valid macroscopic and historical studies. A number of scholars, for example, have asked how studies can best be designed to take intuitions about configurational causation and temporal process seriously. In other words, if historical institutionalists doubt that single, highly general variables have uniform effects across contexts, and regardless of interactions with other factors, how can research designs allow for adequate empirical exploration of hypotheses about contexts and configurations (see Abbott 2001; Mahoney 1999; Hall 2002; Ragin 2000)? If historical institutionalists stress mechanisms rather than simple association in causal arguments, how can process tracing be done in a rigorous way? And what criteria must be met to demonstrate valid arguments about path dependence, critical conjunctures, or sequence effects? Although Pierson (2000a, 2002), Thelen (1999, 2000a), and others have primarily focused on the theoretical characteristics of arguments about temporal causality, their reflections also set empirical standards to be met in case analyses and comparative studies that aim to establish the presence of causally relevant processes or events.

Reflecting on the strengths and limits of hundreds of studies in various important literatures, methodologically oriented historical institutionalists have also made the case for circumstances under which in-depth case studies and small- to medium-n comparisons are an optimal research strategy (Collier 1993; Mahoney 2000a; Munck 1998; Ragin 1987; Rueschemeyer and Stephens 1997; Tilly 1984). Random selection of cases — say, of particular regimes or nations from hundreds across the globe — is often not appropriate; and it is far from the only way to test hypotheses rigorously. Whatever the risks or drawbacks, hypotheses can be rigorously tested even when scholars cannot sample from large numbers of truly independent cases (for an excellent overview of strategies of inference in small-n research, see Mahoney 2000a). Alternative strategies of causal inference have been developed and applied, because there are important intellectual and practical advantages to focusing agendas of research on a small to intermediate number of cases, including instances of substantively compelling outcomes and arrangements we want to understand.

For example, a scholar who wants to understand revolutions is unlikely to be willing to start with a purely random set of times and places; she will want to make sure that clear-cut revolutions are included in her research. But in the best past studies of revolutions — as in many other historical-institutionalist literatures — it has long been standard to test hypotheses with comparisons between positive cases, where phenomena of interest occur, and closely matched negative cases, where the phenomena do not occur (Skocpol 1979; Goodwin 2001). Speaking about comparative studies in many topic literatures—analyses have juxtaposed time periods, regions, and policy sectors, turning what appear to be one or a few national instances into settings for many carefully compared cases. And even within what appear to be single case studies, empirical observations have often been multiplied by formulating and testing hypotheses about the *mechanisms* that connect causes to effects (Bennett and George 1997). All of these strategies of analysis have been used to good effect by scientifically sound historical-institutional studies, and the rapidly developing methodological literatures will make it easier for future scholars to recognize and apply the standards and rationales for best practices in case-based and small-*n* research.

No matter what theories or research methods are deployed, individual studies in isolation never do more than move the scholarly enterprise a step or two forward. Scholarship is an inherently communal enterprise, and so it is appropriate to reflect on how well clusters of scholars do at *accumulating* valid and important findings. Here is where historical institutionalists do quite well, in our view, because substantively compelling, problem-driven research facilitates exactly the sort of intellectual cumulation that allows a community of researchers to make clear progress over time.

Because historical institutionalists tend to tackle big, humanly important questions, scholars are likely to come back to the issues again and again over several academic generations. Within each generation as well, smart people jump in, willing to argue about how best to frame the questions and describe patterns worth explaining, as well as about how to formulate and test hypotheses. Researchers reexamine cases and hypotheses and extend established hypotheses to new sets of cases. A good example is spelled out in James Mahoney's review of several decades of historical-institutionalist research on the origins and dynamics of democratic and authoritarian regimes. In this literature, research took off from pioneering agenda-setting works (i.e, Moore 1966; O'Donnell 1973; Linz 1978), with waves of succeeding scholars executing dozens of historical and comparative-historical studies that served to refute some arguments, refine others, discover new lines of causal argument, and extend findings across eras and continents. Cumulative research now offers a convincing picture of when, why, and how different types of regimes have emerged in various continents over much of modern world history. "Most of our knowledge about the relationship between democracy and various other factors (social classes, international conditions, elite behavior) has been derived through such step-by-step accumulation . . ." Mahoney concludes. "Plainly, if one were to strike all comparative-historical research from the record, most of what we currently know about the causes of democracy and authoritarianism would be lost" (Mahoney 2002). What Mahoney demonstrates about the literature on democracy and authoritarianism holds as well for literatures on revolutions, state building, and varieties of public policymaking, to name just some areas of clear-cut progress in recent decades. In each of these literatures, historical institutionalists have persistently addressed big questions, while collectively examining and reexamining a large variety of cases.

Of course, scholars in other major traditions also think of themselves as savvy practitioners of cumulative social science, and we would hardly suggest that steady progress can occur only in areas where historical institutionalists predominate. But it is worth noting that sets of scholars who define cumulation in theoretically orthodox terms or who let themselves be captured by their methodological tools can lead us up blind alleys.

Rational-choice scholars often focus research agendas on puzzles internally generated by their overarching theory (Green and Shapiro 1994). There is no doubt that this can at times generate significant scientific progress, highlighting new questions, identifying or explaining new phenomena, and generating linkages among subject matters and research communities that had not been visible before. Research on collective action, growing out of Mancur Olson's seminal work (1971) on public goods, probably provides the clearest example. Outside observers have, however, had more doubts about other prominent examples of theory-derived problems, such as the "paradox of voting" or the relative stability (as opposed to Arrow-style "cycling" dynamics) exhibited in Congress. Each of these "problems" has generated a massive amount of published work, and there is no doubt that the answers provided have become more sophisticated over time. What is less clear is whether these agendas have generated knowledge that speaks to major social problems or would be of significant interest to anyone other than enthusiasts of rational-choice theory. How might these bodies of work fare if we asked James Rule's question (1997) for evaluating research programs: Would someone standing outside your research community be likely to acknowledge the usefulness of the knowledge you are providing?

Methods of investigation rigidly tied to theoretical presumptions can also prompt rational-choice research agendas into overly constricted channels. With game theory generally providing the central analytical tool, studies too easily confine themselves to modeling strategic action at the microlevel. Rational choice practitioners prefer to focus on political settings, such as legislatures, that offer favorable conditions for a particular analytical strategy. They look for coherent strategic actors operating in well-bounded contexts where choices are clearly identifiable and payoffs relatively transparent. Efforts to deal with broader social aggregates, whether interrelated organizations or looser social groupings, are often avoided. Or such challenges are handled by simply treating these groups as themselves being coherent strategic actors—a highly questionable move given rational choice's own assumptions. What is more, rational-choice studies typically assume that all major actors and their preferences are present at the outset of the setting to be analyzed, when in the real world, new actors and changed preferences often emerge in later stages of a linked process. Politics ends up sliced and frozen into artificial moments on the slide of a powerful but tightly focused microscope.

The use of one grand theoretical framework and the decision to focus intensively on a restricted range of political phenomena are often justified, at least implicitly, by what could be called the "lego" rationale. This rationale holds that social scientists should focus on developing solid blocks of findings within a presumed whole. Although the findings may in themselves appear small or distant from pressing social concerns, these blocks can then be pieced together to produce robust answers to important questions. Triviality is acceptable if it provides something to build on. But there are strong reasons to doubt that we should place such a heavy bet on the lego approach. As rational-choice scholars, above all, should know, partial actions do not invariably add up to optimal outcomes. More to the point, where is the evidence that a quarter-century of lego-style research has generated ever-broader findings? In certain areas of political science, arguably, instead of the intellectual problems faced by rational choice becoming bigger, the universe of politics deemed suitable for scrutiny gets redefined in ever more diminutive terms. Thus the study of American politics becomes the study of Congress (or, at its most expansive, the study of Congress and administrative agencies). And the study of comparative politics becomes the study of parliaments and government coalitions. Big questions, broader contexts, and long-term transformations recede ever farther from view, and political science risks cutting itself off from concerns important to broad audiences.

Obsession with a single theory for its own sake is not the only way that cumulative research agendas can go awry. Another danger is capture by technique, or overreliance on a single kind of data. Like historical institutionalists, behavioralists are usually more problem focused. But they risk becoming exclusively enamored with social surveys and the statistical manipulations that can be performed on the answers of random samples of individuals. This can lead behavioralists to neglect other kinds of data that might be relevant to the substantive questions at hand. Tendencies in this direction plague some current work on civic engagement, for example. Why should we presume that everything we need to know about civic participation can be discovered from social surveys—usually confined to one moment in time—that ask vast aggregates of people about their attitudes and reported behaviors? Heavy reliance on social surveys has channeled much of the current debate about civic engagement in U.S. democracy toward exploring attitudes of social trust and indications of whether individuals choose to participate in various ways. But data of this sort is available only for the 1970s and after, and key changes in behavior and institutions happened well before that. What is more, we cannot understand the impact of rising or declining individual memberships in voluntary groups unless we know what kinds of groups have increased or decreased and unless we know how groups interact with institutional centers of decision making.

Questions about an important topic like civic engagement and democracy can rarely be adequately addressed with just one type of data or one technique of empirical analysis.

When it comes to avoiding the dangers of capture by theory, technique, or single data sources, historical institutionalists may have an easier time than scholars in the other major political science traditions. Precisely because historical institutionalists are so riveted by big, compelling real-world problems with clear substantive import to audiences beyond fellow academics, they almost never forget that keeping the eye on the substantive prize—remaining determined to understand important phenomena in the real world—is the formula for enduring scholarly achievement. Because the substantive issues at stake are important in their own right, historical institutionalists are often willing to combine theoretical insights, mine various data sources, and stretch the limits of methodological creativity to gain leverage on those issues (for some nice examples, see McAdam 1982; Rueschemeyer, Stephens, and Stephens 1992; and Schickler 2001). Each scholar knows that his or her interim answers may soon be subject to reconsideration by other scholars (or members of educated audiences) who care just as much about explaining the outcome or solving the puzzle. And real-world developments may intervene to change the definition of important issues or bring new dimensions of them into view. Literatures leavened by many historical-institutionalist participants remain, in short, committed to broad conversations and to theoretical and methodological pluralism. This introduces dynamism and reality checks. If the legos are not fitting together to make at least the foundations of a beautiful structure, historical institutionalists won't keep playing with them forever.

■ | Historical Institutionalism in a Pluralistic Political Science

Addressing questions of interest to educated publics as well as academics, historical institutionalists analyze institutional configurations and develop explanations that highlight conjunctures and path-dependent temporal processes. In this overview, we have stressed and illustrated the many comparative advantages of historical-institutionalist scholarship, drawing on recent clarifications of the distinctive theoretical underpinnings and methodological proclivities of this genre of political science. Still, like other analytic strategies, those employed by historical institutionalists also entail certain costs. Critics often characterize historical institutionalism as mired in mere description and marred by intractable methodological limits. In our view, these criticisms are often misdirected or overdrawn, yet it is true that the focus of historical institutionalists on diverse substantive questions can entail intellectual fragmentation. Even though they share theoretical and methodological proclivities, historical-institutionalist scholars in different subfields may not regularly interact—a situation that (at least until recently) has limited theoretical clarity and cross-fertilization of substantive fields, frustrating steady methodological development. What is more, if historical institutionalists themselves are insufficiently clear about shared strategies, then scholars using other approaches may also fail to notice the theoretically and methodologically relevant commonalities among historical institutionalist contributions addressing so many distinct topics and questions. Important modes of analysis, such as ways of conceptualizing and measuring causal processes that play out over a long stretch of time, may thereby recede from view within the discipline. In this respect, recent critiques have had the salutary effect of prodding historical institutionalists to clarify and develop the methodological and theoretical underpinnings of their work.

Each of the leading approaches in contemporary empirical political science—behaviorialism, rational choice, and historical institutionalism—has proven its value. Political science—indeed social science as a whole—benefits from the coexistence and competition of varied approaches to theory and research. And it benefits even more from dialogue that crosses distinct traditions. Not only can external critiques point to blind spots, prompting improvements in scholarship to the degree that practitioners of each approach are prepared to listen and respond—as historical institutionalists have listened and responded of late. In addition to this back and forth of criticism, multiple approaches can set the stage for creative new blends of methodology and theorizing, especially as new generations of young scholars pick and choose and combine ideas from their elders. Breakthrough studies can combine lines of analysis, generating powerful synergies from the complementary strengths of alternative traditions. Indeed, many breakthroughs have already happened, and while we certainly cannot catalogue them here, we can illustrate some of the possibilities through three excellent examples.

Advancing the agenda for legislative studies suggested in "Legislatures as Political Institutions" (Gamm and Huber this volume), Eric Schickler's *Disjointed Pluralism: Institutional Innovation and the Development of the U.S. Congress* (2001) represents a pathbreaking study of institutional innovation in Congress over the past century. In two respects, Schickler's analysis synthesizes contributions from major research approaches. Theoretically, he tests various functional hypotheses about institutional design drawn from rational-choice scholarship, sorting them out and combining them with the aid of historical-institutionalist arguments about the layering of institutional arrangements over time, and about institutional choices as stemming from interacting processes rather than single processes operating in isolation. Methodologically, Schickler combines the quantitative analysis of roll call votes typical of congressional studies with sophisticated process tracing of a large number of institutional innovations drawn from four time periods (each time period lasting a decade or more). The result is the most serious effort yet to test the strength of a number of prominent theories of institutional choice over an extended time period, and the development of some strikingly original insights into the sources of change and continuity in legislative rules.

Across the globe, new democracies are emerging from previously entrenched authoritarian polities. Explaining variations in new institutional rules and in the processes by which they take shape represents a major challenge for students of comparative politics. In her new book on *Institutional Change and Political Continuity in Post-Soviet Central Asia*, Pauline Luong (2002) compares the establishment of electoral systems in Kazakhstan, Kyrgyzstan, and Uzbekistan and, in the process, develops of new and potentially generalizeable theory of "institutions designed under transitional circumstances," blending insights from both rational-choice institutionalism and historical institutionalism. Although historical institutionalists have directed our attention to persistent legacies from the past, new rules of the game can and do emerge from strategic bargains among elites, especially in a period of crisis and uncertainty. Yet rational-choice approaches too easily fall into the trap of assuming that elite bargaining over new arrangements occurs on a tabula rasa, without regard to entrenched understandings and power relationships. In Jones's model, actors change goals and perceptions in response to uncertainty and bargain in a dynamic way, producing different outcomes in three central Asian polities with many prior structural similarities. But elites work from power positions and understandings embedded in inherited arrangements—indeed they try to encode those older meanings and power relationships into seemingly new structures. Luong's work would not have been possible without prior breakthroughs in game theory. At the same time, she is inspired by the theoretical agendas set out by such historical institutionalists as Kathleen Thelen, calling for careful analyses not just of institutional outcomes but of the temporally and structurally embedded *processes* by which actors entrenched in previous institutions maneuver to create modified arrangements that retain many continuities from the past. Methodologically, moreover, Luong makes a powerful case for close comparison of kindred polities within a geocultural region, as a valuable laboratory for working out explanations of institutional change that may have much broader theoretical application.

In different ways, both Schickler and Luong work at the intersection of rational-choice theorizing and historical-institutional analysis. Our third instance of creative synergy, Andrea Campbell's *Shaping Policy, Shaping Citizens: Senior Citizen Activism and the American Welfare State* (forthcoming) exemplifies possibilities for combining strong points of survey-based behavioral analysis with analytic strategies that have been developed by historical institutionalists. Campbell's subject is a traditional focus of behavioralism: citizen participation. Specifically, she is interested in the changing patterns of political behavior of the U.S. elderly, and she ably uses survey results to document aggregate behaviors and attitudes.

At the same time, Campbell draws two major insights from historical institutionalism. First, she stresses the importance of studying participation over time, both to increase variation in her outcome and to identify and assess the contribution of relatively slow moving factors to changing patterns of participation. Second, she highlights the contributions of policy feedbacks—specifically from Social Security and Medicare—to both the level and style of citizen participation among the elderly. Through the painstaking assembly of longitudinal microdata on participation among the elderly and the thoughtful combination of multiple traditions, Campbell demonstrates how major federal programs both raised the level of elderly participation and produced an unusual pattern of participation. Among working-aged U.S. adults, participation is heavily skewed toward better-educated and higher-income groups, but this "upward" bias is largely absent among the elderly, where concerns about Social Security and Medicare have encouraged middle- and lower-strata elders to participate much more fully. Through its creative combination of behavioral and historical-institutional analysis, Campbell's study speaks to major issues of our time. Its findings are highly relevant to ongoing public as well as scholarly debates about entitlement reforms and about civic engagement in U.S. democracy.

None of the exemplary new studies we have just described could have been produced without imaginative efforts to draw on and combine the best of multiple analytical strategies. By featuring these studies, we mean to underline that it has not been our purpose to pit major approaches against one another in any kind of zero-sum game. We have simply sought to clarify the distinctive contributions and advantages of historical-institutionalist scholarship. Indeed, a good reason to clarify distinctions among approaches and highlight potential comparative advantages of each is to facilitate exchanges that combine the strengths of different approaches to maximum effect. We have made the case for historical institutionalism as one of the three research pillars in contemporary political science, and our task has been made easy by the outpouring of so much excellent work in recent years. Historical institutionalism has become, of late, more self-conscious both theoretically and methodologically, in ways we have indicated and illustrated throughout this review essay. Readers who wonder what political science would be like without self-conscious historical institutionalism need only ask what we would have lost if all the works in our bibliography, and many others like them, had not been published. We think the answer is obvious: without historical institutionalism, our discipline would be shorn of much of its ability to tackle major agendas of concern to all political scientists. And without historical institutionalists, political science would have much less to say about questions of great import to people beyond as well as within the ivory tower.

KAREN ORREN AND STEPHEN SKOWRONEK

The Study of American Political Development

The study of American political development (APD) is an inquiry into the temporal attributes of governance. The United States provides the primary setting for this inquiry; U. S. history provides the primary data; and understanding past politics as accurately as possible is a primary concern. But finding out "what happened" in American political history is not the ultimate objective. Rather, practitioners of APD seek knowledge of how governance changes over time; they are interested in specifying the processes by which political innovations are negotiated and new political relationships generated. The aim is to understand these things conceptually, that is to say, in terms that illuminate general features of the polity, over a range of historical instances. Of special interest are dynamics of governance in the past as they affect practices of governance in the present or shed light on its future prospects.

Intellectual currents affecting disciplines closely related to APD research have served in recent years to highlight the field's distinctive concerns. It is often noted, for instance, that APD came into its own as a subfield in political science departments during the 1980s and 1990s, when the study of American political history had lost much of its intellectual currency within history departments (Leuchtenberg 1986).[1] Government and politics, long a centerpiece of the historian's understanding of the United States's past, found itself in the position of a foil against which alternative interests gained ascendancy. Political history was first challenged by social historians who refocused attention on economic power, class relationships, group formation, and demographic trends. Then came the cultural turn in historical writing with its call for narratives of Ameri-

1. Of course, political history never disappeared and there are today encouraging signs of its resurgence. For the purposes of this essay, however, we have concentrated on the work of political scientists. Readers should not read our essay to imply that political scientists have been unaffected by the ongoing work of political historians or to deny the vibrant exchange that has been established between politically minded historians and historically minded political scientists.

cans who were not white, male, or otherwise favored by the state authority and office.

In political science, where government and its public ramifications are more firmly lodged as objects of study, the rise to prominence of alternative perspectives on the past had a different effect. Rather than crowd out interest in high politics and formal institutions, they opened it up. The discovery and exploration of alternative sources of power and authority spurred political scientists to rethink the operations of government and the dynamics of political change. Moreover, when political scientists turned back to history, they did so with the methodological debates of their own discipline in mind. Studies of American political development called attention to interactions over time that were difficult to square with the prevailing assumptions of pluralist theory and behavorial research. Historical approaches, which had been mainstays of the study of constitutional law and political philosophy since the inception of political science as a discipline, were reworked and redeployed to challenge received conceptions of the U.S. state (Skowronek 1982), of the relationship between governing institutions and political action (Huntington 1981) and of the proper angles of research into state-society relations (March and Olsen 1989).

By joining traditional interests in high politics and formal institutions to the wider array of concerns now understood to attend questions of power and authority, APD research has begun to illuminate the distinctive political problems that arise within the categorical realm of rules and operations to which individuals are expected to conform under threat of legal sanction. The study of changes in governance now ranges from investigations of Congress and the Supreme Court to investigations of workplace and family relations; problems of political development are situated in a variety of arenas, public and private, and within institutions that exhibit varying degrees of formal organization. In each domain, analytic attention has focused on the operation of rules that are enforced by socially legitimate authority designated to perform that task. Recognition of the diversity of these rules and their disparate institutional foundations underlies some of the most important questions now being asked, questions about relations between the whole and parts and how transformations in one arena of governance bears on the enforcement of rules elsewhere.

A second intellectual current that has highlighted the distinctiveness of APD's agenda is the collapse of faith in the sufficiency of development as a premise for historical inquiry in the social sciences. Before this, what conceptual apparatus there was for thinking about American politics over time was drawn from theories of world historical forces acting to modernize Western nations. Hegelian idealists, Marxist materialists, Weberian institutionalists, American progressives, modernization theorists—all assumed that progress onward and upward, toward one state of affairs or another, was history's predominant attribute. The rejection of this assumption and the questions that have come to surround the tradition of social theorizing built on it made American political history a field ripe for revision.

That APD came into its own at a time when the central premise it names had been widely discarded in part explains the intensity of the search that has been set in motion for theories and interpretive frameworks that might relate past and present in more compelling ways. The subfield continues to attract scholars convinced of the enduring value of historical strategies for situating American governance comparatively, for identifying common features and particular configurations and for considering the interaction over time of shared elements combined differently in different locales (Katzenelson 1997; Pierson 1994; Evans, Reueschemeyer, and Skocpol 1985; Bright and Harding 1984; Sheingate 2001). What these scholars have carried over from the tradition of theorizing devoted to uncovering natural laws of development is the intuition that one essential, constitutive dimension of governance is the passage of time itself and an accompanying commitment to rethink its implications. But APD research also evidences the challenges that now confront theorizing along these lines and the spadework that needs to be done if we are to formulate compelling explanations of how a nation's past bears on its subsequent politics.

The broadside critique of development unhinged settled notions across the board, not only about politics in the United States but also about politics in the states to which it had traditionally been compared. Relieved of teleological baggage, the search for meaning in change over time has moved closer to the ground and become more attentive to nuance and complication. It has become a more-contested inquiry as well, a forum for debate over whether anything worthy of the term *development* in fact occurs in politics, over what development might be composed of, and over the conditions under which it might happen. With the *d* word under scrutiny, APD has become as the seedbed of a general reconsideration of the character of political history itself.

A final current distinguishing the APD agenda today has been the rise to prominence of rational-choice theory within political science. Rational choice is a deductive theory whose main advances to this point are seen in the elaboration of microfoundations for analyzing political events and in the modeling of comparative statics. Explaining change is a central objective, but change is normally stylized by practitioners for game theoretic purposes, appearing as an exogenous shock to a stable state that induces the search for a new equilibrium of preferences. In this respect at least, the rise of rational-choice theory in political science may be regarded as of a piece with contemporary disillusionment with historical forces as a basis for political theorizing. As a testing ground for the theory, however, history remains inescapable, and increasing numbers of scholars working within the rational-choice tradition have turned to the past to demonstrate and refine the power of their models.

As we shall see below, the historical turn in rational-choice theorizing has opened new channels for collaboration in APD research. The grounds for such an exchange are clear: Political development necessarily concerns the acts of individuals, and APD and rational-choice research share certain assumptions about individual behavior—that individuals are on the whole rational in pursuing goals, that they act within structures and according to rules they understand, and that they have limited responses to coercion. But notwithstanding the potential for mutual advancement on this ground, a chief product of the exchange thus far has been a clarification of the different agendas that political scientists bring to the study the past. Rational-choice theorists approach political history with a set of propositions assumed to be independent of time and place and thus portable in their application to discrete instances. In this way, the past becomes a reservoir of examples. Research in APD assumes, in contrast, that time is constitutive of politics and that direct examination of dynamics emblematic of political history is one of the prime prerequisites for theory building. Other differences follow. Rational-choice theory offers snapshots, episodes of change in exemplary arenas; APD unreels a "motion picture" of governance, its parts' repositioning with diverse rhythms and mechanisms of coordination (Pierson 2000a, b). Rational-choice applications have sought to engage historians in debates about discrete political episodes (Bates et al. 1998); APD scholarship tends to draw historians into a dialogue about how periods relate to one another and how discrete episodes might be connected.

More will be said about each of these currents as we proceed. Suffice it to say here that APD is pursuing its own lines of inquiry among them. The claim that governance in its various aspects exhibits distinctive dynamics over time and that these are best examined over the long term touches a wide range of subject matters and engages scholarship in a number of specialties. Rather than assume a priori one set of dynamics everywhere or extrapolate from some related discipline to the realm of governance, APD has begun a thoroughgoing reassessment of how politics is arranged empirically at given points in time and how politics moves through time in a place. With long-standing assumptions about these matters exposed and interrogated, APD has emerged today as a field of considerable intellectual ferment and creativity.

■ | Culture

One important line of APD research pivots on Louis Hartz's argument (1955) that the United States "has always been a place where the common issues of the West have taken a strange and singular shape." Prior to Hartz, discussion of APD had followed the assumptions of progressive historians in directing attention to the common pressures that economic interest, industrialization, and class conflict exerted on political development throughout the West. Hartz challenged that approach, citing insufficient attention to the peculiarities of American political culture and to the distinctive ways that common pressures played out in particular settings. Recent scholarship has shown that this line of criticism is not easily contained. As contemporary scholarship has broadened and deepened inquiry into the "strange and singular" features of American political culture, it has come to find Hartz's own work wanting, too caught up in the primacy of common influences and the elusive standards of development that lurk behind them.

In fact, Hartz built on what orthodox theories of class conflict had said about developmental problems and prospects. His innovation was to present the United States as an exception to these rules, one that he explained with reference to Tocqueville's insight that Americans had never endured a bourgeois revolution against feudalism but had instead been "born equal." Hartz called attention to the fact that the American puritans had removed themselves from the struggle of liberal principles against the reigning doctrines of the English aristocracy. In so doing, he conjectured, they had bypassed a critical stage in the political development of liberalism itself. Hartz theorized that America's middle-class fragment, having been transplanted from its origins in a larger contest of worldviews but already aligned with the political sympathies of their coreligionists, gave rise to a peculiar political culture, one in which the values of individualism, limited government, and equality were so widely shared as to become irresistible to all serious contenders for political power. A "genuinely revolutionary tradition" never took hold in this environment, he argued, nor did a "genuine tradition of reaction," for never was there a need for American liberals to dislodge an antithetical establishment, to replace one set of ideas with another, or defend their own creation against alternatives. Hartz depicted a polity that acted without any consciousness of conflict as a battle between class antagonists over fundamental principles, and he concluded that, in the absence of class consciousness, the economic antagonisms routinely produced by capitalist development elsewhere were shorn of their potential to generate radical change. Having skipped the middle-class revolution against feudalism, Americans became impervious to the idea of a social revolution against capitalism.

Hartz's "consensus" thesis identified American "exceptionalism" with radically truncated cultural boundaries that constrained political thought, political action, and ultimately political development. In fact, Hartz's analysis went far toward rendering the whole idea of American political development an oxymoron. While he acknowledged pervasive and persistent conflict in American politics, he found no juncture at which these conflicts conjured political alternatives or aspirations robust enough to produce anything genuinely new or different; the United States's political struggles appeared to him mere "shadows" of the momentous struggles played out elsewhere on the world stage. Writing at the height of the cold war, Hartz expressed concern about the anachronistic character of American politics, in particular about problems Americans would face in grappling with the political alternatives with which they were now forced to engage. The limits of their capacity to understand anything beyond the narrow confines of their own experience might, he thought, lead them to exaggerate the threat posed by internal dissent and to underestimate the appeal that alternatives held elsewhere in the world.

With the end of the cold war and the emergence of United States unrivaled on the world stage, the concerns which Hartz expressed about American political development appear about as relevant as the predictions of Karl Marx (Foner 1984b). That said, the new tone in APD research has yet to strike a triumphalist chord. If anything, recent work raises even more serious questions about the proposition that the United States is the vanguard state of political development in the world. Consensus theory has been challenged in the very same terms that consensus theorists themselves challenged prior thinking about APD: it is charged with being too Euro-centric, too economistic, and insufficiently attentive to what makes American politics tick (Smith 1993). Scholars are far less willing now to leap from the relative absence of feudalism and socialism in the United States to the insignificance of ideological differences here or to ignore the choices that have divided the nation and shaped their political history. In place of Hartz's portrait of the United States's liberal naïveté is a new appreciation of the multiple dimensions of political culture and of the pivotal character of the struggles that ensue from the different political visions it has supported. In looking for standards by which to evaluate American political development, today's scholars are less preoccupied by the alternatives generated elsewhere and more attentive to those that have been generated from within (Norton 1986; Ellis 1993).

The immediate concern of the literature on the United States's alternatives is to reclaim the political ideas put forth by the United States's diverse social movements from the dismissive presumptions of American political consensus. To this end, it has undertaken a thoroughgoing reassessment of the programs that ultimately lost out in contests to redirect the course of American politics. The revised narrative of political change in the United States now begins boldly with insurgents who bore robust programs for change and were fully conscious of the fundamental choices being adjudicated in the political decisions at hand. Its conclusions are all the more sober, detailing the sidelining of the insurgent's signal claims and the refortication of their opponents. We have gained from this literature a sharper picture of the Progressive's moral vision and how it was lost (Eisenach 1994); of the "maternalist" ideal of U.S. welfare state and why it was scrapped (Skocpol 1992); of the agrarian theory of the modern political economy and how it was coopted (Sanders 1999; Ritter 1997; James 2000), of the indigenous radicalism of labor's commonwealth ideals and why they were aborted (Hattam 1993), and of class demands as they came to be expressed and organized under conditions of expanding manhood suffrage (Bridges 1984).

Beyond its vigorous reassertion of the generative capacities of American political culture, this work compels attention for two general propositions advanced against prior thinking about American political development. One is that the alternatives that lost out promised to move the nation in a starkly different direction from the ones that actually took hold; the other is that these were plausible alternatives for the United States. As the first proposition dispels the illusion of an overarching political consensus within which choices about development are relatively inconsequential, the second challenges the aura of inevitability and progress that history's winners tend to attribute to their own victories. Indeed, by refusing to diminish these alternative tracts as intellectually shallow or hopelessly backward looking—by treating them as coherent, intelligent, and practical—this literature has called into question all claims of special insight into which ideas, groups, or movements represent the true forces of history (Berk 1994). The effect is not only to displace the consensus view of American political history with fundamental conflict but also to strip the conflicting visions in play of the teleological projections that previous work on APD had brought to the study of change.

There remains the irony that by reclaiming the radicalism and practicality of alternatives that were ultimately frustrated, this literature leaves us in the end with a compromised path of development not all that different from the one Hartz described. As we shall see in a moment, this problem has prompted others to push inquiries into cultural multiplicity in the United States in other directions. But the response found within the literature reclaiming lost alternatives is worth considering on its own terms, for notwithstanding Hartz-like results, the explanations provided here are quite different. With politics from below found to be more authentic and coherent than previously thought, scholars have had to look to arrangements above to account for why these aspirations failed to materialize. Debunking Hartz's charge of a culturally constricted vision, this literature has substituted an analyses of political defeat and, in effect, projected a gaping disjunction between the products of the U.S. state and its full-blown political opposition. Each instance points to a gross imbalance in the distribution of political resources and stiff institutional hurdles that all but foreclose certain courses of action. In other words, it is not consensus that stifles political alternatives but governmental arrangements and elite advantages. American political development now appears to have been constrained not by ideology but by a state apparatus which, for all its divisions and internal conflicts, has absorbed, dissolved, and deflected alternative visions with remarkable consistency.

As suggested, not all efforts to push beyond the Hartzian consensus have proceeded in this way. A different approach to studying the relationship between political culture and political development was suggested by the late J. David Greenstone (1986). Greenstone dismissed the lost-alternatives critique of Hartz, accepted the notion of a pervasive consensus on liberal values in the United States, and urged instead a more direct consideration of possibilities for development within that value system. The central deficiency in Hartz's analysis, Greenstone charged, lay in its inability to account for the emergence of any new ideas affecting the operations of American government. By extension, he saw Hartz's theory as prone to understate the real transformative potential of the ideas Americans had at their disposal. Greenstone pointed out that Hartz had not provided a causal theory of change, that the liberal consensus merely specified a peculiar political universe, a set of boundary conditions within which change in American politics had occurred. To explain change, he recommended an investigation of the ways in which new ideas are constructed from the discursive categories of a common culture, that is to say, from its linguistic tools.

To demonstrate, Greenstone examined the debate over slavery in the northern states of the union during the middle of the nineteenth century, a debate about which Hartz had said next to nothing. In *The Lincoln Persuasion: Remaking American Liberalism* (1993) he examined the words *liberty* and *Union* as these were used by politicians representing all the contending positions. He showed not only that these concepts admitted multiple meanings in different relations to one another but that fundamental differences among those meanings were elaborated in the very process of debating them. Some usages drew upon a secular humanist strand in U.S. liberal thought, employing a negative conception of freedom as an absence of constraint to conceptualize the relationship between these values; others drew on a Puritan, pietistic strand with strong moralistic and positive entailments.

It was Lincoln, Greenstone argued, who found in the United States's storehouse of ideals and aspirations a combination of meanings that focused the fundamental conflict of values gestating within U.S. society at the time, a conflict *within* the United States's liberal culture that, once articulated, could not be deflected, absorbed, or dissolved. Greenstone readily granted that when Lincoln conceptualized the Union as a moral force whose ultimate purpose was to facilitate individual self-improvement, he was working wholly within the boundaries of the established culture. At the same time, he insisted that Lincoln was articulating a radical political alternative, one categorically different from, and far more expansive than, that produced either by Jacksonian understandings (in which the Union was merely an instrument for maximizing the freedom of white men to do as they chose) or Whig understanding (in which liberty derived from the Union and had to be regulated in ways consistent with its preservation). In fact, Lincoln's alternative produced something wholly unaccounted for in Hartz's analysis: a normative revolution that carried a triumphant political revolution in its train.

The claim that the United States's liberal discourse has sufficient nuance and dimension to develop of its own accord has an intuitive appeal. Others have argued in a similar vein that liberalism has not merely been rearranged or readapted from time to time but substantively reinvented and conceptually expanded by people driven to think anew about the meaning of common values (Rodgers 1987; Ericson 2000). But as Greenstone's meticulous argumentation suggests, we have come a long way from any easy invocation of that premise, and on inspection, the claims he made on behalf of these prospects were quite modest. His argument was about a toolbox of legitimate concepts and ideals. He ventured that the United States's stock of liberal ideas can be and has been augmented through interactive processes of debate, that we have not been stuck with the ideas with which we began, and that new ideas, once brought to power, are available for elaboration in the future. Little was said, however, about how closely liberalism's conceptual expansion informs the course taken in American politics, about whether these expanded liberal ideas, even when they seize control of the state and change the Constitution, actually determined the subsequent course of public policy.

In fact, while Greenstone's amendment to Hartz allows for liberalism's advance, the argument for linguistic inventiveness can as easily cut the other way. In a culture that is robust enough to conceptualize alternatives and carry them to power, no alternative is really secure; an expansive idea may dominate at one moment only to be countered and undermined by a newly constrictive conception in the next. The fate of the Lincoln persuasion appears to be a prime case in point. As it happened, the vanguard commitments of the Civil War era on behalf of civil and political rights were progressively abandoned as energies for reform waned and the South was reintegrated into national politics. Apparently, even empowered alternatives can be lost.

This is precisely the point made by Rogers Smith in *Civic Ideals: Conflicting Visions of Citizenship in U.S. History* (1997). While Greenstone criticized Hartz for giving too little credit to American liberalism's developmental potential, Smith criticized Hartz for giving too much. Smith's challenge took direct aim at the proposition that liberalism has been hegemonic in determining the course of American politics. In his analysis, the United States's most potent alternatives have neither been lost nor liberal; he demonstrated that nonliberal and downright illiberal traditions have been prominently displayed in American politics and occasionally ascendant in the high affairs of state. *Civic Ideals* documented the persistence in American politics of cultural values supportive of patriarchy and racism, and it showed that advocates of these values have been politically effective in competing with the advocates of expanded rights for the allegiances of the American people. Smith's book detailed counterarguments promulgated on behalf of these alternatives to pace liberalism's advances and call its guiding assumptions into question, and it identified important domains of state action dominated by these contrary claims for extended periods of time. By dubbing these alternatives traditions in their own right, Smith meant to attribute to them a degree of coherence, distinctiveness, resonance, and staying power comparable to the liberal tradition which Hartz had identified with the whole of the American consciousness.

Though assaults on liberalism in our day are never far from view in his work, Smith directed attention to the late–nineteenth century to illustrate just how potent these alternative traditions can become in redirecting American politics. The about-face negotiated after the Reconstruction on matters relating to the civil and political rights cannot, in Smith's reading, be dismissed as an aberrant loss of cultural bearings, as a momentary hiatus in liberalism's march of progress, or as a time-lag in perceptions of the disparity between ideals and reality; it was rather an emblematic moment in which an alternative set of ideals gained the upper hand in American government. Documenting the success of prominent elites, inside the government and out, in reworking counterthemes with powerful claims on the hearts and minds of the American people, and ultimately, in legitimating a substantial reversal of rights formally achieved and exercised in the 1870s, Smith upended the proposition that American political development has been a series of incremental advances on liberal premises.

By exposing unwarranted assumptions of uniformity and linearity in American political development, Smith accelerated the unraveling of developmental premises that Hartz's consensus thesis had already done much to weaken. The discovery of multiple traditions that are fundamentally at cross-purposes shifts the burden of developmental thinking off the stifling hegemony of liberalism in American politics and onto the tentative status of any liberal, or for that matter nonliberal, change that might happen to occur. The specification of illiberal traditions that can drive potent political movements and control significant sectors of public policy presents the United States as a polity susceptible to swing back and forth between competing standards of fundamental value, a polity prone to move over time in opposite directions and to repeal liberal advances once attained. It is difficult to imagine traveling much further away from the developmental conception of American politics without calling into question the enduring significance of liberal ideals altogether.

■ | **Periodization**

Another line of research in APD may be traced back to V. O. Key's proposition that American politics is periodically punctuated by "sharp and durable" changes. "A Theory of Critical Elections" (Key 1955) was published the same year that Hartz published *The Liberal Tradition in America.* Beyond that, however, the two works might seem to have little in common. While Hartz drew attention to the uniformity of the American political experience and explained why the New Deal had changed so little, Key pointed to large-scale discontinuities like that which ushered in the New Deal and suggested that American politics has not been all of a piece. Specifically, Key argued that some elections in American political history were far more important than others in bringing about political change, and he suggested that these "critical elections" might be the missing link between the everyday operations of democracy in the United States and larger dynamics at work in the transformation of the political system as a whole.

Walter Dean Burnham, who studied at Harvard while Hartz and Key taught there, saw a connection between their two perspectives. Burnham proposed that critical elections were the characteristic product of the United States's exceptional political culture, and with that he set out to resolve a number of riddles implicit in the consensus thesis. If, as Hartz theorized, American politics did not develop in any meaningful sense, what exactly did it do? By registering only the polity's most timeless and encompassing features, consensus theory failed to convey any clear sense of what distinguished one period from the next. Furthermore, the theory failed to explain how a government fit for nothing so much as the preservation of its founding principles could successfully adapt to the rapid pace of change in its economy and society. Hartz had used Marx to identify crucial elements of class consciousness missing in American political culture, but he had failed to contend with Marx's understanding of capitalism itself as an unrelenting engine of social and economic transformation.

Burnham's theory of critical elections addressed these questions by positing a systemic, causal connection between persistence and change in American politics. *The American Party Systems: Stages of Development* (Burnham and Chambers 1967) and *Critical Elections and the Mainsprings of American Democracy* (Burnham 1970) cast electoral realignments as political surrogates for social revolution in a polity culturally impervious to social revolution. At the heart of Burnham's analysis was a Hartzian gloss on the United States's "Lockean cultural monolith," evidenced first and foremost by a Constitution designed to preserve prior consensus and inhibit the power of particular groups to make changes. Burnham proposed that in such a system the new demands on government routinely produced by social and economic change were bound to fester, that as the Constitution intercepted and delayed adaptations to the changing conditions of governance, relations between state and society would drift toward moments of extreme national stress. The characteristic products of this stress were major electoral uprisings, critical elections or election sequences that realigned the coalition base of the contending parties and compelled American government, one way or another, to accommodate the new realities. Such disruptions were likely to be rare and episodic, for the mobilization required would be difficult to sustain. The return to normalcy would feature the new alignment of interests secured by constitutional divisions, and the beginnings of a new cycle.

The orthodox version of this theory highlighted five such transformations coming at intervals of roughly thirty years and centering around the elections of 1800, 1828, 1860, 1896, and 1932. These framed five extended periods of political order, or regimes—the Jeffersonian, the Jacksonian, the Republican, the Progressive, and the New Deal. The theory affirmed that each of these orderings reflected broad cultural commitments to democracy and capitalism but suggested that each also defined a distinctive universe of political and institutional action. They featured different party systems with economic, sectional, and ethnoreligious interests differently divided into national political coalitions, they each brought a different mix of policy debates into government, and each offered economic interests different kinds of institutional services and supports.

Significantly, Burnham himself did not find any particular political trajectory in the movement from one political regime to the next. While he allowed for constitutional changes of the first order and described a mechanism that would periodically reconstruct the relationship between democracy and capitalism in the United States, he was even more explicit than Hartz in raising questions about progress. He dwelled on the realignment of 1896 in particular because he saw in that shift to a more starkly sectional electoral alignment the demobilization of a once-vibrant democratic politics and the insulation of corporate control over processes of industrial consolidation. "When the conflict between industrial capitalism and pre-existing democratic structures came into the open," he charged, "it eventuated in the displacement of democracy, not industrial capitalism" (Burnham 1970, 187, 1965). *Realignment* referred not to development but to change; it identified a tension release mechanism through which the constituent elements of American political culture periodically reconstituted themselves.

Realignment theory transformed the discussion of state-society relations in the United States, introducing new conceptions of time, change, sequence, and regime. Its periodization scheme was widely recognized in the 1970s as the "dominant conceptual picture" of American political history (Bogue 1980), and it inspired literatures not only on electoral politics but on public policy and governmental structure as well (Brady 1988; Ginsberg 1976; Shefter 1978). Its impact is still evident today in a wide range of studies—on party formation (Aldrich 1995), regime formation

(Plotke 1996; Polsky 1997), presidential politics (Skowronek 1993), American political thought (Eisenach 1990), labor politics (Mink 1986), and constitutional law (Ackerman 1991). And yet, recent research, often the very same research that is informed by the periodization scheme, has also become circumspect about limitations of these demarcations and attentive to the value of alternative formulations.

No doubt, the major catalyst to new thinking about periodization has been the elusiveness of realignment since 1932, in particular, the difficulty of squaring classic realignment theory with the twisted and halting course of American politics since 1968 (Shafer 1991). But there are other factors at work as well. The critique of Hartz has played an important role. With more attention's being paid the ideological divisions that have been expressed within American politics, scholars have discovered continuities and breakpoints that don't fit the standard electoral periods. John Gerring, for example, finds that competing party ideologies in the United States have not changed in lockstep with electoral realignments; his periodization of the alternatives offered by mass political organizations in the United States not only crosscuts the realignment divides but also suggests distinct dynamics as work within the different party organizations themselves. Another recent study has taken aim at the claim that the Republican victory in 1896 resolved the most contentious questions about American industrialization by foreclosing effective political challenges to corporate consolidation. Elizabeth Sanders (1999) finds that the agrarian reform agenda not only survived the realignment but refortified itself thereafter. Documenting the implementation of that agenda during the Wilson administration, she argues for extending the moment of the populist insurgency from the 1890s through the 1910s.

Other researchers have been impressed by the changing role of parties themselves, in particular by the secular decline in their relative importance as governing instruments over much of the twentieth century (J. J. Coleman 1996; Milkis 1993). Some work along this line has suggested that the major divide to be drawn in American political history is between the nineteenth century, or party period—when parties were the dominant organizing instruments of governance—and the twentieth century, or bureaucratic period—when administrative instruments began to assume prominence (McCormick 1986; Silbey 1991; Skowronek 1982; Balogh 1991). By calling attention to a twentieth-century shift in the underlying mode of governmental operations, this periodization points to important continuities in American politics before and after the Civil War and before and after the New Deal. It also helps explain why realignments of the sort found in the nineteenth century have been so rare in the twentieth.

Still other challenges have targeted the transformative political significance of seemingly unrelated events—wars, for example—that occurred between realignments (Mayhew 2000; Kryder 2000; Sparrow 1996) or called attention to the critical choices that party realignments left unresolved and contested (Katznelson and Pietrykowski 1991; Katznelson, Geiger, and Kryder 1993; Kryder 2000). At the heart of all of this new thinking about breakpoints and continuities is a recognition of the multiple dimensions of political history, of the difficulties raised by trying to fit everything of significance into a single periodization scheme, of the dangers of simply dichotomizing "normal" politics against transformative "moments." With the explication of alternative schemes, the idea that there is one best periodization has begun to dissipate, and the competition to find out which of those before us synthesizes the most information has lost much of its appeal (but see Burnham, 1986, 1994). In place of the search for a new synthesis, an agenda of sorting out different temporalities at work in political history has emerged (Jillson 1994). By specifying the institutional foundation of each dynamic identified and by considering its operation in light of others, APD scholars have begun to grapple with political interactions among elements of governance differently constituted by time and to employ more complex models of political change in advancing their analytic program. The emergent insight of overriding significance is that different temporalities operate simultaneously in the political construction of governance.

Consider in this regard two recent works that both reflect and delimit the significance of critical elections. In *Presidents, Parties and the State,* Scott James (2000) asked why it was that the central issue contested in the realignment of 1896, the legitimacy of corporate capitalism, was resolved by the losing party to that conflict some two decades after the event. One part of his explanation is that, rather than change in lockstep, the different institutions of American government moved by their own rhythms and at their own pace. In this instance, the Supreme Court, operating with members previously seated, issued a ruling in 1897 that, under the Sherman Anti-Trust Act of 1890, all restraints on trade, not just unreasonable restraints, were unlawful. This decision opened a glaring incongruity between national law and the corporatist commitments of the victorious Republican Party on the central issue which the realignment had presumably resolved. It was not until 1911 that a Court newly constituted to reflect dominant Republican thinking on trusts reestablished the common law standard of reasonableness, but by that time, the issue of how to respond to the radical position staked out by the Court on corporate power had so divided the Republican ranks that they had lost their majority in the political branches to the Democrats, a party committed to a radically anticorporate program of action (see also Sklar 1988).

The second part of James's explanation turns on the operations of the electoral college, and the plight of a minority party in power as it attempted to implement its opposition program under threat of imminent displacement by the reunification of the party system's dominant member. James argues that the national leadership of the Democratic Party, eyeing with trepidation the presidential election of 1916 and desperate to attract coalition allies, gradually pulled its rank and file in Congress toward a position on the trusts that they avowedly opposed. This dynamic ultimately ratified the legitimacy of corporate capitalism and with it the logic of the system of '96, but, James notes, not before new antitrust laws had been enacted and U.S. corporate law had been stamped with a competing set of values.

In *Party and State in America's New Deal,* Kenneth Finegold and Theda Skocpol (1995) compared two emergency programs enacted in 1933, that is, directly in the aftermath of another critical electoral upheaval. As the programs were backed by the same coalition in Congress and aspired to the same aim of raising prices and incomes in their respective sectors, the comparison would seem to be calculated to hold historical variance at bay; and yet, the authors observed that the Agricultural Adjustment Administration (AAA) and the National Industrial Relations Board (NIRB) experienced results that were not only disparate but also in the opposite direction from what strictly sectoral—that is, nonhistorical—factors would have predicted. The farmers should have presented a more difficult problem of coordination than the occupants of workplaces, but in practice, the AAA achieved far higher levels of successful mobilization than the NIRA. To explain this outcome, the authors pointed to the contrasting administrative histories of the two policy domains. The AAA operated within a policy network with origins in the Civil War era and progressive reform. Veterans of earlier federal initiatives in agriculture already possessed a good grasp on the problems to be addressed and the available solutions, and the government officials dealing with these issues were connected by education and experience to their counterparts in private cooperatives and land grant colleges. In contrast, NIRA administrators proceeded on a ground pitted during the past years by private suspicion, public irresolution, and an adverse tradition of antitrust. Understood in this way, the electoral realignment of the 1930s was a multifaceted event, one whose impact varied in accordance with the prior history of reform in the different policy domains it brought up for reexamination.

The question of periodization underlies all assessments of continuity and change in politics. Martin Sklar (1991) has argued that periodization is the historian's method of specifying testable hypotheses about order in human relations and the causes of their transformation, that it is the foundation of the science of history. In taking up the challenge of periodization, recent APD research has added a significant twist. Rather than simply replace one set of breakpoints with another, it has begun to question the underlying conception of American politics as an ordered whole punctuated over time by moments of radical change (Orren and Skowronek 1994). Reckoning with alternative periodizations and the competing temporalities of governance behind them points to a multiple-orders hypothesis, wherein change proceeds through the push and pull of differently constituted elements simultaneously engaged. Considered next to Smith's multiple-traditions thesis, this multiple-orders hypothesis is suggestive of some over-arching themes emerging in APD research today. Before turning to those, however, other lines of research need to be brought into view. The notion of multiple orders rests on a more decidedly institutional view of politics than multiple traditions, and as it turns out, the study of institutions claims the lion's share of attention in APD research today.

∎ | Institutions I: Interest Mediation

The current preoccupation with institutions in APD research follows di-rectly from the field's interest in reexamining the temporal attributes of governance. Institutions are the premier instruments of governance, dura-bility is one of their leading features, and this tendency to persist engenders distinctive political relationships over time. Moreover when institutions do change, they do so in ways that invite rigorous empirical analysis. They are built, dismantled, and rearranged in ways that are readily perceived and easily specified, thus offering researchers a reliable standard of reference in plotting patterns of continuity and change.

If there is a single unifying question behind institutional research in APD today it is about how institutions construct politics—how they shape action, conflict, order, change, and meaning. But this broad concern ad-mits several different lines of investigation. At least three versions of the constructivist thesis can be distinguished in the contemporary literature, each of which elaborates a different conception of the political significance of institutions. We take these up in turn, beginning with the more familiar ones and proceeding to the less so.

Most familiar of all is the idea that governing institutions construct politics by mediating conflicts of interest within society. This notion hews closely to the traditional association of government with institutionally in-duced political order and stability, an association expounded on at length by practical statesmen like James Madison and Martin Van Buren during some of the United States's most important institution-building episodes. In revisiting this idea, APD scholars have paid special attention to the pre-cise mechanisms through which order has been created and sustained and to the political contingencies that underlie it.

One study along these lines explains sectional comity during the ante-bellum years with reference to Congress's balance rule for the admission of slave states and free states to the Union (Weingast 1998). Documenting the potential for the empowerment of a purely Northern, free-labor majority long before one actually appeared, Weingast observes that "nothing inher-ent in the antebellum era inevitably preserved rights in slaves." More to the point, he argues that with the more rapid expansion of the North in both population and territory, neither the arrangements of the Constitution (the Madisonian solution) nor the arrangements of the party organizations (the

Van Buren solution) sufficed in themselves to induce sectional comity institutionally. Central to this argument is the fact that the convention of sectional balance in state admissions had taken hold early on; it was the product of a time when regional economic prospects were more evenly matched and representatives of the North and South perceived themselves as equally vulnerable to one another in matters of material interest. Incorporated into the Missouri compromise of 1820—before the institutionalization of national two-party competition—adherence to the rule became over time an increasingly important signal to Southern slaveholders of a credible commitment by the North not to press its growing political advantages. Weingast's analysis explains the antebellum political order with reference to Northern legislators' willingness to acquiesce to the rule. It was by granting the South an institutional veto over national programs in this way, Weingast argues, that sectional comity and national stability were sustained long after the balance of economic interests that had given rise to it had changed.

As Congress is the branch of American government least insulated from the direct influence of social and economic pressures, congressional rules, norms, and structures bear a heavy burden in explaining how order is constructed out of conflicting interests. But mediation effects are not limited to the Congress, and the Constitution's structure of coequal branches suggests processes that are far more intricate and broad ranging. A recent study of the political architecture of U.S. industrialization has shown just how elaborate these processes can get. In *The Political Economy of American Industrialization* (2000), Richard Bensel asks how the nineteenth century's most-advanced democracy could sustain a course of rapid industrialization when the policies essential to it were fiercely and persistently contested by powerful political interests mobilized in opposition. His answer identifies rapid industrialization as an institutional construct, one produced by interactions among all the various branches and levels of the constitutional system.

Bensel explains this construct with reference to a contingent alignment of triplets: three government policies were essential to the outcome observed—maintenance of an unencumbered national market, maintenance of the gold standard, and maintenance of the protective tariff; contests over these policies were structured by three principle interests—cotton exporters, yeoman settlers, and financial capitalists; and the antithetical designs of these interests were grounded in and politically bolstered by their geographic concentration in three distinct regions—the South, the West, and the Northeast respectively. His model explains how the peculiar tripartite structure of American government interacted with the peculiar tripartite structure of the late-nineteenth-century economy to foster rapid industrialization when that outcome by itself was supported by no social or political consensus, let alone a natural foundation.

As it happened, each branch of American government operated to support one of the three critical policies and to thwart alternatives supported in the others. The Court worked to secure the interests of both national party coalitions in the maintenance of the open market against regulation-prone majorities from the South and West and the incursions of the more populist state legislatures. Congress worked to secure support for tariff protection against Grover Cleveland, a Democratic president committed to freer trade: the legislature logrolled benefits in such a way as to divide support in the South and West for lower rates and to tie the interests of northern labor and industrial capital to the program of finance capital. Finally, the electoral college system of presidential coalition building worked to produce chief executives friendly to New York financial interests and willing to protect those interests in the gold standard against inflationary interests in the South and West which claimed congressional majorities at critical junctures.

Bensel presents a powerful case for the socially constructive impact of a far-flung institutional politics. Rapid industrialization appears in his analysis as a wholly mediated effect, the synthetic product of interactions within and among institutions each of which was motivated in a different way to deal with interests pressing in on it from the outside. A central issue in the study of the institutional construction of politics today, however, concerns the limitations of this outside-in perspective itself. In both the Weingast and Bensel studies, interests press in on government, and government officials fashion responses in accordance with their own rules and motivations; but in neither of these analyses do institutions appear to alter the interests themselves. The concept of mediation contemplates the institutional construction of policy responses to interests, not an institutional construction of interests themselves.

A study by Terry Moe (1987) of the institutional construction of order in relations between business and labor in the middle of the twentieth century breaches this boundary. Moe tied the equilibrium observed in this period to two factors. First was the passing of the electoral volatility of the 1930s and 1940s and the emergence in the 1950s of a new strategic environment facing labor and business interests. Partisan alignments within and across the institutions of the national government made it unlikely that either could prevail in any further attempt to alter the regulatory regime that had been established during the 1930s and 1940s; it also permitted institutional actors in the three branches of government to turn their attention to other priorities. The other factor Moe identified was the emergence at this time of political stalemate of a highly professionalized regulatory agency. The National Labor Relations Board (NLRB), which was charged to execute the mandates of the 1930s and 1940s, staffed itself with lawyers specially trained in the new law of labor and industrial relations, and it was able, by virtue of its professionalism and the relative indifference of the other institutional actors, to deliver a product that assured the contending interests of the integrity and predictability of the regulatory process itself.

Moe argues that by the time the midcentury political impasse gave way, both business and labor had come to value the underlying stability and predictability that NLRB norms and routines afforded. He points out that when, in 1980, political control of the presidency and the Senate aligned for a major offensive against the interests of organized labor at the NLRB, business showed little interest in casting off the NLRB regimen. In fact, the board nominees suggested by the business clientele of the NLRB were passed over by President Ronald Reagan. Rather than select members who might be expected to support business interests within established norms, the president chose appointees who promised to disrupt and displace those norms. Moe's analysis suggests not only that the institutional arrangements of government had over time affected the preferences of the contending economic interests acting within them but that a government actor, eyeing the strategic environment with his own purposes in view, pressed radical action independent of the expressed interests of his economic allies.

Like Weingast and Bensel, Moe is interested in how institutions stabilize relations among antagonistic interests and how the motivations of institutional actors are reflected in the kind of political order constructed. But Moe's analysis maps movement and interaction on all sides of the various relationships arrayed around the NLRB. His analysis challenges not only the Congress-centered view of the institutional construction of order out of interest conflict but also the larger conception of change modeled as comparative statics. In its place, he presents a picture of systemwide dynamics in which there are multiple points of control none of which is fully competent to produce the result observed and each of which depends for its effective operation on all the others. It is a picture in which interest organizations and institutional actors push and pull one another through time, and one in which the causal arrows point in different directions—from economic interests to the institutions of politics and government and from the institutions of government and politics back to economic interests. The presidency, the Senate, and the bureaucracy appear both as a set of constraints that filter the preferences of economic interests and as locations for alternative purposes and aspirations that create and change interests of their own accord. Government actors appear as much interest makers as interest takers.

None of this is to suggest that the mediation of social interests is less significant in governance than previously thought, only that it has become one factor among others that is being considered in the institutional construction of politics. Notwithstanding its more elaborate and precise specification in the current literature, the concept of interest mediation appears limited by its unidirectional conception of relations between society and the state and by an accompanying narrowness in considering the roles and aspirations of institutional actors themselves. Evidence of a wider array of institutional constructions can now be found in a range of historical studies investigating the development of bureaucratic cultures (Carpenter 2000b), of judicial prerogatives and duties (Gilman 1993) and of political entrepreneurship (Milkis 1993). Investigation of the distinctive temporalities of governance move in very different directions once images of a system built from the bottom up by economic interests contending for the use of state power give way to interactions among relatively autonomous streams of institutional activity, each with its own rhythms, purposes, and repertoires.

■ | Institutions II: Policy Selection and Political Feedback

Much of the institutional research in APD today self-consciously seeks to avoid an a priori assignment of privilege to societal interests or state interests in explaining patterns of order and change over time. The polity is understood rather as a realm of mutual influence and dialectical exchange, a realm in which the reciprocities of control and voluntarism, structure and agency, and authority and resistance hold sway. This "polity-centered" perspective (Skocpol 1992) assumes that governing arrangements are always up and running, that no matter where one cuts into politics for analytic purposes, such arrangements are already at work fashioning, to a greater or lesser extent, the interests, motives, and movements that seek to use (or challenge) government authority.

This more-encompassing view of institutional construction links explanations of order and stability more directly to explanations of movement and change. The equilibria momentarily sustained through mediation effects are subsumed in an examination of more-extended sequences of action and reaction. Questions of periodization loom large here, for politics is understood analytically to be propelled through time by the dynamics of institutional selection and interest feedback, and wider temporal horizons are necessary to illuminate the path-dependent qualities of change (Pierson 1993).

Anyone who cares to look back far enough in time will likely find that government has a strong hand in creating the interests it appears to be mediating later on. The point is implicit in Bensel's larger corpus. Prior to his analysis of late-nineteenth-century industrialization, Bensel (1990) did a study that traced the consolidation of a powerful class of financiers concentrated in New York and motivated by far-reaching interests in national politics. That process began, he argued, with national banking legislation passed in the early 1860s by a Republican Congress anxious to meet the demands of fighting a war against Southern secession. Considered in conjunction with this earlier work, Bensel's study of the political economy of the 1890s shows American government under the influence of an economic interest that it had itself brought into being for very different purposes decades before.

Those pursuing this line of research in earnest draw inspiration from the proposition that government policy creates interest politics. The idea is almost as familiar to students of American government as that embodied in the proposition that government mediates conflicts of interest within society (Schattschneider 1935; Lowi 1964, 1972). *Policy* in this proposition refers to the precise terms of control selected by government officials to address particular classes of situations. The categories employed, the forms of control chosen, the procedures set up—all of these are to be understood as formative constructs that intrude more or less radically on existing relations of authority and that have important consequences for politics over the long haul. The effects of governmental interventions on a massive scale, like those associated with war and its aftermath, are staples of the study of political development for the reason that policies adopted at these junctures tend to cut widely and deeply through established relations between state and society, thereby altering relations that are possible in the future.

But exactly how widely and deeply they cut is the critical question. Margaret Weir (1992b) has shown that even in wake of depression and world war, American employment policy maintained sharp divisions both conceptually and institutionally between the social problems and the economic problems posed by idle workers, that these divisions came to delimit American development in both domains, and that they continue to distinguish American policy from its counterparts in other countries. Along similar lines, it has been argued that nonintervention by government may prove to be as consequential for development as decisions to enact sweeping new controls. In a comparative study of health care policy, for example, Jacob Hacker (1998) relates the political power of private health care providers to the timing of government intervention into the development of policy networks. In the United States, the failure of comprehensive reform initiatives in the 1930s, 1940s, and 1960s left private interests largely to their own devices in developing elaborate service networks. These, Hacker argues, came to pose ever more-formidable obstacles to comprehensive governmental action as time went on and compounded the difficulties of implementing a national health insurance scheme in the United States in the 1990s. Even more pointed is Marie Gottschalk's analysis (2000) of how government policy in the 1970s entangled labor in private health care networks and business alliances in the 1980s and ultimately compromised its long-standing commitment to national health insurance in the 1990s.

The effects of government policy, whether it entails positive action or de facto inaction, are of interest in the study of APD not only because they determine who gets what in the here and now but also because they classify the groups, impart the identities, forge the divisions, and strike the alliances that channel future political action. Politics has a correspondingly broad construction in this literature, referring both to the institutional creation of policy clienteles—the interests that come to depend on the government's largesse and thus lend support to it—and to the concomitant construction of political dissonance and interests in opposition. In a recent study of welfare politics, Robert Lieberman (1998) analyzed the dismantling of Aid to Families with Dependent Children (AFDC) in 1996 in just this way. He related the effective assault on AFDC back to strategic policy choices made in the 1930s, showing that care had been taken at the outset to separate poor relief from other forms of welfare and to decentralize its administration. Over time, he argued, these arrangements produced a program clientele that was not only more politically isolated than those produced by other welfare policies but also more provocative of local opposition.

Though interests and institutions are understood to be mutually constituted in this literature, characteristic modalities of politics have been discerned on each side. With regard to the institutional construction of interests, it has been shown, for example, that government officials enact particular conceptions of U.S. society simply by incorporating into their policies the norms of the larger political culture of which they are a part. In this way, prevailing prejudices may enter into the demarcation of spheres of legitimate governmental intervention without any external pressure at all and still serve as formative forces delimiting major transformations of the polity. In particular, it has been observed that social programs framed and implemented during the New Deal to aid the forgotten "man" at the bottom of the economic ladder generally failed to address, or even recognize, the distinctive social and economic interests of women. Their effect was to introduce a new gender divide into social provision, liberalizing, nationalizing, and standardizing programs for males while leaving females to appeal their interests to the state and local institutions of an earlier era (Mettler 1998).

At issue, however, are not just the biases carried around in the heads of governmental officials; politics is shaped just as powerfully by their institutional expertise and on-the-job experience. Recent studies of the origins of affirmative action policy in the 1960s and 1970s, for example, show bureaucrats moving far out ahead of the demands being placed on government by the civil rights insurgency. When, in the late-1960s, civil rights organizations were demanding equal treatment in the pursuit of employment opportunities, government administrators were learning that color-blind hiring practices would not produce the concrete signs of progress desired. Pressured by their superiors to show results, administrators began to experiment with rules that would provide for special treatment of minorities. Affirmative action became a cornerstone of African American political interest in this way; that is, as a product of administrative ingenuity and government policy. The political consequences of this institutionally constructed interest would not be fully revealed until affirmative action was taken up and given wider application by a Republican president alert to its potential for setting key Democratic constituencies—blue-collar workers and African Americans—at each others' throats (Graham 1990; Skrentny 1996).

As policy is a specification of governmental purposes, it almost always engages questions of ideology. An expanded view of official motivations has thus also led to more careful distinctions between those aspects of policy which represent government responsiveness to outside pressure and those which reflect the programmatic ideas of officeholders and their determination to secure control in a way consistent with their own political visions. President Reagan's assault on the NLRB is a case in point. Another is federal recognition of the rights of unions to organize and bargain collectively in the first place. Most agree that the disruptions brought on by labor insurgency of the 1930s made some government response imperative, but the extent to which business or labor dictated the government's response has been hotly debated (Goldfield 1990). Several scholars have argued that the Wagner Act was primarily the work of progressive officeholders in power at the time, politicians who had some clear ideas of their own about how best to secure a new order in industrial relations (Plotke 1996; Skocpol and Finegold 1990). The act accorded unions official recognition and it was vigorously opposed by corporate interests for that reason, but it also made the government the ultimate arbiter of the appropriate units of labor bargaining and implicated labor in broader government concerns with securing political order and economic stability. The American Federation of Labor which had long fought against making government a partner in industrial relations found its unions more dependent on the state after they had secured these rights than they had been before (Tomlins 1985).

Turning the perspective around and examining things from the point of view of political interests, the synergistic effects look a bit different. From this angle, the proposition that policy creates politics has illuminated an institutional construction of access and fit. Interests obtain access to officials in ways that are compatible with officials' goals. By this means, government policies can be expected, as a matter of course, to organize some interests into politics and others out. A politics of access is framed by the correspondence or fit between some interests and prevailing government arrangements and by the mobilization of "misfits" for institutional reform.

Access, seen through the lens of fit, likens the polity to an ecological system where institutions establish an environment, and interests thrive, or not, to the extent that they fill niches within it or discover channels for action made available by it (Pierson 1993; Howard 1995). In *Protecting Soldiers and Mothers*, Theda Skocpol (1992) pointed out that while the nineteenth-century United States's patronage-hungry party state proved indifferent or hostile to the welfare demands of laborers, women, and farmers, it reached out to Union veterans of the Civil War with an expansive pension system to support them and their families. In more recent work, Skocpol, Ganz, and Munson (2000) have shown more generally how American government affected the early formation of civic associations in the United States, in particular how the more successful national interests mimicked the government's federated and representative structure.

Narrowly employed, the ecological metaphor evokes the traditional association of the institutions of government with the establishment of political order: the system is self-reinforcing as interests that don't fit get ignored or crowded out. But even in ecological systems, there are other possibilities. Elements that don't fit may die out, but they may also adapt and on occasion they may alter, even radically transform, the environment on which they intrude. The distinctive thing about institutional politics in this regard is that it produces misfits as a matter of course, that transformative elements are introduced as a natural by-product of the particular selections of policy elites. Incongruities of access may intensify over time as institutions and their clienteles form networks of reciprocal support and perpetuate themselves in circumstances often very different from those in which they first took hold. Policy feedback may thus appear in two very different forms. One is mutually reinforcing: interests able to thrive in the niches and channels provided by the existing institutional environment will serve over time to bolster the governing arrangements that sustain them and sustain them over time. The other is mutually threatening as elements excluded or repressed develop their own sense of interest with reference to institutional limits of the existing political space. In this way, institutions construct order and discord simultaneously.

The barriers to entry into politics are formidable, and the mere existence of incongruous interests is no guarantee of political transformation. Explaining why some new interests gain the leverage to change things while others do not is a primary concern in this literature (Clemens 1997). In general, however, it may safely be ventured that the transformational potential of interests that don't fit is far greater than that of those which do. Interests that fit will characteristically seek to minimize alterations in established arrangements; they can be expected to press only those adaptations which promise to maintain the current course or path. Skocpol (1992) shows that pensions for Union veterans filled a niche in the party politics of the late–nineteenth century and that the incipient institutions of a materalist welfare state filled a niche in the antiparty politics of the Progressive Era, but she also shows that each of these developments was bypassed later on, that these niches disappeared when the political climate changed, and that the further elaboration of these incipient welfare ideas was cut short. Incongruous elements, on the other hand, if they can organize at all, are likely to do so in ways that threaten to change more rather than less of the existing state of affairs; their interests are likely to abrade and challenge received institutional arrangements, to target the vulnerabilities of those arrangements and foster rearrangements that fundamentally alter the mix of interests receiving attention.

Historical institutionalists working on these relationships between policy and politics have begun to close the circle of these dialectics of political reconstruction. They have shown how incongruous interests come to define themselves on a site over a span of time: how interest identities are created by the specific institutional arrangements confronted, how demands are shaped by the limitations of those arrangements, and how organizational strategies are informed by the location of interests within the institutional setting and the immediate challenges of dislodging extant controls. Political conditions around the turn of the twentieth century have provided an especially fertile field for illustrating these formative effects, for at that time a state apparatus organized around courts and parties and geared to the assumptions of a dispersed and decentralized society strained to cope with the wrenching social effects of rapid industrialization and rise of economic interdependence. Under these conditions incompatible elements proliferated, and state indifference to their demands spurred diverse actors to experiment with alternative modes of organization and action.

Scholars have found that those who had the greatest transformative effects were those whose demands fell somewhere between a fit with the interests of institutional elites and a frontal assault on their positions. These interests gained leverage by virtue of their development of innovative techniques of lobbying and networking, techniques that by-passed courts and parties while still compelling the attention of office holders (Hansen 1991; Skocpol 1992; Clemens 1997; Harvey 1998). The characteristic government innovations of the Progressive Era—interest-based representation, administrative independence, issue networks, candidate-centered parties— have, in this way, come to be seen not as natural by-products of modernization but as the strategic inventions of new group forms gotten up in a struggle for access to a government which had been arranged and operated with very different interests and purposes in view.

Path dependence, the overriding theme of this version of institutional construction, reintroduces a sense of trajectory into the study of APD. All the various implications of institutional outreach—selection and division, access and exclusion, and clientelism and opposition—anticipate that politics will be propelled along its own course by frictions and abrasions endogenously generated. Natural disasters, foreign disruptions, economic crises, and the like, may intrude from the outside, but their impact is likely to be processed through identities, cleavages, and alliances that have been institutionally constructed. At the same time, this literature has in its own way elaborated the contemporary theme of multiplicity. Gone from this view of development is a single trajectory for the whole system or stages in the unfolding of a singular ideal. Many paths are being blazed simultaneously within the same polity; each according to its own policy-specific political formations. Today's scholars are less likely to portray institutions and political paths as components of larger historical schemes or destinations than as fragments of polity, individual conduits of action, that will in degrees be coordinated or at odds with one another. A final proposition to be found in the literature on institutional construction draws out these implications even further.

▪ | Institutions III: Intercurrence

When scholars observe that public policy has subjected women to different standards of control than men or African Americans to different standards than European Americans, something more is hinted at than the interests and choices of the policymakers. These are observations about the temporal makeup or historical constitution of government itself. They suggest that prior political changes were targeted, partial, or incomplete and that, as a consequence, the institutions of government are carrying forward and enforcing a variety of different ordering principles simultaneously.

The simultaneous operation of different, often contrary, orderings of authority is a third feature of the institutional construction of politics, and the most novel of those currently being elaborated in the study of APD today. Its conceptual underpinnings in the nonsimultaneity of institutional origins have led to the discovery of still-more intricate and encompassing temporalities of governance. The proposition is that governments regularly juxtapose different forms of authority because even sweeping political changes are unlikely to change all extant relations between state and society at once in accordance with the same organizing principles. Whether political initiatives and institutional innovations are limited deliberately, unconsciously, or out of practical necessity, their effect is to introduce incongruities into the construction and exercise of government authority over time. The devices that order politics at any given moment are going to be a mixed bag of instruments and are likely to weave political contention into their asymmetries and mutual impingements. We have given this dynamic the label of intercurrence (Orren and Skowronek 1996, 1998).

The idea that intercurrence underlies the institutional construction of politics follows on findings throughout the APD literature, but its revisionist entailments are only now under exploration. In documenting the effects of intercurrence, scholars have begun to present institutions less as sites of conflict resolution or dialectical exchange than as sites of ingrained political contestation, where the successive waves of reform have compounded the difficulties of achieving order over time. Students of environmental politics, for example, have pointed out that the different ideas animating reform over the decades have institutionalized conflicting principles of resource management. Nineteenth-century institutions were designed to distribute federal resources and were geared for their local use and private exploitation. In the Progressive Era, new institutions were created to regulate the use of natural resources and were geared for centralized bureaucratic management and planning, but these never entirely displaced the institutions of distribution and private exploitation. Another wave of reform in the 1970s brought institutions designed for environmental protection and geared toward court-enforced protections of whole ecological systems; these challenged but did not entirely displace the institutions of regulated use or local exploitation. Today, disillusioned reformers are promoting community-based conservation, cooperative public-private initiatives at the local level. Another set of institutions geared to these purposes is entering the field with no sign that previously established institutions will be dislodged (Klyza 1996; Moseley 1999).

In a historical-institutional nexus such as this, authorities collide and standards of legitimacy abrade. Purposes accumulate and crowd in on each other. Institutions fall short of their goals, new goals are specified, and more institutions are created. It is easy to see intercurrence in this light as an indictment of the very possibility of effective government, and indeed scholars have implicated it directly in the persistence of institutions that fail to perform effectively by any standards at all.

In one such study Andrew Polsky (1989) follows the "odyssey of the juvenile court," an institution spawned by the professionalization of social work around the turn of the twentieth century. Social work professionals insisted that juvenile offenders be treated in a less adversarial and more therapeutic manner than common criminals. They promoted the creation of special tribunals in which the traditional court proceeding aimed at an impartial rendering of individual guilt or innocence would be modified to accommodate new concerns for correcting the effects of social injustice and protecting children from any further damage from their environment. The result, Polsky argues, was an institution perpetually torn by the competing standards and purposes that its own officers brought to the table. He finds that involving lawyers in social work and social workers in law enforcement kept the juvenile courts suspended in a state of internal turmoil and turned them into an endless source of political controversy within the larger community. And yet, he also shows that these internal divisions proved critical to the institution's tenacity, as every charge of failure was met by an adjustment and reformulation of the different norms competing for dominance within it. The juvenile court, in this analysis, was from the outset an institution at cross-purposes, in constant and ingrained disequilibrium, but it survived, even thrived, in the face of failure by recycling goals that it could not reconcile.

In another study, this one examining the presidency, Jeffrey Tulis (1987) points to the layering of new rules of presidential rhetoric on older structures and considers the consequences of the resultant combination in undermining political legitimacy. Tulis's empirical analysis of rhetorical standards relates modes of speech, audience, and political purposes and reveals two distinct frameworks. One, a nineteenth-century pattern largely congruent with the arrangements of the Constitution, has incumbents speaking in public mainly on official occasions, according to highly formalized modes of address; policy communications were sent in writing primarily to the Congress and were limited to the president's constitutionally prescribed duties. The other, a twentieth-century pattern associated with the progressive critique of the Constitution, has presidential incumbents speaking often and fluently on a variety of policy issues. Talking frequently over the heads of congressional representatives directly to the public at large, modern presidents aim to mobilize national opinion independently behind their own policy goals. Had these new rules of rhetoric followed on a displacement of the institutional structures on which the old rules had been premised, a coherent standard of legitimacy for the modern presidency might have emerged. Instead, the new rules were layered over the old forms. As a result, twentieth-century presidents have been found to promise far more than they can deliver, Congresses have continued to insist on the vitality of powers anchored in the Constitution (like the war power) when presidents act subject only to their standing in public opinion, and a rising tide of public cynicism has come to engulf officials who invoke different and antithetical standards at will to suit the circumstances of the moment (see also Lowi 1985).

The notion of governance as an intercurrence of different systems of authority relations opens several avenues of exploration. One concerns the internal structure of institutions themselves. In a recent study of Congress, Eric Schickler (2001) challenges the notion that there is a single or even dominant institutional set of rules or incentives ordering legislative politics in the United States over time. Documenting the historical proliferation of disjoint mechanisms that can be invoked by actors at will for their different purposes, he presents Congress as a complex of institutions, multilayered and in tension with one another. A related concern has been to figure out how tensions and contradictions within institutions may work to propel change in patterned and productive ways even as they preclude stable equibibria. Again consider the presidency. It is commonly observed that the U.S. president's constitutional duty—to execute the independent powers of his office and to preserve, protect, and defend the whole—clashes with his role as the leader of a national political party—one who has been nominated by a party convention, elected by a party coalition, and tied to an agenda that depends on cross-institutional cooperation for its implementation.

The tensions between these demands stem from the historical fact that the president's role as party leader was not fixed institutionally until some fifty years after the constitutional duties of the office had been established. But what of the practical effects of these tensions? Beyond the common observations that presidents do not make very responsible party leaders and that national leadership without party support is severely handicapped, this intercurrence has been shown to implicate presidential action in a continual transformation of national government and politics. A recent study points out that when established party coalitions have been at their most robust, the independent actions of presidents have repeatedly sent schisms through their own ranks and thrown national political alignments into disarray but that when political coalitions are already in an advanced state of disarray, the independent actions of presidents have repeatedly galvanized new alliances and secured them in power. A sturdy pattern of systemic political change is to be discerned in this interaction, one that has periodically regenerated American government (Skowronek 1993).

A third implication of intercurrence is that wherever periods of stability are observed, government officials must be actively managing the boundaries and jurisdictions of the different institutions they inhabit. That is to say, multiple orders may work in tandem so long as the endemic problems of coordination they present are effectively addressed. More often than not this means holding divergent principles of government within separate institutional domains and policing their interfaces. The balance rule for the admission of slave and free states in the antebellum era was a managerial device of this sort, a convention negotiated by government officials to hold together in the same orbit whole systems of control that would otherwise have been at loggerheads.

A study of labor in American political development examines stable interactions among multiple orderings explicitly (Orren 1991). The analysis begins, contra Hartz, by pointing to the incorporation into the original Constitution of the common law of master and servant, a body of strictures governing workplace relations between employers and employees that had been passed down with remarkably little change from late-medieval England. The common law arranged workplace relations in sharply hierarchical terms. Contract rights and organizational activities of workers were strictly limited and employer prerogatives were upheld through the authority of the courts. The study details the efforts of judges to sustain this authority in a new constitutional setting where provisions for electoral democracy made it possible, in principle, to implement very different sorts of workplace relations through legislation. For nearly a century, the courts' active patrol and enforcement of these boundaries were successful in holding labor relations safe from encroachments by state legislatures and, generally, in keeping this separate sphere of governance separate.

This same study points to a final implication of intercurrence: the changes most likely to be decisive in political development are those which most thoroughly dismantle and replace established authority. The same institutional activism that held labor governance so effectively within its own domain stymied the restoration of order as unions gained greater power to disrupt the national economy. When organized labor's pivotal position in the new industrial economy became manifest and its challenge to the old rules of workplace became a persistent feature of society and politics, the courts responded by pressing their ancient prerogatives more aggressively. Judges continued to void all efforts to legislate an alternative set of rules, and Congress itself proved reluctant to intrude directly on what had long been the court's domain. The Interstate Commerce Act of 1887, for example, explicitly prohibited the railroads from raising labor issues in rate disputes, even though the pressure on rates which caused Congress to act was driven by demands that railroad unions were pressing ever more forcefully on their employers. It was not until 1937, when the Court upheld the National Labor Relations Act of 1935, that the dismantling and replacement of the old rules of the workplace was complete. For six decades, the court's active management of labor relations implicated it in a disintegration of order and precluded the restoration of stability in the industrial United States (see also O'Brien 1998).

GOVERNANCE AND HISTORY

Recent work on political culture, periodization, and institutions points out multiple orders, ingrained incompatibilities, and colliding principles of organization as new premises for the study of American politics. These in turn conjure distinctive conceptions of history. In an essay that is already elaborate, we will limit our conclusion to a brief sketch of two of these emerging conceptions of history, indicating some of the implications for theory building that follow from them.

First, recent APD scholarship has insisted on history as the *site* of governance. The idea conveyed here is something different from, say, history as origins. Whereas origins refer to background and reaches behind to another time, sites occupy the foreground; the reference is to the full spread of extant authority relations that any new state of political affairs must, for better or worse, negotiate. In this view, all political change proceeds on political arrangements, rules, leaders, ideas, practices, attitudes, and so on, that are already in existence. These sites are pitched above the horizon of any discrete actor, at the macrolevel, with the actions of individuals engaging and altering more or less of the larger array of authority relations. The premise of history as a site leads to a conception of political action as an impingement on the authority of others, and it directs attention to those elements in the larger array that are challenged, displaced, transformed, reformed, or unaffected by new political efforts.

Consider, by way of contrast, an ahistorical rendition of the site theme, John Locke's (1960 [1689], 343) statement in *The Second Treatise on Government:* "In the beginning, all the world was America." Locke began by imagining a site "of wild woods and uncultivated waste," a situation before kings and parliaments, a place populated sparsely by individuals who lived without money or property—in other words, an empty place that the word *America* would conjure up in the minds of eighteenth-century English readers. Much of what he said about politics proceeded from this particular proposition about the past. But once actual history becomes the site of action, things look very different. The terrain is filled from the get go, and what already exists defines the problems and substance of change. The proposition "in the beginning all the world was downtown Tokyo" comes closer to the essence of governance as a historical construct.

This image elaborates the notion that governance is always present, even if not in forms we are used to. Wherever we look—at a modern capital like Tokyo, a contested stretch of Arabian desert, an indigenous village in early America, shipboard on the Mayflower—political authority occupies the available space with rules the inhabitants expect will be enforced, and persons assigned to do the job. Vacant lots are few and far between. Constructing something new usually means dislodging something else, and even minor reorganizations are likely to affect impinging activities and installations. This is the essential insight of all those who have detailed the challenges of political development in terms of dismantling and rearrangement (Orren and Skowronek 1998): this includes those who have analyzed antebellum political development as an assault on institutions created by the "regime of local notables" already in place (Shefter 1978; Bridges 1984; Crenson 1975; Wiebe 1995), those who have analyzed the expansion of national administrative capacities in the early–twentieth century with reference to the "state of courts and parties" that had formed in their absence (Skowronek 1982; Clemens 1997), and those who have explored the limitations which U.S. apartheid placed on progressive economic reform (Milkis and Tichenor, 1994, Katznelson, Geiger and Kryder 1993).

Once it is agreed that politics always entails a preexisting where, the question becomes what and after that how and why. In fact, the what question is itself complicated by the difficulty of knowing when a given moment in a course of events constitutes "real" change, and when essentially more of the same. Does the election of a new U.S. president represent "real" change? Only when both houses of Congress change their majority party to his? Always when this happens? To ask such questions is to acknowledge varying magnitudes of change and its combination of different elements. Here a second premise is pertinent, that of history as a matrix. The matrix conveys myriad past experiences pertinent to governance; it presents history as a vessel composed of disparate moving parts out of which all political action emerges and by which it is, in crucial respects, formed.

As we have seen, analysts do not wade into this broth unaided. They begin with topics, problems, and time frames that provide some semblance of coherence, however provisional. Their next move is to identify regularities in behavior or events that are recognizable as patterns. Unlike sites, which signal containment in time and place, patterns express continuities that are, to the degree indicated, impervious to time's passage. Some patterns are smooth, with no internal breaks: Hartz's liberal polity; some that are cyclical or recurrent: Burnham's realignments; and some that oscillate between opposing extremes like hierarchical and democratic traditions (R. M. Smith 1997; Huntington 1981; Morone 1990). Of course, allowing patterns to stand out from time does not in itself recommend thinking about history as a matrix, nor does the search for patterns distinguish APD's research agenda from many others. But just as history as the site conveys the distinct understanding of a world already fully governed, history as a matrix conveys a distinct understanding of patterns (North 1990).

The image conveyed is one of several patterns moving alongside one another, each with its own rhythms and different points of inception and termination. The interconnections that characterize governance and that are built into the structure of all politics are observed in the parallels and collisions, the push and pull, and the alignments and asymmetries of separate patterns. Likewise, the periodization of various starts and stops, whether staggered or coinciding, becomes a standard of the significance of change, distinguishing that which is narrowly contained from that which is likely to have broader political significance. Research in APD has shown that patterns that suggest nothing controversial when regarded singly become problematic when juxtaposed; this is to say they ask for an explanation of how they are reconciled in practice. The juxtaposition in the nineteenth century of liberal principles of representation against hierarchical common law principles of labor relations is one example (Orren 1991). Another is the juxtaposition of expanding welfare services in the mid–twentieth century amidst continued repression along race and gender lines (McDonagh 1993). Another is the expansion in the twentieth century of a national administrative apparatus that has concentrated discretionary power in bureaucracies that are relatively insulated from the people alongside recurrent social movements, fired by the idea of returning power to the people and demonstrably influential in electoral politics (Morone 1990).

Besides the sheer fun of drawing out the implications of a matrix, these examples indicate an important departure in APD research with implications for all empirical studies of politics that also engaged history. In contrast to the methodical isolation of politics in game theoretic models, for instance, APD research has posited the priority of configurations of authority where persons and agencies exchange authority, influence, resources, and ideas with others outside their sphere or jurisdiction. These sometimes incongruous relations may themselves be patterned in ways that distinguish politics in different countries (Katznelson 1997; Pierson 1994; Sheingate 2001). Politics in the United States stands out in this way for the distinctive bundles of patterns it presents: democratization before bureaucratization, slavery within liberalism, a secular market infused by puritan moralism, and a self-adjusting economy segmented by gender and race. Like other patterns, configurations are sometimes analyzed negatively, as in Greenstone's boundary conditions: the absence of feudalism, for instance, associated with the absence of class politics and with judicial review.

Approaching political change through a matrix affects the essential components of explanation. If governance is composed of different elements juxtaposed as they proceed through time, then causation in political affairs will be difficult to capture as variables ordered separately as cause and effect. Causation in the realm of governance takes place in a vortex of mutual influences and reciprocal effects. At any particular moment, outcomes will turn on questions of timing, that is, on the intersection or conjunction of patterns. As several patterns are likely to be at work at every significant juncture, political change will be characterized generally by weak or diffuse causation. At the same time the weak causation found in a matrix is likely to be joined to a strong sense of agency, as all political change comes down to the matter of negotiating contending elements in motion. It is as agents, not causes, that political actions matter.

Reckoning with politics through patterns in a matrix is APD's signal accomplishment to date. In this, it has presented a fundamental challenge to the rest of political science: to elaborate and adopt an idea of time that is appropriate to the organization of the political universe and the study of governance. The matrix image alerts us to a time different from the $t - 1$, $t - 2$ lockstep characteristic of history neatly periodized into separate eras or politics modeled as games. Sites are too diverse in their composition to travel in so linear a fashion. As a substitute, APD poses a time composed of progressions, sequences, and coincidences of governance, as these are discerned individually and assayed for their mutual and cumulative effects.

Robert Powell

Game Theory, International Relations Theory, and the Hobbesian Stylization[1]

■ | Introduction

Strategic interaction is at the center of much of the work that has been done in international relations theory since at least the end of World War II.[2] At that time, a consensus emerged among international relations scholars on at least two broad points. The first was on the domain of the field, and the second was that this domain made the field of international relations theoretically distinct from other fields, including other areas of political science.[3] Writing in 1949, Frederick Dunn summarized the scope of international relations (IR) as it then seemed "to be taking form in the work of leading scholars in the field. . . . The distinguishing characteristic of IR as a separate branch of learning is found in the nature of the questions with which it deals. IR is concerned with the questions that arise in the relations between autonomous political groups in a world system in which power is not centered at one point" (1949, 142, 144). That is, international relations focuses on understanding the relations among actors or groups that interact in an anarchic political system whereas other fields of political science concentrate on the political interaction that takes place in and is conditioned by a more hierarchically ordered system.

This consensus on the scope and distinctiveness of the field defined the challenge that confronted it. As William T. R. Fox concluded from his survey of interwar research in international relations, "A body of political

1. I am grateful to James Alt, James Fearon, Robert Jervis, Helen Milner, James Morrow, and Ira Katznelson for helpful comments and criticisms.

2. See Knutsen 1997 for a general history of international relations theory, Schmidt 1998 for an emphasis on the century between 1850 and World War II, and Kahler 1997 and Milner 1997 for excellent discussions of the period after 1945. Jervis 1997 provides a conceptual discussion of the importance of strategic interaction in international relations theory.

3. See Milner 1998 on the latter point.

theory dealing with a system characterized by an absence of a central authority is yet to be developed. . . ." (1949, 79). Indeed, we can see much of the work that would be done over the next fifty years as an effort to devise just such a theory.

One very important and influential approach to developing this theory begins by trying to abstract away from many of the details of international politics and foreign policy. This approach focuses instead on attempting to understand the strategic logic of a simple, stylized model of the international system. In this stylization, a small number of states interact in a Hobbesian state of nature in which there is no supranational Leviathan to impose order and to protect the states from each other. There is nothing to stop one state from trying to further its interests by using its military means against another state if the former believes that doing so is its best interest.

This approach has been used to investigate problems and questions that have dominated much of the field over the last half-century: Does the anarchy of the Hobbesian state of nature induce states to try to maximize their power (Morgenthau 1948; Herz 1950; Wolfers 1962; Waltz 1979; Mearsheimer 2001)? Can a system composed entirely of security-seeking states that do not want war still break down in war (Butterfield 1950; Schelling 1960; Jervis 1977, 1978; Waltz 1979; Glaser 1992, 1996; Schweller 1996; Kydd 1997a)? Do offensive advantages make the security dilemma more intense and war more likely (Quester 1977; Jervis 1978; Glaser 1992, 1997; Kydd 1997a; Van Evera 1999)? Do secure, second-strike nuclear forces make war less likely (Brodie 1946, 1959; Jervis 1984, 1989; Waltz 1990). Do states balance or at least act in ways that tend to produce balances of power (Morgenthau 1948; Gulick 1955; Wolfers 1962; Waltz 1979; Walt 1987; Schweller 1994)? Is war less likely if there is an even distribution of power or if one state has a preponderance of power (Claude 1962; Wolfers 1962; Organski 1968; Blainey 1973; Organski and Kugler 1980; Kugler and Lemke 1996)?

Do shifts in the distribution of power make war more likely (Organski 1968; Organski and Kugler 1980; Gilpin 1981)? Do the constraints of the international system induce states to be concerned about their relative gains, and, if so, to what extent do these concerns impede international cooperation (Waltz 1979; Grieco 1988, 1990, 1993; Powell 1991, 1999; Snidal 1991; Gowa and Mansfield 1993; Keohane 1993; Morrow 1997)? To what extent can repeated interaction and reputational concerns mitigate states' short-run incentives to exploit each other (Axelrod 1984; Oye 1986b; Fearon 1998a)? Do international regimes and institutions have an independent effect on states' behavior and, in particular, can they facilitate international cooperation (Krasner 1983; Keohane 1984; Krasner 1991; Mearsheimer 1994–95; Morrow 1994a; Chayes and Chayes 1995; Keohane and Martin 1995; Downs, Rocke, and Barsoom 1996)?

Each of these particular questions shares the same general form. Each begins with a setting in which one actor's optimal behavior depends on what the other actors do. It then asks how different environmental features—the state of the offense-defense balance; the distribution of power; the existence of secure, second-strike nuclear forces; the presence of international institutions—affect the way that the states or, more generally, the units interact. Each question is fundamentally about strategic interaction.

Game theory is a tool for analyzing strategic interaction. Not surprisingly, then, international relations theorists have tried at various times over the last half-century to use game theory to advance their understanding of these problems. This essay focuses broadly on how game theory fits into the continuing intellectual development of international relations theory, especially that branch of the field that has tried to understand certain aspects of international politics by examining the strategic logic of very spare stylizations of the international system based on a Hobbesian state of nature. The essay does not review the specific contributions game theoretic analyses have made to international relations theory.[4] Rather, it considers three more general questions: What does game theory have to offer international relations theory? To what extent is what game theory has to offer needed? And, what are some of the effects on international relations theory of adopting a more game theoretic approach likely to be?

To foreshadow the discussion of these questions, this essay emphasizes that game theory is not a theory of international relations. Nor is it a substitute for deep ideas and good intuitions about the workings of international politics. Nor is game theory a substitute for careful, systematic empirical analysis. Game theory is a research tool which complements systematic empirical work and ideally interacts synergistically with it. Game theory provides a formal method of analyzing strategic interaction.

Formalization offers two advantages to the study of strategic interaction. First, specifying or closing a formal model usually requires one to describe the actors and the strategic environment in which they find themselves more clearly and more precisely than ordinary-language arguments typically do.

The relative importance of what game theory has to offer to international relations theory depends on the state of the field and varies as the field evolves. Formalization is less important when a field has already developed clear and coherent theories that make different empirical predictions. In these circumstances, careful empirical evaluation is likely to offer a higher payoff than greater formalization. By contrast, formalization is more important when assumptions and the conclusions that follow from them are unclear, for then there is nothing to test empirically. A review of some of the major debates that have dominated much of international relations theory in recent years suggests that the value added by greater formalization is large at this stage in the development of the field.

---

4. See Morrow 1999b as well as Morrow's contribution to this volume for reviews of some of this work.

Adopting a more game theoretic approach seems likely to have several effects on international relations theory. One of them is what Paul Krugman (1995) calls the "evolution of ignorance." Some theoretical deductions that have been derived from ordinary-language arguments will be lost at least temporarily because they cannot be derived formally. Another effect is that game theory will promote a reintegration of international relations with the rest of political science by showing that the strategic problems that states and other actors face in international politics often have close parallels in other areas of political science like U.S. and comparative politics.

The next section of this essay describes some of the general properties of research methods and some of the particular advantages that game theory has to offer in the study of strategic interaction. The subsequent section examines some of the debates that have dominated international relations theory in recent years and shows that much of the debate arises from weakly or poorly specified connections among the actors' preferences, the strategic setting in which the actors pursue their goals, and the resulting outcomes. The final section centers on some of the consequences of adopting a more formal approach to international relations.

■ | **Game Theory as a Research Tool**

Game theory is not a theory of international politics any more than calculus is a theory of Newtonian dynamics. Newton developed calculus as a tool for helping him analyze the problems that his theory of mechanics posed (Christianson 1984). Similarly, game theory is one of many research tools or methods that can be used to study the problems that international relations theories pose.[5] This section briefly discusses the origins of the most recent efforts to use game theory to understand international politics, the role of research methods in general and of game theory in particular, and some of the advantages and disadvantages of formalization.

DYNAMIC INTERACTIONS, GAME THEORY, AND INTERNATIONAL RELATIONS

The latest concerted attempt to use game theory to advance our understanding of international politics dates from the mid-1980s and draws

5. Game theory, of course, was not developed in order to solve problems in international relations theory. But there are some close connections. The classic example is Thomas Schelling's *The Strategy of Conflict* (1960). Less well known is the fact that the U.S. Arms Control and Disarmament Agency also sponsored work in the 1960s that helped pioneer the study of repeated games with asymmetric information (Aumann and Maschler 1995). O'Neill (1994) reviews the relation between game theory and deterrence theory.

on two technical innovations in game theory that were then beginning to revolutionize economics (Kreps 1990b, 1). The first was due to John Harsanyi. In many situations in international politics, actors are uncertain about the motivations, intentions, or resolve of other actors. For example, Britain in the 1930s was unsure of Hitler's motivations and the extent of his ambitions. As Alexander Cadogan, the permanent undersecretary in the Foreign Office put it shortly after Germany annexed Austria: "I am quite prepared to believe that the incorporation in the Reich of Austrian and Sudentendeutch may only be the first step in a German expansion eastwards. But I do not accept that this is necessarily so, and that we should rush to any hasty conclusions" (quoted in Parker 1993, 135). Harsanyi (1967–68) showed how to model formally situations in which actors are uncertain of each other's intentions, motivation, or resolve.[6]

The second technical innovation was a set of tools designed for analyzing dynamic interactions and the credibility issues inherent in them. A static interaction is one in which no one can respond to anyone else's actions because everyone acts simultaneously or because they are unable to observe what other actors have already done. The prisoner's dilemma or other 2×2 games like chicken or stag hunt are all static games. Each player makes a single decision, and neither actor can react to what the other does. A dynamic interaction, by contrast, is one in which at least some actors can observe the actions of others and react to those actions. The bidding in poker is an example of a dynamic interaction.

Many of the interactions we want to understand better in international politics are fundamentally dynamic. If, for example, one defines a crisis, as Snyder and Diesing (1977, 13) do, as a situation in which one state challenges another state and the latter resists, then crises are dynamic interactions. But the formal analysis of dynamic interactions requires more tools than the analysis of static interactions does, for the latter require us to address credibility problems.

These problems arise in dynamic but not static interactions, because actors can make threats and promises in the former but not the later. By their very nature, threats and promises presuppose a situation in which an actor can react to the behavior of others. A threat, for example, is fundamentally a conditional statement. If one actor behaves in certain ways, then the threatener will react in certain other ways. Thus threats and promises can only arise in dynamic interactions.

Once threats and promises are at issue, credibility considerations arise. Intuitively, actors should respond to credible threats and promises differently than they react to patently incredible threats and promises. Thus in order to be able to analyze dynamic interactions formally, we need to

---

6. More generally, Harsanyi showed how to model situations in which actors have asymmetric information. For example, one actor knows how much risk it is willing to run but not how much risk another is willing to run.

be able to describe formally what it means for a threat or promise to be credible.

In the late 1970s and early 1980s, game theorists devised a set of formal tools for the analyzing the credibility issues inherent in dynamic interactions. The combination of these tools and Harsanyi's earlier work on asymmetric-information games triggered an explosion of work that transformed economics over the next decade.[7] By the mid-1980s the effects of these tools were also beginning to be felt in political science.[8]

RESEARCH METHODS

Good ideas and sharp insights about the various ways that international politics work can come from many places. Sometimes they originate in a deep historical knowledge of particular cases, at other times they arise from spare stylizations, and often they develop through an iterative dialogue that moves back and forth between thick descriptions and thin conceptualizations.[9] Research methods in general and game theory in particular are not a substitute for good ideas.

Research methods have less to do with the origins of good ideas and more to do with evaluating those ideas logically and empirically. Sometimes promising ideas that initially seem deep and insightful turn out to be so, and sometimes they do not. One of the most important functions of research methods—be they formal, statistical, or qualitative—is to help us discipline our thinking about our ideas and intuitions and about the conclusions that seem to follow from them. This discipline plays an essential part in translating those ideas and insights into clear theoretical claims and, ultimately, empirically substantiated findings.

One of the ways that methods provide this kind of discipline is by establishing a set of standards for assessing arguments. To draw an analogy with statistics, these standards ideally reduce the chances of making both type I and type II errors. The latter occur when false claims are mistaken for true ones. The discipline of good research methods reduces the likelihood of this kind of mistake by making it harder to see what, because of motivated or unmotivated biases, we want or expect to see in the data or case studies. For example, Alexander George's method (1979) of "structured, focused comparison" makes it more difficult to accept a causal

---

7. The 1994 Nobel Prize in economics recognized this work along with that of John Nash. Kreps (1990) provides an accessible and nontechnical survey of some of these developments.

8. Among the earliest work to draw on these tools and appear in the *American Political Science Review* are Brito and Intriligator 1985, Palfrey and Rosenthal 1985, Austen-Smith and Riker 1987, Bendor and Mookerjee 1987, Ordeshook and Schwarz 1987, Powell 1987, and Shepsle and Weingast 1987.

9. See Myerson 1992 and Powell 1999 for a discussion of this interative process.

claim that seems to fit a particular case, because it requires a researcher to make a more-controlled comparison across multiple cases in a way that "defines and standardizes the data collection" (George and McKeown 1985, 41).[10] Similarly, research methods can also reduce the chances of making type I errors which occur when true claims are mistaken for false ones. By providing a set of common standards by which arguments are judged, methods make it more difficult to dismiss or discount a finding because one dislikes it or its implications.

THE DISCIPLINE WROUGHT BY FORMALIZATION

Formalization brings a particular kind of discipline. Mathematical models give us "a clear and precise language for communicating insights and notions" in the sense that they

> show that certain precise assumptions lead to other precise conclusions. It also allows us to stretch our analyses and to unify them; once we have worked our way through the logic that assumptions A imply conclusions X, we may see how assumptions A' lead to conclusions X' by the "same basic argument." It allows us to appreciate how critical are certain (often implicit) assumptions: If A leads to X, but a slight change in A to A' leads to not X, then we can appreciate that X or not X depends on the seemingly slight differences between A and A'; hence X is not a very robust conclusion. Taking logical deductions back to the real world, where the satisfaction of assumptions A or A' is a matter of some controversy, our developed intuition concerning what assumptions lead to which conclusions, together with a sense of how closely the real world conforms to A or A', gives us the courage to assert that X will or will not pertain with very high probability. (Kreps 1997, 63–64)

In essence, formal models provide a kind of accounting mechanism that helps us think through some issues more carefully than ordinary-language models can. Accounting schemes make a firm's financial situation more transparent both to those inside the firm and to those outside it. Formal models make arguments more transparent both to those making them and to those to whom the arguments are made.

This improved transparency comes from two sources. First, models must be fully specified or closed before they can be analyzed. Closing a model often reveals that important but previously unappreciated assumptions have to be made in order to support an argument. Models help make critical assumptions more explicit. Second, the links from assumptions to conclusions are clearer in formal models. Indeed, the derivation of conclusions frequently takes the form of mathematical proofs or demonstra-

10. On the comparative case study method, also see Lijphart 1971; Eckstein 1975; Collier 1993; and King, Keohane, and Verba 1994.

tions. These clearer linkages make it easier to trace the effects of changing one or more assumptions.

Game theory is a particular kind of mathematical modeling which disciplines our thinking about strategic interaction in at least two important ways. The first results from defining a game. Specifying a game tree requires us to describe the strategic environment, that is, who the actors are, the order in which they make decisions, what alternatives each actor has to choose from when deciding what to do, and, finally, what each actor knows when it has to make a decision. We also have to specify the actor's preferences over the possible outcomes of their interaction, that is, their ranking of the terminal nodes of the tree. These specifications make the assumptions being made about the actors' strategic environment more transparent.

Second, games are generally analyzed in terms of their perfect equilibria. Solving a game for its perfect equilibria disciplines our predictions about how the game will be played just as defining a game disciplines our thinking about the strategic setting. Equilibrium analysis forces us to look at the situation being modeled from the perspective of each and every actor and to ensure that the prediction makes sense from all of these perspectives.

A perfect equilibrium is a set of strategies—one for each actor—that satisfy two conditions, and meeting these two requirements is what effectively forces us to look at the situation from each actor's position. The first condition is that the set of strategies must be self-reinforcing. That is, no actor can benefit by deviating from its strategy given that that actor believes that all of the other actors are playing according to their strategies. If this condition did not hold, then at least one actor would want to do something other than what he was predicted to do and the prediction as a whole would not make sense. Strategies that satisfy this condition are called *Nash equilibria*.

The second condition is what makes a Nash equilibrium in the modest language of game theory *perfect*. This requirement is important because self-reinforcing strategies beg a prior question. A set of strategies is self-reinforcing if no actor can increase its payoff by altering its strategy *given* that the other actors follow their strategies. But is it reasonable in the first place for an actor to believe that the other actors will play according to the posited strategies? One situation in which it is unreasonable is if the threats and promises implicit in another actor's strategy are inherently incredible. Suppose, for example, that the strategy an actor is presumed to follow relies on a threat which would not be in that actor's own self-interest to carry out if the time came to do so. If other actors know this, then it no longer makes sense for them to assume that the first actor will follow its posited strategy and carry out its threat.

Insisting that a set of self-reinforcing strategies also be perfect helps to resolve this issue formally. Perfection requires that following through on the threats and promises implicit in each actor's strategy be in that actor's self-interest. Thus, no actor has any reason to doubt that any other actor will not play according to its posited strategy.

We can think of the relative advantages and disadvantages of formalization compared to ordinary-language arguments in terms of a trade-off between type I and type II errors. If an ordinary-language argument can be formalized, that formalization generally forges tighter, more transparent, and deductively rigorous links between the initial ideas and insights and the conclusions that follow from them. These clearer, more precise links often reduce the chances of incorrectly accepting a false claim and thereby making a type II error. For example, much of the recent formal work in international relations theory shows that many widely accepted ordinary-language arguments do not go through when they are formalized.[11]

But, moving toward a standard that requires more formalization may increase the chances of making a type I error at least in the short run. It initially may prove to be impossible to study some existing ordinary-language arguments which are fundamentally correct because no one can figure out how to model them formally. Until some one can figure out how to formalize these arguments, they will remain interesting ideas and conjectures but they will not be accepted because they do not "measure up" (to the formal standard). If, however, these ordinary-language analyses are describing a causal argument that is fundamentally correct, then the shift to a more formal standard will have induced a type I mistake at least temporarily.

This kind of mistake is part of what Paul Krugman calls the "evolution of ignorance" that accompanies modeling. Because what we "know" is partly a function of the standards by which we evaluate arguments, imposing a different set of standards may mean that at least at the outset we "know" less that we thought we did.

> Model-building, especially in its early stages, involves the evolution of ignorance as well as knowledge; and someone with powerful intuition, with a deep sense of the complexities of reality, may well feel that from his point of view more is lost than is gained. . . . The cycle of knowledge lost before it can be regained seems to be an inevitable part of formal model building. (Krugman 1995, 79)

In sum, using formalization to filter arguments is likely to screen out ordinary-language analyses that are fundamentally wrong or seriously incomplete as well as those analyses that are fundamentally correct but presently cannot be modeled. Filtering the former reduces the chances of making type II errors, but filtering the latter raises the chances of making type I errors.

11. See, for instance, Fearon 1994b, 1995b and Powell 1999.

However, this trade-off goes beyond the assessment of existing arguments, and this may be the most important effect of a shift from one set of standards to another. What counts in a research community as interesting and important new work is often judged as such relative to some standard for assessing arguments. A shift in these standards may therefore implicitly redefine what constitutes important new work and thereby lead to a redirection or reorientation of the field.

■ | Assessing the Trade-off

Greater formalization entails a trade-off because there are both costs and benefits to applying a more formal standard. Whether the costs outweigh the benefits depends in part on the state of the field. As emphasized above, much of international relations theory centers on strategic interaction. This work proceeds by making assumptions about states and the strategic arena in which they interact and then by tracing the implications of these assumptions. Formalization promotes a clearer and more precise specification of these assumptions and helps to forge tighter and more transparent links between these assumptions and the conclusions claimed to follow from them. But the value of this contribution will be relatively less important if the field already has several clear and internally coherent arguments. In these circumstances, empirical evaluation and testing would be more valuable. If, however, existing formulations are vague or poorly specified so that it is not clear what is being assumed or what follows from what, then the relative risk of making type II errors is large and the value added of formalization is greater.

This section examines three issues in international relations theory. The first is an essential element of the theoretical infrastructure of the field; it is the very notion of what a structural theory is and what structurally induced preferences are. The second issue is representative of many of the controversies that have dominated the field over the years. It is the emerging debate between offensive and defensive realism. The third issue is the theoretical usefulness and adequacy of one of the fundamental assumptions of much of international relations theory—the assumption that states seek to survive. A review of these issues shows that many of the misunderstandings surrounding them can be traced to the failure to make key ideas and concepts clear. These misunderstandings have impeded the development of the field, and this suggests that game theory and formalization have much to offer at this stage in the development of international relations theory.

STRUCTURAL THEORIES AND STRUCTURALLY INDUCED PREFERENCES

The quest for systemic or structural theories has a long history in international relations theory.[12] The self-conscious search for structural theories can be traced back at least as far as Kaplan's *System and Process in International Politics* (1957) and Waltz's discussion of the third image in *Man, the State, and War* (1959). The key insight underlying the third image (which can also be found in Butterfield's brief discussion [1950] of what we now call the security dilemma) is that one of the important effects of strategic interaction is that it may divorce desired outcomes from realized outcomes. To wit, war may occur even though each state is only seeking to ensure its security and none prefer war to peace.

Man, the State, and War provided a typology of existing theories and arguments but did not present a theory. For example, the defining feature of the third image was anarchy (1959, 159). But Waltz never traced an explicit path from anarchy to outcomes. Rather, anarchy served as a permissive cause: wars occurs in anarchic systems because "there is nothing to prevent them" (232). Twenty years later, Waltz proposed such a theory.

Theory of International Politics was one of the most influential books in international relations theory published since World War II. Its emphasis on international structure and its spare definition of that structure sparked an enormous debate about the proper definition of structure and about the ability to infer a state's preferences and behavior from its structural position. Since the degree to which a state's preferences can be derived from its structural position would seem to be inversely related to the importance of domestic politics in explaining international relations, the debate over the power and usefulness of structural explanations also fueled the continuing dispute about the significance of domestic politics. Although debates about structure no longer dominate the field as they once did, the usefulness of structural theories remains important. For example, the ability to infer state preferences from its structural position lies at the center of the growing controversy about the prospects of constructing neorealist or structural theories of foreign policy.[13]

Despite this long quest for and debate about structural explanations, the very notions of what it means for a theory to be "structural" or of what it means for preferences to be induced or inferred from structure remain uncertain. To illustrate the point, suppose we think of structure as defining the strategic arena in which the units interact and of preferences as the ends that the units pursue. Then, both structure and preferences are prim-

12. See Jervis 1997 for a recent overview of systemic approaches in international relations.

13. Elman (1996) and Rose (1998) survey this debate, and Fearon (1998c) offers a critical assessment of the distinction between international politics and foreign policy.

itives in the analysis of the units' interaction; neither entails the other.[14] But if this is so, what does it mean to say that we have a *structural* theory or that we can infer a unit's preferences from its structural position?

Surely, it does not mean that these primitive preferences can be inferred from the structure since these preferences are prior to any deductions. If preferences can be inferred from structure, then these "induced preferences" must be of a different kind. Here it is useful to distinguish between preferences over outcomes and preferences over strategies. The former is an actor's ranking over the terminal nodes of a game tree or over the cells of a game in payoff matrix (i.e., strategic) form. The latter kind of preference is the way that a player ranks its strategies. Because of strategic interdependence, this ranking depends on what strategies the other players intend to follow. For example, the 2×2 game of chicken in figure 1 can end in four ways: mutual compromise if both states submit, mutual disaster if both stand firm, and with one state or the other prevailing if it stands firm while the other submits. Then, the numbers in the cells of the matrix refer to the primitive assumption about the way the players rank the four possible outcomes. However, a player's preferred course of action, that is, whether it stands firm, depends on what it expects the other player to do. In particular, a state prefers to stand firm if it expects its adversary

Figure 1 | Preferences over Outcomes and Strategies in Chicken

	Firm	Submit
Firm	−10, −10	5, −1
Submit	−1, 5	0, 0

14. In a game theoretic model, for example, both the game tree and the actor's preferences, which are defined over the terminal nodes of the tree, are coequal elements that go into the specification of a model.

to submit, and it prefers to submit if it expects its adversary to stand firm.[15]

Preferences over strategies, therefore, are not a primitive of the analysis. At least in principle, they can be derived from the primitives describing the strategic environment and the actors' preferences (over outcomes). Indeed, this is precisely what game theory tries to do. Consequently, efforts to infer "preferences" from structure would seem to be referring to this kind of preference.

What, then, is a structural theory and a structural explanation? James Fearon (1998c) provides a point of departure. In an effort to examine the relation between theories of international politics and of foreign policy, he offers two broad notions of what one might mean by a structural theory. The first sees "states as unitary actors who consider what other states will or might do when they choose their foreign policies" (1998c, 261). That is, a theory is structural by this definition if it treats states as purposive, unitary actors who perceive themselves to be in a strategic environment. The second type of a structural theory is a subset of the first. A theory is structural if it satisfies the first definition by treating states as purposive unitary actors and if it also "adds conditions on which explanatory variables can operate or how they operate. . . ." (1998c, 261).

Waltz, for example, restricts a systemic explanation to be one that relies on only three variables (two of which are moot in international relations): the ordering principle of the system, the functional differentiation or non-differentiation of the units, and the distribution of capabilities among the units (1979, 79–101). Consequently, explanations of international political outcomes that rely on, say, the advent of nuclear weapons or the offense-defense balance are not structural explanations (for him), because they appeal to variables that have been *defined* to be nonstructural.

Of course, there is nothing sacrosanct about this definition, and one could readily add other variables to the list.[16] To illustrate the point, suppose we follow Glaser (2000b) by adding the offense-defense balance to the list of "acceptable" structural variables. Then Christensen and Snyder's (1990) explanation of states' alliance behavior would not be structural according to Waltz but would be according to this amended definition.[17]

15. See Powell 1994, 318–21, for a discussion of preferences over outcomes and strategies. Frieden (1999) discusses different approaches to specifying preferences over outcomes.

16. Indeed, Waltz himself offers a pragmatic defense of his emphasis on the distribution of power and exclusion of other things that can be cast in distributive terms, e.g., "differences in ideology, in internal structure of property relations, or in governmental form." His justification of this emphasis is that "state behavior varies more with differences in power" than with differences in these other things (1986, 329).

17. Presumably, the empirical effects of the offense-defense balance on alliance behavior would not depend on whether we defined this balance as a structural or nonstructural variable.

Fearon's distinction between two types of structural theory makes what constitutes structure entirely a matter of definition. A theory is *defined* to be structural if it treats states as strategically interdependent unitary actors or if, in addition to this, the theory only considers how some predefined set of variables, for example, the distribution of power, affect this interaction. This purely definitional approach is in keeping with much of the literature in international relations theory and does provide a useful way of categorizing both structural and nonstructural theories.[18]

But there is another way to conceive of a structural explanation which is partly a matter of definition and partly a matter of deduction. This other conception is moreover what many international relations theorists seem to have in mind when they discuss structural explanations and the ability to infer state preferences from structure. To develop this alternative, consider why a powerful structural theory would be a useful thing to have in the first place. Structural theories, if they can be devised, "explain why states similarly placed [in the system's structure] behave similarly despite their internal differences" (Waltz 1996, 54). That is, a structural theory *explains* why we can account for at least "a small number of important things" (Waltz 1986, 329) on the basis of the states' structural positions without having to know anything about, say, the states' domestic politics or their internal characteristics except, possibly, that they seek to survive. To draw a loose analogy with statistics again, structural position is akin to a *sufficient statistic* for predicting outcomes; that is, once one knows the units' structural positions, knowing other things about their unitary attributes would not improve on one's ability to predict outcomes.

However, explaining why variation in a set of (possibly arbitrarily defined) structural variables significantly affects state interactions *and* why variation in the other nonstructural variables does not have a significant effect (and therefore can be ignored) is a matter of deduction and not solely one of definition. A theory that does not allow for variation among nonstructural characteristics cannot *explain* why such variation would or would not have any consequential effects. In order to demonstrate theoretically that variation in, say, some attributes of the units has no little or no effect on the outcome, a theory must represent those attributes in some way, allow them to vary, and show *deductively* that this variation has no significant effects. Unless it does these things, then the theory cannot "explain why similarly placed states behave similarly despite" their different unitary tributes.[19]

To put the point more concretely, suppose that a theorist is trying to create a structural theory that accounts for the likelihood of war. She be-

18. The definition of a structural explanation also implicitly defines what constitutes a nonstructural or domestic politics explanation; this is the point Fearon is emphasizing.

19. Of course, all theories leave some things out and therefore are deductively silent on the effects that variation in these features would have.

gins by treating states as purposive, unitary actors and by defining the distribution of power to be the sole structural variable. That is, explanations which link changes in the likelihood of war to changes in the distribution of power are the only kinds of explanation that count as structural. This is in keeping with Fearon's second notion of a structural explanation.

After much toil and trouble, she succeeds in devising a theory that deductively links variations in the distribution of power to changes in the likelihood of war. Should this count as a structural explanation? It surely satisfies the definition above in that it only appeals to variation in what has been defined to be a structural variable. In this purely definitional sense, then, this is a structural explanation. But would this theory support the claim that "states similarly placed behave similarly despite their internal differences" (Waltz 1996, 54)? Would, for example, the theory support the claim that states' internal structures, for example, whether they are democratic or not, have no significant effect on the likelihood of war?

The answer is clearly no, and there are two cases to consider. If, first, there is no way to represent the distinction between democratic and nondemocratic states in the theory—albeit even at a high level of abstraction—then one cannot ask whether this difference has a significant effect on states' interaction in the context of this theory. The question is simply beyond the theory's scope.

If, by contrast, there is a way to distinguish between democratic and nondemocratic states in the theory, one can pose the question. But in order to answer it, that is, to see whether variation in the states' internal attributes affects their interaction, then one must vary this nonstructural variable. If this variation has no significant effect on states' interaction, the theory would provide a structural account of outcomes. That is, knowing states' structural positions would be sufficient to account for the outcome of their interaction. But if this variation in nonstructural elements led to significant variation in the outcomes, then the theory would have undercut a structural explanation. According to the theory, states similarly placed in the structure would not behave similarly depsite their internal differences.

In these circumstances, we would have a structural theory in the purely definitional sense; it links changes in the distribution of power to unambiguous changes in the likelihood of war *as long as one does not consider the effects of variables that have been defined to be nonstructural*. But the theory would not be structural in the sense that it showed that variation in nonstructural variables had no significant effect on the outcomes. And, it is the latter notion of a structural explanation that makes such explanations useful.

In sum, structural explanation is more than a matter of definition. What one takes to constitute *structure* is a definitional issue. But a *structural explanation*, however structure is defined, is also a matter of deduction, for it shows that variation in these structural variables significantly affects outcomes whereas variation in nonstructural variables does not.

Although the importance of structural explanations has been debated and discussed since Waltz published *Theory of International Politics* more than two decades ago, the relation between definition and deduction in the development of structural theories and explanations is still not widely appreciated nor is this lack of appreciation limited to neorealists. Consider, for example, Andrew Moravcsik's recent effort to provide a "liberal theory of international politics" that takes "preferences seriously." He claims that realism and institutionalism believe that variation in state preferences has little or no effect on the outcomes of state interaction (1997, 522). Variation "in state preferences should be treated as if they were irrelevant, secondary, or endogenous. . . . What states do is primarily determined by strategic calculations . . . which in turn reflect their international political environment" (Moravcsik 1997, 522). Liberalism, by contrasts, "reverses this *assumption*" (522, emphasis added) by taking variation in state preferences to be paramount in explaining outcomes. Variation in "interstate political and strategic circumstances" is unimportant (522–23). Thus, whether structural or nonstructural features are consequential is a matter of assumption for Moravscik and not of theoretical deduction.

How is all of this related to game theory and to the value added of forging tighter links between assumptions about actors and their environments and the conclusions that follow from these assumptions? The real issue underlying the debate about structural explanations is not whether some variables are defined to be structural and others are not. The issue is a theoretical effort to trace the effects of changes in certain factors such as the distribution of power, the offense-defense balance, or whether the states are democratic or nondemocratic. Whether or not some of these factors are called structural is theoretically irrelevant. Whether variation in a variable in the context of a given theory significantly affects the outcome is a deductive property of the theory and does not depend on whether this variable is called structural. Whether a statement can be derived from a set of assumptions does not depend on what those assumptions are called. *The appellation* structure *does no theoretical work.*

If the links between assumptions and conclusions were clearer, all of this would be immediately evident. One would not debate whether this or that factor, say, the existence of nuclear weapons or the offense-defense balance, was structural in an effort to piggy back on the "well-known" implications of structure. Rather, one would simply try to incorporate these elements into a formulation and then try to trace their implications. Clearer links between assumptions and conclusions would have saved an enormous amount of scholarly time and energy, time and energy that could have be devoted to testing theoretical implications.

OFFENSIVE VERSUS DEFENSIVE REALISM AND THE PROBLEM OF INFERENCE

As noted above, much of international relations theory has tried to understand certain aspects of international politics by analyzing the strategic logic of a simple stylized system based on a Hobbesian state of nature. One of the latest efforts revolves around offensive and defensive realism.[20] A brief review of this debate shows again the importance of forging tighter, more transparent links between assumptions and the conclusions claimed to follow from them. This, in turn, underscores the high value added that greater formalization offers international relations theory given the current state of development.

At the center of the controversy between offensive and defensive realism is the question: What do certain assumptions about the international system imply about state interactions? In particular, do these assumptions imply that states attempt to maximize their power?

Defensive and offensive realism as well as Waltz's version of structural realism seem to share a consistent set of core assumptions about state preferences and about the strategic arena in which states interact. Recall that Waltz assumes that states are functionally nondifferentiated, purposive unitary actors seeking security and that these states interact in an anarchically ordered system. Call these two core assumptions A_{SR} where the subscript denotes structural realism. The school of defensive realism is still in flux and the core assumptions are still unsettled. Snyder (1991, 10–13), who coined the term, and Grieco (1997, 164–67) seem to posit the same set of core assumptions that structural realism does. Call this set of assumptions A_{DR}, where DR denotes defensive realism, and note that $A_{SR} = A_{DR}$. Glaser (2000b, 6–12), by contrast, explicitly adds the security dilemma and the offense-defense balance to defensive realism's characterization of the states' strategic setting.[21] Call this set of assumptions $A_{OFF\text{-}DEF}$, and observe that $A_{OFF\text{-}DEF}$ is really A_{SR} along with offense-defense assumptions; that is, $A_{OFF\text{-}DEF} = A_{DR} \cup \Omega$, where Ω represents assumptions about the offense-defense balance. Finally, offensive realism assumes that states are purposive unitary actors seeking security in a strategic environment characterized by anarchy, that the presence of some offensive capabilities gives the states "the wherewithal to hurt and possibly destroy each other," and that states are uncertain about other's motivations (Mearsheimer 1994–95, 2000). Call this set of assumptions A_{OR}.

20. Glaser (2000b) provides an excellent overview of this debate. Other contributions and analyses include Herz 1950, Mearsheimer 1990, Snyder 1991, Zakaria 1992, 1998, Grieco 1997, Labs 1997, Lynn-Jones 1998, and Rose 1998.

21. Lynn-Jones (1995), Van Evera (1998, 1999), and others call this offense-defense theory. However, as Glaser (2000b) points out, offense-defense theory often adds many more things than the offense-defense balance, and these additions have led to a great deal of confusion.

Although they do not emphasize it, both structural and defensive realism also seem to assume at least implicitly that the actors have some ability to hurt each other. This is, after all, an important part of what makes the strategic environment *strategic*, that is, why states have to be concerned about what other states are going to do. Similarly, both structural and defensive realism seem to presume some uncertainty about motivations (e.g., Glaser 1996, 127, 1992; Waltz 1979, 165) although they do not always emphasize this assumption. If we make these two stipulations, then structural and offensive as well as the minimalist version of defensive realism appear to be based on the same set of assumptions, which to simplify the subscripts will simply be called A. This set, in turn, is contained in the version of defensive realism that includes offense-defense variables. That is,

$$A = A_{SR} = A_{DR} = A_{OR} \subset A_{OFF\text{-}DEF} = A \cup \Omega$$

But if two or more theories make the same set of assumptions, what does it mean for a field like international relations theory to be debating whether those assumptions imply a particular conclusion? More specifically, what does it mean to debate whether the set of assumptions A implies that states try to maximize their power as offensive realism claims (Mearsheimer 1994–95, 2001; Herz 1950) or that they do not as structural realism and the minimal version of defensive realism claim (Waltz 1979, 126; Greico 1997)?

One possible interpretation of such a debate is that at present no theorist has been able to link these assumptions *deductively* to power maximization or the absence of it. In this account, the debate would be between contending *speculations* about what will eventually be shown to follow from a set of assumptions. This kind of speculation can play an important role in the development of a field because it motivates theorists to work on a problem.

However, this interpretation of the debate as contending speculation about what ultimately may be shown to follow from a set of assumptions does not accurately characterize the growing controversy between structural realism, defensive realism, and offensive realism. Mearsheimer (1994–95, 2001), for example, claims that one can show that power maximization follows from A. By contrast, Waltz (1979) and Grieco (1997) claim that A implies that states do not maximize power. Indeed, A implies that "states balance power rather than maximize it" (Waltz 1979, 127).

Two conclusions do seem to follow from this brief review. First, a consistent set of assumptions cannot imply both X and not X.[22] Assuming,

---

22. A basic result in logic is that if a set of assumptions implies one conclusion, say Y, and its opposite, not Y, then *any* other proposition can be deduced from this set of assumptions. Thus any conclusion can be inferred from a theory built on an inconsistent set of assumptions, and this makes empirical testing of the theory meaningless.

therefore, that A is consistent (something which has not been challenged so far as I know), then A cannot imply that states do maximize power and that they do not.[23] Set A implies either that states maximize power or that they do not, or set A by itself does not imply either of these conclusions. If the latter is the case, then some other assumptions have to be added to A in order to support any deduction about power maximization or the lack of it. And, given the importance attached to the idea of power maximization or balancing, these other assumptions—whatever they might be—would seem to constitute a key part of theory and are too important to be left unstated. Indeed, this is precisely the tack Glaser (1996, 2000b) takes by adding offense-defense assumptions to A.

The second conclusion that follows from this review of offensive and defensive realism is more important for present purposes. The only way that a debate like the one brewing over offensive and defensive realism can exist is if the links between assumptions and the conclusions that do deductively follow from them are very loose and opaque. Once again, the state of the field indicates that there would be a very high value added to being able to forge tighter, more transparent links from assumptions to conclusions.

ON SEEKING SURVIVAL

If a theory takes actors to be purposive, then some assumption must be made about the purposes they pursue. A fundamental assumption underlying much of contemporary international relations theory is that states seek to survive. Waltz, most notably, assumes that "states seek to ensure their survival" (1979, 91), and most subsequent theories or applications have adopted this assumption.[24] But the assumption was commonplace before Waltz made it the foundation for his theory of structural realism (e.g., Herz 1950, 1959; Jervis 1978; Wolfers 1951, 1962). Indeed, the basic idea can be traced back to Hobbes if not Thucydides. Hobbes (1991, esp. 117–21) argued that the fundamental quid pro quo between the sovereign and subject is that the ruler provides security in return for the subject's obedience, whereas Thucydides (1954) believed that the fear and insecurity engendered by the growth of Athenian power was the primary cause of the Peloponnesian War.

23. It is important to separate deductive claims from empirical issues. Whether A implies that states maximize power is a matter of deduction and not of empirical evidence, as Glaser (2000b) points out. Empirically, determining whether states maximize power is relevant for assessing a theory once we know what it implies, but determining what a set of assumptions implies is not an empirical issue.

24. See, for example, Brooks 1997, Elman 1996b, Glaser 1992, 1996, 1997, Grieco 1988, 1990, Lynn-Jones 1995, Mearsheimer 1994–95, 2000, Rose 1998, Sndyer 1991, and Van Evera 1998, 1999. Schweller (1996) discusses this assumption in the context of the historical development of realism.

However, the idea that states seek to survive in their anarchic environment is too poorly specified to serve as a theory's core assumption about preferences. Although this assumption is thought to be important, it generally does not do much theoretical work and little if anything follows from it. The reason it appears to be an important assumption and one sufficient for many theories is that the links from this and other assumptions to the conclusions that are claimed to follow from them are too opaque.

To develop these points, suppose that a theorist uses a game to model some interaction over an issue that a theory purports to explain. As noted above, one of the fundamental primitives of this analysis is the actors' preferences, that is, how the actors rank the terminal nodes of the game tree. A theoretically useful assumption about preferences should provide clear guidance as to what to assume about the way that the actors rank the possible outcomes of the game. In economics, for example, the assumption that firms try to maximize profits is useful because it specifies how firms rank outcomes in a wide variety of circumstances. That is, when defining the firm's preferences over the terminal nodes of a game that models some aspect of their interaction, the firms should rank the possible outcomes in terms of the levels of profits associated with those outcomes.

To see that the assumption that states seek to ensure their survival is too vague to provide clear guidance in ranking outcomes and therefore cannot play a role parallel to that of the assumption of profit maximization, consider the following simple bargaining game. A satisfied state S and a dissatisfied state D are bargaining about revising the territorial status quo. The situation is depicted in figure 2 where the total territory is represented

Figure 2 | Bargaining over Territory

S must withdraw to this point to appease the least resolute type it might be facing.

S must withdraw to this point to appease the least resolute type it might be facing.

Dissatisfied state's capital D

Satisfied state's capital S

0 q $\underline{x}$ $\bar{x}$ 1

as the interval $[0, 1]$. State D currently controls all of the territory to the left of the status quo border q, and state S controls all of the territory to the right of q.

State D, however, claims to be dissatisfied with the status quo and threatens to go to war with state S unless S makes a territorial concession. To keep things simple, suppose that S can deal with this situation by making a single offer of x to D. If D accepts this offer, it acquires control over the territory to the left of x and S retains the territory to the right of x. If D rejects this offer, then D attacks and the interaction ends in war. To specify the payoffs to fighting, assume that S pays a cost c of fighting and that the war can end in one of two ways. Either S prevails and thereby acquires all of the territory, or D prevails and takes all of the territory. The probability that D prevails is p.

Suppose further that S is unsure of D's willingness to fight. At one extreme, D could be very dissatisfied; this means more formally that S would have to make a large concession to D in order to induce it not to attack. Suppose, in particular, that S would have to withdraw to $\bar{x}$ in order to induce this most-dissatisfied type not to attack. At the other extreme, D could be less willing to use force and would be satisfied if it were to control the territory to the left of $\underline{x}$. In this case, the satisfied state has to make a smaller concession in order to "buy" peace. Finally, suppose that S is sure that D's willingness to fight is between these two extremes but that no point between these extremes is any more likely than another (i.e., D's willingness to fight is uniformly distributed over $[\underline{x}, \bar{x}]$).[25]

The outcomes of this interaction can be described simply in terms of three elements. If the satisfied state offers x, this offer will be rejected with probability $w(x)$. If this offer is subsequently accepted, the territorial division will be x for D and $1 - x$ for S. If, however, the dissatisfied state rejects x, war follows and the satisfied state prevails with probability p. Thus, the set of outcomes of this interaction can be characterized as $\{x, w(x), p\}$, where x is any number between 0 and 1 and represents what the satisfied state offers; $w(x)$ is the probability of war or, equivalently, the probability that the satisfied state rejects x; and p is the probability that the satisfied state prevails in the event of war.[26]

These outcomes reflect a number of possible trade-offs that may affect the way that a state ranks the outcomes. For example, the state can *ensure* that it will survive as an independent entity by offering $x = \bar{x}$ (or anything more). Conversely, *any* offer less than $\bar{x}$ entails some risk that the state will be eliminated and not survive. This risk is the probability that the dissatis-

25. For elaborations of this basic model and a complete specification, see Powell 1999. Fearon (1995b) discusses a similar model.

26. Given that the dissatisfied state's minimal acceptable offers are evenly between $\underline{x}$ and $\bar{x}$, the probability of war is $w(x) = 1$ for $x \leq \underline{x}$; $w(x) = (\bar{x} - x)/(\bar{x} - \underline{x})$ for $\underline{x} \leq x \leq \bar{x}$; and $w(x) = 0$ for $x \geq \bar{x}$.

fied state will reject x and subsequently defeat the satisfied state, which is $w(x)(1 - p)$. The risk is inversely related to the size of the concession; that is, the larger x, the lower the probability of war $w(x)$ and of elimination. Thus, there is a trade-off between territorial concessions and the probability of being eliminated. The more the satisfied state offers, that is, the larger x, the lower the risk of war and elimination, but the less territory the satisfied state will have if its offer is accepted.

In light of these trade-offs, how should S rank these outcomes if it seeks to ensure its survival? This assumption has been variously interpreted to mean that states "give priority to ensuring their security" (Glaser 1996, 127), that states are "security maximizers" (Schweller 1996, 99, 114), or that states have "lexicographic preferences" over security (Schweller 1996, 103). Yet, these different interpretations can have very different implications even in the context of the very simple model described here.

To see this variation, suppose for the moment that security refers solely to the probability of surviving as an independent political entity. Waltz seems to have something like this in mind when he says, "Survival is a prerequisite to achieving any goals that states may have, other than the goal of promoting their own disappearance as a political entity" (1979, 92). This construction suggests that the larger the probability that the satisfied state will be eliminated, the less secure it is.[27] Accordingly, a security maximizer would offer $x = \bar{x}$ and thereby avoid any risk of war. Similarly, a state with lexicographic preferences would always prefer one outcome to another if the former offered a higher level of security. A state with these preferences would therefore offer $\bar{x}$ as well.[28]

But defining *security* solely in terms of the probability of surviving regardless of the territorial sacrifice is only one interpretation of this term, and it is an extremely narrow one. An equally narrow but opposite notion would define *security* solely in terms of territorial integrity. In this context, a security seeker tries to preserve its territorial integrity but has no desire to expand. This would seem to be a plausible interpretation of the idea that the "first concern of states is not to maximize their power but to maintain

27. Kydd (1997b, 121) and Lynn-Jones (1995) interpret Waltz this way and explicitly define security in terms of the probability of surviving. Lynn-Jones also observes that "most definitions of security remain vague" (664).

28. As an aside, one implication of this that has generally not been appreciated in the work on realism is worth noting. Even if a security maximizer (or a state with lexicographic preferences) is uncertain of its adversaries willingness to use force, this state effectively makes a worst-case assumption about its adversary, that is, that its adversary is willing to fight unless it receives $\bar{x}$. This is in keeping with some discussions of structural realism which associate worst-case planning with it (e.g., Brooks 1997; Glaser 2000b). But the security-maximizing state then makes a concession sufficient to appease this worst-case adversary (and therefore sufficient to appease any other adversary) and consequently eliminates the risk of war. *Worst-case planning therefore leads to a lower risk of war.*

their positions in the system" (Waltz 1979, 126). This formulation is also keeping with treating security-seeking states as status quo states.[29]

To trace the implications of this interpretation, suppose that we make the extreme assumption that a security-seeking state is willing to fight in order to preserve its territorial integrity but will not accept any risk of war in order to expand its territory.[30] This state's optimal offer is q. Note further that a state that defines *security* in terms of territorial integrity ranks the outcomes of the game in exactly the opposite way than does a security-seeking state that defines *security* in terms of the probability of survival. In the model, a larger territorial concession "buys" a lower probability of war; that is, if $x > y$, then $w(x)(1 - p) < w(y)(1 - p)$. Thus, a security-seeking state (defined in terms of territory) prefers offering y to x whereas a security-seeking state (defined in terms of the probability of survival) prefers x to y!

Of course, *security* need not be defined solely in terms of either of these extremes. A state's security might be related to both the probability of survival and its territorial integrity. Indeed, this is one plausible reading of what it means for a security-seeking state to give the highest priority to its survival. Unfortunately, this reading of the meaning of security seeking is likely to give rise to yet another ranking of the possible outcomes. If a state is concerned with both the probability of survival and the size of any territorial concessions, then it will offer the concession that balances or equates the marginal benefit of offering slightly more (a benefit which is measured in terms of a slightly higher probability of survival) to the marginal cost of offering slightly more (which is measured in terms of the loss of slightly more territory). The resolution of this trade-off typically results in an offer strictly between $\underline{x}$ and $\bar{x}$. This offer is more than a state that defines security in terms of territorial integrity would offer and less than a state that defines security in terms of the probability of survival would offer.

To summarize this discussion of the assumption that states seek survival, there is no consensus on what the key assumption that "states seek to ensure their survival" means. Different theories seem to be based on different interpretations even though they typically claim to be making the same assumption that Waltz makes. Yet, as the simple model above makes clear, different interpretations lead to widely different preference orderings and to widely different predictions. Effectively, then, these theories are not making the same assumptions, and, once again, the assumption claimed to be doing the heavy theoretical work is not. Rather, the specific formulation

29. See Schweller's (1996) discussion of the relation between neorealism and status quo states.

30. As Glaser (1992) and others observe, sometimes a state has to expand in order to improve the chances that it will not lose what it already has, and this possibility has been central to much recent work on expansion (e.g., Snyder 1991; Zakaria 1992, 1998). However, this complexity does not arise in the simple formulation above.

of what it means to try to ensure one's survival is doing the theoretical work. But because ordinary-language formulations frequently do not force a theorist to specify the range of possible outcomes and precisely how the actors rank them, the fact that "seeking to ensure survival" is too vague to provide the needed guidance in specifying these preferences has generally not been appreciated.

The benefits of formalization are that it requires clearer, more precise assumptions about the actors and their strategic environment and tighter, more transparent links between these assumptions and the conclusions claimed to follow from them. Clear links are moreover critically important to the empirical evaluation of theories. Unless we can be confident about what our theories predict, there is really nothing to test.

But, as noted above, the benefits of formalization also bring costs. The resolution of the cost-benefit trade-off depends at least in part on the state of the field and may change as the field does. In general, the more coherent and clearer existing arguments, the less formalization has to offer and the relatively more important empirical assessment and evaluation may be.

The discussion of structural theories and structurally induced preferences, the nascent debate between offensive and defensive realism, and the assumption that states seek to survive shows that key ambiguities lie at the center of these issues. Indeed, one suspects that the debate surrounding these issues would completely disappear if the assumptions and arguments were more transparent. Either it would be clear that the conclusions did not follow from the stated assumptions, in which case more theoretical work would need to be done. Or, clear but different assumptions would have led to different predictions, at which point the issue becomes a matter of empirical assessment. This current lack of clarity indicates that that branch of international relations theory that tries to understand international politics through an explication of simple stylizations of the international system has much to gain from formalization. At this stage in the development of this branch of international relations theory, the potential for making type II errors by incorrectly accepting fundamentally flawed arguments seems much larger than the potential of making type I errors by incorrectly rejecting sound arguments. The benefits of greater formalization appear to overwhelm the costs.

■ | Some Consequences of Formalization

Although moving toward greater formalization appears to have a high value added, this move still entails costs and consequences. As noted above, one of the likely consequences is the evolution of ignorance. Some conclusions that can be supported with ordinary-language arguments because those arguments *sound* convincing may prove impossible to support formally. Another, more important long-run consequence is the likely reintegration of international relations theory with the rest of political science.

The assumption of anarchy has long served as an analytic wall separating international relations theory from the rest of political science. Recall Dunn's comment in 1949 that the "distinguishing characteristic of IR as a separate branch of learning is found in the nature of the questions with which it deals. IR is concerned with the questions that arise in the relations between autonomous political groups in a world system in which power is not centered at one point" (142, 144). Anarchy is also at the heart of Fox's observation and the challenge implicit in it: "A body of political theory dealing with a system characterized by an absence of a central authority is yet to be developed. . . ." (1949, 79). Most succinctly, "Anarchy is the characteristic that distinguishes international politics from ordinary politics" (Wight 1979, 102). Half a century later, this analytical wall has been breached, and exploiting this breach seems likely to lead to a reintegration of international relations with other fields in political science.

In a thoughtful review appearing in the fiftieth anniversary issue of *International Organization*, Helen Milner (1998) discusses what she sees as an "emerging synthesis of international, American, and comparative politics" based on a rational-institutionalist approach.[31] Each of these fields is too diverse to characterize in terms of a single approach. But, "a strain of such rational institutional work now exists in all three fields, and the scholars who are applying it are asking many of the same questions and using the same analytic tools" (762).

The thrust of her argument is twofold. First, the focus on anarchy and the absence of a higher authority leads to a very strong tendency to treat states as purposive *unitary* actors, which in turn has led to the separation and intellectual isolation of international relations. That is, the emphasis on anarchy renders international relations theory a "narrower specialty, one concerned with a specific type of power relationship among particular kinds of units" (764). The unitary-actor assumption "has cut the field off from other areas of political science" (767). Second, relaxing the assumption that states are unitary actors has important consequences for the field. One of the most important of these is that breaking down the unitary-actor assumption allows international relations theory to focus *explicitly* on the effects that different domestic institutions or different substate-actors' preferences have on international outcomes.[32] These issues, in turn, have

31. Also see her excellent discussion of why the field of international relations diverged from political science (Milner 1998, 762–67).

32. In light of the discussion of structural theories above, it should be clear that taking states to be unitary actors does not preclude the study of the effects of differential *state* preferences. One can, for example, consider the effects of different attitudes toward risk or different discount factors or interests in openness and international trade. However, taking states to be unitary actors does prevent the development of an explicit theoretical link from the preferences of domestic actors or

direct parallels in American and comparative politics, and this provides the basis of the emerging synthesis among at least large and significant parts of these three fields (772–79).

I share Milner's view about the possibility of a synthesis and see this as one of the most exciting developments in international relations theory and political science. But the basis of this potential synthesis seems to me to be different from the one she emphasizes. Milner does see game theory as playing a significant part in this emerging synthesis, because it provides a means for analyzing the strategic interaction that is at the center of the rational institutional approach (783). However, the driving forces behind this emerging synthesis for her are efforts to relax the assumptions that states are unitary actors and that states are the most important or sole actors.

In my view, game theory is the primary carrier of this prospective synthesis. Formalization brings greater clarity and transparency, and this has revealed striking parallels between the strategic problems that states face in international politics and the strategic problems that other actors face in American and comparative politics. These parallels will be the foundation of any synthesis that ultimately emerges, and these parallels exist *even when states are treated as unitary actors*. It is not the assumption that states are unitary actors that has led to the isolation of international relations but the inability to see the strategic parallels that transcend the analytic divide of anarchy.

To illustrate these parallels, consider the bargaining that occurs in the shadow of force in the *anarchic* realm of international politics and the bargaining that occurs between potential litigants in the "shadow of the law" (Cooter, Marks, Mnookin 1982) in the *hierarchical* realm of courts and enforced contracts. If the anarchy-hierarchy distinction had much bite, one would expect it to appear here. Yet, research on bargaining in these two domains has led to strikingly similar questions and hypotheses.

A central question in the work on legal disputes is why do cases go to court?[33] Why, that is, does bargaining sometimes break down in costly litigation and result in a court-imposed settlement? Is there, as Priest and Klein (1984) ask, a relationship between the chances that a dispute will go to court and the strength of the case? Are, for example, clear-cut cases in which the court is very likely to find in favor of one of the parties more likely to go to court than a case in which the ultimate verdict is much less clear? These questions have direct analogs in international relations theory. Why do disputes between states sometimes end in war and costly fighting (Fearon 1995b)? What is the relationship between the risk of war and the distribution of power? Is war less likely if there is a preponderance

---

from the institutions in which they interact to preferences assumed in the states-as-unitary-actor models. As Milner emphasizes, forging these links requires one to relax the assumption that states are unitary actors.

33. See Cooter and Rubinfeld 1989 for a review of the work on legal disputes.

of power and the victor seems assured, as the preponderance of power school maintains (Organski and Kugler 1980; Kugler and Lemke 1996). Or, is an even distribution of power more stable as the balance of power school argues (Claude 1962; Morgenthau 1948; Mearsheimer 1990; Wright 1965; Wolfers 1962)?

Parallel questions have led to parallel hypothesis. One explanation for why cases go to trial is that the parties disagree about the expected outcome. At least one of the litigants is too optimistic about its prospects of prevailing or about the size of its award (Cooter, Marks, Mnookin 1982; Gould 1973; Landes 1971; Schweizer 1989). For instance, Priest and Klein (1984) argue that excessive optimism is less likely in clear-cut cases. Thus, the probability of litigation is smallest when one party has a preponderance of legal power on its side. Similarly, Blainey claims that a primary cause of war is that states are uncertain of the distribution of power between them and of the likely verdict of fighting (1973, 122). Such disagreements are moreover less likely when one state preponderates. Consequently, a preponderance of power is more peaceful.[34]

A second example of what may be an emerging parallel centers on the effects of shifts in the distribution of power. Ever since Thucydides ascribed the cause of the Peloponnesian War to the rise of Athenian power, shifts in the distribution of power have been seen as a source of tension and conflict in international politics (e.g., Organski and Kugler 1980; Gilpin 1981; Kennedy 1987). Powell develops a model of the way that (unitary) states cope with shifts in the distribution of power and finds that states will make compromises and avoid war if the distribution of power does not shift too rapidly. However, rapid shifts in the distribution of power are doomed to breakdown in war (Powell 1999, 115–48, esp. 128–31).

The relation between political stability and the rate at which the distribution of power shifts appears to be an important mechanism that underlies problems in American and comparative politics as well as international relations. Fearon (1998b), for example, argues that a shift in the distribution of power between a minority and a majority group may be a significant cause of ethnic conflict. Recent work on democratic transitions also suggests that the ability to consolidate a democratic transition depends on the speed at which the distribution of power is shifting among the factions (Acemoglu and Robinson 2001). And, theoretical as well as empirical work links shifts in the distribution of power to the internal structure of political organizations (de Figueiredo 2000a, b).

In sum, one of the most important and exciting consequences of moving toward a more formal standard is that it will make it easier to see the existence of strong parallels between the strategic problems that unitary actors—be they states or not—face in international relations and the

34. For a more extensive discussion of this and other parallels, see Lake and Powell 1999b, 27–9, and Powell 1999, 217–22.

strategic problems that different actors face in comparative and American politics. These parallels presumably exist regardless of the tools one uses to study the problems.[35] In principle, then, a synthesis could emerge without formalization. In practice, however, these parallels have turned out to be much more difficult to see when the analyses of these problems are cast in ordinary-language arguments. Formalization forces the basic mechanism underlying the interaction to the fore and thereby facilities a more-integrated approach to the study of politics. Although not a substitute for good ideas and deep insights, formalization can serve as an important "intuition pump."

■ | Conclusion

Just as game theory is not a substitute for good ideas and deep insights about international politics, good ideas and deep insights are not a substitute for game theory or, more generally, good research methods. Research methods and substantive ideas complement each other, and theoretical progress requires both.

Good theoretical ideas suggest causal relations between a set of assumptions and some conclusions. Game theory helps forge tighter deductive links between these assumptions and the conclusions believed to follow from them. Game theory tests the internal logic of the basic idea. In so doing, it sometimes shows that other important assumptions must be added in order to sustain some conclusions. It also sometimes reveals a fundamental problem with what initially sounded like a very promising idea. Empirical methods in turn provide a way of assessing the empirical power or content of the deductive links.

However, methods and good substantive ideas are more than complements. They are more intimately and subtlety related, for methods do or at least should partly define what a good idea is. In the fiftieth anniversary issue of *International Organization*, Peter Katzenstein, Robert Keohane, and Stephen Krasner describe the evolution and development of the field of international political economy in terms of competing analytic orientations, paradigms, and "isms". This competition has produced lively debates; "substantive findings, however, remain meager" (1998, 683). Barry Eichengreen in the same volume attributes this state of affairs to the lack of "close connections between theory and empirical work" and observes that "the field needs to move in the direction of formulating more parsimonious models and clearly refutable null hypotheses, and developing em-

---

35. This is largely correct but not entirely so. Looking at different issues through the same analytic lens—a lens which emphasizes some things, like credibility and commitment problems, and deemphasizes other things—will tend to highlight these parallels but not others.

pirical techniques that will allow those theories to be confronted by the data" (1998, 1012). This description applies equally well to international relations theory as a whole. It also suggests that part of what makes an idea interesting is its ability to be formulated in a way that it can be evaluated theoretically and, especially, empirically. Good ideas, therefore, are at least partly defined by the methods we have to develop and evaluate them.

Until the 1980s, ordinary-language arguments were arguably the best analytic tool available for analyzing strategic interaction in a wide range of situations. But better tools are now available, and their application has shown that many widely accepted, ordinary-language arguments are at best incomplete. Formalization has shown too often that the conclusions said to follow from a set of assumptions do not. This, moreover, is not simply a kind of methodological incommensurability, for after seeing the formal result, one can often go back to the ordinary-language argument and find key assumptions that were not previously noticed and that once made explicit greatly weaken the argument. Nevertheless, the extent to which the field of international relations theory will move toward greater formalization over the next decade or so remains uncertain. What is more certain is that the extent to which international relations theory does move in this direction will have an important effect on what will be written about the field in *The State of the Discipline* in 2020.

CHARLES M. CAMERON AND
REBECCA MORTON

Formal Theory Meets Data[1]

■ | Political Methodology: Where Do We Stand?

We begin by providing the reader the context for this essay and that by Donald Green and Alan Gerber in this volume. Our device for doing so is a recent article by Nobel laureate James Heckman (2000) in which he discusses the current state of statistical methodology in our sister discipline, economics. Heckman's astute insights into econometric practice help illuminate the current role of statistical methods in political science, both by underscoring what is similar to economics and by revealing what is different.

CAUSAL ANALYSIS AND THE SEM APPROACH

As Heckman relates the recent history of econometrics, he assigns a central role to the linear simultaneous equations model (SEM), developed during the middle years of the twentieth century. The SEM allowed researchers to translate economic theory into well-posed, causally oriented empirical models. The concepts created by these researchers—exogenous variables, endogenous variables, causal effects, misspecification, omitted variable bias, the identification problem—after some delay entered political science, where they continue to provide the bread and butter of introductory methods training.

But, as Heckman tells the story, by the mid-1960s the SEM "was widely perceived to be an intellectual success but an empirical failure" (2000, 48). A simple example will help explain why. Consider the path

1. We thank Henry Brady, Alan Gerber, Don Green, Ira Katznelson, Gary King, Lisa Martin, Helen Milner, and participants in the 2000 Political Methodology Meetings, 2000 APSA meetings, and the "State of the Discipline" miniconference for very helpful comments on an earlier version. We also thank the more than 200 political scientists and economists who assisted in the literature survey that accompanies this chapter as a web page. Of course, the usual caveat applies.

Figure 1 | A Structural Model

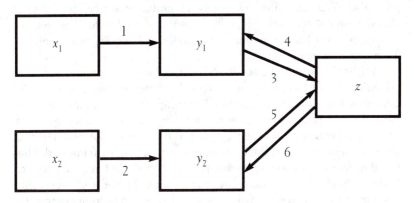

diagram shown in figure 1, which corresponds, to a three-equation model. The path diagram illustrates a structural model, detailing the causal relations between all the variables in the system; it shows how the "shin bone is connected to the knee bone, the knee bone is connected to the thigh bone," and so on. In the diagram, the variables x_1 and x_2 are external, or exogenous, because their values are determined outside the system; the variables y_1, y_2, and z are internal, or endogenous, because their values are determined within the system. Variables like y_1 and y_2 are sometimes called intermediate or intervening variables since their values are determined within the system but in turn determine the value of another variable z. The arrows labeled with numbers indicate the fundamental causal effects of one variable on another. For example, x_1 has a direct causal effect on y_1 via path 1, an indirect effect on z via paths 1 and 3, and an even more indirect effect on y_2 via paths 1, 3, and 6. Direct causal effects are sometimes called structural causal effects. Within the traditional SEM approach, all the structural causal effects in the figure are assumed to be linear, and the task of the empirical analyst is to use data to estimate each of them. Alternatively, if the interest were just variable z, the analyst might use the structural model to justify estimating a reduced form equation $z = z(x_1, x_2)$, relating z only to the two exogenous variables. This is a valid practice since the structural model shows that z ultimately is a function only of the external, or "forcing," variables.

Heckman suggests that the style of thinking illustrated in figure 1 was an intellectual triumph of twentieth-century social science. It's not hard to see why. The concept of stable causal effects is indispensable in most approaches to social science, and the structural approach offers a rigorous yet tractable way to think concretely about causal effects. Because the approach is so grounded in causal thinking, structural parameters are often social-scientifically transparent; they are readily interpretable in terms of theory. Hence, empirical estimates of them can be used to test theory. In addition, empirical estimates of causal parameters can be used for forecasting or performing "what if" policy experiments. Finally, the SEM approach clarifies the limits of purely empirical evidence, by focusing attention on the necessity of identifying assumptions. It is for these reasons that Heckman calls the approach an intellectual success. Most political methodologists would agree.

Yet, as Heckman indicates, the SEM approach soon ran into empirical difficulties, at least in economics. To put the matter simply, only rarely did estimations uncover stable causal relationships (the direct path effects in figure 1). The problem was most notorious in empirical macroeconometrics but, as Heckman documents, widespread in other fields like empirical labor economics. Absent stable structural parameters, the framework illustrated in figure 1 implodes. Heckman suggests that most of what occurred in the methodology of empirical economics since the mid-1960s represents a response to the perceived failure of the SEM program to uncover stable causal parameters.

Post-SEM Developments in Political Science

Political scientists did not suffer the demoralizing failures of the empirical macroeconomists. Nonetheless, many of the new developments in political methodology have followed or even imitated the post-SEM moves in economics, though sometimes the intellectual origins in the SEM approach are overlooked.

Broadly speaking, there are four such moves. The first (and most conservative) locates the failure of the SEM approach in *tools*. Proponents of this approach argue that simple linear models were too rigid or otherwise inappropriate for political data. Their approach emphasizes the development and use of more appropriate, powerful, or flexible tools—duration models, event count models, and general additive models. It also emphasizes more powerful methods for estimation, including computer intensive methods like bootstrapping or Markov Chain Monte Carlo (MCMC) methods from Bayesian statistics. Not surprisingly, the tools approach is extremely popular among political methodologists. This volume does not contain a tools-oriented essay—they tend to be rather technical—but many are available for interested readers.[2]

The second and third approaches are somewhat more radical. The second locates the failure of the SEM approach in *theory*. It argues that the social scientific theories underlying early efforts were too weak or ill

2. Here is a selection of recent essays and monographs for different models: duration models—Box-Steffensmeier 1998, Gordon forthcoming, and Therneau and Grambsch 2000; count models—King 1989 and Cameron and Trivedi 1998; bootstrapping—Davison and Hinckley 1997; general additive models—Hastie and Tibshirani 1990 and Beck and Jackman 1998; and MCMCs—Congdon 2001, Gelman et al. 1995, and S. Jackman 2000.

formed and the link between the empirical analysis and the theories was too tenuous to sustain well-grounded analysis. We pursue this response in the remainder of this chapter. The third approach locates the failure in *data*. It argues that structural estimation with nonexperimental data is often doomed to failure. Consequently, it focuses on acquiring much better data—whether from laboratory experiments, field experiments, or so-called natural experiments. Stronger data can allow one to establish clear causal effects, often without deploying much social scientific theory. The essay by Green and Gerber in this volume pursues this line of thought.

The fourth approach is perhaps the most radical. It takes a step away from the causal thinking at the center of the structural approach. It argues that identifying assumptions making a strong distinction between exogenous and endogenous variables are untenable. Hence, the best one can do is to stay close descriptively to the data and make short-term forecasts. This line of thinking leads to vector autoregression (VAR) approaches in time series and neural net or other highly black-box approaches in cross-sectional data. The fourth approach is not represented in this volume, but interested readers may consult, for example, Beck, King, and Zeng 2000.

The first three approaches tend to have different adherents, who sometimes disagree intensely. But all three approaches are broadly complementary. Few of their adherents would argue against deep theory, closely tied to empirical analyses employing appropriate tools and strong, on-point data. In our view, the fourth approach runs the risk of throwing out the social scientific baby with the methodological bathwater, but data description and forecasting have a place too. In sum, political methodology is more heterogeneous and less naive than it once was. Yet almost all of its practitioners remain strongly committed to the ideal of *causal inference in service to causal reasoning*.

This Essay

The remainder of this essay explores new efforts to link theory and data in what we call (for want of a better term) formal empirical (FE) work. In addition, we have constructed a web page with supplementary material (a link may be found at http://www.columbia.edu/~cmc1). This web page lists hundreds of FE articles, books, and working papers, classified by topical subject in political science. The topics range across voting and elections, international political economy, war studies and international relations, legislative studies, executive studies, judicial politics, democratization, a grab bag of topics in comparative politics, and many, many more. Collectively, these studies give the lie to the claim that formal models are never tested in political science. This canard was an overstated but nonetheless plausible description of the state of the discipline in 1985 or even 1990. It grossly misrepresents the practice of political science ten years later.

The essay has the following organization. In the next section, we explore the empirical content of formal models, using a simplistic model as an expository device. The following section provides thumbnail sketches of some interesting real examples. The last section presents an incomplete and prejudiced overview of the substantive accomplishments of FE work.[3]

◼ | The Empirical Content of Formal Models

When we say "social scientific theories underlying early efforts were too weak or ill formed, and the link between the empirical analysis and the theories too tenuous, to sustain well-grounded analysis," what do we mean? In this section, as a pedagogic device we construct a rather old-fashioned, tinker-toy formal model and show how to use it to structure empirical work. The model and empirical implementation illustrate in bare bones form the SEM approach, thereby providing a benchmark (or, perhaps, straw man). We then discuss why contemporary theorists view models of this kind as inadequate and how they are moving beyond them, and why some FE analysts see this style of empirical work as unsatisfactory and how they are attempting to forge stronger data-theory links. But we also discuss the virtues of inadequate models for structuring empirical work, for at some level, all models are inadequate.

A Motivating Example: Political Outcomes in a Democracy

What is the relationship between voters, interest groups, politicians, and political outcomes in a democracy? This is a central question in modern political science. Even a cursory summary of the many relevant literatures is beyond our scope. However, for purely pedagogic purposes, pluralist "theory" of the 1950s and 1960s affords a starting point. A caricature of pluralist notions is the parallelogram of forces: government policy reflects the vector of forces created by different pressure groups (Truman 1971 [1951]).

How might one formalize this parallelogram and use it to structure empirical work? The Chicago political economy models of pressure group politics represented an early effort to do so (Stigler 1971; Peltzman 1976; Becker 1983).[4] Most formal political theorists now see these models as in-

---

3. Morton's *Methods and Models* (1999) is a book-length exposition of many of the ideas in this chapter. Bates et al.'s *Analytic Narratives* (1998) provides a somewhat different take on FE work, stressing qualitative historical data.

4. Becker's version is rather different from Stigler's and Peltzman's. In particular, in his game theoretic formulation, interest groups are the actors. But both approaches, as well as more recent interest group models in political economy (e.g., Magee, Brock, and Young 1989) and rent-seeking models in public choice economics adopt a broadly similar, black-box approach to elections and political institutions.

adequate. But they afford a relatively painless entree to FE work, because their extremely simple structure allows a clear demonstration of the SEM approach.

In simplest and most schematic form, we imagine a single actor, the government, facing a political support function $s(z; \mathbf{x}_1)$ and a political opposition function $o(z; \mathbf{x}_2)$, where z represents a government policy (e.g., a tax, tariff, subsidy rate, or a liberalism-conservatism score for some complex policy). In addition, both support and opposition are functions of many other variables too ($\mathbf{x}_1$ and $\mathbf{x}_2$ respectively).[5] In the Chicago tradition, these functions are assumed to be everywhere twice continuously differentiable. In this sketch model, we imagine the government setting policy to maximize its net political support, that is, to maximize $n(z; \mathbf{x}_1, \mathbf{x}_2) = s(z; \mathbf{x}_1) - o(z; \mathbf{x}_2)$. Models in this tradition typically assume political support and opposition both increase with the level of the policy, but benefits do so at a decreasing rate while costs do so at an increasing one. Denoting the marginal change in s with respect to z by s' and the marginal change in that change with respect to z as s', and similarly for similar changes in o, it is as-

Figure 2 | Equilibrium in the Expository Example. z_1^* indicates the policy leading to maximum net support (that is, the greatest difference in "support" and "opposition").

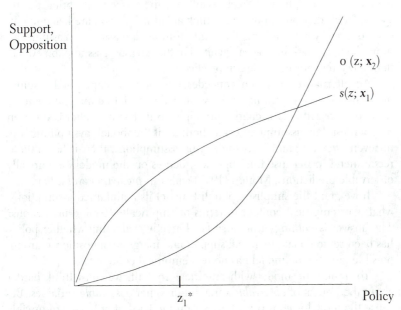

5. The bold notation, e.g., $\mathbf{x}_1$, denotes a vector, that is, a group of variables. In contrast, x_1 denotes a single variable.

sumed that $s' > 0$, $o' > 0$, $s'' < 0$, and $o'' > 0$. Standard techniques from calculus show that the solution to the government's policy-setting problem is characterized by choosing a level of policy z^* that equates marginal political support and marginal political opposition (that is, $s' = o'$) provided $s'' < o'$ at z^* (which is true by assumption). This answer has an intuitive plausibility: if the government set policy lower than z^*, it could increase its net political support by increasing the level of the policy, while if it set it higher than z^* it could increase net political support by lowering the level of the policy. Figure 2 illustrates the solution graphically.

What is the empirical content of this tinker-toy model? On the one hand, it appears to have a great deal of content in the form of extremely strong and highly contestable assumptions. Among these: there is some entity that can be meaningful considered a policy-setting actor, and it seeks to maximize its net political support; there is something that can be meaningfully thought of as political support, which increases in the level of the policy; and so on. From this perspective, a test of the model could come through direct empirical evaluation of the basic assumptions. On some occasions, as discussed in Morton 1999, *assumption evaluation* of formal models is quite feasible, as when basic assumptions are amenable to straightforward empirical evaluation. When practical, assumption evaluation is appealing because of its directness and simplicity. Unfortunately, many assumptions are not amenable to simple empirical evaluation. Moreover, all theorizing involves abstract concepts and maintained assumptions. Direct assaults on these frequently bring the response "it all depends on how you think about it," or "you are being too literal," or even "you are missing the point." Further discussion then assumes an unproductive, quasi-theological quality. For these reasons, assumption evaluation only rarely proves decisive in practice.

An alternative approach concedes the model's maintained assumptions and then asks, *granting these*, what is the model's empirical content? In some sense this is a charity principle. But it is also affords an even tougher test than assumption evaluation, for if the model says nothing useful even *after* we grant it its underlying assumptions, then it has little to recommend it. Because this approach focuses on the model's empirically observable predictions, Morton (1999) calls this *prediction evaluation*.

If we grant the simplistic pluralist model its maintained assumptions, what is its empirical content in terms of empirically testable predictions? The answer is *nothing*, at least so far. Directly evaluating whether policy has been set to equate marginal support and marginal opposition is an impossible task. So the model has no real empirical content yet.

To imbue the model with empirical content, we must think harder about the impact of *observable* variables on other *observable* variables. Because the model is constructed to explain the level of policy—presumably an observable quantity—z is an obvious candidate for one variable. Observable exogenous variables (or observable but logically prior intervening ones) supply the other candidates. Hence, the question the model must answer is, what is the impact of (observable) exogenous variable x on endogenous variable z? More specifically, in this simplistic pressure group model, the logical chain of inference will run: effect of (observable) exogenous variable x on either (unobservable) intervening variable political opposition o or (unobservable) political support s; effect of (unobservable) support s or opposition o on (observable) policy level z; hence, effect of (observable) exogenous variable x on (observable) endogenous variable z.

There is a direct link between this reasoning and the logic of the SEM approach. In fact, the pluralism model has exactly the form shown in figure 1, with s corresponding to y_1 and o corresponding to y_2. A full-scale empirical implementation of the structural model would use data to estimate the direct effects on support and opposition of the exogenous variables and the policy level z, and the direct effects of support and opposition on effect z. However, *given* the theory embodied in the structural model, one is justified in moving to the reduced form policy equation $z^* = z(x_1, x_2)$. This is exactly the logic of the last part of the preceding paragraph.

There are many plausible candidates for exogenous variables that enter the political support and opposition functions. Examples include the size of the groups that support or oppose the policy; the wealth of the members of those groups; the geographic dispersion of group members; the organization and procedural rules of the government, including the control of key proposal and veto points by supporters or opponents of the policy; the electoral rules that select politicians and allow supporters or opponents to reward or punish them for their actions; laws that control the use of money in politics; and so on. The silence of Chicago-style models on these points is their Achilles heel; momentarily, we discuss the consequences for theory and empirics of thinking hard about these matters. But to pursue the immediate pedagogic point, assume for the moment that somehow we specify that variable x_1 increases the government's political support at all positive levels of z while leaving political opposition unaffected.

Figure 3 illustrates the effect of x_1 on the support curve: as x_1 increases, the support curve rotates upward. In turn, this rotation changes the location of the point of maximum difference between the support and opposition curves. Consequently, z^* increases. Thus the theoretical result $\frac{\partial z^*}{\partial x_1} > 0$. (One reads this quotient as, "a marginal increase in x_1 strictly increases policy.") This hypothesis, and others like it, constitutes the empirical content of the model.

The figure illustrates the logic of the result but does not constitute a valid proof. A set of techniques called *comparative statics* supplies mathematical tools for carefully deriving such hypotheses from underlying assumptions.[6] In the interest of economy, we forgo a demonstration.

---

6. Explication of these tools may be found in most textbooks on mathematical economics and in many microeconomics texts. No political science textbook that we know exposits these techniques—a telling omission, perhaps.

Figure 3 | A Simple Comparative Static in the Expository Model. An increase in x_1 leads to a shift upward in the support curve, raising the level of the optimum policy from $z_1{}^*$ to $z_2{}^*$.

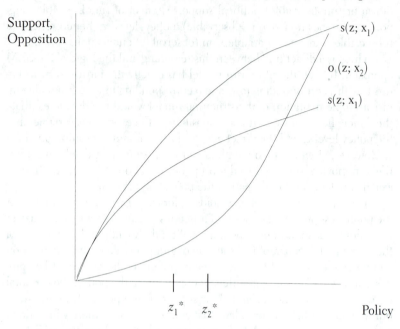

However, it is important to note that the formal comparative static result $\frac{\partial z^*}{\partial x_1} > 0$ is not like the "hypotheses" discussed in statistics texts, which might better be described as empirical conjectures or, bluntly, hunches about data. Rather, within FE work, a hypothesis *is a formal mathematical result derived from the basic assumptions of the model.* In our view, the epistemological status of a formally derived hypothesis is quite distinct from an informal hunch about data, however acute.

How would one use the simplistic pressure model to structure empirical work? Working within the SEM tradition, first one would show that the reduced form policy equation $z^* = z(x_1, x_2, \ldots, x_m)$ is linear in the x's (some might simply assume this). Hence, the theory specifies $z^* = b_0 + b_1 x_1 + b_2 x_2 + \ldots + b_m x_m$. To turn this equation into a stochastic relationship that one could take to actual data, one would add a convenient white noise error term (say, u) to create $z = b_0 + b_1 x_1 + b_2 x_2 + \ldots + b_m x_m + u$. The error term would be rationalized as reflecting omitted variables, measurement error in z, or inherent randomness in society. Given a modest quantity of data, the parameters in this stochastic relationship can be estimated via multiple linear regressions, yielding actual numerical estimates, with standard errors, for each of the parameters, for example, $\hat{b}_1$ for b_1. It is important to note that the formally derived comparative static hypotheses correspond *exactly* to the parameters in the linear reduced form equation; for example, in the linear reduced form equation $\frac{\partial z^*}{\partial x_1} = b_1$. Consequently, the estimated coefficients, for example, $\hat{b}_1$, and their standard errors allow direct statistical tests of the model's formally derived empirical content!

THE VIRTUES OF INADEQUATE MODELS

Before examining the shortcomings of this style of formal model as theory and this methodology as a template for FE work, it is worth pausing briefly to consider the virtues of even inadequate formal models *as devices for structuring empirical work.*[7] These virtues are almost nascent in the simple parallelogram model, which after all is just a pedagogic device. Yet one can still discern their outlines. Three virtues stand out: clarity, rigor, and unity.

1. Testable hypotheses formally derived from explicit assumptions have the advantage of *clarity.* An overt casual mechanism generates the predictions in a transparent way. This transparent chain of logic may lead to surprises. It may uncover unexpected ambiguities. It may even reveal inadequacies in the underlying assumptions and provoke a reformulation of the theory. But in all cases, everything is laid on the table for inspection.

2. Testable hypotheses formally derived from explicit assumptions have the advantage of *rigor.* Reasoning from abstract assumptions to concrete empirical predictions can be extremely difficult, particularly about situations in which strategic interactions, expectations, beliefs, and communication work in subtle ways. The mathematics of comparative statics makes it possible for an analyst to check rigorously for mistakes in his or her own reasoning. It also makes it possible for others to confirm that the analyst's reasoning is correct—the theoretical equivalent of replication in empirical studies.

3. Testable hypotheses formally derived from explicit assumptions have the advantage of *unity.* In nonformal empirical work, analysts frequently sketch the reasoning behind multiple empirical conjectures. But the reasoning behind one conjecture may have little in common with that behind another. The two may even employ contradictory assumptions. Using a formal model to explicitly derive empirical hypotheses prevents this absurd situation.[8] It may also become clear which hypotheses can only be

7. Morton (1999) addresses the issues in this section more carefully, supplying many concrete illustrations.

8. An illustration: Lax and Cameron (2001) present a formal model of opinion assignment on the Supreme Court and formally derive a series of hypotheses. Many of these hypotheses already exist in the nonformal empirical literature but are motivated by a series of ad hoc and sometimes contradictory assumptions. In contrast, Lax and Cameron show that all can be derived from a single set of assumptions (assigners are effort-constrained maximizers of policy) and the same causal mechanisms.

derived from a different set of assumptions, opening the way to a test of competing models.[9]

Paradoxically, many political scientists seem to see the clarity, rigor, and unity of formal modeling as its principal *disadvantage* for empirical work. For some researchers, a fuzzy, possibly erroneous prediction from a nonformal model with unknown assumptions is somehow preferable. The unspoken belief seems to be that if you keep your assumptions implicit or hidden (perhaps even from yourself), you haven't made any assumptions! Of course, this position is utterly mistaken. Behind the selection of facts and narrative strategy of every case study and behind every regression in every quantitative analysis, lie a multitude of assumptions. Refusing to face those assumptions and their logical consequences is no virtue.

TOWARD BETTER THEORY

In our exposition of SEM-like methods using the parallelogram model, we alluded several times to its inadequacy as theory. What's the problem, and what are the implications for FE work of building better theory?

The parallelogram model shoves most of the interesting politics in policymaking into the support and opposition functions, which are severely undertheorized. We concur with theorist David Austen-Smith's evaluation of the result:

> Questions about how and when influence is effective in majoritarian legislatures, about why some groups have "intrinsically more influence" than others, about how and why resources devoted by groups should map deterministically into a legislative decision and subsequent bureaucratic execution, about why groups adopt different patterns of activity (campaign contributions, informational lobbying, grass-roots activism, etc.), and so on, simply cannot be posed with the aggregate framework [i.e., an approach like the parallelogram model]. (1997, 299)

Austen-Smith concludes that better theory must be "micro-oriented" and more firmly grounded institutionally. Absent this kind of theory, it is hardly surprising that empirical estimates of parameters are unstable.

Austen-Smith's conception of better theory is widely shared among formal political theorists. It is exactly the direction contemporary formal theory is developing in American politics, comparative politics, and international relations. Within political economy, some researchers have preferred to retain very austere depictions of politics but embed them within quite elaborate models of economies, for example, of international trade. But others are moving to build models with strong micro- and institutional foundations.

9. Morton (1999) discusses alternative model evaluation at some length.

Models of this kind raise new issues for FE work. They are inevitably game theoretic. Comparative statics becomes subtler and more difficult.[10] The smooth, linear, continuous functions assumed in our expository example often go out the window. For example, in models using spatial theory, there can be distinct regimes. The behavior of political agents may differ dramatically across these regimes, but the conditions separating them may be difficult to observe empirically.[11] Problems like these raise a host of new and difficult methodological issues that need to be addressed in the years ahead.

FORGING STRONGER LINKS BETWEEN THEORY AND EMPIRICAL WORK

Our review of the current state of FE work in political science indicates that the average study consists of a simple formal model, used to gain insight into a phenomenon, followed by some empirical work (a case study or quantitative data analysis) loosely suggested by the model. The empirical work is inspired by the theory because the researcher uses the formal model to suggest relationships to look for and variables to employ. But the logical connection between theory and empirics is rarely closer than that. For example, the analyst may fail to derive formal comparative statics, consider the model's structural form, or ponder restrictions imposed on reduced forms. This inspired-by methodology gains the analyst the power of formal models for theorizing, which is no small matter. But it throws away the virtues of formal models for structuring empirical work. We predict FE work in political science will increasingly move away from the inspired-by methodology toward the SEM-like methods exposited above.

At the cutting edge of FE work, however, analysts are challenging certain elements of the SEM approach. We cannot hope to resolve the issues being raised, especially since many remain unsettled. But we can give the reader at least some sense of the debates.

Broadly speaking, two issues are at play:

- Is the formal model to be viewed as a *complete* model of the data generating process or as a *partial* model of the data in hand? The answer to this question determines the legitimacy of control variables and arbitrary assumptions about functional forms.

- What is the true nature of the stochastic element in the estimating equations, and what is its relationship to the formal model? The an-

10. A selection of essays addressing this point includes Dixit 1986, Fudenberg and Tirole 1984, and Hirshleifer and Rasmusen 1992.

11. A selection of essays addressing or illustrating this point includes Cameron, Segal, and Songer 2000, Lee and Porter 1984, Moraski and Shipan 1999, Segal and Wang 2001, and Spiller and Gely 1992.

swer to this question determines how the empirical evaluation of the formal model is to be interpreted.

Viewing a formal model as, at best, a partial picture of reality seems like common sense. Thus, it may seem natural to include control variables in the empirical analysis (control in the sense of multiple regression, not experimental manipulations), variables missing from the formal model. It may seem equally straightforward to specify tractable functional forms for estimating equations, so one can use standard statistical packages or results, even though one is unsure whether the specified form is compatible with the model's assumptions. But each such move drives a wedge between the formal model and the empirical analysis. At some point, the wedge becomes so large that an analyst is no longer using the formal model and certainly isn't testing it.

These problems have led some researchers to treat formal models *as if* they specify the complete data-generating process. In this view, if a variable isn't important enough to include in the formal model, it shouldn't be in the empirical work. Similarly, estimating equations should be strictly derived from the formal model, whose assumptions must be explicit enough and tractable enough to allow such derivations.

Similar issues arise concerning the stochastic elements in formal models versus estimating equations. Adding white noise error terms to deterministic models seems at best arbitrary and may lead to logical absurdities. For example, if the actors in a political situation understand that their world has a degree of randomness, this understanding is apt to affect their behavior. But if so, a deterministic formal model of the situation is simply wrong, and sprinkling white noise error terms in estimating equations won't fix it. This line of thought leads to incorporating stochastic elements directly in formal models (usually as games of imperfect or incomplete information) and carrying those stochastic elements through into the empirical estimation.[12]

These efforts may seem like an extraordinary effort simply to achieve logical consistency. Whether they are truly necessary remains controversial within the FE community.[13] In addition, such efforts often require considerable technical prowess. But they promise a payoff that political scientists have been slow to grasp. If full-blown, ultrarigorous structural models actually uncover stable causal parameters, *it becomes possible to perform theory-driven, data-sensitive policy experiments.*

12. Signorino (2000) provides a helpful analysis of these and related issues. In addition, Signorino has written software that estimates structural parameters for several commonly encountered strategic models, incorporating explicit, theoretically plausible stochastic elements. This software is currently available at http://www.rochester.edu/College/PSC/signorino/.

13. They have become quite common in economics, however. Illustrative examples are Donald and Paarsch 1996 and Rust 1994.

To see the point, refer again to figure 1. Let x_1 be a novel policy intervention (e.g., a change in a political institution, like voter registration requirements) with uncertain effect on y_1. If the *remaining* parameters in the model are truly stable, then one can use them to predict the effect of the policy intervention on outcome z, under different assumptions about the effect of x_1 on y_1. Theory-driven, data-grounded "what if" experiments about political and institutional reforms might well deserve the attention of citizens and policymakers. Where data and theory allow such "what if" experiments, the possibilities are exciting.

CONCLUSION

Nonformal empirical work can be informative and revealing. However, the move from nonformal empirical work to inspired-by studies lets the analyst tap into the power of formal models for the purposes of theorizing. The move from inspired-by work to SEM-like work gains the analyst clarity, rigor, and unity in empirical hypotheses. The move from SEM-like work to rigorous structural estimation opens the door to theory-driven, data-grounded policy and political analysis. In our view, each of these moves is valuable.

■ | Illustrative Examples

Space prohibits extensive consideration of real examples, which are invariably far more complex than the previous section's simplistic expository device. Instead, we supply some thumbnail sketches of illustrative examples that interested readers might wish to pursue. We group these into three categories. First are works that take seriously Austen-Smith's call for micro-oriented, institutionally rich theory seriously, and then match these models with SEM-like empirical methods. Second are works that retain somewhat summary models of politics but move toward rigorous structural estimation. Third are works that meld micro-oriented, institutionally rich theory with rigorous structural estimation. The selection of these examples is necessarily arbitrary; many more examples in all substantive fields of political science are compiled on the accompanying web page.

MICRO/INSTITUTIONALIST THEORY, SEM-LIKE METHODS

AMERICAN POLITICS EXAMPLE

Filer, Kenny, and Morton (1993) examine the effect of income on voter turnout. They propose a game theoretic model in which highly motivated elites within social networks in turn motivate others to vote. The authors solve the elites' strategic turnout game and then formally derive comparative static predictions about group turnout by income class. They test the formally derived predictions against country-level data from presidential elections.

COMPARATIVE POLITICS EXAMPLE

Huber and Shipan (2001) examine the efforts of legislators to control bureaucrats through the design of statutes, especially their specificity. The authors construct a formal model of statute design, incorporating substantial variation in institutional arrangements. They formally derive a series of comparative statics, focusing on issues like the extent of policy conflict between legislators and bureaucrats, the internal capacity of the legislature, conflict across chambers in bicameral legislatures, and the availability of nonstatutory means for controlling bureaucrats (e.g., legislative vetoes). They test the formally derived hypotheses with remarkable original data on the specificity of statutes. An interesting element of this analysis is its use of comparative data from the U.S. states simultaneously with cross-national data.

INTERNATIONAL RELATIONS EXAMPLE

Schultz (2001) uses FE work to examine information, threats, and war fighting—issues related to the Democratic Peace. The author builds a formal model of a unitary democratic state engaged in crisis bargaining. In the model, the monopoly party's actions convey information to domestic voters and a foreign bargaining partner. The critical comparative static comes from adding a domestic opposition party, whose support or opposition to the governing party also transmits information. Schultz shows that this institutional difference decreases the probability of war, decreases the likelihood that the democratic state makes threatening moves, and increases the effectiveness of the threatening moves it makes. Schultz then tests these and other propositions empirically, focusing on threatening moves and their effectiveness.[14]

INTERNATIONAL POLITICAL ECONOMY EXAMPLE

Mansfield, Milner, and Rosendorff (2000) examine the effect of regime type (democracy, autocracy) on the likelihood of concluding trade agreements. They construct a formal game theoretic model in which a government undertakes international agreements, which strategically convey information to voters about the government. The authors solve the game between the government and voters, allowing variation in the electoral

14. This choice is of methodological interest. The direct empirical evidence on the Democratic Peace appears inherently too weak to make a definitive determination of the existence and origins of this phenomenon (see, e.g., Gartzke 1998). Schultz's solution is to build a formal model that can accommodate the Democratic Peace but can itself be tested with different, less ambiguous data—an excellent demonstration of the power of joining formal models and empirical evaluation.

power of voters (hence, regime type.) They formally derive empirically testable hypotheses using comparative statics, which they test with data from recent trade agreements.

AUSTERE POLITICAL THEORY, STRUCTURAL ESTIMATION

INTERNATIONAL POLITICAL ECONOMY EXAMPLE

Goldberg and Maggi (1999) test one of the best-known models of endogenous tariff formation, the Grossman and Helpman model (1994), a lineal descendant of the early Chicago models. In this model, two interest groups simultaneously offer a government actor a schedule of campaign contributions, in exchange for trade protection. The government then chooses a level of tariffs. This somewhat austere model of politics is embedded in a fairly elaborate model of an economy. Goldberg and Maggi undertake a structural estimation of the Grossman and Helpman model. By solving the game between the groups and the government, they derive a specific functional form for the relationship between protection and key variables in the model. The stochastic element in the model is explicitly rationalized as measurement error. The authors estimate this equation using cross-sectional data from the United States for 1983, collected at the level of 3 digit SIC codes. The extensive use of sensitivity tests is a particularly interesting feature of the analysis.

MICRO-INSTITUTIONALIST THEORY, STRUCTURAL ESTIMATION

AMERICAN POLITICS EXAMPLE

Schachar and Nalebuff (1999) use a structural approach to empirically evaluate a group-voting model with some similarities to Filer, Kenney, and Morton's model. Shachar and Nalebuff use their formal model to construct a maximum likelihood function for estimating turnout levels by state in presidential elections. The maximum likelihood function's form is directly derived from the formal model's equations. It is quite complex, incorporating a multitude of parameters in the formal model. An interesting feature of the analysis is the use of a structural model to conduct a modest "what if" experiment, concerning higher levels of turnout. They argue that if turnout levels had been 100 percent, Republicans would never have gained the presidency in the post–World War II era.

COMPARATIVE POLITICS EXAMPLE

Diermeier and Merlo (1999) consider a formal, stochastic bargaining model of government formation and duration in parliamentary democracies. The authors derive a parametric structural estimating equation that is compatible with the formal model. They estimate this with maximum likelihood. The data come from 236 governments in 9 countries over the period 1947 to 1997. Using the estimated structural causal parameters, the authors undertake a series of policy experiments that examine the effects of different institutional rules (the investiture rule and the constructive vote of no confidence) on negotiation duration, government duration, and government size.

INTERNATIONAL RELATIONS EXAMPLE

Signorino and Tarar (2001) examine a straightforward incomplete information model of extended deterrence (that is, whether a country can prevent others from making war on its allies). They derive an estimating equation compatible with the formal strategic model, including the assumed form of incomplete information. They then structurally estimate the model using standard data sets on war. An interesting element of the paper is the use of the estimated structural causal parameters to interpret specific cases in recent history, for example, the Berlin blockade of 1948.

■ | **Substantive Contributions of Formal Empirical Work**

What are the substantive, as opposed to the methodological, contributions of FE work to political science?—for such is the basis on which FE work must ultimately be judged. We can only offer illustrations, for FE work has become so widespread and diverse that it extends far beyond our ability to evaluate knowledgeably. Nonetheless, these illustrations suggest that substantive accomplishments are relatively abundant and likely to grow.

In evaluating FE work, we use four standards:

1. *Understanding political phenomena and solving empirical puzzles.* Did the empirical work show that a particular formal model affords powerful analytic leverage over an important political phenomenon? In other words, did the FE work show the formal model has empirical punch?
2. *Advancing rich theory and stimulating new theory.* Did the empirical work lend support to a formal model or class of models or lead to the formulation or refinement of new theories or models? In other words, does the FE work lend credence or stimulate formal models with theoretical punch?
3. *Rejecting theory.* Conversely, did the empirical work allow the rejection of a plausible formal model or class of models, as offering relatively little empirical or theoretical leverage over an important political phenomenon?
4. *Improving public policy.* Did the FE work offer convincing grounds for better public policy? Did it work as applied political science?

SOLVING PUZZLES AND UNDERSTANDING THE WORLD OF POLITICS

- *The activity puzzle in congressional studies.* In legislative studies, a puzzle of the 1980s was statistical evidence indicating that congressmen's activities (e.g., constituency service) did not affect their reelection prospects. The FE work in Rivers and Fiorina 1989, employing structural estimation, solved the puzzle.

- *Outlier committees in Congress.* Determining the extent and distribution of outlier committees (ones in which the ideological or policy preferences of members differ significantly from those of the average member) was a central thrust of congressional scholarship in the 1990s. This work was stimulated by Gilligan and Krehbiel's formal models (1990) of legislative organization and Krehbiel's subsequent FE work (1990). The work led to a better understanding of the phenomenon.

- *Duverger's law.* Gary Cox's FE work on party structures remains a touchstone in comparative politics.

- *Veto politics.* Recent FE work on vetoes and veto threats arguably advanced the understanding of the presidential veto and interbranch bargaining in separation of powers systems (C. M. Cameron 2000; Groseclose and McCarty 2001).

- *Gridlock in separation of powers systems.* Krehbiel's FE work (1998) on policymaking in the United States establishes the standard for future work in this area.

- *Legislative delegation to agencies.* Epstein and O'Halloran's FE work (1999) established a coherent theoretical framework, demonstrated the feasibility of systematic empirical study, and documented plausible patterns in legislative delegation to agencies.

- *Referenda and legislative constraints.* E. R. Gerber's FE work (1999) on state referenda shows that the presence of this device forces legislators to remain more proximal to the desires of the median voter in the state.

ADVANCING RICH THEORY

- *The spatial model of elections.* The intellectual elegance of the spatial theory is clear. But FE work helped establish its practical usefulness and in turn further stimulated theorists (Enelow and Hinich 1984). But see "Rejecting Theory," below.

- *Duvergerian conceptions of party structure.* Again, primarily via Cox's landmark work. These theories have become a staple and an intellectual highlight of comparative politics.

- *The monopoly agenda setter model.* Work in FE employing and extending Romer and Rosenthal's monopoly agenda setter model confirms that it is a fundamental tool for thinking about separation of powers systems.

- *Regulatory politics.* The FE work of Chicago political economists fundamentally altered discussions of the subject and exerts considerable influence in IPE studies of tariffs and trade barriers.

- *Informational foundations of war.* Drawing on simple formal theory, Fearon (1995b) argued that war between states is most likely to result from informational, rather than material, factors. This mode of thinking represented a considerable departure from realist views (including ones in early formal models). Ongoing FE work has considerably elaborated and empirically tested these ideas.

Rejecting Theory

- *Downsian models of party politics.* Work in FE has consistently found a substantial degree of policy divergence between candidates, platforms, or policy proposals, even in circumstances that seem to approximate the conditions for the median voter theorem.

- *The separation-of-powers model of judicial independence.* The case is hardly closed, but accumulating evidence suggests that federal courts in the United States are not as responsive to Congress as simple separation-of-powers models seem to suggest (Segal 1997).

- *Political-business-cycle models.* This is a very complex area, but evidence seems to reject early, naïve theories, though the jury is still out on more-sophisticated models.

- *Commitment model of veto threats.* The evidence on veto threats clearly rejects the simplest version of commitment-type veto threats as a general explanation of how veto threats work.

Improving Public Policy

We know of few areas in which contemporary academic political science of any kind has demonstrably affected public policy. Consequently, we simply note a few FE research programs that have the clear *potential* to improve public policy.

- *Juries.* Formal work has suggested that changing jury voting rules might lead to different and perhaps better decision making. Experimental evaluation of different rules is under way (Guarnaschelli et al. 2000). If any of the modifications were adopted, the impact on millions of jurors as well as litigants might be enormous.

- *Campaign finance.* Ongoing FE work (e.g., McCarty and Rothenberg 1996) has obvious policy implications.

- *Sequential elections versus simultaneous elections.* Investigations in FE of sequential elections (e.g., as in presidential primaries sequenced over many states) versus simultaneous elections (e.g., one large national primary) have obvious policy implications (Morton and Williams 2001).

- *Redistricting.* Recent FE work on the policy consequences of racial redistricting has substantial policy implications (Shotts 2001).

- *Extended deterrence in international relations.* Signorino's use (1999) of a structural model to interpret historical cases of extended deterrence raises the possibility of using this and similar structural models for predictive and policy analytic purposes.

SUMMARY: THE TRAJECTORY OF FE WORK

We believe the trajectory of FE work is illustrated by advances in an area one of us knows well, turnout in elections. Turnout is a notoriously difficult topic for formal theory; hence, the growth of FE work in such stony soil provides a kind of critical test.

In this area, theorists first formulated a simple, deterministic model of turnout.[15] This model made stark point predictions, allowing evaluation through simple observation of errant observations. These were notoriously abundant. Yet, the initial, brutal collision between theory and data did not lead theorists to abandon their general framework. Instead, most formal theorists temporarily bracketed their failure to explain turnout and used the same general framework to study electoral choices, where it worked much better. Meanwhile, other theorists developed strategic models of the calculus of voting, incorporating the role of groups and the probabilistic nature of leader influence (see the discussion of Filer, Kenney, and Morton 1993, above). Empirical estimations in the SEM style supported the models' predictions. However, the initial rounds of evaluation of the second-generation models stopped short of rigorous structural estimation. Finally, structural estimation of a formal model—using empirical equations directly derived from the formal model's equations—showed support for the formal model as an explanation of voter turnout decisions, explaining nearly 90 percent of the variation in turnout (see Schachar and Nalebuff 1999, above). The structurally estimated models allowed analysts to make theoretically driven, empirically grounded political and policy predictions. Needless to say, this work is not the last word on the subject, but the trajectory in this difficult area is impressive.

15. For a review of the early turnout literature, see Morton 1991.

■ | Conclusion

We are both assertive and modest about the value of FE work. We are assertive in claiming that a thorough, ongoing confrontation between formal theory and data will improve both theory and empiricism in political science and take the discipline a step closer to a cumulative, sophisticated social science of politics. It will improve formal theory by providing feedback on which models have empirical bite and which do not, and thereby stimulate new theorizing along productive lines. It will improve empirical work by allowing analysts to exploit the clarity, rigor, and unity of formal models as devices for generating hypotheses and help them escape the degenerating inductivism so well parodied by the cognitive scientist Allen Newell in his essay, "You Can't Play 20 Questions with Mother Nature and Win." Finally, by providing the profession with a core of clear, deductive models of proven empirical bite, it will advance the discipline as a whole and gradually open the door to theoretically driven, empirically grounded political analysis.

We are assertive in calling for more (and better) FE work in empirical political science, but we also wish to be modest, for two reasons. First— simply to be clear—we do not claim, or for a moment believe, that FE work is the only way to go. The well-established, older style of descriptive and inductive empirical work—quantitative and qualitative—will continue to be essential for providing knowledge about the world of politics. In our view, the only sensible position is that nonformal and formal empirical analyses both contribute to a more robust political science. Similarly, pure formal theory—theory unaccompanied by data and statistical tests—is a precious commodity. Investing in formal theory is investing in our discipline's basic intellectual infrastructure. In fact, formal theory assumes an even greater importance when political scientists are serious about confronting theory with data. But a second and equally important cause for modesty is the difficulty of the enterprise. Combining theory and data involves more than mastering two different skill sets. It requires new ways of thinking and solutions to new methodological problems, problems that political scientists have hardly begun to face. Solving these problems will be a major challenge for the new century of political science.

Donald P. Green and Alan S. Gerber

Reclaiming the Experimental Tradition in Political Science[1]

The history of political science in the twentieth century is typically recounted as the saga of how behavioralism, statistics, and formal modeling freed the discipline from the clutches of storytellers and preachers. The protagonists are the founders of survey research organizations and research programs that emphasize conceptual rigor. Much of the storyline concerns the rise of various theoretical approaches—modernization, dependency, pluralism, rational choice. A lesser, though still important theme is the diffusion and refinement of quantitative methodology, spurred by the development of new statistical methods and easy availability of high-speed computers. Curiously, the most prominent accounts of political science's ascent from darkness into light scarcely mention the sine qua non of science, experiments (Waldo 1975; Easton 1968; Almond 1996).

Before the advent of surveys, formal models, regression analysis, and many other accouterments of modern political science, there existed a brand of political science that was based on field experimentation, the study of controlled interventions into the political world. An early example of such work was Harold Gosnell's study (1927) of voter registration and turnout in Chicago prior to the 1924 and 1925 elections. Gosnell gathered the names, addresses, and background information of thousands of voting age adults living in various Chicago neighborhoods. He then divided these neighborhoods into blocks, assigning certain blocks to the treatment condition of his experiment, which consisted of a letter urging adults to register to vote. Tabulating the registration and voting rates in his treatment and control group, Gosnell found his letter campaign to have produced a noticeable increase in political participation across a variety of ethnic and

1. The authors would like to thank the Institution for Social and Policy Studies, which helped support this research. We are grateful to Henry Brady, Nancy Burns, Gary King, Rebecca Morton, Karen Orren, and the editors for their helpful comments and suggestions. We are also grateful to Matthew Green, Barry McMillion, David Nickerson, and Jennifer Smith for their assistance.

demographic groups. Similarly, in 1935 George Hartmann conducted a controlled experiment in Allentown, Pennsylvania, in which he distributed 10,000 leaflets bearing either rational or emotional appeals for the Socialist Party. Examining ballot returns, Hartmann (1936–1937) found Socialist voting to be somewhat more common in wards that received emotional leaflets. Underhill Moore and Charles Callahan (1943), seeking to establish a "behavioristic jurisprudence," examined the effects of varying New Haven's parking regulations, traffic controls, and police enforcement in an effort to plot a "behavioral response function" for compliance with the law.

These early studies might be characterized as controlled field experiments, as distinct from randomized field experiments. Using certain decision rules, Gosnell, Hartmann, and Moore determined which blocks or wards were to receive their solicitations; they did not assign observations to treatment and control conditions on a purely random basis. In subsequent decades, as the statistical insights of R. A. Fisher (1935) took root in social science, experimentation became synonymous with randomized experimentation.[2] For example, Hovland, Lumsdaine, and Sheffield (1949), working in the Experimental Section of the Research Division of the War Department during World War II, conducted a series of randomized experiments examining the effectiveness of various training films designed to indoctrinate army personnel. While this type of research became more common in psychology than in political science and, at that, more common in the laboratory than in the field, experimentation in naturalistic settings was not unknown to political scientists. Eldersveld's classic study (1956) of voter mobilization in the Ann Arbor elections of 1953 and 1954 built randomization into the basic design of the Gosnell study. Assigning voters to receive phone calls, mail, or personal contact prior to election day, Eldersveld examined the marginal effects of different types of appeals, both separately and in combination with one another.

Although Eldersveld's research was widely admired, it was seldom imitated.[3] To the limited extent that political scientists thought at all about experiments, their prevailing impression was that field experiments typically involve local samples, very specific types of interventions, and little attention to the psychological mechanisms that mediate cause and effect. Each new development in data analysis, sampling theory, and computing seemed to make nonexperimental research more promising and experimentation less so. Once the principles of probability sampling took root in

2. Rubin offers the following definition of an experiment: "If Treatments E and C were assigned to the 2N units randomly, that is, using some mechanism that assured each unit was equally likely to be exposed to E as to C, then the study is called a randomized experiment or more simply an experiment; otherwise, the study is called a nonrandomized study, a quasi-experiment, or an observational study" (1974, p 689).

3. Blydenburgh (1971), Gertzog (1970), and Reback (1971) follow Eldersveld's lead but do not appear to have randomized their campaign interventions.

the early 1950s, surveys offered an inexpensive means by which to gather information from nationally representative samples. They could inquire whether the respondent had been contacted by parties or campaigns; indeed, they could examine the psychological mechanisms that might explain why canvassing leads to higher rates of political participation. Moreover, survey data could be mined again and again by researchers interested in an array of different questions, not just the causal question that animated a particular experiment. Surveys seemed superior not only as instruments of measurement and description but also as vehicles for causal analysis.

The narrow purview of experiments also ran afoul of the grand ambitions that animated the behavioral revolution in social science. The aims of science were often construed as the complete explanation of particular phenomena, hence the fascination with the R-squared statistic. To students of political behavior, surveys seemed well suited to the task of arranging explanatory variables—economic, demographic, social-psychological —within a "funnel of causality," to borrow a memorable phrase from *The American Voter* (Campbell et al. 1976 [1960]). Experiments, by contrast, could speak to causal questions a few variables at a time. And there could be little hope of using experiments to investigate the big variables that had captured the discipline's imagination—civic culture, identification with political parties, modernization, diffuse support for the political system.

Political science marched on, and field experiments all but fell out of the discipline's methodological kit bag. Riecken et al.'s monograph *Social Experimentation* (1974) mentioned only one field experiment conducted in political science after 1960, Robertson et al.'s study (1974) of the effects of televised public service announcements on behavior. The *Handbook of Political Science* (Brody and Brownstein 1975) devoted a chapter to "Experiments and Simulations." Although the authors praised field experiments, they could point to few examples. Most of these appeared in the young journal *Experimental Study of Politics*, which expired a few years later.

The overwhelming preponderance of empirical work in political science continues to rely on nonexperimental data. To be sure, recent years have witnessed a resurgence of interest in laboratory experiments dealing with topics ranging from media exposure (Iyengar and Kinder 1987; Ansolabehere and Iyengar 1995) to collective action (Dawes et al. 1986) to legislative bargaining (McKelvey and Ordeshook 1990). Surveys with randomized question content and wording have become increasingly common in the study of public opinion, particularly racial attitudes (Sniderman and Grob 1996; Hurwitz and Peffley 1998). Yet, the increasing number and sophistication of such studies has done little to generate interest in field experimentation. Bartels and Brady (1983) make no mention of field experimentation in their synopsis of the discipline's data collection methods. In Donald Kinder and Thomas Palfrey's edited volume *Experi-*

mental Foundations of Political Science (1993), only one of the twenty re-search essays may be described as a field experiment, Cover and Brumberg 1982. From our canvass of the *American Political Science Review, American Journal of Political Science, Journal of Politics,* and *Legislative Studies Quarterly,* it appears that field experiments were altogether absent from po-litical science journals during the 1990s.

Field experimentation is in our view far more valuable than this meager accumulation of scholarship would suggest. Conversely, nonex-perimental research is far more limited in scientific value than its prepon-derant market share would seem to imply. Nonexperimental analysis, after all, is only informative to the extent that nature performs a convenient ran-domization on our behalf or that statistical correctives enable us to approx-imate the characteristics of an actual experiment. Ironically, whether nonexperimental research succeeds in any particular application is diffi-cult to discern empirically without a true experiment against which to compare it.

Our aim is to call attention to the untapped potential of field experi-ments. Randomized intervention into real-world settings should be a prominent methodology in political science, not a curio from the disci-pline's distant past. This essay begins by explicating the essential features of experiments, showing why well-conducted experiments are typically more persuasive arbiters of causality than comparable nonexperimental re-search. Next, we discuss certain important considerations that arise in the design and analysis of experiments, in both the field and the laboratory. We then review the experimental literature in political science, giving special attention to field experiments as distinct from those conducted in artificial settings. After suggesting some potential applications of field experimenta-tion, we review the leading criticisms of experimental social science that have been advanced in other disciplines. Finding these criticisms wanting, we argue that field experimentation should occupy a central place in polit-ical science, particularly in subfields where randomized interventions con-front fewer practical difficulties.

■ | Why Experiments Are Valuable

Empirical investigation comprises an array of activities, and by focusing here on the investigation of cause and effect, we do not mean to disparage other activities of science that have to do with measurement, description, and classification. Case study, formal modeling, and large-*n* statistical analysis may also be fruitful ways to develop hypotheses. Our focus in this essay, however, is causal inference. How can one gauge the extent to which a change in one variable causes change in some other variable?

For concreteness, suppose one were interested in whether contributing money to a candidate's campaign increases an individual's access to a candidate after he or she is elected. One might formulate the hypothesis that, ceteris paribus, the more a person contributes, the greater the likelihood that he or she will be permitted to schedule an extended face-to-face conversation with the recipient of the donation. Suppose that we had data on how much, if anything, people contributed to candidates and whether their request for an extended meeting was granted. What must we assume about these data if we are to draw inferences about the *causal* influence of donations on access?

One key assumption concerns measurement. The amount of money that each donor contributes—the independent variable—must be measured precisely. Simply asking people to recall the size of their political donations might well generate unreliable data that could lead to biased inferences. A second and often more problematic assumption is that the size of the donation is uncorrelated with other factors that affect whether a meeting request is granted. Intuitively, we sense that nonexperimental data on campaign contributions are unlikely to satisfy this requirement. A candidate's friends and relatives are both more likely to donate to the campaign and to be granted a meeting. Even if donations per se had no effect, we might nonetheless observe a correlation between donations and access.

These threats to inference may be handled through statistical fixes of various sorts.[4] To summarize these technical results briefly, the ill effects of errors in variables (Greene 1997) may be corrected if researchers have redundant indicators of the constructs they seek to measure. The problem of spuriousness may be offset by one of two regression techniques. The *multivariate regression approach* introduces control variables, such that donations become uncorrelated with any remaining unmeasured determinants of the dependent variable. The *instrumental variables approach* makes use of variables that have the special property of being correlated with donations but uncorrelated with unobserved causes of the dependent variable. Instrumental variables remedy both spuriousness and measurement error. With the right statistical adjustments, experimentation is unnecessary.

Unfortunately, making the right statistical adjustments requires additional data and knowledge of the true model by which the data were generated. Much as one might like to use instrumental variables regression, finding valid instrumental variables is no mean feat: one must locate a variable that predicts donations but is known to be unrelated to omitted determinants of access. What this variable might be is far from obvious, nor would one necessarily know when one had found it. And much as one might like to build an ordinary least squares regression model that controls for all threats to unbiased inference, one must first know what the threats are and how to measure them. That will not be easy, particularly when what one knows is derived from prior nonexperimental research.

4. These techniques are discussed in any number of texts, such as Greene 1997.

Nonexperimental data analysis rests on stipulations about which statistical models are adequate. No clear stopping rules exist to tell researchers when their statistical manipulations have succeeded. Researchers analyze their data until they feel that the results are presentable. More to the point, no well-defined *procedure* exists by which causality is inferred from nonexperimental data. At best, researchers work to show that their conclusions are robust across a range of alternative models and hope that the true model was among those which they considered.

A quite different approach is to gather data in such a way as to satisfy the requirements for valid inference. The procedure for drawing valid causal inferences involves random assignment of observations to treatment and control groups.[5] To study the effects of campaign donations, one would randomly dole out contributions of varying size, then ask for meetings.[6] One might, for example, ask people who intend to make contributions totaling $50,000 to produce a list of 100 candidates that they might like to support, with the intention of contributing money to a random subset of the list. Randomization ensures that the those in the various experimental conditions differ only due to random chance, the properties of which are well understood in statistical theory. The larger the number of observations, the less likely it is that observed differences between treatment and control groups could be ascribed to chance correlation between the treatment condition and factors outside the researcher's control.

The beauty of experimentation is that one need not possess a complete theoretical model of the phenomenon under study. By assigning the level of contributions at random, one guarantees that the only factors that could give rise to a correlation between donations and other determinants of access occur by chance alone. The experimenter in effect interrupts a causal process of mutual adjustment and interaction among politicians and donors; this greatly simplifies the task of interpreting the experimentally induced correlation between donations and politicians' behavior. Rather than launch a complex multivariate analysis of the flow to and from donations and access, the researcher may obtain an unbiased assessment of the average treatment effect merely by cross-tabulating access by the size of contribution. Rudimentary data analysis replaces scores of regressions,

5. In some instances, random or near-random interventions occur naturally, as when individuals are chosen for jury duty or military service by lottery (Angrist 1988), required to comply with court-ordered desegregation on the basis of the first letter of their last names (Green and Cowden 1992), or assigned a ballot order in a near random sequence (Miller and Krosnick 1998). For a critique of this literature in economics, see Rosenzweig and Wolpin 2000.

6. Whether experiments such as this are ethical is a question to which we return below. To what extent does the research harm the subjects or the society? Of what benefit is the knowledge acquired from the experiment? How do the risks of this and other experiments compare with experiments that are deemed acceptable?

freeing the researcher from the scientific and moral hazards of data mining.

Granted, the design and interpretation of experiments benefit enormously from sound theoretical knowledge. To the extent that we begin the process with intuitions about the conditions under which money buys access, we may design experiments to isolate high-effect and low-effect circumstances. For example, it may be that donations to well-funded candidates buy little gratitude and hence access, whereas donations to candidates who are strapped for cash have greater effect. Theoretical reflection on the conditions under which a treatment is likely to be effective may prevent us from drawing inferences that do not generalize to other situations. The point remains, however, that the experimental method could discover these nuances merely by trial and error, as researchers make sense of why a sequence of experiments produces different results. By clarifying both what experimental results mean and what kinds of experiments are likely to yield the most fruitful parameter estimates, good theories provide a more efficient path to knowledge about the underlying causal process (see Rosenzweig and Wolpin 2000).

Experimentation resolves certain measurement problems, since the experimenter sets the level of contributions. In addition, experimental procedures can rescue the researcher from certain mishaps in the execution of the study. It sometimes happens that some experimental subjects do not receive the treatment (e.g., some letters containing campaign donations are returned due to incorrect addresses). The experimental data remain informative because the *intended* donation is correlated with the actual donation but uncorrelated with other determinants of access. For this reason, intended donations represent an ideal instrumental variable for purposes of regression analysis. Indeed, random assignment may be characterized as a procedure for generating the instrumental variables necessary for the unbiased estimation of causal parameters (Angrist, Imbens, and Rubin 1996).

Randomization, of course, does not rule out threats to inference. Threats to *internal validity* arise when the treatment does not exactly correspond to the construct that is envisioned as the independent variable. In the campaign donation example, the independent variable is the level of financial support from a person or group. If donors present their checks to the candidates in person, while nondonors have no contact with the candidates, the effects of the treatment will be an unknown combination of the effect of the money and the effect of the greeting. Issues of *external validity* concern the connection between the experimental results and the causal processes that operate in other times and places. Laboratory experiments that examine how undergraduate subjects behave in contrived situations may produce results that are deficient in this respect, depending on whether the causal process in question varies greatly across people and context.

The attractiveness of field experimentation stems from the fact that randomization is performed within a naturalistic setting. The field experiment described above, though fanciful, is very different from a corresponding laboratory study or simulation exercise. We are not asking subjects to envision themselves as elected officials deciding how to allocate their time. Nor are we proposing to study how actual officials answer requests for meetings that they know to be fictitious (cf. Chin, Bond, and Geva 2000). Field experiments involve real contributors and real candidates. While the result of this field experiment cannot tell us the influence of money on political access for all times and places, it speaks to the question of causality with far greater clarity and precision than alternative experimental or non-experimental methods.

■ | Field Experimentation In Practice

To this point, we have considered only a hypothetical case of field experimentation, constructed in order to illustrate the distinctiveness of this methodology. To appreciate the relative merits of experimental and nonexperimental research in practice, it is instructive to examine a research literature that features both types of investigation. One such literature concerns voter mobilization. As noted above, this line of research dates back to Gosnell's efforts (1927) to register voters and impel them to vote by mailing them leaflets. The experimental studies of Gosnell (1927) and Eldersveld (1956), as well as the lesser-known works of Adams and Smith (1980) and Miller, Bositis, and Baer (1981), have been overshadowed by a plethora of nonexperimental studies (Caldeira, Clausen, and Patterson 1990; Kramer 1970; Rosenstone and Hansen 1993; Wielhouwer and Lockerbie 1994; Huckfeldt and Sprague 1992). These studies use survey data to gauge whether citizens recall having been contacted by political campaigns. In a typical statistical analysis, voter turnout is regressed on reported campaign contact, controlling for background variables such as partisanship, interest in politics, and demographic characteristics.

This approach has certain inherent drawbacks: the researcher must take the respondent's word that reported contacts actually occurred. In addition, the vague way in which campaign contacts are defined and measured raises further concerns. Little attempt is made to distinguish between personal and phone contacts or between single and multiple contacts. Serious though these measurement concerns may be, they are in some sense eclipsed by even more serious doubts about spuriousness. If parties direct their appeals disproportionately to committed partisans and frequent voters, those most likely to vote will be most likely to receive political contact, and the apparent link between contact and turnout may be spurious.

As noted above, these problems may be corrected statistically. For example, one may use instrumental variables regression to offset biases associated with endogeneity and misreporting. None of the aforementioned studies uses instrumental variables regression. This gap in the literature is not hard to understand. Valid instrumental variables are difficult to think of, let alone find in existing surveys. To the wayward scholar in search of knowledge, the Oracle at Delphi commands: Before you may unlock the secret of mobilization's influence, you must find a survey measure that predicts campaign contact but is uncorrelated with unmodeled determinants of voting. Only very gifted scholars can hope to solve this inscrutable puzzle, and, even then, they will seldom do so to the satisfaction of their critics. The validity of any proposed instrumental variable ultimately rests on theoretical stipulations of one sort or another. Only randomization provides a *procedure* for generating instrumental variables that are valid on their face.

A more common but nonetheless problematic strategy for avoiding bias is to formulate an exhaustive model of voting, hoping that the control variables in the model eliminate any correlation between campaign contacts and the disturbance term. Unlike the instrumental variables approach, this methodological tack fails to address biases arising from mismeasurement. Given the seriousness of the measurement problem in most survey-based studies, this defect may altogether invalidate the results. Holding measurement concerns in abeyance, this statistical approach nonetheless requires a leap of faith. How can one tell whether a given set of control variables performs its appointed task? Sometimes scholars seem prepared to defend their models on theoretical grounds, but their choice of control variables often bears a more-than-coincidental resemblance to the measures that happened to be available in the survey they analyze. In the end, reasonable people may differ about whether a regression model is adequate to ward off bias. In the absence of such Delphic certitudes about the completeness of the model and the integrity of the available measures, the only way to determine the success of one's regression model is to conduct a randomized experiment to use as a benchmark.

In the case of voter mobilization, it would be very difficult to predict ex ante whether experimental and nonexperimental results would coincide. Random errors in survey measures of campaign contacts might lead to an underestimate of their effects; on the other hand, if voters are more likely than nonvoters to report campaign contact when none occurred, regression analysis might overestimate the effects of mobilization. If parties and candidates target likely voters, the effects will also be overestimated. Under these conditions, the sign and magnitude of the biases in nonexperimental research are knotty functions of variances and covariances of observed and unobserved determinants of the vote. Even if by some accident of fate the positive biases were to offset the negative, our ability to compare experimental and nonexperimental findings is hampered by the fact that most surveys fail to gauge the precise nature and frequency of campaign contact. It would be a stretch to call this exercise parameter estimation.

As it turns out, experimental studies have found that the effectiveness of mobilization varies markedly depending on whether voters are contacted by phone, mail, or face-to-face. Building on the earlier experiments of Miller et al. (1981) and Eldersveld (1956), Gerber and Green (2000b) conducted a randomized field experiment using a population of 30,000 registered voters in New Haven. These results indicate that personal canvassing boosts turnout by approximately 9 percentage points, whereas phone calls have no discernible effect. The intensity of the mobilization effort matters as well. Registered voters who were sent a series of mailings urging them to vote were more likely to go to the polls than those who were sent just one piece of mail. It could be said that these results corroborate earlier nonexperimental findings, in that both find statistically significant effects of campaign activities on voter turnout. Experimental studies, however, speak to the issue of causality with far greater clarity and nuance, because the researchers had control over the content of the campaign stimulus. It is fair to say that absent the various field experiments that have been conducted over the years, we simply would not know whether the nonexperimental results were trustworthy or artifactual.

These experiments, to be sure, have important limitations. Unlike survey-based research, which uses nationally representative samples, these field experiments involve just one region. And in contrast to many of the nonexperimental studies, which examine a variety of elections, the extant experimental literature examines certain municipal, primary, and midterm elections. Finally, the experimental intervention in this study was a nonpartisan get-out-the-vote drive, which leaves open the question of whether partisan mobilization efforts work differently.

Notice, however, that these limitations are different in kind from those associated with nonexperimental work. In the latter case, doubts about measurement and endogeneity leave us uncertain about whether correlation implies causation. Mobilization might cause voters to go to the polls, or its apparent influence might be artifactual. The limitations of the field experiments invite us to ask whether the demonstrated causation generalizes to other campaigns, times, and places. These limitations represent testable hypotheses about the conditions under which mobilization campaigns succeed. Thus, the solution to each of these concerns is to conduct additional experiments, gradually broadening the external validity of the experimental findings. Accordingly, Gerber, Green, and Green (2000) report the results of seven follow-up experiments examining the effects of partisan mobilization in off-year legislative and mayoral elections in various states, and follow-up studies involving millions of registered voters were conducted during the 2000 campaign. Through replication and extension, experimentation gradually resolves uncertainties about the scope of external validity. Eventually, this line of investigation will lead to a precise understanding of when and where mobilization works.

■ | Accumulation of Data and Knowledge

Certain crucial field experiments have the capacity to break deadlocks that arise when nonexperimental analyses produce conflicting results. Consider, for instance, the large research literature on campaign spending and election outcomes. By political science standards, this literature addresses a particularly well defined question (How much does campaign spending influence the election outcome?) using relatively straightforward independent and dependent variables (money and votes). This literature spans decades of elections. It focuses not only on House and Senate elections but also on state and local races. Most of the literature examines U.S. legislative races, but some attention is devoted to referenda and elections outside the United States. One noteworthy feature of this literature is that replication seems to do little to advance the ongoing methodological debate over the proper way to estimate the influence of spending on election outcomes. For example, Gary Jacobson (1990) has shown that his ordinary least squares regression model produces more or less the same results regardless of the year or type of election studied. According to Jacobson, challenger spending has a profound effect on the election outcome, while incumbent spending has little influence. Green and Krasno (1990) argue that Jacobson's regressions are not to be trusted because spending is endogenous—incumbents spend more as they become more vulnerable to defeat. Green and Krasno estimate an instrumental variables model instead and find that in election after election both challenger spending and incumbent spending matter greatly. Replicability is not at issue here. Depending on one's perspective, the data either reveal the same lawlike parameters over time or the same debilitating biases. Every election cycle brings a harvest of new data, yet this literature remains at a standstill.

One way to proceed is to argue about the validity of various modeling assumptions. Green and Krasno's answer (1990) to the problem of endogeneous spending is to estimate an instrumental variables regression in which past spending by the incumbent is the instrument. Abramowitz (1991) criticizes this model on the grounds that past incumbent spending might be correlated with omitted determinants of the vote, arguing instead that vulnerability can be measured by expert judgments and controlled statistically. Erikson and Palfrey (1998) argue that total spending by both candidates corrects problems caused by unobserved heterogeneity. Levitt (1994) claims that the best way to deal with endogenous candidate selection and spending proclivities is to focus on repeat races in which the same challenger and incumbent square off in successive elections. Gerber (1998) contends that candidates' personal wealth provides a valid instrument with which to assess the effectiveness of their campaign spending. Theoretical pluralism is reflected in the diversity of empirical findings. Levitt (1994) finds that expenditures by incumbents and challengers have little effect; Abramowitz (1991) says that only challenger spending matters;

Gerber (1998) and Erikson and Palfrey (1998) find both to be influential. These discrepant findings reflect the fact that each researcher makes different assumptions when modeling the relationship between money and votes. One senses that scholars have reached the limits of what they can learn from more modeling exercises of this kind.

The alternative to econometric analysis of nonexperimental data is to estimate the marginal effectiveness of spending through experimental intervention. Find a campaign that is willing to allow its campaign tactics to be randomized, and examine the effectiveness of its tactics on a dollar-per-vote basis. This resulting efficiency estimate may be compared to the econometric estimates derived from nonexperimental data. For example, Gerber (2000) notes that the regression models endorsed by Jacobson (1985) put the rate of return at approximately one vote for every $300 that an incumbent spends. The estimates of Green and Krasno (1988, 1990) and Gerber (2000) are closer to $15. The experimental literature on the effects of personal canvassing suggests a figure of approximately $20 per vote. Furthermore, Gerber's own experiment gauging the cost-effectiveness of an actual direct mail campaign on behalf of incumbents in New Jersey legislative elections estimates a return of one additional vote for each $40 spent. Assuming that the marginal returns of direct mail are not atypical of returns to campaign spending in general (a testable proposition), these results strongly suggest that Jacobson's regression models underestimate the efficacy of incumbent expenditures, while the Green and Krasno results overestimate it. Thus, experimentation offers a way out of deadlock that occurs when nonexperimental analyses produce contradictory results.

The literatures on campaign spending and voting may seem unrelated because they involve very different sorts of data. Studies of campaign spending tend to focus on aggregate data, evaluating the effects of incumbent and challenger expenditures on vote outcomes. Studies of mobilization, on the other hand, use survey data to ascertain whether voters are more likely to go to the polls in the wake of a campaign solicitation. The two literatures seldom cite each other. Yet, as one reflects on the experimental logic underlying the two literatures, it becomes apparent that they are closely intertwined. In some sense, this illustrates the value of experimental results. Once a solid fact is generated through an experiment, one must then reevaluate every theory with which it is inconsistent.

■ | **The Downstream Benefits of Experiments**

For decades, political scientists have argued that, ceteris paribus, acquiring education raises the probability of voting. This causal proposition is confirmed by a wide variety of surveys, most of which are cross-sectional in design. At a given point in time, well-educated people are more likely to vote than those with less education. As with any nonexperimental result, this empirical regularity could be spurious. It could be that unobserved factors that cause one to vote are also correlated with educational attainment. Education could, for example, simply be a marker of one's socioeconomic status, and critics of this proposition have noted that rising levels of education have failed to produce higher levels of voter participation. In an effort to guard against spuriousness, scholars who seek to gauge the effects of education sometimes build elaborate and exhaustive models of voter participation. Have these models expunged all threats to valid inference? Absent some kind of randomized intervention, it would be impossible to know.

An alternative approach would be to examine the consequences of experimental interventions that randomly alter educational attainment. This is not as outlandish as it might at first seem. Scholars outside political science regularly investigate the determinants of educational attainment. For them, educational attainment is a dependent variable of great importance, and from time to time, they launch randomized experiments to see whether they can lower dropout rates, improve college performance, and the like. For political scientists, educational attainment is an independent variable. Any experiment that alters educational attainment provides the wherewithal to assess its effects on voting behavior. Our shared interest in educational attainment creates an opportunity for significant cross-disciplinary collaboration. Returning to these studies, political scientists could graft new information about the subjects' voting behavior and examine whether the treatment and control groups vote at different rates.[7] One such experiment would arguably contribute more to the understanding of education's effects than scores of survey-based regressions.

The larger implications of the previous example bear emphasis. Political scientists would be well advised to take stock of experimentation in other disciplines. Unlike most calls for interdisciplinary collaboration, this one does not rest on the conviction that social sciences should become more theoretically or methodologically ecumenical. The intellectual forces that impel sociologists, psychologists, and economists to conduct randomized experiments are in some sense irrelevant. Any randomized intervention that genuinely produces different outcomes in treatment and control conditions is potentially useful to political scientists. Fortunately for us, other social science disciplines are less benighted about the benefits of randomized field experiments.

This argument also suggests a very different way of looking at the value

7. The estimator used to analyze these data would be an instrumental variables regression of vote on education, using random assignment as the instrument. Note that the key assumption of this model is that nothing about the experimental treatment per se directly affects turnout. This assumption would be violated if the education program in question explicitly advocated civic participation.

of laboratory experiments within political science. Studies that examine the influence of television news on political opinions are frequently criticized on the grounds that the subjects are not watching television in a "naturalistic" setting. (The experimental subjects might not ordinarily watch televised news; in the lab, they watch television news in groups and may have some sense that the experimenter expects them to attend to the content of the shows.) These criticisms lose much of their force when political attitudes, not media viewing, become the independent variable. Consider, for example, the frequently advanced proposition that favorable assessments of the country's economic performance increase the likelihood of voting for and identifying with the incumbent president's party (Kiewiet 1983; MacKuen, Erikson, and Stimson 1989). When a randomized media intervention alters subjects' economic optimism, do their vote intentions and party attachments change also (Cowden and McDermott 2000)? Although some questions remain about the representativeness of the sample of subjects used in laboratory experiments, randomization provides a powerful instrument for gauging the effects of opinion change. *The dependent variables in lab experiments make for highly informative independent variables in subsequent research.*

This way of thinking about experiments greatly expands the range of feasible experiments, because it also corrects for the fact that certain subjects may be unwilling or unable to receive the treatment. The central principle is that if one can intervene in such a way as to alter (randomly) the independent variable, one can study its effects on some dependent variable. Thus, for example, if one were interested in the effects of face-to-face canvassing on voter turnout, one could randomly determine whether a canvasser *attempted* to contact a possible voter. Only some proportion of these attempted contacts would succeed in producing an actual contact.[8] Attempted contact serves as the instrument in an instrumental variables regression of turnout on actual contact. Notice that this estimator provides unbiased estimates even when subjects in the treatment group decide whether to allow a contact to occur.

Having dispelled the commonly held view that experiments are feasible only insofar as the independent variable is under complete control of the experimenter, we briefly describe some potential experiments that might be inspired by recent nonexperimental work.

1. *Ballot structure and passage of school bond measures.* Glaser (2002) argues, in part on the basis of survey experiments, that the passage of ballot measures designed to raise money for schools is facilitated by breaking up an omnibus bond request into a series of smaller bond measures. Rather

---

8. One can then determine the effects of actual contact on voter turnout by comparing turnout rates among those canvassers attempted to contact (T) and those canvassers did not attempt to contact (C), and dividing by the proportion (p) of attempts that led to actual contact: $(T - C)/p$ (see Gerber and Green 2000b).

than ask voters to support a bond package to fund air conditioning, science facilities, and a new gymnasium, present voters with a series of bond measures, each of which funds a different component. A field experiment to test this hypothesis begins with a sample of school districts planning to present a bond measure to voters. This group is then divided randomly into treatment and control groups. School boards in the treatment group are informed of the potential benefits of structuring their bond request to voters in a disaggregated fashion. So long as some positive proportion of the treatment group acts on this information, an experimental assessment is possible.

2. *Deliberation and opinion change.* Fishkin (1995) argues that extended political deliberation over issues causes participants to become more circumspect and knowledgeable, which in turn changes their policy opinions. An experimental design would be to divide those who show up for a deliberative session into groups that discuss different issues. Another possibility, which makes use of the downstream randomization idea, is to select a list of potential invitees and divide it randomly into treatment and control groups. The treatment group receives invitations, while the control group does not. Only some of those who were invited will actually show up. After the deliberative session, survey both the treatment and control groups (disregarding whether someone actually showed up). The differences between the two groups, when divided by the rate at which people acted on the invitations, indicates the effect of deliberation.

3. *Interpersonal influence.* Huckfeldt and Sprague (1995) contend on the basis of survey evidence that friends influence each other's opinions. This proposition could be tested experimentally by drawing a sample of dyadic friendships. In the treatment condition, one member of each dyad is contacted by a political campaign urging them to vote in a particular way. No attempted contacts occur in the control group. After this intervention, the member of each treatment dyad is interviewed, as are members of the control group. By comparing the opinions of those who were contacted directly, those whose friends were contacted, and those who received neither direct nor indirect contact, we can ascertain the extent to which campaign appeals are transmitted through these personal networks.

4. *The consequences of civic engagement.* Putnam (2000) argues that participation in civic organizations increases the trust one places in other people and in political institutions more generally. This proposition could be tested by means of a field experiment in which civic groups (e.g., parent-teacher associations, the League of Women Voters, Rotary clubs) randomize the effort that they devote to recruiting certain prospective members. Only some of those who are recruited will become active participants, but the effects of participation may be gauged nonetheless by surveying the control group and prospective recruits. If Putnam's thesis is correct, after some period of time the treatment group should show higher levels of trust and political involvement.

The unifying idea behind each of these experiments is the notion that randomized interventions create ripple effects. So long as political scientists have at their disposal interventions that really work, such experiments are possible.[9] Thus, for example, one year after randomly increasing voter turnout through a nonpartisan mobilization campaign, Gerber, Green, and Shachar (2000) found that the treatment group continued to vote at higher rates than the control group, suggesting that the act of voting per se increases the likelihood of subsequent participation. Because experimentation is rare, downstream experimentation is very rare. But as the experimental tradition is rekindled, opportunities for downstream analysis will grow.

■ | The Case against Experimentation

Experiments are not without their limitations. Any fair assessment of their strengths must also take into account the many ways that experiments are thought to fall short as a research methodology in political science. Here we summarize the leading criticisms and offer our rejoinders to them.

INTERESTING MANIPULATIONS LIE BEYOND OUR REACH

The drawback that most readily comes to mind is the inability to manipulate key political variables of interest. It is difficult to imagine how one could randomly assign presidential and parliamentary regimes for the purpose of evaluating their relative strengths and weaknesses. Surely, world leaders cannot be persuaded to allow political scientists to randomize their foreign policies, systems of patronage, or prospects for retaining power. The really big social science variables—culture, economic development, ethnic heterogeneity—probably could not be manipulated even if political scientists were permitted to try. For this reason, it is commonly thought that political science can never hope to become an experimental science. And that is where the discussion of experimentation typically ends.

Before dismissing experimentation as impractical or trivial, one should bear in mind that our discipline lacks a clear sense of what kinds of experiments are feasible. Even in the field of political behavior, field experiments are so seldom contemplated, let alone proposed and executed, that the discipline has little track record with randomized interventions in naturalistic settings. The authors' own experience in this regard may be instructive. In

9. If, due to sampling error or threats to internal validity, the experimental intervention only seems to work but does not actually work, the downstream inferences will be misleading.

1998, we conducted a large-scale mobilization experiment using nonpartisan get-out-the-vote appeals. After examining the results, we wondered whether partisan appeals also stimulate voter turnout. On a whim, we contacted a political consulting firm and asked whether they would be willing to randomize a small portion of their mailing lists. Rather than send each household on their mailing list four mailers, the campaign would randomly divide its list so that some households would receive nine pieces of mail, others would receive four pieces, and a small group would receive none at all. On its face, this sounds like an unsuitable proposal. Why would anyone allow political scientists to meddle in this way? The answer is that this consulting firm was curious about how their mailings affected the election outcome, particularly the campaign mail that was negative in tone. Neither campaign managers nor political scientists have the slightest idea whether the most efficient use of their budget is to send four mailers to fellow partisans, nine mailers to a small set of ardent partisan supporters, or two mailers to everyone.

Political scientists have something to offer those who command discretionary resources and take an interest in cause and effect: expertise in designing randomized interventions and analyzing the statistical results. In general, we would argue that, at a minimum, *experimentation is possible whenever decision makers face constrained resources and are indifferent between competing ways of allocating them*. In such cases, decision makers may as well randomize their allocations, since they could then derive some useful information about the consequences of their actions.

Alternatively, they can roll out their intended intervention in stages or regions, again on a random schedule. Suppose that legislators wish to gauge the influence of a new policy, such as the elimination of a national maximum speed limit. One way to craft an experiment would be to phase in the implementation of the new speed limits, starting with randomly selected stretches of roadway. These treatment roads would otherwise be identical to the roads in the control group, and one could examine the consequence of short-term changes in speed limits on fatality rates, congestion, and other dependent variables. Again, randomized phase-ins can be justified on the grounds that administrative capacity does not allow for the simultaneous introduction of new policies everywhere.

The same principle applies to situations in which political actors work their way through lists. Suppose a political campaign seeks to canvass by phone 10,000 registered voters prior to an election. Given constraints of time and money, they do not know ahead of time whether they will be able to call all the numbers on the list. If the list is sorted in random order ahead of time, then any numbers that are not called constitute a randomized control group. If the campaign makes its way through the entire list, no experimental analysis is possible. But if some names are left over, the data become quite valuable. Indeed, even experiments in which only a small number of observations are assigned to the treatment or control group may produce more knowledge than a conventional large-n observational study.[10]

Experiment-minded political scientists, however, must be on hand to propose randomization to the powerful but indifferent. Otherwise, these actors will experiment in the colloquial sense of the term: they will try different courses of action in an effort to guess which one works best. Absent randomization, neither they nor we will be able to draw reliable inferences. So long as political scientists remain oblivious to field experimentation, opportunities for conducting this type of research will be missed.

Sometimes we can do better than merely make decision makers indifferent to our experimental intrusions. Political scientists from time to time acquire knowledge that decision makers would find useful. A good example is Glaser's findings (2002) concerning the disaggregation of school bond referenda. According to Glaser, public officials in Jackson, Mississippi, may have discovered a way to increase the chances of obtaining funds for schools. School boards desperate to win passage of bond issues may welcome the suggestion that they imitate the successful strategy deployed elsewhere. Outside of political science, field experiments routinely grow out of hypotheses about how to reduce domestic violence (Sherman and Berk 1984), increase tax compliance (Perng 1985), or decrease school dropout rates (Crain, Heebner, and Si 1992).

Such experiments are small by political science standards, but they can be used to bolster the investigation of large questions. Big theories hinge on a subsidiary propositions, some of which may be susceptible to experimentation. The microlevel phenomena (e.g., shirking, obedience, conformity) that are thought to undergird aggregate phenomena can be examined experimentally. Big theories may also be tested using institutions or collectivities of different scope and size. Theories that are crafted with an eye toward large units of analysis (e.g., the effects of committee jurisdictions in national legislatures) may be tested using analogous smaller units (e.g., local legislative bodies).[11] To the extent that political science strives to produce theories of general applicability, it makes sense to disaggregate theories and test their constituent parts.

In political science, there is a tendency to dismiss this line of reasoning as reductionist or naive. Our profession encourages students to go after big problems directly, rather than work up to them slowly via bench science.

10. This point may be demonstrated more rigorously by way of a mean-squared error comparison between two estimators, one based on a randomized experiment of size n_1 and the other a potentially spurious regression based on a nonexperimental sample of size n_2. As intuition would suggest, the more serious the expected biases of the latter, the greater the advantages of randomized experimentation.

11. To date, this line of argument has been used to justify decades of laboratory research on legislative behavior. This logic becomes all the more compelling as research moves from the lab into actual legislative arenas.

In fairness, both sides of this question base their methodological strategy on hunches about which type of science works best. It could be that the most fruitful way to learn about the causes of revolution, democracy, or economic development is to study them historically or comparatively. Such studies might produce a dramatic surge in our understanding of these phenomena. Another possibility is that the causes of these phenomena are too complex and intertwined to permit secure causal inference. More reliable inferences may be built up from studies of more basic aspects of these broad-gauged phenomena.

To draw an analogy to biological science, we observe that some leukemia researchers try to ascertain its causes by studying epidemiologic data, linking incidence of this disease to various environmental or genetic risk factors, while others focus their attention on cell biology. The former provides descriptive information about the scope of the problem and hints about its causes. The latter leads down many blind alleys but ultimately leads to an accumulation of secure knowledge about what leukemia is and how it comes about. Both, of course, are important and complementary endeavors, and neither has solved the mysteries of leukemia. But arguably bench science has contributed more to its understanding, as well as to the understanding of cognate phenomena. By investing so much of its resources in broad-gauge research, political science may be missing out on the rewards of basic science.

EXPERIMENTS ARE EXPENSIVE AND DIFFICULT TO EXECUTE

Harold Gosnell's voting experiments (1927) required a complete census of several neighborhoods, the creation and dissemination of direct mail, and the careful examination of voter turnout records. This sort of primary research goes beyond the experience of the typical political scientist. And if one were to contemplate the kind of randomized television campaigns that would test propositions about negative television advertising and opinion change or randomized campaign contributions and access to the legislative agenda, the costs would be astronomical. The benefits of such studies, meanwhile, must be discounted by the probability that something goes awry in the execution of the experimental manipulations. By this view, a cost-benefit analysis of nonexperimental and experimental research comes down in favor of the former.

It is difficult to say in advance what the payoff from field experimentation will be, but we strongly suspect it to be greater than for nonexperimental research, particularly in fields such as political behavior where large-scale randomized interventions are feasible. On the cost side, the overwhelming preponderance of funds flowing to political science supports nonexperimental research or lab experimentation. The situation in our discipline is in no way analogous to that in economics, where large-scale field experiments have in recent decades consumed immense sums of research money. Thus, even if one thought field experimentation promising only in certain subfields of the discipline, one would be forced to conclude that some reallocation of resources in its direction would be desirable.

Beyond this, we hasten to point out that field experiments may not be as expensive as one might think. The very forces that make possible large-n studies of voting behavior—computers, specialized databases, and campaign professionals—also make large scale experimentation easier now than in Gosnell's day. In the weeks leading up to the 1998 election, we conducted randomized experiments in which the people we hired distributed thousands of leaflets, sent tens of thousands of pieces of direct mail, made tens of thousands of phone calls, and visited thousands of addresses. These projects, which spanned three neighboring cities, cost a total of $50,000. In 1999, we worked with political campaigns that used randomized quantities of direct mail advocating the election of certain candidates. In order to gauge the effects of these mailers on vote preference, postelection interviews were conducted with members of the treatment and control groups in two different jurisdictions, again at a cost of $50,000. In 2000, we randomized the mail, phone, and canvassing campaigns of organizations working in more than a dozen states. The cost of these mobilization campaigns was largely borne by these organizations, which in turn hired us to conduct randomized experiments evaluating their efforts. The sums of money involved are not trivial, but taken together, they are less than a typical budget request for political surveys funded by the National Science Foundation.

EXTERNAL VALIDITY

The fact that field experiments are often confined to local areas raises important concerns about external validity. The experiments often purport to examine the consequences of a policy intervention (e.g., a nationwide campaign of mailings urging people to vote), but there may be many reasons why the results of a given experiment fail to generalize across time and place. Appeals to civic duty may seem hollow when elections are uncompetitive or in places where that theme has become hackneyed from overuse. Indeed, the fact that direct mail mobilizes voters once is no assurance that it will do so when repeated over a series of elections. Finally, one must be attentive to issues of scale. If a nationwide mobilization campaign were conducted, the campaign itself might draw attention (either positive or negative) that might augment or undermine the effectiveness of the intervention.[12]

12. Note that some of the nuisances that threaten the assessment of average treatment effects may represent research topics in themselves. For example, if those who are mobilized by the experimenter in turn mobilize others in the control group, these spillover effects will lead to biased inference. On the other hand, the relative size and proximity of those in the treatment and control groups may be varied, in an effort to detect the role of interpersonal influence.

These concerns are properly viewed as empirical questions. As is true for all empirical research projects, experimental studies raise questions that lead to new projects and modifications of the experimental procedures. Rather than assume the portability of experimental findings, researchers should replicate their studies in a variety of settings, devoting special attention to the consequences of repeating the same intervention over time. Before endorsing nationwide implementation, researchers should study interventions of varying magnitudes. The accumulation of knowledge from experiments proceeds by increments. In some sense, impatience for answers and reservations about extrapolation constitute arguments on behalf of experimentation far and wide.

EXPERIMENTAL RESULTS ARE DISJOINTED

There is no guarantee that experiments will generate solid facts. Experiments may generate contradictory results, either due to sampling error or to idiosyncracies in their design (Heckman and Smith 1995). As one looks to the field of social psychology, which has invested heavily in laboratory-based experimental research, one may be concerned about creating a tower of babel in which secure generalizations are reputed to be in short supply. Whether experiments will produce a knot of contradictions in political science is an empirical question that cannot be resolved until more of them are performed. In the meantime, it should be remembered that the reputation of social psychology is shaped in large part by the fact that in recent decades its experiments have been confined to the lab.

At the very least, field experiments offer the prospect of cumulative knowledge about the specific circumstances under investigation. For example, Cover and Brumberg (1982) use a randomized field experiment to demonstrate that baby books sent by members of Congress to new parents improved the standing of these representatives in the eyes of the recipients. Whether this finding speaks solely to the effectiveness of baby books or generalizes to franked mail or to all communications from elected officials, the point remains that this finding shows something important about a particular political tactic. By the same token, Miller, Krosnick, and Lowe's randomized study (2000) of direct mail appeals for campaign contributions shows that one raises the most money by mail that strikes an alarmist tone, claiming that the respondent's values are in jeopardy. Whether this finding generalizes to other instances of political fund-raising or political mobilization remains to be seen, but again it provides useful practical knowledge.

INTERNAL VALIDITY

Every experiment raises questions about the true causal agent at work. Indeed, an infinite supply of challenges might be directed at each experiment. Consider an experiment in which some voters are encouraged to vote through a face-to-face conversation while others are contacted by phone. Even if the scripts that are read to subjects are identical, they could be read in different ways, at different times of day, by different canvassers. Rather than chase down every possibility empirically, theory-based decisions must be made to winnow the range of possible hypotheses to a smaller number of plausible ones. Experimental inference is never entirely inductive, and therefore the contrast between experimental and nonexperimental inference is one of degree rather than kind.

This is a fair criticism. Generalizing from any particular experiment to some broader causal law requires an inherent theoretical leap. But like concerns about external validity, this concern suggests the need for more experimentation. The more ways in which a given experimental result is reproduced, the more implausible internal validity critiques become.

Much the same may be said about problems stemming from publication bias. To the extent that researchers report or journals publish only those results that achieve statistical significance, the research literature will become distorted by unrepresentative findings. Consistent with suspicions of publication bias, Gerber, Green, and Nickerson (2001) find that the larger the sample size, the smaller the reported effect of canvassing on voter turnout, presumably because smaller studies had to report larger effects in order to reach statistical significance. Certainly, when one reads that randomized prayer by outsiders on behalf of (unknowing) coronary patients improved their medical outcomes (Harris et al. 1999), one would like to see the result replicated before generalizations are advanced about the curative powers of prayer. The hypothesis of publication bias would suggest that the replication will find smaller effects than the published study.

Black-Box Causality

One common complaint about experimental research is that it often fails to generate a clear sense of why the intervention produced its effects. Canvassing leads to higher turnout, but why? Is it because people would otherwise forget to vote? Does it pique their interest in the election outcome? Does it evoke a sense of civic obligation? Or something else? None of the published experimental work on voter mobilization addresses these questions.

Although existing research tends to be deficient in this respect, experimentation need not involve black-box causality. Having demonstrated a causal connection between an intervention and an outcome, the researcher may take one of two approaches to figuring out why the effect occurs. The first approach is to vary the stimulus so as to isolate particular mechanisms. For example, if canvassing works because voters would otherwise forget Election Day, phone reminders should produce similar effects to messages delivered face-to-face. The audit experiments designed to measure the conditions under which employers, realtors, and commercial operations discriminate on the basis of race frequently take this approach (Yinger 1995).

An alternative approach is to measure the variables that are thought to mediate the relationship between the intervention and the dependent variable. For example, suppose it were thought that face-to-face canvassing increased voter turnout by fostering an interest in politics among those canvassed. For this proposition to be true, it must be the case that subjects in the treatment group show higher levels of political interest after the canvassing. One way to detect this change is to conduct a survey of those in the treatment and control conditions, examining whether the two groups differ with respect to political interest. If political interest does not differ across treatment and control conditions, it cannot be regarded as a mediating variable that explains why canvassing works. Although one would not invest in this kind of research until one were reasonably sure that interventions such as canvassing really work, in principle nothing prevents experimental researchers from investigating causal mechanisms.[13]

THE SCOPE OF EXPERIMENTAL POLITICAL SCIENCE

Randomized field studies threaten to narrow the range of research questions posed in the discipline. Research will be tailored to coincide with opportunities for experimental intervention, and the discipline will lose sight of the big questions that make the discipline vibrant and interesting. Hazardous though it may be to draw causal inferences from nonexperimental data, we typically have no alternative when studying international affairs, the presidency, or the federal budgetary process. To denigrate nonexperimental political science is tantamount to suggesting that the discipline move away from these important objects of inquiry.

In some sense, this criticism posits a trade-off between the significance of the research question and the reliability with which it can be answered. This distinction is misleading insofar as the discipline has relied almost entirely on nonexperimental research to answer all of its questions, both big and small. Field experiments are rare even in circumstances where they are feasible and well suited to the questions at hand.

Even if we grant the existence of this trade-off, it is far from clear how the discipline's effort ought to be allocated. Reflecting on several decades of scholarship, one might ask what we really *know* as a discipline? What sorts of causal propositions have been established with a high degree of

---

13. From a statistical standpoint, the investigation of causal mechanisms raises an identification problem when the number of randomized interventions is smaller than the number of potential intervening variables. It is useful, therefore, for an experiment to include a range of different treatments.

certainty? We have a great many useful descriptive generalizations, but what do we know about cause and effect? As we reflect on the triumphs that are likely to be reported in other chapters of this volume, it occurs to us that each of them is potentially subject to withering methodological critique. Democracy contributes to international peace. Globalization undermines the welfare state. Closed rules in legislative chambers encourage committee members to gather costly information. Each of these propositions may be true, but it is far from clear that nonexperimental analysis has powerfully shaped our prior intuitions about them.

To put it somewhat differently, suppose you strongly believe one of these propositions to be true. One day, you are presented with a regression based on nonexperimental evidence or the results of a laboratory experiment showing this proposition to be false. Naturally, your first inclination is to find fault with the regression model or the verisimilitude between the laboratory and the real world. Indeed, even a series of such studies might well leave you unpersuaded, since methodological uncertainties cloud them all. By contrast, it would be difficult to maintain a prior view in the face of disconfirmation by a succession of field experiments.

As we noted earlier, political science may be well advised to start small. Using reliable scientific methods such as randomized intervention, first answer basic research questions. Build gradually to larger propositions, as experimental evidence accumulates. We recognize that this vision of progress may be unappealing to a discipline that has long put its faith in two Stachanovite models of science. The first emphasizes the great leaps forward that come as the result of theory-driven breakthroughs. Each generation of political scientists holds out the hope that the right way of looking at politics will lay bare its inner workings. The second emphasizes the importance of asking big questions and throws researchers into the breach armed with nonexperimental data. It requires a combination of genius and good fortune to extract secure causal inferences from theoretical deduction or nonexperimental data. Few rules and procedures guide the scholar through these modes of scientific exploration. Experimentation, on the other hand, is a form of science bounded by procedures that greatly simplify the task of drawing inferences from statistical relationships. Experimentation benefits from genius and good fortune but does not require them.

Ethics

The previous concerns focused on the capacity of experiments to produce secure knowledge about the political world. A quite different kind of concern surrounds the ethics of field experimentation. Because experimentation involves intervention rather than passive observation, experimental researchers bear an ethical burden that nonexperimental researchers do not. Even if we accept that experimental analysis is a superior method for securing valid causal inferences, there remains the question of whether researchers are justified in altering the world in ways that may adversely affect those connected with the experiment.

This question cannot be answered in the abstract or by analogy to medical ethics, since political science experiments vary widely in terms of the risks that they present and the value of the knowledge that they might generate. Unlike medical experimentation, where a consensus of opinion understands risks in terms of health, political science experiments may involve contested values. Suppose one were considering an intervention thought to raise voter turnout. Do higher levels of voter turnout lead to more desirable political outcomes? Does going to the polls make voters themselves better off?[14]

A related concern focuses on the moral culpability of the researcher. Intuitively, we sense that it is acceptable to raise voter turnout but unacceptable to lower it. But suppose one honestly believes that desirable political outcomes follow from *lower* voter turnout, can one ethically perform experiments designed to reduce voter participation? And what about circumstances where one genuinely has no prior sense of whether an intervention is likely to be harmful or beneficial? The same question arises from ambivalent prior beliefs. Can one justify an experiment on the grounds that decision makers seem to be of two minds about the benefits of a particular course of action?

Like visitors to nature preserves, social scientists who seek to conduct randomized experiments in real-world settings should aspire to leave no footprints. Sometimes there is no practical alternative to intrusive intervention, but where possible, they should employ what we would term "minimally intrusive randomized designs." The hallmark of these designs is that randomization is conducted in ways that have no effect on social outcomes. As suggested earlier, such designs emerge naturally in situations where the scope of an intervention confronts resource constraints. Suppose an environmental organization seeks to recruit members from a list of local residents but lacks the resources to call everyone on the list. If the ordering of the names on the list is randomized before they work their way through it sequentially, the names they do not get to constitute a random control group. Similar designs may be devised for the randomization of waiting lists or the sequence in which a policy change is implemented. Experimental protocols still dictate which individuals or political units receive the treatment without affecting the overall flow of resources or risks.

Perhaps because the values associated with the objects of study are often controversial, ethical questions concerning experimentation with human subjects are typically reduced to procedural questions. For example,

---

14. Paradoxically, what harms are likely to befall subjects is itself an empirical question, possibly one that can only be answered satisfactorily through experimentation.

human subject committees generally require that investigators obtain consent waivers from participants in experiments. But unlike laboratory studies, field experiments in political science do not lend themselves to these kinds of contractual arrangements. As a practical matter, it is often impossible to obtain informed consent without irreparably damaging the study itself. It would be hard to envision a real-world voter mobilization experiment that first asked subjects to agree to participate in a study. The problem of informed consent grows even more unwieldy as one considers the possibility that an experiment could sway an election, an outcome that impinges on people outside the treatment and control groups.

One of the many complexities of characterizing ethical problems in procedural terms is that the interventions in some political science experiments (e.g., political expression and voter mobilization) may involve constitutionally protected political activity.[15] As citizens, political scientists have the right to engage in this kind of conduct, regardless of their motives. Yet there remains a lurking sense that scientific motivations render this kind of conduct inauthentic and suspect. Suppose, for example, that a political scientist were to run for public office. Suppose that she made ten or twenty such speeches at various churches in attempt to curry public support. We ordinarily would not question the rectitude of this behavior even if the churches were chosen at random. Now suppose that the political scientist were interested not simply in winning the election but also in figuring out how much these speeches affected the election outcome. Should we now regard this behavior in a fundamentally different moral light? Does it make sense to draw an ethical distinction between sincere interventions and experimental interventions?

Rather than focus on motives, one might contend that the standard for ethical responsibility comes down to the social cost and benefits of the research. Here, the discipline should reflect not only the ethical ramifications of experimentation but also the implications of continuing the current practice of attempting to acquire knowledge through nonexperimental observation. We earlier discussed the criticism that field experiments are incapable of tackling the big questions that most interest political scientists. In some sense, this limitation arises because, as Campbell (1969) laments, neither academics nor policymakers have embraced the ethic of an experimenting society in which proposed innovations are introduced and evaluated systematically. By resisting the idea that political institutions should be changed so that we can study their consequences, we preserve a conception of an organic polity untrammeled by science, but we neither reap the benefits of this potential knowledge nor suffer the social costs of obtaining it. In the meantime, the political world changes in ways

---

15. Another wrinkle is that, in some cases, political scientists themselves do not administer the intervention but rather suggest to other groups how they may structure their activities in ways that make for experimental evaluation.

that are neither informed by rigorous scientific inquiry nor readily interpretable through post hoc investigation.

■ | Conclusion

Political science is bristling with intriguing claims about cause and effect. Participation in church and civic organizations increases one's trust in other people (Putnam 2000). The more education one has, the more likely one is to vote (Wolfinger and Rosenstone 1980). As individuals' finances improve, they become more likely to vote for the incumbent president (Tufte 1978). Propositions such as these lie at the heart of some of the largest research literatures in the discipline. Yet, so far as we know, none of these well-known and extensively researched claims has been tested using field experimentation, and much the same could be said for the bulk of received wisdom in political science. Knowledge about the determinants of political behavior derives almost entirely from nonexperimental investigation.

Nonexperimental research is not valueless. The distinction between experimental and nonexperimental evidence should be viewed as a continuum. At one extreme lie observations that make for clear and direct causal interpretation. Experiments fall in this class when randomization is executed faithfully and precautions are taken to prevent threats to internal validity. Nearby are certain nonexperimental investigations that focus on the consequences of near-random variation, such as unexpected events or policies that divide groups arbitrarily. Toward the center of the spectrum are studies that make use of nonexperimental data but rely on robust statistical analysis. As we move toward the other end of the spectrum, the causal systems become more complex and statistical correctives less robust. Here the state of the discipline resembles monocrop agriculture, efficiently generating prodigious quantities of nonexperimental results but deeply vulnerable to an experimental intrusion that could consume the stock of received wisdom.

By arguing on behalf of field experimentation, we are recommending a fundamental change in the way that political scientists look at research. Not enough attention is paid to the prospects for randomized interventions or to the natural occurrence of near-random variation. At a minimum, political scientists should consider what kind of experiments would *in principle* test the causal propositions they advance. Even in those instances where such experiments are altogether infeasible, this exercise can prove extremely useful, as it clarifies the empirical claims while illustrating how the underlying concepts might be operationalized. Whether or not they are aware of it, social scientists rely on the logic of experimentation even when analyzing nonexperimental data.

Experimentation may also lead political scientists to rethink the way in which they interact with the outside world. Political scientists seek to devise and deploy procedures that lead to valid causal inference; political activists seek to bring about social change; interest groups and those who administer the state seek to understand how policies and programs operate. Each group has an interest in acquiring knowledge (although not necessarily in sharing it). Through collaboration, these groups in some sense strengthen each other. If scholars can demonstrate the practical benefits of science, those who have the discretion and resources to effect change will learn to seize opportunities to acquire knowledge.

The value of experimentation to political science as a profession should not be underestimated. As one reflects on the history of medicine during the last century, it is clear that the status and credibility of the profession soared once doctors began to prevent and cure disease. The demonstrable practical benefits of medicine made it reasonable to instruct an ill person to call a doctor. "Call a political scientist," on the other hand, sounds more like a gag line. Seldom do people in politics look to political scientists for practical advice, and to the extent that we are consulted, political actors have a nagging sense that our advice is scarcely better than their own intuitions. This is not an unreasonable suspicion, because we have seldom deigned to analyze the narrow questions that concern those engaged in day-to-day politics, nor have we attacked these or other problems with sufficient rigor to make the outside world sit up and take notice. Experimentation is not only a secure path to knowledge, it is a secure path to the kind of knowledge that is in great demand.

WORKS CITED

Abbott, Andrew. 1988. "Transcending General Linear Reality." *Sociological Theory* 6: 169–86.

Abbott, Andrew. 1997. "Of Time and Space: The Contemporary Relevance of the Chicago School." *Social Forces* 75: 1149–82.

Abbott, Andrew. 2001. *Time Matters: On Theory and Method*. Chicago: University of Chicago Press.

Abbott, Kenneth W., Robert O. Keohane, Andrew Moravcsik, Anne-Marie Slaughter, and Duncan Snidal. 2000. "The Concept of Legalization." *International Organization* 54 (3): 401–19.

Abelmann, Nancy, and John Lie. 1995. *Blue Dreams: Korean Americans and the Los Angeles Riots*. Cambridge: Harvard University Press.

Abney, Glenn, and Thomas P. Lauth. 1997. "The Item Veto and Fiscal Responsibility." *Journal of Politics* 59: 882–92.

Abram, Michael, and Joseph Cooper. 1968. "The Rise of Seniority in the House of Representatives." *Polity* 1: 52–85.

Abramowitz, Alan I. 1991. "Incumbency, Campaign Spending, and the Decline of Competition in United States House Elections." *Journal of Politics* 53 (1): 34–56.

Abramson, Paul R. 1983. *Political Attitudes in America: Formation and Change*. San Francisco: Freeman.

Abramson, Paul R., and John Aldrich. 1982. "The Decline of Electoral Participation in America." *American Political Science Review* 76: 502–21.

Abramson, Paul R., John Aldrich, and David W. Rohde. 1999. *Change and Continuity in the 1996 and 1998 Elections*. Washington, DC: CQ.

Acemoglu, Daron, and James A. Robinson. 2001. "A Theory of Political Transitions." *American Economic Review* 91 (4): 938–63.

Acemoglu, Daron, Simon Johnson, and James Robinson. 2000. "Colonial Origins of Comparative Development: An Empirical Investigation." NBER Working Paper 7771.

Achen, Christopher H. 1992. "Social Psychology, Demographic Variables, and Linear Regression: Breaking the Iron Triangle in Voting Research." *Political Behavior* 14: 195–211.

Ackerman, Bruce. 1980. *Social Justice in the Liberal State*. New Haven, CT: Yale University Press.

Ackerman, Bruce. 1991. *We The People*. Vol. 1, *Foundations*. Cambridge, MA: Belknap Press of Harvard University Press.

Ackerman, Bruce. 1993. "Crediting the Voters: A New Beginning for Campaign Finance." *American Prospect* 13: 71–80.

Ackerman, Bruce, and James Fishkin. 2000. "Deliberation Day." Delivered at the conference on Deliberating on Deliberative Democracy, 4–6 February, University of Texas, Austin. http://www.la.utexas.edu/conf2000/papers/Deliberation Day.pdf.

Adam, Heribert. 1971. *Modernizing Racial Domination*. Berkeley: University of California Press.

Adams, Julia. 1996. "Principals and Agents, Colonialists and Company Men: The Decay of Colonial Control in the Dutch East Indies." *American Sociological Review* 61: 12–28.

Adams, William C., and Dennis J. Smith. 1980. "Effects of Telephone Canvassing on Turnout and Preferences: A Field Experiment." *Public Opinion Quarterly* 44: 389–95.

Adler, Emanuel. 2002. "Constructivism in International Relations." In *Handbook of International Relations*, ed. W. Carlsnaes, B. Simmons, and T. Risse, 95–118. London: Sage.

Adler, Emanuel, and Michael Barnett, eds. 1998. *Security Communities*. Cambridge: Cambridge University Press.

Adler, Emanuel, and Peter Haas. 1992. "Conclusion: Epistemic Communities, World Order, and the Creation of a Reflective Research Program." *International Organization* 46 (1): 367–90.

Adler, Emanuel. 1997. "Seizing the Middle Ground. Constructivism in World Politics." *European Journal of International Relations* 3 (3): 319–63.

Adorno, Theodor. 1973. *Negative Dialectics*. Trans. E. B. Ashton. New York: Seabury.

Agamben, Giorgio. 1998. *Homo Sacer: Sovereign Power and Bare Life*. Trans. Daniel Heller-Roazen. Stanford, CA: Stanford University Press.

Agor, Westin. 1971. *The Chilean Senate: Internal Distribution of Influence*. Austin: Institute of Latin American Studies, University of Texas Press.

Agüero, Felipe. 1995. *Soldiers, Civilians, and Democracy: Post-Franco Spain in Comparative Perspective*. Baltimore: Johns Hopkins University Press.

Albert, Mathias. 1994. " 'Postmoderne' und Theorie der internationalen Beziehungen." *Zeitschrift für Internationale Bezie-hungen* 1 (1): 45–63.

Albert, Michel. 1993. *Capitalism versus Capitalism*. New York: Four Wall Eight Windows.

Aldrich, John H. 1993. "Rational Choice and Turnout." *American Journal of Political Science* 37: 246–78.

Aldrich, John H. 1994. "Rational Choice Theory and the Study of American Politics." In *The Dynamics of American Politics: Approaches and Interpretations*, ed. Lawrence C. Dodd and Calvin Jillson, 208–33. Boulder, CO: Westview.

Aldrich, John H. 1995. *Why Parties? The Origin and Transformation of Political Parties in America*. Chicago: University of Chicago Press.

Aldrich, John H., and David Rohde. 2001. "The Logic of Conditional Party Government: Revisiting the Electoral Connection." In *Congress Reconsidered*, 7th ed., ed. Lawrence C. Dodd and Bruce I. Oppenheimer. Washington, DC: CQ.

Alesina, Alberto, and Silvia Ardagna. 1999. "Tales of Fiscal Adjustment." *Economic Policy* 27: 487–545.

Alesina, Alberto, Reza Baqir and William Easterly. 1999. "Public Goods and Ethnic Divisions." *Quarterly Journal of Economics* 114: 1243–84.

Alesina, Alberto, and Allan Drazen. 1991. "Why Are Stabilizations Delayed?" *American Economic Review* 81: 1170–88.

Alesina, Alberto, Ricardo Hausmann, Rudolf Hommes, and Ernesto Stein. 1999. "Budget Institutions and Fiscal Performance in Latin America." *Journal of Development Economics* 59(2): 233–53.

Alesina, Alberto, and Eliana La Ferrara. 2000. "Participation in Heterogeneous Communities." *Quarterly Journal of Economics* (August) 847–904.

Alesina, Alberto, and Roberto Perotti. 1996. "Fiscal Discipline and the Budget Process." *American Economic Review* 86 (May): 401–7.

Alesina, Alberto, and Roberto Perotti. 1999. "Budget Deficits and Budget Institutions." In *Fiscal Institutions and Fiscal Performance*, ed. James R. Poterba and Jurgen von Hagen, 13–36. Chicago: University of Chicago Press.

Alesina, Alberto, Roberto Perotti, and Jose Tavares. 1998. "The Political Economy of Fiscal Adjustments." *Brooking Papers on Economic Activity* 1: 197–266.

Alesina, Alberto, and Lawrence H. Summers. 1993. "Central Bank Independence and Macroeconomic Performance: Some Comparative Evidence." *Journal of Money, Credit, and Banking* 25 (May): 151–62.

Alesina, Alberto, and Nouriel Roubini with Gerald D. Cohen. 1997. *Political Cycles and the Macroeconomy*. Cambridge: MIT Press.

Alesina, Alberto, and Enrico Spolaore. "On the Number and Size of Nations." *Quarterly Journal of Economics* 112: 1027–56.

Alesina, Alberto, and Howard Rosenthal. 1995. *Partisan Politics, Divided Government, and the Economy*. New York: Cambridge University Press.

Alesina, Alberto, and Guido Tabellini. 1990. "A Positive Theory of Budget Deficits and Government Debt." *Review of Economic Studies*: 403–14.

Alexander, De Alva Stanwood. 1916. *History and Procedure of the House of Representatives*. Boston: Houghton Mifflin.

Alexander, Gerard. 2000. "The Sources of Democratic Consolidation." Manuscript, University of Virginia, Charlottesville.

Alexander, Gerard. 2002. *The Sources of Democratic Consolidation*. Ithaca: Cornell University Press.

Allison, Graham. 1971. *The Essence of Decision: Explaining the Cuban Missile Crisis*. Boston: Little, Brown.

Allport, Floyd, and D. A. Hartman. 1925. "The Measurement and Motivation of Atypical Opinion in a Cerain Group," *American Political Science Review* 19: 735–60.

Almond, Gabriel A. 1988. "The Return to the State." *American Political Science Review* 82 (September): 853–74.

Almond, Gabriel A. 1990. *A Discipline Divided: Schools and Sects in Political Science*. Newbury Park, CA: Sage.

Almond, Gabriel A. 1996. "Political Science: A History of The Discipline." In *A New Handbook of Political Science*, ed. Robert E. Goodin and Hans-Dieter Klingemann. Oxford: Oxford University Press.

Almond, Gabriel A., S. Flanagan, and R. Mundt. 1973. *Crisis, Choice and Change*. Boston: Little, Brown.

Almond, Gabriel A., and Sidney Verba. 1963. *The Civic Culture*. Princeton, NJ: Princeton University Press.

Alstyne, Marshall Van, and Erik Brynjolfsson. 1997. "Electronic Communities: Global Village or Cyberbalkans." Unpublished manuscript, Massachusetts Institute of Technology, Boston.

Alt, James E., and Alberto Alesina. 1996. "Political Economy: An Overview." In *A New Handbook of Political Science*, ed. Robert E. Goodin and Hans-Dieter Klingemann. Oxford: Oxford University Press.

Alt, James E., and K. Alec Chrystal. 1983. *Political Economics*. Berkeley: University of California Press.

Alt, James, and Michael Gilligan. 1994. "The Political Economy of Trading States: Factor Specificity, Collective Action Problems, and Domestic Political Institutions." *Journal of Political Philosophy* 2 (2): 165–192.

Alt, James E., Margaret Levi, and Elinor Ostrom, eds. 1999. *Competition and Cooperation*. New York: Russell Sage.

Alt, James E., David Dreyer Lassen, and David Skilling. 2001. "Fiscal Transparency and Fiscal Policy Outcomes in OECD Countries." Unpublished paper.

Alt, James E., David Dreyer Lassen, and David Skilling. 2002. "Fiscal Transparency, Popularity, and the Scale of Government: Evidence from the States." *State Politics and Policy Quarterly* 2 (3).

Alt, James E., and Robert C. Lowry. 1994. "Divided Government, Fiscal Institutions, and Budget Deficits: Evidence From the States." *American Political Science Review* 88 (December): 811–28.

Alt, James E., and Robert C. Lowry. 2000. "A Dynamic Model of State Budget Outcomes under Divided Partisan Government." *Journal of Politics* 162: 1035–70.

Alt, James E., and Charles H. Stewart III. 1990. "Parties and the Deficit: Some Historical Evidence." Unpublished paper.

Althusser, Louis. 1969. *For Marx*. New York: Vintage/Random.

Althusser, Louis. 1971. "Ideology and Ideological State Apparatuses." In *Lenin and Philosophy and Other Essays*, ed. Louis Althusser. London: New Left.

Alvarez, Jose E. 2001. "Do Liberal States Behave Better?: A Critique of Slaughter's Liberal Theory." *European Journal of International Law* 12:183–246.

Alvarez, Sonia. 1990. *Engendering Democracy in Brazil: Women's Movements in Transition Politics*. Princeton, NJ: Princeton University Press.

Amenta, Edwin. 2002. "What We Know about the Development of Social Policy: Comparative and Historical Research in Comparative and Historical Perspective." In *Comparative Historical Analysis: Achievements and Agenda*, ed. James Mahoney and Dietrich Rueschemeyer. Cambridge: Cambridge University Press.

American Political Science Association. 1950. "Toward a More Responsible Two-Party System: A Report of the Committee on Political Parties." *American Political Science Review* 44 (Supplement, September): 1–96.

Ames, Barry. 1987. *Political Survival: Politicians and Public Policy in Latin America*. California Series on Social Choice and Political Economy. Berkeley: University of California Press.

Ames, Barry. 1995a. "Electoral Rules, Constituency Pressures, and Pork Barrel: Bases of Voting in the Brazilian Congress." *Journal of Politics* 57: 324–43.

Ames, Barry. 1995b. "Electoral Strategy under Open List Proportional Representation." *American Journal of Political Science* 39: 406–33.

Ames, Barry. 2001. *The Deadlock of Democracy in Brazil.* Ann Arbor: University of Michigan Press.

Amin, Samir. 1997. *Capitalism in the Age of Globalization.* London and New Jersey: Zed.

Aminzade, Ronald. 1992. "Historical Sociology and Time." *Sociological Methods and Research* 20: 456–80.

Amsden, Alice H. 1989. *Asia's Next Giant: South Korea and Late Industrialization.* New York: Oxford University Press.

Amsden, Alice H., ed. 1994. "Special Section on the East Asian Miracle." *World Development* 22 (4): 615–70.

Andersen, Kristi. 1975. "Working Women and Political Participation, 1952–1972." *American Journal of Political Science* 19: 439–53.

Andersen, Kristi. 1996. *After Suffrage: Women in Partisan and Electoral Politics before the New Deal.* Chicago: University of Chicago Press.

Andersen, Kristi, and Elizabeth A. Cook. 1985. "Women, Work, and Political Attitudes." *American Journal of Political Science* 29: 606–25.

Anderson, Benedict. 1991 [1983]. *Imagined Communities.* Rev. ed. London: Verso.

Anderson, Lisa, ed. 1999. *Transitions to Democracy.* New York: Columbia University Press.

Anderson, Lisa. 1986. *The State and Political Transformation in Tunisia and Libya, 1830–1980.* Princeton, NJ: Princeton University Press.

Anderson, Perry. 1974a. *Lineages of the Absolutist State.* London: Verso.

Anderson, Perry. 1974b. *Passages From Antiquity.* London: Verso.

Andrews, David. 1994. "Capital Mobility and State Autonomy: Toward a Structural Theory of International Monetary Relations." *International Studies Quarterly* 38 (2) 193–218.

Andrews, Josephine, and Kathryn Stoner-Weiss. 1995. "Regionalism and Reform in Provincial Russia." *Post-Soviet Affairs* 11: 384–407.

Angrist, Joshua D. 1988. "Estimating the Labor Market impact of Voluntary Military Service Using Social Security Data on Military Applicants." *Econometrica* 66 (2): 249–88.

Angrist, Joshua D., Guido W. Imbens, and Donald B. Rubin. 1996. "Identification of Casual Effects Using Instrumental Variables." *Journal of the American Statistical Association* 91 (June): 444–55.

Ansolabehere, Stephen, and Shanto Iyengar. 1995. *Going Negative: How Political Advertisements Shrink and Polarize the Electorate.* New York: Free Press.

Ansolabehere, Stephen, Shanto Iyengar, Adam Simon, and Nicholas Valentino. 1994. "Does Attack Advertising Demobilize the Electorate?" *American Political Science Review* 88: 829–38.

Antholis, William. 1993. "Liberal Democratic Theory and the Transformation of Sovereignty." Ph.D. diss., Yale University, New Haven, CT.

Appiah, Kwame Anthony. 1996. "Cosmopolitan Patriots." In *For Love of Country: Debating the Limits of Patriotism*, ed. Joshua Cohen. Boston: Beacon Press.

Appiah, Kwame Anthony, and Amy Gutmann. 1996. *Color Conscious: The Political Morality of Race*. Princeton, NJ: Princeton University Press.

Archer, Ronald, and Matthew Shugart. 1997. "The Unrealized Potential of Presidential Dominance in Colombia." In *Presidentialism and Democracy in Latin America*, ed. Scott Mainwaring and Matthew Shugart. Cambridge: Cambridge University Press.

Ardrey, Saundra. 1994. "The Political Behavior of Black Women: Contextual, Structural, and Psychological Factors." In *Black Politics and Black Political Behavior: A Linkage Analysis*, ed. Hanes Walton. Westport, CT: Praeger.

Arendt, Hannah. 1963. *On Revolution*. New York: Viking.

Arendt, Hannah. 1968 [1951]. *The Origins of Totalitarianism*. New York: Harcourt, Brace Jovanovich.

Arendt, Hannah. 1973 [1958] *The Human Condition*. 8th ed. Chicago: University of Chicago Press.

Aristotle. 1954. *Nichomachean Ethics*. Trans. Sir David Ross. London: Oxford University Press.

Aristotle. 1941. *The Basic Works of Aristotle*, ed. Richard McKeon. New York: Random House. 1275a.

Arnesen, Eric. 1994. " 'Like Banquo's Ghost, I Will Not Down': The Race Question and the American Railroad Brotherhoods, 1889–1920." *American Historical Review* 99: 1601–33.

Arreaza, Adriana, Bent E. Sorensen, and Oved Yosha. 1999. "Consumption Smoothing through Fiscal Policy in OECD and EU Countries." In *Fiscal Institutions and Fiscal Performance*, ed. James Poterba and Jurgen von Hagen. Chicago: NBER and University of Chicago Press.

Arrow, Kenneth J. 1963 [1951]. *Social Choice and Individual Values*. 2d ed. New York: Wiley.

Art, Robert J. 1996a. "Why Europe Needs the United States and NATO." *Political Science Quarterly* 11 (spring): 1–39.

Art, Robert J. 1996b. "American Foreign Policy and the Fungibility of Force." *Security Studies* 8 (summer): 7–42.

Art, Robert J. 1998–99. "Geopolitics Updated: The Strategy of Selective Engagement." *International Security* 23 (winter): 79–113.

Arter, David. 1984. *The Nordic Parliaments: A Comparative Analysis*. London: Hurst.

Ashley, Richard K. 1984. "The Poverty of Neorealism." *International Organization* 38 (spring): 225–86.

Aslund, Anders. 1995. *How Russia Became a Market Economy*. Washington, DC: Brookings.

Aspinwall, Mark D., and Gerald Schneider. 2000. "The Institutionalist Turn in Political Science and the Study of European Integration." *European Journal of Political Research* 38: 1–36.

Auerswald, David. 2000. *Disarmed Democracies: Domestic Institutions and the Use of Force.* Ann Arbor: University of Michigan Press.

Aumann, Robert J., and Michael B. Maschler. 1995. *Repeated Games with Incomplete Information.* Cambridge: MIT Press.

Austen-Smith, David, and Jeffrey S. Banks. 1996. "Information Aggregation, Rationality, and the Condorcet Jury Theorem," *American Political Science Review* 90 (March): 34–45.

Austen-Smith, David. 1997. "Interest Groups: Money, Information, and Influence." In *Perspectives on Public Choice,* ed. Dennis Mueller 296–321. Cambridge: Cambridge University Press.

Austen-Smith, David, and Jeffrey Banks. 1988. "Elections, Coalitions, and Legislative Outcomes." *American Political Science Review* 82: 405–22.

Austen-Smith, David, and Jeffrey Banks. 1990. "Stable Governments and the Allocation of Policy Portfolios." *American Political Science Review* 84: 891–906.

Austen-Smith, David, and William H. Riker. 1987. "Asymmetric Information and the Coherence of Legislation." *American Political Science Review* 81: 897–918.

Austen-Smith, David, and Jeffrey Banks. 1999. *Positive Political Theory.* Ann Arbor: University of Michigan Press.

Austen-Smith, David, and John Wright. 1992. "Competitive Lobbying for a Legislator's Vote." *Social Choice and Welfare* 9: 229–57.

Austen-Smith, David, and John Wright. 1994. "Counteractive Lobbying." *American Journal of Political Science* 38: 25–44.

Avant, Deborah. 1994. *Political Institutions and Military Change: Lessons from Peripheral Wars.* Ithaca, NY: Cornell University Press.

Avant, Deborah. 2000. "From Mercenary to Citizen Armies: Explaining Change in the Practice of War." *International Organization* 54 (winter): 41–72.

Avineri, Shlomo, and Avner De-Shalit. 1992. *Communitarianism and Individualism.* Oxford: Oxford University Press.

Axelrod, Robert. 1970. *Conflict of Interest.* Chicago: Markham.

Axelrod, Robert. 1984. *Evolution of Cooperation.* New York: Basic.

Axelrod, Robert, and Robert Keohane. 1985. "Achieving Cooperation under Anarchy: Strategies and Institutions." *World Politics* 38: 226–54.

Ayala, Louis J. 2000. "Trained for Democracy: The Differing Effects of Voluntary and Involuntary Organizations on Political Participation." *Political Research Quarterly* 53: 99–115.

Ayres, Ian. 2000. "Disclosure versus Anonymity in Campaign Finance." In *NOMOS XLII: Designing Democratic Institutions,* ed. Ian Shapiro and Stephen Macedo, 19–54. New York: New York University Press.

Bachrach, Peter. 1967. *The Theory of Democratic Elitism: A Critique.* Boston: Little, Brown.

Bachrach, Peter, and Morton S. Baratz. 1962. "Two Faces of Power." *American Political Science Review* 56 (4, December): 947–52.

Bachrach, Peter, and Morton S. Baratz. 1980. *Power and Poverty.* New York: Oxford University Press.

Bader, Veit. 1995. "Citizenship and Exclusion. Radical Democracy, Community, and Justice. Or, What Is Wrong with Communitarianism?" *Political Theory* 23 (2): 211–46.

Bader, Veit. 1997. "Fairly Open Borders." In *Citizenship and Exclusion,* ed. V. M. Bader, 28–60. London: Macmillan & Co.

Badie, Bertrand. 2000. *The Imported State: The Westernization of the Political Order.* Stanford, CA: Stanford University Press.

Baer, Denise, and David Bositis. 1993. *Politics and Linkage in a Democratic Society.* Englewood Cliffs, NJ: Prentice-Hall.

Bagehot, Sir Walter. 1966 [1867]. *The English Constitution.* With an introduction by R. H. S. Crossman. Ithaca, NY: Cornell University Press.

Bagwell, Kyle, and Robert Staiger. 1999. "An Economic Theory of GATT." *American Economic Review* 89 (1): 215–48.

Bailey, Michael, and David W. Brady. 1998. "Heterogeneity and Representation: The Senate and Free Trade." *American Journal of Political Science* 42: 524–44.

Bailey, Michael, Judith Goldstein, and Barry Weingast. 1997. "The Institutional Roots of American Trade Policy." *World Politics* 49 (3): 309–38.

Bailyn, Bernard. 1967. *The Ideological Origins of the American Revolution.* Cambridge, MA: Harvard University Press.

Baker, Paula. 1984. "The Domestication of Politics: Women and American Political Society, 1780–1920." *American Historical Review* 89: 620–47.

Baldez, Lisa, and John M. Carey. 1999. "Presidential Agenda Control and Spending Policy: Lessons from General Pinochet's Constitution." *American Journal of Political Science* 43: 29–55.

Baldwin, David A. 1989. *Paradoxes of Power.* New York: Blackwell.

Baldwin, David A., ed. 1993. *Neorealism and Neoliberalism: The Contemporary Debate.* New York: Columbia University Press.

Baldwin, Richard E., and Philippe Martin. 1999. Two Waves of Globalisation: Superficial Similarities, Fundamental Differences. NBER Working Paper 6904 (January).

Ball, Terence. 1995. "An Ambivalent Alliance: Political Science and American Democracy." In *Political Science in History: Research Programs and Political Traditions,* ed. James Farr, John S. Dryzek, and Stephen T. Leonard. New York: Cambridge University Press.

Balogh, Brian. 1991. "Reorganizing the Organizational Synthesis: Federal-Professional Relations in Modern America." *Studies in American Political Development* 5 (1): 119–72.

Baloyra, Enrique, ed. 1987. *Comparing New Democracies: Transition and Consolidation in Mediterranean Europe and the Southern Cone.* Boulder, CO: Westview.

Banaszak, Lee Ann. 1996. *Why Movements Succeed or Fail: Opportunity, Culture, and the Struggle for Women's Suffrage.* Princeton, NJ: Princeton University Press.

Baqir, Reza, 1999. "Districts, Spillovers, and Government Overspending." Unpublished paper.

Baran, Paul. 1957. *The Political Economy of Growth.* New York: Monthly Review.

Barber, Benjamin. 1984. *Strong Democracy.* Berkeley: University of California Press.

Barber, Benjamin. 1988. *The Conquest of Politics: Liberal Philosophy in Democratic Times.* Princeton, NJ: Princeton University Press.

Barber, Benjamin. 1995. *Jihad vs. McWorld.* New York: Ballantine Books.

Barber, Benjamin. 1998. *A Passion for Democracy: American Essays.* Princeton, NJ: Princeton University Press.

Barbieri, W. 1998. *Ethics of Citizenship: Immigration and Group Rights in Germany.* Durham, NC: Duke University Press.

Barnes, Harry Elmer. 1925. Introduction to *The History and Prospects of the Social Sciences,* ed. Harry Elmer Barnes, xv–xvi. New York: Knopf.

Barnett, Michael N. 1995. "Sovereignty, Nationalism, and Regional Order in the Arab States System." *International Organization* 49 (summer): 479–510.

Barnett, Michael N., and Jack S. Levy. 1991. "Domestic Sources of Alliances and Alignments: The Case of Egypt, 1962–73. *International Organization* 45 (summer): 369–96.

Baron, David P. 1991. "Spatial Bargaining Theory of Government Formation in Parliamentary Systems." *American Political Science Review.* 85: 137–65.

Baron, David P. 1993. "Government Formation and Endogenous Parties." *American Political Science Review* 87: 34–47.

Baron, David P. 1998. "Comparative Dynamics of Parliamentary Governments." *American Political Science Review* 92: 593–609.

Baron, David P., and John A. Ferejohn. 1989a. "Bargaining in Legislatures." *American Political Science Review* 83: 1181–206.

Baron, David P., and John A. Ferejohn. 1989b. "The Power to Propose." In *Models of Strategic Choice in Politics,* ed. Peter Ordeshook. Ann Arbor: University of Michigan Press.

Baron, Marcia. 1987. "Kantian Ethics and Supererogation." *Journal of Philosophy* 84 (May): 237–62.

Barro, Robert J. 1979. "On the Determination of the Public Debt." *Journal of Political Economy* 97 (October): 940–71.

Barro, Robert J. 1989. "The Ricardian Approach to Budget Deficits." *Journal of Economic Perspectives:* 37–54.

Barro, Robert J. 1991. "Economic Growth in a Cross-Section of Countries." *Quarterly Journal of Economics* 106: 407–43.

Barro, Robert J. 1997. *The Determinants of Economic Growth: A Cross-Country Empirical Study.* Cambridge: MIT Press.

Barro, Robert J. 1999. "Determinants of Democracy." *Journal of Political Economy* 107: 158–83.

Barro, Robert J., and David B. Gordon. 1983. "Rules, Discretion and Reputation in a Model of Monetary Policy." *Journal of Monetary Economics* 12: 101–21.

Barros, Robert. 2000. *Law and Dictatorship: Pinochet, the Junta, and the 1980 Constitution*. Unversidad de San Andreas, Chile.

Barry, Brian. 1989a. "Humanity and Justice in Global Perspective." In *Liberty and Justice: Essays in Political Theory*, ed. Brian Barry, 182–210. Oxford: Clarendon.

Barry, Brian. 1989b. *A Treatise on Social Justice: Theories of Justice*. Berkeley: University of California Press.

Barry, Brian. 1990. *Political Argument*. 2d ed. Herefordshire, UK: Harvester Wheatsheaf.

Barry, Brian. 1995. *A Treatise on Social Justice: Justice as Impartiality*. Oxford: Clarendon.

Barry, Brian. 1998. "Something in the Disputation Not Unpleasant." In *Impartiality, Neutrality and Justice: Re-Reading Brian Barry's Justice as Impartiality*, ed. Paul Kelly, 186–257. Edinburgh: Edinburgh University Press.

Barry, Brian. 2001. *Culture and Equality: An Egalitarian Critique of Multiculturalism*. Cambridge: Polity.

Barry, Brian. Forthcoming. *The Classics and Game Theory* (tentative title).

Bartels, Larry M., and Henry E. Brady. 1983. "The State of Quantitative Methodology." In *The State of the Discipline II*, ed. Ada W. Finifter. Washington, DC: American Political Science Association.

Barth, Fredrik. 1969. Introduction to *Ethnic Groups and Boundaries: The Social Organization of Culture Difference*, ed. Fredrik Barth, 9–38. Boston: Little, Brown.

Barzel, Yoram. 1989. *Economic Analysis of Property Rights*. New York: Cambridge University Press.

Barzel, Yoram. 2001. *A Theory of the State*. New York: Cambridge University Press.

Barzel, Yoram, and Edgar Kiser. 1997. "The Development and Decline of Medieval Voting Institutions: A Comparison of England and France." *Economic Inquiry* 35 (April): 244–60.

Basu, Kaushik. 1996. "Notes on Evolution, Rationality, and Norms." *Journal of Institutional and Theoretical Economics* 152: 739–50.

Bates, Robert. 1981. *Markets and States in Tropical Africa: The Political Basis of Agricultural Policies*. Series on Social Choice and Political Economy. Berkeley: University of California Press.

Bates, Robert. 1983. "Modernization, Ethnic Competition, and the Rationality of Politics in Contemporary Africa." In *State versus Ethnic Claims: African Policy Dilemmas*. Boulder, CO: Westview.

Bates, Robert H. 1988a. "Contra Contractarianism: Some Reflections on the New Institutionalism." *Politics and Society* 16 (2): 387–401.

Bates, Robert H. 1988b. *Towards a Political Economy of Development: A Rational Choice Perspective*. Berkeley and Los Angeles: University of California Press.

Bates, Robert H. 1997a. "Area Studies and the Discipline: A Useful Controversy." *PS: Political Science and Politics* 30 (2): 166–69.

Bates, Robert H. 1997b. *Open Economy Politics: The Political Economy of the World Coffee Trade*. Princeton, NJ: Princeton University Press.

Bates, Robert H. 2000. "The analytic narrative project." *American Political Science Review* 94 (3): 696–702.

Bates, Robert H., Rui J. P. de Figueiredo, and Barry R. Weingast. 1998. "The Politics of Interpretation: Rationality, Culture, and Transition." *Politics and Society* 26: 603–42.

Bates, Robert H., Avner Greif, Margaret Levi, Jean-Laurent Rosenthal, and Barry Weingast. 1998. *Analytic Narratives.* Princeton, NJ: Princeton University Press.

Bates, Robert H., and Anne O. Krueger. 1993. *Political and Economic Interactions in Economic Policy Reform.* Cambridge, MA: Blackwell.

Bates, Robert H., and Da-Hsiang Donald Lien. 1985. "A Note on Taxation, Development and Representative Government." *Politics and Society* 14 (1): 53–70.

Bauboeck, Rainer, 1998. "The Crossing and Blurring of Boundaries in International Migration: Challenges to Social and Political Theory." In *Blurred Boundaries: Migration, Ethnicity, and Citizenship*, ed. Rainer Bauboeck and John Rundell. Vienna: Ashgate Publications.

Bauboeck, Rainer. 1994. *Transnational Citizenship: Membership and Rights in International Migration.* Cornwall, UK: Elgar.

Baumgartner, Frank R., and Bryan D. Jones. 1993. *Agendas and Institutions in American Politics.* Chicago: University of Chicago Press.

Bawn, Kathleen. 1993. "The Logic of Institutional Preferences: German Electoral Law as a Social Choice Outcome." *American Journal of Political Science* 37 (4): 965–89.

Bawn, Kathleen. 1999a. "Constructing 'Us': Ideology, Coalition Politics, and False Consciousness." *American Journal of Political Science* 43: 303–34.

Bawn, Kathleen. 1999b. "Money and Majorities in the Federal Republic of Germany: Evidence for a Veto Players Model of Government Spending." *American Journal of Political Science* 43: 707–36.

Baxter, Sandra, and Marjorie Lansing. 1983. *Women and Politics: The Visible Majority.* Rev. ed. Ann Arbor: University of Michigan Press.

Bayart, Jean-François. 1993. *The State in Africa: The Politics of the Belly.* London and New York: Longman.

Baynes, Kenneth. 1992. *The Normative Grounds of Social Criticism: Kant, Rawls and Habermas.* Albany: State University of New York Press.

Baynes, Kenneth. 2000. "Rights as Critique and the Critique of Rights: Karl Marx, Wendy Brown and the Social Function of Rights." *Political Theory,* 28 (4): 451–69.

Bayoumi, Tamim, and Barry Eichengreen. 1995. "Restraining Yourself: The Implications of Fiscal Rules for Economic Stabilization." *IMF Staff Papers*: 32–48.

Bazenguissa-Ganga, Remy. 1999. "The Spread of Political Violence in Congo-Brazzaville." *African Affairs* 98: 390.

Beard, Charles. 1913. *An Economic Interpretation of the Constitution.* New York: Macmillan Co.

Beardsworth, Richard. 1996. *Derrida and the Political.* London: Routledge.

Beblawi, Hazem, and Giacomo Luciani, eds. 1987. *The Rentier State.* London: Croom Helm.

Beck, Nathaniel L, and Simon Jackman. 1998. "Beyond Linearity by Default: Generalized Additive Models." *American Journal of Political Science* 42 (2): 596–627.

Beck, Nathaniel L., and Jonathan N. Katz. 1995. "What to Do (and Not to Do) with Time-Series-Cross-Section Data." *American Political Science Review* 89: 634–47.

Beck, Nathaniel L., Gary King, and Langche Zeng. 2000. "Improving Quantitative Studies of International Conflict: A Conjecture." *American Political Science Review* 94 (1): 21–35.

Beck, Nathaniel L., and Richard Tucker. 1996. "Conflict in Space and Time." Paper presented at the annual meeting of the American Political Science Association, San Francisco.

Beck, Nathaniel L., and Richard Tucker. 1998. "The Democratic Peace: Monadic or Dyadic?" Paper presented at the annual meeting of the International Studies Association, Minneapolis, MN.

Beck, Ulrich. 1998. *Was Ist Globalisierung?* 2d ed. Frankfurt: Suhrkamp.

Beck, Ulrich, Anthony Giddens, and Scott Lasch. 1994. *Reflexive Modernization: Politics, Tradition and Aesthetics in the Modern Social Order.* Oxford, UK. Polity.

Becker, Gary. 1983. "A Theory of Competition Among Pressure Groups for Political Influence." *Quarterly Journal of Economics* 98: 371–400.

Becker, Gary. 1992. "An Open Door for Immigrants—The Auction." *Wall Street Journal,* 14 October, A14.

Beckwith, Karen. 1986. *American Women and Political Participation: The Impacts of Work, Generation, and Feminism.* New York: Greenwood.

Bederman, Gail. 1995. *Manliness and Civilization: A Cultural History of Gender and Race in the United States, 1880–1917.* Chicago: University of Chicago Press.

Beiner, Ronald, ed. 1995. *Theorizing Citizenship.* New York: State University of New York Press.

Beissinger, Mark R. 2001. *Nationalism and the Collapse of the Soviet State.* New York: Cambridge University Press.

Beitz, Charles. 1988. "Equal Opportunity in Political Representation." In *Equal Opportunity,* ed. Norman E. Bowie, 155–74. Boulder, CO: Westview.

Bellin, Eva. 1994. "The Politics of Profit in Tunisia: Utility of the Rentier Paradigm?" *World Development* 22 (3): 427–36.

Bellin, Eva. 2000. "Contingent Democrats: Industrialists, Labor, and Democratization in Late-Developing Countries." *World Politics* 52 (2): 175–205.

Bellin, Eva. Forthcoming. *Stalled Democracy: Capitalist Industrialization and the Paradox of State Sponsorship in Tunisia, the Middle East, and Beyond.* Ithaca, NY: Cornell University Press.

Bendix, Reinhard. 1967. "Tradition and Modernity Reconsidered." *Comparative Studies in Society and History* 9 (3): 292–346.

Bendix, Reinhard. 1977. *Nation-Building and Citizenship.* Berkeley: University of California Press.

Bendix, Reinhard. 1978. *Kings or People: Power and the Mandate to Rule.* Berkeley: University of California Press.

Bendix, Reinhard. 1962. *Max Weber: An Intellectual Portrait*. Garden City, NY: Anchor.

Bendix, Reinhard. 1964. *Nation-Building and Citizenship*. New York: Wiley.

Bendix, Reinhard, ed. 1973. *State and Society: A Reader in Comparative Political Sociology*. Berkeley: University of California Press.

Bendor, Jonathon, and Dilip Mookerjee. 1987. "Institutional Structure and the Logic of Ongoing Collective Action," *American Political Science Review* 81: 129–54.

Bendyna, Mary E., and Celinda C. Lake. 1994. "Gender and Voting in the 1992 Presidential Election." In *The Year of the Woman: Myths and Realities*, ed. Elizabeth Adell Cook, Sue Thomas, and Clyde Wilcox, Boulder, CO: Westview.

Benedict, Michael Les. 1973. *The Impeachment and Trial of Andrew Johnson*. New York: Norton.

Benhabib, Seyla. 1986. *Critique, Norm, and Utopia: A Study of the Foundations of Critical Theory*. New York: Columbia University Press.

Benhabib, Seyla. 1992. *Situating the Self: Gender, Community and Postmodernism in Contemporary Ethics*. New York: Routledge.

Benhabib, Seyla. 1996a. *The Reluctant Modernism of Hannah Arendt*. Thousand Oaks, CA: Sage.

Benhabib, Seyla. 1996b. "Toward a Deliberative Model of Democratic Legitimacy." In *Democracy and Difference: Contesting the Boundaries of the Political*, ed. Seyla Benhabib. Princeton, NJ: Princeton University Press.

Benhabib, Seyla. 1999a. "Citizens, Residents and Aliens in a Changing World: Political Membership in the Global Era." *Social Research* 66 (fall): 709–44.

Benhabib, Seyla. 1999b. *Kulturelle Vielfalt und demokratische Gleichheit. Die Horkheimer Vorlesungen*. Frankfurt: Fischer Verlag.

Benhabib, Seyla. 2001. *Transformations of Citizenship. Dilemmas of the Nation-State in the Global Age*. Baruch de Spinoza Lectures. Amsterdam: Van Gorcum.

Benhabib, Seyla, Judith Butler, et al. 1995. *Feminist Contentions: A Philosophical Exchange*. New York and London: Routledge.

Benhabib, Seyla, ed. 1996. *Democracy and Difference*. Princeton, NJ: Princeton University Press.

Bennett, Andrew, and Alexander George. 1997. "Process Tracing in Case Study Methods." Paper Presented at the MacArthur Workshop (October), Harvard University, Cambridge, MA.

Bennett, D. Scott, and Allan C. Stam III. 1998. "The Declining Advantages of Democracy." *Journal of Conflict Resolution* 42: 344–66.

Bennett, Jane. 1996. "How Is It, Then, That We Still Remain Barbarians? Foucault, Schiller, and the Aestheticization of Politics." *Political Theory* 24: 653–669.

Bennett, Jane. 2001. *The Enchantment of Modern Life*. Princeton, NJ: Princeton University Press.

Bennett, Linda, and Stephen Earl Bennett. 1986. "Political Participation: Meaning and Measurement." In *Annual Review of Political Science*, ed. Samuel Long. Norwood, NJ: Ablex.

Bennett, Linda, and Stephen Earl Bennett. 1989. "Enduring Gender Differences in Political Interest." *American Politics Quarterly* 17: 105–22.

Bennett, Stephen Earl. 1986. *Apathy in America, 1960–1984: Causes and Consequences of Citizen Political Indifference.* Dobbs Ferry, NY: Transnational.

Bennett, Stephen Earl, and David Resnick. 1990. "The Implications of Nonvoting for Democracy." *American Journal of Political Science* 34: 771–802.

Benoit, Kenneth. 1996. "Democracies Really Are More Peaceful (in General): Re-examining Regime Type and War Involvement." *Journal of Conflict Resolution* 40: 636–57.

Benoit, Kenneth, and John Schiemann. 2001. "Institutional Choice in New Democracies: Bargaining over Hungary's 1989 Electoral Law." *Journal of Theoretical Politics* 13: 153–82.

Bensel, Richard. 1990. *Yankee Leviathan: The Origins of Central State Authority in America, 1859–1877.* New York: Cambridge University Press.

Bensel, Richard. 2000. *The Political Economy of American Industrialization.* New York: Cambridge University Press.

Bentley, Arthur F. 1895. *The Units of Investigation in the Social Sciences.* Philadelphia: American Academy of Political and Social Science.

Bentley, Arthur F. 1908. *The Process of Government.* Chicago: University of Chicago Press.

Bentley, Arthur F. 1969. *Makers, Users, and Masters.* Syracuse, NY: University of Syracuse Press.

Berelson, Bernard, Paul Lazarsfeld, and William McPhee. 1954. *Voting.* Chicago: University of Chicago Press.

Berger, Suzanne, and Ronald Dore, eds. 1996. *National Diversity and Global Capitalism.* Ithaca, NY: Cornell University Press.

Berg-Schlosser, Dirk, and Gisèle De Meur. 1994. "Conditions of Democracy in Interwar Europe: A Boolean Test of Major Hypotheses." *Comparative Politics* 26 (3): 253–80.

Berk, Gerald. 1994. *Alternative Tracks: The Constitution of American Industrial Order, 1865–1917.* Baltimore: Johns Hopkins University Press.

Berlin, Isaiah. 1990. *The Crooked Timber of Humanity: Essays in the History of Ideas.* London: Murray.

Berman, Sheri. 1997a. "Civil Society and the Collapse of the Weimar Republic." *World Politics* 49 (3): 401–29.

Berman, Sheri. 1997b. "Civil Society and Political Institutionalization." *American Behavioral Scientist* 40: 562–74.

Bermeo, Nancy. 2002. *Ordinary People in Extraordinary Times: Citizens and the Collapse of Democracy.* Princeton, NJ: Princeton University Press.

Bernhard, Michael. 1997. "Semipresidentialism, Charisma, and Democratic Institutions in Poland." In *Presidential Institutions and Democratic Politics: Comparing Regional and National Contexts,* ed. Kurt von Mettenheim. Baltimore: Johns Hopkins University Press.

Bernhard, William. 1998. "A Political Explanation of Variations in Central Bank Independence." *American Political Science Review* 92 (2): 311–27.

Bernhard, William, and David Leblang. 1999. "Democratic Institutions and Exchange-Rate Commitments." *International Organization* 53 (1) 71–97.

Bernheim, B. Douglas. 1989. "A Neoclassical Perspective on Budget Deficits." *Journal of Economic Perspectives*: 55–72.

Bernstein, Richard. 1993. *The New Constellation: The Ethical-Political Horizons of Modernity/Postmodernity.* Cambridge: MIT Press.

Bernstein, Richard. 1998. "The Retrieval of the Democratic Ethos." In *Habermas on Law and Democracy: Critical Exchanges,* ed. Michel Rosenfeld and Andrew Arato. Berkeley: University of California Press.

Berry, Jeffrey M. 1999. *The New Liberalism: The Rising Power of Citizen Groups.* Washington, DC: Brookings.

Berry, Jeffrey M., Kent E. Portney, and Ken Thomson. 1993. *The Rebirth of Urban Democracy.* Washington, DC: Brookings.

Bertram, Christoph. 1995. *Europe in the Balance: Securing the Peace Won in the Cold War.* Washington, DC: Carnegie Endowment for International Peace.

Besley, Timothy, and Anne Case. 1995. "Does Electoral Accountability Affect Economic Policy Choices? Evidence from Gubernational Term Limits." *Quarterly Journal of Economics* 110 (August): 769–98.

Besley, Timothy, and Rohini Pande. 1998. "Read My Lips: The Political Economy of Information Transmission." London School of Economics and Political Science Suntory Center Discussion Paper, TE/98/355.

Best, Geoffrey. 1986. *War and Society in Revolutionary Europe, 1770–1870.* New York: Oxford University Press.

Betts, Richard K. 1999. "Must War Find a Way? A Review Essay." *International Security* 24 (fall): 166–98.

Bhagwati, Jagdish N. 1986. "Rethinking Trade Strategy." In *Development Strategies Reconsidered,* ed. John P. Lewis and Valeriana Kallab, 91–104. New Brunswick, NJ: Transaction.

Bianco, William T. 1994. *Trust: Representatives and Constituents.* Ann Arbor: University of Michigan Press.

Bienen, Henry, John Londregan, and Nicolas van de Walle. 1995. "Ethnicity and Leadership Succession in Africa." *International Studies Quarterly* 39:1–25.

Bienen, Henry, and Nicholas Van de Walle. 1991. *Of Time and Power: Leadership Duration in the Modern World.* Stanford, CA: Stanford University Press.

Biersteker, Thomas J. 2002. "Forms of State, States of Sovereignty: The Changing Meanings of State, Sovereignty and Territory in the Theory and Practice of International Relations." In *Handbook of International Relations,* ed. W. Carlsnaes, B. Simmons, and T. Risse. London: Sage.

Biersteker, Thomas J., and Cynthia Weber, eds. 1996. *State Sovereignty as Social Construct.* Cambridge: Cambridge University Press.

Billig, M., and H. Tajfel. 1973. "Social Categorization and Similarity in Intergroup Behavior." *European Journal of Social Psychology* 3: 27–52.

Binder, Sarah A. 1997. *Minority Rights, Majority Rule: Partisanship and the Development of Congress.* Cambridge: Cambridge University Press.

Binder, Sarah A. 1999. "The Dynamics of Legislative Gridlock, 1947–96." *American Political Science Review* 93: 519–33.

Binder, Sarah A., Eric D. Lawrence, and Forest Maltzman. 1999. "Uncovering the Hidden Effect of Party." *Journal of Politics* 61: 815–31.

Binder, Sarah A., and Steven S. Smith. 1997. *Politics or Principle? Filibustering in the United States Senate.* Washington, DC: Brookings.

Blainey, Geoffrey. 1973. *The Causes of War.* New York: Free Press.

Blair, Diane Kincaid, and Ann R. Henry. 1981. "The Family Factor in State Legislative Turnover." *Legislative Studies Quarterly* 6 (February): 55–68.

Blais, Andre, Donald Blake, and Stephane Dion. 1993. "Do Parties Make a Difference: Parties and the Size of Government in Liberal Democracies." *American Journal of Political Science* 37: 40–62.

Blais, Andre, Donald Blake, and Stephane Dion. 1996. "Do Parties Make a Difference: A Reappraisal." *American Journal of Political Science* 40: 514–20.

Blake, Michael. 2000. "Rights for People, Not for Cultures." *Civilization* (August–September): 50–54.

Blank, Stephen. 1978. "Britain: The Politics of Foreign Economic Policy, the Domestic Economy, and the Problem of Pluralistic Stagnation." In *Between Power and Plenty: Foreign Economic Policies of Advanced Industrial Societies,* ed. Peter J. Katzenstein, 89–138. Madison: University of Wisconsin Press.

Blee, Kathleen. 1991. *Women of the Klan: Racism and Gender in the 1920s.* Berkeley: University of California Press.

Block, Fred. 1980. "Beyond Relative Autonomy." In *Socialist Register,* ed. Ralph Miliband and John Saville, 227–42. London: Merlin.

Block, Fred. 1977. "The Ruling Class Does Not Rule." *Socialist Revolution* 33: 6–28.

Blomkvist, Henry, et al. 2001. "Social Capital and Democracy in India." *Economic and Political Weekly,* February 24.

Blondel, Jean. 1973. *Comparative Legislatures.* Englewood Cliffs, NJ: Prentice-Hall.

Blydenburgh, John C. 1971. "A Controlled Experiment to Measure the Effects of Personal Contact Campaigning." *Midwest Journal of Political Science* 15 (May): 365–81.

Bobo, Lawrence D. 1988. "Group Conflict, Prejudice, and the Paradox of Contemporary Racial Attitudes." In *Eliminating Racism: Profiles in Controversy,* ed. Phyllis A. Katz and Dalmas A. Taylor, 85–114. New York: Plenum.

Bobo, Lawrence D. 2000. "Racial Attitudes and Relations at the Close of the Twentieth Century. In *American Becoming: Racial Trends and Their Consequences,* vol. 1, ed. Neil Smelser, William Julius Wilson, and Faith N. Mitchell, tba. Washington, DC: National Academy Press.

Bobo, Lawrence D., and Franklin D. Gilliam Jr. 1990. "Race, Sociopolitical Participation, and Black Empowerment." *American Political Science Review* 84: 377–93.

Bobo, Lawrence D., and James R. Kluegel. 1997. "Status, Ideology, and Dimensions of Whites' Racial Beliefs and Attitudes: Progress and Stagnation." In *Racial Attitudes in the 1990s: Continuity and Change*, ed. Steven A. Tuch and Jack K. Martin. 93–120. Westport, CT: Praeger.

Bogue, Allen. 1980. "The New Political History in the 1970s." In *The Past Before Us: Contemporary Historical Writing in the United States*. Ithaca, NY: Cornell University Press.

Bohman, James, and Matthias Lutz-Bachmann. 1997. *Perpetual Peace. Essays on Kant's Cosmopolitan Ideal.* Cambridge: MIT Press.

Bohman, James, and William Rehg, eds. 1997. *Deliberative Democracy: Essays on Reason and Politics.* Cambridge: MIT Press.

Bohn, Henning, and Robert P. Inman. 1996. "Constitutional Limits and Public Deficits: Evidence From the U.S. States." Carnegie-Rochester Conference Series on Public Policy 4 (December): 13–76.

Boix, Carles. 1998. *Political Parties, Growth and Equality.* New York: Cambridge University Press.

Boles, Janet K. 1994. "Local Feminist Policy Networks in the Contemporary American Interest Group System." *Policy Sciences* 27: 161–78.

Boli, John, and George M. Thomas, eds. 1998. *World Polity Formation since 1875.* Stanford, CA: Stanford University Press.

Boli, John, and George M. Thomas. 1999. "INGOs and the Organization of World Culture." In *Constructing World Culture: International Nongovernmental Organizations since 1875*, ed. J. Boli and G. M. Thomas. Stanford, CA: Stanford University Press.

Bollen, Kenneth. 1993. "Liberal Democracy: Validity and Method Factors in Cross-National Measures." *American Journal of Political Science* 37(4): 1207–30.

Bonk Kathy. 1988. "The Selling of 'The Gender Gap.'" In *The Politics of the Gender Gap*, ed. Carol M. Mueller. Newbury Park, CA: Sage.

Books, John, and Charles Prysby. 1988. "Studying Contextual Effects on Political Behavior: A Research Inventory and Agenda." *American Politics Quarterly* 16: 211–38.

Bordo, Michael, Barry Eichengreen, and Douglas A. Irwin. 1999. "Is Globalization Today Really Different than Globalization a Hundred Years Ago?" NBER Working Paper W7195 (June).

Boring, Edwin G. 1954. "The Nature and History of Experimental Control." *American Journal of Psychology* 67: 573–89.

Borrelli, Stephen A., and Terry J. Royed. 1995. "Government Strength and Budget Deficits in Advanced Democracies." *European Journal of Political Research* 28: 225–60.

Börzel, Tanja A. 2001. *States and Regions in Europe. Institutional Adaptation in Germany and Spain.* Cambridge: Cambridge University Press.

Börzel, Tanja A., and Thomas Risse. 2002. "Die Wirkung internationaler Institutionen: Von der Normanerkennung zur Normeinhaltung." In *Festschrift für Beate Kohler-Koch*, ed. M. Jachtenfuchs and M. Knodt.

Boudon, Raymond. 1998. "Limitations of Rational Choice Theory." *American Journal of Sociology* 104 (3): 817–28.

Bowles, Samuel, and Herbert Gintis. 1986. *Democracy and Capitalism: Property, Community, and the Contradictions of Modern Social Thought*. New York: Basic.

Bowman, John R. 1985. "The Politics of the Market: Economic Competition and the Organization of Capitalists." *Political Power and Social Theory* 5: 35–88.

Box-Steffensmeier, Janet M., Laura W. Arnold, and Christopher J. W. Zorn. 1997. "The Strategic Timing of Position Taking in Congress: A Study of the North American Free Trade Agreement." *American Political Science Review* 91: 324–38.

Box-Steffensmeier, Janet M., and Brad Jones. 1998. "Time Is of the Essence: Event History Models in Political Science." *American Journal of Political Science* 42 (2): 661–89.

Boyd, Richard W. 1989. "The Effects of Primaries and Statewide Races on Voter Turnout." *Journal of Politics* 51: 730–39.

Boyd, Robert, and Peter J. Richerson. 1985. *Culture and the Evolutionary Process*. Chicago: University of Chicago Press.

Boyer, Robert, and J. Rogers Hollingsworth, eds. 1997. *Contemporary Capitalism: The Embeddedness of Institutions*. New York: Cambridge University Press.

Boyte, Harry C. 1980. *The Backyard Revolution: Understanding the New Citizen Movement*. Philadelphia: Temple University Press.

Brace, Kimball, Lisa Handley, Richard G. Niemi, and Harold W. Stanley. 1995. "Minority Turnout and the Creation of Majority-Minority Districts." *American Politics Quarterly* 23: 190–203.

Bradley, David, Evelyne Huber, Stephanie Moller, Francois Nielsen, and John D. Stephens. 2001. "Distributive Processes in Post-Industrial Democracies." Manuscript, University of North Carolina, Chapel Hill.

Brady, David W. 1972. "Congressional Leadership and Party Voting in the McKinley Era: A Comparison to the Modern House." *Midwest Journal of Political Science* 16: 439–59.

Brady, David W. 1973. *Congressional Voting in a Partisan Era: A Study of the McKinley Houses and a Comparison to the Modern House of Representatives*. Lawrence: University Press of Kansas.

Brady, David W. 1978. "Critical Elections, Congressional Parties and Clusters of Policy Changes." *British Journal of Political Science* 8: 79–100.

Brady, David W. 1985. "A Reevaluation of Realignments in American Politics: Evidence from the House of Representatives." *American Political Science Review* 79: 28–49.

Brady, David W. 1988. *Critical Elections and Congressional Policy Making*. Stanford, CA: Stanford University Press.

Brady, David W., and Phillip Althoff. 1974. "Party Voting in the U.S. House of Representatives, 1890–1910: Elements of a Responsible Party System." *Journal of Politics* 36: 753–75.

Brady, David W., and Craig Volden. 1997. *Revolving Gridlock*. Boulder, CO: Westview.

Brady, Henry E. 1999. "Political Participation." In *Measures of Political Attitudes*, ed. John P. Robinson, Phillip R. Shaver, and Lawrence Wrightsman. San Diego, CA: Academic.

Brady, Henry E., and Cynthia S. Kaplan. Forthcoming. "Subjects to Citizens: From Non-Voting to Protesting to Voting in Estonia during the Transition to Democracy." *Journal of Baltic Studies*.

Brady, Henry E., Kay Lehman Schlozman, and Sidney Verba. 1999. "Prospecting for Participants: Rational Expectations and the Recruitment of Political Activists." *American Political Science Review* 93: 153–68.

Brady, Henry E., Kay Lehman Schlozman, Sidney Verba, and Laurel Elms. 2002. "Who Bowls? The (Un)Changing Stratification of Participation." In *Understanding Public Opinion*, ed. Barbara Norrander and Clyde Wilcox. Washington, DC: CQ.

Brand, Laurie A. 1994. *Jordan's Inter-Arab Relations: The Political Economy of Alliance Making*. New York: Columbia University Press.

Brass, Paul R. 1997. *Theft of an Idol: Text and Context in the Representation of Collective Violence*. Princeton,: Princeton University Press.

Brass, Paul R. 2000. "Foucault Steals Political Science." *Annual Review of Political Science* 3: 305–30.

Bratton, Kathleen A., and Kerry L. Haynie. 1999. "Agenda Setting and Legislative Success in State Legislatures: The Effects of Gender and Race." *Journal of Politics* 61 (3, August) 658–79.

Bratton, Michael, and Nicholas Van de Walle. 1997. *Democratic Experiments in Africa: Regime Transition in Comparative Perspective*. Cambridge and New York: Cambridge University Press.

Brehm, John. 1993. *The Phantom Respondents*. Ann Arbor, MI.

Brehm, John, and Wendy Rahn. 1997. "Individual-Level Evidence for the Causes and Consequences of Social Capital." *American Journal of Political Science* 41: 999–1023.

Breitmeier, Helmut, and Klaus Dieter Wolf. 1995. "Analysing Regime Consequences: Conceptual Outlines and Environmental Explorations." In *Regime Theory and International Relations*. ed. V. Rittberger and P. Mayer. Oxford: Clarendon.

Bremer, Stuart A. 1992. "Dangerous Dyads." *Journal of Conflict Resolution* 36: 309–41.

Breuilly, John. 1994. *Nationalism and the State*. 2d ed. Chicago: University of Chicago Press.

Brewer, John. 1989. *The Sinews of Power: War, Money and the English State, 1688–1783*. New York: Knopf.

Bridges, Amy. 1984. *A City in the Republic: Antebellum Politics and the Origins of Machine Politics*. New York: Cambridge University Press.

Brighouse, Harry. "Against Nationalism." *Canadian Journal of Philosophy* (Supplement) 22: 365–405.

Bright, Charles, and Susan Harding, eds. 1984. *State-Making and Social Movements*. Ann Arbor: University of Michigan Press.

Brito, Dagobert L., and Michael Intriligator. 1985. "Conflict, War, and Redistribution." *American Political Science Review* 79: 943–57.

Broder, David. 1971. *The Party's Over*. New York: Harper and Row.

Broder, David. 2000. *Democracy Derailed: Initiative Campaigns and the Power of Money*. New York: Harcourt Brace.

Brodie, Bernard. 1946. *The Absolute Weapon*. New York: Harcourt Brace.

Brodie, Bernard. 1959. *Strategy in the Missile Age*. Princeton: Princeton University Press.

Brody, Richard A. 1978. "The Puzzle of Participation in America." In *The New American Political System*, ed. Anthony King. Washington, DC: American Enterprise.

Brody, Richard A., and Charles Brownstein. 1975. "Experimentation and Simulation." In *Handbook of Political Science*, 7th ed., ed. Fred Greenstein and Nelson Polsby, 211–264. Reading, MA: Addison-Wesley.

Bromwich, David. 1995. "Culturalism, the Euthenasia of Liberalism." *Dissent* (winter): 89–102.

Brooks, Stephen G. 1997. "Dueling Realisms." *International Organization* 51 (summer): 445–78.

Brooks, Stephen G. 1999. "The Globalization of Production and the Declining Benefits of Conquest." *Journal of Conflict Resolution* 43 (October): 646–70.

Brooks, Stephen G., and William C. Wohlforth. 2000–01. "Power, Globalization, and the End of the Cold War: Reevaluating a Landmark Case for Ideas." *International Security* 25 (winter): 5–53.

Brown, Clifford, Lynda Powell, and Clyde Wilcox. 1995. *Serious Money*. Cambridge: Cambridge University Press.

Brown, Michael Barratt. 1963. *After Imperialism*. London: Heinemann.

Brown, Michael K. 1999. *Race, Money and the American Welfare State*. Ithaca, NY: Cornell University Press.

Brown, Robert D., Robert A. Jackson, and Gerald C. Wright. 1999. "Registration, Turnout, and State Party Systems." *Political Research Quarterly* 52: 463–479.

Brown, Wendy. 1995. *States of Injury: Power and Freedom in Late Modernity*. Princeton, NJ: Princeton University Press.

Brown, Wendy. 2000. "Revaluing Critique: A Respond to Kenneth Baynes." *Political Theory* 28: 469–79.

Broz, J. Lawrence. 1997. "The Domestic Politics of International Monetary Order: The Gold Standard." In *Contested Social Orders and International Politics*, ed. David Skidmore, 53–91. Nashville, TN: Vanderbilt University Press.

Broz, J. Lawrence. Forthcoming. "Political System Transparency and Monetary Commitment Regimes." *International Organization*.

Brubaker, Rogers. 1992. *Citizenship and Nationhood in France and Germany.* Cambridge, MA: Harvard University Press.

Brubaker, Rogers. 1996. *Nationalism Reframed: Nationhood and the National Question in the New Europe.* Cambridge and New York: Cambridge University Press.

Brubaker, Rogers, and Frederick Cooper. 2000. "Beyond 'Identity.'" *Theory and Society* 29: 1–47.

Buchanan, Allen E. 1982. *Marx and Justice: The Radical Critique of Liberalism.* Totowa, NJ: Rowman and Littlefield.

Buchanan, James M., and Gordon Tullock. 1962. *The Calculus of Consent: Logical Foundations of Constitutional Democracy.* Ann Arbor: University of Michigan Press.

Buchanan, James M., and Richard Wagner. 1977. *Democracy in Deficit.* New York: Academic.

Bueno de Mesquita, Bruce, and David Lalman. 1992. *War and Reason.* New Haven, CT: Yale University Press.

Bueno de Mesquita, Bruce, James D. Morrow, Randolph M. Siverson, and Alastair Smith. 1999. "An Institutional Explanation of the Democratic Peace." *American Political Science Review* 93: 791–807.

Bueno de Mesquita, Bruce, and Randolph M. Siverson. 1995. "War and the Survival of Political Leaders." *American Political Science Review* 89: 841–55.

Bull, Hedley. 1977. *The Anarchical Society: A Study of Order in World Politics.* New York: Columbia University Press.

Bunce, Valerie. 1999. *Subversive Institutions: The Design and the Destruction of Socialism and the State.* New York: Cambridge University Press.

Bunce, Valerie. 2000. "Comparative Democratization: Big and Bounded Generalizations." *Comparative Political Studies* 33 (August): 703–34.

Burg, Steven L. 1983. *Conflict and Cohesion in Socialist Yugoslavia: Political Decision Making Since 1966.* Princeton: Princeton University Press.

Burke, Peter. 2000. *A Social History of Knowledge.* Oxford, UK: Blackwell.

Burnham, Walter Dean. 1965. "The Changing Shape of the American Political Universe." *American Political Science Review* 59: 7.

Burnham, Walter Dean. 1970. *Critical Elections and the Mainsprings of American Democracy.* New York: Norton.

Burnham, Walter Dean. 1986. "Periodization Schemes and 'Party Systems': The System of 1896 as a Case in Point." *Social Science History* 10.

Burnham, Walter Dean. 1994. "Pattern Recognition and 'Doing' Political History: Art, Science, or Bootless Enterprise." In *The Dynamics of American Politics 4: Approaches and Interpretations,* ed. Lawrence Dodd and Calvin Jilson, 59–82. Boulder, CO: Westview.

Burnham, Walter Dean, and William Nisbet Chambers, eds. 1967. *The American Party Systems: Stages of Development.* New York: Oxford University Press.

Burns, Nancy. 1994. *The Formation of American Local Governments.* New York: Oxford University Press.

Burns, Nancy, Kay Lehman Schlozman, and Sidney Verba. 1997. "The Public Consequences of Private Inequality: Family Life and Citizen Participation." *American Political Science Review* 91: 373–89.

Burns, Nancy, Kay Lehman Schlozman, and Sidney Verba. 2001. *The Private Roots of Public Action: Gender, Equality, and Political Participation*. Cambridge, MA: Harvard University Press.

Burns, Nancy, and Paul Schumaker. 1987. "Gender Differences in Attitudes about the Role of Local Government." *Social Science Quarterly* 68 (1, March): 138–147.

Burrell, Barbara C. 1994. *A Woman's Place is in the House*. Ann Arbor: University of Michigan Press.

Burt, Robert A. 1992. *The Constitution in Conflict*. Cambridge, MA: Belknap.

Burton, Michael, Richard Gunther, and John Higley. 1992. "Introduction: Elite Transformations and Democratic Regimes." In *Elite and Democratic Consolidation in Latin America and Southern Europe*, ed. John Higley and Richard Gunther. Cambridge: Cambridge University Press.

Busch, Marc. 2000. "Democracy, Consultation, and the Paneling of Disputes Under GATT." *Journal of Conflict Resolution* 44 (4): 425–46.

Butler, David, and Donald Stokes. 1969. *Political Change in Britain*. New York: St. Martin's.

Butler, Judith. 1996. "Universality in Culture." In *For the Love of Country: Debating the Limits of Patriotism*, 13th ed., Joshua Cohen. Boston: Beacon.

Butler, Judith. 1990. *Gender Trouble: Feminism and the Subversion of Identity*. New York: Routledge.

Butler, Judith. 2000. "Restaging the Universal: Hegemony and the Limits of Formalism." In *Contingency, Hegemony, Universality*, ed. Judith Butler, Ernesto Laclau, and Slavoj Zizek. London: Verso.

Butterfield, Herbert. 1950. "The Tragic Element in Modern International Conflict." *Review of Politics* 12: 146–67.

Buzan, Barry. 1984. "Economic Structure and International Security: The Limits of the Liberal Case." *International Organization* 38: 597–624.

Buzan, Barry, Charles Jones, and Richard Little. 1993. *The Logic of Anarchy: Neorealism to Structural Realism*. New York: Columbia University Press.

Byman, Daniel L., and Kenneth M. Pollack. 2001. "Let Us Now Praise Great Men: Bringing the Statesman Back In." *International Security* 25 (spring): 107–46.

Cacioppo, John T., and Gary G. Berntson. 2001. "The Affect System and Racial Prejudice." Unpublished manuscript, University of Chicago, Chicago.

Cain, Bruce E., John A. Ferejohn, and Morris P. Fiorina. 1987. *The Personal Vote: Constituency Service and Electoral Independence*. Cambridge, MA: Harvard University Press.

Caldeira, Gregory A., Aage R. Clausen, and Samuel C. Patterson. 1990. "Partisan Mobilization and Electoral Participation." *Electoral Studies* 9 (3): 191–204.

Calder, Kent E. 1993. *Strategic Capitalism: Private Business and Public Purpose in Japanese Industrial Finance*. Princeton, NJ: Princeton University Press.

Calhoun, Craig. 1992. *Habermas and the Public Sphere*. Cambridge: MIT Press.

Calhoun, Craig. 1998. "Explanation in Historical Sociology: Narrative, General Theory and Historically Specific Theory." *American Journal of Sociology* 104 (3): 846–71.

Calhoun-Brown, Allison. 1996. "African American Churches and Political Mobilization: The Psychological Impact of Organizational Resources." *Journal of Politics* 58: 935–53.

Callaghy, Thomas M. 1984. *The State-Society Struggle: Zaire in Comparative Perspective*. New York: Columbia University Press.

Callaghy, Thomas M. 1987. "The State as a Lame Leviathan." In *The African State in Transition*, ed. Zaki Ergas, 87–116. London: Macmillan & Co.

Calmfors, Lars, and John Driffill. 1988. "Centralisation of Wage Bargaining and Economic Performance." *Economic Policy* 6: 13–61.

Calvert, Randall L. 1995a. "Rational Actors, Equilibrium, and Social Institutions." In *Explaining Social Institutions*, ed. J. Knight and I. Sened. Ann Arbor: University of Michigan Press.

Calvert, Randall L. 1995b. "The Rational Choice Theory of Social Institutions." In *Modern Political Economy: Old Topics, New Directions*, ed. J. Banks and E. Hanushek. New York: Cambridge University Press.

Calvert, Randall L., and James Johnson. 1999. "Interpretation and Coordination in Constitutional Politics." In *Lessons in Democracy*, ed. Ewa Hauser and Jacek Wasilewski. Rochester, NY: University of Rochester Press.

Cameron, A. Colin, and Pravin K. Trivedi. 1998. *Regression Analysis of Count Data*. Cambridge: Cambridge University Press.

Cameron, Charles M. 2000. *Veto Bargaining: Presidents and the Politics of Negative Power*. Cambridge: Cambridge University Press.

Cameron, Charles M., Jeffrey Segal, and Donald Songer. 2000. "Strategic Auditing in a Political Hierarchy: An Informational Model of the Supreme Court's Certiorari Decisions," *American Political Science Review* 94: 101–116.

Cameron, David. 1978. "The Expansion of the Political Economy: A Comparative Analysis." *American Political Science Review* 72: 1243–61

Cameron, David. 1984. "Social Democracy, Corporatism, Labour Quiescence, and the Representation of Economic Interest in Advanced Capitalist Society." In *Order and Conflict in Contemporary Capitalism*, ed. J. H. Goldthorpe. London: Oxford University Press.

Campbell, Andrea Louise. Forthcoming. *Shaping Policy, Shaping Citizens: Senior Citizen Activism and the American Welfare State*. Princeton, NJ: Princeton University Press.

Campbell, Angus, Philip E. Converse, Warren E. Miller, and Donald E. Stokes. 1976 [1960]. *The American Voter*. New York: Wiley.

Campbell, Donald T. 1969. "Reforms as Experiments." *American Psychologist* 24: 409–29.

Campbell, Donald T. 1975. " 'Degrees of Freedom' and the Case Study." *Comparative Political Studies* 8: 178–93.

Campbell, Donald T., and Julian C. Stanley. 1966. *Experimental and Quasi-experimental Designs for Research.* Chicago: Rand McNally.

Campillo, Marta, and Jeffrey A. Miron. 1997. "Why Does Inflation Differ Across Countries?" In *Reducing Inflation*, ed. Christina D. Romer and David H. Romer, 335–57. Chicago: University of Chicago Press.

Campos, Jose E., and Hilton Root. 1996. *The Key to the Asian Miracle: Making Shared Growth Credible.* Washington, DC: Brookings.

Canon, David T. 1999. *Race, Redistricting, and Representation: The Unintended Consequences of Black Majority Districts.* Chicago: University of Chicago Press.

Canon, David T., and Charles Stewart, III. 2001. "The Evolution of the Committee System in Congress." In *Congress Reconsidered*, 7th ed., ed. Lawrence C. Dodd and Bruce I. Oppenheimer. Washington, DC: CQ.

Cantril, Hadley. 1946. "The Intensity of an Attitude," *Journal of Abnormal and Social Psychology* 41: 129–35.

Caporaso, James A. 1996. "The European Union and Forms of State: Westphalian, Regulatory or Post-Modern?" *Journal of Common Market Studies* 34 (March): 29–52.

Caporaso, James A. 2000. "Comparative Politics: Diversity and Coherence." *Comparative Political Studies* 33: 6–7, 699–702

Cardoso, Fernando Henrique. 1973a. "Associated-Dependent Development: Theoretical and Practical Implications." In *Authoritarian Brazil: Origins, Policies, and Future*, ed. Alfred Stepan. New Haven, CT: Yale University Press.

Cardoso, Fernando Henrique. 1973b. "Imperialism and Dependency in Latin America." In *Structures and Dependency*, ed. Frank Bonilla and Robert Girling. Stanford, CA: Institute of Political Studies.

Carens, Joseph H. 1995a. "Aliens and Citizens: The Case for Open Borders." In *Theorizing Citizenship*, ed. Beiner, 229–55. Albany: State University of New York Press.

Carens, Joseph H. 1995b. "Immigration, Welfare, and Justice." In *Justice in Immigration*, ed. Warren F. Schwartz. New York: Cambridge University Press.

Carens, Joseph H. 2000. *Culture, Citizenship, and Community.* Oxford: Oxford University Press.

Carey, John M. 1996. *Term Limits and Legislative Representation.* New York: Cambridge University Press.

Carey, John M. 1998. "Institutional Design and Party Systems." In *Consolidating the Third Wave Democracies*, ed. Larry Diamond, Marc Plattner, Yun-han Chu, and Hung-mao Tien. Baltimore: Johns Hopkins University Press.

Carey, John M. 2000. "Parchment, Equilibria, and Institutions." *Comparative Political Studies* 33 (August–September): 735–61.

Carey, John M., and Matthew Soberg Shugart. 1995. "Incentives to Cultivate a Personal Vote: Rank Ordering of Electoral Formulas." *Electoral Studies* 14: 417–39.

Carey, John M., and Matthew Soberg Shugart. 1998a. "Calling Out the Tanks or Filling in the Forms?" In *Executive Decree Authority*, ed. John M. Carey and Matthew Soberg Shugart. Cambridge: Cambridge University Press.

Carey, John M., and Matthew Soberg Shugart. 1998b. "Institutional Design and Executive Decree." In *Executive Decree Authority*, ed. John M. Carey and Matthew Soberg Shugart. Cambridge: Cambridge University Press.

Carey, John M., and Matthew Soberg Shugart, eds. 1998c. *Executive Decree Authority: Calling Out the Tanks or Just Filling Out the Forms.* New York: Cambridge University Press.

Carmines, Edward G., and James Stimson. 1989. *Issue Evolution: Race and the Transformation of American Politics.* Princeton, NJ: Princeton University Press.

Carpenter, Daniel P. 2001. *The Forging of Bureaucratic Autonomy: Reputations, Networks, and Policy Innovation in Executive Agencies, 1862–1928.* Princeton, NJ: Princeton University Press.

Carpenter, Daniel P. 2000a. "What Is the Marginal Value of Analytic Narratives?" *Social Science History* 24 (4): 653–68.

Carpenter, Daniel P. 2000b. "State Building Through Reputation Building: Coalitions of Esteem and Program Innovation in the National Postal System, 1882–1913." *Studies in American Political Development* 14 (2): 121–55.

Carpenter, Jesse T. 1972. *Competition and Collective Bargaining in the Needle Trades.* Ithaca, NY: Cornell University Press.

Carr, Edward Hallet. 1941. *The Future of Nations: Independence or Interdependence?* London: Paul, Trench, Trubner. Reproduced in *Conditions of Peace.* Edward Hallet Carr (New York: Macmillan Co, 1942), 39–69.

Carr, Edward Hallett. 1946. *The Twenty Years Crisis, 1919–1939: An Introduction to the Study of International Relations.* London: Macmillan CO.

Carroll, Susan J. 1985. *Women as Candidates in American Politics.* Bloomington: Indiana University Press.

Carroll, Susan J. 1988. "Women's Autonomy and the Gender Gap: 1980 and 1982." In ed. Carol M. Mueller. *The Politics of the Gender Gap*, Newbury Park, CA: Sage.

Carroll, Susan J. 1989. "The Personal is Political: The Intersection of Private Lives and Public Roles among Women and Men in Elective and Appointive Office." *Women and Politics* 9 (2): 51–67.

Carroll, Susan J., and Linda M. G. Zerilli. 1993. "Feminist Challenges to Political Science." In *Political Science: The State of the Discipline*, vol. II, ed. Ada Finifter. Washington, DC: American Political Science Association.

Carruba, Clifford J., and Craig Volden. 2000. "Coalitional Politics and Logrolling in Legislative Institutions." *American Journal of Political Science* 44: 261–77.

Carsey, Thomas M., and Barry Rundquist. 1999. "Party and Committee in Distributive Politics: Evidence from Defense Spending." *Journal of Politics* 61: 1156–69.

Cassel, Carol A., and Robert C. Luskin. 1988. "Simple Explanations of Turnout Decline." *American Political Science Review* 82: 1321–30.

Ceaser, James. 1979. *Presidential Selection: Theory and Development.* Princeton NJ: Princeton University Press.

Cederman, Lars-Erik. 1997. *Emergent Actors in World Politics*. Princeton, NJ: Princeton University Press.

Chakrabarty, Dipesh. 2000. *Provincializing Europe: Postcolonial Thought and Historical Difference*. Princeton, NJ: Princeton University Press.

Chambers, Simone. 1996. *Reasonable Democracy: Jurgen Habermas and the Politics of Discourse*. Ithaca, NY: Cornell University Press.

Chaney, Carole K., R. Michael Alvarez, and Jonathan Nagler. 1998. "Explaining the Gender Gap in the U.S. Presidential Elections, 1980–1992." *Political Research Quarterly* 51 (2): 211–340.

Chang, Gordon H, ed. 2001. *Asian Americans and Poitics: Perspectives, Experiences, Prospects*. Stanford, CA: Stanford University Press.

Chang, Ha-Joon. 1994. *The Political Economy of Industrial Policy*. New York: St. Martin's.

Chanley, Virginia, Thomas Rudolph, and Wendy Rahn. 2001. "The Origins and Consequences of Public Trust in Government," *Public Opinion Quarterly* 64: 239–56.

Chappell, Henry W., Thomas Havrilesky, and Rob Roy McGregor. 1993. "Partisan Monetary Policies: Presidential Influence Through the Power of Appointment." *Quarterly Journal of Economics* 108: 185–219.

Charrad, Mounira. 2001. *States and Women's Rights: The Making of Postcolonial Tunisia, Algeria, and Morocco*. Berkeley and Los Angeles, University of California Press.

Chase, Kerry. Forthcoming. "Economic Interests and Regional Trading Agreements: The Case of NAFTA." *International Organization*.

Chaudhry, Kiren Aziz. 1994. "Economic Liberalization and the Lineages of the Rentier State." *Comparative Politics* 27 (1): 1–25.

Chaudhry, Kiren Aziz. 1997. *The Price of Wealth: Economies and Institutions in the Middle East*. Ithaca, NY: Cornell University Press.

Chavez, Rebecca Bill. 2000. "The Rule of Law in Processes of Democratization: The Construction of Judicial Autonomy in Latin America." Ph.D. diss., Stanford University, Stanford, CA.

Chayes, Abram, and Antonia Chayes Handler. 1995. *The New Sovereignty, Compliance with International Regulatory Agreements*. Cambridge, MA: Harvard University Press.

Checkel, Jeffrey T. 1997. "International Norms and Domestic Politics: Bridging the Rationalist-Constructivist Divide." *European Journal of International Relations* 3 (4): 473–495.

Checkel, Jeffrey T. 1998. "The Constructivist Turn in International Relations Theory." *World Politics* 50 (2): 324–48.

Checkel, Jeffrey T. 1999. *Why Comply? Constructivism, Social Norms, and the Study of International Institutions*. Oslo: ARENA, University of Oslo.

Checkel, Jeffrey T. 2001. "Why Comply? Social Learning and European Identity Change." *International Organization* 55 (3): 553–88.

Chehabi, H. E., and Juan J. Linz, eds. 1998. *Sultanistic Regimes*. Baltimore: Johns Hopkins University Press.

Cheibub, José. 2002. "Minority Governments, Deadlock Situations, and the Survival of Presidential Democracies." *Comparative Political Studies*. 32 (3): 284–312.

Cheibub, José, and Fernando Limongi. 2000. "Parliamentarism, Presidentialism, Is There a Difference?" Mimeograph, Yale University, New Haven, CT.

Chin, M. L., J. R. Bond, and N. Geva. 2000. "A Foot in the Door: an Experimental Study of Pac and Constituency Effects on Access." *Journal of Politics* 62 (2): 534–49.

Christensen, Thomas J. 1996. *Useful Adversaries: Grand Strategy, Domestic Mobilization, and Sino-American Conflict, 1947–1958*. Princeton, NJ: Princeton University Press.

Christensen, Thomas J. 1997. "Perceptions and Allies in Europe, 1865–1940." *International Organizations* 51: 65–97.

Christensen, Thomas J., and Jack Snyder. 1990. "Chain Gangs and Passed Bucks: Predicting Alliance Patterns in Multipolarity." *International Organization* 44: 137–168.

Christianson, Gale. 1984. *In the Presence of the Creator*. New York: Free Press.

Christy, Carol. 1987. *Sex Differences in Political Participation*. New York: Praeger.

Chubb, John. 1983. *Interest Groups and Democracy*. Stanford, CA: Stanford University Press.

Chwe, Michael Suk-Young. 2001. *Rational Ritual: Culture, Coordination, and Common Knowledge*. Princeton, NJ: Princeton University Press.

Cigler, Allan J., and Burdett A. Loomis, eds. 1995. *Interest Group Politics*. 4th ed. Washington, DC: CQ.

Cioffi-Revilla, Claudio. 2000. "The First International System." Paper prepared for presentation at the Annual Meeting of the International Studies Association (March), Los Angeles, CA.

Cioffi-Revilla, Claudio, and Todd Landman. 1999. "Evolution of Maya Polities in the Ancient Mesoamerican System." *International Studies Quarterly* 43 (December): 559–98.

Citrin, Jack, and Christopher Muste. 1999. "Trust in Government." In *Measures of Political Attitudes*, ed. John P. Robinson, Phillip R. Shaver, and Lawrence Wrightsman. San Diego, CA: Academic.

Clapham, Christopher, ed. 1982. *Private Patronage and Public Power: Political Clientism in the Modern State*. New York: St. Martin's.

Clark, Cal, and Janet Clark. 1986. "Models of Gender and Political Participation in the United States." *Women and Politics* 6: 5–25.

Clark, Terry. 2000. "The New Political Culture: Changing Dynamics of Support for the Welfare State and Other Policies in Postindustrial Societies." In *The New Political Culture*, ed. Terry Clark and Ronald Inglehart, 9–72. Boulder, CO: Westview.

Clark, W., Usha N. Reichert, with S. L. Lomas and K. L. Parker. 1998. "International and Domestic Constraints on Political Business Cycles in OECD Economies." *International Organization* 52: 87–120.

Clark, William Roberts, and Mark Hallerberg. 2000. "Mobile Capital, Domestic Institutions, and Electorally Induced Monetary and Fiscal Policy." *American Political Science Review*, 94 (2, June): 323–46.

Clarke, Wes. 1998. "Divided Government and Budget Conflict in the U.S. States." *Legislative Studies Quarterly* 23: 5–22.

Claude, Innis. 1962. *Power and International Relations*. New York: Random House.

Clemens, Elisabeth S. 1997. *The People's Lobby: Organizational Innovation and the Rise of Interest Group Politics, 1890–1925*. Chicago: University of Chicago Press.

Clifford, James. 1988. *The Predicament of Culture*. Cambridge, MA: Harvard University Press.

Clucas, Richard A. 1997. "Party Contributions and the Influence of Campaign Committee Chairs on Roll-Call Voting." *Legislative Studies Quarterly* 22: 179–94.

Coase, R. H. 1960. "The Problem of Social Cost." *Journal of Law and Economics* 3 (October): 1–46.

Coase, Ronald. 1934. "The Theory of the Firm."

Coase, Ronald. 1937. "The Nature of the Firm." *Economica* 4: 386–405.

Cohen, Benjamin J. 1997. "The Political Economy of Currency Regions." In *The Political Economy of Regionalism*, ed. Edward D. Mansfield and Helen V. Milner, 50–76. New York: Columbia University Press.

Cohen, Benjamin J. 1998. *The Geography of Money*. Ithaca, NY: Cornell University Press.

Cohen, Cathy J. 1999. *The Boundaries of Blackness: AIDS and the Breakdown of Black Politics*. Chicago: University of Chicago Press.

Cohen, G. A. 1997. "Where the Action Is: On the Site of Distributive Justice." *Philosophy and Public Affairs* 26 (spring).

Cohen, G. A. 2000. *If You're an Egalitarian, How Come You're So Rich?* Cambridge, MA: Harvard University Press.

Cohen, Jean. 1999. "Changing Paradigms of Citizenship and the Exclusiveness of the Demos." *International Journal of Sociology* 14 (September): 245–68.

Cohen, Jean, and Arato, Andrew. 1992. *Civil Society and Political Theory*. Cambridge: MIT Press.

Cohen, Linda R., and Matthew L. Spitzer. 1994. "Solving the *Chevron* Puzzle." *Law and Contemporary Problems* 57 (winter): 65–110.

Cohen, Raymond, and Raymond Westbrook. 2000. *Amarna Diplomacy: The Beginnings of International Relations*. Baltimore: Johns Hopkins University Press.

Cohen, Roberta, and Francis M. Deng. 1998. *Masses in Flight: The Global Crisis of Internal Displacement*. Washington, DC: Brookings.

Colburn, Forrest. 1994. *The Vogue of Revolutions in Poor Countries*. Princeton, NJ: Princeton University Press.

Coleman, Doreen Lambelet. 1996. "Individualizing Justice Through Multiculturalism: The Liberals' Dilemma." *Columbia Law Review* 96 (5): 1093–167.

Coleman, James S. 1988. "Social Capital in the Creation of Human Capital." *American Journal of Sociology* 94: 95–120.

Coleman, James S. 1990. "Popular Representation and the Distribution of Information." In *Information and Democratic Processes*, ed. John A. Ferejohn and James H. Kuklinski. Chicago: University of Illinois Press.

Coleman, James S. 1990. *Foundations of Social Theory*. Cambridge, MA: Belknap Press of Harvard University Press.

Coleman, John J. 1996. *Party Decline in America: Policy, Politics, and the Fiscal State*. Princeton, NJ: Princeton University Press.

Coleman, John J. 1999. "Unified Government, Divided Government, and Party Responsiveness." *American Political Science Review* 93: 821–35.

Coleman, Jules. 1982. "The Normative Basis of Economic Analysis: a Critical Review of Richard Posner's The Economics of Justice." *Stanford Law Review* 34: 1105.

Coleman, Jules. 1992. *Risks and Wrongs*. Cambridge: Cambridge University Press.

Coles, Romand. 1992b. *Self/Power/Other: Political Theory and Dialogical Ethics*. Ithaca, NY: Cornell University Press.

Coles, Romand. 1992a. "Communicative Action and Dialogical Ethics: Habermas and Foucault." *Polity* 25: 71–94.

Coles, Romand. 1997. *Rethinking Generosity: Critical Theory and the Politics of Caritas*. Ithaca, NY: Cornell University Press.

Coles, Romand. 2001. "Traditio: Feminists of Color and the Torn Virtues of Democratic Engagement." *Political Theory* 29: 488–516.

Collier, David. 1993. "The Comparative Method." In *Political Science: The State of the Discipline II*, ed. Ada Finifter, 105–19. Washington, DC: American Political Science Association.

Collier, David, and Steven Levitsky. 1997. "Democracy with Adjectives: Conceptual Innovation in Comparative Research." *World Politics* 49: 430–51.

Collier, David, and James Mahoney 1993. "Conceptual Stretching Revisited: Adapting Categories in Comparative Analysis," *American Political Science Review* 87: 845–55.

Collier, David, and James Mahoney. 1996. "Insights and Pitfalls: Selection Bias in Qualitative Research." *World Politics* 49 (1): 56–91.

Collier, David, ed. 1979. *The New Authoritarianism in Latin America*. Princeton, NJ: Princeton University Press.

Collier, Paul, and Anke Hoeffler. 2000. *Greed and Grievance in Civil War*. Washington, DC: World Bank.

Collier, Ruth Berins. 1999. *Paths Toward Democracy: The Working Class and Elites in Western Europe and South America*. Cambridge: Cambridge University Press.

Collier, Ruth Berns and David Collier. 1979. "Inducements versus Constraints: Disaggregating Corporatism." *American Political Science Review* 73 (4): 967–986.

Collier, Ruth Berins, and David Collier. 1991. *Shaping the Political Arena: Critical Junctures, the Labor Movement, and Regime Dynamics in Latin America*. Princeton, NJ: Princeton University Press.

Collins, Patricia Hill. 1998. *Fighting Words. Black Women and the Search for Justice*. Minneapolis: University of Minnesota Press.

Collins, Sharon. 1997. *Black Corporate Executives: The Making and Breaking of a Black Middle Class.* Philadelphia: Temple University Press.

Colomer, Josep. 1995. *Game Theory and the Transition to Democracy: The Spanish Model,* 134. Aldershot, UK: Elgar.

Colomer, Josep. 1997. "Strategies and Outcomes in Eastern Europe." *Journal of Democracy:* 72–86.

Colomer, Josep. 2000. *Strategic Transitions.* Baltimore: Johns Hopkins University Press.

Congdon, Peter. 2001. *Bayesian Statistical Modelling.* New York: Wiley.

Conge, Patrick J. 1996. *From Revolution to War: State Relations in a World of Change.* Ann Arbor: University of Michigan Press.

Connerly, Ward. 1997. "Are Ethnic and Gender-Based Special-Interest Groups Good for America?" *Insight on the News,* July 7, 1997. Lexis Academic Universe, News, General News, Magazines & Journals, Part Symposium, 25. Accessed October 18, 2000.

Connolly, William E. 1991. *Identity/Difference: Democratic Negotiations of Political Paradox.* Ithaca, NY: Cornell University Press.

Connolly, William E. 1993. "Critical Response: Identifying the Difference." *Political Theory* 21: 128–131.

Connolly, William E. 1995. *The Ethos of Pluralization.* Minneapolis: University of Minnesota Press.

Connolly, William E. 1999. *Why I Am Not a Secularist.* Minneapolis: University of Minnesota Press.

Connolly, William E., ed. 1969. *The Bias of Pluralism.* New York: Atherton.

Conover, Pamela Johnston. 1988. "Feminists and the Gender Gap." *Journal of Politics* 50: 985–1010.

Conover, Pamela Johnston, and Virginia Gray. 1983. *Feminism and the New Right.* New York: Praeger.

Conover, Pamela Johnston, and Virginia Sapiro. 1993. "Gender, Feminist Consciousness, and War." *American Journal of Political Science* 37: 1079–99.

Constantini, Edmond, and Julie Davis Bell. 1984. "Women in Political Parties: Gender Differences in Motives Among California Party Activists." In *Political Women: Current Roles in State and Local Government,* ed. Janet Flammang. Beverly Hills, CA: Sage.

Constantini, Edmond, and Kenneth H. Craik. 1977. "Women as Politicians: The Social Background, Personality, and Political Careers of Female Party Leaders." In *A Portrait of Marginality,* ed. Marianne Githens and Jewel L. Prestage. New York: McKay.

Converse, Philip E. 1964. The Nature of Belief Systems in Mass Publics. In *Ideology and Discontent,* ed. David Apter. New York: Free Press. pp. 206–261.

Conway, M. Margaret. 2000. *Political Participation in the United States.* 3d ed. Washington, DC: CQ.

Conway, M. Margaret, Gertrude A. Steuernagel, and David W. Ahern. 1997. *Women and Political Participation.* Washington, DC: CQ.

Conybeare, John. 1984. "Public Goods, Prisoners' Dilemmas, and the International Political Economy." *International Studies Quarterly* 28 (March).

Conybeare, John. 1986. "Trade Wars: A Comparative Study of Anglo-Hanse, Franco-Italian, and Hawley-Smoot Conflicts." In *Cooperation under Anarchy*, ed. Kenneth A. Oye, 147–72. Princeton, NJ: Princeton University Press.

Cook, Elizabeth Adell. 1989. "Measuring Feminist Consciousness." *Women and Politics* 9: 71–88.

Cooper, Joseph. 1962. "The Previous Question: Its Standing as a Precedent for Cloture in the United States Senate." 87th Cong., 2d sess. S. Doc. 104.

Cooper, Joseph. 1970. "The Origins of the Standing Committees and the Development of the Modern House." *Rice University Studies* 56 (3).

Cooper, Joseph, and David W. Brady. 1981a. "Institutional Context and Leadership Style: The House from Cannon to Rayburn." *American Political Science Review* 75: 411–25.

Cooper, Joseph, and David W. Brady. 1981b. "Toward a Diachronic Analysis of Congress." *American Political Science Review* 75: 988–1006.

Cooper, Richard N. 1968. *The Economics of Interdependence*. New York: McGraw-Hill.

Cooter, Robert, Stephen Marks, and Robert Mnookin. 1982. "Bargaining in the Shadow of the Law." *Journal of Legal Studies* 11: 225–51.

Cooter, Robert, and Peter Rappoport. 1984. "Were the Ordinalists Wrong About Welfare Economics?" *Journal of Economic Literature* 22 (June): 507–30.

Cooter, Robert, and Daniel Rubinfeld. 1989. "Economic Analysis of Legal Disputes." *Journal of Economic Literature* 27: 1067–97.

Copeland, Dale C. 1996a. "Neorealism and the Myth of Bipolar Stability: Toward a New Dynamic Realist Theory of Major War." *Security Studies* 5 (spring): 29–89.

Copeland, Dale C. 1996b. "Economic Interdependence and War: A Theory of Trade Expectations." *International Security* 19 (spring): 5–41.

Copeland, Dale C. 1997. "Do Reputations Matter?" *Security Studies* 7 (autumn): 33–71.

Copeland, Dale C. 1999–2000. "Trade Expectations and the Outbreak of Peace: Detente 1970–74 and the End of the Cold War 1985–91." *Security Studies* 9 (autumn–winter): 15–58.

Copeland, Dale C. 2000a. *The Origins of Major War*. Ithaca, NY: Cornell University Press.

Copeland, Dale C. 2000b. "The Constructivist Challenge to Structural Realism: A Review Essay." *International Security* 25 (Fall): 187–212.

Coppedge, Michael, and Wolfgang H. Reinicke. 1990. "Measuring Polyarchy." *Studies in Comparative International Development* 25: 51–72.

Corlett, William. 1998. *Class Action: Reading Labor, Theory, and Value*. Ithaca, NY: Cornell University Press.

Cortell, Andrew P., and James W. Jr. Davis. 2000. "Understanding the Domestic Impact of International Norms: A Research Agenda." *International Studies Review* 2 (1): 65–87.

Coser, Lewis. 1975. "Presidential Address: Two Methods in Search of a Substance." *American Sociological Review* 40: 691–700.

Costain, Anne N. 1992. *Inviting Women's Rebellion*. Baltimore: Johns Hopkins University Press.

Cott, Nancy F. 1977. *The Bonds of Womanhood*. New Haven, CT: Yale University Press.

Cott, Nancy F. 1990. "Across the Great Divide: Women in Politics Before and After 1920." In *Women, Politics, and Change*, ed. Patricia Gurin and Louise A. Tilly. New York: Sage.

Cover, Albert D., and Bruce S. Brumberg. 1982. "Baby Books and Ballots: The Impact of Congressional Mail on Constituent Opinion." *American Political Science Review* 76 (June): 347–59.

Cowden, Jonathan A., and Rose M. McDermott 2000. "Short-Term Forces and Partisanship." *Political Behavior* 22: 197–222.

Cowhey, Peter F. 1995. "The Politics of Foreign Policy in Japan and the United States." In *Structure and Policy in Japan and the United States*, ed. Peter F. Cowhey and Mathew D. McCubbins. Cambridge: Cambridge University Press.

Cox, Robert. 1983. "Gramsci, Hegemony and IR." *Millenium* 12: 162–75.

Cox, Gary W. 1987. *The Efficient Secret: The Cabinet and the Development of Political Parties in Victorian England*. Cambridge: Cambridge University Press.

Cox, Gary W. 1997, 1999. *Making Votes Count*. New York: Cambridge University Press.

Cox, Gary W. and Jonathan N. Katz. 1999. "The Reapportionment Revolution and Bias in U.S. Congressional Elections." *American Journal of Political Science* 43: 812–41.

Cox, Gary W., and Eric Magar. 1999. "How Much Is Majority Status in the U.S. Congress Worth?" *American Political Science Review* 93: 299–309.

Cox, Gary W., and Mathew D. McCubbins. 1993. *Legislative Leviathan: Party Government in the House*. Berkeley and Los Angeles: University of California Press.

Cox, Gary W., and Mathew D. McCubbins. 2001. "The Institutional Determinants of Economic Policy Outcomes." In *Presidents, Parliaments, and Policy*, ed. Stephan Haggard and Mathew D. McCubbins. Cambridge: Cambridge University Press.

Cox, Gary W., and Michael C. Munger. 1989. "Closeness, Expenditures, and Turnout in the 1982 U.S. House Elections." *American Political Science Review* 83: 217–31.

Cox, Gary W., Frances M. Rosenbluth, and Michael F. Thies. 2000. "Electoral Rules, Career Ambitions, and Party Structure: Comparing Factions in Japan's Upper and Lower Houses." *American Journal of Political Science* 44: 115–22.

Cox, Gary, and Matthew Shugart. 1995. "In the Absence of Vote Pooling: Nomination and Vote Allocation Errors in Colombia." *Electoral Studies* 14: 441–60.

Craig, Barbara Hinkson, and David M. O'Brien. 1993. *Abortion and American Politics*. Chatham, NJ: Chatham House.

Crain, R. L., A. L. Heebner, and Y. Si. 1992. *The Effectiveness of New York City's Career Magnet Schools: An Evaluation of Ninth Grade Performance Using an Experimental Design*. Berkeley, CA: National Center for Research in Vocational Education.

Crain, W. Mark. 2000. "Volatile States: A Mean-Variance Analysis of American Political Economy." Paper presented to the annual meeting of the American Economic Association (January), Boston.

Crawford, Neta C. 1994. "A Security Regime among Democracies: Cooperation among Iroquois Nations." *International Organization* 48 (summer): 345–85.

Crawford, Vincent, and Hans Haller. 1990. "Learning How to Cooperate: Optimal Play in Repeated Coordination Games." *Econometrica* 58: 571–95.

Crawford, Vincent, and Joel Sobel. 1982. "Strategic Information Transmission." *Econometrica* 50: 1431–52.

Crenshaw, Kimberlé. 1990. "A Black Feminist Critique of Antidiscrimination Law and Politics." In *The Politics of Law: A Progressive Critique*, ed. David Kairys, 195–218. New York: Pantheon Books.

Crenshaw, Kimberlé. 1992. "Whose Story Is It, Anyway? Feminist and Antiracist Appropriations of Anita Hill." In *Race-ing Justice, En-gendering Power*, ed. Toni Morrison, 402–40. New York: Pantheon.

Crenson, Matthew. 1975. *The Federal Machine: Beginnings of Bureacracy in Jacksonian America*. Baltimore: Johns Hopkins University Press.

Crepaz, Markus. 1992. "Corporatism in Decline?" *Comparative Political Studies* 25: 139–68.

Cress, Daniel M., and David A. Snow. 2000. "The Outcomes of Homeless Mobilization: The Influence of Organization, Disruption, Political Mediation, and Framing." *American Journal of Sociology* 105: 1063–104.

Crick, Bernard. 1969. "Freedom as Politics." In Peter Laslett and W. G. Runciman, *Philosophy, Politics, and Society*, ed. Peter Laslett and W. G. Runciman, Third Series. Oxford, UK: Blackwell.

Crisp, Brian. 2000. *Democratic Institutional Design: The Powers and Incentives of Venezuelan Politicians and Interest Groups*. Stanford, CA: Stanford University Press.

Critchley, Simon. 1992. *The Ethics of Deconstruction: Derrida and Levinas*. Oxford, UK: Blackwell.

Critchley, Simon. 1998. "Metaphysics in the Dark." *Political Theory* 26: 803–17.

Crombez, Christophe. 1996. "Legislative Procedures in the European Community." *British Journal of Political Science* 26: 199–288.

Cronin, Bruce. 1999. *Community Under Anarchy: Transnational Identity and the Evolution of Cooperation*. New York: Columbia University Press.

Crook, Sara Brandes, and John R. Hibbing. 1997. "A Not-So-Distant Mirror: The 17th Amendment and Congressional Change." *American Political Science Review* 91: 845–53.

Crozier, Michael, Samuel Huntington, and Joji Watanuki. 1975. *The Crisis of Democracy*. New York: New York University Press.

Cruikshank, Barbara. 1999. *The Will to Empower: Democratic Citizens and Other Subjects*. Ithaca, NY: Cornell University Press.

Cukierman, Alex, and Francesco Lippi. 1999. "Central Bank Independence, Centralization of Wage Bargaining, Inflation and Unemployment: Theory and Some Evidence." *European Economic Review* 43 (June): 1395–434.

Cukierman, Alex, Steven B. Webb, and Bilin Neyapti. 1992. "Measuring the Independence of Central Banks and Its Effect on Policy Outcomes." *World Bank Economic Review* 6: 353–98.

Curtis, Kimberley. 1999. *Our Sense of the Real*. Ithaca, NY: Cornell University Press.

Cutler, Claire A.. Virginia Haufler, and Tony Porter, eds. 1999. *Private Authority and International Affairs*. Albany: State University of New York Press.

Dahl, Robert A., and Charles Lindblom. 1953. *Politics, Economics and Welfare*. Chicago: University of Chicago Press.

Dahl, Robert A. 1956. *A Preface to Democratic Theory*. Chicago: University of Chicago Press.

Dahl, Robert A. 1957. "The Concept of Power." *Behavioral Science* 2 (June): 201–15.

Dahl, Robert A. 1961. *Who Governs? Democracy and Power in an American City*. New Haven, CT: Yale University Press.

Dahl, Robert A. 1971. *Polyarchy*. New Haven, CT: Yale University Press.

Dahl, Robert A. 1982. *Dilemmas of Pluralist Democracy: Autonomy vs. Control*. New Haven, CT: Yale University Press.

Dahl, Robert A. 1989. *Democracy and its Critics*. New Haven, CT: Yale University Press.

Dahl, Robert A. 1994. "A Democratic Dilemma: System Effectiveness versus Citizen Participation." *Political Science Quarterly* 109: 23–24.

Dahl, Robert A. 1997. *Toward Democracy—A Journey: Reflections, 1940–1997*. Berkeley, CA: Institute of Governmental Studies.

Dahl, Robert A. 1998. *Democracy*. New Haven, CT: Yale University Press.

Dahl, Robert A. 2002. *How Democratic is the American Constitution?* New Haven, CT: Yale University Press.

Dallmayr, Fred. 1992. *Between Frankfurt and Freiburg: Toward a Critical Ontology*. Amherst: University of Massachusetts Press.

Dalton, Russell J., and Richard Eichenberg. 1993. "Europeans and the European Community: The Dynamics of Public Support for European Integration." *International Organization* 47: 507–34.

Dalton, Russell J. 1996. *Citizen Politics*. 2d ed. Chatham, NJ: Chatham House.

Damgaard, Erik, ed. 1992. *Parliamentary Change in Nordic Countries*. Oslo: Scandinavian University Press.

Darcy, R. Robert, Susan Welch, and Janet Clark. 1994. *Women, Elections, and Representation*. 2d ed. Lincoln: University of Nebraska Press.

David, Steven R. 1997. "Internal War: Causes and Cures." *World Politics* 49: 552–76.

David, Steven R. 1991. *Choosing Sides: Alignment and Realignment in the Third World*. Baltimore: John Hopkins University Press.

Davies, James C. 1972. "Toward a Theory of Revolution." In *Anger, Violence, and Politics: Theories and Research*, ed. Ivo K. Feierabend, Rosalind L. Feierabend, and Ted Robert Gurr. Englewood Cliffs, NJ: Prentice-Hall.

Davis, Angela Y. 1981. *Women, Race and Class*. New York: Vintage.

Davis, Lance E., and Robert A. Huttenback. 1986. *Mammon and the Pursuit of Empire: The Political Economy of British Imperialism*. Cambridge: Cambridge University Press.

Davison, A. C., and D. V. Hinkley. 1997. *Bootstrap Methods and Their Application*. Cambridge: Cambridge University Press.

Dawes, Robyn M., John M. Orbell. Randy T. Simmons, and Alphons J. C. van de Kragt. 1986. "Organizing Groups for Collective Action." *American Political Science Review* 80 (December): 117–85.

Dawisha, Karen, and Bruce Parrott, eds. 1997. *The End of Empire? The Transformation of the USSR in Comparative Perspective*. Armonk, NY: Sharpe.

Dawson, Michael C. 1994a. *Behind the Mule: Race, Class, and African American Politics*. Princeton, NJ: Princeton University Press.

Dawson, Michael C. 1994b. "A Black Counterpublic? Economic Earthquakes, Racial Agenda(s), and Black Politics." *Public Culture* 7: 195–223.

Dawson, Michael C. 1997. "Globalization, the Racial Divide, and a New Citizenship." In *The New Majority: Toward a Popular Progressive Politics*, ed. Stanley B. Greenberg and Theda Skocpol, 264–78. New Haven, CT: Yale University Press.

Dawson, Michael C. 2000. "Slowly Coming to Grips with the Effects of the American Racial Order on American Policy Preferences." In *Racialized Politics: The Debate About Racism in America*, ed. David O. Sears, Jim Sidanius, and Lawrence Bobo, 344–57. Chicago: University of Chicago Press.

Dawson, Michael C. 2001. *Black Visions: The Roots of Contemporary African-American Political Ideologies*. Chicago: University of Chicago Press.

Dawson, Michael C., and Ernest J. Wilson, III. 1991. "Paradigms and Paradoxes: Political Science and the Study of African American Politics." In *Political Science: Looking to the Future*, vol. 1, ed. William Crotty, 189–234. Evanston, IL: Northwestern University Press.

Deaux, Kay, and Marianne LaFrance. 1998. "Gender." In *The Handbook of Social Psychology*, ed. Daniel T. Gilbert, Susan T. Fiske, and Gardner Lindzey, 788–827. Boston: McGraw-Hill.

de Figueiredo, Rui. 2000a. "Electoral Competition, Political Uncertainty, and Policy Insulation." Manuscript, Haas School of Business, University of California, Berkeley.

de Figueiredo, Rui. 2000b. "Endogenous Budget Institutions and Political Insulation." Manuscript, Haas School of Business, University of California, Berkeley.

de Figueiredo, Rui, and Barry R. Weingast. 1997. "The Rationality of Fear: Political Opportunism and Ethnic Conflict." In *Military Intervention in Civil Wars*, ed. J. Snyder and B. Walter. New York: Columbia University Press.

de Figueiredo, Rui, and Barry R. Weingast. 1999. "The Rationality of Fear: Political Opportunism and Ethnic Conflict." In *Civil Wars, Insecurity and Intervention*, ed. Barbara Walter and Jack Snyder. New York: Columbia University Press.

De Haan, Jakob, Wim Moessen, and Bjorn Volkerink. 1999. "Budgetary Procedures—Aspects and Changes: New Evidence for Some European Countries." In *Fiscal Institutions and Fiscal Performance*, ed. James Poterba and Jurgen von Hagen. Chicago: NBER and University of Chicago Press.

De Haan, Jakob, and Jan-Egbert Sturm. 1994. "Political and Institutional Determinants of Fiscal Policy in the European Community." *Public Choice*: 157–72.

De Haan, Jakob, and Jan-Egbert Sturm. 1997. "Political and Economic Determinants of OECD Budget Deficits and Government Expenditures: A Reinvestigation." *European Journal of Political Economy*: 739–50.

Dehousse, Renaud. 1998. *European Institutional Architecture after Amsterdam: Parliamentary System or Regulatory Structure?* European University Institute, Working Paper RSC No. 98/11.

de la Garza, Rodolfo O., Louis De Sipio, F. Chris Garcia, John Garcia, and Angelo Falcon. 1992. *Latino Voices: Mexican, Puerto Rican, and Cuban Perspectives on American Politics*. Boulder, CO: Westview.

de la Garza, Rodolfo O., Martha Menchaca, and Louis De Sipio, eds. 1994. *Barrio Ballots*. Boulder, CO: Westview.

Deleuze, Gilles, and Guatarri, Felix. 1983. *Anti-Oedipus*. Minneapolis: University of Minnesota Press.

Deleuze, Gilles, and Felix Guatarri. 1987. *A Thousand Plateaus*. Minneapolis: University of Minnesota Press.

Delli Carpini, Michael X., and Scott Keeter. 1993. "Measuring Political Knowledge: Putting First Things First." *American Journal of Political Science* 37: 1179–206.

Delli Carpini, Michael X., and Scott Keeter. 1996. *What Americans Know about Politics and Why It Matters*. New Haven, CT: Yale University Press.

DeNardo, James. 1985. *Power in Numbers: The Political Strategy of Protest and Rebellion*. Princeton, NJ: Princeton University Press.

Denzau, Arthur, and Douglass C. North. 1994. "Shared Mental Models: Ideologies and Institutions." *Kyklos* 47: 3–31.

Der Derian, James, ed. 1995. *International Theory: Critical Investigations*. London: Macmillan & Co.

Derrida, Jacques, 1992. *The Other Heading: Reflections on Today's Europe*. Bloomington: Indiana University Press.

Derrida, Jacques. 1994. *Specters of Marx: The State of the Debt, the Work of Mourning, and the New International*. London: Routledge.

Desch, Michael C. 1996. "War and Strong States, Peace and Weak States." *International Organization* 50 (spring): 237–68.

Desch, Michael C. 1998. "Culture Clash: Assessing the Importance of Ideas in Security Studies." *International Security* 23 (summer): 141–70.

Desch, Michael C. 1999. *Civilian Control of the Military: The Changing Security Environment.* Baltimore: Johns Hopkins University Press.

DeSipio, Louis, and Rodolfo O. De La Garza. 1998. *Making Americans, Remaking America: Immigration and Immigrant Policy.* Dilemmas in American Politics. Boulder, CO: Westview.

DeSoto, Hernando. 1989. *The Other Path.* New York: Harper and Row.

Desposato, Scott. 2001. "Institutional Theories and Social Realities: Explaining Latin American Party Systems." Ph.D. diss., University of California, Los Angeles.

Destler, I. M., and John S. Odell. 1987. *Anti-Protection: Changing Forces in United States Trade Politics.* Washington, D.C.: Institute for International Economics.

Deudney, Daniel H. 1995. "The Philadelphia System: Sovereignty, Arms Control, and Balance of Power in the American States-Union, circa 1787–1861," *International Organization* 49 (spring): 191–228.

De Winter, Lieven. 1995. "The Role of Parliament in Government Formation and Resignation." In *Parliaments and Majority Rule in Western Europe*, ed. Herbert Döring. New York: St. Martin's.

Diamond, Irene. 1977. *Sex Roles in the State House.* New Haven, CT: Yale University Press.

Diamond, Larry. 1992. "Economic Development and Democracy Reconsidered." *American Behavioral Scientist* 35 (4–5): 450–99.

Diamond, Larry. 1999a. "Consolidating Democracy." In *Developing Democracy*, ed. Larry Diamond. Baltimore: Johns Hopkins University Press.

Diamond, Larry. 1999b. *Developing Democracy: Toward Consolidation.* Baltimore: Johns Hopkins University Press.

Diamond, Larry, Juan J. Linz, and Seymour Martin Lipset, eds. 1988. *Democracy in Developing Countries.* 4 vols. Boulder, CO: Rienner.

Diamond, Larry, Marc F. Plattner, Yun-han Chus, and Hung-mao Tien, eds. 1997. *Consolidating the Third Wave Democracies.* Baltimore: Johns Hopkins University Press.

DiCicco, Jonathan M., and Jack Levy. 1999. "Power Shifts and Problem Shifts: The Evolution of the Power Transition Research Program." *Journal of Conflict Resolution* 43 (December): 675–704.

Diermeier, Daniel. 1995. "Commitment, Deference, and Legislative Institutions." *American Political Science Review* 89: 344–55.

Diermeier, Daniel, and Timothy J. Feddersen. 1998. "Cohesion in Legislatures and the Vote of Confidence Procedure." *American Political Science Review* 92: 611–21.

Diermeier, Daniel, and Timothy J. Feddersen. 2000. "Information and Congressional Hearings." *American Journal of Political Science* 44: 51–65.

Diermeier, Daniel, and Antonio Merlo. 1999. "A Structural Model of Government Formation." Working paper, MEDS, Kellogg School of Management, Northwestern University, Evanston, IL.

Diermeier, Daniel, and Roger B. Myerson. 1999. "Bicameralism and Its Consequences for the Internal Organization of Legislatures." *American Economic Review* 89: 1182–96.

DiMaggio, Paul J., and Walter W. Powell. 1991a. Introduction To *The New Institutionalism in Organizational Analysis*, ed. P. J. DiMaggio and W. W. Powell. Chicago: University of Chicago Press.

DiMaggio, Paul J., and Walter W. Powell. 1991b. "The Iron Cage Revisited: Institutional Isomorphism and Collective Rationality in Organizational Fields." In *The New Institutionalism in Organizational Analysis*, ed. W. W. Powell and P. J. DiMaggio. Chicago: University of Chicago Press.

Dion, Douglas. 1997. *Turning the Legislative Thumbscrew: Minority Rights and Procedural Change in Legislative Politics*. Ann Arbor: University of Michigan Press.

Dion, Douglas, and John D. Huber. 1996. "Procedural Choice and the House Committee on Rules." *Journal of Politics* 58: 25–53.

Disch, Lisa. 1994. *Hannah Arendt and the Limits of Philosophy*. Ithaca, NY: Cornell University Press.

Dixit, Avinash. 1986. "Comparative Statics for Oligopoly," *International Economic Review* 27 (1): 107–22.

Dixon, William. 1994. "Democracy and the Peaceful Settlement of International Conflict." *American Political Science Review* 88: 14–32.

Dobbin, Frank. 1994. *Forging Industrial Policy: The United States, Britain and France in the Railway Age*. New York: Cambridge University Press.

Dodd, Lawrence, and Richard Schott. 1979. *Congress and the Administrative State*. New York: Wiley.

Dolan, Kathleen. 1998. "Voting for Women in the 'Year of the Woman.' " *American Journal of Political Science* 42 (January): 272–93.

Dolan, Kathleen, and Lynne E. Ford. 1997. "Change and Continuity among Women State Legislators: Evidence from Three Decades." *Political Research Quarterly* 50 (1): 137–51.

Donald, David. 1965. *The Politics of Reconstruction, 1863–1867*. Baton Rouge: Louisiana State University Press.

Donald, Stephen, and Harry Paarsch. 1996. "Identification, Estimation, and Testing in Parametric Empirical Models of Auctions Within the Independent Private Values Paradigm." *Econometric Theory* 12: 517–67.

Doner, Richard F. 1991. *Driving a Bargain: Automobile Industrialization and Japanese Firms in Southeast Asia*. Berkeley: University of California Press.

Donnelly, Jack. 2000. *Realism and International Relations*. Cambridge: Cambridge University Press.

Doremus, Paul N., William W. Keller, Louis Pauly, and Simon Reich. *The Myth of the Global Corporation*. Princeton, NJ: Princeton University Press.

Döring, Herbert. 1995a. "Is Government Control of the Agenda Likely to Keep Legislative Inflation at Bay?" In *Parliaments and Majority Rule in Western Europe*, ed. Herbert Döring. New York: St. Martin's.

Döring, Herbert, ed. 1995b. *Parliaments and Majority Rule in Western Europe.* New York: St. Martin's.

Dornbusch, Rudiger. 1992. "The Case for Trade Liberalization in Developing Countries." *Journal of Economic Perspectives* 6: 69–85.

Downing, Brian M. 1992. *The Military Revolution and Political Change: Origins of Democracy and Autocracy in Early Modern Europe.* Princeton, NJ: Princeton University Press.

Downs, Anthony. 1957. *An Economic Theory of Democracy.* New York: Harper and Row.

Downs, George W., and David Rocke. 1995. *Optimal Imperfection? Domestic Uncertainty and Institutions in International Relations.* Princeton, NJ: Princeton University Press.

Downs, George W., David M. Rocke, and Peter N. Barsoom. 1996. "Is the Good News about Compliance Good News about Cooperation?" *International Organization* 50 (3): 379–406.

Doyle, Michael W. 1986a. *Empires.* Ithaca, NY: Cornell University Press.

Doyle, Michael W. 1986b. "Liberalism and World Politics." *American Political Science Review* 80: 1151–69.

Dreifus, Claudia. 2000. "A Life Devoted to Stopping the Suffering of Mutilation: A Conversation with Nawal Nour." *New York Times,* 11 July, F7.

Drezner, Daniel. 1997. "Allies, Adversaries, and Economic Coercion: Russian Foreign Economic Policy." *Security Studies* 6 (spring): 65–111.

Drezner, Daniel. 1999. *The Sanctions Paradox: Economic Statecraft and International Relations.* Cambridge: Cambridge University Press.

Drezner, Daniel. 1999–2000. "The Trouble with Carrots: Transaction Costs, Conflict Expectations and Economic Inducements." *Security Studies* 9 (autumn–winter): 188–218.

Dryzek, John S. 1990. *Discursive Democracy: Politics, Policy, and Political Sciences.* Cambridge: Cambridge University Press.

Dryzek, John S. 1996. *Democracy in Capitalist Times: Ideals, Limits, and Struggles.* Oxford: Oxford University Press.

Dryzek, John S., and Jeffrey Berejikian. 1993. "Reconstructive Democratic Theory." *American Political Science Review* 87: 48–60.

Duerst-Lahti, Georgia. 1998. "The Bottleneck: Women Becoming Candidates." In *Women and Elective Office: Past, Present, and Future,* ed. Sue Thomas and Clyde Wilcox. New York: Oxford University Press.

Duffield, John S. 1995. *Power Rules: The Evolution of NATO's Conventional Force Posture.* Stanford, CA: Stanford University Press.

Dumm, Thomas L. 1987. *Discipline and Democracy: Disciplinary Origins of the United States.* Madison: University of Wisconsin Press.

Dunlavy, Colleen A. 1994. *Politics and Industrialization: Early Railroads in the United States and Prussia.* Princeton, NJ: Princeton University Press.

Dunn, Frederick S. 1949. "The Scope of International Relations." *World Politics* 1: 142–46.

Duverger, Maurice. 1959. *Political Parties*. Trans. Robert North. New York: John Wiley.

Dworkin, Ronald. 1977. *Taking Rights Seriously*. Rev. ed. London: Duckworth.

Dworkin, Ronald. 1978. "Liberalism." In *Public and Private Morality*, ed. Stuart Hampshire, 113–43. Cambridge: Cambridge University Press.

Dworkin, Ronald. 1981a. "What is Equality? Part 1: Equality of Welfare." *Philosophy and Public Affairs* 10 (summer): 185–246.

Dworkin, Ronald. 1981b. "What is Equality? Part 2: Equality of Resources." *Philosophy and Public Affairs* 10 (autumn): 283–345.

Dworkin, Ronald. 1985a. "What Justice Isn't." In *A Matter of Principle*, Ronald Dworkin, 214–20. Cambridge, MA: Harvard University Press.

Dworkin, Ronald. 1985b. "Is Wealth a Value?" In *A Matter of Principle*, Ronald Dworkin, 237–66. Cambridge, MA: Harvard University Press.

Dworkin, Ronald. 1986. *Law's Empire*. Cambridge, MA: Harvard University Press.

Dworkin, Ronald. 2000. *Sovereign Virtue: The Theory and Practice of Equality*. Cambridge, MA: Harvard University Press.

Eagly, Alice. 1987. *Sex Differences in Social Behavior*. Hillsdale, NJ: Erlbaum.

Easter, Gerald. 2000. *Reconstructing the State*. New York: Cambridge University Press.

Easton, David. 1968. "Political Science." In *International Encyclopedia of the Social Sciences*. New York: McMillan Co. and Free Press.

Ebbinghaus, Bernhard, and Philip Manow, eds. 2001. *Comparing Welfare Capitalism: Social Policy and Political Economy in Europe, Japan and the USA*. London: Routledge.

Eccles, Jacquelynne S. 1994. "Understanding Women's Educational and Occupational Choices." *Psychology of Women Quarterly* 18: 585–609.

Echeverri-Gent, John. 1993. *The State and the Poor: Public Policy and Political Development in India and the United States*. Berkeley: University of California Press.

Eckstein, Harry. 1966. *Division and Cohesion in Democracy*. Princeton, NJ: Princeton University Press.

Eckstein, Harry. 1975. "Case Study and Theory in Political Science." In *Handbook of Political Science*, Vol. 1, ed. Fred I. Greenstein and Nelson W. Polsby. Reading, MA: Addison-Wesley.

Edin, Per-Anders, and Henry Ohlsson. 1991. "Political Determinants of Budget Deficits: Coalition Effects versus Minority Effects." *European Economic Review*: 1597–603.

Edwards, Bob, and Michael W. Foley. 1997. "Social Capital and the Political Economy of Our Discontent." *American Behavioral Scientist* 40 (March–April): 669–78.

Edwards, George C., III, Andrew Barrett, and Jeffrey Peake. 1997. "The Legislative Impact of Divided Government." *American Journal of Political Science* 41: 545–63.

Edwards, Rebecca. 1997. *Angels in the Machinery: Gender in American Party Politics from the Civil War to the Progressive Era*. New York: Oxford University Press.

Edwards, Sebastian, and Guido Tabellini. 1991. "Explaining Fiscal Policies and Inflation in Developing Countries." *Journal of International Money and Finance*: S16–S48.

Ehrenhalt, Alan. 1991. *The United States of Ambition.* New York: Times Books.

Eichengreen, Barry. 1994. *International Monetary Arrangements for the 21st Century.* Washington, DC: Brookings.

Eichengreen, Barry. 1996. *Globalizing Capital: A History of the International Monetary System.* Princeton, NJ: Princeton University Press.

Eichengreen, Barry. 1998. "Dental Hygiene and Nuclear War," *International Organization* 52: 993–1012.

Eisenach, Eldon. 1990. "Reconstituting American Political Thought from a Regime-Change Perspective." In *Studies in American Political Development* 4. New Haven, CT: Yale University Press.

Eisenach, Eldon. 1994. *The Lost Promise of Progressivism.* Lawrence: University Press of Kansas.

Ekiert, Grzegorz. 1996. *The State Against Society: Political Crises and Their Aftermath in East Central Europe.* Princeton, NJ: Princeton University Press.

Eldersveld, Samuel J. 1956. "Experimental Propaganda Techniques and Voting Behavior." *American Political Science Review* 50 (March): 154–65.

Ellis, Ellen Deborah. 1927. "Political Science at the Crossroads." *American Political Science Review* 21 (November).

Ellis, Richard J. 1993. *American Politics Cultures.* New York: Oxford University Press.

Ellis, S. D. K. 1999. *Masks of Anarchy.* New York: New York University Press.

Elman, Colin, and Miriam Fendius Elman, eds. 2002. *Progress in International Relations Theory: Metrics and Methods of Scientific Change.* Cambridge: MIT Press.

Elman, Colin. 1996a. "Horses for Courses: Why Not Neorealist Theories of Foreign Policy?" *Security Studies* 6 (autumn): 7–53.

Elman, Colin. 1996b. "Neorealism and Foreign-Policy Theory." *Security Studies* 6: 7–53.

Elman, Colin. 1996c. "Cause, Effect, and Consistency: A Reply to Kenneth Waltz." *Security Studies* 6: 58–61.

Elman, Miriam Fendius, ed. 1997. *Paths to Peace: Is Democracy the Answer?* Cambridge: MIT Press.

Elster, Jon. 1985. *Making Sense of Marx.* Cambridge: Cambridge University Press.

Elster, Jon. 1989a. *Nuts and Bolts for the Social Sciences.* Cambridge: Cambridge University Press.

Elster, Jon. 1989b. *The Cement of Society.* New York: Cambridge University Press.

Elster, Jon. 1999. *Alchemies of the Mind: Rationality and the Emotions.* New York: Cambridge University Press.

Elster, Jon. 2000. "Rational Choice History: A Case of Excessive Ambition." *American Political Science Review* 94: 685–95.

Elster, Jon, ed. 1993. *Constitutionalism and Democracy (Studies in Rationality and Social Change).* Cambridge: Cambridge University Press.

Elster, Jon, ed. 1996. *The Roundtable Talks and the Breakdown of Communism (Constitutionalism in Eastern Europe).* Cambridge: Cambridge University Press.

Elster, Jon, ed. 1998. *Institutional Design in Post-Communist Societies: Rebuilding the Ship at Sea (Theories of Institutional Design).* Chicago: University of Chicago Press.

Ely, John Hart. 1980. *Democracy and Distrust: A Theory of Judicial Review.* Cambridge, MA: Harvard University Press.

Enelow, James M., and Melvin J. Hinich. 1982. "Ideology, Issues, and the Spatial Theory of Elections." *American Political Science Review* 76: 493–501.

Enelow, James M., and Melvin J. Hinich. 1984. *The Spatial Theory of Voting.* New York: Cambridge University Press.

Engerman, Stanley L. 1997. "Cultural Values, Ideological Beliefs, and Changing Labor Institutions: Notes on Their Interactions." In *The Frontiers of the New Institutional Economics*, ed. John N. Drobak and John V. C. Nye, 95–119. New York: Academic.

Ensminger, Jean, and Jack Knight. 1997. "Changing Social Norms: Common Property, Bridewealth, and Clan Exogamy." *Current Anthropology* 38 (February): 1–24.

Epstein, Cynthia Fuchs. 1988. *Deceptive Distinctions.* New Haven, CT: Yale University Press.

Epstein, David, and Sharyn O'Halloran. 1999. *Delegating Powers: A Transaction Cost Politics Approach to Policy Making Under Separate Powers.* Cambridge: Cambridge University Press.

Epstein, Lee, and Jack Knight 1999. *Choices Justices Make.* Washington, DC: CQ.

Epstein, Leon D. 1986. *Political Parties in the American Mold.* Madison: University of Wisconsin Press.

Ericson, David. 2000. *The Debate Over Slavery: Antislavery and Proslavery Liberalism in Antebellum America.* New York: New York University Press.

Erikson, Erik H. 1968. *Identity, Youth, and Crisis.* New York: Norton.

Erikson, Robert S. 1995a. "Reply to Radcliff." *American Politics Quarterly* 23: 404–8.

Erikson, Robert S. 1995b. "State Turnout and Presidential Voting: A Closer Look." *American Politics Quarterly* 23: 387–96.

Erikson, Robert S., and Thomas R. Palfrey. 1998. "Campaign Spending and Incumbency: An Alternative Simultaneous Equations Approach." *Journal of Politics* 60 (2): 355–73.

Ertman, Thomas. 1997. *Birth of the Leviathan: Building States and Regimes in Medieval and Early Modern Europe.* New York: Cambridge University Press.

Eskridge, William N. Jr. 1992. "Overriding Supreme Court Statutory Interpretation Decisions." *Yale Law Journal* 101: 331–455.

Eskridge, William N., Jr., and John Ferejohn. 1992. JLEO

Eskridge, William N., Jr. 1992. "Reneging on History? Playing the Court/Congress/President Civil Rights Game." *California Law Review* 79: 613–84.

Eskridge, William N., Jr., and William Frickey. 1988. *Legislation*. Minneapolis, MN: West.

Esping-Andersen, Gosta. 1992. *The Three Worlds of Welfare Capitalism*. Princeton, NJ: Princeton University Press.

Estevez-Abe, Margarita, Torben Iversen, and David Soskice. 1999. "Social Protection and the Formation of Skills: A Reinterpretation of the Welfare State." Paper Presented at the annual meeting of the American Political Science Association, Atlanta, GA.

Esty, Daniel C., et al. 1995 "Working Papers: State Failure Task Force Report." Contracted Report for the U.S. Government, Central Intelligence Agency, Directorate of Intelligence.

Esty, Daniel C., et al. 1998. "State Failure Task Force Report: Phase II Findings." Contracted Report for the U.S. Government, Central Intelligence Agency, Directorate of Intelligence.

Evans, Peter B. 1979. *Dependent Development: The Alliance of Multinational, State, and Local Capital in Brazil*. Princeton, NJ: Princeton University Press.

Evans, Peter B. 1992. "The State as Problem and Solution: Predation, Embedded Autonomy, and Structural Change." In *The Politics of Economic Adjustment*. ed. S. Haggard and R. Kaufman. Princeton, NJ: Princeton University Press.

Evans, Peter B. 1995. *Embedded Autonomy: States and Industrial Transformation*. Princeton, NJ: Princeton University Press.

Evans, Peter B. 1997. "The Eclipse of the State: Reflections on Stateness in an Era of Globalization." *World Politics* 50 (1): 62–87.

Evans, Peter B., Dietrich Rueschemeyer, and Theda Skocpol, eds. 1985. *Bringing the State Back In*. New York: Cambridge University Press.

Eyerman, Joe, and Robert A. Hart Jr. 1996. "An Empirical Test of the Audience Cost Proposition." *Journal of Conflict Resolution* 40: 597–616.

Farber, Daniel, and William Frickey. 1992. "Forward: Positive Political Theory in the Nineties." *Georgetown Law Rev.* 80 (February): 457–76.

Farber, Henry S., and Joanne Gowa. 1995. "Polities and Peace." *International Security* 20: 123–46.

Farley, Reynolds, and Walter Allen. 1987. *The Color Line and the Quality of Life in America*. New York: Oxford University Press.

Farr, James, John S. Dryzek, and Stephen T. Leonard, eds. 1995. *Political Science in History: Research Programs and Political Traditions*. New York: Cambridge University Press.

Farrell, Theo. 1999. "Correspondence." *International Security* 24 (summer): 161–68.

Faust, Jon, and Lars Svensson. 2001. "Transparency and Credibility: Monetary Policy with Unobservable Goals." *International Economic Review* 2001, 42: 369–399.

Fearon, James D. 1994a. "Domestic Political Audiences and the Escalation of International Disputes." *American Political Science Review* 88: 577–592.

Fearon, James D. 1994b. "Signaling versus the Balance of Power and Interests: An Empirical Test of a Crisis Bargaining Model." *Journal of Conflict Resolution* 38: 236–69.

Fearon, James D. 1994c. "Ethnic Warfare as a Commitment Problem." Manuscript, University of Chicago, Chicago.

Fearon, James D. 1995a. "The Offense-Defense Balance and War Since 1648." Paper presented at the Annual Meeting of the International Studies Association, Chicago.

Fearon, James D. 1995b. "Rationalist Explanations for War." *International Organization* 49: 379–414.

Fearon, James D. 1997. "What Is Identity (As We Now Use the Word)?" Manuscript, Stanford University, Stanford, CA.

Fearon, James D. 1998a. "Bargaining, Enforcement, and International Cooperation." *International Organization* 52: 269–306.

Fearon, James D. 1998b. "Commitment Problems and the Spread of Ethnic Conflict." In *The International Spread of Ethnic Conflict*, ed. David A. Lake and Donald Rothchild. Princeton, NJ: Princeton University Press.

Fearon, James D. 1998c. "Domestic Politics, Foreign Policy, and Theories of International Relations." In *Annual Review of Political Science*, vol. 1, ed. Nelson Polsby. Palo Alto, CA: Annual Reviews.

Fearon, James D. 1999. "Electoral Accountability and the Control of Politicians." In *Democracy, Accountability, and Representation*, ed. Adam Przeworski, Susan Stokes, and Bernard Manin. New York: Cambridge University Press.

Fearon, James D. 2000. "Why Use Elections to Allocate Power?" Working paper, Stanford University, Stanford, CA.

Fearon, James D., and David D. Laitin. 1996. "Explaining Interethnic Cooperation." *American Political Science Review* 90: 715–35.

Fearon, James D., and David D. Laitin. 1999. "Weak States, Rough Terrain, and Large-Scale Ethnic Violence since 1945." Paper presented at the annual meet-ing of the American Political Science Association (2–5 September), Atlanta, GA.

Fearon, James D., and David D. Laitin. 2000. "Violence and the Social Construction of Ethnic Identity." *International Organization* 54 (4): 845–77.

Fearon, James D., and Alexander Wendt. 2002. "Rationalism and Constructivism in International Relations Theory." In *Handbook of International Relations*, ed. W. Carlsnaes, B. Simmons, and T. Risse. London: Sage.

Featherstone, Mike, Scott Lash, and Roland Robertson. 1995. *Global Modernities*. London: Sage.

Feaver, Peter D. 1999. "Civil-Military Relations." *Annual Review of Political Science* 2: 211–41.

Felker, Greg. 1998. "Upwardly Global? The State, Business, and MNCs in Malaysia and Thailand's Technological Transformation." Ph.D. diss., Princeton University, Princeton, NJ.

Fenno, Richard F., Jr. 1962. "The House Appropriations Committee as a Political System: The Problem of Integration." *American Political Science Review* 56: 310–24.

Fenno, Richard F., Jr. 1966. *The Power of the Purse: Appropriations Politics in Congress.* Boston: Little, Brown.

Fenno, Richard F., Jr. 1973. *Congressmen in Committees.* Boston: Little, Brown.

Fenno, Richard F., Jr. 1978. *Home Style: House Members in Their Districts.* Boston: Little, Brown.

Fenno, Richard F., Jr. 1997. *Learning to Govern: An Institutional View of the 104th Congress.* Washington, DC: Brookings.

Fenno, Richard F., Jr. 2000. *Congress at the Grassroots: Representational Change in the South, 1970–1998.* Chapel Hill: University of North Carolina Press.

Ferejohn, John. 1991. "Rationality and Interpretation: Parliamentary Elections in Early Stuart England." In *The Economic Approach to Politics: A Critical Reassessment of the Theory of Rational Action*, ed. Kristen Renwick Monroe. New York: Harper Collins.

Ferejohn, John. 1999. "Accountability and Authority." In *Democracy, Accountability, and Representation*, ed. Adam Przeworski, Susan Stokes, and Bernard Manin. New York: Cambridge University Press.

Ferejohn, John, and Charles Shipan. 1989. "Congressional Influence on Telecommunications." In *Congress Reconsidered*, 4th ed., ed. Larry Dodd and Bruce Oppenheimer. Washington, DC: CQ.

Ferejohn, John, and Charles Shipan. 1990. "Congressional Influence on Bureaucracy." *Journal of Law, Economics and Organization* 6: 1–20.

Ferguson, Niall. 1999. *The Pity of War.* New York: Basic.

Fernandez, Raquel, and Dani Rodrik. 1991. "Resistance to Reform: Status Quo Bias in the Presence of Individual Specific Uncertainty." *American Economic Review* 81: 1146–55

Ferner, Anthony, and Richard Hyman, eds. 1998. *Changing Industrial Relations in Europe.* Malden, MA: Blackwell.

Fett, Patrick J. 1994. "Presidential Legislative Priorities and Legislators' Voting Decisions: An Exploratory Analysis. *Journal of Politics* 56: 502–12.

Filer, John E., Lawrence W. Kenny, and Rebecca B. Morton. 1993. "Redistribution, Income, and Voting." *American Journal of Political Science* 37 (February): 63–87.

Filippov, Mikhail, Peter Ordeshook, and Olga Shvetsova. 1999. "Party Fragmentation and Presidential Elections in Post-Communist Democracies." *Constitutional Political Economy* 10: 1–24.

Finegold, Kenneth, and Theda Skocpol. 1995. *State and Party in America's New Deal.* Madison: University of Wisconsin Press.

Finifter, Ada W., ed. 1983. *Political Science: State of the Discipline.* Washington, D.C.: American Political Science Association.

Finifter, Ada W., ed. 1993. *Political Science: State of the Discipline II.* Washington, D.C.: American Political Science Association.

Finnemore, Martha. 1996a. *National Interests in International Society.* Ithaca, NY: Cornell University Press.

Finnemore, Martha. 1996b. "Norms, Culture, and World Politics: Insights From Sociology's Institutionalism." *International Organization* 50 (2): 325–47.

Finnemore, Martha, and Kathryn Sikkink. 1998. "International Norm Dynamics and Political Change." *International Organization* 52 (4): 887–917.

Fiorina, Morris P. 1976. "The Voting Decision: Instrumental and Expressive Aspects." *Journal of Politics* 38: 390–413.

Fiorina, Morris P. 1977. "An Outline for a Model of Party Choice." *American Journal of Political Science* 21: 601–25.

Fiorina, Morris P. 1980. "The Decline of Collective Responsibility in American Politics." *Daedalus* (summer): 25–45.

Fiorina, Morris P. 1981. "Congressional Control of the Bureaucracy." In *Congress Reconsidered*, 2nd ed., ed. Lawrence C. Dodd and Bruce I. Oppenheimer. Washington: Congressional Quarterly Press.

Fiorina, Morris P. 1994. "Divided Government in the American States: A Byproduct of Legislative Professionalism?" *American Political Science Review* 88: 304–16.

Fiorina, Morris P. 1999a, 1999b. "Extreme Voices: A Dark Side of Civic Engagement." In *Civic Engagement in American Democracy*, ed. Theda Skocpol and Morris Fiorina. Washington, DC: Brookings.

Fiorina, Morris P. 1999c. "Whatever Happened to the Median Voter?" Paper presented at the Annual Meeting of the Midwest Political Science Association, Chicago, April.

Fiorito, Riccardo. 1997. "Stylized Facts of Government Finance in G7." IMF Working Paper 97/142 (October).

Fischer, Markus. 1992. "Feudal Europe, 800–1300: Communal Discourse and Conflictual Practices." International Organization 46 (spring): 427–65.

Fischer, Markus. 1993. "On Context, Facts, and Norms: Response to Hall and Kratochwil." *International Organization* 47 (summer): 493–500.

Fisher, Ronald. 1935. *Design of Experiments.* New York: Hafner.

Fishkin, James S. 1991. *Democracy and Deliberation: New Directions for Democratic Reform.* New Haven, CT: Yale University Press.

Fishkin, James S. 1995. *The Voice of the People: Public Opinion and Democracy.* New Haven, CT: Yale University Press.

Fishlow, Albert. 1978. *Rich and Poor Nations in the World Economy.* New York: McGraw-Hill.

Fishlow, Albert. 1990. "The Latin American State." *Journal of Economic Perspectives* 4 (3): 61–74.

Fishlow, Albert et al. 1994. *Miracle or Design? Lessons from the East Asian Experience.* Washington, DC: Overseas Development Council.

Fiss, Owen. 1998. "The Immigrant as Pariah," *Boston Review* 23 (October–November): 4–6.

Flammang, Janet. 1987. "Women Made a Difference: Comparable Worth in San Jose." In *The Women's Movements of the United States and Western Europe*, ed. Mary Fainsod Katzenstein and Carol McClurg Mueller. Philadelphia: Temple University Press.

Flammang, Janet. 1997. *Women's Political Voice*. Philadelphia: Temple University Press.

Flathman, Richard E. 1992. *Willful Liberalism: Voluntarism and Individuality in Political Theory and Practice*. Ithaca, NY: Cornell University Press.

Flathman, Richard E. 1998. *Reflections of a Would-Be Anarchist: Ideals and Institutions of Liberalism*. Minneapolis: University of Minnesota Press.

Fleron, Frederic J., Jr. 1996. "Post-Soviet Political Culture in Russia: An Assessment of Recent Empirical Investigations." *Europe-Asia Studies* 48: 225–60.

Fleron, Frederic J., Jr. and Erik Hoffman, eds. 1993. *Post-Communist Studies and Political Science: Methodology and Empirical Theory in Sovietology*. Boulder, Co. Westview.

Flexner, Eleanor. 1975. *Century of Struggle*. Cambridge, MA: Harvard University Press.

Flora, Cornelia B., and Naomi B. Lynn. 1974. "Women and Political Socialization: Considerations of the Impact of Motherhood." In *Women in Politics*, ed. Jane S. Jaquette, 37–53. New York: Wiley.

Flora, Peter, and Arnold J. Heidenheimer, eds. 1981. *The Development of Welfare States in Europe and America*. New Brunswick, NJ: Transaction.

Flora, Peter. 1999a. "Introduction and Interpretation." In *State Formation, Nation-Building, and Mass Politics in Europe: The Theory of Stein Rokkan*, ed. Peter Flora. Oxford: Oxford University Press.

Flora, Peter, ed. 1999b. *State Formation, Nation-Building, and Mass Politics in Europe: The Theory of Stein Rokkan*. Oxford: Oxford University Press.

Foley, Michael W., and Bob Edwards. 1997. "Escape from Politics? Social Theory and the Social Capital Debate." *American Behavioral Scientist* 40: 550–61.

Follett, Mary Parker. 1896. *The Speaker of the House of Representatives*. New York: Longmans, Green.

Foner, Eric. 1980. *Politics and Ideology in the Age of the Civil War*. Oxford: Oxford University Press.

Foner, Eric. 1984a. "Reconstruction and the Black Political Tradition." In *Political Parties and the Modern State*, ed. Richard S. McCormick. New Brunswick, NJ: Rutgers University Press.

Foner, Eric. 1984b. "Why Is There No Socialism in America?" *History Workshop Journal* 17 (1984): 57–80.

Foner, Eric. 1988. *Reconstruction: America's Unfinished Revolution, 1863–1877*. New York: Harper and Row.

Forbath, William E. 1998. "Short-Circuit: A Critique of Habermas's Understanding of Law, Politics, and Economic Life." In *Habermas on Law and Democracy: Critical Exchanges*, ed. Michel Rosenfeld and Andrew Arato. Berkeley: University of California Press.

Fording, Richard C. 1997. "The Conditional Effect of Violence as a Political Tactic: Mass Insurgency, Welfare Generosity, and Electoral Context in the American States." *American Journal of Political Science* 41: 1–29.

Forgette, Richard, and Brian R. Sala. 1999. "Conditional Party Government and Member Turnout on Senate Recorded Votes, 1873–1935." *Journal of Politics* 61: 467–84.

Foucault, Michel. 1971. *The Order of Things: An Archeology of the Human Sciences.* New York: Pantheon.

Foucault, Michel. 1972. *The Archeology of Knowledge.* New York: Pantheon.

Foucault, Michel. 1977. *Discipline and Punish: The Birth of the Prison.* New York: Pantheon.

Foucault, Michel. 1980. *Power/Knowledge: Selected Interviews and Other Writings.* Brighton, Sussex, UK: Harvester Wheatsheaf.

Foucault, Michel. 1984. "What is Enlightenment?" In *The Foucault Reader,* ed. Paul Rabinow. New York: Pantheon.

Foucault, Michel. 1986. "Kant on Enlightenment and Revolution." *Economy and Society* 15: 88–96.

Foweraker, Joe. 1998. "Institutional Design, Party Systems and Governability: Differentiating the Presidential Regimes of Latin America." *British Journal of Political Science* 28: 651–76.

Fowlkes, Diane L., Jerry Perkins, and Sue Tolleson Rinehart. 1979. "Gender Roles and Party Roles." *American Political Science Review* 73: 772–80.

Fox, William T. R. 1949. "Interwar International Relations Research." *World Politics* 2: 67–79.

Fozouni, Bahman. 1995. "Confutation of Political Realism." *International Studies Quarterly* 39 (December): 479–508.

Francis, Wayne L., and Lawrence W. Kenny. 1997. "Equilibrium Projections of the Consequences of Term Limits Upon Expected Tenure, Institutional Turnover, and Membership Experience." *Journal of Politics* 59: 240–52.

Franck, Thomas M. 1990. *The Power of Legitimacy Among Nations.* Oxford: Oxford University Press.

Franck, Thomas M. 1995. *Fairness in International Law and Institutions.* Oxford: Clarendon.

Frank, Andre Gunder. 1967. *Capitalism and Underdevelopment in Latin America: Historical Case Studies of Chile and Brazil.* New York: Monthly Review.

Frank, Andre Gunder. 1970. "The Development of Underdevelopment." In *Imperialism and Underdevelopment,* ed. Robert I. Rhodes. New York: Monthly Review.

Frank, Robert. 1988. *Passions within Reason: The Strategic Role of the Emotions.* New York: Norton.

Frankel, Benjamin. 1996. "Restating the Realist Case: An Introduction." In *Realism: Restatements and Renewal,* ed. Benjamin Frankel. London: Cass.

Frankel, Jeffrey A. 1999. *No Single Currency Regime Is Right For All Countries Or At All Times.* Princeton, NJ: Princeton University Department of Economics, International Finance Section.

Frankel, Jeffrey A., and Katharine Rockett. 1988. "International Monetary Policy Coordination When Policy-Makers Do Not Agree on the Model." *American Economic Review* 78 (3): 318–40.

Franklin, Charles H., and John E. Jackson. 1983. "The Dynamics of Party Identification." *American Political Science Review* 77: 957–73.

Franklin, Daniel P., and Eric E. Grier. 1997. "Effects of Motor Voter Legislation: Voter Turnout, Registration, and Partisan Advantage in the 1992 Presidential Election." *American Politics Quarterly* 25: 104–17.

Franklin, Mark N. 1999. "Electoral Engineering and Cross-National Turnout Differences: What Role for Compulsory Voting?" *British Journal of Political Science* 29: 205–24.

Franklin, Mark N., and Wolfgang P. Hirczy de Miño. 1998. "Separated Powers, Divided Government, and Turnout in U.S. Presidential Elections." *American Journal of Political Science* 42: 316–26.

Frankovic, Kathleen. 1982. "Sex and Politics—New Alignments, Old Issues." *Political Science* 15: 439–48.

Franzese, Robert J., Jr. 1998a. "Political Participation, Income Distribution, and Public Transfers in Developed Democracies." Mimeograph, University of Michigan, Ann Arbor.

Franzese, Robert J. Jr. 1998b. "The Positive Political Economy of Public Debt: An Empirical Examination of the OECD Postwar Experience." University of Michigan.

Franzese, Robert J., Jr. 1999. "Partially Independent Central Banks, Politically Responsive Governments, and Inflation." *American Journal of Political Science* 43 (3).

Franzese, Robert J., Jr. 2002. *The Political Economy of Macroeconomic Policy in Developed Democracies.* New York: Cambridge University Press.

Franzese, Robert J., Jr. Forthcoming. "Monetary Policy and Wage/Price Bargaining: Macro-Institutional Interactions in the Traded, Public, and Sheltered Sectors." In *Varieties of Capitalism: The Institutional Foundations of Comparative Advantage*, ed. Peter Hall and David Soskice.

Freedman, Paul. 1999. "Framing the Abortion Debate: Public Opinion and the Manipulation of Ambivalence." Ph.D. diss. University of Michigan, Ann Arbor.

Freeman, Jo. 1975. *The Politics of Women's Liberation.* New York: McKay.

Freeman, Jo. 1987. "Whom You Know versus Whom You Represent: Feminist Influence in the Democratic and Republican Parties." In *The Women's Movements of the United States and Western Europe*, ed. Mary Fainsod Katzenstein and Carol McClurg Mueller, ch. 10. Philadelphia: Temple University Press.

Freeman, Jo. 2000. *A Room at a Time: How Women Entered Party Politics.* Lanham, MD: Roman and Littlefield.

Freer, Regina M. 1999. "From Conflict to Convergence: Interracial Relations in the Liquor Store Controversy in South Central Los Angeles." Ph.D. diss., University of Michigan, Ann Arbor.

Friedberg, Aaron L. 1993–1994. "Ripe for Rivalry: Prospects for Peace in a Multipolar Asia." *International Security* 18 (winter): 5–33.

Friedberg, Aaron L. 2000. *In the Shadow of the Garrison State: America's Anti-Statism and Its Cold War Grand Strategy.* Princeton, NJ: Princeton University Press.

Frieden, Jeffry A. 1991a. *Debt, Development and Democracy: Modern Political Economy and Latin America 1965–1985.* Princeton, NJ: Princeton University Press.

Frieden, Jeffry A. 1991b. "Invested Interests: The Politics of National Economic Policies in a World of Global Finance." *International Organization* 45 (autumn): 425–51.

Frieden, Jeffry A. 1993. "The Dynamics of International Monetary Systems: International and Domestic Factors in the Rise, Reign, and Demise of the Classical Gold Standard." In *Coping with Complexity in the International System,* ed. Robert Jervis and Jack Snyder. Boulder, CO: Westview.

Frieden, Jeffry A. 1999. "Actors and Preferences in International Relations." In *Strategic Choice in International Relations,* ed. David A. Lake and Robert Powell. Princeton, NJ: Princeton University Press.

Friedman, Milton. 1963. *Capitalism and Freedom.* Chicago: University of Chicago Press.

Friedman, Thomas L. 1993. "Friends Like Russia Make Diplomacy a Mess." *New York Times,* March 28, 4: 5.

Friedman, Thomas L. 1999. *The Lexus and the Olive Tree: Understanding Globalization.* New York: Farrar, Straus, & Giroux.

Friedson, Eliot. 1986. *Professional Powers: A Study of the Institutionalization of Formal Knowledge.* Chicago: University of Chicago Press.

Frieze, Irene Hanson, and Maureen C. McHugh, eds. 1997. *Psychology of Women Quarterly* (Special Issue: Measuring Beliefs about Appropriate Roles for Women and Men) 21: 1–170.

Frye, Timothy. 1997. "The Politics of Institutional Choice: Post-Communist Presidencies." *Comparative Political Studies* 30: 523–53.

Frye, Timothy. 2000. *Brokers and Bureaucrats: Building Market Institutions in Russia.* Ann Arbor: University of Michigan Press.

Frymer, Paul. 1999. *Uneasy Alliances: Race and Party Competition in America.* Princeton: Princeton University Press.

Fudenberg, Drew, and Eric Maskin. 1986. "The Folk Theorem in Repeated Games with Discounting and with Incomplete Information." *Econometrica* 54: 533–54.

Fudenberg, Drew, and Jean Tirole. 1984. "The Fat-Cat Effect, the Puppy-Dog Ploy, and the Lean and Hungry Look," *American Economic Review* 74 (May): 361–66.

Fukuyama, Francis. 1995. *Trust.* New York: Basic.

Fulcher, James. 1991. *Labour Movements, Employers and the State: Conflict and Cooperation in Britain and Sweden.* Oxford: Clarendon.

Fulenwider, Clare Knoche. 1981. "Feminist Ideology and the Political Attitudes and Participation of White and Minority Women." *Western Political Quarterly* 34: 17–30.

Fuller, Hubert Bruce. 1909. *The Speakers of the House*. Boston: Little, Brown.

Gabel, Matthew. 2001. "Divided Opinion, Common Currency: The Political Economy of Public Support for EMU." In *The Political Economy of European Monetary Unification*, 2d ed., ed. Barry Eichengreen and Jeffry Frieden. Boulder, CO: Westview.

Gabel, Matthew. 1998. *Interests and Integration: Market Liberalization, Public Opinion, and European Union*. Ann Arbor: University of Michigan Press.

Galloway, George B. 1962. *History of the House of Representatives*. New York: Crowell.

Galston, William. 1993. "Political Theory in the 1980s: Perplexity Amid Diversity." In *Political Science: The State of the Discipline II*, ed. Ada W. Finifter. Washington, DC: American Political Science Association.

Galston, William. 1991. *Liberal Purposes: Goods, Virtues, and Duties in the Liberal State*. Cambridge: Cambridge University Press.

Gamm, Gerald. 1999. *Urban Exodus: Why the Jews Left Boston and the Catholics Stayed*. Cambridge, MA: Harvard University Press.

Gamm, Gerald, and Kenneth A. Shepsle. 1989. "Emergence of Legislative Institutions: Standing Committees in the House and Senate, 1810–1825." *Legislative Studies Quarterly* 14: 39–66.

Gamm, Gerald, and Steven S. Smith. 2000. "Last among Equals: The Senate's Presiding Officer." In *Esteemed Colleagues: Civility and Deliberation in the U.S. Senate*, ed. Burdett A. Loomis. Washington, DC: Brookings.

Gamm, Gerald, and Steven S. Smith. Forthcoming a. "Emergence of Senate Party Leadership." In *Senate Exceptionalism*, ed. Bruce I. Oppenheimer. Columbus: Ohio State University Press.

Gamm, Gerald, and Steven S. Smith. Forthcoming b. "Policy Leadership and the Development of the Modern Senate." In *Theoretical Explorations of the History of Congress*, ed. David W. Brady and Mathew D. McCubbins. Stanford, CA: Stanford University Press.

Gant, Michael M., and William Lyons. 1993. "Democratic Theory, Nonvoting, and Public Policy: The 1972–1988 Presidential Elections." *American Politics Quarterly* 21: 185–204.

Garcia-Bedolla, Lisa. 1999. "Fluid Borders: Latino Identity, Community and Politics in Los Angeles." Ph.D. diss., Yale University, New Haven, CT.

Garnham, David. 1991. "Explaining Middle Eastern Alignments during the Gulf War." *Jerusalem Journal of International Relations* 13 (September): 63–83.

Garrett, Geoffrey. 1998a. "Global Politics and National Markets: Collision Course or Virtuous Circle?" *International Organization* 52 (autumn): 787–824.

Garrett, Geoffrey, 1998b. *Partisan Politics in the Global Economy*. Cambridge: Cambridge University Press.

Garrett, Geoffrey. Forthcoming. "Globalization and Government Spending Around the World." *Studies in Comparative International Development*.

Garrett, Geoffrey, and Peter Lange. 1986. "Performance in a Hostile World." *World Politics* 38: 517–45.

Garrett, Geoffrey, and Deborah Mitchell. 2001. "Globalization, Government Spending, and Taxation in the OECD." *European Journal of Political Research* 39 (2): 145–77.

Garrett, Geoffrey, and Christopher Way. 1999. "The Rise of Public Sector Unions, Corporatism, and Macroeconomic Performance, 1970–1990." *Comparative Political Studies* 32: 411–34.

Garrett, Geoffrey, and Christopher Way. 2000. "Public-Sector Unions, Corporatism, and Wage Determination." In *Unions, Employers, and Central Banks: Macroeconomic Coordination and Institutional Change in Social Market Economies*, ed. T. Iversen, J. Pontusson, and D. Soskice. New York: Cambridge University Press.

Gartzke, Erik. 1998. "Kant We All Just Get Along? Opportunities, Willingness, and the Origins of the Democratic Peace," *American Journal of Political Science*: 1–26.

Gartzke, Erik. 1999. "War Is in the Error Term." *International Organization* 53: 567–87.

Gartzke, Erik, and J. Mark Wrighton. 1998. "Thinking Globally or Acting Locally? Determinants of the GATT Vote in Congress." *Legislative Studies Quarterly* 23: 33–45.

Gasiorowski, Mark, and Timothy Power. 1998. "The Structural Determinants of Democratic Consolidation: Evidence from the Third World." *Comparative Political Studies* 31: 740–71.

Gauthier, David. 1998. "Mutual Advantage and Impartiality." In *Impartiality, Neutrality and Justice: Re-Reading Brian Barry's Justice as Impartiality*, ed. Paul Kelly, 120–36. Edinburgh, UK: Edinburgh University Press.

Gauthier, David. 1986. *Morals by Agreement*. Oxford: Clarendon.

Gaventa, John. 1980. *Power and Powerlessness*. Urbana, IL: University of Illinois Press.

Gavin, Michael, and Roberto Perotti. 1997. "Fiscal Policy in Latin America." *NBER Macroeconomics Annual*: 11–60.

Gay, Claudine. 1998. "Taking Charge: Black Electoral Success and the Redefinition of American Politics." Ph.D. diss., Harvard University, Cambridge, MA.

Geddes, Barbara. 1990. "How the Cases You Choose Affect the Answers You Get." *Political Analysis* 2: 131–49.

Geddes, Barbara. 1991. "Paradigms and Sand Castles in Comparative Politics of Developing Areas." In *Comparative Politics, Policy, and International Relations*, 45–75. Vol. 2 of *Political Science: Looking to the Future*, ed. William Crotty. Evanston, IL: Northwestern University Press.

Geddes, Barbara. 1994. *Politician's Dilemma: Building State Capacity in Latin America*. Berkeley: University of California Press.

Geddes, Barbara. 1995. "A Comparative Perspective on the Leninist Legacy in Eastern Europe," *Comparative Political Studies* 28 (July): 239–74.

Geddes, Barbara. 1996. "The Initiation of New Democratic Institutions in Eastern Europe and Latin America." In *Institutional Design in New Democracies*, ed. Arend Lijphart and Carlos Waisman, 15–41. Boulder, CO: Westview.

Geddes, Barbara. 1999a. "Douglass C. North and Institutional Change in Contemporary Developing Countries." In *Competition and Cooperation*, ed. James Alt, Margaret Levi, and Elinor Ostrom, 200–27. New York: Russell Sage.

Geddes, Barbara. 1999b. "The Effect of Regime Type on Authoritarian Breakdown: Empirical Test of a Game Theoretic Argument." Presented at American Political Science Association meetings.

Geddes, Barbara. 1999c. "What Do We Know about Democratization after Twenty Years?" *Annual Review of Political Science* 2: 115–44.

Geer, John. 1996. *From Tea Leaves to Opinion Polls*. New York: Columbia University Press.

Geering, John. 1998. *Party Ideologies in America, 1828–1996*. New York: Cambridge University Press.

Gelb, Joyce. 1989. *Feminism and Politics*. Berkeley: University of California Press.

Gelb, Joyce, and Marian Lief Palley. 1996. *Women and Public Policies*. Charlottesville: University Press of Virginia.

Gellner, Ernest. 1986. *Nations and Nationalism*. Ithaca, NY: Cornell University Press.

Gellner, Ernest. 1988. "Trust, Cohesion, and the Social Order." In *Trust: Making and Breaking Cooperative Relations*, ed. D. Gambetta. New York: Blackwell.

Gelman, Andrew, John Carlin, Hal Stern, and Donald Rubin. 1995. Bayesian Data Analysis. London: Chapman and Hall.

Gelman, Andrew, and Gary King. 1990. "Estimating Incumbency Advantage Without Bias." *American Journal of Political Science* 34: 1142–64.

Gely, Rafael, and Pablo T. Spiller. 1992. "The Political Economy of Supreme Court Constitutional Decisions: The Case of Roosevelt's Court Packing Plan." *International Review of Law and Economics* 12: 45–67.

George, Alexander L. 1979. "Case Studies and Theory Development," In *Diplomacy*, ed. Paul G. Lauren. New York: Free Press.

George, Alexander L., and Timothy J. McKeown. 1985. "Case Studies and Theories of Organizational Decision Making." In *Advances in Information Processing in Organizations*, ed. Robert F. Coulam and Richard A. Smith. Greenwich, CT: JAI.

Gerber, Alan S. 1996. "African Americans' Congressional Careers and the Democratic House Delegation." *Journal of Politics* 58: 831–45.

Gerber Alan S. 1998. "Estimating the Effect of Campaign Spending on Senate Election Outcomes Using Instrumental Variables." *American Political Science Review* 92 (2) 401–11.

Gerber, Alan S. 2000. "A Tale of Two Literatures: A New Approach to Assessing the Effect of Campaign Spending on Elections." Manuscript, Yale University, New Haven, CT.

Gerber, Alan S., and Donald P. Green. 2000a. "The Effect of a Nonpartisan Get-Out-the-Vote Drive: An Experimental Study of Leafletting." *Journal of Politics* 62: 846–57.

Gerber, Alan S., and Donald P. Green. 2000b. "The Effects of Canvassing, Direct Mail, and Telephone Contact on Voter Turnout: A Field Experiment." *American Political Science Review* 94: 653–63.

Gerber, Alan S., Donald P. Green, and Matthew Green. 2000. "Direct Mail and Voter Turnout: Results from Seven Randomized Field Experiments." Paper Presented at the Annual Meeting of the American Political Science Association, Washington, DC.

Gerber, Alan S., Donald P. Green, and David Nickerson. 2001. "Testing for Publication Bias in Political Science Research." *Political Analysis* 9: 385–92.

Gerber, Alan S., Donald P. Green, and Roni Shachar. 2000. "Voting May Be Habit Forming." Manuscript. New Haven: Yale University.

Gerber, Elisabeth R. 1996. "Legislative Response to the Threat of Popular Initiatives." *American Journal of Political Science* 40: 99–128.

Gerber, Elisabeth R. 1999. *The Populist Paradox: Interest Group Influence and the Promise of Direct Legislation.* Princeton, NJ: Princeton University Press.

Gerschenkron, Alexander. 1962. *Economic Backwardness in Historical Perspective.* Cambridge, MA: Harvard University Press.

Gertzog, Irwin N. 1970. "The Electoral Consequences of a Local Party Organization's Registration Campaign." *Polity* 2: 247–64.

Gertzog, Irwin N. 1995. *Congressional Women.* 2d ed. Westport, CT: Praeger.

Gervasoni, Carlos. 1999. "El Impacto Electoral de las Reformas Economicas en America Latina (1982–1995)." *America Latina, Hoy.* Instituto de Estudios de Iberoamerica y Portugal, Universidad de Salamanca, Spain: 22.

Geuss, Raymond. 2001. *History and Illusion in Politics.* Cambridge: Cambridge University Press.

Giavazzi, Francesco, and Marco Pagano. 1988. "The Advantage of Tying One's Hands: EMS Discipline and Central Bank Credibility." *European Economic Review* 32: 1055–75.

Giavazzi, Francesco, and Marco Pagano. 1990. "Can Severe Fiscal Adjustments Be Expansionary?" In *NBER Macroeconomics Annual,* ed. Olivier Blanchard and Stanley Fischer. Cambridge: MIT Press.

Giavazzi, Francesco, and Marco Pagano. 1996. "Non-Keynesian Effects of Fiscal Policy Changes: International Evidence and the Swedish Experience." *Swedish Economic Policy Review*: 67–103.

Giddens, Anthony. 1984. *The Constitution of Society.* Cambridge, MA: Polity.

Giddings, Paula. 1984. *When and Where I Enter: The Impact of Black Women on Race and Sex in America.* New York: Morrow.

Gilens, Martin. 1999. *Why Americans Hate Welfare: Race, Media, and the Politics of Antipoverty Policy.* Chicago: University of Chicago Press.

Gilliam, Franklin D. 1996. "Exploring Minority Empowerment: Symbolic Politics, Governing Coalitions, and Traces of Political Style in Los Angeles." *American Journal of Political Science* 40: 56–81.

Gilliam, Jr., Franklin D., and Shanto Iyengar. 2000. "Prime Suspects: The Influence of Local Television News on the Viewing Public." *American Journal of Political Science* 44: 560–73.

Gilliam, Franklin D., and Karen Kaufmann. 1998. "Is There an Empowerment Life Cycle? Long-Term Black Empowerment and Its Influence on Voter Participation." *Urban Affairs Review* 33: 741–66.

Gilligan, Thomas W., and Keith Krehbiel. 1987. "Collective Decision-Making and Standing Committees: An Informational Rationale for Restrictive Amendment Procedures." *Journal of Law, Economics, and Organization* 3: 287–335.

Gilligan, Thomas W., and Keith Krehbiel. 1989. "Asymmetric Information and Legislative Rules with a Heterogeneous Committee." *American Journal of Political Science* 33 (2): 459–90.

Gilligan, Thomas W., and Keith Krehbiel. 1990. "Organization of Informative Committees by a Rational Legislature." *American Journal of Political Science* 34: 531–64.

Gilman, Howard. 1993. *The Constitution Beseiged: The Rise and Demise of Lochner Era Police Powers Jurisprudence.* Durham, NC: Duke University Press.

Gilpin, Robert. 1976. *U.S. Power and the Multinational Corporation.* New York: Basic.

Gilpin, Robert. 1981. *War and Change in World Politics.* Princeton, NJ: Princeton University Press.

Gilpin, Robert. 1986. "The Richness of the Tradition of Political Realism." In *Neorealism and Its Critics,* ed. Robert O. Keohane. New York: Columbia University Press.

Gilpin, Robert. 1987. *The Political Economy of International Relations.* Princeton, NJ: Princeton University Press.

Gilpin, Robert. 1996. "No One Loves a Political Realist." In *Realism: Restatements and Renewal,* ed. Benjamin Frankel. London: Cass.

Gilpin, Robert. 2000. *The Challenge of Global Capitalism: The World Economy in the 21st Century.* Princeton, NJ: Princeton University Press.

Gilroy, Paul. 2000. *Against Race: Imagining Political Culture beyond the Color Line.* Cambridge, MA: Harvard University Press.

Ginsberg, Benjamin. 1976. "Elections and Public Policy." *American Political Science Review* 70: 41–50.

Ginsburg, Benjamin, and Martin Shefter. 1990. *Politics by Other Means.* New York: Basic.

Ginsburg, Ruth Bader. 1993. "Speaking in a Judicial Voice." Mimeograph, Madison Lecture, New York University Law School, New York.

Githens, Marianne. 1983. "The Elusive Paradigm, Gender, Politics and Political Behavior: The State of the Art." In *Political Science: The State of the Discipline,* ed. Ada Finifter. Washington, DC: American Political Science Association.

Gitlin, Todd. 1995. *Twilight of Common Dreams.* New York: Holt.

Glaser, Charles L. 1990. *Analyzing Strategic Nuclear Policy.* Princeton, NJ: Princeton University Press.

Glaser, Charles L. 1992. "The Political Consequences of Military Strategy." *World Politics* 44: 497–538.

Glaser, Charles L. 1994–95. "Realists as Optimists: Cooperation as Self-Help." *International Security* 19 (winter): 50–90.

Glaser, Charles L. 1996. "Realists as Optimists." *Security Studies* 5: 122–66.

Glaser, Charles L. 1997. "The Security Dilemma Revisited." *World Politics* 50: 171–210.

Glaser, Charles L. 2000a. "The Causes and Consequences of Arms Races." *Annual Review of Political Science* 3: 251–76.

Glaser, Charles L. 2000b. "Defensive Realism and the IR Theory Landscape." Manuscript, Harris Graduate School of Public Policy Studies, University of Chicago, Chicago.

Glaser, Charles L., and Chaim Kaufmann. 1998. "What is the Offense-Defense Balance and Can We Measure It?" *International Security* 22 (spring): 44–82.

Glaser, James M. 2002. "White Voters, Black Schools: Structuring Racial Choices with a Checklist Ballot." *American Journal of Political Science* 46: 35–46.

Glick, P., and Susan T. Fiske. 1996. "The Ambivalent Sexism Inventory: Differentiating Hostile and Benevolent Sexism." *Journal of Personality and Social Psychology* 70: 491–512.

Gobetti, Daniela. 1996. "Regularities and Innovation in Italian Politics." *Politics and Society* 24: 57–70.

Goertzel, Ted. 1983. "The Gender Gap: Sex, Family Income, and Political Opinions in the 1980s." *Journal of Family and Military Sociology* 11: 209–22.

Goffman, Erving. 1959. *The Presentation of Self in Everyday Life.* Garden City, NJ: Doubleday.

Goffman, Erving. 1977. "The Arrangement between the Sexes." *Theory and Society* 4: 301–31.

Goldberg, Ellis. 1996. "Thinking about How Democracy Works." *Politics and Society* 24: 7–18.

Goldberg, Pinelopi Koujianou, and Giovanni Maggi, "Protection for Sale: An Empirical Analysis," *American Economic Review* 89 (5): 1135–55.

Goldfield, Michael. 1990. "Explaining New Deal Labor Policy." *American Political Science Review* 84: 1277–315.

Goldman, Emily O., and Richard B. Andres. 1999. "Systemic Effects of Military Innovation and Diffusion." *Security Studies* 8 (summer): 79–125.

Goldsmith, Jack L., and Eric A. Posner. 1999. "A Theory of Customary International Law." *University of Chicago Law Review* 66 (fall): 1113–77.

Goldsmith, Jack L., and Eric A. Posner. 2000. "Understanding the Resemblance Between Modern and Traditional Customary International Law." *Virginia Journal of International Law* 40 (winter): 640–72.

Goldstein, Avery. 1991. *From Bandwagoning to Balance-of-Power Politics: Structural Constraints and Politics in China, 1949–1978.* Stanford, CA: Stanford University Press.

Goldstein, Judith. 1993. *Ideas, Interests, and American Trade Policy.* Ithaca, NY: Cornell University Press.

Goldstein, Judith, and Robert O. Keohane. 1993. "Ideas and Foreign Policy: An Analytical Framework." In *Ideas and Foreign Policy: Beliefs, Institutions, and Political Change*, ed. Judith Goldstein and Robert O. Keohane, 3–30. Ithaca, NY: Cornell University Press.

Goldstein, Judith, and Robert O. Keohane, eds. 1993b. *Ideas and Foreign Policy: Beliefs, Institutions, and Political Change*. Ithaca, NY: Cornell University Press.

Goldstein, Judith, and Lisa L. Martin. 2000. "Legalization, Trade Liberalization, and Domestic Politics: A Cautionary Note." *International Organization* 53 (3): 603–32.

Goldstone, Jack A. 1980. "Theories of Revolution: The Third Generation." *World Politics* 32 (3): 425–53.

Goldstone, Jack A. 1991. *Revolution and Rebellion in the Early Modern World*. Berkeley: University of California Press.

Goldstone, Jack A. 1998. "Initial Conditions, General Laws, Path Dependence, and Explanation in Historical Sociology." *American Journal of Sociology* 104 (3): 829–45.

Goldthorpe, J. H. 1991. "The Uses of History in Sociology: Reflections on Some Recent Tendencies." *British Journal of Sociology* 42 (2): 211–30.

Goodin, Robert E., and Hans-Dieter Klingemann, eds. 1996. *A New Handbook of Political Science*. Oxford: Oxford University Press.

Goodman, John, and Louis Pauly. 1993. "The Obsolescence of Capital Controls? Economic Management in an Age of Global Markets." *World Politics* 46 (1): 50–82.

Goodwin, Jeff. 2001. *States and Revolutionary Movements, 1945–1991*. New York: Cambridge University Press.

Gordon, Sanford. Forthcoming. "Stochastic Dependence in Competing Risks," *American Journal of Political Science*.

Gosnell, Harold F. 1927. *Getting Out The Vote: An Experiment in the Stimulation of Voting*. Chicago: University of Chicago Press.

Gottlieb, Gidon. 1993. *Nation Against State: A New Approach to Ethnic Conflicts and the Decline of Sovereignty*. New York: Council on Foreign Relations.

Gottschalk, Marie. 2000. *The Shadow Welfare State: Labor, Business, and the Politics of Health Care in the United States*. Ithaca, NY: Cornell University Press.

Gould, Andrew. 1999. *Origins of Liberal Dominance: State, Church, and Party in Nineteenth Century Europe*. Ann Arbor: University of Michigan Press.

Gould, John. 1973. "The Economics of Legal Conflict," *Journal of Legal Studies* 2: 279–300.

Gourevitch, Peter. 1978. "The Second Image Reversed: The International Sources of Domestic Politics," *International Organization* 32 (4): 881–911.

Gourevitch, Peter. 1986. *Politics in Hard Times*. Ithaca, NY: Cornell University Press.

Gourevitch, Peter. 1998. "The Political Sources of Democracy." In *Democracy, Revolution and History*, ed. Theda Skocpol. Ithaca, NY: Cornell University Press.

Gowa, Joanne. 1986. "Anarchy, Egoism, and Third Images: The Evolution of Co-operation in International Relations." *International Organization* 40 (winter): 167–86.

Gowa, Joanne. 1988. "Public Goods and Political Institutions: Trade and Monetary Policy Processes in the United States." *International Organization* 42 (1): 15–32.

Gowa, Joanne. 1989. "Rational Hegemons, Excludable Goods, and Small Groups: An Epitaph for Hegemonic Stability Theory?" *World Politics* 41 (3): 307–24.

Gowa, Joanne and Edward D. Mansfield. 1993. "Power and Politics and International Trade." *American Political Science Review* 87: 2: 408–420.

Gowa, Joanne. 1994. *Allies, Adversaries, and International Trade*. Princeton, NJ: Princeton University Press.

Gowa. Joanne. 1999. *Ballots and Bullets: The Elusive Democratic Peace*. Princeton, NJ: Princeton University Press.

Graham, Hugh Davis. 1989, 1990. *The Civil Rights Era: Origins and Development of National Policy*. New York: Oxford University Press.

Gramsci, Antonio. 1973. *Letters from Prison*. New York: Harper and Row.

Granovetter, Mark. 1973. "The Strength of Weak Ties." *American Journal of Sociology* 78 (May): 1360–80.

Granovetter, Mark. 1985. "Economic Action and Social Structure: The Problem of Embeddedness." *American Journal of Sociology* 91: 481–510.

Grassi, Davide. 1999. *La democrazia in America Latina: problemi e prospettive del consolidamento democratico*. Milano: Angeli.

Green, Donald Philip, and Jonathan A. Cowden. 1992. "Who Protests: Self-Interest and White Opposition to Busing." *Journal of Politics* 54: 471–96.

Green, Donald Philip, and Jonathan S. Krasno. 1988. "Salvation for the Spendthrift Incumbent: Reestimating the Effects of Campaign Spending in House Elections." *American Journal of Political Science* 32: 884–907.

Green, Donald Philip, Soo Yeon Kim, and David Yoon. 2001. "Dirty Pool." *International Organization* 55: 441–68.

Green, Donald Philip, and Jonathan S. Krasno. 1990. Rebuttal to Jacobson's "New Evidence for Old Arguments." *American Journal of Political Science* 34: 363–72.

Green, Donald Philip, and Ron Shachar. 2000. "Habit Formation and Political Behaviour: Evidence of Consuetude in Voter Turnout." *British Journal of Political Science* 30: 561–73.

Green, Donald Philip, and Ian Shapiro. 1994. *Pathologies of Rational Choice Theory: A Critique of Applications in Political Science*. New Haven, CT: Yale University Press.

Green, Michael J. 2001. *Japan's Reluctant Realism: Foreign Policy Challenges in an Era of Uncertain Peace*. New York: Palgrave.

Greenberg, Anna. 2000. "The Church and the Revitalization of Politics and Community." *Political Science Quarterly* 115: 377–94.

Greenberg, Anna. 2001. "Race, Religiosity, and the Women's Vote." *Women and Politics*, 22: 59–82.

Greene, Jack. 1986. *Peripheries and Center: Constitutional Development in the Extended Polities of the British Empire and the United States, 1607–1788.* Athens: University of Georgia Press.

Greene, William H. 1997. *Econometric Analysis.* Upper Saddle River, NJ: Prentice-Hall.

Greenstein, Fred, and Nelson Polsby. 1975. *Handbook of Political Science.* New York: Addison-Wesley.

Greenstein, Fred. 1965. *Children and Politics.* New Haven, CT: Yale University Press.

Greenstone, J. David. 1986. "Political Culture and Political Developments." In *Studies in American Political Development*, vol. 1, New Haven, CT: Yale University Press.

Greenstone, J. David. 1993. *The Lincoln Persuasion: Remaking American Liberalism.* Princeton, NJ: Princeton University Press.

Greenstone, J. David, and Paul Peterson. 1973. *Race and Authority in Urban Politics.* Chicago: University of Chicago Press.

Greico, Joseph M. 1988. "Anarchy and the Limits of Cooperation," *International Organization* 42: 485–507.

Greico, Joseph M. 1990. *Cooperation Among Nations.* Ithaca, NY: Cornell University Press.

Greico, Joseph M. 1997. "Realist International Theory and the Study of World Politics." In *New Thinking in International Relations*, ed. Michael W. Doyle and G. John Ikenberry. Boulder, CO: Westview.

Greif, Avner. 1994a. "Cultural Beliefs and the Organization of Society: A Historical and Theoretical Reflection on Collectivist and Individualist Societies." *Journal of Political Economy* 102 (5): 912–50.

Greif, Avner. 1994b. "On the Political Foundations of the Late Medieval Commercial Revolution: Genoa During the Twelfth and Thirteenth Centuries." *Journal of Economic History* 54 (4): 271–87.

Greif, Avner. 1997. "Microtheory and Recent Developments in the Study of Economic Institutions through Economic History." In *Advances in Economics and Econometrics: Theory and Applications*, vol. 2, ed. David M Kreps, and Kenneth F. Wallis, 79–113. Cambridge: Cambridge University Press.

Greif, Avner. 1998. "Self-enforcing Political Systems and Economic Growth: Late Medieval Genoa." In *Analytic Narratives*, ed. Robert H. Bates, Avner Greif, Margaret Levi, Jean-Laurent Rosenthal, and Barry R. Weingast. Princeton, NJ: Princeton University Press.

Greif, Avner. Forthcoming. *Culture and the Institutional Foundations of States and Markets: Historical and Comparative Institutional Analysis of Genoa and the Maghribi Traders.* New York: Cambridge University Press.

Greif, Avner, Paul Milgrom, and Barry R. Weingast. 1994. "Commitment, Coordination, and Enforcement: The Case of the Merchant Guilds." *Journal of Political Economy* 102: 745–76.

Grieco, Joseph M. 1988. "Anarchy and the Limits of Cooperation: A Realist Critique of the Newest Liberal Institutionalism." *International Organization* 42 (summer): 485–507.

Grieco, Joseph M. 1990. *Cooperation Among Nations: Europe, America and Non-Tariff Barriers to Trade.* Ithaca, NY: Cornell University Press.

Grieco, Joseph. 1993. "Understanding the Problem of Cooperation." In *Neorealism and Neoliberalism,* ed. David A. Baldwin. New York: Columbia University Press.

Grieco, Joseph M. 1997. "Realist International Theory and the Study of World Politics." In *New Thinking in International Relations Theory,* ed. Michael W. Doyle and G. John Ikenberry. Boulder, CO: Westview.

Griffin, James. 1986. *Well-Being: Its Meaning, Measurement, and Moral Importance.* Oxford: Clarendon.

Grilli, Vittorio, Donato Masciandaro, and Guido Tabellini. 1991. "Political and Monetary Institutions and Public Financial Policies in the Industrial Countries." *Economic Policy* (October): 341–92.

Grofman, Bernard, Robert Griffin, and Gregory Berry. 1995. "House Members Who Become Senators: Learning from a 'Natural Experiment' in Representation." *Legislative Studies Quarterly* 20: 513–29.

Grose, Peter. 2000. *Operation Rollback: America's Secret War behind the Iron Curtain.* Boston: Houghton Mifflin.

Groseclose, Timothy, and Keith Krehbiel. 1994. "Golden Parachutes, Rubber Checks, and Strategic Retirements from the 102d House." *American Journal of Political Science* 38: 75–99.

Groseclose, Timothy, Steven D. Levitt, and James M. Snyder, Jr. 1999. "Comparing Interest Group Scores across Time and Chambers: Adjusted ADA Scores for the U.S. Congress." *American Political Science Review* 93: 33–50.

Groseclose, Timothy, and Nolan McCarty. 2001. "The Politics of Blame: Bargaining Before an Audience," *American Journal of Political Science,* 45: 101–19.

Grossman, Gene M., and Elhanan Helpman. 1994. "Protection for Sale," *American Economic Review* 84 (4, September): 833–50.

Grossman, Gene M., and Elhanan Helpman. 1995. "Trade Wars and Trade Talks." *Journal of Political Economy* 103 (4): 675–708.

Grossman, Gene M., and Elhanan Helpman. 2001. *Special Interest Politics,* Cambridge, MA: MIT Press.

Gruber, Lloyd. 1999. *Ruling the World: Power Politics and the Rise of Supranational Institutions.* Princeton, NJ: Princeton University Press.

Grzymala-Busse, Anna. 2002. *Redeeming the Past: The Regeneration of Communist Successor Parties in East Central Europe after 1989.* Studies in Comparative Politics. New York: Cambridge University Press.

Guarnaschelli, Serena, Richard D. McKelvey, and Thomas R. Palfrey. 2000. "An Experimental Study of Jury Decision Rules," *American Political Science Review* 94 (2): 407–25.

Guéhenno, Jean-Marie. 1995. *The End of the Nation-State.* Minneapolis: University of Minnesota Press.

Guinier, Lani. 1991. "The Triumph of Tokenism: The Voting Rights Act and the Theory of Black Educational Success." *Michigan Law Review* 89: 1077–154.

Guinier, Lani. 1994a. "(E)racing Democracy: The Voting Rights Cases." *Harvard Law Review* 108: 109–37.

Guinier, Lani. 1994b. *The Tyranny of the Majority: Fundamental Fairness in Representative Democracy.* New York: Free Press.

Gulick, Edward. 1955. *Europe's Classical Balance of Power.* Ithaca, NY: Cornell University Press.

Gurin, Patricia. 1985. "Women's Gender Consciousness." *Public Opinion Quarterly* 49: 143–63.

Gurin, Patricia. 1987. "The Political Implications of Women's Statuses." In *Spouse, Parent, Worker,* ed. F. J. Crosby. New Haven, CT: Yale University Press.

Gurin, Patricia, Shirley Hatchett, and James S. Jackson. 1989. *Hope and Independence: Blacks' Response to Electoral and Party Politics.* New York: Russell Sage.

Gurr, Ted Robert. 1993. *Minorities at Risk.* Washington, DC: U.S. Institute of Peace.

Gurr, Ted Robert. 2000. *Peoples versus States.* Washington, DC: U.S. Institute of Peace.

Gutmann, Amy. 1993. "The Challenge of Multiculturalism in Political Ethics." *Philosophy and Public Affairs* 22 (3): 171–206.

Gutmann, Amy. 2000. "Religion and State in the United States: A Defense of Two-Way Protection." In *Religion and Law: Obligations of Citizenship and Demands of Faith,* ed. Nancy L. Rosenblum. Princeton, NJ: Princeton University Press.

Gutmann, Amy, and Thompson, Dennis. 1996. *Democracy and Disagreement.* Cambridge, MA: Harvard University Press.

Guzmán, Eugenio. 1993. "Reflexiones sobre el sistema binominal." *Estudios Públicos* 50: 303–30.

Haas, Peter M. 1992. "Introduction: Epistemic Communities and International Policy Coordination." *International Organization* 46 (1): 1–36.

Habermas, Jürgen. 1971. *Knowledge and Human Interests.* Boston: Beacon.

Habermas, Jürgen. 1975. *Legitimation Crises.* Boston: Beacon.

Habermas, Jürgen. 1979. *Communication and the Evolution of Society.* Boston: Beacon.

Habermas, Jürgen. 1981. *Theorie des kommunikativen Handelns.* 2 vols. Frankfurt/M.: Suhrkamp.

Habermas, Jürgen. 1984. *The Theory of Communicative Action.* Vol. 1. Trans. T. McCarthy. Boston: Beacon.

Habermas, Jürgen. 1987. *The Philosophical Discourse of Modernity.* Cambridge: MIT Press.

Habermas, Jürgen. 1990. *Moral Consciousness and Communicative Action.* Cambridge: MIT Press.

Habermas, Jürgen. 1992. "Further Reflections on the Public Sphere." In *Habermas and the Public Sphere,* ed. Craig Calhoun. Cambridge: MIT Press.

Habermas, Jürgen. 1994. "Three Normative Models of Democracy." *Constellations* 1 (1): 1–10.

Habermas, Jürgen. 1996. *Between Facts and Norms.* Trans. William Regh. Cambridge: MIT Press.

Habermas, Jürgen. 1998a. *The Inclusion of the Other.* In *Studies in Political Theory*, ed. Ciaran Cronin and Pablo de Greiff. Cambridge: MIT Press.

Habermas, Jürgen. 1998b. "Paradigms of Law." In *Habermas on Law and Democracy: Critical Exchanges*, ed. Michel Rosenfeld and Andrew Arato. Berkeley: University of California Press.

Habermas, Jürgen. 1998c. "Reply to Symposium Participants." In *Habermas on Law and Democracy: Critical Exchanges*, ed. Michel Rosenfeld and Andrew Arato. Berkeley: University of California Press.

Hacker, Jacob S. 1998. "The Historical Logic of National Health Insurance: Structure and Sequence in the Development of British, Canadian, and U.S. Medical Policy." *Studies in American Political Development* 12 (spring): 57–130.

Hacker, Jacob S. 2000. "Boundary Wars: The Political Struggle over Public and Private Social Benefits in the United States." Ph.D. diss., Yale University, New Haven, CT.

Hacker, Jacob S. Forthcoming. *The Divided Welfare State: The Battle over Public and Private Social Benefits in the United States.* Cambridge: Cambridge University Press.

Hacker, Jacob S., and Paul Pierson. 2000. "Business Power and Social Policy: Employers and the Formation of the American Welfare State." Paper presented at Paper presented at the annual meeting of the American Political Science Association, Washington, DC.

Hager, Gregory L., and Jeffrey C. Talbert. 2000. "Look for the Party Label: Party Influences on Voting in the U.S. House." *Legislative Studies Quarterly* 25: 75–99.

Haggard, Stephan. 1988. "The Institutional Foundations of Hegemony: Explaining the Reciprocal Trade Agreements Act of 1934." *International Organization* 42 (1): 91–119.

Haggard, Stephan. 1990. *Pathways from the Periphery: The Policies of Growth in Newly Industrializing Countries.* Ithaca, NY: Cornell University Press.

Haggard, Stephan, and Robert R. Kaufman. 1995. *The Political Economy of Democratic Transitions.* Princeton, NJ: Princeton University Press.

Haggard, Stephan, and Robert R. Kaufman, eds. 1992. *The Politics of Economic Adjustment: International Constraints, Distributive Conflicts, and the State.* Princeton, NJ: Princeton University Press.

Hagopian, Frances. 1996. *Traditional Politics and Regime Change in Brazil.* Cambridge and New York: Cambridge University Press.

Hagopian, Frances. 2000. "Political Development, Revisited." *Comparative Political Studies* 33 (August–September): 880–911.

Haldenius, Axel. 1992. *Democracy and Development.* Cambridge: Cambridge University Press.

Hall, John A., and G. John Ikenberry. 1989. *The State.* Minneapolis: University of Minnesota Press.

Hall, Peter A. 1986. *Governing the Economy: The Politics of State Intervention in Britain and France.* New York: Oxford University Press.

Hall, Peter A. 1994. "Central Bank Independence and Coordinated Wage Bargaining: Their Interaction in Germany and Europe." *German Politics and Society:* 1–23.

Hall, Peter A. 1999. "The Political Economy of Europe in an Era of Interdependence." In *Continuity and Change in Contemporary Capitalism,* ed. Herbert Kitschelt, Peter Lange, Gary Marks, and John D. Stephens. New York: Cambridge University Press.

Hall, Peter A. 2002. "Aligning Ontology and Methodology in Comparative Politics." In *Comparative-Historical Analysis: Achievements and Agendas,* ed. James Mahoney and Dietrich Rueschemeyer.

Hall, Peter A., and Robert Franzese. 1998. "Mixed Signals: Central Bank Independence, Co-ordinated Wage Bargaining, and European Monetary Union." *International Organization* 52 (3, Summer): 505–36.

Hall, Peter A., and David Soskice. 2001a. "An Introduction to Varieties of Capitalism." In *Varieties of Capitalism: The Institutional Foundations of Comparative Advantage,* ed. Peter A. Hall and David Soskice. New York and Oxford: Oxford University Press.

Hall, Peter A., and David Soskice, eds. 2001b. *Varieties of Capitalism: The Institutional Foundations of Comparative Advantage.* New York and Oxford: Oxford University Press.

Hall, Peter A., and Rosemary C. R. Taylor. 1996. "Political Science and the Three New Institutionalisms." *Political Studies* 44 (December): 939, 952–73.

Hall, Richard L. 1996. *Participation in Congress.* New Haven, CT: Yale University Press.

Hall, Richard L., and Robert P. van Houweling. 1995. "Avarice and Ambition in Congress: Representatives' Decisions to Run or Retire from the U.S. House." *American Political Science Review* 89: 121–36.

Hall, Rodney Bruce. 1999. *National Collective Identity: Social Constructs and International Systems.* New York: Columbia University Press.

Hall, Rodney Bruce, and Friedrich Kratochwil. 1993. "Medieval Tales: Neorealist 'Science' and the Abuse of History." *International Organization* 47 (summer): 479–91.

Hallerberg, M., and Jurgen von Hagen. 1997. "Electoral Institutions, Cabinet Negotiations, and Budget Deficits within the European Union." CEPR Discussion Paper 1555.

Hamilton, Alexander, James Madison, and John Jay. 1966 [1788]. *The Federalist Papers.* 2d ed. Ed. Roy P. Fairfield. New York: Anchor Books.

Hamilton, W. D. 1963. "The Evolution of Altrustic Behavior." *American Naturalist* 97: Letters to the Editor, 353–56.

Hamilton, W. D. 1964. "The Genetical Evolution of Social Behavior." *Journal of Theoretical Biology* 7: 1–32.

Hamm, Keith E., and Robert Harmel. 1993. "Legislative Party Development and the Speaker System: The Case of the Texas House." *Journal of Politics* 55: 1140–51.

Hanchard, Michael G. 1994. *Orpheus and Power: The Movimento Negro of Rio de Janeiro and Sao Paulo, Brazil, 1945–1988*. Princeton, NJ: Princeton University Press.

Hansen, John Mark. 1991. *Gaining Access: Congress and the Farm Lobby, 1919–1981*. Chicago: University of Chicago Press.

Hansen, Susan B. 1997. "Talking about Politics: Gender and Contextual Effects in Political Proselytizing." *Journal of Politics* 59: 73–103.

Hansen, Susan B., Linda M. Franz, and Margaret Netemeyer-Mays. 1976. "Women's Political Participation and Policy Preferences." *Social Science Quarterly* 56: 576–90.

Hardin, Russell. 1982. *Collective Action*. Baltimore: Johns Hopkins University Press.

Hardin, Russell. 1989. "Why a Constitution?" In *The Federalist Papers and the New Institutionalism*, ed. B. Grofman and D. Wittman. New York: Agathon.

Hardin, Russell. 1995. *One for All: The Logic of Group Conflict*. Princeton, NJ: Princeton University Press.

Hardin, Russell. 1999. *Liberalism, Constitutionalism, and Democracy*. Oxford: Oxford University Press.

Hardin, Russell. 2002. *Trust and Trustworthiness*. New York: Russell Sage.

Hardy-Fanta, Carol. 1993. *Latina Politics, Latino Politics: Gender, Culture and Political Participation in Boston*. Philadelphia: Temple University Press.

Hare, R. M. 1981. *Moral Thinking: Its Levels, Method, and Point*. Oxford: Clarendon.

Harlow, Ralph Volney. 1917. *The History of Legislative Methods in the Period Before 1825*. New Haven, CT: Yale University Press.

Harmon-Martin, Sheila F. 1994. "Black Women in Politics: A Research Note." In *Black Politics and Black Political Behavior: A Linkage Analysis*, ed. Hanes Walton. Westport, CT: Praeger.

Harris, Frederick C. 1999. *Something Within: Religion in African-American Political Activism*. New York: Oxford University Press.

Harris, John. 2001. "How Much Difference Does Politics Make? Regime Types and Trends in Rural Poverty in India." Paper presented at the University of Wisconsin, Madison, October 18.

Harris, William S., et al. 1999. "A Randomized, Controlled Trial of the Effects of Remote, Intercessory Prayer on Outcomes in Patients Admitted to the Coronary Care Unit." *Archives of Internal Medicine* 159 (19): 2273–78.

Harris-Lacewell, Melissa. 1999. "Barbershops, Bibles and B.E.T.: Dialogue and the Development of Black Political Thought." Ph.D. diss., Duke University, Durham, NC.

Harrison, Cynthia. 1988. *On Account of Sex: The Politics of Women's Issues, 1945–1968*. Berkeley: University of California Press.

Harrison, Selig, ed. 1996. *Japan's Nuclear Future: The Plutonium Debate and East Asian Security*. Washington, DC: Carnegie Endowment for International Peace.

Harsanyi, John C. 1967–1968. "Games with Incomplete Information Played by Bayesian Players," Parts I, II, III. *Management Science* 14: 159–82, 320–34, 486–502.

Harsanyi, John C. 1975. "Can the Maximin Principle Serve as a Basis for Morality? A Critique of John Rawls's Theory." *American Political Science Review* 69: 594–606.

Hart, Vivien. 1994. *Bound by Our Constitution: Women, Workers, and the Minimum Wage.* Princeton, NJ: Princeton University Press.

Hartmann, George W. 1936–1937. "Field Experiment on the Comparative Effectiveness of 'Emotional' and 'Rational' Political Leaflets in Determining Election Results." *Journal of Abnormal Psychology* 31: 99–114.

Hartz, Louis. 1955. *The Liberal Tradition in America: An Interpretation of American Political Thought Since the Revolution.* New York: Harcourt, Brace and World.

Harvey, Anna L. 1998. *Votes Without Leverage: Women in American Electoral Politics, 1920–1970.* Cambridge: Cambridge University Press.

Hasenclever, Andreas, Peter Mayer, and Volker Rittberger. 1997. *Theories of International Regimes.* Cambridge: Cambridge University Press.

Haslanger, Sally. 2000. "Gender and Race: (What) Are They? (What) Do We Want Them to Be?" *Nous* 34 (March): 31–55.

Hastie, T. J., and R. J. Tibshirani. 1990. *Generalized Additive Models.* London: Chapman and Hall.

Hattam, Victoria. 1993. *Labor Visions and State Power: Origins of Business Unionism in the United States.* Princeton, NJ: Princeton University Press.

Hayek, F. A. 1976. *The Mirage of Social Justice.* London: Routledge and Paul.

Hayek, Freidrich. 1994 [1944]. *The Road to Serfdom.* Chicago: University of Chicago Press.

Hayward, Clarissa. 2000. *Defacing Power.* Cambridge: Cambridge University Press.

Hechter, Michael. 1975. *Internal Colonialism.* London: Routledge and Paul.

Hechter, Michael. 2000. *Containing Nationalism.* New York: Oxford University Press.

Heckman, James J. 1979. "Sample Selection Bias as a Specification Error." *Econometrica* 47: 153–61.

Heckman, James J. 2000. "Causal Parameters and Policy Analysis in Economics: A Twentieth Century Retrospective." *Quarterly Journal of Economics* (February): 45–97.

Heckman, James J., and Brook S. Payner. 1989. "Determining the Impact of Federal Antidiscrimination Policy on the Economic Status of Blacks: A Study of South Carolina." *American Economic Review* 79: 138–77.

Heckman, James J., and Jeffrey A. Smith. 1995. "Assessing the Case for Social Experiments." *Journal of Economic Perspectives* 9 (spring): 85–110.

Heckman, James J., and Robert Willis. 1977. "A Beta-logistic Model for the Analysis of Sequential Labor Force Participation by Married Women." *Journal of Political Economy* 85 (1): 27–58.

Heclo, Hugh. 1974. *Modern Social Politics in Britain and Sweden.* New Haven: Yale University Press.

Hedlund, Ronald D. 1983. "Organizational Attributes of Legislative Institutions: Structure, Rules, Norms, Resources." In *Handbook of Legislative Research*, ed. Gerhard Loewenberg, Samuel C. Patterson, and Malcolm E. Jewell. Cambridge, MA: Harvard University Press.

Heiberg, Marianne, ed. 1994. *Subduing Sovereignty. Sovereignty and the Right to Intervene*. London: Pinter.

Held, David. 1980. *Introduction to Critical Theory*. Berkeley: University of California.

Held, David, Anthony McGrew, David Goldblatt, and Jonathan Perraton. 1999. *Global Transformations*. Stanford, CA: Stanford University Press.

Helleiner, Eric. 1999. "Sovereignty, Territoriality and the Globalization of Finance." In *States and Sovereignty in the Global Economy*, ed. David A. Smith, Dorothy J. Solinger, and Steven C. Topik. New York: Routledge.

Heller, Patrick. 1999. *The Labor of Development: Workers and the Transformation of Capitalism in Kerala, India*. Ithaca, NY: Cornell University Press.

Heller, William B. 1997. "Bicameralism and Budget Deficits: The Effect of Parliamentary Structure on Government Spending." *Legislative Studies Quarterly* 22: 485–516.

Helliwell, John F. 1998. *How Much Do National Borders Matter?* Washington, DC: Brookings.

Hellman, Gunther, and Reinhard Wolf. 1993. "Neorealism, Neoliberal Institutionalism, and the Future of NATO." *Security Studies* 3 (autumn): 3–43.

Hellman, Joel. 1998. "Winners Take All: The Politis of Partial Reform in Postcommunist Transitions." *World Politics* 50: 203–34.

Henderson-King, Donna, and Abigail J. Stewart. 1994. "Women or Feminists? Assessing Women's Group Consciousness." *Sex Roles* 31 (9–10): 505–16.

Henning, C. Randall. 1994. *Currencies and Politics in the United States, Germany, and Japan*. Washington, DC: Institute for International Economics.

Henning, C. Randall. 1998. "Systemic Conflict and Regional Monetary Integration: The Case of Europe." *International Organization* 52 (3): 537–73.

Herbst, Jeffrey. 1990. *State Politics in Zimbabwe*. Berkeley: University of California Press.

Herbst, Jeffrey. 1993. *Politics of Reform in Ghana, 1982–1991*. Berkeley: University of California Press.

Herbst, Jeffrey. 2000. *States and Power in Africa: Comparative Lessons in Authority and Control*. Princeton, NJ: Princeton University Press.

Hero, Rodney E. 1992. *Latinos and the U.S. Political System: Two-Tiered Pluralism*. Philadelphia: Temple University Press.

Hero, Rodney E., and Caroline J. Tolbert. 1995. "Latinos and Substantive Representation in the U.S. House of Representatives: Direct, Indirect, or Nonexistent?" *American Journal of Political Science* 39: 640–52.

Herrick, Rebekah, Michael K. Moore, and John R. Hibbing. 1994. "Unfastening the Electoral Connection: The Behavior of U.S. Representatives When Reelection Is No Longer a Factor." *Journal of Politics* 56: 214–27.

Herrigel, Gary. 1996. *Industrial Constructions: The Sources of German Industrial Power.* New York: Cambridge University Press.

Herring, Ronald J. 1983. *Land to the Tiller: The Political Economy of Land Reform in South Asia.* New Haven and London: Yale University Press.

Herring, Ronald J. 1999. "Embedded Particularism: India's Failed Developmental State." In *The Developmental State,* ed. Meredith Woo-Cumings, 306–34. Ithaca, NY: Cornell University Press.

Herz, John H. 1950. "Idealist Internationalism and the Security Dilemma." *World Politics* 2: 157–80.

Herz, John H. 1959. *International Politics in the Atomic Age.* New York: Columbia University Press.

Herz, John H. 1976. *The Nation-State and the Crisis of World Politics.* New York: McKay.

Herzog, Don. 1998. *Poisoning the Minds of the Lower Orders.* Princeton, NJ: Princeton University Press.

Hess, Robert D., and Judith V. Torney. 1968. *The Development of Political Attitudes in Children.* Garden City, NY: Doubleday, Anchor Books.

Hibbing, John R. 1999. "Legislative Careers: Why and How We Should Study Them." *Legislative Studies Quarterly* 24: 149–72.

Hibbing, John, and Elizabeth Theiss-Morse. 1995. *Congress as Public Enemy.* New York: Cambridge University Press.

Hibbs, Douglas A. 1973. *Mass Political Violence: A Cross-National Causal Analysis.* New York: Wiley Interscience.

Hibbs, Douglas A. 1977. "Political Parties and Macroeconomic Policy." *American Political Science Review* 71: 1467–87.

Hicks, Alexander M. 1999. *Social Democracy and Welfare Capitalism: A Century of Income Security Politics.* Ithaca, NY: Cornell University Press.

Hicks, Alexander M., and Duane H. Swank. 1992. "Politics, Institutions and Welfare Spending in Industrialized Countries, 1960–82." *American Political Science Review* 86: 658–74.

Higginbotham, Evelyn Brooks. 1990. "In Politics to Stay: Black Women Leaders and Party Politics in the 1920s." In *Women, Politics, and Change,* ed. Louise A. Tilly and Patricia Gurin. New York: Russell Sage.

Higginbotham, Evelyn Brooks. 1992. "African-American Women's History and the Metalanguage of Race." *Signs* 17: 251–74.

Highton, Benjamin. 1997. "Early Registration and Voter Turnout." *Journal of Politics* 59: 565–75.

Hill, Kim Quaile, and Jan E. Leighley. 1994. "Mobilizing Institutions and Class Representation in U.S. State Electorates." *Political Research Quarterly* 47: 137–50.

Hill, Kim Quaile, and Jan E. Leighley. 1996. "Political Parties and Class Mobilization in Comtemporary United States Elections." *American Journal of Political Science* 40: 787–804.

Hill, Kim Quaile, and Jan E. Leighley. 1999. "Racial Diversity, Voter Turnout, and Mobilizing Institutions in the United States." *American Politics Quarterly* 27: 275–95.

Hill, Kim Quaile, Jan E. Leighley, and Angela Hinton-Anderson. 1995. "Lower-Class Mobilization and Policy Linkage in the U.S. States." *American Journal of Political Science* 39: 75–86.

Hinich, Melvin J., and Michael C. Munger. 1997. *Analytical Politics.* New York: Cambridge University Press.

Hinich, Melvin J., and Walker Pollard. 1981. "A New Approach to the Spatial Theory of Electoral Competition." *American Journal of Political Science* 25: 323–41.

Hirschl, Ran. 1999. "Towards Juristocracy: A Comparative Inquiry onto the Origins and Consequences of the New Constitutionalism." Ph.D. diss., Yale University, New Haven, CT.

Hirschl, Ran. 2000. "The Political Origins of Judicial Empowerment through Constitutionalization: Lessons from Four Constitutional Revolutions." *Law and Social Inquiry* 25 (1): 91–147.

Hirshleifer, Jack, and Eric Rasmusen. 1992. "Are Equilibrium Strategies Unaffected By Incentives?" *Journal of Theoretical Politics* 4 (3): 353–67.

Hirschman, Alberto. 1958. *The Strategy of Economic Development.* New Haven, CT: Yale University Press.

Hirschman, Albert O. 1981. "Rise and Decline of Development Economics." In *Essays in Trespassing: Economics to Politics and Beyond,* Albert O. Hirschman. Cambridge and New York: Cambridge University Press.

Hirschmann, Nancy J. 1996. "Revisioning Freedom: Relationship, Context, and the Politics of Empowerment." *Political Theory* 24 (1).

Hirst, Paul, and Grahame Thompson. 1996. *Globalization in Question.* Cambridge, MA: Polity.

Hirst, Paul, and Grahame Thompson, 1999. *Globalization in Question: The International Economy and the Possibilities of Governance.* Cambridge: Polity.

Hiscox, Michael J. 1999. "The Magic Bullet? The RTAA, Institutional Reform, and Trade Liberalization." *International Organization* 53 (4): 669–98.

Hix, Simon. 1999. *The Political System of the European Union.* New York: St. Martin's.

Hobbes, Thomas. 1985 [1651]. *Leviathan.* ed. C.B. MacPherson. London: Penguin.

Hobbes, Thomas. 1991 [1651]. *Leviathan.* New York: Cambridge University Press.

Hobsbawm, E. J. 1992. *Nations and Nationalism since 1780: Programme, Myth, Reality.* 2d ed. Cambridge: Cambridge University Press.

Hobson, John M. 2000. *The State and International Relations.* Cambridge: Cambridge University Press.

Hochschild, Jennifer L. 1984. *The New American Dilemma: Liberal Democracy and School Desegregation.* New Haven, CT: Yale University Press.

Hofer v. Hofer. 1970. S.C.R. 958–92.

Hofstadter, Richard. 1950. "Beard and the Constitution: The History of an Idea." *American Quarterly* 2 (autumn)

Hogan, Robert E. 1999. "Campaign and Contextual Influences on Participation in State Legislative Elections." *American Politics Quarterly* 27: 403–33.

Holborn, Hajo. 1982. *A History of Modern Germany.* Princeton, NJ: Princeton University Press.

Holden, Matthew, Jr. 2000. "The Competence of Political Science: 'Progress in Political Research Revisited.'" *American Political Science Review* 94 (1): 1–20.

Hollifield, James F. 1992. *Immigrants, Markets and States. The Political Economy of Postwar Europe.* Cambridge, MA: Harvard University Press.

Hollinger, David. 1995. *Postethnic America: Beyond Multiculturalism.* New York: Basic.

Hollis, Martin, and Steve Smith. 1990. *Explaining and Understanding International Relations.* Oxford: Clarendon Press.

Holmes, Stephen. 1993. *The Anatomy of Antiliberalism.* Cambridge, MA: Harvard University Press.

Holmes, Stephen. 1995. *Passions and Constraint: On the Theory of Liberal Democracy.* Chicago: University of Chicago Press.

Holmes, Stephen, and Cass Sunstein. 1999. *The Costs of Rights: Why Liberty Depends on Taxes.* New York: Norton.

Holt, Thomas C. 2000. *The Problem of Race in the 21st Century.* Cambridge, MA: Harvard University Press.

Honig, Bonnie. 1993. *Political Theory and the Displacement of Politics.* Ithaca, NY: Cornell University Press.

Honig, Bonnie. 2001. *Democracy and the Foreigner.* Princeton, NJ: Princeton University Press.

Honneth, Axel. 1991. *The Critique of Power: Reflective Stages in Critical Social Theory.* Cambridge: MIT Press.

Honneth, Axel. 1995. "Integrity and Disrespect: Principles of a Conception of Morality Based on a Theory of Recognition." In *The Fragmented World of the Social: Essays in Social and Political Philosophy,* ed. Axel Honneth, 247–60. Albany: State University of New York Press.

Honneth, Axel. 1996. *The Struggle for Recognition: The Moral Grammar of Social Conflicts.* Cambridge: MIT Press.

Hood, M. V., III, and Irwin L. Morris. 1998. "Boll Weevils and Roll-Call Voting: A Study in Time and Space." *Legislative Studies Quarterly* 23: 245–69.

hooks, bell. 1984. *Feminist Theory: From Margin to Center.* Boston: South End.

Hopf, Ted. 1991. "Polarity, the Offense-Defense Balance, and War." *American Political Science Review* 85: 475–93.

Hopf, Ted. 1994. *Peripheral Visions: Deterrence Theory and American Foreign Policy in the Third World, 1965–1980.* Ann Arbor: University of Michigan Press.

Horowitz, Donald L. 1985. *Ethnic Groups in Conflict.* Berkeley: University of California Press.

Horowitz, Donald L. 1990. "Presidents vs. Parliaments: Comparing Democratic Systems." *Journal of Democracy* 1 (4): 73–79.

Horowitz, Donald L. 1991. *A Democratic South Africa? Constitutional Engineering in a Divided Society*. Berkeley: University of California Press.

Horowitz, Donald L. 2000. "Constitutional Design: An Oxymoron?" In *N.M. SXL II: Designing Democratic Institutions*, ed. Ian Shapiro and Stephen Macedo, 253–84. New York: New York University Press.

Hoskin, Gary, Francisco Leal, and Harvey Kline. 1976. *Legislative Behavior in Colombia*. Buffalo: Council on International Studies, State University of New York.

Hough, Jerry F. 1997. *Democratization and Revolution in the USSR, 1985–1991*. Washington, DC, Brookings.

Hough, Jerry. 1974. "The Soviet System: Petrification or Pluralism?" In *Communist Systems in Comparative Perspective*, ed. Lenard Cohen and Jane Shapiro. Garden City, NY: Anchor.

Hovland, Carl I., Arthur A. Lumsdaine, and F. D. Sheffield. 1949. *Experiments on Mass Communication*. Princeton, NJ: Princeton University Press.

Howard, Christopher. 1995. "Protean Lure for the Working Poor: Party Competition and the Earned Income Tax Credit." *Studies in American Political Development* 9 (2): 404–36.

Howard, Christopher. 1997. *The Hidden Welfare State: Tax Expenditures and Social Policy in the United States*. Princeton, NJ: Princeton University Press.

Howell, Chris. 2001. "The Construction of Industrial Relations Institutions: Theoretical and Comparative Perspectives." Paper presented at the meetings of the American Political Science Association, San Francisco, August 30–September 2.

Howell, William, Scott Adler, Charles Cameron, and Charles Riemann. 2000. "Divided Government and the Legislative Productivity of Congress: 1945–94." *Legislative Studies Quarterly* 25: 285–312.

Hoxie, R. Gordon, ed. 1955. *A History of the Faculty of Political Science, Columbia University*. New York: Columbia University Press.

Hritzuk, Natasha, and David K. Park. 2000. "The Question of Latino Participation: From an SES to a Social Structural Explanation." *Social Science Quarterly* 81: 151–66.

Hsiao, Hsin-Huang Michael, and Hagen Koo. 1997. "The Middle Classes and Democratization." In *Consolidating the Third Wave Democracies*, ed. Larry Diamond, Marc F. Plattner, Yun-han Chus, and Hung-mao Tien. Baltimore: Johns Hopkins University Press: 312–33.

Htun, Mala. Forthcoming. *Democracy, Dictatorship, and Gendered Rights*. Cambridge and New York: Cambridge University Press.

Huber, Evelyne, and John D. Stephens. 2001. *Development and Crisis of the Welfare State: Parties and Policies in World Markets*. Chicago: University of Chicago Press.

Huber, John D. 1992. "Restrictive Legislative Procedures in France and the United States." *American Political Science Review* 86: 675–87.

Huber, John D. 1996a. *Rationalizing Parliament: Legislative Institutions and Party Politics in France*. Cambridge: Cambridge University Press.

Huber, John D. 1996b. "The Vote of Confidence in Parliamentary Democracies." *American Political Science Review* 90: 269–82.

Huber, John D. 1998. "How Does Cabinet Instability Affect Political Performance? Portfolio Volatility and Health Care Cost Containment in Parliamentary Democracies." *American Political Science Review* 92: 577–91.

Huber, John D. 2000. "Delegation to Civil Servants in Parliamentary Democracies." *European Journal of Political Research* 37: 397–413.

Huber, John, and Charles Shipan. 2001. *Political Control of the State in Modern Democracies*. Manuscript, Departments of Political Science, Columbia University and University of Iowa.

Huckfeldt, Robert, Eric Plutzer, and John Sprague. 1993. "Alternative Contexts of Political Behavior: Churches, Neighborhoods, and Individuals." *Journal of Politics* 55: 365–81.

Huckfeldt, Robert, and John Sprague. 1992. "Political Parties and Electoral Mobilization: Political Structure, Social Structure, and the Party Canvass." *American Political Science Review* 86 (March): 70–86.

Huckfeldt, Robert, and John Sprague. 1995. *Citizens, Politics, and Social Communication*. Cambridge: Cambridge University Press.

Huddy, Leonie, and Stanley Feldman. 2001. The Intersection of Race and Class in White Opposition to Racial Polices. Prepared for the annual meeting of the American Political Science Association, San Francisco, CA.

Huddy, Leonie, and Nayda Terkildsen. 1993. "Gender Stereotypes and the Perception of Male and Female Candidates." *American Journal of Political Science* 37 (February): 119–47.

Huitt, Ralph K. 1957. "The Morse Committee Assignment Controversy: A Study in Senate Norms." *American Political Science Review* 51: 313–29.

Huitt, Ralph K. 1961a. "Democratic Party Leadership in the Senate." *American Political Science Review* 55: 331–44.

Huitt, Ralph K. 1961b. "The Outsider in the Senate: An Alternative Role." *American Political Science Review* 55: 566–75.

Hunter, Wendy. 1997. *Eroding Military Influence in Brazil: Politicians against Soldiers*. Chapel Hill: University of North Carolina Press.

Huntington, Samuel P. 1965. "Political Development and Political Decay." *World Politics* 17 (3): 378–414.

Huntington, Samuel P. 1966. *Political Order in Changing Societies*. New Haven, CT: Yale University Press.

Huntington, Samuel P. 1968. *Political Order in Changing Societies*. New Haven and London: Yale University Press.

Huntington, Samuel P. 1971. "The Change to Change." *Comparative Politics* 3 (3): 283–322.

Huntington, Samuel P. 1981. *American Politics: The Promise of Disharmony*. Cambridge, MA: Harvard University Press.

Huntington, Samuel P. 1991. *The Third Wave: Democratization in the Late Twentieth Century*. Norman: University of Oklahoma Press.

Hurd, Ian. 1999. "Legitimacy and Authority in International Politics." *International Organization* 53 (2): 379–408.

Hurwitz, Jon, and Mark Peffley, eds. 1998. *Perception Prejudice.* New Haven, CT: Yale University Press.

Husami, Ziyad I. 1978. "Marx on Distributive Justice." *Philosophy and Public Affairs* 8 (autumn): 27–64.

Hutchcroft, Paul D. 1998. *Booty Capitalism: The Politics of Banking in the Philippines.* Ithaca, NY: Cornell University Press.

Hutchings, Vincent L. 1999. "Issue Salience and Support for Civil Rights Legislation among Southern Democrats." *Legislative Studies Quarterly* 23: 521–44.

Huth, Paul K. 1988. *Extended Deterrence and the Prevention of War.* New Haven, CT: Yale University Press.

Huth, Paul K. 1996. *Standing Your Ground: Territorial Disputes and International Conflict.* Ann Arbor: University of Michigan Press.

Huth, Paul. 1997. "Reputations and Deterrence." *Security Studies* 7 (autumn): 72–99.

Huth, Paul K. 1999. "Deterrence and International Conflict: Empirical Findings and Theoretical Debates." *Annual Review of Political Science* 2: 25–48.

Hyndman, Patricia. 1986. "Refugees Under International Law with Reference to the Concept of Asylum." *Australian Law Journal* 60 (3): 148–55.

Hypatia: A Journal of Feminist Philosophy. 12:4 (Fall 1997).

Hypatia: A Journal of Feminist Philosophy. 13:2 (Spring 1998).

Iglitzin, Lynne B. 1974. "The Making of the Apolitical Woman: Feminity and Sex-Stereotyping in Girls." In *Women in Politics,* ed. Jane S. Jaquette. New York: Wiley.

Iida, Keisuke. 1990. "Analytic Uncertainty and International Cooperation: Theory and Application to International Economic-Policy Coordination." *International Studies Quarterly* 37 (4): 431–57.

Iida, Keisuke. 1999. *International Monetary Cooperation Among the United States, Japan, and Germany.* Norwell: Kluwer Academic.

Ikenberry, G. John. 2001. *After Victory: Institutions, Strategic Restraint, and the Rebuilding of Order After Major Wars.* Princeton, NJ: Princeton University Press.

Ikenberry, G. John, David A. Lake, and Michael Mastanduno, eds. 1988. *The State and American Foreign Economic Policy.* Ithaca, NY: Cornell University Press.

Im, Hyug Baeg. 1987. "The Rise of Bureaucratic Authoritarianism in South Korea." *World Politics* 39: 231–57.

Immergut, Ellen. 1992. *Health Politics: Interests and Institutions in Western Europe.* Cambridge: Cambridge University Press.

Inglehart, Margaret L. 1981. "Political Interest in West European Women." *Comparative Political Studies* 14: 299–326.

Inglehart, Ronald. 1990. *Culture Shift in the Advanced Industrial Countries.* Princeton, NJ: Princeton University Press.

Irwin, Douglas, and Randall Kroszner. 1999. "Interests, Institutions, and Ideology in Securing Policy Change: The Republican Conversion to Trade Liberalization after Smoot-Hawley." *Journal of Law and Economics* (October): 643–73.

Isaac, Jeffrey C. 1998. *Democracy in Dark Times*. Ithaca, NY: Cornell University Press.

Iversen, Torben. 1996. "Power, Flexibility and the Breakdown of Centralized Wage Bargaining: The Cases of Denmark and Sweden in Comparative Perspective." *Comparative Politics* 28 (4): 399–436.

Iversen, Torben. 1998a. "The Political Economy of Inflation: Bargaining Structure or Central Bank Independence." *Public Choice* 99: 237–58.

Iversen, Torben. 1998b. "Wage Bargaining, Central Bank Independence, and the Real Effects of Money." *International Organization* 52: 469–504.

Iversen, Torben. 1999. *Contested Economic Institutions: The Politics of Macroeconomics and Wage Bargaining in Advanced Democracies*. Cambridge: Cambridge University Press.

Iversen, Torben, and Thomas R. Cusack. 2000. "The Causes of Welfare State Expansion: Deindustrialization or Globalization?" *World Politics* 52 (April): 313–49.

Iversen, Torben, and Jonas Pontusson. 2000. "Comparative Political Economy: A Northern European Perspective." In *Unions, Employers and Central Banks*, ed. T. Iversen, J. Pontusson, and D. Soskice. New York: Cambridge University Press.

Iversen, Torben, Jonas Pontusson, and David Soskice, eds. 2000. *Unions, Employers, and Central Banks: Macroeconomic Coordination and Institutional Change in Social Market Economies*. New York: Cambridge University Press.

Iversen, Torben, and David Soskice. 2001. "An Asset Theory of Social Policy Preferences." *American Political Science Review* 95 (December): 875–94.

Iversen, Torben, and Anne Wren. 1998. "Equality, Employment and Budgetary Restraint: The Trilemma of the Service Economy." *World Politics* 50 (4): 507–546.

Iyengar, Shanto. 1990. "Shortcuts to Political Knowledge: The Role of Selective Attention and Accessibility." In *Information and Democratic Processes*, ed. John A. Ferejohn and James H. Kuklinski. Chicago: University of Illinois Press.

Iyengar, Shanto, and Donald R. Kinder. 1987. *News That Matters: Television and American Opinion*. Chicago: University of Chicago Press.

Jackman, Mary R. 1994. *The Velvet Glove: Paternalism and Conflict in Gender, Class, and Race Relations*. Berkeley: University of California Press.

Jackman, Robert W., and Ross A. Miller. 1998. "Social Capital and Politics." *Annual Review of Political Science* 1: 47–73.

Jackman, Simon. 2000. "Estimation and Inference via Bayesian Simulation: An Introduction to Markov Chain Monte Carlo," *American Journal of Political Science* 44 (2): 375–404.

Jackson, John E. 1975. "Issues, Party Choices, and Presidential Voting." *American Journal of Political Science* 19: 161–86.

Jackson, Robert A. 1995. "Clarifying the Relationship Between Education and Turnout." *American Politics Quarterly* 23: 279–99.

Jackson, Robert A. 1996. "A Reassessment of Voter Mobilization." *Political Research Quarterly* 49: 331–49.

Jackson, Robert A. 1999. "The Mobilization of State Electorates in the 1988 and 1990 Elections." *Journal of Politics* 59: 520–37.

Jackson, Robert H. 1990. *Quasi-States: Sovereignty, International Relations, and the Third World.* Cambridge: Cambridge University Press.

Jackson, Robert H. 1993. "The Weight of Ideas in Decolonization: Normative Change in International Relations." In *Ideas and Foreign Policy: Beliefs, Institutions and Political Change,* ed. Judith Goldstein and Robert O. Keohane. Ithaca, NY: Cornell University Press.

Jackson, Robert H., and Carl G. Rosberg. 1982. "Why Africa's Weak States Persist: The Empirical and Juridical in Statehood." *World Politics* 35 (1): 1–24.

Jackson, Robert Max. 1984. *The Formation of Craft Labor Markets.* New York: Academic.

Jacobson, David. 1997. *Rights Across Borders. Immigration and the Decline of Citizenship.* Baltimore: Johns Hopkins University Press.

Jacobson, Gary. 1985. "Money and Votes Reconsidered: Congressional Elections, 1972–1982." *Public Choice* 47 (1): 7–62.

Jacobson, Gary. 1990. "The Effects of Campaign Spending in House Elections: New Evidence for Old Arguments." *American Journal of Political Science* 34 (May): 334–62.

James, Patrick. 1995. "Structural Realism and the Causes of War." *Mershon International Studies Review* 39 (October): 181–208.

James, Scott. 2000. *Presidents, Parties and the State: A Party System Perspective on Democratic Regulatory Choice, 1884–1936.* New York: Cambridge University Press.

Jameson, Frederic, and Masao Miyoshi, eds. 1998. *The Cultures of Globalization.* Durham, NC: Duke University Press.

Jay, Martin. 1973. *The Dialectical Imagination.* Boston: Little, Brown.

Jenkins, Jeffery A. 1998. "Property Rights and the Emergence of Standing Committee Dominance in the Nineteenth-Century House." *Legislative Studies Quarterly* 23: 493–519.

Jennings, Jeanette. 1991. "Black Women Mayors: Reflections on Race and Gender." In *Gender and Policymaking,* ed. Debra L. Dodson. New Brunswick: Center for the American Woman and Politics, Eagleton Institute of Politics, Rutgers University.

Jennings, M. Kent, and Barbara G. Farah. 1981. "Social Roles and Political Resources." *American Journal of Political Science* 25 (August): 462–82.

Jennings, M. Kent, and Laura Stoker. 1999. "The Persistence of the Past: The Class of 1965 Turns Fifty." Paper presented at the Midwest Political Science Association Convention, Chicago.

Jennings, M. Kent, and Richard G. Niemi. 1981. *Generations and Politics.* Princeton, NJ: Princeton University Press.

Jennings, M. Kent, Laura Stoker, and Jake Bowers. 1999. "Politics across Generations: Family Transmission Reexamined." Paper presented at the American Political Science Convention, Atlanta, GA.

Jennings, Sir Ivor. 1957. *Parliament*. 2d ed. Cambridge: Cambridge University Press.

Jenson, Jane. 1986. "Gender and Reproduction: Or, Babies and the State." *Studies in Political Economy* 20 (fall): 1–19.

Jepperson, Ronald L. 2000. "The Development and Application of Sociological Institutionalism." In *New Directions in Sociological Theory: The Growth of Contemporary Theories*, ed. J. Berger and M. J. Zelditch. Lanham, MD: Rowman and Littlefield.

Jepperson, Ronald L. 2001. "The Development and Application of Sociological Neoinstitutionalism." European University Institute Working Paper RSC 2001/5.

Jepperson, Ronald L., Alexander Wendt, and Peter J. Katzenstein. 1996. "Norms, Identity, and Culture in National Security." In *The Culture of National Security: Norms and Identity in World Politics*, ed. P. J. Katzenstein, 33–75. New York: Columbia University Press.

Jervis, Robert. 1970. *The Logic of Images in International Relations*. Princeton, NJ: Princeton University Press.

Jervis, Robert. 1976. *Perception and Misperception in International Politics*. Princeton, NJ: Princeton University Press.

Jervis, Robert. 1978. "Cooperation under the Security Dilemma." *World Politics* 30: 167–214.

Jervis, Robert. 1984. *The Illogic of American Nuclear Strategy*. Ithaca, NY: Cornell University Press.

Jervis, Robert. 1989. *The Meaning of the Nuclear Revolution*. Ithaca, NY: Cornell University Press.

Jervis, Robert. 1997. *System Effects*. Princeton, NJ: Princeton University Press.

Jervis, Robert. 1998. "Realism in the Study of World Politics." *International Organization* 52 (autumn): 971–92.

Jervis, Robert. 1999. "Realism, Neoliberalism, and Cooperation: Understanding the Debate." *International Security* 24 (summer).

Jessop, Bob. 1990. *State Theory*. Cambridge: Polity.

Jewell, Malcom E. 1976. "Editor's Introduction." *Legislative Studies Quarterly* 1: 1–9.

Jillson, Calvin. 1994. "Patterns and Periodicity in American National Politics." In *The Dynamics of American Politics: Approaches and Interpretations*, ed. Lawrence Dodd and Calvin Jillson, 24–58. Boulder, CO. Westview.

Jillson, Calvin, and Rick K. Wilson. 1994. *Congressional Dynamics: Structure, Coordination, and Choice in the First American Congress, 1774–1789*. Stanford, CA: Stanford University Press.

Joerges, Christian, and Jürgen Neyer. 1997. "Transforming Strategic Interaction into Deliberative Problem-Solving: European Comitology in the Foodstuffs Sector." *Journal of European Public Policy* 4: 609–25.

Joffe, Josef. 1995. " 'Bismarck' or 'Britain'?: Toward an American Grand Strategy after Bipolarity." *International Security* 19 (spring): 94–117.

Johnson, Chalmers A. 1982. *MITI and the Japanese Miracle: The Growth of Industrial Policy, 1925–1975.* Stanford, CA: Stanford University Press.

Johnson, Chalmers A. 1987. "Political Institutions and Economic Performance: The Government-Business Relationship in Japan, South Korea, and Taiwan." In *The Political Economy of the New Asian Industrialism,* ed. Frederic Deyo, 136–64. Ithaca, NY: Cornell University Press.

Johnson, Chalmers A. 1997. "Perceptions versus Observation, or the Contributions of Rational Choice Theory and Area Studies to Contemporary Political Science." *PS: Political Science and Politics* 30 (2): 170–74.

Johnson, Chalmers A. 1999. "The Developmental State: Odyssey of a Concept." In *The Developmental State,* ed. Meredith Woo-Cumings, 32–60. Ithaca, N.Y.: Cornell University Press.

Johnson, R. W. 1989. "Wars of Religion." *New Statesman and Society* (December 15): 13–14.

Johnston, Alastair Iain. 1995. *Cultural Realism: Strategic Culture and Grand Strategy in Chinese History.* Princeton, NJ: Princeton University Press.

Jomo, K. S., et al. 1997. *Southeast Asia's Misunderstood Miracle: Industrial Policy and Economic Development in Thailand, Malaysia, and Indonesia.* Boulder, CO: Westview.

Jones, Bryan D., James L. True, and Frank R. Baumgartner. 1997. "Does Incrementalism Stem from Political Consensus or from Institutional Gridlock?" *American Journal of Political Science* 41: 1319–39.

Jones, Charles O. 1968. "Joseph G. Cannon and Howard W. Smith: An Essay on the Limits of Leadership in the House of Representatives." *Journal of Politics* 30: 617–46.

Jones, Charles O. 1970. *The Minority Party in Congress.* Boston: Little, Brown.

Jones, Charles O. 1999. *Global Justice: Defending Cosmopolitanism.* Oxford, UK: Oxford University Press.

Jones, Kathleen B., ed. 1997. *Citizenship in Feminism: Identity, Action, and Locale. Hypatia: A Journal of Feminist Philosophy* Special Issue. 12 (4, fall).

Jones, Leroy P., and Il Sakong. 1980. *Government, Business, and Entrepreneurship in Economic Development: The Korean Case.* Cambridge, MA: Council on East Asian Studies, Harvard University Press.

Jones, Mark. 1995. *Electoral Laws and the Survival of Presidential Democracies.* South Bend, IN: University of Notre Dame Press.

Jones, Mark, Pablo Sanguinetti, and Mariano Tommasi. 2000. "Politics, Institutions, and Fiscal Performance in a Federal System: An Analysis of the Argentine Provinces." *Journal of Development Economic* 61: 305–34.

Jones-Correa, Michael. 1998. *Between Two Nations: The Political Predicament of Latinos in New York City.* Ithaca, NY: Cornell University Press.

Jørgenson, Knud Erik. 1998. "The European Union's Performance in World Politics: How Should We Measure Success?" In *Paradoxes of European Foreign Policy,* ed. Jan Zielonka. The Hague: Kluwer Law International.

Jung, Courtney. 2000. "The Myth of the Divided Society and the Case of South Africa." Mimeograph, New School for Social Research, New York.

Jung, Courtney, and Ian Shapiro. 1995. "South Africa's Negotiated Transition: Democracy, Opposition, and the New Constitutional Order." *Politics and Society* 23: 269–308.

Junn, Jane. 1997. "Assimilating or Coloring Participation? Gender, Race, and Democratic Political Participation." In *Women Transforming Politics*, ed. Cathy J. Cohen, Kathleen B. Jones, and Joan C. Tronto. New York: New York University Press.

Kagan, Korina. 1997–98. "The Myth of the European Concert." *Security Studies* 7 (winter): 1–57.

Kagan, Shelly. 1989. *The Limits of Morality*. Oxford: Clarendon.

Kahler, Miles, and David A. Lake. 2000. *Globalization and Governance*. Paper presented at the 2000 Annual Meeting of the American Political Science Association, Washington, DC.

Kahler, Miles. 1984. *Decolonization in Britain and France*. Princeton: Princeton University Press.

Kahler, Miles. 1995. *International Institutions and the Political Economy of Integration*. Washington, DC: Brookings.

Kahler, Miles. 1997. "Inventing International Relations." In *New Thinking in International Relations*, ed. Michael W. Doyle and G. John Ikenberry. Boulder, CO: Westview.

Kahler, Miles. Forthcoming. "The State of the State in World Politics." In *State of the Discipline*, ed. I. Katznelson and H. Milgram.

Kahn, Kim Fridkin. 1992. "Does Being Male Help? An Investigation of the Effects of Candidate Gender and Campaign Coverage on Evaluation of U.S. Senate Candidates." *Journal of Politics* 54 (May): 497–517.

Kahn, Kim Fridkin. 1994a. "The Distorted Mirror: Press Coverage of Women Candidates for Statewide Office." *Journal of Politics* 56 (February): 154–73.

Kahn, Kim Fridkin. 1994b. "Does Gender Make a Difference? An Experimental Examination of Sex Stereotypes and Press Patterns in Statewide Campaigns." *American Journal of Political Science* 38 (February): 162–95.

Kahn, Kim Fridkin, and Patrick J. Kenney. 1999. "Do Negative Campaigns Mobilize or Suppress Turnout? Clarifying the Relationship between Negativity and Participation." *American Political Science Review* 93: 877–89.

Kahneman, Daniel, and Amos Tversky. 1979. "Prospect Theory." *Econometrica* 47: 263–91.

Kalyvas, Stathis N. 1996. *The Rise of Christian Democracy in Europe*. Ithaca, NY: Cornell University Press.

Kalyvas, Stathis N. 1999. "The Decay and Breakdown of Communist One-Party Systems." *Annual Review of Political Science* 2: 323–43.

Kalyvas, Stathis N. Forthcoming. *The Logic of Violence in Civil War*.

Kang, David C. 2002. *Crony Capitalism, Corruption, and Development in South Korea and the Philippines*. Cambridge, MA: Cambridge University Press.

Kant, Immanuel. 1914. "Zum Ewigen Frieden. Ein philosophischer Entwurf." In *Immanuel Kants Werke*, ed. A. Buchenau, E. Cassirer and B. Kellermann. Berlin: Verlag Bruno Cassirer.

Kant, Immanuel. 1996 [1797]. *The Metaphysics of Morals*. Trans. Mary Gregor. Cambridge: Cambridge University Press.

Kant, Immanuel. 1795. "Perpetual Peace." In *On History*, trans. Lewis White Beck. New York: Bobbs-Merrill.

Kanter, Rosabeth Moss. 1977. *Men and Women of the Corporation*. New York: Basic.

Kaplan, Morton. 1957. *System and Process in International Politics*. Chicago: University of Chicago Press.

Kaplow, Louis, and Steven Shavell. 2001. "Fairness Versus Welfare." *Harvard Law Review* 114 (February): 961–1388.

Kapstein, Ethan B. 1994. *Governing the Global Economy: International Finance and the State*. Cambridge, MA: Harvard University Press.

Karl, Terry Lynn. 1997. *The Paradox of Plenty: Oil Booms and Petro-States*. Berkeley and Los Angeles: University of California Press.

Karnig, Albert K., and Susan Welch. 1979. "Sex and Ethnic Differences in Municipal Representation." *Social Science Quarterly* 60 (December): 465–81.

Kateb, George. 1992. *The Inner Ocean*. Ithaca, NY: Cornell University Press.

Kateb, George. 1994. "Notes on Pluralism." *Social Research* 61 (3): 511–37.

Kateb, George. 1998. "The Value of Association." In *Freedom of Association*, ed. Amy Gutmann, 35–63. Princeton, NJ: Princeton University Press.

Kathlene, Lyn. 1994. "Power and Influence in State Legislative Policymaking: The Interaction of Gender and Position in Committee Hearing Debates." *American Political Science Review* 88: 560–76.

Kathlene, Lyn. 1995a. "Alternative Views of Crime." *Journal of Politics* 57: 696–723.

Kathlene, Lyn. 1995b. "Position Power versus Gender Power: Who Holds the Floor?" In *Gender Power, Leadership, and Governance*, ed. Georgia Duerst-Lahti and Rita Mae Kelly, 167–193. Ann Arbor: University of Michigan Press.

Katz, Harry. 1993. "The Decentralization of Collective Bargaining: A Literature Review and Comparative Analysis." *Industrial and Labor Relations Review* 47 (1): 3–22.

Katz, Jonathan N., and Brian R. Sala. 1996. "Careerism, Committee Assignments, and the Electoral Connection." *American Political Science Review* 90: 21–33.

Katzenstein, Mary Fainsod. 1998. *Faithful and Fearless: Moving Feminist Protest inside the Church and Military*. Princeton, NJ: Princeton University Press.

Katzenstein, Mary Fainsod, and Carol McClurg Mueller, eds. 1987. *The Women's Movements of the United States and Western Europe*. Philadelphia: Temple University Press.

Katzenstein, Peter J. 1978. *Between Power and Plenty: Foreign Economic Policies of Advanced Industrial Societies.* Madison: University of Wisconsin Press.

Katzenstein, Peter J. 1984, 1985. *Corporatism and Change.* Ithaca, NY: Cornell University Press.

Katzenstein, Peter J. 1985a. *Small States in World Markets: Industrial Policy in Europe.* Ithaca, NY: Cornell University Press.

Katzenstein, Peter J. 1987. *Policy and Politics in West Germany: The Growth of a Semisovereign State.* Philadelphia: Temple University Press.

Katzenstein, Peter J. 1996a. *Cultural Norms and National Security.* Ithaca, NY: Cornell University Press.

Katzenstein, Peter J., ed. 1996b. *The Culture of National Security. Norms and Identity in World Politics.* New York: Columbia University Press.

Katzenstein, Peter J., Robert Keohane, and Stephen Krasner. 1998. "International Organization and the Study of World Politics." *International Organization* 52: 654–86.

Katznelson, Ira. 1981. *City Trenches: Urban Politics and the Patterning of Class in the United States.* New York: Pantheon Books.

Katznelson, Ira. 1996. *Liberalism's Crooked Circle: Letters to Adam Michnik.* Princeton, NJ: Princeton University Press.

Katznelson, Ira. 1997. "Structure and Configuration in Comparative Politics." In *Comparative Politics: Rationality, Culture, and Structure,* ed. Mark Irving Lichbach and Alan Zuckerman. New York: Cambridge University Press.

Katznelson, Ira. 2002. "Periodization and Preferences: Reflections on Purposive Action in Comparative Historical Social Science." In *Comparative Political Historical Analysis,* ed. James Mahoney and Dietrich Rueschemeyer. New York: Cambridge University Press.

Katznelson, Ira, Kim Geiger and Daniel Kryder. 1993. "Limiting Liberalism: The Southern Veto in Congress." *Political Science Quarterly* 108: 283–306.

Katznelson, Ira, and Bruce Pietrykowski. 1991. "Rebuilding the American State: Evidence from the 1940s." *Studies in American Political Development* 5 (2): 3001–339.

Katznelson, Ira, and Aristide R. Zolberg, eds. 1986. *Working-Class Formation: Nineteenth-Century Patterns in Western Europe and the United States.* Princeton, NJ: Princeton University Press.

Kaufman, Robert G. 1992. "Do Balance or to Bandwagon? Alignment Decisions in 1930s Europe." *Security Studies* 1 (spring): 417–47.

Kaufmann, Chaim D. 1996. "Possible and Impossible Solutions to Ethnic Civil Wars." *International Security* 20 (spring): 136–75.

Kaufmann, Chaim D. 1998. "When All Else Fails: Ethnic Population Transfers and Partitions in the 20th Century." *International Security* 23 (fall): 120–56.

Kaufmann, Chaim D., and Robert A. Pape. 1999. "Explaining Costly International Moral Action: Britain's Sixty-Year Campaign Against the Atlantic Slave Trade." *International Organization* 53: 631–68.

Kaufmann, Karen M., and John R. Petrocik. 1999. "The Changing Politics of American Men: Understanding the Sources of the Gender Gap." *American Journal of Political Science* 43 (3): 864–87.

Kaysen, Carl. 1990. "Is War Obsolete?: A Review Essay." *International Security* 14 (spring): 42–64.

Keck, Margaret E., and Kathryn Sikkink. 1998. *Activists Beyond Borders: Advocacy Networks in International Politics.* Ithaca, NY: Cornell University Press.

Keech, William. 1995. *Economic Politics.* New York: Cambridge University Press.

Keeley, Lawrence H. 1996. *War Before Civilization.* New York: Oxford University Press.

Kegley, Charles W., Jr.. 1993. "The Neoidealist Moment in International Studies: Realist Myths and the New International Realities." *International Studies Quarterly* 37 (June): 131–46.

Kegley, Charles W., Jr. 1995. *Controversies in International Relations Theory: Realism and the Neoliberal Challenge.* New York: St. Martin's.

Keith, Linda Camp. 1999. "The United Nations International Covenant on Civil and Political Rights: Does It Make a Difference in Human Rights Behavior?" *Journal of Peace Research* 36 (1): 95–118.

Keller, Morton. 1977. *Affairs of State: Public Life in 19th Century America.* Cambridge, MA: Harvard University Press.

Kelley, Robin. 1990. *Hammer and Hoe: Alabama Communists During the Great Depression.* Chapel Hill: University of North Carolina Press.

Kelley, Robin. 1994. *Race Rebels: Culture, Politics, and the Black Working Class.* New York: Free Press.

Kelly, Rita Mae, Michelle A. Saint-Germain, and Jody D. Horn. 1991. "Female Public Officials: A Different Voice?" In *American Feminism: New Issues for a Mature Movement,* ed. Janet K. Boles. Newbury Park, CA: Sage.

Kennedy, Paul. 1987. *The Rise and Fall of the Great Powers.* New York: Random House.

Kenski, Henry C. 1988. "The Gender Factor in a Changing Electorate." In *The Politics of the Gender Gap,* ed. Carol M. Mueller. Newbury Park, CA: Sage.

Keohane, Robert O. 1983. "Theory of World Politics: Structural Realism and Beyond." In *Political Science: The State of the Discipline,* ed. Ada P. Finifter. Washington, DC: American Political Science Association.

Keohane, Robert O. 1984. *After Hegemony: Cooperation and Discord in the World Political Economy.* Princeton, NJ: Princeton University Press.

Keohane, Robert O. 1989. "International Institutions: Two Approaches." In *International Institutions and State Power,* ed. Robert O. Keohane. Boulder, CO: Westview.

Keohane, Robert O. 1993. "Institutionalist Theory and the Realist Challenge after the Cold War." In *Neorealism and Neoliberalism,* ed. David A. Baldwin. New York: Columbia University Press.

Keohane, Robert O. 1999. "Ideology and Professionalism in International Institutions: Insights from the Work of Douglass C. North." In *Competition and Coopera-*

tion: Conversations with Nobelists about Economics and Political Science, ed. J. Alt, et al. New York: Russell Sage.

Keohane, Robert O. 2001. "Governance in a Partially Globalized World." *American Political Science Review* 95 (1): 1–13.

Keohane, Robert O., and Marc A. Levy. 1996. *Institutions for Environmental Aid: Pitfalls and Promise*. Cambridge: MIT Press.

Keohane, Robert O., and Lisa L. Martin. 1995. "Promises, Promises: Can Institutions Deliver?" *International Security* 20: 1 (summer): 39–51.

Keohane, Robert O., and Lisa Martin. 2002. "Institutional Theory as a Research Program." In *Progress in International Relations Theory: Metrics and Measures of Scientific Change*, ed. Colin Elman and Miriam Feldman Elman. Cambridge: MIT Press.

Keohane, Robert O., and Helen Milner, eds. 1996. *Internationalization and Domestic Politics*. Cambridge: Cambridge University Press.

Keohane, Robert O., and Joseph Nye. 2000. "Introduction." In *Governance in a Globalizing World*, ed. Joseph S. Nye and John D. Donahue. Washington, D.C.: Brookings Institution Press.

Keohane, Robert O., and Joseph S. Nye. 1977. *Power and Interdependence: World Politics in Transition*. Boston: Little, Brown.

Keohane, Robert O., and Joseph S. Nye. 1987. "Power and Interdependence Revisited." *International Organization* 41 (autumn): 725–53.

Keohane, Robert O., and Joseph S. Nye. 2000. "Globalization: What's New? What's Not (And So What?)?" *Foreign Policy* 118 (spring): 104–19.

Kerber, Linda. 1997. *Women of the Republic. Intellect and Ideology in Revolutionary America*. Chapel Hill: University of North Carolina Press.

Kessler, Daniel, and Keith Krehbiel. 1996. "Dynamics of Cosponsorship." *American Political Science Review* 90: 555–66.

Key, Valdimer O. 1949. *Southern Politics in State and Nation*. New York: Knopf.

Key, Valdimer O. 1955. "A Theory of Critical Elections." *Journal of Politics* 17 (3).

Keyssar, Alexander. 2000. *The Right to Vote*. New York: Basic.

Kiewiet, Roderick D. 1983. *Macroeconomics and Micropolitics: The Electoral Effects of Economic Issues*. Chicago: University of Chicago Press.

Kiewiet, D. Roderick, and Mathew D. McCubbins. 1988. "Presidential Influence on Congressional Appropriations Decisions." *American Journal of Political Science* 32 (Aug): 713–36

Kiewiet, D. Roderick, and Mathew D. McCubbins. 1991. *The Logic of Delegation: Congressional Parties and the Appropriations Process*. Chicago: University of Chicago Press.

Kiewiet, D. Roderick, and Langche Zeng. 1993. "An Analysis of Congressional Career Decisions, 1947–1986." *American Political Science Review* 87: 928–41.

Kim, Claire Jean. 1999. "The Racial Triangulation of Asian Americans." *Politics and Society* 27 (March): 105–38.

Kim, Claire Jean. 2000. *Bitter Fruit: The Politics of Black-Korean Conflict in New York City.* New Haven, CT: Yale University Press.

Kinder, Donald R., and Thomas R. Palfrey. 1993. *Experimental Foundations of Political Science.* Ann Arbor: University of Michigan Press.

Kinder, Donald R., and Lynn Sanders. 1996. *Divided by Color: Racial Politics and Democratic Ideals.* Chicago: University of Chicago Press.

Kinder, Donald R., and David Sears. 1985. "Public Opinion and Political Action." In *Handbook of Social Phychology.* Gardner Lindzey and Elliot Aranson, eds. Hillsdale, NJ: Random House.

Kinder, Donald R., and Nicholas Winter. 2001. "Exploring the Racial Divide: Blacks, Whites, and Opinion on National Policy." *American Journal of Political Science* 45: 439–56.

Kindleberger, Charles Poor. 1975. *The World in Depression, 1929–1939.* Berkeley: University of California Press.

King, Gary. 1989. *Unifying Political Methodology: The Likelihood Theory of Statistical Inference.* New York: Cambridge University Press.

King, Gary, Robert O. Keohane, and Sidney Verba. 1994. *Designing Social Inquiry: Scientific Inference in Qualitative Research.* Princeton, NJ: Princeton University Press.

King, James D. 1994. "Political Culture, Registration Laws, and Voter Turnout Among the American States." *Publius: Journal of Federalism* 24: 115–27.

King, Ronald F., and Susan Ellis. 1996. "Partisan Advantage and Constitutional Change: The Case of the Seventeenth Amendment." *Studies in American Political Development* 10: 69–102.

Kingdon, John W. 1973. *Congressmen's Voting Decisions.* New York: Harper and Row.

Kirkpatrick, Jeane J. 1974. *Political Woman.* New York: Basic.

Kirkpatrick, Jeane J. 1976. *The New Presidential Elite.* New York: Russell Sage.

Kirshner, Jonathan. 1999 "The Political Economy of Realism." In *Unipolar Politics: Realism and State Strategies after the Cold War,* ed. Ethan B. Kapstein and Michael Mastanduno. New York: Columbia University Press

Kiser, Edgar. 1994. "Markets and Hierarchies in Early Modern Tax Systems: A Principal-Agent Analysis." *Politics and Society* 22 (3): 285–316.

Kiser, Edgar. 1999. "Comparing Varieties of Agency Theory in Economics, Political Science, and Sociology: An Illustration from State Policy Implementation." *Sociological Theory* 17 (2): 146–70.

Kiser, Edgar, and Yoram Barzel. 1991. "The Origins of Democracy in England." *Rationality and Society* 3 (4): 396–422.

Kiser, Edgar, and Michael Hechter. 1991. "The Role of General Theory in Comparative-Historical Sociology." *American Journal of Sociology* 97: 1–30.

Kiser, Edgar, and X. X. Tong. 1992. "Determinants of the Amount and Type of Corruption in State Fiscal Bureaucracies—An Analysis of Late Imperial China." *Comparative Political Studies* 25 (3): 300–31.

Kissinger, Henry. 1957. *Nuclear Weapons and Foreign Policy.* New York: Harper.

Kitschelt, Herbert. 1991. "Political Regime Change: Structure and Process-Driven Explanations." *American Political Science Review* 86: 1028–34.

Kitschelt, Herbert, Peter Lange, Gary Marks, and John D. Stephens, eds. 1999. *Continuity and Change in Contemporary Capitalism.* New York: Cambridge University Press.

Klatch, Rebecca E. 1987. *Women of the New Right.* Philadelphia: Temple University Press.

Klein, Ethel. 1984. *Gender Politics.* Cambridge, MA: Harvard University Press.

Klein, Ethel. 1985. "The Gender Gap: Different Issues. Different Answers." *Brookings Review* 3: 33–7.

Kleppner, Paul. 1979. *The Third Electoral System, 1853–1892: Parties, Voters, and Political Cultures.* Chapel Hill: University of North Carolina Press.

Kloppenberg, James T. 1986. *Uncertain Victory: Social Democracy and Progressivism in European and American Thought, 1870–1920.* New York: Oxford University Press.

Klotz, Audie. 1995. *Norms in International Relations: The Struggle against Apartheid.* Ithaca, NY: Cornell University Press.

Klyza, Christopher. 1996. *Who Controls Public Lands? Mining, Forestry and Grazing Policies, 1870–1990.* Chapel Hill: University of North Carolina Press.

Knack, Stephen. 1995. "Does 'Motor Voter' Work? Evidence from State-Level Data." *Journal of Politics* 57: 796–811.

Knack, Stephen, and James White. 1998. "Did States' Motor Voter Programs Help the Democrats?" *American Politics Quarterly* 26: 344–65.

Knight, Jack, and Douglass North. 1997. "Explaining Economic Change: The Interplay Between Cognitive and Institutions." *Legal Theory* 3: 221–226.

Knorr, Klaus, and James N. Rosenau, eds. 1969. *Contending Approaches to International Relations.* Princeton, NJ. Princeton University Press.

Knutsen, Torbjorn. 1997. *A History of International Relations Theory.* 2d ed. New York: Manchester University Press.

Koch, Jeffrey. 1997. "Candidate Gender and Women's Psychological Engagement In Politics." *American Politics Quarterly* 25: 118–33.

Koh, Harold Hongju. 1997. "Why Do Nations Obey International Law?" *Yale Law Journal* 106: 2599–659.

Kohli, Atul. 1987. *The State and Poverty in India: The Politics of Reform.* Cambridge and New York: Cambridge University Press.

Kohli, Atul. 1990. *Democracy and Discontent: India's Growing Crisis of Governability.* Cambridge and New York: Cambridge University Press.

Kohli, Atul. 1993. "Democracy amid Economic Orthodoxy: Trends in Developing Countries." *Third World Quarterly* 14 (4): 671–89.

Kohli, Atul. Forthcoming. *In Search of Development: Creating States and Industry on the Global Periphery.*

Kohli, Atul, ed. 2001. *The Success of India's Democracy.* Cambridge and New York: Cambridge University Press.

Kolko, Gabriel. 1977. *The Triumph of Conservatism.* New York: Free Press.

Kollman, Ken. 1998. *Outside Lobbying: Public Opinion and Interest Group Strategies.* Princeton, NJ: Princeton University Press.

Kontopoulos, John T. 1997. "Fiscal Policy and Electoral Competition." Ph.D. diss., Columbia University, New York.

Kontopoulos, Yianos, and Roberto Perotti. 1999. "Government Fragmentation and Fiscal Policy Outcomes: Evidence from OECD Countries." In *Fiscal Institutions and Fiscal Performance,* ed. James Poterba and Jurgen von Hagen. Chicago: NBER and University of Chicago Press.

Kopits, George, and Jon Craig. 1998. "Transparency in Government Operations." IMF Occasional Paper 158.

Kopits, George, and Steven Symansky. 1998. "Fiscal Policy Rules." IMF Occasional Paper 162.

Koslowski, Rey, and Friedrich V. Kratochwil. 1994. "Understanding Change in International Politics: The Soviet Empire's Demise and the International System." *International Organization* 48 (spring): 215–48.

Kowert, Paul, and Jeffrey Legro. 1996. "Norms, Identity, and Their Limits: A Theoretical Reprise." In *The Culture of National Security: Norms and Identity in World Politics,* ed. P. J. Katzenstein. New York: Columbia University Press.

Kraditor, Aileen S. 1968. *The Ideas of the Women's Suffrage Movement.* New York: Norton.

Kramer, Gerald H. 1970. "The Effects of Precinct-Level Canvassing on Voting Behavior." *Public Opinion Quarterly* 34 (winter): 560–72.

Krasner, Stephen D. 1976. "State Power and the Structure of International Trade." *World Politics* 28 (3): 317–43.

Krasner, Stephen D. 1978. *Defending the National Interest: Raw Materials Investments and U.S. Foreign Policy.* Princeton, NJ: Princeton University Press.

Krasner, Stephen D. 1991. "Global Communications and National Power: Life on the Pareto Frontier." *World Politics* 43 (April): 336–66.

Krasner, Stephen D. 1999. *Sovereignty: Organized Hypocrisy.* Princeton, NJ: Princeton University Press.

Krasner, Stephen D. 2000. *Sovereignty: Organized Hypocrisy.* Princeton: Princeton University Press.

Krasner, Stephen D., ed. 1983. *International Regimes.* Ithaca, NY: Cornell University Press.

Kratochwil, Friedrich. 1989. *Rules, Norms, and Decisions.* Cambridge: Cambridge University Press.

Kratochwil, Friedrich. 1993. "The Embarassment of Riches: Neo-Realism as the Science of Realpolitik without Politics." *Review of International Studies* 19 (January): 63–80.

Kratochwil, Friedrich, and John G. Ruggie. 1986. "International Organization: A State of the Art or an Art of the State." *International Organization* 40 (4): 753–75.

Kraus, Peter. 2000. "Political Unity and Linguistic Diversity in Europe." *Archives Europeennes de Sociologie* 41 (1): 138–63.

Krehbiel, Keith. 1991. *Information and Legislative Organization*. Ann Arbor: University of Michigan Press.

Krehbiel, Keith. 1994. "Where's the Party?" *British Journal of Political Science* 23: 235–66.

Krehbiel, Keith. 1995. "Cosponsors and Wafflers from A to Z." *American Journal of Political Science* 39: 906–23.

Krehbiel, Keith. 1998. *Pivotal Politics: A Theory of U.S. Lawmaking*. Chicago: University of Chicago Press.

Krehbiel, Keith. 1999. "The Party Effect from A to Z and Beyond: Reply to S. Binder et al." *Journal of Politics* 61: 832–40.

Krehbiel, Keith. 2000. "Party Discipline and Measures of Partisanship." *American Journal of Political Science* 44: 212–27.

Kreppel, Amie. 2001. *The Development of the European Parliament and the Supranational Party System*. New York: Cambridge University Press.

Kreps, David, and Robert Wilson. 1982. "Reputation and Imperfect information." *Journal of Economic Theory* 27: 253–79.

Kreps, David. 1990a. "Corporate Culture and Economic Theory." In *Perspectives on Positive Political Economy*, ed. J. Alt and K. Shepsle. New York: Cambridge University Press.

Kreps, David. 1990b. *Game Theory and Economic Modeling*. New York: Oxford University Press.

Kreps, David. 1997. "Economics—The Current Position." *Daedalus* 126: 59–86.

Krieckhaus, Jonathan. 2000. "The Politics of Economic Growth in the Third World: Brazilian Developmentalism in Comparative Perspective." Ph.D. diss., Princeton University.

Kristeva, Julia. 1977. *Powers of Horror: An Essay in Abjection*. New York: Columbia University Press.

Krueger, Anne O. 1974. "The Political Economy of the Rent Seeking Society." *American Economic Review* 64 (3): 291–303.

Krugman, Paul. 1995. *Development, Geography, and Economic Theory*. Cambridge: MIT Press.

Kryder, Daniel. 2000. *Divided Arsenal: Race and the American State During World War II*. New York. Cambridge University Press.

Kugler, Jacek, and David Lemke. 1996. *Parity and War*. Ann Arbor: University of Michigan Press.

Kuhonta, Erik M. Forthcoming. "The Politics of Inequity: State Formation and Political Parties in Thailand and Malaysia." Ph.D. diss., Princeton University, Princeton, NJ.

Kukathas, Chandran. 1992. "Are There Any Cultural Rights?" *Political Theory* 20 (1): 105–39.

Kuper, Andrew. 2000. "Rawlsian Global Justice: Beyond the Law of Peoples to a Cosmopolitan Law of Persons." *Political Theory* 28: 640–74.

Kuran, Timur. 1998. "Ethnic Norms and Their Transformation through Reputational Cascades." *Journal of Legal Studies* 27 (2): 623–59

Kuran, Timur. 1991. "Now Out of Never: The Role of Surprise in the East European Revolution of 1989." *World Politics* 44: 7–48.

Kurth, James. 1979. "Political Consequences of the Product Cycle." *International Organization* 33: 1–34.

Kydd, Andrew. 1997a. "Game Theory and the Spiral Model." *World Politics* 49: 371–400.

Kydd, Andrew. 1997b. "Sheep in Sheep's Clothing: Why Security Seekers Do Not Fight Each Other." *Security Studies* 7 (autumn): 114–54.

Kydland, Finn E., and Edward C. Prescott. 1977. "Rules Rather Than Discretion: The Inconsistency of Optimal Plans." *Journal of Political Economy*: 473–91.

Kymlicka, Will. 1989. *Liberalism, Community, and Culture.* Oxford: Oxford University Press.

Kymlicka, Will, 1995a. "Misunderstanding Nationalism." *Dissent* (winter): 130–37.

Kymlicka, Will. 1995b. *Multicultural Citizenship: A Liberal Theory of Minority Rights.* Oxford: Oxford University Press.

Kymlicka, Will. 1996. "Three Forms of Group-Differentiated Citizenship in Canada." In *Democracy and Difference*, ed. Seyla Benhabib. Princeton, NJ: Princeton University Press.

Kymlicka, Will, and Wayne Norman. 1995. "Return of the Citizen: A Survey of Recent Work on Citizenship Theory." In *Theorizing Citizenship*, ed. Beiner, 283–323.

Kymlicka, Will, and Wayne Norman. 2000. *Citizenship in Diverse Societies.* Oxford: Oxford University Press.

Labs, Eric J. 1992. "Do Weak States Bandwagon?" *Security Studies* 1 (spring): 383–416.

Labs, Eric J. 1997. "Beyond Victory: Offensive Realism and the Expansion of War Aims." *Security Studies* 6 (summer): 1–49.

Laclau, Ernesto. 1990. *New Reflections on the Revolutions of Our Time.* London: Verso.

Laclau, Ernesto, and Chantal Mouffe. 1985. *Hegemony and Socialist Strategy: Towards a Radical Democratic Politics.* London: Verso.

Lacy, Dean, and Barry C. Burden. 1999. "The Vote-Stealing and Turnout Effects of Ross Perot in the 1992 U.S. Presidential Election." *American Journal of Political Science* 43: 233–55.

Ladd, Everett Carll. 1992. "Political Parties, 'Reform,' and American Democracy." In *Challenges to Party Government*, ed. John Kenneth White and Jerome Mileur, 32–36. Carbondale: Southern Illinois University Press.

Ladd, Everett Carll. 1999. *The Ladd Report.* New York: Free Press.

Ladd, Everett Carll, and Karlyn H. Bowman. 1997. *Public Opinion about Abortion*. Washington, DC: AEI.

Laffey, Mark, and Jutta Weldes. 1997. "Beyond Belief: Ideas and Symbolic Technologies in the Study of International Relations." *European Journal of International Relations* 3 (2): 193–237.

Laitin, David D. 1986. *Hegemony and Culture: Politics and Religious Change among the Yoruba*. Chicago: University of Chicago Press.

Laitin, David D. 1992. *Language Repertoires and State Construction in Africa*. New York: Cambridge University Press.

Laitin, David D. 1995. "National Revivals and Violence." *Archives Européennes de Sociologie* 36: 3–43.

Laitin, David D. 1998a. *Identity in Formation: The Russian-Speaking Populations in the Near Abroad*. Ithaca, NY: Cornell University Press.

Laitin, David D. 1998b. "Toward a Political Science Discipline." *Comparative Political Studies* 31 (4): 423–43.

Laitin, David D. 2000. "Language Conflict and Violence." *Archives Européennes de Sociologie* 41: 97–137.

Laitin, David D. Forthcoming. "Comparative Politics: The State of the Subdiscipline." In *State of the Discipline III*, ed. Ira Katznelson and Helen V. Milner. Washington, DC: American Political Science Association.

Laitin, David D., et al. 1994. "Language and the Construction of States: The Case of Catalonia in Spain." *Politics and Society* 22 (1): 5–29.

Lakatos, Imre. 1970. "Falsification and the Methodology of Scientific Research Programmes." In *Criticism and the Growth of Knowledge*, ed. Alan Musgrave. Cambridge: Cambridge University Press.

Lakatos, Imre. 1978. *The Methodology of Scientific Research Programmes*. Cambridge: Cambridge University Press.

Lake, David A. 1984. "Beneath the Commerce of Nations: A Theory of International Economic Structures." *International Studies Quarterly* 28 (June).

Lake, David A. 1992. "Powerful Pacifists." *American Political Science Review* 86: 24–37.

Lake, David A. 1999. *Entangling Relations: American Foreign Policy in Its Century*. Princeton, NJ: Princeton University Press.

Lake, David A., and Robert Powell. 1999a. "International Relations: A Strategic-Choice Approach." In *Strategic Choice and International Relations*, ed. David A. Lake and Robert Powell, 3–38. Princeton, NJ: Princeton University Press.

Lake, David A., and Robert Powell, eds. 1999b. *Strategic Choice and International Relations*. Princeton, NJ: Princeton University Press.

Lake, David A., and Donald Rothchild. 1996. "Containing Fear: The Origins and Management of Ethnic Conflict." *International Security* 21 (fall): 41–75.

Lal, Deepak. 1997. *The Poverty of Development Economics*. London: Institute of Economic Affairs.

Lambert, Rob. 2000. "Globalization and the Erosion of Class Compromise in Contemporary Australia." *Politics and Society* 28 (1): 93–118.

Lambert, Ronald D., James E. Curtis, Barry J. Kay, and Steven D. Brown. 1988. "The Social Sources of Political Knowledge." *Canadian Journal of Political Science* 21: 359–74.

Landes, Joan. 1988. *Women and the Public Sphere in the Age of the French Revolution.* Ithaca, NY: Cornell University Press.

Landes, William M. 1968. "The Economics of Fair Employment Laws." *Journal of Political Economy* 76: 507–52.

Landes, William. 1971. "An Economic Analysis of Courts." *Journal of Law and Economics* 14: 61–107.

Lane, Philip R. 1999. "The Cyclical Behavior of Fiscal Policy: Evidence from the OECD." Mimeograph, Trinity College, Dublin.

Lange, Peter, and Geoffrey Garrett. 1985. "The Politics of Growth." *Journal of Politics* 47: 792–827.

Lange, Peter, Michael Wallerstein, and Miriam Golden. 1995. "The End of Corporatism? Wage Setting in the Nordic and Germanic Countries." In *Workers of Nations: Industrial Relations in a Global Economy,* ed. S. Jacoby. New York: Oxford University Press.

Lapid, Yosef, and Friedrich Kratochwil. 1996a. "Revisiting the 'National': Toward an Identity Agenda in Neorealism?" In *The Return of Culture and Identity in IR Theory,* ed. Yosef Lapid and Friedrich Kratochwil. Boulder, CO: Rienner.

Lapid, Yosef, and Friedrich Kratochwil, eds. 1996b. *The Return of Culture and Identity in IR Theory.* Boulder, CO: Rienner.

LaPorta, R., F. Lopez de Silanes, A. Shleifer, and R. Vishny. 1999. "The Quality of Government." *Journal of Law, Economics, and Organization* 15: 222–79.

Larmore, Charles E. 1987. *Patterns of Moral Complexity.* Cambridge: Cambridge University Press.

Larson, Magali Sarfatti. 1977. *The Rise of Professionalism: A Sociological Analysis.* Berkeley: University of California Press.

Lasswell, Harold. 1936. *Politics: Who Gets What, When, How* (New York: McGraw-Hill).

Lasswell, Harold, and Abraham Kaplan. 1950. *Power and Society.* New Haven, CT: Yale University Press.

Laudan, Larry. 1977. *Progress and Its Problems: Toward a Theory of Scientific Growth.* Berkeley: University of California Press.

Laver, Michael. 1999. "Divided Parties, Divided Government." *Legislative Studies Quarterly* 24: 5–29.

Laver, Michael, and Norman Schofield. 1990. *Multiparty Government.* New York: Oxford University Press.

Laver, Michael, and Kenneth A. Shepsle. 1990. "Coalitions and Cabinet Government." *American Political Science Review* 84: 873–90.

Laver, Michael, and Kenneth Shepsle. 1991. "Divided Government: America Is Not 'Exceptional.' " *Governance* 4: 250–69.

Laver, Michael, and Kenneth A. Shepsle. eds. 1994. *Cabinet Ministers and Parliamentary Government*. Cambridge: Cambridge University Press.

Laver, Michael, and Kenneth A. Shepsle. 1996. *Making and Breaking Governments: Cabinets and Legislatures in Parliamentary Democracies*. Cambridge: Cambridge University Press.

Lax, Jeffrey, and Charles Cameron. 2001. "Opinion Assignment on the U.S. Supreme Court: Theory and Evidence." Paper presented at the 2001 meetings of the American Political Science Association.

Layne, Christopher. 1993. "The Unipolar Illusion: Why New Great Powers Will Rise." *International Security* 17 (spring): 5–51.

Layne, Christopher. 1994. "Kant or Cant: The Myth of the Democratic Peace." *International Security* 19: 5–49.

Layne, Christopher. 1997. "From Preponderance to Offshore Balancing: America's Future Grand Strategy." *International Security* 22 (summer): 86–124.

Lazersfeld, Paul, Bernard Berelson, and Hazel Gaudet. 1944. *The People's Choice: How the Voter Makes up his Mind in a Presidential Election*. New York: Duell, Sloan, and Pearce.

LeBlanc, Steven A. 1999. *Prehistoric Warfare in the American Southwest*. Salt Lake City: University of Utah Press.

Lebow, Richard Ned. 1981. *Between Peace and War: The Nature of International Crisis*. Baltimore: Johns Hopkins University Press.

Lebow, Richard Ned. 1994. "The Long Peace, The End of the Cold War, and the Failure of Realism." *International Organization* 48 (spring): 249–77.

Lee, Frances E. 1998. "Representation and Public Policy: The Consequences of Senate Apportionment for the Geographic Distribution of Federal Funds." *Journal of Politics* 60: 34–62.

Lee, Frances E. 2000. "Senate Representation and Coalition Building in Distributive Politics." *American Political Science Review* 94: 59–72.

Lee, Lung-Fei, and Robert H. Porter. 1984. "Switching Regression Models with Imperfect Sample Separation Information—With an Application to Cartel Stability." *Econometrica* 52: 391–418.

Lee, Marcia Manning. 1976. "Why Few Women Hold Public Office: Democracy and Sex Roles." *Political Science Quarterly* 91 (summer): 297–314.

Lee, Taeku. 1997. "Two Nations, Separate Grooves: Black Insurgency and the Dynamics of Mass Opinion: The United States from 1948–1972." Ph.D. diss. (in progress), University of Chicago, Chicago.

Lees, John D., and Malcolm Shaw, eds. 1979. *Committees in Legislatures: A Comparative Analysis*. Durham, NC: Duke University Press.

Leffler, Melvyn. 1992. *A Preponderance of Power: National Security, the Truman Administration, and the Cold War*. Stanford, CA: Stanford University Press.

Lefort, Claude. 1986. *The Political Forms of Modern Society*. Cambridge: MIT Press.

Legro, Jeffrey W. 1996. "Culture and Preferences in the International Cooperation Two-Step." *American Political Science Review* 90 (1): 118–37.

Legro, Jeffrey W., and Andrew Moravcsik. 1999. "Is Anybody Still a Realist?" *International Security* 24 (fall): 5–55.

Lehoucq, Frabrice E., and Ivan J. Molina. 2002. *Stuffing the Ballot Box: Fraud, Election Reform, and Democratization in Costa Rica*. New York: Cambridge University Press.

Leighley, Jan E. 1995. "Attitudes, Opportunities and Incentives: A Field Essay on Political Participation." *Political Research Quarterly* 48: 181–209.

Leighley, Jan E. 1996. "Group Membership and the Mobilization of Political Participation." *Journal of Politics* 58: 447–63.

Leighley, Jan E. 2001. *Strength in Numbers? The Political Mobilization of Racial and Ethnic Minorities*. Princeton, NJ: Princeton University Press.

Leighley, Jan E., and Jonathan Nagler. 1992a. "Individual and Systematic Influences on Turnout: Who Votes? 1984." *Journal of Politics* 54: 718–40.

Leighley, Jan E., and Jonathan Nagler. 1992b. "Socioeconomic Class Bias in Turnout, 1964–1988: The Voters Remain the Same." *American Political Science Review* 86: 725–36.

Leighley, Jan E., and Arnold Vedlitz. 1999. "Race, Ethnicity, and Political Participation: Competing Models and Contrasting Expectations." *Journal of Politics* 61: 1092–114.

Lerner, Gerda. 1979. *The Majority Finds Its Past: Placing Women in History*. New York: Oxford University Press.

Leuchtenberg, William. 1986. "The Pertinence of Political History: Reflections on the Significance of the State in America." *Journal of American History* 73 (3) 585–600.

Levi, Margaret. 1981. "The Predatory Theory of Rule." *Politics and Society* 10 (4): 431–65.

Levi, Margaret. 1988. *Of Rule and Revenue*. Berkeley: University of California Press.

Levi, Margaret. 1996. "Social and Unsocial Capital: A Review Essay of Robert Putnam's Making Democracy Work." *Politics and Society* 24 (1): 45–56.

Levi, Margaret. 1997a. *Consent, Dissent and Patriotism*. New York: Cambridge University Press.

Levi, Margaret. 1997b. "A Model, a Method, and a Map: Rational Choice in Comparative and Historical Analysis." In *Comparative Politics: Rationality, Culture, and Structure*, ed. Mark Irving Lichbach, and Alan Zuckerman, 19–41. New York: Cambridge University Press.

Levi, Margaret. 1998a. "Conscription: The Price of Citizenship." In *Analytic Narratives*, ed. Robert H. Bates, A. Greif, M. Levi, J.-L. Rosenthal, and B. Weingast, 109–47. Princeton, NJ: Princeton University Press.

Levi, Margaret. 1998b. "A State of Trust." In *Trust and Governance*, ed. Valerie Braithwaite and Margaret Levi, 77–101. New York: Russell Sage.

Levi, Margaret. 2000. "The Economic Turn in Comparative Politics." *Comparative Political Studies* 33: 822–44.

Levine, R., and D. Renelt. 1992. "A Sensitivity Analysis of Cross-Country Growth Regressions." *American Economic Review* 82: 942–64.

Levitt, Steven. 1994. "Using Repeat Challengers to Estimate the Effect of Campaign Spending on Election Outcomes in the House." *Journal of Political Economy* 102: 77–98.

Levy, Brian, and Pablo Spiller. 1994. "Institutional Foundations of Regulatory Commitment: A Comparative Analysis of Telecommunications Regulation." *Journal of Law, Economics, and Organization* 10: 201–46.

Levy, Jack S. 1983. *War in the Modern Great Power System, 1495 to 1975.* Lexington: University Press of Kentucky.

Levy, Jack S. 1984. "The Offensive/Defensive Balance of Military Technology." *International Studies Quarterly* 38: 219–38.

Levy, Jack S. 1998. "The Causes of War and the Conditions of Peace." *Annual Review of Political Science* 1: 139–65.

Levy, Jacobs. 1997. "Classifying Cultural Rights." In *Ethnicity and Group Rights,* ed. Ian Shapiro, 22–66. New York: New York University Press.

Lewis, Peter. 1994. "Economic Statism, Private Control, and the Dilemmas of Accumulation in Nigeria." *World Development* 22 (3): 437–51.

Leys, Colin. 1974. *Underdevelopment in Kenya: The Political Economy of Neo-Colonialism, 1964–1971.* Berkeley: University of California Press.

Liberman, Peter. 1996a. *Does Conquest Pay? The Exploitation of Occupied Industrial Societies.* Princeton, NJ: Princeton University Press.

Liberman, Peter. 1996b. "Trading with the Enemy." *International Security* 21 (summer): 147–75.

Liberman, Peter. 1999–2000. "The Offense-Defense Balance, Interdependence, and War." *Security Studies* 9 (autumn–winter): 59–91.

Lichbach, Mark I. and Alan S. Zuckerman. 1997a. "Research Traditions and theory in Comparative Politics: An Introduction." In *Comparative Politics.* Mark Irving Lichbach and Alan S. Zuckerman, eds. 3–16. New York: Cambridge University Press.

Lichbach, Mark Irving and Alan S. Zuckerman, eds. 1997b. *Comparative Politics.* New York: Cambridge University Press.

Lieber, Keir A. 2000. "Grasping the Technological Peace: The Offense-Defense Balance and International Security." *International Security* 25 (summer): 71–104.

Lieberman, Robert C. 1998. *Shifting the Color Line: Race and the American Welfare State.* Cambridge, MA: Harvard University Press.

Lieberson, Stanley. 1991. "Small N's and Big Conclusions: An Examination of the Reasoning in Comparative Studies Based on a Small Number of Cases." *Social Forces* 70: 307–20.

Liebert, Ulrike, and Maurizio Cotta, eds. 1990. *Parliament and Democratic Consolidation in Southern Europe: Greece, Italy, Portugal, Spain, and Turkey.* London: Pinter.

Liese, Andrea. 2001. "Staaten am Pranger. Zur Wirkung internationaler Regime auf die innerstaatliche Menschenrechtspolitik. "Ph.D. diss, Institut für Politikwissenschaft, Universität Bremen, Bremen.

Lijphart, Arend. 1968. *The Politics of Accommodation*. Berkeley: University of California Press.

Lijphart, Arend. 1969. "Consociational Democracy." *World Politics* 21: 207–25.

Lijphart, Arend. 1971. "Comparative Politics and Comparative Method." *American Political Science Review* 65: 682–98.

Lijphart, Arend. 1977. *Democracy in Plural Societies*. New Haven, CT: Yale University Press.

Lijphart, Arend. 1991. "Constitutional Choices for New Democracies." *Journal of Democracy* 2 (1): 72–84.

Lijphart, Arend, ed. 1992. *Parliamentary versus Presidential Government*. New York: Oxford University Press.

Lijphart, Arend. 1997. "Unequal Participation: Democracy's Unresolved Dilemma." *American Political Science Review* 91: 1–14.

Lin, Ann Chih, and Amaney Jamal. 1998. "Ties of Memory and Experience: Arab Immigrant Political Socialization and Activity." Paper presented at the annual meeting of the American Political Science Association, Washington, DC.

Lindblom, Charles E. 1977. *Politics and Markets*. New York: Basic.

Lindblom, Charles E. 1990. *Inquiry and Change: The Troubled Attempt to Understand and Shape Society*. New Haven, CT: Yale University Press.

Lindblom, Charles E. 1997. "Political Science in the 1940s and 1950s." In *American Academic Culture in Transformation: Fifty Years, Four Disciplines*, ed. Thomas Bender and Carl E. Schorske, 244–70. Princeton, NJ: Princeton University Press.

Lindzey, Gardner and Elliot Aranson, eds. 1985. *Handbook of Social Psychology*. 3d. ed. vol. 2. Hillsdale, NJ: Random House.

Linz, Juan J. 1978. *The Breakdown of Democratic Regimes: Crises, Breakdown and Reequilibration*. Baltimore: Johns Hopkins University Press.

Linz, Juan J. 1990a. "The Perils of Presidentialism." *Journal of Democracy* 1 (1): 51–69.

Linz, Juan J. 1990b. "The Virtues of Parliamentarism." *Journal of Democracy* 1 (4): 84–91.

Linz, Juan J. 1994. "Presidential or Parliamentary Democracy: Does It Make a Difference?" In *The Failure of Presidential Democracy*, ed. Juan J. Linz and Arturo Valenzuela. Baltimore: Johns Hopkins University Press.

Linz, Juan J., and Alfred Stepan, eds. 1978. *The Breakdown of Democratic Regimes*. Baltimore: Johns Hopkins University Press.

Linz, Juan J., and Alfred Stepan. 1992. "Political Identities and Electoral Sequences." *Daedalus* 121 (Spring): 123–39.

Linz, Juan J., and Alfred Stepan. 1996. *Problems of Democratic Transition and Consolidation: Southern Europe, South America, and Post-Communist Europe*. Baltimore: Johns Hopkins University Press.

Linz, Juan J., and Arturo Valenzuela, eds. 1994. *The Failure of Presidential Democracy*. Baltimore: Johns Hopkins University Press.

Lippincott, Benjamin E. 1940. "The Bias of American Political Science." *Journal of Politics* 2: 125–239.

Lippmann, Walter. 1922. *Public Opinion*. New York: Macmillan Co.

Lipset, Seymour Martin. 1959. "Some Social Requisites of Democracy: Economic Development and Political Legitimacy." *American Political Science Review* 53: 69–105.

Lipset, Seymour Martin. 1994. "The Social Prerequisites of Democracy Revisited." *American Sociological Review* 59 (February): 1–22.

Lipset, Seymour Martin, Kyoung-Ryung Seong, and John Charles Torres. 1993. "A Comparative Analysis of the Social Requisites of Democracy." *International Social Science Journal* 45 (2): 155–175.

Lipset, Seymour Martin, and Stein Rokkan. 1967. "Cleavage Structures, Party Systems, and Voter Alignment: An Introduction." In *Party Systems and Voter Alignments*, ed. Seymour Martin Lipset and Stein Rokkan. New York: Free Press.

Lipset, Seymour Martin, and William Schneider. 1983. *The Confidence Gap*. New York: Free Press.

Lipson, Charles. 1986. "Bankers' Dilemmas: Private Cooperation in Rescheduling Sovereign Debts." In *Cooperation under Anarchy*, ed. Kenneth A. Oye, 200–25. Princeton, NJ: Princeton University Press.

Lipton, Michael. 1977. *Why Poor People Stay Poor: Urban Bias in World Development*. Cambridge, MA: Harvard University Press.

Little, Daniel. 1991. *Varieties of Social Explanation: An Introduction to the Philosophy of Social Science*. Boulder, CO: Westview.

Little, I. M. D. 1979. "The Developing Countries and the International Order." In *Challenges to a Liberal International Economic Order*, ed. R. C. Amacher, G. Haberler, and T. D. Willett. Washington, DC: American Enterprise.

Livermore, Seward W. 1966. *Politics Is Adjourned: Woodrow Wilson and the War Congress, 1916–1918*. Middletown, CT: Wesleyan University Press.

Locke, John. 1960 [1689]. *Two Treatises of Government*. Ed. Peter Laslett. New York: Mentor.

Locke, John. 1980 [1689]. *Second Treatise of Government*. Ed. C. B. Macpherson. Indianapolis, IN: Hackett.

Locke, Richard M., and Lucio Baccaro. 1996. "Learning From Past Mistakes? Recent Reforms in Italian Industrial Relations." *Industrial Relations Journal* 27: 289–303.

Loewenberg, Gerhard, Peverill Squire, and D. R. Kiewiet, eds. Forthcoming. *Legislatures: Comparative Perspectives on Representative Assemblies*. Ann Arbor: University of Michigan Press.

Lohmann, Susanne. 1992. "Optimal Commitment in Monetary Policy: Credibility versus Flexibility." *American Economic Review* 82 (1, March): 273–86.

Lohmann, Susanne. 1994. "The Dynamics of Informational Cascades: The Monday Demonstrations in Leipzig, East Germany, 1989–91." *World Politics* 47 (1): 42–101.

Lohmann, Susanne. 1998a. "Federalism and Central Bank Independence: The Politics of German Monetary Policy, 1957–92." *World Politics* 50: 401–46.

Lohmann, Susanne. 1998b. "Institutional Checks and Balances and the Political Control of the Money Supply." *Oxford Economic Papers* 50: 360–77.

Lohmann, Susanne. 1999. "What Price Accountability? The Lucas Island Model and the Politics of Monetary Policy." *American Journal of Political Science* 43: 396–430.

Lohmann, Susanne, and Sharyn O'Halloran. 1994. "Divided Government and the U.S. Trade Policy: Theory and Evidence." *International Organization* 48 (4): 595–632.

Londregan, John. 2000. *Legislative Institutions and Ideology in Chile*. New York: Cambridge University Press.

Londregan, John, and Keith Poole. 1990. "Poverty, the Coup Trap, and the Seizure of Executive Power." *World Politics* 42: 151–83.

Londregan, John, and Keith Poole. 1996. "Does High Income Promote Democracy?" *World Politics* 49: 1–30.

Lowell, A. Lawrence. 1902. "The Influence of Party upon Legislation in England and America." Annual Report of the American Historical Association for the Year 1901 1: 319–542.

Lowenstein, Daniel Hays. 1995. *Election Law: Cases and Materials*. Carolina Academic.

Lowi, Theodore. 1964. "American Business, Public Policy, Case Studies and Political Theory." *World Politics* 16: 677–715.

Lowi, Theodore. 1972. "Four System of Policy Politics and Change." *Public Administration Review* 32: 298–312.

Lowi, Theodore. 1985. *The Personal President: Power Invested Promise Unfulfilled*. Ithaca, NY: Cornell University Press.

Lowry, Robert C., and James E. Alt. 2001. "A Visible Hand? Bond Markets, Political Parties, Balanced Budget Laws, and State Government Debt." *Economics and Politics* (March).

Lowry, Robert C., James E. Alt, and Karen E. Ferree. 1998. "Fiscal Policy Outcomes and Electoral Accountability in American States." *American Political Science Review* 92 (December): 759–74.

Lucas, Robert E., Jr., and Nancy L. Stokey. 1983. "Optimal Fiscal and Monetary Policy in an Economy Without Capital." *Journal of Monetary Economics*: 55–93.

Luebbert, Gregory M. 1991. *Liberalism, Fascism, or Social Democracy: Social Classes and the Political Origins of Regimes in Interwar Europe*. New York: Oxford University Press.

Luker, Kristin. 1984. *Abortion and the Politics of Motherhood*. Berkeley: University of California Press.

Lukes, Steven. 1974. *Power: A Radical View*. London: Macmillan & Co.

Lukes, Steven. 1997. "Toleration and Recognition." *Ratio Juris* 10 (2): 213–22.

Luong, Pauline Jones. 2000. "After the Break-Up: Institutional Design in Transitional States." *Comparative Political Studies* 33: 563–92.

Luong, Pauline Jones. 2002. *Institutional Change and Continuity in Post-Soviet Central Asia.* New York: Cambridge University Press.

Lupia, Arthur, and Matthew McCubbins. 1998. *The Democratic Dilemna.* New York: Cambridge University Press.

Lust-Okar, Ellen. 2001. "Divided They Fall: The Management and Manipulation of Political Opposition." Paper presented at the Conference on Bringing the Middle East Back into the Study of Comparative Politics, Yale University, New Haven, CT.

Lust-Okar, Ellen, and Amaney Ahmad Jamal. 1999. "Rulers and Rules: Reassessing Electoral Laws and Political Liberalization in the Middle East." Paper presented at the American Political Science Association meeting, Atlanta, GA.

Lustick, Ian. 1993. *Unsettled States, Disputed Lands: Britain and Ireland, France and Algeria, Israel and the West Bank–Gaza.* Ithaca, NY: Cornell University Press.

Lustick, Ian. 2000. "Agent-Based Modeling of Collective Identity: Testing Constructivist Theory." *Journal of Artificial Societies and Social Simulations* 3 (1).

Lynch, Michael. 1991. *Scotland: A New History.* London: Pimlico.

Lynn-Jones, Sean. 1995. "Offense-Defense Theory and Its Critics." *Security Studies* 4: 660–94.

Lynn-Jones, Sean. 1998. "Realism and America's Rise: A Review Essay." *International Security* 23 (fall): 157–82.

Lyons, William, and Robert Alexander. 2000. "A Tale of Two Electorates: Generational Replacement and the Decline of Voting in Presidential Elections." *Journal of Politics* 62: 1014–34.

Macedo, Stephen. 1990. *Liberal Virtues: Citizenship, Virtue, and Community.* Oxford: Oxford University Press.

Macedo, Stephen, ed. 1999. *Deliberative Politics: Essays on Democracy and Disagreement.* New York: Oxford University Press.

Machiavelli, Niccolò. 1970 [c. 1517]. *The Discourses.* Trans. Leslie J. Walker, with revisions by Brian Richardson. Harmondsworth, UK: Penguin.

MacIntyre, Aladair. 1990. *Three Rival Versions of Moral Enquiry: Encyclopaedia, Genealogy, and Tradition.* South Bend, IN: University of Notre Dame Press.

MacIntyre, Andrew. 1991. *Business and Politics in Indonesia.* Sydney, AUS: Allen and Unwin.

Mack, Andrew. 1997. "Potential, not Proliferation." *Bulletin of the Atomic Scientists* 53 (July–August): 49–50.

Mack, Eric. 1976. "Distributionism Versus Justice." *Ethics* 86 (January): 145–53.

Mackie, Gerry. 2000. "Is Democracy Impossible? A Preface to Deliberative Democracy." Ph.D. diss., University of Chicago, Chicago.

MacKinnon, Catherine. 1987. *Feminism Unmodified.* Cambridge, MA: Harvard University Press.

MacKuen, Michael B., Robert S. Erikson, and James A. Stimson. 1989. "Macropartisanship." *American Political Science Review* 83: 1125–42.

MacManus, Susan A., and Charles S. Bullock III. 1989. "Women on Southern City Councils: A Decade of Change." *Journal of Political Science* 17: 32–49.

Magar, Eric, Marc Rosenblum, and David Samuels. 1998. "On the Absence of Centripetal Incentives in Double-Member Districts." *Comparative Political Studies* 31: 714–39.

Magee, Stephen, William Brock, and Leslie Young. 1989. *Black Hole Tariffs and Endogenous Policy Theory: Political Economy in General Equilibrium.* Cambridge: Cambridge University Press.

Maggi, Giovanni. 1999. "The Role of Multilateral Institutions in International Trade Cooperation." *American Economic Review* 89 (1): 190–214.

Mahon, Rianne. 1991. "From Solidaristic Wages to Solidaristic Work: A Post-Fordist Historical Compromise for Sweden?" *Economic and Industrial Democracy* 12 (3): 295–325.

Mahoney, James. 1999. "Nominal, Ordinal, and Narrative Appraisal in Macro-causal Analysis." *American Journal of Sociology* 104: 1154–96.

Mahoney, James. 2000a. "Path Dependence in Historical Sociology." *Theory and Society* 29: 507–48.

Mahoney, James. 2000b. "Strategies of Causal Inference in Small-N Analysis." *Sociological Methods and Research* 28: 387–424.

Mahoney, James. 2001. *The Legacies of Liberalism: Path Dependence and Political Regimes in Central America.* Baltimore: Johns Hopkins University Press.

Mahoney, James. 2002. "Knowledge Accumulation in Comparative-Historical Analysis: The Case of Democracy and Authoritarianism." In *Comparative-Historical Analysis: Achievements and Agendas,* ed. James Mahoney and Dietrich Rueschemeyer. Cambridge: Cambridge University Press.

Mainwaring, Scott. 1997. "Multipartism, Robust Federalism, and Presidentialism in Brazil." In *Presidentialism and Democracy in Latin America,* ed. Scott Mainwaring and Matthew Soberg Shugart. Cambridge: Cambridge University Press.

Mainwaring, Scott, and Matthew Soberg Shugart. 1997a. "Presidentialism and Democracy in Latin America: Rethinking the Terms of the Debate" and "Conclusion: Presidentialism and the Party System." In *Presidentialism and Democracy in Latin America,* ed. Scott Mainwaring and Matthew Soberg Shugart. Cambridge: Cambridge University Press.

Mainwaring, Scott, and Matthew Soberg Shugart, eds. 1997b. *Presidentialism and Democracy in Latin America.* Cambridge: Cambridge University Press.

Maioni, Antonia. 1998. *Parting at the Crossroads: The Emergence of Health Insurance in the United States and Canada.* Princeton, NJ: Princeton University Press.

Mallick, Ross. 1993. *Development Policy of a Communist Government: West Bengal since 1977.* Cambridge and New York: Cambridge University Press.

Malloy, James, ed. 1977. *Authoritarianism and Corporatism in Latin America.* Pittsburgh, PA: University of Pittsburgh Press.

Maltzman, Forrest. 1998. "Maintaining Congressional Committees: Sources of Member Support." *Legislative Studies Quarterly* 23: 197–218.

Maltzman, Forrest, and Lee Sigelman. 1996. "The Politics of Talk: Unconstrained Floor Time in the U.S. House of Representatives." *Journal of Politics* 58: 819–30.

Mamdani, Mahmood. 1996. *Citizen and Subject: Contemporary Africa and the Legacy of Late Colonialism.* Princeton, NJ: Princeton University Press.

Mandel, Ruth B., and Debra L. Dodson. 1992. "Do Women Officeholders Make a Difference?" In *The American Woman 1992–93: A Status Report,* ed. Paula Ries and Anne J. Stone. New York: Norton.

Manion, Melanie. 1996a. "Corruption by Design: Bribery in Chinese Enterprise Licensing." *Journal of Law, Economics and Organization* 12: 167–95.

Manion, Melanie. 1996b. "The Electoral Connection in the Chinese Countryside." *American Political Science Review* 90: 376–48.

Manley, John F. 1970. *The Politics of Finance: The House Committee on Ways and Means.* Boston: Little, Brown.

Mann, Michael. 1986. *The Sources of Social Power: A History of Power from the Beginning to A.D. 1760.* Vol. 1. New York: Cambridge University Press.

Mann, Michael. 1993. *The Sources of Social Power: The Rise of Clases and Nation-States, 1760–1914,* vol. 2. New York: Cambridge University Press.

Manow, Philip. 2000. " 'Modell Deutschland' as a Cross-Class Alliance." Cologne, GER: Max Planck Institute for Social Research.

Mansbridge, Jane J. 1980. *Beyond Adversary Democracy.* New York: Basic.

Mansbridge, Jane J. 1986. *Why We Lost the ERA.* Chicago: University of Chicago Press.

Mansbridge, Jane J., ed. 1990. *Beyond Self-Interest.* Chicago: University of Chicago Press.

Mansfield, Edward D. 1994. *Power, Trade, and War.* Princeton, NJ: Princeton University Press.

Mansfield, Edward, Helen V. Milner, and B. Peter Rosendorff. 2000. "Free to Trade: Democracies, Autocracies, and International Trade." *American Political Science Review* 94 (2): 305–21.

Maoz, Ze'ev. 1997. "The Controversy over the Democratic Peace: Rearguard Action or Cracks in the Wall?" *International Security* 22 (summer): 162–98.

Maoz, Ze'ev, 1998. "Realist and Cultural Critiques of the Democratic Peace." *International Interactions* 24: 3–89.

Maoz, Ze'ev, and Bruce M. Russett. 1993. "Normative and Structural Causes of the Democratic Peace." *American Political Science Review* 87: 624–38.

March, James G., and Johan P. Olsen. 1989. *Rediscovering Institutions.* New York: Free Press.

March, James G, and Johan P Olsen. 1998. "The Institutional Dynamics of International Political Orders." *International Organization* 52 (4): 943–69.

Mares, Isabela. 2000. "Strategic Alliances and Social Policy Reform: Unemployment Insurance in Comparative Perspective." *Politics and Society* 28 (2): 223–44.

Margalit, Avishai, and Moshe Halbertal. 1994. "Liberalism and the Right to Culture." *Social Research* 61 (3): 491–510.

Margalit, Avishai, and Joseph Raz. 1994. "National Self-Determination." In *Ethics in the Public Domain*, ed. Joseph Raz, 110–30. Oxford: Clarendon.

Marinucci, Carla. 2000. "GOP to Play Musical Chairs Over Abortion," *San Francisco Chronicle*, May 15, A1.

Marinucci, Carla, and Mark Simon. 2000. "Nader Defends Record on Women's Rights." *San Francisco Chronicle*, September 15, A3.

Marks, Brian A. 1988. "A Model of Judicial Influence on Congressional Policymaking: Grove City College v. Bell," Working Papers in Political Science P-88-7, Hoover Institution.

Marshall, T. H. 1950. *Citizenship and Social Class and Other Essays*, Cambridge: Cambridge University Press.

Marshall, William P. 1991. "In Defense of Smith and Free Exercise Revisionism." *University of Chicago Law Review* 58 (1): 308–28.

Martin, Andrew. 2000. "The Politics of Macroeconomic Policy and Wage Negotiations in Sweden." In *Unions, Employers and Central Banks*, ed. T. Iversen, J. Pontusson, and D. Soskice. New York: Cambridge University Press.

Martin, Cathie Jo. 1995. "Nature or Nurture? Sources of Firm Preference for National Health Reform." *American Political Science Review* 89 (4): 898–913.

Martin, Cathie Jo. 1999. "Business and Politics of Human Capital Investment Policy: A New Institutionalist Perspective." *Polity* 32 (2): 203–32.

Martin, Cathie Jo. 2000. *Stuck in Neutral: Business and the Politics of Human Capital Investment Policy.* Princeton, NJ: Princeton University Press.

Martin, Lisa L. 1992a. *Coercive Cooperation: Explaining Multilateral Economic Sanctions.* Princeton, NJ: Princeton University Press.

Martin, Lisa L. 1992b. "Interests, power, and multilateralism." *International Organization* 46 (4): 765–92.

Martin, Lisa L. 2000. *Democratic Commitments: Legislatures and International Cooperation.* Princeton, NJ: Princeton University Press.

Martin, Lisa L. 2001. "International and Domestic Institutions in the EMU Process and Beyond." In *The Political Economy of European Monetary Unification*, 2d ed., Barry Eichengreen and Jeffry Frieden. Boulder, CO: Westview.

Martin, Lisa L., and Beth Simmons. 1998. "Theories and Empirical Studies of International Institutions." *International Organization* 52 (3): 729–57.

Martinez, Michael D., and David Hill. 1999. "Did Motor Voter Work?" *American Politics Quarterly* 27: 296–315.

Marx, Anthony W. 1998. *Making Race and Nation: A Comparison of South Africa, the United States, and Brazil.* Cambridge: Cambridge University Press.

Marx, Karl. 1972 [1883]. *The Eighteenth Brumaire of Louis Bonaparte.* In *The Marx-Engels Reader*, ed. Robert Tucker. New York: Norton.

Marx, Karl. 1976. *Capital: A Critique of Political Economy.* Vol. 1. Harmondsworth: Penguin.

Marx, Karl. 1977 [1875]. "Critique of the Gotha Programme." In *Karl Marx: Selected Writings*, ed. David McLellan, 569–78. Oxford: Oxford University Press.

Mastanduno, Michael. 1991. "Do Relative Gains Matter? America's Response to Japanese Industrial Policy." *International Security* 16 (summer): 73–113.

Mastanduno, Michael. 1992. *Economic Containment: CoCom and the Politics of East-West Trade*. Ithaca, NY: Cornell University Press.

Mastanduno, Michael. 1999. "Preserving the Unipolar Moment: Realist Theories and U.S. Foreign Policy After the Cold War." In *Unipolar Politics: Realism and State Strategies After the Cold War*, ed. Ethan B. Kapstein and Michael Mastanduno. New York: Columbia University Press.

Masten, Scott. 2000. "Commitment and Political Governance: Why Universities, Like Legislatures, Are Not Organized as Firms." Paper, University of Michigan Business School, Ann Arbor, MI.

Mathews, Donald, and Jane Sherron DeHart. 1992. *Sex, Gender and the Politics of the ERA*. New York: Oxford University Press.

Mathews, Jessica. 1997. "Power Shift: The Rise of Global Civil Society." *Foreign Affairs* 76 (January–February): 50–66.

Mattei, Laura R. Winsky. 1998. "Gender and Power in American Legislative Discourse." *Journal of Politics* 60 (May): 440–61.

Mathews, Donald G., and Jane Sherron De Hart. 1990. *Sex, Gender, and the Politics of ERA: A State and the Nation*. New York: Oxford University Press.

Matthews, Donald R. 1959. "The Folkways of the United States Senate: Conformity to Group Norms and Legislative Effectiveness." *American Political Science Review* 53: 1064–89.

Matthews, Donald R. 1960. *U.S. Senators and Their World*. Chapel Hill: University of North Carolina Press.

Matthews, John. 1996. "Current Gains and Future Outcomes: When Cumulative Relative Gains Matter." *International Security* 21 (summer): 112–46.

Matthews, Steven. 1989. "Veto Threats: Rhetoric in Bargaining." *Quarterly Journal of Economics* 104: 347–69.

Maxfield, Sylvia. 1997. *Gatekeepers of Growth: The International Political Economy of Central Banking in Developing Countries*. Princeton, NJ: Princeton University Press.

Mayhew, David R. 1974a. "Congressional Elections: The Case of the Vanishing Marginals." *Polity* 3: 295–317.

Mayhew, David R. 1974b. *Congress: The Electoral Connection*. New Haven, CT: Yale University Press.

Mayhew, David R. 1986. *Placing Parties in American Politics*. Princeton, NJ: Princeton University Press.

Mayhew, David R. 1991. *Divided We Govern: Party Control, Lawmaking, and Investigations, 1946–1990*. New Haven, CT: Yale University Press.

Mayhew, David R. 2000. "Electoral Realignments," *Annual Review of Political Science* 3: 449–74.

McAdam, Doug. 1982. *Political Process and the Development of Black Insurgency, 1930–1970.* Chicago: University of Chicago Press.

McAdam, Doug, John D. McCarthy, and Mayer N. Zald, eds. 1996. *Comparative Perspectives on Social Movements: Political Opportunities, Mobilizing Structures, and Cultural Framings.* Cambridge: Cambridge University Press.

McAdam, Doug, and Ronnelle Paulsen. 1993. "Specifying the Relationship Between Social Ties and Activism: Mississippi Freedom Summer Project, 1964." *American Journal of Sociology* 99 (November): 640–67.

McAdam, Doug, Sidney Tarrow, and Charles Tilly. 1997. "Toward an Integrated Perspective on Social Movements and Revolutions." In *Comparative Politics: Rationality, Culture, and Structure,* ed. Mark Lichbach and Alan Zukerman, 142–73. New York: Cambridge University Press.

McAdam, Doug, Sidney Tarrow, and Charles Tilly. 2001. *Dynamics of Contention.* Cambridge: Cambridge University Press.

McCarthy, John D., and Mark Wolfson. 1996. "Resource Mobilization by Local Social Movement Organizations: Agency, Strategy, and Organization in the Movement against Drinking and Driving." *American Sociological Review* 61: 1070–88.

McCarthy, Thomas. 1991. *Ideals and Illusions: On Reconstruction and Deconstruction in Contemporary Critical Theory.* Cambridge: MIT Press.

McCarthy, Thomas. 1998. "Legitimacy and Diversity: Dialectical Reflections on Analytic Distinctions." In *Habermas on Law and Democracy: Critical Exchanges,* ed. Michel Rosenfeld and Andrew Arato. Berkeley: University of California Press.

McCarthy, Thomas. 1999. "On Reconciling Cosmopolitan Unity and National Diversity." *Public Culture* 11 (1): 175–210.

McCarty, Nolan M. 2000. "Presidential Pork: Executive Veto Power and Distributive Politics." *American Political Science Review* 94: 117–29.

McCarty, Nolan M., and Keith T. Poole. 1995. "Veto Power and Legislation: An Empirical Analysis of Executive and Legislative Bargaining from 1961 to 1986." *Journal of Law, Economics, and Organization* 11: 282–312.

McCarty, Nolan M., and Rose Razaghian. 1999. "Advice and Consent: Senate Responses to Executive Branch Nominations, 1885–1996." *American Journal of Political Science* 43: 1122–43.

McCarty, Nolan, and Lawrence S. Rothenberg. 1996. "Commitment and Campaign Contribution Contract." *American Journal of Political Science* 40 (3, August): 872–904.

McCloskey, D. N. 1994. *Knowledge and Persuasion in Economics.* Cambridge: Cambridge University Press.

McCloskey, Herbert, Paul Hoffman, and Rosemary O'Hara. 1960. "Issue Conflict and Consensus among Party Leaders and Followers." *American Political Science Review* 54: 406–27.

McConachie, Lauros G. 1898. *Congressional Committees: A Study of the Origins and Development of Our National and Local Legislative Methods.* New York: Crowell.

McConnell, Michael W. 1991. "A Response to Professor Marshall." *University of Chicago Law Review* 58 (1): 329–32.

McConnell, Michael W. 2000. "Believers as Equal Citizens." In *Religion and Law: Obligations of Citizenship and Demands of Faith*, ed. Nancy L. Rosenblum. Princeton, NJ: Princeton University Press.

McCormick, Richard L. 1986. *The Party Period and Public Policy: American Politics from the Age of Jackson to the Progressive Era*. New York. Oxford University Press.

McCubbins, Mathew D. 1991. "Party Governance and U.S. Budget Deficits: Divided Government and Fiscal Stalemate." In *Politics and Economics in the Eighties*, ed. Alberto Alesina and Geoffrey Carliner. Chicago: University of Chicago Press.

McCubbins, Mathew D., Roger G. Noll, and Barry R. Weingast. 1987. "Administrative Procedures as Instruments of Political Control." *Journal of Law, Economics, and Organization* 3: 243–77.

McCubbins, Mathew D., Roger G. Noll, and Barry R. Weingast. 1989. "Structure and Process, Politics and Policy: Administrative Arrangements and the Political Control of Agencies." *Virginia Law Review* 75: 431–82.

McCubbins, Mathew D., and Thomas Schwartz. 1984. "Congressional Oversight Overlooked: Police Patrols vs. Fire Alarms." *American Journal of Political Science* 28: 165–79.

McDermott, C. John, and Robert F. Westcott. 1996. "An Empirical Analysis of Fiscal Adjustments." IMF Staff Papers: 725–53.

McDermott, Monika L. 1997. "Voting Cues in Low-Information Elections: Candidate Gender as a Social Information Variable in Contemporary United States Elections." *American Journal of Political Science* 41 (January): 270–83.

McDonagh, Eileen. 1982. "To Work or Not to Work: The Differential Impact of Achieved and Derived Status upon the Political Participation of Women, 1956–76." *American Journal of Political Science* 26: 280–97.

McDonagh, Eileen. 1993. "The 'Welfare Rights State' and the 'Civil Rights State': Policy Paradox and State Building in the Progressive Era." *Studies in American Political Development* 7: 225–74.

McDonald, Keith M. 1995. *The Sociology of the Professions*. London: Sage.

McDonald, Michael, and Samuel Popkin. 2000. "Rethinking Turnout in America." unpublished manuscript.

McGerr, Michael. 1986. *The Decline of Popular Politics*. New York: Oxford University Press.

McGillivray, Fiona. 1997. "Party Discipline as a Determinant of the Endogenous Formation of Tariffs." *American Journal of Political Science* 41 (2): 584–607.

McGlen, Nancy. 1980. "The Impact of Parenthood on Political Participation." *Western Political Quarterly* 33: 297–313.

McKay, Derek, and H. M. Scott. 1983. *The Rise of the Great Powers, 1648–1815*. London: Longman.

McKelvey, Richard D., and Peter C. Ordeshook. 1990. "Information and Elections: Retrospective Voting and Rational Expectations." In *Information and Demo-*

cratic Processes, ed. J. Ferejohn and J. Kuklinski, 281–312. Urbana-Campaign: University of Illinois Press.

McKim, Robert, and Jeff McMahan, eds. 1997. *The Morality of Nationalism*. Oxford: Oxford University Press.

Mearsheimer, John J. 1990. "Back to the Future: Instability in Europe after the Cold War." *International Security* 15 (summer): 5–56.

Mearsheimer, John J. 1994–1995. "The False Promise of International Institutions." *International Security* 19 (winter): 5–49.

Mearsheimer, John J. 2001. *The Tragedy of Great Power Politics*. New York: Norton.

Mehta, Uday Singh. 1999. *Liberalism and Empire: A Study in Nineteenth-Century British Liberal Thought*. Chicago: University of Chicago Press.

Melnick, R. Shep. 1994. *Between the Lines: Interpreting Welfare Rights*. Washington, DC: Brookings.

Meltzer, Allan, and Scott F. Richard. 1981. "A Rational Theory of the Size of Government." *Journal of Political Economy* 89: 5, 914–927.

Mercer, Jonathan. 1995. "Anarchy and Identity." *International Organization* 49: 229–52.

Mercer, Jonathan. 1996. *Reputation and International Politics*. Ithaca, NY: Cornell University Press.

Merriam, Charles. 1900. *History of the Theory of Sovereignty Since Rousseau*. New York: Columbia University Press.

Merriam, Charles. 1921. "The Present State of the Study of Politics." *American Political Science Review*, 15: 173–185.

Merriam, Charles. 1925. *New Aspects of Politics*. Chicago: University of Chicago Press.

Merriam, Charles. 1926. "Progress in Political Research." *American Political Science Review* 20 (February): 1–13.

Merrill, Horace Samuel, and Marion Galbraith Merrill. 1971. *The Republican Command, 1897–1913*. Lexington: University Press of Kentucky.

Merton, Robert K. 1949. *Social Theory and Social Structure*. Glencoe, Ill.: Free Press.

Mettler, Suzanne. 1998. *Dividing Citizens: Gender and Federalism in New Deal Public Policy*. Ithaca, NY: Cornell University Press.

Meyer, David S., and Suzanne Staggenborg. 1996. "Movements, Countermovements, and the Structure of Political Opportunity." *American Journal of Sociology* 101: 1628–60.

Meyer, John W., John Boli, and George Thomas. 1987. "Ontology and Rationalization in the Western Cultural Account." In *Institutional Structure: Constituting State, Society, and the Individual*, ed. G. Thomas et al. Newbury Park, CA: Sage.

Meyer, John W., John Boli, George M. Thomas, and Francisco O. Ramirez. 1997. "World Society and the Nation-State." *American Journal of Sociology* 103 (1): 144–81.

Meyer, John W., and Brian Rowen. 1991. "Institutionalized Organizations: Formal Structures as Myth and Ceremony." In *The New Institutionalism in Organizational*

Analysis, ed. P. J. DiMaggio and W. W. Powell. Chicago: University of Chicago Press.

Mezey, Michael L. 1979. *Comparative Legislatures.* Durham, NC: Duke University Press.

Mezey, Michael L. 1993. "Legislatures: Individual Purpose and Institutional Performance." In *Political Science: The State of the Discipline II,* ed. Ada W. Finifter. Washington, DC: American Political Science Association.

Mezey, Susan Gluck. 1994. "Increasing the Number of Women in Office: Does it Matter?" In *The Year of the Woman: Myths and Realities,* ed. Elizabeth Adell Cook, Sue Thomas, and Clyde Wilcox. Boulder, CO: Westview.

Micheletti, Michele. 2000. "End of Big Government: Is It Happening in the Nordic Countries?" *Governance* 13 (April): 265–78.

Michels, Roberto. 1927. "Some Reflections on the Sociological Character of Political Parties." *American Political Science Review* 21 (November): 753–772.

Michels, Robert. 1962. *Political Parties: A Sociological Study of the Oligarchical Tendencies of Modern Democracy.* Trans. Eden and Cedar Paul. New York: Free Press.

Midlarsky, Manus. 1999. *The Evolution of Inequality: War, State Survival, and Democracy in Comparative Perspective.* Stanford, CA: Stanford University Press.

Migdal, Joel S. 1988. *Strong Societies and Weak States: State-Society Relations and State Capabilities in the Third World.* Princeton, NJ: Princeton University Press.

Migdal, Joel S. 1994. "The State in Society." In *State Power and Social Forces,* ed. Joel S. Migdal, Atul Kohli, and Vivienne Shue, 7–34. New York: Cambridge University Press.

Migdal, Joel S. 2001. *State in Society: Studying How States and Societies Transform and Constitute One Another.* New York: Cambridge University Press.

Migdal, Joel S., Atul Kohli, and Vivienne Shue, eds. 1994. *State Power and Social Forces Domination and Transformation in the Third World.* New York: Cambridge University Press.

Mignolo, Walter. 2000. *Local Histories/Cosmopolitan Designs: Coloniality, Subaltern Knowledges, and Border Thinking.* Princeton, NJ: Princeton University Press.

Milbrath, Lester W., and M. L. Goel. 1977. *Political Participation: How and Why Do People Get Involved in Politics?* 2d ed. Chicago: Rand McNally.

Milesi-Ferretti, Gian, Roberto Perotti, and Massimo Rostagno. 1999. "Electoral Systems and Public Spending." Unpublished paper.

Mileur, Jerome. 1991. "Party Renewal." In *Political Parties and Elections in the United States,* vol. 2, ed. L. Sandy Maisel, 780–85. New York: Garland.

Milgrom, Paul R., Douglas C. North, and Barry R. Weingast. 1990. "The Role of Institutions in the Revival of Trade: The Medieval Law Merchant, Private Judges, and the Champagne Fairs." *Economics and Politics* 2 (1): 1–23.

Milgrom, Paul R., and John Roberts. 1991. *Economics, Organization, and Management.* Englewood Cliffs, NJ: Prentice-Hall.

Milkis. Sidney. 1993. *The President and the Parties.* New York: Oxford University Press.

Milkis, Sidney, and Daniel Tichenor. 1994. " 'Direct Democracy' and Social Justice: The Progressive Party Campaign of 1912." *Studies in American Political Development*, 8: 225–74.

Mill, John Stuart. 1975. "On the Subjection of Women." In *John Stuart Mill: Three Essays*, ed. Richard Wollheim. Oxford: Oxford University Press.

Mill, John Stuart. 1989. "On Liberty." In *On Liberty and Other Writings*, ed. Stefan Collini. New York: Cambridge University Press.

Miller, Arthur H. 1988. "Gender and the Vote: 1984." In *The Politics of the Gender Gap*, ed. Carol M. Mueller. Newbury Park, CA: Sage.

Miller, Arthur H., Patricia Gurin, Gerald Gurin, and Oksana Malanchuk. 1981. "Group Consciousness and Political Participation." *American Journal of Political Science* 25: 494–511.

Miller, David. 1995. *On Nationality*. New York: Oxford University Press.

Miller, David. 1999. *Principles of Social Justice*. Cambridge, MA: Harvard University Press.

Miller, Joanne M., and Jon A. Krosnick. 1998. "The Impact of Candidate Name Order on Election Outcomes." *Public Opinion Quarterly* 62: 291–330.

Miller, Joanne M., Jon A. Krosnick, and Laura Lowe. 2000. "The Impact of Policy Change Threat on Financial Contributions to Interest Groups." Manuscript.

Miller, Nicholas R. 1993. "Pluralism and Social Choice." *American Political Science Review* 77: 734–47.

Miller, Roy E., David A. Bositis, and Denise L. Baer. 1981. "Stimulating Voter Turnout in a Primary: Field Experiment with a Precinct Committeeman." *International Political Science Review* 2 (4): 445–60.

Miller, Warren E., and J. Merrill Shanks. 1996. *The New American Voter*. Cambridge, MA: Harvard University Press.

Milliken, Jennifer. 1999. "The Study of Discourse in International Relations: A Critique of Research and Methods." *European Journal of International Relations* 5 (2): 225–54.

Milner, Helen V. 1988. *Resisting Protectionism: Global Industries and the Politics of International Trade*. Princeton, NJ: Princeton University Press.

Milner, Helen V. 1991. "The Assumption of Anarchy in International Politics: A Critique." *Review of International Studies* 19 (January): 67–85.

Milner, Helen V. 1997. *Interests, Institutions, and Information: Domestic Politics and International Relations*. Princeton, NJ: Princeton University Press.

Milner, Helen V. 1998. "Rationalizing Politics: The Emerging Synthesis of International, American, and Comparative Politics." *International Organization* 52 (autumn): 759–86.

Milner, Helen V., and B. Peter Rosendorff. 1997. "Democratic Politics and International Trade Negotiations: Elections and Divided Government as Constraints on Trade Liberalization." *Journal of Conflict Resolution* 41 (1): 117–46.

Milner, Helen, and David Yoffie. 1989. "Between Free Trade and Protectionism: Strategic Trade Policy and a Theory of Corporate Trade Demands." *International Organization* 43 (2): 239–272.

Mink, Gwendolyn. 1986. *Old Labor and New Immigrants in American Political Development: Union Party and the State 1875–1920.* Ithaca, NY: Cornell University Press.

Mink, Gwendolyn. 1995. *The Wages of Motherhood: Inequality in the Welfare State, 1917–1942.* Ithaca, NY: Cornell University Press.

Minkoff, Debra C. 1997. "The Sequencing of Social Movements." *American Sociological Review* 62: 779–99.

Mishler, William, and Richard Rose. 1997. "Trust, Distrust, and Skepticism: Popular Evaluations of Civil and Political Institutions in Post-Communist Societies." *Journal of Politics* 59: 419–51.

Mitchell, Glenn E., and Christopher Wlezien. 1995. "The Impact of Legal Constraints on Voter Registration, Turnout, and the Composition of the American Electorate." *Political Behavior* 17: 179–202.

Mitchell, Timothy. 1991. "The Limits of the State: Beyond Statist Approaches and Their Critics." *American Political Science Review* 85 (1): 77–96.

Mitrovich, Gregory. 2000. *Undermining the Kremlin: America's Strategy to Subvert the Soviet Bloc, 1947–1956.* Ithaca, NY: Cornell University Press.

Moe, Terry M. 1980. *The Organization of Interests.* Chicago: University of Chicago Press.

Moe, Terry M. 1987. "Institutions Interests and Positive Theory: The Politics of the NLRB." In *Studies in American Political Development*, vol. 2, 236–302. New Haven, CT: Yale University Press.

Moe, Terry M. 1989. "The Political Structure of Agencies." In *Can the Government Govern?* ed. John E. Chubb and Paul E. Peterson. Washington, DC: Brookings.

Moe, Terry, and William Howell. 1999. "Unilateral Action and Presidential Leadership: A Theory." *Presidential Studies Quarterly* 29: 850–72.

Moene, Karl Ove, and Michael Wallerstein. 1999. "Social Democratic Labor Market Institutions: A Retrospective Analysis." In *Continuity and Change in Contemporary Capitalism*, ed. H. Kitschelt, P. Lange, G. Marks, and J. D. Stephens. New York: Cambridge University Press.

Moene, Karl Ove, and Michael Wallerstein. 2001. "Inequality, Social Insurance, and Redistribution." *American Political Science Review* 95 (December): 859–74.

Monroe, Kristen Renwick. 1996. *The Heart of Altruism: Perceptions of a Common Humanity.* Princeton, NJ: Princeton University Press.

Moon, Donald J. 1993. *Constructing Community: Moral Pluralism and Tragic Conflicts.* Princeton, NJ: Princeton University Press.

Moon, Donald J. 1995. "Practical Discourse and Communicative Ethics." In *The Cambridge Companion to Habermas*, ed. Stephen K. White. Cambridge: Cambridge University Press.

Moore, Barrington. 1966. *The Social Origins of Dictatorship and Democracy: Lord and Peasant in the Making of the Modern World.* Boston: Beacon.

Moore, Michael K., and John R. Hibbing. 1998. "Situational Dissatisfaction in Congress: Explaining Voluntary Departures." *Journal of Politics* 60: 1088–107.

Moore, Underhill, and Charles C. Callahan. 1943. "Law and Learning Theory: A Study in Legal Control." *Yale Law Journal* 53 (December): 1–136.

Moraski, Bryon, and Charles Shipan. 1999. "The Politics of Supreme Court Nominations: A Theory of Institutional Constraints and Choices," *American Journal of Political Science* 43: 1069–95.

Moravcsik, Andrew. 1997. "Taking Preferences Seriously: A Liberal Theory of International Politics." *International Organization* 51 (autumn): 513–53.

Moravcsik, Andrew. 1998a. *The Choice for Europe: Social Purpose and State Power from Messina to Maastricht.* Ithaca, NY: Cornell University Press.

Moravcsik, Andrew. 1998b. "Explaining the Emergence of Human Rights Regimes: Liberal Democracy and Political Uncertainty in Postwar Europe." Working Paper Series No. 98–17, 1–49. Weatherhead Center for International Affairs.

Moravcsik, Andrew. 1999. "A New Statecraft? Supranational Entrepreneurs and International Cooperation." *International Organization* 53 (2): 267–306.

Morgan, T. Clifton, and Sally Howard Campbell. 1991. "Domestic Structure, Decisional Constraints, and War." *Journal of Conflict Resolution* 35: 187–211.

Morgenstern, Scott. 1999. "Organized Factions and Disorganized Parties: Electoral Incentives in Uruguay." Manuscript, Duke University, Durham, NC.

Morgenstern, Scott. 2000. "Explaining Voting Unity in the Legislatures of the United States and Latin America." Paper presented at the Annual Meeting of the American Political Science Association, Washington, DC.

Morgenstern, Scott, and Pilar Domingo. 1999. "Gridlock and Breakdown." Manuscript, Duke University, Durham, NC.

Morgenthau, Hans J. 1946. *Scientific Man vs. Power Politics.* Chicago: University of Chicago Press.

Morgenthau, Hans J. 1948. *Politics Among Nations: The Struggle for Power and Peace.* New York: Knopf.

Morgenthau, Hans J. 1959. "Alliances in Theory and Practice." In *Alliance Policy and the Cold War,* ed. Arnold Wolfers. Baltimore: John Hopkins University Press.

Morone, James. 1990. *Democratic Wish: Popular Participation and the Limits of American Government.* New York. Basic.

Morrell, Michael E. 1999. "Citizens' Evaluations of Participatory Democratic Procedures: Normative Theory Meets Empirical Science." *Political Research Quarterly* 52: 293–322.

Morris, Aldon D., and Carol McClurg Mueller, eds. 1992. *Frontiers of Social Movement Theory.* New Haven: Yale University Press.

Morris, Irwin. 2000. *Congress, the President, and the Federal Reserve.* Ann Arbor: University of Michigan Press.

Morris, Martin. 2001. *Rethinking the Communicative Turn.* Albany: State University of New York Press.

Morrison, Toni. 1992. *Playing in the Dark: Whiteness and the Literary Imagination.* Cambridge, MA: Harvard University Press.

Morrow, James D. 1989. "Capabilities, Uncertainty, and Resolve: A Limited Information Model of Crisis Bargaining." *American Journal of Political Science* 33: 941–72.

Morrow, James D. 1993. "Arms Versus Allies: Trade-offs in the Search for Security." *International Organization* 47: 207–33.

Morrow, James D. 1994a. "Alliances, Credibility, and Peacetime Costs." *Journal of Conflict Resolution* 38: 270–97.

Morrow, James D. 1994b. "Modelling the Forms of International Cooperation: Distribution versus Information." *International Organization* 48 (3): 387–423.

Morrow, James D. 1997. "When Do 'Relative Gains' Impede Trade?" *Journal of Conflict Resolution* 41: 12–37.

Morrow, James D. 1999a. "How Could Trade Affect Conflict?" *Journal of Peace Research* 36: 481–89.

Morrow, James D. 1999b. "The Strategic Setting of Choices: Signaling, Commitment, and Negotiation in International Politics." In *Strategic Choice and International Relations*, ed. David A. Lake and Robert Powell, 77–114. Princeton, NJ: Princeton University Press.

Morrow, James D. 2000. "Alliances: Why Write Them Down?" *Annual Review of Political Science* 3: 63–83.

Morton, Rebecca B. 1991. "Groups in Rational Turnout Models." *American Journal of Political Science* 35: 758–76.

Morton, Rebecca B. 1999. *Methods and Models: A Guide to the Empirical Analysis of Formal Models in Political Science*. Cambridge: Cambridge University Press.

Morton, Rebecca B., and Kenneth Williams. 2001. *Learning by Voting: Sequential Choices in Presidential Primaries and Other Elections*. Ann Arbor: University of Michigan Press.

Mosca, Gaetano. 1939. *The Ruling Class*. New York: McGraw-Hill.

Moscardelli, Vincent G., Moshe Haspel, and Richard S. Wike. 1998. "Party Building through Campaign Finance Reform: Conditional Party Government in the 104th Congress." *Journal of Politics* 60: 691–704.

Moseley, Cassandra. 1999. "New Ideas, Old Institutions: Environment, Community, and State in the Pacific Northwest." Ph.D. diss., Yale University, New Haven, CT.

Moser, Peter. 1997. "A Theory of Conditional Influence of the European Parliament in the Cooperation Procedure." *Public Choice* 91: 333–50.

Moser, Peter. 1999a. "Checks and Balances, and the Supply of Central Bank Independence." *European Economic Review* 43: 1569–93.

Moser, Peter. 1999b. "The Impact of Legislative Institutions on Public Policy: A Survey." *European Journal of Political Economy* 15: 1–34.

Moser, Peter. 2000. *The Political Economy of Democratic Institutions*. Cheltenham, UK: Elgar.

Mosley, Layna. 2000. "Room to Move: International Financial Markets and National Welfare States." *International Organization* 54 (autumn): 737–74.

Mueller, Dennis. 1989. *Public Choice II*. New York: Cambridge University Press.

Mueller, Karl. 1995. "Alignment Balancing and Stability in Eastern Europe." *Security Studies* 5 (autumn): 38–76.

Mufti, Malik. 1996. *Sovereign Creations: Pan-Arabism and Political Order in Syria and Iraq*. Ithaca, NY: Cornell University Press.

Muller, Edward N., and Mitchell A. Seligson. 1994. "Civic Culture and Democracy: The Question of Causal Relationships." *American Political Science Review* 88: 635–52.

Müller, Harald. 1994. "Internationale Beziehungen als kommunikatives Handeln. Zur Kritik der utilitaristischen Handlungstheorien." *Zeitschrift für Internationale Beziehungen* 1 (1): 15–44.

Munck, Gerardo L. 1998. "Canons of Research Design in Qualitative Analysis." *Studies in Comparative International Development* 33: 18–45.

Munck, Gerardo L. 2001a. "Democratic Transitions." In *International Encyclopedia of the Social and Behavioral Sciences*, ed. Neil J. Smelser and Paul B. Bates. Oxford, UK: Pergamon.

Munck, Gerardo L. 2001b. "Game Theory and Comparative Politics: New Perspectives and Old Concerns." *World Politics* 53 (January).

Murillo, Maria Victoria. 2001. *Partisan Coalitions and Labor Competition in Latin America: Trade Unions and Market Reforms*. New York: Cambridge University Press.

Muthu, Sankar. 1999. "Enlightenment and Anti-Imperialism." *Social Research* 66 (4): 959–1007.

Muthu, Sankar. 2000. "Justice and Foreigners: Kant's Cosmopolitan Rights." *Constellations* 7 (1): 23–45.

Myerson, Roger B. 1992. "On the Value of Game Theory in Social Science." *Rationality and Society* 4: 62–73.

Myerson, Roger B., and Robert J. Weber. 1993. "A Theory of Voting Equilibria." *American Political Science Review* 87: 102–14.

Myles, J., and P. Pierson. 2001. "The Comparative Political Economy of Pension Reform." In *The New Politics of the Welfare State*, ed. P. Pierson. Oxford: Oxford University Press.

Myrdahl, Gunnar. 1958. *Economic Theory and Underdeveloped Regions*. Bombay, IND: Vora.

Nadelmann, Ethan. 1990. "Global Prohibition Regimes: The Evolution of Norms in International Society." *International Organization* 44 (4): 479–526.

Nagel, Jack H. 1993. "Lessons of the Impending Electoral Reform in New Zealand." *PEGS Newsletter* 3 (1): 9–10.

Nagel, Jack H., and John E. McNulty. 1996. "Partisan Effects of Voter Turnout in Senatorial and Gubernatorial Elections." *American Political Science Review* 90: 780–93.

Nagel, Jack H., and John E. McNulty. 2000. "Partisan Effects of Voter Turnout in Presidential Elections." *American Politics Quarterly* 28: 408–29.

Nagel, Thomas. 1991. *Equality and Partiality*. New York: Oxford University Press.

Nagler, Jonathan. 1991. "The Effect of Registration Laws and Education on U.S. Voter Turnout." *American Political Science Review* 85: 1393–405.

Nakano Glenn, Evelyn. 1992. "From Servitude to Service Work." *Signs* 18 (autumn): 1–43.

Narayan, Uma, and Sandra Harding, ed. 1998. *Border Crossings: Multicultural and Postcolonial Challenges to Philosophy* (Part I). *Hypatia. A Journal of Feminist Philosophy* (Special Issue) 13 (2, spring).

National Association of State Budget Offices. February 1995 and October 1999. "Budget Processes in the States."

National Conference of State Legislatures. 1998. "Legislative Budget Procedures," June.

Nayar, Baldev Raj. 1995. "Regimes, Power, and International Aviation." *International Organization* 49 (winter): 139–70.

Neblo, Michael. 2000. "Thinking Through Democracy: Deliberative Politics in Theory and Practice." Ph.D. diss., University of Chicago, Chicago.

Nee, Victor, and Rebeccah Matthews. 1996. "Market Transition and Societal Transformation in Reforming State Socialism." *Annual Review of Sociology* 22: 401–35.

Nelson, Joan. 1992. "Poverty, Equity, and the Politics of Adjustment." In *The Politics of Economic Adjustment: International Constraints, Distributive Conflicts, and the State*, ed. Stephan Haggard and Robert Kaufman. Princeton, NJ. Princeton University Press.

Nelson, Michael, ed. 1999. *The Evolving Presidency (Addresses, Cases, Essays, Letters, Reports, Resolutions, Transcripts, and Other Landmark Documents, 1787–1998.* Washington, DC: CQ.

Nettl, J. P. 1968. "The State as a Conceptual Variable." *World Politics* 20 (July): 559–92.

Neuman, Gerald L. 1993. "Buffer Zones Against Refugees: Dublin, Schengen and the German Asylum Amendment." *Virginia Journal of International Law* 33: 503–26.

Neuman, Gerald L. 1996. *Strangers to the Constitution. Immigrants, Borders and Fundamental Law.* Princeton, NJ: Princeton University Press.

Newell, Allen. 1973. "You Can't Play 20 Questions with Mother Nature and Win." In *Visual Information Processing*, ed. William C. Chase, 283–308. New York: Academic.

Newton, Kenneth. 1997. "Social Capital and Democracy." *American Behavioral Scientist* 40 (March–April): 575–86.

Nicholson, Linda. 1994. "Interpreting Gender." *Signs* 20: 79–105.

Nie, Norman H., Sidney Verba, and John R. Petrocik. 1976. *The Changing American Voter.* Cambridge, MA: Harvard University Press.

Nie, Norman H., Jane Junn, and Kenneth Stehlik-Barry. 1996. *Education and Democratic Citizenship in America.* Chicago: University of Chicago Press.

Nino, Carlos Santiago. 1996. *The Constitution of Deliberative Democracy.* New Haven, CT: Yale University Press.

Niou, Emerson M. S., and Peter C. Ordeshook. 1997. "Designing Coherent Government." In *Consolidating the Third Wave Democracies*, ed. Larry Diamond, Marc F. Plattner, Yun-han, Chu, and Hung-mao Tien, 160–73. Baltimore: Johns Hopkins University Press.

Nobles, Melissa. 2000. *Shades of Citizenship: Race and the Census in Modern Politics*. Stanford, CA: Stanford University Press.

Nokken, Timothy P. 2000. "Dynamics of Congressional Loyalty: Party Defection and Roll-Call Behavior, 1947–97." *Legislative Studies Quarterly* 25: 417–44.

Nomos XLII: Designing Democratic Institutions, ed. Ian Shapiro and Stephen Macedo. New York: New York University Press, 2000. 105–46.

Norrander, Barbara. 1991. "Explaining Individual Participation in Primaries." *Western Political Quarterly* 44: 640–55.

Norris, Pippa 1985. "The Gender Gap: America and Britain." *Parliamentary Affairs* 38: 192–201.

North, Douglass C. 1981. *Structure and Change in Economic History*. New York: Norton.

North, Douglass C. 1985. "Transaction Costs in History." *Journal of European Economic History* 14: 557–76.

North, Douglass. 1989a. "Institutions and Economic Growth: An Historical Introduction." *World Development* 17: 1319–32.

North, Douglass. 1989b. "A Transaction Cost Approach to the Historical Development of Polities and Economies." *Journal of Institutional and Theoretical Economics* 145: 661–68.

North, Douglass. 1990. *Institutions, Institutional Change and Economic Performance*. New York: Cambridge University Press.

North, Douglass C., and Robert Thomas. 1972. *Rise of the West*. New York: Norton.

North, Douglass C., and Barry R. Weingast. 1989. "Constitutions and Commitment: The Evolution of Institutions Governing Public Choice in Seventeenth Century England." *Journal of Economic History* 49: 803–32.

Norton, Ann. 1986. *Alternative Americas: A Reading of Antebellum Political Culture*. Chicago: University of Chicago Press.

Norton, Noelle H. 1999. "Uncovering the Dimensionality of Gender Voting in Congress." *Legislative Studies Quarterly* 24: 65–86.

Norton, Noelle. 1995. "Women, It's Not Enough to be Elected: Committee Position Makes a Difference." In *Gender Power, Leadership and Governance*, ed. Georgia Duerst-Lahti and Rita Mae Kelly. Ann Arbor: University of Michigan Press.

Norton, Philip. 1993. *Does Parliament Matter?* New York: Harvester Wheatsheaf.

Nownes, Anthony J. 1992. "Primaries, General Elections, and Voter Turnout: A Multinomial Logit Model of the Decision to Vote." *American Politics Quarterly* 20: 205–26.

Nownes, Anthony J., and Patricia K. Freeman. 1998. "Female Lobbyists: Women in the World of 'Good Ol' Boys.'" *Journal of Politics* 60 (November): 1191–201.

Nozick, Robert. 1974. *Anarchy, State and Utopia*. Oxford, UK: Blackwell.

Nurkse, Ragnar. 1961. *Equilibrium and Growth in the World Economy*. Cambridge, MA: Harvard University Press.

Nussbaum, Martha. 1996. "Patriotism and Cosmopolitanism." In *For Love of Country. Debating the Limits of Patriotism*, ed. Joshua Cohen. Boston: Beacon.

Nussbaum, Martha. 1997a. "Kant and Cosmopolitanism." In *Perpetual Peace: Essays on Kant's Cosmopolitan Ideal*, ed. Bohmann and Lutz-Bachmann, 25–59. Cambridge: MIT Press.

Nussbaum, Martha. 1997b. *Sex and Social Justice*. New York: Oxford University Press.

Nussbaum, Martha, and Jonathan Glover, eds. 1994. *Women, Culture, and Human Development*. Oxford: Clarendon.

Nye, Joseph S. 1995. "East Asian Security: The Case for Deep Engagement." *Foreign Affairs* 74 (July–August): 90–102.

Nye, Joseph, Philip Zelikow, and David King, eds. 1997. *Why People Don't Trust Government*. Cambridge, MA: Harvard University Press.

O'Brien, Kevin J., and Laura M. Luehrmann. 1998. "Institutionalizing Chinese Legislatures: Trade-offs Between Autonomy and Capacity." *Legislative Studies Quarterly* 23: 91–108.

O'Brien, Robert, Anne Marie Goetz, Jan Aart Scholte, and Marc Williams. 2000. *Contesting Global Governance. Multilateral Economic Institutions and Global Social Movements*. Cambridge: Cambridge University Press.

O'Brien, Ruth. 1998. *Worker's Paradox: The Republican Origins of New Deal Labor Policy*. Chapel Hill. University of North Carolina Press.

O'Connor, James. 1973. *The Fiscal Crisis of the State*. New York: St. Martin's.

O'Connor, Julia S., Ann Shola Orloff, and Sheila Shaver. 1999. *States, Markets, Families: Gender, Liberalism and Social Policy in Australia, Canada, Great Britain and the United States*. Cambridge: Cambridge University Press.

O'Donnell, Guillermo O. 1973. *Modernization and Bureaucratic-Authoritarianism: Studies in South American Politics*. Berkeley: Institution of International Studies, University of California.

O'Donnell, Guillermo O. 1978. "Reflections on the Patterns of Change in the Bureaucratic-Authoritarian State." *Latin American Research Review* 13: 3–38.

O'Donnell, Guillermo O. 1979. "Tensions in the Bureaucratic-Authoritarian State and the Question of Democracy." In *The New Authoritarianism in Latin America*, ed., David Collier. Princeton, NJ: Princeton University Press.

O'Donnell, Guillermo O. 1994. "Delegative Democracy." *Journal of Democracy* 5 (1): 55–70.

O'Donnell, Guillermo O. 1997. "Illusions About Consolidation." In *Consolidating the Third Wave Democracies*, ed. Larry Diamond, Marc F. Plattner, Yun-han Chus, and Hung-mao Tien, 40–57. Baltimore: Johns Hopkins University Press.

O'Donnell, Guillermo O. and Philippe C. Schmitter. 1986. *Transitions from Authoritarian Rule: Tentative Conclusions about Uncertain Democracies*. Baltimore: Johns Hopkins University Press.

O'Donnell, Guillermo O., Philippe C. Schmitter, and Laurence Whitehead, eds. 1986a. *Transitions from Authoritarian Rule: Comparative Perspectives*. Baltimore: Johns Hopkins University Press.

O'Donnell, Guillermo O., Philippe C. Schmitter, and Laurence Whitehead, eds. 1986b. *Transitions from Authoritarian Rule: Latin America.* Baltimore: Johns Hopkins University Press.

O'Donnell, Guillermo O., Philippe C. Schmitter, and Laurence Whitehead, eds. 1986c. *Transitions from Authoritarian Rule: Southern Europe.* Baltimore: Johns Hopkins University Press.

O'Neill, Barry. 1990. "The Intermediate Nuclear Force Missiles." *International Interactions* 15: 345–63.

O'Neill, Barry. 1994. "Game Theory Models of Peace and War." In *Handbook of Game Theory,* Vol. 2, ed. Robert Aumann and Sergiu Hart. New York: Elsevier-Science.

Obstfeld, Maurice, and Kenneth Rogoff. 2000. "Perspectives on OECD Economic Integration: Implications for U.S. Current Account Adjustment." Paper presented at the Federal Reserve Bank of Kansas City Symposium, Global Economic Integration: Opportunities and Challenges (24–26 August 2000), Jackson Hole, Wyoming.

Odell, John S. Forthcoming. "Bounded Rationality and the World Political Economy." In *Organizing the World Economy. Essays in Honor of Benjamin J. Cohen,* ed. D. Andrews, R. Henning, and L. Pauly.

Offe, Claus. 1973a. "The Abolition of Market Control and the Problem of Legitimacy, Part 1." *Kapitalstate* 1: 109–16.

Offe, Claus. 1973b. "The Abolition of Market Control and the Problem of Legitimacy, Part 2." *Kapitalstate* 2: 73–75.

Offe, Claus. 1984. *Contradictions of the Welfare State.* London: Hutchinson.

Ohmae, Kenichi. 1995. *The End of the Nation-State: The Rise of Regional Economies.* New York: Free Press.

Okin, Susan Moller. 1989. *Justice, Gender, and the Family.* New York: Basic.

Okin, Susan Moller. 1998. "Gender, the Public, and the Private." In *Feminism and Politics,* ed. Anne Phillips. Oxford: Oxford University Press.

Okin, Susan Moller, et al. 1999. *Is Multiculturalism Bad for Women?* Princeton, NJ: Princeton University Press.

Oliver, J. Eric. 1996. "The Effects of Eligibility Restrictions and Party Activity on Absentee Voting and Overall Turnout." *American Journal of Political Science* 40: 498–513.

Oliver, J. Eric. 2000. "City Size and Civic Involvement in Metropolitan America." *American Political Science Review* 94: 361–73.

Oliver J. Eric. 2001. *Democracy in Suburbia.* Princeton, NJ: Princeton University Press.

Oliver, J. Eric, and Raymond E. Wolfinger. 1999. "Jury Aversion and Voter Registration." *American Political Science Review* 93: 147–52.

Oliver, J. Eric, and Tali Mendelberg. 2000. "Reconsidering the Environmental Determinants of Racial Attitudes." *American Journal of Political Science* 44: 574–89.

Olson, David M., and Michael L. Mezey. 1991. *Legislatures in the Policy Process: The Dilemmas of Economic Policy.* Cambridge: Cambridge University Press.

Olson, Mancur. 1965. *The Logic of Collective Action: Public Goods and the Theory of Groups*. Cambridge, MA: Harvard University Press.

Olson, Mancur. 1971. *The Logic of Collective Action: Public Goods and the Theory of Groups*. Rev. ed. Cambridge, MA: Harvard University Press.

Olson, Mancur. 1993. "Dictatorship, Democracy and Development." *American Political Science Review* 87 (September): 567–76.

Oneal, John R., and Bruce M. Russett. 1997. "The Classical Liberals Were Right." *International Studies Quarterly* 41: 267–93.

Onis, Ziya. 1998. *State and Market: The Political Economy of Turkey in Comparative Perspective*. Istanbul: Bogazici University Press.

Onuf, Nicholas. 1989. *World of Our Making: Rules and Rule in Social Theory and International Relations*. Columbia: University of South Carolina Press.

Ordeshook, Peter C. 1996. "Russia's Party System: Is Russian Federalism Viable?" *Post-Soviet Affairs* 12: 195–217.

Ordeshook, Peter C., and Thomas Schwartz. 1987. "Agendas and The Control of Political Outcomes." *American Political Science Review* 81: 179–200.

Ordeshook, Peter C., and Olga Shvetsova. 1994. "Ethnic Heterogeneity, District Magnitude, and the Number of Parties." *American Journal of Political Science* 38: 100–23.

Organski, A. F. K. 1968. *World Politics*, 2nd ed. New York: Knopf.

Organski, A. F. K., and Jacek Kugler. 1980. *The War Ledger*. Chicago: University of Chicago Press.

Orlie, Melissa A. 1994. "Thoughtless Assertion and Political Deliberation." *American Political Science Review* 88: 684–95.

Orloff, Ann Shola. 1996. "Gender in the Welfare State." *American Sociological Review* 22: 51–78.

Orren, Karen. 1991. *Belated Feudalism: Labor, the Law and Liberal Political Development in the United States*. New York: Cambridge University Press.

Orren, Karen, and Stephen Skowronek. 1994. "Beyond the Iconography of Order: Notes for a 'New' Institutionalism." In *The Dynamics of American Politics*, ed. L. C. Dodd and C. Jillson, 311–32. Boulder, CO: Westview.

Orren, Karen, and Stephen Skowronek. 1996. "Institutions and Intercurrence: Theory Building in the Fullness of Time." *Nomos* 38: 111–46.

Orren, Karen, and Stephen Skowronek. 1998. "Regimes and Regime Building in American Government." *Political Science Quarterly*, 113 (4): 689–702.

Ortner, Sherry. 1996. *Making Gender*. Boston: Beacon.

Orum, Anthony M., Roberta S. Cohen, Sherri Grassmuck, and Amy Orum. 1977. "Sex, Socialization, and Politics." In *A Portrait of Marginality*, ed. Marianne Githens and Jewel L. Prestage. New York: McKay.

Ostrom, Elinor. 1990. *Governing the Commons: The Evolution of Institutions for Collective Action*. New York: Cambridge University Press.

Ostrom, Elinor. 1999. "Coping with Tragedies of the Commons." *Annual Review of Political Science* 2: 493–537.

Overby, L. Marvin, and Kenneth M. Cosgrove. 1996. "Unintended Consequences? Racial Redistricting and the Representation of Minority Interests." *Journal of Politics* 58: 540–50.

Overbye, Einar. 1995. "Making a Case for the Rational, Self-regarding, Ethical Voter . . . and Solving the Paradox of Not Voting in the Process." *European Journal of Political Research* 27: 369–96.

Owen, John M. 1994. "How Liberalism Produces Democratic Peace." *International Security* 19: 87–125.

Oye, Kenneth A. 1986a. "The Sterling-Dollar-Franc Triangle: Monetary Diplomacy 1929–1937." In *Cooperation Under Anarchy*, ed. Kenneth A. Oye, 173–99. Princeton, NJ: Princeton University Press.

Oye, Kenneth A., ed. 1986b. *Cooperation Under Anarchy*. Princeton, NJ: Princeton University Press.

Packenham, Robert A. 1970. "Legislatures and Political Development." In *Legislatures in Developmental Perspective*, ed. Alan Kornberg and Lloyd Musolf. Durham, NC: Duke University Press.

Page, Benjamin, and Robert Shapiro. 1992. *The Rational Public: Fifty Years of Trends in Americans' Policy Preferences*. Chicago: University of Chicago Press.

Palfrey, Thomas R. 1985. "Voter Participation and Strategic Uncertainty." *American Political Science Review* 79: 62–78

Palfrey, Thomas R., and Howard Rosenthal. 1985. "Voter Participation and Strategic Uncertainty." *American Political Science Review* 79:1 (March): 62–78.

Palma, Gabriel. 1978. "Dependency: A Formal Theory of Underdevelopment or a Methodology for the Analysis of Concrete Situations of Underdevelopment?" *World Development* 6: 881–924.

Pampel, Fred C., and John B. Williamson. 1989. *Age, Class, Politics, and the Welfare State*. New York: Cambridge University Press.

Paolino, Phillip. 1995. "Group-Salient Issues and Group Representation: Support for Women Candidates in the 1992 Senate Elections." *American Journal of Political Science* 39 (May): 294–313.

Pape, Robert. 1997. "Why Economic Sanctions Do Not Work." *International Security* 22 (fall): 90–136.

Parikh, Sunita. 2000. "The Strategic Value of Analytic Narratives." *Social Science History* 24 (4): 677–84.

Park, Chan Wook. 1988. "Constituency Representation in Korea: Sources and Consequences." *Legislative Studies Quarterly* 13: 225–42.

Parker, R. A. C. 1993. *Chamberlain and Appeasement*. New York: St. Martin's.

Parry, Geraint. 1972. "The Idea of Political Participation." In *Participation in Politics*, ed. Geraint Parry. Totowa, NJ: Rowman and Littlefield.

Parry, Geraint, George Moyser, and Neil Day. 1992. *Political Participation and Democracy in Britain*. Cambridge: Cambridge University Press.

Pateman, Carole. 1970. *Participation and Democratic Theory*. Cambridge: Cambridge University Press.

Pateman, Carole. 1988. *The Sexual Contract.* Stanford, CA: Stanford University Press.

Patterson, James T. 1967. *Congressional Conservatism and the New Deal: The Growth of the Conservative Coalition in Congress, 1933–1939.* Lexington: University Press of Kentucky.

Pattillo-McCoy, Mary. 1999. *Black Picket Fences: Privilege and Peril Among the Black Middle Class.* Chicago: University of Chicago Press.

Pauly, Louis W., and Simon Reich. 1997. "National Structures and Multinational Corporate Behavior: Enduring Differences in the Age of Globalization." *International Organization* 51 (winter): 1–30.

Payne, Charles M. 1995. *I've Got the Light of Freedom: The Organizing Tradition and the Mississippi Freedom Struggle.* Berkeley: University of California Press.

Peabody, Robert L. 1976. *Leadership in Congress: Stability, Succession, and Change.* Boston: Little, Brown.

Peel, Mark. 1995. *Good Times, Hard Times.* Melbourne, AUS: Melbourne University Press.

Peltzman, Sam. 1976. "Toward a More General Theory of Regulation," *Journal of Law and Economics* 19: 211–40.

Perez, Sofia A. 2000. "From Decentralization to Reorganization: Explaining the Return to National Bargaining in Italy and Spain." *Comparative Politics* 32 (4): 437–58.

Perng, S. S. 1985. "The Accounts Receivable Treatments Study." *New Directions for Program Evaluation* 28: 55–62.

Perotti, Roberto. 1999. "Fiscal Policy in Good Times and Bad." *Quarterly Journal of Economics* 114 (4): 1399–436.

Persson, Torsten, and Leo Svensson. 1989. "Why a Stubborn Conservative Would Run a Deficit; Policy with Time Inconsistent Preferences." *Quarterly Journal of Economics* 104 (2): 325–46.

Persson, Torsten, and Guido Tabellini. 1999. "The Size and Scope of Government: Comparative Politics with Rational Politicians." *European Economic Review* 43: 699–735.

Persson, Torsten, and Guido Tabellini. 2000. *Political Economics.* Cambridge: M.I.T. Press.

Peterson, Mark A. 2000. "The Fate of 'Big Government' in the United States: Not Over, But Undermined?" *Governance* 13 (April): 251–64.

Peterson, Paul. 1981. *City Limits.* Chicago: University of Chicago Press

Peterson, Steven A. 1992. "Church Participation and Political Participation: The Spillover Effect." *American Politics Quarterly* 20: 123–39.

Pettit, Philip. 1997. *Republicanism: A Theory of Freedom and Government.* New York: Oxford University Press.

Pettit, Philip. 2000. "Democracy, Electoral and Contestatory." In *Designing Democratic Institutions*, ed. Ian Shapiro and Stephen Macedo, 105–46. New York: New York University Press (Nomos XLII).

Phelan, Shane. 1993. "Interpretation and Domination: Adorno and the Habermas-Lyotard Debate." *Polity* 25: 597–616.

Phelan, Shane. 1994. *Getting Specific: Postmodern Lesbian Politics.* Minneapolis: University of Minnesota Press.

Phillips, Anne. 1991. *Engendering Democracy.* Cambridge, UK: Polity and Black-well.

Phillips, Anne. 1993. *Democracy and Difference.* Cambridge, UK: Polity.

Phillips, Anne. 1995. *The Politics of Presence.* Oxford and New York: Clarendon.

Pierson, Paul. 1993. "When Effect Becomes Cause: Policy Feedback and Political Change." *World Politics* 45 (4): 595–628.

Pierson, Paul. 1994. *Dismantling the Welfare State? Reagan, Thatcher, and the Politics of Retrenchment.* Cambridge: Cambridge University Press.

Pierson, Paul. 1996. "The New Politics of the Welfare State." *World Politics* 48 (2): 143–79.

Pierson, Paul. 2000a. "Increasing Returns, Path Dependence, and the Study of Politics." *American Political Science Review* 94 (2): 251–67.

Pierson, Paul. 2000b. "The Limits of Design: Explaining Institutional Origins and Change." *Governance* 13 (4): 475–99.

Pierson, Paul. 2000c. "Not Just What But When: Timing and Sequence in Political Processes." *Studies in American Political Development.* 14 (1): 72–92.

Pierson, Paul. 2000d. "Three Worlds of Welfare State Research." *Comparative Political Studies* 33 (August–September): 791–821.

Pierson, Paul. 2002. "Big, Slow, and . . . Invisible: Macro-Social Processes in the Study of Comparative Politics." In *Comparative-Historical Analysis: Achievements and Agendas,* ed. James Mahoney and Dietrich Rueschemeyer. Cambridge: Cambridge University Press.

Pierson, Paul and Theda Skocpol. 2002. "Historical Institutionalism in Contemporary Political Science." *Political Science: The State of the Discipline,* ed. Ira Katznelson and Helen V. Milner. New York: W. W. Norton & Company.

Pinderhughes, Dianne. 1987. *Race and Ethnicity in Chicago Politics.* Urbana: University of Illinois Press.

Plant, Raymond. 1984. *Equality, Markets and the State.* London: Fabian Society.

Plato. 1993. *The Republic.* Trans. Robin Waterfield. Oxford: Oxford University Press.

Pleština, Dijana. 1993. *Regional Development in Communist Yugoslavia: Success, Failure, and Consequences.* Boulder, CO: Westview.

Plotke, David. 1996. *Building a Democratic Political Order: Reshaping American Liberalism in the 1930s and 1940s.* New York: Cambridge University Press.

Pogge, Thomas. 1989. *Realizing Rawls.* Ithaca, NY: Cornell University Press.

Pogge, Thomas. 1994a. "An Egalitarian Law of Peoples." *Philosophy and Public Affairs* 23 (summer): 195–224.

Pogge, Thomas. 1994b. "Cosmopolitanism and Sovereignty." In *Political Restructuring in Europe: Ethical Perspectives,* ed. Chris Brown. London: Routledge.

Polanyi, Karl. 1944. *The Great Transformation*. Boston: Beacon.

Polatnick, M. Rivka. 1996. "Diversity in Women's Liberation Ideology: How a Black and a White Group of the 1960s Viewed Motherhood." *Signs* 21 (3): 679–706.

Pollin, Robert. 2000. "Globalization, Inequality and Financial Instability: Confronting the Marx, Keynes and Polanyi Problems in the Advanced Capitalist Economies." Paper delivered at the Conference on "Globalization and Ethics" (31 March–2 April, 2000), Yale University, New Haven, CT.

Pollins, Brian M. 1989. "Does Trade Still Follow the Flag?" *American Political Science Review* 83: 465–80.

Polsby, Nelson W. 1968. "The Institutionalization of the U.S. House of Representatives." *American Political Science Review* 62: 144–68.

Polsby, Nelson W. 1975. "Legislatures." In *Handbook of Political Science*, vol. 5, ed. Fred Greenstein and Nelson W. Polsby. Reading, MA: Addison-Wesley.

Polsby, Nelson W. 1980. *Community Power and Political Theory*. New Haven, CT: Yale University Press.

Polsby, Nelson W. 1983. *Consequences of Party Reform*. New York: Oxford University Press.

Polsby, Nelson W. 2000. "Toward a More Responsible Two-Party System: Comment." Paper prepared for the 2000 Annual Meetings of the American Political Science Association, Washington, DC, September.

Polsby, Nelson W., Miriam Gallaher, and Barry Spencer Rundquist. 1969. "The Growth of the Seniority System in the U.S. House of Representatives." *American Political Science Review* 63: 787–807.

Polsky, Andrew. 1989. "The Odyessy of the Juvenile Court: Policy Failure and Institutional Persistence in the Therapeutic States." *Studies in American Political Development*, 157–99. New Haven, CT: Yale University Press.

Polsky, Andrew. 1997. "Why Regimes? Ideas, Incentives and Politics in American Political Orders." *Polity* 29 (2): 625–40.

Pontusson, Jonas. 2000. "Labor Market Institutions and Wage Distribution." In *Unions, Employers, and Central Banks*, ed. T. Iversen, J. Pontusson, and D. Soskice. New York: Cambridge University Press.

Pontusson, Jonas, and Peter Swenson. 1996. "Labor Markets, Production Strategies, and Wage Bargaining Institutions." *Comparative Political Studies* 29 (2): 223–50.

Poole, Keith T., and Howard Rosenthal. 1997. *Congress: A Political-Economic History of Roll Call Voting*. New York: Oxford University Press.

Popkin, Samuel. 1979. *The Rational Peasant: The Political Economy of Rural Society in Vietnam*. Berkeley: University of California Press.

Popkin, Samuel. 1991. *The Reasoning Voter*. Chicago: University of Chicago Press.

Posen, Barry R. 1984. *The Sources of Military Doctrine: France, Britain and Germany between the World Wars*. Ithaca, NY: Cornell University Press.

Posen, Barry R. 1993a. "Nationalism, the Mass Army, and Military Power." *International Security* 18 (fall): 80–124.

Posen, Barry R. 1993b. "The Security Dilemma and Ethnic Conflict." *Survival* 35 (spring): 27–47.

Posner, Daniel. 1998. "The Institutional Origins of Ethnic Politics in Zambia." Ph.D. diss., Harvard University, Cambridge, MA.

Posner, Richard A. 1980. "The Ethical and Political Basis of the Efficiency Norm in Common Law Adjudication." *Hofstra Law Review* 8: 487–507

Posner, Richard A. 2001. *Frontiers of Legal Theory.* Cambridge, MA: Harvard University Press.

Posusney, Marsha Pripstein. 2001. "Multi-Party Elections in the Arab World: Institutional Engineering and Oppositional Strategies." *Studies in Comparative International Development* 36: 4.

Poterba, James M. 1994. "State Responses to Fiscal Crisis: The Effects of Budgetary Institutions and Politics." *Journal of Political Economy* 102 (August): 799–821.

Poterba, James M. 1996. "Budget Institutions and Fiscal Policy in the U.S. States." *American Economic Review:* 395–400.

Poterba, James M., and Jurgen von Hagen, eds. 1999. *Fiscal Institutions and Fiscal Performance.* Chicago: NBER and University of Chicago Press.

Poulantzas, Nicos. 1968. *Political Power and Social Classes.* London: New Left.

Poulantzas, Nicos. 1969. "The Problem of the Capitalist State." *New Left Review* 58: 67–78.

Poulantzas, Nicos. 1973. *Political Power and Social Classes.* London: New Left.

Powell, G. Bingham. 1982. *Contemporary Democracies.* Cambridge, MA: Harvard University Press.

Powell, G. Bingham. 1986. "American Voter Turnout in Comparative Perspective." *American Political Science Review* 80: 17–43.

Powell, G. Bingham. 2000. *Elections As Instruments of Democracy: Majoritarian and Proportional Visions.* New Haven, CT: Yale University Press.

Powell, Robert. 1987. "Crisis Bargaining, Escalation, and MAD," *American Political Science Review* 81: 717–36.

Powell, Robert. 1990. *Nuclear Deterrence Theory: The Search for Credibility.* Cambridge: Cambridge University Press.

Powell, Robert. 1991. "Absolute and Relative Gains in International Relations Theory." *American Political Science Review* 85 (December): 1303–20.

Powell, Robert. 1993. "Guns, Butter, and Anarchy." *American Political Science Review* 87: 115–32.

Powell, Robert. 1994. "Anarchy in International Relations Theory." *International Organization* 48: 313–44.

Powell, Robert. 1999. *In the Shadow of Power: States and Strategies in International Politics.* Princeton, NJ: Princeton University Press.

Powell, Robert. Forthcoming. "Game Theory, International Relations Theory, and the Hobbesian Stylization." In *State of the Discipline III,* ed. Ira Katznelson and Helen V. Milner. Washington, DC: American Political Science Association.

Powell, Walter W., and Paul DiMaggio. 1991. *The New Institutionalism in Organizational Analysis.* Chicago: University of Chicago Press.

Power, Timothy, and Mark Gasiorowski. 1997. "Institutional Design and Democratic Consolidation in the Third World." *Comparative Political Studies* 30: 123–55.

Prébisch, Raúl. 1950. *The Economic Development of Latin America and Its Principal Problems.* New York: United Nations.

Price, David E., and Michael Lupfer. 1973. "Volunteers for Gore: The Impact of a Precinct Level Canvass in Three Tennessee Cities." *Journal of Politics* 35 (May): 410–38.

Price, H. Douglas. 1971. "The Congressional Career Then and Now." In *Congressional Behavior,* ed Nelson W. Polsby. New York: Random House.

Price, H. Douglas. 1975. "Congress and the Evolution of Legislative Professionalism." In *Congress in Change: Evolution and Reform,* ed. Norman J. Ornstein. New York: Praeger.

Price, H. Douglas. 1977. "Careers and Committees in the American Congress: The Problem of Structural Change." In *The History of Parliamentary Behavior,* ed. William O. Aydelotte. Princeton, NJ: Princeton University Press.

Price, Richard M. 1997. *The Chemical Weapons Taboo.* Ithaca, NY: Cornell University Press.

Price, Richard M. 1998. "Reversing the Gun Sights: Transnational Civil Society Targets Land Mines." *International Organization* 52 (3): 613–44.

Price, Richard M., and Christian Reus-Smit. 1998. "Dangerous Liaisons? Critical International Theory and Constructivism." *European Journal of International Relations* 4 (3): 259–94.

Price, Robert. 1991. *The Apartheid State in Crisis: Political Transformation in South Africa, 1975–1990.* New York: Oxford University Press.

Price, Vincent. 1999. "Political Information." In *Measures of Political Attitudes,* ed. John P. Robinson, Phillip R. Shaver, and Lawrence Wrightsman. San Diego, CA: Academic.

Priess, David. 1996. "Balance-of-Threat Theory and the Genesis of the Gulf Cooperation Council." *Security Studies* 5 (summer): 143–71.

Priest, George, and Benjamin Klein. 1984. "The Selection of Disputes for Litigation." *Journal of Legal Studies* 13: 1–55.

Princen, Thomas, and Matthias Finger. 1994. *Environmental NGOs in World Politics: Linking the Local and the Global.* London: Routledge.

Przeworski, Adam. 1985. *Capitalism and Social Democracy.* New York: Cambridge University Press.

Przeworski, Adam. 1986. "Some Problems in the Study of the Transition to Democracy." In *Transitions from Authoritarian Rule: Comparative Perspectives,* ed. Guillermo O'Donnell, Philippe Schmitter, and Laurence Whitehead. Baltimore: Johns Hopkins University Press.

Przeworski, Adam. 1991. *Democracy and the Market: Political and Economic Reforms in Eastern Europe and Latin America.* Cambridge: Cambridge University Press.

Przeworski, Adam. 1992. "Games of Transition." In *Issues in Democratic Consolidation,* ed. Scott Mainwaring, Guillermo O'Donnell, and Samuel Valenzuela. South Bend, IN: University of Notre Dame Press.

Przeworski, Adam. 1999. "Minimalist Conception of Democracy: A Defense." In *Democracy's Value,* ed. Ian Shapiro and Casiano Hacker-Cordón. Cambridge: Cambridge University Press.

Przeworski, Adam. 2001. "Democracy as Equilibrium." Paper presented at the Democracy and Development Distinguished Lecture Series, Princeton University, Princeton, NJ, February 28.

Przeworski, Adam, Michael E. Alvarez, José Antonio Cheibub, and Fernando Limongi. 2000. *Democracy and Development: Political Institutions and Well-Being in the World 1950–1990.* Cambridge: Cambridge University Press.

Przeworski, Adam, and Fernando Limongi. 1993. "Political Regimes and Economic Growth." *Journal of Economic Perspectives* 7 (3): 51–69.

Przeworski, Adam, and Fernando Limongi. 1997. "Modernization: Theories and Facts." *World Politics* 49 (2): 155–83.

Przeworski, Adam, Susan Stokes, and Bernard Manin, eds. 1999. *Democracy, Accountability, and Representation.* New York: Cambridge University Press.

Przeworski, Adam, and Michael Wallerstein. 1982. "The Structure of Class Conflicts under Democratic Capitalism." *American Political Science Review* 82: 11–31.

Przeworski, Adam, and Michael Wallerstein. 1986. "Popular Sovereignty, State Autonomy, and Private Property." *Archives Europeenes de Sociologie* 27 (2):

Przeworski, Adam, and Michael Wallerstein. 1988. "Structural Dependence of the State on Capital." *American Political Science Review* 82: 11–30.

Putnam, Robert D. 1988. "Diplomacy and Domestic Politics: The Logic of Two-Level Games." *International Organization* 42: 427–60.

Putnam, Robert D. 1993a. *Making Democracy Work: Civic Traditions in Modern Italy.* Princeton, NJ: Princeton University Press.

Putnam, Robert D. 1993b. "The Prosperous Community: Social Capital and Public Affairs." *American Prospect.* 13: 35–42.

Putnam, Robert D. 1995. "Bowling Alone: America's Declining Social Capital." *Journal of Democracy* 6: 65–78.

Putnam, Robert D. 2000. *Bowling Alone: The Collapse and Revival of American Community.* New York: Simon and Schuster.

Quester, George. 1977. *Offense and Defense in the International System.* New York: Wiley.

Rabkin, Rhoda. 1996. "Redemocratization, Electoral Engineering, and Party Strategies in Chile, 1989–1995." *Comparative Political Studies* 29: 335–56.

Radcliff, Benjamin. 1994. "Turnout and the Democratic Vote." *American Politics Quarterly* 22: 259–76.

Radcliff, Benjamin. 1995. "Turnout and the Vote Revisited: A Reply to Erikson." *American Politics Quarterly* 23: 397–403.

Radcliff, Benjamin, and Patricia Davis. 2000. "Labor Organization and Electoral Participation in Industrial Democracies." *American Journal of Politics* 44: 132–41.

Rae, Douglas W. 1967. *The Political Consequences of Electoral Rules.* New Haven, CT: Yale University Press.

Rae, Douglas W. 1969. "Decision-Rules and Individual Values in Constitutional Choice." *American Political Science Review* 63: 40–56.

Rae, Douglas W. 1975. "The Limits of Consensual Decision." *American Political Science Review* 69: 1270–94.

Rae, Douglas W. 1995. "Using District Magnitude to Regulate Political Party Competition." *Journal of Economic Perspectives* 9 (1): 65–75.

Rae, Douglas W., with Douglas Yates, Jennifer Hochschild, Joseph Morone, and Carol Fessler. 1981. *Equalities.* Cambridge, MA: Harvard University Press.

Ragin, Charles C. 1987. *The Comparative Method: Moving Beyond Qualitative and Quantitative Strategies.* Berkeley: University of California Press.

Ragin, Charles C. 2000. *Fuzzy-Set Social Science.* Chicago: University of Chicago Press.

Rakove, Jack. 1996. *Original Meanings: Politics and Ideas in the Making of the Constitution.* New York: Knopf.

Rakove, Jack, Andrew Rutten, and Barry R. Weingast. 2000. "Ideas, Institutions, and Credible Commitments in the American Revolution." Working paper, Hoover Institution, Stanford University, Stanford, CA.

Rakowski, Eric. 1991. *Equal Justice.* Oxford: Clarendon.

Ramseyer, J. Mark, and Frances Rosenbluth. 1993. *Japan's Political Marketplace.* Cambridge, MA: Harvard University Press.

Ranade, Sudhanshu. 1991. "Competitive Democracies: The Case of Targeted Transfers in India." Ph.D. diss., Princeton University, Princeton, NJ.

Rangan, Subramanian, and Robert Z. Lawrence. 1999. *A Prism on Globalization: Corporate Responses to the Dollar.* Washington, DC: Brookings.

Ranney, Austin. 1954. *The Doctrine of Responsible Party Government.* Urbana: University of Illinois Press.

Ranney, Austin. 1975. *Curing the Mischiefs of Faction: Party Reform in America.* Berkeley: University of California Press.

Ransby, Barbara. 1996. "Ella J. Baker and the Black Radical Tradition." Doctoral dissertation, University of Michigan.

Rapoport, Ronald B. 1982. "Sex Differences in Attitude Expression: A Generational Explanation." *Public Opinion Quarterly* 46: 86–96.

Rapoport, Ronald B. 1985. "Like Mother, Like Daughter: Intergenerational Transmission of DK Response Rates." *Public Opinion Quarterly* 49: 198–208.

Rasch, Bjørn Erik. 2000. "Parliamentary Floor Voting Procedures and Agenda Setting in Europe." *Legislative Studies Quarterly* 25: 3–24.

Rasler, Karen A., and William R. Thompson. 1985. "War Making and State Making: Governmental Expenditures, Tax Revenues, and Global Wars." *American Political Science Review* 79 (June): 491–507.

Ratner, Sidney, and James Altman, eds. 1964. *John Dewey and Arthur F. Bentley: A Philosophical Correspondence, 1932–1951.* New Brunswick, NJ: Rutgers University Press.

Rauch, James, and Alessandra Casella, eds. 2001. *Networks and Markets.* New York: Russell Sage.

Raustiala, Kal, and Anne-Marie Slaughter. 2002. "Considering Compliance." In *Handbook of International Relations,* ed. W. Carlsnaes, B. Simmons, and T. Risse. London: Sage.

Rawls, John. 1971. *A Theory of Justice.* Oxford: Oxford University Press.

Rawls, John. 1980. "Kantian Constructivism in Moral Theory." *Journal of Philosophy* 77 (September): 515–72.

Rawls, John. 1985. "Justice as Fairness: Political Not Metaphysical." *Philosophy and Public Affairs* 14 (summer): 223–51.

Rawls, John. 1995. "Political Liberalism: Reply to Habermas." *Journal of Philosophy.* 92 (March): 132–80

Rawls, John. 1996 [1993]. *Political Liberalism.* New York: Columbia University Press.

Rawls, John. 1999a. *The Law of Peoples.* Cambridge, MA: Harvard University Press.

Rawls, John. 1999b. *A Theory of Justice.* Rev. ed. Cambridge, MA: Harvard University Press.

Rawls, John. 2001. *Justice as Fairness: A Restatement.* Ed. Erin Kelly. Cambridge, MA: Harvard University Press.

Ray, James Lee. 1995. *Democracy and International Conflict.* Columbia, SC: University of South Carolina Press.

Ray, James Lee. 1998. "Does Democracy Cause Peace?" *Annual Review of Political Science* 1: 27–46.

Reback, Gary L. 1971. "The Effects of Precinct-Level Voter Contact Activities on Voting Behavior." *Experimental Study of Politics* 1: 65–97.

Reed, Adolph L., Jr. 1999. *Stirrings in the Jug: Black Politics in the Post-Segregation Era.* Minneapolis: University of Minnesota Press.

Reed, William. 2000. "A Unified Model of Conflict Onset and Escalation." *American Journal of Political Science* 44: 84–93.

Reef, Mary Jo, and David Knoke. 1999. "Political Alienation and Efficacy." In *Measures of Political Attitudes,* ed. John P. Robinson, Phillip R. Shaver, and Lawrence Wrightsman. San Diego, CA: Academic.

Reeves, Jesse S. 1929. "Perspectives in Political Science." *American Political Science Review* 23: 1–12.

Regini, Marino. 1997. "Still Engaging in Corporatism? Recent Italian Experiences in Comparative Perspective." *European Journal of Industrial Relations* 3: 259–78.

Regini, Marino, and Ida Regalia. 1997. "Employers, Unions and the State: The Resurgence of Concertation in Italy?" *West European Politics* 25: 210–230.

Reid, John. 1995. *Constitutional History of the American Revolution.* Abridged ed. Madison: University of Wisconsin Press.

Reingold, Beth. 1996. "Conflict and Cooperation: Legislative Strategies and Concepts of Power among Female and Male State Legislators." *Journal of Politics* 58 (May): 464–85.

Reingold, Beth. 2000. *Representing Women: Sex, Gender, and Legislative Behavior in Arizona and California.* Chapel Hill: University of North Carolina Press.

Reinhardt, Eric. 1999. *Adjudication without Enforcement in GATT Disputes*. Cambridge, MA: Harvard University Conference on Institutional Design, Dispute Settlement, and International Trade, Cambridge, MA.

Reinhardt, Mark. 1997. *The Art of Being Free: Taking Liberties with Tocqueville, Marx, and Arendt*. Ithaca, NY: Cornell University Press.

Reinicke, Wolfgang H. 1998. *Global Public Policy. Governing without Government?* Washington, DC: Brookings.

Reiter, Dan, and Allan C. Stam III. 1998. "Democracy, War Initiation, and Victory." *American Political Science Review* 92: 377–89.

Remington, Thomas, and Steven Smith. 1995. "The Development of Parliamentary Parties in Russia." *Legislative Studies Quarterly.*

Remington, Thomas, and Steven Smith. 1996. "Political Goals, Institutional Context, and the Choice of an Electoral System: The Russian Parliamentary Election Law." *American Journal of Political Science* 404 (4): 1253–79.

Remington, Thomas, and Steven Smith. 1998a. "Decrees, Laws, and Inter-Branch Relations in the Russian Federation." *Post-Soviet Affairs* 14: 287–322.

Remington, Thomas, and Steven Smith. 1998b. "Theories of Legislative Institutions and the Organization of the Russian Duma." *American Journal of Political Science* 42: 545–72.

Remmer, Karen L. 1989. *Military Rule in Latin America*. Boston: Unwin Hyman.

Remmer, Karen L. 1991a. "New Wine or Old Bottlenecks? The Study of Latin American Democracy." *Comparative Politics* 23 (4): 479–95.

Remmer, Karen L. 1991b. "The Political Impact of Economic Crisis in Latin America in the 1980s." *American Political Science Review* 85 (3): 777–800.

Remmer, Karen L. 1995. "New Theoretical Perspectives on Democratization," *Comparative Politics* (October): 103–22.

Remmer, Karen L. 1997. "Theoretical Decay and Theoretical Development: The Resurgence of Institutional Analysis." *World Politics* 50 (1): 34–61.

Rendell, Matthew. 2000. "Russia, the Concert of Europe and Greece, 1821–1829." *Security Studies* 9 (summer): 52–90.

Reno, William. 1995. *Corruption and State Politics in Sierra Leone*. Cambridge: Cambridge University Press.

Reno, William. 1998. *Warlord Politics and African States*. Boulder, CO: Rienner.

Resende-Santos, Joao. 1996. "Anarchy and the Emulation of Military Systems: Military Organization and Technology in South America, 1870–1914." *Security Studies* 5 (spring): 193–260.

Resnik, Judith. 1989. "Dependent Sovereigns: Indian Tribes: States, and the Federal Courts." *University of Chicago Law Review* 56 (1): 671–759.

Reus-Smit, Christian. 1997. "The Constitutional Structure of International Society and the Nature of Fundamental Institutions." *International Organization* 51 (4): 555–89.

Reus-Smit, Christian. 1999. *The Moral Purpose of the State*. Princeton, NJ: Princeton University Press.

Reuveny, Rafael, and Heejoon Kang. 1996. "International Trade, Political Conflict/Cooperation, and Granger Causality." *American Journal of Political Science* 40: 943–70.

Rhine, Staci L. 1995. "Registration Reform and Turnout Change in the American States." *American Politics Quarterly* 23: 409–26.

Richards, Alan, and John Waterbury. 1990. *A Political Economy of the Middle East: State, Class, and Economic Development.* Boulder, CO: Westview.

Richardson, J. David. 1990. "The Political Economy of Strategic Trade Policy." *International Organization* 44 (winter): 107–35.

Ridgeway, Cecilia L., and Lynn Smith-Lovin. 1999. "The Gender System and Interaction." *Annual Review of Sociology* 25: 195.

Riecken, Henry W., and Robert F. Boruch. 1974. *Social Experimentation: A Method for Planning and Evaluating Social Intervention.* New York: Academic.

Riker, William H. 1962. *The Theory of Political Coalitions.* Westport, CT: Greenwood.

Riker, William H. 1980. "Implications from the Disequilibrium of Majority Rule for the Study of Institutions." *American Political Science Review* 74: 432–46.

Riker, William H. 1982. *Liberalism Against Populism: A Confrontation Between the Theory of Democracy and the Theory of Social Choice.* San Francisco: Freeman.

Riker, William H. 1986. *The Art of Political Manipulation.* New Haven, CT: Yale University Press.

Riker, William H. 1990. "Political Choice and Rational Choice," in *Perspectives on Positive Political Economy,* ed. James Alt and Kenneth Shepsle. New York: Cambridge University Press.

Riker, William H., and Peter C. Ordeshook. 1968. "A Theory of the Calculus of Voting." *American Political Science Review* 62: 25–42.

Riker, William H., and Barry R. Weingast. 1988. "Constitutional Regulation of Legislative Choice: The Political Consequences of Judicial Deference to Legislatures." *Virginia Law Review* 74: 373–401.

Ringer, Fritz K. 1969. *The Decline of the German Mandarins: The German Academic Community, 1890–1933.* Cambridge, MA: Harvard University Press.

Ringer, Fritz K. 1979. *Education and Society in Modern Europe.* Bloomington: Indiana University Press.

Ringer, Fritz K. 1992. *Fields of Knowledge: French Academic Culture in Comparative Perspective, 1890–1920.* Cambridge: Cambridge University Press.

Ringquist, Evan J., Kim Quaile Hill, Jan E. Leighley, and Angela Hinton-Anderson. 1997. "Lower-Class Mobilization and Policy Linkage in the U.S. States: A Correction." *American Journal of Political Science* 41: 339–44.

Riordan, William, ed. 1963. *Plunkitt of Tammany Hall.* New York: Dutton.

Ripley, Randall B. 1967. *Party Leaders in the House of Representatives.* Washington, DC: Brookings.

Ripley, Randall B. 1969a. *Majority Party Leadership in Congress.* Boston: Little, Brown.

Ripley, Randall B. 1969b. *Power in the Senate.* New York: St. Martin's.

Ripstein, Arthur. 1994. "Equality, Luck, and Responsibility." *Philosophy and Public Affairs* 23 (winter): 3–23.

Risse, Thomas. 1999. "International Norms and Domestic Change: Arguing and Communicative Behavior in the Human Rights Area." *Politics and Society* 27 (4): 526–56.

Risse, Thomas. 2000. "'Let's Argue!' Communicative Action in International Relations." *International Organization* 54 (1): 1–39.

Risse, Thomas. 2002. "Transnational Actors and World Politics." In *Handbook of International Relations*, ed. W. Carlsnaes, T. Risse and B. Simmons. London: Sage.

Risse, Thomas, Stephen C. Ropp, and Kathryn Sikkink, eds. 1999. *The Power of Human Rights: International Norms and Domestic Change.* Cambridge: Cambridge University Press.

Risse-Kappen, Thomas. 1995. "Cooperation among Democracies." In *The European Influence on U.S. Foreign Policy.* Princeton, NJ: Princeton University Press.

Risse-Kappen, Thomas. 1996. "Exploring the Nature of the Beast: International Relations Theory and Comparative Policy Analysis Meet the European Union." *Journal of Common Market Studies* 34 (March): 53–80.

Rittberger, Volker. 1994. *Internationale Organisationen: Politik und Geschichte.* (Grundwissen Politik Bd. 10) Opladen: Leske und Budrich.

Ritter, Gretchen. 1997. *Goldbugs and Greenbacks: The Antimonopoly Tradition and the Politics of Finance in America.* New York: Cambridge University Press.

Rivers, Douglas, and Morris P. Fiorina. 1989. "Constituency Service, Reputations, and the Incumbency Advantage." In *Home Style and Washington Work: Studies of Congressional Politics*, ed. Fiorina and David Rohde, 17–45. Ann Arbor: University of Michigan Press.

Roach, Hannah Grace. 1925. "Sectionalism in Congress (1870–1890)." *American Political Science Review* 19: 500–526.

Robertson, L. S., A. B. Kelley, B. O'Neill, C. W. Wixom, R. S. Eiswirth, and W. Haldon. 1974. "Controlled-Study of Effect of Television Messages on Safety Belt Use." *American Journal of Public Health* 64: (11) 1071–80.

Robinson, John P., Phillip R. Shaver, and Lawrence S. Wrightsman, eds. 1999. *Measures of Political Attitudes.* San Diego: Academic Press.

Robinson, Michael. 1976. "Public Affairs Television and the Growth of Political Malaise: The Case of 'The Selling of the Pentagon.'" *American Political Science Review* 70: 409–32.

Rodgers, Daniel. 1987. *Contested Truths: Keywords in American Politics Since Independence.* New York: Basic.

Rodriguez, Daniel, and Barry R. Weingast. 1995. "Legislative Rhetoric, Statutory Interpretation, and the History of the 1964 Civil Rights Act." Working paper, Hoover Institution, Stanford University, Stanford, CA.

Rodríguez, Francisco, and Dani Rodrik. 2001. "Trade Policy and Economic Growth: A Skeptic's Guide to the Cross-National Evidence." In *NBER Macroeconomics Annual 2000*, ed. Ben Bernanke and Kenneth S. Rogoff. Cambridge: MIT Press for NBER.

Rodrik, Dani. 1992. "The Limits of Trade Policy Reform in Developing Countries." *Journal of Economic Perspectives* 6: 87–105.

Rodrik, Dani. 1994. In *Voting for Reform: Democracy, Political Liberalization, and Economic Adjustment*, ed. Stephan Haggard and Steven Webb. New York: Oxford University Press.

Rodrik, Dani. 1996. "Understanding Economic Policy Reform." *Journal of Economic Literature* 34: 9–41.

Rodrik, Dani. 1997. *Has Globalization Gone Too Far?* Washington, DC: Institute for International Economics.

Rodrik, Dani. 1998. "Why Do More Open Economies Have Bigger Governments?" *Journal of Political Economy* 106 (5): 997–1032.

Roeder, Philip. 1993. *Red Sunset*. Princeton, NJ: Princeton University Press.

Rogers, Lindsay. 1949. *The Pollsters: Public Opinion, Politics, and Democratic Leadership*. New York: Knopf.

Rogers, Ruel. 2000. "Between Race and Ethnicity: Afro-Caribbean Immigrants, Afro-Americans, and the Politics of Incorporation." Ph.D. diss., Princeton University, Princeton, NJ.

Rogoff, Kenneth. 1985. "The Optimal Degree of Commitment to an Intermediate Monetary Target." *Quarterly Journal of Economics* 11: 1169–88.

Rogowski, Ronald. 1987a. "Political Cleavages and Changing Exposure to Trade." *American Political Science Review* 81 (4): 1121–37.

Rogowski, Ronald. 1987b. "Trade and the Variety of Democratic Institutions." *International Organization* 41: 203–24.

Rogowski, Ronald. 1989. *Commerce and Coalitions: How Trade Affects Domestic Political Alignments*. Princeton, NJ: Princeton University Press.

Rogowski, Ronald. 1993. "Comparative Politics." In *Political Science: State of the Discipline II*, ed. Ada W. Finifter, 431–49. Washington, DC: American Political Science Association.

Rogowski, Ronald. 1998. "Globalization and Convergence: Getting the Theory and the Evidence Right." *Society For Comparative Research*, http://www.sscnet. ucla.edu/soc/groups/scr/global.htm.

Rogowski, Ronald. 1999. "Institutions as Constraints on Strategic Choice." In *Strategic Choice and International Relations*, ed. David A. Lake and Robert Powell, 115–36. Princeton, NJ: Princeton University Press.

Rohde, David W. 1991. *Parties and Leaders in the Postreform House*. Chicago: University of Chicago Press.

Romer, Thomas, and Howard Rosenthal. 1978. "Political Resource Allocation, Controlled Agendas, and the Status Quo." *Public Choice* 33: 27–43.

Romer, Thomas, and Howard Rosenthal. 1979. "Bureaucrats and Voters: On the Political Economy of Resource Allocation by Direct Democracy". *Quarterly Journal of Economics* 93: 563–88.

Root, Hilton L. 1989. "Tying the King's Hands: Credible Commitments and Royal Fiscal Policy During the Old Regime." *Rationality and Society* 1: 240–58.

Rorty, Richard. 1989. *Contingency, Irony, Solidarity*. Cambridge: Cambridge University Press.

Rorty, Richard. 1996. "Global, Utopias, History and Philosophy." In *Cultural Pluralism, Identity, and Globalization*. Rio de Janeiro: Unesco/Issc/Educam.

Rorty, Richard. 1998. *Achieving Our Country: Leftist Thought in Twentieth Century America*. Cambridge, MA: Harvard University Press.

Rosati, Jerel A. 2000. "The Power of Human Cognition in the Study of World Politics." *International Studies Review* 2: 45–75.

Rose, Gideon. 1998. "Neoclassical Realism and Theories of Foreign Policy." *World Politics* 51 (October): 144–72.

Rose, Harold M., and Paula D. McClain. 1990. *Race, Place, and Risk: Black Homicide in Urban America*. Albany: State University of New York Press.

Rose, John C. 1906. "Negro Suffrage: The Constitutional Point of View." *American Political Science Review* 17: 25–27.

Rose, Richard. 1994. "Postcommunism and the Problem of Trust." *Journal of Democracy* 5 (3): 18–30.

Rose, Richard, William Mishler, and Christian Haerpfer. 1998. *Democracy and Its Alternatives: Understanding Post-Communist Societies*. Baltimore: Johns Hopkins University Press.

Rose, William. 2000. "The Security Dilemma and Ethnic Conflict." *Security Studies* 9 (summer): 1–51.

Rosecrance, Richard. 1999. *The Rise of the Virtual State: Wealth and Power in the Coming Century*. New York: Basic.

Rosecrance, Richard, and Arthur A. Stein. 1993. "Beyond Realism: The Study of Grand Strategy." In *The Domestic Bases of Grand Strategy*, ed. Richard Rosecrance and Arthur A. Stein. Ithaca, NY: Cornell University Press.

Rosen, Stanley. 1987. *Hermeneutics and Politics*. Oxford: Oxford University Press.

Rosenau, James. 1997. *Along the Domestic-Foreign Frontier: Exploring Governance in a Turbulent World*. Cambridge: Cambridge University Press.

Rosenblum, Nancy L. 1998a. "Compelled Association: Public Standing, Self-Respect, and the Dynamics of Exclusion." In *Freedom of Association*, ed. Amy Gutmann, 75–108. Princeton, NJ: Princeton University Press.

Rosenblum, Nancy L. 1998b. *Membership and Morals: The Personal Uses of Pluralism in America*. Princeton, NJ: Princeton University Press.

Rosenblum, Nancy L. 1999. "The Moral Uses of Pluralism." In *Civil Society, Democracy, and Civic Renewal*, ed. Robert K. Fullinwider. Lanham, MD: Roman and Littlefield.

Rosenblum, Nancy L., ed. 2000. *Religion and Law: Obligations of Citizenship and Demands of Faith*. Princeton, NJ: Princeton University Press.

Rosenbluth, Frances. 1993. "Financial Deregulation and Interest Intermediation." In *Political Dynamics in Contemporary Japan*, ed. Gary Allinson and Yasunori Sone. Ithaca, NY: Cornell University Press.

Rosenfeld, Michel, and Andrew Arato. 1998. *Habermas on Law and Democracy: Critical Exchanges*. Berkeley: University of California Press.

Rosenstone, Steven J., and John Mark Hansen. 1993. *Mobilization, Participation, and Democracy in America*. New York: Macmillan Co.

Rosenthal, Cindy Simon. 1998. *When Women Lead*. New York: Oxford University Press.

Rosenthal, Howard. 1990. "The Setter Model." In *Advances in the Spatial Theory of Voting*, ed. James M. Enelow and Melvin J. Hinich. Cambridge: Cambridge University Press.

Rosenthal, Jean-Laurent. 1998. "The Political Economy of Absolutism Reconsidered." In *Analytic Narratives*, ed. Robert H. Bates et al., 64–108. Princeton, NJ: Princeton University Press.

Rosenzweig, Mark R., and Kenneth I. Wolpin. 2000. "Natural 'Natural Experiments' in Economics." *Journal of Economic Literature* 38 (December): 827–74.

Ross, Dorothy. 1991. *The Origins of American Social Science*. New York: Cambridge University Press.

Ross, Michael. Forthcoming. *World Politics*.

Rothenberg, Lawrence S., and Mitchell S. Sanders. 2000. "Severing the Electoral Connection: Shirking in the Contemporary Congress." *American Journal of Political Science* 44: 316–25.

Rothman, David J. 1966. *Politics and Power: The United States Senate, 1869–1901*. Cambridge, MA: Harvard University Press.

Rothstein, Bo. 1990. "Marxism, Institutional Analysis and Working-Class Power: The Swedish Case." *Politics and Society* 18 (3): 317–45.

Rothstein, Bo. 1992. "Social Justice and State Capacity." *Politics and Society* 20 (1): 101–26.

Rothstein, Bo. 1998. *Just Institutions Matter*. London: Cambridge University Press.

Roubini, Nouriel. 1991. "Economic and Political Determinants of Budget Deficits in Developing Countries." *Journal of International Money and Finance*: S49–S72.

Roubini, Nouriel, and Jeffrey Sachs. 1989a. "Government Spending and Budget Deficits in the Industrial Countries." *Economic Policy*: 100–32.

Roubini, Nouriel, and Jeffrey Sachs. 1989b. "Political and Economic Determinants of Budget Deficits in the Industrial Countries." *European Economic Review* 33 (May): 903–33.

Rousseau, David L., Christopher Gelpi, Dan Reiter, and Paul K. Huth. 1996. "Assessing the Dyadic Nature of the Democratic Peace, 1918–88." *American Political Science Review* 90: 512–33.

Rousseau, David L., and Karl Mueller. 1995. "Democratic Idealists or Pragmatic Realists?: Reassessing the Iroquois League." Paper presented at the annual meeting of the American Political Science Association.

Rousseau, Jean-Jacques. 1968 [1762]. *The Social Contract*. Harmondsworth, UK: Penguin.

Roy, Denny. 1994. "Hegemon on the Horizon? China's Threat to East Asian Security." *International Security* 19 (summer): 149–68.

Royo, Sebastian. 2000. " 'Still the Century of Corporatism?' Corporatism in South-ern Europe, Spain and Portugal in Comparative Perspective." Paper presented at Twelfth Biennial Conference of Europeanists (30 March–2 April) Chicago.

Rubin, Donald B. 1974. "Estimating Causal Effects of Treatments in Randomized and Non-randomized Studies." *Journal of Educational Psychology* 66: 688–701.

Ruddick, Sara. 1989. *Maternal Thinking: Toward a Politics of Peace.* Boston: Bea-con.

Rudolph, Lloyd I., and Susanne Hoeber Rudolph. 1967. *The Modernity of Tradi-tion: Political Development in India.* Chicago: University of Chicago Press.

Rudolph, Lloyd I., and Susanne Hoeber Rudolph. 1987. *In Pursuit of Lakshmi: The Political Economy of the Indian State.* Chicago. University of Chicago Press.

Rueben, Kim. 1995. "Tax Limitations and Government Growth: The Effect of State Tax and Expenditure Limits on State and Local Government." Mimeograph, MIT, Cambridge, MA.

Rueschemeyer, Dietrich A., Evelyne Huber Stephens, and John D. Stephens. 1992. *Capitalist Development and Democracy.* Chicago: University of Chicago Press.

Rueschemeyer, Dietrich A., and John D. Stephens. 1997. "Comparing Historical Sequences: A Powerful Tool for Causal Analysis." *Comparative Social Research* 17: 55–72.

Ruggie, John Gerard. 1983a. "International Regimes, Transactions, and Change: Embedded Liberalism in the Postwar Economic Order." In *International Regimes,* ed. Stephen D. Krasner, 195–232. Ithaca, NY: Cornell University Press.

Ruggie, John Gerard. 1983b. "Continuity and Transformation in the World Polity: Toward a Neorealist Synthesis." *World Politics* 35 (January): 261–385.

Ruggie, John Gerard. 1996. *Winning the Peace: America and World Order in the New Era.* New York: Columbia University Press.

Ruggie, John Gerard. 1998. "What Makes the World Hang Together? Neo-Utilitarianism and the Social Constructivist Challenge." *International Organiza-tion* 52 (autumn): 855–86.

Rule, James B. 1997. *Theory and Progress in Social Science.* Cambridge: Cam-bridge University Press.

Rule, Wilma. 1981. "Why Women Don't Run: The Critical Contextual Factors in Women's Legislative Recruitment." *Western Political Quarterly* 34: 60–77.

Rule, Wilma. 1990. "Why More Women are State Legislators." *Western Political Quarterly* 43: 437–48.

Rule, Wilma. 1992. "Multimember Legislative Districts: Minority and Anglo Women's and Men's Recruitment Opportunity." In *United States Electoral Systems: Their Impact on Women and Minorities,* ed. Wilma Rule and Joseph F. Zimmer-man. New York: Praeger.

Rummel, Rudolph J. 1983. "Libertarianism and International Violence." *Journal of Conflict Resolution* 27: 27–72.

Russett, Bruce M. 1993. *Grasping the Democratic Peace.* Princeton, NJ: Princeton University Press.

Russett, Bruce M. 1995. "Correspondence: And Yet It Moves." *International Security* 19 (spring): 164–75.

Rust, John. 1994. "Structural Estimation of Markov Decision Processes." In *Handbook of Econometrics*, Vol. 4, ed. R. F. Engle and D. McFadden, ch. 51. Elsevier Science B. V.

Sabato, Larry. 1991. *Feeding Frenzy*. New York: Free Press.

Sabetti, Filippo. 1996. "Path Dependency and Civic Culture: Some Lessons from Italy About Interpreting Social Experiments." *Politics and Society* 24: 19–44.

Sachs, Jeffrey. 1985. "External Debt and Macroeconomic Performance in Latin America and East Asia." *Brookings Papers on Economic Activity* 2: 523–73.

Sachs, Jeffrey. 1986. "The Bolivian Hyperinflation and Stabilization." NBER Working Paper 2073.

Sachs, Jeffrey. 1993. *Poland's Jump to the Market Economy*. Cambridge: MIT Press.

Sachs, Jeffrey, Aaron Tornell, and Andres Velasco. "Financial Crises in Emerging Markets: The Lessons from 1995." NBER Working Paper 5576.

Sagan, Scott. 1986. "1914 Revisited." *International Security* 11 (2): 151–76.

Saideman, Stephen. 2001. *The Ties That Divide: Ethnic Politics: Foreign Policy, and International Conflict*. New York: Columbia University Press.

Saint-Germain, Michelle A. 1989. "Does Their Difference Make a Difference? The Impact of Women on Public Policy in the Arizona Legislature." *Social Science Quarterly* 70 (December): 956–68.

Salisbury, Robert H. 1969. "An Exchange Theory of Interest Groups." *Midwest Journal of Political Science* 13: 1–32.

Samuels, David. Forthcoming. *Ambassadors of the States: Federalism, Ambition, and Congressional Politics in Brazil*. Cambridge: Cambridge University Press.

Sanbonmatsu, Kira. 2000. "Gender Stereotypes and Vote Choice." Paper presented at the Annual Meetings of the American Political Science Association, Washington, D.C.

Sanchez, George J. 1993. *Becoming Mexican American: Ethnicity, Culture and Identity in Chicano Los Angeles, 1900–1945*. New York: Oxford University Press.

Sandbrook, Richard. 1985. *Politics of Africa's Economic Stagnation*. Cambridge and New York: Cambridge University Press.

Sandel, Michael. 1982. *Liberalism and the Limits of Justice*. Cambridge: Cambridge University Press.

Sandel, Michael. 1996. *Democracy's Discontent: America in Search of a Public Philosophy*. Cambridge, MA: Harvard University Press.

Sanders, Elizabeth. 1999. *Roots of Reform: Farmers, Workers and the American State, 1877–1917*. Chicago: University of Chicago Press.

Sanders, Lynn M. 1995. "The Racial Legacy of American Values." Ph.D. diss., University of Michigan, Ann Arbor.

Santa Clara Pueblo v. Martinez. 1978. 436 U.S. 49.

dos Santos, Theotônio. 1970. "The Structure of Dependence." *American Economic Review* 60: 235–46.

Sapiro, Virginia. 1981. "When Are Interests Interesting? The Problem of Political Representation of Women." *American Political Science Review* 75: 701–16.

Sapiro, Virginia. 1983. *The Political Integration of Women.* Urbana: University of Illinois Press.

Sapiro, Virginia, and Pamela Johnston Conover. 1997. "The Variable Gender Basis of Electoral Politics: Gender and Context in the 1992 U.S. Election." *British Journal of Political Science* 27: 497–523.

Sartori, Giovanni. 1976. *Parties and Party Systems.* Cambridge: Cambridge University Press.

Sassen, Saskia. 1999. *Guests and Aliens.* New York: The New Press.

Sassen, Saskia. 1991. *The Global City, New York, London, Tokyo.* Princeton, NJ: Princeton University Press.

Sassen, Saskia. 1996. "Losing Control? Sovereignty in an Age of Globalization." In *The 1995 Columbia University Leonard Hastings Schoff Memorial Lectures.* New York: Columbia University Press.

Savage, Barbara Dianne. 1999. *Broadcasting Freedom: Radio, War, and the Politics of Race, 1938–1948.* Chapel Hill: University of North Carolina Press.

Sbragia, Alberta M. 2000. "Governance, the State, and the Market: What Is Going On?" *Governance* 13 (April): 243–50.

Scanlon, T. M. 1998. *What We Owe to Each Other.* Cambridge, MA: Harvard University Press.

Schacher, Ron, and Barry Nalebuff. 1999. "Follow the Leader: Theory and Evidence on Political Participation." *American Economic Review* 89: 525–47.

Schaffer, Frederic C. 1998. *Democracy in Translation.* Ithaca, NY: Cornell University Press.

Scharpf, Fritz W. 1991. *Crisis and Choice in European Social Democracy.* Ithaca, NY: Cornell University Press.

Scharpf, Fritz W. 1997. *Games Real Actors Play.* New York: Westview.

Scharpf, Fritz W. 1999. *Governing in Europe: Effective and Democratic.* New York: Oxford University Press.

Scharpf, Fritz W., and Vivien A. Schmidt, eds. 2000. *Welfare and Work in the Open Economy: Diverse Responses to Common Challenges.* Vol. 2. Oxford: Oxford University Press.

Schattschneider, E. E. 1935. *Politics, Pressures and the Tariff.* New York: Prentice-Hall.

Schattschneider, E. E. 1942. *Party Government* (New York: Farrar & Rinehart).

Schattschneider, E. E. 1965. *The Semi-Sovereign People: A Realist's View of Democracy in America.* New York: Holt, Rinehart, and Winston.

Scheffler, Samuel. 1982. *The Rejection of Consequentialism: A Philosophical Investigation of the Considerations Underlying Rival Moral Conceptions.* Oxford: Clarendon.

Scheffler, Samuel. 1992. "Responsibility, Reactive Attitudes, and Liberalism in Philosophy and Politics." *Philosophy and Public Affairs* 21 (autumn): 299–323.

Schelling, Thomas C. 1960. *The Strategy of Conflict*. Cambridge, MA: Harvard University Press.

Schelling, Thomas C. 1978. *Micromotives and Macrobehavior*. New York: Norton.

Scheve, Kenneth, and Matthew Slaughter. 2001a. "What Explains Individual Trade-Policy Preferences?" *Journal of International Economics* 54 (2): 267–92.

Scheve, Kenneth, and Matthew Slaughter. 2001b. "Labor-Market Competition and Individual Preferences over Immigration Policy." *Review of Economics and Statistics* 83 (1): 133–45.

Schickler, Eric. 1997. "Collective Interests, Institutional Innovation, and the Development of the United States Congress." Ph.D. diss., Yale University, New Haven, CT.

Schickler, Eric. 2001. *Disjointed Pluralism: Institutional Innovation and the Development of the U.S. Congress*. Princeton, NJ: Princeton University Press.

Schiemann, John. 2001. "Hedging against Uncertainty: Regime Change and the Adoption of a Mixed Electoral System in Hungary." In *Mixed-Member Electoral Systems*, ed. Matthew Shugart and Martin Wattenberg. Oxford: Oxford University Press.

Schiffrin, Steven. 1999. *Dissent, Injustice and the Meanings of America*. Princeton, NJ: Princeton University Press.

Schiller, Wendy J. 1995. "Senators as Political Entrepreneurs: Using Bill Sponsorship to Shape Legislative Agendas." *American Journal of Political Science* 39: 186–203.

Schiller, Wendy J. 2000. *Partners and Rivals: Representation in U.S. Senate Delegations*. Princeton, NJ: Princeton University Press.

Schimmelfennig, Frank. 1997. "Rhetorisches Handeln in der internationalen Politik." *Zeitschrift für internationale Beziehungen* 4 (2): 219–54.

Schimmelfennig, Frank. 2000. "International Socialization in the New Europe: Rational Action in an Institutional Environment." *European Journal of International Relations* 6 (1): 109–39.

Schlichting, Kurt, Peter Tuckel, and Richard Maisel. 1998. "Racial Segregation and Voter Turnout in the Urban America." *American Politics Quarterly* 26: 218–36.

Schlozman, Kay Lehman. 1990. "Representing Women in Washington: Sisterhood and Pressure Politics." In *Women, Politics, and Change*, ed. Louis A. Tilly and Patricia Gurin, ch. 15. New York: Russell Sage.

Schlozman, Kay Lehman, Henry E. Brady, Sidney Verba, and Jennifer Erkulwater. 2001. "Growing Up, Settling Down, and Becoming Active: Political Participation over the Life Cycle." Paper presented at the annual meeting of the Midwest Political Science Association.

Schlozman, Kay Lehman, Nancy Burns, and Sidney Verba. 1999. "What Happened at Work Today? A Multi-Stage Model of Gender, Employment, and Political Participation." *Journal of Politics* 61: 29–54.

Schlozman, Kay Lehman, Nancy Burns, Sidney Verba, and Jesse Donahue. 1995. "Gender and Citizen Participation: Is There a Different Voice?" *American Journal of Political Science* 39: 267–93.

Schlozman, Kay Lehman, and Sidney Verba. 1979. *Injury to Insult: Unemployment, Class, and Political Response*. Cambridge, MA: Harvard University Press.

Schlozman, Kay Lehman, and John Tierney. 1986. *Organized Interests and American Democracy*. New York: Harper and Row.

Schlozman, Kay Lehman, Sidney Verba, and Henry E. Brady. 1995. "Participation's Not a Paradox: The View from American Activists." *British Journal of Political Science* 25: 1–36.

Schlozman, Kay Lehman, Sidney Verba, and Henry E. Brady. 1999. "Civic Participation and the Equality Problem." In *Civic Engagement in American Democracy*, ed. Theda Skocpol and Morris Fiorina. Washington, DC: Brookings.

Schmidt, Brian C. 1998. *The Political Discourse of Anarchy*. Albany: State University of New York Press.

Schmitter, Philippe C. 1973. "The Portugalization of Brazil?" In *Authoritarian Brazil*, ed. Alfred Stepan. New Haven, CT: Yale University Press.

Schmitter, Philippe C. 1974. "Still the Century of Corporatism?" *Review of Politics* 36 (1): 85–121.

Schmitter, Philippe C. 1981. "Interest Intermediation and Regime Governability in Contemporary Western Europe and North America." In *Organizing Interests in Western Europe*, ed. S. Berger. Cambridge: Cambridge University Press.

Schmitter, Philippe C. 1997. "Civil Society East and West." In *Consolidating the Third Wave Democracies*, ed. Larry Diamond, Marc F. Plattner, Yun-han Chus, and Hung-mao Tien, 239–62. Baltimore: Johns Hopkins University Press.

Schmitter, Philippe C., and Gerhard Lehmbruch, eds. 1979. *Trends toward Corporatist Intermediation*. Beverly Hills, CA: Sage.

Schneider, Ben Ross. 1999. "The *Desarrollista* State in Brazil and Mexico." In *The Developmental State*, ed. Meredith Woo-Cumings, 276–305. Ithaca, N.Y.: Cornell University Press.

Schofield, Norman. 1999. "Constitutional Political Economy: On the Possibility of Combining Rational Choice Theory and Comparative Politics." Working paper, Washington University.

Scholz, John T. 1998. "Trust, Taxes, and Compliance." In *Trust and Governance*, ed. Valerie Braithwaite and Margaret Levi, 135–66. New York: Russell Sage.

Schonhardt-Bailey, Cheryl. 1991. "Specific Factors, Capital Markets, Portfolio Diversification, and Free Trade: Domestic Determinants of the Repeal of the Corn Laws." *World Politics* 43, (4, July): 545–69.

Schoolman, Morton. 1997. "Toward a Politics of Darkness: Individuality and Its Politics in Adorno's Aesthetics." *Political Theory* 25: 57–93.

Schoolman, Morton. 2001. *Reason and Horror: Critical Theory, Democracy, and Aesthetic Individuality*. New York: Routledge.

Schorr, Juliet. 1993. *The Overworked American*. New York: Basic.

Schotter, A. 1981. *The Economic Theory of Social Institutions*. Cambridge: Cambridge University Press.

Schroeder, Paul W. 1994a. "Historical Reality vs. Neorealist Theory." *International Security* 19 (summer): 108–48.

Schroeder, Paul W. 1994b. *The Transformation of European Politics, 1763–1848*. Oxford: Clarendon.

Schudson, Michael. 1998. *The Good Citizen: A History of American Civic Life*. New York: Free Press.

Schuessler, Alexander A. 2000. "Expressive Voting." *Rationality and Society* 12: 87–119.

Schultz, Kenneth. 2001. *Democracy and Coercive Diplomacy*. New York: Cambridge University Press.

Schultz, Kenneth A. 1998. "Domestic Opposition and Signaling in International Crises." *American Political Science Review* 92: 829–44.

Schultz, Kenneth A. 1999. "Do Democratic Institutions Constrain or Inform? Contrasting Two Institutional Perspectives on Democracy and War." *International Organization* 53: 233–66.

Schultz, Kenneth A. 2001. *Democracy and Coercive Diplomacy*. New York: Cambridge University Press.

Schumaker, Paul, and Nancy Elizabeth Burns. 1988. "Gender Cleavages and the Resolution of Local Policy Issues." *American Journal of Political Science* 32: 1070–95.

Schumpeter, Joseph. 1942. *Capitalism, Socialism, and Democracy*. New York: Harper.

Schurmann, Franz. 1966. *Ideology and Organization in Communist China*. Berkeley: University of California Press.

Schweizer, Urs. 1989. "Litigation and Settlement Under Two-Sided Incomplete Information." *Review of Economic Studies* 18: 163–78.

Schweller, Randall L. 1994. "Bandwagoning for Profit: Bringing the Revisionist State Back In." *International Security* 19 (summer): 72–107.

Schweller, Randall L. 1996. "Neo-realism's Status Quo Bias: What Security Dilemma?" *Security Studies* 5 (spring): 90–121.

Schweller, Randall L. 1998. *Deadly Imbalances: Tripolarity and Hitler's Strategy for World Conquest*. New York: Columbia University Press.

Schweller, Randall L., and David Priess. 1997. "A Tale of Two Realisms: Expanding the Institutions Debate." *Mershon International Studies Review* 41 (May): 1–32.

Schweller, Randall L., and William C. Wohlforth. 2000. "Power Test: Evaluating Realism in Response to the End of the Cold War." *Security Studies* 9 (spring): 60–107.

Scott, Anne Firor. 1984. *Making the Invisible Woman Visible*. Urbana: University of Illinois Press.

Scott, James C. 1976. *The Moral Economy of the Peasant*. New Haven, CT: Yale University Press.

Scott, James C. 1990. *Domination and the Arts of Resistance*. New Haven, CT: Yale University Press.

Scott, James C. 1998. *Seeing Like A State: How Certain Schemes to Improve the Human Condition Have Failed*. New Haven, CT: Yale University Press.

Scott, Joan. 1988. *Gender and the Politics of History*. New York: Columbia University Press.

Scully, Timothy. 1994. *Rethinking the Center: Party Politics in 19th and 20th Century Chile*. Stanford, CA: Stanford University Press.

Searing, Donald. 1994. *Westminster's World: Understanding Political Roles*. Cambridge, MA: Harvard University Press.

Sears, David O., Jim Sidanius, and Lawrence Bobo, eds. 2000. *Racialized Politics: The Debate About Racism in America*. Chicago: University of Chicago Press.

Segal, Jeffrey. 1997. "Separation-of-Powers Games in the Positive Theory of Congress and Courts," *American Political Science Review* 91 (1): 28–44.

Segal, Jeffrey, and Cheng-Lung Wang. 2001. "Inducing Apparently Strategic Behavior in Models of Bounded Discretion: The Case of Regime-Change Switching Regressions." Paper prepared for the annual meeting of the American Political Science Association, Department of Political Science, SUNY Stony Brook.

Sen, Amartya K. 1978. "Rational Fools: A Critique of the Behavioural Foundations of Economic Theory." In *Scientific Models and Men*, ed. H. Harris. London: Oxford University Press.

Sen, Amartya K. 1982. "Equality of What?" In *Choice, Welfare and Measurement*, 353–69. Cambridge: MIT Press.

Serra, Jose. 1979. "Three Mistaken Theses Regarding the Connection between Industrialization and Authoritarian Regimes." In *The New Authoritarianism in Latin America*, ed. David Collier, 99–163. Princeton, NJ: Princeton University Press.

Sewell, William H., Jr. 1992. "A Theory of Structure: Duality, Agency, and Transformation." *American Journal of Sociology* 98: 1–29.

Sewell, William H., Jr. 1996. "Three Temporalities: Toward an Eventful Sociology." In *The Historic Turn in the Human Sciences*, ed. Terrence J. McDonald, 245–80. Ann Arbor: University of Michigan Press.

Shafer, Byron. 1991. *The End of Realignment: Interpreting American Electoral Eras*. Madison: University of Wisconsin Press.

Shalev, Michael. 1998. "Limits and Alternatives to Multiple Regression in Macro-Comparative Research." Paper Presented at the Second Conference on the Welfare State at the Crossroads, Stockholm.

Shapiro, Ian. 1993. "Democratic Innovation: South Africa in Comparative Context." *World Politics* 46: 121–50.

Shapiro, Ian. 1996. *Democracy's Place*. Ithaca, NY: Cornell University Press.

Shapiro, Ian. 1999. *Democratic Justice*. New Haven, CT: Yale University Press.

Shapiro, Ian 2001. *Abortion: The Supreme Court Decisions 1965–2000*. 27 ed. Indianapolis, IN: Hackett.

Shapiro, Ian and Casiano Hacker-Cordón, ed. 1999a. *Democracy's Value*. Cambridge, UK: Cambridge University Press.

Shapiro, Ian, and Casiano Hacker-Cordón, ed. 1999b. *Democracy's Edges*. Cambridge, UK: Cambridge University Press.

Shapiro, Ian, and Courtney Jung. 1996. "South African Democracy Revisited: A Reply to Koelble and Reynolds." *Politics and Society* 24: 237–47.

Shapiro, Martin. 1981. *Courts: A Comparative And Political Analysis*. Chicago: Chicago University Press.

Shapiro, Michael. 1997. *Violent Cartographies: Mapping Cultures of War*. Minneapolis: University of Minnesota Press.

Shapiro, Robert Y., and Harpreet Mahajan. 1986. "Gender Differences in Policy Preferences: A Summary of Trends from the 1960s to the 1980s." *Public Opinion Quarterly* 50: 42–61.

Shaw, Brian J. 1999. "Habermas and Religious Inclusion: Lessons from Kant's Moral Theory." *Political Theory* 27: 634–66.

Sheetz, Mark. 1999. "Exit Strategies: American Grand Designs for Postwar European Security." *Security Studies* 8 (summer): 1–43.

Shefter, Martin. 1977. "Party and Patronage: Germany, England, and Italy." *Politics and Society* 7: 403–52.

Shefter, Martin. 1978. "Party Bureaucracy and Political Change in the United States." In *Political Parties: Development and Decay*, ed. Louis Maisel and Joseph Cooper, 211–66. Beverly Hills, CA: Sage Publications.

Sheingate, Adam. 2001. *The Rise of the Agricultural Welfare State: Institutions and Interest Group Power in the United States, France, and Japan*. Princeton, NJ: Princeton University Press.

Shepard, Walter James. 1925. "Political Science." In *The History and Prospects of the Social Sciences*, ed. Harry Elmer Barnes. New York: Knopf.

Shepsle, Kenneth A. 1979. "Institutional Arrangements and Equilibrium in Multidimensional Voting Models." *American Journal of Political Science* 23: 27–59.

Shepsle, Kenneth A. 1986. "Institutional Equilibrium and Equilibrium Institutions." In *Political Science: The Science of Politics*, ed. Herbert Weisberg. New York: Agathon.

Shepsle, Kenneth A. 1989. "The Changing Textbook Congress." In *Can the Government Govern?* ed. John E. Chubb and Paul E. Peterson. Washington, DC: Brookings.

Shepsle, Kenneth A., and Mark S. Bonchek. 1997. *Analyzing Politics: Rationality, Behavior, and Institutions*. New York: Norton.

Shepsle, Kenneth A., and Barry R. Weingast. 1981. "Political Preferences for the Pork Barrel: A Generalization." *American Journal of Political Science* 25: 96–111.

Shepsle, Kenneth A., and Barry R. Weingast. 1987. "The Institutional Foundations of Committee Power," *American Political Science Review* 81: 85–104.

Shepsle, Kenneth A., and Barry R. Weingast, eds. 1995. *Positive Theories of Congressional Institutions*. Ann Arbor: University of Michigan Press.

Sherman, L. W., and R. A. Berk. 1984. "The Specific Deterrent Effects of Arrest for Domestic Assault." *American Sociological Review* 49: 261–72.

Shields, Todd G., and Robert K. Goidel. 1997. "Participation Rates, Socioeconomic Class Biases, and Congressional Elections: A Cross Validation." *American Journal of Political Science* 41: 683–91.

Shields, Todd G., and Robert K. Goidel. 2000. "Who Contributes? Checkbook Participation, Class Biases, and the Impact of Legal Reforms, 1952–1994." *American Politics Quarterly* 28: 216–33.

Shimko, Keith. 1992. "Realism, Neorealism, and American Liberalism." *Review of Politics* 54 (spring): 281–301.

Shimshoni, Jonathan. 1990–1991. "Technology, Military Advantage, and World War I: A Case for Military Entrepreneurship." *International Security* 3 (winter): 187–215.

Shin, Doh Chull. 1994. "On the Third Wave of Democratization: A Synthesis and Evaluation of Recent Theory and Research." *World Politics* 47 (1): 135–70.

Shin, Doh Chull, and Peter McDonough. 1999. "The Dynamics of Popular Reactions to Democratization in Korea." *Journal of Public Policy.* 19 (1): 1–32.

Shingles, Richard D. 1981. "Black Consciousness and Political Participation: The Missing Link." *American Political Science Review* 75: 76–91.

Shipan, Charles R. 1997. *Designing Judicial Review: Interest Groups, Congress, and Communications Policy.* Ann Arbor: University of Michigan Press.

Shively, W. Phillips. 1979. "The Development of Party Identification among Adults: Exploration of a Functional Model." *American Political Science Review* 73: 1039–54.

Shklar, Judith N. 1991. *American Citizenship: The Quest for Inclusion.* Cambridge, MA: Harvard University Press.

Shklar, Judith N. 1998. *Redeeming American Political Thought.* ed. Dennis F. Thompson. Chicago. University of Chicago Press.

Shleifer, Andrei, and Daniel Treisman. 2000. *Without a Map: Political Tactics and Economic Reform in Russia.* Boston: MIT Press.

Shleifer, Andrei, and Robert Vishny. 1993. "Corruption." *Quarterly Journal of Economics* 108 (3, August): 599–617.

Shleifer, Andrei, and Robert Vishny. 1998. *The Grabbing Hand: Government Pathologies and Their Cures.* Cambridge, MA: Harvard University Press.

Shotts, R. W. 2001. "The Effect of Majority-Minority Mandates on Partisan Gerrymandering." *American Journal of Political Science* 45 (1, January): 120–35.

Shue, Henry. 1988. "Mediating Duties." *Ethics* 98 (July): 687–704.

Shue, Vivienne. 1988. *The Reach of the State: Sketches of the Chinese Body Politic.* Stanford, CA: Stanford University Press.

Shugart, Matthew. 1995. "The Electoral Cycle and Institutional Sources of Divided Government." *American Journal of Political Science* 89: 327–43.

Shugart, Matthew. 1998. "The Inverse Relationship Between Party Strength and Executive Strength: A Theory of Politicians' Constitutional Choices." *British Journal of Political Science* 28: 1–29.

Shugart, Matthew, and John M. Carey. 1992. *Presidents and Assemblies: Constitutional Design and Electoral Dynamics.* New York: Cambridge University Press.

Shultz, Kenneth A. 1999. "Do Democratic Institutions Constrain or Inform?" *International Organization* 53 (spring): 233–66.

Sigel, Roberta S. 1996. *Ambition and Accommodation: How Women View Gender Relations.* Chicago: University of Chicago Press.

Signorino, Curtis. 1999. "Strategic Interaction and the Statistical Analysis of International Conflict." *American Political Science Review* 93 (2, June): 279–97.

Signorino, Curtis. 2000. "Theoretical Sources of Uncertainty in Discrete Choice Models." Manuscript, Department of Political Science, University of Rochester, Rochester, NY.

Signorino, Curtis, and Ahmer Tarar. 2001. "A Unified Theory and Test of Immediate Extended Deterrence." Manuscript, Department of Political Science, University of Rochester, Rochester, NY.

Silbey, Joel H. 1967. *The Shrine of Party: Congressional Voting Behavior, 1841–1852.* Pittsburgh, PA: University of Pittsburgh Press.

Silbey, Joel H. 1991. "Beyond Realignment and Realignment Theory." In *The End of Realignment? Interpreting American Electoral Eras,* ed. Byron Shafer. Madison: University of Wisconsin Press.

Simmons, Beth A. 1993. *Who Adjusts? Domestic Sources of Foreign Economic Policy During the Interwar Years.* Princeton, NJ: Princeton University Press.

Simmons, Beth. 1994. *Who Adjusts?* Princeton: Princeton University Press.

Simmons, Beth A. 2000. "The Legalization of International Monetary Affairs." *International Organization* 54 (3): 573–602.

Simmons, Beth A., and Zachary Elkins. 2000. *Globalization and Policy Diffusion: Explaining Three Decades of Liberalization.* Berkeley.

Simon, Herbert A. 1982. *Models of Bounded Rationality,* Vol. I, *Economic Analysis and Public Policy,* Vol. 2. *Behavioral Economics and Business Organization.* 2 vols. Cambridge: MIT Press.

Simon, Herbert A. 1985. "Human Nature in Politics: The Dialogue of Psychology with Political Science." *American Political Science Review* 79: 293–304.

Simpson, Andrea Y. 1998. *The Tie That Binds: Identity and Political Attitudes in the Post-Civil Rights Generation.* New York: New York University Press.

Sinclair, Barbara Deckard. 1977. "Party Realignment and the Transformation of the Political Agenda: The House of Representatives, 1925–1938." *American Political Science Review* 71: 940–53.

Sinclair, Barbara Deckard. 1978. "The Policy Consequences of Party Realignment: Social Welfare Legislation in the House of Representatives, 1933–1954." *American Journal of Political Science* 22: 83–105.

Sinclair, Barbara Deckard. 1982. *Congressional Realignment, 1925–1978.* Austin: University of Texas Press.

Sinclair, Barbara Deckard. 1989. *The Transformation of the U.S. Senate.* Baltimore: Johns Hopkins University Press.

Sinclair, Barbara Deckard. 1999. "Transformational Leader or Faithful Agent? Principal-Agent Theory and House Majority Party Leadership." *Legislative Studies Quarterly* 24: 421–49.

Singer, Hans. 1950. "The Distribution of Gains Between Investing and Borrowing Countries." *American Economic Review* 40: 472–99.

Singer, Peter. 1999. "The Singer Solution To World Poverty." *New York Times Sunday Magazine*, 5 September 1999, 60.

Sirianni, Carmen, and Lewis Friedland. 2001. *Civic Innovation in America: Community Empowerment, Public Policy, and the Movement for Civic Renewal.* Berkeley: University of California Press.

Sisson, Richard. 1973. "Comparative Legislative Institutionalization: A Theoretical Exploration." In *Legislatures in Comparative Perspective,* ed. Allen Kornberg. New York: McKay.

Siverson, Randolph M. 1995. "Democracies and War Participation." *European Journal of International Relations* 1: 481–90.

Skilling, Gordon. 1966. "Interest Groups and Communist Politics." *World Politics* 18: 435–51.

Skilling, Gordon, and Franklyn Griffiths, eds. 1971. *Interest Groups in Soviet Politics.* Princeton, NJ: Princeton University Press.

Sklar, Martin. 1988. *The Corporate Reconstruction of American Capitalism, 1890–1916.* New York: Cambridge University Press.

Sklar, Martin. 1991. "Periodization and Historiography: Studying American Political Development in the Progressive Era." *Studies in American Political Development* 5 (2): 173–213.

Skocpol, Theda. 1979. *States and Social Revolutions: A Comparative Analysis of France, Russia, and China.* Cambridge: Cambridge University Press.

Skocpol, Theda. 1992. *Protecting Soldiers and Mothers: The Political Origins of Social Policy in the United States.* Cambridge MA: Belknap Press of Harvard University Press.

Skocpol, Theda. 1994. *Social Revolutions in the Modern World.* Cambridge and New York: Cambridge University Press.

Skocpol, Theda. 1996. "Unraveling from Above." *American Prospect* 25 (March–April): 20–25.

Skocpol, Theda. 1997. "The Tocqueville Problem: Civic Engagement in American Democracy." *Social Science History* 21 (4): 455–79.

Skocpol, Theda. 1999. "How Americans Became Civic." In *Civic Engagement in American Democracy,* ed. Theda Skocpol and Morris Fiorina. Washington, DC: Brookings.

Skocpol, Theda. 2000. "Commentary: Theory Tackles History." *Social Science History* 24 (4): 669–76.

Skocpol, Theda, Marjorie Abend-Wein, Christopher Howard, and Susan Goodrich Lehmann. 1993. "Women's Associations and the Enactment of Mothers' Pensions in the United States." *American Political Science Review* 87: 686–701.

Skocpol, Theda, and Kenneth Finegold, 1990. "Explaining New Deal Labor Policy." *American Political Science Review* 84: 1282–310.

Skocpol, Theda, Marshall Ganz, and Ziad Munson. 2000. "A Nation of Organizers: Institutional Origins of Civic Voluntarism in the United States." *American Political Science Review* 94 (3): 527–46.

Skocpol, Theda, and Margaret Somers. 1980. "The Uses of Comparative History in Macrosocial Inquiry." *Comparative Studies in Society and History* 22 (2): 174–97.

Skowronek, Stephen. 1982. *Building a New American State: The Expansion of National Administrative Capacities, 1877–1920.* New York: Cambridge University Press.

Skowronek, Stephen. 1993. *The Politics Presidents Make: Leadership from John Adams to Bill Clinton.* Cambridge, MA: Belknap Press of Harvard University Press.

Skrentny, John David. 1996. *The Ironies of Affirmative Action: Politics Culture and Justice in America.* Chicago: University of Chicago Press.

Slemrod, Joel. 1995. "What Do Cross-Country Studies Teach about Government Involvement, Prosperity, and Economic Growth?" *Brookings Papers on Economic Activity* 2: 373–431.

Small, Melvin, and J. David Singer. 1976. "The War-Proneness of Democratic Regimes, 1816–1965." *Jerusalem Journal of International Relations* 1: 50–69.

Smart, Alan. 1999. "Predatory Rule and Illegal Economic Practices." In *States and Illegal Practices,* ed. Josiah McC. Heyman, 99–128. Oxford, UK: Berg.

Smith, Alastair. 1998. "International Crises and Domestic Politics," *American Political Science Review* 92: 623–38.

Smith, Alastair. 1999. "Testing Theories of Strategic Choice: The Example of Crisis Escalation." *American Journal of Political Science* 43: 1254–83.

Smith, Anna Marie. 1998. *Laclau and Mouffe: The Radical Democratic Imaginary.* New York: Routledge.

Smith, James McCall. 2000. "The Politics of Dispute Settlement Design: Explaining Legalism in Regional Trade Pacts." *International Organization* 54 (1): 137–80.

Smith, Mark A. 1997. "The Nature of Party Governance: Connecting Conceptualization and Measurement." *American Journal of Political Science* 41: 1042–56.

Smith, Munroe. 1886. "Introduction: The Domain of Political Science." *Political Science Quarterly,* 1 (March).

Smith, Rogers M. 1993. "Beyond, Toqueville, Mydal and Hartz: Multiple Traditions in America." *American Political Science Review* 87 (3).

Smith, Rogers M. 1997. *Civic Ideals: Conflicting Visions of Citizenship in America.* New Haven, CT: Yale University Press.

Smith, Steven Rathgeb, and Michael Lipsky. 1993. *Nonprofits for Hire: The Welfare State in the Age of Contracting.* Cambridge, MA: Harvard University Press

Smith, Steven S. 1989. *Call to Order: Floor Politics in the House and Senate.* Washington, DC: Brookings.

Smith, Steven S. 2000. "Positive Theories of Congressional Parties." *Legislative Studies Quarterly* 25: 193–216.

Smith, Tony. 1979. "The Underdevelopment of Development Literature: The Case of Dependency Theory." *World Politics* 31 (2): 247–88.

Smith-Lovin, Lynn, and J. Miller McPherson. 1991. "You Are Who You Know: A Network Approach to Gender." In *Theory on Gender/Feminism on Theory,* ed. Paula England. New York: Aldine.

Snidal, Duncan. 1985. "The Limits of Hegemonic Stability Theory." *International Organization* 39: 579–614.

Snidal, Duncan. 1991. "Relative Gains and the Pattern of International Cooperation." 85 (September): 701–26.

Sniderman, Paul M., and Douglas B. Grob. 1996. "Innovations in Experimental Design in Attitude Surveys." *Annual Review of Sociology* 22: 377–99.

Snyder, Glenn H. 1984. "The Security Dilemma in Alliance Politics." *World Politics* 36 (July): 461–95.

Snyder, Glenn H. 1997. *Alliance Politics.* Ithaca, NY: Cornell University Press.

Snyder, Glenn H., and Paul Diesing. 1977. *Conflict Among Nations.* Princeton, NJ: Princeton University Press.

Snyder, Jack L. 1984. *The Ideology of the Offensive.* Ithaca, NY: Cornell University Press.

Snyder, Jack L. 1991. *Myths of Empire: Domestic Politics and International Ambition.* Ithaca, NY: Cornell University Press.

Snyder, Jack L. 1993a. "East-West Bargaining over Germany: The Search for Synergy in a Two-Level Game." In *Double-Edged Diplomacy: International Bargaining and Domestic Politics,* ed. Peter B. Evans, Harold Karan Jacobson, and Robert D. Putnam, 104–27. Berkeley: University of California Press.

Snyder, Jack L. 1993b. "Nationalism and the Crisis of the Post-Soviet State." *Survival* 35 (1): 5–26.

Snyder, James M., Jr., and Tim Groseclose. 2000. "Estimating Party Influence in Congressional Roll-Call Voting." *American Journal of Political Science* 44: 193–211.

Snyder, Richard. 1998. "Paths Out of Sultanistic Regimes: Combining Structural and Voluntarist Perspectives." In *Sultanistic Regimes,* ed. H. E. Chehabi and Juan J. Linz, 49–81. Baltimore: Johns Hopkins University Press.

Snyder, Richard. 2001. *Politics after Neoliberalism Reregulation in Mexico.* New York: Cambridge University Press.

Solnick, Steven. 1998. *Stealing the State.* Cambridge, MA: Harvard University Press.

Somers, Margaret R. 1998. " 'We're No Angels:' Realism, Rational Choice, and Relationality in Social Science." *American Journal of Sociology* 104 (3): 722–84.

Soskice, David. 1990a. "Reinterpreting Corporatism and Explaining Unemployment: Co-ordinated and Non-co-ordinated Market Economies." In *Labour Relations and Economic Performance,* ed. R. Brunetta and C. Dell'Aringa. New York: New York University Press.

Soskice, David. 1990b. "Wage Determination: The Changing Role of Institutions in Advanced Industrialized Countries." *Oxford Review of Economic Policy* 6 (4): 36–61.

Soskice, David. 1991. "The Institutional Infrastructure for International Competitiveness: A Comparative Analysis of the UK and Germany." In *The Economics of the New Europe,* ed. A. B. Atkinson and R. Brunetta. London: MacMillan & Co.

Soskice, David. 1996. "German Technology Policy: Innovation, and National Institutional Frameworks." WZB Discussion Paper *FSI 96–319* (Wissenschaftszentrum Berlin für Sozialforschung, September 1996).

Soskice, David. 1997. "The Future Political Economy of EMU: Rethinking the Effects of Monetary Integration on Europe." Discussion paper, *Wissenschaftszentrum-Berlin*, Berlin.

Soskice, David. 1999. "Divergent Production Regimes: Coordinated and Uncoordinated Market Economies in the 1980s and 1990s." In *Change and Continuity in Contemporary Capitalism*, ed. Herbert Kitschelt, Peter Lange, Gary Marks, and John D. Stephens, 101–34. New York and Cambridge: Cambridge University Press.

Soskice, David, and Torben Iversen. 1998. "Multiple Wage Bargaining Systems in the Single European Currency Area." *Oxford Review of Economic Policy.*

Solnich, Steven. 1998. *Stealing the State.* Cambridge, MA: Harvard University Press.

Soss, Joe. 2000. *Unwanted Claims: The Politics of Participation in the U.S. Welfare System.* Ann Arbor: University of Michigan Press.

Soule, John W., and Wilma E. McGrath. 1977. "A Comparative Study of Male-Female Political Attitudes at Citizen and Elite Levels." In *A Portrait of Marginality*, ed. Marianne Githens and Jewel L. Prestage. New York: McKay.

Southwell, Priscilla L. 1991. "Voter Turnout in the 1986 Congressional Elections: The Media as a Demobilizer?" *American Politics Quarterly* 19: 96–108.

Southwell, Priscilla L., and Justin I. Burchett. 2000. "The Effect of All-Mail Elections on Voter Turnout." *American Politics Quarterly* 28: 72–79.

Soysal, Yasemin. 1994. *Limits of Citizenship: Migrants and Postnational Membership in Europe.* Chicago: University of Chicago Press.

Sparrow, Bartholomew A. 1996. *From the Outside In: World War II and the American State.* Princeton, NJ: Princeton University Press.

Spero, Joan Edelman. 1994. *The Politics of International Economic Relations.* New York: St. Martin's.

Spiller, Pablo T., and Rafael Gely. 1992. "Congressional Control or Judicial Independence: The Determinants of U.S. Supreme Court Labor-Relations Decisions 1949–1988." *RAND Journal of Economics* 23: 463–92.

Spiro, David. 1994. "The Insignificance of the Liberal Peace." *International Security* 19: 50–86.

Spiro, David. 1998. *The Hidden Hand of American Hegemony: Petrodollar Recycling and International Markets.* Ithaca, NY: Cornell University Press.

Spragens, Thomas A., Jr. 2000. *Civic Liberalism: Reflections on Our Democratic Ideals.* New York: Rowman and Littlefield.

Spruyt, Hendrik. 1994. *The Sovereign State and Its Competitors.* Princeton, NJ: Princeton University Press.

Spykman, Nicholas. 1942. *America's Strategy in World Politics: The United States and the Balance of Power.* New York: Harcourt Brace.

Squire, Peverill. 1998. "Membership Turnover and the Efficient Processing of Legislation." *Legislative Studies Quarterly* 23: 23–32.

Stallings, Barbara, ed. 1995. *Global Change, Regional Response: The New International Context of Development*. Cambridge and New York: Cambridge University Press.

Stark, David, and L. Bruszt. 1998. *Postsocialist Pathways: Transforming Politics and Property in East Central Europe*. Cambridge: Cambridge University Press.

Stein, Arthur A. 1980. "The Politics of Linkage." *World Politics* 33 (October): 62–81.

Stein, Arthur A. 1990. *Why Nations Cooperate: Circumstances and Choice in International Relations*. Ithaca, NY: Cornell University Press.

Stein, Ernesto, Ernesto Talvi, and Alejandro Grisanti. 1999. "Institutional Arrangements and Fiscal Performance: The Latin American Experience." In *Fiscal Institutions and Fiscal Performance*, ed. James Poterba and Jurgen von Hagen. Chicago: NBER and University of Chicago Press.

Steinmo, Sven. 1996. *Taxation and Democracy: Swedish, British, and American Approaches to Financing the Modern State*. New Haven, CT: Yale University Press.

Stenner, Karen. 2001. "Betsy, Beverly and Monica: The Impact of Female Candidates and Role Models on Women's and Men's Political Engagement." Manuscript, Princeton University, Princeton, NJ.

Stepan, Alfred. 1978. *The State and Society: Peru in Comparative Perspective*. Princeton, NJ: Princeton University Press.

Stepan, Alfred. 1988. *Rethinking Military Politics: Brazil and the Southern Cone*. Princeton, NJ: Princeton University Press.

Stephenson, Gilbert Thomas. 1909. "Separation of the Races in Public Conveyances." *American Political Science Review* 3: 180–204.

Sterling-Folker, Jennifer. 1997. "Realist Environment, Liberal Process, and Domestic-Level Variables." *International Studies Quarterly* 41 (March): 1–25.

Steunenberg, Bernard. 1994. "Decision Making under Different Institutional Arrangements: Legislation by the European Community." *Journal of Institutional and Theoretical Economics* 150: 642–69.

Stevens, Jacqueline. 1999. *Reproducing the State*. Princeton, NJ: Princeton University Press.

Stewart, Charles H., III. 1989. *Budget Reform Politics: The Design of the Appropriations Process in the House of Representatives, 1865–1921*. Cambridge: Cambridge University Press.

Stewart, Charles H., III, and Barry R. Weingast. 1992. "Stacking the Senate, Changing the Nation: Republican Rotten Boroughs, Statehood Politics, and American Political Development." *Studies in American Political Development* 6: 223–71.

Stewart, Richard. 1975. "The Reformation of American Administrative Law." *Harvard Law Review* 88: 1169–813.

Stigler, George. 1971. "The Theory of Economic Regulation," *Bell Journal of Economics and Management Science* 2: 3–21.

Stinchcombe, Arthur L. 1968. *Constructing Social Theories*. Chicago: University of Chicago Press.

Stinchcombe, Arthur. 1997. "On the Virtues of the Old Institutionalism." *Annual Review of Sociology* 23: 1–18.

Stoker, Laura, and M. Kent Jennings. 1995. "Life-Cycle Transitions and Political Participation: The Case of Marriage." *American Political Science Review* 89: 421–33.

Stokes, Susan C. 2001a. *Markets, Mandates, and Democracy: Neoliberalism by Surprise in Latin America.* New York: Cambridge University Press.

Stokes, Susan C. 2001b. *Public Support for Market Reforms in New Democracies.* New York: Cambridge University Press.

Stoler, Ann Laura. 1996. "Carnal Knowledge and Imperial Power: Gender, Race, and Morality in Colonial Asia." In *Feminism and History,* ed. Joan Wallach Scott. Oxford: Oxford University Press.

Stone, Walter J., Lonna Rae Atkeson, and Ronald B. Rapoport. 1992. "Turning On or Turning Off? Mobilization and Demobilization Effects of Participation in Presidential Nomination Campaigns." *American Journal of Political Science* 36: 665–91.

Stoper, Emily. 1977. "Wife and Politician: Role Strain Among Women in Public Office." In *A Portrait of Marginality,* ed. Marianne Githens and Jewel L. Prestage. New York: McKay.

Strange, Susan. 1996. *The Retreat of the State: The Diffusion of Power in the World Economy* Cambridge: Cambridge University Press.

Strate, John M., Charles J. Parrish, Charles D. Elder, and Coit Ford III. 1989. "Life Span Civic Development and Voting Participation." *American Political Science Review* 83: 443–64.

Strauch, Rolf, and Jurgen von Hagen, eds. 1999. *Institutions, Politics and Fiscal Policy.* Kluwer Academic.

Streeck, Wolfgang. 1991. "On the Institutional Conditions of Diversified Quality Production." In *Beyond Keynesianism,* ed. E. Matzner and W. Streeck. Aldershot, UK: Elgar.

Streeck, Wolfgang. 1992. *Social Institutions and Economic Performance.* Newbury Park, CA: Sage.

Streeck, Wolfgang. 1997. "Beneficial Constraints: On the Economic Limits of Rational Voluntarism." In *Contemporary Capitalism: The Embeddedness of Institutions,* ed. J. R. Hollingsworth and R. Boyer. New York: Cambridge University Press.

Streeck, Wolfgang. 2001. "Introduction: Explorations into the Origins of Non-Liberal Capitalism in Germany and Japan." In *The Origins of Nonliberal Capitalism: Germany and Japan in Comparison,* ed. Wolfgang Streeck and Kozo Yamamura. Ithaca, NY: Cornell University Press.

Streeck, Wolfgang, and Kozo Yamamura. Forthcoming. *Germany and Japan in the 21st Century: Strengths into Weaknesses?*

Strom, Kaare. 1984. "Minority Governments in Parliamentary Democracies: The Rationality of Non-winning Solutions." *Comparative Political Studies* 17: 199–227.

Strom, Kaare. 1990. *Minority Government and Majority Rule.* Cambridge: Cambridge University Press.

Strom, Kaare. 2000. "Delegation and Accountability in Parliamentary Democracies." *European Journal of Political Research* 37: 261–89.

Strom, Kaare, Ian Budge, and Michael J. Laver. 1994. "Constraints on Cabinet Formation in Parliamentary Democracies." *American Journal of Political Science* 38: 303–35.

Strom, Kaare, Wolfgang C. Müeller and Torbjörn Bergman, eds. Forthcoming. *Rulers, Rules, and Coalitions: Cabinet Governance in European Democracies.* New York: Oxford University Press.

Sugden, Robert. 1986. *The Economics of Rights, Co-operation, and Welfare.* Oxford, UK: Blackwell.

Sundquist, James. 1981. *The Decline and Resurgence of Congress.* Washington, DC: Brookings.

Sunkel, Osvaldo. 1973. "Transnational Capitalism and National Disintegration in Latin America." *Social and Economic Studies* 22: 132–76.

Sunstein, Cass, 2000. "The Law of Group Polarization." http://www.la.utexas.edu/conf2000/papers/LawofGroupPolarization.pdf.

Suny, Ronald. 1993. *Revenge of the Past.* Stanford, CA: Stanford University Press.

Suppe, Frederick. 1977. Afterword to *The Structure of Scientific Theories,* ed. Frederick Suppe. Urbana: University of Illinois Press.

Swank, Duane H. 2001a. "Political Institutions and Welfare State Restructuring: The Impact of Institutions on Social Policy Change in Developed Democracies." In *The New Politics of the Welfare State,* ed. Paul Pierson. Oxford: Oxford University Press.

Swank, Duane H. 2001b. "Withering Welfare? Globalization, Political Economic Institutions, and the Foundations of Contemporary Welfare States." In *States in the Global Economy: Bringing Domestic Institutions Back In,* ed. L. Weiss. New York: Cambridge University Press.

Swank, Duane H. 2002. *Global Capital, Political Institutions, and Policy Change in Developed Welfare States.* New York: Cambridge University Press.

Swenson, Peter. 1989. *Fair Shares: Unions, Pay, and Politics in Sweden and West Germany.* Ithaca, NY: Cornell University Press.

Swenson, Peter. 1991. "Bringing Capital Back In, or Social Democracy Reconsidered: Employer Power, Cross-Class Alliances, and Centralization of Industrial Relations in Denmark and Sweden." *World Politics* 43 (4): 513–44.

Swenson, Peter. 1997. "Arranged Alliance: Business Interests in the New Deal." *Politics and Society* 25 (1): 66–116.

Swenson, Peter. Forthcoming. *Capitalists Against Markets.* Oxford: Oxford University Press.

Swers, Michele L. 1998. "Are Women More Likely to Vote for Women's Issue Bills Than Their Male Colleagues?" *Legislative Studies Quarterly* 23: 435–48.

Swift, Elaine K. 1996. *The Making of an American Senate: Reconstitutive Change in Congress, 1787–1841.* Ann Arbor: University of Michigan Press.

Sztompka, Piotr. 1999. *Trust.* New York: Cambridge University Press.

Taagepera, Rein, and Matthew Shugart. 1989. *Seats and Votes.* New Haven, CT: Yale University Press.

Tabellini, Guido. 1991. "The Politics of Intergenerational Redistribution." *Journal of Political Economy*: 335–57.

Tabellini, Guido, and Alberto Alesina. 1990. "Voting on the Budget Deficit." *American Economic Review*: 37–49.

Tajfel, Henri, and John C. Turner. 1986. "The Social Identity Theory of Intergroup Behavior." In *Psychology of Intergroup Relations*, ed. Stephen Worchel and William C. Austin. 2d ed. Chicago: Nelson-Hall.

Taliaferro, Jeffrey W. 2000–2001. "Security Seeking under Anarchy: Defensive Realism Revisited." *International Security* 25 (winter): 128–61.

Talvi, Ernesto, and Carlos A. Vegh. 2000 "Tax Base Variability and Procyclical Fiscal Policy." NBER Working Paper 7499.

Tamerius, Karin L. 1995. "Sex, Gender, and Leadership in the Representation of Women." In *Gender Power, Leadership, and Governance*, ed. Georgia Duerst-Lahti and Rita Mae Kelly, 93–112. Ann Arbor: University of Michigan Press.

Tamir, Yael. 1993. *Liberal Nationalism.* Princeton, NJ: Princeton University Press.

Tangian, A. S. 2000. "Unlikelihood of Condorcet's Paradox in a Large Society." *Social Choice and Welfare* 17: 337–65.

Tannenwald, Nina. 1999. "The Nuclear Taboo: The United States and the Normative Basis of Nuclear Non-Use." *International Organization* 53 (3): 433–68.

Tanzi, Vito. 1998. "The Demise of the Nation State?" Washington, DC: International Monetary Fund Working Paper 120 (August).

Tarrow, Sidney. 1994. *Power in Movement.* Cambridge: Cambridge University Press.

Tarrow, Sidney. 1998. *Power in Movement: Social Movements and Contentious Politics.* 2d ed. Cambridge: Cambridge University Press.

Tarrow, Sidney. 2000. "Mad Cows and Activists: Contentious Politics in the Trilateral Democracies." In *Disaffected Democracies: What's Troubling the Trilateral Democracies*, ed. Susan Pharr, and Robert Putnam, 270–90. Princeton, NJ: Princeton University Press.

Tate, Katherine. 1991. "Black Political Participation in the 1984 and 1988 Presidential Elections." *American Political Science Review* 85: 1159–76.

Tate, Katherine. 1993, 1994. *From Protest to Politics: The New Black Voters in American Elections.* Cambridge, MA: Harvard University Press.

Taylor, Charles. 1971. "Interpretation and the Sciences of Man." *Review of Metaphysics* 25: 3–51.

Taylor, Charles. 1969. "Neutrality in Political Science." In *Philosophy, Politics, and Society*, ed. Peter Laslett and W. G. Runciman, 26–57. Third Series. Oxford, UK: Blackwell.

Taylor, Charles. 1984. "Foucault on Freedom and Truth." *Political Theory* 12: 152–83.

Taylor, Charles. 1993. *Reconciling the Solitudes. Essays on Canadian Federalism and Nationalism.* Montreal: McGill Queen's University Press.

Taylor, Charles. 1994. "The Politics of Recognition." In *Multiculturalism: Examining the Politics of Recognition*, ed. Amy Gutmann, 25–73. Princeton, NJ: Princeton University Press.

Taylor, Charles. 1995. "Response (to Bromwich)." *Dissent* (winter): 103–4.

Taylor, Michael. 1969. "Proof of a Theorem on Majority Rule." *Behavioral Science* 14: 228–31.

Taylor, Michael. 1976. *Anarchy and Cooperation*. London: Wiley.

Taylor, Michael. 1982. *Community, Anarchy, and Liberty*. Cambridge: Cambridge University Press.

Taylor, Michael. 1987 [1976] *The Possibility of Cooperation*. Cambridge: Cambridge University Press.

Taylor, Michael, ed. 1988. *Rationality and Revolution*. Cambridge and New York: Cambridge University Press.

Taylor, Michelle. 1992. "Formal versus Informal Incentive Structures and Legislator Behavior: Evidence from Costa Rica." *Journal of Politics* 54: 1055–73.

Teixeira, Ruy A. 1992. *The Disappearing American Voter*. Washington, DC: Brookings.

Tellis, Ashley J. 1995–1996. "Reconstructing Political Realism: The Long March to Scientific Theory." *Security Studies* 5 (winter): 3–102.

Tellis, Ashley J., Janice L. Bially, Christopher Layne, and Melissa McPherson. 2000. *Measuring National Power in the Post-Industrial Age*. Santa Monica, CA: RAND.

Tendler, Judith. 1997. *Good Government in the Tropics*. Baltimore: Johns Hopkins University Press.

Thayer, Bradley. 2000. "Bringing in Darwin: Evolutionary Theory, Realism, and International Politics." *International Security* 25 (fall): 124–51.

Thelen, Kathleen. 1991. *Union of Parts: Labor Politics in Postwar Germany*. Ithaca, NY: Cornell University Press.

Thelen, Kathleen. 1993. "European Labor in Transition: Sweden and Germany Compared." *World Politics* 46 (1): 23–49.

Thelen, Kathleen. 1994. "Beyond Corporatism: Toward a New Framework for the Study of Labor in Advanced Capitalism." *Comparative Politics* 27: 107–24.

Thelen, Kathleen. 1999. "Historical Institutionalism in Comparative Politics." *Annual Review of Political Science* 2: 369–404.

Thelen, Kathleen. 2000a. "Time and Temporality in the Analysis of Institutional Evolution and Change." *Studies in American Political Development* 14.

Thelen, Kathleen. 2000b. "Why German Employers Cannot Bring Themselves to Dismantle the German Model." In *Unions, Employers and Central Banks: Macroeconomic Coordination and Institutional Change in Social Market Economies*, ed. T. Iversen, J. Pontusson, and D. Soskice. New York: Cambridge University Press.

Thelen, Kathleen. 2001. "Varieties of Labor Politics in the Developed Democracies." In *Varieties of Capitalism: The Institutional Foundations of Comparative Advantage*, ed. Peter A. Hall and David Soskice. New York and Oxford: Oxford University Press.

Thelen, Kathleen. 2002. "How Institutions Evolve: Insights from Comparative Historical Analysis." In *Comparative Historical Analysis: Achievements and Agendas,* ed. James Mahoney and Dietrich Reuschemeyer. Cambridge: Cambridge University Press.

Thelen, Kathleen, and Ikuo Kume. 1999. "The Effects of Globalization on Labor Revisited: Lessons from Germany and Japan." *Politics and Society* 27 (4): 477–506.

Thelen, Kathleen, and Sven Steinmo. 1992. "Historical Institutionalism in Comparative Politics." In *Structuring Politics: Historical Institutionalism in Comparative Analysis,* ed. S. Steinmo, K. Thelen, and F. Longstreth. New York and Cambridge: Cambridge University Press.

Thelen, Kathleen, and Christa van Wijnbergen. 2000. "The Paradox of Globalization: Turning the Tables on Labor and Capital in German Industrial Relations." Institute for Policy Research Working Paper Series. Evanston, IL: Northwestern University.

Theriault, Sean. 2001. "Congress, Institutional Design, and the Politics of Pressure." Ph.D. diss., Stanford University, Stanford, CA.

Therneau, Terry M., and Patricia M. Grambsch. 2000. *Modeling Survival Data: Extending the Cox Model.* New York: Springer-Verlag.

Thies, Michael F. 1998. "When Will Pork Leave the Farm? Institutional Bias in Japan and the United States." *Legislative Studies Quarterly* 23: 467–92.

Thomas, George M., John W. Meyer, Francisco Ramirez, and John Boli, eds. 1987. *Institutional Structure: Constituting State, Society, and the Individual.* Newbury Park, CA: Sage.

Thomas, Sue. 1991. "The Impact of Women on State Legislative Policies." *Journal of Politics* 53 (November): 958–76.

Thomas, Sue. 1994. *How Women Legislate.* New York: Oxford University Press.

Thomas, Sue, and Susan Welch. 1991. "The Impact of Gender on Activities and Priorities of State Legislators." *Western Political Quarterly* 44: 445–56.

Thompson, William R., and Karen Rasler. 1999. "War, the Military Revolution(s) Controversy, and Army Expansions." *Comparative Political Studies* 32 (February): 3–31.

Thompson, William R., and Richard Tucker. 1997. "A Tale of Two Democratic Peace Critiques." *Journal of Conflict Resolution* 41: 428–54.

Thomson, Janice E. 1994. *Mercenaries, Pirates, and State Sovereignty.* Princeton, NJ: Princeton University Press.

Thorne, Barrie. 1993. *Gender Play: Girls and Boys in School.* New Brunswick, NJ: Rutgers University Press.

Thucydides. 1954. *The Peloponnesian War.* Trans. Rex Warner. New York: Penguin.

Tiebout, Charles. 1956. "A Pure Theory of Local Expenditures." *Journal of Political Economy* 64: 416–24.

Tilly, Charles. 1978. *From Mobilization to Revolution.* New York: Random House.

Tilly, Charles. 1984. *Big Structures, Large Processes, Huge Comparisons.* New York: Russell Sage.

Tilly, Charles. 1986. *The Contentious French: Four Centuries of Popular Struggle.* Cambridge, MA: Harvard University Press.

Tilly, Charles. 1990. *Coercion, Capital, and European States, AD 990–1990.* Cambridge, MA: Blackwell.

Tilly, Charles. 1992. "Futures of European States." *Social Research* 59: 705–17.

Tilly, Charles. 1996. "The State of Nationalism." *Critical Review* 10 (spring): 299–306.

Tilly, Charles. 1998a. *Durable Inequality.* Berkeley: University of California Press.

Tilly, Charles. 1998b. "International Communities, Secure or Otherwise." In *Security Communities*, ed. Emanuel Adler and Michael Barnett. Cambridge: Cambridge University Press.

Tilly, Charles, ed. 1975. *The Formation of National States in Western Europe.* Princeton, NJ: Princeton University Press.

Timpone, Richard J. 1995. "Mass Mobilization or Government Intervention? The Growth of Black Registration in the South." *Journal of Politics* 57: 425–42.

Timpone, Richard J. 1998. "Structure, Behavior, and Voter Turnout in the United States." *American Political Science Review* 92: 145–58.

Tocqueville, Alexis de. 1966 [1832]. *Democracy in America.* Vol. I. ed. J. P. Mayer. Trans. George Lawrence. New York: Harper and Row.

Tocqueville, Alexis de. 1990 [1835]. *Democracy in America.* Vol. II. New York: Vintage.

Toft, Monica. 1998. "The Geography of Ethnic Conflict." Ph.D. diss., University of Chicago, Chicago.

Tolleson Rinehart, Sue. 1992. *Gender Consciousness and Politics.* New York: Routledge.

Tollison, Robert. 1982. "Rent Seeking: A Survey." *Kyklos* 35: 28–47.

Tomlins, Christopher. 1985. *The State and the Unions: Labor Relations, Law and the Organized Labor Movement, 1880–1960.* New York: Cambridge University Press.

Trachtenberg, Marc. 1991. *History and Strategy.* Princeton, NJ: Princeton University Press.

Trachtenberg, Marc. 1999. *A Constructed Peace: The Making of the European Settlement.* Princeton, NJ: Princeton University Press.

Trachtenberg, Marc. 2001. "Realism as a Theory of Peace." Manuscript.

Traugott, Michael W., and John B. Katosh. 1979. "Response Validity in Surveys of Voting Behavior." *Public Opinion Quarterly.* 43: 359–77.

Treisman, Daniel. 1999a. "Political Decentralization and Economic Reform: A Game-Theoretic Analysis." *American Journal of Political Science* 43: 488–517.

Treisman, Daniel. 1999b. "Russia's Tax Crisis: Explaining Falling Revenues in a Transitional Economy." *Economics and Politics* 11: 145–69.

Treisman, Daniel, 2000a. "The Causes of Corruption: A Cross-National Study." *Journal of Public Economics* 76: 399–457.

Treisman, Daniel. 2000b. "Decentralization and Inflation: Commitment, Collective Action, or Continuity?" *American Political Science Review* 94: 837–57.

Truman, David B. 1959. *The Congressional Party: A Case Study.* New York: Wiley.

Truman, David B. 1971 [1951]. *The Governmental Process.* 2d. ed. New York: Knopf.

Tsebelis, George. 1990. *Nested Games.* Berkeley: University of California Press.

Tsebelis, George. 1994. "The Power of the European Parliament as a Conditional Agenda Setter." *American Political Science Review* 88: 128–42.

Tsebelis, George. 1995. "Decision Making in Political Systems: Veto Players in Presidentialism, Parliamentarism, Multicameralism, and Multipartyism." *British Journal of Political Science* 25: 289–325.

Tsebelis, George. 1999. "Veto Players and Law Production in Parliamentary Democracies: An Empirical Analysis." *American Political Science Review* 93: 591–608.

Tsebelis, George, and Jeannette Money. 1995. "Bicameral Negotiations: The Navette System in France." *British Journal of Political Science* 25: 101–29.

Tsebelis, George, and Jeannette Money. 1997. *Bicameralism.* Cambridge: Cambridge University Press.

Tudor, Rani. Forthcoming. "Does Local Governance Matter for Improving Social Well-Being? Case Studies of the Indian Panchayat System in Action." Ph.D. diss., Princeton University, Princeton, NJ.

Tufte, Edward R. 1978. *Political Control of the Economy.* Princeton, NJ: Princeton University Press.

Tulis, Jeffrey. 1987. *The Rhetorical Presidency.* Princeton, NJ: Princeton University Press.

Tully, James. 1995. *Strange Multiplicity: Constitutionalism in an Age of Diversity.* Cambridge: Cambridge University Press.

Turner, Lowell. 1998. *Fighting for Partnership: Labor and Politics in Unified Germany.* Ithaca, NY: Cornell University Press.

Tushnet, Mark. 1999. *Taking the Constitution Away From the Courts.* Princeton, NJ: Princeton University Press.

Twomey, Christopher P. 2000. "Japan, A Circumscribed Balancer: Building on Defensive Realism to Make Predictions about East Asian Security." *Security Studies* 9 (summer): 167–205.

Tyler, Tom R. 1998. "Trust and Democratic Government." In *Trust and Governance,* ed. Valerie Braithwaite and Margaret Levi, 269–94. New York: Russell Sage.

Tyler, Tom R. 1990. *Why People Obey The Law.* New Haven, CT: Yale University Press.

Uhlaner, Carole J. 1989. "Rational Turnout: The Neglected Role of Groups." *American Journal of Political Science* 38: 390–422.

Ulbert, Cornelia. 1997. "Die Konstruktion von Umwelt." In *Der Einfluss von Ideen, Institutionen und Kultur auf Internationale Klimapolitik in den USA und der Bundesrepublik.* Baden-Baden, GER: Nomos.

Ullman-Margalit, Edna. 1977. *The Emergence of Norms.* Oxford, UK: Clarendon.

Ulman, Lloyd. 1955. *The Rise of the National Trade Union.* Cambridge, MA: Harvard University Press.

Underdal, Arild. 1998. "Explaining Compliance and Defection: Three Models." *European Journal of International Relations* 4 (1): 5–30.

Vail, Leroy, ed. 1989. *The Creation of Tribalism in South Africa.* Berkeley: University of California Press.

Valenzuela, Arturo. 1978. *The Breakdown of Democratic Regimes: Chile.* Baltimore: Johns Hopkins University Press.

Valenzuela, J. Samuel. 2000. "Class Relations and Democratization: A Reassessment of Barrington Moore's Model." In *The Other Mirror: Grand Theory Through the Lens of Latin America,* ed. Miguel Angel Centeno and Fernando Lopez-Alves. Princeton, NJ: Princeton University Press.

Van Creveld, Martin. 1999. *The Rise and Decline of the State.* Cambridge: Cambridge University Press.

Van de Walle, Nicholas. 2001. *African Economies and the Politics of Permanent Crisis, 1979–1999.* Cambridge and New York: Cambridge University Press.

Van Evera, Stephen. 1984. "The Cult of the Offensive and the Origins of the First World War." *International Security* 9 (summer): 58–107.

Van Evera, Stephen. 1985. "Why Cooperation Failed in 1914." *World Politics* 38 (October): 80–117.

Van Evera, Stephen. 1990–1991. "Primed for Peace: Europe after the Cold War." *International Security* 15 (winter): 7–57.

Van Evera, Stephen. 1997. *Guide to Methods for Students of Political Science.* Ithaca, NY: Cornell University Press.

Van Evera, Stephen. 1998. "Offense, Defense and The Causes of War." *International Security* 22 (spring): 5–43.

Van Evera, Stephen. 1999. *Causes of War. Vol. 1. The Structure of Power and the Roots of Conflict.* Ithaca, NY: Cornell University Press.

Van Parijs, Philippe. 1991. "Why Surfers Should be Fed: The Liberal Case for an Unconditional Basic Income." *Philosophy and Public Affairs* 20 (spring): 101–31.

Van Parijs, Philippe. 1995. *Real Freedom for All: What (If Anything) Can Justify Capitalism.* Oxford: Clarendon.

Van Parijs, Philippe. 1996. "Justice and Democracy: Are They Incompatible?" *Journal of Political Philosophy* 4 (2): 101–17.

Vanberg, Georg. 1998. "Abstract Judicial Review, Legislative Bargaining, and Policy Compromise." *Journal of Theoretical Politics* 10: 299–326.

Vanhanen, Tatu. 1997. *Prospects of Democracy: A Study of 172 Countries.* London: Routledge.

Varshney, Ashutosh. 2002. *Ethnic Conflict and Civic Life: Hindus and Muslims in India.* New Haven, CT: Yale University Press.

Vasquez, John A. 1997. "The Realist Paradigm and Degenerative versus Progressive Research Programs: An Appraisal of Neotraditional Research on Waltz's Balancing Proposition." *American Political Science Review* 91 (December): 899–912.

Vega, Arturo, and Juanita M. Firestone. 1995. "The Effects of Gender on Congressional Behavior and the Substantive Representation of Women." *Legislative Studies Quarterly* 20: 213–22.

Velasco, Andres. 1997. "A Model of Endogenous Fiscal Deficits and Delayed Fiscal Reforms." NBER Working Paper 6336.

Verba, Sidney. 1996. "The Citizen as Respondent: Sample Surveys and American Democracy." *American Political Science Review* 90: 1–7.

Verba, Sidney, Nancy Burns, and Kay Lehman Schlozman. 1997. "Knowing and Caring about Politics: Gender and Political Engagement." *Journal of Politics* 59: 1051–72.

Verba, Sidney, and Norman H. Nie. 1972. *Participation in America*. New York: Harper and Row.

Verba, Sidney, Norman H. Nie, Jae-on Kim, and Goldie Shabad. 1978. "Men and Women: Sex-Related Differences in Political Activity." In *Participation and Political Equality*, ed. Sidney Verba, Norman H. Nie, and Jae-on Kim. Cambridge: Cambridge University Press.

Verba, Sidney, and Gary R. Orren. 1985. *Equality in America: The View from the Top*. Cambridge, MA: Harvard University Press.

Verba, Sidney, Kay Lehman Schlozman, and Henry E. Brady. 1995. *Voice and Equality: Civic Voluntarism in American Politics*. Cambridge, MA: Harvard University Press.

Verba, Sidney, Kay Lehman Schlozman, Henry E. Brady, and Norman H. Nie. 1993. "Race, Ethnicity, and Political Resources: Participation in the United States." *British Journal of Political Science* 23: 453–97.

Verba, Sidney, Kay Lehman Schlozman, and Henry E. Brady. 2000. "Rational Action and Political Activity," *Journal of Theoretical Politics* 12: 243–68.

Villa, Dana. 1996. *Arendt and Heidegger: The Fate of the Political*. Princeton, NJ: Princeton University Press.

Vogel, David. 1978. "Why Businessmen Distrust Their State: The Political Consciousness of American Corporate Executives." *British Journal of Political Science* 8: 45–78.

von Drehle, David. 2000. "No Stone Left Unturned for Turnout." *MSNBC*. www.msnbc.com/news. Accessed 11/7/00.

von Hagen, Jurgen. 1992. "Budgeting Procedures and Fiscal Performance in the European Community." *EEC Economic Papers* 96.

von Hagen, Jurgen. 1998. "Budgeting Institutions for Aggregate Fiscal Discipline." ZEI Policy Paper B98-01.

von Hagen, Jurgen, and Ian Harden. 1994. "National Budget Processes and Fiscal Performance. *European Economy, Reports and Studies* 3: 311–418.

von Hagen, Jurgen, and Ian Harden. 1995. "Budget Processes and Commitment to Fiscal Discipline." *European Economic Review:* 771–79.

Voss, D. Stephen. 2001. "Cultural Backlash and the Structural Foundation of Racial Attitudes." Paper prepared for the annual meeting of the American Political Science Association, San Francisco, CA.

Wade, Robert. 1990. *Governing the Market: Economic Theory and the Role of Government in East Asian Industrialization*. Princeton, NJ: Princeton University Press.

Wade, Robert. 1992. "East Asia's Economic Success: Conflicting Perspectives, Partial Insights, Shaky Evidence." *World Politics* 44 (January): 270–320.

Wade, Robert. 2000. "Wheels within Wheels: Rethinking the Asian Crisis and the Asian Model." *Annual Review of Political Science* 3: 85–115.

Wagner, R. Harrison. 1993. "What Was Bipolarity?" *International Organization* 47 (winter): 77–106.

Wagner, R. Harrison. 1994. "Peace, War, and the Balance of Power." *American Political Science Review* 88: 593–607.

Wagner, R. Harrison. 2000. "Bargaining and War." *American Journal of Political Science* 44: 469–84.

Wahlke, John C., H. Eulau, W. Buchanan, and L. C. Fergusen. 1962. *The Legislative System: Explorations in Legislative Behavior*. New York: Wiley.

Waldner, David. 1999. *State Building and Late Development*. Ithaca, NY: Cornell University Press.

Waldo, Dwight. 1975. "Political Science: Tradition, Discipline, Profession, Science, Enterprise." In *Handbook of Science*, Vol. 1, ed. Fred Greenstein and Nelson Polsby, 1–130. Reading, MA: Addison-Wesley.

Waldron, Jeremy. 1992. "Superseding Historic Injustice." *Ethics* 103 (October): 4–28.

Waldron, Jeremy. 1993a. *Liberal Rights: Collected Papers 1981–1991*. Cambridge: Cambridge University Press.

Waldron, Jeremy. 1993b. "Special Ties and Natural Duties." *Philosophy and Public Affairs* 22 (winter): 3–30.

Waldron, Jeremy. 1995. "Minority Cultures and the Cosmopolitan Alternative." In *The Rights of Minority Cultures*, ed. Will Kymlicka, 93–119. Oxford: Oxford University Press.

Waldron, Jeremy. 1999. *Law and Disagreement*. Oxford: Oxford University Press.

Walker, Jack L., Jr. 1991. *Mobilizing Interest Groups in America*. Ann Arbor: University of Michigan Press.

Walker, R. B. J. 1993. *Inside/Outside: International Relations as Political Theory*. Cambridge: Cambridge University Press.

Wallander, Celeste. 1999. *Mortal Friends, Best Enemies*. Ithaca, NY: Cornell University Press.

Waller, Christopher J. 1992. "A Bargaining Model of Partisan Appointments to the Central Bank." *Journal of Monetary Economics* 29: 411–28.

Wallerstein, Michael, and Miriam Golden. 1997. "The Fragmentation of the Bargaining Society: Wage Setting in the Nordic Countries, 1950 to 1992." *Comparative Political Studies* 30 (6): 699–731.

Wallerstein, Michael, Miriam Golden, and Peter Lange. 1997. "Unions, Employers' Associations, and Wage-Setting Institutions in Northern and Central Europe, 1950–1992." *Industrial and Labor Relations Review* 50 (3): 379–402.

Walt, Stephen M. 1987. *The Origins of Alliances*. Ithaca, NY: Cornell University Press.

Walt, Stephen M. 1988. "Testing Theories of Alliance Formation: The Case of Southwest Asia." *International Organization* 42 (spring): 275–316.

Walt, Stephen M. 1989. "The Case for Finite Containment: Analyzing U.S. Grand Strategy." *International Security* 14 (summer): 5–49.

Walt, Stephen M. 1992. "Alliances, Threats, and U.S. Grand Strategy: A Reply to Kaufman and Labs." *Security Studies* 1 (spring): 448–82.

Walt, Stephen M. 1996. *Revolution and War*. Ithaca, NY: Cornell University Press.

Walt, Stephen M. 1997a. "The Progressive Power of Realism." *American Political Science Review* 91 (December): 931–35.

Walt, Stephen M. 1997b. "Why Alliances Endure or Collapse." *Survival* 39 (spring): 156–79.

Walt, Stephen M. 1998. "International Relations: One World, Many Theories." *Foreign Policy* 110 (spring): 29–45.

Walt, Stephen M. 1998–99. "The Ties That Fray: Why Europe and America are Drifting Apart." *National Interest* 54 (winter): 3–11.

Walt, Stephen M. 1999. "Rigor or Rigor Mortis? Rational Choice and Security Studies." *International Security* 23 (spring): 5–48.

Walter, Barbara F. 1997. "The Critical Barrier to Civil War Settlement." *International Organization* 51: 335–64.

Walter, Barbara F., and Jack Snyder, eds. 1999. *Civil Wars, Insecurity, and Intervention*. New York: Columbia University Press.

Walters, Ronald W. 1988. *Black Presidential Politics in America: A Strategic Approach* Albany: State University of New York Press.

Walton, Hanes, Jr. 1972. *Black Political Parties*. New York: Free Press.

Walton, Hanes, Jr. 1985. *Invisible Politics: Black Political Behavior*. Albany: State University of New York Press.

Walton, Hanes., Jr. 1988. "The National Democratic Party of Alabama and Party Failure in America." In *When Parties Fail: Emerging Alternative Organizations*, ed. Kay Lawson and Peter H. Merkl. Princeton, NJ: Princeton University Press.

Walton, Hanes, Jr., Cheryl M. Miller, and Joseph P. McCormick II. 1995. "Race and Political Science: The Dual Traditions of Race Relations Politics and African-American Politics." In *Political Science*, ed. Farr, Dryzek, and Leonard, 144–74.

Waltz, Kenneth N. 1959. *Man, the State, and War*. New York: Columbia University Press.

Waltz, Kenneth N. 1967. *Foreign Policy and Democratic Politics*. Boston: Little, Brown.

Waltz, Kenneth N. 1979. *Theory of International Politics*. Reading, MA: Addison-Wesley.

Waltz, Kenneth N. 1986. "Reflections on Theory of International Politics: A Response to My Critics." In *Neorealism and Its Critics*, ed. Robert O. Keohane. New York: Columbia University Press.

Waltz, Kenneth N. 1990. "Nuclear Myths and Political Realities," *American Political Science Review* 87: 731–45.

Waltz, Kenneth N. 1991. "Realist Thought and Neorealist Theory." In *The Evolution of Theory in International Relations: Essays in Honor of William T. R. Fox*, ed. Robert L. Rothstein. Columbia: University of South Carolina Press.

Waltz, Kenneth N. 1993. "The Emerging Structure of International Politics." *International Security* 18 (fall): 44–79.

Waltz, Kenneth N. 1996. "International Politics is Not Foreign Policy." *Security Studies* 6 (autumn): 54–7.

Waltz, Kenneth N. 2000a. "Structural Realism after the Cold War." *International Security* 25 (summer): 5–41.

Waltz, Kenneth N. 2000b. "Globalization and Governance." *PS: Political Science and Politics* 32 (December): 693–700.

Walzer, Michael. 1983. *Spheres of Justice: A Defense of Pluralism and Equality.* New York: Basic.

Walzer, Michael. 1992. *What It Means to Be An American.* New York: Marsilio.

Walzer, Michael. 1995. "Response (to Bromwich)." *Dissent* (winter): 105–6.

Walzer, Michael. 1997. *On Toleration.* New Haven, CT: Yale University Press.

Warren, Mark E. 1998. "Democracy and Associations: An Approach to the Contributions of Associations to Democracy." Paper prepared for the annual meeting of the Western Political Science Association, Los Angeles.

Warren, Mark E. 2001. *Democracy and Associations.* Princeton, NJ: Princeton University Press.

Warren, Mark R. 2001. *Dry Bones Rattling: Community Building to Revitalize American Democracy.* Princeton: Princeton University Press.

Warwick, Paul. 1994. *Government Survival in Parliamentary Democracies.* New York: Cambridge University Press.

Waterbury, John. 1983. *The Egypt of Nasser and Sadat: The Political Economy of Two Regimes.* Princeton, NJ: Princeton University Press.

Waterbury, John. 1993. *Exposed to Innumerable Delusions: Public Enterprise and State Power in Egypt, India, Mexico, and Turkey.* New York: Cambridge University Press.

Waters, Mary C. 1999. *Black Identities: West Indian Immigrant Dreams and American Realities.* Cambridge, MA: Harvard University Press.

Watkins, Frederick Mundell. 1934. *The State as a Concept of Political Science.* New York: Harper and Brothers.

Watkins, Frederick Mundell. 1968. "State." In *International Encyclopedia of the Social Science*, Vol. 15, ed., David Sills. New York: Macmillan Co.

Wattenberg, Martin P., and Craig Leonard Brians. 1999. "Negative Campaign Advertising: Demobilizer or Mobilizer?" *American Political Science Review* 93: 891–99.

Weber, Katja. 1997. "Hierarchy Amidst Anarchy: A Transactions Costs Approach to International Security Cooperation." *International Studies Quarterly* 41(2): 321–40.

Weber, Max. 1946. *From Max Weber.* Trans. and ed. Hans H. Gerth and C. Wright Mills. New York: Oxford University Press.

Weber, Max. 1958. "Science As a Vocation." In *From Max Weber: Essays in Sociology.* Trans. and ed. Hans H. Gerth and C. Wright Mills. New York: Oxford University Press.

Weber, Max. 1978 [1956]. *Economy and Society.* Ed. Guenther Roth and Claus Wittich. Berkeley: University of California Press. (A translation of Max Weber, *Wirtschaft und Gesellschaft. Grundriss der verstehenden Soziologie,* ed. Johannes Winckelmann [Tuebingen: J. C. B. Mohr, 1956].)

Wedeen, Lisa. 1999. *Ambiguities of Domination: Politics, and Rhetoric, and Symbols in Contemporary Syria.* Chicago: University of Chicago Press.

Weiler, Joseph H. 1995. "Does Europe Need a Constitution? Demos, Telos and the German Maastricht Decision." *European Law Journal* 1 (3): 219–58.

Weiner, Jonathan. 1976. "Review of Reviews: The Barrington Moore Thesis and its Critics." *History and Theory* 15: 146–75.

Weiner, Myron. 1991. *The Child and the State in India: Child Labor and Education Policy in Comparative Perspective.* Princeton, NJ: Princeton University Press.

Weiner, Myron. 1995. *The Global Migration Crisis: Challenge to States and to Human Rights.* New York: HarperCollins.

Weingast, Barry R. 1984. "The Congressional-Bureaucratic System: A Principal-Agent Perspective (with applications to the SEC)." *Public Choice* 44: 147–91.

Weingast, Barry R. 1995. "The Economic Role of Political Institutions: Market-Preserving Federalism and Economic Development." *Journal of Law, Economics, and Organization* 11: 1–31.

Weingast, Barry R. 1997. "The Political Foundations of Democracy and the Rule of Law." *American Political Science Review* 91 (June): 245–63.

Weingast, Barry R. 1998. "Constructing Trust: The Politics and Economics of Ethnic and Regional Conflict." In *Where is the New Institutionalism Now?*, ed. Virginia Haufler, Karol Soltan, and Eric Uslaner. Ann Arbor: University of Michigan Press.

Weingast, Barry R. 1998. "Political Stability and Civil War: Institutions, Commitment, and American Democracy." In *Analytic Narratives,* ed. Robert Bates, Avner Greif, Margaret Levi, Jean-Laurent Rosenthal, and Barry R. Weingast. Princeton, NJ: Princeton University Press.

Weingast, Barry R. Forthcoming. "Constructing Self-Enforcing Democracy in Spain." In *Politics and Rational Choice,* ed. Joe Oppenheimer and Irwin Morris.

Weingast, Barry R., and William J. Marshall. 1988. "The Industrial Organization of Congress; Or, Why Legislatures, Like Firms, Are Not Organized as Markets." *Journal of Political Economy* 96: 132–63.

Weingast, Barry R., and Mark J. Moran. 1983. "Bureaucratic Discretion or Congressional Control: Regulatory Policymaking by the FTC." *Journal of Political Economy* 91: 765–800.

Weingast, Barry R., Kenneth A. Shepsle, and Christopher Johnsen. 1981. "The Political Economy of Benefits and Costs: A Neoclassical Approach to Distributive Politics." *Journal of Political Economy* 89: 642–64.

Wilcox, Clyde. 1997. "Racial and Gender Consciousness Among African-American Women: Sources and Consequences." *Women and Politics* 17: 73–94.

Wilensky, Harold L. 1976. *The 'New Corporatism': Centralization and the Welfare State.* Beverly Hills, CA: Sage.

Wilkinson, Steven I. 1998. "The Electoral Incentives for Ethnic Violence: Hindu-Muslim Riots in India." Paper prepared for delivery at the annual meeting of the American Political Science Association, Boston.

Wilkinson, Steven I. 2001. "Weak States and Low Violence? Explaining State Variations in Hindu-Muslim Riots." Paper presented at the Annual Meeting of the American Political Science Association, San Francisco, CA, August 30–September 2.

Will, George. 1986. "In Defense of Nonvoting." *The Morning After,* ed. George Will, 229–31. New York: Free Press.

Williams, Melissa. 1998. *Voice, Trust, and Memory.* Princeton, NJ: Princeton University Press.

Williamson, John. 1998. "The Emergent Development Policy Consensus." In *Development at a Crossroads: Uncertain Paths to Sustainability after the Neo-Liberal Revolution,* eds. Michael R. Carter, Jeffrey Cason, and Frederic Zimmerman. 33–46. Madison: Global Studies Program, University of Wisconsin.

Williamson, Oliver. 1985. *The Economic Institutions of Capitalism.* New York: Free Press.

Williamson, Oliver. 1996. *Mechanisms of Governance.* Oxford: Oxford University Press.

Willoughby, Westel Woodbury. 1896. *An Examination of the Nature of the State: A Study in Political Philosophy.* New York: Macmillan Co.

Wilson, Graham. 2000. "In a State?" *Governance* 13 (April): 235–42.

Wilson, James Q. 1973. *Political Organizations.* New York: Basic.

Wilson, William J. 1980. *The Declining Significance of Race.* 2d ed. Chicago: University of Chicago Press.

Wilson, William J. 1987. *The Truly Disadvantaged: The Inner City, The Underclass and Public Policy.* Chicago: University of Chicago Press.

Wilson, Woodrow. 1885. *Congressional Government: A Study in American Politics.* Boston: Houghton Mifflin.

Wilson, Woodrow. 1887. "The Study of Administration." *Political Science Quarterly* 2 (July): 197–222.

Wilson, Woodrow. 1919. *The Wisdom of Woodrow Wilson: Being Selections from his Thoughts and Comments on Political, Social, and Moral Questions.* Comp. Charles J. Herald. New York: Brentano's.

Wingrove, Elizabeth. 1999. "Interpellating Sex," *Signs* 24 (4): 869–93.

Winsor, Hugh. 1989. "Compromise Eases French Disputes on Muslim Veils in Schools." *New York Times,* 3 December, L17.

Winsor, Hugh. 1996. "Out of Canada: Sikh 'Mountie' Makes History in the New World." *The Independent,* 18 May.

Wirls, Daniel. 1986. "Reinterpreting the Gender Gap." *Public Opinion Quarterly* 50: 316–30.

Wirls, Daniel. 1999. "Regionalism, Rotten Boroughs, Race, and Realignment: The Seventeenth Amendment and the Politics of Representation." *Studies in American Political Development* 13: 1–30.

Wittman, Donald A. 1973. "Parties as Utility Maximizers." *American Political Science Review* 67: 490–98.

Wohlforth, William C. 1987. "The Perception of Power: Russia in the Pre-1914 Balance." *World Politics* 39 (April): 353–81.

Wohlforth, William C. 1993. *The Elusive Balance: Power and Perceptions during the Cold War.* Ithaca, NY: Cornell University Press.

Wohlforth, William C. 1994–95. "Realism and the End of the Cold War." *International Security* 19 (winter): 91–129.

Wohlforth, William C. 1999. "The Stability of a Unipolar World." *International Security* 24 (summer): 5–41.

Wolbrecht, Christina. 2000. *The Politics of Women's Rights.* Princeton, NJ: Princeton University Press.

Wolfe, Alan. 1997. "Is Civil Society Obsolete?" *Brookings Review*, 9–12. Washington, DC: Brookings.

Wolfers, Arnold. 1951. "The Pole of Power and the Pole of Indifference." *World Politics* 4: 39–63.

Wolfers, Arnold. 1962. *Discord and Collaboration.* Baltimore: Johns Hopkins University Press.

Wolfinger, Raymond E., and Steven J. Rosenstone. 1980. *Who Votes?* New Haven, CT: Yale University Press.

Wollheim, Richard. 1962. "A Paradox in the Theory of Democracy." In *Philosophy, Politics, and Society, Second Series*, ed. Peter Laslett and W.G. Runciman.

Wong, Cara. 1998. "Group Closeness." Report for the 1997 National Election Studies Pilot Study, www.umich.edu/~nes.

Wong, Janelle S. 2001. "Political Participation among Asian Americans: Mobilization or Selective Recruitment?" Paper prepared for the annual meeting of the American Political Science Association, San Francisco, CA.

Woo-Cumings, Meredith, ed. 1999. *The Developmental State.* Ithaca, NY: Cornell University Press.

Woo, Jung-en. 1991. *Race to the Swift: State and Finance in Korea's Industrialization.* New York: Columbia University Press.

Wood, Gordon S. 1966. "Rhetoric and reality in the American Revolution." *William and Mary Quarterly*, 3d. ser., 23: 3.

Woodruff, David. 2000. "Rules for Followers: Institutional Theory and the New Politics of Economic Backwardness in Russia." *Politics and Society* 28 (4): 437–82.

World Bank. 1991. *World Development Report 1991: The Challenge of Development.* New York: Oxford University Press.

World Bank. 1993. *The East Asian Miracle: Economic Growth and Public Policy.* New York: Oxford University Press.

Wright, Erik Olin, D. A. Gold, and C. Y. H. Lo. 1975. "Recent Developments in Marxist Theories of the Capitalist State." *Monthly Review* 27 (5, 6): 29–43, 36–51.

Wright, Quincy. 1965. *A Study of War.* Chicago: University of Chicago Press.

Wright, Robert. 2000. "Continental Drift." *New Republic* (4, 17 January): 435.

Wuthnow, Robert. 1989. *Communities of Discourse: Ideology and Social Structure in the Reformation, the Enlightenment, and European Socialism.* Cambridge, MA: Harvard University Press.

Wuthnow, Robert., ed. 1991. *Between States and Markets.* Princeton, NJ: Princeton University Press.

Yashar, Deborah J. 1997. *Demanding Democracy: Reform and Reaction in Costa Rica and Guatamala, 1870s–1950s.* Stanford, CA: Stanford University Press.

Yashar, Deborah. Forthcoming. *Contesting Citizenship: Indigenous Movements and the Postliberal Challenge in Latin America.*

Yinger, John. 1995. *Closed Doors, Opportunities Lost: The Continuing Costs of Housing Discrimination.* New York: Russell Sage.

Young, Iris Marion. 1989. "Polity and Group Difference. A Critique of the Ideal of Universal Citizenship." *Ethics.* 99: 250–74.

Young, Iris Marion. 1990. *Justice and the Politics of Difference.* Princeton, NJ: Princeton University Press.

Young, Iris Marion. 1992. "Books in Review: Identity/Difference, by William Connolly." *Political Theory* 20: 511–14.

Young, Iris Marion. 1994. "Gender as Seriality: Thinking about Women as a Social Collective." *Signs* 19: 713–38.

Young, Iris Marion. 1997. *Intersecting Voices: Dilemmas of Gender, Political Philosophy, and Policy.* Princeton, NJ: Princeton University Press.

Young, Iris Marion. 2000. *Inclusion and Democracy.* New York and Oxford: Oxford University Press.

Young, M. Crawford. 1976. *The Politics of Cultural Pluralism.* Madison: University of Wisconsin Press.

Young, M. Crawford. 1994. *The African Colonial State in Comparative Perspective.* New Haven, CT: Yale University Press.

Young, Oran R. 1991. "Political Leadership and Regime Formation: On the Development of Institutions in International Society." *International Organization* 45 (3): 281–308.

Young, Oran R. 1994. *International Governance. Protecting the Environment in a Stateless Society.* Ithaca, NY: Cornell University Press.

Young, Oran R., ed. 1997. *Global Governance: Drawing Insights from the Environmental Experience.* Cambridge: MIT Press.

Zacher, Mark. 2000. "The Territorial Integrity Norm: International Boundaries and the Use of Force." Unpublished paper, University of British Columbia.

Zakaria, Fareed. 1992. "Realism and Domestic Politics," *International Security* 17: 177–98.

Zakaria, Fareed. 1998. *From Wealth to Power: The Unusual Origins of America's World Role.* Princeton, NJ: Princeton University Press.

Zaller, John. 1992. *The Nature and Origins of Mass Opinion.* Cambridge: Cambridge University Press.

Zartman, William I., ed. 1995. *Collapsed States: The Disintegration and Restoration of Legitimate Authority.* Boulder, CO: Rienner.

Zechman, Martin J. 1979. "Dynamic Models of the Voter's Decision Calculus." *Public Choice* 34: 297–315.

Zielonka, Jan. 1998. "Constraints, Opportunities, and Choices in European Foreign Policy." In *Paradoxes of European Foreign Policy,* ed. Jan Zielonka. The Hague: Kluwer Law International.

Zuckert, Catherine, H. 1996. *Postmodern Platos.* Chicago: University of Chicago Press.

Zürn, Michael. 1992. *Interessen und Institutionen in der internationalen Politik: Grundlegung und Anwendung des situationsstrukturellen Ansatzes.* Opladen, GER: Leske und Budrich.

Zürn, Michael, and Christian Joerges, eds. Forthcoming. *Compliance in Modern Political Systems.*

Zürn, Michael. 1997. " 'Positives Regieren' jenseits des Nationalstaates." *Zeitschrift fur Internationale Beziehungen* 4 (1): 41–68.

Zysman, John. 1977. *Political Strategies for Industrial Order: State, Market, and Industry in France.* Berkeley: University of California Press.

Zysman, John. 1983. *Governments, Markets, and Growth.* Ithaca, NY: Cornell University Press.

Zysman, John. 1994. "How Institutions Create Historically Rooted Trajectories of Growth." *Industrial and Corporate Change* 3 (1): 243–83.

Zysman, John. 1996. "The Myth of a 'Global' Economy: Enduring National Foundations and Emerging Regional Realities." *New Political Economy* 1 (2):157–84.

Index of Names

Numbers in **boldface** refer to essay selections included in this volume.

Abbott, Andrew, 367, 711, 714, 715
Abbott, Kenneth W., 616
Abney, Glenn, 327, 339
Abram, Michael, 317
Abramowitz, Alan, 815
Abramson, Paul R., 440n, 453n, 537
Acemoglu, Daron, 365, 781
Achen, Christopher H., 464n
Ackerman, Bruce, 242, 243, 247, 262, 268, 419, 734
Adam, Heribert, 647
Adams, Julia, 468
Adams, William, 812
Adler, Emanuel, 598, 599, 606, 612, 615
Adorno, Theodor, 286, 289, 297, 298, 303
Agor, Westin, 358
Agüero, Felipe, 681
Ahern, David W., 475, 477
Albert, Mathias, 598
Albert, Michel, 385
Aldrich, John, 19, 318, 331, 353, 453n, 459, 537, 577, 706n, 733
Alesina, Alberto, 62, 135, 147, 151, 152, 158, 164, 165, 166, 167, 168, 169, 170, 359, 450n, 499, 631n, 655
Alexander, De Alva Stanwood, 313
Alexander, Gerard, 681
Alexander, William, 453n
Allen, Walter, 492n
Allison, Graham, 23
Allport, Floyd, 528
Almond, Gabriel A., 1, 2, 11, 18, 21, 805
Alstyne, Marshall Van, 499
Alt, James, 17, 24, 31, 127, 129, 132, **147–71**, 147, 159, 162, 163, 164, 166, 167, 168–69, 170, 327, 371n, 631n, 655, 755n
Althoff, Phillip, 317
Althusser, Louis, 37, 87
Altman, James, 12
Alvarez, Jose E., 228
Alvarez, Sonia, 101
Amenta, Edwin, 694n, 698

Ames, Barry, 327, 353, 358, 368
Aminzade, Ronald, 702
Amsden, Alice H., 38, 88, 111, 114, 349
Andersen, Joel, 313, 316
Andersen, Kristi, 460n, 467n, 469, 474, 480, 481
Anderson, Lisa, 694n, 695, 700, 707, 709
Anderson, Perry, 37
Andrews, David, 122
Andrews, Josephine, 360
Angrist, Joshua, 810n, 811
Ansolabehere, Stephen, 449n, 807
Antholis, William, 244
Appiah, Kwame Anthony, 543
Arato, Andrew, 14, 291–92, 405
Ardrey, Saundra, 440n, 475, 482
Arendt, Hannah, 286, 303, 304, 411, 418n, 423n
Aristotle, 4, 270, 410
Arneson, Eric, 494
Arnold, Laura W., 326, 338
Arreaza, Adriana, 166
Arrow, Kenneth J., 17, 18, 237, 260, 702
Art, Robert J., 223, 228, 230
Arter, David, 320
Ashley, Richard K., 203, 229
Aslund, Anders, 350, 359
Aspinwall, Mark D., 597
Atkeson, Lonna Rae, 449n
Auerswald, David, 77
Aumann, Robert J., 758n
Austen-Smith, David, 18, 22, 669, 760n, 794, 797
Avant, Deborah, 70, 79
Avineri, Shlomo, 411
Axelrod, Robert, 19, 670, 672, 674, 756
Ayala, Louis J., 451n
Ayres, Ian, 247

Baccaro, Lucio, 375, 380
Bachrach, Peter, 14, 15, 45, 437n
Bader, Veit, 404n, 411, 424
Badie, Bertrand, 71

Baechler, Jean, 62
Baer, Denise, 521, 522, 524n, 812
Bagehot, Sir Walter, 320, 323
Bagwell, Kyle, 143
Bailey, Michael, 133, 326, 338
Bailyn, Bernard, 687
Baldez, Lisa, 322, 339, 358
Baldwin, David A., 14, 16, 57, 60
Ball, Terence, 10
Balogh, Brian, 734
Baloyra, Enrique, 694n
Banaszak, Lee Ann, 694n
Banks, Jeffrey, 18, 669
Baqir, Reza, 162, 499
Baran, Paul, 347
Baratz, Morton S., 14, 15, 45
Barber, Benjamin, 14, 406, 514, 540
Barbieri, W., 244
Bard, Charles, 5
Barnes, Harry Elmer, 10–11
Barnett, Michael, 72, 212, 606
Baron, David P., 18, 19, 322, 330 , 669
Barrett, Andrew, 327
Barro, Robert J., 18, 24, 152, 154, 159,
        164, 351, 359, 365
Barros, Robert, 677
Barry, Brian, 14, 242, 273, 275, 276,
        422n, 558
Barsoom, Peter N., 214, 616, 756
Bartels, Larry, 807
Barth, Fredrik, 464n
Barzel, Yoram, 37, 38
Basu, Kaushik, 595n
Bates, Robert H., 17, 37, 44, 50, 52, 54,
        110, 115, 143, 344, 362, 364, 368,
        388, 584, 590, 598, 630n, 705, 710,
        725, 788n
Bauboeck, Rainer, 411, 420
Baumgartner, Frank R., 327, 703, 707
Bawn, Kathleen, 322, 324, 575, 577, 578,
        579, 580, 581, 582, 588, 591, 594,
        595, 669
Baxter, Sandra, 481, 482
Bayart, Jean-François, 646
Baynes, Kenneth, 139, 290, 306, 307, 308
Bayoumi, Tamim, 147, 166
Bazenguissa-Ganga, Remy, 647

Beard, Charles, 25
Beardsworth, Richard, 301
Beblawi, Hazern, 114
Beck, Nathaniel, 163, 178, 179, 786n, 787
Becker, Gary, 424n, 788
Beckwith, Karen, 480, 481
Bederman, Gail, 468, 473
Beer, Samuel, 632
Beiner, Ronald, 406, 412, 413, 428
Beissinger, Mark R., 48, 646
Beitz, Charles, 260
Bell, Julie Davis, 484
Bellin, Eva, 100, 114
Bendix, Reinhard, 18, 86, 87, 88, 89
Bendor, Jonathon, 760n
Bendyna, Mary E., 477
Benedict, Michael Les, 317
Benhabib, Seyla, 14, 289, 294–95, 303,
        399, **404–32**, 405, 416, 417n, 418n,
        419, 422, 427, 428
Bennett, Andrew, 699
Bennett, D. Scott, 182
Bennett, Jane, 286, 303
Bennett, Linda, 433n, 440n, 481
Bennett, Stephen Earl, 433n, 440n, 446n,
        481
Benoit, Kenneth, 177, 359
Bensel, Richard, 738, 739, 740, 741
Bentley, Arthur, 11–12, 25
Berejikian, Jeffrey, 596n
Berelson, Bernard, 22, 518
Berger, Suzanne, 65, 379, 656
Berg-Schlosser, Dirk, 258
Berk, Gerald, 728
Berk, R. A., 822
Berlin, Isaiah, 14
Berman, Sheri, 84, 101, 437n
Bermeo, Nancy, 88, 98
Bernhard, Michael, 134, 157, 158, 359
Bernhard, William, 335
Bernheim, B. Douglas, 164
Bernstein, Richard, 293, 294, 296
Berntson, Gary G., 497
Berry, Gregory, 326
Berry, Jeffrey M., 437n, 452, 456
Bertram, Christoph, 230
Besley, Timothy, 171

Best, Geoffrey, 184
Betts, Richard K., 205
Bhagwati, Jagdish N., 110
Bianco, William T., 328
Bienen, Henry, 96, 365, 366
Biersteker, Thomas J., 69, 606
Billig, M., 568n
Binder, Sarah A., 326, 327, 332, 336
Bismarck, Otto von, 520
Blainey, Geoffrey, 756, 781
Blair, Diane Kincaid, 467, 468
Blais, Andre, 163–64
Blake, Donald, 163–64
Blake, Michael, 551
Blank, Stephen, 653
Blee, Kathleen, 475
Bliss, Ray, 525
Block, Fred, 37
Blomkvist, Henry, 101
Blondel, Jean, 320
Blydenburgh, John, 806n
Bobo, Lawrence D., 449n, 496, 505, 506
Bodin, 33
Bogue 1980, 733
Bohman, James, 292
Bohn, Henning, 162, 166
Boix, Carles, 51
Boles, Janet K., 474
Boli, John, 598, 606, 611
Bollen, Kenneth, 634n
Bonchek, Mark S., 660
Bond, J. R., 812
Bonk, Kathy, 476
Books, John, 447n
Bordo, Michael, 60
Borrelli, Stephen A., 167
Börzel, Tanja, 597n, 615, 616, 617, 618
Bositis, David, 521, 522, 524n, 812
Boudon, Raymond, 54
Bowers, Jake, 470
Bowles, Samuel, 299
Bowman, John R., 377
Bowman, Karlyn H., 477
Box-Steffensmeier, Janet, 326, 338, 786n
Boyd, Richard W., 449n
Boyd, Robert, 594n
Boyer, Robert, 379, 385

Boyte, Harry C., 456
Brace, Kimball, 450n
Bradley, David, 394
Brady, David W., 317, 326, 327, 336, 338, 662n, 667, 669, 733
Brady, Henry E., 433n, 434n, 436n, 439, 440n, 441n, 442, 444n, 445n, 446n, 450n, 451n, 456, 458n, 460n, 527, 528, 784n, 805n, 807
Brand, Laurie A., 212
Brass, Paul R., 39, 648, 650
Bratton, Kathleen A., 485
Bratton, Michael, 88, 103, 694n
Brehm, John, 455n, 519
Breitmeier, Helmut, 616
Bremer, Stuart A., 177
Breuilly, John, 69
Brewer, John, 50
Brians, Craig Leonard, 449n
Bridges, Amy, 728, 752
Bright, 724
Brito, Dagobert L., 760n
Brock, William, 788n
Broder, David, 520, 521
Brodie, Bernard, 756
Brody, Richard A., 452, 807
Bromwich, David, 551n
Brooks, Stephen G., 197, 199, 205, 209, 217, 223, 773n, 776n
Brown, Clifford, 532
Brown, Michael Barratt, 347
Brown, Michael K., 496, 509
Brown, Robert D., 447n
Brown, Ronald, 506
Brown, Wendy, 306, 307, 308
Brownlee, Jason, 84
Brownstein, Charles, 807
Broz, J. Lawrence, 135, 140
Brubaker, Rogers, 361, 411, 542, 547
Brumberg, Bruce, 808, 825
Bruszt, L. 709
Brynjolfsson, Erik, 499
Buchanan, James M., 241, 242, 246, 249, 274, 279
Budge, Ian, 339
Bueno de Mesquita, Bruce, 23, 76, 174, 177, 179, 182

Bukovansky, Mlada, 197
Bull, Hedley, 605
Bullock, Charles S., III, 484
Bunce, Valerie, 48, 49, 648
Burchett, Justin I., 447n
Burden, Barry C., 447n, 449n
Burg, Steven L., 685n
Burke, Peter, 8
Burnham, Walter Dean, 521, 732, 733, 735
Burns, Arthur, 22, 151
Burns, Nancy E., 400, 433n, 440n, 444n, 449n, 450n, 455n, 462–87, 466, 467, 468, 472, 474, 477, 478, 480, 481, 482, 484, 485, 518, 805n
Burrell, Barbara C., 483, 485
Burt, Robert A., 240, 260, 261, 262
Burton, Michael, 679, 682
Busch, Marc, 144
Bush, George W., 535, 536n
Butler, David, 571, 575
Butler, Judith, 286, 294, 300, 405
Butterfield, Herbert, 756, 765
Buzan, Barry, 67, 203, 226
Byman, Daniel L., 211

Cacioppo, John T., 497, 498, 502
Cadogan, Alexander, 759
Cain, Bruce E., 320
Caldeira, Gregory, 1, 812
Calder, Kent E., 111
Calhoun, Craig, 54
Calhoun-Brown, Allison, 450n
Callaghy, Thomas M., 88, 112, 646
Callahan, Charles, 806
Calmfors, Lars, 154, 155, 156, 383
Calvert, Randall, 16, 150, 313, 402, 568–96, 578, 596n, 599, 609, 660n, 674
Cameron, A. Colin, 786n
Cameron, Charles, 17, 20, 321, 327, 328–29, 337–38, 339, 628, 662n, 663n, 784–804, 793n, 795n, 801
Cameron, David, 160, 163, 375, 376n, 652
Campbell, Andrea, 460, 710, 720, 721
Campbell, Angus, 568n, 575, 807
Campbell, Donald, 21, 22, 191, 194, 830

Campbell, Sally Howard, 179
Campillo, Marta, 153
Campos, Jose-E, 47
Canon, David T., 336, 509
Cantril, Hadley, 528
Caporaso, James A., 74, 631
Cardoso, Fernando Henrique, 87, 344, 347
Carens, Joe, 278, 406, 413, 415, 428, 432, 542
Carey, John M., 20, 42, 52, 53, 313, 322, 334–35, 339, 355, 357, 358, 368, 642
Carmines, Edward G., 705
Carpenter, Daniel P., 45, 54, 336
Carpenter, Jesse T., 377, 741
Carr, Edward Hallett, 56, 71, 198, 202, 203, 204, 210, 211
Carroll, Susan, 462, 467, 468, 478, 483, 484
Carruba, Clifford J., 335
Carsey, Thomas M., 327
Carterm Jimmy, 537
Casella, Alessandra, 61
Cassel, Carol A., 452n
Ceaser, James, 517
Cederman, Lars-Erik, 68, 70, 81
Chambers, Simone, 290
Chambers, William, 732
Chandra, Kanchan, 630n
Chang, Gordon H., 504n
Chang, Ha-Joon, 111
Chanley, Virginia, 513
Chappell, Henry W., 157
Charrad, Mounira, 694n, 697
Chase, William C., 127
Chaudhry, Kiren Aziz, 96, 114
Chavez, Rebecca Bill, 677
Chayes Handler, Antonia, 616, 756
Chayes, Abram, 616, 756
Checkel, Jeffrey T., 602, 606, 609, 616, 618, 619, 620
Chehabi, H. E., 96, 694n
Cheibub, José Antonio, 256, 357
Chin, M. L., 812
Chomsky, Noam, 659
Christensen, Thomas J., 183, 184, 185, 187, 188, 208, 211, 213, 222, 767

Christianson, Gale, 758
Christy, Carol, 479
Chrystal, K. Alec, 159
Chubb, John E., 22
Chwe, Michael Suk-Young, 592n
Cigler, Allan J., 546
Cioffi-Revilla, Claudio, 68
Citrin, Jack, 440n
Clapham, Christopher, 96
Clark, Cal, 472, 480
Clark, Janet, 472, 480, 484n
Clark, Terry, 541
Clark, William Rogers, 64, 135, 158
Clarke, Wes, 339
Clausen, Aage, 812
Clemens, Elisabeth S., 711, 745, 746, 752
Cleveland, Grover, 739
Clifford, James, 564
Clinton, Bill, 513
Clucas, Richard A., 326
Coase, Ronald, 660
Cohen, Benjamin J., 79, 138, 147, 151,
    152, 158, 164, 166, 168, 169
Cohen, Cathy J., 401, 473, **488–510**, 489,
    503
Cohen, G. A., 275, 404n, 405, 422
Cohen, Jean, 14, 22, 64, 292
Cohen, Linda R., 676n
Cohen, Raymond, 68
Cohen, Roberta S., 421, 469
Colburn, Forrest, 84, 95
Coleman, D. L., 431
Coleman, James S., 39, 437n, 515
Coleman, John J., 327, 734
Coleman, Jules, 282, 284
Coles, Romand, 14, 232, 233, **286–312**,
    293, 295, 298, 299
Collier, David, 87, 88, 97, 98, 367, 371n,
    630n, 633, 634n, 687, 693, 699,
    702, 703, 704, 714, 761n
Collier, Paul, 644, 649
Collier, Ruth Berns, 87, 88, 98, 100, 633,
    637, 638, 639, 687, 693, 699, 702,
    704
Collins, Patricia Hill, 501
Collins, Sharon, 500
Colombani, Jean-Marie, 428

Colomer, Josep, 359, 641, 669, 679n
Congdon, Peter, 786n
Connerly, Ward, 544
Connolly, William, 15, 300, 301–302, 303,
    305, 306, 567
Conover, Pamela Johnston, 449n, 467,
    468, 474, 475, 477, 478, 481
Constantini, Edmond, 484
Converse, Philip E., 21, 22, 575
Conway, M. Margaret, 433n, 475, 477
Conybeare, John, 138, 139
Cook, Elizabeth, A., 467n, 480
Cooper, Frederick, 542, 547
Cooper, Joseph, 317, 332, 336
Cooper, Richard N., 59, 121
Cooter, Robert, 282, 780, 781
Copeland, Dale C., 197, 204, 206, 208,
    215, 222, 224, 226
Coppedge, Michael, 634n
Cortell, Andrew P., 616, 618
Coser, Lewis, 697
Cosgrove, Kenneth M., 326, 338
Costain, Anne N., 474, 475
Cott, Nancy F., 473, 474, 481
Cotta, Maurizio, 320
Cover, Albert, 808, 825
Cowden, Jonathan A., 459n, 810n, 818
Cowhey, Peter F., 77
Cox, Gary W., 77, 313, 319, 325, 328, 330,
    335, 338, 449n, 577, 578, 642, 669,
    801
Cox, Robert, 15, 18, 19
Craig, Barbara Hinkson, 477
Craig, Jon, 166
Craik, Kenneth H., 484
Crain, R. L., 822
Crain, W. Mark, 147, 166
Crawford, Vincent, 67, 140, 595n
Crenshaw, Kimberlé, 465, 489, 501
Crenson, Matthew, 752
Crepaz, Markus, 375
Cress, Daniel M., 459n
Critchley, Simon, 301, 303
Crombez, Christophe, 322
Cronin, Bruce, 600, 606
Crook, Sara Brandes, 327, 336
Crozier, Michael, 523

Cruikshank, Barbara, 307
Cukierman, Alex, 152, 155, 156
Curtis, Kimberley, 286, 304
Cusack, Thomas R., 63, 653
Cutler, Claire A., 604

Dahl, Robert A., 1, 5, 14, 15, 79, 240,
    241, 245, 263, 461, 509, 634n, 640
Dallmayr, Fred, 298
Dalton, Russell J., 127, 434n
Damgaard, Erik, 320
Darcy, R. Robert, 484n
David, 172
Davies, James C., 644
Davis, Angela Y., 481
Davis, James W. Jr., 616, 618
Davis, Patricia, 450n
Davison, A. C., 786n
Dawes, Robyn, 807
Dawisha, Karen, 71
Dawson, 22
Dawson, Michael C., 401, 462n, 475, 476,
    488–510, 495, 496, 501, 502, 504,
    505, 506
Day, Neil, 436n
de Figueiredo, Rui J. P., 388, 584, 590,
    660n, 680, 683, 688, 781
De Haan, Jakob, 165, 167
de la Garza, Rodolfo O., 444n, 450n, 507,
    508
De Meur, Gisèle, 258
Deaux, Kay, 463, 479
DeHart, Jane Sherron, 472, 473, 478
Dehousse, Renaud, 74
Deleuze, Gilles, 286, 305
Delli Carpini, Michael X., 440n, 481, 514
DeNardo, James, 95, 650
Deng, Francis M., 421
Der Derian, James, 598
Derrida, Jacques, 286, 300, 302, 303, 311
Desch, Michael C., 197, 219, 227
De-Shalit, Avner, 411
DeSipio, Louis, 450n, 508
DeSoto, Hernando, 47
Desposato, Scott, 357
Destler, 129
Deudney, Daniel, 73

Dewey, John, 12
DeWinter, Lieven, 339
Diamond, Irene, 484
Diamond, Larry, 100, 101, 635, 679, 694n
DiCicco, Jonathan M., 200
Diermeier, Daniel, 313, 326, 332, 333–34,
    335, 799
Diesing, Paul, 175, 759
DiMaggio, Paul, 470, 608, 609, 611
Dion, Douglas, 321, 336
Dion, Stephanie, 163–64
Disch, Lisa, 304
Dixit, Avinash, 795n
Dixon, William, 179
Dobbin, Frank, 381
Dodd, Lawrence, 518
Dodson, Debra L., 484
Dolan, Kathleen, 477, 483
Donald, David, 317
Donald, Stephen, 796n
Doner, Richard F., 88
Donnelly, Jack, 199
Donohue, Jesse, 477
Dore, Ronald, 65, 379, 656
Döring, Herbert, 324, 339
Dornbusch, Rudiger, 350
dos Santos, Theotônio, 347
Downing, Brian M., 12, 38, 694, 707
Downs, Anthony, 19, 246, 458, 524, 569,
    571, 575n, 576
Downs, George W., 125, 214, 616, 756
Doyle, Michael W., 23, 177, 178, 694n,
    707
Drazen, Allan, 164, 359
Dreifus, Claudia, 551n
Drezner, Daniel, 215
Driffill, John, 154, 155, 156, 383
Dryzek, John S., 310, 596n
Duerst-Lahti, Georgia, 483
Duffield, John S., 143
Dumm, Thomas L., 307
Dunn, Frederick, 755, 778
Duverger, Maurice, 18, 354
Dworkin, Ronald, 262, 268, 271, 272,
    282, 284, 619

Eagly, Alice, 470, 471

Easter, Gerald, 48
Easterly, William, 499
Easton, David, 805
Ebbinghaus, Bernhard, 376, 384
Eccles, Jacqueline, 470, 472
Echeverri-Gent, John, 108
Eckstein, Harry, 18, 630n, 761n
Edin, Per-Anders, 167
Edwards, Bob, 436n, 437n
Edwards, George C., III, 327
Edwards, Rebecca, 474
Edwards, Sebastian, 168
Ehrenhalt, Alan, 518
Eichenberg, Richard, 127
Eichengreen, Barry, 60, 63–64, 122, 147, 166, 782
Eisenach, Eldon, 727–28, 734
Ekiert, Grzegorz, 694n
Elazar, Daniel, 450n
Elder, Charles D., 445n
Eldersveld, Samuel, 806, 812, 814
Elkins, Zachary, 141
Ellis, S. D. K., 647, 727
Ellis, Susan, 327, 336
Elman, Colin, 197, 201, 220, 228, 765, 773n
Elman, Miriam Fendium, 197, 201
Elms, Laurel, 456
Elster, Jon, 405, 474n, 589, 594n, 670, 692, 705
Ely, John Hart, 260
Emcke, Carolin, 404n
Enelow, James M., 575n, 576, 801
Engels, Friedrich, 36
Engerman, Stanley L., 46
Ensminger, Jean, 46
Epstein, Cynthia Fuchs, 470
Epstein, David, 20, 328, 339, 669, 801
Epstein, Lee, 676n
Epstein, Leon D., 247
Ericson, David, 730
Erikson, Erik H., 568n, 586
Erikson, Robert S., 446n, 815, 816, 818
Erkulwater, Jennifer, 445n
Ertman, Thomas, 12, 38, 50, 693, 699, 700, 701, 702, 703, 704, 707
Eskridge, William N. Jr., 667, 668n, 676n

Esping-Andersen, Gosta, 24, 651, 694n, 707, 710
Estevez-Abe, Margarita, 709
Esty, Daniel C., 645
Evans, Peter B., 35, 37, 44, 50, 57, 58, 63, 84, 87, 88, 90, 113, 344, 347, 660, 724
Eyerman, Joe, 177

Falcon, Angelo, 507
Farah, Barbara G., 484
Farber, Daniel, 676n
Farber, Henry, 180, 181, 220
Farley, Reynolds, 492n
Farrell, Theo, 220, 229
Faust, Jon, 170, 171
Fearon, James D., 23, 137, 148, 173, 175, 176, 177, 181, 189, 200, 216, 224, 228, 362, 544, 582, 583, 584, 587, 590, 598, 599, 604, 644, 645, 649, 679n, 683, 755n, 756, 763n, 765n, 767, 769, 775n, 780, 781, 802
Feaver, Peter D., 172
Feddersen, Timothy J., 326, 335
Feldman, Stanley, 495
Felker, Greg, 111
Fenno, Richard F., Jr., 316, 317, 318, 337
Ferejohn, John A., 18, 148, 162, 320, 322, 330, 591, 669n, 676n
Ferguson, Niall, 186
Fernandez, Raquel, 359
Ferner, Anthony, 379
Ferree, Karen E., 168
Fett, Patrick J., 326
Filer, John, 797, 799, 803
Filippov, Mikhail, 355
Finegold, Kenneth, 736, 744
Finger, Matthias, 613
Finnemore, Martha, 78, 604, 606, 609, 611, 613, 617
Fiorina, Morris, 19, 320, 339, 401, 437n, 511–41, 521, 525n, 530, 537, 571, 572, 573, 574, 576, 579, 590, 669, 801
Fiorito, Riccardo, 165
Firestone, Juanita M., 326
Fischer, Markus, 197, 216, 217

Fisher, R.A., 806
Fishkin, James M., 238, 242, 243, 288
Fishkin, James, 819
Fishlow, Albert, 112, 114, 346
Fiske, Susan T., 479
Flammang, Janet, 440n, 485
Flanagan, S., 18
Flathman, Richard E., 287
Fleron, Frederic J., Jr., 342, 359
Flora, Peter, 24, 694n, 704
Foley, Michael W., 436n, 437n
Follett, Mary Parker, 313
Foner, Eric, 501, 727
Forbath, William E., 299
Ford, Coit, III, 445n
Ford, Lynne E., 483
Fording, Richard C., 461n
Forgette, Richard, 326
Foucault, Michel, 14, 15, 239, 286, 300–301, 303, 307
Foweraker, Joe, 256
Fowlkes, Diane L., 484
Fox, William T. R., 755, 779
Fozouni, Bahman, 229
Francis, Wayne L., 339
Franck, Thomas M., 617, 619
Frank, Andre Gunder, 87, 347
Frank, Robert, 594n
Frankel, Benjamin, 199
Frankel, Jeffrey A., 64, 140
Franklin, Charles H., 576n
Franklin, Daniel P., 448n
Franklin, Mark N., 447n, 449n
Frankovic, Kathleen, 476
Franz, Linda M., 475
Franzese, Robert J., 48, 153, 155, 156, 161, 163, 164, 165, 168, 169, 376n
Fraser, Nancy, 404n
Freeman, Jo, 460n, 473, 474, 476
Freeman, Patricia, 485
Freer, Regina M., 504
Frickey, William, 668n, 676n
Friedberg, Aaron L., 218–19, 694n
Frieden, Jeffry A., 1, 24, 30–31, 118–46, 56, 59, 129, 140, 364, 767n
Friedland, Lewis, 456, 458n

Friedman, Milton, 24
Friedman, Thomas L., 226, 229
Friedson, Eliot, 3
Frye, Timothy, 360
Frymer, Paul, 509
Fudenberg, Drew, 595n, 795n
Fukuyama, Francis, 46
Fulcher, James, 377, 381n
Fulenwider, Clare Knoche, 482
Fuller, Hubert Bruce, 313

Gabel, Matthew, 127
Gallaher, Mirriam, 317
Galloway, George B., 317
Galston, William, 404, 411
Gamm, Gerald, 20, 233, 313–41, 335–36, 694, 719
Gant, Michael M., 446n
Ganz, Marshall, 460n, 707, 744
Garcia, F. Chris, 507
Garcia, John A., 507
Garcia-Bedolla, Lisa, 508
Garnham, David, 212
Garrett, Geoffrey, 24, 51, 59, 63, 122, 156, 158, 163, 380, 652, 654
Gartzke, Erik, 176, 194, 326, 798n
Gasiorowksi, Mark, 365, 366
Gaudet, Hazel, 22
Gauthier, David, 276
Gaventa, John, 14
Gavin, Michael, 165
Gay, Claudine, 449n
Geddes, Barbara, 23, 38, 52, 69, 99, 115, 233, 313, 342–70, 343, 359, 360, 364, 631n, 633, 643, 713
Geer, John, 519
Geiger, Kim, 735, 752
Gellner, Ernest, 44, 69
Gelman, Andrew, 517, 786n
Gely, Rafael, 795n
George, Alexander, 699, 715, 760, 761
Gerber, Alan S., 17, 326, 338, 441n, 453n, 628, 784, 787, 805–32, 814, 815, 816, 818n, 820, 826
Gerber, Elisabeth R., 339, 801
Gerring, John, 734

Gerschenkron, Alexander, 651n, 700, 702
Gertzog, Irwin N., 483, 806n
Gervasoni, Carlos, 351
Geuss, Raymond, 26
Geva, N., 812
Giavazzi, Francesco, 140, 168
Giddens, Anthony, 463, 500
Giddings, Paula, 481
Gilens, Martin, 505, 506
Gilliam, Franklin D., 449n, 498, 505
Gilligan, Thomas W., 127, 132, 140, 329, 669, 801
Gilman, Howard, 741
Gilpin, Robert, 24, 62, 199, 206, 215, 226, 229, 756, 781
Gilroy, Paul, 500
Ginsberg 1976, 733
Ginsburg, Benjamin, 536
Ginsburg, Ruth Bader, 261
Gintis, Herbert, 299
Githens, Marianne, 462
Gitlin, Todd, 299
Glaser, Charles L., 172, 177, 183, 184, 186, 190, 197, 204, 205, 223, 756, 767, 771, 772, 773, 776, 777n, 818, 822
Glick, P., 479
Glover, Jonathan, 553n
Gobetti, Daniela, 260
Goel, M. L., 433n, 440n
Goertzel, Ted, 476
Goffman, Erving, 470, 472, 475
Goidel, Robert K., 455n
Gold, D. M., 87
Goldberg, Ellis, 260
Goldberg, Pinelopi Koujianou, 799
Golden, Miriam, 375, 379, 395, 652
Goldfield, Michael, 744
Goldsmith, Jack L., 228
Goldstein, Judith, 122, 133, 139, 140, 144, 599, 694
Goldstone, Jack A., 54, 93, 644, 694n, 703, 704
Goldthorpe, J. H., 713
Goldwater, Barry, 517
Goodin, Robert E., 2
Goodman, John, 122

Goodnow, Frank, 6, 25
Goodwin, Jeff, 694n, 712, 714
Goodwin, Jeff, 95
Gorbachev, Mikhail, 404
Gordon, 152, 154
Gordon, Sanford, 786n
Gore, Al, 529, 536n
Gosnell, Harold, 11, 433, 805, 806, 812, 823, 824
Gottlieb, Gidon, 83
Gottschalk, Marie, 697, 742
Gould, Andrew, 694n
Gould, John, 781
Gourevitch, Peter, 129, 377, 630n, 643n, 651, 655, 694n
Gowa, Joanne, 130, 138, 180, 181, 213, 214, 220, 756
Graham, Hugh Davis, 668n, 743
Grambsch, Patricia, 786n
Granovetter, Mark, 471, 594n
Grassi, Davide, 640
Grassmuck, Sherri, 469
Gray, Virginia, 475
Green, Donald Philip, 17, 178, 181, 220, 237, 246, 368, 441n, 445n, 453n, 459n, 628, 630n, 716, 784, 787, 805–32, 810n, 814, 815, 816, 818n, 820, 826
Green, Matthew, 805n, 814
Green, Michael J., 230
Greenberg, Anna, 450n, 481
Greene, Jack, 687
Greene, William, 809
Greenstein, Fred, 149, 469
Greenstone, J. David, 518, 729, 730, 753
Greenstone, P. David, 4
Greif, Avner, 17, 39, 79, 150, 388, 598, 672, 686, 687
Grieco, Joseph M., 199, 213, 214, 756, 771, 772, 773n
Grier, Eric E., 448n
Griffin, James, 280–81
Griffin, Robert, 326
Griffiths, Franklyn, 343
Grilli, Vittorio, 135, 147, 152
Grisanti, Alejandro, 163, 166
Grob, Douglas, 807

Grofman, Bernard, 326
Grose, Peter, 217
Groseclose, Timothy, 326, 801
Grossman, Gene M., 125, 169, 799
Gruber, Lloyd, 214
Grzymala-Busse, Anna, 38, 48
Guarnaschelli, Serena, 802
Guatarri, Felix, 286, 305
Guéhenno, Jean-Marie, 57
Guinier, Lani, 252
Gulick, Edward, 756
Gunther, Richard, 679, 682
Gurin, Gerald, 440n, 475
Gurin, Patricia, 440n, 467, 472, 474, 475, 506
Gurr, Ted Robert, 644, 645
Gutmann, Amy, 14, 238, 242, 288, 401, 402, 404n, 418n, 542–67, 550n
Guzmán, Eugenio, 355

Haas, Peter M., 140, 612, 615
Habermas, Jürgen, 14, 37, 260, 269, 289, 290, 291–92, 293, 294, 295–96, 297, 299, 307, 309, 310, 419, 508, 563, 596n, 602
Hacker, Jacob S. 381, 393, 694n, 697, 699, 700, 701, 707, 710, 742
Hacker-Cordón, Casiano, 243, 244
Haerpfer, Christian, 635n
Hager, Gregory L., 326
Haggard, Stephan, 38, 88, 102, 103, 112–13, 114, 133, 349, 350, 351, 694n
Hagopian, Frances, 35, 88, 344
Halbertal, Moshe, 553, 554
Haldenius, Axel, 24
Hall, Peter A., 16, 38, 51, 54, 75, 149, 155, 156, 372, 373, 376, 384, 385, 388n, 597, 650, 652, 653, 656, 657, 660, 691, 693, 699, 706, 707, 709, 711, 714
Hall, Richard L., 326, 328, 338
Hall, Rodney Bruce, 217, 600, 606
Haller, Hans, 595n
Hallerberg, Mark, 64, 135, 165, 167
Hamilton, Alexander, 245, 533
Hamilton, W. D., 594n

Hamm, Keith E., 327, 335
Hanchard, Michael G., 509
Handley, Lisa, 450n
Hansen, John Mark, 441, 453, 454, 475, 514, 693, 694, 746, 812
Hansen, Susan B., 449n, 455n, 475, 481
Harden, Ian, 147, 165
Hardin, Russell, 47, 53, 151, 258, 555n, 582, 585, 587, 588, 589, 590, 591, 594, 595, 669
Harding, 724
Hardy-Fanta, Carol, 482
Hare, R. M., 280
Harlow, Ralph Volney, 313
Harmel, Robert, 327, 335
Harmon-Martin, Sheila F., 482
Harris, Frederick C., 450n, 481, 826
Harris-Lacewell, Melissa, 495, 500, 504, 507
Harrison, Selig, 230, 474
Harsanyi, John C., 280, 281, 759, 760
Hart, Robert A., Jr., 177
Hart, Vivien, 694
Hartman, D. A., 528
Hartmann, George, 806
Hartz, Louis, 4, 725, 726, 727, 728, 729, 730, 731, 732, 733, 734, 750, 752
Harvey, Anna L., 471, 474, 475, 476, 485, 579, 580, 581, 582, 586, 589, 590, 591, 594, 595, 706n, 746
Hasenclever, Andreas, 610, 611
Haslanger, Sally, 465
Haspel, Moshe, 338
Hastie, T. J., 786n
Hattam, Victoria. 694n, 695, 728
Hauck, Robert, xiv
Haufler, Virginia, 604
Havrilesky, Thomas, 157
Hayek, Friedrich A., 23, 24, 267, 271, 274, 277, 279
Haynie, Kerry L., 485
Hayward, Clarissa, 239
Hechter, Michael, 45, 54, 70, 71
Heckman, James J., 466, 499, 784, 785, 786, 825
Heclo, Hugh, 710
Hedlund, Ronald D., 314

Heebner, A. L., 822
Hegel, Georg Wilhelm Friedrich, 548
Heidenheimer, Arnold J., 24, 694n
Held, David, 289, 407, 427
Helleiner, Eric, 64
Heller, William B., 322
Helliwell, John F., 62, 63
Hellman, Gunther, 213
Helpman, Elhanan, 125, 169, 799
Henderson-King, Donna, 475
Henning, C. Randall, 128
Henning, R., 138
Henry, Ann R., 467, 468
Herbst, Jeffrey, 72, 83, 84, 112, 646
Hero, Rodney E., 326, 509
Herrick, Rebekah, 326, 484
Herrigel, Gary, 657
Herring, Ronald J., 108, 112
Herz, John H., 56, 57, 73, 756, 771n, 772, 773
Herzog, Don, 473
Hess, Robert D., 469
Hibbing, John R., 326, 327, 336, 477, 520, 537, 538
Hibbs, Douglas A., 644n, 651n, 652
Hicks, Alexander M., 162, 163, 394, 694n
Higginbotham, Evelyn Brooks, 465, 474, 493, 501
Highton, Benjamin, 448n
Higley, John, 679, 682
Hill, David, 448n, 450n, 461n
Hinich, Melvin J., 575n, 576, 579, 660, 801
Hinkley, D. V., 786n
Hinton-Andersson, Angela, 461n
Hirczy de Miño, Wolfgang P., 449n
Hirschl, Ran, 263
Hirschman, Albert O., 109, 346
Hirschmann, Nancy, 465
Hirshleifer, Jack, 795n
Hirst, Paul, 62, 226
Hiscox, Michael J., 133
Hitler, Adolf, 759
Hix, Simon, 80
Hobbes, Thomas, 33, 36, 43, 198, 227, 239, 245, 773
Hobsbawm, E. J., 69, 411
Hobson, John M., 38

Hochschild, Jennifer L., 509
Hoeffler, Anke, 644, 649
Hoffman, Erik, 342
Hoffman, Paul, 525
Hoffman, Stanley, 229
Hogan, Robert E., 449n
Holborn, Hajo, 21
Holden, Matthew, Jr., 17
Hollinger, David, 566
Hollingsworth, J. Rogers, 379, 385
Hollis, Martin, 598
Holmes, Stephen, 14, 242, 245
Holt, Thomas C., 492, 493, 494
Honig, Bonnie, 15, 286, 301, 303, 309–10, 511n
Honneth, Axel, 289, 548, 557n
Hood, M. V., III, 326
hooks, bell, 465
Hopf, Ted, 187, 224
Horn, Jody D., 484
Horowitz, Donald L., 103, 250, 253, 254, 352, 644, 683
Hoskin, Gary, 358
Hough, Jerry F., 343, 646
Hovland, Carl, 806
Howard, Christopher, 694n, 697, 744
Howell, Chris, 371n, 374
Howell, William, 321, 536
Hritzuk, Natasha, 444n
Hsiao, Hsin-Huang Michael, 638n
Htun, Mala, 694n, 697
Huber, Evelyne, 376, 391, 392, 393, 694n, 699, 702, 707, 710, 719, 798
Huber, John D., 20, 313–41, 321, 322, 328, 332, 335, 339
Huber, John, 371n, 660n
Huckfeldt, Robert, 441n, 447n, 472, 812, 819
Huddy, Leonie, 477, 481, 495
Huitt, Ralph K., 316, 317
Humboldt, Wilhelm von, 423
Hume, David, 36
Humphrey, Hubert, 517
Hunter, Wendy, 364
Huntington, Samuel P., 87, 92, 93, 94, 97, 98, 101, 103, 246, 255, 257, 343, 523, 646, 723, 752

Hurd, Ian, 619
Hurwitz, John, 807
Husami, Ziyad I., 274
Hutchcroft, Paul D., 88
Hutchings, Vincent L., 326
Huth, Paul K., 172, 173, 190, 192, 224
Huttenback, 72
Hyman, Richard, 379
Hyndman, Patricia, 422n

Iglitzin, Lynne B., 469
Iida, Keisuke, 140
Ikenberry, G. John, 38, 57, 75, 694n
Im, Hyug Baeg, 98, 694n
Imbens, Guido, 811
Immergut, Ellen, 694n, 695, 707
Inglehart, Ronald, 635
Inman, Robert P., 147, 166
Intriligator, Michael, 760n
Irwin, Douglas A., 60, 133
Isaac, Jeffrey C., 304, 405
Iversen, Torben, , 51, 63, 154, 155, 156,
    162, 374, 376n, 380, 381, 382, 386,
    394n, 651, 652, 653, 709
Iyengar, Shanto, 440n, 449n, 498, 505, 807

Jackman, Mary R., 464, 465, 467, 471,
    475, 479
Jackman, Robert W., 437n
Jackman, Simon, 786n
Jackson, James, 506
Jackson, John E., 576
Jackson, Robert A., 442n, 447n, 448n, 449n
Jackson, Robert H., 72, 91
Jackson, Robert Max, 377
Jacobson, David, 416
Jacobson, Gary, 815, 816
Jamal, Amaney Ahmad, 352, 482
James, Patrick, 199
James, Scott, 336, 728, 735, 736
Jay, John, 245
Jay, Martin, 289
Jefferson, Thomas, 412
Jenkins, Jeffery A., 335–36
Jennings, Jeanette, 485
Jennings, M. Kent, 444n, 470, 472, 480,
    484

Jennings, Sir Ivor, 320
Jenson, James, 694n, 697
Jepperson, Ron, 78, 597n, 604, 606, 611,
    707
Jervis, Robert, 16, 173, 183, 204, 205,
    214, 229, 755n, 756, 765n, 773
Jessop, Bob, 37
Jewell, Malcolm E., 315
Jillson, Calvin, 336, 735
Joerges, Christian, 619
Johnsen, Christopher, 160, 165, 533
Johnson, Chalmers A., 88, 110, 111, 115
Johnson, James, 596n
Johnson, Simon, 365
Johnston, Alastair Iain, 78
Jomo, K. S., 111
Jones, Bryan D., 327, 703, 707
Jones, Charles O., 67, 203, 277, 316, 317,
    318
Jones, Leroy P., 111
Jones, Mark, 361, 368
Jones-Correa, Michael, 508
Jørgenson, Knud Erik, 74
Jung, Courtney, 250
Junn, Jane, 443, 482

Kagan, Korina, 217
Kagan, Shelly, 275
Kahler, Miles, 13, 29–30, 42, **56–83**, 57,
    65, 72, 74, 755n
Kahn, Kim Fridkin, 449n, 481, 482
Kahneman, Daniel, 692
Kalyvas, Stathis N., 342, 644, 648
Kang, David C., 38, 48
Kang, Heejoon, 181
Kant, Immanuel, 177, 178, 303, 416, 419
Kanter, Rosabeth Moss, 471
Kaplan, Abraham, 17
Kaplan, Cynthia S., 442n
Kaplan, Morris, 404n, 765
Kaplow, Louis, 285
Kapstein, Ethan B., 215
Karl, Terry Lynn, 694n
Karl, Terry R., 96
Karnig, Albert K., 484
Kateb, George, 287, 557, 562
Kathlene, Lyn, 327, 471, 485, 486

Katz, Harry, 379
Katz, Jonathan N., 163, 335, 336
Katzenstein, Mary Fainsod, 462n, 471, 474, 475, 476
Katzenstein, Peter J., 16, 19, 37, 57, 78, 87, 375n, 396, 600, 604, 630n, 651, 655, 657, 694n, 782
Katznelson, Ira, xiii–xv, 1–26, 16, 24, 286, 313, 371n, 404n, 462n, 597n, 630n, 687n, 694n, 711, 724, 735, 752, 753, 755n, 784n
Kaufman, Robert A., 694n
Kaufman, Robert G., 102, 206, 212, 350
Kaufman, Robert R., 103, 114, 351
Kaufmann, Chaim D., 183, 184, 186, 205, 216, 218, 223, 648
Kaufmann, Karen M., 449n, 477, 478
Kaunda, Kenneth, 584
Kaysen, Carl, 205
Keck, Margaret E., 60, 61, 62, 612, 613, 620, 693
Keech, William, 152, 159
Keeley, Lawrence, 67
Keeter, Scott, 440n, 481, 514
Kefauver, Estes, 517
Kegley, Charles W., Jr., 197, 199
Keith, Linda Camp, 617
Keller, Morton, 531n
Kelley, Robin, 500, 501
Kelly, Rita Mae, 484
Kennedy, John F., 517
Kennedy, Paul, 781
Kenney, Patrick J., 449n
Kenny, Lawrence W., 339, 797, 799, 803
Kenski, Henri, 477
Keohane, Robert O., xiii, 23, 46, 56, 57, 59, 60, 121, 140, 142, 143, 197, 199, 200, 203, 213, 214, 220, 223, 597, 599, 602, 604, 605, 611, 672, 674, 713, 756, 761n, 782
Kerber, Linda, 410
Kessler, Daniel, 326, 338
Key, Valdimer O., 19, 541n, 732
Keyssar, Alexander, 460
Kiewiet, D. Roderick, 167, 314, 323, 326, 328, 338, 663, 818
Kim, Claire Jean, 462n, 465, 492, 494, 503
Kim, Jae-on, 479
Kimber, MaryLee, 630n
Kinder, Donald, 462n, 465, 478, 498, 499, 505, 506, 526, 807
Kindleberger, Charles Poor, 138
King, David, 513
King, Gary, 194, 517, 713, 761n, 784n, 786n, 787, 805n
King, James D., 450n
King, Ronald F., 327, 336
Kirkpatrick, Jeane J., 483, 484
Kirshner, Jonathan, 213, 214, 225
Kiser, Edgar, 38, 54
Kissinger, Henry, 23
Kitschelt, Herbert, 48, 386, 704, 707
Klatch, Rebecca E., 472, 478
Klein, Benjamin, 780, 781
Klein, Ethel, 440n, 475, 476
Kleppner, Paul, 525
Kline, Harvey, 358
Klingeman, Hans-Dieter, 2
Kloppenberg, James T., 4
Klotz, Audie, 612, 621
Kluegel, James R., 506
Klyza, Christopher, 748
Knack, Stephen, 448n
Knight, Jack, 46, 676n, 692
Knoke, David, 440n
Knorr, Klaus, 172
Knutsen, Torbjorn, 755n
Koch, Jeffrey, 449n
Koh, Harold Hongju, 619
Kohli, Atul, 18, 30, 39, 84–117, 88, 102, 103, 115
Kolko, Gabriel, 391n
Kollman, Ken, 22, 475, 476
Kontopoulos, John T., 163, 168
Kontopoulos, Yianos, 162, 165, 166, 167
Koo, Hagen, 638n
Kopits, George, 166
Koslowski, Rey, 197
Kowert, Paul, 78
Kramer, Gerald, 812
Krasner, Stephen D., 23, 37, 69, 78, 138, 142, 214, 604, 610, 694n, 756, 782
Krasno, Jonathan, 815, 816

Kratochwil, Friedrich V., 69, 217, 599, 600, 604, 605, 618

Krehbiel, Keith, 20, 21, 140, 321, 326, 328, 329–30, 338, 662n, 667, 669, 801

Kreppel, Amie, 48

Kreps, David M., 140, 148, 151

Kreps, David, 578, 579n, 759, 760n, 761

Krieckhaus, Jonathan, 112

Kristeva, Julia, 304

Krosnick, Jon, 810n, 825

Kroszner, Randall, 133

Krueger, Anne O., 43–44

Krugman, Paul, 758, 763

Kryder, Daniel, 694n, 734, 735, 752

Kugler, Jacek, 756, 781

Kuhonta, Erik M., 84, 108

Kukathas, Chandran, 553n

Kume, Ikuo, 387, 395, 397, 656

Kuper, Andrew, 310

Kuran, Timur, 194, 592n, 649

Kurth, James, 700, 702, 704

Kydd, Andrew, 177, 190, 200, 205, 210, 223, 756, 776n

Kydland, Finn E., 151

Kymlicka, William, 14, 406, 413, 428, 429, 546, 549, 552, 553n, 559n, 562

La Ferrara, Eliana, 450n

Labs, Eric J., 206, 207, 212, 771n

Laclau, Ernesto, 239, 299, 405

Lacy, Dean, 447n, 449n

Ladd, Everett Carll, 260, 455n, 477, 514, 521

Laffey, Mark, 598

LaFrance, Marianne, 463, 479

Laitin, David D., 1, 17, 45, 69, 71, 83, 172, 344, 352, 362, 363, 369, 545, 580, 585, 586, 587, 588, 589, 591, 594, 595, 599, 625, 626, **630–659**, 644, 645, 649, 683

Lakatos, Imre, 201, 570, 572

Lake, Celinda C., 477

Lake, David A., 56, 57, 65, 73, 81, 137, 138, 182, 200, 216, 781

Lal, Deepak, 346, 349

Lalman, David, 177, 179

Lambert, Rob, 652, 657n

Landes, Joan, 410

Landes, William M., 499, 781

Landman, Todd, 68

Lane, Philip R., 165

Lane, Robert, 466

Lange, Peter, 158, 375, 379, 630n, 652, 707

Lansing, Marjorie, 481, 482

Lapid, Yosef, 69, 600

LaPorta, R., 365

Larson, Magali Sarfatti, 3

Lassen, David Dreyer, 162, 167

Lasswell, Harold, 11, 17

Laudan, Larry, 201

Lauth, Thomas P., 327, 339

Laver, Michael J., 19, 134, 321, 324, 328, 332, 335, 338, 339, 669

Lawrence, Eric D., 326

Lawrence, Robert Z., 63

Lax, Jeffrey, 793n

Layne, Christopher, 180, 213, 218, 220, 228

Lazarsfeld, Paul, 21, 22, 518

Leal, Francisco, 358

LeBlanc, Steven A., 67

Leblang, 134

Lebow, Richard Ned, 173, 197

Lee, Frances E., 327

Lee, Lung-Fei, 795n

Lee, Marcia Manning, 467

Lee, Taeku, 507

Lees, John D., 320, 334

Leffler, Melvyn, 217

LeFort, Claude, 307

Legro, Jeffrey W., 78, 199, 200, 221, 616

Lehmbruch, Gerhard, 652

Lehoucq, Frabrice E., 48

Leighley, Jan, 433n, 440n, 441n, 442n, 444n, 448n, 450, 455n, 461n

Lemke, David, 756, 781

Leng, Russell, 194

Lerner, Gerda, 481

Leuchtenberg, William, 722

Levi, Margaret, 13, 17, 29, **33–55**, 48, 50, 54, 56, 79, 260, 365, 388, 598

Levinas, 302

Levine, R., 366

Levitsky, Steven, 634n

Levitt, Steven D., 326
Levitt, Steven, 815
Levy, Brian, 676n, 677
Levy, Jack S., 172, 183, 189, 200, 205, 212
Levy, Jacobs, 550
Levy, Marc A., 143
Lewis, Peter, 112
Leys, Colin, 347
Liberman, Peter, 206, 214, 215, 225
Lichbach, Mark I., 630n, 632
Lieber, Keir A., 197, 205
Lieberman, Robert C., 509, 743
Lieberson, Stanley, 367, 713
Liebert, Ulrike, 320
Lien, Da-Hsiang Donald, 37
Lien, Pei-te 504, 507
Liese, Andrea, 617, 621
Lijphart, Arend, 19, 103, 249, 434n, 446n, 447n, 540n, 630n, 761n
Limongi, Fernando, 18, 49, 100, 256
Lin, Ann Chih, 482
Lincoln, Abraham, 729, 730
Lindblom, Charles, 1, 2, 5, 15, 24, 25
Linz, Juan J., 19, 96, 98, 101, 103, 256, 636, 640, 642, 679, 681n, 694n, 715
Lippi, Francesco, 155, 156
Lippincott, Benjamin, 4
Lippmann, Walter, 21
Lipset, Seymour Martin, 18, 92, 93, 100, 101, 255, 512, 633, 634, 635
Lipsky, Michael, 43
Lipson, Charles, 139
Lipton, Michael, 110
Little, Daniel, 707
Little, I. M. D., 349
Little, Richard, 67, 203
Livermore, Seward W., 317
Lo, C. Y. H., 87
Locke, John, 20, 36, 550n, 750
Locke, Richard M., 375, 380
Lockerbie, Brad, 441n, 812
Loewenberg, Gerhard, 313, 314
Lohmann, Susanne, 134, 147, 153, 158, 362, 646
Londregan, John, 328, 351, 358, 365, 366, 368, 643, 663, 664n, 666n, 677
Loomis, Burdett A., 546

Lowe, Laura, 825
Lowell, A. Lawrence, 313, 340
Lowenstein, 246
Lowi, Theodore, 22, 742, 749
Lowry, Robert C., 147, 163, 164, 166, 168–69, 170, 327
Lucas, Robert E., Jr., 164
Luciani, Giacomo, 114
Luebbert, Gregory M., 12, 377n, 637, 638, 639, 643, 702, 704, 709
Luehrmann, Laura M., 327
Luker, Kristin, 472, 478
Lukes, Steven, 14, 15, 550
Lumsdaine, Arthur, 806
Luong, Pauline Jones, 38, 359, 694, 720
Lupia, 147
Luskin, Robert C., 452n
Lustick, Ian, 631n, 694n
Lust-Okar, Ellen, 352, 370
Lynch, 70
Lynn-Jones, Sean, 183, 197, 204, 205, 211, 223, 771n, 773n, 776n
Lyons, William, 446n, 453n

Macedo, Stephen, 238, 411
Machiavelli, Niccolò, 198, 211, 240, 263, 264
MacIntyre, Aladair, 77, 299
MacIntyre, Andrew, 88, 296
Mack, Andrew, 230
Mack, Eric, 267
Mackie, Gerry, 237
MacKinnon, Catherine, 464, 465, 467n, 565
MacKuen, Michael, 818
MacManus, Susan A., 484
Madison, James, 245, 437, 540, 546, 737
Magar, Eric, 338, 355
Magee, Stephen, 788n
Maggi, Giovanni, 143, 799
Mahajan, Harpreet, 477
Mahon, Rianne, 380
Mahoney, James, 637n, 639, 694n, 699, 714, 715, 84, 97, 99, 367
Mainwaring, Scott, 357, 360, 368
Maioni, Antonia, 694n
Maisel, Richard, 450n

Malanchuk, Oksana, 440n, 475
Mallick, Ross, 108
Malloy, James, 343
Maltzman, Forrest, 326, 338
Mamdani, Mahmood, 257, 646
Mandel, Ruth B., 484
Manion, Melanie, 370
Manley, John F., 316
Mann, Michael, 37
Manow, Philip, 376, 378, 384
Mansbridge, Jane J., 238, 436n, 472, 473, 478, 535n, 594n
Mansfield, Edward D., 77, 125, 138, 756, 798
Maoz, Ze'ev, 177, 178, 179, 180, 220
March, James G., 600, 601, 604, 607, 608, 611, 614, 660, 723
Mares, Isabela, 378, 379, 381, 382
Margalit, Avishai, 547n, 548, 553, 554
Marinucci, Carla, 525n, 536n
Marks, Brian A., 676n, 707
Marks, Stephen, 780, 781
Marshall, T. H., 410, 411
Marshall, William J., 330, 387n
Martin, 23, 24, 60
Martin, Andrew, 375
Martin, Cathie Jo, 77, 371n, 376, 391, 392
Martin, Lisa L, 23, 30–31, 118–46, 122, 123, 124, 142, 143, 144, 200, 220, 605, 610, 630n, 756, 784n
Martinez, Julia, 564, 565
Martinez, Michael D., 448n
Marx, Anthony W., 107, 361, 694n
Marx, Karl, 15, 23, 33, 86, 92, 94, 239, 274, 307, 412, 727, 732
Maschler, Michael, 758n
Masciandaro, Donato, 135
Maskin, Eric, 595n
Mastanduno, Michael, 57, 197, 212, 214, 219, 225
Masten, Scott, 150, 151
Mathews, Donald, 472, 473, 478
Mathews, Jessica, 225
Mattei, Laura R. Winsky, 486
Matthews, Donald R., 316
Matthews, John, 214, 225
Matthews, Steven, 663n

Maxfield, Sylvia, 64, 153
Mayer, Peter, 610, 611
Mayhew, David R., 21, 317, 318, 325, 327, 337, 338, 339, 511n, 517, 532, 734
McAdam, Doug, 45, 459n, 471, 473, 614, 694n, 703, 718
McCain, John, 529
McCarthy, John D., 459n, 525n, 614
McCarthy, Thomas, 293, 296, 299
McCarty, Nolan M., 339., 663n, 801, 803
McClain, Paula D., 509
McCloskey, D. N., 201
McCloskey, Herbert, 525
McConachie, Lauros G., 313
McConnell, Michael W., 550n
McCormick, Richard L., 5, 734
McCubbins, Mathew D., 77, 147, 167, 168, 319, 323, 325, 328, 330, 663, 669, 676n
McDermott, Monika L., 481
McDermott, Rose, 818
McDonagh, Eileen, 753
McDonald, Keith M., 3
McDonald, Michael, 514
McDonough, Peter, 635n
McGerr, Michael, 533, 534n
McGillivray, Fiona, 132, 134
McGlen, Nancy, 467
McGovern, George, 517
McGrath, Wilma E., 481
McGregor, Rob Roy, 157
McKay, Derek, 189
McKelvy, Richard, 807
McKeown, Timothy J., 761
McMillion, Barry, 805n
McNulty, John E., 446n
McPhee, William, 518
McPherson, J. Miller, 471
Mearsheimer, John J., 197, 200, 204, 206, 207, 208, 209, 210, 213, 218, 219, 220, 222, 225, 228, 756, 771, 772, 773n, 781
Mehta, Pratap, 404n
Meinecke, Friedrich, 198
Melnick, R. Shep, 536, 707
Meltzer, Allan, 128, 159

Menchaca, Martha, 450n
Mendelberg, Tali, 505, 506
Mercer, Jonathan, 173, 224, 227
Merlo, Antonio, 799
Merriam, Charles, 11, 12, 25
Merrill, Horace Samuel, 317
Merrill, Marion Galbraith, 317
Merton, Robert K., 46, 494
Mettler, Suzanne, 468, 485, 694n, 743
Meyer, David S., 459n
Meyer, John W., 606, 611, 617
Mezey, Michael L., 314, 319, 320, 484
Micheletti, Michele, 35
Michels, Roberto, 21, 46, 239
Midlarsky, Manus, 68
Migdal, Joel S., 39, 40, 48, 53, 84, 88, 115, 646
Mignolo, Walter, 310, 311
Milbrath, Lester W., 433n, 440n
Milesi-Ferretti, Gian, 163
Mileur, Jerome, 521
Milgrom, Paul R., 39, 660, 670, 672, 673
Milkis, Sidney, 734, 741, 752
Mill, John Stuart, 36, 239, 437, 555n, 630
Miller, Arthur H., 440n, 475, 477, 5, 21, 22
Miller, David, 271, 272
Miller, Joanne, 810n, 825
Miller, Nicholas R., 249
Miller, Ross A., 437n
Miller, Roy, 812, 814
Miller, Steven, 197
Miller, Warren E., 453, 575
Milliken, Jennifer, 598
Milner, Helen V., xiii–xv, 1–26, 23, 60, 77, 79, 81, 121, 124, 125, 127, 129, 204, 313, 371n, 404n, 462n, 511n, 597n, 617, 630n, 755n, 779, 780n, 784n, 798
Milosevic, Slobodan, 584, 585
Mink, Gwendolyn, 496, 509, 734
Minkoff, Debra C., 459n
Miron, Jeffrey A., 153
Mishler, William, 48, 635n
Mitchell, Glenn E., 448n
Mitchell, Timothy, 115
Mitrovich, Gregory, 217
Mnookin, Robert, 780, 781

Moe, Terry, 536, 546, 570, 592n, 669, 739, 740
Moene, Karl Ove, 162, 375
Molina, Ivan J., 48
Money, Jeanette, 322, 324, 328
Monroe, Kristin Renwick, 594n
Mookerjee, Dilip, 760n
Moon, Donald J., 287, 293, 299
Moore, Barrington, 12, 18, 92, 93, 94, 99, 100, 255, 632, 634, 637, 638, 639, 640, 643, 703, 715
Moore, Michael K., 326
Moore, Underhill, 806
Moran, Mark J., 669
Moraski, Bryon, 795n
Moravcsik, Andrew, 38, 50, 52, 74, 140, 143, 199, 200, 221, 770
Morgan, Glyn, 404n
Morgan, T. Clifton, 179
Morgenstern, Scott, 339
Morgenthau, Hans J., 22–23, 198, 202, 203, 204, 207, 210, 211, 212, 756, 781
Morone, James, 752, 753
Morrell, Michael E., 436n
Morris, Aldon D., 459n
Morris, Irwin L., 157, 326
Morris, Martin, 298
Morrison, Toni, 494
Morrow, James D., 23, 31–32, 137, 140, 172–96, 172, 173, 176, 177, 181, 186, 188, 660n, 755n, 756, 757n
Morton, Rebecca B., 17, 459n, 462n, 628, 784–804, 788n, 790, 793n, 794n, 797, 799, 803, 805n
Mosca, Gaetano, 239
Moscardelli, Vincent G., 338
Moseley, Cassandra, 669, 748
Moser, Peter, 159, 314, 322
Mosley, Layna, 59
Mouffe, Chantal, 239, 299
Moyser, George, 436n
Mueller, Carol McClurg, 459n, 475
Mueller, Dennis, 161, 237, 242
Mueller, Karl, 213, 220
Mufti, Malik, 72
Muller, Edward N., 258, 635

Müller, Harald, 602
Munck, Gerald, 630n, 639, 705, 714
Mundt, R., 18
Munger, Michael C., 449n, 660
Munson, Ziad, 460n, 707, 744
Murillo, Maria Victoria, 48
Muste, Christopher, 440n
Myerson, Roger B., 333–34, 576, 577, 578, 760n
Myles, J., 657
Myrdahl, Gunnar, 347

Nadelmann, Ethan, 612
Nader, Ralph, 535n, 536n
Nagel, Jack H., 255, 446n
Nagel, Thomas, 274
Nagler, Jonathan, 448n, 455n
Nakano Glenn, Evelyn, 465
Nalebuff, Barry, 799, 803
Nash, John, 760n
Nayar, Baldev Raj, 214
Neblo, Michael, 498, 505
Nedelsky, Jennifer, 404n
Nelson, Joan, 351
Nelson, Michael, 537
Netemeyer-Mays, Margaret, 475
Nettl, J. P., 29, 33, 55, 57, 66, 82
Neuman, Gerald L., 420, 432
Newell, Allen, 804
Newton, Isaac, 758
Newton, Kenneth, 436n
Neyer, Jürgen, 619
Nicholson, Linda, 463
Nickerson, David, 805n, 826
Nie, Norman H., 22, 440n, 442, 444n, 450n, 457, 474n, 479
Niemi, Richard G., 450n, 480
Niou, Emerson M. S., 643
Nobles, Melissa, 509
Nokken, Timothy P., 326
Noll, Roger G., 676n
Norman, Wayne, 413, 428
Norrander, Barbara, 449n
Norris, Pippa, 477
North, Douglass C., 24, 35, 37, 39, 43, 44, 50, 151, 331, 360, 660, 661, 670, 672, 673, 692, 706n, 753

Norton, Noelle H., 326, 485, 727
Norton, Philip, 320
Nownes, Anthony J., 449n, 453n, 485
Nozick, Robert, 267, 270, 277, 278, 279, 280
Nurkse, Ragnar, 346
Nussbaum, Martha, 415, 553n
Nye, Joseph H., 57, 59, 60, 121, 215, 513

O'Brien, David M., 477
O'Brien, Kevin J., 327
O'Brien, Robert, 613, 620
O'Brien, Ruth, 751
Obstfeld, Maurice, 63
O'Connor, James, 37
O'Connor, Julia S., 694n
Odell, John S., 129, 608, 609
O'Donnell, Guillermo O., 37, 87, 97, 98, 101–102, 342, 354, 634n, 635, 641, 681n, 682, 715
Offe, Claus, 37
O'Halloran, Sharyn, 20, 134, 328, 339, 669, 801
O'Hara, Rosemary, 525
Ohlsson, Henry, 167
Ohmae, Kenichi, 225
Okin, Susan Moller, 275, 467, 553n, 566
Oliver, J. Eric, 447n, 450, 459n, 505, 506
Oliver, Melvin L., 492
Olsen, Johan P., 600, 601, 604, 607, 608, 611, 614, 660, 723
Olson, David M., 320
Olson, Mancur, 22, 38, 49–50, 129, 458, 546, 569, 570, 716
Oneal, John R., 181
O'Neill, Barry, 183
Onis, Ziya, 112
Onuf, Nicholas, 599
Opal, Barb, 462n
Ordeshook, Peter C., 355, 360, 571, 643, 681n, 760n, 807
Organski, J. F. K., 756, 781
Orlie, Melissa A., 303
Orloff, Ann Shola, 470, 694n
Orren, Karen, 16, 54, 462n, 627, 702, 722–54, 736, 747, 750, 752, 753, 805n

Ortiz, Anna Maria, 462n
Orum, Amy, 469
Orum, Anthony M., 469
Ostrom, Elinor, 17, 39, 44, 388
Overby, L. Marvin, 326, 338
Overbye, Einar, 570, 573, 574, 575, 577, 579, 588, 589, 591, 594, 595
Owen, John M., 180
Oye, Kenneth A., 137, 605, 611, 756

Paarsch, Harry, 796n
Packenham, Robert A., 320, 358
Pagano, Marco, 140
Page, Benjamin, 21
Palfrey, Thomas, 760n, 807, 815, 816
Palma, Gabriel, 87
Pampel, Fred C., 163
Pande, Rohini, 171
Paolino, Phillip, 477
Pape, Robert, 215, 218
Parikh, Sunita, 54
Park, David K., 444n
Parker, R. A. C., 759
Parrish, Charles J., 445n
Parrott, Bruce, 71
Parry, Geraint, 436n, 437n
Pateman, Carole, 14, 437n
Patillo-McCoy, Mary, 500, 503
Patterson, James T., 317
Patterson, Samuel, 812
Paulsen, Ronnelle, 471
Pauly, Louis W., 62, 122
Payne, Charles M., 473, 476, 482
Payner, Brook S., 499
Peabody, Robert L., 316, 317
Peake, Jeffrey, 327
Peel, 48
Peffley, Mark, 807
Peltzman, Sam, 127, 788
Perez, Sofia A., 375, 380
Perkins, Jerry, 484
Perng, S. S., 822
Perot, H. Ross, 449n
Perotti, Roberto, 147, 162, 165, 166, 167
Persson, Torsten, 164, 167, 169
Peterson, Mark A., 35
Peterson, Paul, 495, 496, 518

Peterson, Steven A., 450n
Petrocik, John M., 22
Petrocik, John R., 477, 478
Pettit, Philip, 241, 263
Phelan, Shane, 298, 300
Phillips, Anne, 427
Pierson, Paul, 1, 16, 37, 313, 371n, 373, 374, 381, 390, 391, 393, 607, 608, 626, 627, 656, 657, 687, **693–721**, 694n, 695, 698, 699, 701, 703, 708, 710, 712, 714, 724, 725, 741, 744, 753
Pietrykowski, Bruce, 735
Pinderhughes, Dianne, 509
Plant, Raymond, 277
Plato, 239, 274
Pleština, Dijana, 360
Plotke, David, 734, 744
Pogge, Thomas, 244, 276–77, 310
Polanyi, Karl, 23, 24, 377n
Polatnick, M. Rivka, 478
Pollack, Kenneth M., 211
Pollard, Walker, 576
Pollins, Brian M., 181
Polsby, Nelson W., 14, 20, 149, 317, 318, 320, 517, 522, 524
Polsky, Andrew, 734, 748
Pontusson, Jonas, 371n, 374, 375, 376n, 380, 382, 386, 389, 394n
Poole, Keith T., 319, 351, 365, 661, 663n
Popkin, Samuel, 21, 344, 364, 514
Porter, Robert, 795n
Porter, Tony, 604
Portney, Kent E., 437n, 452
Posen, Barry R., 649, 70, 216, 222
Posner, Daniel, 362, 369
Posner, Eric A., 228
Posner, Richard A., 282, 284
Posusney, Marsha Pripstein, 352
Poterba, James M., 147, 166
Poterba, James R., 162, 166, 167, 168
Poulantzas, Nicos, 37, 87
Powell, G. Bingham, 447, 642
Powell, Lynda, 532
Powell, Robert, 172, 173, 183, 200, 204, 214, 609, 627, 628, **755–83**, 760n, 763n, 767n, 775n, 781

Powell, Walter W., 16, 19, 137, 249, 470, 608, 609, 611
Power, Timothy, 365, 366
Prébisch, Raúl, 347
Prescott, Edward C., 151
Price, H. Douglas, 317
Price, Richard M., 598, 611, 612, 613
Price, Robert, 87, 88
Price, Vincent, 440n
Priess, David, 212, 219
Priest, George, 780, 781
Princen, Thomas, 613
Prysby, Charles, 447n
Przeworski, Adam, 18, 37, 49, 50, 100, 101, 237, 246, 255, 256, 257–58, 350, 351, 362, 630n, 634, 635, 636, 637, 638n, 640, 641, 642, 643, 669, 679n, 680, 681n
Putnam, Robert D., 21, 39, 101, 123, 258–60, 434n, 436n, 437n, 454, 455, 456, 514, 516, 567, 636, 705, 819, 831

Quester, George, 187, 205, 756

Rabkin, Rhoda, 355
Radcliff, Benjamin, 446n, 450n
Rae, Douglas W., 242, 249
Ragin, Charles C., 640, 644, 711, 714
Rahn, Wendy, 455n, 513
Rakove, Jack, 687, 688
Rakowski, Eric, 272
Ramseyer, J. Mark, 323, 324, 328
Ranade, Sudhanshu, 108, 63
Ranney, Austin, 249, 516
Ransby, Barbara, 501
Rapoport, Ronald B., 449n, 481
Rappoport, Peter, 282
Rasch, Bjørn Erik, 314, 322
Rasler, Karen A., 38
Rasmusen, Eric, 795n
Ratner, Sidney, 12
Rauch, James, 61
Raustiala, Kal, 615, 616
Rawls, John, 14, 232, 262, 266–67, 268, 269, 270, 271, 272, 273, 274, 275–76, 277, 280, 281, 285, 287,

288, 290, 291, 293, 294, 308, 414, 415, 431, 543, 563
Ray, James Lee, 177, 178, 180
Raz, Joseph, 547n, 548
Razaghian, Rose, 339
Reagan, Ronald, 740, 744
Reback, Gary, 806n
Reed, Adolph L., Jr., 509
Reed, William, 193
Reef, Mary Jo, 440n
Reeves, Jesse S., 6
Regalia, Ida, 375
Regini, Marino, 375
Rehg, William, 292
Reich, Simon, 62
Reichert, Usha N., 135, 158
Reid, John, 687
Reid, Pam Trotman, 462n
Reingold, Beth, 471, 485
Reinhardt, E., 144
Reinicke, Wolfgang H., 225, 623, 634n
Reiter, Dan, 182
Remington, Thomas, 327, 328, 358, 369
Remmer, Karen L., 36, 50, 52, 98, 102, 342, 635n
Rendell, Matthew, 217
Renelt, D., 366
Reno, William, 114, 646
Resnick, David, 446n
Resnik, Judith, 565
Reus-Smit, Christian 598, 600, 606, 67
Reuveny, Rafael, 181
Rhine, Staci L., 448n
Ricardo, David, 36, 127
Richard, Scott F., 128, 159
Richards, Alan, 98, 694n
Richardson, J. David, 127
Richerson, Peter J., 594n
Ridgeway, Cecilia L., 471
Rieken, Hanry, 807
Riker, William H., 16, 19, 39, 571, 660, 661, 669, 708, 760n
Ringer, Fritz K., 8
Ringquist, Evan J., 461n
Riordan, William, 532
Ripley, Randall B., 316, 317

Risse, Thomas, 17, 402, 403, **597–623**, 600, 602, 603, 613, 615, 617, 619, 620
Risse-Kappen, Thomas, 612, 74
Rittberger, Volker, 604, 610, 611
Ritter 1997, 728
Rivers, Douglas, 801
Roach, Hannah Grace, 5
Roberts, John, 660
Robertson, L. S., 807
Robinson, James, 365, 781
Robinson, John P., 440n
Robinson, Michael, 513n
Rocke, David M., 125, 214, 616, 756
Rockett, Katharine, 140
Rodden, Jonathan, 159
Rodgers, 730
Rodriguez, Daniel, 668n
Rodríguez, Fernando, 113, 348, 359
Rodrik, Dani, 24, 61, 63, 113, 122, 162, 348, 350, 359, 360, 364, 652
Roeder, Philip, 646
Rogers, Lindsay, 21
Rogers, Ruel, 495
Rogoff, Kenneth S., 63, 152
Rogowski, Ronald, 18, 19, 75, 121, 132, 377n, 617, 632n, 650, 651, 655
Rohde, David W., 318, 319, 330–31, 353, 453n
Romer, Thomas, 18, 150, 321, 802
Root, Hilton L., 47, 50
Ropp, Stephen C. 620
Rorty, Richard, 288, 291, 299
Rosati, Jerel A., 172
Rosberg, Carl G., 91
Rose, Gideon, 210, 765n, 771n, 773n
Rose, Harold M., 509
Rose, John C., 5, 48
Rose, Richard, 635n
Rose, William, 216
Rosecrance, Richard, 62, 197
Rosen, Stanley, 299
Rosenau, James N., 172, 407, 415
Rosenblum, Marc, 355
Rosenblum, Nancy L., 436n, 437n, 559n, 560, 561n, 562
Rosenbluth, Frances M., 132, 323, 324, 328, 335

Rosendorff, B. Peter, 23, 124, 125, 798
Rosenfeld, Michel, 291, 292
Rosenstone, Steven J., 441, 442, 446, 447, 448n, 453, 454, 455n, 475, 514, 531n, 812, 831
Rosenthal, Howard, 17, 18, 150, 171, 319, 321, 484, 661, 802
Rosenthal, Jean-Laurent, 598
Rosenzweig, Mark, 810n, 811
Ross, Dorothy, 12
Ross, Michael, 365
Rothchild, Donald, 216
Rothenberg, Lawrence S., 326, 338, 803
Rothman, David J., 317
Rothstein, Bo, 45, 46, 48
Roubini, Nouriel, 147, 151, 152, 158, 163, 164, 166, 167, 168, 169
Rousseau, David L., 177, 220
Rousseau, Jean-Jacques, 13, 36, 236–37, 238, 260, 412, 418, 548
Rowen, Brian, 617
Roy, Denny, 218–19
Royed, Terry J., 167
Royo, Sebastian, 375
Rubin, Donald, 806n, 811
Rubinfeld, Daniel, 780n
Rudder, Catherine, xiv
Ruddick, Sara, 478
Rudolph, Lloyd I., 87, 88
Rudolph, Susanne Hoeber, 87, 88
Rudolph, Thomas, 513
Rueben, Kim, 162
Rueschemeyer, Dietrich A., 637, 638, 639, 660, 694n, 699, 703, 704, 714, 718, 724, 37, 87, 99–100, 255, 367
Ruggie, John Gerard, 67, 197, 200, 203, 604, 605, 653
Rule, James, 716
Rule, Wilma, 483
Rummel, Rudolph J., 177, 178
Rundquist, Barry Spencer, 317, 327
Russett, Bruce M., 23, 177, 179, 181, 220
Rust, John, 796n
Rutten, Andrew, 687, 688

Sabato, Larry, 513n
Sabetti, Filippo, 260

Sachs, Jeffrey, 110, 163, 164, 167, 350
Sagan, Scott, 186
Saideman, Stephen, 645
Saint-Germain, Michelle A., 484
Sakong, Il, 111
Sala, Brian R., 326, 336
Salisbury, Robert H., 570, 592n
Samuels, David, 355, 357, 360
Samuelson, 127
Sanbonmatsu, Kira, 479
Sanchez, George J., 501
Sandbrook, Richard, 111
Sandel, Michael, 14, 269, 411, 416, 426
Sanders, Elizabeth, 336, 734
Sanders, Lynn M., 478, 495, 500, 506, 728
Sanders, Mitchell S., 326, 338
Sanguinetti, Pablo, 361
Sapiro, Virginia, 449n, 463, 467, 472, 474, 475, 477, 478, 480, 481
Sartori, Giovanni, 19, 98
Sassen, Saskia, 419, 420, 426
Savage, Barbara Dianne, 501
Sayres, Wallace, 535n
Sbragia, Alberta M., 35
Scalia, Antonin, 539n
Scanlon, T. M., 273
Schachar, Roni, 799, 803, 820
Schaffer, Frederic C., 634n
Scharpf, Fritz W., 50, 51, 52, 607, 608, 612, 622, 652
Schattschneider, E. E., 15, 22, 128, 129, 539n, 541n, 742
Scheffler, Samuel, 271, 272, 275
Schelling, Thomas C., 16, 124, 125, 257, 572, 579, 580, 586, 756, 758n
Scheve, Kenneth, 127
Schickler, Eric, 336, 708, 709, 718, 719, 720, 749
Schiemann, John, 359
Schiffrin, Steven, 240
Schiller, Wendy J., 326, 328, 338
Schimmelfennig, Frank, 603, 619
Schlichting, Kurt, 450n
Schlozman, Kay Lehman, 21, 399, 433–61, 434n, 436n, 439, 440n, 441n, 442, 444n, 445n, 446n,

449n, 450n, 451n, 455n, 456, 458n, 460n, 462n, 466, 467, 468, 472, 474, 477, 478, 480, 481, 482, 485, 519, 527, 528
Schmidt, Brian C., 51, 755n
Schmitter, Philippe C., 375, 376n, 636, 641, 652, 681n, 682, 87, 102
Schneider, Ben Ross, 112
Schneider, Gerald, 597
Schneider, William, 512
Schofield, Norman, 687
Scholz, John T., 48
Schonhardt-Bailey, Cheryl, 128
Schoolman, Morton, 298
Schorr, Juliet, 514
Schott, Richard, 518
Schotter, A., 150
Schroeder, Paul W., 203, 209, 217
Schudson, Michael, 452
Schuessler, Alexander A., 572, 573, 580, 586, 590
Schultz, Kenneth A., 23, 76, 181, 182, 224, 798
Schumaker, Paul, 477, 484, 485
Schumpeter, Joseph, 23, 231, 235, 244–45, 246, 634n
Schurmann, Franz, 88
Schwartz, Thomas, 669, 760n
Schweizer, Urs, 781
Schweller, Randall L., 197, 203, 204, 206, 211, 213, 219, 222, 756, 773n, 776, 777n
Scott, Anne Firor, 481
Scott, H. M., 189
Scott, James C., 15, 36, 39, 44, 70, 88, 115, 647
Scott, Joan, 410
Scully, Timothy, 355
Searing, Donald, 320
Sears, David O., 496, 505, 526
Secret, Philip, 482
Segal, Jeffrey, 795n, 802
Seligson, Mitchell A., 258, 635
Sen, Amartya K., 272, 594n
Seong, Kyoung-Ryung, 100
Sewell, William H., Jr., 491, 702
Shabad, Goldie, 479

Shachar, Ron, 445n

Shafer, Byron, 734

Shalev, Michael, 711

Shanks, J. Miller, 453

Shapiro, Ian, 14, 17, 21, 231, 232, **235–65**,
    237, 238, 240, 243, 244, 246, 249,
    250, 254, 255, 258–59, 260, 262,
    264, 368, 404n, 716

Shapiro, Martin, 675

Shapiro, Michael, 300, 302, 309

Shapiro, Robert Y., 433n, 477

Shapiro, Thomas M., 492

Shavell, Steven, 285

Shaver, Phillip R., 440n

Shaver, Shiela, 694n

Shaw, Brian J., 293, 294

Shaw, Malcolm, 320, 334

Sheetz, Mark, 217

Sheffield, F. D., 806

Shefter, Martin, 536, 699, 700, 702, 703,
    733, 752

Sheingate, Adam, 724, 753

Shepard, Walter James, 11

Shepsle, Kenneth A., 18, 19, 134, 150,
    160, 162, 165, 313, 314, 318, 321,
    324, 328, 330, 332, 335–36, 338,
    533, 660, 661, 669, 702, 760n

Sherman, L. W., 822

Shields, Todd G., 455n

Shimko, Keith, 229

Shimshoni, Jonathan, 185, 205

Shin, Doh Chull, 632n, 635n, 99

Shingles, Richard D., 440n

Shipan, Charles R., 18, 328, 669n, 795n,
    798

Shively, W. Phillips, 576n

Shklar, Judith, 412, 413, 494

Shleifer, Andrei, 360–61

Shotts, R. W., 803

Shuck, Peter, 404n

Shue, Henry, 275

Shue, Vivienne, 39, 88, 115

Shugart, Matthew Soberg, 20, 256,
    334–35, 357, 368

Shugart, Matthew, 642

Shvetsova, Olga, 355

Si, Y., 822

Sidanius, Jim, 505

Sidgwick, Henry, 416

Sigel, Roberta, 465, 468, 471, 475, 477,
    478, 479

Sigelman, Lee, 338, 477

Signorino, Curtis, 796n, 800, 803

Sikkink, Kathryn, 56, 60, 61, 62, 78,
    597n, 604, 606, 612, 613, 617,
    620, 693–94

Silbey, Joel H., 317, 734

Simmons, Beth, 23, 137, 141, 142, 143,
    605, 610, 694n

Simon, Adam, 449n

Simon, Herbert A., 497, 608

Simon, Mark, 536n

Sinclair, Barbara Deckard, 315, 318, 326,
    327

Singer, Hans, 347

Singer, J. David, 177, 192

Singer, Peter, 275

Sirriani, Carmen, 456, 458n

Sisson, Richard, 320

Siverson, Randolph M., 23, 174, 182

Skilling, David, 162

Skilling, Gordon, 167, 343

Sklar, Martin, 735, 736

Skocpol, Theda, 16, 37, 45, 54, 87, 88, 93,
    94, 95, 96, 327, 336, 371n, 373,
    374, 390, 391, 392n, 393, 436n,
    460n, 468, 470, 486n, 607, 626,
    627, 630n, 644, 660, 687, **693–721**,
    694, 703, 704, 707, 709, 714, 724,
    736, 741, 744, 745, 746

Skowronek, Stephen, 16, 54, 336, 627, 693,
    702, 703, 707, 710, 711, **722–54**,
    723, 728, 734, 736, 747, 750, 752

Skretny, David, 743

Slaughter, Anne-Marie, 615, 616

Slaughter, Matthew, 127

Sleeper, James, 404n

Slemrod, Joel, 164

Small, Melvin, 177, 192

Smith, Adam, 36, 44

Smith, Alastair, 175, 193, 195

Smith, Dennis, 812

Smith, James McCall, 144

Smith, Jeffrey, 825

Smith, Jennifer, 805n
Smith, Mark A., 327
Smith, Munroe, 9, 23
Smith, R. H., 4, 244
Smith, Rogers M., 430, 431, 432, 490n, 494, 496, 509, 727, 730, 731, 752
Smith, Steve, 598
Smith, Steven Rathgeb, 43, 358
Smith, Steven S., 314, 318, 327, 328, 336, 369
Smith, Tony, 87
Smith-Lovin, Lynn, 471
Snidal, Duncan, 138, 213, 214, 756
Sniderman, Paul M., 498, 499, 505, 807
Snow, David A., 459n
Snyder, Glenn H., 43, 48, 175, 212, 213, 759
Snyder, Jack L., 183, 187, 188, 197, 208, 213, 221, 222, 649, 767, 771, 773n, 777n
Snyder, James L., 123, 185
Snyder, James M., Jr., 326
Sobel, Joel, 140
Solnick, Steven, 646
Somers, Margaret R., 54, 630n
Songer, Donald, 795n
Soskice, David, 371n, 372, 376, 383, 384, 385, 386, 387, 388, 396, 653, 656, 657, 694n, 707, 709, 51, 162
Soss, Joe, 454
Soule, John W., 481
Souter, David, 486
Southwell, Priscilla L., 441n, 447n, 449n
Soysal, Yasemin, 411, 415
Sparrow, Bartholomew A., 694n, 734
Spero, Josh, 118
Spiller, Pablo, 676n, 677, 795n
Spiro, David, 178, 220, 223
Spitzer, Matthew L., 676n
Spolaore, Enrico, 62
Spragens, Thomas A., Jr., 299
Sprague, John, 441n, 447n, 472, 812, 819
Spruyt, Hendrik, 12, 38, 68
Spykman, Nicholas, 206
Squire, Peverill, 314, 339
Staggenborg, Suzanne, 459n
Staiger, Robert, 143

Stallings, Barbara, 112
Stam, Allan C., III, 182, 197
Stanley, Harold W., 450n
Stanley, Julian C., 191
Stark, David, 709
Stehlik-Barry, Kenneth, 443
Stein, Arthur A., 197, 223, 611
Stein, Ernesto, 163, 166
Steinmo, Sven, 367, 371n, 373, 609, 651n, 694n
Stenner, Karen, 481, 482
Stepan, Alfred, 19, 87, 88, 98, 103, 343, 636, 640, 679, 681n
Stephens, Evelyne Huber, 99–100, 255, 367, 637, 638, 694n, 703, 704, 718
Stephens, John D., 99–100, 255, 367, 376, 391, 392, 393, 637, 638, 694n, 699, 702, 703, 704, 707, 710, 714, 718
Stephenson, Gilbert Thomas, 5
Sterling-Folker, Jennifer, 215, 222
Steuernagel, Gertrude A., 475, 477
Steunenberg, Bernard, 322, 323
Stevens, Jacqueline, 464
Stewart, Abigail J., 462n, 475
Stewart, Charles H., 661
Stewart, Charles H., III, 167, 168, 327, 336
Stewart, Richard, 518
Stigler, George, 127, 788
Stilz, Annie, 404n
Stimson, James, 705, 818
Stinchcombe, Arthur L., 36, 53, 54, 331
Stinchcombe, Arthur, 700
Stoker, Laura, 444n, 470, 471
Stokes, Donald, 571, 575
Stokes, Susan C., 21, 22, 48
Stokey, Nancy L., 164
Stoler, Ann Laura, 465
Stolper, 127
Stone, Walter J., 449n
Stoner-Weiss, Kathryn, 360
Stoper, Emily, 467, 483
Strange, Susan, 226
Strate, John M., 445n
Streeck, Wolfgang, 376, 384, 387, 393, 694n
Strom, Kaare, 19, 323, 324, 339
Studlar, Donley T., 483

Sturm, Jan-Egbert, 167
Sugden, Robert, 582, 585
Summers, Lawrence H., 135, 147
Sundquist, James, 525
Sunkel, Osvaldo, 347
Sunstein, Cass, 239, 242
Suny, Ronald, 646
Svensson, Lars, 170, 171
Svensson, Leo, 164, 169
Swank, Duane H., 394n, 704, 51, 162, 163
Swenson, Peter, 371n, 372, 375, 376, 377, 378, 379, 380, 382, 389, 391, 392n, 651
Swers, Michele L., 326
Swift, Elaine K., 336
Symansky, Steven, 166
Sztompka, Piotr, 48

Taagepera, Rein, 642n
Tabellini, Guido, 135, 163, 164, 167, 168, 169
Tajfel, H., 568n
Talbert, Jeffrey C., 326
Taliaferro, Jeffrey W., 204
Talvi, Ernesto, 163, 165, 166
Tamerius, Karin L., 485
Tangian, A. S., 237
Tannenwald, Nina, 610, 612
Tanzi, Vito, 61
Tarar, Ahmer, 800
Tarrow, Sidney, 45, 459n, 460, 475, 694n
Tate, Katherine, 440n, 449n, 481, 506
Tavares, Jose, 167
Taylor, Charles, 406, 427, 548, 551n, 562, 594n
Taylor, Michael, 38–39, 44, 54, 95, 242, 582, 585, 670
Taylor, Rosemary C. R., 373, 597, 660, 691, 706, 75, 149, 299
Teixeira, Ruy A., 434n, 446n, 448n, 452, 459n, 514
Tellis, Ashley J., 223, 227
Tendler, Judith, 108
Terkildsen, Nayda, 477, 481
Teune, 630n
Thayer, Bradley, 227
Theiss-Morse, Elizabeth, 520, 537, 538

Thelen, Kathleen, 16, 37, 54, 234, 363, 367, 371–97, 373, 374n, 386, 387, 395, 396, 397, 609, 651n, 656, 660, 694n, 706, 708, 709, 714, 720
Theriault, Sean, 336
Therneau, Terry, 786n
Thies, Michael F., 335, 339
Thomas, George M., 598, 606, 611
Thomas, Robert, 661
Thomas, Sue, 484, 485
Thompson, Dennis F., 238, 242, 288
Thompson, Grahame, 226
Thompson, William R., 38, 62, 180
Thomson, Janice E., 38
Thomson, Ken, 437n, 452
Thorne, Barrie, 470, 472
Thucydides, 198, 210, 211, 773, 781
Tibshirani, R. J., 786n
Tichenor, Daniel, 752
Tiebout, Charles, 360
Tierney, John, 519
Tilly, Charles, 12, 16, 37, 45, 68, 411, 465n, 467, 476, 644, 694n, 707, 714
Timpone, Richard J., 447n, 448n
Tirole, Jean, 795n
Tocqueville, Alexis de, 21, 45, 46, 239, 255, 262, 263, 515
Toft, Monica, 645
Tolbert, Caroline J., 326
Tolleson Rinehart, Sue, 440n, 472, 474, 475, 476, 477, 478, 479, 480, 481, 484
Tollison, Robert, 43
Tomlins, Christopher, 744
Tommasi, Mariano, 361
Tong, X. X., 38
Tornell, Aaron, 350
Torney, Judith V., 469
Torres, John Charles, 100
Trachtenberg, Marc, 186, 197, 203, 208, 209, 217
Treisman, Daniel, 360–61, 364, 636
Trivedi, Pravin, 786n
True, James L., 327
Truman, David B., 5, 22, 530, 546, 788
Tsebelis, George, 20, 21, 77, 167, 322, 324, 328, 616, 643, 669

Tuckel, Peter, 450n
Tucker, Richard, 178, 179
Tudjman, Franjo, 585
Tudor, Rani, 108
Tufte, Edward, 831
Tulis, Jeffrey, 748
Tullock, Gordon, 241, 242, 246, 249
Tully, James, 311, 406, 428, 548
Turner, John C., 568n
Turner, Lowell, 379
Tushnet, Mark, 263
Tversky, Amos, 692
Twomey, Christopher P., 219
Tyler, Tom R., 48

Uhlaner, Carole J., 459n
Ulbert, Cornelia, 618
Ullman-Margalit, Edna, 582, 585
Ulman, Lloyd, 377
Underdal, Arild, 616
Urbanati, Nadia, 404n

Vail, Leroy, 250
Valentino, Nicholas, 449n
Valenzuela, Samuel, 637n, 642, 681
Van Buren, Martin, 737
Van Creveld, Martin, 57, 71
Van de Walle, Nicholas, 694n, 88, 96, 103, 112, 365, 366
Van Evera, Stephen, 75, 183, 184, 185, 187, 189, 199, 201, 203, 204, 205, 210, 221, 223, 756, 771n, 773n
Van Houweling, Robert P., 326
Van Parijs, Philippe, 254, 272–73
van Wijnbergen, Christa, 387, 395n
Vanberg, Georg, 322
Vanhanen, Tatu, 640
Varshney, Ashutosh, 101, 644, 648, 650, 694n
Vasquez, John A., 197, 212, 221, 229
Vedlitz, Arnold, 440n, 444n
Vega, Arturo, 326
Vegh, Carlos A., 165
Velasco, Andres, 165, 350
Verba, Sidney, 1, 21, 22, 433n, 434n, 436n, 439, 440n, 441n, 442, 444n, 445n, 446n, 449n, 450n, 451n,

455n, 456, 457, 458n, 460n, 462n, 466, 467, 468, 472, 474, 477, 478, 479, 480, 481, 482, 527, 528, 713, 761n
Villa, Dana, 303
Viner, 127
Vishny, Robert, 360
Vogel, David, 694n
Volden, Craig, 335, 662n, 667, 669
von Drehle, David, 513
von Hagen, Jurgen, 147, 162, 164, 165, 166, 167
Voss, D. Stephen, 495

Wade, Robert, 38, 88, 111, 114, 215, 349
Wagner, R. Harrison, 161, 175, 184, 204
Wahlke, John C., 320
Waldner, David, 701, 88
Waldo, Dwight, 805
Waldron, Jeremy, 13, 232, **266–85**, 274, 279, 548
Walker, Jack L., Jr., 22, 452n, 519
Walker, R. B. J., 598
Waller, Christopher J., 158
Wallerstein, Michael, 37, 50, 162, 375, 379, 395, 643, 652
Walt, Stephen M., 22, 32, **197–234**, 201, 204, 212, 213, 218, 221, 223, 228, 756
Walter, Barbara F., 176, 216, 649
Walters, Ronald W., 509
Walton, Hanes, Jr., 5. 440n, 481, 509
Waltz, Kenneth N., 23, 32, 57, 173, 194, 198, 200, 202–203, 204, 206, 207, 210, 212, 215, 218, 219, 222, 225, 226, 227–28, 756, 765, 767, 768, 769, 770, 771, 772, 773, 776, 777
Walzer, Michael, 14, 268, 413, 416, 417, 431, 551n
Wang, Cheng-Lung, 795n
Warren, M. E., 436n, 458n
Warren, Mark R., 456
Warwick, Paul, 19
Watanuki, Joji, 523
Waterbury, John, 43, 88, 98, 113, 694n
Waters, Mary C., 494
Watkins, Frederick Mundell, 9, 15

Wattenberg, Martin P., 449n
Way, Christopher, 156, 380
Weber, Cynthia, 69, 606
Weber, Katja, 73
Weber, Max, 14–15, 33, 40, 86, 94, 347, 408
Weber, Robert J., 576, 577, 578
Wedeen, Lisa, 647, 658n
Weiler, Joseph H., 422
Weiner, Jonathan, 637n
Weiner, Myron, 61, 87
Weingast, Barry R., 1, 16, 17, 24, 39, 50, 133, 150, 151, 160, 162, 165, 245, 314, 318, 321, 327, 330, 331, 360, 387n, 388, 533, 584, 590, 598, 626, 641, 642, **660–92**, 661, 668n, 670, 672, 673, 676n, 679, 680, 681, 682, 683, 685n, 687, 688, 737, 738, 739, 740, 760n
Weinstein, James, 391n
Weir, Margaret, 390, 511n, 707, 710, 742
Weisberg, Herbert F., 440n
Welch, Susan, 469, 477, 480, 482, 483, 484, 485
Weldes, Jutta, 598
Wellmer, Albrecht, 297, 298
Wendt, Alexander, 15, 57, 78, 174, 200, 204, 244, 598, 599, 600, 604, 606
West, Candace, 472
Westbrook, Raymond, 68
Western, Bruce, 45
Weyland, Kurt, 108
Whalen, Barbara, 668n
Whalen, Charles, 668n
White, Byron, 565
White, James, 448n
White, Lynn T., 88
White, Stephen K., 303, 305
White, William S., 316
Whitehead, Laurence, 102, 641
Whiteley, Paul F., 458n
Whiting, Susan, 38, 48
Wibbels, Erik, 159
Wickham-Crowley, Timothy P., 95. 694n, 712
Wiebe, Robert, 752
Wielhouwer, Peter W., 441n, 812

Wiener, Antje, 598
Wight, Martin, 206, 779
Wilcox, Clyde, 440n, 475, 532
Wike, Richard S., 338
Wilde, Oscar, 540n
Wilensky, Harold L., 375
Wilkinson, Steven I., 648
Will, George, 515n
Williams, Kenneth, 803
Williams, Melissa, 404n, 550
Williamson, John B., 110, 163
Williamson, Oliver, 660, 670
Willis, Robert, 466
Willoughby, Westel Woodbury, 12
Wilson, Ernest J., III, 506
Wilson, Graham, 35, 140
Wilson, James Q., 533, 592n
Wilson, Rick K., 336
Wilson, William Julius, 489
Wilson, Woodrow, 8, 9, 19, 23, 313, 340, 516, 521
Wingrove, Elizabeth, 465
Winsor, Hugh, 550
Winter, Nicholas, 465
Wirls, Daniel, 327, 336
Wittman, Donald A., 247
Wlezien, Christopher, 448n
Wohlforth, Christine, 197, 218
Wohlforth, William C., 197, 211, 217, 218, 222, 225
Wolbrecht, Christina, 486
Wolf, Klaus Dieter, 616
Wolf, Reinhard, 213
Wolfe, Alan, 515
Wolfers, Arnold, 756, 773, 781
Wolfinger, Raymond E., 442, 446, 447, 448n, 459n, 531n, 831
Wolfson, Mark, 459n
Wollheim, Richard, 258
Wolpin, Kenneth, 810n, 811
Wong, Cara, 474
Wong, Janelle S., 495, 507, 508
Woo, Jung-en, 111
Woo-Cumings, Meredith, 88
Wood, Gordon S., 687
Woodruff, David, 641
Wren, Anne, 651, 652

Wright, Erik Olin, 87
Wright, Gerald C., 447n
Wright, Quincy, 11, 22, 781
Wrighton, J. Mark, 326
Wrightsman, Lawrence, 440n
Wuthnow, Robert, 435n, 707

Yamamura, Kozo, 384
Yashar, Deborah J., 694n, 84, 99, 107, 367
Yinger, John, 827
Yoffie, 127
Yoon, David H., 220
Young, Iris Marian, 14, 88, 295, 300, 302, 303–306, 309, 312, 427, 465, 475, 495, 500
Young, Leslie, 788n
Young, M. C., 646
Young, M. Crawford, 112, 352

Young, Oran R., 614

Zakaria, Fareed, 75, 206, 207, 211, 771n, 777n
Zald, Mayer N., 459n, 614
Zaller, John, 21, 440n
Zartman, William I., 114
Zechman, Martin J., 576
Zelikow, Philip, 513
Zeng, Langche, 326, 338, 787
Zerilli, Linda, 462
Zielonka, Jan, 74
Zimmerman, Don H., 472
Zolberg, Aristide R., 694n
Zorn, Christopher J. W., 326, 338
Zuckerman, Alan S., 630n, 632
Zuckert, Catherine H., 299
Zürn, Michael, 605, 611, 616, 619
Zysman, John, 373, 379, 655, 694n